UNIVERSITY CASEBOOK SERIES®

INTERNATIONAL INTELLECTUAL PROPERTY LAW

CASES AND MATERIALS

FIFTH EDITION

PAUL GOLDSTEIN
Lillick Professor of Law
Stanford University

MARKETA TRIMBLE
Samuel Lionel Professor of Law
University of Nevada, Las Vegas

FOUNDATION
PRESS

The publisher is not engaged in rendering legal or other professional advice, and this publication is not a substitute for the advice of an attorney. If you require legal or other expert advice, you should seek the services of a competent attorney or other professional.

University Casebook Series is a trademark registered in the U.S. Patent and Trademark Office.

© 2001 FOUNDATION PRESS
© 2008, 2012 THOMSON REUTERS/FOUNDATION PRESS
© 2015 LEG, Inc. d/b/a West Academic
© 2019 LEG, Inc. d/b/a West Academic
    444 Cedar Street, Suite 700
    St. Paul, MN 55101
    1-877-888-1330

Printed in the United States of America

ISBN: 978-1-64020-631-1

To Jan and Lizzy

To Gary

PREFACE

Increasingly, the practice of intellectual property law has an international reach. A U.S. pharmaceutical company will time its patent disclosures with not only American grace periods in mind, but also foreign statutory bars. A French book publisher, if well-counselled, will accommodate its licensing arrangements to the different rules on rights and ownership that may obtain under foreign law. Trademark ownership acquired by use in the United States may lose out to trademark ownership acquired by registration abroad. Legislators must be alert to intellectual property treaty obligations, particularly since the 1994 TRIPs Agreement gave teeth to many of these obligations.

This book has two objectives. One is to equip law students with the tools they will need to engage in international intellectual property practice, whether transactional or litigation. The second is to expose the social, economic and cultural considerations that underpin intellectual property laws around the world. The division between developed and developing economies is doubtless the most salient source of conflict in contemporary policy discussions, but this book also explores the division between common law and civil law approaches to intellectual property protection.

Chapter I considers the private and public international law topics— territoriality, national treatment, choice of forum, choice of law, recognition and enforcement of foreign judgments, treaties and trade— that frame the substantive rules of intellectual property law. Chapter II considers the substantive rules themselves—copyright, patent, trademark, unfair competition, trade secrets and design protection— from the perspective of comparative law. Chapter II also discusses the rules concerning databases, plant varieties, Internet domain names, geographical indications and designs. Throughout, the text offers the viewpoint not only of the practitioner whose domestic client wants to obtain, license or enforce intellectual property rights abroad, but also the practitioner whose foreign client wants to obtain, license or enforce intellectual property rights in the practitioner's home country.

It would of course be impossible to capture the relevant details of all national intellectual property laws in a single volume. Nonetheless, a book this size can convey more than just the flavor of national practice around the world. The great bulk of intellectual property norms are in fact strikingly similar from country to country. Applicable treaties and trade agreements have gone far toward establishing universal norms and, at least across developed economies, legislators have struck pretty much the same balances between the interests of producers and consumers of intellectual goods. Also, regional institutions such as the European Union have adopted common rules for large areas; EU directives and regulations, several of which are considered in these pages, have played an important role in establishing intellectual property norms not only inside the European Union, but outside as well.

Stakeholder challenges to the norms of intellectual property treaties and agreements, and to the policy choices and compromises they embody, are to a great extent also global in nature.

Academic perspective and practical insight animate international intellectual property law, and we are grateful for the guidance of friends and colleagues. Jorge Contreras, John Duffy, Adela Faladova, Amalia Kessler, Mary LaFrance, Marshall Leaffer, Jiarui Liu, Péter Mezei, Neil Netanel, Tyler Ochoa, Margaret Jane Radin, Piet Jan Slot and Toshiko Takenaka provided helpful comments on all or portions of the book. Research assistants at Stanford Law School and the William S. Boyd School of Law at the University of Nevada, Las Vegas, devoted long hours to compiling bibliographies, checking references and proofreading manuscript. At Stanford we are grateful to Rey Barcelò, Simona Kiritsov Jankowski, Julia Martin, Corynne McSherry, Laura Nowell, Phil Poirier and David Walker. A bequest from the Clare and Michael Brown Estate supported their work. At the University of Nevada, Las Vegas, Wonhee (Elizabeth) Do, Christiana T. Dupont, Melissa L. Flatley, Lindsay L. Liddell, Stacy M. Newman and Miriam Shumway provided valuable research support. The book also benefited greatly from the services of the superb Stanford Law Library Information Services staff, and of Jeanne Price, the Director of the Wiener-Rogers Law Library at the University of Nevada, Las Vegas, and the Library's faculty, especially David McClure, Youngwoo Ban, Elizabeth Manriquez and Library Fellows James Rich and Lena Rieke.

P.G.
M.T.

Stanford, California
Las Vegas, Nevada
July, 2019

SUMMARY OF CONTENTS

TABLE OF CONTENTS

TABLE OF CASES

The principal cases are in bold type.

UNIVERSITY CASEBOOK SERIES®

INTERNATIONAL INTELLECTUAL PROPERTY LAW

CASES AND MATERIALS

FIFTH EDITION

CHAPTER I

PRINCIPLES AND INSTITUTIONS

A. LEGAL PRINCIPLES

1. TERRITORIALITY

Curtis Bradley, Territorial Intellectual Property Rights in an Age of Globalism[*]

37 Virginia Journal of International Law 505, 520–531 (1997).

III. Extraterritorial Application of Intellectual Property Law

In this Part, I examine the current state of the law regarding the extraterritorial application of federal intellectual property statutes. This examination shows that, absent some act of infringement within the United States, courts generally refuse to apply the patent and copyright statutes to conduct abroad. By contrast, courts apply the trademark statute in some cases to conduct that occurs abroad even in the absence of any domestic act of infringement. This extraterritorial treatment of trademark law can be traced largely to a 1952 Supreme Court decision, *Steele v. Bulova Watch Co.*[68] . . .

A. Patent Law

A patent is a government grant that entitles the recipient to exclude others from making, using, or selling an invention. Congress first enacted a federal patent statute in 1790. . . . The latest Patent Act was adopted in 1952. . . . This Act contains language suggesting that its scope is limited to the U.S. territory. It provides that the grant of a patent confers a "right to exclude others from making, using, offering for sale, or selling the invention *throughout the United States*." . . . Thus, "whoever without authority makes, uses or sells any patented invention, *within the United States* during the term of the patent therefore, infringes the patent." . . . Similar territorial language can be found as far back as the Patent Act of 1870. . . .

Even before the adoption of this language, courts consistently held that patent law is territorial in scope. One of the earliest decisions is *Brown v. Duchesne*.[74] There, the Court held that U.S. patent law did not apply to an improvement used in constructing the gaff of a foreign sailing vessel. The Court described the issue as one involving "the construction

---

[*]   Copyright © 1997 Curtis A. Bradley.

[68]   344 U.S. 280 (1952).

[74]   60 U.S. (19 How.) 183 (1856).

of the patent laws."[75] The Court acknowledged that the words of the patent statute "taken by themselves, and literally construed, without regard to the object in view, would seem to sanction the claim of the plaintiff."[76] But the Court stated categorically that the patent laws "do not, and were not intended to, operate beyond the limits of the United States."[77] The Court further stated that it would not give the statute an extraterritorial construction "unless plain and express words indicated that such was the intention of the Legislature."[78]

The strict territorial approach was applied again early in this century in *Dowagiac Manufacturing Co. v. Minnesota Moline Plow Co.*[79] In that case, third parties had manufactured grain drills that infringed the plaintiff's patents. The defendants purchased the drills from the third parties and then sold them in the United States and Canada. There was no question that the defendants' sale of the drills in the United States constituted infringement. The Court held, however, that the patent laws did not reach the defendants' sale of the drills in Canada. . . . The Court said that "[t]he right conferred by a patent under our law is confined to the United States and its Territories . . . and infringement of this right cannot be predicated of acts wholly done in a foreign country."[81]

More recently, the Supreme Court applied the territorial approach in *Deepsouth Packing Co. v. Laitram Corp.*[82] In that case, the defendant was exporting U.S.-made components of a shrimp deveiner for assembly outside the country. The plaintiff held combination patents . . . on certain mechanisms in the deveiner. In a five-to-four decision, the Court held that there was no violation of the patents. . . . Consistent with earlier lower court decisions, the Court held that a good protected by a combination patent is only "made" when it is fully assembled. . . . Because this assembly occurred outside the United States, the Court concluded that the U.S. patent laws were inapplicable. Quoting *Brown v. Duchesne*, the Court emphasized that "[o]ur patent system makes no claim to extraterritorial effect; 'these acts of Congress do not, and were not intended to, operate beyond the limits of the United States.' "[86] The Court also stated that, to the extent that a U.S. inventor needs protection in foreign markets, the wording of the patent statute suggests "a congressional intent to have him seek it abroad through patents secured in countries where his goods are being used."[87]

---

[75]   Id. at 194.

[76]   Id.

[77]   Id. at 195.

[78]   Id.

[79]   235 U.S. 641 (1915).

[81]   Id.

[82]   406 U.S. 518 (1972).

[86]   Id. at 531 (quoting Brown v. Duchesne, 60 U.S. (19 How.) 183, 195 (1856)).

[87]   Id. Congress eventually amended the patent statute to overrule the specific holding of *Deepsouth*. See 35 U.S.C. § 271(f).

Despite this territorial approach, there are two scenarios in which courts nevertheless give patent law what could be called an extraterritorial effect. The first is under the doctrine of contributory infringement.... Courts have held that conduct abroad can be reached under U.S. patent law if it actively induces or contributes to infringement occurring within the U.S. territory.... These cases recognize that, even though U.S. patent law applies only to infringements occurring within the U.S. territory, the cause of an infringement may emanate from outside the territory. The second situation concerns the recovery of profits received as a result of an infringement. The Federal Circuit has indicated (without much explanation) that, so long as the defendant infringes the patent in the United States (for example by making the patented invention here), then the recoverable damages may include the profits received by the defendant from *foreign* sales of the invention.[90] Importantly, in both of these situations, liability is premised on the existence of an infringement of the patent in the United States. Absent an infringement occurring within the U.S. territory, there can be no violation of the patent laws.... As discussed below, this is also the general rule in copyright law, but not in trademark law.

on condition of
domestic
infringement

B. Copyright Law

Copyright law protects "original works of authorship fixed in any tangible medium of expression."[92] As with patent law, there has been a federal copyright statute in the United States since 1790.... After a variety of revisions and amendments, the statute was comprehensively recodified in 1909.... The 1909 Act remained in place until the enactment of the current 1976 Act.... In contrast to the patent statute, there is no language in the copyright statute suggesting that its scope is generally limited to the U.S. borders. The "exclusive rights" of copyright listed in Section 106 of the Act do not mention any particular territory.... Nor does the general infringement provision, Section 501(a), state that it applies only within the United States.... Nevertheless, courts consistently have held that U.S. copyright law, at least as a general matter, does not apply beyond U.S. territorial boundaries.

The Supreme Court applied this principle early in this century in *United Dictionary Co. v. G. & C. Merriam Co.*[98] There, in an opinion by Justice Holmes, the Court held that a requirement under U.S. copyright law that a notice of copyright be inserted "in the several copies of every edition published"[99] did not extend to publications outside the United States.... The Court acknowledged that Congress "could attach what

---

[90] AG v. SciMed Life Sys., 39 U.S.P.Q.2d (BNA) 1596, 1598 (Fed.Cir. 1995) (per curiam); Datascope Corp. v. SMEC, Inc., 879 F.2d 820, 826–27 (Fed.Cir. 1989).

[92] 17 U.S.C. § 102(a) (1994).

[98] 208 U.S. 260 (1908).

[99] [Copyright] Act of June 18, 1874, ch. 3, § 4962, 18 Stat. 965, 967.

conditions it saw fit to its grant."[101] However, in language reflecting a territorial conception of copyrights, the Court said it was "unlikely that [Congress] would make requirements of personal action beyond the sphere of its control. Especially is it unlikely that it would require a warning to the public against the infraction of a law beyond the jurisdiction where that law was in force."[102]

The territorial nature of copyright law was recently reaffirmed in strong terms by the Ninth Circuit in *Subafilms, Ltd. v. MGM-Pathe Communications Co.*[103] In that case, the court held that the mere authorization within the United States of acts of infringement occurring outside of the United States does not violate U.S. copyright law. Overruling an earlier decision, . . . the court held that an "authorization" only violates the Copyright Act if the conduct authorized itself violates the Act. . . . The court then proceeded to hold, consistent with earlier decisions, that the Act does not apply to activities occurring outside the United States. The court invoked the general presumption against the extraterritorial application of federal statutes and observed that "[t]here is no clear expression of congressional intent in either the 1976 Act or other relevant enactments to alter the preexisting extraterritoriality doctrine."[106] The court also expressed concern about interfering with efforts by Congress to achieve multilateral intellectual property protection. . . . Finally, the court noted that extraterritorial application of copyright law would embroil the courts in difficult choice-of-law questions. . . .

Consistent with *Subafilms*, courts in recent years have stated categorically that the copyright laws do not have extraterritorial effect. . . . As in the patent area, there are what could arguably be called exceptions to this rule for situations involving contributory infringement . . . and extraterritorial profits. . . . Some courts have also adopted a related exception for situations in which an infringement in the United States permits further infringement abroad.[112] But, as under patent law, the courts have held that there can be no violation of U.S. copyright law without an act of infringement within the United States. . . . As discussed below, this is not the case with respect to U.S. trademark law.

C. Trademark Law

Trademark law protects the use of designations that identify and distinguish goods or services in commerce. The first federal trademark statute was enacted in 1870, but it was held unconstitutional because it was not limited to interstate commerce, and it was found to be beyond

---

[101] 208 U.S. at 264.

[102] Id.

[103] 24 F.3d 1088 (9th Cir. 1994) (en banc).

[106] 24 F.3d at 1096.

[112] See, e.g., Update Art, Inc. v. Modiin Publ'g, Ltd., 843 F.2d 67, 73 (2d Cir. 1988); DeBardossy v. Puski, 763 F.Supp. 1239, 1243 (S.D.N.Y. 1991); P & D Int'l v. Halsey Publ'g Co., 672 F. Supp. 1429, 1432 (S.D.Fla. 1987).

Congress's powers under the copyright and patent clause. . . . After subsequently enacting a statute in 1881 applicable only to marks used in commerce with foreign nations and Indian tribes, Congress in 1905 relied on its commerce clause powers to enact the "first modern federal trademark registration statute."[115] The 1905 statute was replaced by the current federal trademark statute, the Lanham Trade-Mark Act, which was enacted in 1946. . . .

In contrast to patent and copyright law, courts apply trademark law to conduct abroad even in some cases where no act of infringement has taken place within the United States. This differential treatment can be traced in large part to a 1952 Supreme Court decision, *Steele v. Bulova Watch Co.* . . . There, the defendant Steele, a U.S. citizen, had been purchasing unbranded watch components from Switzerland and the United States, assembling the watches in Mexico, and there stamping the watches with the name "Bulova." Although Steele sold the watches only in Mexico, a significant number of the watches had filtered across the border into the United States. . . . The Bulova Watch Company, a U.S. corporation, brought suit against Steele in federal district court in Texas seeking injunctive and monetary relief under the Lanham Act. The company had registered the name "Bulova" as a trademark in the United States, but had not registered the mark in Mexico. By contrast, Steele, many years before the lawsuit, had registered the mark in Mexico. . . .

In holding that the Lanham Act applied to the defendant's conduct, the Supreme Court began by stating that it is well settled that Congress has the power to prescribe rules of conduct for its nationals that extend beyond the country's territorial boundaries. . . . Although the Court acknowledged that "legislation of Congress will not extend beyond the boundaries of the United States [absent] a contrary legislative intent,"[121] it noted that the Lanham Act purports to extend to "all commerce which may lawfully be regulated by Congress."[122] The Court described this as a "broad jurisdictional grant."[123]

In addition to relying on the commerce language of the Act, the Court emphasized that Steele was a U.S. citizen and that his conduct had effects in the United States—he had been buying watch components from the United States and his watches were filtering into the United States. The Court rejected the argument that the place where Steele affixed the infringing mark and sold the watches was determinative of the choice of law: "[W]e do not think that petitioner by so simple a device can evade the thrust of the laws of the United States in a privileged sanctuary beyond our borders."[124] Finally, the Court found no conflict with foreign law, because, while the case had been pending before the Court, the

---

[115]   Restatement (Third) of Unfair Competition § 9 cmt. e (1995).

[121]   344 U.S. at 285.

[122]   Id. at 284.

[123]   Id. at 286.

[124]   Id. at 287.

Mexican government canceled Steele's registration of the mark in that country. . . .

The Court's decision left a number of unanswered questions. What if none of the watches had turned up in the United States? What if Steele had not purchased component parts in the United States? What if Steele had not been a U.S. citizen? What if Steele's Mexican trademark registration had not been canceled? Not only did the Court not answer these questions, its analysis did not even suggest how these questions were to be resolved. In particular, the Court did not explain which of the facts of the case, if any, were essential to liability or how such facts were to be weighed.

The lower courts have struggled with these and similar questions after *Steele*. Despite the "broad jurisdictional grant" in the Lanham Act, the courts have not applied the Act to the full reaches of Congress's commerce power. Instead, they have applied a variety of balancing tests to limit the Lanham Act's extraterritorial effect. Most circuits apply some version of a three-part test that considers the effects of the defendant's conduct on U.S. commerce, the citizenship of the defendant, and the likelihood of a conflict between U.S. law and foreign law. . . . The Ninth Circuit, however, applies a more complicated balancing test that it developed for the extraterritorial application of antitrust law:

> [F]irst, there must be some effect on American foreign commerce; second, the effect must be sufficiently great to present a cognizable injury to plaintiffs under the federal statute; and third, the interests of and links to American foreign commerce must be sufficiently strong in relation to those of other nations to justify an assertion of extraterritorial authority.[127]

In evaluating the third part of the test, the Ninth Circuit considers and balances seven "comity" factors.[128]

The differences in the tests used and the uncertain nature of these tests have meant that the extraterritorial scope of the Lanham Act varies to some extent from circuit to circuit. For example, the Ninth Circuit has taken a relatively broad view of the Lanham Act's extraterritorial scope, and the Second Circuit has taken a relatively narrow view. The key point for present purposes is that the courts in some situations apply the

---

[127] Reebok Int'l, Ltd. v. Marnatech Enters., Inc., 970 F.2d 552, 554 (9th Cir. 1992) (quoting Star-Kist Foods, Inc. v. P.J. Rhodes & Co., 769 F.2d 1393, 1395 (9th Cir. 1985)).

[128] These factors are:

> [T]he degree of conflict with foreign law or policy, the nationality or allegiance of the parties and the locations or principal places of business of corporations, the extent to which enforcement by either state can be expected to achieve compliance, the relative significance of effects on the United States as compared with those elsewhere, the extent to which there is explicit purpose to harm or affect American commerce, the foreseeability of such effect, and the relative importance to the violations charged of conduct within the United States as compared with conduct abroad.

Reebok, 970 F.2d at 555 (quoting *Timberlane*, 549 F.2d at 614).

Lanham Act to conduct abroad even in the absence of an act of infringement within the United States. Trademark infringement under the Lanham Act requires, among other things, that there be a likelihood of confusion. . . . Nevertheless, there have been a number of decisions applying the Act to the exportation and sale abroad of allegedly infringing merchandise, despite the lack of any showing that the merchandise was likely to reenter the United States or cause any confusion within the United States. Recently, a court even applied it to the performance of services in another country. . . .

The distinction between the approach taken in the trademark area and the one taken in the patent and copyright areas is highlighted by a decision from the Fourth Circuit, *Nintendo of America, Inc. v. Aeropower Co.*[132] In that case, the defendants were found to have sold counterfeit Nintendo video games not only in the United States, but also in Mexico and Canada. Although "[t]he cartridges and video game software also display[ed] several registered trademarks of Nintendo's," the principal intellectual property protection for the content of the video games was copyright law.[133] Nevertheless, in considering the validity of an injunction directed at the foreign conduct, the Fourth Circuit looked only to trademark law rather than copyright law. The court stated that, whereas "the Copyright Act is generally considered to have no extraterritorial application,"[134] the power to regulate extraterritorial conduct "is more extensive under the Lanham Act,"[135] in that it extends to "any [conduct] which has a significant effect on United States Commerce."[136]

NOTES   *Territ'ly defm*

1. *Origins of Territoriality Doctrine.* The seventeenth-century Dutch scholar Ulrich Huber identified three precepts of modern territoriality doctrine: (a) a state's laws have force only within the state's boundaries; (b) anyone found within the state's boundaries is subject to the state's authority; and (c) comity will discipline one sovereign's exercise of authority to respect the territorial competence of other sovereigns. As synthesized by Professor Harold Maier, these precepts "state that acts of foreign sovereigns should, when appropriate, be given effect within another state's territory and that courts of all nations should indulge a presumption against the extraterritorial impact of law." Harold G. Maier, Extraterritorial Jurisdiction at a Crossroads: An Intersection Between Public and Private International Law, 76 Am. J. Int'l. L. 280, 282 (1982).

Contemporary territoriality doctrine was formulated at a time when the effects of commercial behavior were largely local and the occasions for

---

[132] 34 F.3d 246 (4th Cir. 1994).
[133] Id. at 248.
[134] Id. at 249 n. 5.
[135] Id. at 249.
[136] Id. at 249–50 n. 5.

conflict with the doctrine were few. One early exception from strict territoriality doctrine was the "nationality principle" which gave states the competence to regulate certain foreign conduct of their nationals and citizens, so long as the regulation did not violate foreign law. A more recent exception, followed principally in the United States, and criticized by many other countries, is the so-called "effects doctrine" under which Country *A* may assert legislative competence over conduct occurring in Country *B* if the conduct has, or is intended to have, substantial effects within the borders of Country *A*; examples include application of United States antitrust and securities regulations to conduct abroad. *See* generally, Restatement (Third) of Foreign Relations Law of the United States §§ 402–403.

2.   *Territoriality and Intellectual Property Law*. The globalized nature of current intellectual property activities forces parties and courts to seek the expanded application of national laws to cover complex transnational transactions. Does the presumption against extraterritoriality create unreasonable restrictions on the application of U.S. law? Congress rarely expresses its intent regarding the territorial scope of U.S. statutes; it passes legislation primarily for domestic purposes—as do other national legislatures.

In RJR Nabisco, Inc. v. European Community, 136 S.Ct. 2090 (2016), a case that involved the Racketeer Influenced and Corrupt Organizations Act, the U.S. Supreme Court formulated a two-step framework for analyzing the territorial scope of the application of U.S. statutes: First, a court should ask "whether the presumption against extraterritoriality has been rebutted—that is, whether the statute gives a clear, affirmative indication that it applies extraterritorially." If the presumption against extraterritoriality is rebutted, "[t]he scope of an extraterritorial statute . . . turns on the limits Congress has (or has not) imposed on the statute's foreign application . . . ." 136 S.Ct. 2101. When assessing the territorial reach of the Lanham Act, courts will apply a test—such as the Ninth Circuit's *Timberlane* test quoted in the Bradley article, above—to determine whether the Lanham Act's phrase "all commerce which may lawfully be regulated by Congress" "sweeps foreign activities into the Act's prescriptive reach." Trader Joe's Company v. Hallatt, 835 F.3d 960 (9th Cir. 2016).

Second, under *RJR Nabisco*, if the presumption against extraterritoriality has not been rebutted, the court should determine whether the case involves a domestic or an extraterritorial application of the statute by considering the statute's "focus." "[I]f the conduct relevant to the [statute's] focus occurred in a foreign country, then the case involves an impermissible extraterritorial application regardless of any other conduct that occurred in U.S. territory." 136 S.Ct. at 2101. What is the "focus" of an intellectual property statute? In Spanski Enterprises, Inc. v. Telewizja Polska, S.A., 883 F.3d 904 (D.C.Cir. 2018), the defendant, a Polish television station, argued that holding it liable under the U.S. Copyright Act for publicly performing copyright-protected content on its website outside the United States was an impermissible extraterritorial application of the Act. The Court of Appeals for the District of Columbia Circuit ruled for the plaintiff, observing that the "focus" of the Copyright Act is on "protecting the exclusivity of the rights it guarantees." Because "the infringing performances—and consequent violation of [plaintiff's] copyrights—occurred on computer screens in the United States," "the conduct relevant to the statute's focus occurred in the United States [and the case therefore] involves a permissible domestic application of the Copyright Act." 883 F.3d at 914.

Will pressures for extraterritorial application of intellectual property laws ease to the extent that international arrangements such as the TRIPs Agreement succeed in harmonizing national laws? Can pressures for extraterritorial application of national law be separated from another issue in private international law—the choice of forum? If the patent owner in *Deepsouth*, discussed in the Bradley article, could have brought an action under foreign law in a U.S. court for the direct infringement abroad, might the patent owner have been less reluctant to proceed under foreign law? *See London Film*, page 25, below.

3. *Patent.* Congress legislatively overruled *Deepsouth v. Laitram* in 1984 by adding section 271(f) to the Patent Act providing that "[w]hoever without authority supplies or causes to be supplied in or from the United States all or a substantial portion of the components of a patented invention, where such components are uncombined in whole or in part, in such manner as to actively induce the combination of such components outside of the United States in a manner that would infringe the patent if such combination occurred within the United States, shall be liable as an infringer." Pub. L. No. 98–622, § 101(a), 98 Stat. 3383.

Would it constitute patent infringement under section 271(f) for Company *Z* in the United States to deliver a master disk, or an electronic transmission embodying software, that, when copied and installed abroad in a foreign-made computer, would have infringed Company Y's patent on an apparatus for digitally encoding and compressing recorded speech if all of the relevant conduct had instead occurred inside the United States? Observing that "[p]lausible arguments can be made for and against extending § 271(f) to the conduct charged in this case," and "[r]ecognizing that § 271(f) is an exception to the general rule that our patent law does not apply extraterritorially," the U.S. Supreme Court ruled that the provision did not apply. Microsoft Corp. v. AT & T Corp., 550 U.S. 437, 442 (2007). The opinion in the *Microsoft* case appears at page 422 below.

Four years after adding section 271(f) to the Patent Act, Congress plugged an even larger hole in United States patent protection—the importation of *products*, mainly pharmaceuticals, produced through *processes* that, though patented in the United States, were not patented in the country of manufacture. Section 271(g) of the Patent Act, as subsequently amended, provides that "[w]hoever without authority imports into the United States or offers to sell, sells, or uses within the United States a product which is made by a process patented in the United States shall be liable as an infringer, if the importation, offer to sell, sale, or use of the product occurs during the term of such process patent." Pub. L. No. 100–418, § 9003, 102 Stat. 1563–1564; amended by Public Law 103–465, sec. 533(a), 108 Stat. 4988.

See Donald Chisum, Normative and Empirical Territoriality in Intellectual Property: Lessons from Patent Law, 37 Va. J. Int'l L. 603 (1997); Timothy R. Holbrook, Extraterritoriality in U.S. Patent Law, 49 Wm. & Mary L. Rev. 2119 (2008).

4. *Copyright.* The Ninth Circuit's *en banc* decision in *Subafilms,* discussed in the Bradley article, rests on a straightforward syllogism: acts occurring outside the United States do not constitute infringement under the U.S. Copyright Act; there can be no contributory infringement without direct infringement; therefore, there can be no contributory liability under the U.S. Copyright Act for acts of direct infringement occurring outside the United States. Are there any flaws in this logic? Does the syllogism honor the *Steele v. Bulova* guidelines under which territoriality requires only that some relevant conduct occur in the protecting country? Why were the acts of authorization in the United States in *Subafilms* insufficient for this purpose? Is it relevant that the Lanham Act, applied in *Bulova,* encompasses "all commerce which may lawfully be regulated by Congress" while the 1976 Copyright Act contains no such inclusive terms? Would the outcome in *Subafilms* have been the same if the two-step extraterritoriality framework outlined in *RJR Nabisco* (note 2, above) had been employed?

Would the *Subafilms* court have reached a different result if the facts were reversed and the direct infringement had occurred in the United States while the alleged contributory infringement had occurred abroad? Some U.S. courts have acknowledged that an act occurring abroad may constitute contributory infringement under U.S. law if the extraterritorial act was intended—and did—have effects in the United States and resulted in direct copyright infringement in the United States. ITSI T.V. Productions, Inc. v. California Authority of Racing Fairs, 785 F.Supp. 854 (E.D.Ca. 1992), *rev'd in part on other grounds,* 3 F.3d 1289 (9th Cir. 1993); Armstrong v. Virgin Records, Ltd., 91 F.Supp.2d 628 (S.D.N.Y. 2000).

The opinion in *Subafilms* appears at page 191 below.

5. *Trademark.* The Supreme Court's holding in *Steele v. Bulova* that the Lanham Act may be applied extraterritorially rested significantly on the finding that the defendant's conduct had a substantial effect on United States commerce. In Atlantic Richfield Co. v. Arco Globus International Co., 150 F.3d 189 (2d Cir. 1998), the court, finding no substantial effect on U.S. commerce, declined to apply the Lanham Act against defendant AGI's use of plaintiff's registered ARCO mark abroad—in the former Soviet Union—even though plaintiff allegedly used the ARCO mark in the former Soviet Union and defendant engaged in some activities in the United States. "AGI has only two employees in the United States, no American customers, and no plans to expand its petroleum operations into the United States. To be sure, there is evidence of other domestic activities in which AGI has engaged: escorting oil refinery managers on tours of United States refineries, attempting to participate in a joint venture, and depositing money from foreign sales in a New York bank. However, these activities are in no sense essential to AGI's allegedly infringing activities abroad." 150 F.3d at 193.

Would a global Internet website maintained by a Japanese retailer and featuring goods that bear plaintiff's name have "substantial effects" in the United States if, though accessible from the United States, the website was in Japanese and did not facilitate sales of goods in the United States? In McBee v. Delica Co., 417 F.3d 107, 123–124 (1st Cir. 2005), the court ruled that "[t]o hold that any website in a foreign language, wherever hosted, is automatically reachable under the Lanham Act so long as it is visible in the United States would be senseless." Just as "the mere existence of a website that is visible in a forum and that gives information about a company and its products is not enough, by itself, to subject a defendant to personal jurisdiction in that forum," so it is insufficient to confer subject matter jurisdiction under the Lanham Act.

The opinion in the *McBee* case is reproduced at page 582, below. *[handwritten: Lanham]*

6. *Remedies.* In copyright and patent cases, U.S. courts will award profits for connected infringements that occur in other countries if the predicate act of infringement occurred on United States soil. For example, in Los Angeles News Service v. Reuters Television Int'l, Ltd., 149 F.3d 987 (9th Cir. 1998), *[handwritten: copyright]* clarified in 340 F.3d 926 (9th Cir. 2003), the court held that plaintiff could recover profits arising from foreign exploitation of copyrighted footage where the exploitation was made possible by the reproduction of the footage in the United States. The 2003 opinion in *LA News Service* appears at page 362, below.

In WesternGeco LLC v. ION Geophysical Corp., 138 S.Ct. 2129 (2018), *[handwritten: patent]* the U.S. Supreme Court addressed the question whether a "damages award for lost profits was a permissible domestic application" of the Patent Act's damages provision in section 284 of the Patent Act. 138 S.Ct. at 2139. Respondent ION supplied components abroad that were specially adapted for the patented invention, which was assembled abroad. The district court found infringement under section 271(f)(2) of the Patent Act and awarded WesternGeco, the patent owner, damages in royalties and lost profits. On appeal, the Supreme Court rejected respondent's argument that the award of profits for foreign sales amounted to an impermissible extraterritorial application of the Patent Act. Applying the second step of its two-step *[handwritten: ION's domestic]* extraterritoriality analysis, the Court identified "infringement" as the focus *[handwritten: act of supplying]* of section 284. Because the focus of section 271(f)(2) is "the domestic act of *[handwritten: the components]* 'suppl[ying] in or from the United States'," the Court concluded that the focus *[handwritten: that infringed]* of section 284 in a case involving infringement under section 271(f)(2) is the *[handwritten: W.geco's patents]* domestic infringement. Therefore, the Court held that "the lost-profits *[handwritten: clearly occurred]* damages that were awarded to WesternGeco were a domestic application of *[handwritten: in the U.S.]* § 284." 138 S.Ct. at 2138.

Foreign courts have also awarded monetary relief to account for the foreign effects of domestic infringements. In Schmid Bros. Inc. v. Genossenschaft der Franziskanerinnen von Siessen e.V. (Hummel Christmas 1971 Plate), I ZR 110/74, December 19, 1975, 8 IIC 276 (1977), the German Federal Supreme Court ruled that monetary recovery should encompass an accounting for unauthorized goods that, though manufactured in Germany, were distributed in the United States; the accounting was to be "without any territorial limitations since defendants' royalty receipts payable by Goebel [its U.S. licensee] have been reduced through plaintiff's distribution abroad." 8 IIC 280.

Does it violate the territoriality principle to allow an act of infringement in Country *A* to trigger liability for profits earned and damages suffered in Country *B*? If the defendant's conduct in Country *B* would not give rise to a cause of action under Country *B*'s law, how can it give rise to remedies? Would these cases on monetary relief also support an award of injunctive relief in Country *B*? Even if the acts in issue in fact infringed rights under the law of Country *B*, what justification is there for applying to these acts the remedies prescribed by the law of Country *A* rather than those prescribed by the law of Country *B*?

On the treatment of the predicate act doctrine in various U.S. circuits see Tire Engineering and Distribution, LLC v. Shandong Linglong Rubber Co., Ltd., 682 F.3d 292, 306–309 (4th Cir. 2012), *cert. denied,* 568 U.S. 1087, 133 S.Ct. 846 (2013). On extraterritorial remedies in intellectual property cases see Marketa Trimble, The Territorial Discrepancy between Intellectual Property Rights Infringement Claims and Remedies, 23 Lewis & Clark L. Rev. 501 (2019).

7. *Territoriality in the Digital Environment.* Intellectual property by its very nature challenges the principle of territoriality. Unlike real property, and even chattels, intellectual property rights in a single object can simultaneously exist, and be exploited, in dozens of countries. If in Country *A* copyrighted television signal is transmitted to a satellite, and the signal is received from the satellite in Countries *B, C, D* and *E*, does it make practical sense to divide liability among the laws of five different countries? What if the law of Country *A* provides that receipt, but not transmission, of a signal constitutes infringement, while the laws of Countries *B–E* treat transmission, but not receipt as infringement?

Digital communications have seriously complicated the territoriality question in intellectual property law, and not just for copyrighted works; there is also a regular traffic in trademarks and patents on the Internet. Extraterritoriality—the prescriptive competence of Country *A* to export its law to govern conduct occurring in Country *B*—is but one of the legal questions that arise in these contexts. Choice of forum and choice of law also present hard questions: What country's courts are competent to decide these cases? What country's laws should they apply in deciding them?

For detailed inquiries, see Marketa Trimble, Advancing National Intellectual Property Policies in a Transnational Context, 74 Md. L. Rev. 203 (2015); Teresa Scassa, Robert J. Currie, New First Principles? Assessing the Internet's Challenges to Jurisdiction, 42 Geo. J. Int'l L. 1017 (2011); Graeme B. Dinwoodie, Developing A Private International Intellectual Property Law: The Demise of Territoriality?, 51 Wm. & Mary L. Rev. 711 (2009); Symposium, Intellectual Property Online: The Challenge of Multi-Territorial Disputes, 30 Brook. J. Int'l L. 813 (2005); Jane Ginsburg, Global Use/Territorial Rights: Private International Law Questions of the Global Information Infrastructure, 42 J. Copyr. Soc'y 318 (1995).

8. *Territoriality and Piracy.* The international expansion of enforceable intellectual property rights, most notably through the TRIPs Agreement, promises to reduce conflicts between countries that are more and less avid about enforcing intellectual property norms. Nonetheless, infringement havens in which pirates commit acts that would be barred elsewhere—while exploiting their products worldwide—are likely to be an enduring feature of international intellectual property law. Would it be appropriate for countries in which these pirated products are received to redefine infringement to include this otherwise noninfringing conduct? To narrowly—and extraterritorially—extend their domestic rules to infringement havens?

Steele v. Bulova weighed considerations of comity in observing that, because defendant's "Bulova" registration had already been cancelled in Mexican proceedings, there was "no conflict which might afford petitioner a pretext that such relief would impugn foreign law." 344 U.S. at 289. Can the principle behind this observation, that domestic laws may be applied extraterritorially if application produces no conflict with foreign law, properly be applied to control conduct in pirate havens that, though having no substantial markets of their own, effectively flood foreign markets with goods made through infringing activities? In *RJR Nabisco*, Justice Alito observed that "[a]lthough a risk of conflict between the American statute and a foreign law is not a prerequisite for applying the presumption against extraterritoriality, where such a risk is evident, the need to enforce the presumption is at its apex." 136 S.Ct. at 2107.

PROBLEM 1

Your client, E-Journal Publishing (EJP), publishes *E-Journal*, an Internet news magazine with 200,000 subscribers around the world. EJP is based in Cambridge, Massachusetts, where the 25–30 news articles for each issue are loaded onto EJP's server located there. Subscriptions to *E-Journal* are free and the company derives its revenues from advertising placed in a 1″ frame surrounding each page of text as it appears on the computer screen; the logo, "*E-Journal,*" appears in the center of each frame. Computer software developed for EJP enables subscribers to flip through "pages" of *E-Journal* in a manner comparable to browsing a hard copy magazine. The software is the subject of a United States patent owned by EJP. No patent for the software has issued in any other country.

X-Journal S.A. (XSA), a French company based in Marseilles where it maintains its web server, provides a free news service, *X-Journal*, to subscribers around the world. *X-Journal* has no original content of its own. Rather, a subscriber will use links provided at the *X-Journal* website to sample the contents of dozens of web-based news journals such as *E-Journal*. When an *X-Journal* subscriber clicks on links to the *E-Journal* site, she sees the full editorial contents of the then-current issue of *E-Journal*; however, the advertising content and *E-Journal* logo in the 1″ border surrounding each *E-Journal* page are automatically replaced with advertising secured by XSA. The *X-Journal* link effectively interoperates with the patented *E-Journal* browsing feature and provides this feature's full functionality to *X-Journal* subscribers.

EJP would like to take legal action against XSA, but at this point does not want to engage in litigation outside the United States or to pay for research on foreign law. Please advise EJP on its rights, if any, against XSA under U.S. law.

2. NATIONAL TREATMENT

The national treatment principle, embodied in all the major intellectual property conventions as well as in the TRIPs Agreement, is a rule of nondiscrimination, promising foreign intellectual property owners that they will enjoy in a protecting country at least the same treatment as the protecting country gives to its own nationals. In Stephen Ladas's phrase, national treatment provides for "the complete assimilation of foreigners to nationals, without condition of reciprocity." Stephen P. Ladas, 1 The International Protection of Literary and Artistic Property 365 (1938). So, for example, since the Paris Convention for the Protection of Industrial Property imposes a national treatment obligation on its adherents, and since both Switzerland and the United States are parties to the Convention, a Swiss inventor will receive patent protection in the United States on the same terms as a U.S. inventor.

The terms in which intellectual property treaties formulate the national treatment rule vary. Article 5(1) of the Berne Convention, 1971 Paris Text, provides that authors shall enjoy in protecting countries "the rights which their respective laws do now or may hereafter grant to their nationals, as well as the rights specially granted by this Convention." The Paris Convention for the Protection of Industrial Property, as revised at Stockholm in 1967, provides in Article 2(1) that "[n]ationals of any country of the Union shall, as regards the protection of industrial property, enjoy in all the other countries of the Union the advantages that their respective laws now grant, or may hereafter grant, to nationals; all without prejudice to the rights specially provided for by this Convention. Consequently, they shall have the same protection as the latter, and the same legal remedy against any infringement of their rights, provided that the conditions and formalities imposed upon nationals are complied with."

The TRIPs Agreement, which builds on the foundation of existing intellectual property treaties, provides in Article 3(1) that "[e]ach Member shall accord to the nationals of other Members treatment no less favourable than that it accords to its own nationals with regard to the protection of intellectual property, subject to the exceptions already provided in, respectively, the Paris Convention (1967), the Berne Convention (1971), the Rome Convention and the Treaty on Intellectual Property in Respect of Integrated Circuits."

Advances in technology sometimes present hard challenges for the national treatment principle. Doubt may arise whether a new form of creative production is a "work" under the Berne Convention, "industrial property" under the Paris Convention, or "intellectual property" under the TRIPs Agreement, obligating one treaty member to extend to nationals of another treaty member the same protection that it gives to its own nationals. So, for example, it required extended debate before a consensus emerged that computer programs should be treated as literary works within the terms of the Berne Convention. Similarly, some authorities once viewed the then-new technology of sound recordings as musical adaptations, and thus entitled to national treatment under the terms of the Berne Convention; more recent commentary and practice hold that sound recordings are (not) "works" subject to the national treatment obligation. Consequently, unless it is obligated to give national treatment to right holders with regard to sound recordings under another international treaty, Country A, a Berne Union member, is free to extend sound recording protection to its own nationals while denying protection to nationals of Country B, another Berne member, even though Country B extends copyright protection to sound recordings that originate in Country A.

The Paris Convention nowhere defines the pivotal term, "industrial property," and in Article 1(2) refers only to the "object" of industrial property protection—for example, patents, industrial designs and trademarks. The treaty states in Article 1(3) that "[i]ndustrial property shall be understood in the broadest sense. . . ." (The original 1883 text of the Paris Convention was more explicit: "The subjects or citizens of each contracting state shall, as regards patents, industrial designs, trademarks and trade names, enjoy the advantages that their respective laws now grant, or may hereafter grant, to nationals.") Is a law that protects semiconductor chips an "industrial property" law for purposes of the national treatment obligation? Even though this subject matter may fall substantively within the category of industrial design referred to in Article 1(2) of the Paris Convention, the United States Congress evidently thought not when it passed the Semiconductor Chip Protection Act of 1984 imposing reciprocity as a condition to protection for foreign semiconductor chip designs.

New technological means for exploiting creative works may also raise questions for one or more of the "rights" contemplated by the Berne Convention's national treatment provision, the "advantages" envisioned by the Paris Convention, or the "protection" contemplated by the TRIPs Agreement. Government grants and other direct and indirect subsidies to authors clearly fall outside the Berne Convention because they differ structurally from the "rights" contemplated by Article 5(1), with the result that a country will not be obligated to make such grants available to foreign authors. However, other remuneration systems, such as the public lending right for libraries and home taping levies that compensate musical composers for the private copying of their works, come closer to the traditional contours of copyright and raise the question whether a Berne member country is free to deny revenues from these royalty systems to nationals of other Berne Union countries.

Bibliographic Note. On the question of national treatment, see The Principle of National Treatment in International Economic Law: Trade, Investment and Intellectual Property (Anselm Kamperman Sanders ed., 2014); Peter Burger, The New Photocopy Remuneration Provisions in the Federal Republic of Germany and their Application to Foreign Authors Under International Copyright Law, 19 IIC 319, 448 (1988); Walter Dillenz, The Remuneration for Home Taping and the Principle of National Treatment, 26 Copyright 186 (1990); Elizabeth Steup, The Rule of National Treatment for Foreigners and its Application to New Benefits for Authors, 25 Bull. Copr. Soc'y. 279, 287 (1978); David Vaver, The National Treatment Requirements of the Berne and Universal Copyright Conventions (pts. 1 & 2), 17 IIC 577, 715 (1986).

Phil Collins v. Imtrat Handelsgesellschaft mbH

Court of Justice of the European Communities, 1993.
Joined cases C-92/92 and C-326/92.

Judgment

1   By order of 4 March 1992, received at the Court on the following 23 March and registered under number C-92/92, the Landgericht München I (Regional Court Munich I) referred to the Court for a preliminary ruling under Article 177 of the EEC Treaty two questions on the interpretation of the first paragraph of Article 7 of the EEC Treaty.

2   By order of 30 April 1992, received at the Court on the following 30 July and registered under number C-326/92, the Bundesgerichtshof (Federal Supreme Court) also referred to the Court for a preliminary ruling under Article 177 of the Treaty two questions on the interpretation of that same provision.

3   The questions which the Landgericht München I submitted in Case C-92/92 were raised in proceedings between Phil Collins, singer and composer of British nationality, and a phonogram distributer, Imtrat Handelsgesellschaft mbH ('Imtrat'), relating to the marketing, in Germany, of a compact disk containing the recording, made without the singer's consent, of a concert given in the United States.

4   According to Paragraphs 96(1) and 125(1) of the German Copyright Act of 9 September 1965 (Urheberrechtsgesetz, hereinafter 'the UrhG') performing artists who have German nationality enjoy the protection granted by Paragraphs 73 to 84 of the UrhG in respect of all their performances. In particular, they may prohibit the distribution of those performances which are reproduced without their permission, irrespective of the place of performance. In contrast, the effect of the provisions of Paragraph 125(2) to (6) of the UrhG, relating to foreign performers, as interpreted by the Bundesgerichtshof and the Bundesverfassungsgericht (Federal Constitutional Court), is that those performers cannot avail themselves of the provisions of Paragraph 96(1), where the performance was given outside Germany.

[handwritten: ECJ European + Court Jur]

5   Phil Collins applied to the Landgericht München I for an interim injunction prohibiting the marketing of the compact disk in question. The national court considered that the provisions of Paragraph 125 of the UrhG were applicable to the proceedings, to the exclusion, in particular, of the terms of the international Rome Convention of 26 October 1961 for the Protection of Performers, Producers of Phonograms and Broadcasting Organizations (Treaties Series, volume 496, No 7247), to which the United States, where the performance had taken place, had not acceded. It questioned, however, the conformity of those national provisions with the principle of non-discrimination laid down by the first paragraph of Article 7 of the [EEC] Treaty.

[handwritten margin note: Rome Convent.]

[handwritten margin note: US not a Rome country, so under Rome Convent., Germany doesn't have to enforce (?)]

6   In those circumstances, the Landgericht München I stayed the proceedings and referred the following questions to the Court for a preliminary ruling:

    '1.   Is copyright law subject to the prohibition of discrimination laid down in the first Paragraph of Article 7 of the EEC Treaty?

    2.   If so: does that have the (directly applicable) effect that a Member State which accords protection to its nationals for all their artistic performances, irrespective of the place of performance, also has to accord that protection to nationals of other Member States, or is it compatible with the first paragraph of Article 7 to attach further conditions (i.e. Paragraph 125(2) to (6) of the German Urheberrechtsgesetz of 9 September 1965) to the grant of protection to nationals of other Member States?'

[handwritten margin note: was there in fact discrimination?]

[handwritten margin note: Is Phil Collins entitled to invoke that principle of nondiscrimination?]

[handwritten margin note: Is this notion directly applicable]

[The Court's summary of case 326/92 is omitted.]

The subject-matter of the references for a preliminary ruling

[handwritten: EEC Treaty]

13   In proceedings under Article 177 of the Treaty the Court may rule neither on the interpretation of national laws or regulations nor on the conformity of such measures with Community law. Consequently, it may neither interpret the provisions of the UrhG nor may it assess their conformity with Community law. The Court may only provide the national court with criteria for interpretation based on Community law which will enable that court to solve the legal problem with which it is faced. . . .

[handwritten margin note: He can invoke non-discrimination provision of Article VII b/c he is an EU resident]

14   The orders for reference mention the national rules applicable to copyright, and also Paragraph 125 of the UrhG which governs the rights of performers, known as 'rights related to copyright'. It is not for the Court to determine within which of those two categories of rights the disputes in the main proceedings fall. As the Commission has proposed, the questions referred to the Court should be regarded as relating to the rules which apply to both of those categories of rights.

15   Those questions concern the first paragraph of Article 7 of the Treaty which lays down the general principle of non-discrimination on the

grounds of nationality. As is expressly provided in that paragraph, the prohibition of discrimination contained in it applies only within the scope of application of the Treaty.

16   The questions referred to the Court must accordingly be regarded as seeking, essentially, to ascertain:

— whether copyright and related rights fall within the scope of application of the Treaty within the meaning of the first paragraph of Article 7, and consequently, if the general principle of non-discrimination laid down by that article applies to those rights;

— if so, whether the first paragraph of Article 7 of the Treaty precludes the legislation of a Member State from denying to authors or performers from other Member States, and those claiming under them, the right, accorded by that legislation to the nationals of that State, to prohibit the marketing, in its national territory, of a phonogram manufactured without their consent, where the performance was given outside its national territory;

— whether the first paragraph of Article 7 of the Treaty may be directly relied upon before a national court by an author or performer from another Member State, or by those claiming under them, in order to claim the benefit of the protection reserved to nationals.

The application of the provisions of the Treaty to copyright and related rights

17   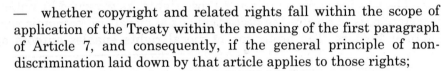The Commission, the German Government, the United Kingdom, Phil Collins and EMI Electrola maintain that copyright and related rights, inasmuch as they constitute, in particular, economic rights which determine the conditions in which an artist's works and performances may be exploited in return for payment, fall within the scope of application of the Treaty; this, they maintain, is apparent, moreover, from the judgments of the Court in which Articles 30, 36, 59, 85 and 86 of the Treaty were applied to those rights, and also from the intense legislative activity of which those rights are the subject within the Communities. On the rare occasions where a specific provision of the Treaty does not apply, the general principle of non-discrimination laid down by the first paragraph of Article 7 of the Treaty, must, in any event, do so.

18   Imtrat maintains, to the contrary, that the conditions for the grant of copyright and related rights, which concern the existence, and not the exercise, of those rights, do not, according to Article 222 of the Treaty and well-established case law of the Court, fall within the scope of application of the Treaty. Taking up the findings of the Bundesgerichtshof on that point, Patricia and Mr. Kraul submit in particular that at the material time in the main proceedings copyright and related rights were not, in the absence of Community rules or harmonization measures, governed by Community law.

19 As Community law now stands, and in the absence of Community provisions harmonizing national laws, it is for the Member States to establish the conditions and detailed rules for the protection of literary and artistic property, subject to observance of the applicable international conventions. . . .

20 The specific subject-matter of those rights, as governed by national legislation, is to ensure the protection of the moral and economic rights of their holders. The protection of moral rights enables authors and performers, in particular, to object to any distortion, mutilation or other modification of a work which would be prejudicial to their honour or reputation. Copyright and related rights are also economic in nature, in that they confer the right to exploit commercially the marketing of the protected work, particularly in the form of licences granted in return for payment of royalties (*see* the judgment in Joined Cases 55/80 and 57/80 *Musik-Vertrieb membran v GEMA* [1981] ECR 147, paragraph 12).

21 As the Court pointed out in the last-mentioned judgment (paragraph 13), whilst the commercial exploitation of copyright is a source of remuneration for the owner, it also constitutes a form of control of marketing, exercisable by the owner, the copyright management societies and the grantees of licences. From this point of view, the commercial exploitation of copyright raises the same problems as does the commercial exploitation of any other industrial and commercial property right.

Answer to Q1

22 Like the other industrial and commercial property rights, the exclusive rights conferred by literary and artistic property are by their nature such as to affect trade in goods and services and also competitive relationships within the Community. For that reason, and as the Court has consistently held, those rights, although governed by national legislation, are subject to the requirements of the Treaty and therefore fall within its scope of application.

Court's reasons to Q.3 on 18 PJ

23 Thus they are subject, for example, to the provisions of Articles 30 and 36 of the Treaty relating to the free movement of goods. According to the case-law of the Court, musical works are incorporated into phonograms which constitute goods the trade in which, within the Community, is governed by the above provisions. . . .

24 Furthermore, the activities of copyright management societies are subject to the provisions of Articles 59 and 66 of the Treaty relating to the freedom to provide services. As the Court stated in its judgment in Case 7/82 *GVL v. Commission* [1983] ECR 483, paragraph 39, those activities should not be conducted in such a way as to impede the free movement of services, and particularly the exploitation of performers' rights, to the extent of partitioning the common market.

25 Finally, the exclusive rights conferred by literary and artistic property are subject to the provisions of the Treaty relating to competition. . . .

26   It is, moreover, precisely in order to avoid the risk of hindrances to trade and the distortion of competition that the Council has, since the disputes in the main proceedings arose, adopted Directive 92/100/EEC of 19 November 1992 on rental right and lending right and on certain rights related to copyright in the field of intellectual property, on the basis of Article 57(2) and Articles 66 and 100a of the Treaty. . . .

27   It follows that copyright and related rights, which by reason in particular of their effects on intra-Community trade in goods and services, fall within the scope of application of the Treaty, are necessarily subject to the general principle of non-discrimination laid down by the first paragraph of Article 7 of the Treaty, without there even being any need to connect them with the specific provisions of Articles 30, 36, 59 and 66 of the Treaty.

28   Accordingly, it should be stated in reply to the question put to the Court that copyright and related rights fall within the scope of application of the Treaty within the meaning of the first paragraph of Article 7; the general principle of non-discrimination laid down by that article therefore applies to those rights.

Discrimination within the meaning of the first paragraph of Article 7 of the Treaty

29   Imtrat and Patricia maintain that the differentiation which is made between German nationals and nationals of the other Member States in the cases referred to it by the national courts is objectively justified by the disparities which exist between national laws and by the fact that not all Member States have yet acceded to the Rome Convention. That differentiation is not, in those circumstances, contrary to the first paragraph of Article 7 of the Treaty.

30   It is undisputed that Article 7 is not concerned with any disparities in treatment or the distortions which may result, for the persons and undertakings subject to the jurisdiction of the Community, from divergences existing between the laws of the various Member States, so long as those laws affect all persons subject to them, in accordance with objective criteria and without regard to their nationality. . . .

31   Thus, contrary to what Imtrat and Patricia maintain, neither the disparities between the national laws relating to the protection of copyright and related rights nor the fact that not all Member States have yet acceded to the Rome Convention can justify a breach of the principle of non-discrimination laid down by the first paragraph of Article 7 of the Treaty.

32   In prohibiting 'any discrimination on the grounds of nationality', Article 7 of the Treaty requires, on the contrary, that persons in a situation governed by Community law be placed on a completely equal footing with nationals of the Member State concerned. . . . In so far as that principle is applicable, it therefore precludes a Member State from

making the grant of an exclusive right subject to the requirement that the person concerned be a national of that State.

33 Accordingly, it should be stated in reply to the question put to the Court that the first paragraph of Article 7 of the Treaty must be interpreted as precluding legislation of a Member State from denying, in certain circumstances, to authors and performers from other Member States, and those claiming under them, the right, accorded by that legislation the nationals of that State, to prohibit the marketing, in its national territory of a phonogram manufactured without their consent, where the performance was given outside its national territory.

The effects of the first paragraph of Article 7 of the Treaty

34 The Court has consistently held that the right to equal treatment laid down by the first paragraph of Article 7 of the Treaty, is conferred directly by Community law. . . . That right may, therefore, be relied upon before a national court as the basis for a request that it disapply the discriminatory provisions of a national law which denies to nationals of other Member States the protection which they accord to nationals of the State concerned.

35 Accordingly, it should be stated in reply to the question put to the Court that the first paragraph of Article 7 of the Treaty should be interpreted as meaning that the principle of non-discrimination which it lays down may be directly relied upon before a national court by an author or performer from another Member State, or by those claiming under them, in order to claim the benefit of protection reserved to national authors and performers. . . .

NOTES

1. *The Phil Collins Decision: Effect on Obligations Under International Intellectual Property Treaties.* Article 7 of the 1961 Convention for the Protection of Performers, Producers of Phonograms and Broadcasting Organizations, commonly called the Rome Convention, requires member countries to protect performers against the unauthorized fixation of their performances. Germany, though a party to the Rome Convention, was under no obligation to extend this protection to Collins (a national of Great Britain, another party to the Rome Convention) in the case above because, while Article 4 of the Convention requires contracting states to grant national treatment to performers for performances that take place in other countries that are parties to the Convention, the Collins performance in issue occurred in the United States, which is not a party to the Rome Convention. Would the result have been different if Germany protected performances not under neighboring rights but under copyright, for which the governing treaties require reference only to the country of domicile or of publication?

In the view of one leading scholar, the *Phil Collins* decision "has had the effect of a landslide in international copyright." Herman Cohen Jehoram, The Law of the European Community and Copyright, in Paul Edward Geller, (ed.), International Copyright Law and Practice § 1[2][e][iii] (1995). One effect of the decision is presumably to bar European Union countries from relying on certain exceptions carved out from the national treatment obligation imposed by intellectual property treaties.

Does the TRIPs Agreement's most-favored nation provision give *Phil Collins* a comparable impact *outside* the European Union? *See* note 5, below.

2. *TRIPs and National Treatment.* Article 3(1) of the TRIPs Agreement requires each member to "accord to the nationals of other Members treatment no less favourable than it accords to its own nationals with regard to the protection of intellectual property." Article 1(2) defines "intellectual property" for these purposes as the categories encompassed by the Agreement—copyright and related rights, trademarks, geographical indications, industrial designs, patents, integrated circuit topographies and undisclosed information, or trade secrets. A footnote to Article 3 adds that "'protection' shall include matters affecting the availability, acquisition, scope, maintenance and enforcement of intellectual property rights as well as those matters affecting the use of intellectual property rights specifically addressed in this Agreement."

Article 3(1) subjects its national treatment obligation to the exceptions already provided in the Paris, Berne and Rome Conventions and the Treaty on Intellectual Property in Respect of Integrated Circuits. The provision would, for example, permit WTO members to require material reciprocity as a condition to protection for the resale royalty right under Article 14*ter* of the Berne Convention. Would it allow WTO members to require material reciprocity as a condition to protection for nonoriginal collections of data in databases? *See* TRIPs Article 9(2) excepting certain elements from copyright protection and Article 39 defining the scope of trade secret protection; Berne Article 2 defining the scope of copyright subject matter; and Article 10*bis* of the Paris Convention dealing with unfair competition.

3. *What Law Characterizes Protected Subject Matter and Rights for Purposes of National Treatment?* If, for purposes of its own nationals, Country *A* defines particular intellectual property rights or subject matter as falling within the rights or subject matter covered by an applicable treaty, while Country *B,* another treaty party, does not, is Country *A* obligated to extend national treatment respecting these rights or subject matter to nationals of Country *B*? The United States Copyright Act characterizes sound recordings as copyrightable works (even though they are not literary or artistic works under the Berne Convention) while France does not. Must the United States extend copyright protection to sound recordings of French nationals, even though it could have legitimately avoided this result, as did France, by protecting sound recordings under discrete neighboring rights legislation, separate from copyright?

Under one view, "[a] state that defines works more broadly than required under the RBC [Revised Berne Convention] is neither obliged nor entitled by the RBC to extend national treatment for these works, nor is it obliged or entitled to claim national treatment for these in another RBC state." David Vaver, The National Treatment Requirements of the Berne and Universal Copyright Conventions, 17 IIC 577, 591 (1986). Under the opposing view, "it devolves solely upon the national jurisdiction of that country of protection to decide whether or not specific products originating from a person's intellectual creation are to be regarded as 'literary or artistic works' within the meaning of the law of the country of protection. If they are to be so regarded, then the country of protection is *obliged* to grant national treatment to the authors from other member countries of the Convention; for they enjoy, according to Article 5(1) of the Berne Convention (Paris Act) in all countries 'the rights which their respective laws do now or may hereafter grant to their nationals,' and according to Article II of the UCC (Paris Act) the 'same protection' as the national of the country of protection." Wilhelm Nordemann, The Principle of National Treatment and the Definition of Literary and Artistic Works, 25 Copyright 300, 301 (1989).

4. *The Trade Economics of National Treatment.* For purposes of its own economic well-being, why would Country *A* pass a law that surpasses an intellectual property treaty's minimum standards on rights, remedies or subject matter if national treatment obligates it to give this same level of protection to authors from Country *B*, when Country *B* will give authors from Country *A* no more than the same minimum treaty level of protection that it gives to its own authors?

In the case of a country that is a substantial net exporter of intellectual goods, granting higher than minimum levels of intellectual property protection may help to ensure the continued abundant production of the copyrighted goods that generate its export revenues. Also, where the difference between levels of protection offered in exporting and importing countries is narrow, but the imbalance in world intellectual property trade is great, the net intellectual property exporter can expect its total revenues, even from countries adhering only to minimum standards, to more than offset the revenues it sends to net importing countries.

Why would a country that is a net *importer* of intellectual goods exceed the minimum required levels of protection or, for that matter, even decide to adhere to the treaty? One answer may be that the community of interest that exists between intellectual property owners in both net export and net import countries can overcome political and economic arguments based on the intellectual property balance of trade. It was, for example, an alliance of interests between British and American publishers that led to the first initiatives in 1891 to protect foreign works under United States copyright. *See* James Barnes, Authors, Publishers, and Politicians: The Quest for an Anglo-American Copyright Agreement, 1815–1854 (1974).

5. *Most-Favored Nation Treatment.* The most-favored nation obligation, embodied in Article 4 of the TRIPs Agreement, closely parallels the national treatment obligation. Where national treatment bars a member state from treating the nationals of other member states less favorably than it treats its own nationals, the most-favored nation obligation bars a member state from treating the nationals of other member states less favorably than it treats the nationals of any other country (including a non-WTO member country).

As a practical matter, compliance with the national treatment requirement will in most cases duplicate the effects of compliance with the most-favored nation obligation. However, there are differences. For example, national treatment under the Paris Convention bars a country from unilaterally insisting on reciprocity, but does not exclude the possibility that the country will secure reciprocity through a separate agreement under Article 19 of the Convention. As a rule, the most-favored nation principle of TRIPs Article 4 would effectively block such exclusive bilateral or multilateral intellectual property agreements by requiring that their benefits be conferred on all WTO members.

Historically, the most favored nation principle has been a feature of trade agreements, not intellectual property agreements, and the TRIPs Agreement represented the first time that it has been included in a multilateral intellectual property agreement. The innovation may have unforeseen consequences. After the *Phil Collins* decision, does Article 4 of the TRIPs Agreement require a member country of the European Union to extend to nationals of all TRIPs partners the same treatment that the Court of Justice has said the EU law requires it to extend to nationals of other European Union countries? Does Article 4(d) of the TRIPs Agreement support or reject such a result?

See generally, Herman Cohen Jehoram, The E.C. Copyright Directives, Economics and Author's Rights, 25 IIC 821, 827 (1994); Paul Katzenberger, TRIPs and Traditional International Copyright Conventions, in Freidrich-Karl Beier & Gerhard Schricker, (eds.), From GATT to TRIPs 59, 78–79 (1996).

6. *The Principle of Non-Discrimination.* The Treaty Establishing the European Economic Community (the EEC Treaty in the *Phil Collins* decision), one of the founding treaties of the European Union, since replaced by newer EU treaties, is not the only international treaty that includes a provision on non-discrimination; human rights treaties typically also provide for non-discrimination. For example, Article 7 of the Universal Declaration of Human Rights (1948) states that "[a]ll are equal before the law and are entitled without any discrimination to equal protection of the law." Does the principle of non-discrimination embodied in human rights treaties apply to intellectual property rights? Article 17 of the Universal Declaration of Human Rights mandates that countries ensure that "everyone has the right to own property" and that "no one shall be arbitrarily deprived of his property."

See Silke von Lewinski, Intellectual Property, Nationality, and Non-Discrimination, a document prepared for the Panel Discussion to Commemorate the 50th Anniversary of the Universal Declaration of Human Rights, 1998. For the current non-discrimination provisions of the European Union see Article 18 of the Treaty on the Functioning of the European Union and Article 21 of the Charter of Fundamental Rights of the European Union. On the intersection of human rights and intellectual property see, generally, Research Handbook on Human Rights and Intellectual Property (Christophe Geiger ed. 2015); Ruth L. Okediji, Intellectual Property in the Image of Human Rights: A Critical Review, in Framing Intellectual Property Law in the 21st Century 234 (Rochelle Cooper Dreyfuss & Elizabeth Siew-Kuan Ng eds., 2018).

3. CHOICE OF FORUM AND CHOICE OF LAW

a. CHOICE OF FORUM

London Film Productions Ltd. v. Intercontinental Communications, Inc.

United States District Court, Southern District of New York, 1984.
580 F.Supp. 47, 223 U.S.P.Q. 381.

CARTER, DISTRICT JUDGE.

This case presents a novel question of law. Plaintiff, London Film Productions, Ltd. ("London"), a British corporation, has sued Intercontinental Communications, Inc. ("ICI"), a New York corporation based in New York City, for infringements of plaintiff's British copyright. The alleged infringements occurred in Chile and other South American countries. In bringing the case before this Court, plaintiff has invoked the Court's diversity jurisdiction. 28 U.S.C. § 1332(a)(2). Defendant has moved to dismiss plaintiff's complaint, arguing that the Court should abstain from exercising jurisdiction over this action.

British P

US D

Background

London produces feature motion pictures in Great Britain, which it then distributes throughout the world.[1] ICI specializes in the licensing of motion pictures, produced by others, that it believes are in the public domain. London's copyright infringement claim is based mainly on license agreements between ICI and Dilatsa S.A., a buying agent for Chilean television stations. The agreements apparently granted the latter the right to distribute and exhibit certain of plaintiff's motion pictures on television in Chile. London also alleges that ICI has marketed several of its motion pictures in Venezuela, Peru, Equador, Costa Rica and Panama, as well as in Chile.

p's claim basis

what D did

Plaintiff alleges that the films that are the subjects of the arrangements between Dilatsa S.A. and defendant are protected by copyright in Great Britain as well as in Chile and most other countries (but not in the United States) by virtue of the terms and provisions of the Berne Convention. The license agreements, it maintains, have unjustly enriched defendants and deprived plaintiff of the opportunity to market its motion pictures for television use.

unjust enrichment

Defendant questions this Court's jurisdiction because plaintiff has not alleged any acts of wrongdoing on defendant's part that constitute

D's position

---

[1]   These include: "The Private Life of Henry VIII," "Things To Come," and "Jungle Book," all of which are subjects of this suit.

[2]   The Berne Convention is a shorthand designation for the "International Union for the Protection of Literary and Artistic Works", signed in Berne, Switzerland on September 9, 1886, as amended. Chile adhered to the Convention on June 5, 1970, but the United States has never become a party thereto. . . . (The United States acceded to the Berne Convention effective March 1, 1989. *Ed.*).

violations of United States law,[3] and, therefore, defendant claims that this Court lacks a vital interest in the suit. In addition, assuming jurisdiction, defendant argues that because the Court would have to construe "alien treaty rights," with which it has no familiarity, the suit would violate, in principle, the doctrine of *forum non conveniens*. In further support of this contention, defendant maintains that the law would not only be foreign, but complex, since plaintiff's claims would have to be determined with reference to each of the South American states in which the alleged copyright infringements occurred.

Determination

There seems to be no dispute that plaintiff has stated a valid cause of action under the copyright laws of a foreign country. Also clear is the fact that this Court has personal jurisdiction over defendant; in fact, there is no showing that defendant may be subject to personal jurisdiction in another forum. Under these circumstances, one authority on copyright law has presented an argument pursuant to which this Court has jurisdiction to hear the matter before it. M. Nimmer, 3 *Nimmer on Copyright* (1982). It is based on the theory that copyright infringement constitutes a transitory cause of action, . . . and hence may be adjudicated in the courts of a sovereign other than the one in which the cause of action arose. . . . That theory appears sound in the absence of convincing objections by defendant to the contrary.

Although plaintiff has not alleged the violation of any laws of this country by defendant, this Court is not bereft of interest in this case. The Court has an obvious interest in securing compliance with this nation's laws by citizens of foreign nations who have dealings within this jurisdiction. A concern with the conduct of American citizens in foreign countries is merely the reciprocal of that interest. An unwillingness by this Court to hear a complaint against its own citizens with regard to a violation of foreign law will engender, it would seem, a similar unwillingness on the part of a foreign jurisdiction when the question arises concerning a violation of our laws by one of its citizens who has since left our jurisdiction. This Court's interest in adjudicating the controversy in this case may be indirect, but its importance is not thereby diminished.

Of course, not every violation of foreign law by a citizen of this country must be afforded a local tribunal, and defendants cite several cases in which, basically under general principles of comity, it would be inappropriate for this Court to exercise its jurisdiction. . . . This is not one of those. The line of cases on which defendants rely can be distinguished on significant points. The Court in *Vanity Fair Mills, Inc. v. T. Eaton Co.*, 234 F.2d 633 (2d Cir. 1956) cert. denied, 352 U.S. 871, 1 L.Ed. 2d 76, 77 S.Ct. 96 (1956), the principal case of those cited, found that the district

---

[3]   The films named, although formerly subject to United States copyrights, are no longer so subject.

court had not abused its discretion in declining to assume jurisdiction over a claim for acts of alleged trademark infringement and unfair competition arising in Canada under Canadian law. As defendant here has acknowledged, the complaint raised a "crucial issue" as to the validity of Canadian trademark law. This factor weighed heavily in the Court's decision.

> We do not think it the province of United States district courts to determine the validity of trademarks which officials of foreign countries have seen fit to grant. To do so would be to welcome conflicts with the administrative and judicial officers of the Dominion Canada.

Id. at 647. But as Nimmer has noted, "[i]n adjudicating an infringement action under a foreign copyright law there is . . . no need to pass upon the validity of acts of foreign government officials," 3 Nimmer, *supra* at § 1703, since foreign copyright laws, by and large, do not incorporate administrative formalities which must be satisfied to create or perfect a copyright. *Id.*

The facts in this case confirm the logic of Nimmer's observation. The British films at issue here received copyright protection in Great Britain simply by virtue of publication there. . . . Chile's adherence to the Berne Convention in 1970 automatically conferred copyright protection on these films in Chile. Therefore, no "act of state" is called into question here. Moreover, there is no danger that foreign courts will be forced to accept the inexpert determination of this Court, nor that this Court will create "an unseemly conflict with the judgment of another country." *See Packard Instrument Co. v. Beckman Instruments, Inc.*, 346 F. Supp. 408, 410 (N.D.Ill. 1972). The litigation will determine only whether an American corporation has acted in violation of a foreign copyright, not whether such copyright exists, nor whether such copyright is valid.[5]

With respect to defendant's *forum non conveniens* argument, it is true that this case will likely involve the construction of at least one, if not several foreign laws.[6] However, the need to apply foreign law is not in itself reason to dismiss or transfer the case. . . . Moreover, there is no foreign forum in which defendant is the subject of personal jurisdiction, and an available forum is necessary to validate dismissal of an action on

---

[5]   It should also be noted that application of foreign law in this jurisdiction creates no conflicts in public policy with our own laws. . . . Although the United States is not a party to the multilateral copyright treaty known as the Berne Convention, American nationals obtain copyright protection under foreign laws by virtue of the Universal Copyright Convention. The principle of the U.C.C. is the same as that of the Berne Convention. Under both treaties "an author who is a national of one of the member states . . . or one who publishes his work in any such member state, is entitled to the same copyright protection in each other member state as such other state accords its own nationals." 3 Nimmer, *supra* at § 12.05. (The United States adhered to the Berne Convention, effective March 1, 1989. *Ed.*).

[6]   Plaintiff has alleged infringements in Chile, Venezuela, Peru, Ecuador, Costa Rica and Panama. Since, under the Berne Convention, the applicable law is the copyright law of the state in which the infringement occurred, defendant seems correct in its assumption that the laws of several countries will be involved in the case. 3 Nimmer, *supra* at § 17.05.

the ground of *forum non conveniens*, for if there is no alternative forum "the plaintiff might find himself with a valid claim but nowhere to assert it." *Farmanfarmaian v. Gulf Oil Corp.*, 437 F. Supp. 910, 915 (S.D.N.Y. 1977) (Carter, J.), aff'd, 588 F.2d 880 (2d Cir. 1978).

While this Court might dismiss this action subject to conditions that would assure the plaintiff of a fair hearing, ... neither plaintiff nor defendant has demonstrated the relative advantage in convenience that another forum, compared to this one, would provide. ... The selection of a South American country as an alternative forum, although it would afford greater expertise in applying relevant legal principles, would seem to involve considerable hardship and inconvenience for both parties. A British forum might similarly provide some advantages in the construction of relevant law, however, it would impose additional hardships upon defendant, and would raise questions, as would the South American forum, regarding enforceability of a resulting judgment. ... Where the balance does not tip strongly in favor of an alternative forum it is well-established that the plaintiff's choice of forum should not be disturbed.

For all of the above reasons, the Court finds it has jurisdiction over the instant case and defendant's motion to dismiss is denied, as is its motion to have the Court abstain from exercising its jurisdiction here. ...

IT IS SO ORDERED.

NOTES

1.   *Justiciability*. If intellectual property rights are territorial and countries must afford national treatment, is it appropriate for courts to decide a party's rights or liabilities under foreign intellectual property laws? Some but not all U.S. courts have followed *London Film* when deciding whether foreign copyright infringements are justiciable in U.S. courts. One court remarked that "American courts should be reluctant to enter the bramble bush of ascertaining and applying foreign law without an urgent reason to do so." ITSI T.V. Productions, Inc. v. California Authority of Racing Fairs, 785 F.Supp. 854, 866 (E.D.Ca. 1992), *rev'd on other grounds* 3 F.3d 1289 (9th Cir. 1993).

In Lucasfilm Ltd. v. Ainsworth, [2011] UKSC 39, [2011] 3 WLR 487 (U.K. Supreme Court, 2011), the question of justiciability in the United Kingdom of a copyright infringement claim under a foreign law became particularly pressing because the answer determined whether the plaintiffs had any remedy at all. The plaintiffs had secured a judgment against the English defendants in the United States where a court found copyright infringement under the U.S. Copyright Act. However, when the plaintiffs asked an English court to recognize and enforce the U.S. judgment against the English defendants, the English court refused to do so (*id.*, ¶ 7; *see* page 84, below, for a discussion of recognition and enforcement of judgments), and additionally held that there could be no copyright infringement under U.K. law because the objects at issue were not protectible under U.K. copyright

The US Plaintiff sued British D in UK court, for Infringement under US copyright law

law (*id.*, ¶ 49). The plaintiffs then requested that the English court adjudicate copyright infringement under U.S. law. The U.K. Supreme Court held that a claim of infringement of copyright under U.S. law was justiciable in the United Kingdom. *Id.*, ¶ 105. *oyay*

2. *The Transitory Cause of Action.* Under the old English common law rule courts had no jurisdiction to determine the title to or the right of possession of foreign-located immovable property or to decide actions for trespass to such immovable property; such actions were considered purely "local." Other actions were "transitory," meaning courts could adjudicate the actions even if they concerned claims that were based on foreign laws. Because of the territorial nature of intellectual property rights, courts once considered these rights, particularly registered rights, to have "a definite locality," and therefore claims concerning these rights were also held to be "local" and not "transitory" causes of action. Lucasfilm Ltd. v. Ainsworth, [2011] UKSC 39, [2011] 3 WLR 487 (U.K. Supreme Court, 2011), ¶¶ 54–55, 61, 71–76.

3. *The Act of State Doctrine.* To respect national sovereignty, the act of state doctrine precludes courts from "sit[ting] in judgment on the acts of the government of another done within its own territory." Underhill v. Hernandez, 168 U.S. 250, 252 (1897). Is a grant of a patent an expression of a country's sovereignty that should be protected by the act of state doctrine, or is it a purely ministerial act? *no registration required.*

The court in *London Film* reasoned that copyright actions are transitory because, unlike patent and trademark actions, they do not require a court to second-guess the administrative decisions of a foreign government. Should a registration of copyright with the U.S. Copyright Office trigger the application of the doctrine? In *Lucasfilm* the U.K. Supreme Court conceded that "copyright can involve delicate political issues" but ruled that the concerns over "the maintenance of comity and the avoidance of conflict with foreign jurisdictions" do not bar the justiciability of a claim of copyright infringement under a foreign law. Lucasfilm Ltd. v. Ainsworth, [2011] UKSC 39, [2011] 3 WLR 487 (U.K. Supreme Court, 2011), ¶ 106. The Court also ruled that because registration is not a prerequisite to subsistence of copyright under U.S. law, the act of registration is not protected by the act of state doctrine. *Id.*, ¶ 107. For a discussion of copyright registration requirements see page 211, below. *International Comity doesn't bar justiciability of copyright infringement claim.*

4. *Justiciability of Claims Involving Foreign Patents.* Donald Chisum has observed that "[t]he issue of the validity of a patent—that is, whether the patent defines an invention that is patentable under the applicable legal standards—is frequently raised in infringement litigation in the United States, and assessing validity may involve complex issues of law and fact. Courts assume that similar complexities will arise in assessing the validity of a foreign patent. In fact, such difficulties will not often arise. The *why?* patentability requirements in other countries are usually more straightforward and less dependent on issues of historic fact than those in the United States." Donald Chisum, Normative and Empirical Territoriality for Intellectual Property: Lessons from Patent Law, 37 Va. J. Int'l L. 603, 610–11 (1997). Should the potential complexity of the application of a foreign law be a factor in determining justiciability? Should actions for a declaration of patent invalidity be treated differently from patent infringement actions?

In the European Union, Article 24(4) of the Brussels I Regulation (recast) vests exclusive jurisdiction "in proceedings concerned with the registration or validity of patents, trade marks, designs, or other similar rights required to be deposited or registered" in "the courts of the Member State in which the deposit or registration has been applied for, has taken place or is under the terms of an instrument of the Union or an international convention deemed to have taken place." Regulation (EU) No. 1215/2012 of the European Parliament and of the Council of 12 December 2012 on jurisdiction and the recognition and enforcement of judgments in civil and commercial matters (the "Brussels I Regulation (recast)"), Article 24(4).

In a much-discussed 2006 ruling concerning the interpretation of the predecessor of the Brussels I Regulation (recast), the Court of Justice of the European Communities held that the issuing country has exclusive jurisdiction not only in actions for the declaration of invalidity of a patent but also with regard to any decisions on patent validity, even when the validity issue arises as a defense or counterclaim in a patent infringement action. In the court's view, "to allow, within the scheme of the [Regulation], decisions in which courts other than those of a State in which a particular patent is issued [to] rule indirectly on the validity of that patent would also multiply the risk of conflicting decisions which the [Regulation] seeks specifically to avoid." Gesellschaft für Antriebstechnik mbH & Co. KG v. Lamellen und Kupplungsbau Beteiligungs KG, ECJ, C-4/03, 2006, ¶ 29. The ruling prompted the inclusion in Article 24(4) of the Brussels I Regulation (recast) (and in the corresponding provision of the Lugano II Convention) of a clause according to which the exclusive jurisdiction rule applies "irrespective of whether the issue [of registration or validity] is raised by way of an action or as a defence." Convention on Jurisdiction and the Enforcement of Judgments in Civil and Commercial Matters (the "Lugano II Convention"), Article 22(4).

In Voda v. Cordis Corp., 476 F.3d 887 (Fed.Cir. 2007), the U.S. Court of Appeals for the Federal Circuit reached a comparable result, holding that the Judicial Code's provision for supplemental jurisdiction, 28 U.S.C. § 1367, did not support the district court's exercise of jurisdiction over infringement actions based on British, Canadian, French and German patents, as well as U.S. patents. "[C]onsiderations of comity, judicial economy, convenience, fairness, and other exceptional circumstances constitute compelling reasons to decline jurisdiction under section 1367(c) in this case." 476 F.3d at 898. Although the court characterized the district court's error as an abuse of discretion, its exhaustive catalogue of reasons for denying jurisdiction over foreign patent claims raises the question whether a foreign patent claim could ever be entertained under section 1367.

If courts were to decide the validity of patents granted by foreign countries, what kind of repercussions might be expected? When Dr. Abdullah Ali Bahattab filed suit in Dubai against Juniper Networks, Inc. for infringement of his U.S. patent, Juniper countered by filing a declaratory judgment action in the U.S. District Court for the District of Columbia seeking declarations of invalidity, unenforceability and non-infringement. The U.S. court denied Dr. Bahattab's motion to dismiss because, among other reasons, the court "decline[d] to defer the consideration of the issues related to the [U.S.] patent to a foreign jurisdiction even though the suit in the United Arab Emirates was 'first-filed.' " Juniper Networks, Inc. v. Abdullah Ali Bahattab, 92 U.S.P.Q.2d 1736, 1742 (D.D.C. 2009). The magistrate judge explained that "[b]ecause Dr. Bahattab's suit on a United States patent in the United Arab Emirates is novel—indeed Juniper believes it to be the *first-ever* patent infringement case in that country . . .—and because United States patent law is intended to operate only domestically, it would be imprudent for this Court to decline jurisdiction in favor of a resolution of the validity of a United States patent in a foreign jurisdiction." *Id.*, 1743. Ultimately, however, the Dubai courts did not address the question of patent validity and held, consistently with the U.S. court's decision on the merits, that Juniper did not infringe Mr. Bahattab's U.S. patent. Abdullah Ali Bahattab v. Juniper Networks Middle East, Court of Cassation, Dubai, 2012; Juniper Networks, Inc. v. Bahattab, 2009 WL 1310842 (D.D.C. 2009).

Should a court exercise jurisdiction in a case involving a foreign patent infringement if the case does not require the court to decide on patent validity? In Actavis UK Ltd v. Eli Lilly & Co, [2017] UKSC 48, the U.K. courts ruled on infringements of foreign patents (in this case national designations of a European patent) because the alleged infringer, who brought the case for a declaration of non-infringement, undertook not to challenge patent validity in the U.K. proceedings. In the words of Justice Birss, the decision marked "a significant shift in practice in that it is now clear that there can be situations in which the UK court will hear and determine cross-border patent cases." Eli Lilly & Co v. Genentech Inc., [2017] EWHC 3104 (Pat), ¶ 54. The *Actavis v. Eli Lilly* decision is excerpted on page 555, below. For a French decision on the justiciability of foreign patent infringements when there is no patent validity dispute see Global ATS v. CTP Environment, Tribunal de Grande Instance de Paris, No. 15/06637, 2016.

5. *Forum Non Conveniens*. As a rule, common law jurisdictions will entertain the discretionary stay or dismissal of an intellectual property lawsuit on the ground of *forum non conveniens*. U.K. practice has been a partial exception to the common law rule; although English courts originally formulated the *forum non conveniens* doctrine, EU rules on jurisdiction exclude the defense, with the result that U.K. courts do not apply the doctrine in cases that are subject to EU rules. *See* Owusu v. Jackson, ECJ, C-281/02, 2005; Allianz SpA v. West Tankers, Inc., ECJ, C-185/07, 2009.

The American version of *forum non conveniens* has two requirements. First, a court will dismiss a claim only if the defendant can show that an adequate alternative forum exists to hear the dispute; the defense will fail if the defendant cannot show that it is subject to process in another forum or if the alternative forum would not give the plaintiff a satisfactory remedy. Second, the defendant must show that the balance of private and public interests favors dismissal. Private interest factors include relative access to evidence, availability of process to compel attendance of hostile witnesses, the cost of transporting friendly witnesses, and any other factors affecting a prompt and economical trial. Public interest factors include court congestion, local interest in the controversy, a forum's preference for applying familiar law and avoidance of choice of law problems.

In assessing the availability of an adequate alternative forum, should a U.S. court assume that a foreign court will adjudicate a case under U.S. law, or under a third country's law? Or that a foreign court will apply its own law but grant extraterritorial remedies to cover activities in the United States? In Creative Technology, Ltd. v. Aztech System Pte Ltd., 61 F.3d 696 (9th Cir. 1995), plaintiff and defendant, both Singaporean nationals, manufactured computer sound cards in Singapore, marketing them in the United States through wholly-owned subsidiaries. Plaintiff, which owned the United States copyrights in a series of sound cards, filed suit for infringement in the Northern District of California, alleging the unauthorized manufacture and distribution of clones of its sound cards. The U.S. Court of Appeals for the Ninth Circuit determined that, under the first *forum non conveniens* requirement, Singapore was an adequate alternative forum for the lawsuit because the defendants were amenable to process there and because the Singapore Copyright Act's "lack of extraterritorial reach" should not prevent the High Court of Singapore from applying United States copyright law to plaintiff's claims or "from subsuming the amount of damages incurred by Aztech Labs' alleged illegal distribution of pirated sound cards within the United States in the amount of damages awarded under the Singapore Copyright Act for Aztech's alleged infringing acts occurring in Singapore." Under the second requirement, the court found that private factors (parallel litigation in Singapore, location of records and witnesses there) and public interest factors (neither American goods nor American companies were involved) weighed in favor of dismissal.

Judge Warren Ferguson dissented in *Creative Technology*, arguing that because all the claimed acts of infringement had occurred in the United States, and because only U.S. law applied, it was wrong to dismiss the case on the ground of *forum non conveniens*. Citing the Berne Convention's national treatment requirement for the proposition that "where a copyright has been infringed in a particular country, the author has a right to pursue a remedy in that country," Ferguson concluded that "the first part of the *forum non conveniens* test requires us to retain this action because the principle of national treatment precludes Singapore from being an adequate alternative forum." On the second part of the test, weighing public and private interest factors, Judge Ferguson observed that the lower court "utterly ignored the public interest in having the federal courts of this country apply American copyright law to resolve this controversy." 61 F.3d at 707.

In Halo Creative & Design Ltd. v. Comptoir des Indes Inc., 816 F.3d 1366 (Fed.Cir. 2016), the U.S. Court of Appeals for the Federal Circuit chose not to assume that Canadian courts would apply U.S. copyright law. The plaintiff, a Hong Kong company, sued a Canadian defendant in a U.S. district court for copyright, patent, and trademark infringements under U.S. law. The district court had dismissed the case on the defense of *forum non conveniens*, concluding that the Federal Court of Canada would be a better forum and could probably apply U.S. law because "the United States has recognized the potential of applying the copyright laws of other nations . . . [and] perhaps Canada could do likewise." The Court of Appeals for the Federal Circuit rejected this "mere speculation" regarding the Canadian courts' application of U.S. law and pointed out that "[t]he Berne Convention does not require that member countries provide remedies for extraterritorial infringing activity [or] that Canada apply its laws extraterritorially." 816 F.3d at 1371.

6. *Plaintiffs' Choice of Forum.* American courts will generally indulge a presumption in favor of the plaintiff's choice of forum, but will give this presumption less force than otherwise in cases where the plaintiff is a foreign national. *See*, for example, Piper Aircraft Co. v. Reyno, 454 U.S. 235, 255–56 (1981). Does this weakened presumption offend the national treatment obligation imposed by intellectual property treaties to which the United States is a party? *See* Murray v. British Broadcasting Corp., 81 F.3d 287, 293 (2d Cir. 1996) (there is no obligation of access to courts unless the treaty expressly requires it; "the Berne Convention's national treatment principle insures that no matter where Murray brings his claim, United States copyright law would apply to exploitation of the character in this country."). *See* also the order in B.P. Chemicals Ltd. v. Jiangsu Sopo Corp., 429 F.Supp.2d 1179 (E.D. Mo. 2006), reproduced at page 761, below.

7. *Choice of Court Agreements.* The parties to a license or other transfer of intellectual property can obtain some degree of certainty about the forum in which their disputes will be resolved by specifying the forum in the agreement. Civil law countries generally honor forum selection agreements, but will decline to enforce them if doing so would violate a strong domestic public policy. Common law jurisdictions are only slightly more likely than civil law jurisdictions to overturn forum selection agreements, usually for reasons comparable to those entertained under *forum non conveniens* doctrine. A widely followed English case, The Eleftheria, 2 All E.R. 641 (1969), held that an English court should as a rule stay a local action in order to allow the parties to proceed in the contractually designated foreign forum unless the plaintiff could show compelling reasons for proceeding locally. The United States Supreme Court has ruled that a forum selection clause would be enforced in the absence of a showing that enforcement would be unreasonable and unjust. M/S Bremen v. Zapata Off-Shore Co., 407 U.S. 1, 10 (1972).

What if the selected forum has no connection to the subject matter of the agreement, parties to the agreement, territorial scope of the agreement, potentially applicable law, or the location of evidence? In Skype Technologies SA v. Joltid Ltd., [2009] EWHC 2783 (Ch), the parties, one incorporated in Luxembourg and the other in the British Virgin Islands, selected the English courts to have exclusive jurisdiction over "any claims arising under or relating" to their copyright licensing agreement, with world-wide application. *Id.*, ¶ 3. Justice Lewison refused to dismiss the case and noted that "what one might call the standard considerations that arise in arguments about *forum non conveniens* should be given little weight in the face of an exclusive jurisdiction clause where the parties have chosen the courts of a neutral territory in the context of an agreement with world-wide application. Otherwise the exclusive jurisdiction clause would be deprived of its intended effect. Indeed, the more 'neutral' the chosen forum was the less the importance the parties must have placed on the convenience of the forum for any particular dispute. If the standard considerations that arise in arguments about *forum non conveniens* were to be given full weight, they would almost always trump the parties' deliberate selection of a neutral forum." *Id.*, ¶ 33.

Should courts adopt a different approach when the agreement is not concluded between businesses but between a business and a consumer? An imbalance of power might be particularly pronounced when the agreement is concluded in the form of a clickwrap or shrinkwrap agreement. Some jurisdictions limit the enforceability of such agreements or disregard the choice of venue made in such agreements. For example, a French court held that the choice of U.S. courts in Facebook's terms of use violated the European Convention on Human Rights and the French consumer protection law. Monsieur X v. Facebook, Paris Court of First Instance, 2015, *aff'd* Facebook v. Durand, Cour d'Appel de Paris, 2016-58, 2016. The Supreme Court of Canada has held that policy concerns—"[t]he grossly uneven bargaining power between the parties and the importance of adjudicating quasi-constitutional . . . rights in the province"—weighed heavily in favor of unenforceability of the clause. Douez v. Facebook, Inc., 2017 SCC 33, 2017, ¶ 4 (the case involved a privacy rights claim).

Section 202(2)(a) of the A.L.I.'s Intellectual Property: Principles Governing Jurisdiction, Choice of Law, and Judgments in Transnational Disputes, approved May 14, 2007, makes a "choice-of-court" agreement "valid as to form and substance if it is valid under the law of the designated forum state," following the approach generally taken by Article 5 of The Hague Convention on Choice of Court Agreements, concluded June 30, 2005. According to Comment *b* to section 202, "the forum chosen must have subject-matter jurisdiction under local law. If it does not, then the plaintiff may choose another court consistent with these Principles." Section 202(3) makes special provision for choice of court clauses in "mass-market agreements," such as Internet clickwrap agreements, and validates them "only if the choice-of-court clause was reasonable and readily accessible to the nondrafting party at the time the agreement was concluded, and is available for subsequent reference by the court and the parties."*

See generally, Mathias Reimann, Conflict of Laws in Western Europe: A Guide Through the Jungle 76 (1995); J.J. Fawcett, General Report, in Declining Jurisdiction in Private International Law 1, 47–58 (J.J. Fawcett, ed. 1995); Dai Yokomizo, Choice-of-Court and Choice-of-Law Clauses in International Trademark Transactions, in The Law and Practice of Trademark Transactions: A Global and Local Outlook (Irene Calboli & Jacques de Werra, eds., 2016), pp. 276–292.

Mecklermedia Corp. v. D.C. Congress GmbH

Chancery Division, 1997.
[1998] Ch. 40, [1998] 1 All ER 148, [1997] 3 WLR 479.

JACOB J. handed down the following judgment. This is an application by the defendant, D.C. Congress G.m.b.H. ("D.C."), for an order setting aside the writ on the grounds that this court does not have jurisdiction to hear and determine the claim made against it under the provisions of the Civil Jurisdiction and Judgments Act 1982. Alternatively D.C. seeks an order staying this action or declining jurisdiction on the grounds that the Landgericht München I is first seised of a related action in which D.C. is plaintiff and a corporation called Messe Berlin G.m.b.H. is defendant. Further or alternatively D.C. seeks an order striking out the claim under the provisions of the R.S.C., Ord. 18, r. 19 or the inherent jurisdiction of the court.

The claim

The plaintiffs allege that D.C. is committing the English tort of passing off. The relief sought is in relation to the activities of D.C. in and from Germany said to lead to that tort being committed. It is said that the plaintiffs have a goodwill in England and Wales, that D.C. is making a misrepresentation within the jurisdiction and that that misrepresentation has caused and will cause the plaintiffs damage within the jurisdiction—the trinity of elements constituting passing off.

It is convenient to consider the strength of this claim first, for if D.C. can show that the claim has no prospect of success it should be struck out on purely English law principles. Further, it is common ground that the strength of the claim is relevant to jurisdiction under the relevant provisions of the Convention on Jurisdiction and the Enforcement of Judgments in Civil and Commercial Matters ("the Brussels Convention") which apply by virtue of the Civil Jurisdiction and Judgments Act 1982. In particular it is common ground that a higher standard than that for a strike out is required: it is for the plaintiff to satisfy the court that there is "a serious question which calls for a trial for its proper determination:" *per* Dillon LJ in *Mölnlycke A.B. v. Procter & Gamble Ltd.* [1992] 1 W.L.R. 1112, 1121, quoting from Nicholls L.J. in *Tesam Distribution Ltd. v. Schuh Mode Team G.m.b.H.* [1990] I.L.Pr. 149,158, 160. Clearly a foreign, even a European Union, defendant should not be brought before our courts unless there is a serious question to be tried.

I turn to the first element of the trinity. The first plaintiff, Mecklermedia Corporation, is incorporated in Delaware. The second plaintiff, Mecklermedia Ltd, is its English subsidiary. The second plaintiff has, since 1994, been involved in the organisation of three trade shows in the United Kingdom. These were called "Internet World and Document Delivery World" (1994) and "Internet World International" (1995–96). It is said that these trade shows were widely advertised and attended. The trade shows were organised in conjunction with a licensee company. It is said that it was specifically agreed that all goodwill in the name "Internet World" should vest in the first plaintiff, which I will henceforth call "Mecklermedia."

Mecklermedia has, since 1993, published in the United States a magazine called "Internet World." This is claimed to have some circulation within the U.K., but this must be essentially of the "spillover" variety. In the autumn of 1996 an English version of the magazine was launched under the same name. It is published by V.N.U. Business Publications but claims association, correctly, with the US magazine by saying:

> "*Internet World* is already the most popular Internet magazine in the U.S. Now *Internet World* is to be published in the U.K. by the people who bring you *Personal Computer World*."

The first edition was given away free with "Personal Computer World" and there was no dispute but that that magazine has a substantial U.K. circulation. It is claimed that V.N.U. publishes the English edition under licence from Mecklermedia and that it is specifically agreed by V.N.U. that the goodwill in the name "Internet World" should belong to Mecklermedia.

Finally it is claimed that Mecklermedia owns two web sites having the addresses "http://www.internet-world.com" and "http://www.iworld.com." It is said that anyone "visiting" these sites would see prominent use of the name "Internet World" and promotion of the plaintiff's trade shows and magazines. Not much information is given about these sites—for instance their date of establishment and the number of English visitors—and I do not place reliance on them.

The upshot of these activities is said to be that the plaintiffs own an "extensive goodwill" in England. I certainly think that the plaintiffs have established that there is a "serious question" that they do own such a goodwill. . . .

The next element of the trinity is misrepresentation. D.C. has organised its own trade shows, also calling them "Internet World." The shows have been in Düsseldorf (26–28 November 1996) and Vienna (11–13 February 1997). To promote these shows D.C., based in Germany, has prepared an English language letter and brochure and sent them out to prospective visitors and exhibitors. I have no information about other language promotional material, but I expect there is at least a German brochure. It is clear from what D.C. has done that it does not regard its shows as purely national affairs—it seeks business internationally, including from here. D.C. has also established a German web site under the domain name "http://www.internet-world.de."

So far as this country is concerned, D.C. specifically puts onto its database the names and addresses of people and companies who appeared in the plaintiffs' "Internet World" trade show catalogue in London. D.C. openly so admitted in a fax of 12 August 1996. Actually the fax is a little ambiguous (it speaks of the "congress visitors"). I was told, and there seems to be no dispute, that the trade show brochure contained a list of exhibitors and those visitors who had booked their tickets in advance. So D.C. has deliberately targeted those particularly interested in the plaintiffs' shows. Moreover D.C. has asked the Overseas Department of the Department of Trade and Industry to promote its "Internet World" exhibitions. D.C. is clearly drumming up business from the U.K.

I think there is certainly a serious question to be tried as to whether what D.C. has been doing would mislead the interested public here. It is true that D.C. uses the name "dc conferences" in small type. I cannot see how that would help those who spotted that use. The show here was organised with a local company and I rather think that quite a number of recipients of the defendant's material would expect the two shows advertised to be connected with the plaintiffs by much the same sort of arrangement. True it is that evidence of misrepresentation at this stage does not include evidence from deceived or confused persons (I disregard the thin evidence that the second plaintiff's managing director has received calls from confused customers as too vague). But I do not think that matters. After all the names are the same and I am entitled to form my own view of the matter.

What about the third element of the trinity, damage? Miss Jones [(appearing on behalf of D.C.)] says none has been proved. Now in some cases one does indeed need separate proof of damage. This is particularly so, for example, if the fields of activity of the parties are wildly different: *e.g. Stringfellow v. McCain Foods (G.B.) Ltd.* [1984] R.P.C. 501, nightclub and chips. But in other cases the court is entitled to infer damage, including particularly damage by way of dilution of the plaintiff's goodwill. Here I think the natural inference is that Mecklermedia's goodwill in England will be damaged by the use of the same name by D.C. To a significant extent Mecklermedia's reputation in this country is in the hands of D.C.—people here will think there is a trading connection between the German and Austrian fairs and the Mecklermedia fairs.

It is to be noted that all the activities of D.C. take place in Germany and Austria—none take place within the territorial jurisdiction of this court. But I cannot think that matters so far as the English law of passing off is concerned. To do acts here which lead to damage of goodwill by misleading the public here is plainly passing off. To do those same acts from abroad will not avoid liability. Whether the court can assume jurisdiction—in the sense of becoming seised of an action—over a defendant abroad is another matter. That depends upon the extent to which the court has the power to make a person abroad party to an action. The Brussels Convention regulates that power for members of the Convention.

I therefore think that there is a serious question to be tried. That disposes of the strike-out application and gets the plaintiffs over the first hurdle to justify service out of the jurisdiction. I now turn to the remaining points, which concern the Brussels Convention.

Is service out of the jurisdiction justified under the Convention?

The convention

Article 2 of the Convention sets out the basic rule: "Subject to the provisions of this Convention, persons domiciled in a contracting state shall, whatever their nationality, be sued in the courts of that state." In footballing terms the plaintiff must "play away." Section 2 of the Convention provides for "Special Jurisdiction," under which a plaintiff is given a choice of other forums in the circumstances defined. The relevant provision here is article 5(3):

> "A person domiciled in a contracting state may, in another contracting state, be sued . . . 3. In matters relating to tort, delict or quasi-delict, in the courts for the place where the harmful event occurred."

Section 8 of the Convention deals with co-pending proceedings under the general title "Lis pendens—related actions." It provides:

> "Article 21. Where proceedings involving the same cause of action and between the same parties are brought in the courts of different contracting states, any court other than the court first seised shall of its own motion stay its proceedings until such time as the jurisdiction of the court first seised is established. Where the jurisdiction of the court first seised is established, any court other than the court first seised shall decline jurisdiction in favour of that court.

> "Article 22. Where related proceedings are brought in the courts of different contracting states, any court other than the court first seised may, while the actions are pending at first instance, stay its proceedings. A court other than the court first seised may also, on the application of one of the parties, decline jurisdiction if the law of that court permits the consolidation of related actions and the court first seised has jurisdiction over both actions. For the purposes of this article, actions are deemed to be related where they are so closely connected that it is expedient to hear and determine them together to avoid the risk of irreconcilable judgments resulting from separate proceedings."

The contentions

The plaintiffs say that by virtue of article 5(3) they are entitled to sue the defendant in England for the English tort of passing off. D.C. says it should be sued in Germany for a variety of reasons. It contends that: (1) the circumstances do not fall within article 5(3); alternatively, (2) article 21 is applicable and there should be a mandatory stay of this action; alternatively, (3) article 22 is applicable, so that the court has a discretion to order a stay and should exercise that discretion.

Is the case within article 5(3)?

It is settled, and self-evident from the Convention, that where article 5(3) applies the plaintiff is given an option to sue either in the forum of the defendant's domicile or forum (or forums) of the place (or places) where the harmful event occurred. For the present I will assume that article 2 would permit an action in Germany in respect of the passing off in England (though as to this see below). That does not prevent an action in England if the "harmful event" occurs here. . . .

D.C. asserts that in this case Germany is the place of the harmful event. I do not accept that submission. So far as the English tort of passing off is concerned, the harm is to the goodwill in England, and is the effect on the reputation in England. That is a direct effect on the plaintiffs' claimed English property.

I am confirmed in that view by the last-quoted paragraph from the *Dumez France* case [1990] E.C.R. I-49. All the components of liability of the tort take place in England. A trial would require proof of goodwill, misrepresentation and damage in England. It would not matter whether or not what D.C. was doing in Germany was, so far as German law and facts were concerned, lawful or not.

I find further support for the proposition that in relation to the English law claim it is in England that the harmful event is occurring from the decision of Knox J in *Modus Vivendi Ltd v British Products Sanmex Co Ltd* [1996] F.S.R. 790. Knox J had to consider the Convention (as adapted in respects immaterial in the present case by Schedule 4 to the Act of 1982) in the context of a choice between England and Scotland as the appropriate forum. The defendants were in Scotland, where they filled butane containers. These were transported through England to Hong Kong and China. The artwork was deceptive in the ultimate markets. An argument that the harmful event occurred in England failed. Knox J said that the place where the damage occurred was the place where the deception occurred, namely Hong Kong and China. Knox J said, at p 802:

> "If one supposes that the passing off in the present case was effected in a Convention country, say, for example, France . . . there would in my view be seen to be close connecting factors with France where, to put it neutrally, the illicit incursion into the plaintiff's goodwill . . . occurred."

In this case the deception alleged is in England. On that reasoning there are close connecting factors with England.

D.C. puts its case in an alternative way. Assume, it says, that the German court is prepared to consider the English passing off claim. Then there would be a risk of inconsistent judgments, the very thing that the

Dumez France case [1990] E.C.R. I-49 says it is an object of the Convention to avoid. There are, I think, several answers to that.

First, avoiding a possibility of conflict is not a matter with which article 5(3), as such, is concerned. All one derives from the desire to avoid conflicting decisions in relation to article 5(3) is, as the court said in the *Dumez France* case and in other cases, that the exceptions to the general principle should be recognised as such and confined accordingly. It is articles 21 and 22 which are directly concerned with the possibility of conflict.

Second, it is clear that each of the derogations from article 2 gives the plaintiff the possibility of an alternative forum from that of the defendant's domicile. If the argument were right, then there would never be alternatives. Putting the point another way, implicit in the argument is that there is only one possible forum. Once that is made explicit one can see it is fallacious. The fallacy is even more apparent when one considers the important case of *Shevill v. Presse Alliance SA* (Case C-68/93) [1995] 2 A.C. 18. The plaintiffs, an individual and some companies, sued in England in respect of an alleged libel in daily newspaper "France Soir." "France Soir" had a limited circulation here and in several other European countries, but its main distribution was in France. The court accepted that there was a possible multiplicity of jurisdictions. The "place where the harmful event occurred" was any place where damage was directly caused, namely the place where the publisher was established, *i.e.* France, and the place where the publication was distributed, *i.e.* England, and possibly other countries too. If the action was brought in a state where the publisher was established, the courts of that state had jurisdiction to award damages in respect of all the harm caused by the publication. If the action was brought "locally" the courts of the state concerned had jurisdiction to award damages for the publication in that state. The case is of great importance if it also governs parallel infringements of intellectual property rights and governs the grant of injunctions as well as damages. It would mean that a plaintiff could not forum-shop around Europe for a Europe-wide injunction. He could only seek such an injunction in the state of the source of the allegedly infringing goods or piratical activity. I say no more here. For present purposes *Shevill's* case is as clear a case as one could find that article 5(3) does not exclude the possibility of action in several states.

I think the plaintiffs are within article 5(3).

Article 21

This requires that there be proceedings *for the same cause of action* and *between the same parties*. D.C. says that is the position here. Prior to the present action, in Germany D.C. commenced trade mark infringement proceedings against Mecklermedia's German licensees. It is submitted that those licensees should be regarded as the "same party" as Mecklermedia itself. I do not see why. I can understand that a wholly-owned subsidiary might be so regarded. . . . But a mere licensee, a wholly different enterprise which happens to be working with the plaintiff, is simply not the same party. What if the licensee decided not to contest the proceedings? Or decided to fight them in some way contrary to the plaintiff's interest, *e.g.*, attacking the trade mark on the grounds of descriptiveness when the plaintiff contends that it is distinctive but means it? There is nothing Mecklermedia could do to stop this—because the licensee is not the same party.

Further I think that the causes of action are different. The cause of action in Germany is alleged infringement of the German registration. Hardly any of the facts relevant to the present action are relevant there: not English goodwill, not English reputation and not damage to goodwill or trade in or from England. And many facts, and all the law, which will be relevant to the German dispute are not relevant here. The situation is not as described by the Court of Justice as necessary for article 21 to apply: "For the purposes of article 21 of the Convention, the 'cause of action' comprises the facts and the rule of law relied on as the basis of the action:" see *The Maciej Rataj* (Case C-406/92) [1995] All E.R. (E.C.) 229, 254, para 39.

I reject the article 21 argument.

Article 22

There are a number of points here. Before the discretion to order a stay or decline jurisdiction arises, the case must come within the terms of the article. Here there are three points in issue. (1) Is the German court seised of a "related action?" (2) If so, is there a German action pending "at first instance?" (3) Can the German court assume jurisdiction in respect of passing off in England?

I must first set out in more detail what proceedings are on foot in Germany. I have already said that there are infringement proceedings by D.C. against Messe Berlin, Mecklermedia's licensees. D.C. sought provisional relief preventing Messe Berlin from advertising "Internet World Berlin 1997" in respect of trade shows. Relief was refused and an appeal is pending. Mecklermedia here has now—on 30 January 1997—started its own German proceedings seeking an order to prevent D.C. from using the marks "Internetworld" and "Internet World" and for cancellation of the German registered trade mark. It was suggested that those proceedings included a claim to prevent passing off in England. I have been shown a rough translation of the pleading, prepared by D.C.'s solicitors, and am not convinced that that is so. In addition (although this is irrelevant save possibly on the question of discretion) Mecklermedia has started proceedings in the US to prevent use of "Internet World" in the US.

(1)   *Related action?*

So the only proceeding prior to the present claim is the infringement action in Germany. Article 22 effectively defines the term "related actions" as those in respect of which it is expedient to hear them together to avoid the risk of irreconcilable judgments. I fail to see how there is such a risk. It may be—if the German registration is valid—and there is no defence of prior use made out, that D.C. could win in Germany. I do not know. But whether it does or not could not affect the English proceedings, concerned as they are with the goodwill here. There is no risk of conflicting decisions, that being the relevant test under *The Maciej Rataj* (Case C-406/92) [1995] All E.R. (E.C.) 229. 256, para. 58.

Miss Jones submits that this is really all about an international dispute. That is true in a sense. But that does not mean that there cannot be different results in different countries. Much depends on the local goodwill and the extent to which the mark has been used locally. Indeed the argument is inconsistent with the proposition advanced earlier that the mark may be wholly descriptive in England, but not in Germany.

(2) *Action at first instance?*

The evidence as to the nature of the German proceedings is as follows. The application for an injunction in Germany does not take place within the context of a "main" action, *i.e.* a legal proceeding for a final determination on the merits. It takes place outside of such proceedings. If the plaintiff obtains an injunction, then the defendant can, but does not have to, require the plaintiff to start a main action. If no injunction is obtained, that is an end of the matter. The procedure sounds quite sensible and may be worth considering for adoption here as a way of obtaining an "early view" on the merits of some cases. Mecklermedia says that accordingly there are no first instance proceedings on foot. D.C. says that the possibility of full proceedings is a live issue in Germany, though it would be premature to take any further steps towards a main hearing.

I decline to come to any conclusion on this point. It seems to me perfectly arguable that the German procedure is in substance an interim measure in an action. It would be odd if what is procedurally somewhat different but in substance not significantly different between Germany and here could really matter. . . .

(3) *English passing off triable in Germany?*

This takes the extreme form of an attack on "related proceedings." It is also directly relevant to the question of whether the English court should exercise its discretion under the second paragraph of article 22 to decline jurisdiction or, under the first paragraph, to stay the action. Mecklermedia says that, although by article 2 the German court is given jurisdiction over an action against D.C. because D.C. is of German domicile, article 2 goes no further. It does not make passing off in England actionable in Germany. Mecklermedia's expert on German law asserts that:

> "The plaintiffs cannot rely in Germany on their rights generated in the U.K. and similarly the defendant cannot rely on the right granted by their German trade mark registration outside Germany. Accordingly the plaintiffs would be unable to bring

these proceedings in Germany against the defendant because they cannot base their claim in Germany on U.K. trade mark rights acquired by use. The German courts are neither permitted nor competent to hear the action."

D.C.'s expert on German law does not answer this as a matter of German national law. He points to the Convention. He says that this not only provides for the appropriate forums, but, as a consequence, makes matters assigned to a particular forum justiciable there. Unless this is so, he argues, there would be no need for article 16, and other articles, providing for exclusive jurisdiction in limited and defined classes of case. Now all this is a matter of E.U. law. Unlike foreign law, which is treated by our law as a question of fact, E.U. law is part of our law. So this court needs no evidence and is competent and under a duty, where it is necessary to do so, to decide the point itself.

The point is of considerable importance. If D.C.'s contention is correct, the Convention provides that a defendant can be sued in his state of domicile for a tort committed in another member state according to the law of that member state. The domestic law of the state of domicile would be irrelevant. In other words, article 2 is concerned with more than questions of proper service: it requires the courts of one state to apply the law of another state in relation to events in that other state. If right, then it would seem that the recent abolition of the double actionability rule of English law was irrelevant so far as Convention states were concerned. It would have already been abolished by the Convention, which in providing for where cases were to be heard also was conferring on the courts given jurisdiction under the Convention powers and duties to consider matters which may not, prior to the Convention, have been within their competence. If that is so, the only qualification on a possibly wide scope for forum shopping in intellectual property cases—bearing in mind the possibilities of suing distributors as well as originators of products—would be the principles of *Shevill's* case [1995] 2 A.C. 18, especially if applied as I indicate above.

It is clear that this point is too important to be decided without full argument. In this case it is raised only as an extra argument under article 22 and I do not think it right to decide it.

Discretion

Finally, even if the case did come within article 22, it is for the defendant to persuade the court that it should stay the action or decline jurisdiction. . . . I certainly would not take either of those steps when I think, as I do, that normally the most convenient forum for deciding an English trade mark or passing off case is this court. In many cases a question of deceptive resemblance involving language may be involved. Then I think it would be very difficult for a court which uses a language other than English to form a reliable view on the question, especially if it was marginal. In this case the question of a deceptive resemblance hardly arises. But even so the German court would have to import both the evidence and the law, whereas neither of those things would be necessary if the action proceeds here.

It is submitted that it would be better if all questions were decided by a single court and that multiple litigation should be avoided. That, as a generality, is of course always true, but on the other hand when an enterprise wants to use a mark or word throughout the world—and that may include an Internet address or domain name—it must take into account that in some places, if not others, there may be confusion. Here it is clear that D.C. knew that Mecklermedia used the name "Internet World" and I do not think it is surprising that it is met with actions in places where confusion is considered likely. So I decline to set aside service.

Application dismissed.

NOTES

1.   *Choice of Forum.* Because the law of the forum may govern several critical issues, choice of forum can significantly affect the outcome of an intellectual property case. Among other issues, the law of the forum will govern the availability and scope of personal jurisdiction over the defendant and other procedural incidents such as the extent and availability of discovery, jury trial, *res judicata* and enforcement of judgments. It is also the forum's choice of law rules that will determine what country's law will be applied to resolve one or more substantive aspects of a case.

The Brussels Convention (formally, the Convention on Jurisdiction and the Enforcement of Judgments in Civil and Commercial Matters), which was applied in the *Mecklermedia* decision, was concluded in 1968 among the member countries of the European Communities and has, since *Mecklermedia*, been replaced first by a Council Regulation in 2000 ("Brussels I Regulation") and later by the "Brussels I Regulation (recast). The Convention has effectively been replicated in the countries of the European Free Trade Association by the 1988 European Communities—European Free Trade Association Convention on Jurisdiction and the Enforcement of Judgments in Civil and Commercial Matters, which has itself since been revised in its new 2007 version (the "Lugano II Convention").

See generally, James Fawcett & Paul Torremans, Intellectual Property and Private International Law, 142–258 (2nd ed., 2011).

2.   *Preemptive Strikes: Torpedoes.* The Brussels Convention, applied in *Mecklermedia*, the successor provisions of the Brussels I Regulation and the Brussels I Regulation (recast), and the Lugano II Convention extend jurisdiction over parties in cases of "tort, delict or quasi-delict" to the courts of the contracting state in which the harmful events occurred. At the same time, general jurisdiction over parties exists in the courts of the state of their domicile. Under these rules, a potential infringement defendant can try to beat the intellectual property owner to court—and choose the forum for litigation—by filing a lawsuit for a declaration of non-infringement before the owner files an infringement lawsuit. One attraction of such a "torpedo" is to bar the prosecution of a later-filed infringement action in a less friendly forum; the courts of choice for non-infringement actions have been courts in countries like Italy with crowded dockets and slow procedures, thus inspiring the name given to the strategy: "Italian torpedoes."

The growing torpedo practice in Europe precipitated reactions from national courts. In one case, a French court refused to suspend its own proceedings on the ground that an Italian torpedo was an abuse of procedural law. Société The General Hospital v. S.A. Société Laboratoires Byk France, Paris Dist. Ct. 2000, 33 IIC 69 (2002). *See* Mario Franzosi, Torpedoes Are Here to Stay, 33 IIC 154 (2002). Some courts in Europe declined to exercise jurisdiction in actions for non-infringement based on the provision that confers jurisdiction on the courts in the place of the tortious activity. Defendants in these actions—the right holders—argued that if plaintiffs alleged that no infringement occurred, the plaintiffs could not claim the place of the allegedly non-harmful events as the jurisdictional basis. Eventually, the Court of Justice of the European Union held that "an action for a negative declaration seeking to establish the absence of liability in tort, delict, or quasi-delict falls within the scope" of the provision establishing jurisdiction in the place of a tort, delict, or quasi-delict. Folien Fischer AG and Fofitec AG v. RITRAMA SpA, CJEU, C-133/11, 2012, ruling of the Court.

3. *Preemptive Strikes: Anti-Suit Injunctions.* American parties maneuvering for forum advantage may also seek to enjoin a foreign proceeding. In Microsoft Corp. v. Lindows.Com, Inc., 319 F.Supp. 2d 1219 (W.D. Wash. 2004), Lindows sought to enjoin Microsoft from pursuing trademark actions against it for infringement of the registered "Windows" mark in the European Union and elsewhere. Noting that "[i]t is with grave reluctance that this Court approaches the request to inject itself into the proceedings of another nation," the court denied the request on the ground that "[a]n injunction is appropriate only in cases where the parties are the same, the issues are the same, and resolution of the U.S. action will be dispositive of the action to be enjoined." In the court's view, "a trademark dispute is not the 'same' for purposes of an anti-suit injunction" because trademark rights have a separate existence under the laws of each country. 319 F.Supp. 2d 1221–22.

In Zynga, Inc. v. Vostu USA, Inc., 816 F.Supp.2d 824 (N.D. Cal. 2011) Vostu argued that when deciding whether to issue anti-suit injunctions, courts should treat copyright disputes and trademark disputes differently. Faced with parallel suits in the United States and Brazil for infringements of copyright to online games, Vostu asked the U.S. court to issue a preliminary injunction to prohibit Zynga from litigating in Brazil. Vostu argued that the copyright laws of Brazil and the United States are essentially the same with respect to the issues involved in the case. Vostu supported its argument with an expert's declaration and comparative analysis of the two countries' copyright laws; however, the court rejected Vostu's argument, and citing an older case reiterated that "[i]ntellectual property issues . . . involve separate and independent rights arising from the unique laws of each nation." What role, if any, should differences in countries' copyright laws play in a decision concerning an anti-suit injunction?

Would the court's decision in *Zynga* have been different if Zynga had claimed the same causes of action under both U.S. and Brazilian laws in both the U.S. and Brazilian suits? Assuming that Brazilian and U.S. courts could adjudicate copyright infringements under the laws of both countries, Vostu would have to demonstrate that additional factors would support the issuance of an anti-suit injunction; the threshold showing that the parties and issues in the U.S. and foreign suits are the same and that the U.S. action is dispositive of the foreign action is not on its own sufficient for an anti-suit injunction. Additionally, courts will consider whether the foreign litigation "would (1) frustrate a policy of the forum issuing the injunction; (2) be vexatious or oppressive; (3) threaten the issuing court's *in rem* or *quasi in rem* jurisdiction; or (4) . . . prejudice other equitable considerations." E. & J. Gallo Winery v. Andina Licores S.A., 446 F.3d 984, 990 (9th Cir. 2006).

4. *Forum Non Conveniens and Anti-Suit Injunctions.* Are a dismissal based on *forum non conveniens* and the issuance of an anti-suit injunction two sides of the same coin? If a court does not dismiss a case based on *forum non conveniens* while foreign litigation is pending, should it issue an anti-suit injunction? In Skype Technologies SA v. Joltid Ltd., [2009] EWHC 2783 (Ch), Justice Lewison observed that "the test for the grant of a stay of domestic proceedings on the one hand, and the restraint of foreign proceedings on the other, is not exactly the same. No question of comity arises in the first case; but comity plays an important part in the second." *Id.*, ¶ 27.

In the European Union a court that has jurisdiction based on the Brussels I Regulation (recast) may not dismiss a case based on *forum non conveniens*, but neither may it issue an anti-suit injunction to prevent litigation in another court in the European Union. The court may, however, issue an anti-suit injunction against litigation in a court outside the European Union. Such was the result in the *Skype* case; the court had jurisdiction under the Brussels I Regulation, and it issued an anti-suit injunction preventing the parties from litigating in the U.S. District Court for the Northern District of California.

5. *Personal Jurisdiction on the Internet: Targeting in the United States.* The ubiquity of the Internet seriously complicates personal jurisdiction in intellectual property cases. If it is a sufficient basis for personal jurisdiction that the defendant has made an infringing work available over the Internet so that users in the forum have access to it, then not only direct infringers, but also secondary infringers such as Internet service providers, would be subject to suit in virtually every forum in the world.

In ALS Scan, Inc. v. Digital Service Consultants, Inc., 293 F.3d 707 (4th Cir. 2002) the defendant, a Georgia-based Internet service provider, argued that it conducted no business and had no offices, contracts, income, or advertising (other than through its website) in Maryland. Plaintiff, a Maryland corporation, countered that, by enabling a third-party website operator to publish infringing photographs in Maryland, defendant had subjected itself to specific jurisdiction in the state. The court ruled for the defendant. "If we were to conclude as a general principle that a person's act of placing information on the Internet subjects that person to personal jurisdiction in each State in which the information is accessed, then the defense of personal jurisdiction, in the sense that a State has geographically limited judicial power, would no longer exist."

The *ALS* court formulated a general rule that would govern personal jurisdiction in at least some of these cases: "a State may, consistent with due process, exercise judicial power over a person outside of the State when that person (1) directs electronic activity into the State, (2) with the manifested intent of engaging in business or other interactions within the State, and (3) that activity creates, in a person within the State, a potential cause of action cognizable in the State's courts." The court added, however, that "[u]nder this standard, a person who simply places information on the Internet does not subject himself to jurisdiction in each State into which the electronic signal is transmitted and received." 293 F.3d 712–714.

6. *Personal Jurisdiction on the Internet: Targeting in the European Union.* The Court of Justice of the European Union approved targeting as a factor in determining personal jurisdiction under the Brussels I Regulation in matters involving consumer contracts. Peter Pammer v. Reederei Karl Schlüter GmbH & Co KG, CJEU, C-585/08, 2010. Consumer contracts may include, for example, end-user licensing agreements that cover intellectual property rights issues. The Court of Justice rejected, however, targeting as a requirement for specific personal jurisdiction in cases involving infringements of registered trademarks. In Wintersteiger AG v. Products 4U Sondermaschinenbau GmbH the Court ruled that such cases "may be brought before . . . the courts of the Member State in which the trade mark is registered." CJEU, C-523/10, 2012.

Later, the Court explicitly rejected targeting as a requirement for specific personal jurisdiction in copyright infringement cases: "Article 5(3) [of the Brussels I Regulation] . . . does not require . . . that the activity concerned . . . be 'directed to' the Member State in which the court seised is situated." Peter Pinckney v. KDG Mediatech AG, CJEU, C-170/12, 2013, ¶ 42. *See* also Pez Hejduk v. EnergieAgentur.NRW GmbH, CJEU, C-441/13, 2015. Is there justification for analyzing conditions for personal jurisdiction differently depending on whether the case concerns consumer contract matters or intellectual property rights infringements?

Should targeting be a factor in assessing personal jurisdiction over the defendant or in choosing applicable law? In L'Oreal SA v. eBay International AG, CJEU, C-324/09, 2011, the Court of Justice of the European Union ruled that a targeting inquiry will be conducted to determine whether a trademark owner may prevent the sale, offer for sale, or advertising on the Internet of trademark infringing goods based on the rules set out in the EU trademark legislation. *See* also Donner, CJEU, C-5/11, 2012 (in the context of copyright); Football Dataco Ltd v. Sportradar GmbH, CJEU, C-173/11, 2012, ¶ 36 (in the context of the *sui generis* database right). *See* note 11 below for a discussion of connections among personal jurisdiction, subject matter jurisdiction, and the territorial scope of applicable law.

National courts in the EU member states have used targeting to determine personal jurisdiction under national law in cases of non-EU defendants. *See*, for example, Sohlen für Sportschuhe, Düsseldorf Landgericht, 4a O 33/01, Feb. 5, 2002; eBay Europe v. SARL Maceo, Cour de Cassation, W 10-12.272, Mar. 29, 2011. The interpretation by the Court of Justice of the European Union of the Brussels I Regulation (recast) and of its predecessors does not formally mandate the same interpretation of national rules of jurisdiction over non-EU defendants.

7.   *Jurisdiction and Localization.* Localization—the determination of the location of parties, their acts, and the effects of their acts—is central to jurisdictional analyses and other conflict-of-laws applications. As the *Mecklermedia* court observed, under *Shevill* the "place where the harmful event occurred . . . cover[s] both the place where the damage occurred and the place of the event giving rise to it." Shevill v. Presse Alliance SA, ECJ, C-68/93, March 7, 1995.

When a seller sells through its website a product from country *A* to customers in country *B* and then ships the product from *A* to *B*, where does the infringing sale take place? Following the U.S. Supreme Court's rejection of the notion that personal jurisdiction should turn on "mechanical tests" or "conceptualistic . . . theories of the place of contracting or of performance," the U.S. Court of Appeals for the Federal Circuit held that to sell a patent-infringing product from *A* to *B* "is to commit a tort [in *B*] (though not necessarily only there)." North American Philips Corp. v. American Vending Sales, Inc., 35 F.3d 1576 (Fed.Cir. 1994).

Should the location of servers hosting content ever be relevant for the personal jurisdiction inquiry? U.S. courts have found jurisdiction in the location of a computer server when the server itself was the location of the tortious conduct or of its effects, such as when the data that were the object of a trade secrets misappropriation were stored on the server, and the defendant knew where the server was located. MacDermid, Inc. v. Deiter, 702 F.3d 725, 726–730 (2d Cir. 2012).

When infringing conduct consists of posting content on the Internet by an infringer, courts typically locate the infringing activity where the infringer acted or where the act had effects, or in both of these places, rather than where the servers that happened to be involved in the transmission of the content are located. Wintersteiger AG v. Products 4U Sondermaschinenbau GmbH, CJEU, C-523/10, 2012, ¶ 36; Pez Hejduk v. EnergieAgentur.NRW GmbH, CJEU, C-441/13, 2015, ¶ 24.

8.   *Concentration of Proceedings in a Single Court.* In Penguin Group (USA) Inc. v. American Buddha, 16 N.Y.3d 295, 946 N.E.2d 159 (2011), the Court of Appeals of New York localized the injury from a copyright infringement in New York, which was where the copyright holder was located. The Court explained that "the role of the Internet in cases alleging the uploading of copyrighted books distinguishes them from traditional commercial tort cases where courts have generally linked the injury to the place where sales or customers are lost." Ultimately, no personal jurisdiction was found over the defendant because the plaintiff did not satisfy one of the prongs of New

York's long-arm statute that requires a showing that "the defendant derived substantial revenue from interstate or international commerce." Penguin Grp. (USA) v. American Buddha, 106 U.S.O.Q.2d 1306 (S.D.N.Y. 2013).

The Court of Justice of the European Union declined to extend to intellectual property cases the rule applicable in the European Union to jurisdiction in cases of infringements of personality rights, according to which an action for infringement of the rights can be brought in a single court for all damage caused if the court is either in the member state where the publisher is established or in the member state where the right holder's center of interests is. Explaining why the rule does not apply in copyright infringement cases, the Court noted that "the place where the alleged damage occurred . . . may vary according to the nature of the right allegedly infringed." Peter Pinckney v. KDG Mediatech AG, CJEU, C-170/12, 2013, ¶ 32.

However, alternatives exist for EU unitary rights. For example, under the EU Trademark Regulation, cases concerning the validity of EU trademarks and their infringements in any EU member state may be brought not only where the Brussels I Regulation (recast) allows, but also in the courts of the plaintiff's domicile or establishment (if the defendant's domicile or establishment is outside the European Union) or in the courts where the European Union Intellectual Property Office has its seat (if neither the plaintiff nor the defendant has domicile or establishment in the European Union). Regulation (EU) 2017/1001 of the European Parliament and of the Council of 14 June 2017 on the European Union trade mark, Article 125(2) and (3).

See, generally, Marketa Trimble, The Multiplicity of Copyright Laws on the Internet, 25 Fordham Intell. Prop., Media & Entertainment L. Rev. 339 (2015). On the jurisdiction of the Unified Patent Court see Stefan Luginbuehl & Dieter Stauder, Application of Revised Rules on Jurisdiction under Brussels I Regulation to Patent Lawsuits, 10(2) J. Intell. Property Law & Practice 135 (2015).

9. *Personal Jurisdiction on the Internet: Proposals for Solutions.* Section 204 of the American Law Institute's Intellectual Property: Principles Governing Jurisdiction, Choice of Law, and Judgments in Transnational Disputes, approved May 14, 2007, proposes a three-tiered approach to jurisdiction on and off the Internet. Section 204(1) "addresses the case in which the forum is a staging area for the nonresident defendant's activities," and gives courts there "authority to hear all claims arising out of these activities without geographic limitation." Section 204(2) subjects a nonresident defendant whose connection to the forum is more attenuated— but who has "intentionally directed an infringement into the forum State from outside and causes harm"—to relief only for injuries sustained in the forum State. Section 204 Comment a.

What if, to escape liability, a prospective defendant locates its business in a pirate haven whose laws fall below international intellectual property norms? Section 204(3) of the A.L.I. *Principles* provides:

A person who cannot be sued in a WTO-member State* with respect to the full territorial scope of the claim through the application of §§ 201–204(1) may be sued in any State in which that person's activities give rise to an infringement claim if:

    (a)   that person directed those activities to that State, and

    (b)   that person solicits or maintains contacts, business, or an audience in that State on a regular basis, whether or not such activity initiates or furthers the infringing activity.

The court's jurisdiction extends to claims respecting injuries arising out of conduct outside the State that relates to the alleged infringement in the State, wherever the injuries occur.**

10. *Geoblocking.* Can the Internet provide a technical solution to the localization problem? Many website operators use geolocation tools to determine users' locations, and some also employ geoblocking tools to limit users' access to certain content based on the particular country, region or location from which users connect to the Internet.

Should geoblocking become *the* required means of territorial delineation of activities on the Internet? In Plixer Intl., Inc. v. Scrutinizer GmbH, 905 F.3d 1 (1st Cir. 2018), the plaintiff alleged that the German defendant's use of the term "Scrutinizer" on defendant's website caused confusion with the plaintiff's registered U.S. trademark in the United States. Plaintiff argued that the German defendant purposefully availed itself of the U.S. forum because it did not use geoblocking to prevent customers from the United States from accessing its website. The court of appeals ruled that "[i]f a defendant tries to limit U.S. customers' ability to access its website, . . . that is surely relevant to its intent not to serve the United States." 905 F.3d at 9. While not holding that a lack of geoblocking would be dispositive for a finding of jurisdiction, the court concluded that "Scrutinizer's failure to implement such restrictions, coupled with its substantial U.S. business, provides an objective measure of its intent to serve customers in the U.S. market and thereby profit." 905 F.3d at 9.

Two recent regulations limit, but do not completely eliminate, the use of geoblocking in the European Union: Regulation (EU) 2017/1128 of the European Parliament and of the Council of 14 June 2017 on cross-border portability of online content services in the internal market, and Regulation (EU) 2018/302 of the European Parliament and of the Council of 28 February 2018 on addressing unjustified geo-blocking and other forms of discrimination based on customers' nationality, place of residence or place of establishment within the internal market.

On geoblocking, users' circumvention of geoblocking, and EU limitations on geoblocking see Marketa Trimble, Copyright and Geoblocking: The Consequences of Eliminating Geoblocking, 25 B.U. J. Sci. & Tech. L. (2019);

---

    *   The WTO is the World Trade Organization, and membership requires adherence to the Agreement on Trade-Related Aspects of Intellectual Property Rights, which imposes internationally-accepted norms of intellectual property protection. *Ed.*

    **   Copyright 2007 by the American Law Institute. Reprinted with permission. All rights reserved. *Ed.*

Marketa Trimble, The Future of Cybertravel: Legal Implications of the Evasion of Geolocation, 22 Fordham Intell. Prop. Media & Ent. L. J. 567 (2012); Dan Jerker B. Svantesson, Borders On, or Borders Around—The Future of the Internet, 16 Alb. L.J. Sci. & Tech. 343 (2006).

11. *Personal Jurisdiction, Subject Matter Jurisdiction, and the Territorial Scope of Applicable Law.* What connections exist among personal jurisdiction, subject matter jurisdiction, and the territorial scope of applicable law? Although they are three separate concepts, an inquiry into the territorial scope of applicable law can arise in analyses of personal jurisdiction and subject matter jurisdiction.

Determination of personal jurisdiction will be linked to the territorial scope of an applicable law when personal jurisdiction arises in the place of the tortious activity, as is the case under Article 7(2) of the Brussels I Regulation (recast) (Article 5(3) of the Brussels Convention in the *Mecklermedia* decision) and under the provisions of U.S. state long-arm jurisdiction statutes (in the United States, the exercise of personal jurisdiction must also comport with Constitutional due process requirements). Although whether infringement occurred or not will be decided only on the merits, for the purposes of determining specific personal jurisdiction, courts must assess whether the alleged tortious activity can be localized within a territory.

Subject matter jurisdiction is typically not confined territorially. When the U.S. Patent Act makes a sale of a patented invention within the United States a patent infringement, does the prepositional phrase "within the United States" impose territorial limits on the subject matter jurisdiction of the U.S. federal district courts, or does the phrase define the territorial reach of the patent statute? The Federal Judicial Code confers subject matter jurisdiction on U.S. federal district courts in "any civil action arising under any *Act of Congress* relating to patents, plant variety protection, copyrights and trademarks." 28 U.S.C. § 1338(a) (emphasis added).

In Litecubes, LLC v. Northern Light Products, Inc., 523 F.3d 1353 (Fed.Cir. 2008), the defendant argued that because it acted outside the United States—where the U.S. Patent Act does not apply—U.S. courts could not have had subject matter jurisdiction to decide a dispute concerning the acts. The U.S. Court of Appeals for the Federal Circuit disagreed and held that in the absence of statutory language to the contrary, "whether the allegedly infringing act happened in the United States is an element of the claim for patent infringement, not a prerequisite for subject matter jurisdiction." 523 F.3d at 1366. Similarly, the court held that the issue of applicability of the U.S. Copyright Act to the defendant's acts "is properly treated as an element of the claim which must be proven before relief can be granted, not a question of subject matter jurisdiction." 523 F.3d at 1368.

Other U.S. circuit courts have agreed that "the extraterritorial reach of the Lanham Act is a merits question that does not implicate federal courts' subject-matter jurisdiction," and that "the Copyright Act's insistence that infringing conduct be domestic offers an essential element of a copyright infringement plaintiff's claim, not of jurisdiction." Trader Joe's Company v.

Hallatt, 835 F.3d 960, 968 (9th Cir. 2016). *See* also Geophysical Service, Inc. v. TGS-NOPEC Geophysical Company, 850 F.3d 785, 791 (5th Cir. 2017).

12. *Arbitrability of Intellectual Property Disputes.* As one commentator noted, "the difficulties of litigating international intellectual property disputes before state courts," such as the difficulties caused by the limitations on the courts' jurisdiction, "explain why commercial arbitration has emerged as an attractive alternative for solving international intellectual property disputes." Jacques de Werra, Global Policies for Arbitrating Intellectual Property Disputes, in Research Handbook on Intellectual Property Licensing (Jacques de Werra ed., 2013), pp. 353–377, at pp. 353–354. Arbitration has advantages; for example, it provides the possibility of centralizing in a single venue the proceedings concerning parallel intellectual property rights, such as patents on the same invention issued in several countries. What are some of the limitations of arbitration? In many countries an arbitration tribunal may not render a decision on the validity of registered intellectual property, such as a patent, with *erga omnes* effects. In general, arbitration deprives future parties of reasoned case law in the form of published opinions.

On arbitration of intellectual property disputes in general see François Dessemontet, The Specificity of Intellectual Property Arbitration, in Research Handbook on Cross-Border Enforcement of Intellectual Property (Paul Torremans ed., 2014), pp. 607–641; Jacques de Werra, Alternative Dispute Resolution Mechanisms for Solving Trademark Disputes (Mediation, UDRP, Arbitration), in The Law and Practice of Trademark Transactions: A Global and Local Outlook (Irene Calboli & Jacques de Werra, 2016), pp. 304–322.

b.   CHOICE OF LAW

Itar-Tass Russian News Agency
v. Russian Kurier Inc.

United States Court of Appeals, Second Circuit, 1998.
153 F.3d 82, 47 U.S.P.Q.2d 1810.

JON O. NEWMAN, CIRCUIT JUDGE:

This appeal primarily presents issues concerning the choice of law in international copyright cases and the substantive meaning of Russian copyright law as to the respective rights of newspaper reporters and newspaper publishers. The conflicts issue is which country's law applies to issues of copyright ownership and to issues of infringement. The primary substantive issue under Russian copyright law is whether a newspaper publishing company has an interest sufficient to give it standing to sue for copying the text of individual articles appearing in its newspapers, or whether complaint about such copying may be made only by the reporters who authored the articles. Defendants-appellants Russian Kurier, Inc. ("Kurier") and Oleg Pogrebnoy (collectively "the Kurier defendants") appeal from the March 25, 1997, judgment of the

District Court for the Southern District of New York (John G. Koeltl, Judge) enjoining them from copying articles that have appeared or will appear in publications of the plaintiffs-appellees, mainly Russian newspapers and a Russian news agency, and awarding the appellees substantial damages for copyright infringement.

On the conflicts issue, we conclude that, with respect to the Russian plaintiffs, Russian law determines the ownership and essential nature of the copyrights alleged to have been infringed and that United States law determines whether those copyrights have been infringed in the United States and, if so, what remedies are available. We also conclude that Russian law, which explicitly excludes newspapers from a work-for-hire doctrine, vests exclusive ownership interests in newspaper articles in the journalists who wrote the articles, not in the newspaper employers who compile their writings. We further conclude that to the extent that Russian law accords newspaper publishers an interest distinct from the copyright of the newspaper reporters, the publishers' interest, like the usual ownership interest in a compilation, extends to the publishers' original selection and arrangement of the articles, and does not entitle the publishers to damages for copying the texts of articles contained in a newspaper compilation. We therefore reverse the judgment to the extent that it granted the newspapers relief for copying the texts of the articles. However, because one non-newspaper plaintiff-appellee is entitled to some injunctive relief and damages and other plaintiffs-appellees may be entitled to some, perhaps considerable, relief, we also remand for further consideration of this lawsuit.

Background

The lawsuit concerns *Kurier*, a Russian language weekly newspaper with a circulation in the New York area of about 20,000. It is published in New York City by defendant Kurier. Defendant Pogrebnoy is president and sole shareholder of Kurier and editor-in-chief of *Kurier*. The plaintiffs include corporations that publish, daily or weekly, major Russian language newspapers in Russia and Russian language magazines in Russia or Israel; Itar-Tass Russian News Agency ("Itar-Tass"), formerly known as the Telegraph Agency of the Soviet Union (TASS), a wire service and news gathering company centered in Moscow, functioning similarly to the Associated Press; and the Union of Journalists of Russia ("UJR"), the professional writers union of accredited print and broadcast journalists of the Russian Federation.

The Kurier defendants do not dispute that *Kurier* has copied about 500 articles that first appeared in the plaintiffs' publications or were distributed by Itar-Tass. The copied material, though extensive, was a small percentage of the total number of articles published in *Kurier*. . . . The Kurier defendants also do not dispute how the copying occurred: articles from the plaintiffs' publications, sometimes containing headlines, pictures, bylines, and graphics, in addition to text, were cut out, pasted on layout sheets, and sent to *Kurier*'s printer for photographic reproduction and printing in the pages of *Kurier*.

Most significantly, the Kurier defendants also do not dispute that, with one exception, they had not obtained permission from any of the plaintiffs to copy the articles that appeared in *Kurier*. Pogrebnoy claimed at trial to have received permission from the publisher of one newspaper, but his claim was rejected by the District Court at trial. . . . Pogrebnoy also claimed that he had obtained permission from the authors of six of the copied articles. The District Court made no finding as to whether this testimony was credible, since authors' permission was not pertinent to the District Court's view of the legal issues. . . .

Discussion

I.   Choice of Law

The threshold issue concerns the choice of law for resolution of this dispute. That issue was not initially considered by the parties, all of whom turned directly to Russian law for resolution of the case. Believing that the conflicts issue merited consideration, we requested supplemental briefs from the parties and appointed Professor William F. Patry as Amicus Curiae. . . . Prof. Patry has submitted an extremely helpful brief on the choice of law issue.

Choice of law issues in international copyright cases have been largely ignored in the reported decisions and dealt with rather cursorily by most commentators. Examples pertinent to the pending appeal are those decisions involving a work created by the employee of a foreign corporation. Several courts have applied the United States work-for-hire doctrine, . . . without explicit consideration of the conflicts issue. . . . Other courts have applied foreign law. . . . In none of these cases, however, was the issue of choice of law explicitly adjudicated. The conflicts issue was identified but ruled not necessary to be resolved in *Greenwich Film Productions, S.A. v. D.R.G. Records, Inc.*, 1992 Copr.L.Dec. P 27004, 25 U.S.P.Q.2D, 1992 WL 279357 (S.D.N.Y. 1992).

The Nimmer treatise briefly (and perhaps optimistically) suggests that conflicts issues "have rarely proved troublesome in the law of copyright." *Nimmer on Copyright* § 17.05 (1998) ("*Nimmer*"). Relying on the "national treatment" principle of the Berne Convention . . . and the Universal Copyright Convention . . . ("U.C.C."), *Nimmer* asserts, correctly in our view, that "an author who is a national of one of the member states of either Berne or the U.C.C., or one who first publishes his work in any such member state, is entitled to the same copyright protection in each other member state as such other state accords to its own nationals." *Id. Nimmer* then somewhat overstates the national treatment principle: "The applicable law is the copyright law of the state in which the infringement occurred, not that of the state of which the author is a national, or in which the work is first published." *Id.* . . . The difficulty with this broad statement is that it subsumes under the phrase "applicable law" the law concerning two distinct issues—ownership and substantive rights, *i.e.*, scope of protection.[8] Another commentator has also broadly stated the principle of national treatment, but described its application in a way that does not necessarily cover issues of ownership. "The principle of national treatment also means that both the question of whether the right exists and the question of the scope of the right are to be answered in accordance with the law of the country where the protection is claimed." S.M. Stewart, *International Copyright and Neighboring Rights* § 3.17 (2d ed. 1989). We agree with the view of the Amicus that the Convention's principle of national treatment simply assures that if the law of the country of infringement applies to the scope of substantive copyright protection, that law will be applied uniformly to foreign and domestic authors. . . .

Source of conflicts rules. Our analysis of the conflicts issue begins with consideration of the source of law for selecting a conflicts rule. Though *Nimmer* turns directly to the Berne Convention and the U.C.C., we think that step moves too quickly past the Berne Convention Implementation Act of 1988, Pub. L. 100 § 568, 102 Stat. 2853, 17 U.S.C. § 101 note. Section 4(a)(3) of the Act amends Title 17 to provide: "No right or interest in a work eligible for protection under this title may be claimed by virtue of . . . the provisions of the Berne Convention. . . . Any rights in a work eligible for protection under this title that derive from this title . . . shall not be expanded or reduced by virtue of . . . the provisions of the Berne Convention." . . . 17 U.S.C. § 104(c).

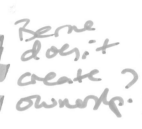

We start our analysis with the Copyright Act itself, which contains no provision relevant to the pending case concerning conflicts issues. . . . We therefore fill the interstices of the Act by developing federal common law on the conflicts issue. . . . In doing so, we are entitled to consider and apply principles of private international law, which are " 'part of our law.' " *Maxwell Communication Corp. v. Societe Generale*, 93 F.3d 1036, 1047 (2d Cir. 1996) (quoting *Hilton v. Guyot*, 159 U.S. 113, 143, 40 L.Ed. 95, 16 S.Ct. 139 (1895)).

The choice of law applicable to the pending case is not necessarily the same for all issues. *See* Restatement (Second) of Conflict of Laws § 222 ("The courts have long recognized that they are not bound to decide all issues under the local law of a single state."). We consider first the law applicable to the issue of copyright ownership.

Conflicts rule for issues of ownership. Copyright is a form of property, and the usual rule is that the interests of the parties in property are determined by the law of the state with "the most significant relationship" to the property and the parties. . . . The Restatement

---

[8]   Prof. Patry's brief, as Amicus Curiae, helpfully points out that the principle of national treatment is really not a conflicts rule at all; it does not direct application of the law of any country. It simply requires that the country in which protection is claimed must treat foreign and domestic authors alike. Whether U.S. copyright law directs U.S. courts to look to foreign or domestic law as to certain issues is irrelevant to national treatment, so long as the scope of protection would be extended equally to foreign and domestic authors.

recognizes the applicability of this principle to intangibles such as "a literary idea." . . . Since the works at issue were created by Russian nationals and first published in Russia, Russian law is the appropriate source of law to determine issues of ownership of rights. That is the well-reasoned conclusion of the Amicus Curiae, Prof. Patry, and the parties in their supplemental briefs are in agreement on this point. In terms of the United States Copyright Act and its reference to the Berne Convention, Russia is the "country of origin" of these works, see 17 U.S.C. § 101 (definition of "country of origin" of Berne Convention work); Berne Convention, Art. 5(4), although "country of origin" might not always be the appropriate country for purposes of choice of law concerning ownership.[11]

To whatever extent we look to the Berne Convention itself as guidance in the development of federal common law on the conflicts issue, we find nothing to alter our conclusion. The Convention does not purport to settle issues of ownership, with one exception not relevant to this case. . . .

Selection of Russian law to determine copyright ownership is, however, subject to one procedural qualification. Under United States law, an owner (including one determined according to foreign law) may sue for infringement in a United States court only if it meets the standing test of 17 U.S.C. § 501(b), which accords standing only to the legal or beneficial owner of an "exclusive right."

Conflicts rule for infringement issues. On infringement issues, the governing conflicts principle is usually *lex loci delicti*, the doctrine generally applicable to torts. . . . We have implicitly adopted that approach to infringement claims, applying United States copyright law to a work that was unprotected in its country of origin. . . . In the pending case, the place of the tort is plainly the United States. To whatever extent *lex loci delicti* is to be considered only one part of a broader "interest" approach, . . . United States law would still apply to infringement issues, since not only is this country the place of the tort, but also the defendant is a United States corporation.

lex loci delicti for infringt

The division of issues, for conflicts purposes, between ownership and infringement issues will not always be as easily made as the above discussion implies. If the issue is the relatively straightforward one of which of two contending parties owns a copyright, the issue is unquestionably an ownership issue, and the law of the country with the closest relationship to the work will apply to settle the ownership dispute. But in some cases, including the pending one, the issue is not simply who owns the copyright but also what is the nature of the ownership interest. Yet as a court considers the nature of an ownership interest, there is some risk that it will too readily shift the inquiry over to the issue of

---

[11]   In deciding that the law of the country of origin determines the ownership of copyright, we consider only initial ownership, and have no occasion to consider choice of law issues concerning assignments of rights.

whether an alleged copy has infringed the asserted copyright. Whether a copy infringes depends in part on the scope of the interest of the copyright owner. Nevertheless, though the issues are related, the nature of a copyright interest is an issue distinct from the issue of whether the copyright has been infringed. . . . The pending case is one that requires consideration not simply of who owns an interest, but, as to the newspapers, the nature of the interest that is owned.

II.   Determination of Ownership Rights Under Russian Law

Since United States law permits suit only by owners of "an exclusive right under a copyright," 17 U.S.C. § 501(b), we must first determine whether any of the plaintiffs own an exclusive right. That issue of ownership, as we have indicated, is to be determined by Russian law.

Determination of a foreign country's law is an issue of law. . . . Even though the District Court heard live testimony from experts from both sides, that Court's opportunity to assess the witness's demeanor provides no basis for a reviewing court to defer to the trier's ruling on the content of foreign law. In cases of this sort, it is not the credibility of the experts that is at issue, it is the persuasive force of the opinions they expressed. . . .

[The [District] Court noted that under Russian copyright law authors of newspaper articles retain the copyright in their articles unless there has been a contractual assignment to their employer or some specific provision of law provides that the author's rights vest in the employer. . . . Since the defendants alleged no claim of a contractual assignment, the Court next considered the provision of the 1993 Russian Federation Law on Copyright and Neighboring Rights ("Russian Copyright Law") (World Intellectual Property Organization (WIPO) translation) concerning what the United States Copyright Act calls "works made for hire," 17 U.S.C. § 201(b). *See* Russian Copyright Law, Art. 14(2). That provision gives employers the exclusive right to "exploit" the "service-related work" produced by employees in the scope of their employment, absent some contractual arrangement. However, the Court noted, Article 14(4) specifies that subsection 2 does not apply to various categories of works, including newspapers. . . . Accepting the view of plaintiffs' expert, Professor Vratislav Pechota, Judge Koeltl therefore ruled that the Russian version of the work-for-hire doctrine in Article 14(2), though exempting newspapers, applies to press agencies, like Itar-Tass. . . .

Turning to the rights of the newspapers, Judge Koeltl relied on Article 11, captioned "Copyright of Compiler of Collections and Other Works." This Article contains two sub-sections. Article 11(1) specifies the rights of compilers generally:

The author of a collection or any other composite work (compiler) shall enjoy copyright in the selection or arrangement of subject matter that he [sic] has made insofar as that selection or arrangement is the result of a creative effort of compilation.

The compiler shall enjoy copyright subject to respect for the rights of the authors of each work included in the composite work.

Each of the authors of the works included in the composite work shall have the right to exploit his own work independently of the composite work unless the author's contract provides otherwise. . . .

Russian Copyright Law, Art. 11(1). Article 11(2), the interpretation of which is critical to this appeal, specifies the rights of compilers of those works that are excluded from the work-for-hire provision of Article 14(2):

The exclusive right to exploit encyclopedias, encyclopedic dictionaries, collections of scientific works—published in either one or several installments—newspapers, reviews and other periodical publications shall belong to the editor[1] thereof. The editor shall have the right to mention his name or to demand such mention whenever the said publications are exploited.

The authors of the works included in the said publications shall retain the exclusive rights to exploit their works independently of the publication of the whole work.

Id., Art. 11(2). In another translation of the Russian Copyright Law, which was in evidence at the trial, the last phrase of Article 11(2) was rendered "independently from the publication as a whole." Russian Copyright Law, Art. 11(2) (Newton Davis translation). Because the parties' experts focused on the phrase "as a whole" in the Davis translation of Article 11(2), we will rely on the Davis translation for the rendering of this key phrase of Article 11(2), but all other references to the Russian Copyright Law will be to the WIPO translation.

The District Court acknowledged, as the plaintiffs' expert had stated, that considerable scholarly debate existed in Russia as to the nature of a publisher's right "in a work as a whole." . . . Judge Koeltl accepted Professor Pechota's view that the newspaper could prevent infringing activity "sufficient to interfere with the publisher's interest in the integrity of the work." . . . Without endeavoring to determine what extent of copying would "interfere with" the "integrity of the work," Judge Koeltl concluded that a preliminary injunction was warranted because what *Kurier* had copied was "the creative effort of the newspapers in the compilation of articles including numerous articles for the same issues, together with headlines and photographs." . . . The Court's preliminary injunction opinion left it unclear whether at trial the plaintiffs could obtain damages only for copying the newspapers' creative efforts as a compiler, such as the selection and arrangement of articles, the creation

---

[1]   The Newton Davis translation, which was an exhibit at trial, renders this word "publisher."

of headlines, and the layout of text and graphics, or also for copying the text of individual articles.

Expert testimony at trial. At trial, this unresolved issue was the focus of conflicting expert testimony. The plaintiffs' expert witness at trial was Michael Newcity, coordinator for the Center for Slavic, Eurasian and East European Studies at Duke University and an adjunct member of the faculty at the Duke University Law School. He opined that Article 11(2) gave the newspapers rights to redress copying not only of the publication "as a whole," but also of individual articles. He acknowledged that the reporters retained copyrights in the articles that they authored, but stated that Article 11(2) created a regime of parallel exclusive rights in both the newspaper publisher and the reporter. He rejected the contention that exclusive rights could not exist in two parties, pointing out that co-authors shared exclusive rights to their joint work. . . .

Defendants' experts presented a very different view of the rights of newspapers. Professor Peter B. Maggs of the University of Illinois, Urbana-Champaign, College of Law, testifying by deposition, pointed out that Article 11(2) gives authors the exclusive rights to their articles and accords newspaper publishers only the "exclusive rights to the publication as a whole, because that's the only thing not reserved to the authors." He opined that a newspaper's right to use of the compiled work "as a whole" would be infringed by the copying of an entire issue of a newspaper and probably by copying a substantial part of one issue, but not by the copying of a few articles, since the copyright in the articles belongs to the reporters. He also disagreed with Newcity's contention that exclusive rights to individual articles belonged simultaneously to both the newspaper and the reporter. Exclusive rights, he maintained, cannot be held by two people, except in the case of co-authors, who have jointly held rights against the world. . . .

Trial ruling. The District Court resolved the dispute among the experts by accepting Newcity's interpretation of Russian copyright law. . . . As he had previously ruled in granting the preliminary injunction, Judge Koeltl recognized that newspapers acquire no rights to individual articles by virtue of Article 14 since the Russian version of the work-for-hire doctrine is inapplicable to newspapers. Nevertheless, Judge Koeltl accepted Newcity's view of Article 11, relying on both the movement of the phrase "as a whole" from the first paragraph of Article 11(2) to the second paragraph of Article 11(2), and the opinion of the Informational Disputes Chamber. He also reasoned that publishers have "the real economic incentive to prevent wholesale unauthorized copying," and that, in the absence of assignments of rights to individual articles, widespread copying would occur if publishers could not prevent *Kurier*'s infringements. . . .]

Having considered all of the views presented by the expert witnesses, we conclude that the defendants' experts are far more persuasive as to the meaning of Article 11. In the first place, once Article

14 of the Russian Copyright Law explicitly denies newspapers the benefit of a work-for-hire doctrine, which, if available, would accord them rights to individual articles written by their employees, it is highly unlikely that Article 11 would confer on newspapers the very right that Article 14 has denied them. Moreover, Article 11 has an entirely reasonable scope if confined, as its caption suggests, to defining the "Copyright of Compilers of Collections and Other Works." That article accords compilers copyright "in the selection and arrangement of subject matter that he has made insofar as that selection or arrangement is the result of a creative effort of compilation." Russian Copyright Law, Art. 11(1). Article 11(2) accords publishers of compilations the right to exploit such works, including the right to insist on having its name mentioned, while expressly reserving to "authors of the works included" in compilations the "exclusive rights to exploit their works independently of the publication of the whole work." *Id.* As the defendants' experts testified, Article 11 lets *authors* of newspaper articles sue for infringement of their rights in the text of their articles, and lets *newspaper publishers* sue for wholesale copying of all of the newspaper or for copying any portions of the newspaper that embody their selection, arrangement, and presentation of articles (including headlines)—copying that infringes their ownership interest in the compilation. . . .

Relief. Our disagreement with the District Court's interpretation of Article 11 does not mean, however, that the defendants may continue copying with impunity. In the first place, Itar-Tass, as a press agency, is within the scope of Article 14, and, unlike the excluded newspapers, enjoys the benefit of the Russian version of the work-for-hire doctrine. Itar-Tass is therefore entitled to injunctive relief to prevent unauthorized copying of its articles and to damages for such copying, and the judgment is affirmed as to this plaintiff.

Furthermore, the newspaper plaintiffs, though not entitled to relief for the copying of the text of the articles they published, may well be entitled to injunctive relief and damages if they can show that Kurier infringed the publishers' ownership interests in the newspaper compilations. . . . Because the District Court upheld the newspapers' right to relief for copying the text of the articles, it had no occasion to consider what relief the newspapers might be entitled to by reason of *Kurier*'s copying of the newspapers' creative efforts in the selection, arrangement, or display of the articles. Since *Kurier*'s photocopying reproduced not only the text of articles but also headlines and graphic materials as they originally appeared in the plaintiffs' publication, it is likely that on remand the newspaper plaintiffs will be able to obtain some form of injunctive relief and some damages. On these infringement issues, as we have indicated, United States law will apply. . . .

Conclusion

Accordingly, we affirm the judgment to the extent that it granted relief to Itar-Tass, we reverse to the extent that the judgment granted relief to the other plaintiffs, and we remand for further proceedings. . . .

NOTES

1. *Choice of Law: International Intellectual Property Treaties.* The national treatment obligation imposed by international intellectual property treaties assures foreign authors, inventors, and businesses that they will enjoy the same intellectual property rules as nationals of the forum state. Does this principle mandate that they also be subject to the same choice-of-law rules as are nationals of the forum state in matters of intellectual property?

Are Berne Convention Articles 5(2) and 14*bis*(2) choice of law rules, or are they solely expressions of the principle of non-discrimination? Do the laws of the protecting country to which the provisions refer include the country's choice of law rules? *See* Paul Goldstein & Bernt Hugenholtz, International Copyright: Principles, Law, and Practice 131–138 (3d ed., 2013); Sam Ricketson & Jane C. Ginsburg, International Copyright and Neighbouring Rights: The Berne Convention and Beyond §§ 20.17–20.28 (2d ed. 2005). On choice-of-law issues in international instruments concerning cross-border access to orphan works for the visually impaired see Marketa Trimble, The Marrakesh Puzzle, 45(7) IIC 768 (2014).

2. *Choice of Law: Unitary Rights.* Is there a role for choice-of-law rules when an international instrument creates unitary law that is applicable in all countries that are parties to the instrument? Although Part II of the European Patent Convention sets substantive patent law, the Convention leaves a number of issues to national laws. Articles 60(1) and 64(3) of the Convention contain rules for the choice of law applicable to determine the right to a European patent and infringement.

European Union instruments that have created unitary trademarks, designs, and patents provide for some of the substantive law that governs the rights but also include choice-of-law rules for issues that are left to national laws. *See* Regulation (EU) 2017/1001 of the European Parliament and of the Council of 14 June 2017 on the European Union trade mark, Article 129; Council Regulation (EC) No 6/2002 of 12 December 2001 on Community designs, Article 88; Regulation (EU) No 1257/2012 of the European Parliament and of the Council of 17 December 2012 implementing enhanced cooperation in the area of the creation of unitary patent protection; *see* also Agreement on a Unified Patent Court, Article 7.

3. *Choice of Law: Initial Ownership.* As a rule, the main intellectual property conventions prescribe neither choice-of-law rules nor minimum standards for determining original ownership of intellectual goods, and national rules on the choice of law applicable to ownership may differ. *Itar-Tass* formulates one such choice of law rule for determining initial ownership of copyrighted works.

Some commentators would alternatively determine authorship and initial ownership under the law of the protecting country—the country in which the alleged infringement occurred. *See* Eugen Ulmer, Intellectual Property Rights and the Conflict of Laws 36–37 (1978). Under this approach, if *A*, a U.S. national, creates and first publishes in the United States a work that the U.S. Copyright Act would characterize as a work for hire, making *A*'s corporate employer, *B*, the work's "author" and initial copyright owner, *A* would nonetheless be considered the first owner of copyright in an infringement action in Germany, for example, which recognizes only flesh-and-blood creators as a work's author. This approach, using the law of the protecting country, has been adopted in countries other than Germany as well; for example, according to Article 48 of the Law of the People's Republic of China on the Laws Applicable to Foreign-Related Civil Relations the law of the place where protection is claimed governs the ownership and content of intellectual property rights.

Other commentators argue that authorship and initial ownership should be determined according to the law of the work's country of origin. *See* Georges Koumantos, Private International Law and the Berne Convention, 24 Copyright 415, 423–428 (1988). Under this approach, since the United States is the work's country of origin, another country would treat corporate employer *B*, and not creative employee *A*, as the work's author and initial copyright owner. For example, under Article 48 of the Portuguese Civil Code, author's rights are governed by the law of the place of the first publication and, if the work has not been published, by the law of the country of the author's nationality, unless a special law provides otherwise.

Does application of the "most significant relationship" rule of the Restatement (Second) of Conflict of Laws, referred to in the *Itar-Tass* decision, above, effectively mean choice of the law of the country of origin? Of the law of the protecting country? One author has suggested that the result of the application of the Restatement (Second) rule is that "the United States has effectively adopted a lex loci originis rule on copyright authorship." Graeme B. Dinwoodie, Developing a Private International Intellectual Property Law: The Demise of Territoriality?, 51 Wm. & Mary L. Rev. 711 (2009).

What happens to the ownership of copyright to a foreign work in a country that changes its choice-of-law rule for copyright ownership after the work was created? France previously applied the law of the work's country of origin but the Court of Cassation changed course in 2013 when it decided that the law of the protecting country, and not the law of the country of origin, determines copyright ownership. MX v. ABC News, Cour de Cassation, Civil Division 1, Case No. 11-12508, Apr. 10, 2013. As a result in France the copyright to the works at issue in the case was not owned by the producers, who owned copyright in the United States under the work for hire doctrine, but by the individual authors-journalists, who owned copyright under French law which, with a minor exception, does not have a work for hire doctrine. *See* page 230 below for a discussion of differences in national rules on initial copyright ownership.

4.   *Choice of Law: Ownership—Copyright Versus Other Types of Intellectual Property.* Questions on initial intellectual property ownership most commonly arise in copyright cases. Which, if any, of the three copyright choice of law approaches—law of the country with the most significant relationship, law of the protecting country, or law of the country of origin—best fits the interests at stake in patent, trademark and unfair competition cases?

In the case of employee inventions, several commentators, and Article 60(1) of the European Patent Convention, take the position that patent ownership is to be determined under the law of the country where the employment relationship exists; other commentators argue that ownership should be controlled by the law of the protecting country. Eugen Ulmer, Intellectual Property Rights and the Conflict of Laws 73 (1978). Article 93 of the Belgian Code of Private International Law refers to the law of the closest connection to the inventing activity to determine the original owner of an industrial right, such as a patent; however, if "the activity takes place in the context of contractual relations" the Code establishes a presumption that the law applicable to the contractual relations applies.

Sections 311–313 of A.L.I., Intellectual Property: Principles Governing Jurisdiction, Choice of Law, and Judgments in Transnational Disputes, approved May 14, 2007, differentiate in their choice of law rules on initial ownership between registered rights, unregistered trademark and trade dress rights, and other rights that do not arise out of registration. As a rule, section 311 makes the law of the country of registration govern initial title to rights arising out of registration and section 312 determines initial title to unregistered trademarks and trade dress according to "the law of each state in which the trademark or trade dress identifies and distinguishes the source of the goods or the services." In the case of other rights, principally copyright, not arising out of registration, section 313 generally assigns initial title according to the law of the creator's residence at the time the subject matter was created or, if the subject matter was created in an employment relationship, according to the law of the country governing the relationship.

The European Max Planck Group on Conflict of Laws in Intellectual Property, in its Principles for Conflict of Laws in Intellectual Property, has adopted a single approach to choice of law for initial ownership of intellectual property rights. Article 3:201(1) of the Principles establishes "the law of the State for which protection is sought" as the governing law for initial ownership and entitlement to intellectual property rights. Special rules are proposed for rights to a work made for hire and for rights to claim a registered right that arise within a contractual relationship, such as employment. Conflict of Laws in Intellectual Property: The CLIP Principles and Commentary (2013), p. 11.

5.   *Choice of Law: Issues Other than Ownership.* Apart from questions of initial ownership and ownership by transfer, and absent a dispositive treaty rule, the law of the protecting country will typically control substantive aspects of an intellectual property dispute such as protectibility of the subject matter, and the scope of the rights in issue. This general preference for the law of the protecting country doubtless stems from the historic principle that

intellectual property is territorial: To apply the law of Country *A* to an alleged infringement occurring in Country *B* would effectively violate the territoriality principle by exporting the law of one country to the territory of another.

What other reasons are there to apply the law of the protecting country to questions of rights and subject matter? Is it relevant that rules on protectible subject matter and enforceable rights will invariably have a greater impact on a country's intellectual property balance of trade than rules on initial ownership? That questions of protectible subject matter and scope of rights—particularly exceptions from rights—may bear directly on a country's political and cultural traditions? *See* generally, Paul Edward Geller, Conflicts of Laws in Copyright Cases: Infringement and Ownership Issues, 51 J. Copyr. Soc'y U.S.A. 315 (2004); Christopher Wadlow, Trade Secrets and the Rome II Regulation on the Law Applicable to Non-Contractual Obligations, 30(8) EIPR 309 (2008).

What country is the protecting country when the intellectual property right in dispute is a unitary regional right? Matters not governed by the regional law establishing the unitary right will be governed by the law of the protecting country. But which country is the protecting country when the infringement spans multiple countries in which the unitary right exists? The Rome II Regulation directs EU member states' courts to apply "the law of the country for which protection is claimed" in cases of infringements of national intellectual property rights, but it provides for the application of "the law of the country in which the act of infringement was committed" for infringements of EU unitary rights. Regulation (EC) No 864/2007 of the European Parliament and of the Council of 11 July 2007 on the law applicable to non-contractual obligations (the "Rome II Regulation"), Article 8(1) and (2).

It will not always be easy to identify "the country in which the act of infringement was commited." In Nintendo Co. Ltd. v. BigBen Interactive GmbH, CJEU, C-24/16 and 25/16, 2017, Nintendo brought an action in a German court against BigBen France and its subsidiary, BigBen Germany, for infringements of Nintendo's registered designs in its Wii video game accessories that the defendant companies committed in several EU member states when they sold the infringing accessories through their websites. Nintendo argued that German law should apply to its claims relating to BigBen Germany but that French law should apply to its claims relating to BigBen France. The CJEU held that "Where the same defendant is accused of various acts of infringement in various Member States, the correct approach for identifying the event giving rise to the damage is not to refer to each alleged act of infringement, but to make an overall assessment of that defendant's conduct in order to determine the place where the initial act of infringement at the origin of that conduct was committed or threatened by it." *Id.*, holding of the court.

Generally on choice-of-forum and choice-of-law issues concerning unitary rights see Annette Kur, Enforcement of Unitary Intellectual Property Rights: International Jurisdiction and Applicable Law, 10(6) JIPLP 468 (2015); Eleonora Rosati, International Jurisdiction in Online EU Trade

Mark Infringement Cases: Where Is the Place of Infringement Located?, 38(8) EIPR 482 (2016).

6. *Choice of Law for Intellectual Property Contracts.* Well-counseled parties to international intellectual property transactions commonly designate in their agreement the law that will govern the agreement. *See* note 7, below. What law will govern in the absence of such a clause? In the United States, on issues such as contract legality and construction, section 188 of the Restatement (Second) of Conflict of Laws would determine the rights and duties of the parties by "the local law of the state which, with respect to that issue, has the most significant relationship to the transaction and to the parties." In determining what state possesses the "most significant relationship," a court is to evaluate at least five contacts "according to their relative importance with respect to the particular issue": "(a) the place of contracting, (b) the place of negotiation of the contract, (c) the place of performance, (d) the location of the subject matter of the contract, and (e) the domicil, residence, nationality, place of incorporation and place of business of the parties." Section 206 would determine issues relating to the details of performance under the local law of the place of performance.

Regulation (EC) No. 593/2008 of the European Parliament and of the Council of 17 June 2008 on the law applicable to contractual obligations (the "Rome I Regulation"), which replaced the 1980 Convention on the Law Applicable to Contractual Obligations, commonly known as the Rome Contracts Convention, provides in Article 4 that, absent choice of law by the parties, the determination of the applicable law will be based on the category of the contract, such as a contract for the sale of goods or a contract for the provision of services. If the contract does not fall within one or a multiple of the categories listed, the contract will be "governed by the law of the country with which it is most closely connected." Article 4(4). Special rules apply to consumer contracts, which are "governed by the law of the country where the consumer has habitual residence." Article 6.

How difficult is it to apply the above rules to determine the law applicable to licenses that concern the creation of computer programs by developers who reside in multiple countries? How will the rules apply to non-negotiated instruments, such as the GNU General Public License or Creative Commons licenses? On choice of law and contracts in general see Pedro A. de Miguel Asensio, The Law Governing International Intellectual Property Licensing Agreements (A Conflict of Laws Analysis), in Research Handbook on Intellectual Property Licensing (Jacques de Werra ed., 2013), pp. 312–336.

7. *Contract Choice of Law Clauses.* Parties to an intellectual property agreement that has connections to more than one country can reduce uncertainty over judicial choice of law by including a governing law clause that designates the law applicable to the contract. In the European Union, Article 3(1) of the Rome I Regulation provides that parties may select the law to be applied to all or part of their contract. In the United States, section 187 of the Restatement (Second) of Conflict of Laws, provides that "[t]he law of the state chosen by the parties to govern their contractual rights and duties will be applied if the particular issue is one which the parties could have resolved by an explicit provision in their agreement directed to that issue."

Party choice of law will not, however, always control judicial choice of law. Article 3(3) of the Rome I Regulation effectively provides that if the contract's relevant elements are rooted in some country other than the country designated by the governing law clause, that country's "mandatory rules"—antitrust laws for example—will supersede the law selected by the parties. Further, Article 21 provides that the "application of a provision of the law of any country specified by this Regulation may be refused only if such application is manifestly incompatible with the public policy (*ordre public*) of the forum." Special protection is afforded to consumer contracts; choice of law in the contracts "may not . . . have the result of depriving the consumer of the protection afforded to him by provisions that cannot be derogated from by agreement by virtue of the law which, in the absence of choice would have been applicable." Article 6(2).

The Restatement (Second) of Conflict of Laws, section 187, requires enforcement of a governing law clause unless the state whose law is chosen "has no substantial relationship to the parties or the transaction and there is no other reasonable basis for the parties' choice," or applying the chosen law would violate "a fundamental policy of a state which has a materially greater interest than the chosen state in the determination of the particular issue" and whose law would govern in the absence of the governing law clause.

Section 302 of A.L.I., Intellectual Property: Principles Governing Jurisdiction, Choice of Law, and Judgments in Transnational Disputes, approved May 14, 2007, allows parties to designate the law that will govern all or part of their dispute, but, in section 302(2), excludes from party choice the law governing "(a) the validity and maintenance of registered rights; (b) the existence, attributes, transferability, and duration of rights, whether or not registered; and (c) formal requirements for recordation of assignments and licenses." Also, as in the case of choice of forum agreements, section 302(5) provides that "choice-of-law clauses in mass-market agreements are valid only if the choice-of-law clause was reasonable and readily accessible to the nondrafting party at the time the agreement was concluded, and is available for subsequent reference by the court and the parties."*

See generally, James Fawcett & Paul Torremans, Intellectual Property and Private International Law, 2nd ed., 745–797 (2011); Rome I Regulation: The Law Applicable to Contractual Obligations in Europe (Franco Ferrari, & Stefan Leible eds. 2009).

8. *Conflicts of the Applicable Intellectual Property Law and the Law Applicable to the Transfer of Right.* The law governing an intellectual property contract will sometimes conflict with the law that governs the rights the contract purports to convey; a right that may be freely transferred under the law of one country may in other countries be subject to mandatory rules that limit its transferability. Campbell Connelly & Co. Ltd. v. Noble, 1

---

* Copyright 2007 by The American Law Institute. Reprinted with permission. All rights reserved.

W.L.R. 252 (1963), is the leading case on the methodology to be employed in resolving these conflicts. Under *Campbell Connelly,* the court is first to consult the law of the country in which the right is to be exploited (under the facts of the case, the United States renewal copyright) to determine whether the right is transferable (under U.S. law it is) and then to consult the law of the contract (in this case English law since it was a "purely English contract") to determine whether the contract in fact assigned the American renewal right. (The court held that, under English rules of construction, it did.)

Consider how the following conflict should be resolved using the *Campbell Connelly* methodology: Under a contract ostensibly governed by U.S. law, writer-director John Huston and his co-writer Ben Maddow assigned worldwide rights to the black-and-white film *Asphalt Jungle* to defendant's predecessor in interest; when defendant sought to perform a colorized version of the film in France (presumably in violation of France's moral right of integrity), Huston's heirs and Maddow sued. Under U.S. law, rights are freely alienable; under French law, moral rights are not.

The Paris Court of Appeal ruled for the defendant, holding that authorship and ownership were to be determined under the law of the United States, as the work's country of origin, a decision that "compels denying the parties Huston and Maddow any possibility of asserting their moral rights." Turner Entertainment v. Huston, Court of Appeal, Paris 4th Chamber, July 6, 1989, 143 R.I.D.A. 329, 335 (1989). The Court of Cassation set aside the decision. Attaching no weight to the possible applicability of U.S. law, the court relied on Article 6 of the French Copyright Act, the Law of March 11, 1957, which makes moral rights inalienable. Consorts Huston et. autres v. Sté Turner Entertainment, Court of Cassation, 1st Civ. Chamber, May 28, 1991, 149 R.I.D.A. 197 (1991). Would a French court resolve the issue differently under the current French rule for choice of law applicable to initial copyright ownership? *See* note 3, above.

In *Salvador Dalí*, French rules applicable to copyright, specifically the resale right, conflicted with Spanish inheritance rules. In his will Dalí appointed the Spanish State to be the sole legatee of his intellectual property rights. However, when the French collecting society ADAGP collected resale royalties for sales of his works in France after his death, ADAGP did not pay the royalties to the Spanish State but to Dalí's intestate heirs, because under Article L. 123–7 of the French Intellectual Property Code "legatees and successors in title" are not entitled to benefit from the resale right following the death of the author. After the Court of Justice of the European Union confirmed that EU law provided no solution to the problem, the High Court of Paris held that Spanish law applied and the testamentary heir—the Spanish State—was the beneficiary of Dalí's resale right. Fundación Gala-Salvador Dalí v. ADAGP, CJEU, C-518/08, 2010; High Court of Paris, 2011.

The *Huston* case is discussed in Bernard Edelman, Applicable Legislation Regarding Exploitation of Colourized U.S. Films in France: The "John Huston" Case, 23 IIC 629 (1992); Jane C. Ginsburg & Pierre Sirinelli, Authors and Exploitation in International Private Law: The French Supreme Court and the Huston Film Colorization Controversy, 15 Colum.-VLA J.L. & Arts 135 (1991). For a provocative discussion of this class of conflicts generally, see Paul Edward Geller, Harmonizing Copyright-Contract Conflicts Analyses, 25 Copyright 49 (1989).

9.   *A Single Law Applicable to Multi-Jurisdictional Infringements.* Is it possible to identify the law of one jurisdiction that could apply to infringements globally? The place from which an alleged infringement originates, the place of a right owner's domicile, and the place of a server or servers hosting infringing content have all been proposed as possible candidates. The proposals for intellectual property law cases parallel similar approaches adopted in other areas of law: The place from which an alleged infringement originates resembles the approach taken by the EU E-Commerce Directive; the place of a right owner's domicile has been used in the United States as the place in which an injury for defamation is located.

The "emission principle" was adopted in the EU Satellite and Cable Directive, according to which "[t]he act of communication to the public by satellite" is localized where "the programme-carrying signals are introduced into an uninterrupted chain of communication leading to the satellite and down towards the earth." Council Directive 93/83/EEC of 27 September 1993 on the coordination of certain rules concerning copyright and rights related to copyright applicable to satellite broadcasting and cable retransmission, Article 1(2)(b).

An attempt in the European Union to extend the emission principle broadly to "ancillary online services offered by broadcasting organisations" failed; a compromise resulted in the emission principle being extended only to (1) radio programs and (2) television programs that are either "news and current affairs" or a content provider's own productions (not licensed content). Directive (EU) 2019/789 of the European Parliament and of the Council of 17 April 2019 laying down rules on the exercise of copyright and related rights applicable to certain online transmissions of broadcasting organisations and retransmissions of television and radio programmes, Article 3(1).

10.   *Choice of Law on the Internet.* Section 321(1) of A.L.I., Intellectual Property: Principles Governing Jurisdiction, Choice of Law, and Judgments in Transnational Disputes, approved May, 14, 2007, guides choice of law in cases where "the alleged infringing activity is ubiquitous and the laws of multiple States are pleaded" by authorizing courts to "apply to the issues of existence, validity, duration, attributes, and infringement of intellectual property rights, and remedies for their infringement, the law or laws of the State or States with close connections to the dispute." As examples of "close connections," the Principles suggest: "(a) where the parties reside; (b) where the parties' relationship, if any, is centered; (c) the extent of the activities and the investment of the parties; and (d) the principal markets toward which the parties directed their activities."[**]

Consider how this principle would apply to a case in which *A*, a website operator in Country *X*, posts on her site, for global distribution, a 1930 motion picture, the worldwide rights to which are owned by *B* a resident of

---

Country *Y*. The duration of motion picture rights in Countries *X* and *Y* is 95 years from publication, but in Country *Z*, where the rights are also infringed, the term is fifty years from publication. On these facts, taken from an illustration in the A.L.I. Principles, the court could apply the law of Country *Y* because *B* is a resident of Country *Y* and its filmmaking activities are centered there. While it would be appropriate under this approach to award *B* monetary relief for its losses in Countries *X* and *Y*, where its rights continue to subsist, a monetary award for Country *Z*, where the movie is now in the public domain, would overcompensate *B*. Section 321(2) of the *Principles* addresses this possibility by providing that "[n]otwithstanding the State or States designated pursuant to subsection (1), a party may prove that, with respect to particular States covered by the action, the solution provided by any of those States' laws differs from that obtained under the law(s) chosen to apply to the case as a whole. The court must take into account such differences in fashioning the remedy." Thus, in the example given, a court could reduce *B*'s award to exclude recovery for the film's exploitation in Country *Z*.

11. *Choice of Law on the Internet and Secondary Liability.* Suppose that in the example above *A* does not have her own website but utilizes the services of *A-Load*, which enable her to post the motion picture on the *A-Load* website for global distribution. In some countries and under certain conditions, *A-Load*'s liability for *A's* conduct will be limited; however, even if safe harbors exist that protect Internet service providers from secondary liability, the standards of the safe harbors can vary from country to country. Which country's law should be applied to determine *A-Load*'s secondary liability? *See* Graeme B. Dinwoodie, Rochelle C. Dreyfuss, Annette Kur, The Law Applicable to Secondary Liability in Intellectual Property Cases, 42 N.Y.U.J. Int'l L. & Pol. 201 (2009).

The European Max Planck Group on Conflict of Laws in Intellectual Property has proposed an exception to the general rule that any secondary infringement will be governed by the law applicable to a direct infringement. The exception would benefit Internet service providers, such as *A-Load*, as long as they provided services with some non-infringing uses, took no part in the infringing activity, had no actual knowledge of any directly infringing activities by their users, and did not actively induce acts of direct infringement. If the conditions are met, any secondary liability of the service providers would be governed by "the law of the State where the centre of gravity of [their] activities relating to [their] services is located." Conflict of Laws in Intellectual Property: The CLIP Principles (2013), pp. 15–16, Article 3:604 (2) and (3). Would this exception permit *A-Load* to arrange its operation in a manner that would avoid secondary liability? Is the rule proposed in the Principles a choice-of-law rule or a substantive law rule? What is the rationale behind creating a special rule for Internet service providers but not for other parties that may be exposed to claims of secondary liability?

12. *Choice of Law: Arbitration.* One of the possible advantages of resolving a transnational dispute in an arbitration proceeding is the possibility that the arbitration tribunal will apply a single country's law to govern the dispute. As one commentator noted, "[i]n an international arbitration, . . . parties should . . . be in a position to decide that all contractual and non-contractual issues shall be governed by a single law. . . [T]he choice of law could also cover issues regarding the validity of the relevant intellectual property rights . . . [a]s long as a decision to be made by an arbitral tribunal as to the validity of a certain [registered intellectual] property right would only have an *inter partes* effect . . ." Jacques de Werra, Global Policies for Arbitrating Intellectual Property Disputes, in Research Handbook on Intellectual Property Licensing (Jacques de Werra ed., 2013), pp. 353–377, at p. 367.

c.   RES JUDICATA AND COLLATERAL ESTOPPEL

Cuno Inc. v. Pall Corporation

United States District Court, Eastern District, New York, 1989.
729 F.Supp. 234, 14 U.S.P.Q.2d 1815.

WEINSTEIN, DISTRICT JUDGE.

The production of microporous nylon membrane filters generates hundreds of millions of dollars in worldwide revenues. It is vital to pharmaceutical, microchip and other industries requiring filtration of impurities the size of the smallest microbes. Plaintiff Cuno and defendants Pall and its associated companies are major competitors in this field. They press claims and counterclaims relating to the validity, infringement and enforceability of a number of key patents teaching methods of producing these filters.

Defendants move for partial summary judgment based on the collateral estoppel effect of factual findings made by a Justice of the United Kingdom Court of Chancery, Patent Division, in a prior adjudication between the parties. The European Patent Office's counterpart of defendants' United States patent at issue here was there found to be valid and noninfringing. Defendants argue that the findings of fact made by the foreign court are entitled to preclusive effect since the patent issued by the European Patent Office on behalf of the countries of the European Economic Community describes the same technological invention and makes claims that are in all material ways identical to those contained in defendants' United States patent.

Plaintiff argues that the traditional requirements for granting collateral estoppel are not present here and that the application of preclusive effect to findings made by a foreign court runs counter to policies underlying both domestic and foreign patent law. For the reasons noted below, the court denies defendants' motion.

I.   Facts

At issue are six patents. Five of the patents—four of which are held by plaintiff—relate to the membrane filters themselves. One—also held by plaintiff—covers a process for producing microporous membrane filters. Closely analogous counterpart patents for the membranes have been issued to both plaintiff and defendants in a number of foreign countries. . . .

In addition to opposing Pall's various patent applications abroad, Cuno brought the instant lawsuit in September of 1986 [alleging infringements of its patents; in response, Pall alleged that Cuno's patents were invalid and that Cuno infringed Pall's patent]. . . . Cuno [then] also challenged the validity of Pall's patent . . . [and] Pall counterclaimed for infringement of its [patent.] . . . Included in [Pall's] claims are allegations and counterallegations of [Cuno's] fraudulent failure to disclose information to the United States Patent Office.

While discovery was proceeding in the United States action, Pall initiated a lawsuit in Great Britain in 1987 against Cuno and two of its European subsidiaries, claiming that Cuno's Zetapor membranes infringed key claims made in Pall's newly-granted EPC patent. Discovery for the United States case was used in the British action. That case was tried in London for four weeks in the late spring and summer of 1989. Some of the testimony, and many of the witnesses from the British case are expected to be utilized in the upcoming United States trial.

On July 25, 1989 the British judge, Justice Falconer, ruled in Pall's favor, making extensive findings and construing critical terms in the claims made in Pall's EPC patent. In a 64-page opinion, he concluded, inter alia, 1) that Pall's patent was valid; 2) that Cuno's Zetapor membranes infringed claims in Pall's EPC patent; 3) that there was no merit to the . . . defense raised by Cuno [concerning the validity of Pall's patent]; and 4) that there had been no invalidating prior public use [that would have invalidated Pall's patent]. An order enjoining Cuno from infringing the Pall EPC patent was entered on August 1, 1989. Shortly thereafter Cuno filed a notice of appeal.

Cuno continues to prosecute its opposition to the Pall EPC patent in the European Patent Office. It is unclear what, if any, effect a decision revoking or modifying Pall's EPC patent would have on the British court's ruling should Cuno's opposition prove successful. The court's order contained a "liberty to apply" provision, which apparently allows either party to return to the court to make further applications in the event that matters are elicited "concerning or arising out of [Cuno's] Opposition in the [European Patent Office]." In any event, the parties have informed the court that the European Patent Office may not render a decision for years.

This court originally ordered a jury trial to begin in September. As a result of the United Kingdom decision, the court tentatively suggested that collateral estoppel might permit shortening of the trial. It became apparent, however, that the procedural and technical problems associated with a motion for application of collateral estoppel on the basis of findings made in the English judgment were so difficult and required so much further briefing and argument that it would be impossible to start the jury trial as scheduled.

In support and opposition to the motion for partial summary judgment, several days of hearings were conducted at which experts on patent and procedural law from the United States, the United Kingdom and Germany testified. Experts from both sides described the technology and development of a variety of patents in this field over the last 20 years. Extensive briefing and argument followed.

II.   Law

A motion for summary judgment pursuant to Rule 56 of the Federal Rules of Civil Procedure is appropriate in a patent case. . . .

The application of collateral estoppel to patent cases is similarly appropriate. *See, e.g., Blonder-Tongue Laboratories, Inc. v. University of Illinois Foundation*, 402 U.S. 313, 333, 91 S.Ct. 1434, 1445, 28 L.Ed.2d 788 (1971) (collateral estoppel applied to issue of validity of patent where patent was declared invalid in prior proceeding in which patentee had full and fair chance to litigate); *Hartley v. Mentor Corp.*, 869 F.2d 1469, 1471 (Fed.Cir. 1989) ("Issue preclusion in patent litigation may arise under same conditions as in any litigation. . . ."); *Molinaro v. Fannon/Courier Corp.*, 745 F.2d 651, 655 (Fed.Cir. 1984) (granting summary judgment on basis of collateral estoppel); *Mississippi Chemical Corp. v. Swift Agricultural Chemicals Corp.*, 717 F.2d 1374 (Fed.Cir. 1983) (where no evidence existed that patentee had been deprived of full and fair opportunity to litigate in earlier case, it was appropriate to issue writ of mandamus ordering district court judge to grant summary judgment based on application of collateral estoppel to prior finding of invalidity).

Nevertheless, the Federal Circuit has shown a general antipathy to applying collateral estoppel as a basis for a judgment in circumstances arguably similar to those present in this case. *See, e.g., Ethicon, Inc. v. Quigg*, 849 F.2d 1422, 1428–29 (Fed.Cir. 1988) ("[A] court's decision upholding a patent's validity is not ordinarily binding on another challenge to the patent's validity . . . in . . . the courts. . . .") . . . ; *A.B. Dick Co. v. Burroughs Corp.*, 713 F.2d 700 (Fed.Cir. 1983) (in order to apply collateral estoppel to judicial statements in prior proceeding regarding scope of patent claims, such statements must be narrowly construed and must have been essential to final judgement on question of either validity or infringement). . . .

Where the prior adjudication was by a foreign nation's court applying its patent law to its patents, the barriers to reliance on the foreign judgment for collateral estoppel purposes become almost insurmountable. Differences in the law of the two nations and in the detailed language of the patent are emphasized to avoid issue preclusion in a patent case pending in this country even where the invention, the technological and economic competition between the parties, and the consequences of the judgments are for all practical purposes the same. *See, e.g., Medtronic, Inc. v. Daig Corp.*, 789 F.2d 903, 907–08 (Fed.Cir.), *cert. denied*, 479 U.S. 931, 107 S.Ct. 402, 93 L.Ed.2d 355 (1986) (prior conclusion of German tribunal as to obviousness of counterpart German patent does not control issue of obviousness in action involving United States patent); *Stein Associates, Inc. v. Heat and Control, Inc.*, 748 F.2d 653 (Fed.Cir. 1984) (denying motion to enjoin efforts to enforce British patent in Britain where U.S. counterpart patent had been deemed invalid). As Chief Judge Markey remarked in *Stein Associates v. Heat and Control, Inc.*, 748 F.2d 653 (Fed.Cir. 1984):

> British law being different from our own, and British and United States courts being independent of each other, resolution of the question of whether the United States patents are valid could have no binding effect on the British court's decision.

Id. at 658. The converse is equally true.

Even if this court were to apply collateral estoppel to certain factual findings made by the British court—as opposed to importing its legal conclusions wholesale—it is not clear that trial time would be significantly shortened. Furthermore, the Federal Circuit's reluctance to give collateral estoppel effect to foreign judgments would seem to apply here to foreign findings of fact insofar as those findings involve mixed questions of fact and foreign law.

[handwritten margin note: ground for denial ① ②]

It is a quiddity of our law that a well and thoroughly reasoned decision reached by a highly skilled and scientifically informed justice of the Patent Court, Chancery Division, in the High Court of Justice of Great Britain after four weeks of trial must be ignored and essentially the same issues with the same evidence must now be retried by American jurors with no background in science or patents, whose average formal education will be no more than high school. This curious event is the result of the world's chauvinistic view of patents.

The law's absurdity as revealed by this case lends force to recommendations for a universal patent system that recognizes that ours is a worldwide technological and economic community. . . . Obviously there are grave difficulties in devising a system that will not disadvantage the old fashioned single craftsman-inventor or citizens of countries with patent offices that are careful in investigating before issuing patents. But the European Patent Office furnishes a model that appears to be working. Perhaps paragraph (1) of Article 4bis of the Paris Convention, with its emphasis on nationality, needs to be reconsidered. It reads:

[handwritten margin note: Paris Convention]

> (1) Patents applied for in the various countries of the Union by nationals of countries of the Union shall be independent of patents obtained for the same invention in other countries, whether members of the Union or not.

Convention of Paris for the Protection of Industrial Property, article 4bis(1). . . .

There would appear to be no constitutional inhibition against a reconsideration of international patent policy. Clause 8 of Article I of the Constitution grants Congress power over patents. But, just as Congress delegates much of its patenting power to the patent office and the courts, the government may, under Article II, section 2, clause 2 of the Constitution, provide a role for international bodies through the treaty making powers. . . .

III. Other Grounds for Summary Judgment

As an alternative ground for summary judgment the court could rely on the evidence produced on the motion for summary judgment. It includes extensive affidavits, testimony before this court of scientific and legal experts, the transcript of the trial in Great Britain, patent files and extensive materials for judicial notice. Taken together this mass of evidence still depends somewhat on evaluation of the credibility of prospective witnesses. The issue must be left for the jury.

Should the jury decide in a way inconsistent with the United Kingdom court's decision or the record, the court could, after the trial, grant what would be in effect a delayed summary judgment motion. . . .

IV. Conclusion

The motion for summary judgment is denied. . . .

So ordered.

NOTES

1. *Collateral Estoppel.* Will collateral estoppel, or issue preclusion, ever play a role in a case concerning intellectual property? Parallel patents are patents granted in different countries for the same invention; often the patents stem from a single international patent application. If a court decides that one of the national parallel patents is invalid because the invention was not novel, is it necessary to have patent offices or courts in other countries decide on the validity of each of the corresponding parallel patents individually?

Courts in the United States have adopted the factual findings that were made in foreign proceedings, as long as the issue was identical, the issue was actually litigated, the fact finding was necessary for the court's final decision, and the foreign proceedings were fundamentally fair. Oneac Corp. v. Raychem Corp., 20 F.Supp.2d 1233, 1243 (N.D. Ill. 1998). However, courts have refused to adopt the conclusions of foreign courts as to the validity of the corresponding parallel patents. *See* Medtronic, Inc. v. Daig Corp., 789 F.2d 903 (Fed.Cir. 1986) (decision of a German tribunal on the validity of a German parallel patent); Merck & Co., Inc. v. Teva Pharmaceuticals USA, Inc., 288 F.Supp.2d 601 (D. Del. 2003) (decision of a British court on the validity of a European patent).

Should the courts' approach be different if two parallel patents stemming from a single European patent application are at issue? Although courts in such instances will not apply collateral estoppel to decisions on foreign patent validity, they may attach some weight to the decisions that courts in other European countries render with regard to parallel patents. In HTC Europe Co. Ltd. v. Apple, Inc., [2011] EWHC 2396 (Pat), the plaintiff requested that an English court expedite three patent actions concerning U.K. patents in order for the plaintiff to use the findings made by the English court in the expedited actions to defeat a presumption of validity of the parallel German patents in proceedings pending before the German courts. The connection with the German proceedings was not considered the main factor for the decision by the English court but it did provide additional support for the request for expediting the English proceedings, which was ultimately granted in the case. *Id.*, ¶ 19.

In *Roller Forming Machinery* the German Federal Supreme Court noted that although the German Federal Patent Court is not bound by earlier decisions of the European Patent Office concerning eligibility for protection of the same invention, such decisions by the European Patent Office "are of considerable importance in that they contain an opinion on a legal issue which arises in an identical or similar manner in proceedings before the Federal Patent Court or the Federal Supreme Court." Therefore, if the German Federal Patent Court reaches a decision that differs from an earlier decision by the European Patent Office concerning the same invention, the Court must, "in the interest of the uniform application of the law," address the difference. Roller Forming Machinery, Bundesgerichtshof, Xa ZB 10/09, 2010; 42(3) IIC 363–367 (2011).

Once the Unified Patent Court becomes operational in Europe, it will be competent to decide the validity of European patents with unitary effect as well as the validity of European patents granted under the European Patent Convention. The court will issue decisions based on either an action for revocation or a counterclaim for revocation, and its decisions will be effective in all countries in which the particular European patent has effect. Agreement on a Unified Patent Court, Articles 34 and 65. For a discussion of European patents and European patents with unitary effect see page 490, below.

2.   *Identical Issues.* Courts do not view infringements of parallel intellectual property rights as presenting identical issues when the rights exist and the infringements arise under the laws of different countries. *See* the examples of disputes concerning parallel trademarks and copyrights in *Microsoft Corp. v. Lindows.Com, Inc.* and *Zynga, Inc. v. Vostu USA, Inc.* at page 45, above.

Could the same acts concerning the same patents present different issues depending on the proceedings? In Sanofi-Aventis Deutschland G.m.b.H. v. Genentech Inc., 716 F.3d 586 (Fed.Cir. 2013), Genentech sought to stop Sanofi-Aventis from pursuing arbitration in Europe concerning Sanofi-Aventis's two U.S. patents that a U.S. court held that Genentech had not infringed. In the arbitration Sanofi-Aventis maintained that Genentech had committed a breach of contract when it refused to pay royalties for the two patents. The U.S. Court of Appeals for the Federal Circuit declined to issue an anti-suit injunction against the arbitration and opined that the meaning of infringement in the two proceedings was "not functionally the same." 716 F.3d at 593. Does it make a difference that the U.S. court applied U.S. patent law but the arbitrator was to apply German contract law, French procedural law, and the rules of the International Chamber of Commerce? 716 F.3d at 592.

3.   *Identical Parties.* Can the identity of parties become the subject of a dispute? In a dispute between Eli Lilly and Actavis, Actavis filed a suit in England for declaration of non-infringement of several of Eli Lilly's parallel patents, including a German patent (a German designation of Eli Lilly's European patent). Subsequently Eli Lilly filed a suit in Germany claiming that Actavis infringed Eli Lilly's German patent. Actavis then asked the German court to stay its proceedings under either Article 27 or Article 28 of the Brussels I Regulation. The German court refused to stay its proceedings under Article 27, finding that the parties to the dispute were not identical. While the plaintiff in the German proceedings was identical to the defendant in the English proceedings, the defendants in the German proceedings were not identical to the plaintiffs in the English proceedings. The German court explained that it did not matter that the plaintiff in the English proceedings was the parent company of the companies that were sued in Germany. Referring to Eli Lilly's "legitimate interests in a speedy and effective decision," the German court used its discretion to also refuse to stay its proceedings under Article 28. Oberlandesgericht Düsseldorf, I-2 W 6/13, Mar. 4, 2014, ¶ 38. For the parallel English proceedings see Actavis UK Ltd v. Eli Lilly, High Court of Justice, [2014] EWHC 1511 (Pat), May 15, 2014.

4.   *Extraterritorial Effects of a Territorially Limited Decision.* If a dispute involves the same invention, same parties, and same actions, such as an infringing activity that spreads across multiple countries, multiple parallel actions might be necessary to enforce intellectual property rights, particularly if registered intellectual property rights are at issue and the issue of their validity is raised. However, pursuing parallel litigation in several countries may be infeasible for a plaintiff.

Will a judgment rendered in one country have no practical effect in other countries? As the English Court of Appeal noted, "[w]inning in one [EU] member state may indeed be enough as a practical matter for the whole of Europe—some companies market products only Europe-wide. A hole, say in Germany, of a Europe-wide business in a particular product may make the whole of that business impractical." Research in Motion UK Ltd. v. Visto Corp., [2008] EWCA Civ. 153, ¶ 15. Will this effect also extend beyond European borders?

Should practical effects be considered when assessing whether decisions on parallel national patents pose the risk of producing irreconcilable judgments? The Court of Justice of the European Communities explained that, in the context of Article 28 of the Brussels I Regulation (formerly Article 22 of the Brussels Convention and now Article 30 of the Brussels I Regulation (recast)), irreconcilable judgments are any "conflicting decisions, even if the judgments can be separately enforced and their legal consequences are not mutually exclusive." Tatry v. Maciej Rataj, ECJ, C-406/92, 1995, ¶ 52.

James Fawcett opined that it is an "old-fashioned view that, in litigation involving parallel rights, the actions are based on different rights and there would not be a risk of irreconcilable judgments." James Fawcett & Paul Torremans, Intellectual Property and Private International Law, 200 (2d ed. 2011).

For a discussion of the *lis pendens* provisions in the EU see the decision in *Mecklermedia* which appears at page 24, above. On influences—actual and potential—of foreign patent law and foreign decisions in patent matters see Timothy R. Holbrook, Should Foreign Patent Law Matter?, 34(3) Campbell L. Rev. 581 (2012).

4. RECOGNITION AND ENFORCEMENT OF FOREIGN JUDGMENTS

Sarl Louis Feraud International, S.A. v. Viewfinder, Inc.

United States Court of Appeals, Second Circuit, 2007.
489 F.3d 474.

POOLER, CIRCUIT JUDGE.

Plaintiffs-appellants Sarl Louis Feraud International ("Feraud") and S.A. Pierre Balmain ("Balmain") appeal from the September 29, 2005, order of the United States District Court for the Southern District of New York (Lynch, J.) dismissing plaintiffs' action to enforce two judgments issued by the Tribunal de grande instance de Paris ("the French Judgments") against defendant-appellee Viewfinder, Inc. ("Viewfinder"). Plaintiffs challenge the district court's conclusion that enforcement of the French Judgments would be repugnant to the public policy of New York under N.Y. C.P.L.R. § 5304(b)(4) because it would violate Viewfinder's First Amendment rights. Because the district court did not conduct the full analysis necessary to reach this conclusion, we vacate its order and remand for further proceedings consistent with this opinion.

BACKGROUND

Plaintiffs-appellants Feraud and Balmain are French corporations that design high-fashion clothing and other items for women. Defendant-appellee Viewfinder is a Delaware corporation with a principal place of business in New York. Viewfinder operates a website called "firstView.com," on which it posts photographs of fashion shows held by designers around the world, including photographs of plaintiffs' fashion shows. Donald Ashby, the president of Viewfinder, is a professional fashion photographer. Viewfinder styles itself as an Internet fashion magazine akin to the online version of Vogue. The firstView website contains both photographs of the current season's fashions, which may be viewed only upon subscription and payment of a fee, and photographs of past collections, which are available for free. An annual subscription to firstView costs $999. . . . Users can also view the content for one hour for $5.95. Viewfinder does not sell clothing or designs. . . .

In January 2001, Feraud and Balmain, along with several other design houses, each filed suit against Viewfinder in the Tribunal de grande instance de Paris seeking money damages from Viewfinder for alleged unauthorized use of their intellectual property and unfair competition. These civil actions stemmed from Viewfinder displaying photographs of the designers' fashion shows, which revealed designs from their upcoming collection, on the firstView.com website. Viewfinder was served in New York in accordance with the terms of The Hague Convention on the Service of Judicial and Extrajudicial Documents in Civil or Commercial Matters. Viewfinder failed to respond to the complaints, however, and therefore, on May 2, 2001, the French court issued default judgment against Viewfinder. The French court found that plaintiffs' "ready-to-wear" and "haute couture" collections from 1996–2001 were available on the firstView.com website. The court further found that Viewfinder's posting of these photographs of plaintiffs' designs was "without the necessary authorization" and thus "constitute[d] counterfeit and violation of royalties pursuant to articles L 716–1 and L 122–4 of the Intellectual [P]roperty Code." The court also found with respect to each of the plaintiffs that Viewfinder had committed "parasitism" under French law because it had "take[n] advantage of plaintiff's reputation and commercial efforts creating confusion between the two companies." The French court ordered Viewfinder to remove the offending photographs, and awarded damages of 500,000 francs for each plaintiff, costs of the action, and a fine ("*astreinte*") of 50,000 francs a day for each day Viewfinder failed to comply with the judgment.[1]

On October 6, 2003, Viewfinder appealed these judgments to the Cour d'appel de Paris, but subsequently withdrew its appeal without opposition after plaintiffs filed their brief. The French appellate court accordingly dismissed the appeal in February 2004. In December 2004, plaintiffs filed separate complaints in the United States District Court for the Southern District of New York to enforce the French Judgments. Plaintiffs sought enforcement under New York's Uniform Foreign Money Judgment Recognition Act, which provides that, subject to certain exceptions, foreign judgments that are "final, conclusive and enforceable" in the country where rendered are deemed conclusive between the parties and enforceable by U.S. courts. N.Y. C.P.L.R. §§ 5302, 5303. The district court consolidated these actions and also granted plaintiffs' request for an order of attachment. Federal jurisdiction is based on diversity of citizenship.

---

[1]   In the district court, Viewfinder argued that the French Judgments were not final because of the *astreinte*. Plaintiffs then commenced proceedings before the Juge de l'exécution of the French court to reduce the *astreinte* to a fixed amount. Viewfinder no longer contends that the French Judgments are not final.

On January 18, 2005, Viewfinder filed a motion to dismiss or, in the alternative, a motion for summary judgment and a motion to vacate the attachment order. Viewfinder raised a variety of arguments in its motion papers, one of which was found meritorious by the district court. . . . The district court found that enforcing the French Judgments would be repugnant to the public policy of New York because it would violate Viewfinder's First Amendment rights. . . . Specifically, the district court found that the fashion shows at issue were public events and Viewfinder had a First Amendment right to publish the photographs at issue. . . . Thus, as the district court concluded, the "First Amendment simply does not permit plaintiffs to stage public events in which the general public has a considerable interest, and then control the way in which information about those events is disseminated in the mass media." [406 F.Supp. 2d at 285.] The district court also stated that to the extent that plaintiffs' designs were protected by copyright, "the copyright law similarly provides, as a matter of First Amendment necessity, a 'fair use' exception for the publication of newsworthy matters." . . . Based on its conclusion that enforcing the judgment would impinge upon Viewfinder's free speech rights, the district court dismissed the action and vacated the order of attachment. *Id.* at 285. Plaintiffs filed a timely notice of appeal.

DISCUSSION

The question presented by this appeal is whether the district court properly found that the French Judgments were unenforceable under New York law. In order to address this question, we begin with the language of the relevant state statute: "A foreign country judgment need not be recognized if . . . the *cause of action* on which the judgment is based is repugnant to the public policy of this state." N.Y. C.P.L.R. § 5304(b)(4) (emphasis added). As the plain language of the statute makes clear, the first step in analyzing whether a judgment is unenforceable under Section 5304(b)(4) is to identify the "cause of action on which the judgment is based." The district court never identified the French statutes that underlie the judgments at issue in this case. Nor does Viewfinder do so in its submission. In fact, Viewfinder contends that "there is simply no way for this Court to know what substantive law was actually applied in France and on what grounds Defendant was found liable." We find this argument curious considering that Viewfinder, as the party invoking Section 5304(b), had the burden to prove that the public policy exception applied. . . . In any event, we cannot agree with Viewfinder's contention that it is impossible to discern the causes of action on which the French Judgments were based. The default judgments issued by the French court explicitly state that Viewfinder's actions violated "articles L 716–1 and L 122–4 of the Intellectual Property Code." Article L 122–4 is in Book I, Title II, Chapter II of the French Intellectual Property Code, which are entitled "Copyright," "Authors' Rights," and "Patrimonial Rights," respectively. . . . Article L 122–4 provides: "Any complete or partial performance or reproduction made without the consent of the author or of his successors in title or assigns shall be unlawful." . . . This is analogous to the United States Copyright Act, which defines a copyright infringer as one "who violates any of the exclusive rights of the copyright owner," 17 U.S.C. § 501, including the rights of reproduction, performance, and public display. 17 U.S.C. § 106. Under French copyright law, the "creations of the seasonal industries of dress and articles of fashion" are entitled to copyright protection. Code de la propriete intellectuelle art. L 112–2 (Fr.). . . . The French court found that Viewfinder's publication of numerous photographs depicting plaintiffs' design collections violated plaintiffs' copyrights. Furthermore, the French Judgments concluded that Viewfinder's reproduction and publication of plaintiffs' designs were "without the necessary authorization." Thus, it is apparent that the French Judgments were based in part on a finding of copyright infringement.

We cannot second-guess the French court's finding that Viewfinder's actions were "without the necessary authorization." Viewfinder had the opportunity to dispute the factual basis of plaintiffs' claims in the French court, but it chose not to respond to the complaint. As this court has held: "By defaulting [in the foreign adjudication], a defendant ensures that a judgment will be entered against him, and assumes the risk that an irrevocable mistake of law or fact may underlie that judgment." *Ackermann v. Levine,* 788 F.2d 830, 842 (2d Cir. 1986). . . . Thus, for the purposes of this action, we must accept that Viewfinder's conduct constitutes an unauthorized reproduction or performance of plaintiffs' copyrighted work infringing on plaintiffs' intellectual property rights, and the only question to consider is whether a law that sanctions such conduct is repugnant to the public policy of New York.

The "public policy inquiry rarely results in refusal to enforce a judgment unless it is inherently vicious, wicked or immoral, and shocking to the prevailing moral sense." *Sung Hwan Co. v. Rite Aid Corp.,* 7 N.Y.3d 78, 82, 817 N.Y.S.2d 600, 850 N.E.2d 647 (N.Y. 2006). . . . Furthermore, "it is well established that mere divergence from American procedure does not render a foreign judgment unenforceable." *Pariente v. Scott Meredith Literary Agency, Inc.,* 771 F.Supp. 609, 616 (S.D.N.Y. 1991). "Under New York law[,] . . . foreign decrees and proceedings will be given respect . . . even if the result under the foreign proceeding would be different than under American law." *Id.* . . .[3] . . .

---

[3]   For this reason, we reject the argument advanced by Viewfinder and amici that holding Viewfinder liable under French copyright laws would be repugnant to public policy because plaintiffs' dress designs are not copyrightable in the United States. While it is true that United States law does not extend copyright protection to dress designs . . . , Viewfinder presents no argument as to why this distinction would offend the public policy of New York. As the district court found in rejecting this argument below—which Viewfinder has not challenged on appeal—copyright laws are not "matters of strong moral principle" but rather represent "economic legislation based on policy decisions that assign rights based on assessments of what legal rules will produce the greatest economic good for society as a whole." *Viewfinder,* 406 F.Supp.2d at 281.

Laws that are antithetical to the First Amendment will create such a situation. Foreign judgments that impinge on First Amendment rights will be found to be "repugnant" to public policy. . . . The district court in this case reached the conclusion that the French Judgments were unenforceable because they impinged on Viewfinder's First Amendment rights. In doing so, however, it appears not to have conducted the full analysis for us to affirm its decision.

The district court's decision appears to rest on the assumption that if Viewfinder is a news magazine reporting on a public event, then it has an absolute First Amendment defense to any attempt to sanction such conduct. The First Amendment does not provide such categorical protection. Intellectual property laws co-exist with the First Amendment in this country, and the fact that an entity is a news publication engaging in speech activity does not, standing alone, relieve such entities of their obligation to obey intellectual property laws. While an entity's status as a news publication may be highly probative on certain relevant inquiries, such as whether that entity has a fair use defense to copyright infringement, it does not render that entity immune from liability under intellectual property laws. In rejecting a First Amendment defense to a lawsuit by a confidential informant against a newspaper under a promissory estoppel theory, the Supreme Court stated:

> This case . . . is . . . controlled . . . by the . . . well-established line of decisions holding that generally applicable laws do not offend the First Amendment simply because their enforcement against the press has incidental effects on its ability to gather and report the news. . . . The press may not with impunity break and enter an office or dwelling to gather news. . . . The press, like others interested in publishing, may not publish copyrighted material without obeying the copyright laws. . . . It is, therefore, beyond dispute that [t]he publisher of a newspaper has no special immunity from the application of general laws. He has no special privilege to invade the rights and liberties of others. . . .
>
> . . .
>
> . . . The dissenting opinions suggest that the press should not be subject to any law, including copyright law for example, which in any fashion or to any degree limits or restricts the press' right to report truthful information. The First Amendment does not grant the press such limitless protection.

Cohen v. Cowles Media Co., 501 U.S. 663, 669–671, 111 S.Ct. 2513, 115 L.Ed.2d 586 (1991). . . . Because the First Amendment does not provide news entities an exemption from compliance with intellectual property laws, the mere fact that Viewfinder may be characterized as a news magazine would not, standing alone, render the French Judgments repugnant to public policy.

Rather, because Section 5304(b) requires courts to examine the cause of action on which the foreign judgment was based, the district court should have analyzed whether the intellectual property regime upon which the French Judgments were based impinged on rights protected by the First Amendment. This is consistent with the two-step analysis courts apply in deciding whether foreign libel judgments are repugnant to public policy: (1) identifying the protections deemed constitutionally mandatory for the defamatory speech at issue, and (2) determining whether the foreign libel laws provide comparable protection. . . . For instance, in *Bachchan,* the defamatory speech at issue related to a matter of public concern. Because the First Amendment requires a plaintiff to bear the burden of proving falsity when the speech involves matters of public concern, the New York court refused to enforce a British libel judgment because the British laws failed to provide this protection, placing the burden of proof on the defendant to prove the truth. *Bachchan,* 585 N.Y.S.2d at 664. The same analysis is appropriate here. In deciding whether the French Judgments are repugnant to the public policy of New York, the district court should first determine the level of First Amendment protection required by New York public policy when a news entity engages in the unauthorized use of intellectual property at issue here. Then, it should determine whether the French intellectual property regime provides comparable protections.[4]

With regard to the protections provided by the First Amendment for the unauthorized use of copyrighted material, this court has held that absent extraordinary circumstances, "the fair use doctrine encompasses all claims of first amendment in the copyright field." *Twin Peaks Prods., Inc. v. Publ'ns Int'l, Ltd.,* 996 F.2d 1366, 1378 (2d Cir. 1993). . . . Because the fair use doctrine balances the competing interests of the copyright laws and the First Amendment, some analysis of that doctrine is generally needed before a court can conclude that a foreign copyright judgment is repugnant to public policy. Factors that must be considered in determining fair use are:

(1)   the purpose and character of the use, including whether such use is of a commercial nature or is for nonprofit educational purposes;

(2)   the nature of the copyrighted work;

(3)   the amount and substantiality of the portion used in relation to the copyrighted work as a whole; and

(4)   the effect of the use upon the potential market for or value of the copyrighted work.

17 U.S.C. § 107. As the Supreme Court has explained: "The task [of applying the fair use doctrine] is not to be simplified with bright-line

---

[4]   We note that in some circumstances the repugnancy of the foreign judgment may be so patently obvious that a court need not engage in a detailed analysis of the foreign law at issue. This case, however, does not present such a scenario.

rules, for the statute, like the doctrine it recognizes, calls for case-by-case analysis. . . . Nor may the four statutory factors be treated in isolation, one from another. All are to be explored, and the results weighed together, in light of the purposes of copyright." *Campbell v. Acuff-Rose Music, Inc.,* 510 U.S. 569, 577–578, 114 S.Ct. 1164, 127 L.Ed.2d 500 (1994). . . .

In this case, the district court dispensed with the issue of fair use in a single sentence: "Similarly, even were plaintiffs' designs copyrightable, the copyright law similarly provides, as a matter of First Amendment necessity, a 'fair use' exception for the publication of newsworthy matters." . . . To the extent the district court believed that Viewfinder's use was necessarily fair use because it was publishing "newsworthy matters," this was erroneous. . . . Whether the material is newsworthy is but one factor in the fair use analysis.

While both parties urge this court to resolve the issue of fair use, the record before us is insufficient to determine fair use as a matter of law. . . . For instance, the record is unclear as to the percentage of plaintiffs' designs that were posted on firstView.com. While the French Judgments do provide some information as to the number of photographs posted by Viewfinder, that information is both incomplete and unclear because it does not indicate what proportion of plaintiffs' designs were revealed by these photographs. . . . Such factual findings are relevant in determining whether Viewfinder's use would constitute "fair use" under United States law. If the publication of photographs of copyrighted material in the same manner as Viewfinder has done in this case would not be fair use under United States law, then the French intellectual property regime sanctioning the same conduct certainly would not be repugnant to public policy. Similarly, if the sole reason that Viewfinder's conduct would be permitted under United States copyright law is that plaintiffs' dress designs are not copyrightable in the United States, the French Judgment would not appear to be repugnant. However, without further development of the record, we cannot reach any conclusions as to whether Viewfinder's conduct would fall within the protection of the fair use doctrine.

The record is similarly unclear as to the manner of protection afforded plaintiffs' fashion shows by French law as well as the protections afforded to alleged infringers generally, and photographers specifically, under French law. The minutes of the French criminal judgment contained in the record . . . suggest that photographers may well enjoy some protection. These minutes indicate that the "Law covers a right to the benefit of the fashion designers that coexists with *that of the photographers.*" . . . (emphasis added). Moreover, Article L 122–5(3) of the French Intellectual Property Code permits unauthorized use of copyrighted material in limited circumstances similar to uses deemed "fair use" under United States law. *See* Code de la propriete intellectuelle art. L 122–5(3) (Fr). . . . Whether such protections are sufficiently comparable to that required by the public policy of New York is a question best addressed in the first instance by the district court on a fully-developed record.

CONCLUSION

For the foregoing reasons, we vacate the judgment of the district court and remand for further proceedings consistent with this opinion. Because we remand for a new analysis by the district court, we do not address the other grounds of alleged error raised by plaintiffs.

NOTES

1.   *Extraterritorial Enforcement.* If in *Viewfinder* plaintiffs had filed their lawsuit not in France, but as a diversity action in federal district court in the Southern District of New York, seeking the application of French law to the alleged infringements that occurred in France, would *London Film*, page 25 above, have required the U.S. court to apply French law to the French elements of the action? Would or should the U.S. court have dismissed the case on grounds of *forum non conveniens* or rejected the application of French law on public policy grounds?

The Supreme Court of Japan held that Japanese courts could not apply the U.S. Patent Act provision on inducement of patent infringement to acts committed in Japan. The Court stated that "[t]o order prohibition of the act of actively inducing infringement of a U.S. patent and destruction of the infringing goods located in Japan by applying the U.S. Patent Act is contrary to the meaning of [public policy]." Saikō Saibansho [Sup. Ct.] Sept. 26, 2002, 56 SAIKŌ SAIBANSHO MINJI HANREISHŪ [MINSHŪ], 1551 (Fujimoto v. Neuron Co. (Card Reader)). Should different standards apply depending on whether an action is one for application of foreign law or for enforcement of a foreign judgment?

2.   *Recognition and Enforcement of Foreign Judgments in the United States.* Thirty-one states, the District of Columbia and the U.S. Virgin Islands enacted the 1962 Uniform Foreign Money-Judgments Recognition Act, and Sections 5301–5309 of the N.Y.C.P.L.R., applied in the *Viewfinder* case, represent one of the state enactments. The 1962 Uniform Act was revised by the 2005 Foreign-Country Money Judgments Recognition Act, which has been or is being enacted by numerous states. The Uniform Acts obligate local courts to recognize non-U.S. money judgments with the exception of judgments in cases where the foreign court had no personal jurisdiction over the defendant or subject matter jurisdiction over the cause of action, or where the defendant failed to receive due process. Additionally, courts have discretion to refuse to recognize foreign judgments in other cases, for example when the underlying cause of action or the claim for relief are repugnant to local public policy, or where the judgment conflicts with another final and conclusive judgment.

3.   *Recognition and Enforcement of U.S. Judgments Abroad.* Most countries ostensibly apply many of the same standards in determining whether to recognize and enforce foreign judgments as are embodied in the Uniform Acts. Nonetheless, a 2001 survey of recognition practices among a broad

sample of U.S. trading partners found that "the relevant substantive and procedural laws themselves, or more precisely the variances found in them between the United States and the states surveyed, constitute significant hurdles to efficient recognition. While at first glance many of the differences may appear minimal, in the actual reality of daily practice they constitute significant obstacles to the efficient recognition of foreign judgments. These substantive and procedural differences result both from historical and cultural factors and from conscious domestic policy choices, and while their existence is understandable, their impact on international commercial activity is indisputable." Committee on Foreign and Comparative Law of the Association of the Bar of the City of New York, Survey on Foreign Recognition of U.S. Money Judgments 2 (July 31, 2001). *See* also Samuel P. Baumgartner, Understanding the Obstacles to the Recognition and Enforcement of U.S. Judgments Abroad, 45 Int'l Law & Politics 965 (2013).

The principal variation among foreign countries appears to stem from differences in general legal norms. For example, while all of the states surveyed considered whether the court in which the judgment originated had jurisdiction over the defendant, "[m]ost of the states surveyed have concepts of jurisdiction which are inconsistent or incompatible with U.S. concepts of long-arm jurisdiction and are not prepared to see such U.S. concepts expanded into their countries." In *Lucasfilm Ltd. v. Ainsworth*, the English Court of Appeal refused to recognize a judgment of the U.S. District Court for the Central District of California because it found that the U.S. court did not have sufficient grounds for personal jurisdiction as defined by the English rule for a recognizable foreign judgment, which requires that foreign court jurisdiction be based on at least a temporary physical presence by the defendant. The court rejected the argument that an Internet "presence" by the defendant in the United States through his website was sufficient to satisfy the rule. Lucasfilm Ltd. v. Ainsworth, [2009] EWCA Civ. 1328. For a discussion of the U.K. Supreme Court decision in the case, which did not concern the issue of recognition of the U.S. judgment, see page 28, above.

Some of the surveyed states required reciprocity as a condition to recognition, a hurdle that presents particular problems in the case of U.S. judgments in intellectual property cases. Since, at least in the case of patent and copyright, the U.S. judgment will be from a federal court, and since as a rule, there is no federal law or treaty on recognition of foreign judgments, a country could decline recognition on the ground that no reciprocity exists.

For an overview of the rules on recognition and enforcement in the United States, the European Union, and China see Ronald A. Brand, New Challenges in the Recognition and Enforcement of Judgments, in The Continuing Relevance of Private International Law and Its Challenges (F.Ferrari & Diego P. Fernandez Arroyo eds., 2019).

4. *Non-Money Judgments.* In the European Union, the Brussels I Regulation (recast) requires that, subject to limited exclusions (which include the usual exception for public policy), member states recognize judgments originating in other member states to monetary as well as non-monetary judgments, most notably injunctions. By contrast, the original common law rule is to confine recognition to final money judgments. The position in countries that apply the original common law rule presents a challenge to intellectual property owners, for injunctive and other coercive relief will often be their preferred—and sometimes their only—effective remedy.

In Pro Swing Inc. v. ELTA Golf Inc., [2006] 2 S.C.R. 612, 2006 SCC 52, which involved a U.S. trademark owner's effort to enforce in Canada a contempt order issued by an Ohio federal district court against a Canadian company's breach of a consent decree earlier issued by the district court, the Supreme Court of Canada recognized "the need for a new rule" that would extend recognition to foreign judgments for non-monetary relief—"[t]he advent of the Internet has heightened the need for appropriate tools"—but ultimately concluded that the instant case was not the right one for implementing such a change. The Court's majority started with the rationale for the common law rule confining recognition to money judgments: "The foreign judgment is evidence of a debt. All the enforcing court needs is proof that the judgement was rendered by a court of competent jurisdiction and that it is final, and proof of its amount." However, enforcement of non-money judgments will "move beyond triggering mechanisms necessary to collect a debt," and will often require the recognizing court to interpret and apply the originating jurisdiction's law, as for example, the scope of conduct encompassed by a foreign injunctive decree. For the majority, the decree in the instant case presented too many such uncertainties—whether, for example, the parties and the U.S. court intended the consent decree to apply extraterritorially—for a Canadian court properly to recognize the contempt order.

Since *Pro Swing*, Canadian courts have recognized and enforced a number of foreign-issued injunctions. For an example where a U.S. court issued an injunction in a copyright infringement case and a Canadian court subsequently recognized the U.S. court decision and enforced the injunction see Blizzard v. Simpson, 2012 ONSC 4312; Dish v. Shava, 2018 ONSC 2867.

5. *The Public Policy Exception.* Do international intellectual property norms have a legitimate place in a court's evaluation of local public policy in deciding whether to enforce a foreign judgment? American fair use doctrine, one of the *Viewfinder* court's policy touchstones, provides a far broader excuse for otherwise infringing conduct than does copyright law in other countries. Is it appropriate for a U.S. court to refuse to enforce a copyright judgment that most other countries in the world would not find offensive and that is based on a national law that complies with international copyright treaties?

Intellectual property laws may conflict with other laws, as discussed in note 8 on page 66, above. Does the Berne Convention dictate that the other laws ultimately yield to copyright law? Or does it require that the law that prevails be the law that provides more protection to the copyright owner? In SAS Institute Inc. v. World Programming Ltd., [2013] EWCA Civ 1482, SAS argued in both a U.K. court and a U.S. court that World Programming's ("WPL") reverse-engineering of SAS's software violated the terms of SAS's clickwrap license. The license provided for the law of North Carolina to be the applicable law, but the parties agreed before the U.K. court that there was no difference between the laws of England and the laws of North Carolina and the United States. However, as opposed to North Carolina law and U.S. law, English law, which implemented an EU directive, invalidates contractual provisions that prevent reverse engineering of computer programs. The U.K. court therefore held for WPL.

Subsequently, WPL moved in the U.S. court for the U.K. judgment to be recognized and given preclusive effect in the U.S. proceedings. The U.S. Court of Appeals for the Fourth Circuit held that the U.K. judgment could not have preclusive effect because it was contrary to North Carolina's public policy: "North Carolina public policy and E.U. public policy are in clear conflict in this case . . . [T]he United States has taken an approach that is more protective of intellectual property, and North Carolina courts have taken an approach that is more protective of the sanctity of contract . . . Granting the U.K. judgment preclusive effect would frustrate these policy goals by barring a North Carolina company from vindicating its rights under North Carolina law on the bases of E.U.'s contrary policies." SAS Institute, Inc. v. World Programming Ltd., 874 F.3d 370, 379–380 (4th Cir. 2017), *cert. denied.*

Whose public policy gets the final word? Having prevailed in the U.S. District Court for the Eastern District of North Carolina on its claims that WPL fraudulently induced SAS to contract (based on SAS's claim that WPL fraudulently gained access to SAS's "Learning Edition" of the software), SAS brought an action in a U.K. court to have the U.S. judgment enforced against SAS in the United Kingdom. Justice Cockerill found that issue estoppel barred the enforcement of the U.S. judgment because "the existence of the terms of the contract was a fundamental block for the Fraud Claim and that without it that claim—as it was formulated in the US—could not have been run," and concluded that "it would have been appropriate in this case to refuse enforcement on the grounds of public policy because of conflict with the [EU] Directive" and the earlier U.K. judgment. SAS Institute Inc. v. World Programming Ltd., [2018] EWHC 3452 (Comm), ¶¶ 73 and 190.

6. *Punitive Awards.* In declining to recognize the U.S. federal court contempt order in *Pro Swing*, the Canadian Supreme Court relied in part on its perception that the U.S. court's contempt order was, at least under Canadian law, "quasi-criminal in nature"; "it is well established that Canadian courts will not enforce a penal order, either directly or indirectly." 2 S.C.R.612 ¶ 34.

The rule that, apart from specific treaty undertakings, courts of one country will not recognize or enforce penal judgments or decrees rendered by another country is sometimes part of the public policy exception to recognition of foreign judgments, but other times operates as an independent principle. It encompasses not only penal sanctions such as imprisonment and fines, but any remedy, such as treble damages, that the enforcing court views as punitive in nature.

As it is in the case of non-money judgments, the blanket rule against recognition of punitive awards is, in some countries at least, being replaced with a more nuanced approach. For example, the Spanish Supreme Court

[handwritten margin note: "Internal Comity"]

[handwritten margin note: "Not → contrary to Public Policy"]

held that a U.S. award of punitive damages could be recognized even when the damages awarded to the plaintiffs in the U.S. proceeding were in excess of that which could be calculated as compensatory damages in Spain. The Court "acknowledge[d, first,] that U.S. courts are prudent in policing the proportionality of damages amounts awarded in their courts. Second, and most importantly, it reasoned that a particular Spanish doctrine permits minimal overlap between civil and criminal concepts of compensation for injuries, and thus the concept of punitive damages was not completely counter to public policy in Spain. Third, it acknowledged a common desire to protect intellectual property rights among those countries with market economies. Such conclusions led the Court to hold that, in taking into account 'the intentionality and gravity of the defendant's conduct,' the U.S. judgment was not contrary to public policy in Spain even though its punitive damages portion had the effect of tripling the amount of compensatory damages." Scott R. Jablonski, Enforcing U.S. Punitive Damages Awards in Foreign Courts—A Recent Case in the Supreme Court of Spain, 24 J. L. & Com. 225, 229–230 (2005).

The intellectual property laws of some countries in which punishment is otherwise traditionally left to the purview of criminal law provide for the possibility of increased royalty payments as remedies in civil intellectual property rights infringement cases. *See*, for example, Polish Law on Copyright and Related Rights, Article 79(1)(3)(b); Slovenian Copyright and Related Rights Act, Article 168(3). *See* also Stowarzyszenie Olawska Telewizja Kablowa v. Stowarzyszenie Filmowcow Polskich, CJEU, C-367/15, 2017; John Y. Gotanda, Charting Developments Concerning Punitive Damages: Is the Tide Changing? 45 Colum. J. Transnat'l L. 507 (2007).

7. *Territorial Scope of Remedies.* What territory do remedies granted by national courts cover? Does an injunction that a U.S. court has issued in a trade secrets case in which the court has applied California law cover only the territory of California, or the entire United States? Or does the injunction apply worldwide? *See* Restatement (Third) of Unfair Competition, § 44, cmt. d (1995). Does the fact that a court has applied the law of a particular country dictate or imply the territorial scope of the remedy granted? How far did the French order in *Viewfinder* reach?

In Google Inc. v. Equustek Solutions Inc., 2017 SCC 34, a Canadian court ordered Google, a non-party to the original litigation concerning a theft of trade secrets, to de-list from its search results links pointing to websites of the party that infringed Equustek's rights. Google offered to delist the links from the Canadian version of its search engine (google.ca) but the court ordered Google to de-list the links globally. Google then brought an action in the U.S. District Court for the Northern District of California seeking a declaration that the Canadian order was "unenforceable in the United States because it directly conflicts with the First Amendment, disregards [a U.S. federal statute's] immunity for interactive service providers, and violates principles of international comity." In an unreported order the district court issued a preliminary injunction barring the enforcement of the Canadian order, finding that it was likely that Google would prevail on the merits, that it would be "harmed because the Canadian order restricts activity that [the

U.S. federal statute] protects," and that "the balance of equities favors Google because the injunction would deprive it of the benefits of U.S. federal law." Google LLC v. Equustek Solutions Inc., 2017 WL 5000834 (N.D.Ca. 2017).

Armed with the preliminary injunction from the U.S. court, Google returned to Canada to request an amendment of the Canadian order, but Justice Smith of the Supreme Court of British Columbia dismissed the application. Justice Smith noted that (1) "[t]he U.S. decision does not establish that the injunction requires Google to violate American law," (2) "Google has not demonstrated that the injunction violates core American values," and (3) "the effect of the U.S. order is that no action can be taken against Google to enforce the injunction in U.S. courts [but it] does not restrict the ability of this Court to protect the integrity of its own process through orders directed to parties over whom it has personal jurisdiction." Equustek Solutions Inc. v. Jack, 2018 BCSC 610 (Supreme Court of British Columbia, 2018), ¶¶ 20–22.

In *Viewfinder,* would it have sufficed for compliance with the French order if Viewfinder had employed geoblocking tools to deny access to its website to users connecting from France? Would the imposition of an obligation to geoblock be contrary to the free speech protections afforded by U.S. law? On geoblocking see note 10 on page 50, above.

An injunction issued by a court of an EU member state with regard to an EU unitary right, such as an EU trademark (formerly a Community trademark), has effects throughout the European Union. However, the court must limit the territorial scope of the injunction if "it finds that the acts of infringement or threatened infringement of [the] Community trade mark are limited to a single Member State or to a part of the territory of the European Union." DHL Express France SAS v. Chronopost SA, CJEU, C-235/09, 2011, ¶ 48. "[I]t is for the defendant to prove that the use of the sign does not affect, and is not liable to affect, the functions of the trade mark in Member States other than the State where the Community trade mark court is located." Supreme Petfoods Ltd v. Henry Bell & Co., High Court of Justice, [2015] EWHC 256 (Ch), ¶ 150; combit Software GmbH v. Commit Business Solutions Ltd, CJEU, C-223/15, 2016, ¶¶ 31–32. For a discussion of the EU trademark system see page 669, below.

PROBLEM 2

Since completing your initial research for EJP in connection with Problem 1 on page 13, you have learned that although some *E-Journal* articles are written by full-time EJP employees, others are written by freelancers in Asia, Europe and the United States with whom EJP has entered into agreements that in part provide: "All contributions to *E-Journal* shall be works made for hire under the terms of the 1976 U.S. Copyright Act, as amended, and EJP shall be the exclusive copyright owner of these contributions." You have also learned that EJP's agreement with *E-Journal* subscribers, concluded electronically over the Internet, provides in part: "Subscriber agrees not to reproduce or distribute any *E-Journal* content and not to delete any *E-Journal* advertising without EJP's written permission, except to the extent that such acts would be excused under applicable U.S. law, and U.S. law shall govern all aspects of this contract." An XSA employee executed one of these agreements in the course of establishing the link between *X-Journal* and *E-Journal*.

EJP is now willing to give you a budget for at least initial research into applicable foreign law and, although it would prefer to litigate in the United States, is willing to consider filing suit in a foreign jurisdiction. Based on the newly discovered facts, and the facts already considered in connection with Problem 1, please advise EJP on what law is likely to apply to each of its claims, if any, against XSA or XSA's subscribers, and on where litigation for each such claim may be instituted.

B. ECONOMICS, TECHNOLOGY AND DEVELOPMENT

1. INTELLECTUAL PROPERTY: WHO BENEFITS? WHO PAYS?

Carlos Primo Braga, The Developing Country Case for and Against Intellectual Property Protection

Wolfgang E. Siebeck, (ed.), Strengthening Protection of Intellectual Property in Developing Countries (112 World Bank Discussion Papers) 69–87 (1990).

The literature on the economics of intellectual property, particularly patents, says little about the implications of intellectual property rights for developing countries, a gap pointed out by several authors. Over the last few years, however, interest in the subject has increased significantly, pushed by the "marriage of convenience"[1] between trade law and intellectual property rights in the developed countries. Under the threat of trade retaliations, many developing countries have begun to reevaluate their intellectual property systems. At the same time, "trade-related intellectual property" concerns (TRIPs) have become a major negotiating topic at the Uruguay Round.

The present chapter reviews the state of discussion on intellectual property directly relevant to developing countries. Following a brief historical account of arguments advanced and positions taken, it traces the discussion on the costs and benefits facing a country when it strengthens protection of intellectual property.

Changing Perceptions

Perceptions of the economic significance of intellectual property for a developing country have not remained static over the last few decades. For most of this period, however, economists have been rather negative about the benefits a developing country might expect to extract from intellectual property rights. The conventional wisdom presented in the

---

[1] Gadbaw, R.M. 1989. "Intellectual Property and International Trade: Merger or Marriage of Convenience?" *Vanderbilt Journal of Transnational Law* 22, 2:223–242.

pre-1970 literature is well captured in this statement by Penrose ". . . non-industrialized countries and countries in the early stages of industrialization gain nothing from granting foreign patents since they themselves do little, if any patenting abroad.[2] These countries receive nothing for the price they pay for the use of foreign inventions or for the monopoly they grant to foreign patentees." She concluded her analysis by suggesting that developing countries "should be exempt from any international patent arrangements."[3]

Implicit in this type of criticism was the assumption that innovative activities in developing countries were not particularly sensitive to domestic intellectual property protection. Even so, the World Intellectual Property Organization and its predecessor organization (the United International Bureaux for the Protection of Intellectual Property-BIRPI) developed model intellectual property legislation for developing nations during the 1960s. Experts from developing countries contributed to these texts, which were widely circulated.

A major qualification to this approach was developed in the context of the broader issue of technology transfer to developing countries. A United Nations document on the relationship between patents and technology transfer, for instance, pointed out that when the "technical services, management experience and capital resources as well as other connexions of the foreign patentee himself are essential for the introduction of the patented process in the under-developed country, basically the situation is that in one form or other the minimum terms and conditions of the foreign patentee must be met if the innovation is to be brought to the under-developed country."[4] Accordingly, even though this situation was perceived as "a one-sided relationship," the potentially positive role of intellectual property protection in the process of acquiring foreign technology had been recognized.

In the 1970s, the negative attitude toward intellectual property protection in developing countries grew stronger amid a general movement in favor of regulation of technology transfers and of foreign capital in the Third World. The literature on the subject became particularly critical of the benefits for the Third World of the existing systems of protection. Some authors, such as Greer[5] bluntly suggested the complete abandonment of the patent system by developing countries.

The discussion was accompanied by much debate over technology licensing agreements under which technology is transferred from a multinational corporation to a local firm or affiliate. The literature

---

[2]   Penrose, E. 1951. *The Economics of the International Patent System.* Baltimore: Johns Hopkins University Press, 220.

[3]   Penrose, E. 1951. *The Economics of the International Patent System.* Baltimore: Johns Hopkins University Press, 233.

[4]   United Nations. 1964. *The Role of Patents in the Transfer of Technology to Developing Countries.* Report of the Secretary General. New York: United Nations, 50.

[5]   Greer, D.F. 1973. "The Case Against the Patent System in Less-Developed Countries," *Journal of International Law and Economics* 8, 2.

indicated that developing nations paid a rather high price for such transfers. Rents were extracted in the form of profits, transfer pricing favorable to the firm, and management or training contracts, as well as in the stated royalties.

Following these studies, and in imitation of Japan's Ministry of International Trade and Industry, a number of developing nations, including those of the Andean Pact, enacted technology-transfer legislation during the 1970s. Such legislation typically required that a government office review all technology-transfer contracts. In some cases, royalty rates could not exceed a specified ceiling and efforts were made to curtail hidden payments. Nearly all such laws restricted the use of specific restrictive clauses, particularly those that might hinder the technological competitiveness of the local affiliate or prevent the exportation of products to the developing world.

This trend also significantly influenced the North—South debate on the so-called New International Economic Order (NIEO), with developing countries seeking the establishment of an International Code of Conduct on the Transfer of Technology. This code would have affirmed the right of nations to review technology-transfer contracts and, depending on the specific terms selected for incorporation into national law, made it more difficult to include various restrictive clauses then in common use.

In the international arena, the main result of these developments was growing pressure by developing countries for revision of the Paris Convention. The gist of the proposed reform was "to weaken the international standards of industrial property protection."[6] The developing countries were not successful in their attempts at reform, mainly because of the firm opposition of the United States.

By the second half of the 1980s, developed countries had regained the initiative in the international debate on intellectual property rights. The use of trade laws by the United States and the European Community in their war against "piracy," and the evolution of the discussions on TRIPs in multilateral trade negotiations, played an important role in this process. External pressures, in the context of this new climate, were particularly effective in fostering reforms in several developing countries. Several developing nations modified their technology-transfer laws or enforced them less strictly. For example, the Andean Pact weakened certain of its restrictions on direct investment, and Mexico issued new regulations in January 1990 that radically weakened that country's 1972 and 1982 legislation on technology transfer, patents, and trademarks. At the same time, technological developments have enhanced the economic value of knowledge-appropriation as the world economy becomes more R & D intensive, economic globalization evolves, copying becomes easier, and the prevailing jurisprudence on intellectual property rights is

---

[6]   Kunz-Hallstein, H.P. 1989. "The United States Proposal for a GATT Agreement on Intellectual Property and the Paris Convention for the Protection of Industrial Property." *Vanderbilt Journal of Transnational Law* 22, 2: 269.

challenged. In view of these parallel developments, the growing concern of developed countries with intellectual property is not surprising.

It is equally true that the attitudes of developing countries toward foreign investments and technology transfers have changed significantly over the 1980s. The foreign debt crisis, decreasing private capital flows to developing countries, negative experiences with the regulatory approach, outward-oriented development strategies, and the ongoing "technological revolution" are some of the possible explanations for the more liberal posture adopted by many developing countries on intellectual property. Yet for a developing country the economic implications of the trade-off between static and dynamic aspects of the production and allocation of knowledge remain open to debate.

There is a renewed academic interest in assessing the potential advantages of strengthening intellectual property in the Third World. Mansfield, although recognizing that it is not "always socially beneficial to strengthen intellectual property rights, regardless of other factors," points out that "a reasonable amount of respect for intellectual property rights" is fundamental for stimulating technological change. Accordingly, the "widespread resistance to a strengthening of intellectual property rights" in developing countries should be evaluated not only in terms of its implications for local innovative activity, but also in terms of its impact "on R & D and innovation in developed countries." According to Mansfield, there is good reason to believe that worldwide R & D investments are below their socially optimal level and that "weak protection of intellectual property rights in developing countries aggravates this important problem. What is unknown is whether this is a major or a minor aggravation from the point of view of the developing countries, the developed countries, and the world as a whole."[7]

Sherwood, in turn, claims that important benefits of strengthening intellectual property systems occur at a micro level and are not easily captured by conventional economic analysis. He emphasizes the positive influence of strong intellectual property protection on the accumulation and diffusion of corporate business practices that contribute to welfare in the form of training offered by companies, the productivity of research parks, and interactions between universities and the business community, and by fostering "an inventive habit of mind in the population and, more specifically, in the workforce."[8] In the same vein, he suggests that "much of the [negative] effect of non-protection is

[7]   Mansfield, E. 1988. "Intellectual Property Rights, Technological Change, and Economic Growth." In *Intellectual Property Rights and Capital Formation in the Next Decade*. See Walker and Bloomfield, 1988, 24–26; 29.

Mansfield, E. 1989. "Protection of Intellectual Property Rights in Developing Countries." Washington, D.C.: The World Bank.

[8]   Sherwood, R.M. 1990b. *Intellectual Property and Economic Development*. Boulder, Colo.: Westview Press, 138.

invisible," and therefore difficult to measure.[9] His evaluation is built upon a series of case studies from Mexico and Brazil, and as such provides a more "hands-on" perspective on the economics of intellectual property rights than is typically found in the conventional literature.

Sherwood also emphasizes the need to adopt a comprehensive approach when evaluating a country's intellectual property rights system. His analysis suggests that weak protection is the equivalent of no protection. Accordingly, Sherwood questions the soundness of attempting to strengthen the intellectual property system in step with economic development.

The pages that follow review the costs and benefits that can be identified as befalling a developing country strengthening its intellectual property rights system. Among the costs are the administrative and enforcement costs associated with the reform; the increase in payments for foreigners' proprietary knowledge; the costs of economic displacement of "pirates;" the opportunity cost of additional domestic R & D; and the loss in consumer surplus generated by the anticompetitive aspect of such measures. The main benefits are the cost savings derived from additional domestic R & D and the disclosure of new knowledge; positive contributions to global technological dynamism; benefits from additional technology transfers; and more capital formation in knowledge-intensive sectors.

Costs

Administration and Enforcement

The administrative costs of implementing an effective intellectual property system are not trivial. The United States spends over $300 million each year to operate the Patent and Trademark Office. Such costs are highly correlated with the size of the domestic market and the R & D intensity of the economy. Nonetheless, as reflected in WIPO's Industrial Property Statistical Report, many developing countries' systems already deal with a significant number of patents, which are the most expensive form of protection from an administrative point of view.

Brazil spends approximately US $30 million per year to support its National Institute of Industrial Property (INPI). INPI is the government agency responsible not only for patents, trademarks, computer software registrations, but also for the regulation of technology transfers. It employs approximately 800 people, including 110 patent examiners. INPI has historically operated with a sizable backlog of patent applications. By 1980, there was a record number of applications pending: 150,000. The situation has since improved, but the period of patent protection in Brazil is significantly reduced by the delay in processing applications.

---

[9]   Sherwood, R.M. 1990b. *Intellectual Property and Economic Development.* Boulder, Colo.: Westview Press 152–155.

Other developing countries with sizable patent offices include Mexico with approximately 330 employees in its patent examination division; India, which in addition to clerical staff and administrative personnel, works with 35 patent examiners and South Korea, which operates its Office of Patent Administration with a staff of 380 including 20 trial and appellate trial examiners, 15 trademark examiners, 72 patent and utility model examiners, and 11 design examiners.

The typical situation in many developing countries is well captured by Yamaguchi: "Some of these patent offices receive several hundred or several thousand patent applications, filed mostly from foreign countries such as Japan and the United States. There are about ten examiners in each of these patent offices to examine this large number of patent applications . . ."[10]

The administrative costs of strengthening patent systems in developing countries may be significant for some of them. However, there are many ways to improve the effectiveness of these systems without imposing a major financial burden on these countries. User fees, international cooperation (for example, the Patent Cooperation Treaty, the International Patent Documentation Centre, and the African regional arrangements described in chapter 2), and networking with patent offices in developed countries are some of the available alternatives. And by choosing a registration system (in which the application undergoes only a superficial review) instead of an examination system (in which detailed technical evaluation is performed) a country can significantly reduce the administrative costs of its patent office. Needless to say, the latter advantage may be superseded by higher enforcement costs, particularly, in terms of court litigation. Besides, as Machlup points out, a pure registration system may allow "a mass of worthless, conflicting, and probably invalid patents, onerous to the public as well as to bona fide owners of valid patents."[11]

The costs of administering other instruments of protection tend to be much smaller than is the case for patents. The protection of trade secrets, for instance, does not entail any administrative cost. Furthermore, the registration and search of trademarks and, eventually, copyrights are being revolutionized by computer techniques. Some countries have indirectly increased the administrative costs of their copyright systems by adopting discretionary regulations for the registration of computer software. (For example, Brazil's "similarity" requirement allows imported software to be marketed only if there is no "similar" domestic substitute.)

In summary, although administrative costs must be taken into account by any country interested in strengthening its intellectual

---

[10]   Yamaguchi, Y. 1989. "Remarks." Vanderbilt Journal of Transnational Law 22, 2:327.

[11]   Machlup, F. 1958, "An Economic Review of the Patent System." Subcommittee on Patents, Trademarks and Copyrights, Committee on the Judiciary, U.S. Senate, Study no. 15. Washington, D.C.: U.S. Government Printing Office, 8.

property system, they do not seem to impose a major constraint. The improving conditions of access to international information networks on intellectual property rights suggest that developing countries may well face decreasing costs in this area. On the other hand, the domestic availability of human resources may, in some cases, be a binding constraint. Griliches, for instance, has shown that in the case of the United States the number of patent examiners explains much of the variance in the number of patents examined and granted each year.[12] WIPO educational programs and international cooperation are two possible responses to this problem.

The enforcement component of a "mature" intellectual property rights system, in turn, is not something easy to emulate in Third World countries. Surveys on systems of intellectual property rights, taking US standards as the basis for analysis, tend to list a large number of enforcement inadequacies in developing countries. Problems often mentioned include: the slowness of the enforcement process; discrimination against foreigners; biased court decisions; inadequate civil and or criminal remedies; and corruption.

It is true the enforcement of intellectual property rights is often laden with uncertainty in the developed countries as well. Nonetheless, such problems seem to be much more pervasive in developing countries. Unfortunately, there are no available estimates of the costs that developing countries would face in bringing enforcement up to the levels prevailing in industrialized countries. The establishment of specialized intellectual property courts, for instance, could play a role in improving these systems. It would be naive, however, to expect developing countries to implement highly effective enforcement systems in the short run. The recognition of this limitation, in turn, qualifies the benefits one should expect from intellectual property reforms.

Increased Royalty Payments

Because developing countries are net importers of both embodied and disembodied knowledge, strengthening their intellectual property rights systems would tend to increase the level of payments abroad for proprietary knowledge. Patent statistics, for instance, show that "only one per cent of existing patents [are] held by nationals of developing countries."[13] Furthermore, patenting activity in developing countries is dominated by nonresident patentees.

It is reasonable to expect that a reform in a developing country—for instance, an expansion of the degree of coverage of patents or of the term of protection—would result in higher payments for foreign technology. The long-term impact of the reform in terms of the balance of payments

---

[12] Griliches, Z. 1989. "Patents: Recent Trends and Puzzles," in Brookings Papers on Economic Activity: Microeconomics: 5.

[13] OECD. 1989. "Economic Arguments for Protecting Intellectual Property Rights Effectively," TC/WP(88) 70. Paris: OECD, 21.

is not easy to forecast given its potential effect on foreign investment flows and on exports of technology. Abstracting from these other effects, it remains to be determined if such an increase would be significant.

This type of consideration has always been present in the analyses of intellectual property rights in developing countries. The United Nations, for instance, pointed out that ". . . . as long as we are concerned merely with the role of the patent system as such in creating these balance of payments burdens, it seems irrefutable that its particular role in the circumstances can only be called a minor one."[14] Some recent analyses, tend on the other hand to significantly overestimate this burden, as the quotation illustrates: "If the United States succeeds [in changing the GATT rules to accommodate intellectual property protection] countries will be expected to pay, annually, additional royalty charges that could be equivalent to 5% of global trade and which could double or even triple the foreign exchange outflow caused by Third World annual debt repayments (about US $60 billion in 1988)."[15] These numbers reflect additional technology-related payments that would be made both by developing and developed countries. It seems, however, that they were estimated based on evaluations by U.S. industries of their worldwide revenue loss. Accordingly, they cover not only royalty payments, but other "loss factors," such as export losses, reduced profit margins, foregone research opportunities, and so on.

In order to keep these numbers in perspective, it is worth mentioning that a country like Brazil—which is usually listed as a "problem country"—spent an average of US $214 million per year on disembodied technology in 1980–88. This represented approximately 1.3 percent of Brazilian expenditures on imported services over this period, suggesting that even a steep increase in technology imports following an intellectual property reform in Brazil would have a relatively slight impact on the country's balance of payments. Currently, restrictive technology acquisition regulations play a more important role than "defective" intellectual property laws in explaining Brazil's technology import performance.

Displacement of "Pirates"

Imitation is understood differently by economists and lawyers. The latter tend to equate imitation with infringement of intellectual property rights whereas the former are often more concerned with any imitation, whether legal or not, as imitation constitutes an important part of competition at the national and international levels. As used in this survey, the term "pirate" denotes an economic agent riding free on the intellectual property of another economic agent, irrespective of legality.

---

[14]   United Nations. 1964. The Role of Patents in the Transfer of Technology to Developing Countries, Report of the Secretary General. New York: United Nations, 44.

[15]   Rural Advancement Fund International. 1989. *RAFI Communique* (May/June): 8.

From a social perspective the displacement of "pirates" may not entail a welfare loss. As MacLaughlin, Richards, and Kenny point out the "transfer of sales or royalty payments to other nationals would represent merely a transfer of income from one member of society to another and therefore, from the nation's perspective, would represent *no* net loss at all."[16] Assuming, however, that all excess demand generated by the war on "piracy" would be captured by foreign intellectual property owners, one can estimate the impact of a reform. MacLaughlin, Richards, and Kenny have estimated the additional revenue that intellectual property owners would enjoy in the event of a reform (by different industries and developing countries, and assuming that "pirate" supply would disappear completely after the reform).[17]

The estimates of revenues foregone due to lack of intellectual property protection vary significantly among industries and countries, reaching (for the year 1985) record levels in the case of the pharmaceutical industry in India (US $953.7 million) and Argentina (US $241.2 million), and of the software industry in Brazil (US $220.9 million).[18]

These results can be criticized on several grounds, including their underlying assumptions with respect to price elasticities of demand, ad hoc estimates of the role played by price controls in the process, and extensive recourse to extrapolations in estimating market size and pirate sales. However, even if one accepts these figures at face value, it is quite clear that they overestimate the social cost of displacing "pirate" firms. First of all, they reflect the extreme assumption that these companies would be wiped out entirely. As suggested by the experience of several countries that have undergone some intellectual property rights reform, this is usually not the case. In Singapore, for instance, with the new Copyright Act of 1987 "the large volume audio cassette and video tape pirates quickly switched to legitimate businesses, such as producing blank cassettes and cassette parts, primarily for exports."[19] Second, to use "pirate" sales as a proxy for the cost of displacement is tantamount to assuming that the factors of production displaced from the affected industry would not find employment in other sectors of the economy.

Maskus describes an evaluation of the economic impact of "piracy" on U.S. products developed by Feinberg and Rousslang based on data from the U.S. International Trade Commission. This analysis deals

---

[16]   MacLaughlin, J.H., T.J. Richards, L.A. Kenny. 1988. "The Economic Significance of Piracy," in Intellectual Property Rights: Global Consensus, Global Conflict?

[17]   MacLaughlin, J.H., T.J. Richards, L.A. Kenny. 1988. "The Economic Significance of Piracy." In Intellectual Property Rights: Global Consensus, Global Conflict?

[18]   Revenues foregone are estimated by subtracting the revenue currently being earned by intellectual property owners in a given market from the estimated revenue that would be earned if "pirate" sales were eliminated. The estimates reflect market conditions and intellectual property systems prevailing in 1985.

[19]   Hoay, T.B. 1988. "The 1987 Singapore Copyright Act and Its Economic Consequences." *APLA* [Asia-Pacific Lawyers Association] Journal, no. 4 (December: 111–115).

explicitly with the welfare of the infringers. "Their estimates suggest that in 1986 U.S. legitimate producers lost some $2.3 billion in profits, while consumers (U.S. and foreign) gained $3 billion and infringers profited by $0.6 billion."[20] As in the case of the previous estimates, the robustness of these results is untested. However, according to Maskus, the Feinberg and Rousslang figures "suggest that global welfare [from a static perspective] is enhanced by the current state of piracy."

Opportunity Cost of Increased R & D

If national and foreign corporations in a developing country strengthening its intellectual property regime respond with some additional investment in R & D, the opportunity costs of these activities should be assessed.

An intellectual property rights reform would primarily stimulate R & D financing by the private sector. In economies characterized by a relatively low endowment of human capital, additional demand for this scarce resource could bid its price up and "even have a negative short term impact in terms of income distribution."[21]

Combined with existing distortions in the foreign trade regime, strengthened intellectual property protection could also lead to potentially inefficient R & D investments. As Nogués suggests, an intellectual property reform could lead to wasteful R & D ("reinventing the wheel") in economies characterized by high levels of trade protection.[22]

Anticompetitive Effects

A major concern in developing countries over strengthening intellectual property is that it would not only bring significant increases in prices, but would also impair the process of technological diffusion.

It is difficult to assess the impact that an intellectual property reform would have on prices in economies characterized by high levels of foreign trade protection and price distortions, as is often the case in the Third World. The estimates of MacLaughlin, Richards, and Kenny (which should be seen as educated guesses), suggest that price increases would be substantial—in excess of 100 percent in some countries—in the case of audio and video products as well as software.[23] Royalty payments *per se* constitute only part of the cost of strengthened intellectual property rights. Increased market power enables the seller to reduce output and

---

[20]   Maskus, K.E. 1989. "The Economics of International Protection of Intellectual Property Rights: Background and Analysis." International Labor Affairs Bureau, U.S. Department of Labor, Washington, D.C., 96.

[21]   Primo Braga, C.A. 1989. "The Economics of Intellectual Property Rights and the GATT: A View from the South." Vanderbilt Journal of Transnational Law 22, 2:257.

[22]   Nogués, Julio. 1990a. "Patents, Distortions, and Development." PRE Working Paper Series no.315. Washington, D.C.: The World Bank, 22–25.

[23]   Among other things, MacLaughlin, Richards and Kenny (1988: Appendix) assume that the impact of the reform on the prices of pharmaceutical products would not exceed 5 percent because governments would apply price controls to avoid any steeper increases.

raise prices, resulting in a greater producer surplus (which is typically repatriated), and driving a larger wedge between price and marginal cost, increasing static welfare losses. The economic significance of the price effort, however, can only be adequately evaluated once other factors such as quality considerations and informational benefits—for example, those conveyed to consumers by trademarks—are also taken into account.

Evidence from developed countries suggests that patents "in most cases do not prevent imitation—and thus may not slow down diffusion to any great extent."[24] It is recognized, however, that intellectual property rights may affect learning economies and increase entry barriers. The role played by brand identification on the consumer side and by firm-specific knowledge on the supply side immediately comes to mind. It may be argued that brand loyalty will be a more effective barrier to entry under a strengthened intellectual property rights system. Analogously, trade secrets legislation may constrain the movement of knowledge embodied in the labor force.

The discussion on intellectual property and technology diffusion must be seen within the context of the pattern of technological activities in developing countries. Most of these activities can be classified as adaptive and associated with minor innovations. Furthermore, they are typically implemented via " 'blue-collar' or informal R & D."[25] In such an environment, trade secrets and petty patents may have a greater role to play in fostering domestic technology production than conventional invention patents.

The impact on technological progress of strengthening trade secret legislation, for instance, will depend "on how minor innovations are generated" in a developing country.[26] If, as the works of Katz and Sherwood suggest, minor innovations require specific efforts by producers, then the negative impact of protection on diffusion may be balanced by the spurt of innovative activities. But if minor innovations basically reflect learning by doing, then protection would impair diffusion alone and would not have any major impact on the introduction of such innovations. Even then, one could argue that weak protection would affect the quality of the learning process—as training activities might evolve at a slower pace—and with it the economic significance of diffusion.

---

[24] Stoneman, Paul. 1983. The Economic Analysis of Technological Change. New York: Oxford University Press, 17.

[25] Deolalikar, A.B., and R.E. Evenson. 1990. "Private Inventive Activity in Indian Manufacturing: Its Extent and Determinants." In Science and Technology: Lessons for Development Policy. See Evenson and Ranis, 1990, 233.

[26] Frischtak, C.R. 1989. "The Protection of Intellectual Property Rights and Industrial Technology Development in Brazil." World Bank Industry Series Paper no. 13. Washington, D.C.: The World Bank, 16.

Other common concerns include "patent non-use or their use as import monopolies".[27] Some form of compulsory licensing is the traditional response to this type of problem. Developed countries tend to suggest that "these regulations should be invoked only in exceptional circumstances to correct patent abuses which cannot be dealt with through anti-trust and competition laws".[28] It is quite true that in many cases patents are not used because patentees conclude that economic exploitation would not be feasible. Yet, as the trend toward a more "stringent" environment for international technology transfer evolves, concerns over nonuse tend to become more influential and are often voiced in the context of the debate over "dependency."

Benefits

Domestic Research and Development

As noted in chapter 4, there is very little empirical evidence of the impact of stronger intellectual property protection on domestic R & D in developing countries. In part, this reflects the fact that major reforms introduced during the 1980s have not been in effect long enough to be firmly evaluated. The evidence presented by those who support intellectual property reform tends to be based on questionnaires treating the hypothetical reaction of companies to stronger protection.

Analyses of the elasticity of R & D investments to changes in the protection of intellectual property in developing countries generated considerable skepticism for many years. For example, in 1970 Grundmann asserted "that by far the most efficient way for developing countries (and also industrialized countries) of encouraging the production of new technology is an increase in education in the technical and science field and not a law on the protection of inventions."[29] The same author continued his analysis by pointing out that "inventors" in developing countries faced so many other obstacles (for example, lack of capital and higher levels of uncertainty than those prevailing in developed countries), that inventor's certificates and exploitation of the invention by the state would be more efficient than conventional intellectual property rights. The several cases in which nations have eliminated protection do not suggest that weak intellectual property rights lead, ipso facto, to more competition or to the substitution of exogenous technology for domestic R & D investment.

Even analysts who believe that the drive toward internationalization of intellectual property could "deter or block imitation and leap-frogging in technology" recognize the importance of intellectual property protection for "developing countries wishing to

---

[27] UNCTAD. 1988. "Technology-Related Policies and Legislation in a Changing Economic and Technological Environment." TD/B/C.6/146 Geneva: UNCTAD, 22.

[28] OECD. 1989. "Economic Arguments for Protecting Intellectual Property Rights Effectively," TC/WP(88) 70. Paris: OECD, 8.

[29] Grundmann, H.E. 1970. "The Economic Arguments for Patents and Their Validity for Developing Countries," Indian Economic Journal 19, 2:198.

develop their scientific and technological capacity and benefit from the accelerated rate of technological progress."[30] In his analysis of the Brazilian intellectual property rights system, Frischtak points out that strengthening intellectual property rights "could contribute to firms making R & D a more systematic activity with an overall stronger commitment to innovation," although he cautions against overstating its role "in explaining the technological performance of Brazilian industrial firms."[31]

In summary, the protection of intellectual property rights is considered by most authorities to be neither necessary nor sufficient for strong technological activity. South Korea and Taiwan are often mentioned as examples of countries that significantly increased their technological efforts (as measured by the relative R & D-intensity of their economies) before reforming their intellectual property rights systems. From a historical perspective, one can also find episodes of "vigorous inventive activity" under weak intellectual property rights protection— for example, Switzerland during the patentless era between 1850 and 1888.[32] However, there is growing appreciation for the role that intellectual property rights can play in the development process, particularly under dynamic technological circumstances. The qualitative implications of intellectual property rights—*i.e.*, the degree to which they foster genuine innovation as opposed to mere imitation—are also receiving more attention, even though most evidence remains at the anecdotal level. A balanced evaluation of intellectual property reform in developing countries would also have to take into account its influence on informal R & D.

Disclosure of New Knowledge

One of the oldest arguments in favor of patents is the exchange-for-secrets thesis mentioned in chapter 3. Grundmann criticizes the relevance of this argument for developed and developing countries alike. In the case of developing countries, his criticism runs as follows: To the extent that most patents granted in developing countries "cover inventions already patented abroad, . . . a good library of published letters patent" would perform the same function [of disclosure] at a lower cost. That "the published information is usually insufficient, taken by itself, to be of much use . . ." would further lower the value of disclosure per se in developing countries.[33]

[30]   Bifani, P. "Intellectual Property Rights and International Trade," in The Uruguay Round: Papers on Selected Issues, UNCTAD/ITP/10. New York: United Nations, 179–80.

[31]   Frischtak, C.R. 1989. "The Protection of Intellectual Property Rights and Industrial Technology Development in Brazil." World Bank Industry Series Paper no. 13. Washington, D.C.: The World Bank, 179–80.

[32]   Schiff, Eric. 1971. Industrialization without National Patents. Princeton: Princeton University Press.

[33]   Grundmann, H.E. 1970. "The Economic Arguments for Patents and Their Validity for Developing Countries," Indian Economic Journal 19, 2:196.

However, despite the fact that the drive toward stricter protection of intellectual property rights around the world has a clear bias in favor of secrecy, disclosure continues to receive attention, particularly as an instrument to enhance the efficiency of technology transfers. As Ullrich points out, "since patent claims are clearly defined, they allow the technical and territorial scope of any technology transfer transaction to be precisely defined, as well as the technology to be transferred to be clearly distinguished from any other technical knowledge of which a partner may learn during the transfer contracts."[34]

It is also interesting to mention that "governments in some developing countries have taken action to make the information disclosed in patent applications readily available to their nationals."[35] Deolalikar and Evenson point to the correlation between U.S. patent grants and Indian inventive activity, suggesting broadly that disclosure stimulates inventive activity.[36]

Global Technological Dynamism

The thesis that reform of intellectual property rights in developing countries could have an impact on global technology trends may be developed along two different lines of argument. The first rests on the proposition that domestic R & D fostered by the reform would lead to technological innovations otherwise not available or that would take longer to be introduced in the international market if the reform had not been implemented. It is difficult to envisage such a scenario, but to the extent that leapfrogging into new technologies—particularly, biotechnology—is considered a possibility, one cannot completely discard this proposition.

The second argument is the one examined by Mansfield.[37] Industries for which intellectual property rights protection is fundamental may curtail their R & D projects because of weak protection in developing countries. Vernon long ago called attention to this possibility in observing "that inventors in the industrialized areas of the world may need some special incentive to concentrate their talents on products of special utility to underdeveloped areas."[38] The performance of First World research into tropical diseases, for example, is a natural topic for investigation.

---

[34] Ullrich, H. 1989. "The Importance of Industrial Property Law and Other Legal Measures in the Promotion of Technological Innovation," Industrial Property (March): 110.

[35] Sherwood, R.M. 1990, Intellectual Property and Economic Development. Boulder, Colo.: Westview Press, 56.

[36] Deolalikar, A.B., and R.E. Evenson. 1990. "Private Inventive Activity in Indian Manufacturing: Its Extent and Determinants," In Science and Technology: Lessons for Development Policy.

[37] Mansfield, E. 1989. "Protection of Intellectual Property Rights in Developing Countries." Washington, D.C.: The World Bank.

[38] Vernon, R. 1957, The International Patent System and Foreign Policy. Study of the Subcommittee on Patents, Trademarks and Copyrights of the Committee on the Judiciary, U.S. Senate. Washington, D.C.: Government Printing Office, 12.

Technology Transfer

This is the most traditional argument for intellectual property rights protection in developing countries. Since the 1964 UN report discussed above, several studies have analyzed the link between intellectual property protection and technology transfers to developing countries. The argument rests on the proposition that technology owners do not have an incentive to transfer their proprietary knowledge to countries with weak intellectual property rights systems, in view of the potential for "piracy."

There is evidence that many technology exporters consider inadequate protection of intellectual property to be a strong disincentive to technology transfer to developing countries. A survey conducted by the OECD listed intellectual property problems among the most significant barriers to licensing in developing countries.[39] However, as the case of South Korea suggests, weak intellectual property systems can coexist with intense licensing activity.

The need for a developing country to be more aware of the potential role of intellectual property protection in attracting foreign technology through licensing has recently been pointed out by Sherwood[40] and Frischtak.[41] As Frischtak suggests, in a less benign yet more competitive global trading environment, it is indispensable for a developing country to revise its regulatory environment, including its intellectual property regime, so as to attract foreign expertise of the kind most beneficial to it.

Capital Formation

A common argument linking intellectual property rights and investments focuses on foreign direct investment. According to this view, "it is common knowledge that [if] intellectual property rights are not adequately protected in particular markets, foreign firms will tend to *avoid selling licenses in these countries and investing there*" (emphasis in the original).[42] The magnitude of the problem is debatable. Surveys conducted with multinational executives suggest that the impact of weak intellectual property systems, although often referred to as a problem, is overshadowed by other considerations—particularly the overall economic environment of the country. Furthermore, as UNCTC data suggest, insecure intellectual property rights were not enough to deter foreign

---

[39]   Exchange controls (88 percent) and prior government approval (80 percent) were the only significant disincentives to score higher than inadequate intellectual property protection, which was mentioned by 75 percent of survey respondents. The survey covered 109 executives in manufacturing firms.

[40]   Sherwood, R.M. 1989, "New Theory of Conductivity in Licensing," Les Nouvelles 24, 4 (December): 186–189.

Sherwood, R.M. 1990, Intellectual Property and Economic Development. Boulder, Colo.: Westview Press.

[41]   Frischtak, C.R. 1989. "The Protection of Intellectual Property Rights and Industrial Technology Development in Brazil." World Bank Industry Series Paper no. 13. Washington, D.C.: The World Bank.

[42]   OECD. 1989, "Economic Arguments for Protecting Intellectual Property Rights Effectively," TC/WP(88) 70, Paris: OECD, 1.

direct investment in manufacturing in many developing countries.[43] In such cases, transnational corporations account for the same proportion of output and employment in developing countries as they do in developed economies. Still, it can plausibly be argued that the influence of intellectual property rights protection as a determinant of foreign direct investment is bound to increase as the world economy becomes more knowledge-intensive. If this is true, weak systems of intellectual property rights will have a negative effect on the composition of foreign direct investment in a developing country. Present evidence is inadequate to permit a definitive analysis, however.

Other Benefits

The literature contains references to other benefits in addition to those discussed above. These include encouragement of international trade incentives to additional human-capital formation—through better training practices and an environment more conducive to R & D procompetitive effects such as "patenting around" existing technology (thereby increasing marginal innovation, at least in theory, and preventing any single invention from taking on a dominant role by providing close substitutes); and an increase in the introduction of inventions; for the protection of cultural identity—for example, by fostering truth in "appellation of origin" labels such as Champagne and Bordeaux and consumer benefits through greater variety and quality of products and services. Some of these benefits can be understood as by-products of the impacts discussed above—mainly, the potential stimulus to innovation in developing countries that undertake intellectual property reform. Their importance for individual countries may vary greatly.

Trade Considerations

For developing countries, the possibility of trade retaliation against their intellectual property rights systems must be included in the economic analysis of the costs and benefits reform. Primo Braga suggests that expected "export revenue losses . . . should be included among the variables considered in the benefit function," a variable that could easily affect the economic assessment of intellectual property reform for countries with significant trade links to the industrialized world.[44]

Bilateral disputes and negotiations under the threat of unilateral trade sanctions have become the norm over the last few years. U.S. trade laws have been expanded to include evaluation of the intellectual property protection offered by a foreign nation in establishing that nation's status under the U.S. Generalized System of Preferences (GSP) or to justify investigation under Section 301 of U.S. law on unfair trade

---

[43]   UN Centre on Transnational Corporations, 1988, Transnational Corporations in World Development: Trends and Prospects. New York: UNCTC, 1.

[44]   Primo Braga, C.A. 1989, "The Economics of Intellectual Property Rights and the GATT: A View from the South," Vanderbilt Journal of Transnational Law 22, 2:262.

practices. The Omnibus Trade and Competitiveness Act of 1988 went a step further by creating the possibility of accelerated "301 investigations" against countries identified as "the most egregious intellectual property rights transgressors . . . that do not undertake or make progress in negotiations" with the United States.[45] The European Community has also developed new commercial policy instruments to deal with intellectual property rights issues. Accordingly, developing countries with "weak" intellectual property rights systems have been exposed to growing pressures to reform their systems under the threat of trade sanctions. The United States, for instance, has "secured major changes in the intellectual property rights regimes of Korea, Taiwan, and Singapore."[46] Trade sanctions have been imposed in some instances: in December 1987, the European Community suspended its GSP benefits for Korean products as a response to Korean practices favoring "intellectual property rights of U.S. nationals under the terms of a Section 301 agreement"[47]; in October 1988, the United States "imposed 100 percent [punitive] tariffs against $39 million of Brazilian goods" as a result of a Section 301 investigation of Brazil's refusal to grant patent protection to pharmaceutical products (this investigation was sparked by a complaint from the U.S. Pharmaceutical Manufacturers' Association).[48]

QUESTIONS

If Edwin Mansfield is right that worldwide research and development investment probably falls short of its socially optimal level, and that "weak protection of intellectual property rights in developing countries aggravates this important problem," does it necessarily follow that developing countries should pay the price for increased levels of intellectual property protection? Intellectual property policy traditionally focuses on a single economy and asks a single question: Should private property rights be extended to public goods? Consider whether the global setting increases the pertinence of two additional questions: Who benefits from protection? Who pays for it?

Would a transfer of wealth from developed to less developed economies in return for vigorous intellectual property enforcement be likely to bring research and development expenditures closer to optimal levels? How, if at all, would such a wealth transfer differ from bilateral or multilateral trade measures under which resource-and product-importing countries forego some trade advantages in return for rigorous intellectual property protection in technology-importing countries? Consider whether this line of analysis

---

[45] Abbott, F.M. 1989, "Protecting First World Assets in the Third World: Intellectual Property Negotiations in the GATT Multilateral Framework," Vanderbilt Journal of Transnational Law 22, 4:708.

[46] Gadbaw, R.M. 1989, "Intellectual Property and International Trade: Merger or Marriage of Convenience?" Vanderbilt Journal of Transnational Law 22, 2:229.

[47] Brueckmann, W. 1990 "Intellectual Property Protection in the European Community," In Intellectual Property Rights in Science, Technology, and Economic Performance: International Comparisons.

[48] U.S. Trade Representative. 1989. The National Trade Estimate Report on Foreign Trade Barriers. Washington, D.C.: Office of the U.S. Trade Representative, 20.

explains Primo Braga's statement that "[f]or developing countries, the possibility of trade retaliation against their intellectual property systems must be included in the economic analysis of costs and benefits."

Can trade agreements take account of political, legal and cultural traditions that may affect intellectual property enforcement? At the time it was promulgated, the TRIPs Agreement—the preeminent multilateral trade instrument for establishing global norms of intellectual property enforcement—postponed implementation of these norms in developing and least-developed countries. *See* TRIPs Agreement Articles 65–66.

Most analyses of the costs and benefits of intellectual property protection in economically developing countries center on patent law and, to a lesser extent, on laws protecting know-how and trade secrets. Can the methodologies used in these studies be usefully applied to questions of copyright and trademark protection, or are the interests that underlie these two bodies of law too different for analogies to be instructive? Consider, for example, that rigorously enforced trademarks—unlike patents and copyrights—may benefit local consumers by securing expectations about the source and quality of goods and services, and that the production of copyrighted goods characteristically entails far less infrastructure investment than the production of patented goods. Consider, too, that unlike patent and trademark, copyright enforcement will often touch on aspirations and values—education, culture, free speech—that patents and trademarks rarely encounter. *See* Juan Terán, International Copyright Developments—A Third World Perspective, 30 J. Copyr. Soc'y 129 (1982). *See* also, Haochen Sun, Copyright Law Under Siege: An Inquiry into the Legitimacy of Copyright Protection in the Context of the Global Digital Divide, 36 IIC 36 192 (2005).

For a superb collection of essays on the general issues, see Keith E. Maskus & Jerome H. Reichman, eds., International Public Goods and Transfer of Technology Under a Globalized Intellectual Property Regime (2005). *See* also Jayashree Watal, Intellectual Property Rights in the WTO and Developing Countries (2001); Malcom Rowat, An Assessment of Intellectual Property Protection in LDC's from Both a Legal and Economic Perspective—Case Studies of Mexico, Chile and Argentina, 21 Denv. J. Int'l L. & Policy 401 (1992); A. Samuel Oddi, The International Patent System and Third World Development: Reality or Myth? 1987 Duke L.J. 831.

2. TRADITIONAL KNOWLEDGE, FOLKLORE AND GENETIC RESOURCES

Nancy Kremers, Speaking With a Forked Tongue in the Global Debate on Traditional Knowledge and Genetic Resources: Are U.S. Intellectual Property Law and Policy Really Aimed at Meaningful Protection for Native American Cultures?

15 Fordham Intellectual Property, Media and Entertainment Law Journal
1, 10–29 (2004).

I.   An Overview: What is TKGRF [Traditional Knowledge, Genetic Resources, Folklore], How Does It Differ From Other Intellectual Property, and What Are Some of the TKGRF—Related Legal Controversies and Proposed Solutions that Have Arisen in Recent Years?

A.   Defining and Differentiating TKGRF

The lack of agreed legal definitions for "traditional knowledge," "folklore," or "genetic resources" has presented problems for many international groups and non-governmental organizations ("NGOs") examining the TKGRF protection issue in recent years. Some groups believe definitional clarity is a precondition to substantive discussion and have spent a great deal of time examining the limits of terminology. Others have bypassed the definitional issue altogether, only to find that formulating solutions is impossible when the objects of protection remain indeterminate. WIPO [World Intellectual Property Organization] takes a more pragmatic approach: it continuously develops and refines definitions of TKGRF, while simultaneously exploring potential protection mechanisms. Proposed definitions and potential protections are works in progress, continually adjusted as understanding of the relevant concepts grow.

For the purposes of this Article, "genetic resources" refers to plant, animal, and human genetic material owned, cultivated, or otherwise arising out of the custodianship of individuals or collective groups within an indigenous society. Though genetic material may be the most easily definable category of TKGRF, it recently has engendered numerous ownership and use controversies. For example, several disputes have arisen surrounding patent applications filed by the U.S. National Institutes of Health for T-cell lines used to combat leukemia and hepatitis. Some of these cell lines were originally developed from blood samples taken from Papua New Guineans, Solomon Islanders, and Pandilla tribespeople. Many of the original donors have alleged that their prior informed consent was not obtained before the U.S. government used and patented—for its exclusive benefit—derivatives from their genetic material. Similarly, agricultural germplasm banks, many of which were established to support food crop experimentation by indigenous farmers, have generated controversy. Agribusinesses have become embroiled in a variety of patent infringement and licensing disputes involving indigenous farmers' seed storage and reuse, as well as contractual disputes concerning required farmer repurchase of genetically modified seed. At the heart of many agriculture-related conflicts lies the fact that often the newly patented plant material involved was developed directly from landraces husbanded by indigenous farmers for hundreds, and sometimes thousands, of years.

The definition of "traditional knowledge" is somewhat more problematic than "genetic resources," and controversies surrounding its appropriate use are even more numerous. In this Article, "traditional knowledge" means those systems of tradition-based knowledge developed over time by indigenous peoples or local communities in any sphere of scientific or artistic application, regardless of whether such knowledge is collected and conveyed through written, oral, or other form. This could apply to indigenous peoples' inventions, discoveries (such as plant usage, for example), designs, symbols, and secret or sacred knowledge, but it is not by any means limited only to these areas. Often, traditional knowledge has scientific or practical application, such as knowledge about the healing properties of medicinal plants or the growth and reproductive habit of food plants. It extends, for example, to such matters as the particular suitability of certain types of animal pelts for human clothing, such as the waterproof properties of seal intestine for rain gear or the frost-resistant properties of wolverine fur for lining the facial openings of winter parkas.

There is no commonly accepted definition of "traditional knowledge," in part because it covers such a diverse body of information and in part because traditional knowledge tends to be holistic by nature. It is often intimately tied not just to the material object of the knowledge itself, but also to the larger environmental context of the knowledge. Traditional knowledge also is often deeply interwoven with spiritual or sacred concepts, and it is regularly expressed and preserved via ritualistic or artistic traditions that, unlike Western artistic habit, may be executed and passed down through generations only within firmly fixed parameters of expression.

It is this holistic quality of traditional knowledge that defies its neat categorization into any distinct body of Western intellectual property law and invites reconsideration of some of the basic Western definitions of intellectual property. In TKGRF, many of the legal concepts involved are novel and not yet well-understood in any sophisticated way by anyone other than the members of the relevant indigenous societies. Such concepts may not be easily reduced to a few clear and succinct legal principles. Thus it is not surprising that many of the qualities embodied in traditional knowledge cannot be effectively protected within the present reach of established intellectual property law in the industrialized Western world.

Some of the more subtle and original legal thinking concerning the nature of traditional knowledge is surfacing at WIPO. In a seminar last year, one leading scholar asked his audience members to consider the inherent nature of traditional knowledge by asking themselves a series of questions: What characteristics, if any, make traditional knowledge different from other known forms of intellectual property? Might the legal means to protect it be sui generis? Or is this type of knowledge itself sui generis? If so, what makes it that way—its epistemological nature, or something else? Is it "intellectual?" What makes it "knowledge?" Is it actually a completely different knowledge system—cosmological, for example?

If defining traditional knowledge is difficult, establishing the legal parameters of "folklore" or "traditional cultural expression" is at least equally challenging. Just as with traditional knowledge, the parameters of folkloric terminology are frequently under discussion in a wide variety of international forums. WIPO has not settled on a definition yet, but WIPO experts explain that any definition of traditional cultural expression would have to cover all works characteristic of an indigenous society or local community that reflect its own social and cultural experiences, using the vehicle of its own particular artistic expectations and habits. This would include, but would not be limited to, works of art, handicraft, and design; written and oral verbal works, including songs, poetry, stories, and riddles; music; and works expressed through action, such as dances, rituals, and plays. Increasingly, as WIPO notes, traditional cultural expressions are viewed as a subset of the larger concept of traditional knowledge, and these folkloric expressions often consist of both tangible and intangible components.

For example, a largely unpublicized but typical case of cultural encroachment worldwide involves the Tuareg nomads of Saharan Africa, whose traditional range spans several countries and who possess rich folkloric traditions that are currently under siege. Distinctive Tuareg tribal jewelry has been repeatedly copied, allegedly without authorization, for sale to tourists in North and West Africa by Japanese and Senegalese entrepreneurs. Tuareg traditional music has similarly been recorded and produced in CDs widely sold in Europe and the United States. Since national patent and copyright systems are often not developed enough to provide any protection for the Tuareg, and because the U.N. Declaration of Human Rights gives only the broadest of IP protection guarantees, they, like other citizens of third-world countries, now feel that WIPO is the only realistic forum in which they can petition for help.

How to define TKGRF and identify its unique attributes, then, are two threshold questions facing legal scholars in this field. Western lawmakers and legal scholars should widely discuss these issues with as many indigenous community representatives as possible, so that nonindigenous thinkers can begin to understand more about the true nature of TKGRF. Constructing a flexible legal interface between established intellectual property law and customary law might then become possible—a tool that is vitally important if this creative material is not to be either permanently lost or so far removed from its original context that it loses its meaning and usefulness.

B. Summary of the Legal Issues and Disputes to Date in TKGRF

Like the definitional difficulties, the legal and social issues relating to TKGRF are extremely complex and diverse. Disputes are rapidly arising in a variety of venues. As a result, national legislatures, private businesses, trade associations, international organizations, and, increasingly, indigenous groups themselves, are all experimenting with a variety of potential solutions.

1. Complexity of TKGRF Legal Issues

A statement given on behalf of the Saami Council at a recent WIPO conference illustrates the complexity of legal issues common to TKGRF discussions. The speaker, from the border area of Finland and Norway, addressed various troubling aspects of the exploitation of traditional Saami culture by other, non-Saami Scandinavians. One example of this exploitation occurs when outsiders inaccurately copy and wear the distinctive Saami national dress, usually for commercial reasons. When authentically designed and appropriately worn, this clothing is used within Saami culture to convey extensive and specific nonverbal information about the wearer's family of origin, clan, geographic location, marital status, and other identity factors. When inappropriately worn and inauthentically designed by outsiders, it is robbed of the communication characteristics integral to its design and use in the indigenous society in which it originates. Many members of Saami society find this offensive, but are unsure how to remedy the situation.

Similarly, Saamis view emulation of their customs and religious rites by non-Saami travel agencies as demeaning and disrespectful of their culture. They are concerned not only about unauthorized and handicraft counterfeiting and the loss of tourist income to genuine Saamis, but about the impact of these cultural abuses on young Saamis. The Saamis are typical of growing indigenous populations searching for self-determination and for protection of their traditional cultures (part of which constitutes intellectual property) from widespread adaptation and unauthorized use.

Many isolated ethnic communities have developed unique and complex visual art, music, and storytelling cultures that have been recently "discovered" by the outside world. Allegedly, indigenous cultural creations, like so many other artistic and musical works, are regularly being illegally copied and resold by commercial entities, often via new technologies such as digital sampling. Researchers commonly misuse (perhaps unwittingly) and improperly disseminate material gleaned from indigenous cultural traditions. Labor-intensive local textiles, jewelry, and cultural artifacts are commonly copied and passed off as the work of indigenous craftspeople by entrepreneurs with access to capital and labor-saving machinery, and the duplicates are usually mass-produced and of poor quality. When cheap knockoffs flood local and export markets, the original artisans may cease working altogether. Traditional skills, methods, and designs, as well as the cultures they reflect, are thus permanently lost.

A more widely publicized example of the same problem involves pharmaceutical and agribusinesses' "bioprospecting" among indigenous societies for unfamiliar genetic material and associated traditional knowledge. This practice, now commonplace, has alarmingly and destructively invaded the world of traditional medical knowledge and indigenous local plants. Bioprospecting activity, legitimate and otherwise, is now a routine and widely accepted industrial practice and is pursued aggressively by private, and occasionally public, actors all over the world. Illegal acquisition activity is also increasing, occasionally including the outright stealing of genetic material and knowledge; the term "biopiracy" was thus coined to refer to the illegitimate appropriation and commercialization of human, plant, and other genetic material without the informed consent of its owners or traditional custodians.

TKGRF, and the diverse legal questions they entail, are inextricably intertwined with a larger debate over whether intellectual property law contributes positively to economic development in poor countries, or whether it predominantly protects the interests of developed countries. Contentious debate about TKGRF is underway, not only at WIPO, but in a variety of international forums, including the World Trade Organization ("WTO"), the Food and Agriculture Organization ("FAO"), the UN Working Group on Indigenous Peoples ("UN Working Group"), United Nations Educational, Cultural, and Social Organization ("UNESCO"), the Organization of American States ("OAS"), and the Convention on Biological Diversity ("CBD"). . . .

Developing countries realize that intellectual property laws, however distasteful, are now an unavoidable part of the international trade landscape; instead of objecting to them, they increasingly believe they must use the system to their benefit, by seeking intellectual property protection for TKGRF. For this to occur, TKGRF need global recognition as legitimate forms of intellectual property, and its custodians need clear and enforceable means by which to protect their ownership and development interests.

Undoubtedly the most important single event relating to widespread recognition of these interests and to formal legal protection of TKGRF was the creation and signature of the Convention on Biological Diversity ("CBD") in 1992. The United States signed the CBD a number of years ago, but it has not been ratified by the Senate, primarily due to opposition from biotechnology and agrochemical industries.

The CBD demonstrates international recognition of the need to protect and preserve the global natural environment through the conservation and preservation of biological diversity and through the use of environmentally sustainable methods of development. In particular, Article 8(j) expresses the vital importance of traditional knowledge and resources held by indigenous peoples, and it emphasizes the need for indigenous peoples' active involvement towards reaching these goals. Obtaining prior informed consent from indigenous custodians before using their traditional knowledge or genetic resources is mandatory for contracting parties under the CBD, and users are required to share any resultant benefits with the relevant source communities, including economic benefits arising from commercialization. A set of working guidelines for implementing these requirements, known as the "Bonn Guidelines," has been drafted and approved for member use. These guidelines recommend that each member state establish a national "clearing-house mechanism" to oversee and ensure compliance with CBD terms for all contractual relationships involving access to, use, and commercialization of genetic material in the custodianship of indigenous communities. . . .

2.   Representative Sampling of TKGRF Disputes

A number of interesting and unusual copyright and patent disputes have arisen over the last decade relating to TKGRF, and courts and government agencies have begun to grapple with these conflicts, sometimes in creative and interesting ways.

a)   Copyright Disputes

A recent Australian copyright case involved the importation into Australia of printed fabric using unauthorized designs derived from a local Aboriginal artist's painting, "Magpie Geese and Water Lilies at the Waterhole." Both the painter and his tribe's representative separately sued the foreign textile manufacturer for copyright infringement in 1996. The Federal Court of Australia for the Northern Territory District examined customary Aboriginal law to determine the factual nature of the relationship between the painter and his tribe, as well as the painter's authority to use sacred information and designs belonging to the tribe in making his painting. The court determined that under Australian law the painter had a fiduciary duty to the tribe to ensure that his artistic work would not be exploited in a manner contrary to tribal law and custom. Since the painter had successfully brought an infringement action against the textile manufacturer, however, he had appropriately discharged his fiduciary obligations to the tribe, and the tribe thus had no right to any further cause of action against the manufacturer.

In another landmark case, an Australian federal judge determined that an award of collective damages to a group of Aboriginal artists was appropriate redress for "cultural harm" caused by a Vietnamese carpets importer who was found to have infringed the artists' copyrighted painting designs.

In an earlier case, Yumbulul v. Reserve Bank of Australia, an Aboriginal artist created a Morning Star Pole, which is a sculptural work generally created for and used in Aboriginal ceremonies memorializing the death of important tribe members. The artist in this case was authorized by his tribe to create the work, and he held a valid copyright in the work. When the Bank of Australia reproduced an image of the work on its ten-pound note, however, the artist sued the bank, claiming he had no authority from his tribe to allow reproduction not in accordance with customary law. In addressing the juncture of customary law and Australian copyright law, the court ultimately found that the latter does not recognize protection of artistic works that are communal in origin.

b)   Patent Disputes

In the patent arena, patents and patent applications for derivations (developments from, or processes relating to, genetic material originating with indigenous custodians) have sparked increasingly frequent disputes. Most commonly, these have involved plant substances that have been long used by traditional societies for healing and other properties, but are new to the industrialized world, where they are subsequently patented by third parties who profess to have "discovered" them.

Probably the most famous example of this to date occurred in 1995, when the USPTO issued a U.S. patent for turmeric, a cooking and healing substance used for these purposes for centuries in India. The Indian Council for Scientific and Industrial Research opposed the patent, claiming prior art based on an ancient Sanskrit text and an Indian Medical Association paper published in 1953. The controversy resulted eventually in the revocation of the patent by the USPTO, but the "turmeric incident" has become a celebrated instance of TKGRF misuse and has contributed to widespread criticism of U.S. patent examination procedures.

Presently, over 400 patents based on various uses of turmeric can now be found in the USPTO patent database, including some for such age-old uses as breath-fresheners, for curing warts, and as a nutritional supplement for fending off colds and sore throats—uses that would be unlikely to surprise any householder in India. Questioning the novelty and nonobviousness of such products and uses by those long familiar with them is certainly legitimate, as is the inquiry concerning whether such products and uses should be given monopoly commercial status in any country. These inquiries seem particularly legitimate when no disclosure is made in the patent application regarding the existence or source of the traditional knowledge lying at the heart of the patent in question, and where the patent holder does not share any of the eventual commercial benefits with the original knowledge-holding community.

Bulun Bulun v. R & T Textiles Pty Ltd

Northern Territory District Registry, 1998.
86 FCR 244.

[The applicants were leading Aboriginal artists. The first applicant was the legal owner of copyright in an artistic work known as "Magpie Geese and Water Lilies at the Waterhole" (the artwork). The second applicant brought proceedings in his own right and as a representative of the traditional Aboriginal owners of the Ganalbingu country situated in Arnhem Land in the Northern Territory. The second applicant asserted that the Ganalbingu people were the equitable owners of the copyright in the artwork or, alternatively, that the first applicant's copyright was held in trust for or created fiduciary obligations in favour of the Ganalbingu people, in that the artwork incorporated subject matter regarded by the Ganalbingu people as sacred and important to them, being derived from the corpus of their ritual knowledge. The respondent admitted a breach of the first applicant's copyright. However, the respondent refused to admit the second applicant's claim to equitable ownership in the artwork and the matter proceeded to trial (although the respondent, having since been placed in receivership, did not appear). The Federal Minister for Aboriginal and Torres Strait Islander Affairs and the Northern Territory Attorney-General intervened to argue that if the claim to equitable ownership in the artwork involved an assertion of native title rights over the Ganalbingu country, the Court could not make any determination of such rights in the absence of an application in proper form under s 74 of the *Native Title Act 1993* (Cth).]

VON DOUSSA J.

These proceedings arise out of the importation and sale in Australia of printed clothing fabric which infringed the copyright of the first applicant Mr Bulun Bulun, in the artistic work known as "Magpie Geese and Water Lilies at the Waterhole" (the artistic work).

The proceedings were commenced on 27 February 1996 by Mr Bulun Bulun and the second applicant, Mr George Milpurrurru. Both applicants are leading Aboriginal artists. The respondents were at that time R & T Textiles Pty Ltd (the respondent) and its three directors. Mr Bulun Bulun sued as the legal owner of the copyright pursuant to the *Copyright Act 1968* (Cth) for remedies for the infringement, for contraventions of sections of Pt V of the *Trade Practices Act 1974* (Cth) dealing with misleading or deceptive conduct, and for nuisance. Mr Milpurrurru brought the proceedings in his own right and as a representative of the traditional Aboriginal owners of Ganalbingu country which is situated in Arnhem Land, in the Northern Territory of Australia. He claims that the traditional Aboriginal owners of Ganalbingu country are the equitable owners of the copyright subsisting in the artistic work.

These proceedings represent another step by Aboriginal people to have communal title in their traditional ritual knowledge, and in particular in their artwork, recognised and protected by the Australian legal system. The inadequacies of statutory remedies under the *Copyright Act* as a means of protecting communal ownership have been noted in earlier decisions of this Court. . . .

Mr Bulun Bulun's claim

As soon as the proceedings were served the respondent admitted infringement of Mr Bulun Bulun's copyright in the artistic work, and pleaded that the infringement had occurred in ignorance of the copyright. The respondent immediately withdrew the offending fabric from sale. At that time approximately 7,600 metres of the fabric had been imported and approximately 4,231 metres sold in Australia.

On 27 June 1996 an administrator of the respondent was appointed under Pt 5.3A of the *Corporations Law*, and on 5 July 1996 receivers and managers were appointed.

On 20 January 1997 the applicants were granted leave by consent to proceed against the respondent pursuant to s 440D of the *Corporations Law*. The applicants informed the Court that the proceedings would be discontinued against the directors of the respondent, and leave was given to the applicants to file an amended application and statement of claim. The respondent then consented to final declarations and orders on the claim by Mr Bulun Bulun. These included a declaration that the respondent had infringed Mr Bulun Bulun's legal title to the copyright in the artistic work, and comprehensive permanent injunctions against future infringement.

The amended application and amended statement of claim continued to plead a claim by George Milpurrurru on his own behalf and in a representative capacity for the Ganalbingu people in respect of equitable ownership of the copyright in the artistic work. The claims under the *Trade Practices Act* were abandoned. A claim in nuisance was repleaded, but that claim was also abandoned before trial.

In its defence filed to the original statement of claim the respondent pleaded that Mr Bulun Bulun had full legal rights under the *Copyright Act* to recover in respect of any infringement of copyright in the artistic work, and that it was therefore unnecessary to consider whether the Ganalbingu people or any of them were equitable owners of the copyright. In any event the respondent did not admit the allegations concerning equitable ownership of the copyright.

Counsel for the applicants informed the Court that the artistic work incorporates within its subject matter much that is sacred and important to the Ganalbingu people about their heritage. Counsel emphasised that copyright infringements of artworks such as the artistic work affect interests beyond those of the copyright owner, and that the Ganalbingu people considered it to be of great importance that the Court recognise the rights of the Ganalbingu people and the injury caused to them by the respondent's infringement. Counsel said that Mr Milpurrurru therefore proposed to continue with his claim notwithstanding the consent orders in favour of Mr Bulun Bulun.

Accordingly, on 20 January 1997 directions were given for the filing of affidavit evidence, and generally to bring the claims pleaded by Mr Milpurrurru to readiness for trial.

Evidence in Mr Milpurrurru's claim

It will be necessary to return in due course to consider procedural matters relating to the state of the proceedings when they came on for trial, but it is convenient first to record the nature of the case and the evidence which Mr Milpurrurru filed in support of the claim that he and the Ganalbingu people are equitable owners of the copyright in the artistic work.

Much of the evidence in these proceedings relates to customary rights and obligations recognised and observed by the individual members of the Ganalbingu people and the group as a whole. For a discussion of the reception of customary law into evidence see *Delgmuukw v British Columbia* (1997) 153 DLR (4th) 193 at [81–87], per Lamer CJ. Counsel for the Minister submitted that customary rights and interests are not enforceable in Australian courts. As Lamer CJ in the Supreme Court of Canada observed in *Delgmuukw v British Columbia*, customary rights and obligations are not easily explicable and definable in terms of ordinary western jurisprudential analysis or common law concepts. The High Court's decision in *Mabo v Queensland (No 2)* (1992) 175 CLR 1 shows that customary indigenous law has a role to play within the Australian legal system. Indeed the conclusion that native title survived the Crown's acquisition of sovereignty was dependent upon the Court's acceptance of antecedent traditional laws and customs acknowledged and observed by the indigenous inhabitants of the land claimed. Whilst Mason CJ observed in *Walker v New South Wales* (1994) 182 CLR 45 at 49–59, that it is not possible to use evidence about indigenous customs and traditions to operate as "customary law" in opposition to or alongside Australian law, Australian courts cannot treat as irrelevant the rights, interests and obligations of Aboriginal people embodied within customary law. Evidence of customary law may be used as a basis for the foundation of rights recognised within the Australian legal system. Native title is a clear example. In *Milpurrurru v Indofurn* the Court took into account the effect of the unauthorised reproduction of artistic works under customary Aboriginal laws in quantifying the damage suffered. In my opinion the evidence about Ganalbingu law and customs is admissible.

The amended application in this case alleges that the Ganalbingu people are the traditional Aboriginal owners of Ganalbingu country who have the right to permit and control the production and reproduction of the artistic work under the law and custom of the Ganalbingu people. It is pleaded that the traditional owners of Ganalbingu country comprise:

(i)   Members of the Ganalbingu people;

(ii) The Yolngu people (Aboriginal people of Arnhem Land) who are the children of the women of the Ganalbingu people;

(iii) The Yolngu people who stand in a relationship of mother's-mother to the members of the Ganalbingu people under Ganalbingu law and custom;

(iv) Such other Yolngu people who are recognised by the applicants according to Ganalbingu law and custom as being traditional Aboriginal owners of Ganalbingu country.

The amended statement of claim pleads that the Ganalbingu people are the traditional Aboriginal owners of the corpus of ritual knowledge from which the artistic work is derived, including the subject matter of the artistic work and the artistic work itself.

Mr Milpurrurru is the most senior person of all the Ganalbingu people. The Ganalbingu people are divided into "top" and "bottom" people as is the Ganalbingu country. Mr Milpurrurru is a "top" Ganalbingu. Mr Bulun Bulun is the most senior person of the "bottom" Ganalbingu and is second in line to Mr Milpurrurru of the Ganalbingu people generally.

Djulibinyamurr is the site of a waterhole complex situated close to the eastern side of the Arafura Swamp between the Glyde and Goyder river systems and the Woolen River. Djulibinyamurr, along with another waterhole site, Ngalyindi, are the two most important sites on Ganalbingu country for the Ganalbingu people. Mr Bulun Bulun describes Djulibinyamurr as the ral'kal for the lineage of the bottom Ganalbingu people. In his affidavit evidence Mr Bulun Bulun says:

"Ral'kal translates to mean the principal totemic or clan well for my lineage. Ral'kal is the well spring, life force and spiritual and totemic repository for my lineage of the Ganalbingu people. It is the place from where my lineage of the Ganalbingu people are created and emerge. It is the equivalent of my 'warro' or soul.

Djulibinyamurr is the place where not only my human ancestors were created but according to our custom and law emerged, it is also the place from which our creator ancestor emerged. Barnda, or Gumang (long neck tortoise) first emerged from inside the earth at Djulibinyamurr and came out to walk across the earth from there. It was Barnda that caused the natural features at Djulibinyamurr to be shaped into the form that they are now. . . .

The creation of artworks such as 'at the Waterhole' is part of my responsibility in fulfilling the obligations I have as a traditional Aboriginal owner of Djulibinyamurr. I am permitted by my law to create this artwork, but it is also my duty and responsibility to create such words, as part of my traditional Aboriginal land ownership obligation. A painting such as this is not separate from my rights in my land. It is a part of my bundle of rights in the land and must be produced in accordance with Ganalbingu custom and law. Interference with the painting or another aspect of the Madayin associated with Djulibinyamurr is tantamount to interference with the land itself as it is an essential part of the legacy of the land, it is like causing harm to the spirit found in the land, and causes us sorrow and hardship. The land is the life force of our people. It sustains and nurtures us, as it has done for countless generations. We are very troubled by harm caused to the carrying out of the rituals which are such an essential part of the management of our land, like the making of paintings or performances of ceremony. It is very important that ceremonies are carried out precisely as directed by Barnda, and that the ceremonies are respected.

'At the Waterhole' is the number one item of Madayin for Djulibinyamurr—it is the number one Madayin for Ganalbingu—Gurrumba Gurrumba people. It has all the inside meaning of our ceremony, law and custom encoded in it. 'At the Waterhole' has inside meaning encoded in it. Only an initiate knows that meaning and how to produce the artwork. It is produced in an outside form with encoded meaning inside. It must be produced according to specific laws of the Ganalbingu people, our ritual, ceremony and our law. These things are not separate from the manner in which this painting is produced. To produce 'at the Waterhole' without strict observance of the law governing its production diminishes its importance and interferes adversely with the relationship and trust established between myself, my ancestors and Barnda. Production without observance of our law is a breach of that relationship and trust. The continuance of that relationship depends upon the continuance and observance of our customs and law, it keeps the people and land healthy and strong. This work has within it much that is sacred and important to our people about heritage and right to claim Djulibinyamurr as our land. It is like the title of our people to his land.

Unauthorised reproduction of 'at the Waterhole' threatens the whole system and ways that underpin the stability and continuance of Yolngu society. It interferes with the relationship between people, their creator ancestors and the land given to the people by their creator ancestor. It interferes with our custom and ritual, and threatens our rights as traditional Aboriginal owners of the land and impedes in the carrying out of the obligations that go with this ownership and which require us to tell and remember the story of Barnda, as it has been passed down and respected over countless generations." . . .

Why the claim is confined to one for recognition of an equitable interest

The submissions of counsel for the applicants reflected a wide ranging search for a way in which the communal interests of the traditional Aboriginal owners in cultural artworks might be recognised under Australian law. This exercise was painstakingly pursued by counsel for the applicants (and later by counsel for the Minister). That the claim was ultimately confined to one for recognition of an equitable interest in the legal copyright of Mr Bulun Bulun is an acknowledgment that no other possible avenue had emerged from the researchers of counsel.

Whilst it is superficially attractive to postulate that the common law should recognise communal title, it would be contrary to established legal principle for the common law to do so. . . .

In this case no evidence was led to suggest that anyone other than Mr Bulun Bulun was the creative author of the artistic work. A person who supplies an artistic idea to an artist who then executes the work is not, on that ground alone, a joint author with the artist: *Kenrick & Co v Lawrence & Co* (1890) 25 QBD 99. Joint authorship envisages the contribution of skill and labour to the production of the work itself: *Fylde Microsystems Ltd v Key Radio Systems Ltd* (1998) 39 IPR 481 at 486.

In *Coe v Commonwealth* at 200 Mason CJ rejected the proposition that Aboriginal people are entitled to rights and interests other than those created or recognised by the laws of the Commonwealth, its States and the common law: see also *Walker v New South Wales* at 45–50 and Kirby J in *Wik Peoples v Queensland* at 214. To conclude that the Ganalbingu people were communal owners of the copyright in the existing work would ignore the provisions of s 8 of the *Copyright Act*, and involve the creation of rights in indigenous peoples which are not otherwise recognised by the legal system of Australia.

Do the circumstances in which the artistic work was created give rise to equitable interests in the Ganalbingu people?

The statement of claim alleges

"on the reduction to material form of a part of the ritual knowledge of the Ganalbingu people associated with Djulibinyamurr by the creation of the artistic work, the First Applicant held the copyright subsisting in the artistic work as a fiduciary and/or alternatively on trust, for the second applicant and the people he represents."

The foundation for this contention is expanded in written submissions made on Mr Milpurrurru's behalf. It is contended that these rights arise because Mr Milpurrurru and those he represents have the power under customary law to regulate and control the production and reproduction of the corpus of ritual knowledge. It is contended that the customs and traditions regulating this use of the corpus of ritual knowledge places Mr Bulun Bulun as the author of the artistic work in the position of a fiduciary, and, moreover, make Mr Bulun Bulun a trustee for the artwork, either pursuant to some form of express trust, or pursuant to a constructive trust in favour of the Ganalbingu people. The right to control the production and reproduction of the corpus of ritual knowledge relating to Djulibinyamurr is said to arise by virtue of the strong ties which continue to exist between the Ganalbingu people and their land.

Was there an express trust?

The possibility that an express trust was created in respect of the artistic work or the copyright subsisting in it was not at the forefront of the applicants' submissions. In my opinion that possibility can be dismissed on the evidence in this case. . . .

Did Mr Bulun Bulun hold the copyright as a fiduciary? . . .

The relationship between Mr Bulun Bulun as the author and legal title holder of the artistic work and the Ganalbingu people is unique. The "transaction" between them out of which fiduciary relationship is said to arise is the use with permission by Mr Bulun Bulun of ritual knowledge of the Ganalbingu people, and the embodiment of that knowledge within the artistic work. That use has been permitted in accordance with the law and customs of the Ganalbingu people.

The grant of permission by the Djungayi and other appropriate representatives of the Ganalbingu people for the creation of the artistic work is predicated on the trust and confidence which those granting permission have in the artist. The evidence indicates that if those who must give permission do not have trust and confidence in someone seeking permission, permission will not be granted.

The law and customs of the Ganalbingu people require that the use of the ritual knowledge and the artistic work be in accordance with the requirements of law and custom, and that the author of the artistic work do whatever is necessary to prevent any misuse. The artist is required to act in relation to the artwork in the interests of the Ganalbingu people to preserve the integrity of their culture, and ritual knowledge.

This is not to say that the artist must act entirely in the interests of the Ganalbingu people. The evidence shows that an artist is entitled to consider and pursue his own interests, for example by selling the artwork, but the artist is not permitted to shed the overriding obligation to act to preserve the integrity of the Ganalbingu culture where action for that purpose is required.

In my opinion, the nature of the relationship between Mr Bulun Bulun and the Ganalbingu people was a fiduciary one which gives rise to fiduciary obligations owed by Mr Bulun Bulun.

The conclusion that in all the circumstances Mr Bulun Bulun owes fiduciary obligations to the Ganalbingu people does not treat the law and custom of the Ganalbingu people as part of the Australian legal system. Rather, it treats the law and custom of the Ganalbingu people as part of the factual matrix which characterises the relationship as one of mutual trust and confidence. It is that relationship which the Australian legal system recognises as giving rise to the fiduciary relationship, and to the obligations which arise out of it. . . .

The fiduciary obligation

Central to the fiduciary concept is the protection of interests that can be regarded as worthy of judicial protection. The evidence is all one way. The ritual knowledge relating to Djulibinyamurr embodied within the artistic work is of great importance to members of the Ganalbingu people. I have no hesitation in holding that the interest of Ganalbingu people in the protection of that ritual knowledge from exploitation which is contrary to their law and custom is deserving of the protection of the Australian legal system.

Under the *Copyright Act*, the owner of the copyright has the exclusive right to reproduce the work in a material form, and to publish the work. The copyright owner is entitled to enforce copyright against the world at large. In the event of infringement, the copyright owner is entitled to sue and to obtain remedies of the kind actually obtained by Mr Bulun Bulun in this case.

Having regard to the evidence of the law and customs of the Ganalbingu people under which Mr Bulun Bulun was permitted to create the artistic work, I consider that equity imposes on him obligations as a fiduciary not to exploit the artistic work in a way that is contrary to the laws and custom of the Ganalbingu people, and, in the event of infringement by a third party, to take reasonable and appropriate action to restrain and remedy infringement of the copyright in the artistic work.

Whilst the nature of the relationship between Mr Bulun Bulun and the Ganalbingu people is such that Mr Bulun Bulun falls under fiduciary obligations to protect the ritual knowledge which he has been permitted to use, the existence of those obligations does not, without more, vest an equitable interest in the ownership of the copyright in the Ganalbingu people. Their primary right, in the event of a breach of obligation by the fiduciary, is a right in personam to bring action against the fiduciary to enforce the obligation.

In the present case Mr Bulun Bulun has successfully taken action against the respondent to obtain remedies in respect of the infringement. There is no suggestion by Mr Milpurrurru and those whom he seeks to represent that Mr Bulun Bulun should have done anything more. In these circumstances there is no occasion for the intervention of equity to provide any additional remedy to the beneficiaries of the fiduciary relationship.

However, had the position been otherwise equitable remedies could have been available. The extent of those remedies would depend on all the circumstances, and in an extreme case could involve the intervention of equity to impose a constructive trust on the legal owner of the copyright in the artistic work in favour of the beneficiaries. Equity will not automatically impose a constructive trust merely upon the identification of a fiduciary obligation. Equity will impose a constructive trust on property held by a fiduciary where it is necessary to do so to achieve a just remedy and to prevent the beneficiary from retaining an unconscionable benefit. By way of example, had Mr Bulun Bulun merely failed to take action to enforce his copyright, an adequate remedy might be extended in equity to the beneficiaries by allowing them to bring action in their own names against the infringer and the copyright owner, claiming against the former, in the first instance, interlocutory relief to restrain the infringement, and against the latter orders necessary to ensure that the copyright owner enforces the copyright. Probably there would be no occasion for equity in these circumstances to impose a constructive trust.

On the other hand, were Mr Bulun Bulun to deny the existence of fiduciary obligations and the interests of the parties asserting them, and refuse to protect the copyright from infringement, then the occasion might exist for equity to impose a remedial constructive trust upon the copyright owner to strengthen the standing of the beneficiaries to bring proceedings to enforce the copyright. This may be necessary if the copyright owner cannot be identified or found and the beneficiaries are unable to join the legal owner of the copyright.

It is well recognised that interlocutory injunctive relief can be claimed by a party having an equitable interest in copyright, although as a matter of practice injunctive relief will not be granted without the legal owner of copyright being joined.

I do not consider Mr Milpurrurru and those he seeks to represent have established an equitable interest in the copyright in the artistic work. In my opinion they have established that fiduciary obligations are owed to them by Mr Bulun Bulun, but as Mr Bulun Bulun has taken appropriate action to enforce the copyright, he has fulfilled those obligations and there is no occasion to grant any additional remedy in favour of the Ganalbingu people. However, in other circumstances if the copyright owner of an artistic work which embodies ritual knowledge of an Aboriginal clan is being used inappropriately, and the copyright owner fails or refuses to take appropriate action to enforce the copyright, the Australian legal system will permit remedial action through the courts by the clan.

For these reasons, the proceedings by Mr Milpurrurru must be dismissed.

NOTES

1. *Models for Legislation.* Proposals to protect folklore and traditional knowledge usually start from one or more models for intellectual property, such as copyright, patent or trademark, making adjustments as deemed necessary. The advantage of this approach, particularly if it absorbs folklore and traditional knowledge protection into the existing fabric of copyright, patent and trademark doctrine, is that it ensures that they will receive from all member countries of the international intellectual property community the national treatment and minimum standards of protection required by the Berne Convention for the Protection of Literary and Artistic Works, the Paris Convention for the Protection of Industrial Property and the TRIPs Agreement.

A disadvantage of starting from the traditional intellectual property model is that it may encumber protection of folklore and traditional knowledge with doctrines that fail to fit. Intellectual property is preeminently the product of Western traditions rooted in individualism—not only individual creation of art and invention, but also individual ownership—while creativity and ownership in other traditions are often the subject of collective enterprise with time horizons longer than the limited terms associated with patent and copyright. Some traditional forms of intellectual property for collective activity will bridge the gap better than others. *See* Daniel Gervais, Traditional Knowledge: Are We Closer to the Answers(s)? The Potential Role of Geographical Indications, 15 ILSA J. of Int'l & Comp. Law 551 (2009); Deepa Varadarajan, A Trade Secret Approach to Protecting Traditional Knowledge, 36 Yale J. Int'l Law 371 (2011).

2. Bulun Bulun. What if the defendant in the *Bulun Bulun* case had copied not the copyrighted "Magpie Geese and Water Lilies at the Waterhole," but only those elements of the art work that were "sacred and important to the Ganalbingu people about their heritage," elements on which any copyright protection under Australian law had long ago expired? What procedural or remedial advantage, if any, did the court's finding of fiduciary duty confer on the traditional Aboriginal owners of the Ganalbingu country? Would the artist's breach of his fiduciary duty, for example by failing to prosecute infringements, deprive him of copyright in his work?

Australian courts have been particularly creative in adapting copyright principles, particularly those affecting ownership and remedies, to the protection of aboriginal art. *See* generally Jane E. Anderson, Law, Knowledge, Culture: The Production of Indigenous Knowledge in Intellectual Property Law 89–156 (2009); J. Janewa OseiTutu, A Sui Generis Regime for Traditional Knowledge: The Cultural Divide in Intellectual Property Law, 15 Marq. Intell. Prop. L. Rev. 147 (2011).

3. *Non-Intellectual Property Approaches.* Intellectual property remains at the center of contemporary discussions of protection for traditional knowledge, folklore and genetic resources, but other approaches have proliferated as well, notably in the context of the ongoing work of the World Intellectual Property Organization's Intergovernmental Committee on Intellectual Property and Genetic Resources, Traditional Knowledge and Folklore. The 1992 Convention on Biological Diversity, signed but not ratified by the United States, has stimulated local measures regulating access to genetic resources, and the 2001 International Treaty on Plant Genetic Resources for Food and Agriculture requires member countries to protect "Farmer's Rights," including "protection of traditional knowledge relevant to plant genetic resources for food and agriculture."

Two UNESCO Conventions, the 2003 Convention for the Safeguarding of the Intangible Cultural Heritage, and the 2005 Convention on the Protection and Promotion of the Diversity of Cultural Expressions, though widely adopted, are more aspirational than operational. The Declaration on the Rights of Indigenous Peoples, adopted by the U.N. General Assembly in 2007, frames the issue essentially as one of human rights, declaring in Article 31 that "[i]ndigenous peoples have the right to maintain, control, protect and develop their cultural heritage, traditional knowledge and traditional cultural expressions." Professor Lawrence Helfer has observed of this and a related instrument that "a human rights-inspired analysis of traditional knowledge views intellectual property as one of the problems facing indigenous communities, and, only perhaps, as part of a solution to those problems." Lawrence Helfer, Toward a Human Rights Framework for IP, 40 U.C. Davis L. Rev. 973, 984 (2007).

4. *Bibliographic Note. See* generally Indigenous Intellectual Property: A Handbook of Contemporary Research (Matthew Rimmer ed. 2015); Sharon B. Le Gall, Intellectual Property, Traditional Knowledge and Cultural Property Protection (2016); Naomi Mezey, The Paradoxes of Cultural Property, 107 Colum. L. Rev. 2004 (2007); Jonathan Curci, The Protection of Biodiversity and Traditional Knowledge in International Law of Intellectual Property (2010); Daphne Zografos, Intellectual Property and Traditional Cultural Expressions (2010); Silke von Lewinski, ed., Indigenous Heritage and Intellectual Property: Genetic Resources, Traditional Knowledge and Folklore (2003).

C. TRADE PRINCIPLES AND PROCESSES

For more than a century, treaties defined the multilateral intellectual property obligations among nations. The 1883 Paris Convention for the Protection of Industrial Property, followed in 1886 by the Berne Convention for the Protection of Literary and Artistic Works, set minimum standards for the protection that member countries must extend to nationals of other member countries and adopted national treatment as their central norm. By early in the twenty-first century, the World Intellectual Property Organization administered twenty-six intellectual property treaties, some establishing substantive norms in the fields of patent, copyright, trademark and neighboring rights, others creating procedures for intellectual property registration and prosecution, and still others systematizing the classification of protected subject matter. These treaties have shaped domestic intellectual property norms no less than they have been shaped by them, and are considered at relevant points in Chapter II of this book.

Even as revisions of the Berne Convention, and to a lesser extent of the Paris Convention, regularly increased minimum standards of protection, additional treaties were introduced to fill normative gaps created by new technologies and markets. At the same time, shifting economic and political realities sometimes tempted treaty members to cheat on their obligations by failing to extend national treatment or minimum standards to nationals of other treaty countries. Although treaties themselves will sometimes specify procedures for correcting such violations, by the latter part of the twentieth century it was painfully evident that these procedures were both too cumbersome and too ineffectual to bring reneging treaty members into line.

The international trade process, which had long offered relatively quick and effective procedures for remedying breaches of trade agreements respecting goods and commodities, was a natural candidate to correct the deficiencies in the enforcement of international intellectual property norms. The 1994 Agreement on Trade-Related Aspects of Intellectual Property Rights was the first multilateral step in this direction, expressly incorporating into its text the substantive intellectual property norms of the Paris and Berne Conventions and annexing to them the dispute resolution machinery of the World Trade Organization.

1. MULTILATERAL ARRANGEMENTS: THE TRIPS AGREEMENT

Charles McManis, Intellectual Property and International Mergers and Acquisitions
66 University of Cincinnati Law Review 1283, 1286–1297 (1998).

The TRIPS Agreement is unquestionably the most important development in international intellectual property law since the adoption, over a century ago, of the 1883 Paris Convention for the Protection of Industrial Property, and the 1886 Berne Convention for the Protection of Literary and Artistic Works. Although milestones in their own day, neither the Paris Convention nor the Berne Convention succeeded in establishing universally acknowledged international minimum standards for intellectual property protection, nor did they contain effective international dispute-settlement procedures. Indeed, by the mid-twentieth century, even as the administration of the two great conventions was being consolidated in a single international agency, the World Intellectual Property Organization (WIPO), the consensus needed to amend the Paris and Berne Conventions and strengthen intellectual property protection internationally was breaking down, in the face of growing opposition by the many newly independent developing countries which had become members of the two conventions in the years after World War II.

The Paris Convention is important primarily for having obligated its Member Countries to offer "national [that is, nondiscriminatory] treatment" to the nationals of other Member Countries with respect to "industrial property" protection that the Member Country chooses to provide for its own citizens. It also established an international priority system for the registration of industrial property. The only substantive minimum standards contained in the Paris Convention, however, are those governing the protection that Member Countries are to provide against unfair competition.

The Berne Convention, in addition to imposing national-treatment obligations on its Member Countries with respect to any protection that a Member Country provides for the literary and artistic works of its own nationals, establishes certain substantive minimum standards for the protection of literary and artistic works. However, a number of countries, including the United States, long objected to certain of these minimum standards and, thus, refused to adhere to the Berne Convention. Eventually, nonadhering countries opted for the more minimal national-treatment obligations contained in the Universal Copyright Convention of 1952. Not until 1988, faced with a ballooning trade deficit and a need to restore U.S. competitiveness in world markets, did the United States grudgingly become a member of the Berne Convention, and then only as a part of its larger strategy to use the Uruguay Round of multilateral trade negotiations to strengthen international intellectual property protection.

To the surprise of virtually everyone, the U.S. strategy worked—albeit not before substantial compromises were reached among the various parties to the negotiations. The result, of course, is the TRIPS Agreement. Along with other multilateral trade agreements negotiated during the Uruguay Round, the TRIPS Agreement comes within the enforcement authority of the newly-established World Trade Organization (WTO), the successor to the stopgap international agency that administered the General Agreement on Tariffs and Trade (GATT).

TRIPS is important for four interrelated reasons: (1) it establishes for all WTO Member Countries a detailed set of substantive minimum standards governing the availability, scope and use of intellectual property rights; (2) it specifies an equally detailed set of civil and criminal enforcement obligations, including border measures, which all WTO Member Countries must implement; (3) it establishes certain procedural requirements governing the administrative acquisition and maintenance of intellectual property rights; and (4) it incorporates by reference a new GATT/WTO dispute-settlement process for the resolution of any disputes between WTO Member Countries over the implementation of the TRIPS Agreement.

In one of the few concessions to the developing world, the TRIPS Agreement does provide a minimum five-year transition period for developing countries and countries making the transition from a centrally planned to a market economy to come into compliance with most requirements of TRIPS. However, by the beginning of the year 2000, all but the least developed countries of the world must be in compliance with TRIPS. Only then will the global economic consequences of the TRIPS Agreement begin to be felt.

Exactly what these economic consequences will be is difficult to predict. For intellectual property owners, of course, the TRIPS Agreement should enhance the aggregate value of intellectual property assets worldwide. Equally clear, however, is that implementation of TRIPS will lead to a transfer of wealth from the developing countries to the industrialized world—at least in the short run. Because the essence of intellectual property rights is the right to exclude others from utilizing the protected asset, enhancing the value of the intellectual property assets of one company—or country—will necessarily lead to increased intellectual property liability of other companies or countries. Indeed, the whole purpose of TRIPS was to induce the developing world to incur these liabilities in return for other agreements contained in the WTO Treaty, promising reductions in agricultural export subsidies, concessions on the import of tropical products, and a gradual phasing out of textile import quotas in the industrialized world.

Far less clear is what impact the TRIPS Agreement will have on global economic development in the long term. Notwithstanding the bland assurances of proponents of the TRIPS Agreement, there is little empirical support for the proposition that increased levels of intellectual property protection in the developing world will necessarily lead to increased levels of foreign investment in developing countries. Nor is there any clear theoretical presumption that stronger standards of intellectual property will always be welfare enhancing. Indeed, in the view of one leading commentator, there is ample cause for concern that higher levels of intellectual property protection "will lead to or embed a stratification and concentration" of intellectual property rights ownership in industrialized-world enterprises, with public consequences for both developing and industrialized countries.[41]

In the developing world, the danger is that the global economic system will become even more sharply divided between technology "have" and "have not" countries. This could provoke a political and social backlash, ranging from a reversion to import substitution policies, market closure, and economic stagnation in the developing world, to possible widescale threats to security and social order.

---

[41]   [Frederick M. Abbott, The WTO TRIPs Agreement and Global Economic Development, in Public Policy and Global Technological Integration 46 (Frederick M. Abbott & David J. Gerber eds., 1997).]

By way of illustration, one need only recall the vehemence of the reaction in India in 1993 to the mere prospect that the TRIPS Agreement would be adopted. Not even an earthquake, which had rocked the state of Karnataka in southern India in early October, prevented 500,000 farmers from turning out two weeks later in Bangalore (the capital of Karnataka and India's emerging "Silicon Valley") to protest against the patenting of agricultural products. These anti-GATT protests grew progressively more violent as the Uruguay Round came to a successful conclusion, and eventually resulted in the destruction of a seed processing plant owned by the U.S.-based Cargill Company and the ransacking of the Bangalore offices of both Cargill and a subsidiary of the U.S. multinational, Union Carbide.

These protests occurred at a time when India was in fact experiencing a surge in economic growth, and well before TRIPS would have any adverse impact on the prices of agricultural products in India. Those who have expressed concerns over a possible backlash in the developing world, once the economic impact of TRIPS begins to be felt after the year 2000, all did so well before the recent and dramatic financial collapse in some of the most promising and rapidly developing economies in East Asia.

In the industrialized world, the corresponding risk is that developed economies "will become more highly stratified among those enterprises that can afford to incur large-scale research and development expenses, as well as global advertising expenses, and those that cannot."[48] At a time when Microsoft dominates the market for personal computer operating systems (and is being investigated by the Antitrust Division of the United States Department of Justice), "Intel dominates the market for microprocessors for personal computers," and a few large Japanese companies dominate the market for "[t]he high-definition flat panel color displays used in almost all notebook computers," such concerns cannot be dismissed as idle.

The most comprehensive recent survey of the state of economic research on the impact of higher levels of intellectual property protection on global economic development comes to a decidedly guarded conclusion:

> The strengthening of IPRs protection will have different welfare implications depending on the characteristics of each country. Generalizations can only be made if strong assumptions are adopted. For example, if one assumes that the supply of innovations in the South (*i.e.* in the developing world) is rather inelastic and that IPRs regimes are of limited relevance in influencing trade, foreign direct investment and technology transfer then it follows that the [TRIPS] Agreement is in essence an exercise in rent transfer. A much more optimistic view of its welfare implications for developing countries,

---

[48] [*Id.* at] 49.

however, can be put together if the opposite assumptions are held.[50]

An earlier study that focussed specifically on the impact of rising global intellectual property rights on countries in Asia, came to a similar conclusion. Citing a still earlier empirical study which found that variations in intellectual property protection have little impact on foreign investment, and a theoretical model indicating that a "developing country never gains from stronger intellectual property regimes until it is ready to engage in research and development at the frontiers of knowledge," this study concluded that "foreign pressure to strengthen IPR laws may benefit some more-advanced developing countries, such as Singapore and South Korea," but that for other countries, such as Indonesia, "foreign pressure to adopt a stronger IPR regime may be premature, as no sector has the potential to develop new frontier technologies."[54]

At least one commentator predicts that the TRIPS Agreement will eventually lead to a global equilibrium between the industrialized and developing worlds—though subject to two important qualifications.[55] First, the international institutions responsible for securing compliance with the TRIPS Agreement must successfully manage the clash of interests that will inevitably arise between developed and developing countries in the short and medium terms, as the developed world continues to seek ever higher levels of intellectual property protection, and the developing world resists. Second, entrepreneurs in developing countries—and the developing countries themselves—must begin to think more like, and actually develop ties with, those who manage small- and medium-sized firms in the developed world. In the view of this commentator, the developing world and its allies among small-and medium-sized firms in the developed world might well play a constructive role in the global economy, by combating the market distorting effects of oligopoly and incipient cartellization of research and development in industrialized countries.

In addition to the disparate impact that TRIPS implementation will likely have on countries at different stages of economic development, TRIPS will affect the value of intellectual property in various sectors of the global economy in disparate ways. Some sectors stand to gain much more than others. That disparity in relative gains, in turn, could intensify demands for higher levels of intellectual property protection for sectors that benefit only marginally or not at all from TRIPS implementation.

---

[50]   [Carlos A. Primo Braga & Carsten Fink, The Economic Justifications for the Grant of Intellectual Property Rights: Patterns of Convergence and Conflict, in Abbott & Gerber, id, at 103.]

[54]   [Sumner J. La Croix, The Rise of Global Intellectual Property Rights and Their Impact on Asia, in Asia Pacific Issues 1995 #4# (Analysis from the East-West Center Series Nov. 23, 1995).]

[55]   See J.H. Reichman, From Free Riders to Fair Followers: Global Competition Under the TRIPS Agreement, 29 N.Y.U. J. Int'l L. & Pol. 11, 17 (1997).

Examples drawn from the copyright and patent provisions of TRIPS will suffice to make the point.

Article 10 of TRIPS, entitled "Computer Programs and Compilations of Data," begins with the statement that "[c]omputer programs, whether in source or object code, shall be protected as literary works under the Berne Convention (1971)." The second section of Article 10 then goes on to state that "[c]ompilations of data or other material, whether in machine readable or other form, which by reason of the selection or arrangement of their contents constitute intellectual creations shall be protected as such." However, such protection is not to extend "to the data or material itself." On its face, Article 10 might seem to be treating the computer software and database industries comparably. In reality, however, Article 10 offers substantially more benefits to the computer software industry than it does to the database industry.

For the software industry, Article 10 clearly establishes that, regardless of the particular form in which a computer program is embodied, it is subject to the full panoply of copyright protection mandated by the Berne Convention for literary works. True, considerable leeway remains for individual WTO Member Countries to determine for themselves whether the scope of copyright protection for computer programs should be defined broadly, as it is for more traditional nonfunctional and nonfactual literary and artistic works, or more narrowly, as it often (but not always) is for more functional or factual works. But Member Countries are no longer free to decide that computer programs are not copyrightable subject matter at all, or that only human-readable versions of software should be protected as copyrightable subject matter, or that software should be protected instead by some lesser sui generis form of protection, similar to that which TRIPS mandates for semiconductor chip designs and permits as an alternative to patent protection for plant varieties.

The computer software industry scored a major victory in establishing the Berne Convention standard of copyright protection as the international minimum standard for the protection of computer programs, and the industry stands to gain even more value for its intellectual property if individual WTO Member Countries can be persuaded to define the scope of that copyright protection as broadly as the Berne Convention permits.

The database industry, on the other hand, received little, if any, real benefit from the TRIPS Agreement. To be sure, Article 10 of TRIPS specifies that, under certain conditions, compilations of data or other material are to be protected as copyrightable works. However, the standard that databases must meet to qualify for protection also seems to limit the scope of permissible copyright protection to the selection and arrangement of the data, while specifically excluding copyright protection for the data itself. Indeed, the TRIPS standard for protection of compilations is virtually lifted from the United States Supreme Court's decision in *Feist Publications, Inc. v. Rural Telephone Service Co., Inc.*,[67] a decision widely interpreted as a major defeat for the database industry, as it firmly rejected the "sweat of the brow" theory of copyright protection for compilations of data and held that the alphabetical listings in a telephone directory did not constitute a sufficiently original work of authorship to qualify for copyright protection.

In marked contrast to the *Feist* standard, which governs the protection of databases in the United States, is the recently promulgated European Union Directive on Database Protection,[68] which obliges its Members to adopt a sui generis form of database protection for the uncopyrightable contents of databases. Although the wisdom of extending protection to database contents is the subject of intense debate, the new form of intellectual property created by the Database Directive poses no particular conflict with TRIPS. Article 1 of the TRIPS Agreement states that "Members may, but shall not be obligated to, implement in their law more extensive protection than is required by this Agreement, provided that such protection does not contravene the provisions of this Agreement."

More controversial, however, are provisions in the Database Directive that condition protection of databases originating in countries outside the European Union on the reciprocal grant of protection in those countries for databases of European nationals or habitual residents. This "material reciprocity" requirement is one of the very devices the national treatment obligations of the Paris and Berne Conventions (which were incorporated by reference in, and strengthened by, various provisions in the TRIPS Agreement) were designed to eliminate from the national intellectual property laws of Member Countries.

In the hands of countries with sufficient dominance in a particular technology or a sufficiently important market for the technology, material reciprocity provisions can function as a potent tool for pressuring other countries to adopt similar legislation. The United States successfully employed this tactic when it enacted sui generis protection for semiconductor-chip designs and conditioned protection of foreign designs on the grant of equivalent protection for chips originating in the United States. Now, the European Union is utilizing the same strategy to create sui generis protection for databases.

The Database Directive was obviously drafted with the aim of keeping database protection outside the reach of the national treatment obligations of either the TRIPS Agreement or the Berne Convention. However, it has been suggested that the new data right might nevertheless fall within the meaning of "industrial property," as defined in Article 1(3) of the Paris Convention, and thus might be subject to the

---

[67]   499 U.S. 340 (1991).

[68]   Directive 96/9/EC of the European Parliament and of the Council of 11 March 1996 on the Legal Protection of Databases, 1996 O.J. (L77) . . . .

national treatment obligations imposed by the Paris Convention.[77] Thus, just as the substantive protection mandated by the Database Directive offers an example of a block of industrialized countries attempting to raise the level of intellectual property protection above the minimum prescribed by TRIPS, so the legality of the reciprocity provision contained in the Directive offers an example of the kind of issue that is likely to be brought before the WTO for dispute settlement.

With respect to patent protection, Article 27 of TRIPS states that, subject to various specific exceptions, "patents shall be available for any inventions, whether products or processes, in all fields of technology, provided that they are new, involve an inventive step and are capable of industrial application." Although the language of Article 27 is facially neutral, the principal beneficiaries of this provision will in fact be multinational chemical and pharmaceutical companies. Prior to the TRIPS Agreement, these industries often had to contend, in many countries, with subject-matter exclusions either for chemical compositions, generally (as opposed to chemical processes), or for pharmaceutical compositions, specifically.

If the chemical and pharmaceutical industries are the clearest winners under Article 27, the software and biotechnology industries turn out to be the clearest losers. The problem for the software industry is that, although Article 27 states that the subject matter of patent protection is to extend to any inventions, whether products or processes, in all fields of technology, Article 27 adopts the European standard of patentability as the international minimum standard—that is, inventions must be new, involve an inventive step, and be capable of industrial application. A footnote states that "[f]or purposes of Article 27, the terms 'inventive step' and 'capable of industrial application' may be deemed by a Member to be synonymous with the terms 'non-obvious' and 'useful' respectively," which is the American standard for patentability. However, by negative implication, the footnote also seems to suggest that a Member Country need not deem the required TRIPS standard to be synonymous with the American standard.

This negative implication has particularly important consequences for what in the United States at least, is the burgeoning field of "pure software" patents—patents that "specifically disclose and claim software technology without referring to hardware, other than a computer and typical peripheral devices." Although any patented software that causes a computer to function in a useful way would seem to meet the American requirement of usefulness, it does not necessarily follow that such patented software is capable of an industrial application.

To be sure, in the seminal United States Supreme Court case of *Diamond v. Diehr*,[84] which held that a patent claim drawn to subject

---

[77]   See Paul E. Geller, Intellectual Property in the Global Marketplace: Impact of TRIPS Dispute Settlements?, 29 Int'l Law. 99, 110 (1995). . . .

[84]   450 U.S. 175 (1981).

matter otherwise statutory does not become nonstatutory simply because it uses a mathematical formula, computer program, or digital computer, the Court was in fact confronted with a process for curing synthetic rubber that included in several of its steps the use of a mathematical formula and a programmed digital computer. However, many of the "pure software" patents issued by the United States Patent and Trademark Office and held enforceable by the lower federal courts arguably have no "industrial" application whatsoever. Thus, although they may meet the American standard for patentability, they do not necessarily meet the European standard.

The problem for biotechnology (and to a lesser extent, medical technology) companies is that Article 27 specifically allows for two subject-matter exclusions—one for "diagnostic, therapeutic and surgical methods for the treatment of humans or animals," and a second for "plants and animals other than microorganisms, and essentially biological processes for the production of plants or animals other than non-biological and microbiological processes." To be sure, the latter exclusion is qualified by the requirement that Members "provide for the protection of plant varieties either by patents or by an effective sui generis system, or by any combination thereof." However, if the most widely adopted version of the International Convention for the Protection of New Varieties of Plants (commonly called the UPOV Convention, the French acronym for the treaty) is found to be the standard for what is an "effective sui generis system" of protection, this form of intellectual property in plant varieties will be far weaker than full-blown patent protection. For biotechnology inventions claiming genetically engineered animals, or for that matter, claiming any genetically engineered living matter other than microorganisms, TRIPS creates no international obligation to provide any patent protection at all.

Article 27 does require that this permitted subject-matter exclusion be reviewed by the year 2000, which will give the biotechnology industry a second chance to bring its technology within the international patent regime. But, given the gap between what is currently patentable in the United States and what is patentable in Europe and the rest of the world, it is difficult to predict what this review will conclude.

Peter K. Yu, TRIPS and Its Achilles' Heel

18 Journal of Intellectual Property Law 483–484; 504–521 (2011).

Although the TRIPS Agreement ushered in new and higher standards on international intellectual property enforcement, these standards have yet to strengthen intellectual property enforcement to the satisfaction of the *demandeur* countries in the developed world. Thus, many developed countries and their supportive industries consider these standards primitive, constrained, inadequate, and ineffective. These deficiencies were indeed a primary reason for the developed countries' aggressive push for the establishment of new and higher international benchmarks through the Anti-Counterfeiting Trade Agreement (ACTA) and other bilateral, plurilateral, or regional trade and investment agreements.

The TRIPS Agreement's lack of success in the enforcement area is, indeed, interesting. After all, developed countries, by most accounts, have imposed their higher intellectual property protection standards on their less developed trading partners. As Jacques Gorlin observed in retrospect, the Intellectual Property Committee—an ad hoc coalition of major U.S. corporations he directed in an effort to push for the establishment of the TRIPS Agreement—got ninety-five percent of what it wanted and was particularly pleased with the enforcement provisions.[15] . . . .

III. Post-TRIPS Responses

Given the TRIPS Agreement's failure to achieve a global consensus on international intellectual property enforcement norms, countries have actively pushed for the acceptance of their preferred norms in the international intellectual property system since the adoption of the Agreement. The recent developments in the enforcement area range from the negotiation of ACTA among developed and like-minded countries to the staunch resistance of TRIPS-plus standards by less developed countries in meetings at the Council for Trade-Related Aspects of Intellectual Property Rights (TRIPS Council). This Part highlights some of these developments.

A. DEVELOPED COUNTRIES

1. TRIPS Council Although developed countries were well aware of the fact that they did not get all of their preferred enforcement terms in the TRIPS Agreement, and they remained deeply dissatisfied with the continuous piracy and counterfeiting problems in less developed countries, they did not push for stronger international intellectual property enforcement norms until the mid-2000s. The reasons were twofold. First, while the TRIPS Agreement requires WTO members to fully implement the Agreement within a year after its entering into force on January 1, 1995, Article 65 delays such implementation in less developed and transition countries for another four years. As a result, these countries did not need to comply with the TRIPS enforcement standards until January 1, 2000.

Second, the Doha Development Round of Trade Negotiations was launched during the fourth WTO ministerial meeting in Qatar in November 2001. Amid post-September 11 sentiments and in the wake of the growing need for cooperation between the United States and the less developed world, the WTO members adopted the Doha Declaration on

---

15 [Susan K. Sell, Private Power, Public Law: The Globalization of Intellectual Property Rights 115 (2003) (citing interview with Jacques Gorlin).]

the TRIPS Agreement and Public Health (Doha Declaration). In that climate, the European Union, Japan, the United States, and other *demandeur* countries understandably were reluctant to push for higher intellectual property enforcement standards in the WTO.

In the mid-2000s, however, the landscape changed. During the TRIPS Council meeting in June 2006, the European Union called for an "in-depth discussion" of enforcement issues. Together with two earlier proposals, the Union's effort to push for greater discussion of intellectual property enforcement in the TRIPS Council represented the first attempts by a WTO member to revive such discussion since a flurry of exchanges among WTO members in 1997, during the Council's review of TRIPS-related laws and regulations from developed countries. The European Union proposals, unsurprisingly, were strongly opposed by less developed countries.

In the follow-up TRIPS Council meeting in October 2006, the European Union, with formal support from Japan, Switzerland, and the United States, tabled a joint communication seeking to strengthen the implementation of the TRIPS enforcement provisions. As the document declared: "The TRIPS Council is an appropriate forum to examine and assist Members in the implementation of enforcement provisions of the TRIPS Agreement. The work of the TRIPS Council in this regard should complement Members' efforts to use other cooperative mechanisms to address IPR enforcement." Citing ongoing challenges in the area, the European Union and the paper's cosponsors:

— Invite other Members to engage in a constructive discussion of how to implement the enforcement provisions of TRIPS in a more effective manner.

— Invite other Members to engage in a constructive discussion of accompanying measures which could enhance the effectiveness of national implementing legislation and enforcement efforts, such as for example promoting interagency co-operation, fostering a higher public awareness, and reinforcing institutional frameworks.

— Ask the Secretariat to prepare a synopsis of Members' contributions to the Checklist of Issues on Enforcement that would serve as a basis for the above-mentioned discussion.

— Stand ready, in cooperation with recipients of technical assistance and with relevant international organizations, to better focus the technical assistance they provide in favour of developing countries in order to facilitate the implementation of enforcement provisions.

Although the EU proposal again met with strong opposition from less developed countries, developed countries refused to give up. During the next TRIPS Council meeting in January 2007, the United States took its turn to circulate another paper, sharing its experience on the border enforcement of intellectual property rights. The document discussed the various techniques that the United States found helpful in addressing intellectual property infringement. The United States also called on the TRIPS Council to "make a positive contribution to addressing [intellectual property enforcement] problems through a constructive exchange of views and experiences. Although less developed countries found the United States' approach procedurally acceptable, they insisted that their position "had not changed, and they still [did] not believe [the enforcement issue] belongs in the TRIPS Council." China, with the support of Argentina, Brazil, Cuba, India, and South Africa, stated specifically that "enforcement could not be a permanent agenda item in the council."

In June 2007, Switzerland introduced another paper on enforcement, suggesting ways to implement the TRIPS enforcement provisions and to improve the overall enforcement of intellectual property rights. The paper underscored the need to develop well-functioning communication and coordination structures in the area of border measures. A few months later, Japan introduced its own paper, sharing its experiences in the border enforcement of intellectual property rights while outlining the recent trends in intellectual property infringement. Shortly after the release of these papers, the ACTA negotiations were announced, and developed countries did not table any new papers on enforcement in the TRIPS Council.

2.   *Dispute Settlement Body.* At the WTO, developed countries have also explored the use of the dispute settlement process to shape TRIPS enforcement standards. In the first few years of the organization's existence, there were very few disputes in the area. In fact, most of the TRIPS disputes—enforcement-related or otherwise—were disputes between the United States and the European Communities. TRIPS enforcement disputes were no exception. In May 1998, the United States filed complaints against Greece and, by extension, the European Communities for Greece's failure to provide effective enforcement of intellectual property rights under Part III of the TRIPS Agreement. Those complaints were quickly settled.

The lack of developing country targets for WTO disputes over inadequate intellectual property enforcement, however, changed when China joined the WTO in December 2001. Although the United States had repeated disputes with China over piracy and counterfeiting since the mid-1980s, the United States Trade Representative (USTR) did not seriously consider the filing of a WTO complaint against China until the mid-2000s. There were several reasons. First, the USTR, and, to some extent, the United States intellectual property industries, were willing to be patient in the first few years following China's accession to the WTO. Indeed, the USTR did not put China back on to the priority watch list until April 2005 after its out-of-cycle review. Moreover, the USTR was busy collecting evidence on inadequate intellectual property protection and enforcement in China while exploring the best strategy to challenge China's noncompliance with the TRIPS Agreement. The existence of Article 41.5, the many ambiguities that have been built into the TRIPS enforcement provisions, and the repeatedly-extended moratorium on non-violation complaints certainly did not help the United States' case.

In April 2007, the United States finally requested consultations with China concerning the latter's failure to protect and enforce intellectual property rights pursuant to the TRIPS Agreement. The complaint focused on four particular issues: (1) the high thresholds for criminal procedures and penalties in the intellectual property area; (2) the failure of the Chinese customs authorities to properly dispose of infringing goods seized at the border; (3) the denial of copyright protection to works that have not been authorized for publication or dissemination within China; and (4) the unavailability of criminal procedures and penalties for infringing activities that involved either reproduction or distribution, but not both.

After consultations between the two parties failed to resolve the dispute, leading to the resolution of only the last claim, the Dispute Settlement Body (DSB) established a panel to examine the three unresolved claims. In January 2009, the DSB released its long-awaited panel report on *China—Measures Affecting the Protection and Enforcement of Intellectual Property Rights*. While China prevailed on the claim on criminal thresholds, the United States won the censorship claim. The remaining customs claim was somewhat divided between the two parties, with each side declaring victory.

The limited length and scope of this Article do not allow me to address in full the key arguments made by both parties and the panel report's major findings—a task I have already undertaken elsewhere. Nevertheless, it is fair to view the dispute's outcome as a tie between the two parties. It is also worth noting that none of the parties appealed the report. Thus, the dispute effectively ended after China amended its copyright law and customs regulations in spring 2010.

From the standpoint of WTO jurisprudence, this dispute is important; it represents the first time a WTO panel focused primarily on the interpretation and implementation of the TRIPS enforcement provisions. The report not only provides certainty and clarity to a WTO member's TRIPS enforcement obligations, but also enables the United States to receive redress of some of its complaints over inadequate intellectual property protection and enforcement in China. Nevertheless, the panel's narrow focus and the limited scope of its findings clearly revealed the TRIPS Agreement's shortcomings in the enforcement area. Such revelation, in turn, provided the momentum needed for developed countries to push for stronger international intellectual property enforcement norms both within and without the WTO. While the negotiation of ACTA had already begun more than a year before the release of this panel report, the outcome of the dispute most certainly has strengthened the ACTA *demandeurs'* resolve to develop higher international benchmarks for the enforcement of intellectual property rights.

3. ACTA. For the first fifteen years of the WTO's existence, developed countries have had very limited success in pushing for higher international intellectual property enforcement standards within the organization—through either the TRIPS Council or the mandatory dispute settlement process. Although WTO members sought to make a similar push in WIPO, the other traditional forum for setting international intellectual property norms, that forum was equally hostile. With the establishment of the WIPO Development Agenda in October 2004 and the adoption of forty-five recommendations for the agenda three years later, WIPO does not provide an ideal forum for developing new and higher international intellectual property enforcement norms.

On October 23, 2007, two weeks after the adoption of these recommendations, USTR Susan Schwab formally announced the United States' intent to negotiate a new Anti-Counterfeiting Trade Agreement with its key trading partners. The European Union and Japan made similar but independent announcements. In addition to Japan, the United States, and the European Union—the usual trilateral alliance for heightened intellectual property protection—the initial negotiating parties included Canada, Mexico, New Zealand, South Korea, and Switzerland. As the USTR press release declared: "[T]he goal [of the agreement] is to set a new, higher benchmark for enforcement that countries can join on a voluntary basis. . . . The envisioned ACTA will include commitments in three areas: (1) strengthening international cooperation, (2) improving enforcement practices, and (3) providing a strong legal framework for IPR enforcement."

Since the announcement, eleven rounds of negotiations have been held. Thirty-seven countries participated in the negotiations for close to four years, with Jordan and the United Arab Emirates joining them initially in the first round of negotiations. Although the ACTA negotiation process was unprecedentedly secret, leading to widespread criticism by policymakers, academic commentators, consumer advocates, and civil liberty groups, the negotiation documents slowly leaked onto the internet. In April 2010, the negotiating governments finally agreed to release a mutually-vetted draft agreement text.

As shown in this draft text, as well as other texts that have since been officially released, ACTA contains six different chapters: (1) initial provisions and definitions; (2) legal framework for enforcement of intellectual property rights; (3) enforcement practices; (4) international cooperation; (5) institutional arrangements; and (6) final provisions. Chapter II, which is the most controversial and longest part of the agreement, is subdivided into five different sections: (a) general obligations; (b) civil enforcement; (c) border measures; (d) criminal enforcement; and (e) enforcement of intellectual property rights in the digital environment. While countries continue to explore ACTA's consistency with their existing domestic laws and international treaty obligations, the agreement was finally adopted on April 15, 2011, and is now open for signature.

To a great extent, the ACTA negotiations make salient the TRIPS Agreement's failure to meet the enforcement needs of developed countries, which already existed before the beginning of the Uruguay Round. Toward the end of the Tokyo Round of Trade Negotiations, the previous round of GATT talks, the United States, with strong support from Levi Strauss, pushed for the development of an anti-counterfeiting code. Although the United States' late-developing effort failed in the end, earning support from only the European Communities, Canada, Japan, and Switzerland, it led to the negotiation of the TRIPS Agreement in the Uruguay Round. The Punta del Este Declaration stated specifically that "[n]egotiations shall aim to develop a multilateral framework of principles, rules and disciplines dealing with *international trade in counterfeit goods.*"

Interestingly, despite the *demandeur* countries' success in establishing the TRIPS Agreement, the Agreement has failed to satisfactorily address those issues that precipitated the negotiations in the first place. As a result, countries now need to develop ACTA in part to address some of those challenging issues. This time, the *demandeur* countries opted for a plurilateral Anti-Counterfeiting Trade Agreement among like-minded countries, in lieu of a multilateral anti-counterfeiting code within the GATT/WTO framework. The use of this "country club" approach has been particularly controversial; it has raised difficult questions concerning the future efforts by less developed countries to shape international intellectual property enforcement norms. It has also instilled doubts about the legitimacy of many of the new norms created through ACTA or other bilateral, plurilateral, or regional trade and investment agreements.

To be certain, the ACTA negotiating parties did not sidestep the WTO without trying to strengthen enforcement norms within the forum. As Part III.A has shown, at one time or another, all the key ACTA negotiating parties—Japan, the United States, the European Union, and Switzerland—tabled their own papers on enforcement in the TRIPS Council. Nevertheless, the willingness of these countries to negotiate outside this traditional multilateral forum when they did not achieve their preferred outcome does raise challenging questions about the WTO's future role in the development of international intellectual property enforcement norms.

B.   LESS DEVELOPED COUNTRIES

1.   TRIPS Council Although less developed countries have always preferred enforcement standards that are better tailored to their resource-deficient environments, until recently they were reluctant to take proactive efforts in pushing for their preferred international intellectual property enforcement norms. Instead, they merely registered their concerns over high enforcement norms while resisting the developed countries' attempt to push for the establishment of these standards in the TRIPS Council.

For example, at the June 2006 TRIPS Council meeting discussed earlier, leading developing countries, such as Argentina, Brazil, China, and India, responded by strongly opposing the EU proposal, citing distractions from the WTO trade talks, which they claimed were "supposed to focus on development." As noted by a Chinese official, the TRIPS Council is "not the right time or right place" to discuss enforcement. In China's view, the DSB should handle intellectual property enforcement issues at the WTO instead.

In the follow-up meeting in October 2006, less developed countries again noted their strong opposition to the European Union's joint communication with Japan, Switzerland, and the United States—this time, largely on procedural grounds. As a result, the European Union did not have an opportunity to make a formal presentation of its proposal. Instead, it made a statement, and its proposal was subsequently rejected.

The negative reactions to the EU proposals from less developed countries were understandable. These countries already had great difficulty in complying with the high standards required by the TRIPS Agreement following the expiration of the transitional periods. In effect, they were dealing with what Bernard Hoekman and Petros Mavroidis described as the "Uruguay Round 'hangover'—or, more specifically in the intellectual property context, "TRIPS Veisalgia." It is, therefore, understandable why these countries were very concerned when developed countries sought to push for the establishment of new and higher TRIPS-plus and TRIPS-extra standards through ACTA and other bilateral, plurilateral, or regional trade and investment agreements.

Less developed countries also feared that a greater discussion of the implementation of the TRIPS Agreement would eventually open them up to future challenges over non-compliance in the enforcement area. To many of these countries, compliance issues should be addressed only through the use of the mandatory WTO dispute settlement process. Some less developed countries also feared that a greater discussion of enforcement issues in the TRIPS Council would lead to unconstructive "finger pointing" that would slow down the Council's work while creating unnecessary distractions.

2. Dispute Settlement Body. Similar to the disappointing stance taken by less developed countries in the TRIPS Council, their participation in the WTO dispute settlement process has been largely on the defensive end. The first TRIPS dispute that led to the establishment of a WTO panel, for example, involved India as a respondent. In this dispute, the United States and later the European Communities successfully challenged, through parallel proceedings, India's failure to establish a mailbox system in its patent law pursuant to Article 70.8 of the TRIPS Agreement. The result was a clear-cut victory for the United States and the European Communities.

Similarly, in *Brazil—Measures Affecting Patent Protection*, a case concerning the local working requirement in patent law, Brazil served as a respondent. This complaint, however, was settled a year later, shortly after Brazil filed a retaliatory complaint challenging United States patent law for violations of Articles 27 and 28 of the TRIPS Agreement. Brazil's complaint marked the first time a less developed country filed a TRIPS complaint against a developed country. Nevertheless, the two disputes were quickly settled, and Brazil lost its opportunity to use the WTO dispute settlement process to shape the interpretation and implementation of the TRIPS Agreement.

Apart from Brazil and India, Argentina, China, Indonesia, and Pakistan all have appeared on the respondent side of the TRIPS-related complaints in the WTO's first fifteen years of existence. Although all of these complaints were filed by either the United States or the European Union, developing countries in recent years have made more frequent use of the WTO dispute settlement process to resolve non-TRIPS disputes. Their ability to take advantage of the process also has improved greatly.

For example, in the U.S.-China dispute, although China was still a respondent, it was able to defend its position admirably before the DSB. Given the dispute's serious ramifications for the less developed world, six developing countries—Argentina, Brazil, India, Mexico, Thailand, and Turkey—also participated in the panel proceedings as third parties. Except for India and Turkey, all of them either provided a written submission to or made an oral statement before the WTO panel. Perhaps because of their more active participation, less developed countries seemed to have had greater success in this dispute than in the earlier ones.

As the panel report has shown, less developed countries were able to score some important points that are likely to influence the future interpretation and implementation of the TRIPS Agreement. For example, the panel report underscores both the importance of having minimum standards and flexibilities in the TRIPS Agreement and the longstanding treatment of intellectual property rights as private rights. It also rejects the use of bilateral, plurilateral, or regional trade agreements to divine meaning in the TRIPS language. In addition, the report demonstrates an appreciation of the divergent local market conditions in each WTO member while continuing the use of an evidence-based approach for resolving WTO disputes. The panel's discussion of Article 41.5 also hints at its willingness to consider evidence in cases where resource demands in the area of intellectual property enforcement have exceeded those in other areas of law enforcement. Thus, as I observed in another article, although policymakers, industries, and commentators have largely focused on the gains and losses of China and the United States, the less developed world—whether intended or not—may very well have become the dispute's ultimate winner.

A year after the release of this panel report, India and Brazil filed complaints against the European Union and the Netherlands over the repeated seizure of in-transit generic drugs. These complaints marked the second time less developed countries used the WTO dispute settlement process to address TRIPS concerns. They also represent the first attempt by less developed countries to challenge TRIPS-plus standards—enforcement or otherwise.

It remains to be seen whether any of these complaints will lead to the establishment of a WTO panel, and therefore further interpretation and implementation of the TRIPS Agreement. However, the European Union's recent agreement with India to amend its regulation on customs border measures already suggests the growing ability of less developed countries to take advantage of the WTO dispute settlement process—and in this case, to negotiate in the shadow of a WTO complaint. Even if India ultimately settles with the European Union, the dispute between Brazil and the European Union could still remain.

3. *TRIPS Council: Part Deux.* Although less developed countries initially were rather defensive in the TRIPS Council and before the DSB, their positions changed significantly last year. In addition to the complaints India and Brazil filed against the European Union and the Netherlands, both China and India made important interventions at the TRIPS Council meeting in June 2010, largely in response to the release of the draft ACTA text, as well as the highly disturbing trend concerning TRIPS-plus enforcement standards.

As China explained, TRIPS-plus enforcement standards could cause a wide variety of systemic problems within the international trading system. For example, they could raise potential legal conflicts with the TRIPS Agreement as well as other agreements within the WTO. By increasing the complexity of intellectual property rules, they could also make the international legal framework highly unpredictable, thus posing barriers to legitimate trade. In addition, the TRIPS-plus standards may upset the delicate balance struck in the TRIPS Agreement through an arduous multiyear negotiation process. The standards could also build harmful technological barriers while raising concerns about resource misallocation, an issue that was raised in the U.S.-China TRIPS enforcement dispute. China concluded its intervention by advancing a proposal on specific safeguard principles against the ongoing push for TRIPS-plus enforcement standards.

Supporting China's position, India followed up by drawing attention to these and other systemic problems created by TRIPS-plus standards. Of primary concern to India was the push for ACTA and other TRIPS-plus standards, which it claimed would upset the balance in the TRIPS Agreement. The second sentence of Article 1.1 of the TRIPS Agreement states specifically that "Members may, but shall not be obliged to, implement in their law more extensive protection than is required by this Agreement, provided that such protection does not contravene the provisions of this Agreement." To India, as well as other policymakers and commentators, this particular sentence delineates one of the Agreement's maximum standards, or the so-called "ceilings." Article 1.1 therefore prohibits members from implementing more extensive protection than required by the Agreement if such additional protection contravenes the Agreement.

India further claimed that the introduction of TRIPS-plus standards "could short-change legal processes, impede legitimate competition and shift the escalated costs of enforcing private commercial right to governments, consumers and tax payers." In its view, the standards represent "a systemic threat to the rights of legitimate traders and producers of goods and fundamental rights of due process for individuals." These standards may also upset resource allocation while having strong trade-distorting effects.

In addition, India lamented the fact that "IPR negotiations in [regional trade agreements] and plurilateral processes like ACTA completely bypassed the existing multilateral processes." These negotiations have harmed multilateral trade by undermining the "systemic checks" against trade protectionism that had been built into the WTO framework. Through cross referencing, the resulting bilateral and plurilateral trade agreements may also implicate non-signatory members of the WTO. India concluded its intervention with a trenchant critique of ACTA, covering issues that ranged from customs seizure of in-transit generic drugs to the restriction of TRIPS flexibilities to the inconsistencies between ACTA and the Doha Declaration.

Compared to the earlier passive resistance put up by less developed countries in the TRIPS Council, the interventions recently made by China and India signaled a more active agenda on the enforcement front. Their positions were not only well-conceived, but also strongly supported by both the text and the negotiating history of the TRIPS Agreement. For example, the Punta del Este Declaration stated clearly that the goal of the TRIPS negotiations was to "ensure that measures and procedures to enforce intellectual property rights do not themselves become barriers to legitimate trade." During the TRIPS negotiations, Brazil registered concern over three sets of issues that it believed "should receive priority attention in the discussions":

> (1) The extent to which rigid and excessive protection of IPRs impedes the access to latest technological developments, restricting, therefore, the participation of developing countries to international trade?

> (2) The extent to which abusive use of IPRs gives rise to restrictions and distortions in international trade?

(3) The risks that a rigid system of IPRs protection implies for international trade.

A year later, India reminded the delegates that "it was only the restrictive and anti-competitive practices of the owners of the IPRs that could be considered to be trade-related because they alone distorted or impeded international trade."

In the end, the first recital of the preamble of the TRIPS Agreement echoes the negotiating mandate outlined in the Punta del Este Declaration. It states explicitly that the drafters desired "to reduce distortions and impediments to international trade, and taking into account the need to . . . ensure that measures and procedures to enforce intellectual property rights do not themselves become barriers to legitimate trade." As Carlos Correa reminded us, "higher levels of IPR protection may create barriers to legitimate trade"—a key concern of both the WTO and the TRIPS Agreement.

In sum, the TRIPS Council interventions from China and India, along with the WTO complaints that India and Brazil filed against the European Union and the Netherlands, have suggested a more proactive approach on the part of less developed countries to shaping the development of international intellectual property enforcement norms. This approach is highly promising, considering the fact that Brazil, China, and India represent the three leading voices in the less developed world. As their economic strengths—and therefore political leverage—grow, the evolution of the international intellectual property regime is likely to be more dynamic and multidirectional. Such evolution will become even more intriguing if these countries are willing to establish a united front that negotiates on behalf of the less developed world.

WTO TRIPs Disputes, May 2019*

Year**	Respondents	Complainants	Issue	Status
1996	Japan	U.S.	Measures Concerning Sound Recordings	Mutually agreed solution (1997).
1996	Portugal	U.S.	Patent Protection under the Industrial Property Act	Mutually agreed solution (1996).
1996	Pakistan	U.S.	Patent Protection for Pharmaceutical and Agricultural Chemical Products	Mutually agreed solution (1997).
1996	Japan	EC	Measures Concerning Sound Recordings	Mutually agreed solution (1997).
1996	India	U.S.	Patent Protection for Pharmaceutical and Agricultural Chemical Products	Appellate report (1997); implementation notified (1999).

---

*   This table is drawn from information on the WTO website (http://www.wto.org/english/tratop_e/dispu_e/dispu_agreements_index_e.htm?id=A26) as of May 1, 2019.

**   The year in which the Request for Consultations was sent.

Year**	Respondents	Complainants	Issue	Status
1996	Indonesia	U.S.	Certain Measures Affecting the Automobile Industry	Arbitration report (1998); implementation notified (1999).
1997	India	EC	Patent Protection for Pharmaceutical and Agricultural Chemical Products	Panel report (1998); implementation notified (1999).
1997	Denmark	U.S.	Measures Affecting the Enforcement of Intellectual Property Rights	Mutually agreed solution (2001).
1997	Ireland	U.S.	Measures Affecting the Grant of Copyright and Neighboring Rights	Mutually agreed solution (2000).
1997	Sweden	U.S.	Measures Affecting the Enforcement of Intellectual Property Rights	Mutually agreed solution (1998).
1997	Canada	EC	Patent Protection of Pharmaceutical Products	Arbitration report (2000); implementation notified (2000).
1998	EC	U.S.	Measures Affecting the Grant of Copyright and Neighboring Rights	Mutually agreed solution (2000).
1998	Greece	U.S.	Enforcement of Intellectual Property Rights for Motion Pictures and Television Programs	Mutually agreed solution (2001).
1998	EC	U.S.	Enforcement of Intellectual Property Rights for Motion Pictures and Television Programs	Mutually agreed solution (2001).
1998	EC	Canada	Patent Protection for Pharmaceutical and Agricultural Chemical Products	In consultations.
1999	U.S.	EC	Section 110(5) of US Copyright Act	Arbitration report (2001); mutually satisfactory temporary arrangement (2003).
1999	Argentina	U.S.	Patent Protection for Pharmaceuticals and Test Data Protection for Agricultural Chemicals	Mutually agreed solution (2002).
1999	Canada	U.S.	Term of Patent Protection	Arbitration report (2001); implementation notified (2001).
1999	EC	U.S.	Protection of Trademarks and Geographical Indications for Agricultural Products and Foodstuffs	Panel report (2005); implementation notified (2006).
1999	U.S.	EC	Section 211 Omnibus Appropriations Act of 1998	Appellate report (2002).
2000	U.S.	EC	Section 337 of the Tariff Act of 1930 and Amendments Thereto	In consultations.

First-entry of a developing country boycotts — issue [handwritten annotation]

Year**	Respondents	Complainants	Issue	Status
2000	Argentina	U.S.	Certain Measures on the Protection of Patents and Test Data	Mutually agreed solution (2002).
2000	Brazil	U.S.	Measures Affecting Patent Protection	Mutually agreed solution (2001).
2001	U.S.	Brazil	US Patents Code	In consultations.
2003	EC	Australia	Protection of Trademarks and Geographical Indications for Agricultural Products and Foodstuffs	Panel report (2005); implementation notified (2006).
2007	China	U.S.	Measures Affecting the Protection and Enforcement of Intellectual Property Rights	Panel report (2009); implementation notified (2010).
2008	China	EC	Measures Affecting Financial Information Services and Foreign Financial Information Suppliers	Mutually agreed solution (2008).
2010	EU, Netherlands	India	Seizure of Generic Drugs in Transit	In consultations.
2010	EU, Netherlands	Brazil	Seizure of Generic Drugs in Transit	In consultations.
2012	Australia	Ukraine	Certain Measures Concerning Trademarks, Geographical Indications and Other Plain Packaging Requirements Applicable to Tobacco Products and Packaging	Authority for panel lapsed (2016).
2012	Australia	Honduras	Certain Measures Concerning Trademarks, Geographical Indications and Other Plain Packaging Requirements Applicable to Tobacco Products and Packaging	Panel report under appeal (2018); consolidated with Australia—Tobacco Plain Packaging, DS435 and DS441 (complaints by Honduras and the Dominican Republic).
2012	Australia	Dominican Republic	Certain Measures Concerning Trademarks, Geographical Indications and Other Plain Packaging Requirements Applicable to Tobacco Products and Packaging	Panel report under appeal (2018).
2013	Australia	Cuba	Certain Measures Concerning Trademarks, Geographical Indications and Other Plain Packaging Requirements Applicable to Tobacco Products and Packaging	Report adopted (2018).

Year**	Respondents	Complainants	Issue	Status
2013	Australia	Indonesia	Certain Measures Concerning Trademarks, Geographical Indications and Other Plain Packaging Requirements Applicable to Tobacco Products and Packaging	Report adopted (2018).
2017	United Arab Emirates	Qatar	Measures Relating to Trade in Goods and Services, and Trade-Related Aspects of Intellectual Property Rights	Panel composed.
2017	Bahrain	Qatar	Measures Relating to Trade in Goods and Services, and Trade-Related Aspects of Intellectual Property Rights	In consultations.
2017	Saudi Arabia	Qatar	Measures Relating to Trade in Goods and Services, and Trade-Related Aspects of Intellectual Property Rights	In consultations.
2018	China	United States	Certain Measures Concerning the Protection of Intellectual Property Rights	Panel composed.
2018	China	European Union	Certain Measures on the Transfer of Technology	In consultations.
2018	Saudi Arabia	Qatar	Measures Concerning the Protection of Intellectual Property	Panel composed.
2019	Turkey	European Union	Certain Measures Concerning the Production, Importation and Marketing of Pharmaceutical Products	In consultations.

NOTES

1. *Origins of TRIPs.* The institutional origins of the Agreement on Trade-Related Aspects of Intellectual Property Rights trace to the closing days of the 1979 Tokyo Round of the General Agreement on Tariffs and Trade when, frustrated by the reluctance of developing countries to adopt heightened standards for protection under the principal intellectual property conventions, the European Community and the United States sought to obtain an "Agreement on Measures to Discourage the Importation of Counterfeit Goods." Behind this failed initiative—and subsequent, more successful efforts to place intellectual property on the agenda of the GATT Uruguay Round—was the belief that the trade process could extract developing country concessions on increased minimum standards and that the GATT dispute settlement process could inject a measure of rigor into international intellectual property enforcement.

In June 1986 the European Community, the United States, Japan and several other industrialized countries presented an informal declaration of GATT mandates, intellectual property rights among them. Several developing countries, led by Argentina, Brazil and India, argued against introducing intellectual property issues into the GATT framework. Not surprisingly, the ultimate decision to include intellectual property on the agenda of the Uruguay Round failed to end the conflict between the industrialized and developing countries. Australia, supported by the industrialized countries, proposed that the TRIPs Agreement incorporate the standards of protection embodied in the Berne, Paris, Rome and Geneva Conventions. India, representing the views of many developing countries, proposed instead that negotiations be limited to practices that distort international trade; that the national treatment and most favored nation principles not be applied to intellectual property rights; and that developing nations receive more favorable treatment in the fields of patents and trademarks.

By the time the Agreement Establishing the World Trade Organization was concluded at Marrakesh, Morocco on April 15, 1994, the national treatment and most-favored nation principles had obtained a secure place in the TRIPs Agreement. The Agreement also introduced extensive remedial requirements, including measures for interdicting infringing goods at national borders. Concessions to developing and least-developed country members included, respectively, an extra four-year and ten-year transition period to bring their intellectual property laws into compliance with all but a handful of TRIPs standards.

For background on the history of the TRIPs Agreement, see Daniel Gervais, The TRIPs Agreement: Drafting History and Analysis (1998); Terence Stewart, The GATT Uruguay Round: A Negotiating History (1986–1992) 2270–2272 (1993); William Cornish & Kathleen Liddell, The Origins and Structure of the TRIPS Agreement, in TRIPS Plus 20: From Trade Rules to Market Principles (Hanns Ullrich et al. eds. 2016), pp. 3–51. *See also* A. Jane Bradley, Intellectual Property Rights, Investment and Trade in Services in the Uruguay Round: Laying the Foundation, 23 Stan. J. Int'l. L. 57 (1987). On developments under the TRIPs Agreement, see Symposium, The First Ten Years of the TRIPs Agreement, 10 Marq. Int. Prop. L. Rev. 155 (2006).

2. *Enforcement Against Member States; TRIPs and Dispute Settlement.* What recourse does Country *A*, a party to the Berne and Paris Conventions, have against Country *B*, also a party to one or both Conventions, when it believes that Country *B* has failed to comply with a convention standard? One of the deficiencies of the Berne and Paris Conventions that precipitated the TRIPs Agreement was their lack of an effective mechanism for resolving disputes between members; although both treaties provided for dispute settlement before the International Court of Justice, no member country ever pursued it.

Annex 2 to the WTO Agreement, the Understanding on Rules and Procedures Governing the Settlement of Disputes, establishes a comprehensive system of rules for dispute settlement, and Article III of the Agreement states that administration of the Understanding is one of its principal functions. With the incorporation of existing intellectual property treaty norms into the TRIPs Agreement, systematic and effective dispute resolution now exists for the first time in international intellectual property relations.

The Understanding on Dispute Settlement (DSU) replaces earlier, less formal GATT dispute resolution mechanisms with a precise adjudicatory procedure including appellate review and effective economic sanctions. Under the DSU a WTO member that believes another member has breached its obligations will initiate consultations with the offending member (Article 4). If consultations fail, the parties may pursue mediation, good offices or conciliation within the WTO (Article 5) or, alternatively, proceed directly to the panel phase in which the Dispute Settlement Body (DSB), charged with administering WTO dispute settlement, will form a panel of three—or where the parties agree, five—members to hear the dispute and establish the panel's terms of reference (Articles 6–8). Following hearings and deliberations, the panel is to submit its report to the DSB, and the report will then be automatically adopted unless the DSB decides against adoption or unless a party appeals for review, limited to issues of law, by the seven-member Appellate Body (Articles 12–18). A report from the Appellate Body is similarly subject to automatic adoption by the DSB unless the DSB makes a consensus decision against adoption. If the member is found to be in breach of its obligations and fails to conform to the required standard within a "reasonable amount of time," the complaining member may request negotiations for compensation and, if those fail, may request the DSB to authorize appropriate retaliatory measures (Articles 19–22).

3. *The Role of Private Rights Owners in TRIPs Enforcement.* Some countries treat the TRIPs Agreement as self-executing and consequently enforceable by private parties even apart from any implementing legislation. For example, in Merck Genericos v. Merck & Co., 41 IIC 614 (2010), Portugal's Supreme Court ruled that although plaintiff's patent would have expired on April 9, 1996 under Portugal's 15-year patent term then in effect, the WTO Agreement's entry into force in Portugal on January 1, 1995 effectively extended the patent's term by five years under TRIPs Article 33's provision for a minimum 20-year term of protection from the date of filing. Against the defendant's objection that the significant enforcement flexibilities embodied in the TRIPs Agreement—such as the possibility of countervailing sanctions—made direct enforcement impracticable, the court ruled that the Agreement's direct application was not impaired by the fact that it might reduce the country's legislative or executive discretion in dealing with TRIPs violations. Further, "Art. 33 TRIPs is precise and unconditional, prerequisites for its direct application."

Other countries, including the United States, take the position that the TRIPs Agreement establishes rights and obligations only among member countries, and not among individual rights owners. Nonetheless, intellectual property rights owners, particularly in industrialized countries, can be expected to play an important role in determining what disputes individual governments present for resolution. The former General Counsel in the Office of the United States Trade Representative has observed that "the absence of a private right of action has major implications for the use and development of the WTO dispute settlement process, including for TRIPs disputes. Acting as gatekeepers to the process, an administration's trade lawyers will use prosecutorial discretion to select among competing claims using a range of criteria to establish priorities. Private parties will be limited in the extent to which they can determine which cases to bring, on which TRIPs provisions to focus, and what aspects of TRIPs rules to seek to develop through the dispute settlement process. On the cases they select, however, the government's trade lawyers will collaborate closely with legal counsel for the private parties most directly affected by the foreign government practices being challenged." Judith Bello, Some Practical Observations About WTO Settlement of Intellectual Property Disputes, 37 Va. J. Int'l L. 357, 361 (1997).

On TRIPs dispute settlement procedures generally, see Rochelle Cooper Dreyfuss & Andreas Lowenfeld, Two Achievements of the Uruguay Round: Putting TRIPs and Dispute Settlement Together, 37 Va. J. Int'l L. 275 (1997); Paul Edward Geller, Intellectual Property in the Global Marketplace: Impact of TRIPs Dispute Settlements? 29 Int'l Lawyer 99 (1995); Matthijs Geuze & Hannu Wager, WTO Dispute Settlement Practice Relating to the TRIPs Agreement, 2 J. Int'l Econ. L. 347 (1999); John Jackson, Dispute Settlement and the WTO: Emerging Problems, 1 J. Int'l Econ. L. 329 (1998); Silke von Lewinski, The WTO/TRIPS Dispute Settlement Mechanism: Experiences and Perspectives, in TRIPS Plus 20: From Trade Rules to Market Principles (Hanns Ullrich et al. eds. 2016), pp. 603–620; Matthew Kennedy, WTO Dispute Settlement and the TRIPS Agreement (2016). For a possible change to the self-executing status of TRIPs in EU member states in light of a 2013 decision by the Court of Justice of the European Union, see Miquel Montana I Mora, The Practical Consequences of the CJEU Judgment of 18 July 2013 Changing Its Doctrine on the Respective Competences of the EU and Its Member States to Apply the TRIPS Agreement, 48(7) IIC 784 (2017).

4. *TRIPs and Judicial Remedies.* The Berne and Paris Conventions center almost exclusively on substantive norms, leaving the question of judicial and administrative remedies to local decision. One of the TRIPs Agreement's major contributions was to adopt a code of enforcement procedures; as Jerome Reichman has observed, "[r]ights holders who cannot translate substantive victories into effective remedial action at the local level may eventually trigger the WTO's dispute-settlement machinery if their own states choose to question the good faith of the accused state's judicial and administrative organs." J.H. Reichman, Enforcing the Enforcement Procedures of the TRIPs Agreement, 37 Va. J. Int'l L. 335, 339 (1997).

According to TRIPs Article 41, which summarizes the enforcement rules prescribed more specifically in Articles 42–61, member countries are to ensure the availability of enforcement procedures, including monetary relief, provisional and permanent coercive relief and border measures, "so as to permit effective action against any act of infringement of intellectual property rights covered by this Agreement." Procedures should be "fair and equitable," embodying fundamental notions of due process; decisions on the merits "shall be based only on evidence in respect of which parties were offered the opportunity to be heard" and "shall preferably be in writing and reasoned"; and there must be some form of appellate review of administrative or trial court decisions.

Article 41(5) states two important limiting principles: the enforcement provisions do not "create any obligation to put in place a judicial system for the enforcement of intellectual property rights distinct from that for the enforcement of laws in general," and the provisions do not create "any obligation with respect to the distribution of resources as between enforcement of intellectual property rights and the enforcement of laws in general." Nonetheless, as Professor Reichman has astutely observed, over the short and medium terms the new enforcement procedures may create serious inroads on national autonomy, particularly in states that have only recently become economically and politically independent: "we must imagine how the U.S. Congress would react if other countries told the United States when injunctions had to be made available, what the scope of U.S. discovery and appellate review procedures should be, what actions to criminalize, and how U.S. Customs agents should treat cultural and manufactured goods at the point of entry to this country. Yet, that is precisely what the TRIPs Agreement does in considerable detail." J.H. Reichman, Enforcing the Enforcement of Procedures of the TRIPs Agreement, 37 Va. J. Int'l L. 335, 339–40 (1997).

Although TRIPs does not require the establishment of special intellectual property courts, some countries have created them. For an example, established in response to pressures from the United States and the European Community, see Vichai Ariyanuntaka, TRIPs and the Specialised Intellectual Property Court in Thailand, 30 IIC 360 (1999).

5. *TRIPs and Developing and Least-Developed Countries*. Negotiations for the TRIPs Agreement had barely been concluded when it became evident that the Agreement's concessions to the special needs of developing and least developed country members would fall short of the legal leeway needed to meet these needs. The Doha Round of WTO negotiations, initiated in 2001, focused on the plight of developing and least developed countries and, in the case of intellectual property and TRIPs, on the need for access to medicines in these epidemic-ravaged regions. In its Declaration on the TRIPs Agreement and Public Health, WT/MIN (01)/DEC 2, 20 November 2001, the Ministerial Conference, recognizing "the gravity of the public health problems afflicting many developing and least-developed countries, especially those resulting from HIV/AIDS, tuberculosis, malaria and other epidemics," and the difficulties faced by countries "with insufficient or no manufacturing capacities in the pharmaceutical sector," instructed the TRIPs Council to find an "expeditious" solution by the end of 2002.

As a first step, the 2001 Declaration postponed until 2016 the deadline for least-developed member countries to comply with TRIPs patent and trade secret standards for pharmaceutical products, a decision endorsed by the TRIPs Council in 2002, WTO, IP/C/25, 1 July 2002. Decisions of the WTO General Council in 2003 and 2005 created a framework—through a waiver and an amendment to TRIPs, respectively—to loosen the substantive restrictions on patent compulsory licenses and enable the export of pharmaceuticals produced under compulsory license to countries that themselves lack the capacity to produce the pharmaceutical. In June 2013 the TRIPs Council extended the transition period for least-developed member countries under Article 66.1 from July 2013 to July 2021; the extension was "without prejudice" to the Council's 2016 deadline for pharmaceutical products. These developments are further considered at page 541, below.

See Duncan Matthews, TRIPs Flexibilities and Access to Medicines in Developing Countries: The Problem with Technical Assistance and Free Trade Agreements, 27 EIPR 420 (2005); Elizabeth Henderson, TRIPs and the Third World: Pharmaceutical Patents in India, 19 EIPR 652 (1997); Jerome Reichman, Securing Compliance with the TRIPs Agreement After U.S. v. India, 1 J. Int'l Econ. L. 585 (1998). The fact that developing and least developed countries acted jointly to secure intellectual property concessions in the Uruguay Round does not imply that their interests under TRIPs will be the same. For some views on TRIPs implementation in several countries see Michael Blakeney, The Impact of the TRIPs Agreement in the Asia Pacific Region, 18 EIPR 544 (1996); Carlos Correa, Implementation of the TRIPs Agreement in Latin America and the Caribbean, 19 EIPR 435 (1997); Ruth Gana, Two Steps Forward: Reconciling Nigeria's Accession to the Berne Convention and the TRIPs Agreement, 27 IIC 476 (1996).

2. REGIONAL ARRANGEMENTS

THE INSTITUTIONS OF THE EUROPEAN UNION

The European Union is a major shaping force in world intellectual property law. EU directives, regulations and judicial decisions have reconfigured large parts of the intellectual property law of countries representing most of Western Europe; with the successive enlargements of the European Union, the reach of these rules now extends beyond Western Europe. The EU also plays an often decisive role in negotiating international intellectual property agreements. Authority for these and related measures is vested principally in the Council (formerly the EC Council of Ministers), the European Commission (formerly the Commission of the European Communities), the European Parliament and the Court of Justice of the European Union (commonly referred to as the ECJ prior to December 1, 2009, and as the CJEU thereafter).

The European Economic Community was constituted by the 1957 Treaty of Rome to guide the economic integration of the countries of Western Europe. Together with the European Atomic Energy Community, created at the same time, and the earlier-created European Coal and Steel Community, it formed the European Communities. The Treaty on European Union, which was concluded at Maastricht in December, 1991 and entered into force on November 1, 1993, structured the European Union around three locii, or "pillars," of activity: at the center were the European Communities, consisting of the European Economic, Atomic Energy and Coal and Steel Communities; the other two pillars were a framework for unified action in security and foreign policy matters, and arrangements for cooperation in police and justice activities. The Treaty of Lisbon, concluded in 2007 and in force sinc

2009, further deepened the integration of the European Union by abandoning the three-pillar structure, introducing the posts of the President of the European Council and the External Relations Commissioner, strengthening the power of the European Parliament, and moving from unanimity to qualified majority voting in several areas.

The European Economic Community's founding members were Belgium, France, West Germany, Italy, Luxembourg and the Netherlands. They were joined over the course of four decades by Denmark, Ireland, and the United Kingdom; Greece; Spain and Portugal; and Sweden, Finland and Austria. (East Germany joined in 1990 as part of the reunified German state.) Subsequent enlargements increased the Union to twenty-eight members. Until their admission to the Union, Sweden, Finland and Austria—together with Iceland, Liechtenstein, Norway and Switzerland—belonged to the European Free Trade Association, EFTA, under the terms of the European Economic Area Agreement, and were subject in many respects to EC norms. Partnership and Cooperation Agreements have also been made with countries of the former Soviet bloc aimed at establishing free trade areas and possible future Union membership.

The principal institutions that directly affect the formation and administration of intellectual property law in the European Union are the European Commission, the Council, the European Parliament and the Court of Justice of the European Union. Although elaborate systems of checks and balances frame the relations between these institutions, there is no strict separation of powers between legislative and executive functions of the sort commonly found in national constitutions, and the Council, the Commission and the European Parliament variously participate in the prescription of rules and norms affecting intellectual property. Depending on the issue at hand, and the governing provision of the Treaty, the Council may adopt legislation together with the Parliament in a complex "ordinary legislative procedure," formerly referred to as "co-decision"; or the Council may adopt legislation through other procedures calling only for the Parliament's consultation or "consent." The Council alone or together with the Parliament will empower the Commission to promulgate detailed regulations in the manner of an administrative agency. For most legislation affecting the internal market and intellectual property, the ordinary legislative procedure applies.

The Commission. The European Commission plays a pivotal role in the operation of the European Union, exercising functions that are variously legislative (as in its initiative power to propose legislation); administrative (overseeing the national implementation of directives); executive (representing the Union in negotiating trade agreements and participating in the affairs of international organizations) or related to enforcement (as in its determination, subject to review, of violations of competition law rules). The President of the Commission has the power to influence the direction of Commission, and consequently EU, policy. Individual commissioners—one from each member country—have their own staff, or "cabinet," and portfolio for which they are directly responsible. The Commission's bureaucracy divides into Directorates General, each covering a different, but often overlapping, subject matter area.

The Council. The Council meets in various configurations, with member states represented by one or more government ministers depending on the configuration. (The Council is to be distinguished from the European Council, which is composed of heads of state of the member states, the President of the European Council and the President of the Commission.) The Council's principal role in formulating intellectual property norms is to determine whether to approve legislative initiatives, such as directives, proposed by the Commission. The Council may itself shape the legislative agenda by requesting the Commission to study and propose legislation in designated areas.

Parliament. The European Parliament is a legislative body, directly elected by voters in member states, whose members sit according to political, rather than national, blocs. Originally a powerless, strictly consultative body, the Parliament has over time become a substantive participant in the Community legislative process, often through the ordinary legislative procedure. It may adopt or amend legislation in several areas and participate in conciliation procedures with the object of aligning its position with those of the Council. One source of the Parliament's new strength is its political power over the Commission— not only to take part in the appointment of the Commission, but also to censure and require the Commission's resignation and to approve the nomination of the Commission President.

The Court of Justice of the European Union (CJEU). The CJEU (formerly the Court of Justice of the European Communities, or the ECJ) most commonly adjudicates intellectual property disputes in cases where a question of EU law is raised before the national court of a member state and the national court refers the case to the CJEU. The CJEU comprises two courts: the Court of Justice and the General Court. The Court of Justice consists of one judge from each member state, and may sit as a full court, as a Grand Chamber of fifteen judges, or in Chambers of three or five judges. Advocates General, appointed by member states, play an important role in Court of Justice decisionmaking by providing the Court with an objective and reasoned evaluation of the case and a recommendation for decision (that is followed more often than not).

The General Court, formerly the Court of First Instance, was established in 1988 to relieve the ECJ of some of its workload by taking direct appeals by natural or legal persons and cases of less general significance. The General Court consists of at least one judge from each member state. The court's jurisdiction has expanded over the years, and it maintains a substantial intellectual property docket because it decides matters brought against the European Union Intellectual Property Office and against the Community Plant Variety Office. Appeals on legal questions may be taken from the General Court to the Court of Justice.

For intellectual property, the EU's focus on the creation of a single internal market has principally taken the form of directives, such as the 1991 Software Directive (now the 2009 Directive) and the 1996 Database Directive, and regulations, such as the 1993 Regulation on the Community Trade Mark, establishing uniform norms among member states (now the 2017 Regulation). Directives establish specific objects to be implemented under national law, leaving the precise method and language of implementation to national legislation. Regulations, by contrast, are under Article 288 of the Treaty on the Functioning of the European Union (formerly Article 249 of the EC Treaty) "directly applicable," meaning that they become part of national law immediately, without legislative intervention or implementation. (Regulations may also be "directly applicable" in the sense of international law, and vest rights in individuals that can be pursued in national courts without further action by the national legislature.) Decisions of the Court of Justice, most notably on questions of exhaustion of rights, have also significantly influenced intellectual property law within the Community.

Bibliographic Note. On the general structure and operations of the European Union, see Walter van Gerven, The European Union: A Polity of States and Peoples (2005); Julio Baquero Cruz & Carlos Close Montero, European Integration from Rome to Berlin: 1957–2007 (2009); Paul Craig & Gráinne de Búrca, EU Law: Text, Cases and Materials (1998); Paul Craig & Carol Harlow (eds.), Lawmaking in the European Union (1998); P.J.G. Kapteyn & P. VerLoren van Themaat, Introduction to the Law of the European Communities (3rd ed. 1998).

On the particular institutions of the European Union see, L. Neville Brown & Tom Kennedy, The Court of Justice of the European Communities (1994); Martin Westlake, A Modern Guide to the European Parliament (1994); Francis Jacobs, Richard Corbett & Michael Shackleton, The European Parliament (1995); Geoffrey Edwards & David Spence, (eds.), The European Commission (1997); Martin Westlake, The Council of the European Union (1995).

Jan Corbet, The Law of the EEC and Intellectual Property

13 Journal of Law and Commerce 328–336, 343–345, 359–369 (1994).

A. Overview of the Treaty

The objectives and activities of the EEC are set forth generally in Article 2 of the [EEC] Treaty, which states:

By establishing a common market and progressively approximating the economic policies of Member States, the Community shall promote the harmonious development of economic activities, the continuous and balanced expansion, an increase in stability, an accelerated raising of the standard of living and closer relations between the States belonging to it.

To achieve these goals, Article 3 provides, inter alia, for the following activities:

(a) the elimination, as between Member States, of customs duties and of quantitative restrictions on the import and export of goods, and of all other measures having equivalent effect;

. . . .

(c) the abolition, as between Member States, of obstacles to freedom of movement for persons, services and capital;

. . . .

(f) the institution of a system ensuring that competition in the common market is not distorted;

. . . .

(h) the approximation of the laws of Member States to the extent required for the proper functioning of the common market.

. . . .

Specific articles of the EEC Treaty are relevant to intellectual property. In particular, Article 3 is given specific effect in various Treaty provisions.

For example, the activity mentioned under Article 3(a) has been implemented in Articles 30 through 36 of the Treaty. Article 30 prohibits quantitative restrictions on imports and "all measures having equivalent effect." In contrast, Article 36 contains an exception which has been the source of much litigation brought before the Court of Justice. Article 36 states that "[t]he provisions of Articles 30 to 34 shall not preclude prohibitions or restrictions on imports, exports or goods in transit justified on grounds of . . . the protection of industrial and commercial property." The second sentence of Article 36 states that "such prohibitions or restrictions shall not, however, constitute a means of arbitrary discrimination or a disguised restriction on trade between Member States."

The objective set forth in Article 3(c) has resulted in the promulgation of Article 59, which recognizes the Community-wide freedom to provide services. This provision has been invoked in the context of copyright infringement actions for the unauthorized retransmission of television broadcasts by cable networks.

Moreover, the objective stated in Article 3(f) has resulted in the adoption of Articles 85 and 86, which address the distortion of competition and the abuse of dominant positions within the Common Market. In this context, the Commission, the Court of First Instance and the Court of Justice have handed down many judgments which concern licensing contracts, as well as the abuse of dominant market positions by royalty-collecting societies.

Finally, Article 3(h) mentions the "approximation" of the laws of Member States which is examined in Article 100 of the Treaty. This provision provides the legal basis for the Commission to formulate proposals which will harmonize intellectual property laws within the European Communities.

B.   The Supranational Character of EEC Law

An entire body of law has been created pursuant to the Treaty. Unlike the law which has resulted from international copyright conventions, this law is not typical private international law. The word "supranational" characterizes the legal superstructure which, in the European Common Market, has developed along with its own institutions, namely the Parliament, the Council of Ministers (Council), the Commission, the Court of First Instance and the Court of Justice of the European Communities in Luxembourg. This supranational law and its institutions must be examined in order to determine the general effect upon the national laws and the judicial practices of the Member States, and more specifically its effect on intellectual property law.

In cases of conflict with national laws, as have arisen repeatedly with respect to intellectual property, the Treaty and the applicable law take precedence. In 1964, the Court of Justice ruled to this effect in *Costa v. ENEL.*[12] The court based its judgment on the second paragraph of Article 5 of the Treaty which clearly states that Member States "shall abstain from any measure which could jeopardize the attainment of the objectives of this Treaty." The phrase "any measure" has been construed to include the enforcement of national law in private suits. Consequently, the Treaty precludes national law when the two conflict. EEC law, therefore, can directly affect not only acts of Member States, but also the rights and obligations of individual citizens under their respective national laws.

Moreover, EEC law takes precedence over treaties between Member States. The issue, however, becomes muddled when nations entered into treaties prior to the enactment of the EEC Treaty. For example, Article 23 renders the Treaty powerless with respect to the rights and obligations of third countries which have concluded conventions or treaties with Member States prior to the inception of the EEC Treaty. A related issue is whether the Treaty, namely Articles 30 through 36, 59, 85 and 86, is directly binding within national jurisdictions. If answered in the affirmative, a subsequent issue is whether a citizen of a Member State may invoke these provisions as dispositive law in private litigation before a national court.

---

[12]   Case 6/64, Costa v. Ente Nazionale Energia Elettrica (ENEL), 1964 E.C.R. 585, 3 C.M.L.R. 425 (1964).

The wording of Articles 85 and 86 regarding undistorted competition leaves little doubt with respect to an affirmative answer to that question. The respective headings of these sections of the Treaty, "Rules applying to undertakings," indicates that these Articles are binding upon individual parties. Additionally, in its first ruling on intellectual property law in 1966, the Court of Justice affirmed the direct applicability of Article 85. Subsequent case law, moreover, has upheld this precedent and has established a firm doctrine which applies both Articles 85 and 86.

The issues regarding Articles 30 through 36 of the Treaty on the free movement of goods are more complex. In the past, it was argued that these provisions, namely Article 36, must be viewed in context as part of the chapter entitled "Elimination of Quantitative Restrictions Between Member States." In light of this contextual reading, these provisions were not addressed to individual parties, but to Member States. This reading implied that an individual citizen or company had no recourse to the defense implicit in the first sentence of Article 36 when attacked under Article 85 or 86 for acts that distort competition. Moreover, in accordance with the second sentence of Article 36, the individual citizen or company could not be attacked for arbitrary discrimination in, or disguised restriction of, intra-Community trade. This opinion was supported somewhat by the Court's ruling in *Etablissements Consten*;[20] it was, however, progressively destroyed in later cases. Under the case law, it is now well established that not only Articles 85 and 86, but also Articles 30, 36 and 59 of the Treaty, can be directly applied by national courts in legal disputes between individuals. It is important to note that several European judicial authorities apply EEC law, not only in the national courts of the Member States, but also in Community institutions.

The Commission of the European Communities (Commission) exercises a judicial function by investigating and adjudicating complaints under Articles 85 and 86 which address the distortion of competition and the abuse of dominant market positions. In this field, the Court of First Instance of the European Communities acts as a Court of Appeals for decisions of the Commission. Furthermore, the Court of Justice of the European Communities, as the final appellate court, rules on decisions of the Court of First Instance.

Another important provision of the Treaty is Article 177 which enables lower national courts, and obliges the highest national judicial authorities for particular disputes, to refer questions of EEC law to the Court of Justice for an interlocutory, but binding, ruling. Therefore, the Court is in a position to insure the uniform and correct interpretation of EEC law by the national judicial authorities of the Member States. These national authorities are in turn obliged to follow the precedents established by the Court.

---

[20] Etablissements Consten, 1966 E.C.R. 299, 5 C.M.L.R. 418.

II.   The Relevant EEC Freedoms

A.   The Freedom of Movement of Goods

Considering the aforementioned provisions of Article 3(a), as well as Articles 30 through 36 of the EEC Treaty which are intended to ensure the free movement of goods throughout the Common Market, circumstances exist in which intellectual property rights asserted under the law of a Member State may threaten to hinder the free movement of goods. It is important to analyze, therefore, how the Court of Justice, both doctrinally and in practice, has attempted to reconcile conflicts between the EEC's notion of freedom of commerce in goods and nationally-granted intellectual property rights. In some cases, the Court has precluded the exercise of such rights. Such conflicts have arisen in cases where unauthorized parallel imports of products prompted the assertion of claims to control exclusively the distribution of products within a national market.

The doctrinal basis of the claims in question is an important matter to consider. Two concepts are indispensable to understanding the problem before the Court in all these cases, namely, the principle of territoriality and the first-sale doctrine.

The principle of territoriality limits the scope of intellectual property rights such that their existence is limited to national jurisdictions. This principle provides the necessary line of demarcation between varied national jurisdictions in the field of intellectual property law. In essence, territoriality acts as a choice-of-law rule. Intellectual property rights, for example, are effective only within the individual territorially-isolated jurisdiction which has granted the rights. In practice, this principle has been broadly interpreted so that all too often the facts which form the basis for asserting rights or defenses in any given jurisdiction are also viewed as occurrences which are territorially isolated within that jurisdiction. A course of conduct which ostensibly infringes copyrights in several countries at once will be analyzed individually. Moreover, the action will be broken down into geographically discrete sets of infringing acts, with each set being governed by the copyright law of that country.

In the copyright situation, the first-sale doctrine generally limits a copyright owner's right to control distribution of a given copy of a work once that copy is "first" sold. The distribution right of that one copy is then said to be, to some degree, "exhausted." The holder of the distribution right can no longer fully control the fate of the first-sold copy which, after having lawfully entered into the relevant market, may be resold freely one thousand times over. The larger task involves defining the relevant market in which a copy of a copyright-protected work, a patented work, or a trademark protected product is "first" sold and where distribution rights are then "exhausted."

To understand the response to this issue before the formation of the EEC, it is necessary to recall the interpretation of territoriality, in which both claims of right and the underlying facts were seen as territorially isolated within national jurisdictions. To the extent that this view prevailed, there was a tendency to view the exhaustion of a right, and the first sale that triggered that exhaustion, as occurring in only one country at a time. Consequently, the relevant market was exclusively national in scope.

Interestingly, the extent by which territoriality limits the first-sale doctrine differs according to the intellectual property right involved. While in patent law the doctrine is universally accepted, in trademark law it is absent in many jurisdictions. The first national sale of a product bearing a trademark is most often regarded as exhausting the trademark-based right to control further international distribution of the product. This effect cannot be attenuated by any contrary contractual clause. Similarly, with respect to copyrights, the prevailing opinion is that the first sale of a copy of a work should exhaust the right to control the further sales of that copy worldwide. This view, however, may not apply when confronted with an express contractual clause designed to circumvent it.

Territorial restrictions to the first-sale doctrine seem to be at odds with the EEC Treaty. For example, territorial restrictions to the first-sale doctrine can be used to compartmentalize national markets. Yet, the EEC Treaty aims to unite twelve long-established national markets into a single Common Market. Specifically, territorial restrictions might directly conflict with Articles 30 through 36 of the Treaty which implement the principle of Community-wide free movement of goods. Inherent in this conflict lies the crux of the problem faced by the Court of Justice in a series of cases involving intellectual property.

It is important to understand the balancing of EEC law and national intellectual property rights. A solution to this conflict may be found in Article 36 of the Treaty, which discusses the principle of the free movement of goods with respect to intellectual property. According to Article 36, the provisions of Articles 30 through 34 shall not preclude prohibitions or restrictions on imports, exports, or goods in transit if they are justified on the grounds of, inter alia, the protection of "industrial and commercial property." As previously illustrated, such property has been deemed to include intellectual property rights, including copyrights. Nonetheless, Article 36 also limits prohibitions or restrictions that might be ostensibly "justified" insofar as they protect requisite property interests. Article 36 states that such restrictions "shall not, however, constitute a means of arbitrary discrimination or a disguised restriction on trade between Member States." Even if a certain restriction passes initial scrutiny because it is justified, its concrete application in a certain case may still amount to forbidden arbitrary discrimination or disguised intercommunity restrictions on trade, which was the situation in the trademark cases of *Terrapin*[26] and *Hoffman-La Roche*.[27]

A provision of Article 36 has forced the Court of Justice to perform a tightrope-walking act between EEC law and intellectual property law. In order to maintain its balance on this tightrope walk, the Court itself has given several pairs of names to the two ends of the pole onto which it has been holding. In its judgment in *Etablissements Consten* in 1966, the Court distinguished between the national "grant" of intellectual property rights, in itself inviolable, and the "exercise" of such rights which could be limited to the extent necessary to effectuate EEC objectives.[28] In the subsequent *Parke, Davis* judgment, the Court spoke in terms of the "existence" of intellectual property rights, which are in principle safeguarded, and of the "exercise" of such rights, which might at times be forced to yield to EEC law.[29] In its fourth, and most crucial, judgment on this problem, the Court in the *Deutsche Grammophon / Metro* decision, began to speak not only of the "existence," but also of the "specific object" or "substance," of an intellectual property right which is reserved under Article 36 of the Treaty. Interestingly, however, the "exercise" of such a right could, in some cases, be precluded under the Treaty.[30]

Another important factor to consider is the Community-wide exhaustion of rights after the first sale in any Member State. The outcome of the Court's evaluation of "the substance" of intellectual property rights, as balanced against EEC objectives, has been identical in cases concerning copyrights, so-called neighboring rights, patents and trademarks. The Court no longer isolates the relevant market to the national territory of the location of the first sale of the copy or product. The location of the first sale might trigger the exhaustion of the right to control further distribution of that copy or product. This haphazard approach yields to the EEC principle of the free movement of goods. The relevant market for finding a first sale sufficient to exhaust such a right is the entire Common Market. Thus, any party marketing a copy or product which has already been first-sold on the Common Market can raise the "Eurodefense" of Community-wide exhaustion against a holder of rights suing in order to control distribution in the EEC. The cases, however, must be examined in order to determine the extent and limits of the circumstances in which this defense has been, and might continue to be, effective.

---

[26]   Case 119/75, Terrapin (Overseas) Ltd. v. Terranova Industrie C.A. Kapferer & Co., 1976 E.C.R. 1039, 2 C.M.L.R. 482 (1976).
[27]   Case 102/77, Hoffman-LaRoche & Co. AG v. Centrafarm, 1978 E.C.R. 1139, 3 C.M.L.R. 217 (1978).
[28]   Etablissements Consten, 1966 E.C.R. 299, 5 C.M.L.R. 418.
[29]   Case 24/67, Parke, Davis & Co. v. Reese, 1968 E.C.R. 55, 7 C.M.L.R. 47 (1968).
[30]   Case 78/70, Deutsche Grammophon, 1971 E.C.R. 487, C.M.L.R. 631 (1971).

B.   The Freedom to Provide Services

Copyrights can be "exercised" so as to restrict the freedom to provide services. This practice was highlighted in the first *Coditel* decision of the Court of Justice.[65] Since the Court held that the exercise of the copyright implemented an "essential function" of the copyright, the Court did not preclude the exercise of the right in this case.

In *Coditel*, Cine Vog Films acquired an exclusive license to show the French film, "Le Boucher," in Belgium as both cinema performances and television broadcasts. Under the license, the right to broadcast the film could not be exercised in Belgium until forty months after the first cinema performance. The French copyright owner also licensed a German television broadcasting station to broadcast the film in Germany. The broadcast in Germany took place and a Belgian cable television operator, Coditel, picked up this broadcast and retransmitted the film to its subscribers.

Acting without any authorization from the holder of rights, Coditel infringed upon the copyright of the film. Coditel relied on Article 59 of the EEC Treaty, which establishes the freedom to provide services across intra-Community borders, to raise a "Eurodefense" to the infringement suit. The intermediate Belgian Cour d'Appel submitted the following question to the Court of Justice: Did Articles 59 and 60 of the Treaty prohibit an assignment of the copyright in a film limited to the territory of a Member State, in view of the fact that a series of such assignments might result in the partitioning of the Common Market in regard to the undertaking of economic activity in the film industry? In response, the Court stated:

> A cinematographic film belongs to the category of literary and artistic works made available to the public by performances which may be infinitely repeated. In this respect the problems involved in the observance of copyright in relation to the requirements of the Treaty are not the same as those which arise in [connection] with literary and artistic works the placing of which at the disposal of the public is inseparable from the circulation of the material form of the works, as in the case of books or records.[68]

The Court emphasized that the copyright owners and their assignees "have a legitimate interest in calculating the fees due in respect of the authorization to exhibit the film on the basis of the actual or probable number of performances and in authorizing a television broadcast of the film only after it has been exhibited in cinemas."[69] According to the Court, "the right of a copyright owner and his assigns to require fees for

---

[65]   Coditel I, 1980 E.C.R. 881, 2 C.M.L.R. 362 (1981).

[68]   Id. [at 902, 2 C.M.L.R. at 399.]

[69]   Id. at 902–03, 2 C.M.L.R. at 399.

any showing of a film is part of the essential function of copyright in this type of literary and artistic work."[70]

Thus, the Community-wide exhaustion of a copyright applies only to parallel imports of material copies of a work, and not to the immaterial performances of a work. This ruling is in conformity with intellectual property law in the case where the first-sale doctrine applies exclusively to the physical embodiments of a work, rather than to its less tangible forms. . . .

IV. Harmonization of National Laws

The purpose of merging twelve[*] national markets into one Common Market, as outlined by the EEC Treaty, cannot be attained completely as long as national intellectual property rights substantially differ in scope and modes of protection. The Treaty, therefore, anticipates the process of harmonizing these laws. According to Article 100 of the EEC Treaty, the Council of Ministers is under a mandate to approximate national laws within the European Communities. Here, the word "approximate" means to bring the legislation of the Member States in line with each other, that is, to reduce discrepancies between the Member States that work against the purposes of the Communities. Directives may be issued to this end, but are not intended to replace national statutes with a uniform European legal text. Rather, regulations may serve that purpose.

A. The Problem in the Case Law

In order to effectuate harmonization, the Court of Justice removed the obstacle of territorially-restricted exhaustions of rights. As explained above, rather than fictitiously-isolated national territories, the Common Market is now the only relevant market in which the first-sale of a material copy of an item exhausts the right to control its further distribution in the EEC. The Court, however, has acquiesced in other areas by following the lines of national markets that result from the exercise of diverse intellectual property rights. In some cases, the prohibition of such an exercise affects the guaranteed "substance" of the intellectual property rights that are being asserted. Moreover, in many cases, the Court of Justice has indicated that some of the remaining problems should be solved by Community harmonization of laws, as indicated in Article 100 of the EEC Treaty. Several Directives that are intended to harmonize national laws are in the process of being issued.

B. Binding Council Directives and Regulations

1. Copyright-Rental Rights, Lending Rights and Neighboring Rights

Adopted on November 19, 1992,[133] the final text of Directive 92/100 is somewhat longer than the Commission's original proposal. The

---

[70]   Id. at 903, 2 C.M.L.R. at 400.

[*]   Presently 15. *Ed.*

[133] Council Directive 92/100 on Rental Right and Lending Right and on Certain Rights Related to Copyright in the Field of Intellectual Property, 1992 O.J. (L 346) 61.

Directive provides more detail on the assignment of rights and it addresses the issue of identifying authors of works, namely films. The Directive does not, however, include the Commission's proposal on moral rights. Nor does the Directive cover the availability of records or films for the purpose of public performance, which normally requires a copyright license. Rather, the Directive is aimed essentially at commercial rentals for private-use public lending. The Directive will, inter alia, ensure that portions of the money made by video rental shops will be paid to the author of the work.

Acknowledging the fact that the copying of rented works occurs, the Directive specifically states that it is without prejudice to any future legislation on remuneration for reproduction for private use. The door remains open for a future Commission proposal in this field, and the discussion of the merits of a blank tape levy will continue.

Under the Directive, authors, performing artists, and record and film producers will have the exclusive right to authorize or prohibit the rental and lending of originals and copies of their copyrighted works. Further, authors and performing artists will have an unwaivable right to equitable remuneration for rentals. The use of collecting societies, however, is left to individual Member State regulation.

For audio-visual works, the principal director is deemed to be the author; however, individual Member States may provide that others be considered as co-authors. In other respects the Directive does not define "author" but relies upon existing national legislation.

Rightholders may transfer or assign their exclusive rental and lending rights. In a contract concerning film production concluded by performers with a film producer, the performers will be presumed to have transferred their rental right, but not their right to remuneration, subject to any contrary contractual clauses. Member States may make similar presumptions in film production contracts with respect to authors. Moreover, Member States also retain the option to provide in contracts with performers a presumption that the performer authorizes the rental and the performance of the other exclusive rights set out in the Directive. These other rights include the fixation of performances or broadcasts, the reproduction, the broadcast and communication to the public, and the distribution . . . right.

Under the Directive, Member States may derogate from the exclusive lending right for public lending purposes, that is, lending by an establishment accessible to the public which gives rise to a payment which only covers the operating costs of the establishment. In such situations, remuneration for authors must be introduced. Certain categories of establishments may be exempted totally from the payment of remuneration. The Commission intends to report to the Council and European Parliament on public lending in the Community before July 1, 1997. Ultimately, the rights related to copyrights that are covered by the

Directive may be limited by the Member States for private and teaching use, and in particular, for the reporting of current events.

2.   Trademarks

    a.   Prohibition on the Release of Counterfeit Goods

Regulations which implemented measures to prohibit the release for the free circulation of counterfeit goods were promulgated on December 1, 1986.[142] Among other things, the Regulations allow for action by the customs authorities. These actions consist of suspending the release of goods suspected of being counterfeit for as long as is necessary to determine whether the goods were actually counterfeited.

    b.   Directive to Approximate the Laws of the Member States Relating to Trademarks

Promulgated on December 21, 1988,[143] the sole purpose of Directive 89/104 is to gather and to organize the laws of Member States which most directly affect the functioning of the internal market. The preamble reaffirms the domain in which the Member States maintain their full freedom. The Directive, therefore, only concerns trademarks which are acquired by registration. The Member States retain their rights to protect trademarks acquired through use in their nation. Additionally, the Member States remain free to change the procedures regarding the registration, the revocation and invalidity of the trademark. The application of other provisions of law, such as the provisions relating to unfair competition, civil liability or consumer protection, are not excluded from this Directive. Based on this information, therefore, the Directive clearly serves only a limited purpose with respect to trademarks.

The conditions for obtaining and continuing to hold a registered trademark must be identical in all Member States. The Directive, therefore, lists examples of symbols which may constitute a trademark. The Directive also lists the grounds for refusing or invalidating the trademarks including, for example, the absence of any distinctive character or the existence of earlier rights. This is done with the understanding that Member States will be able to maintain the grounds for refusing or invalidating trademarks for which there is no specific provision in the Directive, namely the renewal of the trademark, rules on fees and procedural rules. The Directive states, in part, that "in order to reduce the total number of trademarks registered and protected in the Community and, consequently, the number of conflicts which arise between them, it is essential to require that registered trademarks must actually be used or, if not used, be subject to revocation. . . ."

In order to facilitate the free movement of goods, trademarks must enjoy the same protection under the legal systems of all Member States.

---

[142] Commission Regulation 3842/86 on Laying Down Measures to Prohibit the Release for Free Circulation of Counterfeit Goods, 1986 O.J. (L 357) 1.

[143] Council Directive 89/104 to Approximate the Laws of the Member States Relating to Trademarks, 1989 O.J. (L 40) 1.

However, the Directive provides that Member States should not be curtailed in providing protection to trademarks with wide reputations. The protection that is afforded to the registered trademark must be "absolute in the case of identity between the mark and the sign and goods or services; . . . the protection applies also in case of similarity between the mark and the sign and the goods or services. . . ." The concept of similarity of trademarks, therefore, must be interpreted in relation to the likelihood of confusion.

The Directive also governs the situation where a trademark holder permits possible infringing behavior and then later attempts to have this infringement declared unlawful. The Directive states, in part, that, for reasons of legal certainty . . . a proprietor of an earlier trade mark . . . may no longer request a declaration of invalidity nor may he oppose the use of a trade mark subsequent to his own of which he has knowingly tolerated the use for a substantial length of time, unless the application for the subsequent trade mark was made in bad faith. . . .[153]

NOTES

1. *Intellectual Property in the European Union.* As indicated in the Corbet excerpt, national intellectual property laws of EU member countries regularly come into conflict with supranational rules on free movement of goods and on fair competition. For example, national intellectual property rules intersect EU interests in the free movement of goods to the extent that they enable copyright, patent and trademark owners to partition markets. The conflict in these cases frequently centers on Article 34 of the Treaty on the Functioning of the European Union (formerly Article 28 of the EC Treaty), prohibiting "[q]uantitative restrictions on imports and all measures having equivalent effect," and Article 36 (formerly Article 30), excepting from this prohibition those restrictions justified on grounds of "the protection of industrial and commercial property." *See* Stefan Enchelmaier, The Inexhaustible Question-Free Movement of Goods and Intellectual Property in the European Court of Justice's Case Law, 2002–2006, 38 IIC 453 (2007).

National intellectual property rules will also sometimes conflict with EU intellectual property policy, specifically the European Union's program to "approximate"—harmonize—the intellectual property laws of member countries through directives and regulations. The premise behind harmonization is that investment and trade patterns will be more fluent in the single market if such important aspects of intellectual property protection as protectable subject matter, scope of rights and terms of protection are substantially similar, if not identical, from country-to-country.

In 2004, after intense debate, the EC adopted the Directive on the Enforcement of Intellectual Property Rights, 2004/48/EC, effectively a set of TRIPs-plus measures harmonizing remedies for all forms of intellectual property infringement. The Directive borrows procedures from national legal systems and extends them across the European Union—for example, British

---

[153] Id.

and French practice on ex parte seizure of evidence; German and Dutch procedures enabling a right holder to demand information on the origin and distribution of infringing goods; and Belgian practice on the removal of infringing goods from commercial distribution. The Directive encompasses only civil remedies, not criminal sanctions, and confines some remedies, such as the right of access to financial documents, to commercial-scale infringements.

See generally, Bryan Harris, Intellectual Property Law in the European Union (2006).

2.   *Regional Intellectual Property Arrangements.* Countries in several regions have harmonized aspects of their intellectual property laws, and some regional blocs have also centralized the administration of patent and trademark grants. The European Patent Convention, which entered into force in 1977, established the European Patent Office, headquartered in Munich, which processes and grants European patents effective for any one or more member countries designated by the patent applicant. *See* page 490, below. Following the collapse of the Soviet Union and the dissolution of the Soviet patent system, the 1994 Eurasian Patent Convention created the Eurasian Patent Organization and the Eurasian Patent Office, to examine patent applications and grant patent for the entire region.

The Benelux countries (Belgium, the Netherlands and Luxembourg) have adopted the Benelux Convention on Trademarks (effective 1969) and the Benelux Convention on Designs (effective 1974) as well as uniform trademark and design laws (effective 1971 and 1975, respectively). A Benelux Trademark Office and a Benelux Designs Office, headquartered in The Hague, have taken on the registration and deposit functions of the national offices.

In Latin America, the 1969 Andean Pact (also called the Cartagena Agreement) empowered the Commission of the Andean Group countries (Bolivia, Columbia, Ecuador, Peru, Venezuela) to make "decisions" regulating intellectual property within the region. Its Decision 1994 extensively harmonized the Andean Group countries' industrial property laws—patents, utility models, industrial designs, trade secrets, trademarks and geographical indications—and Decision 351 significantly harmonized rules on copyright and neighboring rights. The 1968 Central American Agreement for the Protection of Industrial Property establishes uniform rules on trademarks, geographical indications and unfair competition for member countries, Costa Rica, Guatemala, El Salvador and Nicaragua.

In Africa, two organizations promote intergovernmental cooperation on intellectual property matters. The African Regional Industrial Property Organization (ARIPO), with headquarters in Harare, Zimbabwe, was established by the 1978 Agreement on the Creation of an Industrial Property Organization for English—Speaking Africa. ARIPO's objectives include development and harmonization of intellectual property laws among its members. Under a protocol that entered into force in 1984, ARIPO processes applications for patents and industrial designs; the patents it grants and the designs it registers generally enjoy the same effect as patents and designs granted under the national laws of member countries. The African Intellectual Property Organization (OAPI) provides even more extensive coordination of intellectual property relations among its twelve constituent French-speaking African countries, administering not only patents and industrial designs, but also trademarks, copyrights, utility models, geographical indications and unfair competition. Industrial property grants made at OAPI's headquarters in Yaoundé, Cameroon, are effective in all member states.

See generally, WIPO, Introduction to Intellectual Property: Theory and Practice 505–514 (1997).

3. *Regional Trade Arrangements.* As indicated in Professor Yu's article, *TRIPs and Its Achilles' Heel*, more economically developed countries have pressed for higher intellectual property standards through regional agreements that, by design, need not accommodate the demands of less developed economies.

NAFTA. The intellectual property provisions of The North American Free Trade Agreement (NAFTA), which entered into force between Canada, Mexico and the United States on January 1, 1994, borrowed concepts and language from the TRIPs Agreement. (The NAFTA negotiations began well after the start of the TRIPs discussions, but were completed one year before the TRIPs Agreement.) Chapter 17 of NAFTA encompassed, among other objects, protection of copyrights, sound recordings, encrypted program-carrying satellite signals, trademarks, patents, integrated circuit designs, trade secrets, geographical indications and industrial designs. Provision was also made for effective enforcement measures.

A trade agreement called the United States-Mexico-Canada Agreement in the United States—and called the Canada-United States-Mexico Agreement in Canada and the Tratado entre Mexico, Estados Unidos y Canada in Mexico—and informally called NAFTA 2.0, was signed in November 2018. Most of the intellectual property changes required by the agreement fall on Mexico (including removal of certain exceptions from the patent grace period; addition of patent term adjustment provisions; imposition of Internet safe harbors from copyright liability) and on Canada (including patent term adjustment and extension of copyright term to the author's life plus 70 years).

3. BILATERAL ARRANGEMENTS (AND UNILATERAL INITIATIVES)

Memorandum of Understanding Between the People's Republic of China and the United States on the Protection of Intellectual Property

Done at Washington, January 17, 1992.
34 International Legal Materials 676 (1995).

In the spirit of cooperation embodied in their bilateral Agreement on Trade Relations and consistent with the principles of the relevant international agreements, the Government of the People's Republic of China (Chinese Government) and the Government of the United States of America (U.S. Government) have reached a mutual understanding on the following provisions:

Article 1

1. The Chinese Government will provide the following levels of protection under the Patent Law of the People's Republic of China:

(a) Patentable Subject Matter

Patents shall be available for all chemical inventions, including pharmaceuticals and agricultural chemicals, whether products or processes.

(b) Rights Conferred

A patent shall confer the right to prevent others not having the patent owner's consent from making, using, or selling the subject matter of the patent. In the case of a patented process, the patent shall confer the right to prevent others not having the patent owner's consent from using that process and from using, selling, or importing the product obtained directly by that process.

(c) Term of Protection

The term of protection for a patent of invention will be 20 years from the date of filing of the patent application.

(d) Compulsory Licenses

(i) Patent rights shall be enjoyable without discrimination as to the place of invention, the field of technology and whether products are imported or locally produced.

(ii) Where China's law allows for use of the subject matter of a patent without the authorization of the right holder, including use by the government or third parties authorized by the government, the following provisions shall be respected:

(1) authorization of such use shall be considered on its individual merits;

(2) such use may only be permitted if, prior to such use, the proposed user has made efforts to obtain authorization from the right holder on reasonable commercial terms and conditions and that such efforts have not been successful within a reasonable period of time. This requirement may be waived by the government in the case of a national emergency or other circumstances of extreme urgency or in cases of public non-commercial use. In situations of national emergency or other circumstances of extreme urgency, the right holder shall, nevertheless, be notified as soon as reasonably practicable. In the case of public non-commercial use, where the government or contractor, without making a patent search, knows or has demonstrable grounds to know that a valid patent is or will be used by or for the government, the right holder shall be informed promptly;

(3) the scope and duration of such use shall be limited to the purpose for which it was authorized;

(4) such use shall be non-exclusive;

(5) such use shall be non-assignable, except with that part of the enterprise or goodwill which enjoys such use;

(6) any such use shall be authorized predominantly for the supply of China's domestic market;

(7) authorization for such use shall be liable, subject to adequate protection of the legitimate interests of the persons so authorized, to be terminated if and when the circumstances which led to it cease to exist and are unlikely to recur. The competent authority shall have the authority to review, upon motivated request, the continued existence of these circumstances;

(8) the right holder shall be paid adequate remuneration in the circumstances of each case, taking into account the economic value of the authorization;

(9) the legal validity of any decision relating to the authorization of such use shall be subject to judicial review or other independent review by a distinct higher authority;

(10) any decision relating to the remuneration provided in respect of such use shall be subject to judicial review or other independent review by a distinct higher authority;

(11) the conditions set forth in sub-paragraphs (2) and (6) above are not required to be applied where such use is permitted to remedy a practice determined after judicial or administrative process to be anti-competitive. The need to correct anti-competitive practices may be taken into account in determining the amount of remuneration in such cases. Competent authorities shall have the authority to refuse termination of authorization if and when the conditions which led to such authorization are likely to recur;

(12) where such use is authorized to permit the exploitation of a patent ("the second patent") which cannot be exploited without infringing another patent ("the first patent"), the following additional conditions shall apply:

(A) the invention claimed in the second patent shall involve an important technical advance of considerable economic significance in relation to the invention claimed in the first patent;

(B) the owner of the first patent shall be entitled to a cross-license on reasonable terms to use the invention claimed in the second patent; and

(C) the use authorized in respect of the first patent shall be non-assignable except with the assignment of the second patent.

2.   The Chinese Government will submit a bill to provide the levels of protection specified in subparagraph 1 of this Article to its legislative body and will exert its best efforts to have enacted and to implement the amended patent law by January 1, 1993.

3.   Both Governments reaffirm their commitments to each other under the Paris Convention for the Protection of Industrial Property (Stockholm 1967) and their continued commitment to observe the principle of national treatment with respect to providing patent protection for the natural and legal persons of the other Party.

4.   If the U.S. Government becomes a party to an international convention that requires the United States to provide a patent term of at least 20 years from the date of filing of the patent application, the United States will amend its laws to satisfy this obligation.

Article 2

Both Governments reaffirm that the principle of territoriality and independence of patents with regard to protection of patents as provided in the Paris Convention for the Protection of Industrial Property should be respected.

The Chinese Government agrees to provide administrative protection to U.S. pharmaceutical and agricultural chemical product inventions which:

(i)   were not subject to protection by exclusive rights prior to the amendment of current Chinese laws;

(ii)   are subject to an exclusive right to prohibit others from making, using or selling it in the United States which were granted after January 1, 1986 and before January 1, 1993;

(iii) have not been marketed in China.

The owner of the exclusive right in the United States regarding such a product invention that meets the above requirements shall provide the competent Chinese authorities with an application for administrative protection including the following documents:

(1) a copy of the certificate issued by the competent authorities of the United States granting such exclusive right;

(2) a copy of the document issued by the competent authorities of the United States for the approval for manufacturing or sale of such product; and

(3) a copy of a contract for the manufacture and/or sale entered into between the owner of the exclusive right and a Chinese legal person (including foreign capital enterprises, joint venture enterprises, or cooperative enterprises) with respect to the manufacture and/or sale of the product in China.

The competent Chinese authorities will, in accordance with published Chinese laws and regulations relating to obtaining manufacturing or marketing approval, examine such application. No special rules or additional requirements for approval will be imposed. After examination and approval, which shall occur promptly, a certificate for administrative protection, which will provide the right to manufacture or sell the subject product, will be issued to the person seeking such protection. The competent Chinese authorities will prohibit persons who have not obtained a certificate for administrative protection from manufacturing or selling the subject product during the term of administrative protection. The term of administrative protection begins from the date on which the certificate for administrative protection of the product is obtained and remains in force for seven years and six months. The above administrative protection will become available on January 1, 1993.

Article 3

1.   The Chinese Government will accede to the Berne Convention for the Protection of Literary and Artistic Works (Berne Convention) (Paris 1971). The Chinese Government will submit a bill authorizing accession to the Berne Convention to its legislative body by April 1, 1992 and will use its best efforts to have the bill enacted by June 30, 1992. Upon enactment of the authorizing bill, the Chinese Government's instrument of accession to the Berne Convention will be submitted to the World Intellectual Property Organization with accession to be effective by October 15, 1992.

2.   The Chinese Government will accede to the Convention for the Protection of Producers of Phonograms Against Unauthorized Duplication of Their Phonograms (Geneva Convention) and submit a bill to its legislative body authorizing accession by June 30, 1992. The Chinese Government will use its best efforts to have the bill enacted by February 1, 1993. The Chinese Government will deposit its instrument of ratification and the Convention will come into effect by June 1, 1993.

3.   Upon China's accession to the Berne Convention and the Geneva Convention, these Conventions will be international treaties within the meaning of Article 142 of the General Principles of the Civil

Code of the People's Republic of China. In accordance with the provisions of that Article, where there is an inconsistency between the provisions of the Berne Convention and the Geneva Convention on the one hand, and Chinese domestic law and regulations on the other hand, the international Conventions will prevail subject to the provisions to which China has declared a reservation, which is permitted by those Conventions.

4.   In so far as China's copyright law and its implementing regulations are inconsistent with the Berne Convention, the Geneva Convention or this Memorandum of Understanding (MOU), the Chinese Government will issue new regulations to comply with these Conventions and the MOU by October 1, 1992. These new regulations will also clarify the existing regulations and in particular will explain that the exclusive right of distribution that applies to all works and sound recordings includes making copies available by rental and that this exclusive right survives the first sale of copies. Regulations implementing the Conventions and this MOU will prevail over regulations for domestic works where there is an inconsistency between the new regulations and existing regulations.

In addition to applying to works created by nationals of Berne Union members, these new regulations will apply to all works created in the context of a contractual relationship, joint venture, or commission from foreign capital enterprises, foreign joint venture enterprises, or cooperative enterprises in which such nationals, individually or jointly with others, are intended to be owners of copyright in the resulting works.

The Chinese Government will submit a bill to amend its copyright law to its legislative body and use its best efforts to have enacted and to implement this legislation within a reasonable period of time.

5.   Both Governments will indicate the status of the Berne Convention and the Geneva Convention in their respective laws and notify judicial and administrative bodies responsible for the enforcement of the copyright law and regulations of the provisions of the Conventions within 30 days after signature of this MOU or 30 days after accession to each Convention, which ever is later.

Both Governments will publish and provide to each other copies of any guidance provided to administrative or judicial bodies regarding the administration or interpretation of any laws and regulations related to the implementation of the Conventions or this MOU no later than 30 days after such guidance is issued.

6.   No later than the effective date of China's accession to the Berne Convention, the Chinese Government agrees to recognize and protect computer programs as literary works under the Berne Convention, and consistent with the protection provided under that Convention shall

impose no formalities on the protection of computer programs and provide a term of 50 years.

7.   After China's accession to the Berne Convention, all works originating in a member of the Berne Union that are not in the public domain in their country of origin will be protected in China.

(i)   With regard to any uses of an original or a copy of a U.S. work on a commercial scale undertaken before establishment of bilateral copyright relations between China and the United States, there will be no liability.

(ii) With regard to such uses undertaken after establishment of bilateral copyright relations, the provisions of the law and regulations will fully apply. With regards to a natural or legal person who owned and used a particular copy of a work for a particular purpose prior to establishment of bilateral copyright relations between China and the United States, that person may continue to make such use of that copy of the work without liability, provided that such copy is neither reproduced nor used in any manner that unreasonably prejudices the legitimate interests of the copyright owner of that work.

8.   The principles of paragraph 7 above, including the limitations on liability, shall apply to sound recordings.

9.   The Chinese Government will recognize this MOU as an agreement under Article 2 of the Copyright Law of the People's Republic of China which shall provide a basis for protection of works, including computer programs, and sound recordings of U.S. nationals published outside of China until such time as China accedes to the Berne Convention and the Geneva Convention. Such protection shall become effective 60 days after signature of this MOU.

Based on the commitments set forth in this MOU, the U.S. Government will take the necessary steps to secure to Chinese nationals and their works eligibility for protection under the copyright law of the United States which shall become effective no later than 60 days after signature of this MOU.

Article 4

1.   For the purpose of ensuring effective protection against unfair competition as provided for in Article 10bis of the Paris Convention for the Protection of Industrial Property, the Chinese Government will prevent trade secrets from being disclosed to, acquired by, or used by others without the consent of the trade secret owner in a manner contrary to honest commercial practices including the acquisition, use or disclosure of trade secrets by third parties who knew, or had reasonable grounds to know, that such practices were involved in their acquisition of such information.

2.   The term of protection for trade secrets shall continue so long as the conditions for protection are met.

3. The competent authorities of the Chinese Government will submit the bill necessary to provide the levels of protection specified in this Article to its legislative body by July 1, 1993 and will exert its best efforts to enact and implement this bill before January 1, 1994.

Article 5

Both Governments will provide effective procedures and remedies to prevent or stop, internally and at their borders, infringement of intellectual property rights and to deter further infringement. In applying these procedures and remedies, both Governments will provide safeguards against abuse and shall avoid creating obstacles to legitimate trade.

Article 6

Both Governments agree, at the request of either Party, to consult promptly on matters relating to the protection and enforcement of intellectual property rights, in particular with respect to the obligations of this MOU. Both Governments agree that the first consultations pursuant to this MOU will include discussions on the new implementing regulations for the Berne Convention and this MOU and that these discussions will be taken into consideration in the drafting of the regulations.

Article 7

In recognition of the progress in improving the protection of intellectual property rights that the Chinese Government has made and of the further progress that will result from the steps that the Chinese Government has agreed to take, and in the expectation that these commitments will be fully implemented, the U.S. Government will terminate the investigation initiated pursuant to the "special 301" provisions of U.S. trade law and China's designation as a priority foreign country will be revoked effective on the date of signature of this MOU.

Signed in Washington, D.C., this seventeenth day of January, one thousand nine hundred and ninety-two, in two copies in the Chinese and English languages, both texts being equally authentic.

China-United States: Agreement Regarding Intellectual Property Rights

February 26, 1995.
34 International Legal Materials 881 (1995).

February 26, 1995

United States

U.S. Trade Representative

Ambassador Michael Kantor

Dear Ambassador Kantor:

I have the honor to refer to the consultations between representatives of the Government of the People's Republic of China (China) and the Government of the United States of America (United States) which were conducted in the spirit of the 1992 Memorandum of Understanding between our governments concerning the protection of intellectual property rights. Both of our governments are committed to providing adequate and effective protection and enforcement of intellectual property rights and have agreed to provide this to each other's nationals.

China's actions in this respect show considerable progress and determination to achieve effective enforcement of intellectual property rights through judicial and administrative procedures. China has created specialized intellectual property courts to hear these cases and I can confirm that the Civil and Criminal Procedure Laws of the People's Republic of China empower the courts to address infringement of intellectual property rights through measures to stop infringement, preserve property before and during litigation, and to order the infringer to provide compensation to right owners for infringement of their intellectual property rights. In addition, the courts also act to preserve evidence to permit effective litigation.

China's Supreme People's Court has issued a circular instructing courts at various levels to address intellectual property cases expeditiously, including cases involving foreign right holders. In respect of taking criminal action against infringers, our procuratorates are actively pursuing criminal infringement cases.

I have attached to this letter a State Council Intellectual Property Enforcement Action Plan of the State Council's Intellectual Property Working Conference (Annex) that will be carried out immediately. This Action Plan strengthens the enforcement efforts that China has already taken and establishes a long term enforcement structure so that the people's governments in the provinces, directly administered municipalities, autonomous regions and cities meet the requirements of that Plan and China will actively implement it. Under Chinese law, each administrative authority mentioned in the Action Plan is fully empowered to take the specified steps to effectively enforce intellectual property rights.

Chinese authorities have recently taken effective actions to enforce intellectual property rights. Recently seven plants producing infringing products have been closed, or their business licenses revoked, and more than two million infringing CDs, LDs and copies of computer software have been seized and destroyed. Under the Chinese government's action plan, this effort will intensify and by July 1, 1995, investigation of all production lines suspected of producing infringing CDs, LDs and CD-ROMs will be completed. Factories that have engaged in infringing activities will be punished through seizure and forfeiture of infringing products and all infringing copies will be destroyed and the materials and implements directly and predominantly used to make the infringing product will be seized, forfeited and destroyed. Business licenses and permits will also continue to be revoked in appropriate cases.

Exports of infringing products have been banned. The establishment of a copyright verification system and the use of unique identifiers on CDs, CD-ROMs and LDs will provide a vital tool to prevent the production of infringing goods and export of those goods. Permits to engage in activities related to audio-visual products will not be issued without copyright verification and imprint of the unique identifier. More than one violation of this condition will result in revocation of the permit and repeat serious offenders will have their business licenses revoked.

Retail establishments will be inspected under the Action Plan and enterprises will keep records of inventories and other information to strengthen enforcement. Recent raids on computer software enterprises are an example of China's effective enforcement of intellectual property rights.

Another aspect of China's decision to develop its economy and open its markets further is increased cooperation and trade in products protected by intellectual property rights.

China has recently approved the establishment of a representative office for the International Federation of Phonogram Industries (IFPI) and will examine and approve, when published requirements are met, the pending application of the relevant entity for the verification of motion picture copyright, as well as other entities involved in copyright verification. Obtaining this approval does not prejudice the ability of these offices to engage in other activities in accord with Chinese laws and regulations.

China confirms that it will not impose quotas, import license requirements, or other restrictions on the importation of audio-visual and published products, whether formal or informal. China will permit U.S. individuals and entities to establish joint ventures with Chinese entities in China in the audio-visual sector for production and reproduction. These joint ventures will be permitted to enter into contracts with

Chinese publishing enterprises to, on a nationwide basis, distribute, sell, display and perform in China. China will immediately permit such joint ventures to be established in Shanghai, Guangzhou, and moreover, other major cities, and will then expand the number of cities, in an orderly fashion, to thirteen (13) by the year 2000. U.S. individuals and entities will be permitted to enter into exclusive licensing arrangements with Chinese publishing houses to exploit the entire catalogue of the licensor and to decide what to release from that catalogue. China will also permit U.S. individuals and entities to establish computer software joint ventures and those joint ventures will be permitted to produce and sell their computer software and computer software products in China.

China will continue to permit U.S. individuals and entities to enter film products into revenue sharing arrangements with Chinese entities. Permissible arrangements will include, for example, licensing agreements under which the U.S. entity receives a negotiated percentage of revenues.

China will adopt or enforce measures necessary to protect public morals or to maintain public order, as long as such measures are applied consistently and in a non-discriminatory, non-arbitrary manner and do not operate as a disguised restriction on trade. By October 1, 1995, China will publish all laws, rules, regulations, administrative guidance, or other official documents concerning any limitation on, regulation, or permission required to engage in all activities identified above.

The audio-visual departments under the State Council will intensify their efforts to formulate the regulatory rules on audio-visual products which will clarify the specific censorship regulations for publication and importation of audio-visual products. For audio-visual products that meet the provisions of the censorship requirements, their publication and import will be approved without any restrictions in terms of quantity. The censorship regulations will be open, transparent and published. Determinations as to censorship requirements will normally be made within ten days, but in no event longer than sixty days from receipt of an application.

In light of China's policies of market opening, representatives of U.S. enterprises are invited to begin discussions on their establishment in China, including possible licensing arrangements, as soon as possible.

It is my understanding that the United States will provide assistance to China with respect to the protection and enforcement of intellectual property rights. This work will be implemented mainly through the U.S. Customs Service, U.S. Department of Justice and the United States Patent and Trademark Office.

The U.S. Customs Service is prepared to provide cooperative and reciprocal assistance to China on providing improved enforcement of intellectual property rights. This assistance and coordination effort could include: (1) providing training, in China, by U.S. customs personnel, of

Chinese customs officers with responsibility for enforcing intellectual property rights, (2) providing mutually agreed relevant technical equipment to assist in the enforcement of intellectual property rights, and (3) training will likely include: how to identify infringing merchandise through physical examination, verification of documents, and laboratory testing, and assistance in building a centralized system of intellectual property rights recordations.

The U.S. Patent and Trademark Office will also assist in training Chinese personnel, including through providing training and documents for the people who work on verification of well-known marks and mechanisms for establishing an administrative appeals process.

China and the United States will exchange information and statistics on a quarterly basis beginning on June 1, 1995, on intellectual property enforcement activities in their two countries. Beginning on January 1, 1996, this exchange will be carried out on a semi-annual basis for the next two years, and on a schedule to be agreed thereafter.

Under these exchanges, China will provide information and statistics concerning enforcement, throughout the country, of intellectual property rights of U.S. nationals and joint ventures with U.S. nationals, by type of intellectual property, establishments raided, and the value and disposition of infringing products and machinery and implements. Information and statistics on prosecutions and administrative and court decisions will also be provided.

Under these exchanges, the United States will provide to China, on the same schedule, information and statistics concerning the customs seizure value of infringing goods by commodity, the seizure value of infringing goods by type of intellectual property right, the seizure value of Chinese infringing goods by commodity, and the seizure quantities of infringing goods by commodity. The United States will also provide information and statistics on federal intellectual property enforcement activities, including information on prosecutions for copyright infringement and trademark counterfeiting and court decisions in intellectual property cases. The United States will also provide information and statistics on Chinese products that are infringed in the United States.

China and the United States will, upon request, consult and exchange information on the license verification system set out in the Action Plan and particular applications of that system. China and the United States require that public entities in both countries shall not use unauthorized copies of computer software in their computer systems and legitimate software will be used. They likewise require that adequate resources shall be provided to permit the acquisition only of authorized computer software.

In addition, China and the United States will consult promptly at the request of either government with respect to any matter affecting the operation or the implementation of the provision of this letter, including its annex. In addition, both governments agree to consult, during the first year on a quarterly basis, semi-annually for the following two years and then on a schedule to be agreed, on the implementation of the Action Plan and its effectiveness.

On the basis of the foregoing, the United States will immediately revoke China's designation as a "special 301" priority foreign country and will terminate the section 301 investigation of China's enforcement of intellectual property rights and market access for persons who rely on intellectual property protection and rescind the order issued by the U.S. Trade Representative on February 4, 1995, imposing increased tariffs on Chinese exports.

Please confirm that this letter, including its annex, and your letter in reply constitute an Understanding between our two Governments.

With assurances of my highest consideration,

Wu Yi, Minister of Ministry of Foreign Trade and Economic Cooperation.

NOTES

1.   *China: The Second Track.* China joined the World Trade Organization in 2001 and, starting in 2006, the U.S. Trade Representative added to the earlier bilateral efforts a second track—the possibility of engaging the WTO dispute settlement mechanism to resolve U.S. intellectual property disputes with China. On April 10, 2007 the USTR filed requests with the WTO for consultation on Chinese intellectual property practices, the first step in the WTO's dispute settlement process. One request targeted China's high quantitative threshold—requiring "relatively large" and allegedly "huge" numbers of offending copies—as a condition to criminal prosecution of trademark counterfeiting and copyright piracy; the request also complained of the suspension of infringement proceedings while copyrighted works were being subjected to censorship review. Another request challenged the discriminatory treatment of foreign distributors of movies, DVDs, music and printed publications. On August 13, 2007, following months of unsuccessful consultations, the USTR asked the WTO to appoint a dispute resolution panel to consider its claim, and in late September, 2007 the WTO's dispute settlement body established a panel for this purpose.

In January 2009, the WTO panel made public its decision in favor of China on the first claim. In ruling that the United States had failed to show that China's thresholds for prosecuting infringement cases violated TRIPs Article 61's requirement that members prosecute counterfeiting and piracy "on a commercial scale," the panel observed that "commercial scale" is a relative, contextual standard and that the evidence offered by the United States failed to "provide data regarding products and markets or other factors, that would demonstrate what constituted a 'commercial scale' in the specific situation of the Chinese marketplace." Not only was the evidence "too little and too random"; the documents were "printed in US or other foreign English-language media that are not claimed to be authoritative sources of information on prices and markets in China." Report of the Panel, China—Measures Affecting the Protection and Enforcement of Intellectual Property Rights WT/DS362IR ¶¶ 7.545, 7.614, 7.617, 7.628 (26 January 2009).

On the second claim, the panel ruled in favor of the United States that Article 4 of China's Copyright Law, providing that "[w]orks the publication and/or dissemination of which are prohibited by law shall not by protected by this Law," violated TRIPs Articles 9.1 and 41. "Part III of the TRIPs Agreement includes a multilaterally-agreed minimum set of enforcement procedures that Members must make available to right holders against any infringement of intellectual property rights covered by the TRIPs Agreement. Where a member chooses to make available other procedures—for enforcement of intellectual property rights or for enforcement of other policies with respect to certain subject matter—that policy choice does not diminish the Member's obligation under Article 41.1 of the TRIPs Agreement to ensure that enforcement procedures as specified in Part III are available." Panel Report, ¶ 7.180.

Neither side appealed the Panel decision. *See* Weijun Zhang & Yanbing Li, Content Review and Copyright Protection in China After the 2009 *U.S. v. China* WTO Panel Ruling, 62 J. Copyr. Soc'y of U.S.A. 437 (2015).

2. *China: A Closing Circle?* China's first, halting steps toward international intellectual property relations took the form of bilateral commercial agreements with Great Britain, Japan and the United States in 1902 and 1903. The treaties centered on trademarks—the 1903 treaty with the United States also covered patents—but in only the sketchiest terms, reflecting China's lack of a national trademark law. Intellectual property law in China evolved slowly, sporadically and with a clear bias against foreigners. According to Professor William Alford, "although the Chinese had committed themselves in 1903 to provide patent protection for certain American inventions, more than two decades passed before foreigners received even the nominal protection first accorded Chinese nationals in 1912, which itself produced fewer than 1,000 patents over its first thirty years." William Alford, To Steal a Book Is an Elegant Offense 41–42 (1995).

What does the long history of U.S. efforts to secure intellectual property enforcement in China reveal about the relative capacity of legal rules and threats of legal sanctions to effect legal change? While provisions of the China-U.S. Memorandum of Understanding paralleled provisions of the roughly contemporaneous TRIPs Agreement, the lengthy Enforcement Action Plan annexed to the 1995 Agreement imposed more detailed procedural obligations than could be provided in a multilateral agreement such as TRIPs.

Some observers anticipated that, within the first two decades of the twenty-first century, China's domestic intellectual property industries would have matured to the point at which the country's economic self-interest would for the first time dictate strong enforcement measures against piracy of intellectual goods. To what extent can external pressures to enforce domestic intellectual property rights be expected to foster such economic development?

3. *TRIPs-Plus.* Bilateral trade agreements have provided a vehicle for establishing intellectual property obligations between nations at least since the tariff treaties of mid-nineteenth century Europe. These arrangements have enjoyed a bustling revival since adoption of the TRIPs Agreement, and it is not only mature industrialized powers that have used bilateral trade negotiations to persuade developing economies to adopt higher standards of intellectual property protection and enforcement than required by TRIPs. Singapore, South Korea and Taiwan, among other emerging industrial powers, have initiated free-trade agreements with developing countries in Latin America, Europe, Africa and Asia.

The United States has been particularly active in pursuing free trade agreements with less developed countries. Although bilateralism offers the opportunity, not present in the case of multilateral arrangements like TRIPs, to tailor norms to a trading partner's particular economic conditions, American free trade agreements generally hew to a standard pattern. Among the topics covered are expanded patent protection for pharmaceuticals, including patentability of life forms and patent term extensions to compensate for time spent obtaining drug approval; limitations on parallel imports for the gray market; and protection of program-carrying satellite signals.

See generally Assafa Endeshaw, Free Trade Agreements as Surrogates for TRIPS-Plus, 28 EIPR 374 (2006).

4. *ACTA.* In October 2007 several countries, principally from industrialized economies, launched negotiations that, after three years and eleven rounds of discussions, produced the final text of the Anti-Counterfeiting Trade Agreement. Although ACTA ostensibly aimed at combating the significant health perils presented by global drug and food counterfeiting, the agreement in fact mainly represents an attempt by these countries to entrench their intellectual property enforcement standards as norms to be adopted by less advanced economies in the context of bilateral negotiations. ACTA builds on the minimum enforcement standards established by TRIPs Articles 41–61, with more specific and rigorous provisions on such matters as border enforcement, litigation discovery and provisional and monetary remedies. According to one study of the instrument's origins, ACTA "was born out of the frustration of the major industrialized economies with progress on monitoring and norm-setting on the enforcement of intellectual property rights in multilateral fora. In the WTO Council for TRIPs ('TRIPs Council'), Brazil, India and China have consistently blocked the inclusion of enforcement as a permanent agenda item. At the World Intellectual Property Organisation (WIPO), enforcement issues were relegated to a purely advisory committee." European Union, Directorate-General for External Policies, Policy Dept. The Anti-Counterfeiting Trade Agreement (ACTA): an Assessment 8 (2011).

Complaints about exclusivity and lack of transparency dogged the ACTA negotiation process almost from the beginning. Neither the major emerging economies nor countries associated with counterfeiting and piracy were invited to participate, and the EU study observed that "the decision to maintain secrecy until the release of draft text in mid-2010 was to prove a significant handicap to public understanding and support for the treaty. The secrecy allowed significant misapprehensions to develop, while making it difficult for negotiators to communicate the actual scale and content of what was being achieved." p. 6. To date, ACTA has not obtained the ratification by six states required for it to enter into force.

ACTA and its context are further discussed in the article by Peter Yu, TRIPS and Its Achilles' Heel, excerpted at page 134, above.

5. *ISDS, Expropriation and Intellectual Property.* Hundreds of bilateral and multilateral investor-state dispute settlement agreements have been concluded around the world to secure foreign private investment from local expropriation. Most commonly these agreements give foreign investors the opportunity to proceed against a host country in a private arbitral tribunal not only for direct expropriation, such as a government takeover of a foreign factory, but for indirect expropriations, such as a government's decision to ban nuclear energy plants on its territory or to restrict shale gas extraction.

More recently, foreign businesses have sought relief under ISDS agreements against government actions affecting their intellectual property rights in the host country—for example, a tobacco company claiming that local plain packaging legislation for cigarettes has undermined trademark rights in its brand, or a pharmaceutical company challenging a local court's invalidation of the patents on two of its drugs. For an intellectual property owner, one advantage of an ISDS proceeding is that the owner can proceed directly against the foreign government, and not have to wait on the political will of the intellectual property owner's home government. Also, these proceedings can be far quicker than the protracted dispute resolution before a trade body such as a WTO panel.

Can an intellectual property owner challenge the limitations or exceptions in a host country's intellectual property law—a compulsory license, say, or an unusually broad exemption—as constituting a prohibited expropriation of its rights? Even if the governing ISDS agreement immunizes local law from expropriation claims so long as the law complies with TRIPs or other applicable intellectual property norms, can private arbitrators, whose decisions are often shielded from public scrutiny, be expected to give the same balanced treatment to intellectual property norms as a WTO panel?

See Peter Yu, Crossfertilizing ISDS with TRIPS, 49 Loyola U. Chicago L. J. 321 (2017); Rochelle Dreyfuss & Susy Frankel, From Incentive to Commodity to Asset: How International Law is Reconceptualizing Intellectual Property, 36 Mich. J. Int'l L. (2015). *See* generally, Andrew Newcombe & Luís Paradell, Law and Practice of Investment Treaties (2009).

6. *Section 301.* The United States Trade Representative's use of Section 301 and Special 301 procedures played a central role in concluding the 1992 MOU and the 1995 Intellectual Property Rights Agreement with China. Originally included in the Trade Act of 1974, Pub. L. No. 93–618, 88 Stat.

1978, 2401, section 301 was amended by the 1984 Trade Act, Pub. L. No. 98–573, 98 Stat. 2948, 3000, to authorize the President to impose trade sanctions against countries that failed adequately to protect intellectual property rights, and was further amended by the 1988 Omnibus Trade and Competitiveness Act, Pub. L. No. 100–418, 102 Stat. 1107, to divide between two main procedures, "Regular 301," and "Special 301."

Regular 301 authorizes retaliatory sanctions against "unjustifiable" or "unreasonable" foreign practices; retaliation is mandatory in the case of unjustifiable practices and discretionary in the case of unreasonable practices. Among other obligations, Special 301 requires the United States Trade Representative to identify countries that deny effective protection or market access to U.S. intellectual property owners, singling out for the most immediate action "priority foreign countries" that are the most egregious violators with the "greatest adverse impact on the relevant U.S. products." (Less serious violators might appear on a "Watch List" or a "Priority Watch List.")

The USTR's 2018 Special 301 Report illustrates the extent of the procedure's reach and the nature of its concerns. The 2018 Report put twelve countries, including perennial offenders China and Russia, and less obvious targets like Canada, on its Priority Watch List, and twenty-four countries, including Switzerland, on the lower level Watch List. Among the concerns were not just small-scale counterfeiting of luxury designer goods, but the mass production and distribution of counterfeit consumer goods and pharmaceuticals and piracy over the Internet and digital piracy generally.

See generally, Myles Getlan, TRIPs and the Future of Section 301: A Comparative Study in Trade Dispute Resolution, 34 Colum. J. Transnat'l L. 173 (1994); C. O'Neal Taylor, The Limits of Economic Power: Section 301 and the World Trade Organization Dispute Settlement System, 30 Vand. J. Transnat'l L. 209 (1997).

7.   *Glass Houses.* As indicated by Canada and Switzerland's inclusion on the 2018 Watch List, developing countries are not the only target of complaints of deficient intellectual property protection; economically developed countries also regularly level these charges against each other. The United States Trade Representative's 1998 Special 301 Watch List identified several European Union countries as falling short in their protection of intellectual property: Denmark, for failing to make *ex parte* provisional relief available against ongoing copyright infringements; Italy, for failing to pass legislation adequately protecting computer programs, sound recordings and films; and Greece for failing to act against audiovisual piracy. The European Commission responded in kind with its fifteenth annual "Report on United States Barriers to Trade and Investment" charging, among other derelictions, the failure of the United States to protect moral rights of authors as required by Article 6*bis* of the Berne Convention and to protect EU appellations of origin and geographical indication for wine. *See* 13 World Intel. Prop. Rep. (BNA) 165, 339 (1999).

PROBLEM 3

Some U.S. database companies arrange to have the data that go into their databases electronically converted by workers in Southeast Asian countries where labor costs are significantly lower than in the United States. Typically, local workers will scan or key the material delivered to them in analog form by U.S. companies into digital format and double-check the compilation before returning it to the U.S. company to be incorporated into the company's proprietary database.

Three of these Southeast Asian countries, all of which belong to the WTO and adhere to the Berne (1971) and Paris (1967) Conventions, recently formed an alliance, the Southeast Asian Intellectual Property Group (SAIPG), to pursue regional interests. Under SAIPG's leadership, each of the three countries has enacted legislation, called the Data Labor Protection Act (DLPA), with the express object of "redressing the imbalance between economically developed and economically developing countries by vesting ownership of intellectual goods in those who produce the goods."

Section 1(1) of the DLPA protects "compilations of data or other material, whether in machine-readable or other form, which by reason of the selection or arrangement of their contents constitute intellectual creations" and extends its protection to anyone who is a national of, or domiciled in, a country that is a member of the WTO. Section 1(2) vests joint ownership of section 1(1) subject matter in the individual or entity that selects or arranges the contents and "the individual or individuals who contribute to the compilation through the digital conversion of data for the compilation," and further provides that these ownership interests are inalienable. Section 1(3) makes protection last for fifty years from the date the compilation is first fixed.

Section 2(1) of the DLPA provides protection for data, "whether or not part of a compilation protected by section 1," and extends protection to nationals or domiciliaries of a SAIPG country or of any country that extends comparable protection to nationals or domiciliaries of SAIPG countries. Section 2(2) vests joint ownership of the data in the individual or entity that collected and organized the data and the individual or entity that converted the data to digital form. Under section 2(3) protection lasts for fifteen years from the date the data are entered into a database. Section 2(4) subjects protection to a compulsory license for government use.

SAIPG has retained you as counsel to advise it on the legality of the DLPA under governing international agreements. Please advise SAIPG.

CHAPTER II

PROTECTION UNDER NATIONAL LAW

A. COPYRIGHT AND NEIGHBORING RIGHTS

Two traditions have historically dominated the protection of literary and artistic works around the world: the *copyright* tradition associated with the common law system of England, its former colonies (including the United States) and the countries of the British Commonwealth, and the *author's right* tradition associated with the civil law systems of the countries of the European Continent and their former colonies in Latin America, Africa and Asia. (Protection for authors in France is traditionally not labelled copyright but rather *droit d'auteur*; in Germany, *Urheberrecht*; in Italy, *diritto d'autore*.) Civil law countries generally use *neighboring rights* rather than author's right to protect subject matter such as sound recordings and television broadcasts that lack a flesh and blood author; the common law approach is to assimilate these productions to the subject matter of copyright.

Copyright's origins in the common law world trace to the establishment of the first printing plant in England, in 1476, and the issuance of Crown licenses to print books. With the decline of licensing in the late seventeenth century, printers and publishers, who had benefited from the licensed printing monopolies, pressed for statutory relief. Their efforts led to the world's first copyright act, the Statute of Anne, 8 Anne c. 19 (1710), entitled "An Act for the Encouragement of Learning, by vesting the Copies of Printed Books in the Authors or Purchasers of such copies, during the Times therein mentioned." The first national American copyright statute, the Act of May 31, 1790, was closely patterned after the Statute of Anne and conferred a fourteen-year copyright, renewable once, on books, maps and charts; the exclusive rights were limited to printing, reprinting, publishing or vending.

On the European continent, as in England, sovereign printing privileges preceded statutory protection for authors. In France, where the printing monopolies ended with the Revolution, a 1791 law laid the statutory foundation for protection by giving authors the exclusive right to perform their works; a 1793 law gave authors a broad-based right against unauthorized reproduction of their works. In the German territorial states, the printing privileges lasted well into the nineteenth century. The first German legislation was an 1837 Prussian statute granting a right that lasted for the author's life and thirty years and protected against unauthorized reproduction.

187

A sturdy utilitarian thread runs through the intellectual history of copyright's common law tradition, and a similarly strong natural rights thread runs through the fabric of the civil law author's right tradition. On the utilitarian, copyright side, Adam Smith recognized that statutory protection was needed "as an encouragement to the labours of learned men,"* and Samuel Johnson observed that "no man but a blockhead ever wrote, except for money."** The rationale for author's right is usually traced to Otto von Gierke who, expanding on Immanuel Kant's connection of literary creation to the personality of the author, argued for a natural right that vested the author with control over every aspect, personal as well as material, of his work's exploitation. But these philosophic points are emphases only. A vigorous natural rights strain can be found in the common law materials, and a utilitarian theme can be traced in author's rights laws. Professor Jane Ginsburg's observation that "mixed motives underlay the French revolutionary copyright laws (as well as their U.S. counterparts"),*** applies with equal accuracy to contemporary civil and common law doctrine.

Early copyright statutes either denied protection to foreign nationals, as did the United States Copyright Act or, as in Britain and Germany, conditioned protection for foreigners on compliance with one or more formalities such as publication within the country. By the middle of the nineteenth century, however, European countries had begun entering into bilateral copyright treaties. These treaties rested on a principle either of *material reciprocity*—Country *A* would protect works coming from Country *B* only if Country *B* gave comparable protection to works coming from Country *A*—or national treatment—Country *A* would protect works originating in Country *B* on the condition that Country *B* would protect works originating in Country *A* on the same terms it applied to works originating in Country *B*.

Even before the first bilateral copyright treaty was concluded, France, invoking the principle of natural right, called for a universal law of copyright. Although the movement for universal copyright ultimately failed on its own terms, it did succeed in spurring diplomatic conferences on the formation of an international copyright union. These conferences culminated in the Convention for the Protection of Literary and Artistic Works, signed in 1886 in Berne, Switzerland by ten countries—Belgium, France, Germany, Haiti, Italy, Liberia, Spain, Switzerland, Tunisia and the United Kingdom. Adopting national treatment as its pivotal principle, the Berne Convention also obligated member countries to honor two of the three rights generally protected under national laws of the time, the rights of translation and public performance. (The reproduction right was omitted.) The Berne Union established by the

---

*   Adam Smith, Lectures on Jurisprudence 83 (1762).

**   James Boswell, II The Life of Samuel Johnson 12 (April 5, 1776) (Everyman's Library 1992).

***   Jane C. Ginsburg, A Tale of Two Copyrights: Literary Property in Revolutionary France and America, 64 Tulane L. Rev. 991, 1014 (1990).

treaty was structured to exist separate and apart from any particular revision of the treaty so that, as the treaty was revised over time to meet changing conditions, no Union member would be required to adhere to the revised act as a condition to remaining in the Union.

Until 1891, the United States Copyright Act extended protection only to works of authors who were citizens or residents of the United States. That year, under particular pressure from the English, whose books were being widely copied without payment in the United States, Congress passed the Chace Act authorizing international copyright relations for the first time. (Among the earliest bilateral copyright treaties were agreements with the United Kingdom, France and Germany). Pressures to join the Berne Union mounted over the course of the twentieth century and finally, on March 1, 1989, the United States adhered to the 1971 Paris Text of the Berne Convention. (Under Article 34 of the Convention any country may join the Union at any time, but only by adhering to the most recent text of the Convention.)

The Berne Convention has been significantly revised at roughly twenty-year intervals, in 1908 (Berlin), 1928 (Rome), 1948 (Brussels), and 1971 (Paris). In Autumn, 1989 the WIPO Governing Bodies agreed to lay the groundwork for a possible protocol to the Berne Convention. The Diplomatic Conference addressed not only questions left open since the Paris revision, but also questions raised by copyright's new digital environment, and ultimately established not a protocol but a new agreement, the 1996 WIPO Copyright Treaty establishing new norms for the digital era, including a "right of making available to the public" that encompasses online, on-demand delivery of copyrighted works. The Marrakesh Treaty to Facilitate Access to Published Works for Persons Who are Blind, Visually Impaired, or Otherwise Print Disabled, which was signed in Marrakesh, Morocco in 2013 and came into force in 2016, requires contracting parties to carve out prescribed limitations and exceptions from the exclusive rights under copyright to enable the reproduction and distribution of published works in formats accessible to blind, visually impaired and otherwise print-disabled persons.

As late as the mid-twentieth century the Berne Union was still a relatively exclusive club, and it was by no means clear that many countries—not only the United States, but also the then Soviet Union and countries in Latin America, Africa, Asia—would ever join. The Universal Copyright Convention, signed by thirty-six states in Geneva in 1952, aimed to secure at least some level of multilateral copyright relations between these countries and the countries of the Berne Union. The U.C.C.'s conditions were less stringent than those of the text of Berne Convention then in effect, allowing formalities as a condition of protection and requiring no minimum standards of protection beyond the general prescription of "adequate and effective protection."

Regional copyright norms sometimes provide an important supplement or alternative to bilateral and multilateral arrangements. Of these, the most robust by far are the directives implemented by member states of the European Union, as supplemented by decisions of the Court of Justice of the European Union. Regional arrangements were the preferred alternative in much of North and South America well into the twentieth century. The first of the regional American copyright treaties was the 1889 Montevideo Treaty which, unlike the treaties that followed, was open to adherence by countries outside the Americas. Later treaties included the 1911 Caracas Convention, the 1908 Washington Treaty among Central American republics and, beginning in 1902, a series of Pan-American Conventions modelled after the Berne Convention. The third Pan-American Convention, concluded in Buenos Aires in 1910, drew the largest number of adherents, including the United States.

Neighboring rights, as distinct from copyright or author's right, began to emerge in the early part of the twentieth century in the form of national laws protecting creative contributions to phonograms and broadcasts. The International Convention for the Protection of Performers, Producers of Phonograms and Broadcasting Organizations, commonly called the Rome Convention, is the premier neighboring rights treaty. Signed on October 26, 1961, it operates on the principle of national treatment subject to minimum standards. The other principal neighboring rights treaties are the 1971 Convention for the Protection of Producers of Phonograms Against Unauthorized Duplication of their Phonograms, commonly called the Geneva Phonograms Convention; the 1996 WIPO Performances and Phonograms Treaty, the 2012 Beijing Treaty on Audiovisual Performances, and the 1974 Convention Relating to the Distribution of Programme-Carrying Signals Transmitted by Satellite, commonly called the Brussels Satellite Convention.

Contemporary trade agreements, most notably the 1994 TRIPs Agreement, have brought national compliance with copyright norms into the arena of trade sanctions. Article 9 of the TRIPs Agreement effectively embraces the norms of the 1971 Paris Text of the Berne Convention (except for moral rights). Other provisions establish new norms, such as protection of computer programs and intellectually creative compilations of data and other materials. Article 14 of the TRIPs Agreement establishes minimum standards for neighboring rights of performers, phonogram producers and broadcasting organizations.

Bibliographic Note. On international and comparative copyright generally, see Paul Goldstein & Bernt Hugenholtz, International Copyright: Principles, Law and Practice (4th ed. 2019); Wilhelm Nordemann, Kai Vinck, Paul Hertin & Gerald Meyer, International Copyright and Neighboring Rights Law (1990). Paul Edward Geller, (ed.), International Copyright Law and Practice (1995), provides an introductory overview of international copyright together with individual chapters on the copyright laws of several countries, as does Hamish Sandison & Stephen Stewart, International Copyright and Neighbouring

Rights (2d ed. 1989). Irini Stamatoudi & Paul Torremans, EU Copyright Law (2014) is a commentary on European Union law in the area.

Sam Ricketson & Jane C. Ginsburg, International Copyright and Neighbouring Rights: The Berne Convention and Beyond (2d ed. 2006) is the indispensable text on the Berne Convention. *See* also W.I.P.O., Guide to the Berne Convention for the Protection of Literary and Artistic Works (Paris Act 1971) (1978). On the so-called WIPO Internet treaties, see Jörge Reinbothe & Silke von Lewinski, The WIPO Treaties 1996 (2002). Arpad Bogsch, The Law of Copyright Under the Universal Convention (3d rev. ed. 1968), though somewhat dated, is the authoritative work on the Universal Copyright Convention.

For historical background on national copyright laws and international copyright relations, see Stephen Ladas, The International Protection of Literary and Artistic Property (1975). On copyright's early history in England, see Mark Rose, Authors and Owners: The Invention of Copyright (1993), and in England and the United States, see Bruce Bugbee, Genesis of American Patent and Copyright Law (1967) and Lyman Ray Patterson, Copyright in Historical Perspective (1968). On the early history of French copyright, see Elizabeth Armstrong, Before Copyright: The French Book—Privilege System 1498–1526 (1990); David Saunders, Authorship and Copyright (1992); Jane Ginsburg, A Tale of Two Copyrights: Literary Property in Revolutionary France and America, 64 Tulane L. Rev. 991 (1990); Carla Hesse, Enlightenment Epistemology and the Laws of Authorship in Revolutionary France, 1777–1793, 30 Representations 109 (1990).

1. TERRITORIAL REACH OF COPYRIGHT LAW

Subafilms, Ltd. v. MGM-Pathe Communications Co.

United States Court of Appeals, Ninth Circuit, *en banc*, 1994.
24 F.3d 1088, 30 U.S.P.Q.2d 1746.

D.W. NELSON, CIRCUIT JUDGE:

In this case, we consider the "vexing question"[1] of whether a claim for infringement can be brought under the Copyright Act, 17 U.S.C. § 101 et seq. (1988), when the assertedly infringing conduct consists solely of the authorization within the territorial boundaries of the United States of acts that occur entirely abroad. We hold that such allegations do not state a claim for relief under the copyright laws of the United States.

Factual and Procedural Background

In 1966, the musical group The Beatles, through Subafilms, Ltd., entered into a joint venture with the Hearst Corporation to produce the animated motion picture entitled "Yellow Submarine" (the "Picture"). Over the next year, Hearst, acting on behalf of the joint venture (the

---

[1]   Paul Goldstein, Copyright: Principles, Law and Practice § 6.1, at 705 n.4 (1989).

"Producer"), negotiated an agreement with United Artists Corporation ("UA") to distribute and finance the film. Separate distribution and financing agreements were entered into in May, 1967. Pursuant to these agreements, UA distributed the Picture in theaters beginning in 1968 and later on television.

In the early 1980s, with the advent of the home video market, UA entered into several licensing agreements to distribute a number of its films on videocassette. Although one company expressed interest in the Picture, UA refused to license "Yellow Submarine" because of uncertainty over whether home video rights had been granted by the 1967 agreements. Subsequently, in 1987, UA's successor company, MGM/UA Communications Co. ("MGM/UA"), over the Producer's objections, authorized its subsidiary MGM/UA Home Video, Inc. to distribute the Picture for the domestic home video market, and, pursuant to an earlier licensing agreement, notified Warner Bros., Inc. ("Warner") that the Picture had been cleared for international videocassette distribution. Warner, through its wholly owned subsidiary, Warner Home Video, Inc., in turn entered into agreements with third parties for distribution of the Picture on videocassette around the world.

In 1988, Subafilms and Hearst ("Appellees") brought suit against MGM/UA, Warner, and their respective subsidiaries (collectively the "Distributors" or "Appellants"), contending that the videocassette distribution of the Picture, both foreign and domestic, constituted copyright infringement and a breach of the 1967 agreements. The case was tried before a retired California Superior Court Judge acting as a special master. The special master found for Appellees on both claims, and against the Distributors on their counterclaim for fraud and reformation. Except for the award of prejudgment interest, which it reversed, the district court adopted all of the special master's factual findings and legal conclusions. Appellees were awarded $2,228,000.00 in compensatory damages, split evenly between the foreign and domestic home video distributions. In addition, Appellees received attorneys' fees and a permanent injunction that prohibited the Distributors from engaging in, or authorizing, any home video use of the Picture.

A panel of this circuit, in an unpublished disposition, affirmed the district court's judgment on the ground that both the domestic and foreign distribution of the Picture constituted infringement under the Copyright Act. With respect to the foreign distribution of the Picture, the panel concluded that it was bound by this court's prior decision in Peter Starr Prod. Co. v. Twin Continental Films, Inc., 783 F.2d 1440 (9th Cir. 1986), which it held to stand for the proposition that, although " 'infringing actions that take place entirely outside the United States are not actionable' [under the Copyright Act, an] 'act of infringement within the United States' [properly is] alleged where the illegal authorization of international exhibitions takes place in the United States." Because the Distributors had admitted that the initial authorization to distribute the

Picture internationally occurred within the United States, the panel affirmed the district court's holding with respect to liability for extraterritorial home video distribution of the Picture.

We granted Appellants' petition for rehearing en banc to consider whether the panel's interpretation of *Peter Starr* conflicted with our subsequent decision in Lewis Galoob Toys, Inc. v. Nintendo of Am., Inc., 964 F.2d 965 (9th Cir. 1992), cert. denied, 507 U.S. 985 (1993), which held that there could be no liability for authorizing a party to engage in an infringing act when the authorized "party's use of the work would not violate the Copyright Act," id. at 970. Because we conclude that there can be no liability under the United States copyright laws for authorizing an act that itself could not constitute infringement of rights secured by those laws, and that wholly extraterritorial acts of infringement are not cognizable under the Copyright Act, we overrule *Peter Starr* insofar as it held that allegations of an authorization within the United States of infringing acts that take place entirely abroad state a claim for infringement under the Act. Accordingly, we vacate the panel's decision in part and return the case to the panel for further proceedings.

Discussion

I. The Mere Authorization of Extraterritorial Acts of Infringement does not State a Claim under the Copyright Act

As the panel in this case correctly concluded, *Peter Starr* held that the authorization within the United States of entirely extraterritorial acts stated a cause of action under the "plain language" of the Copyright Act. *Peter Starr*, 783 F.2d at 1442–43. Observing that the Copyright Act grants a copyright owner "the exclusive rights to do and to authorize" any of the activities listed in 17 U.S.C. § 106 (1)–(5), and that a violation of the "authorization" right constitutes infringement under section 501 of the Act, the *Peter Starr* court reasoned that allegations of an authorization within the United States of extraterritorial conduct that corresponded to the activities listed in section 106 "allege[d] an act of infringement within the United States," id. at 1442–43. Accordingly, the court determined that the district court erred "in concluding that 'Plaintiff allege[d] only infringing acts which took place outside of the United States,'" and reversed the district court's dismissal for lack of subject matter jurisdiction. Id. at 1443.

The *Peter Starr* court accepted, as does this court, that the acts authorized from within the United States themselves could not have constituted infringement under the Copyright Act because "[i]n general, United States copyright laws do not have extraterritorial effect," and therefore, "infringing actions that take place entirely outside the United States are not actionable." *Peter Starr*, 783 F.2d at 1442 (citing Robert Stigwood Group, Ltd. v. O'Reilly, 530 F.2d 1096, 1101 (2d Cir.), cert. denied, 429 U.S. 848, 50 L.Ed. 2d 121, 97 S.Ct. 135 (1976)). The central premise of the *Peter Starr* court, then, was that a party could be held liable as an "infringer" under section 501 of the Act merely for authorizing a third party to engage in acts that, had they been committed within the United States, would have violated the exclusive rights granted to a copyright holder by section 106.

Since *Peter Starr*, however, we have recognized that, when a party authorizes an activity not proscribed by one of the five section 106 clauses, the authorizing party cannot be held liable as an infringer. In *Lewis Galoob*, we rejected the argument that "a party can unlawfully authorize another party to use a copyrighted work even if that party's use of the work would not violate the Copyright Act," *Lewis Galoob*, 964 F.2d at 970, and approved of Professor Nimmer's statement that " 'to the extent that an activity does not violate one of th[e] five enumerated rights [found in 17 U.S.C. § 106], authorizing such activity does not constitute copyright infringement,' " id. (quoting 3 David Nimmer & Melville B. Nimmer, Nimmer on Copyright § 12.04[A][3][a], at 12–80 n. 82 (1991)). Similarly, in *Columbia Pictures*, we held that no liability attached under the Copyright Act for providing videodisc players to hotel guests when the use of that equipment did not constitute a "public" performance within the meaning of section 106 of the Act, see Columbia Pictures [v. Professional Real Estate Investors], 866 F.2d at 279–81.

The apparent premise of *Lewis Galoob* was that the addition of the words "to authorize" in the Copyright Act was not meant to create a new form of liability for "authorization" that was divorced completely from the legal consequences of authorized conduct, but was intended to invoke the preexisting doctrine of contributory infringement. *See Lewis Galoob*, 964 F.2d at 970 ("Although infringement by authorization is a form of direct infringement [under the Act], this does not change the proper focus of our inquiry; a party cannot authorize another party to infringe a copyright unless the authorized conduct would itself be unlawful."). We agree.

Contributory infringement under the 1909 Act developed as a form of third party liability. Accordingly, there could be no liability for contributory infringement unless the authorized or otherwise encouraged activity itself could amount to infringement. Indeed, the Supreme Court in Sony Corp. of Am. v. Universal City Studios, Inc., 464 U.S. 417 (1984), although expressly noting that it addressed an extraordinary claim of vicarious or contributory infringement under the 1976 Act for which there was "no precedent in the law of copyright," id. at 439, inquired whether the machines sold by Sony ultimately were capable of a "substantial noninfringing use[ ]," id. at 442 (emphasis added).

As the Supreme Court noted in *Sony*, and this circuit acknowledged in *Peter Starr*, under the 1909 Act courts differed over the degree of involvement required to render a party liable as a contributory infringer. Viewed with this background in mind, the addition of the words "to authorize" in the 1976 Act appears best understood as merely clarifying that the Act contemplates liability for contributory infringement, and that the bare act of "authorization" can suffice. This view is supported by the legislative history of the Act:

> The exclusive rights accorded to a copyright owner under section 106 are "to do and to authorize" any of the activities specified in the five numbered clauses. *Use of the phrase "to authorize" is intended to avoid any questions as to the liability of contributory infringers.* For example, a person who lawfully acquires an authorized copy of a motion picture would be an infringer if he or she engages in the business of renting it to others for purposes of unauthorized public performance.

H.R. Rep. No. 1476, 94th Cong., 2d Sess. 61, reprinted in 1976 U.S.C.C.A.N. 5659, 5674 (emphasis added).

Consequently, we believe that " 'to authorize' [wa]s simply a convenient peg on which Congress chose to hang the antecedent jurisprudence of third party liability." 3 Nimmer, *supra*, § 12.04[A][3][a] at 12–84 n. 81.

Although the *Peter Starr* court recognized that the addition of the authorization right in the 1976 Act "was intended to remove the confusion surrounding contributory . . . infringement," *Peter Starr*, 783 F.2d at 1443, it did not consider the applicability of an essential attribute of the doctrine identified above: that contributory infringement, even when triggered solely by an "authorization," is a form of third party liability that requires the authorized acts to constitute infringing ones. We believe that the *Peter Starr* court erred in not applying this principle to the authorization of acts that cannot themselves be infringing because they take place entirely abroad. Accepting the proposition that a direct infringement is a prerequisite to third party liability, the further question arises whether the direct infringement on which liability is premised must take place within the United States. Given the undisputed axiom that United States copyright law has no extraterritorial application, it would seem to follow necessarily that a primary activity outside the boundaries of the United States, not constituting an infringement cognizable under the Copyright Act, cannot serve as the basis for holding liable under the Copyright Act one who is merely related to that activity within the United States.

Appellees resist the force of this logic, and argue that liability in this case is appropriate because, unlike in *Lewis Galoob* and *Columbia Pictures*, in which the alleged primary infringement consisted of acts that were entirely outside the purview of 17 U.S.C. § 106 (1)–(5) (and presumably lawful), the conduct authorized in this case was precisely that prohibited by section 106, and is only uncognizable because it occurred outside the United States. Moreover, they contend that the conduct authorized in this case would have been prohibited under the copyright laws of virtually every nation.

Even assuming arguendo that the acts authorized in this case would have been illegal abroad, we do not believe the distinction offered by Appellees is a relevant one. Because the copyright laws do not apply extraterritorially, each of the rights conferred under the five section 106 categories must be read as extending "no farther than the [United States'] borders." 2 Goldstein, supra, § 16.0, at 675. In light of our above conclusion that the "authorization" right refers to the doctrine of contributory infringement, which requires that the authorized act itself could violate one of the exclusive rights listed in section 106(1)–(5), we believe that "it is simply not possible to draw a principled distinction" between an act that does not violate a copyright because it is not the type of conduct proscribed by section 106, and one that does not violate section 106 because the illicit act occurs overseas. Danjaq, S.A. v. MGM/UA Communications Co., 773 F.Supp. 194, 203 (C.D. Cal. 1991). In both cases, the authorized conduct could not violate the exclusive rights guaranteed by section 106. In both cases, therefore, there can be no liability for "authorizing" such conduct.

To hold otherwise would produce the untenable anomaly, inconsistent with the general principles of third party liability, that a party could be held liable as an infringer for violating the "authorization" right when the party that it authorized could not be considered an infringer under the Copyright Act. Put otherwise, we do not think Congress intended to hold a party liable for merely "authorizing" conduct that, had the authorizing party chosen to engage in itself, would have resulted in no liability under the Act.

Appellees rely heavily on the Second Circuit's doctrine that extraterritorial application of the copyright laws is permissible "when the type of infringement permits further reproduction abroad." Update Art, Inc. v. Modiin Publishing, Ltd., 843 F.2d 67, 73 (2d Cir. 1988). Whatever the merits of the Second Circuit's rule, and we express no opinion on its validity in this circuit, it is premised on the theory that the copyright holder may recover damages that stem from a direct infringement of its exclusive rights that occurs within the United States. In these cases, liability is not based on contributory infringement, but on the theory that the infringing use would have been actionable even if the subsequent foreign distribution that stemmed from that use never took place. These cases, therefore, simply are inapplicable to a theory of liability based merely on the authorization of noninfringing acts.

Accordingly, accepting that wholly extraterritorial acts of infringement cannot support a claim under the Copyright Act, we believe that the *Peter Starr* court, and thus the panel in this case, erred in concluding that the mere authorization of such acts supports a claim for infringement under the Act.

II. The Extraterritoriality of the Copyright Act

Appellees additionally contend that, if liability for "authorizing" acts of infringement depends on finding that the authorized acts themselves are cognizable under the Copyright Act, this court should find that the United States copyright laws do extend to extraterritorial acts of infringement when such acts "result in adverse effects within the United States." Appellees buttress this argument with the contention that failure to apply the copyright laws extraterritorially in this case will have a disastrous effect on the American film industry, and that other remedies, such as suits in foreign jurisdictions or the application of foreign copyright laws by American courts, are not realistic alternatives.

We are not persuaded by Appellees' parade of horribles. More fundamentally, however, we are unwilling to overturn over eighty years of consistent jurisprudence on the extraterritorial reach of the copyright laws without further guidance from Congress.

The Supreme Court recently reminded us that "[i]t is a long-standing principle of American law 'that legislation of Congress, unless a contrary intent appears, is meant to apply only within the territorial jurisdiction of the United States.'" EEOC v. Arabian American Oil Co. (Aramco), 499 U.S. 244 (1991) (quoting Foley Bros. v. Filardo, 336 U.S. 281, 285,(1949)). Because courts must "assume that Congress legislates against the backdrop of the presumption against extraterritoriality," unless "there is 'the affirmative intention of the Congress clearly expressed'" congressional enactments must be presumed to be " 'primarily concerned with domestic conditions.'" Id. 499 U.S. at 248.

The "undisputed axiom," 3 Nimmer, *supra*, § 12.04[A][3][b], at 12–86, that the United States' copyright laws have no application to extraterritorial infringement predates the 1909 Act, and, as discussed above, the principle of territoriality consistently has been reaffirmed. There is no clear expression of congressional intent in either the 1976 Act or other relevant enactments to alter the preexisting extraterritoriality doctrine. Indeed, the *Peter Starr* court itself recognized the continuing application of the principle that "infringing actions that take place entirely outside the United States are not actionable in United States federal courts." *Peter Starr*, 783 F.2d at 1442 (citing *Robert Stigwood*, 530 F.2d at 1101).

Furthermore, we note that Congress chose in 1976 to expand one specific "extraterritorial" application of the Act by declaring that the unauthorized importation of copyrighted works constitutes infringement even when the copies lawfully were made abroad. *See* 17 U.S.C.A. § 602(a). Had Congress been inclined to overturn the preexisting doctrine that infringing acts that take place wholly outside the United States are not actionable under the Copyright Act, it knew how to do so. Accordingly, the presumption against extraterritoriality, "far from being overcome here, is doubly fortified by the language of [the] statute," Smith v. United States, 507 U.S. 197 (1993) (quoting United States v. Spelar, 338 U.S. 217, 222 (1949)), as set against its consistent historical interpretation.

Appellees, however, rely on dicta in a recent decision of the District of Columbia Circuit for the proposition that the presumption against extraterritorial application of U.S. laws may be "overcome" when denying such application would "result in adverse effects within the United States." Environmental Defense Fund, Inc. v. Massey, 986 F.2d 528, 531 (D.C.Cir. 1993) (noting that the Sherman Act, Lanham Act, and securities laws have been applied to extraterritorial conduct). However, the *Massey* court did not state that extraterritoriality would be demanded in such circumstances, but that "the *presumption is generally not applied* where the failure to extend the scope of the statute to a foreign setting will result in adverse [domestic] effects." 986 F.2d at 531 (emphasis added). In each of the statutory schemes discussed by the *Massey* court, the ultimate touchstone of extraterritoriality consisted of an ascertainment of congressional intent; courts did not rest solely on the consequences of a failure to give a statutory scheme extraterritorial application. More importantly, as the *Massey* court conceded, application of the presumption is particularly appropriate when "it serves to protect against unintended clashes between our laws and those of other nations which could result in international discord," *Aramco*, 111 S.Ct. at 1230.

We believe this latter factor is decisive in the case of the Copyright Act, and fully justifies application of the *Aramco* presumption even assuming arguendo that "adverse effects" within the United States "generally" would require a plenary inquiry into congressional intent. At the time that the international distribution of the videocassettes in this case took place, the United States was a member of the Universal Copyright Convention ("UCC"), and, in 1988, the United States acceded to the Berne Convention for the Protection of Literary and Artistic Works ("Berne Conv."). The central thrust of these multilateral treaties is the principle of "national treatment." A work of an American national first generated in America will receive the same protection in a foreign nation as that country accords to the works of its own nationals. Although the treaties do not expressly discuss choice-of-law rules, it is commonly acknowledged that the national treatment principle implicates a rule of territoriality. Indeed, a recognition of this principle appears implicit in Congress's statements in acceding to Berne that "the primary mechanism for discouraging discriminatory treatment of foreign copyright claimants is the principle of national treatment," H.R. Rep. No. 609, 100th Cong., 2d Sess. 43 [hereinafter House Report], and that adherence to Berne will require "careful due regard for the[ ] values" of other member nations, id. at 20.

In light of the *Aramco* Court's concern with preventing international discord, we think it inappropriate for the courts to act in a manner that might disrupt Congress's efforts to secure a more stable international intellectual property regime unless Congress otherwise clearly has expressed its intent. The application of American copyright law to acts of infringement that occur entirely overseas clearly could have this effect.

Extraterritorial application of American law would be contrary to the spirit of the Berne Convention, and might offend other member nations by effectively displacing their law in circumstances in which previously it was assumed to govern. Consequently, an extension of extraterritoriality might undermine Congress's objective of achieving " 'effective and harmonious' copyright laws among all nations.' " House Report, *supra*, at 20. Indeed, it might well send the signal that the United States does not believe that the protection accorded by the laws of other member nations is adequate, which would undermine two other objectives of Congress in joining the convention: "strengthening the credibility of the U.S. position in trade negotiations with countries where piracy is not uncommon" and "raising the likelihood that other nations will enter the Convention." S. Rep. 352, 100th Cong., 2d Sess. 4–5.

Moreover, although Appellees contend otherwise, we note that their theory might permit the application of American law to the distribution of protected materials in a foreign country conducted exclusively by citizens of that nation. A similar possibility was deemed sufficient in *Aramco* to find a provision that, on its face, appeared to contemplate that Title VII would be applied overseas, insufficient to rebut the presumption against extraterritoriality. Of course, under the Berne Convention, all states must guarantee minimum rights, and it is plausible that the application of American law would yield outcomes roughly equivalent to those called for by the application of foreign law in a number of instances. Nonetheless, extending the reach of American copyright law likely would produce difficult choice-of-law problems, cf. House Report, *supra*, at 43 ("[Berne] does not, however, require all countries to have identical legal systems and procedural norms."), dilemmas that the federal courts' general adherence to the territoriality principle largely has obviated. Even if courts, as a matter of comity, would assert extraterritorial jurisdiction only when the effects in the United States and the contacts of the offending party with this country are particularly strong, that the assertion of such jurisdiction would engender new and troublesome choice-of-law questions provides a compelling reason for applying the *Aramco* presumption.

Accordingly, because an extension of the extraterritorial reach of the Copyright Act by the courts would in all likelihood disrupt the international regime for protecting intellectual property that Congress so recently described as essential to furthering the goal of protecting the works of American authors abroad, we conclude that the *Aramco* presumption must be applied. Because the presumption has not been overcome, we reaffirm that the United States copyright laws do not reach acts of infringement that take place entirely abroad. It is for Congress, and not the courts, to take the initiative in this field.

III. Other Arguments

Appellees raise a number of additional arguments for why the district court's judgment should be affirmed. Relying upon the Second

Circuit's doctrine described above, Appellees maintain that they may recover damages for international distribution of the Picture based on the theory that an act of direct infringement, in the form of a reproduction of the negatives for the Picture, took place in the United States. Appellees also suggest that they may recover, under United States law, damages stemming from the international distribution on the theory that the distribution was part of a larger conspiracy to violate their copyright that included actionable infringement within the United States. In addition, they maintain that Appellants are liable for the international distribution under foreign copyright laws. Finally, Appellees argue that the district court's damage award can be sustained under the breach of contract theory not reached by the panel.

We resolve none of these questions, but leave them for the panel, in its best judgment, to consider. A remand to the district court might well be necessary to permit further factual development in light of our decision to overrule aspects of *Peter Starr*. The panel, however, is free to take whatever action it views as appropriate that is consistent with our mandate.

Conclusion

We hold that the mere authorization of acts of infringement that are not cognizable under the United States copyright laws because they occur entirely outside of the United States does not state a claim for infringement under the Copyright Act. *Peter Starr* is overruled insofar as it held to the contrary. Accordingly, we vacate Part III of the panel's disposition, in which it concluded that the international distribution of the film constituted a violation of the United States copyright laws. We also vacate that portion of the disposition that affirmed the damage award based on foreign distribution of the film and the panel's affirmance of the award of attorneys' fees. Finally, we vacate the district court's grant of injunctive relief insofar as it was based on the premise that the Distributors had violated the United States copyright laws through authorization of the foreign distribution of the Picture on videocassettes.

The cause is remanded to the panel for further proceedings consistent with the mandate of this court.

Vacated in Part and Remanded.

NOTES

1. *Territoriality and Statutory Construction.* Territoriality is a rule of statutory interpretation, not a rule of law. Courts will presume that the legislature did not intend the rights it creates to have effect outside the country's borders, and will give a right an extraterritorial reach only if the legislature has made that intention clear. Thus, the U.S. Congress could have expressly provided in the 1976 Copyright Act that the newly-created authorization right encompassed secondary liability for foreign as well as

domestic acts of direct infringement, and it was Congress's failure to do so that, according to the Ninth Circuit *en banc,* dictated the result in *Subafilms.*

Consider whether the Second Circuit Court of Appeals adhered to this principle of statutory construction in National Football League v. PrimeTime 24 Joint Venture, 211 F.3d 10 (2d Cir. 2000), *cert. denied,* 532 U.S. 941 (2001). Defendant satellite carrier had, without permission from plaintiff copyright owner, retransmitted U.S.-originated football broadcasts to the carrier's subscribers in Canada. The carrier argued that uplinking copyrighted material in the United States and transmitting it to a satellite does not constitute a public performance in the United States, and that the only performance occurred in Canada where the signal was received. The court disagreed. "[T]he most logical interpretation of the Copyright Act is to hold that a public performance or display includes 'each step in the process by which a protected work wends its way to its audience.' " It was clear to the court that "PrimeTime's uplink transmission of signals captured in the United States is a step in the process by which NFL's protected work wends its way to a public audience." 211 F.3d at 13.

There is little doubt that the U.S. Copyright Act's definition of "to perform"—"to recite, render, play, dance, or act it [the work], either directly or by means of any device or process, or in the case of a motion picture or other audiovisual work, to show its images in any sequence or to make the sounds accompanying it audible"—encompasses each "step in the process" by which a work may "wend its way to a public audience." But to be actionable under the statute it is not enough that the defendant perform the work; it must perform it to the public. If that public is entirely outside the United States, can it be said that Congress intended to bring the foreign impact of a defendant's conduct within the public performance right any more than it intended to bring foreign direct infringements within the authorization right under the facts of *Subafilms?*

2. *Territoriality on the Internet.* Differing local rules on territoriality present a particular challenge for Internet service providers that daily transmit uncounted infringing signals into dozens of countries. In Society of Composers, Authors and Music Publishers of Canada v. Canadian Assn. of Internet Providers, [2004] 2 S.C.R. at ¶ 427, 2004 SCC 45, plaintiff collecting society sought to collect royalties for its Canadian composer, author and publisher members and foreign affiliates from Internet service providers located in Canada on the ground that, without permission, the service providers had communicated, and authorized the communication of, copyrighted musical works to the public. Defendant, a coalition of service providers, answered that they were merely conduits that did not regulate the content they transmitted, and consequently neither communicated, nor authorized the communication of, any copyrighted works.

The Canadian Supreme Court ruled that the Canadian Copyright Board, to which SOCAN had applied for approval of a royalty from the service providers, had erred in holding that a service provider would be subject to copyright liability in Canada only if its communications originated from a server located in Canada. Writing for the majority, Justice Binnie rejected this as "too rigid and mechanical a test"; all that is required to support application of the Canadian Copyright Act to international Internet transmissions is a "real and substantial" connection to Canada as evidenced by the location of the content provider, the host server, the intermediaries and the end users. The Court acknowledged that its conclusion "raises the spectre of imposition of copyright duties on a single telecommunication in both the State of transmission and the State of reception, but as with other fields of overlapping liability (taxation for example), the answer lies in the making of international or bilateral agreements, not in national courts straining to find some jurisdictional infirmity in either State." [2004] 2 S.C.R. at ¶ 78.

Justice LeBel dissented as to the appropriate test for determining the location of an Internet communication under the Copyright Act, and would have affirmed the Copyright Board's determination that an Internet communication "occurs within Canada when it originates from a server located in Canada." By contrast, the "real and substantial connection test" fails to meet the need of Internet stakeholders "to know with a degree of certainty whether they will be liable in Canada for a communication of copyrighted works." Further, in Justice LeBel's view, the real and substantial connection test "is inconsistent with the territoriality principle in that it may reach out and grasp content providers located in Bangalore who post content on a server in Hong Kong based only on the fact that the copyrighted work is retrieved by end users in Canada." [2004] 2 S.C.R. at ¶ 152.

2. ENTITLEMENT TO PROTECTION

Paul Goldstein, International Copyright: Principles, Law, and Practice*

§§ 4, 4.1 (2001).

§ 4 Protectibility of Foreign Works.

As a rule, a country's obligation to protect foreign works—a work by a foreign national, for example, or a work first published in another country—will turn on the terms of its copyright relations with the country in which the work originated. Only rarely, and selectively, will a country extend copyright or neighboring rights protection to a foreign work in the absence of some general or reciprocal treaty relationship with the work's country of origin. One example is the unconditional and universal extension, as in France and Germany, of protection for at least some of an author's moral rights. Another is the United States Copyright Act's protection of unpublished works without regard to the author's nationality.

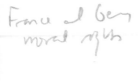 France and Germany moral rights

The first step in determining whether, and to what extent, a work will be protected in a particular country is to determine the requirements

---

that the country's legislation imposes as a condition to protection and, if the governing treaty is self-executing, to determine the requirements imposed by the treaty. If the work in question was created or published before the effective date of the applicable legislation or treaty, it will often be necessary to inquire as well into the requirements for protection imposed by statute or treaty at the earlier time.

§ 4.1   Protectibility of United States Works in Other Countries

Four questions face a United States copyright owner that plans to exploit a work through licensing or enforcement in another country, commonly called the "protecting country." First, the United States copyright owner must determine whether it will qualify as the owner of rights in the work under the law of the protecting country. Applicable choice of law rules in some fora will designate the law of the protecting country, and not the law of the United States, as controlling on the question of ownership, and that law may identify someone other than the United States owner as the work's copyright owner.

Second, the United States copyright owner must determine into what subject matter class the work falls—is it a musical work, say, or a sound recording—and whether the protecting country extends protection to works of this class that originate outside its borders. As a rule, this inquiry entails a determination whether the protecting country has adhered to a treaty and, if necessary, enacted legislation requiring it to protect this class of works and, if so, whether under the terms of the treaty a point of attachment exists to connect the work to the protecting country. Third, the United States copyright owner should determine the scope of its rights under foreign law and, fourth, it must determine when the term of protection for those rights expires.

These four questions intersect in more or less obvious ways. A negative answer to the first question will obviate inquiry into the remaining three; a negative answer to the second question will obviate inquiry into the last two; and a negative answer to the third, will obviate inquiry into the fourth. Further, the fact that the United States work falls into one class rather than another in the protecting country will in some cases control whether a point of attachment exists entitling the work to protection. It may also control the rights that the protecting country will grant. For example, a sound recording produced and protected in the United States as a copyrighted work will in many other countries be viewed as neither a literary nor an artistic work and so will be protected only under neighboring rights doctrine. As a consequence, the existence of a point of attachment in any of these countries will turn not on one of the copyright treaties—Berne or the Universal Copyright Convention—but on one or more neighboring rights treaties—the Rome Convention for the Protection of Performers, Producers of Phonograms and Broadcasting Organizations, the Geneva Phonograms Convention, or the WIPO Performances and Phonograms Treaty—that prescribe different minimum rights for phonograms.

NOTES

1. *Points of Attachment Under the Berne, Rome and Universal Copyright Conventions*. As a rule, copyright and neighboring rights treaties require one country to protect a creative work originating in another country only if there is a point of attachment—also called a "connecting factor"—linking the work to a country that has adhered to the treaty. Article 3(1) of the 1971 Berne Convention, Paris Text provides that a point of attachment exists if the foreign author is a national of a Berne Union country or, alternatively, if the work was first published in a Berne Union country, "or simultaneously in a country outside the Union and in a country of the Union." Under Article 4, a work that enjoys neither of these two points of attachment will nonetheless receive Berne protection if, in the case of a cinematographic work, its maker has its headquarters or habitual residence in a Union country or, in the case of an architectural work, it has been erected in a Union country.

Article II of the 1971 Paris Text of the Universal Copyright Convention makes the author's nationality in a U.C.C. country a point of attachment for both published and unpublished works, and makes publication in a U.C.C. country an added point of attachment for published works. Articles 4, 5 and 6 of the International Convention for the Protection of Performers, Producers of Phonograms and Broadcasting Organizations—commonly called the Rome Convention—respectively provide points of attachment for performers (the performance takes place in another Contracting State, is fixed in a protected phonogram, or is carried by a protected broadcast); producers of phonograms (the producer is a national of another contracting state, or the phonogram was first fixed or published in another contracting state); and broadcasting organizations (the broadcaster has its headquarters in, or the broadcast was transmitted from another contracting state).

Before the United States adhered to the Berne Convention, on March 1, 1989, American copyright owners regularly obtained Berne protection by strategically arranging for the first or simultaneous publication of their works in a Berne Union country—the so-called "back door to Berne." Although the United States is not a party to the Rome Convention, can an American record company similarly arrange its activities so that its phonograms will qualify for protection under the Convention?

2. *Points of Attachment Under the U.S. Copyright Act*. Section 104 of the 1976 Copyright Act divides its points of attachment between published and unpublished works. Following the approach taken under state common law copyright before the 1976 Act, section 104(a) provides that all works coming within the subject matter of copyright, "while unpublished, are subject to protection under this title without regard to the nationality or domicile of the authors." Section 104(b)(1) and (2) respectively incorporate the two basic Berne and U.C.C. points of attachment: (1) nationality or domicile and (2) first publication in the United States or in a foreign country that is a "treaty party." (Section 101 effectively defines "treaty party" to include parties to the Berne, Universal Copyright, and Geneva Phonogram Conventions, the WTO Agreement, the WIPO Copyright and Performances and Phonograms

Treaties and "any other copyright treaty to which the United States is a party.")

Apart from the universal protection given to unpublished works, the determination whether a foreign work will enjoy copyright protection in the United States will turn on the law in force in the United States at the time of the work's first publication, as well as on the treaty relations between the United States and the work's country of origin at that time. For example, unlike the 1976 Copyright Act, the 1909 Copyright Act made only nationality, and not first publication in the United States, a point of attachment; also, before the United States adhered to the Berne Convention, neither nationality nor first publication in a Berne Union country would have, of themselves, provided a point of attachment for protection in the United States.

3. *Retroactivity.* In a provision that dates to the original 1886 Berne Text, the Berne Paris Act obligates member countries to give retroactive protection to foreign works in existence at the time the Convention comes into effect between the protecting country and the work's country of origin so long as the work has not yet fallen into the public domain "in the country of origin through expiry of the terms of protection." Art. 18(1).

In 1994, Congress added section 104A to the U.S. Copyright Act to restore copyright in works coming from Berne Union and WTO member countries if copyright had been lost—or never obtained—because of non-compliance with U.S. formalities or lack of a requisite point of attachment. Section 104A automatically restores copyright in any "original work of authorship" that meets three requirements: the work cannot be in the public domain in its source country through expiration of its term of protection there; the work must have at least one author or right holder "who was, at the time the work was created, a national or domiciliary of an eligible country"; and, if the work was published, it must have been "first published in an eligible country and not published in the United States during the 30-day period following publication in such eligible country."

In 2012 the U.S. Supreme Court upheld section 104A against charges that it exceeded congressional power under the Copyright Clause and infringed free speech rights under the First Amendment. Golan v. Holder, 565 U.S. 302 (2012).

See generally Arpad Bogsch, WIPO Views of Article 18, 43 J. Copyr. Soc'y 181 (1995); Irwin Karp, Final Report, Berne Article 18 Study on Retroactive United States Copyright Protection for Berne and Other Works, 20 Colum.-V.L.A. J.L. & Arts 157 (1996).

4. *What Treaty Governs?* Over the course of its several revisions, the Berne Convention has retained some old Union members, lost others and won new ones. (Countries that are already Union members have no obligation to adhere to new texts of the Convention but, under Article 34(1), a new Union member can adhere only to the current text of the treaty.) At one time, it sometimes became necessary to determine which text controlled the obligations between two Union members when the protecting country and the country providing the point of attachment had each adhered to a different text of the Convention, but the TRIPs Agreement's establishment of the 1971 Paris Act as the norm for all WTO members should eliminate this issue over time.

What treaty controls when the protecting country and the country providing the point of attachment have adhered to two or more separate treaties that impose conflicting standards? The Berne Convention is supreme within its domain and Article 20 of the 1971 Paris Text allows members to enter into "special agreements" among themselves only to the extent that these agreements give authors greater rights than those granted by Berne and are not otherwise contrary to Berne. Article XVII(1) of the U.C.C. expressly subordinates U.C.C. obligations to those imposed by Berne but, as a rule, the U.C.C. is otherwise superior within its domain to other copyright treaties; the one exception, carved out in Article XVIII, is that the U.C.C. "[s]hall not abrogate multilateral or bilateral copyright conventions or arrangements that are or may be in effect exclusively between two or more American republics."

3.   PROTECTED SUBJECT MATTER

a.   CLASSES OF SUBJECT MATTER

Berne Convention for the Protection of Literary and Artistic Works, Paris, 1971

Article 2

(1)   The expression "literary and artistic works" shall include every production in the literary, scientific and artistic domain, whatever may be the mode or form of its expression, such as books, pamphlets and other writings; lectures, addresses, sermons and other works of the same nature; dramatic or dramatico-musical works; choreographic works and entertainments in dumb show; musical compositions with or without words; cinematographic works to which are assimilated works expressed by a process analogous to cinematography; works of drawing, painting, architecture, sculpture, engraving and lithography; photographic works to which are assimilated works expressed by a process analogous to photography; works of applied art; illustrations, maps, plans, sketches and three-dimensional works relative to geography, topography, architecture or science.

(2)   It shall, however, be a matter for legislation in the countries of the Union to prescribe that works in general or any specified categories of works shall not be protected unless they have been fixed in some material form.

(3)   Translations, adaptations, arrangements of music and other alterations of a literary or artistic work shall be protected as original works without prejudice to the copyright in the original work.

(4)   It shall be a matter for legislation in the countries of the Union to determine the protection to be granted to official texts of a legislative, administrative and legal nature, and to official translations of such texts.

(5)   Collections of literary or artistic works such as encyclopedias and anthologies which, by reason of the selection and arrangement of their contexts, constitute intellectual creations shall be protected as such, without prejudice to the copyright in each of the works forming part of such collections.

(6)   The works mentioned in this Article shall enjoy protection in all countries of the Union. This protection shall operate for the benefit of the author and his successors in title. *⇒ successors, so forever? no 50 years after death of the author*

(7)   Subject to the provisions of Article 7(4) of this Convention, it shall be a matter for legislation in the countries of the Union to determine the extent of the application of their laws to works of applied art and industrial designs and models, as well as the conditions under which such works, designs and models shall be protected. Works protected in the country of origin solely as designs and models shall be entitled in another country of the Union only to such special protection as is granted in that country to designs and models; however, if no such special protection is granted in that country, such works shall be protected as artistic works.

(8)   The protection of this Convention shall not apply to news of the day or to miscellaneous facts having the character of mere items of press information.

Article 2*bis*

(1)   It shall be a matter for legislation in the countries of the Union to exclude, wholly or in part, from the protection provided by the preceding Article political speeches and speeches delivered in the course of legal proceedings.

(2)   It shall also be a matter for legislation in the countries of the Union to determine the conditions under which lectures, addresses and other works of the same nature which are delivered in public may be reproduced by the press, broadcast, communicated to the public by wire and made the subject of public communication as envisaged in Article 11*bis*(1) of this Convention, when such use is justified by the informatory purpose.

(3)   Nevertheless, the author shall enjoy the exclusive right of making a collection of his works mentioned in the preceding paragraphs.

International Convention for the Protection of Performers, Producers of Phonograms and Broadcasting Organizations (Rome Convention, 1961)

Article 1

Protection granted under this Convention shall leave intact and shall in no way affect the protection of copyright in literary and artistic works. Consequently, no provision of this Convention may be interpreted as prejudicing such protection.

Article 3

For purposes of this Convention:

(a) "Performers" means actors, singers, musicians, dancers, and other persons who act, sing, deliver, declaim, play in, or otherwise perform literary or artistic works;

(b) "Phonogram" means any exclusively aural fixation of sounds of a performance or of other sounds;

(c) "Producer of phonograms" means the person who, or the legal entity which, first fixes the sounds of a performance or other sounds;

(d) "Publication" means the offering of copies of a phonogram to the public in reasonable quantity;

(e) "Reproduction" means the making of a copy or copies of a fixation;

(f) "Broadcasting" means the transmission by wireless means for public reception of sounds or of images and sounds;

(g) "Rebroadcasting" means the simultaneous broadcasting by one broadcasting organisation of the broadcast of another broadcasting organisation.

NOTES

1. *What Is a "Literary" or "Artistic" Work?* According to one authoritative source, the phrase "literary and artistic works" in Article 2(1) of the Berne Paris Act "must be taken as including all works capable of being protected." WIPO, Guide to the Berne Convention for the Protection of Literary and Artistic Works (Paris Act, 1971) 13 (1978). Article 2(1) establishes a floor, not a ceiling, for protectible subject matter, and national courts and legislators have assimilated new forms and content of expression, such as digital code and computer programs, to the general category of literary and artistic works. Berne Union members may disagree on what is a literary or artistic work. For example, the United States Copyright Act protects sound recordings, broadcasts and other fixed performances as copyright subject matter—and presumably literary and artistic works—while many other countries, principally in the civil law world, protect these creations only under neighboring rights. Do the national treatment requirements of the

TRIPs Agreement and the Berne and Universal Copyright Conventions require United States courts to give full copyright protection to sound recordings originating in France, even though France will extend only more limited neighboring rights protection to sound recordings originating in the United States?

2. *Computer Programs.* The United States was the first country to extend copyright to computer programs—the U.S. Copyright Office registered its first computer program in 1964—and was at the head of the international campaign to treat computer programs as literary works within the meaning of the Berne Convention, barring lower level *sui generis* protection. The campaign bore fruit in Article 10(1) of the TRIPs Agreement, providing that computer programs "whether in source or object code shall be protected as literary works under the Berne Convention," and Article 4 of the WIPO Copyright Treaty providing that "[c]omputer programs are protected as literary works within the meaning of Article 2 of the Berne Convention." For a fascinating study of the considerations affecting one nation's choice between copyright and *sui generis* protection for software, see Dennis Karjala, Lessons from the Computer Software Protection Debate in Japan, 1984 Ariz. St. L.J. 53.

What reason would the United States, the world's leading exporter of computer programs, have to insist that software be protected under the Berne Convention rather than under a *sui generis* regime?

In bringing computer programs into copyright, courts and legislators have fitted traditional copyright doctrine to the unique contours of this subject matter. The EC Directive on the Legal Protection of Computer Programs, 2009/24/EC; commonly referred to as the Software Directive, is one example. The Software Directive brings computer programs within the rubric of literary works but carves out exceptions for specified exigent uses of software, including research analysis and decompilation to develop programs that are interoperable with the copyrighted program. According to a report of the European Commission, "[t]he Directive has been used as a model in a significant number of Central and Eastern European States as well as in Hong Kong, the Philippines and Australia," and it "appears to provide a similar scope of protection to that provided in the legislation of the Community's major trading partners." Report from the Commission to the Council, the European Parliament and the Economic and Social Committee on the Implementation and Effects of Directive 91/250/EEC on the Legal Protection of Computer Programs, COM (2000) 199 final at p. 16.

On the history of the Software Directive's evolution, see Bridget Czarnota & Robert Hart, Legal Protection of Computer Programs in Europe: A Guide to the E.C. Directive 3-25 (1991). *See* generally, Handbook of European Software Law (Michael Lehmann & Colin Tapper, eds., 1993).

3. *Newer Forms of Subject Matter.* Historically, copyright subject matter attracts either or both of two human senses, sight and hearing. As a matter of principle or policy, is there a good reason not also to bring within the realm of copyright protection subject matter that appeals to the sense of smell, taste or touch?

Article 10 of the Dutch Copyright Act concludes its non-exhaustive list of protectible works with the phrase, "and in general every product in the field of literature, science or art, in whichever way or in whichever form it has been expressed." In 2006, the Dutch Supreme Court ruled that this catch-all encompassed the scent of a perfume. "This implies that as to the question whether a (particular) scent qualifies for protection under copyright law or not, it is decisive whether this concerns a product which is open to human perception and whether it has an original character and bears the personal imprint of the maker." Lancôme Parfums et Beauté et Cie S.N.C. v. Kecofa B.V., June 16, 2006, Case No. C04/327HR 37 IIC 997 (2006).

Plaintiff Lancôme enjoyed less success against counterfeiters of its Trésor perfume in France, where the high court ruled that fragrances are not copyrightable under the French Intellectual Property Code. Lancôme Parfums et Beauté & Cie v. MX, unreported (Cass (F)), December 10, 2013, 45 IIC 829, 852 (2014) (Theodoros Chiou).

What of taste? In Levola Hengelo BV v. Smilde Foods BV, CJEU, C-310/17, 2018, the Court of Justice of the European Union, on a reference from an intermediate Dutch appellate court, ruled that the 2001 EC Copyright Directive barred protection for the taste of a food product—in this case a spreadable dip containing cream cheese and fresh herbs—since, to be a "work" as referred to in the Directive, "the subject matter protected by copyright must be expressed in a manner which makes it identifiable with sufficient precision and objectivity, even though that expression is not necessarily in permanent form." With an eye to the division between the Dutch and French high courts on the question for fragrances, the Court underlined that "for a uniform interpretation of the concept of a 'work' throughout the European Union, it must also be concluded that Directive 2001/29 prevents national legislation from being interpreted in such a way that it grants copyright protection to the taste of a food product."

See generally Carl Christian von Scholten Illum, On Copyright Protection of Smell, Taste and Texture, 34 EIPR 704 (2014).

4.   *The Idea-Expression Distinction.* The universal precept that copyright protects expression but not ideas reflects the belief that literary and artistic creativity can flourish only if such building blocks as plot and theme, musical notes and harmony, color and perspective remain free for all to use. Article 9(2) of the TRIPs Agreement and Article 2 of the WIPO Copyright Treaty each provide that copyright protection extends to "expressions and not to ideas, procedures, methods of operation or mathematical concepts as such." Article 1(2) of the EC Software Directive applies the same principle to computer programs: "Ideas and principles which underlie any element of a computer program, including those which underlie its interfaces, are not protected by copyright under this Directive."

The Berne Convention nowhere categorically bars protection for ideas, but Article 2(8) provides that "[t]he protection of this Convention shall not apply to the news of the day or to miscellaneous facts having the character of mere items of press information." According to the Records of the 1967 Stockholm Revision Conference, "the Convention does not protect mere items of information on news of the day or miscellaneous facts, because such material does not possess the attributes needed to constitute a work. That implies *a fortiori* that news items or the facts themselves are not protected." II Records of the 1967 Stockholm Revision Conference 1155.

5.   *Official Texts.* National legislatures have taken strikingly different approaches to the question of copyright for official texts, a division reflected in Article 2(4) of the 1971 Berne Paris Text which provides that "[i]t shall be a matter for legislation in the countries of the Union to determine the protection to be granted to official texts of a legislative, administrative and legal nature, and to official translations of such texts."

Article 5(1) of the German Copyright Act withholds protection from "[l]aws, ordinances, official decrees and notices and also decisions and official grounds of decisions." Article 13 of the Japanese Copyright Act denies protection to "the Constitution and other laws and regulations," as well as judicial and administrative decisions. Courts in the United States have long withheld copyright from judicial opinions and legislative enactments. *See* Paul Goldstein 1 Copyright § 2.5.2.1 (2019).

By contrast, British Commonwealth countries employ the concept of Crown and Parliamentary copyright to protect official publications, including governmental reports and legislation, usually subject to generous provision for free use. Professor W.R. Cornish has observed, "[t]he United Kingdom is not a country in which ideas of free access to, and free use of, government information flourish with any vigour. Were this so, there would have developed, as in the United States, much more embracing notions of public domain material in which no copyright may be claimed." W.R. Cornish, Intellectual Property 480 (3rd ed. 1996). *See* also David Vaver, Copyright and the State in Canada and the United States, 10 Int. Prop. J. 187 (1996).

6.   *Formalities.* Until the 1908 Berlin Act of the Berne Convention, national copyright legislation sometimes made protection depend upon compliance with formalities such as registration, deposit and affixation of notice of the author's claim of copyright. However, starting with the 1908 Act, every text of the Convention has provided that "[t]he enjoyment and the exercise" of rights guaranteed by the Convention "shall not be subject to any formality." The prohibition against formalities is presently embodied in Article 5(2) of the Paris Text. Many countries continue to impose some form of deposit or registration requirement, albeit not as a condition to copyright. French law, for example, requires the deposit of copies of works in national repositories, principally the National Museum. Copies of books published in the United Kingdom must be deposited in the British Library. The German Copyright Act provides for a Register of Authors where the author's true name can be filed in the case of anonymous or pseudonymous works. *See* generally Paul Goldstein & Bernt Hugenholtz, International Copyright § 6.1.3.2 (4th ed. 2019).

If affixation of copyright notice is no longer a requirement for protection in countries of the Berne Union, why do copyright owners nonetheless affix notice to copies of their works? *See* Article III(1) of the 1971 Paris Text of the

U.C.C. for one possible answer. Do practical considerations provide another? Would it violate Article 5(2) of the 1971 Berne Paris Act for a Union member to enact legislation requiring all copyright owners to register their claim to ownership every twenty years as a condition to preserving their rights? To preserving certain remedies?

b. THE ORIGINALITY REQUIREMENT

CCH Canadian Ltd. v. Law Society of Upper Canada

Supreme Court of Canada, 2004.
2004 SCC 13, 236 D.L.R. (4th) 395, 317 N.R. 107, 30 C.P.R. (4th) 1.

THE CHIEF JUSTICE:

I.   Introduction—The Issues To Be Determined

1   The appellant, the Law Society of Upper Canada, is a statutory non-profit corporation that has regulated the legal profession in Ontario since 1822. Since 1845, the Law Society has maintained and operated the Great Library at Osgoode Hall in Toronto, a reference and research library with one of the largest collections of legal materials in Canada. The Great Library provides a request-based photocopy service (the "custom photocopy service") for Law Society members, the judiciary and other authorized researchers. Under the custom photocopy service, legal materials are reproduced by Great Library staff and delivered in person, by mail or by facsimile transmission to requesters. The Law Society also maintains self-service photocopiers in the Great Library for use by its patrons.

2   The respondents, CCH Canadian Ltd., Thomson Canada Ltd. and Canada Law Book Inc., publish law reports and other legal materials. In 1993, the respondent publishers commenced copyright infringement actions against the Law Society, seeking a declaration of subsistence and ownership of copyright in eleven specific works and a declaration that the Law Society had infringed copyright when the Great Library reproduced a copy of each of the works. The publishers also sought a permanent injunction prohibiting the Law Society from reproducing these eleven works as well as any other works that they published.

3   The Law Society denied liability and counterclaimed for a declaration that copyright is not infringed when a single copy of a reported decision, case summary, statute, regulation or a limited selection of text from a treatise is made by the Great Library staff or one of its patrons on a self-service photocopier for the purpose of research.

4   The key question that must be answered in this appeal is whether the Law Society has breached copyright by either (1) providing the custom photocopy service in which single copies of the publishers' works are reproduced and sent to patrons upon their request or by (2) maintaining self-service photocopiers and copies of the publishers' works

in the Great Library for use by its patrons. To answer this question, the Court must address the following sub-issues:

> (1) Are the publishers' materials "original works" protected by copyright?
>
> (2) Did the Great Library authorize copyright infringement by maintaining self-service photocopiers and copies of the publishers' works for its patrons' use?
>
> (3) Were the Law Society's dealings with the publishers' works "fair dealing[s]" under s. 29 of the *Copyright Act*, R.S.C. 1985, c. C-42, as amended?
>
> (4) Did Canada Law Book consent to have its works reproduced by the Great Library? . . . .

6   With respect to the main appeal, I conclude that the Law Society did not infringe copyright by providing single copies of the respondent publishers' works to its members through the custom photocopy service. Although the works in question were "original" and thus covered by copyright, the Law Society's dealings with the works were for the purpose of research and were fair dealings within s. 29 of the *Copyright Act*. I also find that the Law Society did not authorize infringement by maintaining self-service photocopiers in the Great Library for use by its patrons. I would therefore allow the appeal. . . .

II.   Analysis on Appeal

8   Copyright law in Canada protects a wide range of works including every original literary, dramatic, musical and artistic work, computer programs, translations and compilations of works: see s. 5 and ss. 2 and 2.1 of the *Copyright Act*. Copyright law protects the expression of ideas in these works; it does not protect ideas in and of themselves. Thorson P. explained it thus in *Moreau v. St. Vincent*, [1950] Ex. C.R. 198 (Can. Ex. Ct.), at p. 203:

> It is, I think, an elementary principle of copyright law that an author has no copyright in ideas but only in his expression of them. The law of copyright does not give him any monopoly in the use of the ideas with which he deals or any property in them, even if they are original. His copyright is confined to the literary work in which he has expressed them. The ideas are public property, the literary work is his own.

It flows from the fact that copyright only protects the expression of ideas that a work must also be in a fixed material form to attract copyright protection. . . .

[handwritten margin note: works "original" but within Copyright Act b/c they're "fair dealings" ⇒ used for research]

(1) Are the Publishers' Materials "Original Works" Covered by Copyright?

(a) The Law

14   Section 5 of the *Copyright Act* states that, in Canada, copyright shall subsist "in every *original* literary, dramatic, musical and artistic work" (emphasis added). Although originality sets the boundaries of copyright law, it is not defined in the *Copyright Act*. Section 2 of the *Copyright Act* defines "every original literary . . . work" as including "every original production in the literary . . . domain, whatever may be the mode or form of its expression". Since copyright protects only the expression or form of ideas, "the originality requirement must apply to the expressive element of the work and not the idea": S. Handa, *Copyright Law in Canada* (2002), at p. 209.

15   There are competing views on the meaning of "original" in copyright law. Some courts have found that a work that originates from an author and is more than a mere copy of a work is sufficient to ground copyright. This approach is consistent with the "sweat of the brow" or "industriousness" standard of originality, which is premised on a natural rights or Lockean theory of "just desserts", namely that an author deserves to have his or her efforts in producing a work rewarded. Other courts have required that a work must be creative to be "original" and thus protected by copyright. See, for example, *Feist Publications Inc. v. Rural Telephone Service Co.* (1991), 499 U.S. 340 (U.S. Kan.); *Tele-Direct (Publications) Inc. v. American Business Information Inc.* (1997), [1998] 2 F.C. 22 (Fed.C.A.). This approach is also consistent with a natural rights theory of property law; however it is less absolute in that only those works that are the product of creativity will be rewarded with copyright protection. It has been suggested that the "creativity" approach to originality helps ensure that copyright protection only extends to the expression of ideas as opposed to the underlying ideas or facts.

16   I conclude that the correct position falls between these extremes. For a work to be "original" within the meaning of the *Copyright Act*, it must be more than a mere copy of another work. At the same time, it need not be creative, in the sense of being novel or unique. What is required to attract copyright protection in the expression of an idea is an exercise of skill and judgment. By skill, I mean the use of one's knowledge, developed aptitude or practised ability in producing the work. By judgment, I mean the use of one's capacity for discernment or ability to form an opinion or evaluation by comparing different possible options in producing the work. This exercise of skill and judgment will necessarily involve intellectual effort. The exercise of skill and judgment required to produce the work must not be so trivial that it could be characterized as a purely mechanical exercise. For example, any skill and judgment that might be involved in simply changing the font of a work to produce "another" work would be too trivial to merit copyright protection as an "original" work.

17   In reaching this conclusion, I have had regard to: (1) the plain meaning of "original"; (2) the history of copyright law; (3) recent jurisprudence; (4) the purpose of the *Copyright Act*; and (5) that this constitutes a workable yet fair standard.

(i)   The Plain Meaning of "Original"

18   The plain meaning of the word "original" suggests at least some intellectual effort, as is necessarily involved in the exercise of skill and judgment. The *Concise Oxford Dictionary* (7th ed. 1982), at p. 720, defines "original" as follows:

> 1. *a*. . . . existing from the first, primitive, innate, initial, earliest; . . . 2. that has served as pattern, of which copy or translation has been made, not derivative or dependant, first-hand, not imitative, novel in character or style, inventive, creative, thinking or acting for oneself.

"Original's" plain meaning implies not just that something is not a copy. It includes, if not creativity *per se*, at least some sort of intellectual effort. As Professor Gervais has noted, "[w]hen used to mean simply that the work must originate from the author, originality is eviscerated of its core meaning. It becomes a synonym of 'originated,' and fails to reflect the ordinary sense of the word": D.J. Gervais, "*Feist* Goes Global: A Comparative Analysis of the Notion of Originality in Copyright Law" (2002), *49 J. Copyright Soc'y U.S.A.* 949, at p. 961.

(ii)   History of Copyright

19   The idea of "intellectual creation" was implicit in the notion of literary or artistic work under the *Berne Convention for the Protection of Literary and Artistic Works* (1886), to which Canada adhered in 1923, and which served as the precursor to Canada's first *Copyright Act*, adopted in 1924. *See* S. Ricketson, *The Berne Convention for the Protection of Literary and Artistic Works: 1886–1986* (1987), at p. 900. Professor Ricketson has indicated that in adopting a sweat of the brow or industriousness approach to deciding what is original, common law countries such as England have "depart[ed] from the spirit, if not the letter, of the [Berne] Convention" since works that have taken time, labour or money to produce but are not truly artistic or literary intellectual creations are accorded copyright protection: Ricketson, *supra*, at p. 901.

20   In the international context, France and other continental civilian jurisdictions require more than mere industriousness to find that a work is original. "Under the French law, originality means both the intellectual contribution of the author and the novel nature of the work as compared with existing works": Handa, *supra*, at p. 211. This understanding of originality is reinforced by the expression "*le droit d'auteur*"—literally the "*author's*" right"—the term used in the French title of the *Copyright Act*. The author must contribute something

intellectual to the work, namely skill and judgment, if it is to be considered original.

(iii) Recent Jurisprudence

21   Although many Canadian courts have adopted a rather low standard of originality, *i.e.*, that of industriousness, more recently, some courts have begun to question whether this standard is appropriate. For example, the Federal Court of Appeal in *Tele-Direct (Publications) Inc.*, *supra*, held, at para. 29, that those cases which had adopted the sweat of the brow approach to originality should not be interpreted as concluding that labour, in and of itself, could ground a finding of originality. As Décary J.A. explained: "If they did, I suggest that their approach was wrong and is irreconcilable with the standards of intellect and creativity that were expressly set out in NAFTA and endorsed in the 1993 amendments to the *Copyright Act* and that were already recognized in Anglo-Canadian law."

22   The United States Supreme Court explicitly rejected the "sweat of the brow" approach to originality in *Feist Publications Inc.*, *supra*. In so doing, O'Connor J. explained at p. 353 that, in her view, the "sweat of the brow" approach was not consistent with the underlying tenets of copyright law:

> The "sweat of the brow" doctrine had numerous flaws, the most glaring being that it extended copyright protection in a compilation beyond selection and arrangement—the compiler's original contributions—to the facts themselves. Under the doctrine, the only defense to infringement was independent creation. A subsequent compiler was "not entitled to take one word of information previously published," but rather had to "independently wor[k] out the matter for himself, so as to arrive at the same result from the same common sources of information." . . . "Sweat of the brow" courts thereby eschewed the most fundamental axiom of copyright law—that no one may copyright facts or ideas.

As this Court recognized in *Compo Co., supra*, at p. 367, U.S. copyright cases may not be easily transferable to Canada given the key differences in the copyright concepts in Canadian and American copyright legislation. This said, in Canada, as in the United States, copyright protection does not extend to facts or ideas but is limited to the expression of ideas. As such, O'Connor's J. concerns about the "sweat of the brow" doctrine's improper extension of copyright over facts also resonate in Canada. I would not, however, go as far as O'Connor J. in requiring that a work possess a minimal degree of creativity to be considered original. *See Feist, supra*, at pp. 345 and 358.

(iv) Purpose of the Copyright Act

23   As mentioned, in *Galerie d'art du Petit Champlain Inc. c. Théberge*, [(2002) 2 S.C.R. 336] this Court stated that the purpose of copyright law

was to balance the public interest in promoting the encouragement and dissemination of works of the arts and intellect and obtaining a just reward for the creator. When courts adopt a standard of originality requiring only that something be more than a mere copy or that someone simply show industriousness to ground copyright in a work, they tip the scale in favour of the author's or creator's rights, at the loss of society's interest in maintaining a robust public domain that could help foster future creative innovation. By way of contrast, when an author must exercise skill and judgment to ground originality in a work, there is a safeguard against the author being overcompensated for his or her work. This helps ensure that there is room for the public domain to flourish as others are able to produce new works by building on the ideas and information contained in the works of others.

(v)   Workable, Yet Fair Standard

24   Requiring that an original work be the product of an exercise of skill and judgment is a workable yet fair standard. The "sweat of the brow" approach to originality is too low a standard. It shifts the balance of copyright protection too far in favour of the owner's rights, and fails to allow copyright to protect the public's interest in maximizing the production and dissemination of intellectual works. On the other hand, the creativity standard of originality is too high. A creativity standard implies that something must be novel or non-obvious—concepts more properly associated with patent law than copyright law. By way of contrast, a standard requiring the exercise of skill and judgment in the production of a work avoids these difficulties and provides a workable and appropriate standard for copyright protection that is consistent with the policy objectives of the *Copyright Act*.

(vi)   Conclusion

25   For these reasons, I conclude that an "original" work under the *Copyright Act* is one that originates from an author and is not copied from another work. That alone, however, is not sufficient to find that something is original. In addition, an original work must be the product of an author's exercise of skill and judgment. The exercise of skill and judgment required to produce the work must not be so trivial that it could be characterized as a purely mechanical exercise. While creative works will by definition be "original" and covered by copyright, creativity is not required to make a work "original".

(b)   Application of the Law to these Facts

26   At trial, the respondent publishers claimed copyright in eleven works: three reported judicial decisions; the three headnotes preceding these decisions; the Annotated *Martin's Ontario Criminal Practice 1999*; a case summary; a topical index; the textbook *Economic Negligence* (1989); and the monograph "Dental Evidence", being chapter 13 in *Forensic Evidence in Canada* (1991). Gibson J. held that the publishers' works should be judged against a standard of intellect and creativity in

order to determine if they were original. Based on this standard of originality, the trial judge found that the publishers only had copyright in the Annotated *Criminal Practice*, the textbook and the monograph. He concluded that the remaining eight works were not original and, therefore, were not covered by copyright.

27 On appeal, the Law Society did not challenge the trial judge's findings with respect to the three works in which he found copyright did exist, with the exception of questioning whether the monograph constituted a "work" within the meaning of the *Copyright Act*. The Federal Court of Appeal adopted the "sweat of the brow" approach to originality and found that if a work was more than a mere copy, it would be original. On this basis, Linden J.A., writing for the majority, held that all of the remaining works were original and therefore covered by copyright. The Law Society appeals, contending that the headnotes, case summary, topical index and reported judicial decisions are not "original" within the meaning of the *Copyright Act* and, therefore, are not covered by copyright.

28 As stated, in order to be original, a work must have originated from the author, not be copied, and must be the product of the exercise of skill and judgment that is more than trivial. Applying this test, all of the works in question are original and therefore covered by copyright.

(i)   Headnotes

29 The Federal Court of Appeal held that "headnotes", defined as including the summary of the case, catchlines, statement of the case, case title and case information, are more than mere copies and hence "original" works in which copyright subsists. It found that the headnotes are more than simply an abridged version of the reasons; they consist of independently composed features. As Linden J.A. explained, the authors of the headnotes could have chosen to make the summaries "long or short, technical or simple, dull or dramatic, well written or confusing; the organization and presentation might have varied greatly".

30 Although headnotes are inspired in large part by the judgment which they summarize and refer to, they are clearly not an identical copy of the reasons. The authors must select specific elements of the decision and can arrange them in numerous different ways. Making these decisions requires the exercise of skill and judgment. The authors must use their knowledge about the law and developed ability to determine legal *ratios* to produce the headnotes. They must also use their capacity for discernment to decide which parts of the judgment warrant inclusion in the headnotes. This process is more than just a mechanical exercise. Thus the headnotes constitute "original" works in which copyright subsists.

(ii) Case Summary

31 For substantially the same reasons as given for headnotes, the case summary is also covered by copyright. A summary of judicial reasons is

not simply a copy of the original reasons. Even if the summary often contains the same language as the judicial reasons, the act of choosing which portions to extract and how to arrange them in the summary requires an exercise of skill and judgment.

(iii) Topical Index

32   The topical index is part of the book *Canada GST Cases* (1997). It provides a listing of cases with short headings to indicate the main topics covered by the decision and very brief summaries of the decisions. The Federal Court of Appeal held that the index was original in that it required skill and effort to compile. I agree. The author of the index had to make an initial decision as to which cases were authorities on GST. This alone is a decision that would require the exercise of skill and judgment. The author also had to decide which headings to include and which cases should fall under which headings. He or she had to distill the essence of the decisions down to a succinct one-phrase summary. All of these tasks require skill and judgment that are sufficient to conclude that the topical index is an "original" work in which copyright subsists.

(iv) Reported Judicial Decisions

33   The reported judicial decisions, when properly understood as a *compilation* of the headnote and the accompanying edited judicial reasons, are "original" works covered by copyright. Copyright protects originality of *form* or expression. A compilation takes existing material and casts it in a different form. The arranger does not have copyright in the individual components. However, the arranger may have copyright in the form represented by the compilation. "It is not the several components that are the subject of copyright, but the over-all arrangement of them which the plaintiff through his industry has produced": *Slumber-Magic Adjustable Bed Co. v. Sleep-King Adjustable Bed Co.* (1984), 3 C.P.R. (3d) 81 (B.C. S.C.), at p. 84.

34   The reported judicial decisions here at issue meet the test for originality. The authors have arranged the case summary, catchlines, case title, case information (the headnotes) and the judicial reasons in a specific manner. The arrangement of these different components requires the exercise of skill and judgment. The compilation, viewed globally, attracts copyright protection.

35   This said, the judicial reasons in and of themselves, without the headnotes, are not original works in which the publishers could claim copyright. The changes made to judicial reasons are relatively trivial; the publishers add only basic factual information about the date of the judgment, the court and the panel hearing the case, counsel for each party, lists of cases, statutes and parallel citations. The publishers also correct minor grammatical errors and spelling mistakes. Any skill and judgment that might be involved in making these minor changes and additions to the judicial reasons are too trivial to warrant copyright protection. The changes and additions are more properly characterized

as a mere mechanical exercise. As such, the reported reasons, when disentangled from the rest of the compilation—namely the headnote—are *not* covered by copyright. It would not be copyright infringement for someone to reproduce only the judicial reasons.

36 In summary, the headnotes, case summary, topical index and compilation of reported judicial decisions are all works that have originated from their authors and are not mere copies. They are the product of the exercise of skill and judgment that is not trivial. As such, they are all "original" works in which copyright subsists. The appeal of these findings should be dismissed.

[The Court's analysis of the liability issues, omitted here, is reproduced beginning at pages 319, 348, below.]

Gerhard Schricker, Farewell to the "Level of Creativity" (Schöpfungshöhe) in German Copyright Law?*

26 International Review of Industrial Property and Copyright Law 41–48 (1995).**

I.   Introduction

The considerations expressed in this article commence from the viewpoint of European copyright law, a law which is becoming increasingly clearly outlined in the Directives of the Union. The issue concerns the concept of the "work." Without providing a general definition of this term, Council Directives do in fact determine individual categories of works. The question arises as to whether the conventional concept of "work" in German law is still appropriate according to European standards in the areas regulated, and, moreover, whether it should not undergo general revision. The critical point at issue is the so-called "level of creativity" *(Schöpfungshöhe).*

II.   Level of Creativity as a Prerequisite for Protection Under German Law

The concept of the level of creativity is a relatively recent one in German copyright law. The emergence of this concept is documented in a report written by Eugen Ulmer on the 1958 Freiburg Conference on Comparative Law, discussing "The Protection of Industrial Design."[1] Ulmer writes: "Just as in patent law one speaks of the 'inventive step' *[Erfindungshöhe]*, it is possible to speak of the level of creativity *[Schöpfungshöhe]*, to use an expression coined by Frau Dr. Meissner. This is a good suggestion, which met with unanimous agreement at the Freiburg Conference."

---

*   Reprinted from International Review of Industrial Property and Copyright Law with permission of the Editors.

**   Translated by Catriona Thomas.

[1]   1959 GRUR Int. 1, 2.

This suggestion made copyright law history. Ulmer adopted the concept of a "level of artistic creativity" into the second edition of his treatise.[2] Subsequently, the concept of the level of originality or creativity was adopted in both literature and case law. Today it is one of the terms employed when one endeavors to clarify the cryptic formula of a "personal intellectual creation," contained in Sec. 2(2) of the German Copyright Act.

In the meantime, however, the role of the criterion for the level of creativity has altered. Ulmer always spoke of the "level of artistic creativity," denoting the degree of artistic achievement required for works of applied art in order to attract copyright protection. If the required level of creativity was not reached, then at the most design protection came into consideration. Thus, the level of creativity represented a concept contributing towards solving the specific problem of drawing a borderline between artistic protection and design protection; the scope of the concept was limited to a specific category of works, namely works of applied art.

However, in later teaching and practice this concept became generalized. Without much discussion, the "standard of the necessary level of creativity" is now applied to all kinds of works in order to answer the question whether the degree of individuality in the work is sufficient to qualify for copyright protection. "A work must ... rise above craftsmanship, above the average, by means of a certain level of creativity;"[3] here the level of creativity as the "minimum level of intellectual-creative achievement" is combined with individuality as the latter's "quantitative aspect."[4]

Transposing the concept of the level of creativity from its original field of application to other categories of works engendered far-reaching consequences. In the area of works of applied art, the postulate of the level of creativity entailed a reduction of copyright protection as a result of stricter requirements regarding artistic achievement. From a systematic viewpoint, this stricter treatment is justified by referring to the safety net offered by design protection for minor creations.

Generalizing the concept of the level of creativity has opened the gate for the introduction of stricter standards in relation to other categories of works as well, apparently without a similar systematic cause. Some authors have simply established higher standards for all works. The most obvious example of such "stricter requirements" can be found in the commentary by von Gamm. According to his suggested "gradual scale," the "ability of an average creator" remains unprotected.

---

[2]   "Urheber-und Verlagsrecht" 131, on Sec. 25 11 2c (2d ed. 1960), and in the 3d ed. at 150, on Sec. 25 1114. The term does not appear in the first edition; here only a "difference in degree" is mentioned, at 92, Sec. 19 11 lb.

[3]   Hubmann & Rehbinder, "Urheber-und Verlagsrecht, Kommentar" 83, Sec. 12 II 3a (7th ed.).

[4]   See Loewenheim, in: Schricker, "Urheberrecht. Kommentar," point 16, Sec. 2.

Creative achievement above this standard qualifies for design protection; it is "at a considerable distance that the lowest level of copyrightability starts."[5]

The German Federal Supreme Court applied these "strict standards" to a somewhat incomprehensible selection of individual, but not to all, categories of works. The greatest upheaval was prompted by the requirement of "considerably surpassing the average," applied in relation to computer programs.[6] In addition, other scientific works of literature were subjected to this wording, whereas, strangely enough, in relation to scientific-technical illustrations the traditionally "low requirements" as regards originality continue to apply.

The limitation of copyright protection in respect of certain scientific works currently manifesting itself in case law and legal literature has proved to be misguided. In the case of computer programs, European harmonization of laws has compelled reconsideration of the issue. Yet in relation to other scientific works as well, in recent practice the phrase, "considerably surpass the average," has correctly been avoided. The words "according to the circumstances involved, a lower level of intellectual activity can suffice" indicate that protection of so-called "small change" has regained recognition. Protection of "small change" under copyright was never called into doubt in other areas, in particular in music and in the area of cinematographic works.

III. Prerequisites for Protection Under European Law

The level of creativity is a concept based in German copyright law. Without embarking on a detailed comparative discussion, it can be said that a similar, general criterion is not common in the laws of other European states.[7] For the most part, the field is governed by the concepts of individuality, which can be regarded as congruent, or at least as overlapping to a large extent. In some laws explicit emphasis is placed on the fact that protection should be independent of the value of the work.[8] This results in the "generous grant of copyright protection where only minimal creative achievement is involved."[9] Copyright protection is not only accorded to elitist creations, but benefits the whole breadth of

---

[5]   Von Gamm, Urheberrecht, Kommentar at 181, point 16, Sec. 2.

[6]   Federal Supreme Court decision, 1985 GRUR 1041, 1048.

[7]   In Austrian law the "quality of the work" can be found as regards works of fine art. *See* Dittrich. "Urheberrecht, Kommentar," Sec. 1 E 14 (2d ed., Vol. 1). On the reaction to the "level of creativity" in Swedish literature. *see* Strömholm, 1989 GRUR Int. 15, 16. An express rejection in relation to the level of creativity in German law is Troller, "Immaterialgüterrecht" 367, Vol. 1, Chap. 6, Sec. 19 VI 2 (3d ed. Vol. 1): individuality was deemed sufficient.

[8]   *See* on Art. 2 of the French Law of 1957, Dreier, in: "Quellen des Urheberrechts, Frankreich I" 6 *et seq.* for Portugal, Art. 2 No. 1 of the Law of 1985, *see* "Quellen des Urheberrechts, Portugal II"; for Switzerland, *see* Art. 2(1) of the Act of 1992, 1993 GRUR Int. 149.

[9]   According to the comparative resumé provided by Dietz, "Das Urheberrecht in der Europäischen Gemeinschaft" 62. Dietz argues in favor of raising the standard protection, excluding so-called "small change," which would enjoy special protection, *see op. cit.* at 62, 65 *et. seq.*

individual creative activity in literature, science and the arts. Hence, the foundation of economic development is guaranteed for the authors and users working in the relevant professional branches; copyright law is not only cultural law, but also economic law.

This approach is confirmed in the current harmonization of copyright law within the European Union. In particular, the Directive on the Legal Protection of Computer Programs of 1991[10] rejects the restrictive position adopted by the German Federal Supreme Court, which postulated a level of creativity lying considerably above an average achievement: "in respect of the criteria to be applied in determining whether or not a computer program is an original work, no tests as to the qualitative or aesthetic merits of the program should be applied."[11] Consequently, Art. 1(3) of the Directive states: "A computer program shall be protected if it is original in the sense that it is the author's own intellectual creation. No other criteria shall be applied to determine its eligibility for protection."

Section 69(a) of the German Copyright Act, enacted in order to implement the Directive, repeats this wording and also adds the exclusion of the qualitative and aesthetic criteria mentioned in the Recitals of the Directive. The previous case law handed down by the Federal Supreme Court is thus "clearly rejected;" it is established that the "small change" in the field of computer programs also enjoys protection. "Simple individuality" will suffice in order to enjoy protection.

The Directive on the Harmonization of the term of copyright protection and certain related rights of 1993[12] lays down the requirements of protection for photographs correspondingly: "Photographs which are original in the sense that they are the author's own intellectual creation shall be protected in accordance with Article 1. No other criteria shall be applied to determine their eligibility for protection. Member States may provide for the protection of other photographs" (Art. 6).

The manner in which the provision is constructed makes it clear that the possibility of introducing related rights' protection for simple photographs, as indicated in the last sentence, does not alter the fact that protection under copyright law requires individuality and nothing else. Hence, the existence of related rights' protection for simple photographs, cannot serve as an excuse to introduce the requirement of a level of originality for protection of photographic works.[13]

Finally, the draft Database Directive of 1992[14] includes a similar definition for protection of databases under copyright law, in defense

---

[10]   1991 GRUR Int. 545.

[11]   According to the Recitals.

[12]   1994 GRUR Int. 141, OJ EC L 290/12 (24 November 1993).

[13]   Consequently, in German law protection of photographic works pursuant to Sec. 2(*l*)(5), Copyright Act, can no longer be dependent on the level of creativity so frequently postulated.

[14]   1992 GRUR Int. 759.

against additional protection prerequisites. Article 2(3) of the draft Directive provides:

> A database shall be protected by copyright if it is original in the sense that it is a collection of works or material which, by reason of their selection or their arrangement, constitutes the author's own intellectual creation. No other criteria shall be applied to determine the eligibility of a database for this protection.

Computer programs, photographic works, databases—the copyright concept of a work is gradually being harmonized from the outer borders and thus removed from the criterion of the level of creativity. It is hard to imagine that this process will be discontinued. The principle of equal treatment of all categories of works in copyright law would appear to contradict the idea that higher barriers could be erected for individual kinds of work. Where such generous protection is granted in marginal regions of copyright, it will be impossible to be more persnickety in the focal areas of the arts and literature. It remains to be seen whether individuality or originality will constitute the primary criterion; however, no room will remain for a "level of creativity."

IV. Implications for German Law

The above discussion has shown that the concept of the level of creativity derived from the protection of applied arts, where it is at the most worthy of consideration, and that in the process of conceptual analogy it was transferred to other categories of works and was pronounced, without further reflection, to be the central criterion of copyrightability. Viewed from the perspective of comparative law, the "level of creativity" appears to be a dubious construction of German law; European harmonization of laws precludes this prerequisite of protection for a growing number of types of work.

The German Copyright Act of 1965 does not contain any indication of a criterion of the level of creativity. The explanatory report on the Act explicitly rejects the suggestion of requiring "a creation of individual character" in order to attract protection, because this could lead to the conclusion that works of minor creative merit would not enjoy protection in future; "such an alteration in relation to the law currently in force is not intended."[15]

Today, the production and utilization of copyrighted works is focused mainly on creations of a rather modest level. This holds true for the field of music and for the written word, in particular for the press, as well as for radio and television broadcasting. To exclude "small change" from protection would result in a considerable reduction in substance in the field of copyright. From an economic point of view, only a significantly reduced number of items would remain; important sectors of the copyright industries would be deprived of their foundations. Even if "small change" were compensated with the grant of a neighboring right,

---

[15]   Published in M. Schulze, "Materialien zum Urheberrechtsgesetz" 86 (1993).

it would be dropped from the protection system provided by international conventions. The separation of "small change" from the core of copyright would create new problems, resulting in an enormous burden for the collecting societies.

The lengthy 70-year term of protection p.m.a. [*post mortem auctoris*], often used as an argument against protection of "small change," frequently runs dry in relation to higher ranking creations as well. In practice, moral rights are invoked extremely rarely. They are an essential part of copyright protection, but the latter cannot depend upon the extent to which the rights are required in practice. These arguments have often been voiced and discussed. In summary, it can be said that proposals to raise the minimum protection level in copyright from "small change" up to the level of more respectable cultural goods reveals an idealism that is indeed laudable, but not very realistic. Today, such a step would soon be countered by an EU Directive on the reintroduction of a modest standard of protection throughout the Union.

Yet if the decision is made to retain protection of "small change," then the criterion of the level of creativity as a general prerequisite for protection can be thrown overboard: individuality is decisive. Individuality represents a criterion of evaluation and can as such distinguish between everyday, routine production and a minimum of individual character, at which stage the work attracts protection. In this respect the *"de minimis non curat praetor"* is inherent in the criterion of individuality and distinguishes itself from mere statistical uniqueness. For qualification as a work, the additional criterion of a certain level of creativity is not necessary. Such a criterion entails the risk of missing the point and indicates a tendency towards raising the standard of protection, a tendency that is unjustified both *de lege lata* and *de lege ferenda*.

Consequently, it is clear that the level of creativity should be pushed back into the area where it originated: the issue of the protection of applied art. This article does not leave enough scope to discuss the demand for a "significantly higher" standard in this field; yet obvious reservations do exist. The terminological parallels made to patent law, where there is a different, competitive emphasis, are hardly convincing from an objective point of view. Yet harmonization of European design law could, although the relationship to copyright were left aside during this process, lead to a reform of the systematic argument in the copyright protection of applied art and to a lasting farewell to the level of creativity.

NOTES

1. *Originality or Creativity?* Collections of fact such as telephone directories and price lists have long presented a special challenge to intellectual property lawmakers. Should protection for these compilations of data, often gathered and created at considerable expense, be brought under copyright law (and, consequently, the Berne Convention) or unfair

competition doctrine (the Paris Convention), or should it be made the subject of *sui generis* legislation? Since national treatment will be required in the first two cases, but not the third, the choice of legal regimes has important implications for a country's balance of intellectual trade.

It is one of the ironies of international copyright law that at the same time continental countries were—as described in the excerpt from the Schricker article—turning away from a rigorous showing of creativity as a condition to copyright protection for borderline works, courts in the common law world, such as the Canadian Supreme Court in *CCH Canadian*, were systematically approximating the creativity measure, or a variant, for the first time. Similarly, the United States Supreme Court ruled in *Feist Publications, Inc. v. Rural Telephone Service Co.*, 499 U.S. 340, 345 (1991), that alphabetized telephone directory white pages were uncopyrightable, observing that, to be protected, a work must possess "at least some minimal degree of creativity." The court added that the requisite level of creativity is extremely low; "even a small amount will suffice." Because electronic databases will typically entail substantial selection, arrangement and coordination of facts, most if not all such databases will probably meet this modest standard.

Differences among national copyright thresholds are probably more notional than real. Notwithstanding the protestations of the *CCH* Court to the contrary, it is hard to find a substantive difference between the standard adopted there and the one adopted by the U.S. Supreme Court in *Feist*. Standards in fact appear to be barometers more than they are thresholds, reflecting current attitudes towards copyright's proper domain. Starting in 2009, the Court of Justice of the European Union returned copyright in Europe to its earlier, higher standard, holding that, for a work to be protected, it must embody the "author's own intellectual creation." Infopaq Int'l v. Danske Dagblades Forening, ECJ, C-5/08, 2009.

For a penetrating overview of originality standards around the world, see William W. Fisher III, Recalibrating Originality, 54 Houston L. Rev. 437 (2016).

2. *Database Protection.* The 1996 EC Database Directive, 96/9/EC, seeks to rationalize European protection for collections of data by establishing two tiers of protection. Chapter II of the Directive sets the terms for copyright protection of databases, providing that "databases which, by reason of the selection or arrangement of their contents, constitute the author's own intellectual creation shall be protected as such by copyright," and adding that copyright protection for databases "shall not extend to their contents." Art. 3(1), (2). (Article 5 of the WIPO Copyright Treaty substantially parallels this formulation, as does Article 10(2) of the TRIPs Agreement.)

For the *contents* of databases, Chapter III establishes a *sui generis* right "for the maker of a database which shows that there has been qualitatively and/or quantitatively a substantial investment in either the obtaining, verification or presentation of the contents to prevent extraction and/or re-utilization of the whole or of a substantial part, evaluated qualitatively and/or quantitatively, of the contents of that database." Art. 7(1). Chapter

III permits prescribed exceptions from the right and provides for a fifteen-year term of protection.

In Football Dataco v. Yahoo! UK Ltd., CJEU, C-604/10, 2012, plaintiff claimed that defendants' unauthorized use of its English and Scottish football league schedules infringed both its copyright in the lists under Article 3 of the Database Directive, and its *sui generis* database rights under Article 7. The Court of Justice of the European Union ruled that the "selection and arrangement" required by Chapter II's copyright tier means the "selection and the arrangement of data through which the author of the database gives the database its structure"; this standard is "not satisfied when the setting up of the database is dictated by technical considerations, rules or constraints which leave no room for creative freedom." Further, the Directive precludes national legislation granting copyright protection to databases other than on these limited terms.

Unlike Chapter II, which falls under the Berne Convention and that treaty's requirement of national treatment, Chapter III restricts protection for non-EU nationals or domiciliaries, other than those that maintain active businesses within the EU, to international arrangements "concluded by the Council acting on a proposal from the Commission." EC Database Directive Art. 11. If the rights granted under Chapter III were viewed as akin to those given by unfair competition law, would this provision violate the Paris Convention's national treatment obligation? The most-favored-nation requirement of the TRIPs Agreement?

See generally, Estelle Derclaye, The Legal Protection of Databases: A Comparative Analysis (2008); Eleonora Rosati, Originality in a Work, or a Work of Originality: The Effects of the *Infopaq* Decision, 33 EIPR. 746 (2011); Guido Westkamp, Protecting Databases Under U.S. and European Law— Methodical Approaches to the Protection of Investments Between Unfair Competition and Intellectual Property Concepts, 34 IIC 772 (2003). *See* also Mark J. Davison & P. Bernt Hugenholtz, Football Fixtures, Horseraces and Spin Offs: The ECJ Domesticates the Database Right, 27 EIPR 113 (2005).

4. OWNERSHIP AND TERM

Paul Geller, Worldwide "Chain of Title" to Copyright*

4 World Intellectual Property Report 103–107 (1990).

Who may exploit copyright in a work? Monies earned from the work in markets around the world could turn on this question. Due diligence in checking title to copyright internationally requires a reasonably systematic answer.

The image of a chain of title, at first blush, seems applicable to copyright in the United States. Section 201 of the U.S. Copyright Act

---

spells out in whom U.S. copyright initially vests, and section 205 refers to the priority of recordation in the U.S. Copyright Office in governing the priority of transfers of U.S. copyright subsequent to vesting. But the law regarding the initial vesting and subsequent transfer of copyright is far from uniform worldwide, and the United States is among a minority of jurisdictions with public recording systems specifically designed for copyright transfers.

By force of habit, we may continue to speak in terms of a "chain of title," but subject to a number of caveats. Most importantly, we borrow the image of a "chain" from real property, but it rather oversimplifies what happens to "title" in copyright worldwide. Title to real property pertains to but one tangible thing fixed in space and, normally, is governed by the law of the place where the property is located. But any work in which copyright can be vested and transferred is likely to be disseminated worldwide, sometimes at the speed of light. And a variety of laws may affect entitlement in that work in the course of its travels.

Thus the question of chain of title to copyright in a work worldwide largely turns on issues that cannot be decided without answering threshold questions concerning the choice of law. This article will briefly outline the full range of these issues and indicate the most important of these conflicts questions.

1. What Rights, If Any, Are In Effect?

If a work is in the public domain in a country, the question of who owns rights to exploit it there is moot. But, if it is protected, the law and treaties of the country will tell us what rights are available there, that is, to what rights there may be entitlement.

Analysis at this point has to proceed country by country for the simple reason that copyright is territorial. Territoriality means that the law of each national jurisdiction where the work is to be used—including all the treaty obligations of that country—governs the rights available in the work there. Thus, for example, most works first published in the Soviet Union before 1973 will be in the public domain in most of the world since the laws of most countries did not include any copyright treaty with the Soviet Union until it joined the Universal Copyright Convention (UCC) on May 27, 1973. The situation may be far more complex for older works originating in the United States because most countries have protected U.S. works under a variety of treaties and like arrangements in the course of the last hundred years.

Two different cases involving the same works, silent film classics of Buster Keaton published in the United States, illustrate just how closely protection depends on the law and treaties of the country where protection is sought. In the Federal Republic of Germany, protecting U.S. works under a bilateral copyright agreement since 1893 and the UCC since 1955, Keaton's film works were protected even though they had fallen into the public domain in the United States before the time of

German infringement.[1] Thus, in the Federal Republic, as a result of the combined effect of both the earlier and later treaty, the rights available in Keaton's works included the full panoply of rights a German author could have exercised in comparable works. In France, however, where only the UCC came into play, Keaton's works had fallen into the public domain prior to suit.[2]

Thus, to determine whether a work originating in one country is protected in another country, and to what extent it is protected there, it is necessary to see whether it satisfies the conditions of the domestic law or treaty obligations of that country. Most works created by U.S nationals or first published in the U.S.A. today, for example, are either protected abroad on the grounds of reciprocal domestic provisions or, in most countries, by virtue of at least one of a number of treaties. In particular, in most countries, including the USA since March 1, 1989 the dispositive treaty for protecting works of foreign origin will be one of the Acts of the Berne Convention.

Just as copyright arises in a work under the laws and treaties of each country where it is exploited, these laws may affect title to that copyright in a variety of ways. These ways will now be considered.

2.   Is Presumptive Title to the Rights Sufficient?

Once we know copyright in a work exists in a given country, we may then ask: for what purposes is chain of title to copyright needed there? It will sometimes not be necessary to provide as complete a showing of title to obtain standing to assert copyright in court as for other purposes, notably profiting from copyright uses.

For example, Article 15 of the Berne Convention establishes minimum rights to standing in terms of certain presumptions. If a work is protected under the Berne Convention, Article 15 allows the person named on the work in customary fashion as its author, absent proof to the contrary, to bring suit for infringement. Similarly where the author is not so named, as on an anonymous work, Article 15 allows the publisher, presumptively that named on the work, to commence an infringement suit and to represent the author's interests in that suit. Although, as explained below, the meaning of the term author may not always be clear in international copyright, Article 15 has been liberally construed to allow for standing in less than clear cases. On the same reasoning, the usual credits on a motion picture could be argued to include all of the possible authors of the work among the contributors they mentioned.

---

[1]   The Buster Keaton decision, Bundesgerichtshof, Jan. 27, 1978. Case no. I ZR 97/76. 1979 Gewerblicher Rechtschutz und Urheberrecht (GRUR)-Internationaler Teil 50, in English translation in 10 International Review of Industrial Property and Copyright Law (IIC) 358 (1979).

[2]   S.A. Galba Films c. M. Friedman, Cour d'appel. Paris, Ire ch., April 24, 1974. 83 Revue internationale du droit d'auteur (RIDA) 126 (19975), in English translation in 7 IIC 130 (1976), aff'd,.Cbss. civ., Ire ch., Dec 15,1975, 88 RIDA 115 (1976).

But what if the exploiting or suing party is not the "author" or "publisher" named on a work? More precisely, should a party claiming copyright by virtue of a contract with the named author or publisher benefit from a presumption of standing akin to theirs? The Berne Convention does not directly answer this question, and it becomes even more of an open issue where the Berne Convention is not invoked to protect the work in question. Answering it in the negative, the British High Court, Chancery Division, seemed to require a contractual claimant to make proof through every "link" of its chain of title in order to bring a civil infringement suit.[3] By contrast, the Argentine Supreme Court allowed a party, which sought protection under the U.C.C. and based its entitlement on contract, to have a criminal infringement action prosecuted upon a showing of title to the work at issue that merely withstood any attempt at rebuttal.[4]

Similarly, some national laws will sometimes authorize a collecting society to collect royalties without its necessarily having an authorization, much less a formal assignment for the purposes of collection, from every claimant ultimately entitled to pocket these royalties. Nonetheless, the High Court of Austria reasoned that the international treaties entitling foreign authors to royalties in Austria, while allowing a national statute to empower a domestic society to collect such royalties, precluded it from authorizing that society to use foreign claimants' royalties for the benefit of their domestic members.[5] Accordingly, proof of "adequate" title for purposes of establishing standing to sue or to collect royalties on behalf of copyright claimants, on the one hand, is not necessarily tantamount to establishing an entitlement to dispose of monies from copyright uses, on the other.

We now have to turn to analyzing chain of title in that latter, more absolute sense of who gets the money. Here, the image of a chain may be more appropriate in that we can proceed from a starting point, the initial vestees of rights in a work, and follow out the fate of those rights through a series of transfers.

3.   In Whom Do Rights Initially Vest?

The starting point for chains of title in any one work will not necessarily be the same for all purposes worldwide. In some cases, the same work might start with different holders of rights in different countries, depending on what law defines "author" or specifies other

---

[3]   Columbia Pictures Industries v. Robinson (1986) Fleet Street Reports 367, 378. The High Court also noted that "pirates may justifiably have some optimism that, if challenged, their challenger will fail to establish its copyright title." Id. One might well question this approach to standing to the extent its effect is to encourage piracy.

[4]   In re S.A. Editorial Noguer, S.C.J.N., May 16, 1962. Fallos 252. This approach would seem more appropriate at least where it is a matter of stopping piracy on the spot, a goal supported by public policy, or where defendant's interests may be protected by conditioning plaintiff's preliminary relief on the posting of a bond.

[5]   The Einbehaltungsverpflichtung decision, Obersten Gerichtshof, July 14, 1987, Case no. 4 Ob 361/86, 1988 GRUR Int.365.

initial holders of right in each country. To some extent, contractual arrangements can nonetheless anchor chains of title in the same party worldwide.

For example, in both the United States and the Federal Republic of Germany, copyright initially vests in authors, However, the U.S. definition of the "author" of so-called works for hire easily includes corporate employers, while the West German definition of "author" is limited to natural persons. French law, as a matter of principle, only considers each of the flesh-and-blood creators of a work as an "author"; at the same time, it exceptionally vests copyright in the possibly corporate editor or publisher of a so-called collective work, defining such a work by the very difficulty of attributing authorship of its entirety to those natural persons who contribute to its creation.

Nonetheless, in the case in which one natural person authors a work outside any master-servant relationship, all possibly applicable laws will initially vest copyright in that author. Thus only beyond that classic case, most often in cases of works for hire, collective works, joint and team works, especially audiovisual works, and software, will the problem of choosing the law to govern the initial vesting of rights arise. As a rule of thumb, expect judges, if they apply the principle of national treatment set out in international copyright treaties, to be prone to apply the definition of "author" effective for domestic works in the country where copyright is used. But that rule of thumb is not a rule of law, nor do the international treaties or national authorities uniformly establish any clear-cut conflicts rule to control the choice of varying definitions of "author" or other initial holders of rights in a given case. Indeed, there is dispute concerning the Berne Convention, some commentators insisting that the Convention text only allows for recognizing flesh-and-blood authors, not corporate authors of works for hire.

Fortunately, it is often possible to short-circuit such uncertainty, by using proper contracts with all those parties who contribute to the original creation of a work. Consider a feature film created by a team of contributors. Assume that all the members of the team and their principals work under written agreements, some of them as employees and some as independent contractors. These contracts, as the source of the work, may clearly allocate to one party whatever rights of economic exploitation will vest in all the potentially creative contributors as their principals and, therefore, in all possible "authors" and other initial holders of rights by whatever copyright law applies. If these contracts are enforced to the letter, even economic rights variably vested from one country to another will either at once vest in, or be transferred to, a single party, effectively anchoring chain of title in that party.

It may be desirable, in appropriate cases, in order to avoid the effect of the provisions allowing for terminating transfers as to U.S. rights, to use work-for-hire language relative to U.S. rights and comparable language in jurisdictions where such reversion similarly occurs. It may be preferable to consider using irrevocable transfer for rights, which by law, including article 14bis(2)(a) of the Paris Act of the Berne Convention, may vest in different parties in different protecting countries. Article 14bis(2)(a), however, should not be relied upon in lieu of written contracts allocating rights specifically in film works.

Optimally, the contracts relative to our hypothetical feature film will all have the same choice-of-law clause. In the case of foreign coproductions, where the factors bearing on the choice of law are likely to point toward a variety of jurisdictions, the need for choosing the same law to the effect of all such contracts is all the more acute.

Even with the same, enforceable choice-of-law clause, however, the contracts are not sure to have the same law, that spelled out as chosen by the parties, govern their effect on all points. This possibility brings us to the next phase of inquiry into chain of title: the effect of any contract purporting to transfer title.

4.   Do Any Contracts Transfer Title?

How are we to know which rules of law govern the enforcement of a given copyright contract? Consider any one contract which purports to transfer copyright worldwide in a feature film made in the United States. When, if at all, will U.S. copyright rules, most notably those allowing termination of transfers or vesting rights in works for hire, come into play? Or, for example, will French rules against the alienation of moral rights restrict the transferee's options for adapting the film work for French shows? Suppose that the contract includes a clause stating that California law is to govern its effect. To what extent will California contract rules then apply?

Any contract purporting to transfer copyright may be subject to two different types of choice-of-law approaches. On the one hand, the copyright treaties for the most part require country-by-country application of the law of each country where rights are exploited. On the other hand, contracts are usually subject to the contract rules of the law freely chosen by the parties, that is, the law which the parties decide to write into their agreement as governing it. To avoid a larger conflict between these different choice-of-law approaches, a judge may employ the method of analysis called "problem selection" or *depecage* of issues, which allows different rules drawn from different laws to dispose of different issues raised as regards the same contract. Thus, in the case of a copyright contract, possibly subject to copyright and contract laws at the same time, such analysis would disentangle the issues on which copyright rules should be dispositive and those which contract rules should govern.

An English case illustrates such analysis.[6] There the court had to decide what law disposed of the issue: could an assignment of "the full copyright for all countries" in a song effectively convey U.S. renewal

---

[6]   Campbell Connelly & Co., Ltd. v. Noble (1963) 1 Weekly Law Reports 252.

copyright? The court immediately referred to U.S. law to ascertain "the precise nature of that to which it [the contract] is claimed to apply," since that law would establish whether U.S. renewal copyright by definition was susceptible of transfer at all. The fact that the court held U.S. law, that of the country defining the right in question, to be dispositive of the assignability of that right contrasted with its finding that the "agreement was a purely English contract and must be interpreted according to English law."[7] However, in the law which superseded that of U.S. renewal copyright after 1976, there are rules allowing an author to terminate transfers: these rules, by their statutory definition cannot be contractually waived or transferred. Here the statute makes clear that, as purely copyright rules, they only affect a contract insofar as it transfers U.S. copyright and may not be invoked against that contract insofar as it transfers foreign rights. Contracts rules, for example, governing construction, would apply to that contract irrespective of the rights it transferred.

One issue, in particular, can be critical to chain of title: where different third parties claim to benefit, respectively, from different conveyances which purport to transfer to each of these parties the same rights to exploit the same work, which party's claims will prevail? The most authoritative commentators conclude that each protecting country is free to fashion a rule of priority effective within its national territory in accord with its perception of interests in regulating copyright commerce within that territory. Jurisdictions such as the United States might and do choose to maintain systems of recordation because their territories are so large, and copyright commerce so multifarious within national borders, that only recordation, rather than common knowledge within the local trade, will protect third parties acquiring rights. Other jurisdictions, however, apply the rule that the first transfer in time prevails over all subsequent transfers, so that recordation simply provides evidence of which transfer was made first. The law of each country thus has to be consulted to follow out chain of title in this regard.

Throughout the best of all possible worlds there would be but one system for assuring chain of title to copyright. The film industry has begun to move toward this goal in providing for national recordation systems where none existed before and in contemplating an international recordation system. Under the auspices of the World Intellectual Property Organization, a Treaty to establish a proposed International Register of Audiovisual Works was concluded on April 20, 1989: its Article 4(*l*) would have adhering countries deem statements recorded in the International Register to be true until proof to the contrary. It should be noted that such recognition may well be decisive for jurisdictions which give priority domestically to the first transfer in real time, assuming that any presumption of a specific date of transfer raised by international recordation is not rebutted. But it need not in itself have

---

7   Id. at 255.

legal effect against a local recordation to the extent a jurisdiction deems the priority of transfers to be domestically secured only by actually recording them in the national system.

The commentators also reach some consensus to the effect that rules of form, notably rules requiring copyright transfers to be in writing, are contract rules. Thus, in one much-cited French case, a copyright conveyance in conformity with U.S., not French, requirements of form, but concluded in France, was nonetheless held to be contractually valid, ostensibly on the premise that the parties had chosen U.S. law to govern it as a contract.[8] It is, however, less certain that rules of construction requiring contractual language to make express mention of each right to be transferred, or rules precluding rights for unknown media from being transferred, will be considered as mere contract rules.

The situation regarding the contractual waiver of moral rights is still less settled. The case law is even conflicted in France where, in article 6 of the French Copyright Law of March 11, 1957, such rights are categorically declared to be "inalienable." Indeed, the Court of Cassation, the highest court of appeal for private cases in France, may soon have to deal with at least one of the ostensibly conflicting responses which lower courts have given to the question: should a waiver of moral rights be enforced in France when it is contractually valid under foreign contract law?[9]

5.   Has There Been Any Transfer By Law?

Various kinds of laws can effectuate transfers of copyright to third parties without any intervening contractual or like relation. Such laws include laws governing the allocation of assets in marriage, laws governing the attachment of assets by creditors, and inheritance laws. Unfortunately, there is no uniform and clearcut set of choice-of-law rules to govern how such laws might apply to copyright interests worldwide. The best that can be done here is to raise some typical issues.

In California, one court has deemed copyright to fall within the marital community but, only focusing on U.S. copyright, did not make clear whether it covered foreign as well as U.S. copyright.[10] Seminal case law in France held copyright to fall outside the marital community only insofar as the author's moral rights included within French copyright are not property interests, thus allowing French courts to subject the economic value of copyright in a work, notably eventual proceeds from

---

[8]   Ste'Les Films Richebe' c. Ste' Roy Export Charlie Chaplin, Cass. civ., Ire ch., May 28, 1963, 41 RIDA 134 (1963).

[9]   Compare Bragance c. Michel de Grece, Cour d'appel, Paris, Ire ch., I February 1989, 142 RIDA 301 (1989) (contract, validly subject to U. S. contract law, held ineffective to waive French moral right, notably the right to credit for authorship), with La Cinq c. Huston, Cour d'appel, Paris, 4e ch., 6 July 1989, Gazette du Palais, 29 Sept. 1989 (such a waiver enforced to allow French telecast of a colorized Asphalt Jungle in the face of the right to integrity). See also supra note 17.

[10]   In re Marriage of Worth, 195 Cal. App. 3d 768, 241 Cal Rptr. 135, 136, 139–140 (1987) (only the preemption issue, peculiar to U.S. copyright, decided).

exploitation or damages for infringement, to community allocation.[11] Whether including foreign copyrights within the marital community involves a possible conflict with foreign copyright laws may thus depend on what the order in a case actually says. If it merely divides up monies actually or potentially earned from copyright exploitation abroad, there may be no real conflict of laws to resolve. The same reasoning might be extended to including foreign rights within a debtor author's estate.

Conclusion

In tracing chain of title to copyright worldwide, three points should be kept in mind. To begin with, if the work in question has fallen into the public domain where it is to be used, the question of title is moot. Further, if it is a matter of simply asserting copyright, for example, to combat piracy, there are arguments that in some cases presumptive title should suffice. Finally, where it is a matter of exploiting copyright in a country, choice-of-law questions may arise both at the starting point of, and at each link in, the chain of title to rights exercisable in that country.

a.   WHO IS AN AUTHOR?

Adolf Dietz, The Concept of Author Under the Berne Convention

155 Revue Internationale du Droit d' Auteur 2–10 (1993).

In pursuance of decisions taken by its Governing Bodies, the World Intellectual Property Organization (WIPO) has set itself the target of proposing "Model Provisions for Legislation in the Field of Copyright" which are intended to make the protection of intellectual property more effective throughout the world. A Committee of Experts was set up to this end and has already held three sessions (February/March 1989, November 1989 and July 1990) to discuss WIPO's proposals and comments.

One of the controversial issues which gave rise to impassioned debates at the sessions of the Committee of Experts was the definition of the concept of "author". Although the Model Provisions are based explicitly on the letter and spirit of the Berne Convention for the Protection of Literary and Artistic Works (hereinafter "Berne Convention") as last revised in 1971 (Paris Act), this reference is not of much help here because the Berne Convention contains no explicit definition of the concept of "author". It is widely considered that the definition is thus a matter for individual Member States. However, viewed correctly, it does not follow that recognition of authorship is optional but, at the very most, that "possible national differences in the criteria for determining author status in borderline cases between co-

---

[11]   See L'affaire Lecocq, Cass. civ., June 25, 1902, Dalloz, 1903, 1, 5, concl. Beaudoin. note A. Colin. L'al' faire Jamin-Canal, Trib. civ., Seine, April 1, 1936, Cass. civ., May 14, 1945, Dalloz, 1945, 285, note Desbois.

authorship and assistance and between those who provide ideas and those who act as executants" must be accepted. Nevertheless, a definition of the concept of "author" is attempted in Section 1 (definitions) of the Draft Model Provisions (later called the Draft Model Law on Copyright). In the initial version of the Draft Model Provisions, "author" was defined as follows:

> "Author" is the physical person who has created the work. Reference to "author" also means the successors in title of the author as well as the original owner of rights other than the author, where applicable.

Not surprisingly, this definition triggered off a great deal of discussion and opposition both inside and outside the Committee of Experts, not only because it threatened to generate serious confusion between the problems of authorship and of copyright ownership by virtue of a transfer of rights, but also because it would have had dangerous implications as regards the question of whether other *original copyright owners* can also be included in the concept of "author".

Following the discussions which took place at the first two sessions of the Committee of Experts, the International Bureau of WIPO changed the definition slightly and the amended version was then submitted to the Committee for consideration at its third session. The new text is worded as follows:

> "Author" is the physical person who has created the work. Reference to "author" includes, in addition to the author, where applicable, also the successors in title of the author and, where the original owner of the rights in the work is a person other than the author, such a person.

In view of the foregoing danger of an extension of the concept of "author" beyond the scope of the *jus conventionis*, this amended wording is also disquieting. Hence it is not surprising that international copyright circles should have expressed their concern as seen, for example, in the following resolution of the International Literary and Artistic Association (ALAI) which was adopted by its Executive Committee at a meeting in Helsinki on 30 May 1990. The text reads:

AFFIRMS that the definition of the concept of author and the determination of ownership of rights constitute two questions of basic importance to the very structure of copyright;

RECALLS that the Berne Convention has consistently, in both letter and spirit, limited its recognition of the status of author to the actual physical person who creates a work;

RECALLS also that it appears clearly from the provisions of the Berne Convention that it is the author who is the original owner of the economic rights in the work he has created, even though these rights may be transferred by contract or otherwise to another with the limited exception of Article 14bis, paragraph 2;

CONSIDERS that granting ownership of economic rights to a person other than the creator should not have the effect of conferring the status of author upon that person;

1) NOTES that the definition of the word "author" appearing in the WIPO Model Provisions for Legislation in the Field of Copyright entails an unfortunate confusion between the very distinct concepts of author and owner of economic rights, a confusion which should be denounced rather than perpetuated;

RECOMMENDS in consequence that the definition of the word "author" appearing in the aforementioned document should read as follows: "The author is the physical person who creates a work"; this does not exclude the application of certain provisions of the law to persons other than the author;

2) NOTES that the propositions in the WIPO Model Provisions concerning original ownership of the economic rights are not wholly in conformity with the Berne Convention;

RECOMMENDS in consequence that original ownership of the economic rights not be granted to any person other than the author, save for the exception in Article 14bis, paragraph 2, of the Berne Convention.

In view of the confrontation that can be observed worldwide between the two schools of thought and legal traditions in the field of authors' rights, namely the continental European "droit d'auteur" tradition and the Anglo-American "copyright" one, this is in fact a question of utmost significance, especially as the adherence of the United States to the Berne Convention on 1 March 1989 appreciably strengthened the group of countries—which was already represented by Great Britain and others—within the Union whose laws are based on the Anglo-American legal tradition. The idea, which is also expressed in the WIPO proposals, that the two copyright traditions should co-exist within the Berne Convention and are each entitled to mutual respect, is no reason—unless the text of the Convention itself were to be amended accordingly—for simply departing from the basic postulates of the *jus conventionis*.

France, Intellectual Property Code

Articles L.111–1; 113–1–113–9.

Nature of Copyright

Article L. 111–1. The author of a work of the mind shall enjoy in that work, by the mere fact of its creation, an exclusive incorporeal property right which shall be enforceable against all persons.

This right shall include attributes of an intellectual and moral nature as well as attributes of an economic nature, as determined by Books I and III of this Code.

The existence or conclusion of a contract for hire or of service by the author of a work of the mind shall in no way derogate from the enjoyment of the right afforded by the first paragraph above . . .

Owners of Copyright

Berne 15

Article L. 113–1. Authorship shall belong, unless proved otherwise, to the person or persons under whose name the work has been disclosed.

Article L. 113–2. "Work of collaboration" shall mean a work in the creation of which more than one natural person has participated.

Romeo and Juliet ≠ West Side Story

"Composite work" shall mean a new work in which a preexisting work is incorporated without the collaboration of the author of the latter work.

"Collective work" shall mean a work created at the initiative of a natural or legal person who edits it, publishes it and discloses it under his direction and name and in which the personal contributions of the various authors who participated in its production are merged in the overall work for which they were conceived, without it being possible to attribute to each author a separate right in the work as created.

Article L. 113–3. A work of collaboration shall be the joint property of its authors.

100% unanimity
they ask if it's reasonable

The joint authors shall exercise their rights by common accord.

In the event of failure to agree, the civil courts shall decide.

Where the contribution of each of the joint authors is of a different kind, each may, unless otherwise agreed, separately exploit his own personal contribution without, however, prejudicing the exploitation of the common work.

Article L. 113–4. A composite work shall be the property of the author who has produced it, subject to the rights of the author of the preexisting work.

Article L. 113–5. A collective work shall be the property, unless proved otherwise, of the natural or legal person under whose name it has been disclosed.

The author's rights shall vest in such person.

Article L. 113–6. The authors of pseudonymous and anonymous works shall enjoy in such works the rights afforded by Article L. 111–1.

They shall be represented in the exercise of those rights by the original editor or publisher, until such time as they reveal their true identity and prove their authorship.

The declaration referred to in the preceding paragraph may be made by will; however, any rights previously acquired by other persons shall be maintained.

The provisions in the second and third paragraphs above shall not apply if the pseudonym adopted by the author leaves no doubt as to his true identity.

Article L. 113–7. Authorship of an audiovisual work shall belong to the natural person or persons who have carried out the intellectual creation of the work.

Unless proved otherwise, the following are presumed to be the joint authors of an audiovisual work made in collaboration:

1. The author of the script;

2. The author of the adaptation;

3. The author of the dialogue;

4. The author of the musical compositions, with or without words, specially composed for the work;

5. The director.

If an audiovisual work is adapted from a preexisting work or script which is still protected, the authors of the original work shall be assimilated to the authors of the new work.

Article L. 113–8. Authorship of a radio work shall belong to the natural person or persons who carried out the intellectual creation of the work.

The provisions of the final paragraph of Article L. 113–7 and those of Article L. 121–6 shall apply to radio works.

Article L. 113–9. Unless otherwise provided by statutory provision or stipulation, the economic rights in the software and its documentation created by one or more employees in the execution of their duties or following the instructions given by their employer shall be the property of the employer and he exclusively shall be entitled to exercise them.

Any dispute concerning the application of this Article shall be submitted to the first instance court of the registered place of business of the employer.

The first paragraph of this Article shall also apply to servants of the State, of local authorities and of public establishments of an administrative nature.

Germany, Act on Copyright and Related Rights
Sections 7–10.

Section 7. Author

The author is the creator of the work.

Section 8. Joint Authors

(1) Where several persons have jointly created a work without it being possible to separately exploit their individual shares in the work, they are joint authors of the work.

(2) The right of publication and of exploitation of the work accrues jointly to the joint authors; alterations to the work shall be permissible only with the consent of the joint authors. However, a joint author may not refuse his consent to publication, exploitation or alteration contrary to the principles of good faith. Each joint author shall be entitled to assert claims arising from violations of the joint copyright; he may, however, demand performance only to all of the joint authors.

(3) Proceeds derived from the use of the work shall be due to the joint authors according to the extent of their involvement in the creation of the work, unless otherwise agreed between the joint authors.

(4) A joint author may waive his share of the exploitation rights (section 15). He shall make a declaration of waiver to the other joint authors. Upon his declaration his share shall accrue to the other joint authors.

Section 9. Authors of compound works

Where several authors have combined their works for the purpose of joint exploitation, each may require the consent of the others to the publication, exploitation or alteration of the compound works if the consent of the others may be reasonably expected in good faith.

Section 10. Presumption of authorship and ownership

(1) The person designated as the author in the usual manner on the copies of a released work or on the original of an artistic work shall be regarded as the author of the work in the absence of proof to the contrary; the same shall apply to any designation which is known to be a pseudonym or stage name of the author.

(2) Where the author has not been named according to subsection (1), it shall be presumed that the person designated as the editor on the copies of the work is entitled to assert the rights of the author. Where no editor has been named, it shall be presumed that the publisher is entitled to assert such rights.

(3) The presumption in subsection (1) shall apply mutatis mutandis to the holder of exclusive rights of use in the event of proceedings for temporary relief or injunctive relief. The presumption shall not apply in the relationship to the author or the original holder of the related right.

United Kingdom, Copyright, Designs and Patents Act

Sections 9–11.

Authorship and ownership of copyright

9.   Authorship of work.

(1) In this Part "author," in relation to a work, means the person who creates it.

(2) That person shall be taken to be—

(aa) in the case of a sound recording, the producer;

(ab) in the case of a film, the producer and the principal director;

(b) in the case of a broadcast, the person making the broadcast (see section 6(3)) or, in the case of a broadcast which relays another broadcast by reception and immediate re-transmission, the person making that other broadcast;

(c)*

(d) in the case of the typographical arrangement of a published edition, the publisher.

(3) In the case of a literary, dramatic, musical or artistic work which is computer-generated, the author shall be taken to be the person by whom the arrangements necessary for the creation of the work are undertaken.

(4) For the purposes of this Part a work is of "unknown authorship" if the identity of the author is unknown or, in the case of a work of joint authorship, if the identity of none of the authors is known.

(5) For the purposes of this Part the identity of an author shall be regarded as unknown if it is not possible for a person to ascertain his identity by reasonable inquiry; but if his identity is once known it shall not subsequently be regarded as unknown.

10. Works of joint authorship.

(1) In this Part a "work of joint authorship" means a work produced by the collaboration of two or more authors in which the contribution of each author is not distinct from that of the other author or authors.

(1A) A film shall be treated as a work of joint authorship unless the producer and the principal director are the same person.

(2) A broadcast shall be treated as a work of joint authorship in any case where more than one person is to be taken as making the broadcast (see section 6(3)).

---

*   Section 9(2)(c) was repealed. *Ed.*

(3)   References in this Part to the author of a work shall, except as otherwise provided, be construed in relation to a work of joint authorship as references to all the authors of the work.

10A. Works of co-authorship.

(1)   In this Part a "work of co-authorship" means a work produced by the collaboration of the author of a musical work and the author of a literary work where the two works are created in order to be used together.

(2)   References in this Part to a work or the author of a work shall, except as otherwise provided, be construed in relation to a work of co-authorship as references to each of the separate musical and literary works comprised in the work of co-authorship and to each of the authors of such works.

11.   First ownership of copyright.

(1)   The author of a work is the first owner of any copyright in it, subject to the following provisions.

(2)   Where a literary, dramatic, musical or artistic work, or a film, is made by an employee in the course of his employment, his employer is the first owner of any copyright in the work subject to any agreement to the contrary.

(3)   This section does not apply to Crown copyright or Parliamentary copyright (see section 163 and 165) or to copyright which subsists by virtue of section 168 (copyright of certain international organisations).

United States of America, Copyright Act

17 U.S.C. §§ 101, 201.

§ 101. Definitions

A "joint work" is a work prepared by two or more authors with the intention that their contributions be merged into inseparable or interdependent parts of a unitary whole.

A "work made for hire" is—

(1)   a work prepared by an employee within the scope of his or her employment; or

(2)   a work specially ordered or commissioned for use as a contribution to a collective work, as a part of a motion picture or other audiovisual work, as a translation, as a supplementary work, as a compilation, as an instructional text, as a test, as answer material for a test, or as an atlas, if the parties expressly agree in a written instrument signed by them that the work shall be considered a work made for hire. For the purpose of the foregoing sentence, a "supplementary work" is a work prepared for publication as a secondary adjunct to a work by another author for the purpose of introducing, concluding, illustrating,

[handwritten margin notes: In German law, you need consent of all. In US, any co-author can licence the work, subject to a duty to the others]

explaining, revising, commenting upon, or assisting in the use of the other work, such as forewords, afterwords, pictorial illustrations, maps, charts, tables, editorial notes, musical arrangements, answer material for tests, bibliographies, appendixes, and indexes, and an "instructional text" is a literary, pictorial, or graphic work prepared for publication and with the purpose of use in systematic instructional activities.

§ 201. Ownership of copyright

(a) Initial Ownership.—Copyright in a work protected under this title vests initially in the author or authors of the work. The authors of a joint work are co-owners of copyright in the work.

(b) Works Made for Hire.—In the case of a work made for hire, the employer or other person for whom the work was prepared is considered the author for purposes of this title, and, unless the parties have expressly agreed otherwise in a written instrument signed by them, owns all of the rights comprised in the copyright.

(c) Contributions to Collective Works.—Copyright in each separate contribution to a collective work is distinct from copyright in the collective work as a whole, and vests initially in the author of the contribution. In the absence of an express transfer of the copyright or of any rights under it, the owner of copyright in the collective work is presumed to have acquired only the privilege of reproducing and distributing the contribution as part of that particular collective work, any revision of that collective work, and any later collective work in the same series.

(d) Transfer of Ownership.—

(1) The ownership of a copyright may be transferred in whole or in part by any means of conveyance or by operation of law, and may be bequeathed by will or pass as personal property by the applicable laws of intestate succession.

(2) Any of the exclusive rights comprised in a copyright, including any subdivision of any of the rights specified by section 106, may be transferred as provided by clause (1) and owned separately. The owner of any particular exclusive right is entitled, to the extent of that right, to all of the protection and remedies accorded to the copyright owner by this title.

(e) Involuntary Transfer.—When an individual author's ownership of a copyright, or of any of the exclusive rights under a copyright, has not previously been transferred voluntarily by that individual author, no action by any governmental body or other official or organization purporting to seize, expropriate, transfer, or exercise rights of ownership with respect to the copyright, or any of the exclusive rights under a copyright, shall be given effect under this title, except as provided under Title 11.

Copyright Law of the People's Republic of China

Section 2

Ownership of Copyright

Article 11.   Except where otherwise provided in this Law, the copyright in a work shall belong to its author.

The author of a work is the citizen who has created the work.

Where a work is created according to the intention and under the supervision and responsibility of a legal entity or other organization, such legal entity or other organization shall be deemed to be the author of the work.

The citizen, legal entity or other organization whose name is mentioned in connection with a work shall, in the absence of proof to the contrary, be deemed to be the author of the work.

Article 12.   Where a work is created by adaptation, translation, annotation or arrangement of a preexisting work, the copyright in the work thus created shall be enjoyed by the adapter, translator, annotator or arranger, provided that the exercise of such copyright shall not prejudice the copyright in the original work.

Article 13.   Where a work is created jointly by two or more co-authors, the copyright in the work shall be enjoyed jointly by those co-authors. Co-authorship may not be claimed by anyone who has not participated in the creation of the work.

If a work of joint authorship can be separated into independent parts and exploited separately, each co-author shall be entitled to independent copyright in the parts that he has created, provided that the exercise of such copyright shall not prejudice the copyright in the joint work as a whole.

Article 14.   A work created by a compilation of several works, parts of works, data that do not constitute a work or other materials and having originality in the selection or arrangement of its contents is a work of compilation. The copyright in a work of compilation shall be enjoyed by the compiler, provided that the exercise of such copyright shall not prejudice the copyright in the preexisting works.

Article 15.   The copyright in a cinematographic work and any work created by an analogous method of film production shall be enjoyed by the producer of the work, but the scriptwriter, director, cameraman, lyricist, composer and other authors thereof shall enjoy the right of authorship in the work and have the right to receive remuneration pursuant to the contract concluded with the producer.

The authors of the screenplay, musical works and other works that are incorporated in a cinematographic work, and work created by an analogous method of film production, than can be exploited separately, shall be entitled to exercise their copyright independently.

Article 16.   A work created by a citizen in the fulfillment of tasks assigned to him by a legal entity or other organization shall be deemed to be a work created in the course of employment. The copyright in such work shall be enjoyed by the author, subject to the provisions of the second paragraph of this Article, provided that the legal entity or other organization shall have a priority right to exploit the work within the scope of its professional activities. During the two years after the completion of the work, the author shall not, without the consent of the legal entity or other organization, authorize a third party to exploit the work in the same way as the legal entity or other organization does.

In any of the following cases the author of a work created in the course of employment shall enjoy the right of authorship, while the legal entity or other organization shall enjoy the other rights included in the copyright and may reward the author:

(1)   drawings of engineering designs and product designs and maps, computer software and other works created in the course of employment mainly with the material and technical resources of the legal entity or other organization and under its responsibility;

(2)   works created in the course of employment where the copyright is, in accordance with laws, administrative regulations or contracts, enjoyed by the legal entity or other organization.

Article 17.   The ownership of the copyright in a commissioned work shall be agreed upon in a contract between the commissioning and the commissioned parties. In the absence of a contract or of an explicit agreement in the contract, the copyright in such a work shall belong to the commissioned party.

Le Brun v. SA Braesheather

Court of Cassation (France) 1st Civil Chamber, Oct. 18, 1994.
164 Revue Internationale Du Droit D'Auteur 304 (1995).

On the three arguments combined, taken in their various branches:

Whereas, according to the judges dealing with the facts of the case, the company Braesheather, which runs an art gallery in Paris called "Paris Art Center," organized an exhibition in 1989 which was devoted to Donatien-Aldonze-François de Sade and for which a book/catalogue was published, entitled "Petits et Grands Théâtres du Marquis de Sade," containing texts by seventeen authors preceded by an introduction by Mrs. A. Le Brun, the person in charge of organizing the exhibition, who acted as the Paris Art Center's artistic adviser: whereas Mrs. Le Brun, claiming authorship of the work in question, brought an action for payment of proportional remuneration and for infringement:

Whereas Mrs. Le Brun objects to the ruling being challenged (Paris Court of Appeal, 15 April 1992), in a first argument, for having termed the catalogue a collective work of which Braesheather was the author, when it was a work of collaboration in which several natural persons, who were named, had participated as such through separate contributions; when the latter label was to be inferred, moreover, from the fact that the work was not distributed under the name of Braesheather but under the trade name "Paris Art Center" and was not created on its initiative and under its direction, as Mrs. Le Brun had been entirely responsible for its conception and production; whereas, in a second argument, the Court of Appeal is reproached for having declared Mrs. Le Brun's claim for payment of proportional remuneration inadmissible as being new when this claim had been formulated before the initial judges and when, whatever the case, it was merely the extension and accessory of the main claim for recognition of her copyrights; whereas the third argument criticizes the ruling being challenged for having rejected Mrs. Le Brun's claim for payment of her royalties and of damages for infringement when it was found that no remuneration had been paid to Mrs. Le Brun for the 5,000 copies of the work in respect of which she had given her agreement;

But whereas the Court of Appeal noted on a sovereign basis that the work taken as a whole was not the result of a concerted creative effort undertaken jointly by several authors and that Mrs. Le Brun had been responsible for coordinating the various contributions and directing the publication; whereas, therefore, having accepted the absence of any cooperation between the various authors and the role of initiative and direction played by Mrs. Le Brun as an employee of Braesheather, the Court of Appeal correctly inferred that the authors could not claim a joint right in the whole formed by the final work and that the catalogue was to be termed a collective work in which the copyrights belonged to Braesheather as the legal entity under whose name it was disclosed, through the use of its trade name "Paris Art Center";

And whereas, in the case of a collective work, none of the authors of the various contributions may claim a right in the whole formed by the final work so that the Court of Appeal's decision is justified in law as regards Mrs. Le Brun's claims concerning proportional remuneration and compensation for infringement;

Whereas none of the arguments can thus be accepted;

ON THESE GROUNDS:

REJECTS the appeal.

Orders Mrs. Le Brun to pay Braesheather's costs and those of executing this ruling.

NOTES

1. *Authorship.* Why do courts and commentators, principally in civil law countries, insist that a work's author be a flesh and blood human being? Is it that a "work" for purposes of the Berne Convention cannot exist without an "author" and that the impress of the author's personality distinguishes the work from the less elevated fare of neighboring rights? Does Article 113–5 of the French Intellectual Property Code provide that the legal person under whose name a collective work is published is presumptively its author, or only its copyright owner? What of Article 113–9, which deals with computer programs? As a practical or legal matter, what difference is there between treating a legal entity as no more than the original owner of rights in a work and treating it as the work's author as well? *See* generally, Sam Ricketson, People or Machines: The Berne Convention and the Changing Concept of Authorship, 16 Colum.-V.L.A. J. L. & Arts 1 (1991).

2. *Copyright Chain of Title.* Identifying a work's author and source of title for purposes of analyzing the chain of copyright title to the work is as important as it is frequently complex. One reason determinations of authorship are often so vexed and uncertain is that the copyright treaties are virtually silent on the question of authorship and original ownership. Another reason is that the Berne Convention's one effort at defining ownership—Article 14*bis* dealing with ownership of rights in cinematographic works—is complex and confused; the leading commentator on the Berne Convention has called the provision "the most obscure and least useful in the whole Convention." Sam Ricketson, The Berne Convention for the Protection of Literary and Artistic Works: 1986–1986, 582 (1987).

3. *Joint Works.* What differences can you discern between the definitions of joint works under British, Chinese, French, German and U.S. law? Would a Gilbert and Sullivan operetta, for which W.S. Gilbert wrote the words and Arthur Sullivan wrote the music, qualify as a joint work under the German requirement that the "contributions cannot be separately exploited"? Under the British requirement that "the contribution of each author is not distinct from that of the other author or authors"? Under the U.S. Act's requirement that the work be "prepared by two or more authors with the intention that their contributions be merged into inseparable or interdependent parts of a unitary whole"?

As a rule, for a work to qualify as a collaborative work, each joint author must have contributed creative expression to the work. The contributions need not be equal, however, and Professor Hugenholtz has written of a Dutch Supreme Court decision in which the court ruled that a stylist who assisted a photographer by creatively arranging a needlework display for the photograph was a coauthor with the photographer of the resulting works. P. Bernt Hugenholtz, Dutch Copyright Law, 1990–1995, 169 R.I.D.A. 129, 173 (1996).

4. *Works for Hire.* Civil law and most common law jurisdictions differ in how they assign rights to works made in the course of an employment relationship. Common law countries provide that, absent an agreement to the contrary, copyright in works created in the course of employment initially vests in the employer, not the employee. Section 13(3) of the Canadian Copyright Act, for example, provides that where a work's author "was in the employment of some other person under a contract of service or apprenticeship and the work was made in the course of his employment by that person, the person by whom the author was employed shall, in the absence of any agreement to the contrary, be the first owner of the copyright." (The Canadian legislation creates a narrow privilege for contributions to newspapers, magazines and similar periodicals where, absent agreement to the contrary, the author is deemed to reserve a right to restrain the work's publication other than as part of a newspaper, magazine or similar periodical.)

Civil law countries generally reverse the common law presumption and provide that copyright in works created in the course of employment vests in the employee-author, so that a transfer by the employee is required for the employer to obtain copyright. This approach works fluently in such civil law countries as Belgium and France that treat economic rights in literary and artistic works as freely alienable; an employee can expressly or impliedly transfer economic rights to his employer in the employment agreement or otherwise. But in countries such as Austria and Germany that treat author's rights as inalienable, the employer must in the employment agreement secure to itself the power to exploit the employee's economic rights on his behalf.

Consider how Article 2(3) of the EC Directive on the Legal Protection of Computer Programs accommodates the civil law and common law approaches: "[W]here a computer program is created by an employee in the execution of his duties or following the instructions given by his employer, the employer exclusively shall be entitled to exercise all economic rights in the program so created, unless otherwise provided by contract."

Section 201(b) of the U.S. Copyright Act converts presumptions respecting *ownership* into a rule respecting *authorship*. The rule may have international consequence. For example, if *A*, a national or domiciliary of the United States, writes a novel while in the employ of *B*, a national or domiciliary of a country that does not belong to the Berne Convention, and *B* first publishes the work in that country, will the work enjoy a Berne point of attachment? Will the answer turn on whether the United States is the protecting country? The forum country?

On choice of law problems created by the American work for hire doctrine see Jan Bernd Nordemann, The U.S. "Work-for-Hire" Doctrine Before German Courts—Rejection and Reception, 53 J. Copyr. Soc'y U.S.A. 603 (2006).

5.   *Freedom of Contract.* National laws vary, sometimes widely, on the freedom parties enjoy in making copyright contracts. Professor Eugen Ulmer's observation on the diverse treatment of copyright contracts, though made in 1976, remains accurate today: "[I]n some instances we find detailed statutory regulation; in others the laws contain but a few general provisions and regulate only specific types of contracts; in still others, statutory provisions on this subject are almost totally absent. Only a few rules are

[handwritten margin note: Different rules on alienability.]

[handwritten margin note: Suba films problem ⇒ didn't contemplate arrival of video technology]

generally recognized, for example, the principle that an author who has sold the original of his work may not be assumed to have transferred the copyright exploitation rights." Eugen Ulmer, Some Thoughts on the Law of Copyright Contracts, 7. IIC 202 (1976).

Limits on contractual freedom are usually associated with the civil law countries' paternalistic concern for author welfare—provisions such as the twenty-year ceiling on publication contracts imposed by Article 122 of the Italian Copyright Act, the Spanish Copyright Act's bar in Article 43 against the transfer of rights not yet in existence, and the Belgian Copyright Act's bar in Article 3(1) on the transfer of rights to exploitation by technologies not yet in existence.

Civil law countries also sometimes regulate remuneration under copyright contracts. French Intellectual Property Code Art. L. 131–4 prohibits lump sum payments in all but a limited number of situations, and requires instead that the author participate proportionately, through royalties. The German Copyright Act, Art. 32(1), provides that if the remuneration contractually agreed upon between author and publisher is not equitable, the author may obtain equitable remuneration through judicial proceedings, as does the "bestseller" provision of Article 25d of the Dutch Copyright Contract Act, which enables redress of serious imbalances between the publisher's profits and the author's contracted-for remuneration. *See* generally, Karsten Gutsche, New Copyright Contract Legislation in Germany: Rules on Equitable Remuneration Provide 'Just Rewards' to Authors and Performers, 25 EIPR 366 (2003); Thomas Dysart, Author-Protective Rules and Alternative Licences: A Review of the Dutch Copyright Contract Act, EIPR 601 (2015).

But civil law systems have no monopoly on paternalism and common law courts and legislators have also been solicitous of authors' interests. For example, in O'Sullivan v. Management Agency & Music Ltd. [1985] Q.B. 428, [1985] 3 All E.L.R. 351 (Court of App. Civ. Div.), an English court overturned as an "unreasonable restraint of trade" a contract in which it was evident that the publisher had overreached an economically weaker author. Section 203 of the U.S. Copyright Act gives authors and their statutory successors the nonwaivable power to terminate the transfer of a copyright interest thirty-five years after the transfer was made.

6. *Collecting Societies.* Societies organized to enforce and license decentralized, economically modest uses of copyrighted works trace to the mid-nineteenth century with the organization of SACEM, the *Société des Auteurs, Compositeurs et Editeurs de Musique*, to license, collect and distribute revenues under the musical performance right. National copyright collecting societies, also called collective management organizations, have since formed to license exploitation not only of musical performances, but also uses of dramatic and literary works, visual art, choreography and phonograms. *See* generally Daniel Gervais, Collective Management of Copyright and Related Rights (3d ed. 2015); David Sinacore-Guinn, Collective Administration of Copyrights and Neighboring Rights: International Practices, Procedures and Organizations (1993).

A collecting society in Country *A* will often enter into reciprocal arrangements with collecting societies in Countries *B, C* and *D* under which each represents the authors belonging to the other, collecting royalties from the local exploitation of foreign works and remitting them for distribution to the author's national collecting society. Professor Gunnar Karnell has observed that a fundamental provision in most of these agreements is that all holders of rights in each country, regardless of the organization to which they belong, are treated in exactly the same way. "Thus, the organizations apply the national treatment principle proclaimed by both the Berne Convention and the Universal Copyright Convention." Gunnar Karnell, The Relations Between Authors and Organizations Administering Their Rights, 22 Copyright 45, 49 (1986).

PROBLEM 4

In 1988, Ann Autry, a British national domiciled in Britain, compiled a cookbook, *One-Hour Gourmet,* that she self-published in Britain later that year. The book consists of recipes for 75 dishes that can be prepared in less than 60 minutes, a 15-page introduction explaining Autry's philosophy of efficient cooking and 20 photographs illustrating Autry's kitchen techniques. Autrey compiled and updated, but did not write, the recipes, all of which are either in the public domain or are the subject of licenses to her from their copyright owners. The photographs were taken for Autry by a friend, Bernard Berton, a French national domiciled in France; Autry reimbursed Berton for his film and processing expenses.

Autry's book has been a great success, and your client, FoodCable, would like to produce for distribution in the United States a 20-part television series, "One-Hour Gourmet," with each program in the series devoted to an American chef preparing a different recipe from Autry's book. FoodCable has asked you to determine whether it needs to obtain rights from anyone involved with the *One-Hour Gourmet* cookbook and, if so, from whom. Please advise FoodCable. Would your advice change if FoodCable told you that it will seek international distribution of the series if the show proves successful in the United States?

b.   COPYRIGHT TERM

Atlas Film + AV GmbH & Co. Verleih u. Vertrieb v. Janus Film u. Fernsehen Vertriebgesellschaft mbH

Federal Supreme Court (Germany), 1978.
I ZR 97/76, 10 International Review of Industrial Property and
Copyright Law 358 (1979).

From the Facts:

The plaintiff Janus, by contract dated February 11, 1972, obtained an exclusive license from Raymond Rohauer, who on his part, by contract dated September 18, 1970, had purchased from the trustee of Buster

Keaton Production Inc. all rights in the Buster Keaton films listed in the pleading. The license covered the period . . . to December 31, 1979 and was granted for the exploitation of these films in the formats 16 mm and 35 mm in the Federal Republic of Germany and in other German-speaking countries.

The defendant Atlas, which had formerly been authorized to exploit Buster Keaton films in the formats 16 mm and 35 mm for a specified period, and, according to its statement, had entered into a contract with Raymond Rohauer for the exploitation in the super-8 format, intends to exploit the films in 16 mm and 35 mm films also in the future, claiming that it is entitled to do so even without concluding a pertinent license contract.

The films, in their original version, were made in the years 1921 to 1928 in the United States by Buster Keaton, who had American citizenship. They were published there in those years. An extension beyond the initial 28-year term of protection in the United States, which commences on the date of the first publication of a work, was not applied for. Buster Keaton died on February 1, 1966.

In the opinion of the plaintiff, the Buster Keaton films which are in the public domain in the United States, are still protected by copyright in the Federal Republic of Germany, in West Berlin and East Berlin, in East Germany, in the German-speaking area of Switzerland, and in Liechtenstein. The plaintiff relies on the Agreement Between the German *Reich* and the United States of America Concerning the Reciprocal Protection of Copyrights of January 15, 1892. The plaintiff further claims copyright protection under the revised Berne Convention for the films "The General," "College," "Three Ages" and "Steamboat Bill Junior," stating that, a few weeks prior to their first publication in the United States, these films were exhibited for the first time in a Convention country, namely in Great Britain, "The General" also in Japan.

The District Court dismissed the complaint. . . .

From the Opinion:

I.   The Court of Appeals left open the question whether the films "The General," "College," "Three Ages" and "Steamboat Bill Junior" were first published in a Convention country of the Revised Berne Convention and therefore enjoy copyright protection under this Convention. In the opinion of the Court of Appeals, all films are protected in the Federal Republic of Germany under the Agreement of January 15, 1892 between the German Reich and the United States of America.

II.1. The validity of the Agreement Between the Reich and the United States of America Concerning the Reciprocal Protection of Copyrights, of January 15, 1892, as the Court of Appeals rightly determined, remained unaffected by the World Wars (German Law of May 18, 1922) and Proclamation of the President of the United States of

May 25, 1922; further, the exchange of notes of February 6, 1950 and June 20, 1950 with respective memoranda.

2. Under Art. 1 of the Agreement of January 15, 1892:

> Citizens of the United States of America shall enjoy, in the German Empire, the protection of copyright as regards works of literature and art, as well as photographs, against illegal reproduction, on the same basis on which such protection is granted to subjects of the Empire.

Citizens of the United States are thus granted copyright protection in Germany in accordance with domestic law for all works for which nationals are granted protection under the domestic law. Domestic protection is, therefore, also granted for cinematographic works, although such works were only included in copyright protection after the Agreement of January 15, 1892 had been concluded.

The duration of domestic protection is determined according to domestic law. The Agreement of January 15, 1892 contains no express provision as to whether the duration of protection granted under domestic law is dependent on the work in question still enjoying copyright protection in the United States, as the country of origin. For this reason, it was accepted in Germany—prior to the entry into force of the Universal Copyright Convention of September 6, 1952—that works of American citizens are governed exclusively by the German term of protection, *i.e.*, domestic protection was to be allowed independently of a comparison of terms of protection in the United States and in Germany. There is no reason for deviating from this rule. The Court of Appeals could thus, without legal error, in regard to domestic protection for the Buster Keaton films under the Agreement of January 15, 1892 (in conjunction with the domestic copyright law), regard it as irrelevant that these film productions are no longer protected by copyright in the United States. Under the applicable domestic law, the term of protection which began to apply only with the death of the author (February 1, 1966), has not yet expired.

III.1. In the opinion of the Court of Appeals, the Universal Copyright Convention of September 6, 1952, which became effective for the United States and for the Federal Republic of Germany on September 16, 1955, in the version of 1952 and in the revised version of July 24, 1971 on July 10, 1974, does not affect the domestic protection which these Buster Keaton films acquired under the Agreement of January 15, 1892. This cannot be objected to legally.

2. The Universal Copyright Convention pursuant to its Art. XIX, cl. 1, in principle leaves bilateral agreements—such as the Agreement between the United States and Germany of January 15, 1892—unaffected; only where a provision of such an agreement differs from the provisions of the Universal Copyright Convention, the latter provisions shall prevail, Art. XIX, cl. 2.

Such differences are present in the instant case. The determination of the period of protection—and thus the term of protection of the copyright granted—differs in the two agreements. According to the Agreement of January 15, 1892, for domestic protection only the domestic law applies in determining the period of protection, without regard to whether the work in question is still protected in the United States as the country of origin.

Under the Universal Copyright Convention (Art. IV in conjunction with Art. II), the term of protection is also determined according to domestic law, however, under Art. IV No. 4 UCC no Contracting State shall be obliged to grant protection to a work for a period longer than that fixed for works of this class in the Contracting State in which the work has been first published. Under Sec. 140 of the German Copyright Act, this rule of comparison of terms of protection shall be applied so that only the shorter term is to be granted under the law of the country of origin if domestic copyright protection is claimed on the basis of the Universal Copyright Convention. However, this leads to the determination of differing terms of protection—under the Agreement of January 15, 1892, on the one hand, and the Universal Copyright Convention on the other hand; both represent deviations within the meaning of Art. XIX cl. 2 UCC. Contrary to the opinion of Bolla (8 UNESCO Copyright Bulletin No. 1, p. 20 *et seq.* (1955)), "deviation" within the meaning of Art. XIX cl. 2 UCC cannot be confined to the case that the Universal Copyright Convention grants the author a more favorable legal position than the prior bilateral agreement. The Universal Copyright Convention does not differentiate in this regard, even though—according to Bolla—only this case was discussed during the deliberations.

[handwritten margin note: Rule of the shorter term]

3.   The Appeal also proceeds from this thought. However, the appellant improperly objects to the position taken by the Court of Appeals that the comparison of terms of protection and thus the shorter term as provided by the American law—because of the proviso contained in Art. XIX cl. 3 UCC—is in any event not applicable to domestic protection for the older Buster Keaton film productions involved here and that still enjoyed domestic protection under the Agreement of January 15, 1892 at the time the World Copyright Agreement took effect.

Under Art. XIX cl. 3 UCC, the rights in a work acquired in any Contracting State under existing agreements, before the date on which the Universal Copyright Convention came into force, shall not be affected. Rights acquired on the basis of such an agreement, as the Court of Appeals rightly held, are also such rights as were acquired in Germany by American authors for their works on the basis of the Agreement of January 15, 1892. The provision of Art. XIX cl. 3 requires neither a legal transaction, nor even the special intention of legal acquisition. Art. XIX cl. 3 UCC speaks only very generally of rights that have been acquired.

Acquired rights in this general sense, as used in Art. XIX cl. 3 UCC include rights acquired by a legislative act. Therefore, the granting of domestic protection under the bilateral Agreement of January 15, 1892 (existing at the time the Universal Copyright Convention became effective) is also subject to the provision of Art. XIX cl. 3 UCC; for it was only by virtue of this agreement (in connection with domestic copyright legislation) that the American author was granted copyright protection in Germany for his work that was first published in the USA; he acquired this right by virtue of this legal regulation.

The copyright in the Buster Keaton films—acquired under the Agreement of January 15, 1892 prior to the coming into force of the Universal Copyright Convention—thus (according to Art. XIX cl. 3 UCC) remains unaffected by the precedence in principle to be accorded the World Copyright Agreement. This means that the right retains its status as legally granted (at the time the World Copyright Agreement became effective). This includes the term of protection. The term of protection limits the duration of the right and determines the period of time this status is to be maintained. It is, as the Federal Constitutional Court recognized in its decision of July 8, 1976 (31 BVerfGE 275; 1972 NJW 145, 147; 1972 GRUR 491, 494), an integral part of the legal position granted by copyright law and protected by the guarantee of ownership of Art. 14(*l*) cl. 1 GG (Basic Law). However, under Art. XIX cl. 3 UCC, this legal position is to be preserved for the author in its entire scope. It therefore follows that the determination of the term of protection according to the Agreement of January 15, 1892 also remains unaffected, since otherwise, the duration of the right would be changed. A comparison of terms of protection as provided by Art. IV No. 4 UCC would result in a reduction of the duration of protection so that the right—contrary to the provision of Art. XIX cl. 3 UCC—would no longer remain unaffected.

The appellant erroneously contends that, with respect to the term of protection, the Agreement of January 15, 1892 did not create a vested right for the author within the meaning of Art. XIX cl. 3 UCC because the term of protection is not a right in a work; that, on the contrary, the copyright expires by operation of law with the expiry of the term of protection and that the term of protection is merely a durational limitation of a right. As stated, the copyright acquired under the law by the American citizen under the Agreement of January 15, 1892 in its legally determined status is the acquired right within the meaning of Art. XIX cl. 3 UCC. This acquired right would, however, be affected—contrary to the provision of Art. XIX cl. 3 UCC—if the period of protection is shortened pursuant to a comparison of terms of protection periods under Art. IV, No. 4. The differing opinion of the appellant would, furthermore, lead to a result that is also regarded inequitable by Ulmer namely, that rights acquired by third persons in reliance on the existing legal position in Germany would be invalidated (without indemnification) with the very purpose of Art. XIX cl. 3 UCC being to avoid such a result.

Protection of reliance is not required only insofar as the German legislature at the time it provided for a comparison of terms of protection under Art. IV, Nos. 4 to 6, UCC (Sec. 140 UrhG), extended the term of protection from 50 to 70 years after the death of the author (See 64(*l*), 129(*l*) UrhG). This domestic extension of the term of protection does not inure to the benefit of an author whose work was no longer protected in the United States, as the country of origin, at the time the German copyright law became effective on January 1, 1966.

4.   Finally, the appellant can also not use the argument that other countries which had entered into bilateral agreements with the United States prior to the time the Universal Copyright Convention took effect, are said to have proceeded in all cases on the basis of a comparison of terms of protection and applied the proviso contained in Art. IV No. 4 UCC after the Universal Copyright Convention became effective. This has no bearing on the legal situation under the Agreement of January 15, 1892, between the United States and Germany.

NOTES

1.   Under the *Atlas Film* decision, when would the German copyright in the Buster Keaton films expire? Protection for a period measured by the author's life plus fifty years, assured to American works by the 1892 German-American treaty, formed the basis for the vested interests that the *Atlas Film* court honored in the face of the U.C.C.'s provision for comparison of terms. Under the approach taken by the court, would the 1966 German legislation extending the term of copyright by twenty years have had the effect of extending the term of copyright in the Keaton films? In Tele-Cine Film Produktion GmbH v. Constantin Film GmbH, Case: I ZR 4/77 (German Federal Supreme Court 1978) 10 IIC 363 (1979), plaintiff, which had acquired the film rights to American novelist Jack London's novel, *White Fang*, sought a declaration that the rights were still protected in Germany. The Federal Supreme Court ruled that, since London had died in 1916, the novel was no longer protected in Germany even though the copyright, secured under the 1892 German-American Treaty, had not expired before January 1, 1966 when 1965 amendments to the German Copyright Act extended the term of copyright protection from fifty to seventy years after the author's death.

Recognizing that under the reasoning of *Atlas Film* it did not matter that protection for the work had ended in the United States, the *White Fang* court ruled that, although the 1965 legislation extended the copyright term of works not yet in the public domain, it also made comparison of terms under U.C.C. Article IV decisive for domestic protection of a work first published in a U.C.C. country. "The result is, under the applicable domestic law for granting protection, that the extension of the period of protection in favor of works protected under the Universal Copyright Convention or the bilateral Agreement of 1892 in connection with Article XIX U.C.C., will take place only to the extent that these works were still protected under domestic law at the time of the effective date of the Copyright Act of January 1, 1966, provided the period of protection had not yet expired in the country of origin. However, since under the findings of the Court of Appeals, 'White Fang' by Jack London was no longer protected on January 1, 1966 in the United States, the country of origin, an extension of the period of protection under domestic law can no longer apply." 10 IIC at 366.

2.   *Comparison of Terms.* Like Article IV of the U.C.C., Article 7(8) of the Berne Convention, Paris Text, prescribes a rule of comparison of terms, also called the rule of the shorter term: "In any case, the term shall be governed by the legislation of the country where protection is claimed; however, unless the legislation otherwise provides, the term shall not exceed the term fixed in the country of origin of the work." Article 5(4) of the Paris Text establishes the rules for determining a work's country of origin.

The term fixed for protection in the country of origin will not always be self-evident. In the United States, for example, works created before January 1, 1978 received an initial 28-year term of copyright followed by a second term—originally 28 years, presently 67 years—upon compliance with a renewal registration formality. Is the American copyright term for these works 28 years or is it 95 years? According to the Deputy Director General of the World Intellectual Property Organization, "the term affixed in country of origin of the work should be considered that term which would be applicable provided that the formalities would have been fulfilled (or would not have existed)" and this is the term—95 years—that Berne and WTO members should apply under Berne Article 7(8). Letter of Shozo Uemura, Deputy Director General, World Intellectual Property Organization, reprinted in 47 J. Copr. Soc'y 91, 93 (1999).

3.   *Country of Origin on the Internet.* For published works, Article 5(4) of the Berne Convention makes the country of origin "in the case of works first published in a country of the Union, that country; in the case of works published simultaneously in several countries of the Union which grant different terms of protection, the country whose legislation grants the shortest term of protection;" and "in the case of works published simultaneously in a country outside the Union and in a country of the Union, the latter country." Under these rules, what is the country of origin of a work that is first published on the Internet, and thus published simultaneously in every country in the world that has regular access to the Internet? Is it possible that every country in which the work is published is its "country of origin"?

The answer is important because comparison of terms is but one of the consequences that pivot on a work's country of origin. For example, under Article 5(1) and (3), Berne members are obligated to extend the treaty's minimum standards only to works originating in other Berne members, and are free to impose whatever requirements or exceptions they wish on works of domestic origin.

If a Swedish photographer who first published his works on a German website brings suit in the United States against other website proprietors for infringing the copyrights in his works, must he first register his claim to copyright in the U.S. Copyright Office on the ground that the works were published simultaneously in the United States so that the works are "United States works" and subject to a requirement of registration as a condition to filing suit? The court in Håkam Moberg v. 33T LLC, 666 F.Supp.2d 415 (D. Del. 2009), ruled that plaintiff's photographs were not United States works because "acceptance of defendants' position would overextend and pervert the United States copyright laws, and would be contrary to the Berne Convention." But another district court held that in comparable circumstances such works would be United States works subject to the registration requirement. Kernal Records Oy v. Mosley, 794 F.Supp.2d 1355 (S.D. Fla. 2011) ("Moberg's contextual and policy-driven analysis is reasonable and sound but is, in our opinion, wholly untethered to the actual statutory and treaty language that governs this dispute.").

Would it resolve the dilemma posed by worldwide simultaneous publication on the Internet to hold that Internet publication is not in fact "publication" for purposes of Berne Article 5(4)? The result would be that these works are "unpublished," and Article 5(4)(c) provides that in the case of unpublished works, the country of origin is the "country of the Union of which the author is a national." Would the author's nationality be a preferable determinant of country of origin for works disseminated on the Internet? *See* Sam Ricketson & Jane Ginsburg, International Copyright and Neighboring Rights: The Berne Convention and Beyond 285 (2d ed. 2006).

4. *EU Term Directive.* Directive 2006/116 EC of the European Parliament and of the Council of 12 December 2006 on the term of protection of copyright and certain related rights harmonizes several aspects of copyright term in the European Union: Article 1(1) requires a term measured by the author's life and 70 years after his death; Article 2(2) measures the term of protection for cinematographic and audiovisual works by 70 years from the death of the last to survive of the film's director, screenwriter, dialogue writer and composer, "whether or not these persons are designated as co-authors"; Article 6 extends the 70-year *post mortem auctoris* term to original, creative photographs, but gives member states discretion to "provide for protection of other photographs"; and Article 7 obligates member countries to apply the rule of comparison of terms to foreign works. In September 2011, over the objection of several member countries, the Council adopted a directive extending the terms of protection for performers and phonogram producers of musical recordings from 50 to 70 years. Directive 2011/77/EU of the European Parliament and of the Council of 27 September 2011 amending Directive 2006/116/EC on the term of protection of copyright and certain related rights.

See generally Herman Cohen Jehoram, The E.C. Copyright Directives, Economics and Authors' Rights, 25 IIC 821 (1994); Gerald Dworkin & J.A.L. Sterling, Phil Collins and the Term Directive, 16 EIPR 187 (1994).

5. *Orphan Works.* Copyrights last for generations, and even the Berne Convention's minimum term of the author's life plus fifty years will often make it costly for potential copyright users to track down a copyrighted work's current owners in order to negotiate a license. As a result, valuable copyright uses will too often be foregone, even though the copyright owner, once located, would have gladly licensed the use at reasonable cost. One

solution, shortening the duration of protection, is barred by the Berne minimum term. Berne minimum standards stand in the way of other solutions as well. A requirement that owners periodically register their interests as a condition to maintaining their copyrights would presumably violate Article 5(2)'s prohibition on formalities as a condition to protection. Similarly, the grant of a compulsory license to use works whose owners cannot be found runs the risk of violating Berne's pervasive limitations on such compulsory licenses.

These hurdles have not, however, stopped legislators around the world from trying to solve the orphan works problem. Following an extensive inquiry, the U.S. Copyright Office in 2006 issued a report and a legislative proposal that would have generally limited the copyright owner's remedies to reasonable compensation from any user who conducted a reasonably diligent, but ultimately unsuccessful, ownership search prior to making its infringing use of the copyrighted work. Orphan Works Act of 2006, H.R. 5439. Where the proposed U.S. approach would have allowed the infringing use and awaited a claim by the copyright owner before requiring payment by the copyright user, the Canadian system, which also provides for reasonable compensation, requires the copyright user to pay before it makes the use and before any infringement claim is made. Under Copyright Act, R.S., 1985, C-42, 70.7, the Canadian Copyright Board determines whether the applicant has made a reasonable search and, if it has, will set the royalty and prescribe the terms of use. The Board then holds the royalty payment for distribution in the event the copyright owner later comes forward.

In the European Union, the Orphan Works Directive, Directive 2012/28/EU of the European Parliament and of the Council of 25 October 2012 on certain permitted uses of orphan works, contemplates national exceptions or limitations to the reproduction and making available rights to enable the use of works first published or broadcast in a member state by libraries, schools, museums, archives and other nonprofit, publicly accessible institutions to achieve aims related to their public service mission. "Diligent search" is the pivot on which the Directive turns, and Article 3(1) requires that the search be "carried out in good faith in respect of each work or other protected subject-matter, by consulting the appropriate sources for the category of works" in question. Articles 5 and 6(5) respectively ensure rightholders the right to terminate the orphan status of their works and to be awarded "fair compensation" for their use.

See Simone Schroff, Marcella Favale, Aura Bertoni, The Impossible Quest—Problems with Diligent Search for Orphan Works, 48 IIC 286 (2017).

The problem of orphan works is particularly severe when a single or small handful of such works can effectively frustrate the assembly of a digital archive of many thousands of works. One solution, considered in the context of the EU's Digital Libraries Initiative, is to borrow the concept of the "extended collective license," introduced by the Nordic collecting societies, which binds a copyright owner to a collecting society's blanket license whether it is a member of the society or not, so that licensees face no risk of liability for using a non-member's work. The system entitles non-members to the same treatment, including remuneration, as is enjoyed by society members and, typically, the opportunity to opt out of the blanket license.

In what ways, if any, might the American, Canadian and Nordic models fall short of Berne's requirements? For a glimpse of various solutions to the orphan works problem, see Stef van Gompel, Unlocking the Potential of Pre-Existing Content: How to Address the Issue of Orphan Works in Europe? 38 IIC 669 (2007).

5. ECONOMIC RIGHTS AND REMEDIES

a. COPYRIGHT

i. *Dissemination in Intangible Form*

American Broadcasting Corp., Inc. v. Aereo, Inc.

Supreme Court of the United States, 2014.
134 S.Ct. 2498, 189 L.Ed. 2d 476, 110 U.S. P.Q. 2d 1961.

JUSTICE BREYER delivered the opinion of the Court.

The Copyright Act of 1976 gives a copyright owner the "exclusive righ[t]" to "perform the copyrighted work publicly." The Act's Transmit Clause defines that exclusive right as including the right

> to transmit or otherwise communicate a performance . . . of the [copyrighted] work . . . to the public, by means of any device or process, whether the members of the public capable of receiving the performance . . . receive it in the same place or in separate places and at the same time or at different times.

We must decide whether respondent Aereo, Inc., infringes this exclusive right by selling its subscribers a technologically complex service that allows them to watch television programs over the Internet at about the same time as the programs are broadcast over the air. We conclude that it does.

I.

A.

For a monthly fee, Aereo offers subscribers broadcast television programming over the Internet, virtually as the programming is being broadcast. Much of this programming is made up of copyrighted works. Aereo neither owns the copyright in those works nor holds a license from the copyright owners to perform those works publicly.

Aereo's system is made up of servers, transcoders, and thousands of dime-sized antennas housed in a central warehouse. It works roughly as follows: First, when a subscriber wants to watch a show that is currently being broadcast, he visits Aereo's website and selects, from a list of the local programming, the show he wishes to see.

Second, one of Aereo's servers selects an antenna, which it dedicates to the use of that subscriber (and that subscriber alone) for the duration of the selected show. A server then tunes the antenna to the over-the-air broadcast carrying the show. The antenna begins to receive the broadcast, and an Aereo transcoder translates the signals received into data that can be transmitted over the Internet.

Third, rather than directly send the data to the subscriber, a server saves the data in a subscriber-specific folder on Aereo's hard drive. In other words, Aereo's system creates a subscriber-specific copy that is, a "personal" copy—of the subscriber's program of choice.

Fourth, once several seconds of programming have been saved, Aereo's server begins to stream the saved copy of the show to the subscriber over the Internet. (The subscriber may instead direct Aereo to stream the program at a later time, but that aspect of Aereo's service is not before us.) The subscriber can watch the streamed program on the screen of his personal computer, tablet, smart phone, Internet-connected television, or other Internet-connected device. The streaming continues, a mere few seconds behind the over-the-air broadcast, until the subscriber has received the entire show.

Aereo emphasizes that the data that its system streams to each subscriber are the data from his own personal copy, made from the broadcast signals received by the particular antenna allotted to him. Its system does not transmit data saved in one subscriber's folder to any other subscriber. When two subscribers wish to watch the same program, Aereo's system activates two separate antennas and saves two separate copies of the program in two separate folders. It then streams the show to the subscribers through two separate transmissions—each from the subscriber's personal copy.

B.

Petitioners are television producers, marketers, distributors, and broadcasters who own the copyrights in many of the programs that Aereo's system streams to its subscribers. They brought suit against Aereo for copyright infringement in Federal District Court. They sought a preliminary injunction, arguing that Aereo was infringing their right to "perform" their works "publicly," as the *Transmit Clause* defines those terms.

The District Court denied the preliminary injunction. Relying on prior Circuit precedent, a divided panel of the Second Circuit affirmed. In the Second Circuit's view, Aereo does not perform publicly within the meaning of the Transmit Clause because it does not transmit "to the public." Rather, each time Aereo streams a program to a subscriber, it sends a *private* transmission that is available only to that subscriber. The Second Circuit denied rehearing en banc, over the dissent of two judges. We granted certiorari.

II.

This case requires us to answer two questions: First, in operating in the manner described above, does Aereo "perform" at all? And second, if so, does Aereo do so "publicly"? We address these distinct questions in turn.

Does Aereo "perform"? *See* § 106(4)("[T]he owner of [a] copyright . . . has the exclusive righ[t] . . . to perform the copyrighted work publicly" (emphasis added)); § 101 ("To perform . . . a work 'publicly' means [among other things] to transmit . . . a performance . . . of the work . . . to the public . . ." (emphasis added)). Phrased another way, does Aereo "transmit . . . a performance" when a subscriber watches a show using Aereo's system, or is it only the subscriber who transmits? In Aereo's view, it does not perform. It does no more than supply equipment that "emulate[s] the operation of a home antenna and [digital video recorder (DVR)]." Like a home antenna and DVR, Aereo's equipment simply responds to its subscribers' directives. So it is only the subscribers who "perform" when they use Aereo's equipment to stream television programs to themselves.

Considered alone, the language of the Act does not clearly indicate when an entity "perform[s]" (or "transmit[s]") and when it merely supplies equipment that allows others to do so. But when read in light of its purpose, the Act is unmistakable: An entity that engages in activities like Aereo's performs.

A.

History makes plain that one of Congress' primary purposes in amending the Copyright Act in 1976 was to overturn this Court's determination that community antenna television (CATV) systems (the precursors of modern cable systems) fell outside the Act's scope. In *Fortnightly Corp. v. United Artists Television, Inc.*, 392 U.S. 390, 88 S.Ct. 2084, 20 L.Ed.2d 1176 (1968), the Court considered a CATV system that carried local television broadcasting, much of which was copyrighted, to its subscribers in two cities. The CATV provider placed antennas on hills above the cities and used coaxial cables to carry the signals received by the antennas to the home television sets of its subscribers. The system amplified and modulated the signals in order to improve their strength and efficiently transmit them to subscribers. A subscriber "could choose any of the . . . programs he wished to view by simply turning the knob on his own television set." The CATV provider "neither edited the programs received nor originated any programs of its own."

Asked to decide whether the CATV provider infringed copyright holders' exclusive right to perform their works publicly, the Court held that the provider did not "perform" at all. The Court drew a line: "Broadcasters perform. Viewers do not perform." And a CATV provider "falls on the viewer's side of the line."

The Court reasoned that CATV providers were unlike broadcasters:

> Broadcasters select the programs to be viewed; CATV systems simply carry, without editing, whatever programs they receive. Broadcasters procure programs and propagate them to the public; CATV systems receive programs that have been released to the public and carry them by private channels to additional viewers.

Instead, CATV providers were more like viewers, for "the basic function [their] equipment serves is little different from that served by the equipment generally furnished by" viewers. "Essentially," the Court said, "a CATV system no more than enhances the viewer's capacity to receive the broadcaster's signals [by] provid[ing] a well-located antenna with an efficient connection to the viewer's television set." Viewers do not become performers by using "amplifying equipment," and a CATV provider should not be treated differently for providing viewers the same equipment.

In *Teleprompter Corp. v. Columbia Broadcasting System, Inc.*, 415 U.S. 394, 94 S.Ct. 1129, 39 L.Ed.2d 415 (1974), the Court considered the copyright liability of a CATV provider that carried broadcast television programming into subscribers' homes from hundreds of miles away. Although the Court recognized that a viewer might not be able to afford amplifying equipment that would provide access to those distant signals, it nonetheless found that the CATV provider was more like a viewer than a broadcaster. It explained: "The reception and rechanneling of [broadcast television signals] for simultaneous viewing is essentially a viewer function, irrespective of the distance between the broadcasting station and the ultimate viewer."

The Court also recognized that the CATV system exercised some measure of choice over what to transmit. But that fact did not transform the CATV system into a broadcaster. A broadcaster exercises significant creativity in choosing what to air, the Court reasoned. In contrast, the CATV provider makes an initial choice about which broadcast stations to retransmit, but then " 'simply carr[ies], without editing, whatever programs [it] receive[s].' "

B.

In 1976 Congress amended the Copyright Act in large part to reject the Court's holdings in *Fortnightly* and *Teleprompter*. See H.R.Rep. No. 94–1476, pp. 86–87 (1976)(hereinafter H.R. Rep.) Congress enacted new language that erased the Court's line between broadcaster and viewer, in respect to "perform [ing]" a work. The amended statute clarifies that to "perform" an audiovisual work means "to show its images in any sequence or to make the sounds accompanying it audible." § 101; (defining "[a]udiovisual works" as "works that consist of a series of related images which are intrinsically intended to be shown by the use of machines . . . , together with accompanying sounds"). Under this new language, both the broadcaster and the viewer of a television program "perform," because they both show the program's images and make audible the program's sounds. *See* H.R. Rep., at 63 ("[A] broadcasting network is performing when it transmits [a singer's performance of a song] . . . and any individual is performing whenever he or she . . . communicates the performance by turning on a receiving set").

Congress also enacted the Transmit Clause, which specifies that an entity performs publicly when it "transmit[s] . . . a performance . . . to the public." § 101; (defining "[t]o 'transmit' a performance" as "to communicate it by any device or process whereby images or sounds are received beyond the place from which they are sent"). Cable system activities, like those of the CATV systems in *Fortnightly* and *Teleprompter*, lie at the heart of the activities that Congress intended this language to cover. *See* H.R. Rep., at 63 ("[A] cable television system is performing when it retransmits [a network] broadcast to its subscribers"); ("[T]he concep[t] of public performance . . . cover[s] not only the initial rendition or showing, but also any further act by which that rendition or showing is transmitted or communicated to the public"). The Clause thus makes clear that an entity that acts like a CATV system itself performs, even if when doing so, it simply enhances viewers' ability to receive broadcast television signals. . . .

<h2 style="text-align:center">C.</h2>

This history makes clear that Aereo is not simply an equipment provider. Rather, Aereo, and not just its subscribers, "perform[s]" (or "transmit[s]"). Aereo's activities are substantially similar to those of the CATV companies that Congress amended the Act to reach. Aereo sells a service that allows subscribers to watch television programs, many of which are copyrighted, almost as they are being broadcast. In providing this service, Aereo uses its own equipment, housed in a centralized warehouse, outside of its users' homes. By means of its technology (antennas, transcoders, and servers), Aereo's system "receive[s] programs that have been released to the public and carr[ies] them by private channels to additional viewers." It "carr[ies] . . . whatever programs [it] receive[s]," and it offers "all the programming" of each over-the-air station it carries.

Aereo's equipment may serve a "viewer function"; it may enhance the viewer's ability to receive a broadcaster's programs. It may even emulate equipment a viewer could use at home. But the same was true of the equipment that was before the Court, and ultimately before Congress, in Fortnightly and Teleprompter.

We recognize, and Aereo and the dissent emphasize, one particular difference between Aereo's system and the cable systems at issue in *Fortnightly* and *Teleprompter*. The systems in those cases transmitted constantly; they sent continuous programming to each subscriber's television set. In contrast, Aereo's system remains inert until a subscriber indicates that she wants to watch a program. Only at that moment, in automatic response to the subscriber's request, does Aereo's system activate an antenna and begin to transmit the requested program.

This is a critical difference, says the dissent. It means that Aereo's subscribers, not Aereo, "selec[t] the copyrighted content" that is "perform[ed]," and for that reason they, not Aereo, "transmit" the performance. Aereo is thus like "a copy shop that provides its patrons with a library card." A copy shop is not directly liable whenever a patron uses the shop's machines to "reproduce" copyrighted materials found in that library. And by the same token, Aereo should not be directly liable whenever its patrons use its equipment to "transmit" copyrighted television programs to their screens.

In our view, however, the dissent's copy shop argument, in whatever form, makes too much out of too little. Given Aereo's overwhelming likeness to the cable companies targeted by the 1976 amendments, this sole technological difference between Aereo and traditional cable companies does not make a critical difference here. The subscribers of the *Fortnightly* and *Teleprompter* cable systems also selected what programs to display on their receiving sets. Indeed, as we explained in Fortnightly, such a subscriber "could choose any of the . . . programs he wished to view by simply turning the knob on his own television set." The same is true of an Aereo subscriber. Of course, in *Fortnightly* the television signals, in a sense, lurked behind the screen, ready to emerge when the subscriber turned the knob. Here the signals pursue their ordinary course of travel through the universe until today's "turn of the knob"—a click on a website—activates machinery that intercepts and reroutes them to Aereo's subscribers over the Internet. But this difference means nothing to the subscriber. It means nothing to the broadcaster. We do not see how this single difference, invisible to subscriber and broadcaster alike, could transform a system that is for all practical purposes a traditional cable system into "a copy shop that provides its patrons with a library card."

In other cases involving different kinds of service or technology providers, a user's involvement in the operation of the provider's equipment and selection of the content transmitted may well bear on whether the provider performs within the meaning of the Act. But the many similarities between Aereo and cable companies, considered in light of Congress' basic purposes in amending the Copyright Act, convince us that this difference is not critical here. We conclude that Aereo is not just an equipment supplier and that Aereo "perform[s]."

III.

Next, we must consider whether Aereo performs petitioners' works "publicly," within the meaning of the Transmit Clause. Under the Clause, an entity performs a work publicly when it "transmit[s] . . . a performance . . . of the work . . . to the public." § 101. Aereo denies that it satisfies this definition. It reasons as follows: First, the "performance" it "transmit[s]" is the performance created by its act of transmitting. And second, because each of these performances is capable of being received by one and only one subscriber, Aereo transmits privately, not publicly. Even assuming Aereo's first argument is correct, its second does not follow.

We begin with Aereo's first argument. What performance does Aereo transmit? Under the Act, "[t]o 'transmit' a performance . . . is to communicate it by any device or process whereby images or sounds are received beyond the place from which they are sent." And "[t]o 'perform'" an audiovisual work means "to show its images in any sequence or to make the sounds accompanying it audible."

Petitioners say Aereo transmits a *prior* performance of their works. Thus when Aereo retransmits a network's prior broadcast, the underlying broadcast (itself a performance) is the performance that Aereo transmits. Aereo, as discussed above, says the performance it transmits is the *new* performance created by its act of transmitting. That performance comes into existence when Aereo streams the sounds and images of a broadcast program to a subscriber's screen.

We assume *arguendo* that Aereo's first argument is correct. Thus, for present purposes, to transmit a performance of (at least) an audiovisual work means to communicate contemporaneously visible images and contemporaneously audible sounds of the work. When an Aereo subscriber selects a program to watch, Aereo streams the program over the Internet to that subscriber. Aereo thereby "communicate[s]" to the subscriber, by means of a "device or process," the work's images and sounds. And those images and sounds are contemporaneously visible and audible on the subscriber's computer (or other Internet-connected device). So under our assumed definition, Aereo transmits a performance whenever its subscribers watch a program.

But what about the Clause's further requirement that Aereo transmit a performance "to the public"? As we have said, an Aereo subscriber receives broadcast television signals with an antenna dedicated to him alone. Aereo's system makes from those signals a personal copy of the selected program. It streams the content of the copy to the same subscriber and to no one else. One and only one subscriber has the ability to see and hear each Aereo transmission. The fact that each transmission is to only one subscriber, in Aereo's view, means that it does not transmit a performance "to the public."

In terms of the Act's purposes, these differences do not distinguish Aereo's system from cable systems, which do perform "publicly." Viewed in terms of Congress' regulatory objectives, why should any of these technological differences matter? They concern the behind-the-scenes way in which Aereo delivers television programming to its viewers' screens. They do not render Aereo's commercial objective any different from that of cable companies. Nor do they significantly alter the viewing experience of Aereo's subscribers. Why would a subscriber who wishes to watch a television show care much whether images and sounds are delivered to his screen via a large multisubscriber antenna or one small dedicated antenna, whether they arrive instantaneously or after a few seconds' delay, or whether they are transmitted directly or after a personal copy is made? And why, if Aereo is right, could not modern CATV systems simply continue the same commercial and consumer-oriented activities, free of copyright restrictions, provided they substitute such new technologies for old? Congress would as much have intended to protect a copyright holder from the unlicensed activities of Aereo as from those of cable companies.

The text of the Clause effectuates Congress' intent. Aereo's argument to the contrary relies on the premise that "to transmit . . . a performance" means to make a single transmission. But the Clause suggests that an entity may transmit a performance through multiple, discrete transmissions. That is because one can "transmit" or "communicate" something through a *set* of actions. Thus one can transmit a message to one's friends, irrespective of whether one sends separate identical e-mails to each friend or a single e-mail to all at once. So can an elected official communicate an idea, slogan, or speech to her constituents, regardless of whether she communicates that idea, slogan, or speech during individual phone calls to each constituent or in a public square.

The fact that a singular noun ("a performance") follows the words "to transmit" does not suggest the contrary. One can sing a song to his family, whether he sings the same song one-on-one or in front of all together. Similarly, one's colleagues may watch a performance of a particular play—say, this season's modern-dress version of "Measure for Measure"—whether they do so at separate or at the same showings. By the same principle, an entity may transmit a performance through one or several transmissions, where the performance is of the same work.

The Transmit Clause must permit this interpretation, for it provides that one may transmit a performance to the public "whether the members of the public capable of receiving the performance . . . receive it . . . at the same time or at different times." Were the words "to transmit . . . a performance" limited to a single act of communication, members of the public could not receive the performance communicated "at different times." Therefore, in light of the purpose and text of the Clause, we conclude that when an entity communicates the same contemporaneously perceptible images and sounds to multiple people, it transmits a performance to them regardless of the number of discrete communications it makes.

We do not see how the fact that Aereo transmits via personal copies of programs could make a difference. The Act applies to transmissions "by means of any device or process." And retransmitting a television program using user-specific copies is a "process" of transmitting a performance. A "cop[y]" of a work is simply a "material objec[t] . . . in which a work is fixed . . . and from which the work can be perceived, reproduced, or otherwise communicated." So whether Aereo transmits from the same or separate copies, it performs the same work; it shows the same images and makes audible the same sounds. Therefore, when Aereo streams the same television program to multiple subscribers, it "transmit[s] . . . a performance" to all of them.

Moreover, the subscribers to whom Aereo transmits television programs constitute "the public." Aereo communicates the same contemporaneously perceptible images and sounds to a large number of people who are unrelated and unknown to each other. This matters because, although the Act does not define "the public," it specifies that an entity performs publicly when it performs at "any place where a substantial number of persons outside of a normal circle of a family and its social acquaintances is gathered." The Act thereby suggests that "the public" consists of a large group of people outside of a family and friends.

Neither the record nor Aereo suggests that Aereo's subscribers receive performances in their capacities as owners or possessors of the underlying works. This is relevant because when an entity performs to a set of people, whether they constitute "the public" often depends upon their relationship to the underlying work. When, for example, a valet parking attendant returns cars to their drivers, we would not say that the parking service provides cars "to the public." We would say that it provides the cars to their owners. We would say that a car dealership, on the other hand, does provide cars to the public, for it sells cars to individuals who lack a pre-existing relationship to the cars. Similarly, an entity that transmits a performance to individuals in their capacities as owners or possessors does not perform to "the public," whereas an entity like Aereo that transmits to large numbers of paying subscribers who lack any prior relationship to the works does so perform.

Finally, we note that Aereo's subscribers may receive the same programs at different times and locations. This fact does not help Aereo, however, for the Transmit Clause expressly provides that an entity may perform publicly "whether the members of the public capable of receiving the performance . . . receive it in the same place or in separate places and at the same time or at different times." In other words, "the public" need not be situated together, spatially or temporally. For these reasons, we conclude that Aereo transmits a performance of petitioners' copyrighted works to the public, within the meaning of the Transmit Clause.

IV.

Aereo and many of its supporting *amici* argue that to apply the Transmit Clause to Aereo's conduct will impose copyright liability on other technologies, including new technologies, that Congress could not possibly have wanted to reach. We agree that Congress, while intending the Transmit Clause to apply broadly to cable companies and their equivalents, did not intend to discourage or to control the emergence or use of different kinds of technologies. But we do not believe that our limited holding today will have that effect.

For one thing, the history of cable broadcast transmissions that led to the enactment of the Transmit Clause informs our conclusion that Aereo "perform[s]," but it does not determine whether different kinds of providers in different contexts also "perform." For another, an entity only transmits a performance when it communicates contemporaneously perceptible images and sounds of a work.

Further, we have interpreted the term "the public" to apply to a group of individuals acting as ordinary members of the public who pay primarily to watch broadcast television programs, many of which are copyrighted. We have said that it does not extend to those who act as owners or possessors of the relevant product. And we have not considered whether the public performance right is infringed when the user of a service pays primarily for something other than the transmission of copyrighted works, such as the remote storage of content. In addition, an entity does not transmit to the public if it does not transmit to a substantial number of people outside of a family and its social circle.

We also note that courts often apply a statute's highly general language in light of the statute's basic purposes. Finally, the doctrine of "fair use" can help to prevent inappropriate or inequitable applications of the Clause.

We cannot now answer more precisely how the Transmit Clause or other provisions of the Copyright Act will apply to technologies not before us. We agree with the Solicitor General that "[q]uestions involving cloud computing, [remote storage] DVRs, and other novel issues not before the Court, as to which 'Congress has not plainly marked [the] course,' should await a case in which they are squarely presented." And we note that, to the extent commercial actors or other interested entities may be concerned with the relationship between the development and use of such technologies and the Copyright Act, they are of course free to seek action from Congress.

In sum, having considered the details of Aereo's practices, we find them highly similar to those of the CATV systems in *Fortnightly* and *Teleprompter*. And those are activities that the 1976 amendments sought to bring within the scope of the Copyright Act. Insofar as there are differences, those differences concern not the nature of the service that Aereo provides so much as the technological manner in which it provides the service. We conclude that those differences are not adequate to place Aereo's activities outside the scope of the Act.

For these reasons, we conclude that Aereo "perform[s]" petitioners' copyrighted works "publicly," as those terms are defined by the Transmit Clause. We therefore reverse the contrary judgment of the Court of Appeals, and we remand the case for further proceedings consistent with this opinion.

It is so ordered.

Svensson v. Retriever Sverige AB

Court of Justice of the European Union, 2014.
Case C-466/12.

Judgment

1   This request for a preliminary ruling concerns the interpretation of Article 3(1) of Directive 2001/29/EC of the European Parliament and of the Council of 22 May 2001 on the harmonisation of certain aspects of copyright and related rights in the information society (OJ 2001 L 167, p. 10).

2   The request has been made in proceedings between Mr Svensson, Mr Sjogren, Ms Sahlman and Ms Gadd, the applicants in the main proceedings, and Retriever Sverige AB ('Retriever Sverige') concerning compensation allegedly payable to them for the harm they consider they have suffered as a result of the inclusion on that company's website of clickable Internet links (hyperlinks) redirecting users to press articles in which the applicants hold the copyright.

Legal context

International law

The WIPO Copyright Treaty

3   The World Intellectual Property Organisation (WIPO) adopted the WIPO Copyright Treaty ('the WIPO Copyright Treaty') in Geneva on 20 December 1996. It was approved on behalf of the European Community by Council Decision 2000/278/EC of 16 March 2000 (OJ 2000 L 89, p. 6).

4   Article 1(4) of the WIPO Copyright Treaty provides that the contracting parties are to comply with Articles 1 to 21 of the Convention for the Protection of Literary and Artistic Works, signed at Berne on 9 September 1886 (Paris Act of 24 July 1971), as amended on 28 September 1979 ('the Berne Convention').

The Berne Convention

5   Article 20 of the Berne Convention, entitled 'Special Agreements Among Countries of the Union', states: 'The Governments of the countries of the Union reserve the right to enter into special agreements among themselves, in so far as such agreements grant to authors more extensive rights than those granted by the Convention, or contain other provisions not contrary to this Convention. The provisions of existing agreements which satisfy these conditions shall remain applicable.'

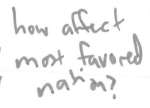

how affect most favored nation?

European Union law

6   Recitals 1, 4, 6, 7, 9 and 19 in the preamble to Directive 2001/29 state:

(1) The Treaty provides for the establishment of an internal market and the institution of a system ensuring that competition in the internal market is not distorted. Harmonisation of the laws of the Member States on copyright

and related rights contributes to the achievement of these objectives. . . .

(4) A harmonised legal framework on copyright and related rights, through increased legal certainty and while providing for a high level of protection of intellectual property, will foster substantial investment in creativity and innovation, including network infrastructure, and lead in turn to growth and increased competitiveness of European industry, both in the area of content provision and information technology and more generally across a wide range of industrial and cultural sectors. . . .

(6) Without harmonisation at Community level, legislative activities at national level which have already been initiated in a number of Member States in order to respond to the technological challenges might result in significant differences in protection and thereby in restrictions on the free movement of services and products incorporating, or based on, intellectual property, leading to a refragmentation of the internal market and legislative inconsistency. The impact of such legislative differences and uncertainties will become more significant with the further development of the information society, which has already greatly increased trans-border exploitation of intellectual property. This development will and should further increase. Significant legal differences and uncertainties in protection may hinder economies of scale for new products and services containing copyright and related rights.

(7) The Community legal framework for the protection of copyright and related rights must, therefore, also be adapted and supplemented as far as is necessary for the smooth functioning of the internal market. To that end, those national provisions on copyright and related rights which vary considerably from one Member State to another or which cause legal uncertainties hindering the smooth functioning of the internal market and the proper development of the information society in Europe should be adjusted, and inconsistent national responses to the technological developments should be avoided, whilst differences not adversely affecting the functioning of the internal market need not be removed or prevented. . . .

(9) Any harmonisation of copyright and related rights must take as a basis a high level of protection, since such rights are crucial to intellectual creation. Their protection helps to ensure the maintenance and development of creativity in the interests of authors, performers, producers, consumers, culture, industry and the public at large. . . .

(19) The moral rights of rightholders should be exercised according to the legislation of the Member States and the

provisions of the Berne Convention . . . [,] the WIPO Copyright Treaty and of the WIPO Performances and Phonograms Treaty. . . .'

7   Article 3 of Directive 2001/29 provides:

1.   Member States shall provide authors with the exclusive right to authorise or prohibit any communication to the public of their works, by wire or wireless means, including the making available to the public of their works in such a way that members of the public may access them from a place and at a time individually chosen by them. . . .

3.   The rights referred to in paragraphs 1 and 2 shall not be exhausted by any act of communication to the public or making available to the public as set out in this Article.'

The dispute in the main proceedings and the questions referred for a preliminary ruling

8   The applicants in the main proceedings, all journalists, wrote press articles that were published in the *Goteborgs-Posten* newspaper and on the *Goteborgs-Posten* website. Retriever Sverige operates a website that provides its clients, according to their needs, with lists of clickable Internet links to articles published by other websites. It is common ground between the parties that those articles were freely accessible on the *Goteborgs-Posten* newspaper site. According to the applicants in the main proceedings, if a client clicks on one of those links, it is not apparent to him that he has been redirected to another site in order to access the work in which he is interested. By contrast, according to Retriever Sverige, it is clear to the client that, when he clicks on one of those links, he is redirected to another site.

9   The applicants in the main proceedings brought an action against Retriever Sverige before the Stockholms tingsratt (Stockholm District Court) in order to obtain compensation on the ground that that company had made use, without their authorisation, of certain articles by them, by making them available to its clients.

10   By judgment of 11 June 2010, the Stockholms tingsratt rejected their application. The applicants in the main proceedings then brought an appeal against that judgment before the Sveahovratt (Svea Court of Appeal).

11   Before that court, the applicants in the main proceedings claimed, inter alia, that Retriever Sverige had infringed their exclusive right to make their respective works available to the public, in that as a result of the services offered on its website, Retriever Sverige's clients had access to the applicants' works.

12   Retriever Sverige contends, in defence, that the provision of lists of Internet links to works communicated to the public on other websites does not constitute an act liable to affect the copyright in those works.

Retriever Sverige also contends that it did not carry out any transmission of any protected work; its action is limited to indicating to its clients the websites on which the works that are of interest to them are to be found.

13 In those circumstances, the Svea hovratt decided to stay the proceedings and to refer the following questions to the Court of Justice for a preliminary ruling:

> (1) If anyone other than the holder of copyright in a certain work supplies a clickable link to the work on his website, does that constitute communication to the public within the meaning of Article 3(1) of Directive [2001/29]?

> (2) Is the assessment under question (1) affected if the work to which the link refers is on a website on the Internet which can be accessed by anyone without restrictions or if access is restricted in some way?

> (3) When making the assessment under question 1, should any distinction be drawn between a case where the work, after the user has clicked on the link, is shown on another website and one where the work, after the user has clicked on the link, is shown in such a way as to give the impression that it is appearing on the same website?

> (4) Is it possible for a Member State to give wider protection to authors' exclusive right by enabling communication to the public to cover a greater range of acts than provided for in Article 3(1) of Directive 2001/29?'

Consideration of the questions referred

The first three questions

14 By its first three questions, which it is appropriate to examine together, the referring court asks, in essence, whether Article 3(1) of Directive 2001/29 must be interpreted as meaning that the provision, on a website, of clickable links to protected works available on another website constitutes an act of communication to the public as referred to in that provision, where, on that other site, the works concerned are freely accessible.

15 In this connection, it follows from Article 3(1) of Directive 2001/29 that every act of communication of a work to the public has to be authorised by the copyright holder.

16 It is thus apparent from that provision that the concept of communication to the public includes two cumulative criteria, namely, an 'act of communication' of a work and the communication of that work to a 'public.'

17 As regards the first of those criteria, that is, the existence of an 'act of communication', this must be construed broadly, in order to ensure, in accordance with, inter alia, recitals 4 and 9 in the preamble to Directive 2001/29, a high level of protection for copyright holders.

18   In the circumstances of this case, it must be observed that the provision, on a website, of clickable links to protected works published without any access restrictions on another site, affords users of the first site direct access to those works.

19   As is apparent from Article 3(1) of Directive 2001/29, for there to be an 'act of communication', it is sufficient, in particular, that a work is made available to a public in such a way that the persons forming that public may access it, irrespective of whether they avail themselves of that opportunity.

20   It follows that, in circumstances such as those in the case in the main proceedings, the provision of clickable links to protected works must be considered to be 'making available' and, therefore, an 'act of communication', within the meaning of that provision.

21   So far as concerns the second of the abovementioned criteria, that is, that the protected work must in fact be communicated to a 'public', it follows from Article 3(1) of Directive 2001/29 that, by the term 'public', that provision refers to an indeterminate number of potential recipients and implies, moreover, a fairly large number of persons.

22   An act of communication such as that made by the manager of a website by means of clickable links is aimed at all potential users of the site managed by that person, that is to say, an indeterminate and fairly large number of recipients.

23   In those circumstances, it must be held that the manager is making a communication to a public.

24   None the less, according to settled case-law, in order to be covered by the concept of 'communication to the public', within the meaning of Article 3(1) of Directive 2001/29, a communication, such as that at issue in the main proceedings, concerning the same works as those covered by the initial communication and made, as in the case of the initial communication, on the Internet, and therefore by the same technical means, must also be directed at a new public, that is to say, at a public that was not taken into account by the copyright holders when they authorised the initial communication to the public.

25   In the circumstances of this case, it must be observed that making available the works concerned by means of a clickable link, such as that in the main proceedings, does not lead to the works in question being communicated to a new public.

26   The public targeted by the initial communication consisted of all potential visitors to the site concerned, since, given that access to the works on that site was not subject to any restrictive measures, all Internet users could therefore have free access to them.

27   In those circumstances, it must be held that, where all the users of another site to whom the works at issue have been communicated by means of a clickable link could access those works directly on the site on

which they were initially communicated, without the involvement of the manager of that other site, the users of the site managed by the latter must be deemed to be potential recipients of the initial communication and, therefore, as being part of the public taken into account by the copyright holders when they authorised the initial communication.

28   Therefore, since there is no new public, the authorisation of the copyright holders is not required for a communication to the public such as that in the main proceedings.

29   Such a finding cannot be called in question were the referring court to find, although this is not clear from the documents before the Court, that when Internet users click on the link at issue, the work appears in such a way as to give the impression that it is appearing on the site on which that link is found, whereas in fact that work comes from another site.

30   That additional circumstance in no way alters the conclusion that the provision on a site of a clickable link to a protected work published and freely accessible on another site has the effect of making that work available to users of the first site and that it therefore constitutes a communication to the public. However, since there is no new public, the authorisation of the copyright holders is in any event not required for such a communication to the public.

31   On the other hand, where a clickable link makes it possible for users of the site on which that link appears to circumvent restrictions put in place by the site on which the protected work appears in order to restrict public access to that work to the latter site's subscribers only, and the link accordingly constitutes an intervention without which those users would not be able to access the works transmitted, all those users must be deemed to be a new public, which was not taken into account by the copyright holders when they authorised the initial communication, and accordingly the holders' authorisation is required for such a communication to the public. This is the case, in particular, where the work is no longer available to the public on the site on which it was initially communicated or where it is henceforth available on that site only to a restricted public, while being accessible on another Internet site without the copyright holders' authorisation.

32   In those circumstances, the answer to the first three questions referred is that Article 3(1) of Directive 2001/29 must be interpreted as meaning that the provision on a website of clickable links to works freely available on another website does not constitute an act of communication to the public, as referred to in that provision.

The fourth question

33   By its fourth question, the referring court asks, in essence, whether Article 3(1) of Directive 2001/29 must be interpreted as precluding a Member State from giving wider protection to copyright holders by laying

down that the concept of communication to the public includes a wider range of activities than those referred to in that provision.

34   In this connection, it is apparent, in particular, from recitals 1, 6 and 7 in the preamble to Directive 2001/129 that the objectives of the directive are, inter alia, to remedy the legislative differences and legal uncertainty that exist in relation to copyright protection. Acceptance of the proposition that a Member State may give wider protection to copyright holders by laying down that the concept of communication to the public also includes activities other than those referred to in Article 3(1) of Directive 2001/29 would have the effect of creating legislative differences and thus, for third parties, legal uncertainty.

35   Consequently, the objective pursued by Directive 2001/29 would inevitably be undermined if the concept of communication to the public were to be construed in different Member States as including a wider range of activities than those referred to in Article 3(1) of that directive.

36   It is true that recital 7 in the preamble to the directive indicates that the directive does not have the objective of removing or preventing differences that do not adversely affect the functioning of the internal market. Nevertheless, it must be observed that, if the Member States were to be afforded the possibility of laying down that the concept of communication to the public includes a wider range of activities than those referred to in Article 3(1) of the directive, the functioning of the internal market would be bound to be adversely affected.

37   It follows that Article 3(1) of Directive 2001/29 cannot be construed as allowing Member States to give wider protection to copyright holders by laying down that the concept of communication to the public includes a wider range of activities than those referred to in that provision.

38   Such a conclusion is not affected by the fact, highlighted by the applicants in the main proceedings in their written observations, that Article 20 of the Berne Convention stipulates that the signatory countries may enter into 'special agreements' among themselves with a view to granting copyright holders more extensive rights than those laid down in that Convention.

39   In this connection, suffice it to recall that, when an agreement allows, but does not require, a Member State to adopt a measure which appears to be contrary to Union law, the Member State must refrain from adopting such a measure.

40   Since the objective of Directive 2001/29 would inevitably be undermined if the concept of communication to the public were construed as including a wider range of activities than those referred to in Article 3(1) of that directive, a Member State must refrain from exercising the right granted to it by Article 20 of the Berne Convention.

41   Therefore, the answer to the fourth question is that Article 3(1) of Directive 2001/29 must be interpreted as precluding a Member State from giving wider protection to copyright holders by laying down that the

concept of communication to the public includes a wider range of activities than those referred to in that provision.

Costs

42   Since these proceedings are, for the parties to the main proceedings, a step in the action pending before the national court, the decision on costs is a matter for that court. Costs incurred in submitting observations to the Court, other than the costs of those parties, are not recoverable.

On those grounds, the Court (Fourth Chamber) hereby rules:

> 1.   Article 3(1) of Directive 2001/29/EC of the European Parliament and of the Council of 22 May 2001 on the harmonisation of certain aspects of copyright and related rights in the information society, must be interpreted as meaning that the provision on a website of clickable links to works freely available on another website does not constitute an 'act of communication to the public', as referred to in that provision.
>
> 2.   Article 3(1) of Directive 2001/29 must be interpreted as precluding a Member State from giving wider protection to copyright holders by laying down that the concept of communication to the public includes a wider range of activities than those referred to in that provision.

NOTES

1.   *Communication to the Public.* Copyright legislation in some countries defines the right to exploit copyrighted works through intangible means in the most general terms, as an exclusive right to communicate, while legislation in other countries creates discrete rights of performance, recitation, broadcasting and display. Legislation in all countries requires that, to be actionable, the exploitation must be to the public. Most definitions of "public" for this purpose include mass broadcasting and performances in public places, and exclude performances that take place exclusively within a circle of family or friends.

New communications technologies enabling individuals to receive performances on command in the privacy of their homes promise to challenge traditional notions of mass performance. Article 8 of the WIPO Copyright Treaty aims to bring these individualized performances within copyright control by providing not only that "authors of literary and artistic works shall enjoy the exclusive right of authorizing any communication to the public of their works by wire or wireless means," but by including within that right "the making available to the public of their works in such a way that members of the public may access these works from a place and at a time individually chosen by them." The provision has been hailed as one of the treaty's "main achievements." Jörg Reinbothe, Maria Martin-Prat, Silke von Lewinski, The New WIPO Treaties: A First Résumé, 19 EIPR 171, 173 (1997). *See* also Mihály Ficsor, Copyright for the Digital Era: The WIPO "Internet" Treaties, 21 Colum.-VLA J. L. & Arts 197 (1997). *See* also Association Littéraire et Artistique Internationale (ALAI), Report and

Opinion on the Making Available and Communication to the Public in the Internet Environment: Focus on Linking Techniques on the Internet, 36 EIPR 149 (2014).

2. *"Performance," "Communication," "Making Available" and "Volition."* The traditional copyright terms, "perform" and "communicate," imply physical action to a greater degree than does the WIPO Copyright Treaty's newer phrase, "making available." Do the traditional terms also imply a higher standard of volition as the threshold for copyright liability? In his dissenting opinion on *Aereo*, Justice Antonin Scalia observed that the U.S. Copyright Act "defines 'performing' in active, affirmative terms," and concluded that "[i]n sum, Aereo does not 'perform' for the sole and simple reason that it does not make the choice of content." 134 S.Ct. 2514. Would defendant's provision of clickable links in the *Svensson* case have passed Scalia's test for volition? The test for volition adopted by the *Aereo* majority?

3. *What Is a "New Public"?* Articles on the *Göteborgs-Posten* website in the *Svensson* case were evidently freely accessible to all. According to the Court, users of defendant's service would constitute a "new public," and defendant would be liable for infringing the making available right "where a clickable link makes it possible for users of the site . . . to circumvent restrictions put in place by the site on which the protected work appears in order to restrict public access to that work to the latter site's subscribers only. . . ." Presumably passwords or other technical measures would have met the Court's requirement of limited access. Would terms of use that prohibited access from another website suffice for these purposes? Did the Court effectively hold that the plaintiff had given an implied license to linked access?

The history behind the *Aereo* case suggests that the U.S. Supreme Court, no less than the CJEU, made liability turn on the question whether the public that received the contested communication was "taken into account by the copyright holders when they authorized the initial communication to the public." The Court of Appeals in *Aereo* had relied on its earlier decision in Cartoon Network LP, LLP v. Cablevision, Systems Corp., 536 F. 3d 121 (2d Cir. 2008), which had excused defendant cable company's remote DVR system that enabled cable subscribers to record programming delivered by the cable provider. Unlike Aereo, which had no contractual relationship with the broadcasters whose signal it carried, Cablevision did have an ongoing relationship with its program suppliers, and these suppliers could have consequently taken these activities "into account when they authorized the initial communication to the public," charging the cable system accordingly.

Is the line drawn by American courts between cases where revenue opportunities do and do not exist more or less practical than the line drawn by the CJEU in *Svensson*? In a case presenting facts closely comparable to those in *Aereo*—retransmission of terrestrial broadcast signals over the Internet—the CJEU ruled that because "the making of works available through the retransmission of a terrestrial television broadcast over the internet uses a specific technical means different from that of the original communication, that retransmission must be considered to be a 'communication' within the meaning of the Directive." Further, since "the retransmission in question is aimed at an indeterminate number of potential recipients and implies a large number of persons . . . it must be held that, by the retransmission in question, the protected works are indeed communicated to a 'public' within the meaning of Article 3(1) of Directive 2001/29." ITV Broadcasting v. TV Catchup Ltd., Case C-607/11 (2013).

4. *Communication to the Public and Derivative Liability.* In GS Media BV v. Sanoma Media Netherlands BV, CJEU, C-160/15, 2016, defendant had provided hyperlinks to photographs placed in a digital locker without the copyright owner's permission. Recognizing that *Svensson's* "new public" rule would not exonerate hyperlinks to unlawfully posted works, the Court of Justice sought some other mechanism for striking a "fair balance" between authors and users on the Internet. It found its balance wheel in proof of knowledge or financial motive: if the party responsible for the hyperlink acted without knowledge of the illicit content or financial motive, it was not "intervening" so that no act of communication occurred; if, however, the actor's linking enterprise was in pursuit of financial gain, knowledge is presumed and a communication to the public has occurred.

Two subsequent Court of Justice decisions further reshaped the communication right around factors—knowledge, financial gain—that are more commonly found in the rules governing derivative or secondary copyright liability. In Stichting Brein v. Wullems, CJEU, C-527/15, 2017, the Court held that it constituted infringement of the communication right for defendant to sell media players containing pre-installed hyperlinks to infringing content, and in Stichting Brein v. Ziggo BV, CJEU, C-610/15, 2017, the Court held that The Pirate Bay, which facilitated large-scale file sharing of music and movies without permission from copyright owners, was directly liable for communicating these works to the public.

See Jane C. Ginsburg & Luke Ali Budiardjo, Liability for Providing Hyperlinks to Copyright-Infringing Content: International and Comparative Law Perspectives, 41 Colum. J. Law & Arts 153 (2018).

5. *Public Display and Exhibition Right.* The public display right has been far less widely adopted than the public performance right. Section 106(5) of the U.S. Copyright Act grants an extensive right "to display the copyrighted work publicly," and section 101 defines "display" as meaning "to show a copy of it, either directly or by means of a film, slide, television image, or any other device or process or, in the case of a motion picture or other audiovisual work, to show individual images nonsequentially." Article 18 of the German Copyright Act prescribes a narrower exhibition right—"the right to place on public view the original or copies of an unpublished work of fine art or of an unpublished photographic work." In some countries, artists will receive compensation for exhibition of their works through noncopyright arrangements instituted by national or local governments.

For an excellent study of the exhibition right, see Wladimir Duchemin, Thoughts on the Exhibition Right, 156 R.I.D.A. 14 (1993).

ii.   Dissemination in Tangible Form

Kirtsaeng v. John Wiley & Sons, Inc.

Supreme Court of the United States, 2013.
568 U.S. 519.

JUSTICE BREYER delivered the opinion of the Court.

Section 106 of the Copyright Act grants "the owner of copyright under this title" certain "exclusive rights," including the right "to distribute copies . . . of the copyrighted work to the public by sale or other transfer of ownership." 17 U.S.C. § 106(3). These rights are qualified, however, by the application of various limitations set forth in the next several sections of the Act, §§ 107 through 122. Those sections, typically entitled "Limitations on exclusive rights," include, for example, the principle of "fair use" (§ 107), permission for limited library archival reproduction, (§ 108), and the doctrine at issue here, the "first sale" doctrine (§ 109).

Section 109(a) sets forth the "first sale" doctrine as follows:

"Notwithstanding the provisions of section 106(3) [the section that grants the owner exclusive distribution rights], the owner of a particular copy or phonorecord *lawfully made under this title* . . . is entitled, without the authority of the copyright owner, to sell or otherwise dispose of the possession of that copy or phonorecord." (Emphasis added.)

Thus, even though § 106(3) forbids distribution of a copy of, say, the copyrighted novel Herzog without the copyright owner's permission, § 109(a) adds that, once a copy of Herzog has been lawfully sold (or its ownership otherwise lawfully transferred), the buyer of that *copy* and subsequent owners are free to dispose of it as they wish. In copyright jargon, the "first sale" has "exhausted" the copyright owner's § 106(3) exclusive distribution right.

What, however, if the copy of Herzog was printed abroad and then initially sold with the copyright owner's permission? Does the "first sale" doctrine still apply? Is the buyer, like the buyer of a domestically manufactured copy, free to bring the copy into the United States and dispose of it as he or she wishes?

To put the matter technically, an "importation" provision, § 602(a)(1), says that

"[i]mportation into the United States, without the authority of the owner of copyright under this title, of copies . . . of a work that have been acquired outside the United States is an infringement of the exclusive right to distribute copies . . . *under section 106. . .*" (emphasis added).

Thus § 602(a)(1) makes clear that importing a copy without permission violates the owner's exclusive distribution right. But in doing so, § 602(a)(1) refers explicitly to the *§ 106(3)* exclusive distribution right. As we have just said, § 106 is by its terms "[s]ubject to" the various doctrines and principles contained in §§ 107 through 122, including § 109(a)'s "first sale" limitation. Do those same modifications apply—in particular, does the "first sale" modification apply—when considering whether § 602(a)(1) prohibits importing a copy?

In Quality King Distributors, Inc. v. L'anza Research Int'l, Inc., 523 U.S. 135, 145, 118 S.Ct. 1125, 140 L.Ed.2d 254 (1998), we held that § 602(a)(1)'s reference to § 106(3)'s exclusive distribution right incorporates the later subsections' limitations, including, in particular, the "first sale" doctrine of § 109. Thus, it might seem that, § 602(a)(1) notwithstanding, one who buys a copy abroad can freely import that copy into the United States and dispose of it, just as he could had he bought the copy in the United States.

But *Quality King* considered an instance in which the copy, though purchased abroad, was initially manufactured in the United States (and then sent abroad and sold). This case is like *Quality King* but for one important fact. The copies at issue here were manufactured abroad. That fact is important because § 109(a) says that the "first sale" doctrine applies to "a particular copy or phonorecord *lawfully made under this title*." And we must decide here whether the five words, "lawfully made under this title," make a critical legal difference.

Putting section numbers to the side, we ask whether the "first sale" doctrine applies to protect a buyer or other lawful owner of a copy (of a copyrighted work) lawfully manufactured abroad. Can that buyer bring that copy into the United States (and sell it or give it away) without obtaining permission to do so from the copyright owner? Can, for example, someone who purchases, say at a used bookstore, a book printed abroad subsequently resell it without the copyright owner's permission?

In our view, the answers to these questions are, yes. We hold that the "first sale" doctrine applies to copies of a copyrighted work lawfully made abroad.

I.

A.

Respondent, John Wiley & Sons, Inc., publishes academic textbooks. Wiley obtains from its authors various foreign and domestic copyright assignments, licenses and permissions—to the point that we can, for present purposes, refer to Wiley as the relevant American copyright owner. Wiley often assigns to its wholly owned foreign subsidiary, John Wiley & Sons (Asia) Pte Ltd., rights to publish, print, and sell Wiley's English language textbooks abroad. Each copy of a Wiley Asia foreign edition will likely contain language making clear that the copy is to be sold only in a particular country or geographical region outside the United States.

For example, a copy of Wiley's American edition says, "Copyright © 2008 John Wiley & Sons, Inc. All rights reserved. . . . Printed in the United States of America." J. Walker, Fundamentals of Physics, p. vi (8th ed. 2008). A copy of Wiley Asia's Asian edition of that book says:

> "Copyright © 2008 John Wiley & Sons (Asia) Pte Ltd[.] All rights reserved. This book is authorized for sale in Europe, Asia, Africa, and the Middle East only and may be not exported out of these territories. Exportation from or importation of this book to another region without the Publisher's authorization is illegal and is a violation of the Publisher's rights. The Publisher may take legal action to enforce its rights. . . . Printed in Asia." J. Walker, Fundamentals of Physics, p. vi (8th ed. 2008 Wiley Int'l Student ed.).

Both the foreign and the American copies say:

> "No part of this publication may be reproduced, stored in a retrieval system, or transmitted in any form or by any means . . . except as permitted under Sections 107 or 108 of the 1976 United States Copyright Act." Compare, *e.g., ibid.* (Int'l ed.), with Walker, *supra,* at vi (American ed.).

The upshot is that there are two essentially equivalent versions of a Wiley textbook, each version manufactured and sold with Wiley's permission: (1) an American version printed and sold in the United States, and (2) a foreign version manufactured and sold abroad. And Wiley makes certain that copies of the second version state that they are not to be taken (without permission) into the United States.

Petitioner, Supap Kirtsaeng, a citizen of Thailand, moved to the United States in 1997 to study mathematics at Cornell University. He paid for his education with the help of a Thai Government scholarship which required him to teach in Thailand for 10 years on his return. Kirtsaeng successfully completed his undergraduate courses at Cornell, successfully completed a Ph.D. program in mathematics at the University of Southern California, and then, as promised, returned to Thailand to teach. While he was studying in the United States, Kirtsaeng asked his friends and family in Thailand to buy copies of foreign edition English-language textbooks at Thai book shops, where they sold at low prices, and mail them to him in the United States. Kirtsaeng would then sell them, reimburse his family and friends, and keep the profit.

B.

In 2008 Wiley brought this federal lawsuit against Kirtsaeng for copyright infringement. Wiley claimed that Kirtsaeng's unauthorized importation of its books and his later resale of those books amounted to an infringement of Wiley's § 106(3) exclusive right to distribute as well as § 602's related import prohibition. Kirtsaeng replied that the books he had acquired were " 'lawfully made' " and that he had acquired them legitimately. Thus, in his view, § 109(a)'s "first sale" doctrine permitted him to resell or otherwise dispose of the books without the copyright owner's further permission.

The District Court held that Kirtsaeng could not assert the "first sale" defense because, in its view, that doctrine does not apply to "foreign-manufactured goods" (even if made abroad with the copyright owner's permission). The jury then found that Kirtsaeng had willfully infringed Wiley's American copyrights by selling and importing without authorization copies of eight of Wiley's copyrighted titles. And it assessed statutory damages of $600,000 ($75,000 per work).

On appeal, a split panel of the Second Circuit agreed with the District Court. It pointed out that § 109(a)'s "first sale" doctrine applies only to "the owner of a particular copy . . . *lawfully made under this title.*" (emphasis added). And, in the majority's view, this language means that the "first sale" doctrine does not apply to copies of American copyrighted works manufactured abroad. A dissenting judge thought that the words "lawfully made under this title" do not refer "to a place of manufacture" but rather "focu[s] on whether a particular copy was manufactured lawfully under" America's copyright statute, and that "the lawfulness of the manufacture of a particular copy should be judged by U.S. copyright law."

We granted Kirtsaeng's petition for certiorari to consider this question in light of different views among the Circuits.

II.

We must decide whether the words "lawfully made under this title" restrict the scope of § 109(a)'s "first sale" doctrine geographically. The Second Circuit, the Ninth Circuit, Wiley, and the Solicitor General (as *amicus*) all read those words as imposing a form of *geographical* limitation. The Second Circuit held that they limit the "first sale" doctrine to particular copies "made in territories *in which the Copyright Act is law,*" which (the Circuit says) are copies "manufactured domestically," not " outside of the United States." (emphasis added). Wiley agrees that those five words limit the "first sale" doctrine " to copies made in conformance with the [United States] Copyright Act *where the Copyright Act is applicable,*" which (Wiley says) means it does not apply to copies made "outside the United States" and at least not to "foreign production of a copy for distribution exclusively abroad." Similarly, the Solicitor General says that those five words limit the "first sale" doctrine's applicability to copies " '*made subject to* and in compliance with [the Copyright Act],' " which (the Solicitor General says) are copies "made in the United States." And the Ninth Circuit has held that those words limit the "first sale" doctrine's applicability (1) to copies lawfully made in the United States, and (2) to copies lawfully made outside the United States but initially sold in the United States with the copyright owner's permission. Denbicare U.S.A. Inc. v. Toys "R" Us, Inc., 84 F.3d 1143, 1149–1150 (1996).

Under any of these geographical interpretations, § 109(a)'s "first sale" doctrine would not apply to the Wiley Asia books at issue here. And, despite an American copyright owner's permission to *make* copies abroad, one who *buys* a copy of any such book or other copyrighted work—whether at a retail store, over the Internet, or at a library sale—could not resell (or otherwise dispose of) that particular copy without further permission.

Kirtsaeng, however, reads the words "lawfully made under this title" as imposing a *non*-geographical limitation. He says that they mean made "in accordance with" or "in compliance with" the Copyright Act. In that case, § 109(a)'s "first sale" doctrine would apply to copyrighted works as long as their manufacture met the requirements of American copyright law. In particular, the doctrine would apply where, as here, copies are manufactured abroad with the permission of the copyright owner.

In our view, § 109(a)'s language, its context, and the common-law history of the "first sale" doctrine, taken together, favor a *non*-geographical interpretation. We also doubt that Congress would have intended to create the practical copyright-related harms with which a geographical interpretation would threaten ordinary scholarly, artistic, commercial, and consumer activities. We consequently conclude that Kirtsaeng's nongeographical reading is the better reading of the Act.

A.

The language of § 109(a) read literally favors Kirtsaeng's nongeographical interpretation, namely, that "lawfully made under this title" means made "in accordance with" or "in compliance with" the Copyright Act. The language of § 109(a) says nothing about geography. The word "under" can mean "[i]n accordance with." 18 Oxford English Dictionary 950 (2d ed.1989). And a nongeographical interpretation provides each word of the five-word phrase with a distinct purpose. The first two words of the phrase, "lawfully made," suggest an effort to distinguish those copies that were made lawfully from those that were not, and the last three words, "under this title," set forth the standard of "lawful[ness]." Thus, the nongeographical reading is simple, it promotes a traditional copyright objective (combatting piracy), and it makes word-by-word linguistic sense.

The geographical interpretation, however, bristles with linguistic difficulties. It gives the word "lawfully" little, if any, linguistic work to do. (How could a book be *un*lawfully "made under this title"?) It imports geography into a statutory provision that says nothing explicitly about it. And it is far more complex than may at first appear.

To read the clause geographically, Wiley, like the Second Circuit and the Solicitor General, must first emphasize the word "under." Indeed, Wiley reads "under this title" to mean "in conformance with the Copyright Act *where the Copyright Act is applicable*." Wiley must then take a second step, arguing that the Act "is applicable" only in the United States. And the Solicitor General must do the same.

One difficulty is that neither "under" nor any other word in the phrase means "where." See, *e.g.,* 18 Oxford English Dictionary, *supra,* at 947–952 (definition of "under"). It might mean "subject to," but as this Court has repeatedly acknowledged, the word evades a uniform, consistent meaning.

A far more serious difficulty arises out of the uncertainty and complexity surrounding the second step's effort to read the necessary geographical limitation into the word "applicable" (or the equivalent). Where, precisely, is the Copyright Act "applicable"? The Act does not instantly *protect* an American copyright holder from unauthorized piracy taking place abroad. But that fact does not mean the Act is *inapplicable* to copies made abroad. As a matter of ordinary English, one can say that a statute imposing, say, a tariff upon "any rhododendron grown in Nepal" applies to *all* Nepalese rhododendrons. And, similarly, one can say that the American Copyright Act is *applicable* to *all* pirated copies, including those printed overseas. Indeed, the Act itself makes clear that (in the Solicitor General's language) foreign-printed pirated copies are "subject to" the Act. § 602(a)(2) (2006 ed., Supp. V) (referring to importation of copies "the making of which either constituted an infringement of copyright, or which would have constituted an infringement of copyright if this title had been applicable").

The appropriateness of this linguistic usage is underscored by the fact that § 104 of the Act itself says that works "*subject to protection under this title* " include unpublished works "without regard to the nationality or domicile of the author," and works "first published" in any one of the nearly 180 nations that have signed a copyright treaty with the United States. §§ 104(a), (b) (2006 ed.) Thus, ordinary English permits us to say that the Act "applies" to an Irish manuscript lying in its author's Dublin desk drawer as well as to an original recording of a ballet performance first made in Japan and now on display in a Kyoto art gallery.

The Ninth Circuit's geographical interpretation produces still greater linguistic difficulty. As we said, that Circuit interprets the "first sale" doctrine to cover both (1) copies manufactured in the United States and (2) copies manufactured abroad but first sold in the United States with the American copyright owner's permission. *Denbicare U.S.A.*, 84 F.3d, at 1149–1150.

We can understand why the Ninth Circuit may have thought it necessary to add the second part of its definition. As we shall later describe, see Part II-D, *infra,* without some such qualification a copyright holder could prevent a buyer from domestically reselling or even giving away copies of a video game made in Japan, a film made in Germany, or a dress (with a design copyright) made in China, *even* if the copyright holder has granted permission for the foreign manufacture, importation, and an initial domestic sale of the copy. A publisher such as Wiley would be free to print its books abroad, allow their importation and sale within the United States, but prohibit students from later selling their used texts at a campus bookstore. We see no way, however, to reconcile this half-geographical/half-nongeographical interpretation with the language of the phrase, "lawfully made under this title." As a matter of English, it would seem that those five words either do cover copies lawfully made abroad or they do not.

In sum, we believe that geographical interpretations create more linguistic problems than they resolve. And considerations of simplicity and coherence tip the purely linguistic balance in Kirtsaeng's, nongeographical, favor.

B.

Both historical and contemporary statutory context indicate that Congress, when writing the present version of § 109(a), did not have geography in mind. In respect to history, we compare § 109(a)'s present language with the language of its immediate predecessor. That predecessor said:

> "[N]othing in this Act shall be deemed to forbid, prevent, or restrict the transfer of any copy of a copyrighted work *the possession of which has been lawfully obtained.*" Copyright Act of 1909, § 41, 35 Stat. 1084 (emphasis added).

The predecessor says nothing about geography (and Wiley does not argue that it does). So we ask whether Congress, in changing its language implicitly *introduced* a geographical limitation that previously was lacking.

A comparison of language indicates that it did not. The predecessor says that the "first sale" doctrine protects "the transfer of any copy *the possession of which has been lawfully obtained.*" The present version says that "*the owner* of a particular copy or phonorecord lawfully made under this title is entitled to sell or otherwise dispose of the possession of that copy or phonorecord." What does this change in language accomplish?

The language of the former version referred to those *who are not owners* of a copy, but mere possessors who "lawfully obtained" a copy. The present version covers only those who are *owners* of a "lawfully made" copy. Whom does the change leave out? Who might have lawfully *obtained* a copy of a copyrighted work but not *owned* that copy? One answer is owners of movie theaters, who during the 1970's (and before) often *leased* films from movie distributors or filmmakers. Because the theater owners had "lawfully obtained" their copies, the earlier version could be read as allowing them to sell that copy, *i.e.,* it might have given them "first sale" protection. Because the theater owners were lessees, not owners, of their copies, the change in language makes clear that they (like bailees and other lessees) cannot take advantage of the "first sale" doctrine.

This objective perfectly well explains the new language of the present version, including the five words here at issue. Section 109(a) now makes clear that a lessee of a copy will *not* receive "first sale" protection but one who *owns* a copy *will* receive "first sale" protection, *provided,* of course, that the copy was "*lawfully made* " and not pirated. The new language also takes into account that a copy may be "lawfully made under this title" when the copy, say of a phonorecord, comes into its owner's possession through use of a compulsory license, which "this title" provides for elsewhere, namely, in § 115. . . .

Finally, we normally presume that the words "lawfully made under this title" carry the same meaning when they appear in different but related sections. But doing so here produces surprising consequences. Consider:

(1) Section 109(c) says that, despite the copyright owner's exclusive right "to display" a copyrighted work (provided in § 106(5)), the owner of a particular copy "lawfully made under this title" may publicly display it without further authorization. To interpret these words geographically would mean that one who buys a copyrighted work of art, a poster, or even a bumper sticker, in Canada, in Europe, in Asia, could not display it in America without the copyright owner's further authorization.

(2) Section 109(e) specifically provides that the owner of a particular copy of a copyrighted video arcade game "lawfully made under this title" may "publicly perform or display that game in coin-operated equipment" without the authorization of the copyright owner. To interpret these words geographically means that an arcade owner could not ("without the authority of the copyright owner") perform or display arcade games (whether new or used) originally made in Japan.

(3) Section 110(1) says that a teacher, without the copyright owner's authorization, is allowed to perform or display a copyrighted work (say, an audiovisual work) "in the course of face-to-face teaching activities"—unless the teacher knowingly used "a copy that was not lawfully made under this title." To interpret these words geographically would mean that the teacher could not (without further authorization) use a copy of a film during class if the copy was lawfully made in Canada, Mexico, Europe, Africa, or Asia.

(4) In its introductory sentence, § 106 provides the Act's basic exclusive rights to an "owner of a copyright under this title." The last three words cannot support a geographic interpretation.

Wiley basically accepts the first three readings, but argues that Congress intended the restrictive consequences. And it argues that context simply requires that the words of the fourth example receive a different interpretation. Leaving the fourth example to the side, we shall explain in Part II-D, *infra,* why we find it unlikely that Congress would have intended these, and other related consequences. . . .

D.

Associations of libraries, used-book dealers, technology companies, consumer-goods retailers, and museums point to various ways in which a geographical interpretation would fail to further basic constitutional copyright objectives, in particular "promot[ing] the Progress of Science and useful Arts."

The American Library Association tells us that library collections contain at least 200 million books published abroad (presumably, many were first published in one of the nearly 180 copyright-treaty nations and enjoy American copyright protection under 17 U.S.C. § 104; that many others were first published in the United States but printed abroad because of lower costs; and that a geographical interpretation will likely require the libraries to obtain permission (or at least create significant uncertainty) before circulating or otherwise distributing these books.

How, the American Library Association asks, are the libraries to obtain permission to distribute these millions of books? How can they find, say, the copyright owner of a foreign book, perhaps written decades ago? They may not know the copyright holder's present address. And, even where addresses can be found, the costs of finding them, contacting owners, and negotiating may be high indeed. Are the libraries to stop circulating or distributing or displaying the millions of books in their collections that were printed abroad?

Used-book dealers tell us that, from the time when Benjamin Franklin and Thomas Jefferson built commercial and personal libraries of foreign books, American readers have bought used books published and printed abroad. The dealers say that they have "operat[ed] . . . for centuries" under the assumption that the "first sale" doctrine applies. But under a geographical interpretation a contemporary tourist who buys, say, at Shakespeare and Co. (in Paris), a dozen copies of a foreign book for American friends might find that she had violated the copyright law. The used-book dealers cannot easily predict what the foreign copyright holder may think about a reader's effort to sell a used copy of a novel. And they believe that a geographical interpretation will injure a large portion of the used-book business.

Technology companies tell us that "automobiles, microwaves, calculators, mobile phones, tablets, and personal computers" contain copyrightable software programs or packaging. Many of these items are made abroad with the American copyright holder's permission and then sold and imported (with that permission) to the United States. A geographical interpretation would prevent the resale of, say, a car, without the permission of the holder of each copyright on each piece of copyrighted automobile software. Yet there is no reason to believe that foreign auto manufacturers regularly obtain this kind of permission from their software component suppliers, and Wiley did not indicate to the contrary when asked. Without that permission a foreign car owner could not sell his or her used car. . . .

Neither Wiley nor any of its many *amici* deny that a geographical interpretation could bring about these "horribles"—at least in principle. Rather, Wiley essentially says that the list is artificially invented. It points out that a federal court first adopted a geographical interpretation more than 30 years ago. *CBS, Inc. v. Scorpio Music Distributors, Inc.,* 569 F.Supp. 47, 49 (E.D.Pa.1983), summarily aff'd, 738 F.2d 424 (C.A.3 1984) (table). Yet, it adds, these problems have not occurred. Why not? Because, says Wiley, the problems and threats are purely theoretical; they are unlikely to reflect reality.

We are less sanguine. For one thing, the law has not been settled for long in Wiley's favor. The Second Circuit, in its decision below, is the first Court of Appeals to adopt a purely geographical interpretation. The Third Circuit has favored a nongeographical interpretation. *Sebastian Int'l,* 847 F.2d 1093. The Ninth Circuit has favored a modified geographical interpretation with a nongeographical (but textually unsustainable) corollary designed to diminish the problem. *Denbicare U.S.A.,* 84 F.3d 1143. And other courts have hesitated to adopt, and have cast doubt upon, the validity of the geographical interpretation.

For another thing, reliance upon the "first sale" doctrine is deeply embedded in the practices of those, such as booksellers, libraries, museums, and retailers, who have long relied upon its protection. Museums, for example, are not in the habit of asking their foreign counterparts to check with the heirs of copyright owners before sending, *e.g.,* a Picasso on tour. That inertia means a dramatic change is likely necessary before these institutions, instructed by their counsel, would begin to engage in the complex permission-verifying process that a geographical interpretation would demand. And this Court's adoption of the geographical interpretation could provide that dramatic change. These intolerable consequences (along with the absurd result that the copyright owner can exercise downstream control even when it authorized the import or first sale) have understandably led the Ninth Circuit, the Solicitor General as *amicus,* and the dissent to adopt textual readings of the statute that attempt to mitigate these harms. But those readings are not defensible, for they require too many unprecedented jumps over linguistic and other hurdles that in our view are insurmountable.

Finally, the fact that harm has proved limited so far may simply reflect the reluctance of copyright holders so far to assert geographically based resale rights. They may decide differently if the law is clarified in their favor. Regardless, a copyright law that can work in practice only if unenforced is not a sound copyright law. It is a law that would create uncertainty, would bring about selective enforcement, and, if widely unenforced, would breed disrespect for copyright law itself.

Thus, we believe that the practical problems that petitioner and his *amici* have described are too serious, too extensive, and too likely to come about for us to dismiss them as insignificant—particularly in light of the ever-growing importance of foreign trade to America. See The World Bank, Imports of goods and services (% of GDP) (imports in 2011 18% of U.S. gross domestic product compared to 11% in 1980), online at http:// data.worldbank. org/indicator/NE.IMP.GNFS.ZS? (as visited Mar. 15, 2013, and available in Clerk of Court's case file). The upshot is that copyright-related consequences along with language, context, and interpretive canons argue strongly against a geographical interpretation of § 109(a). . . .

III.

. . . *Third,* Wiley and the dissent claim that a nongeographical interpretation will make it difficult, perhaps impossible, for publishers (and other copyright holders) to divide foreign and domestic markets. We concede that is so. A publisher may find it more difficult to charge different prices for the same book in different geographic markets. But we do not see how these facts help Wiley, for we can find no basic principle of copyright law that suggests that publishers are especially entitled to such rights.

The Constitution describes the nature of American copyright law by providing Congress with the power to "secur[e]" to "[a]uthors" "for limited [t]imes" the *"exclusive [r]ight to their . . . [w]ritings."* Art. I, § 8, cl. 8. The Founders, too, discussed the need to grant an author a limited right to exclude competition. But the Constitution's language nowhere suggests that its limited exclusive right should include a right to divide markets or a concomitant right to charge different purchasers different prices for the same book, say to increase or to maximize gain. Neither, to our knowledge, did any Founder make any such suggestion. We have found no precedent suggesting a legal preference for interpretations of copyright statutes that would provide for market divisions.

To the contrary, Congress enacted a copyright law that (through the "first sale" doctrine) limits copyright holders' ability to divide domestic markets. And that limitation is consistent with antitrust laws that ordinarily forbid market divisions. Whether copyright owners should, or should not, have more than ordinary commercial power to divide international markets is a matter for Congress to decide. We do no more here than try to determine what decision Congress has taken.

Fourth, the dissent and Wiley contend that our decision launches United States copyright law into an unprecedented regime of "international exhaustion." But they point to nothing indicative of congressional intent in 1976. The dissent also claims that it is clear that the United States now opposes adopting such a regime, but the Solicitor General as *amicus* has taken no such position in this case. In fact, when pressed at oral argument, the Solicitor General stated that the consequences of Wiley's reading of the statute (perpetual downstream control) were "worse" than those of Kirtsaeng's reading (restriction of market segmentation). . . .

IV.

For these reasons we conclude that the considerations supporting Kirtsaeng's nongeographical interpretation of the words "lawfully made under this title" are the more persuasive. The judgment of the Court of Appeals is reversed, and the case is remanded for further proceedings consistent with this opinion.

It is so ordered.

[The concurring opinion of Justice Kagan and the dissenting opinion of Justice Ginsburg, omitted here, are summarized in note 3, below.]

NOTES

1. *Public Distribution Right.* Until late in the twentieth century, the United States was one of only a handful of countries with legislation expressly granting a public distribution right—the 1976 Copyright Act's grant in section 106(3) of the exclusive right to distribute "copies or phonorecords of the copyrighted work to the public by sale or other transfer of ownership, or by rental, lease or lending." Section 602(a) of the 1976 Act annexes an importation right, encompassing both piratical and gray market goods, to section 106(3)'s distribution right. Section 602(b), which covers only piratical goods—"where the making of the copies or phonorecords would have constituted an infringement of copyright if this title had been applicable"— authorizes the United States Customs Service to bar the importation of these goods.

The 1996 WIPO Copyright Treaty formulated a broad public distribution right, providing in Article 6 that "[a]uthors of literary and artistic works shall enjoy the exclusive right of authorizing the making available to the public of the original and copies of their works through sale or other transfer of ownership." According to an Agreed Statement of the Diplomatic Conference on Article 6 and 7, "the expressions 'copies' and 'original and copies,' being subject to the right of distribution and the right of rental under said Articles, refer exclusively to fixed copies that can be put into circulation as tangible objects."

Article 7(1) of the WIPO Copyright Treaty, granting an exclusive right of commercial rental to the public of the originals or copies of computer programs, cinematographic works and works embodied in phonograms, carves out exceptions tailored to local political and economic exigencies of rental rights in these works. Article 7(2)(ii) for example, allows member countries to withhold the rental right from cinematographic works "unless such commercial rental has led to widespread copying of such works materially impairing the exclusive right of reproduction." Articles 11 and 14(4) of the TRIPs Agreement parallel Article 7 of the WIPO Copyright Treaty in requiring member states to grant a qualified rental right to computer programs, cinematographic works and phonograms.

On the distribution right generally, see Stig Strömholm, The "Right of Putting into Circulation" in Relation to Copyright: A Study of Comparative Law, 3 Copyright 266 (1967); Dietrich Reimer, The Right of Distribution with Special Reference to the Hiring and Lending of Books and Records, 9 Copyright 56 (1973). On an analogous, largely theoretical doctrine approximating the distribution right, see Frank Gotzen, The Right of Destination in Europe, 25 Copyright 218 (1989).

2.   *Local or International Exhaustion?* The rationale for the first sale, or exhaustion, doctrine applied in the *Kirtsaeng* case is that once a copyright owner has parted with title to a particular copy of his work, successive possessors of the copy should not be put to the trouble of negotiating with him each time they contemplate a further transfer of the copy. The rationale implies that the price of the copy when first sold will roughly cumulate, and discount to present value, the license fees that could have been charged each time the copy was sold if the doctrine did not apply.

Many industrialized countries follow the principle of local exhaustion, under which first sale exhausts the distribution right only in the country where the sale occurred. Other countries follow the principle of international exhaustion, under which the first sale of a copy of a work anywhere in the world exhausts the distribution right in the protecting country as well. The European Union adopts a position of Union-wide exhaustion after a copy's first sale in a member state, but local exhaustion for sales outside the Union. The United States had generally been thought to follow the rule of local exhaustion, and *Kirtsaeng's* effective interpretation of the 1976 Copyright Act's to embody the principle of international exhaustion came as a surprise to many.

The question of local or international exhaustion was the focus of contentious debate in the GATT Uruguay Round. Article 6 of the TRIPs Agreement, providing that, subject to national treatment and most-favored-nation provisions, "nothing in this Agreement shall be used to address the issue of the exhaustion of intellectual property rights," was the result. The Diplomatic Conference on the WIPO Copyright Treaty also failed to agree on the scope of exhaustion. *See* WIPO Copyright Treaty Art. 6(2).

3.   *Kirtsaeng.* Justice Kagan, joined by Justice Alito, concurring, agreed that "[n]either the text nor the history of 17 U.S.C. § 109(a) supports removing first-sale protection from every copy of a protected work manufactured abroad," and saw any problem with the Court's decision as resulting "not from our reading of § 109(a) here, but from *Quality King's* holding that § 109(a) limits § 602(a)(1)." Had *Quality King* been decided differently, "§ 602(a)(1) would allow a copyright owner to restrict the importation of copies irrespective of the first sale doctrine. That result would enable the copyright owner to divide international markets in the way John Wiley claims Congress intended when enacting § 602(a)(1). But it would do so without imposing downstream liability on those who purchase and resell in the United States copies that happen to have been manufactured abroad."

Justice Ginsburg, joined by Justices Kennedy and Scalia, directly challenged the majority's reading of the words "lawfully made under this title": "[T]he word 'under' commonly signals a relationship of subjection, where one thing is governed or regulated by another"; "[o]nly by disregarding this established meaning of 'under' can the Court arrive at the conclusion that Wiley's foreign-manufactured textbooks were lawfully made under U.S. copyright law, even though the law did not govern their creation. It is anomalous, however, to speak of particular conduct as 'lawful' under an inapplicable law."

Does *Kirtsaeng* violate the principle that a statute should be construed to apply extraterritorially only when Congress has clearly expressed its intention to that effect? To be sure, the decision would not alter primary legal relationships on foreign soil, the usual concern of the territoriality presumption, but it does have the effect of displacing foreign law from its role in characterizing local conduct, something Congress knows how to do expressly when it so desires. *See*, for example, section 602(a)(3)(B) of the U.S. Act.

4. *The Economics of Parallel Imports.* The main argument against international exhaustion is that restrictions on parallel imports enable intellectual property owners to price-discriminate, capturing different levels of demand—and consequently price—across different cultures and economies. A videocassette of a Bollywood motion picture drama from India might command a smaller audience and a higher price in the United States than in India, and restrictions on parallel imports enable the copyright owner to price copies in the two markets accordingly. Proponents of international exhaustion respond that, whatever its benefits, price discrimination leads to monopolistic abuses. Their opponents counter that the highly substitutable nature of copyrighted goods—if one Indian film is priced too high, audiences will reject it for a lower-priced alternative—will keep prices in all markets at competitive levels.

Copyright is regularly employed to price-discriminate domestically without objection: novels are sold in paperback a year after the higher-priced hardcover version; films are first released in theatres, where the price is highest, before being released for pay-per-view and, later, broadcast television. Should the desirability of price discrimination be measured in terms of local or global welfare? One study concluded that "[i]f parallel imports are prevented . . . firms could offer lower prices to lower income (more elastic) countries without fear of the products resurfacing in high-price markets. Absent . . . such segmentation, firms may well choose relatively high uniform prices, at which many low-demand countries are likely to go unserved." David Mauleg & Marius Schwartz, Parallel Imports, Demand Dispersion, and International Price Discrimination, Economic Analysis Group, Antitrust Division, U.S. Dept. of Justice, Paper 93-6, 17–18 n.13 (August, 1993).

On the arguments for and against international exhaustion, see Claude Barfield & Mark Groombridge, The Economic Case for Copyright Owner Control Over Parallel Imports, 1 J. World Int. Prop. 903 (1998); Frederick M. Abbott, First Report (Final) to the Committee on International Trade Law of the International Law Association on the Subject of Parallel Importation

(April, 1997). *See* also Shubha Ghosh, Gray Markets in Cyberspace, 7 J. Int. Prop. L. 1 (1999).

5. *Exhaustion and Electronic Transfers.* As its name implies, the first sale doctrine traditionally applies to sales, not leases or licenses of copies. In Vernor v. Autodesk, Inc., 621 F.3d 1102 (9th Cir. 2010), the court held that, because the software agreement under review identified itself as a license, restricted the transfer of copies, and limited the use of the software, it constituted a license, not a sale, so that the first sale defense was not available.

Exhaustion doctrine also contemplates the transfer of a *copy,* a species that promises to become increasing endangered as software and other content migrate from physical discs to transmissions from the cloud. In UsedSoft GmbH v. Oracle International Corp, CJEU, C-128/11, 2012, the Court of Justice of the European Union applied the exhaustion rule to software "distributed" in intangible form from an Internet server. According to the Court, "the right of distribution of a copy of a computer program is exhausted if the copyright holder who has authorized, even free of charge, the downloading of that copy from the internet onto a data carrier has also conferred, in return for payment of a fee intended to enable him to obtain remuneration corresponding to the economic value of the copy of the work of which he is the proprietor, a right to use that copy for an unlimited period."

Two careful readers of the *UsedSoft* opinion have observed that "the application of the first sale doctrine to software is dealt with in one piece of legislation—the EC Software Directive—and its application to other forms of digital content is dealt with in another—the Information Society Directive. The two Directives use different language. In *UsedSoft*, the court was able to rule that the first sale doctrine applies equally whether software is distributed in hard or soft copy form, because the language of the Software Directive allows for this. (The Directive refers to software in any form). However, the Information Society Directive refers to 'tangible articles.'" David Naylor & Emily Parris, After ReDigi: Contrasting the EU and US Approaches to the Re-Sale of Second-Hand Digital Assets, 35 EIPR 487 (2013).

See generally, Lothar Determann, Digital Exhaustion—New Law from the Old World, 33 Berkeley Tech. L. J. 177 (2018).

6. *Resale Royalty Right.* Copyright may under-reward the production of fine art whose value characteristically lies in the original work rather than in its mass exploitation through reproduction or display. Should visual artists have a right to share in the proceeds each time their works are resold? Many countries have enacted some form of artist's resale royalty right, or *droit de suite. Droit de suite* originated in France, and the 1948 Brussels Revision of the Berne Convention introduced the concept as an international norm, but made the right optional for member states and subject to a condition of material reciprocity. *See* Berne Convention 1971 Paris Act Art. 14ter.

Directive 2001/84/EC of the European Parliament and the Council of 27 September 2001 on the Resale Right for the Benefit of the Author of an

Original Work of Art obligated EU member states to adopt a resale royalty right no later than January 1, 2006. Under the Directive, the right is inalienable, nonwaivable, and lasts for the EU term of copyright; it applies only to transactions involving professional art dealers as buyers, sellers or intermediaries. The prescribed royalty rates start at 4% (or 5% at the discretion of the member country) on sales of up to 50,000, and decline to .25% for the portion of the sale price exceeding EUR 500,000. The total amount of the royalty cannot exceed EUR 12,500. The right applies to artists who are nationals of, or habitually reside in, an EU member state and, subject to reciprocity, to nationals of other countries.

See generally, Jonathan Collins, Droit de Suite: An Artistic Stroke of Genius? A Critical Exploration of the European Directive and Its Resultant Effects, 34 EIPR 305 (2012); Charles Lewis, Implementing the Artist's Resale Right Directive, 2 J. Int. Prop. L. & Pract. 298 (2007); Pierre Valentin, Droit de Suite, 28 EIPR 268 (2006); Report of the Register of Copyrights of the Library of Congress, Droit de Suite: The Artist's Resale Royalty (1992); Liliane de Pierredon-Fawcett, The Droit de Suite in Literary and Artistic Property: A Comparative Law Study (1991).

7. *Public Lending Right.* Should authors have a right to remuneration each time their works are borrowed from public libraries? These free uses will sometimes cut into revenue-producing markets, and the notion of compensating authors has won support in a growing number of countries, mostly in Europe. The British public lending right, introduced in 1982, entitles qualifying authors to a payment of funds, provided by the government, proportioned to the number of times their books are borrowed from public libraries. The 1992 EC Rental Right and Lending Right Directive, codified (and replaced) by Directive 2006/115/EC of the European Parliament and of the Council of 2 December 2006, obligates member states to adopt a public lending right, but allows for substantial derogation from the rights.

Does the public lending right come within the national treatment obligation, so that countries that are party to the Berne Convention or the TRIPs Agreement must extend the right to works coming from other member countries? Can a country confine compensation to its own nationals on the theory that compensation for public lending is a social welfare system for authors rather than a form of intellectual property right?

See generally, International Federation of Library Associations and Institutions, 2005 Background Paper on Public Lending Right; Silke von Lewinski, Public Lending Right: General and Comparative Survey of the Existing Systems in Law and Practice, 154 R.I.D.A. 3 (1992); Jennifer Schneck, Closing the Book on the Public Lending Right, 63 N.Y.U. L. Rev. 878 (1988); Herman Cohen Jehoram, (ed.), Public Lending Right (1983).

8. *Reproduction Right.* Article 9(1) of the 1971 Berne Paris Text provides, "Authors of literary and artistic works protected by this Convention shall have the exclusive right of authorizing the reproduction of these works, in any manner or form." Although the reproduction right dates to copyright's very beginnings, it was not until the 1967 Stockholm Revision that the

Convention prescribed reproduction as a minimum right. The original Berne text probably omitted the right not because it was unimportant, but because the national exceptions to the right were so varied. The problem addressed in Stockholm "was to find a formula wide enough to cover all reasonable exceptions but not so wide as to make the right illusory." WIPO, Guide to the Berne Convention for the Protection of Literary and Artistic Works (Paris Act, 1971) 54 (1978).

Modern technologies for transmitting copyrighted works have presented a new challenge to an international norm for the reproduction right: Should the right encompass the ephemeral copies that are inevitably made as a work travels electronically through a digital network? An early proposal on the agenda that ultimately produced the WIPO Copyright Treaty would have brought ephemeral copies within the reproduction right. The Diplomatic Conference sidestepped the proposal: "The reproduction right, as set out in Article 9 of the Berne Convention, and the exceptions permitted thereunder, fully apply in the digital environment, in particular to the use of works in digital form. It is understood that the storage of a protected work in digital form in an electronic medium constitutes a reproduction within the meaning of Article 9 of the Berne Convention." Diplomatic Conference on Certain Copyright and Neighboring Rights Questions, Agreed Statements Concerning the WIPO Copyright Treaty, WIPO Document CNR DC/96, Concerning Article 1(4) (Dec. 23, 1996).

Article 5(1) of the EU's 2001 Information Society Directive, promulgated in part to implement the WIPO Copyright Treaty, exempts "[t]emporary acts of reproduction . . . which are transient or incidental, which are an integral and essential part of a technological process and the sole purpose of which is to enable (a) a transmission in a network between third parties by an intermediary, or (b) a lawful use . . . and which have no independent economic significance." The CJEU has held that copies cached in a hard drive or made on a computer screen in the course of viewing a website meet these conditions. Public Relations Consultants Ass'n Ltd. v. The Newspaper Licensing Agency, Ltd., CJEU, C-360/13, 2014.

9. *Adaptation Right.* Section 106(2) of the United States Copyright Act grants copyright owners the exclusive right "to prepare derivative works based upon the copyrighted work," and section 101 of the Act defines "derivative work" as "a work based upon one or more preexisting works, such as a translation, musical arrangement, dramatization, fictionalization, motion picture version, sound recording, art reproduction, abridgment, condensation, or any other form in which a work may be recast, transformed or adapted."

Japan and Britain are among the countries that, like the United States, treat adaptation as a discrete right. *See* Japan, Copyright Act Art. 27; United Kingdom, Copyright Designs & Patents Act 1988 § 16(1)(e). The French statute, by contrast, treats adaptation as an aspect of the reproduction right and the German statute effectively assimilates unpublished adaptations into the basic reproduction right. *See* France, Intellectual Prop. Code Arts. L. 122–1, 122–4; Germany Copyright Act Art. 15(1). At least three provisions of the Berne Convention, 1971 Paris Act, touch on the scope and conditions of the adaptation right: Article 8, ensuring authors the right "of making and of authorizing the translation of their works"; Article 12 ensuring that authors of literary and artistic works "shall enjoy the exclusive right of authorizing adaptations, arrangements and other alterations of their works"; and Article 14(1) prescribing the exclusive right of authorizing "the cinematographic adaptation and reproduction of these works."

Where the copyright owner of a painting has authorized the production and sale of posters that reproduce the painting, would it infringe the adaptation right—or the reproduction or distribution right—for the owner of a copy of the poster to transfer the ink from the poster, intact and without making another copy, to a sheet of canvas and then selling the canvas? *See* Art & Allposters International BV v. Stichting Pictoright, Court of Justice of the European Union, Case C-419/13 (2015). (The "replacement of the medium . . . results in the creation of a new object incorporating the image of the protected work, whereas the poster itself ceases to exist. Such an alteration of the copy of the protected work, which provides a result closer to the original, is actually sufficient to constitute a new reproduction of that work, within the meaning of Article 2(a) of Directive 2001/29, which is covered by the exclusive right of the author and requires his authorisation.").

See generally, Paul Goldstein, Adaptation Rights and Moral Rights in the United Kingdom, the United States and the Federal Republic of Germany, 14 IIC 43 (1983).

iii. Limitations on Rights

(A) The Three-Step Test

United States—Section 110(5) of the U.S. Copyright Act

Report of the Panel, World Trade Organization, WT/DS160/R June 15, 2000.

I. INTRODUCTION

1.1 On 26 January 1999, the European Communities and their member States (hereafter referred to as the European Communities) requested consultations with the United States under Article 4 of the Understanding on Rules and Procedures Governing the Settlement of Disputes ("DSU") and Article 64.1 of the Agreement on Trade-Related Aspects of Intellectual Property Rights ("TRIPS Agreement") regarding Section 110(5) of the United States Copyright Act as amended by the "Fairness in Music Licensing Act" enacted on 27 October 1998.

1.2 The European Communities and the United States held consultations on 2 March 1999, but failed to reach a mutually satisfactory solution. On 15 April 1999, the European Communities requested the establishment of a panel under Article 6 of the DSU and Article 64.1 of the TRIPS Agreement.

1.3   At its meeting on 26 May 1999, the Dispute Settlement Body ("DSB") established a panel in accordance with Article 6 of the DSU with the following standard terms of reference:

"To examine, in the light of the relevant provisions of the covered agreements cited by the European Communities in document WT/DS160/5, the matter referred to the DSB by the European Communities in that document and to make such findings as will assist the DSB in making the recommendations or in giving the rulings provided for in those agreements."

1.4   Australia, Brazil, Canada, Japan and Switzerland reserved their rights to participate in the panel proceedings as third parties.

1.5   On 27 July 1999, the European Communities made a request, with reference to Article 8.7 of the DSU, to the Director-in-charge to determine the composition of the Panel. On 6 August 1999, the Panel was composed as follows:

Chairperson: Mrs. Carmen Luz Guarda

Members: Mr. Arumugamangalam V. Ganesan

Mr. Ian F. Sheppard

1.6   The Panel met with the parties on 8–9 November 1999 and 7 December 1999. It met with the third parties on 9 November 1999.

1.7   On 15 November, the Panel sent a letter to the International Bureau of the World Intellectual Property Organization (WIPO), that is responsible for the administration of the Berne Convention for the Protection of Literary and Artistic Works. In that letter, the Panel requested factual information on the provisions of the Paris Act of 1971 of that Convention ("Berne Convention (1971)"), incorporated into the TRIPS Agreement by its Article 9.1, relevant to the matter. The International Bureau of WIPO provided such information in a letter, dated 22 December 1999. The parties to the dispute provided comments on this information by means of letters, dated 12 January 2000.

1.8   The Panel submitted its interim report to the parties on 14 April 2000.

VI.   FINDINGS

. . . .

A.   CLAIMS

6.1   As mentioned above, the European Communities allege that the exemptions provided in subparagraphs (A) and (B) of Section 110(5) of the U.S. Copyright Act* are in violation of the United States' obligations

---

*   17 U.S.C. § 110(5) provides:

Notwithstanding the provisions of section 106, the following are not infringements of copyright: . . .

under the TRIPS Agreement, and requests the Panel to find that the United States has violated its obligations under Article 9.1 of the TRIPS Agreement together with Articles 11*bis*(1)(iii) and 11(1)(ii) of the Berne Convention (1971) and to recommend that the United States bring its domestic legislation into conformity with its obligations under the TRIPS Agreement.

6.2 The United States contends that Section 110(5) of the U.S. Copyright Act is fully consistent with its obligations under the TRIPS Agreement, and requests the Panel to find that both subparagraphs (A) and (B) of Section 110(5) of the US Copyright Act meet the standard of Article 13 of the TRIPS Agreement and the substantive obligations of the Berne Convention (1971). Accordingly, the United States requests the Panel to dismiss the claims of the European Communities in this dispute. . . .

---

(5)(A) except as provided in subparagraph (B), communication of a transmission embodying a performance or display of a work by the public reception of the transmission on a single receiving apparatus of a kind commonly used in private homes, unless—

(i) a direct charge is made to see or hear the transmission; or

(ii) the transmission thus received is further transmitted to the public;

(B) communication by an establishment of a transmission or retransmission embodying a performance or display of a nondramatic musical work intended to be received by the general public, originated by a radio or television broadcast station licensed as such by the Federal Communications Commission, or, if an audiovisual transmission, by a cable system or satellite carrier, if—

(i) in the case of an establishment other than a food service or drinking establishment, either the establishment in which the communication occurs has less than 2,000 gross square feet of space (excluding space used for customer parking and for no other purpose) and—

(I) if the performance is by audio means only, the performance is communicated by means of a total of not more than 6 loudspeakers, of which not more than 4 loudspeakers are located in any 1 room or adjoining outdoor space; or

(II) if the performance or display is by audiovisual means, any visual portion of the performance or display is communicated by means of a total of not more than 4 audiovisual devices, of which not more than 1 audiovisual device is located in any 1 room, and no such audiovisual device has a diagonal screen size greater than 55 inches, and any audio portion of the performance or display is communicated by means of a total of not more than 6 loudspeakers, of which not more than 4 loudspeakers are located in any 1 room or adjoining outdoor space;

(ii) in the case of a food service or drinking establishment, either the establishment in which the communication occurs has less than 3,750 gross square feet of space (excluding space used for customer parking and for no other purpose), or the establishment in which the communication occurs has 3,750 gross square feet of space or more (excluding space used for customer parking and for no other purpose) and—

(I) if the performance is by audio means only, the performance is communicated by means of a total of not more than 6 loudspeakers, of which not more than 4 loudspeakers are located in any 1 room or adjoining outdoor space; or

(II) if the performance or display is by audiovisual means, any visual portion of the performance or display is communicated by means of a total of not more than 4 audiovisual devices, of which not more than one audiovisual device is located in any 1 room, and no such audiovisual device has a diagonal screen size greater than 55 inches, and any audio portion of the performance or display is communicated by means of a total of not more than 6 loudspeakers, of which not more than 4 loudspeakers are located in any 1 room or adjoining outdoor space;

(iii) no direct charge is made to see or hear the transmission or retransmission;

(iv) the transmission or retransmission is not further transmitted beyond the establishment where it is received; and

(v) the transmission or retransmission is licensed by the copyright owner of the work so publicly performed or displayed. *Ed.*

. . . .

C.   Burden Of Proof

6.9   Before turning to the substantive aspects of this dispute, we also discuss the issue of burden of proof.

6.10 We note that the United States does not dispute that subparagraphs (A) and (B) of Section 110(5) implicate Articles 11 and 11*bis* of the Berne Convention (1971) as incorporated into the TRIPS Agreement. But we also recall the U.S. statement that the question of whether these subparagraphs are consistent with those Articles cannot be determined without looking both to the scope of the rights that they afford and to the exceptions which are permitted to those rights. In the view of the United States, only if subparagraphs (A) and (B) of Section 110(5) do not fall within the confines of the relevant exceptions under the TRIPS Agreement, will a finding of inconsistency be possible.

6.11 We further recall the European Communities' contention that it merely needs to establish an inconsistency of Section 110(5) with any provision of the TRIPS Agreement (including those of the Berne Convention (1971) incorporated into it). Once such inconsistency is established by the complainant (or admitted by the respondent), in the view of the European Communities, the burden rests on the United States to invoke and prove the applicability of an exception.

6.12 Recalling the principles set out in the Appellate Body report on *United States—Shirts and Blouses*, we note that the burden of proof rests upon the party, whether complaining or defending, who asserts the affirmative of a particular claim or defence. If that party adduces evidence sufficient to raise a presumption that what is claimed is true, the burden then shifts to the other party, who will fail unless it adduces sufficient evidence to rebut the presumption.

6.13 Consistent with past WTO dispute settlement practice, we consider that the European Communities bears the burden of establishing a *prima facie* violation of the basic rights that have been provided under the copyright provisions of the TRIPS Agreement, including its provisions that have been incorporated by reference from the Berne Convention (1971). By the same token, once the European Communities has succeeded in doing so, the burden rests with the United States to establish that any exception or limitation is applicable and that the conditions, if any, for invoking such exception are fulfilled.

6.14 The same rules apply where the existence of a specific fact is alleged. We note that a party who asserts a fact, whether the claimant or the respondent, is responsible for providing proof thereof. It is for the party alleging the fact to prove its existence. It is then for the other party to submit evidence to the contrary if it challenges the existence of that fact.

6.15 While a duty rests on all parties to produce evidence and to cooperate in presenting evidence to the Panel, this is an issue that has to be distinguished from the question of who bears the ultimate burden of proof for establishing a claim or a defence.

6.16 Thus we conclude that it is for the European Communities to present a *prima facie* case that Section 110(5)(A) and (B) of the U.S. Copyright Act is inconsistent with the provisions of the TRIPS Agreement (including those of the Berne Convention (1971) incorporated into it). Should the European Communities fail in establishing such violation, it goes without saying that the United States would not have to invoke any justification or exception. However, we also consider that the burden of proving that any exception or limitation is applicable and that any relevant conditions are met falls on the United States as the party bearing the ultimate burden of proof for invoking exceptions. In view of the statements made by both parties at the first substantive meeting to the Panel, it is our understanding that the parties do not disagree with our interpretation concerning the allocation of the burden of proof as described above.

D.   Substantive aspects of the dispute

1.   General considerations about the exclusive rights concerned and limitations thereto

(a)   Exclusive rights implicated by the EC claims

6.17 Articles 9–13 of Section 1 of Part II of the TRIPS Agreement entitled "Copyright and Related Rights" deal with the substantive standards of copyright protection. Article 9.1 of the TRIPS Agreement obliges WTO Members to comply with Articles 1–21 of the Berne Convention (1971) (with the exception of Article 6*bis* on moral rights and the rights derived therefrom) and the Appendix thereto. The European Communities alleges that subparagraphs (A) and (B) of Section 110(5) are inconsistent primarily with Article 11*bis*(1)(iii) but also with Article 11(1)(ii) of the Berne Convention (1971) as incorporated into the TRIPS Agreement.

6.18 We note that through their incorporation, the substantive rules of the Berne Convention (1971), including the provisions of its Articles 11*bis*(1)(iii) and 11(1)(ii), have become part of the TRIPS Agreement and as provisions of that Agreement have to be read as applying to WTO Members. . . .

(b)   Limitations and exceptions

(i)   Introduction

6.30 A major issue in this dispute is the interpretation and application to the facts of this case of Article 13 of the TRIPS Agreement. The U.S. defense is firmly based upon it. The United States submits that the Article clarifies and articulates the "minor exceptions" doctrine applicable under certain provisions of the Berne Convention (1971) and incorporated into the TRIPS Agreement. But the determination of the dispute raises other questions, for instance questions concerning the relationship between Article 13 and the "minor exceptions" doctrine developed in relation to Articles 11 and 11*bis*(1) and (2) of the Berne Convention (1971) and incorporated into the TRIPs Agreement by Article 9.1 thereof. So although the U.S. case rests on Article 13, the determination of the questions at issue between the parties involves considerations beyond those that arise from the mere application of Article 13 to the facts of this case.

6.31 Article 13 of the TRIPS Agreement, entitled "Limitations and Exceptions", is the general exception clause applicable to exclusive rights of the holders of copyright. It provides:

> "Members shall confine limitations or exceptions to exclusive rights to certain special cases which do not conflict with a normal exploitation of the work and do not unreasonably prejudice the legitimate interests of the right holder."

6.32 We discuss the scope of Article 13 of the TRIPS Agreement in subsection (iv) of this section (paragraphs 6.71ff). In the second part of this report (paragraphs 6.97ff), we will apply the three conditions contained in that Article to subparagraphs (A) and (B) of Section 110(5) of the U.S. Copyright Act.

(ii) Summary of the arguments raised by the parties. . . .

6.74 Apart from the difference in the use of the terms "permit" and "confine",[1] the main difference between Article 9(2) of the Berne Convention (1971) and Article 13 of the TRIPS Agreement is that the former applies only to the reproduction right. The wording of Article 13 does not contain an express limitation in terms of the categories of rights under copyright to which it may apply. It states that limitations or exceptions to exclusive rights can only be made if three conditions are met: (1) the limitations or exceptions are confined to certain special cases; (2) they do not conflict with a normal exploitation of the work; and (3) they do not unreasonably prejudice the legitimate interests of the right holder. As both parties agree, these three conditions apply cumulatively; a limitation or an exception is consistent with Article 13 only if it fulfils each of the three conditions.

6.75 The European Communities argues that Article 13 of the TRIPS Agreement applies only to those rights that were added to the TRIPS Agreement, and, therefore, it does not apply to those provisions of the Berne Convention (1971), including its Articles 11(1) and 11*bis*(1), that were incorporated into the TRIPS Agreement by reference.

6.76 In the view of the European Communities, Article 20 of the Berne Convention (1971) speaks against the interpretation of Article 13 as providing a basis for exceptions to the Berne rights incorporated into the

---

[1] Article 9(2) of the Berne Convention (1971) provides that "[i]t shall be a matter for legislation in the countries of the Union to permit the reproduction", while Article 13 of the TRIPS Agreement provides that "Members shall confine limitations and exceptions to exclusive rights".

TRIPS Agreement, because Article 20 of the Convention only allows "countries of the Berne Union to enter into special agreements among themselves, insofar as such agreements grant to authors more extensive rights than those granted by the (Berne) Convention". In other words, the European Communities contends that parties to the Berne Convention cannot agree in another treaty to reduce the Berne Convention level of protection.

6.77 Furthermore, the European Communities adds that Article 20 of the Berne Convention (1971) is mirrored in the TRIPS Agreement by Article 2(2), which reads as follows:

> "Nothing in Parts I to IV of this Agreement shall derogate from existing obligations that Members may have to each other under the Paris Convention, the Berne Convention, the Rome Convention and the Treaty on Intellectual Property in Respect of Integrated Circuits."

6.78 In the alternative to its principal argument, the European Communities contends that, even if Article 13 of the TRIPS Agreement were given a role in the context of exceptions to exclusive rights under the Berne Convention (1971), a principle should be respected according to which the objective of the TRIPS Agreement is to reduce or eliminate existing exceptions, rather than to grant new or extend existing ones. The European Communities refers to the difference in the wording between Article 13 ("Members *shall confine* limitations or exceptions") and Articles 17, 26(2) and 30 of the TRIPS Agreement ("Members *may provide* limited exceptions"). We recall, however, that under its principal argument the European Communities takes the view that Article 13 provides exceptions to new rights, rather than reduce the scope of any existing limitations.

6.79 The United States contends that "[t]he text of Article 13 is straightforward and applies to 'limitations or exceptions to exclusive rights'. Not *some* limitations, not limitations to *some* exclusive rights". The United States adds that the application of Article 13 of the TRIPs Agreement to the rights provided under Article 11(1) and 11*bis*(1) of the Berne Convention (1971) does not derogate from the obligations under the Berne Convention in violation of Article 2.2 of the TRIPS Agreement or Article 20 of the Berne Convention, because Article 13 of the TRIPS Agreement articulates the standard applicable to minor exceptions under the Berne Convention (1971) as far as these Articles are concerned.

6.80 In our view, neither the express wording nor the context of Article 13 or any other provision of the TRIPS Agreement supports the interpretation that the scope of application of Article 13 is limited to the exclusive rights newly introduced under the TRIPS Agreement.

6.81 The application of Article 13 of the TRIPS Agreement to the rights provided under Articles 11(1) and 11*bis*(1) of the Berne Convention (1971) as incorporated into the TRIPS Agreement need not lead to different standards from those applicable under the Berne Convention (1971), given that we have established that the possibility of providing minor exceptions forms part of the context of these articles. Taking into account this contextual guidance, we will examine the scope for permissible minor exceptions to the exclusive rights in question by applying the conditions of Article 13 of the TRIPS Agreement.

6.82 In regard to the argument of the European Communities that the U.S. interpretation of Article 13 is incompatible with Article 20 of the Berne Convention (1971) and Article 2.2 of the TRIPS Agreement because it treats Article 13 of the TRIPS Agreement as providing a basis for exceptions that would be inconsistent with those permitted under the Berne Convention (1971), we note that the United States is not arguing this but rather that Article 13 clarifies and articulates the standards applicable to minor exceptions under the Berne Convention (1971). Since the EC arguments in relation to these provisions would only be relevant if a finding that would involve inconsistency with the Berne Convention (1971) were being advocated, we do not feel it is necessary to examine them further. . . .

(2)   The three criteria test under Article 13 of the TRIPS Agreement

(a)   General introduction

6.97 Article 13 of the TRIPS Agreement requires that limitations and exceptions to exclusive rights (1) be confined to certain special cases, (2) do not conflict with a normal exploitation of the work, and (3) do not unreasonably prejudice the legitimate interests of the right holder. The principle of effective treaty interpretation requires us to give a distinct meaning to each of the three conditions and to avoid a reading that could reduce any of the conditions to "redundancy or inutility". The three conditions apply on a cumulative basis, each being a separate and independent requirement that must be satisfied. Failure to comply with any one of the three conditions results in the Article 13 exception being disallowed. Both parties agree on the cumulative nature of the three conditions. The Panel shares their view. It may be noted at the outset that Article 13 cannot have more than a narrow or limited operation. Its tenor, consistent as it is with the provisions of Article 9(2) of the Berne Convention (1971), discloses that it was not intended to provide for exceptions or limitations except for those of a limited nature. The narrow sphere of its operation will emerge from our discussion and application of its provisions in the paragraphs which follow. . . .

6.99 The parties have largely relied on similar factual information in substantiating their legal arguments under each of the three conditions of Article 13. We are called upon to evaluate this information from different angles under the three conditions, which call for different requirements for justifying exceptions or limitations. We will look at the defined and limited scope of the exemptions at issue under the first condition, and focus on the degree of conflict with normal exploitation of works under the second condition. In relation to the third condition, we will examine the extent of prejudice caused to the legitimate interests of the right holder in the light of the information submitted by the parties.

6.100 In providing such factual information, the United States has focused on describing the immediate and direct impact on copyright holders caused by the introduction of the exemptions into its law; this can be characterized as the *actual* effects of the exemptions. The United States argues that while both actual losses and potential losses may be relevant to the analysis, the key is a realistic appraisal of the conditions that prevail in the market; the only way to avoid the danger of arbitrariness is to base the analysis on realistic market conditions.

6.101 The European Communities emphasizes the importance of taking into account the way that the exemptions affect the right holders' opportunities to exercise their exclusive rights as well as the indirect impact of the exemptions; this can be characterized as the *potential* effects of the exemptions. We will address below the question to what extent we should focus on the actual impact on the right holder and to what extent we should also take into account the potential impact.

(b) "Certain special cases"

(i) General interpretative analysis

6.102 In invoking the exception of Article 13, as an articulation and clarification of the minor exceptions doctrine, the United States claims that both subparagraphs (A) and (B) of Section 110(5) meet the standard of being confined to "certain special cases".

6.103 The United States submits that the fact that the TRIPS Agreement does not elaborate on the criteria for a case to be considered "special" provides Members flexibility to determine for themselves whether a particular case represents an appropriate basis for an exception. But it acknowledges that the essence of the first condition is that the exceptions be well-defined and of limited application.

6.104 In the view of the European Communities, an exception has to be well-defined and narrow in scope to meet the requirements under the first condition. In the EC's view, in the case at hand, such significant numbers of establishments are excepted from the duty to pay fees for the use of exclusive rights under subparagraph (A) and (B) of Section 110(5) that the exemptions contained therein constitute a rule rather than an exception.

6.105 The European Communities argues that, in the light of the wording of the first condition in Article 9(2) of the Berne Convention (1971), which forms part of the context of Article 13, an exemption should serve a "special purpose". For the European Communities, in the case of Section 110(5), no such special public policy or other exceptional circumstance exists that would make it inappropriate or impossible to enforce the exclusive rights conferred by Articles 11 and 11*bis* of the Berne Convention (1971). In the EC view, the subparagraphs of Section 110(5) do not pursue legitimate public policy objectives.

6.106   In the U.S. view, if the purpose of an exception is relevant at all, the TRIPs Agreement only requires that an exception has a specific policy objective. It does not impose any requirement as to the legitimacy of the policy objectives that a particular country might consider special in the light of its own history and national priorities. . . .

6.112   In our view, the first condition of Article 13 requires that a limitation or exception in national legislation should be clearly defined and should be narrow in its scope and reach. On the other hand, a limitation or exception may be compatible with the first condition even if it pursues a special purpose whose underlying legitimacy in a normative sense cannot be discerned. The wording of Article 13's first condition does not imply passing a judgment on the legitimacy of the exceptions in dispute. However, public policy purposes stated by law-makers when enacting a limitation or exception may be useful from a factual perspective for making inferences about the scope of a limitation or exception or the clarity of its definition.

6.113   In the case at hand, in order to determine whether subparagraphs (B) and (A) of Section 110(5) are confined to "certain special cases", we first examine whether the exceptions have been clearly defined. Second, we ascertain whether the exemptions are narrow in scope, *inter alia*, with respect to their reach. In that respect, we take into account what percentage of eating and drinking establishments and retail establishments may benefit from the business exemption under subparagraph (B), and in turn what percentage of establishments may take advantage of the homestyle exemption under subparagraph (A). On a subsidiary basis, we consider whether it is possible to draw inferences about the reach of the business and homestyle exemptions from the stated policy purposes underlying these exemptions according to the statements made during the U.S. legislative process.[2]

(ii)   The business exemption of subparagraph (B)

6.114   As noted above, the United States argues that the essence of the first condition of Article 13 of the TRIPS Agreement is that exceptions be well-defined and of limited application. It claims that the business exemption of subparagraph (B) meets the requirements of the first condition of Article 13, because it is clearly defined in Section 110(5) of the U.S. Copyright Act by square footage and equipment limitations.

6.115   In the U.S. view, if at all the purpose of an exception is relevant, the first condition only requires that the exception has a specific policy objective, but it does not impose any requirements on the policy objectives that a particular country might consider special in the light of its own history and national priorities. As regards the business exemption, the United States claims that the specific policy objective pursued by this

---

[2]   We discuss the business exemption of subparagraph (B) first because most of the arguments raised by the parties focus on this exception. In turn, we then examine the homestyle exemption in its current form as contained in subparagraph (A).

exemption is fostering small businesses and preventing abusive tactics by CMOs.**

6.116 The European Communities contends that the business exemption is too broad in its scope to pass as a "certain special case", given the large number of establishments which potentially may benefit from it. For the European Communities, it is irrelevant that the size of establishments and the type of equipment are clearly defined, when the broad scope of the business exemption turns an exception into the rule.

6.117 It appears that the European Communities does not dispute the fact that subparagraph (B) is clearly defined in respect of the size limits of establishments and the type of equipment that may be used by establishments above the applicable limits. The primary bone of contention between the parties is whether the business exemption, given its scope and reach, can be considered as a "special" case within the meaning of the first condition of Article 13.

6.118 The Congressional Research Service ("CRS") estimated in 1995 the percentage of the U.S. eating and drinking establishments and retail establishments that would have fallen at that time below the size limits of 3,500 square feet and 1,500 square feet respectively. Its study found that:

(d)   65.2 per cent of all eating establishments;

(e)   71.8 per cent of all drinking establishments; and

(f)   27 per cent of all retail establishments

would have fallen below these size limits. . . .

6.133 The factual information presented to us indicates that a substantial majority of eating and drinking establishments and close to half of retail establishments are covered by the exemption contained in subparagraph (B) of Section 110(5) of the U.S. Copyright Act. Therefore, we conclude that the exemption does not qualify as a "certain special case" in the meaning of the first condition of Article 13.

6.134 The European Communities warns that the potential coverage of both exemptions contained in Section 110(5) could become even larger because subparagraphs (A) and (B) could arguably exempt the transmission of musical works over the Internet. Given that we have found that the business exemption does not meet the first condition of Article 13 regardless of whether it potentially implicates transmission of works over the Internet, we see no need to address this question in the context of subparagraph (B). However, we will take up this question when we examine the homestyle exemption of subparagraph (A) in relation to the first condition of Article 13.

** "CMOs" are collective management organizations, specifically, in this context, performing rights societies. *Ed.*

(iii) The homestyle exemption of subparagraph (A)

6.135 We examine now whether the homestyle exemption in subparagraph (A), in the form in which it is currently in force in the United States, is a "certain special case" in the meaning of the first condition of Article 13 of the TRIPS Agreement.

6.136 The United States submits that the exemption of subparagraph (A) is confined to "certain special cases", because its scope is limited to the use involving a "homestyle" receiving apparatus. In the U.S. view, in the amended version of 1998 as well, this is a well-defined fact-specific standard. The essentially identical description of the homestyle exemption in the original Section 110(5) of 1976 was sufficiently clear and narrow for U.S. courts to reasonably and consistently apply the exception—including square footage limitation since the *Aiken* case—in a number of individual decisions. For the United States, the fact that judges have weighed the various factors slightly differently in making their individual decisions is simply a typical feature of a common-law system.

6.137 The European Communities contends that the criteria of the homestyle exemption in subparagraph (A) are ambiguously worded because the expression "a single receiving apparatus of a kind commonly used in private homes" is in itself imprecise and a "moving target" due to technological development. Also the variety of approaches and factors used by U.S. courts in applying the original version of the homestyle exemption are proof for the European Communities that the wording of subparagraph (A) of Section 110(5) is vague and open-ended. . . .

6.142 We note that the parties have submitted quantitative information on the coverage of subparagraph (A) with respect to eating, drinking and other establishments. The 1995 CRS study found that:

    (a)   16 per cent of all U.S. eating establishments;

    (b)   13.5 per cent of all U.S. drinking establishments; and

    (c)   18 per cent of all U.S. retail establishments

were as big as or smaller than the *Aiken* restaurant (1,055 square feet of total space), and could thus benefit from the homestyle exemption. These figures are not disputed between the parties. The United States expressly confirms these figures as far as eating and drinking establishments are concerned.

6.143 We believe that from a quantitative perspective the reach of subparagraph (A) in respect of potential users is limited to a comparably small percentage of all eating, drinking and retail establishments in the United States.

6.144 We are mindful of the above-mentioned EC argument alleging a judicial trend towards broadening the homestyle exemption of 1976 in recent years. We cannot exclude the possibility that in the future U.S. courts could establish precedents that would lead to the expansion of the scope of the currently applicable homestyle exemption as regards covered establishments. But we also note that since 1976 U.S. courts have in the vast majority of cases applied the homestyle exemption in a sufficiently consistent and clearly delineated manner. Given the sufficiently consistent and narrow application practice of the homestyle exemption of 1976, we see no need to hypothesise whether at some point in the future U.S. case law might lead to a *de facto* expansion of the homestyle exemption of 1998.

Homestyle equipment

6.145   We note that what is referred to as homestyle equipment (*i.e.*, "a single receiving apparatus of a kind commonly used in private homes") might vary between different countries, is subject to changing consumer preferences in a given country, and may evolve as a result of technological development. We thus agree in principle with the European Communities that the homestyle equipment that was used in U.S. households in 1976 (when the original homestyle exemption was enacted) is not necessarily identical to the equipment used in 1998 (when U.S. copyright legislation was amended) or at a future point in time. However, we recall that the term "*certain* special case" connotes "known and particularised, but not explicitly identified". In our view, the term "homestyle equipment" expresses the degree of clarity in definition required under Article 13's first condition. In our view, a Member is not required to identify homestyle equipment in terms of exceedingly detailed technical specifications in order to meet the standard of clarity set by the first condition. While we recognize that homestyle equipment may become technologically more sophisticated over time, we see no need to enter into speculations about potential future developments in the homestyle equipment market. At any rate, we recall that our factual determinations are invariably limited to what currently is being perceived as homestyle equipment in the U.S. market. . . .

6.159   Taking into account the specific limits imposed in subparagraph (A) and its legislative history, as well as in its considerably narrow application in the subsequent court practice on the beneficiaries of the exemption, permissible equipment and categories of works, we are of the view that the homestyle exemption in subparagraph (A) of Section 110(5) as amended in 1998 is well-defined and limited in its scope and reach. We, therefore, conclude that the exemption is confined to certain special cases within the meaning of the first condition of Article 13 of the TRIPS Agreement. . . .

(iv) Need to examine the other two conditions. . . .

(c)   "Not conflict with a normal exploitation of the work"

(i)   General interpretative analysis

6.176   That leaves us with the question of how to determine whether a particular use constitutes a normal exploitation of the exclusive rights provided under Articles 11*bis*(1)(iii) and 11(1)(ii) of the Berne Convention

(1971). In academic literature, one approach that has been suggested would be to rely on "the ways in which an author might reasonably be expected to exploit his work in the normal course of events."[3]

6.177   The main thrust of the U.S. argumentation is that, for judging "normal exploitation", Article 13's second condition implies an economic analysis of the degree of "market displacement" in terms of foregone collection of remuneration by right owners caused by the free use of works due to the exemption at issue. In the U.S. view, the essential question to ask is whether there are areas of the market in which the copyright owner would ordinarily expect to exploit the work, but which are not available for exploitation because of this exemption. Under this test, uses from which an owner would not ordinarily expect to receive compensation are not part of the normal exploitation.

6.178   In our view, this test seems to reflect the empirical or quantitative aspect of the connotation of "normal", the meaning of "regular, usual, typical or ordinary". We can, therefore, accept this U.S. approach, but only for the empirical or quantitative side of the connotation. We have to give meaning and effect also to the second aspect of the connotation, the meaning of "conforming to a type or standard". We described this aspect of normalcy as reflecting a more normative approach to defining normal exploitation, that includes, *inter alia*, a dynamic element capable of taking into account technological and market developments. The question then arises how this normative aspect of "normal" exploitation could be given meaning in relation to the exploitation of musical works.

6.179   In this respect, we find persuasive guidance in the suggestion by a study group, composed of representatives of the Swedish Government and the United International Bureaux for the Protection of Intellectual Property ("BIRPI"), which was set up to prepare for the Revision Conference at Stockholm in 1967 ("Swedish/BIRPI Study Group"). In relation to the reproduction right, this Group suggested to allow countries:

> "[to] limit the recognition and the exercising of that right, for specified purposes and *on the condition that these purposes should not enter into economic competition with these works*" in the sense that "*all forms of exploiting a work, which have, or are likely to acquire, considerable economic or practical importance, must be reserved to the authors.*"[4] (emphasis added)

6.180   Thus it appears that one way of measuring the normative connotation of normal exploitation is to consider, in addition to those forms of exploitation that currently generate significant or tangible revenue, those forms of exploitation which, with a certain degree of

---

[3]   Ricketson, The Berne Convention, op.cit., p. 483.

[4]   Document S/1: Berne Convention; Proposals for Revising the Substantive Copyright Provisions (Articles 1–20). Prepared by the Government of Sweden with the assistance of BIRPI.

likelihood and plausibility, could acquire considerable economic or practical importance.

6.181 In contrast, exceptions or limitations would be presumed not to conflict with a normal exploitation of works if they are confined to a scope or degree that does not enter into economic competition with non-exempted uses. . . .

(iii) The homestyle exemption of subparagraph (A)[***]

6.212 The United States argues that the homestyle exemption, even before nondramatic musical works were removed from its scope through the 1998 Amendment, was limited to the establishments that were not large enough to justify a subscription to a commercial background music service. As noted in the House Report (1976), the United States Congress intended that this exemption would merely codify the licensing practices already in effect. The original homestyle exemption of 1976 was intended to affect only those establishments that were not likely otherwise to enter into a licence, or would not have been licensed under the practices at that time. The United States contends that subparagraph (A) of the amended Section 110(5) does not conflict with the expectation of right holders concerning the normal exploitation of their works.

6.213 As regards the permissible equipment, we note that, according to the House Report (1976), the purpose of the exemption in its original form was to exempt from copyright liability "anyone who merely turns on, in a public place, an ordinary radio or television receiving apparatus of a kind commonly sold to members of the public for private use". "[The clause] would impose liability where the proprietor has a commercial 'sound system' installed or converts a standard home receiving apparatus (by augmenting it with sophisticated or extensive amplification equipment) into the equivalent of a commercial sound system." We also recall the rationale behind the homestyle exemption as expressed in the legislative history relating to its original version: "The basic rationale of this clause is that the secondary use of the transmission by turning on an ordinary receiver in public is so remote and minimal that no further liability should be imposed."

6.214 In other words, the provision is intended to define the borderline between two situations: a situation where one listens to the radio or watches the television—this is clearly not covered by the scope of copyright and, hence, outside normal exploitation of works—and a situation where one uses appropriate equipment to cause a new public performance of music contained in a broadcast or other transmission. This borderline is defined by laying emphasis on "turning on an ordinary receiver", albeit that members of the public might also hear the transmission.

[***] The Panel's discussion of section 110(5)(B)'s business exemption and its conclusion that the exemption conflicts with a normal exploitation of the work under Article 13 are omitted. *Ed.*

6.215   As regards the beneficiaries of the homestyle exemption, we note that its legislative history reveals the intention that the exemption should affect only those establishments that were not likely otherwise to enter into a licence, or would not have been licensed under the practices at that time. As pointed out above, according to the 1995 CRS study, the number of establishments that were as big or smaller than the *Aiken* restaurant and could benefit from the homestyle exemption is limited to a comparatively small percentage of all eating, drinking and retail establishments in the United States.

6.216   The United States argues that the homestyle exemption of 1998 is even less capable of being in conflict with normal exploitation of works because its scope is now limited to works other than nondramatic musical works. While a collective licensing mechanism for nondramatic musical works exists in the United States, there is no such mechanism for "dramatic" musical works and there is little or no direct licensing by individual right holders of the establishments in question. Therefore, in the U.S. view, authors might not reasonably expect to exploit "dramatic" musical works in the normal course of events through licensing public performances or communications thereof to the establishments that may invoke subparagraph (A).

6.217   We recall that it is the common understanding of the parties that the operation of subparagraph (A) is limited, as regards musical works, to the public communication of transmissions embodying dramatic renditions of "dramatic" musical works, such as operas, operettas, musicals and other similar dramatic works. Consequently, performances of, *e.g.*, individual songs from a dramatic musical work outside a dramatic context would constitute a rendition of a nondramatic work and fall within the purview of subparagraph (B).

6.218   It is our understanding that the parties agree that the right holders do not normally license or attempt to license the public communication of transmissions embodying dramatic renditions of "dramatic" musical works in the sense of Article 11*bis*(1)(iii) and/or 11(1)(ii). We have not been provided with information about any existing licensing practices concerning the communication to the public of broadcasts of performances of dramatic works (*e.g.*, operas, operettas, musicals) by eating, drinking or retail establishments in the United States or any other country. In this respect, we fail to see how the homestyle exemption, as limited to works other than nondramatic musical works in its revised form, could acquire economic or practical importance of any considerable dimension for the right holders of musical works.

6.219   Therefore, we conclude that the homestyle exemption contained in subparagraph (A) of Section 110(5) does not conflict with a normal exploitation of works within the meaning of the second condition of Article 13.

(d) "Not unreasonably prejudice the legitimate interests of the right holder"

(i)   General interpretative analysis

6.220   The United States defines "prejudice [to] the legitimate interests of the right holder" in terms of the economic impact caused by subparagraphs (A) and (B) of Section 110(5). In the U.S. view, while the second condition of Article 13 of the TRIPS Agreement looks to the degree of market displacement caused by a limitation or exception, the "unreasonable prejudice" standard measures how much the right holder is harmed by the effects of the exception. Given that any exception to exclusive rights may technically result in some degree of prejudice to the right holder, the key question is whether that prejudice is unreasonable.

6.221   The European Communities submits that the legitimate interests of a right holder consist in being able to prevent all instances of a certain use of his or her work protected by a specific exclusive right undertaken by a third party without his or her consent. The legitimate interests include, at a minimum, all commercial uses by a third party of the right holder's exclusive rights. For the European Communities, both empirical and normative elements are relevant for the examination of the third condition of Article 13. In practice, economic prejudice to right holders should be assessed primarily on the basis of the economic effects in the country applying the exception. In the EC's view, it is sufficient to demonstrate the potentiality to prejudice; it is not necessary to quantify the actual financial losses suffered by the right holders concerned. . . .

Legitimate interests of right holders of EC, U.S. and third-country origin

6.230   We note the EC argument that, in respect of all conditions of Article 13, the effect on all right holders from all WTO Members must be taken into account. For the European Communities, the specific impact on EC right holders is not at issue at this stage of the dispute settlement process, but could become relevant only in the context of Article 22 of the DSU concerning compensation or the suspension of concessions or other obligations equivalent to nullification or impairment suffered. The United States has limited its estimations of the economic impact of subparagraph (B) to the actual losses caused by it to the EC right holders.

6.231   This raises the question who may enforce the legitimate interests of right holders of various WTO Members in panel proceedings within the WTO dispute settlement system. In *EC-Bananas III*, the Appellate Body agreed with the panel that no DSU provision contains a requirement that a complaining party show its legal interest as a prerequisite for requesting a panel. This rejection of a "legal interest" requirement does not necessarily imply that, in the context of the third condition of Article 13, prejudice to the legitimate interests of right holders other than EC right holders should be relevant. But we cannot find any indication in the express wording of the third condition of Article

13 that the assessment of whether the prejudice caused by an exception or limitation to the legitimate interests of the right holder is of an unreasonable level should be limited to the right holders of the Member that brings forth the complaint. For such a limitation to exist, the third condition of Article 13 would have to refer exclusively to the right holders who are nationals of the complaining party, not to "the right holder" as such. . . .

Summary of the general interpretative analysis

6.236   We will now examine subparagraphs (B) and (A) of Section 110(5) in the light of these general considerations. What is at stake in our examination of the third condition of Article 13 of the TRIPS Agreement is whether the prejudice caused by the exemptions to the legitimate interests of the right holder is of an unreasonable level. We will consider the information on market conditions provided by the parties taking into account, to the extent feasible, the actual as well as the potential prejudice caused by the exemptions, as a prerequisite for determining whether the extent or degree of prejudice is of an unreasonable level. In these respects, we recall our consideration above that taking account of actual as well as potential effects is consistent with past GATT/WTO dispute settlement practice. . . .

(iii) The homestyle exemption of subparagraph (A)[****]

6.267   The United States submits that the economic effect of the original homestyle exemption of Section 110(5) of 1976 was minimal. Its intent was to exempt from liability small shop and restaurant owners whose establishments would not have justified a commercial licence. Given that such establishments are not a significant licensing market, they could not be significant sources of revenue for right holders. Where no licences would be sought or issued in the absence of an exception, there was literally no economic detriment to the right holder from an explicit exception. Exempted establishments with small square footage and elementary sound equipment are the least likely to be aggressively licensed by the CMOs and licensing fees for these establishments would likely be the lowest in the range. Given their size and that the playing of music is often incidental to their services, these establishments are among those most likely simply to turn off the radio if pressed to pay licensing fees. The 1998 Amendment has only decreased the economic relevance of the exemption by reducing its scope to "dramatic" musical works. Therefore, in the U.S. view, the homestyle exemption as contained in subparagraph (A) of Section 110(5) does not prejudice the legitimate interests of the right holder.

6.268   The European Communities responds that the vast body of case law on the pre-1998 homestyle exemption makes it clear that very significant economic interests were at stake. Already under the *Aiken*

[****] The Panel's discussion of section 110(5)(B)'s business exemption and its conclusion that the exemption does not meet the requirements of Article 13's third condition are omitted. *Ed.*

scenario, a considerable number of U.S. establishments were covered by the exemption. According to the European Communities, the *Aiken* surface limitations were doubled by U.S. Courts before the 1998 Amendment.

6.269   We recall our discussion concerning the legislative history of the original homestyle exemption in connection with the first and second conditions of Article 13. In particular, as regards the beneficiaries of the exemption, the Conference Report (1976) elaborated on the rationale of the exemption by noting that the intent was to exempt a small commercial establishment "which was not of sufficient size to justify, as a practical matter, a subscription to a commercial background music service". We also recall the estimations on the percentages of establishments covered by the exemption. Moreover, the exemption was applicable to such establishments only if they use homestyle equipment. The House Report (1976) noted that "[the clause] would impose liability where the proprietor has a commercial 'sound system' installed or converts a standard home receiving apparatus (by augmenting it with sophisticated or extensive amplification equipment) into the equivalent of a commercial sound system." In this respect, we refer to our discussion on permissible equipment as well as the applicability of the exemption to Internet transmissions in connection with the first and second conditions of Article 13.

6.270   Furthermore, we recall the common understanding of the parties that the operation of the homestyle exemption as contained in the 1998 Amendment has been limited, as regards musical works, to the public communication of transmissions embodying dramatic renditions of "dramatic" musical works (such as operas, operettas, musicals and other similar dramatic works). We have not been presented with evidence suggesting that right holders would have licensed or attempted to license the public communication, within the meaning of Article 11(1)(ii) or 11*bis*(1)(iii) of the Berne Convention (1971), of broadcasts of performances embodying dramatic renditions of "dramatic" musical works either before the enactment of the original homestyle exemption or after the 1998 Amendment. We also fail to see how communications to the public of renditions of entire dramatic works could acquire such economic or practical importance that it could cause unreasonable prejudice to the legitimate interests of right holders.

6.271   We note that playing music by the small establishments covered by the exemption by means of homestyle apparatus has never been a significant source of revenue collection for CMOs. We recall our view that, for the purposes of assessing unreasonable prejudice to the legitimate interests of right holders, potential losses of right holders, too, are relevant. However, we have not been presented with persuasive information suggesting that such potential effects of significant economic or practical importance could occur that they would give rise to an unreasonable level of prejudice to legitimate interests of right holders. In particular, as regards the exemption as amended in 1998 to exclude from its scope nondramatic musical works, the European Communities has not explicitly claimed that the exemption would currently cause any prejudice to right holders.

6.272   In the light of the considerations above, we conclude that the homestyle exemption contained in subparagraph (A) of Section 110(5) does not cause unreasonable prejudice to the legitimate interests of the right holders within the meaning of the third condition of Article 13.

VII. CONCLUSIONS AND RECOMMENDATIONS

7.1   In the light of the findings in paragraphs 6.92–6.95, 6.133, 6.159, 6.211, 6.219, 6.266 and 6.272 above, the Panel concludes that:

> (a) Subparagraph (A) of Section 110(5) of the U.S. Copyright Act meets the requirements of Article 13 of the TRIPS Agreement and is thus consistent with Articles 11*bis*(1)(iii) and 11(1)(ii) of the Berne Convention (1971) as incorporated into the TRIPS Agreement by Article 9.1 of that Agreement.

> (b) Subparagraph (B) of Section 110(5) of the U.S. Copyright Act does not meet the requirements of Article 13 of the TRIPS Agreement and is thus inconsistent with Articles 11*bis*(1)(iii) and 11(1)(ii) of the Berne Convention (1971) as incorporated into the TRIPS Agreement by Article 9.1 of that Agreement.

7.2   The Panel *recommends* that the Dispute Settlement Body request the United States to bring subparagraph (B) of Section 110(5) into conformity with its obligations under the TRIPS Agreement.

NOTES

1.   *The "Three-Step Test"*. The "three-step test" applied in the section 110(5) proceeding was first introduced into international copyright discussions at the 1967 Stockholm Conference to revise the Berne Convention in order to balance Article 9(1)'s newly-added reproduction right with a general limitation that captured the detailed exceptions to the right already embodied in national laws. The formulation has since found its way not only into Article 13 of the TRIPs Agreement (where the "legitimate interests" protected under the third step are assigned to the "right holder" rather than to the "author" of Berne Article 9(2)), but also into Article 10 of the WIPO Copyright Treaty and Article 16 of the WIPO Performances and Phonograms Treaty, and from these sources into several EU copyright directives, from which in turn they have been transposed into national law in member countries. Other countries have similarly made the three-step test's regulation of limitations and exceptions part of their copyright law. Nor has the test been confined to copyright limitations and exceptions. TRIPs incorporates versions of the test into its provisions on trademarks (Article 17), industrial design (Article 26), and patents (Article 30).

For a close comparison of the three-step test in its various settings, see Andrew F. Christie & Robin Wright, A Comparative Analysis of the Three-

Step Tests in International Treaties, 45 IIC 409 (2014). *See* generally, Martin Senftleben, Copyright, Limitations and the Three-Step Test (2004); P. Bernt Hugenholtz & Ruth Okediji, Conceiving an International Instrument on Limitations and Exceptions to Copyright (2008); Matthew Kennedy, The "Three-Step Test" and the Burden of Proof in Disputes Under the TRIPs Agreement, 45 IIC 161 (2014).

2.   Under the first condition imposed by TRIPs Article 13, confining limitations or exceptions "to certain special cases," is it sufficient, as the United States argued in the WTO Panel proceedings on section 110(5), that the exception have a "specific policy objective," or must the objective also be principled and demonstrably legitimate? Is the objective that the United States claimed for section 110(5)(B)'s business exceptions—"fostering small businesses and preventing abusive tactics by CMOS"—legitimate? Plausible? Did the Panel construe Article 13's third condition any differently than it did the second condition?

Was the Panel's decision on section 110(5)(B) adverse to U.S. interests generally, or adverse only to certain U.S. interests? For example, what reaction would American composers and music publishers be likely to have to the Panel Report? To what extent does the WTO dispute settlement process offer a second chance at success to suitors who failed to win their cause in lobbying the national legislature?

Apparently the economic consequences of the Panel decision were relatively slight since the U.S. has not sought to amend section 110(5) to comply with the order, and the EU has been desultory in seeking compensation for lost benefits. According to a summary report from the USTR, in October 2000 the EU requested arbitration to set a deadline for the U.S. to implement the Panel's decision; the resulting arbitration specified July 27, 2001 as the deadline; and on July 24 of that year, the D.S.B. approved a U.S. proposal to extend the deadline to the earlier of the end of the then-current session of the U.S. Congress or December 31, 2001. On July 23, 2001, the U.S. and EU requested arbitration to determine section 110(5)(B)'s impact on the EU, and in a decision circulated in November, 2001, the arbitrators determined that the annual value of benefits lost to the EU was $1.1 million. On June 23, 2005 the U.S. and EU notified the WTO that the U.S. would make a $3.3 million payment to the EU to cover the three-year period ending December 21, 2004. No payments were subsequently made, and in monthly reports by the U.S. to the WTO under Article 21.6 of the Understanding on Rules and Procedures Governing the Settlement of Disputes, the U.S. stated that "[t]he US administration will work closely with the US Congress and will continue to confer with the European Union in order to reach a mutually satisfactory resolution of this matter." *See* WT/DS 160)24/Add. 79 (8 July 2011).

See generally, Rebecca Ullman, Enhancing the WTO Tool Kit: The Case for Financial Compensation, 9 Rich. J. Global L. & Bus. 167 (2010); Bernard O'Connor & Margarita Djordjevic, Practical Aspects of Monetary Compensation: The US-Copyright Case, 8 J. Int'l Econ. L. 127 (2005).

3. *"Minor Exceptions."* The minor exception rule, relied on by the WTO Panel in reconciling its interpretation of TRIPs Article 13 with the requirements of the Berne Paris Text, traces to the 1948 Brussels Conference at which public performance rights were added as a minimum Berne standard. Professor Herman Cohen Jehoram recounts the history: "These rights had already existed before in many national legislations and had been subject there to a wide variety of exceptions, like 'musical performances made in the course of religious worship,' the famous Italian 'concerts given by military bands', a clear example of 'pork barrel,' charitable performances and concerts on particular festivals or holidays. The question in Brussels now was what to do with all these existing restrictions. They could not be suppressed, because each country defended its own traditions here like the gold in the vaults of its national bank. It was inadvisable to enumerate all existing restrictions in the convention. This left then the idea of a general clause, permitting member states to maintain their existing exceptions. This was however deemed to be too much of an invitation to national legislators to extend their national list of derogations. The end result of this debate was that no clause would be inserted in the text of the convention but that the Report of the Conference would contain a passage on rather indefinite 'minor exceptions' to the new rights." Herman Cohen Jehoram, Restrictions on Copyright and Their Abuse, 27 EIPR 359 (2005).

Since section 110(5) of the 1976 U.S. Act limits the public performance right, the WTO Panel's assimilation of the minor exception rule into TRIPs Article 13 was defensible. But, would a future Panel be justified in subjecting some other right, such as the translation right, which has no connection to the minor exception rule, to Article 13?

See Jane C. Ginsburg, Toward Supranational Copyright Law? The WTO Panel Decision and the "Three-Step Test" for Copyright Exceptions, 187 R.I.D.A. 3 (2001); Matthew Kennedy, The "Three-Step Test" and the Burden of Proof Under the TRIPs Agreement, 45 IIC 161 (2014).

4. *The Third Step.* It is generally assumed that, under the third step, equitable remuneration will cure otherwise unreasonable prejudice. According to the drafting committee report on Article 9(2): "If it is considered that reproduction conflicts with the normal exploitation of the work, reproduction is not permitted at all. If it is considered that reproduction does not conflict with the normal exploitation of the work, the next step would be to consider whether it does not unreasonably prejudice the legitimate interests of the author. Only if such is not the case would it be possible in certain special cases to introduce a compulsory license, or to provide for use without payment. A practical example may be photocopying for various purposes. If it consists of producing a very large number of copies, it may not be permitted, as it conflicts with a normal exploitation of the work. If it implies a rather large number of copies for use in industrial undertakings, it may not unreasonably prejudice the legitimate interests of the author, provided that, according to national legislation, an equitable remuneration is paid. If a small number of copies is made, photocopying may be permitted without payment, particularly for individual or scientific use." Report on the Work of Main Committee I (Substantive Provisions of the Berne Convention:

Articles 1 to 20), paragraph 85, in Records of the Intellectual Property Conference of Stockholm, June 11–July 14, 1967, 1971, Vol. II, pp. 1145–1146.

What if each individual use—typically a private use—of a copyrighted work is sufficiently minor to be harmless, but would in the aggregate unreasonably prejudice the legitimate interests of the author? Many countries impose private copy levies on photocopiers and other reproduction devices, as well as on blank audio and video media, to compensate authors for small private uses. In Padawan SL v. Sociedad General de Autores y Editores de Espana, CJEU, C-467/08, 2010, the Court of Justice of the European Union considered whether Spain's levy on digital media conformed to Information Society Directive Art. 5(2)(b)'s provision for fair compensation for private copying, and concluded that "a link is necessary between the application of the levy intended to finance fair compensation with respect to digital reproduction equipment, devices and media and the deemed use of them for the purposes of private copying. Consequently, the indiscriminate application of the private copying levy, in particular with respect to digital reproduction equipment, devices and media not made available to private users and clearly reserved for uses other than private copying, is incompatible with Directive 2001/29."

The *Padawan* Court left no doubt that "the final user who carries out, on a private basis, the reproduction of a protected work must, in principle, be regarded as the person responsible for paying the fair compensation provided for in Article 5(2)(b)," although "it is open to the Member States to establish a private copying levy chargeable to the persons who make reproduction equipment, devices and media available to that final user." Must proportionality in payments also be observed at the receiving end? What if national practice allocates a portion of the levies collected from private copying not to authors or other right holders but to more general social or cultural objects chosen by the government? *See* A.E. Pardo & A. Lucas-Schloetter, Compensation for Private Copying in Europe, 35 EIPR 463 (2013).

5. *The Marrakesh Treaty and the Three-Step Test.* The Treaty to Facilitate Access to Published Works for Persons Who Are Blind, Visually Impaired, or Otherwise Print Disabled, concluded at Marrakesh on June 27, 2013, is the first international agreement to establish intellectual property norms aimed exclusively at limitations and exceptions, rather than at minimum standards of protection. As such, it is no surprise that the three-step test so thoroughly pervades the treaty's terms—in its preamble (reaffirming "the importance and flexibility of the three-step test" of Berne Article 9(2)), in its Agreed Statements, and in Article 11's explicit incorporation of the formula of Berne Article 9(2), TRIPs Article 13 and WIPO Copyright Treaty Article 10. In the words of one close observer, "the three-step test practically haunted the treaty negotiations and put considerable strain on the arduous work to be accomplished," and "despite legitimate concerns to the contrary, the three-step test was capable of enough flexibility for the 'Marrakesh Miracle' to take place." Simonetta Vezzoso, The Marrakesh Spirit—A Ghost in Three Steps? 45 IIC 796 (2014).

Apart from establishing mandatory norms for exceptions and limitations, Marrakesh differs from earlier intellectual property treaties in requiring member countries to facilitate cross-border access to permitted copies of works in accessible formats, a requirement that may place strains on an individual country's particular accommodation of the three-step test in its own copyright law. The treaty eases the possible strain by giving member countries considerable leeway, including permission to condition the specified limitations or exceptions on a work's commercial nonavailability in an accessible format on "reasonable terms" (Article 4(4)) or on payment of remuneration to the copyright owner (Article 4(5)). *See* Marketa Trimble, The Marrakesh Puzzle, 45 IIC 768 (2014).

(B) Exemptions, Fair Dealing (and Fair Use)

CCH Canadian Ltd. v. Law Society of Upper Canada

Supreme Court of Canada, 2004.
2004 SCC 13, 236 D.L.R. (4th) 395, 317 N.R. 107, 30 C.P.R. (4th) 1, 2004.

THE CHIEF JUSTICE:

I. Introduction—The Issues To Be Determined

1   The appellant, the Law Society of Upper Canada, is a statutory non-profit corporation that has regulated the legal profession in Ontario since 1822. Since 1845, the Law Society has maintained and operated the Great Library at Osgoode Hall in Toronto, a reference and research library with one of the largest collections of legal materials in Canada. The Great Library provides a request-based photocopy service (the "custom photocopy service") for Law Society members, the judiciary and other authorized researchers. Under the custom photocopy service, legal materials are reproduced by Great Library staff and delivered in person, by mail or by facsimile transmission to requesters. The Law Society also maintains self-service photocopiers in the Great Library for use by its patrons.

2   The respondents, CCH Canadian Ltd., Thomson Canada Ltd. and Canada Law Book Inc., publish law reports and other legal materials. In 1993, the respondent publishers commenced copyright infringement actions against the Law Society, seeking a declaration of subsistence and ownership of copyright in eleven specific works and a declaration that the Law Society had infringed copyright when the Great Library reproduced a copy of each of the works. The publishers also sought a permanent injunction prohibiting the Law Society from reproducing these eleven works as well as any other works that they published.

3   The Law Society denied liability and counterclaimed for a declaration that copyright is not infringed when a single copy of a reported decision, case summary, statute, regulation or a limited

selection of text from a treatise is made by the Great Library staff or one of its patrons on a self-service photocopier for the purpose of research.

4   The key question that must be answered in this appeal is whether the Law Society has breached copyright by either (1) providing the custom photocopy service in which single copies of the publishers' works are reproduced and sent to patrons upon their request or by (2) maintaining self-service photocopiers and copies of the publishers' works in the Great Library for use by its patrons. To answer this question, the Court must address the following sub-issues:

> (1)   Are the publishers' materials "original works" protected by copyright?
>
> (2)   Did the Great Library authorize copyright infringement by maintaining self-service photocopiers and copies of the publishers' works for its patrons' use?
>
> (3)   Were the Law Society's dealings with the publishers' works "fair dealing [s]" under s. 29 of the *Copyright Act*, R.S.C. 1985, c. C-42, as amended?
>
> (4)   Did Canada Law Book consent to have its works reproduced by the Great Library?

5   The publishers have filed a cross-appeal in which they submit that, in addition to infringing copyright by reproducing copies of their works, the Law Society infringed copyright both by faxing and by selling copies of the publishers' copyrighted works through its custom photocopy service. The publishers also contend that the Great Library does not qualify for the library exemption under the *Copyright Act* and, finally, that they are entitled to an injunction to the extent that the Law Society has been found to infringe any one or more of their copyrighted works. The four sub-issues that the Court must address on this cross-appeal are:

> (1)   Did the Law Society's fax transmissions of the publishers' works constitute communications "to the public" within s. 3(1)(*f*) of the *Copyright Act* so as to constitute copyright infringement?
>
> (2)   Did the Law Society infringe copyright by selling copies of the publishers' works contrary to s. 27(2) of the *Copyright Act*?
>
> (3)   Does the Law Society qualify for an exemption as a "library, archive or museum" under ss. 2 and 30.2(1) of the *Copyright Act*?
>
> (4)   To the extent that the Law Society has been found to infringe any one or more of the publishers' copyrighted works, are the publishers entitled to a permanent injunction under s. 34(1) of the *Copyright Act*?

6   With respect to the main appeal, I conclude that the Law Society did not infringe copyright by providing single copies of the respondent publishers' works to its members through the custom photocopy service. Although the works in question were "original" and thus covered by copyright, the Law Society's dealings with the works were for the purpose

of research and were fair dealings within s. 29 of the *Copyright Act*. I also find that the Law Society did not authorize infringement by maintaining self-service photocopiers in the Great Library for use by its patrons. I would therefore allow the appeal.

7   On the cross-appeal, I conclude that there was no secondary infringement by the Law Society; the fax transmissions were not communications to the public and the Law Society did not sell copies of the publishers' works. In light of my finding on appeal that the Law Society's dealings with the publishers' works were fair, it is not necessary to decide whether the Great Library qualifies for the library exemption. This said, I would conclude that the Great Library does indeed qualify for this exemption. Finally, in light of my conclusion that there has been no copyright infringement, it is not necessary to issue an injunction in this case. I would dismiss the cross-appeal. . . .

[The Court's analysis of originality, omitted here, is reproduced beginning at page 212, above.]

11   Canada's *Copyright Act* sets out the rights and obligations of both copyright owners and users. Part I of the Act specifies the scope of a creator's copyright and moral rights in works. For example, s. 3 of the Act specifies that only copyright owners have the right to copy or to authorize the copying of their works:

> (1) For the purposes of this Act, "copyright", in relation to a work, means the sole right to produce or reproduce the work or any substantial part thereof in any material form whatever, to perform the work or any substantial part thereof in public or, if the work is unpublished, to publish the work or any substantial part thereof . . .
>
> . . . .
>
> and to authorize any such acts.

12   Part III of the *Copyright Act* deals with the infringement of copyright and exceptions to infringement. Section 27(1) states generally that "[i]t is an infringement of copyright for any person to do, without the consent of the owner of the copyright, anything that by this Act only the owner of the copyright has the right to do". More specific examples of how copyright is infringed are set out in s. 27(2) of the Act. The exceptions to copyright infringement, perhaps more properly understood as users' rights, are set out in ss. 29 and 30 of the Act. The fair dealing exceptions to copyright are set out in ss. 29–29.2. In general terms, those who deal fairly with a work for the purpose of research, private study, criticism, review or news reporting, do not infringe copyright. Educational institutions, libraries, archives and museums are specifically exempted from copyright infringement in certain circumstances: see ss. 29.4–30 (educational institutions), and ss. 30.1–30.5. Part IV of the *Copyright Act* specifies the remedies that may be awarded in cases where copyright has

been infringed. Copyright owners may be entitled to any number of different remedies such as damages and injunctions, among others.

13   This case requires this Court to interpret the scope of both owners' and users' rights under the *Copyright Act*, including what qualifies for copyright protection, what is required to find that the copyright has been infringed through authorization and the fair dealing exceptions under the Act. . . .

(3)   The Law Society and Fair Dealing

47   The Great Library provides a custom photocopy service. Upon receiving a request from a lawyer, law student, member of the judiciary or authorized researcher, the Great Library staff photocopies extracts from legal material within its collection and sends it to the requester. The question is whether this service falls within the fair dealing defence under s. 29 of the *Copyright Act* which provides: "Fair dealing for the purpose of research or private study does not infringe copyright."

(a)   The Law

48   Before reviewing the scope of the fair dealing exception under the *Copyright Act*, it is important to clarify some general considerations about exceptions to copyright infringement. Procedurally, a defendant is required to prove that his or her dealing with a work has been fair; however, the fair dealing exception is perhaps more properly understood as an integral part of the *Copyright Act* than simply a defence. Any act falling within the fair dealing exception will not be an infringement of copyright. The fair dealing exception, like other exceptions in the *Copyright Act*, is a user's right. In order to maintain the proper balance between the rights of a copyright owner and users' interests, it must not be interpreted restrictively. As Professor Vaver, *supra*, has explained, at p. 171: "User rights are not just loopholes. Both owner rights and user rights should therefore be given the fair and balanced reading that befits remedial legislation."

49   As an integral part of the scheme of copyright law, the s. 29 fair dealing exception is always available. Simply put, a library can always attempt to prove that its dealings with a copyrighted work are fair under s. 29 of the *Copyright Act*. It is only if a library were unable to make out the fair dealing exception under s. 29 that it would need to turn to s. 30.2 of the *Copyright Act* to prove that it qualified for the library exemption.

50   In order to show that a dealing was fair under s. 29 of the *Copyright Act*, a defendant must prove: (1) that the dealing was for the purpose of either research or private study and (2) that it was fair.

51   The fair dealing exception under s. 29 is open to those who can show that their dealings with a copyrighted work were for the purpose of research or private study. "Research" must be given a large and liberal interpretation in order to ensure that users' rights are not unduly constrained. I agree with the Court of Appeal that research is not limited to non-commercial or private contexts. The Court of Appeal correctly

noted, at para. 128, that "[r]esearch for the purpose of advising clients, giving opinions, arguing cases, preparing briefs and factums is nonetheless research". Lawyers carrying on the business of law for profit are conducting research within the meaning of s. 29 of the *Copyright Act*.

52   The *Copyright Act* does not define what will be "fair"; whether something is fair is a question of fact and depends on the facts of each case. Lord Denning explained this eloquently in *Hubbard v. Vosper* (1971), [1972] 1 All E.R. 1023 (Eng. C.A.), at p. 1027:

> It is impossible to define what is 'fair dealing'. It must be a question of degree. You must consider first the number and extent of the quotations and extracts. Are they altogether too many and too long to be fair? Then you must consider the use made of them. If they are used as a basis for comment, criticism or review, that may be a fair dealing. If they are used to convey the same information as the author, for a rival purpose, that may be unfair. Next, you must consider the proportions. To take long extracts and attach short comments may be unfair. But, short extracts and long comments may be fair. Other considerations may come to mind also. But, after all is said and done, it must be a matter of impression. As with fair comment in the law of libel, so with fair dealing in the law of copyright. The tribunal of fact must decide.

53   At the Court of Appeal, Linden J.A. acknowledged that there was no set test for fairness, but outlined a series of factors that could be considered to help assess whether a dealing is fair. Drawing on the decision in *Hubbard, supra*, as well as the doctrine of fair use in the United States, he proposed that the following factors be considered in assessing whether a dealing was fair: (1) the purpose of the dealing; (2) the character of the dealing; (3) the amount of the dealing; (4) alternatives to the dealing; (5) the nature of the work; and (6) the effect of the dealing on the work. Although these considerations will not all arise in every case of fair dealing, this list of factors provides a useful analytical framework to govern determinations of fairness in future cases.

(i)   The Purpose of the Dealing

54   In Canada, the purpose of the dealing will be fair if it is for one of the allowable purposes under the *Copyright Act*, namely research, private study, criticism, review or news reporting: see ss. 29, 29.1 and 29.2 of the *Copyright Act*. As discussed, these allowable purposes should not be given a restrictive interpretation or this could result in the undue restriction of users' rights. This said, courts should attempt to make an objective assessment of the user/defendant's real purpose or motive in using the copyrighted work. Moreover, as the Court of Appeal explained, some dealings, even if for an allowable purpose, may be more or less fair than others; research done for commercial purposes may not be as fair as research done for charitable purposes.

(ii) The Character of the Dealing

55   In assessing the character of a dealing, courts must examine how the works were dealt with. If multiple copies of works are being widely distributed, this will tend to be unfair. If, however, a single copy of a work is used for a specific legitimate purpose, then it may be easier to conclude that it was a fair dealing. If the copy of the work is destroyed after it is used for its specific intended purpose, this may also favour a finding of fairness. It may be relevant to consider the custom or practice in a particular trade or industry to determine whether or not the character of the dealing is fair. For example, in *Sillitoe v. McGraw-Hill Book Co. (U.K.) Ltd.*, [1983] F.S.R. 545 (Eng. Ch.), the importers and distributors of "study notes" that incorporated large passages from published works attempted to claim that the copies were fair dealings because they were for the purpose of criticism. The court reviewed the ways in which copied works were customarily dealt with in literary criticism textbooks to help it conclude that the study notes were not fair dealings for the purpose of criticism.

(iii) The Amount of the Dealing

56   Both the amount of the dealing and importance of the work allegedly infringed should be considered in assessing fairness. If the amount taken from a work is trivial, the fair dealing analysis need not be undertaken at all because the court will have concluded that there was no copyright infringement. As the passage from *Hubbard* indicates, the quantity of the work taken will not be determinative of fairness, but it can help in the determination. It may be possible to deal fairly with a whole work. As Vaver points out, there might be no other way to criticize or review certain types of works such as photographs: see Vaver, *supra*, at p. 191. The amount taken may also be more or less fair depending on the purpose. For example, for the purpose of research or private study, it may be essential to copy an entire academic article or an entire judicial decision. However, if a work of literature is copied for the purpose of criticism, it will not likely be fair to include a full copy of the work in the critique.

(iv) Alternatives to the Dealing

57   Alternatives to dealing with the infringed work may affect the determination of fairness. If there is a non-copyrighted equivalent of the work that could have been used instead of the copyrighted work, this should be considered by the court. I agree with the Court of Appeal that it will also be useful for courts to attempt to determine whether the dealing was reasonably necessary to achieve the ultimate purpose. For example, if a criticism would be equally effective if it did not actually reproduce the copyrighted work it was criticizing, this may weigh against a finding of fairness.

(v) The Nature of the Work

58 The nature of the work in question should also be considered by courts assessing whether a dealing is fair. Although certainly not determinative, if a work has not been published, the dealing may be more fair in that its reproduction with acknowledgement could lead to a wider public dissemination of the work—one of the goals of copyright law. If, however, the work in question was confidential, this may tip the scales towards finding that the dealing was unfair. *See Beloff v. Pressdram Ltd.*, [1973] 1 All E.R. 241 at p. 264.

(vi) Effect of the Dealing on the Work

59 Finally, the effect of the dealing on the work is another factor warranting consideration when courts are determining whether a dealing is fair. If the reproduced work is likely to compete with the market of the original work, this may suggest that the dealing is not fair. Although the effect of the dealing on the market of the copyright owner is an important factor, it is neither the only factor nor the most important factor that a court must consider in deciding if the dealing is fair.

60 To conclude, the purpose of the dealing, the character of the dealing, the amount of the dealing, the nature of the work, available alternatives to the dealing and the effect of the dealing on the work are all factors that could help determine whether or not a dealing is fair. These factors may be more or less relevant to assessing the fairness of a dealing depending on the factual context of the allegedly infringing dealing. In some contexts, there may be factors other than those listed here that may help a court decide whether the dealing was fair.

(b) Application of the law to these facts. . . .

62 At trial, the Law Society claimed that its custom photocopy service does not infringe copyright because it is a fair dealing within the meaning of s. 29 of the *Copyright Act*. The trial judge held that the fair dealing exception should be strictly construed. He concluded that copying for the custom photocopy service was not for the purpose of either research or study and therefore was not within the ambit of fair dealing. The Court of Appeal rejected the argument that the fair dealing exception should be interpreted restrictively. The majority held that the Law Society could rely on the purposes of its patrons to prove that its dealings were fair. The Court of Appeal concluded, however, that there was not sufficient evidence to determine whether or not the dealings were fair and, consequently, that the fair dealing exception had not been proven.

63 This raises a preliminary question: is it incumbent on the Law Society to adduce evidence that every patron uses the material provided for in a fair dealing manner or can the Law Society rely on its general practice to establish fair dealing? I conclude that the latter suffices. Section 29 of the *Copyright Act* states that "[f]air dealing for the purpose of research or private study does not infringe copyright". The language is general. "Dealing" connotes not individual acts, but a practice or system.

This comports with the purpose of the fair dealing exception, which is to ensure that users are not unduly restricted in their ability to use and disseminate copyrighted works. Persons or institutions relying on the s. 29 fair dealing exception need only prove that their own dealings with copyrighted works were for the purpose of research or private study and were fair. They may do this either by showing that their own practices and policies were research-based and fair, or by showing that all individual dealings with the materials were in fact research-based and fair.

64   The Law Society's custom photocopying service is provided for the purpose of research, review and private study. The Law Society's Access Policy states that "[s]ingle copies of library materials, required for the purposes of research, review, private study and criticism . . . may be provided to users of the Great Library". When the Great Library staff make copies of the requested cases, statutes, excerpts from legal texts and legal commentary, they do so for the purpose of research. Although the retrieval and photocopying of legal works are not research in and of themselves, they are necessary conditions of research and thus part of the research process. The reproduction of legal works is for the purpose of research in that it is an essential element of the legal research process. There is no other purpose for the copying; the Law Society does not profit from this service. Put simply, its custom photocopy service helps to ensure that legal professionals in Ontario can access the materials necessary to conduct the research required to carry on the practice of law. In sum, the Law Society's custom photocopy service is an integral part of the legal research process, an allowable purpose under s. 29 of the *Copyright Act*.

65   The evidence also establishes that the dealings were fair, having regard to the factors discussed earlier.

(i)   Purpose of the Dealing

66   The Access Policy and its safeguards weigh in favour of finding that the dealings were fair. It specifies that individuals requesting copies must identify the purpose of the request for these requests to be honoured, and provides that concerns that a request is not for one of the legitimate purposes under the fair dealing exceptions in the *Copyright Act* are referred to the Reference Librarian. This policy provides reasonable safeguards that the materials are being used for the purpose of research and private study.

(ii)   Character of the Dealing

67   The character of the Law Society's dealings with the publishers' works also supports a finding of fairness. Under the Access Policy, the Law Society provides single copies of works for the specific purposes allowed under the *Copyright Act*. There is no evidence that the Law Society was disseminating multiple copies of works to multiple members

of the legal profession. Copying a work for the purpose of research on a specific legal topic is generally a fair dealing.

(iii) Amount of the Dealing

68   The Access Policy indicates that the Great Library will exercise its discretion to ensure that the amount of the dealing with copyrighted works will be reasonable. The Access Policy states that the Great Library will typically honour requests for a copy of one case, one article or one statutory reference. It further stipulates that the Reference Librarian will review requests for a copy of more than five percent of a secondary source and that, ultimately, such requests may be refused. This suggests that the Law Society's dealings with the publishers' works are fair. Although the dealings might not be fair if a specific patron of the Great Library submitted numerous requests for multiple reported judicial decisions from the same reported series over a short period of time, there is no evidence that this has occurred.

(iv) Alternatives to the Dealing

69   It is not apparent that there are alternatives to the custom photocopy service employed by the Great Library. As the Court of Appeal points out, the patrons of the custom photocopying service cannot reasonably be expected to always conduct their research on-site at the Great Library. Twenty per cent of the requesters live outside the Toronto area; it would be burdensome to expect them to travel to the city each time they wanted to track down a specific legal source. Moreover, because of the heavy demand for the legal collection at the Great Library, researchers are not allowed to borrow materials from the library. If researchers could not request copies of the work or make copies of the works themselves, they would be required to do all of their research and note-taking in the Great Library, something which does not seem reasonable given the volume of research that can often be required on complex legal matters.

70   The availability of a licence is not relevant to deciding whether a dealing has been fair. As discussed, fair dealing is an integral part of the scheme of copyright law in Canada. Any act falling within the fair dealing exception will not infringe copyright. If a copyright owner were allowed to license people to use its work and then point to a person's decision not to obtain a licence as proof that his or her dealings were not fair, this would extend the scope of the owner's monopoly over the use of his or her work in a manner that would not be consistent with the *Copyright Act*'s balance between owner's rights and user's interests.

(v) Nature of the Work

71   I agree with the Court of Appeal that the nature of the works in question—judicial decisions and other works essential to legal research— suggests that the Law Society's dealings were fair. As Linden J.A. explained, at para. 159: "It is generally in the public interest that access to judicial decisions and other legal resources not be unjustifiably

restrained." Moreover, the Access Policy puts reasonable limits on the Great Library's photocopy service. It does not allow all legal works to be copied regardless of the purpose to which they will be put. Requests for copies will be honoured only if the user intends to use the works for the purpose of research, private study, criticism, review or use in legal proceedings. This further supports a finding that the dealings were fair.

(vi) Effect of the Dealing on the Work

72   Another consideration is that no evidence was tendered to show that the market for the publishers' works had decreased as a result of these copies having been made. Although the burden of proving fair dealing lies with the Law Society, it lacked access to evidence about the effect of the dealing on the publishers' markets. If there had been evidence that the publishers' markets had been negatively affected by the Law Society's custom photocopying service, it would have been in the publishers' interest to tender it at trial. They did not do so. The only evidence of market impact is that the publishers have continued to produce new reporter series and legal publications during the period of the custom photocopy service's operation.

(vii) Conclusion

73   The factors discussed, considered together, suggest that the Law Society's dealings with the publishers' works through its custom photocopy service were research-based and fair. The Access Policy places appropriate limits on the type of copying that the Law Society will do. It states that not all requests will be honoured. If a request does not appear to be for the purpose of research, criticism, review or private study, the copy will not be made. If a question arises as to whether the stated purpose is legitimate, the Reference Librarian will review the matter. The Access Policy limits the amount of work that will be copied, and the Reference Librarian reviews requests that exceed what might typically be considered reasonable and has the right to refuse to fulfill a request. On these facts, I conclude that the Law Society's dealings with the publishers' works satisfy the fair dealing defence and that the Law Society does not infringe copyright. . . .

NOTES

1.   *Civil Law and Common Law Models for Exceptions and Limitations.* The several texts of the Berne Convention have generally confined their limitations on minimum rights to specific exemptions—such as Article 10(1)'s permission to quote from published works consistent with fair practice and to an extent justified by its purpose—and specific compulsory licenses. Commentary on the 1948 Brussels Text added the relatively open-ended minor exception rule for the public performance right, and the 1971 Paris Text added an uncharacteristically open-ended exception in Article 9(2)'s three-step test for exceptions to the reproduction right. The trend in recent international arrangements, such as TRIPs Article 13 and WIPO

Copyright Treaty Article 10, is to frame permitted exceptions in terms modeled after Article 9(2) of the Berne Paris Act.

The tradition among civil law countries has been to provide a long list of narrow exceptions, and in the United Kingdom and Commonwealth countries the tradition has been to accompany narrow exceptions with a more generalized fair dealing defense, such as the "research or private study" exception considered in the *CCH* decision.

The contemporary trend in common law countries has been to extend copyright exemptions by lengthening the list of narrow statutory exceptions, as the United Kingdom did in its 2013 legislation adding or enlarging exceptions for, among other objects, copying, quotation, and teaching, or by judicial expansion of fair dealing, as happened in the *CCH* decision, establishing the concept of "user rights." By giving at least some of these user rights a "large and liberal interpretation," Canada's Supreme Court laid the foundation for decisions, among others, that characterized 30–90 second previews of musical works for purposes of possible purchase as "research," SOCAN v. Bell Canada, 2012 SCC 36, and held that teachers' photocopying from textbooks for their students was fair and for "research or private study." Alberta v. Canadian Copyright Licensing Agency, 2012 SCC 37. *See* generally Michael Geist, ed., The Copyright Pentalogy: How the Supreme Court of Canada Shook the Foundations of Canadian Copyright Law (2013). On contemporary legislative initiatives in Canada, see Ysolde Gendreau, The Reform of the Canadian Copyright Act: In the Spirit of the Times? 239 R.I.D.A. 188 (2014).

2. *The American Model: Fair Use.* U.S. practice departs from historical civil law and common law norms for copyright exceptions by providing a flexible, factor-based formula that can potentially excuse any form of use—including commercial uses—of any kind of work. In addition to the many specific exceptions prescribed in section 108–122 of the 1976 Copyright Act, section 107's fair use doctrine provides:

> Notwithstanding the provisions of sections 106 and 106A, the fair use of a copyrighted work, including such use by reproduction in copies or phonorecords or by any other means specified by that section, for purposes such as criticism, comment, news reporting, teaching (including multiple copies for classroom use), scholarship, or research, is not an infringement of copyright. In determining whether the use made of a work in any particular case is a fair use the factors to be considered shall include—
>
> > (1) the purpose and character of the use, including whether such use is of a commercial nature or is for nonprofit educational purposes;
> >
> > (2) the nature of the copyrighted work;
> >
> > (3) the amount and substantiality of the portion used in relation to the copyrighted work as a whole; and
> >
> > (4) the effect of the use upon the potential market for or value of the copyrighted work.

The fact that a work is unpublished shall not itself bar a finding of fair use if such finding is made upon consideration of all the above factors.

The fair use doctrine encompasses not only much of the conduct excused under the civil law and common law traditions, but conduct as far afield from these as systematic home videotaping of entertainment programs and the reproduction of concert posters in a musical group's biography. *See* Paul Goldstein, Goldstein on Copyright, Chapter 12 (3rd ed. 2019). One long-time observer has bluntly noted that "[t]he open American 'fair use' system in fact violates the Berne Convention with its specific restrictions which serve to guarantee the rights of authors and the interests of users by providing them with legal certainty." Herman Cohen Jehoram, Restrictions on Copyright and their Abuse, 27 EIPR 359 (2005). *See* also Paul Edward Geller, A German Approach to Fair Use: Test Cases for TRIPS Criteria for Copyright Limitations? 57 J. Copyright Soc'y U.S.A. 553 (2010).

American-style fair use is gaining traction outside the United States, principally in common law countries. Section 19 of Israel's Copyright Act closely tracks American fair use doctrine, and section 35(2) of Singapore's Copyright Act supplements the statute's fair dealing provisions with a general provision that adopts the American four-factor test and supplements it with a fifth factor: "the possibility of obtaining the work or adaptation within a reasonable time at an ordinary commercial price."

After careful scrutiny, Australia declined to adopt a U.S.-style fair use provision, but did add "parody or satire" to the pre-existing specified exceptions for research or study, criticism or review, news reporting and legal advice. *See* Graeme W. Austin, Four Questions About the Australian Approach to Fair Dealing Defenses to Copyright Infringement, 57 J. Copyright Society U.S.A. 611 (2010).

See generally, Jonathan Band & Jonathan Gerafi, Fair Use/Fair Dealing Handbook (2013). For a comparative study, see Giuseppina D'Agostino, Healing Fair Dealing? A Comparative Copyright Analysis of Canada's Fair Dealing to U.K. Fair Dealing and U.S. Fair Use, 53 McGill L.J. 309 (2008).

3. *Press Uses.* Article 10*bis*(2) of the Berne Paris Text makes it a matter of legislation for member countries "to determine the conditions under which, for the purpose of reporting current events by means of photography, cinematography, broadcasting or communication to the public by wire, literary or artistic works seen or heard in the course of the event may, to the extent justified by the informatory purpose, be reproduced and made available to the public." According to the WIPO Guide, "[t]his is a matter of allowing the reporting of news, within reasonable limits. It often happens that, during the reporting of current events by film or broadcast, protected works are seen or heard. Their appearance is fortuitous and subsidiary to the report itself. For example, military music and other tunes are played on the occasion of a State visit or a sporting event; a microphone cannot avoid picking them up, even if only part of the ceremony or event is covered. It would be impossible to seek the composer's consent in advance." WIPO Guide to the Berne Convention for the Protection of Literary and Artistic Works (Paris Act, 1971) 62 (1978).

4. *Parody.* The Berne Paris Text provides no exception for parodies, and its guarantee of the moral right of integrity in Article 6*bis* would seem to curtail such uses that may undermine an author's honor and reputation. Nonetheless, legislation and judicial decisions in many countries of the Berne Union have excused parody, and Article 5(3)(k) of the 2001 EU Information Society Directive expressly allows member states to excuse uses "for the purpose of caricature, parody or pastiche."

In Deckmyn v. Vandersteen, CJEU, C-201/13, 2014, the Grand Chamber of the CJEU, on a reference for a preliminary ruling from a Belgian court, ruled that parody under Article 5(3)(k) was an "autonomous concept" of European Union law to be interpreted uniformly across the Union, and that its interpretation required that the accused work both "evoke an existing work, while being noticeably different from it," and "constitute an expression of humor or mockery." Apart from these requirements, the Court's definition was notably broad. Although the defendant used plaintiff's work for purposes of satire—lampooning a government official—rather than parody—lampooning plaintiff's work itself—the Court assimilated the former into the latter, a step the United States Supreme Court declined to take in its own, much-cited decision in Campbell v. Acuff-Rose Music, Inc. 510 U.S. 569, 580–81(1994) ("Parody needs to mimic an original to make its point and so has some claim to use the creation of its victim's . . . imagination, whereas satire can stand on its own two feet and so requires justification for the very act of borrowing.").

See generally, Eleonora Rosati, Just a Matter of a Laugh? Why the CJEU Decision in *Deckmyn* is Broader than Parody, 52 Common Market Law Rev. 511 (2015).

5. *Copyright and Fundamental Rights.* Courts in the United States have long, and explicitly, reconciled copyright's exclusive rights with the U.S. Constitution's free speech guarantee. As Justice Sandra Day O'Connor observed in Harper & Row, Publishers, Inc. v. Nation Enterprises, 471 U.S. 539, 558 (1985), "In our haste to disseminate news, it should not be forgotten that the Framers intended copyright itself to be the engine of free expression. By establishing a marketable right to the use of one's expression, copyright supplies the economic incentive to create and disseminate ideas."

In the much-discussed *Metall auf Metall* decision, BVerfG, 1BvR 1585/13 (2016), Germany's Federal Constitutional Court overturned a decision of the German Federal High Court that defendant's appropriation and continuous repetition in its own recording of a two-second sample from plaintiff's phonogram, "Metall auf Metall," infringed plaintiff's rights in the phonogram. The Constitutional Court characterized the dispute as one between two fundamental rights under the German Copyright Act—the property guarantee embodied in section 85(1)'s exclusive reproduction and distribution right and the guarantee of artistic freedom embodied in section 24(1)'s provision for free use—and ruled that the lower courts had given insufficient weight to artistic freedom when balancing it against the phonogram producer's property right. The Court returned the case to the Federal High Court for reconsideration in light of the newly-explicated balance, including consideration of whether the unauthorized sampling had severely impaired the economic interests of the phonogram producers.

See Marc D. Mimler, "Metall auf Metall"—German Federal Constitutional Court Discusses the Permissibility of Sampling of Music Tracks, 7 Queen Mary J. of Int. Prop. 119 (2017). See also Stijn van Deursen & Thom Snijders, The Court of Justice at the Crossroads: Clarifying the Role for Fundamental Rights in the EU Copyright Framework, 49 IIC 1080 (2018).

6.   *Software.* Computer software presents a particular challenge to the Berne Convention's general requirement that rights be exclusive. Because copyright owners typically disseminate their programs in the form of unreadable object code rather than human-readable source code, a competitor that wishes to discover a program's interface specification in order to achieve interoperability with the program must disassemble or decompile the object code into human-readable form, a process that invariably requires the competitor to make a temporary copy of the copyrighted program. Would legislation permitting decompilation for purposes of achieving interoperability meet the requirements of Article 9(2)?

In the United States, courts have relied on fair use doctrine to excuse copying of computer programs for the purpose of achieving interoperability. In one case, a court ruled in favor of a defendant that had copied and then disassembled the object code version of plaintiff's videogame in order to determine the functional specifications that would enable its own games to operate on plaintiff's console. The court held that "where disassembly is the only way to gain access to the ideas and functional elements embodied in a copyrighted computer program and where there is a legitimate reason for seeking such access, disassembly is a fair use of the copyrighted work as a matter of law." Sega Enterprises Ltd. v. Accolade, Inc., 977 F.2d 1510, 1527–28 (9th Cir. 1992).

In the European Union, Article 5(3) of the Software Directive, 2009/24/EC, entitles a person who has the right to use a copy of a computer program to observe, study or test the functioning of the program in order to determine the ideas and principles that underlie an element of the program, if he does so "while performing any of the acts of loading, displaying, running, transmitting or storing the program which he is entitled to do." Article 6, dealing with decompilation, defines the freely discoverable ideas more narrowly, but more extensively privileges the conduct aimed at discovering them. Article 6(1) excuses the discovery only of "parts of the original program which are necessary to achieve interoperability," but allows the reproduction of code, "and translation of its form," when "indispensable to obtain the information necessary to achieve interoperability of an independently created computer program with other programs."

See generally, Michael Lehmann & Colin Tapper, eds., A Handbook of European Software Law (1995); Bridget Czarnota & Robert Hart, Legal

Protection of Computer Programs In Europe: A Guide to the E.C. Directive (1991).

7. *Internet Uses.* The Internet has placed new stresses on copyright law's exclusive rights, and courts have employed old as well as new techniques to accommodate them. In the United States, courts have applied fair use doctrine to excuse the reproduction and display of thumbnail illustrations by search engines for purposes of locating images and linking from one website to another; although the reproductions were exact, one court reasoned that they were smaller in scale and served an entirely different function than the copyrighted images. Perfect 10, Inc. v. Google Inc., 508 F.3d 1146 (9th Cir. 2007).

Civil law courts, confined as they are by narrow statutory limitations, have had to be more creative in negotiating copyright obstacles on the Internet. The German Federal Supreme Court excused Google's use of thumbnails for purposes of image search on the ground that, by placing their images on the web, the rights holders impliedly consented to their being made available to users in Germany; further, only the right holder's use of technological measures to block the image search would suffice to negate the implied license. Vorschaubilder, Bundesgerichtshof, I ZR 69/08, April 29, 2010, GRUR 628. *See* Matthias Leistner, The German Federal Supreme Court's Judgment on Google's Image Search—A Topical Example of the "Limitations" of the European Approach to Exceptions and Limitations, 42 IIC 417 (2011).

In France, the Paris Civil Court of First Instance excused the use of thumbnails accessed from the *google.fr* website on the ground that decision was controlled by the law of the place where the proximate cause of the infringement occurred—the U.S. where Google was headquartered and had its servers—and not the law of the place—France—where the harm occurred; U.S. fair use doctrine, the court concluded, would exonerate the use. The Paris Court of Appeal subsequently rejected the court's choice of law analysis and used instead the more traditional choice of law rule that applies the law of the country where the harm was sustained. Although French law consequently applied, with the result that fair use doctrine offered no excuse, the court further ruled that the Google search engine qualified as a neutral intermediary and so was not liable under French law. Société des Auteurs des Arts Visuels et de l' Image Fixe, Paris Court of Appeal, Chamber 1 (Jan. 26, 2011). *See* Kate Spelman & Brent Caslin, *La Société des Auteurs des Arts Visuels et de l' Image Fixe* (SAIF): A Parisian Story of the Berne Convention and Online Infringement Claims, 19 Calif. Int'l. L.J. 3 (Spring 2011).

(C) Abuse of Right (or Dominant Position)

Radio Telefis Eireann (RTE) and Independent Television Publications Ltd. (ITP) v. Commission of the European Communities

Court of Justice of the European Communities, 1995.
Joined cases C-241/91 and C-242/91.

Judgment

. . .

6   According to the judgments of the Court of First Instance, most households in Ireland and 30% to 40% of households in Northern Ireland can receive television programmes broadcast by RTE, ITV and BBC.

7   At the material time, no comprehensive weekly television guide was available on the market in Ireland or in Northern Ireland. Each television station published a television guide covering exclusively its own programmes and claimed, under Irish and United Kingdom legislation, copyright protection for its own weekly programme listings in order to prevent their reproduction by third parties.

8   RTE itself published its own weekly television guide, while ITV did so through ITP, a company established for that purpose.

9   ITP, RTE and BBC practised the following policy with regard to the dissemination of programme listings. They provided their programme schedules free of charge, on request, to daily and periodical newspapers, accompanied by a licence for which no charge was made, setting out the conditions under which that information could be reproduced. Daily listings and, if the following day was a public holiday, the listings for two days, could thus be published in the press, subject to certain conditions relating to the format of publication. Publication of "highlights" of the week was also authorized. ITP, RTE and the BBC ensured strict compliance with the licence conditions by instituting legal proceedings, where necessary, against publications which failed to comply with them.

10 Magill TV Guide Ltd ("Magill") attempted to publish a comprehensive weekly television guide but was prevented from doing so by the appellants and the BBC, which obtained injunctions prohibiting publication of weekly television listings.

11 Magill lodged a complaint with the Commission on 4 April 1986 under Article 3 of Regulation No 17 of the Council of 6 February 1962, the First Regulation implementing Articles 85 and 86 of the Treaty ("Regulation No 17") seeking a declaration that the appellants and the BBC were abusing their dominant position by refusing to grant licences for the publication of their respective weekly listings. The Commission decided to initiate a proceeding, at the end of which it adopted Decision 89/205/EEC of 21 December 1988 relating to a proceeding under Article

86 of the EEC Treaty ("the decision"), which was the subject-matter of the proceedings before the Court of First Instance.

12 In that decision the Commission found that there had been a breach of Article 86* of the EEC Treaty and ordered the three organizations to put an end to that breach, in particular "by supplying . . . third parties on request and on a non-discriminatory basis with their individual advance weekly programme listings and by permitting reproduction of those listings by such parties". It was also provided that, if the three organizations chose to grant reproduction licences, any royalties requested should be reasonable.

13 By order of 11 May 1989 in Joined Cases 76, 77 and 91/89 R RTE and Others v. Commission 1989 ECR 1141, the President of the Court of Justice, at the request of the applicants, ordered suspension "of the operation of Article 2 of the . . . decision in so far as it obliges the applicants to bring the infringement found by the Commission to an end forthwith by supplying each other and third parties on request and on a non-discriminatory basis with their individual advance weekly programme listings and by permitting reproduction of those listings by such parties".

14 At first instance the two appellants sought annulment of the Commission decision and an order requiring it to pay the costs of the proceedings.

15 The Court of First Instance dismissed the appellants' applications and ordered them to pay the costs. . . .

The existence of an abuse of a dominant position

24 So far as the existence of a dominant position is concerned, the Court of First Instance held that "ITP enjoyed, as a consequence of its copyright in ITV and Channel 4 programme listings, which had been transferred to it by the television companies broadcasting on those channels, the exclusive right to reproduce and market those listings. It was thus able, at the material time, to secure a monopoly over the publication of its weekly listings in the TV Times, a magazine specializing in the

---

*   Article 86, now Article 102 of the Treaty on the Functioning of the European Union, provides:

Any abuse by one or more undertakings of a dominant position within the common market or in a substantial part of it shall be prohibited as incompatible with the common market in so far as it may affect trade between member States.

Such abuse may, in particular consist in:

(a) directly or indirectly imposing unfair purchase or selling prices or other unfair trading conditions;

(b) limiting production, markets or technical development to the prejudice of consumers;

(c) applying dissimilar conditions to equivalent transactions with other trading parties, thereby placing them at a competitive disadvantage;

(d) making the conclusion of contracts subject to acceptance by the other parties of supplementary obligations which, by their nature or according to commercial usage, have no connection with the subject of such contracts. *Ed.*

programmes of ITV and Channel 4". Consequently, in the opinion of the Court of First Instance, "the applicant clearly held at that time a dominant position both on the market represented by its weekly listings and on the market for the magazines in which they were published in Ireland and Northern Ireland. Third parties such as Magill who wished to publish a general television magazine were in a situation of economic dependence on the applicant, which was thus in a position to hinder the emergence of any effective competition on the market for information on its weekly programmes." With regard to RTE, the Court of First Instance reached the same conclusion in nearly identical terms.

25 So far as the existence of an abuse of that dominant position was concerned, the Court of First Instance considered that it was necessary to interpret Article 86 in the light of copyright in programme listings. It pointed out that, in the absence of harmonization of national rules or Community standardization, determination of the conditions and procedures under which copyright was protected was a matter for national rules. The relationship between national intellectual property rights and the general rules of Community law was governed expressly by Article 36** of the EEC Treaty, which provided for the possibility of derogating from the rules relating to the free movement of goods on grounds of the protection of industrial or commercial property, subject to the conditions set out in the second sentence of Article 36. Article 36 thus emphasized that the reconciliation between the requirements of the free movement of goods and the respect to which intellectual property rights were entitled had to be achieved in such a way as to protect the legitimate exercise of such rights, which alone was justified within the meaning of that article, and to preclude any improper exercise thereof likely to create artificial partitions within the market or pervert the rules governing competition within the Community. The Court of First Instance took the view that the exercise of intellectual property rights conferred by national legislation had consequently to be restricted as far as was necessary for that reconciliation.

26 The Court of First Instance found, in the light of the case-law of the Court of Justice, that it followed from Article 36 of the Treaty that only those restrictions on freedom of competition, free movement of goods or freedom to provide services which were inherent in the protection of the actual substance of the intellectual property right were permitted in Community law. It based its view in particular on the judgment of the Court of Justice in Case 78/70 Deutsche Grammophon v Metro 1971 ECR

**   Article 36, now Article 36 of the Treaty on the Functioning of the European Union, provides:

> The provisions of Articles 30 to 34 [new Articles 28 and 29] shall not preclude prohibitions or restrictions on imports, exports or goods in transit justified on grounds of public morality, public policy or public security; the protection of health and life of humans, animals or plants; the protection of national treasures possessing artistic, historic or archaelogical value; or the protection of industrial and commercial property. Such prohibitions or restrictions shall not, however, constitute a means of arbitrary discrimination or a disguised restriction on trade between Member States. *Ed.*

487, paragraph 11, in which the Court of Justice held that, although it permitted prohibitions or restrictions on the free movement of products which were justified for the purpose of protecting industrial and commercial property, Article 36 only admitted derogations from that freedom to the extent to which they were justified for the purpose of safeguarding rights which constituted the specific subject-matter of such property.

27 The Court of First Instance then observed that in principle the protection of the specific subject-matter of a copyright entitled the copyright-holder to reserve the exclusive right to reproduce the protected work.

28 However, the Court of First Instance took the view that, while it was plain that the exercise of the exclusive right to reproduce a protected work was not in itself an abuse, that did not apply when, in the light of the details of each individual case, it was apparent that that right was being exercised in such ways and circumstances as in fact to pursue an aim manifestly contrary to the objectives of Article 86. In that event, the Court of First Instance continued, the copyright was no longer being exercised in a manner which corresponded to its essential function, within the meaning of Article 36 of the Treaty, which was to protect the moral rights in the work and ensure a reward for the creative effort, while respecting the aims of, in particular, Article 86. From this the Court of First Instance concluded that the primacy of Community law, particularly as regards principles as fundamental as those of the free movement of goods and freedom of competition, prevailed over any use of a rule of national intellectual property law in a manner contrary to those principles.

29 In the present case, the Court of First Instance noted that the applicants, by reserving the exclusive right to publish their weekly television programme listings, were preventing the emergence on the market of a new product, namely a general television magazine likely to compete with their own magazines. The applicants were thus using their copyright in the programme listings produced as part of the activity of broadcasting in order to secure a monopoly in the derivative market of weekly television guides in Ireland and Northern Ireland. The Court of First Instance also regarded it as significant in that regard that the applicants had authorized, free of charge, the publication of their daily listings and highlights of their weekly programmes in the press in both Ireland and the United Kingdom.

30 The Court of First Instance accordingly took the view that conduct of that type, characterized by preventing the production and marketing of a new product for which there was potential consumer demand, on the ancillary market of weekly television guides and thereby excluding all competition from that market solely in order to secure the applicants' respective monopolies clearly went beyond what was necessary to fulfil the essential function of the copyright as permitted in Community law.

The applicants' refusal to authorize third parties to publish their weekly listings was, in this case, the Court of First Instance ruled, arbitrary in so far as it was not justified by the requirements peculiar to the activity of publishing television magazines. It was thus possible for the applicants to adapt to the conditions of a television magazine market which was open to competition in order to ensure the commercial viability of their weekly publications. The applicants' conduct could not, in those circumstances, be covered in Community law by the protection conferred by their copyright in the programme listings.

31 In the light of the foregoing considerations, the Court of First Instance found that, although the programme listings were at the material time protected by copyright as laid down by national law, which still determined the rules governing that protection, the conduct at issue could not qualify for such protection within the framework of the necessary reconciliation between intellectual property rights and the fundamental principles of the Treaty concerning the free movement of goods and freedom of competition. The aim of that conduct was clearly incompatible with the objectives of Article 86.

32 The Court of First Instance accordingly dismissed the plea in law based on breach of Article 86. . . .

(a) *Existence of a dominant position*

46 So far as dominant position is concerned, it is to be remembered at the outset that mere ownership of an intellectual property right cannot confer such a position.

47 However, the basic information as to the channel, day, time and title of programmes is the necessary result of programming by television stations, which are thus the only source of such information for an undertaking, like Magill, which wishes to publish it together with commentaries or pictures. By force of circumstance, RTE and ITP, as the agent of ITV, enjoy, along with the BBC, a de facto monopoly over the information used to compile listings for the television programmes received in most households in Ireland and 30% to 40% of households in Northern Ireland. The appellants are thus in a position to prevent effective competition on the market in weekly television magazines. The Court of First Instance was therefore right in confirming the Commission's assessment that the appellants occupied a dominant position.

(b) *Existence of abuse*

48 With regard to the issue of abuse, the arguments of the appellants and IPO wrongly presuppose that where the conduct of an undertaking in a dominant position consists of the exercise of a right classified by national law as "copyright", such conduct can never be reviewed in relation to Article 86 of the Treaty.

49 Admittedly, in the absence of Community standardization or harmonization of laws, determination of the conditions and procedures

for granting protection of an intellectual property right is a matter for national rules. Further, the exclusive right of reproduction forms part of the author's rights, so that refusal to grant a licence, even if it is the act of an undertaking holding a dominant position, cannot in itself constitute abuse of a dominant position.

50   However, it is also clear from that judgment that the exercise of an exclusive right by the proprietor may, in exceptional circumstances, involve abusive conduct.

51   In the present case, the conduct objected to is the appellants' reliance on copyright conferred by national legislation so as to prevent Magill or any other undertaking having the same intention, from publishing on a weekly basis information (channel, day, time and title of programmes) together with commentaries and pictures obtained independently of the appellants.

52   Among the circumstances taken into account by the Court of First Instance in concluding that such conduct was abusive was, first, the fact that there was, according to the findings of the Court of First Instance, no actual or potential substitute for a weekly television guide offering information on the programmes for the week ahead. On this point, the Court of First Instance confirmed the Commission's finding that the complete lists of programmes for a 24-hour period and for a 48-hour period at weekends and before public holidays, published in certain daily and Sunday newspapers, and the television sections of certain magazines covering, in addition, "highlights" of the week's programmes, were only to a limited extent substitutable for advance information to viewers on all the week's programmes. Only weekly television guides containing comprehensive listings for the week ahead would enable users to decide in advance which programmes they wished to follow and arrange their leisure activities for the week accordingly. The Court of First Instance also established that there was a specific, constant and regular potential demand on the part of consumers.

53   Thus the appellants who were, by force of circumstance, the only sources of the basic information on programme scheduling which is the indispensable raw material for compiling a weekly television guide, gave viewers wishing to obtain information on the choice of programmes for the week ahead no choice but to buy the weekly guides for each station and draw from each of them the information they needed to make comparisons.

54   The appellants' refusal to provide basic information by relying on national copyright provisions thus prevented the appearance of a new product, a comprehensive weekly guide to television programmes, which the appellants did not offer and for which there was a potential consumer demand. Such refusal constitutes an abuse under heading (b) of the second paragraph of Article 86 of the Treaty.

55 Second, there was no justification for such refusal either in the activity of television broadcasting or in that of publishing television magazines.

56 Third, and finally, as the Court of First Instance also held, the appellants, by their conduct, reserved to themselves the secondary market of weekly television guides by excluding all competition on that market since they denied access to the basic information which is the raw material indispensable for the compilation of such a guide.

57 In the light of all those circumstances, the Court of First Instance did not err in law in holding that the appellants' conduct was an abuse of a dominant position within the meaning of Article 86 of the Treaty.

58 It follows that the plea in law alleging misapplication by the Court of First Instance of the concept of abuse of a dominant position must be dismissed as unfounded. It is therefore unnecessary to examine the reasoning of the contested judgments in so far as it is based on Article 36 of the Treaty. . . .

The Berne Convention

72 So far as the Berne Convention ("the Convention") is concerned, RTE had submitted before the Court of First Instance that Article 9(1) thereof conferred an exclusive right of reproduction and that Article 9(2) allowed a signatory State to permit reproduction only in certain special cases, provided that such reproduction did not conflict with normal exploitation of the work and did not unreasonably prejudice the legitimate interests of the author. From this RTE deduced that Article 2 of the contested decision was incompatible with the Convention inasmuch as it conflicted with the normal exploitation of RTE's copyright in the programme listings and seriously prejudiced its legitimate interests.

73 In response to those arguments, the Court of First Instance considered whether the Convention was applicable. Its first finding was that the Community was not a party to it. After reviewing Article 234 of the EEC Treaty and the case-law of the Court of Justice, the Court of First Instance pointed out that "In the present case concerning Ireland and the United Kingdom, . . . under Article 5 of the Act of Accession, Article 234 of the EEC Treaty applies to agreements or conventions concluded before . . . 1 January 1973." From this it deduced that "In intra-Community relations, therefore, the provisions of the Berne Convention, ratified by Ireland and the United Kingdom before 1 January 1973, cannot affect the provisions of the Treaty. . . . The argument that Article 2 of the decision is in conflict with Article 9(1) of the Berne Convention must therefore be dismissed, without there even being any need to inquire into its substance." With regard to Article 9(2) of the Convention, the Court of First Instance observed that this provision "was introduced by the Paris revision of 1971, to which the United Kingdom has been a party since 2 January 1990 and which Ireland has not yet ratified." The Court of First Instance then pointed out that an agreement or a

convention concluded subsequent to accession without recourse to the procedure set out in Article 236 of the EEC Treaty cannot affect a provision of the Treaty.

74   The Court of First Instance accordingly dismissed as unfounded the plea alleging infringement of the Convention. . . .

83   It is appropriate to observe at the outset, as the Court of First Instance did, that the Community is not a party to the Convention for the Protection of Literary and Artistic Works.

84   Next, so far as the United Kingdom and Ireland are concerned, it is true that they were already parties to the Convention when they acceded to the Community and that Article 234 of the Treaty therefore applies to that Convention, in accordance with Article 5 of the Act of Accession. It is, however, settled case-law that the provisions of an agreement concluded prior to entry into force of the Treaty or prior to a Member State's accession cannot be relied on in intra-Community relations if, as in the present case, the rights of non-member countries are not involved.

85   Finally, the Paris Act, which amended Article 9(1) and (2) of the Convention (the provisions relied on by RTE), was ratified by the United Kingdom only after its accession to the Community and has still not been ratified by Ireland.

86   The Court of First Instance was therefore correct to hold that Article 9 of the Convention cannot be relied on to limit the powers of the Community, as provided for in the EEC Treaty, since the Treaty can be amended only in accordance with the procedure laid down in Article 236.

87   It follows that the plea that the Court of First Instance failed to have proper regard to the Convention must be dismissed as unfounded.

The powers conferred on the Commission by Article 3 of Regulation No 17

88   The first limb of ITP's second plea is that the Court of First Instance misconstrued Article 3 of Regulation No 17 in holding that that provision enabled the Commission to impose compulsory licensing, on conditions approved by it, relating to intellectual property rights conferred by the laws of the Member States. Relying on the judgment in Case 144/81 Keurkoop v Nancy Kean Gifts 1982 ECR 2853, ITP submits that only the Parliaments of Ireland and the United Kingdom may take away or replace the copyrights which they have conferred.

89   The second limb alleges infringement of the principle of proportionality in so far as the Court of First Instance held that the Commission's decision was not contrary to that principle. ITP contends that the Court of First Instance should have taken account of a number of considerations: the decision removed not only ITP's exclusive right of reproduction, but also its right of first marketing, particularly important where, as in this case, the product has a useful life of 10 days; there is no reciprocity between ITP and the competitors (other than the BBC and RTE) to whom it is required to grant licences; many of those competitors,

particularly the national newspapers, have turnovers and profits greatly in excess of those of ITP and they also possess valuable copyrights which they protect from reproduction.

90   It is appropriate to observe that Article 3 of Regulation No 17 is to be applied according to the nature of the infringement found and may include an order to do certain acts or things which, unlawfully, have not been done as well as an order to bring an end to certain acts, practices or situations which are contrary to the Treaty.

91   In the present case, after finding that the refusal to provide undertakings such as Magill with the basic information contained in television programme listings was an abuse of a dominant position, the Commission was entitled under Article 3, in order to ensure that its decision was effective, to require the appellants to provide that information. As the Court of First Instance rightly found, the imposition of that obligation with the possibility of making authorization of publication dependent on certain conditions, including payment of royalties was the only way of bringing the infringement to an end.

92   The Court of First Instance was also entitled to dismiss, on the basis of the same findings of fact, the allegation that the principle of proportionality had been infringed.

93   As the Court of First Instance correctly pointed out, in the context of the application of Article 3 of Regulation No 17, the principle of proportionality means that the burdens imposed on undertakings in order to bring an infringement of competition law to an end must not exceed what is appropriate and necessary to attain the objective sought, namely re-establishment of compliance with the rules infringed.

94   In holding, at paragraph 81 of the ITP judgment, that, in the light of the above findings, the order addressed to the applicant was an appropriate and necessary measure to bring the infringement to an end, the Court of First Instance did not commit an error of law. . . .

104 It follows that the appeals must be dismissed in their entirety.

NOTES

1.   If, following the decision in RTE v. Commission of the European Communities (commonly called the *Magill* decision), a European Union country imposed a compulsory license or exemption in circumstances comparable to those involved in *Magill*, would the legislation survive scrutiny by a WTO panel after *United States—Section 110(5)*, page 296 above?

In a subsequent decision, IMS Health GmbH & Co. OHG v. NDC Health GmbH & Co. KG, ECJ, C-418/01, 2004, the European Court of Justice interpreted *Magill* to hold that it would constitute an abuse of dominant position for a copyright owner to decline to license its widely-adopted— indeed, indispensable—data structure if three conditions coincided: "that the refusal is preventing the emergence of a new product for which there is potential consumer demand, that it is unjustified and such as to exclude any competition on a secondary market."

Is it relevant that the subject matter in both *Magill* and *IMS Health*—program listings in one, data structures in the other—lay on the borderline of literary and artistic works, and under rigorous tests of originality might not have been protected at all? Would Article 9(2) of the Berne Convention, Paris Text, allow compulsory licensing as a solution to the problem presented in *Magill* or *IMS Health*? *See* Burton Ong, Anticompetitive Refusals to Grant Copyright License: Reflections on the IMS Saga, 26 EIPR 505 (2004).

2. In Microsoft v. Commission, ECJ, T-201/04, 2007, the European Court of First Instance upheld a European Commission decision that Microsoft abused a dominant position by refusing to supply interface specifications to competitors that needed them to develop and distribute competing products capable of interoperating on Microsoft's operating system platform, and by conditioning the availability of its Windows PC operating system on the acquisition of Windows Media Player software. The Commission had ordered as a remedy for the first abuse that Microsoft make interoperability information available to competitors on reasonable and non-discriminatory terms and, for the abusive tying practice, that the company offer a fully-functioning version of the Windows PC operating system that did not incorporate the Media Player.

Responding to Microsoft's argument, based in part on *Magill* and *IMS Health*, that its refusal to supply interoperability information was not an abuse of dominant position, the court found that several factors confirmed the correctness of the Commissioner's finding that interoperability with the client PC operating system was of significant competitive importance in the relevant market. For example, as the Windows operating system was present on virtually all client PCs installed within organizations, "non-Windows work group server operating systems cannot continue to be marketed if they are incapable of achieving a high degree of interoperability with Windows." ¶ 368. Also, in the court's view, consumer prejudice from the suppression of new products, a factor considered in *Magill* and *IMS Health*, "may arise where there is a limitation not only of production or markets, but also of technical development," as was the case under the instant facts. ¶ 647.

The court also rejected Microsoft's argument that the Commission's interpretation of Article 82 violated Article 13 of TRIPs. Recognizing that the European Court of Justice has ruled that "the primacy of international agreements concluded by the Community over provisions of secondary Community legislation means that such provisions must, so far as is possible, be interpreted in a manner that is consistent with those agreements," the court held "that the principle of consistent interpretation thus invoked by the Court of Justice applies only where the international agreement at issue prevails over the provision of Community law concerned. Since an international agreement, such as the TRIPs Agreement, does not prevail over primary Community law, that principle does not apply where, as here, the provision which falls to be interpreted is Article 82 E.C." ¶¶ 797–98.

See Sujitha Subramanian, EU Obligation to the TRIPs Agreement: E.U. Microsoft Decision, 21 European J. Int'l Law 997 (2011).

(D) Developing Countries

Robert Hadl, Toward International Copyright Revision, Report of the Meetings in Paris and Geneva, September, 1970

18 Bulletin of the Copyright Society of the U.S.A. 183–189, 207–208 (1971).

International copyright was plunged into crisis in 1967 at the Stockholm Intellectual Property Conference. One of the objectives of this Conference was the revision of the Berne Convention including special provisions for the benefit of developing countries. These provisions were annexed to the draft text of the Convention as a Protocol Regarding Developing Countries (hereafter, "Protocol", or "Stockholm Protocol"). During the Conference, however, it became apparent that the developing countries were not satisfied with the concessions proposed in the draft text. Led by India, they were able to orchestrate a chorus of protest which sought much wider gains. The developed countries, unprepared for this onslaught and without strong leadership, found themselves in disarray and unable to silence the developing countries. As a result, the final text of the Protocol adopted by the Conference gave developing countries very broad and uncontrolled privileges with respect to works copyrighted in Berne Union countries. For the most part, these privileges were considered unacceptable by the developed countries.

The Stockholm victory won by the developing countries proved, however, to be a hollow one. They had left one loophole, namely, the provision that unless a developed country agreed to accept the Stockholm Protocol, it could not be bound by it. To this day, no major developed country has ratified or acceded to the Stockholm Protocol, and none is expected to do so in the future. In the aftermath of Stockholm what became apparent was that the developing countries had won the opening battle, but they had not won the war.

For their part, the developing countries were not without recourse against the refusal of the developed countries to accept the Stockholm Protocol. They had two substantial weapons in their arsenal. First, they could renounce their international copyright obligations completely by withdrawing from the UCC and Berne Convention. Second, they could alter their membership in the two major multilateral copyright conventions by resigning from one but maintaining membership in the other. At this point, the existence of two different copyright conventions with different levels of protection and a large overlap in membership created added complexities to the crisis produced by the Stockholm Protocol.

The UCC [Universal Copyright Convention], to which the United States is a party, is characterized chiefly by the principle of national treatment: even if a country's domestic legislation provides for relatively low-level protection, it can still belong to the UCC. The Berne Convention requires its parties to provide a specified minimum of copyright protection for other Berne works in their domestic legislation, and that minimum establishes a standard providing for a high level of copyright protection.

The situation is further complicated by the fact that the original Berne Convention of 1886 has been revised a number of times, and there are, as a result, several different "Berne texts," each providing for different standards of protection. Protection in Berne Convention countries will vary depending upon which text the particular country has accepted. Moreover, some of the texts permit reservations on particular points, and others do not. In addition, the UCC contains the so-called "Berne safeguard clause"—Article XVII and its Appendix Declaration— a provision prohibiting a Berne Convention country from denouncing Berne and relying on the UCC for protection of its works in Berne Union countries. Thus, under this clause, a country resigning from the Berne Union but remaining in the UCC would continue to have obligations under the UCC, but would have no protection for its own works under either convention.

Under these circumstances, the developing countries wishing to leave the Berne Convention for the lower level UCC were frustrated by the existence of the "Berne safeguard clause." To remove this difficulty, they launched a counter-offensive designed to suspend the effectiveness of the "Berne safeguard clause." They argued that without such a suspension their only practical alternative was denunciation of both major copyright conventions. The latter prospect was not appealing to the developed countries, despite their displeasure with the Stockholm Protocol.

It was with this background that the Register of Copyrights announced to a meeting of the IGCC [Intergovernmental Copyright Committee] and Berne Permanent Committee in December, 1967, that it would be impossible for the United States to join the Berne Convention if it had to accept the Stockholm Protocol, and that he viewed with very great concern the confusion and erosion in standards of international copyright protection resulting from the Stockholm Conference. He urged that the representatives of both developed and developing countries join together to restudy the whole international copyright situation, including practical ways of meeting the needs of developing countries.

Underlying the Register's remarks were two policy goals. The first was to renegotiate the concessions for developing countries contained in the Stockholm Protocol. The second was to maintain the structure of international copyright and the balance between the two major multilateral copyright conventions. In both of these he had to overcome the opposition of the developing countries. In the second, he also had to persuade some of the developed countries, members of the Berne Union, that Stockholm did not justify a reorganization of the international copyright system. In their view, Stockholm proved the danger to the developed countries of keeping the developing countries in the Berne Convention. The clear answer was to pave the way for the renunciation of Berne in favor of the UCC by suspension of the "Berne safeguard clause."

Time was needed, however, to review the ramifications of Stockholm and to consider new policies. Thus, it was early 1969 before the curtain rose on the next act of the diplomatic melodrama. At this point the representatives were ready to accept the suggestion made by the Register in December, 1967. The IGCC and Berne Permanent Committee adopted resolutions establishing an International Copyright Joint Study Group, and upon the invitation of the United States, agreed that the Joint Study Group would meet in Washington in September, 1969.

At that meeting, attended by representatives from twenty-five countries, a proposal to end the international copyright crisis was presented and adopted. Dubbed the "Washington Recommendation," this proposal called for the simultaneous revision of both the UCC and Berne Convention to achieve the following objectives:

(1) In the UCC the level of protection would be improved by the adoption of certain minimum rights. These would include the rights of reproduction, public performance, and broadcasting. At the same time, special provisions would be included in the UCC for the benefit of developing countries. Finally, the "Berne safeguard clause" would be suspended to permit developing countries to leave the Berne Convention without penalty under the UCC.

(2) In the Berne Convention, the Protocol would be separated from the Stockholm Act and, in turn, the developing countries would be able to substitute the special provisions included for their benefit in the UCC. This would mean that the developing countries could remain in the Berne Convention and would not be forced to exercise the option provided by the suspension of the "Berne safeguard clause." As a protective measure, it was provided that the Stockholm Protocol could not be separated from the Stockholm text until such time as France, Spain, the United Kingdom and the United States had ratified the revised text of the UCC. Furthermore, developing countries would be relieved of the obligation to pay assessments to the Berne Union if they continued their membership after the new revision.

The Washington Recommendation won the general support of all the countries that attended the meeting. While it was a sound proposal on paper, the unresolved question was whether it could be implemented successfully. The meetings that have taken place since then have all addressed themselves to this problem.

In December, 1969, the IGCC and Berne Permanent Committee met to consider the results of the Washington meeting. With the exception of France, they agreed that the preparations for revision of each Convention should be made "in accordance with the considerations stated in the preamble to the Washington Recommendation and the specific recommendations contained therein, including, in particular, the recommendation that the Universal Copyright Convention and the Berne Convention be revised in revision conferences to be held at the same time and place. . . ." In addition they scheduled several preparatory meetings to consider draft texts.

Pursuant to these arrangements, two Ad Hoc Preparatory Committees met in Paris and Geneva in May, 1970. Based largely upon a proposal for revision of the UCC submitted by the United States, draft texts were prepared for the two conventions. As contrasted with the trend represented by the Stockholm Protocol, several important demands of the developing countries were abandoned at this meeting. These included the concessions respecting the term of copyright, the exclusive right of broadcasting, and the broad right to restrict the protection of literary and artistic works for "teaching, study and research in all fields of education." Accordingly, the concessions for developing countries were limited to restricting the rights of translation and reproduction. The major negotiations in May concerned these points.

The draft texts produced in May were then circulated to governments and interested international non-governmental organizations. As recommended by the resolutions adopted in December, 1969, the IGCC and Berne Permanent Committee met in extraordinary sessions in September, 1970, to consider the draft texts and to make final preparations for the revision conferences. . . .

Conclusion

The international copyright crisis started by the Stockholm Protocol seems headed for a successful resolution. At Stockholm, the developing countries had won concessions relating to the term of copyright, the rights of broadcasting, translation and reproduction. They had also gained broad power to restrict the protection of literary and artistic works for "teaching, study and research in all fields of education." The possible economic benefits from all of these concessions were further enhanced by exceptionally loose provisions concerning the export of copies made under compulsory licenses and royalty payments.

In the final texts of the draft Conventions adopted by the two Committees, the concessions relating to the term of copyright and the right of broadcasting have been eliminated. The broad power to restrict the protection of literary and artistic works for "teaching, study and research in all fields of education" has also disappeared. The export of copies made under compulsory licenses has been prohibited and the payment provisions and standards for determining royalties have been improved considerably. Furthermore, the translation and reproduction provisions are now more realistic and generally represent the kind of concessions which the copyright owners in the developed countries are ready and willing to make.

Moreover, the level of protection in the UCC has been improved by the introduction of certain minimum rights. This will guarantee a minimum level of protection in the UCC which had previously been subject, under the national treatment standard, to any level the particular country wished to set.

With respect to maintaining the equilibrium between the two Conventions, the final texts carry out the thrust of the Washington Recommendation by duplicating the concessions for developing countries in each Convention. While some substantive differences exist because of differences in structure, they should not lead to a wholesale defection by developing countries from the Berne Convention to the UCC. Thus, the Berne Convention will continue to maintain its historic role of improving the level of copyright protection throughout the world, and the United States can continue to look with hope upon the day when it may become a member.

Given the results of the September, 1970 meetings, it would seem that the chances are good for successful diplomatic conferences next July. As contrasted with the Stockholm situation, the developing countries have moderated their demands, the developed countries have had an affirmative program, there have been careful preparations beforehand, firm leadership, and the discussions have taken place in a more rational and less emotionally charged atmosphere. All of these are the ingredients for success, and the United States has contributed substantially to each of them.[*]

iv.   *Secondary Liability*

CCH Canadian Ltd. v. Law Society of Upper Canada

Supreme Court of Canada, 2004.
2004 SCC 13, 236 D.L.R. (4th) 395, 317 N.R. 107, 30 C.P.R. (4th) 1, 2004.

THE CHIEF JUSTICE:

I.   Introduction—The Issues To Be Determined

1   The appellant, the Law Society of Upper Canada, is a statutory non-profit corporation that has regulated the legal profession in Ontario since 1822. Since 1845, the Law Society has maintained and operated the Great Library at Osgoode Hall in Toronto, a reference and research library with one of the largest collections of legal materials in Canada.

---

[*]   With amendments, the 1970 draft texts of the UCC and Berne Convention were adopted at the Paris conferences. The revised UCC was signed at Paris on July 24, 1971 by the United States and twenty-five other member countries. The United States ratified the Paris revision in September, 1972. The UCC and Berne revisions came into force on July 10, 1974. *Ed.*

The Great Library provides a request-based photocopy service (the "custom photocopy service") for Law Society members, the judiciary and other authorized researchers. Under the custom photocopy service, legal materials are reproduced by Great Library staff and delivered in person, by mail or by facsimile transmission to requesters. The Law Society also maintains self-service photocopiers in the Great Library for use by its patrons. . . .

[The parts of the Court's opinion dealing with originality and direct liability are reproduced at pages 212 and 319, above.]

(2)   Authorization: The Self-Service Photocopiers

(a)   The Law

37   Under s. 27(1) of the *Copyright Act*, it is an infringement of copyright for anyone to do anything that the Act only allows owners to do, including authorizing the exercise of his or her own rights. It does not infringe copyright to authorize a person to do something that would not constitute copyright infringement. The publishers argue that the Law Society is liable for breach of copyright under this section because it implicitly authorized patrons of the Great Library to copy works in breach of the *Copyright Act.*

38   "Authorize" means to "sanction, approve and countenance": *Muzak Corp. v. Composers, Authors & Publishers Assn. (Canada)*, [1953] 2 S.C.R. 182 (S.C.C.), at p. 193; *de Tervagne v. Beloeil (Town)*, [1993] 3 F.C. 227 (Fed. T.D.). Countenance in the context of authorizing copyright infringement must be understood in its strongest dictionary meaning, namely, "give approval to, sanction, permit, favour, encourage": see *The New Shorter Oxford English Dictionary* (1993), vol. 1, at p. 526. Authorization is a question of fact that depends on the circumstances of each particular case and can be inferred from acts that are less than direct and positive, including a sufficient degree of indifference. However, a person does not authorize infringement by authorizing the mere use of equipment that could be used to infringe copyright. Courts should presume that a person who authorizes an activity does so only so far as it is in accordance with the law. This presumption may be rebutted if it is shown that a certain relationship or degree of control existed between the alleged authorizer and the persons who committed the copyright infringement.

(b)   Application of the Law to these Facts

39   For several decades, the Law Society has maintained self-service photocopiers for the use of its patrons in the Great Library. The patrons' use of the machines is not monitored directly. Since the mid-1980s, the Law Society has posted the following notice above each machine:

> The copyright law of Canada governs the making of photocopies or other reproductions of copyright material. Certain copying may be an infringement of the copyright law. This library is not

responsible for infringing copies made by users of these machines.

At trial, the Law Society applied for a declaration that it did not authorize copyright infringement by providing self-service photocopiers for patrons of the Great Library. No evidence was tendered that the photocopiers had been used in an infringing manner.

40   The trial judge declined to deal with this issue, in part because of the limited nature of the evidence on this question. The Federal Court of Appeal, relying in part on the Australian High Court decision in *Moorehouse v. University of New South Wales*, [1976] R.P.C. 151 (Australia H.C.), concluded that the Law Society implicitly sanctioned, approved or countenanced copyright infringement of the publishers' works by failing to control copying and instead merely posting a notice indicating that the Law Society was not responsible for infringing copies made by the machine's users.

41   With respect, I do not agree that this amounted to authorizing breach of copyright. *Moorhouse, supra,* is inconsistent with previous Canadian and British approaches to this issue. *See* D. Vaver, *Copyright Law* (2000), at p. 27, and McKeown, *supra*, at p. 21–108. In my view, the *Moorhouse* approach to authorization shifts the balance in copyright too far in favour of the owner's rights and unnecessarily interferes with the proper use of copyrighted works for the good of society as a whole.

42   Applying the criteria from *Muzak Corp., supra,* and *de Tervagne, supra*, I conclude that the Law Society's mere provision of photocopiers for the use of its patrons did not constitute authorization to use the photocopiers to breach copyright law.

43   First, there was no evidence that the photocopiers had been used in a manner that was not consistent with copyright law. As noted, a person does not authorize copyright infringement by authorizing the mere use of equipment (such as photocopiers) that could be used to infringe copyright. In fact, courts should presume that a person who authorizes an activity does so only so far as it is in accordance with the law. Although the Court of Appeal assumed that the photocopiers were being used to infringe copyright, I think it is equally plausible that the patrons using the machines were doing so in a lawful manner.

44   Second, the Court of Appeal erred in finding that the Law Society's posting of the notice constitutes an express acknowledgement that the photocopiers will be used in an illegal manner. The Law Society's posting of the notice over the photocopiers does not rebut the presumption that a person authorizes an activity only so far as it is in accordance with the law. Given that the Law Society is responsible for regulating the legal profession in Ontario, it is more logical to conclude that the notice was posted for the purpose of reminding the Great Library's patrons that copyright law governs the making of photocopies in the library.

45   Finally, even if there were evidence of the photocopiers having been used to infringe copyright, the Law Society lacks sufficient control over the Great Library's patrons to permit the conclusion that it sanctioned, approved or countenanced the infringement. The Law Society and Great Library patrons are not in a master-servant or employer-employee relationship such that the Law Society can be said to exercise control over the patrons who might commit infringement: see, for example, *De Tervagne, supra.* Nor does the Law Society exercise control over which works the patrons choose to copy, the patron's purposes for copying or the photocopiers themselves.

46   In summary, I conclude that evidence does not establish that the Law Society authorized copyright infringement by providing self-service photocopiers and copies of the respondent publishers' works for use by its patrons in the Great Library. I would allow this ground of appeal.

Scarlet Extended SA v. Société Belge des Auteurs, Compositeurs et Editeurs SCRL (SABAM)

Court of Justice of the European Communities, 2011.
Case C-70/10.

Judgment

1   This reference for a preliminary ruling concerns the interpretation of Directives:

— 2000/31/EC of the European Parliament and of the Council of 8 June 2000 on certain legal aspects of information society services, in particular electronic commerce, in the Internal Market ('Directive on electronic commerce') (OJ 2000 L 178, p. 1);

— 2001/29/EC of the European Parliament and of the Council of 22 May 2001 on the harmonisation of certain aspects of copyright and related rights in the information society (OJ 2001 L 167, p. 10);

— 2004/48/EC of the European Parliament and of the Council of 29 April 2004 on the enforcement of intellectual property rights (OJ 2004 L 157, p. 45, and corrigendum OJ 2004 L 195, p. 16);

— 95/46/EC of the European Parliament and of the Council of 24 October 1995 on the protection of individuals with regard to the processing of personal data and on the free movement of such data (OJ 1995 L 281, p. 31); and

— 2002/58/EC of the European Parliament and of the Council of 12 July 2002 concerning the processing of personal data and the protection of privacy in the electronic communications sector (Directive on privacy and electronic communications) (OJ 2002 L 201, p. 37).

2   The reference has been made in proceedings between Scarlet Extended SA ('Scarlet') and the Société Belge des auteurs, compositeurs et éditeurs SCRL ('SABAM') concerning Scarlet's refusal to install a

system for filtering electronic communications which use file-sharing software ('peer-to-peer'), with a view to preventing file sharing which infringes copyright. . . .

The dispute in the main proceedings and the questions referred for a preliminary ruling

15 SABAM is a management company which represents authors, composers and editors of musical works in authorising the use of their copyright-protected works by third parties.

16 Scarlet is an internet service provider ('ISP') which provides its customers with access to the internet without offering other services such as downloading or file sharing.

17 In the course of 2004, SABAM concluded that internet users using Scarlett services were downloading works in SABAM's catalogue from the Internet, without authorisation and without paying royalties, by means of peer-to-peer networks, which constitute a transparent method of file sharing which is independent, decentralised and features advanced search and download functions.

18 On 24 June 2004, SABAM accordingly brought interlocutory proceedings against Scarlet before the President of the Tribunal de premiere instance, Brussels, claiming that that company was the best-placed, as an ISP, to take measures to bring to an end copyright infringements committed by its customers.

19 SABAM sought, first, a declaration that the copyright in musical works contained in its repertoire had been infringed, in particular the right of reproduction and the right of communication to the public, because of the unauthorised sharing of electronic music files by means of peer-to-peer software, those infringements being committed through the use of Scarlet's services.

20 SABAM also sought an order requiring Scarlet to bring such infringements to an end by blocking, or making it impossible for its customers to send or receive in any way, files containing a musical work using peer-to-peer software without the permission of the rightholders, on pain of a periodic penalty. Lastly, SABAM requested that Scarlet provide it with details of the measures that it would be applying in order to comply with the judgment to be given, on pain of a periodic penalty.

21 By judgment of 26 November 2004, the President of the Tribunal de premiere instance, Brussels, found that copyright had been infringed, as claimed by SABAM, but, prior to ruling on the application for cessation, appointed an expert to investigate whether the technical solutions proposed by SABAM were technically feasible, whether they would make it possible to filter out only unlawful file sharing, and whether there were other ways of monitoring the use of peer-to-peer software, and to determine the cost of the measures envisaged.

22   In his report, the appointed expert concluded that, despite numerous technical obstacles, the feasibility of filtering and blocking the unlawful sharing of electronic files could not be entirely ruled out.

23   By judgment of 29 June 2007, the President of the Tribunal de premiere instance, Brussels, accordingly ordered Scarlet to bring to an end the copyright infringements established in the judgment of 26 November 2004 by making it impossible for its customers to send or receive in any way files containing a musical work in SABAM's repertoire by means of peer-to-peer software, on pain of a periodic penalty.

24   Scarlet appealed against that decision to the referring court, claiming, first, that it was impossible for it to comply with that injunction since the effectiveness and permanence of filtering and blocking systems had not been proved and that the installation of the equipment for so doing was faced with numerous practical obstacles, such as problems with the network capacity and the impact on the network. Moreover, any attempt to block the files concerned was, it argued, doomed to fail in the very short term because there were at that time several peer-to-peer software products which made it impossible for third parties to check their content.

25   Scarlet also claimed that that injunction was contrary to Article 21 of the Law of 11 March 2003 on certain legal aspects of information society services, which transposes Article 15 of Directive 2000/31 into national law, because it would impose on Scarlet, de facto, a general obligation to monitor communications on its network, inasmuch as any system for blocking or filtering peer-to-peer traffic would necessarily require general surveillance of all the communications passing through its network.

26   Lastly, Scarlet considered that the installation of a filtering system would be in breach of the provisions of European Union law on the protection of personal data and the secrecy of communications, since such filtering involves the processing of IP addresses, which are personal data.

27   In that context, the referring court took the view that, before ascertaining whether a mechanism for filtering and blocking peer-to-peer files existed and could be effective, it had to be satisfied that the obligations liable to be imposed on Scarlet were in accordance with European Union law.

28   In those circumstances, the cour d'appel de Bruxelles decided to stay the proceedings and to refer the following questions to the Court for a preliminary ruling:

> '(1) Do Directives 2001/29 and 2004/48, in conjunction with Directives 95/46, 2000/31 and 2002/58, construed in particular in the light of Articles 8 and 10 of the European Convention on the Protection of Human Rights and Fundamental Freedoms, permit Member States to authorise a national court, before which substantive proceedings have been brought and on the

basis merely of a statutory provision stating that: 'They [the national courts] may also issue an injunction against intermediaries whose services are used by a third party to infringe a copyright or related right', to order an [ISP] to install, for all its customers, in abstracto and as a preventive measure, exclusively at the cost of that ISP and for an unlimited period, a system for filtering all electronic communications, both incoming and outgoing, passing via its services, in particular those involving the use of peer-to-peer software, in order to identify on its network the movement of electronic files containing a musical, cinematographic or audio-visual work in respect of which the applicant claims to hold rights, and subsequently to block the transfer of such files, either at the point at which they are requested or at which they are sent?

(2)   If the answer to the [first] question . . . is in the affirmative, do those directives require a national court, called upon to give a ruling on an application for an injunction against an intermediary whose services are used by a third party to infringe a copyright, to apply the principle of proportionality when deciding on the effectiveness and dissuasive effect of the measure sought?'

Consideration of the questions referred

29   By its questions, the referring court asks, in essence, whether Directives 2000/31, 2001/29, 2004/48, 95/46 and 2002/58, read together and construed in the light of the requirements stemming from the protection of the applicable fundamental rights, must be interpreted as precluding an injunction imposed on an ISP to introduce a system for filtering

— all electronic communications passing via its services, in particular those involving the use of peer-to-peer software;

— which applies indiscriminately to all its customers;

— as a preventive measure;

— exclusively at its expense; and

— for an unlimited period,

which is capable of identifying on that provider's network the movement of electronic files containing a musical, cinematographic or audio-visual work in respect of which the applicant claims to hold intellectual property rights, with a view to blocking the transfer of files the sharing of which infringes copyright ('the contested filtering system').

30   In that regard, it should first be recalled that, under Article 8(3) of Directive 2001/29 and the third sentence of Article 11 of Directive 2004/48, holders of intellectual property rights may apply for an injunction against intermediaries, such as ISPs, whose services are being used by a third party to infringe their rights.

31   Next, it follows from the Court's case-law that the jurisdiction conferred on national courts, in accordance with those provisions, must allow them to order those intermediaries to take measures aimed not only at bringing to an end infringements already committed against intellectual-property rights using their information-society services, but also at preventing further infringements.

32   Lastly, it follows from that same case-law that the rules for the operation of the injunctions for which the Member States must provide under Article 8(3) of Directive 2001/29 and the third sentence of Article 11 of Directive 2004/48, such as those relating to the conditions to be met and to the procedure to be followed, are a matter for national law.

33   That being so, those national rules, and likewise their application by the national courts, must observe the limitations arising from Directives 2001/29 and 2004/48 and from the sources of law to which those directives refer.

34   Thus, in accordance with recital 16 in the preamble to Directive 2001/29 and Article 2(3)(a) of Directive 2004/48, those rules laid down by the Member States may not affect the provisions of Directive 2000/31 and, more specifically, Articles 12 to 15 thereof.

35   Consequently, those rules must, in particular, respect Article 15(1) of Directive 2000/31, which prohibits national authorities from adopting measures which would require an ISP to carry out general monitoring of the information that it transmits on its network.

36   In that regard, the Court has already ruled that that prohibition applies in particular to national measures which would require an intermediary provider, such as an ISP, to actively monitor all the data of each of its customers in order to prevent any future infringement of intellectual-property rights. Furthermore, such a general monitoring obligation would be incompatible with Article 3 of Directive 2004/48, which states that the measures referred to by the directive must be fair and proportionate and must not be excessively costly.

37   In those circumstances, it is necessary to examine whether the injunction at issue in the main proceedings, which would require the ISP to install the contested filtering system, would oblige it, as part of that system, to actively monitor all the data of each of its customers in order to prevent any future infringement of intellectual-property rights.

38   In that regard, it is common ground that implementation of that filtering system would require

   — first, that the ISP identify, within all of the electronic communications of all its customers, the files relating to peer-to-peer traffic;

   — secondly, that it identify, within that traffic, the files containing works in respect of which holders of intellectual-property rights claim to hold rights;

— thirdly, that it determine which of those files are being shared unlawfully; and

— fourthly, that it block file sharing that it considers to be unlawful.

39 Preventive monitoring of this kind would thus require active observation of all electronic communications conducted on the network of the ISP concerned and, consequently, would encompass all information to be transmitted and all customers using that network.

40 In the light of the foregoing, it must be held that the injunction imposed on the ISP concerned requiring it to install the contested filtering system would oblige it to actively monitor all the data relating to each of its customers in order to prevent any future infringement of intellectual-property rights. It follows that that injunction would require the ISP to carry out general monitoring, something which is prohibited by Article 15(1) of Directive 2000/31.

41 In order to assess whether that injunction is consistent with European Union law, account must also be taken of the requirements that stem from the protection of the applicable fundamental rights, such as those mentioned by the referring court.

42 In that regard, it should be recalled that the injunction at issue in the main proceedings pursues the aim of ensuring the protection of copyright, which is an intellectual-property right, which may be infringed by the nature and content of certain electronic communications conducted through the network of the ISP concerned.

43 The protection of the right to intellectual property is indeed enshrined in Article 17(2) of the Charter of Fundamental Rights of the European Union ('the Charter'). There is, however, nothing whatsoever in the wording of that provision or in the Court's case-law to suggest that that right is inviolable and must for that reason be absolutely protected.

44 As paragraphs 62 to 68 of the judgment in Case C-275/06 Promusicae [2008] ECR1–271 make clear, the protection of the fundamental right to property, which includes the rights linked to intellectual property, must be balanced against the protection of other fundamental rights.

45 More specifically, it follows from paragraph 68 of that judgment that, in the context of measures adopted to protect copyright holders, national authorities and courts must strike a fair balance between the protection of copyright and the protection of the fundamental rights of individuals who are affected by such measures.

46 Accordingly, in circumstances such as those in the main proceedings, national authorities and courts must, in particular, strike a fair balance between the protection of the intellectual property right enjoyed by copyright holders and that of the freedom to conduct a business enjoyed by operators such as ISPs pursuant to Article 16 of the Charter.

47   In the present case, the injunction requiring the installation of the contested filtering system involves monitoring all the electronic communications made through the network of the ISP concerned in the interests of those rightholders. Moreover, that monitoring has no limitation in time, is directed at all future infringements and is intended to protect not only existing works, but also future works that have not yet been created at the time when the system is introduced.

48   Accordingly, such an injunction would result in a serious infringement of the freedom of the ISP concerned to conduct its business since it would require that ISP to install a complicated, costly, permanent computer system at its own expense, which would also be contrary to the conditions laid down in Article 3(1) of Directive 2004/48, which requires that measures to ensure the respect of intellectual-property rights should not be unnecessarily complicated or costly.

49   In those circumstances, it must be held that the injunction to install the contested filtering system is to be regarded as not respecting the requirement that a fair balance be struck between, on the one hand, the protection of the intellectual-property right enjoyed by copyright holders, and, on the other hand, that of the freedom to conduct business enjoyed by operators such as ISPs.

50   Moreover, the effects of that injunction would not be limited to the ISP concerned, as the contested filtering system may also infringe the fundamental rights of that ISP's customers, namely their right to protection of their personal data and their freedom to receive or impart information, which are rights safeguarded by Articles 8 and 11 of the Charter respectively.

51   It is common ground, first, that the injunction requiring installation of the contested filtering system would involve a systematic analysis of all content and the collection and identification of users' IP addresses from which unlawful content on the network is sent. Those addresses are protected personal data because they allow those users to be precisely identified.

52   Secondly, that injunction could potentially undermine freedom of information since that system might not distinguish adequately between unlawful content and lawful content, with the result that its introduction could lead to the blocking of lawful communications. Indeed, it is not contested that the reply to the question whether a transmission is lawful also depends on the application of statutory exceptions to copyright which vary from one Member State to another. Moreover, in some Member States certain works fall within the public domain or can be posted online free of charge by the authors concerned.

53   Consequently, it must be held that, in adopting the injunction requiring the ISP to install the contested filtering system, the national court concerned would not be respecting the requirement that a fair balance be struck between the right to intellectual property, on the one

hand, and the freedom to conduct business, the right to protection of personal data and the freedom to receive or impart information, on the other.

54   In the light of the foregoing, the answer to the questions submitted is that Directives 2000/31, 2001/29, 2004/48, 95/46 and 2002/58, read together and construed in the light of the requirements stemming from the protection of the applicable fundamental rights, must be interpreted as precluding an injunction made against an ISP which requires it to install the contested filtering system.

Costs

55   Since these proceedings are, for the parties to the main proceedings, a step in the action pending before the national court, the decision on costs is a matter for that court. Costs incurred in submitting observations to the Court, other than the costs of those parties, are not recoverable.

On those grounds, the Court (Third Chamber) hereby rules:

Directives:

— 2000/31/EC of the European Parliament and of the Council of 8 June 2000 on certain legal aspects of information society services, in particular electronic commerce, in the Internal Market ('Directive on electronic commerce');

— 2001/29/EC of the European Parliament and of the Council of 22 May 2001 on the harmonisation of certain aspects of copyright and related rights in the information society;

— 2004/48/EC of the European Parliament and of the Council of 29 April 2004 on the enforcement of intellectual property rights;

— 95/46/EC of the European Parliament and of the Council of 24 October 1995 on the protection of individuals with regard to the processing of personal data and on the free movement of such data; and

— 2002/58/EC of the European Parliament and of the Council of 12 July 2002 concerning the processing of personal data and the protection of privacy in the electronic communications sector (Directive on privacy and electronic communications), read together and construed in the light of the requirements stemming from the protection of the applicable fundamental rights, must be interpreted as precluding an injunction made against an internet service provider which requires it to install a system for filtering

— all electronic communications passing via its services, in particular those involving the use of peer-to-peer software;

— which applies indiscriminately to all its customers;

— as a preventive measure;

— exclusively at its expense; and

— for an unlimited period,

— which is capable of identifying on that provider's network the movement of electronic files containing a musical, cinematographic or audio-visual work in respect of which the applicant claims to hold intellectual-property rights, with a view to blocking the transfer of files the sharing of which infringes copyright.

NOTES

1. *Secondary Liability.* The great challenge to copyright in the twenty-first century is to bring under copyright control the widely dispersed, uncounted millions of copyright uses that will often displace revenues from more traditional sources. Simply bringing dispersed, private conduct within the scope of copyright will not suffice to bring the conduct within the copyright owner's economic control if the cost of pursuing individual infringers is too high to justify the effort. Copyright owners will often seek to economize on enforcement in these situations by employing theories of joint, contributory or vicarious liability to pursue those who contribute to these private infringements. In some cases the alleged contributory conduct will take the form of providing premises or services. In other cases, the alleged contributory conduct will consist of providing equipment that is capable of infringement. The *CCH* case provides an example of both.

Like the Canadian Copyright Act, Section 106 of the 1976 U.S. Copyright Act grants the exclusive rights not only to "do" its six prescribed acts, but also to "authorize" them. Section 16(2) of the British Copyright, Designs & Patents Act makes it an act of primary, direct infringement not only to commit an act covered by copyright, but to authorize someone else to commit a restricted act. Sections 22–26 of the Act make a person who knew, or had reason to know, of the underlying infringement secondarily liable for importing, possessing or dealing with an infringing copy; providing means for making infringing copies; permitting use of premises for an infringing performance; and providing the apparatus for an infringing performance.

Secondary copyright liability in the civil law tradition is somewhat less defined. Contributory and vicarious liability under German law, for example, derives from provisions of the German Civil Code imposing joint and several liability on tortfeasors, and has been imposed on such activities as promoting a concert of unauthorized performances and selling copying equipment that lacks any substantial noninfringing use. *See* Alexander Liegl, Andreas Leupold & Peter Bräutigam, Germany, in Susan Cotter, (ed.), Copyright Infringement 119, 162–164 (1997). *See* also Weixiao Wei, The Liability of Internet Service Providers for Copyright Infringement and Defamation Actions in the United Kingdom and China: A Comparative Study, 28 EIPR 528 (2006). For an excellent overview of the subject, see Gerald Spindler & Matthias Leistner, Secondary Copyright Infringement—New Perspectives in Germany and Europe, 37 IIC 788 (2006).

A 2015 study commissioned by the U.K. Intellectual Property Office compared approaches to online copyright infringement in nine countries belonging to both the common law and civil law tradition—among them, graduated response letters, slowing down of Internet connections, termination of access, fines, notice and takedown, blocking of access to sites—and concluded that "despite clear differences in how copyright is defined within the two different legal traditions, it is hard to identify a determining influence that the different legal traditions have in terms of the policies that countries have adopted to enforce copyright online, as countries that share some similarities in terms of their legal system ... have completely different approaches in tackling online copyright infringement." Intellectual Property Office, International Comparison of Approaches to Online Copyright Infringement, Final Report 4 (2015).

2. *Internet Safe Harbors.* Rules on secondary liability have been inadequate to allay the concerns of copyright owners over their inability to police infringing activities in the digital marketplace or the concerns of service providers, such as telephone companies and search services, that are unable to monitor and control infringing activities of their subscribers. Section 512 of the U.S. Copyright Act, added as part of the Digital Millennium Copyright Act in 1998, aims to reconcile the competing interests of copyright owners and service providers by carving out safe harbors to immunize the qualifying activities of defined "service providers" from monetary relief and limit the availability of injunctive relief in prescribed circumstances. The provision covers five categories of online activity: transitory digital network communications, system caching, storage of information at the direction of users, use of information location tools, and specified activities of nonprofit educational institutions.

The European Union's Directive on Electronic Commerce, 2000/31/EC, considered in the *Scarlet* case, limits the liability of intermediary service providers for three classes of "information society service" that generally correspond to the U.S. legislation's safe harbors for transitory network communications, system caching and storage of information at the direction of users: "mere conduit service," for which the service provider does not select the recipient of the transmission or select or modify the information contained in the transmission; "caching"—the automatic, intermediate, and temporary storage of information for its more efficient onward transmission to other recipients; and "hosting"—"the storage of information provided by a recipient of the service." Articles 12(3), 13 and 14(3) respectively qualify the three limitations on liability by providing that they "shall not affect the possibility for a court or administrative authority, in accordance with Member States' legal systems, of requiring the service provider to terminate or prevent an infringement." Article 15 bars Member States from imposing a general obligation on service providers, when providing conduit, caching or hosting services, "to monitor the information which they transmit or store," or "actively to seek facts or circumstances indicating illegal activity." Unlike the U.S. legislation, the Electronic Commerce Directive applies to a wide range of potential liability, not just copyright liability.

Would the directives, along with the "fundamental rights" of an ISP's customers, considered in the *Scarlet* case bar an Internet service provider from *voluntarily* undertaking the sort of filtering measures that the copyright owners were seeking to impose on it? What reasons would a service provider have for adopting such measures? On Internet safe harbors generally, see Victoria McEvedy, The DMCA and the E-Commerce Directive, 24 EIPR (2002); Jane Strachan, The Internet of Tomorrow: The New-Old Communication Tools of Control, 26 EIPR (2004); Rosa Julia-Barceló, On-line Intermediary Liability Issues: Comparing E.U. and U.S. Legal Frameworks, 22 EIPR 105 (2000).

3. *Technological Measures.* Challenged by electronic copying and dissemination technologies, copyright owners have turned to encryption to bar physically what copyright cannot stop legally. The 1996 WIPO Internet Treaties—the WIPO Copyright Treaty and the WIPO Performances and Phonograms Treaty—would give these self-help measures the force of law. Article 11 of the WIPO Copyright Treaty, for example, requires contracting parties "to provide adequate legal protection and effective legal remedies against the circumvention of effective technological measures that are used by authors in connection with the exercise of their rights under this Treaty or the Berne Convention and that restrict acts, in respect of their works, which are not authorized by the authors concerned or permitted by law."

In the United States, section 1201 of Title 17, of the U.S. Code added by the Digital Millennium Copyright Act, P.L. No. 105–304 (Oct. 28, 1998), implements Article 11 of the WIPO Copyright Treaty by prohibiting the manufacture, distribution and traffic in products or services that are used to circumvent technological measures controlling access to copyrighted works or protecting a right of a copyright owner. The offending device must have circumvention as its primary purpose, must have only a limited commercial purpose other than circumvention, or must be a marketed for use in circumvention. Several exceptions aim to approximate traditional copyright exemptions and defenses. Section 1201(f), for example, carves out a reverse engineering exemption, allowing software developers to identify elements of a computer program that need to be embodied in an independently created program if the program is to interoperate with other programs.

For an overview of legal anticircumvention measures in the EU and elsewhere, see Institute of Information Law, University of Amsterdam, Study on the Implementation and Effect in Member States' Laws of Directive 2001/29/EC on the Harmonisation of Certain Aspects of Copyright and Related Rights in the Information Society (2007). *See* also Stefan Bechtold, Digital Rights Management in the United States and Europe, 52 Am. J. Comp. L. 323 (2004); Li Luo, Legal Protection of Technological Measures in China, 28 EIPR 200 (2006); Mihály Ficsor, Copyright for the Digital Era: The WIPO "Internet" Treaties, 21 Colum.-VLA J.L. & Arts 197 (1997).

v.   Remedies

Los Angeles News Service v. Reuters Television International, Limited

United States Court of Appeals for the Ninth Circuit, 2003.
340 F.3d 926, 67 U.S.P.Q.2d. 1677.

O'SCANNLAIN, CIRCUIT JUDGE:

We must decide whether a news organization may recover actual damages under the Copyright Act for acts of infringement that mostly occurred outside the United States.

I

The copyrighted works at issue here ("the works") are two video recordings, "The Beating of Reginald Denny" and "Beating of Man in White Panel Truck," which depict the infamous events at Florence Ave. and Normandie Blvd. during the 1992 Los Angeles riots. Los Angeles News Service ("LANS"), an independent news organization which produces video and audio tape recordings of newsworthy events and licenses them for profit, produced the works (and two other videotapes not at issue here) while filming the riots from its helicopter. LANS copyrighted the works and sold a license to rebroadcast them to, among others, the National Broadcasting Company ("NBC") network, which used them on the *Today Show*.

Visnews International (USA), Ltd. ("Visnews") is a joint venture among NBC, Reuters Television Ltd., and the British Broadcasting Company ("BBC"). Pursuant to a news supply agreement between NBC and Visnews, NBC transmitted the *Today Show* broadcast by fiber link to Visnews in New York; Visnews made a videotape copy of the works, which it then transmitted via satellite to its subscribers in Europe and Africa and via fiber link to the New York office of the European Broadcast Union ("EBU"), a joint venture of Visnews and Reuters. The EBU subsequently made another videotape copy of the works, and transmitted it to Reuters in London, which in turn distributed the works via video "feed" to its own subscribers.

LANS sued Reuters Television International, Inc., Reuters America Holdings, Inc., Reuters America, Inc. (collectively, "Reuters"), and Visnews for copyright infringement and certain other claims not relevant here. The district court subsequently granted Reuters and Visnews partial summary judgment on the issue of extraterritorial infringement, holding that no liability could arise under the Copyright Act for acts of infringement that occurred outside the United States. However, the district court held that Visnews's act of copying the works in New York was a domestic act of infringement[1] and rejected a claimed defense of fair use. *Id.* at 1269, 1271–74.

The district court further concluded that LANS had failed to prove any actual damages arising domestically and that damages arising extraterritorially were unavailable under the Act, which meant that LANS was limited to statutory damages. After a bench trial on the issue of statutory damages, the district court awarded LANS a total of $60,000. *L.A. News Serv. v. Reuters TV Int'l, Ltd. (Reuters II)*, 942 F. Supp. 1275, 1283–84 (C.D. Cal. 1996).

LANS appealed the district court's ruling on actual damages, and Reuters and Visnews cross-appealed the fair use ruling and the statutory damages calculation. We subsequently reversed the district court's actual damages ruling, disagreeing with its interpretation of the Copyright Act's extraterritorial application. *L.A. News Serv. v. Reuters TV Int'l, Ltd. (Reuters III)*, 149 F.3d 987, 992 (9th Cir. 1998). We concluded that although the district court was correct to hold that the Copyright Act does not apply extraterritorially, an exception may apply where an act of infringement is completed entirely within the United States and that such infringing act enabled further exploitation abroad. Relying on *Sheldon v. Metro-Goldwyn Pictures Corp.*, 106 F.2d 45 (2d Cir. 1939), *aff'd*, 309 U.S. 390, 84 L.Ed. 825, 60 S.Ct. 681 (1940), which held that profits from overseas infringement can be recovered on the theory that the infringer holds them in a constructive trust for the copyright owner, we reversed the grant of summary judgment. We held that "LANS [was] entitled to recover damages flowing from exploitation abroad of the domestic acts of infringement committed by defendants."

Turning to the other issues, we affirmed the fair use ruling and the statutory damages calculation. However, we vacated the award of statutory damages so that LANS could make a new election on remand. After the Supreme Court denied certiorari, the case returned to the district court, where Reuters and Visnews moved for summary adjudication of the claim for actual damages. They asserted that the *Reuters III* decision permitted LANS to recover only Defendants' profits attributable to extraterritorial infringement—not actual damages for injuries the infringements caused LANS overseas. Reuters and Visnews further asserted that no factual dispute remained as to the amount of such profits.

After a hearing, the district court agreed with Reuters and Visnews on both points and granted the motion. The court concluded that *Reuters III* had held only that LANS could recover any profits or unjust enrichment from domestic infringers, on the theory that the infringers held such profits in a constructive trust for LANS. "To permit [LANS] to recover damages other than Defendants' profits or unjust enrichment,"

---

[1]   Visnews's transmission of the works to the EBU New York office was not infringement, however. *Id.* at 1270–71.

the court stated, "would . . . effectively permit [LANS] to recover damages for extraterritorial acts of infringement."

Having determined that LANS could recover only Defendants' profits, if any, the district court concluded that Reuters and Visnews had reaped no such profits from their infringement. The court held that LANS's "speculative" testimony about the competitive advantage that exclusive footage gives a subscription broadcaster was insufficient to create a factual dispute. It accordingly granted the motion for summary adjudication. In its order, the district court stated that LANS could elect to take the $60,000 in statutory damages awarded in *Reuters II* and affirmed in *Reuters III*. In its haste, LANS timely appealed to this court, but failed to make the required election as to statutory damages. Because there was no "final decision," we dismissed for lack of jurisdiction. LANS subsequently cured the jurisdictional defect by making such election, and refiled its appeal with this court.

II

LANS claims that the district court erred by disallowing recovery for actual damages. LANS, however, does not challenge the court's further conclusion that LANS had failed to show that Reuters and Visnews had earned any profits from the overseas infringement. Summary adjudication was therefore appropriate if the district court correctly concluded that LANS could not recover actual damages for overseas effects of Defendants' infringement.

A

Both parties engage in detailed exegesis of our opinion in *Reuters III*. On LANS's reading, the *Reuters III* court's use of the term "damages" is dispositive. The statute uses "actual damages" and "profits" separately and distinctly, and provides that an infringer may recover both (in the ordinary case). LANS asserts therefore that the *Reuters III* court should be read as having meant what it said: "damages" means actual damages.

But LANS's interpretation does not fit with the context in which the *Reuters III* court discussed the recoverability of "damages." There, we relied on Judge Learned Hand's opinion in *Sheldon* and discussed damages entirely in the context of that case, which dealt exclusively with the recovery of the defendants' profits.

The *Sheldon* court had previously affirmed the defendants' liability for infringing the plaintiffs' copyright by incorporating their play into a movie. After a remand, the defendants appealed the district court's decision to award the plaintiffs all the defendants' profits from exhibiting the motion picture. The Second Circuit, inter alia, determined that the profits traceable to overseas exhibition of the infringing movie should be included. Although "at first blush it [seemed] that [the overseas profits] should be excluded" because the overseas exhibition of the infringing movie was not tortious under American copyright law, the court nonetheless concluded that the plaintiffs could recover the overseas profits under a different theory, based on one defendant's having made the negatives in the U.S. The court elaborated:

> The negatives were "records" from which the work could be "reproduced," and it was a tort to make them in this country. The plaintiffs acquired an equitable interest in them as soon as they were made, which attached to any profits from their exploitation, whether in the form of money remitted to the United States, or of increase in the value of shares of foreign companies held by the defendants. . . . As soon as any of the profits so realized took the form of property whose situs was in the United States, our law seized upon them and impressed them with a constructive trust, whatever their form.

The *Sheldon* court relied exclusively on this rationale in holding that the plaintiffs could recover the defendants' profits from overseas exhibition.

As *Sheldon* considered only an award of profits, it is counter-intuitive that a court applying Sheldon's rationale, but using the word "damages" as the *Reuters III* court did, was referring consciously to "actual damages" as opposed to "profits." Indeed our prior holding in *Reuters III*, based on the *Sheldon* constructive trust theory, demonstrates that we did not use the term "damages" in that formal sense. Rather, we used "damages" as a shorthand either for both the forms of relief that 17 U.S.C. § 504(b) makes available, *i.e.*, actual damages and defendants' profits, or only the recovery of defendants' profits. Understanding which applies requires closer analysis of *Sheldon* and its progeny.

B

Of course, *Sheldon* did not explicitly deal with the issue of actual damages. But as LANS points out, there is some support in the Second Circuit's post-*Sheldon* case law for the recovery of extraterritorial actual damages once an act of domestic infringement is proven.

The most direct support for such position comes from *Update Art, Inc. v. Modiin Publ'g, Ltd.*, 843 F.2d 67 (2d Cir. 1988), in which the Second Circuit considered an Israeli newspaper's unauthorized reproduction of a poster copyrighted in the United States. *Update Art* held, albeit without much discussion, that the defendants had failed to make any showing that the initial copying of the poster had occurred abroad; thus, in the case's procedural context, the court concluded that the "predicate act" of domestic infringement had occurred and that Update Art had stated a viable copyright claim. *Id.* at 73. The court also affirmed the award of "damages accruing from the illegal infringement in the Israeli newspapers." *Id.*

Update Art, however, is distinguishable from LANS's claim in a couple of important respects. First, several issues of the newspaper in which the infringing reproduction appeared were circulated in the United States. Second, and more importantly, the amount of damages awarded by the district court was based on defendants' profits. Finally, the panel did not even discuss the distinction between damages and profits, much less cite *Sheldon*. Rather, it merely concluded that the damages award could stand despite the extraterritoriality issue, which the magistrate judge had not considered in calculating the amount. . . .

On the whole, we conclude that *Reuters III* adhered very closely to our decision in *Subafilms, Ltd. v. MGM-Pathe Communs. Co.*, 24 F.3d 1088 (9th Cir. 1994) (en banc). *Subafilms* reaffirmed that the copyright laws have no application beyond the U.S. border, and expressly took no position on the merits of the *Update Act* court's apparent willingness to award damages. LANS's appeal thus presents the precise question that *Subafilms* reserved, and as the prior panel recognized, such question should be resolved in light of the principles the en banc court laid down.

The import of such principles counsel a narrow application of the adoption in *Reuters III* of the *Sheldon* exception to the general rule. In particular, the *Sheldon* constructive trust rationale includes a territorial connection that preserves consistency with Congress's decision to keep the copyright laws—presumably including § 504, which prescribes remedies—territorially confined. Moreover, no rational deterrent function is served by making an infringer whose domestic act of infringement—from which he earns no profit—leads to widespread extraterritorial infringement, liable for the copyright owner's entire loss of value or profit from that overseas infringement, particularly if the overseas infringement is legal where it takes place. Moreover, the resulting over-deterrence might chill the fair use of copyrighted works in close cases.

LANS counters that the assessment of damages based on a domestic act of infringement having had consequences in foreign territories is legitimate under "traditional tort principles." However, it offers no direct support for the proposition that those principles compel the extension of relief—legal or equitable—beyond the boundaries where Congress declared that liability stops. Its policy arguments to the contrary seem largely a complaint about the failure of Congress to make the copyright laws—those creating both rights and remedies—applicable extraterritorially.

III

Accordingly we read *Reuters III* to allow only a narrow exception for the recovery of the infringer's profits to *Subafilms*'s general rule against extraterritorial application. We conclude therefore that the Copyright Act does not provide LANS recovery for actual damages resulting from Reuters's and Visnews's infringement.

SILVERMAN, CIRCUIT JUDGE, dissenting:

In our previous decision, *L.A. News Serv. v. Reuters Television Int'l, Ltd. (Reuters III)*, 149 F.3d 987 (9th Cir. 1998), we decided the very issue the majority now re-decides the other way. At that time, we identified the issue as whether "a plaintiff may recover actual damages accruing from the unauthorized exploitation abroad of copyrighted work infringed in the United States." *Id.* at 989. We held that it could. Our mandate said, "We REVERSE the ruling barring the claim for extraterritorial damages and REMAND for a trial on actual damages, with directions that if LANS elects to recover actual damages, the award of statutory damages be vacated." *Id.* at 997.

The majority now holds that when we said "actual damages," we didn't mean actual damages, but only whatever profits the infringer might have realized. This new holding is not only at odds with our previous holding, but it fails to take account of the fact that the Copyright Act itself specifically uses the terms "actual damages" and "profits" separately and distinctly.[1] The district court should have allowed LANS to do what we said it could do—prove its actual damages. For that reason, I respectfully dissent.

At this stage of the case, the majority's reliance on *Sheldon v. Metro-Goldwyn Pictures Corp.*, 106 F.2d 45 (2d Cir. 1939), is puzzling. In *Sheldon*, the question of what constitutes "actual damages" wasn't an issue or even discussed. *Sheldon* was an appeal from an accounting. The sole question was whether the plaintiff could recover the profits earned by the defendant from its foreign exploitation of a motion picture that infringed the plaintiff's stage play, profits that were *discovered* during the accounting. The court held that the plaintiff could, on a constructive trust theory. "Actual damages" had nothing to do with the case.

SubaFilms Ltd. v. MGM-Pathe Communs. Co., 24 F.3d 1088 (9th Cir. 1994) doesn't shed light on this problem, either. It merely holds that there is no recovery under American copyright law for infringements that do not occur within the United States. True enough, but as we previously held in *Reuters III*, "actual damages" *can* be recovered when the infringement occurs wholly within the United States. That's exactly what happened here, and why we reversed for a trial at which LANS would be allowed to prove its actual damages, if any. This is not a novel concept. *See Update Art, Inc. v. Modiin Publ'g, Ltd.*, 843 F.2d 67, 70 n.4 (2d Cir. 1988); *Famous Music Corp. v. Seeco Records, Inc.*, 201 F. Supp. 560 (S.D.N.Y. 1961).

There are any number of ways to compute actual damages. Neither the Copyright Act, nor our prior decision in *this* case, nor any *other* case, limits the calculation of actual damages to only the infringer's ill-gotten profits. LANS should have been allowed to put on its proof of its actual damages, as we previously held it could. I would remand for a trial on actual damages (just as we did *last* time) except *this* time, I would add that we really, really mean it.

---

[1]   17 U.S.C. § 504(b):

(b) Actual Damages and Profits.—The copyright owner is entitled to recover the actual damages suffered by him or her as a result of the infringement, and any profits of the infringer that are attributable to the infringement and are not taken into account in computing the actual damages.

Annette Kur, The Enforcement Directive— Rough Start, Happy Landing?

35 International Review of Intellectual Property and Competition Law
821, 824–830 (2004).

1.   Overview

The scope of the directive [Directive 2004/48/EC on the Enforcement of Intellectual Property Rights (June 22, 2004)] is defined in Art. 2. It shall apply to all intellectual property rights "as provided for by Community law and/or by the national law of the Member State concerned". National provisions may be maintained if and to the extent that they are more favourable to right holders. In addition, it is pointed out in recital No. 13 that member states may also choose to apply the provisions of the directive to "acts involving unfair competition, including parasitic copies, or similar activities." Apart from the still open question of legislative competence, the provision itself as well as the recitals fail to give an indication as to what exactly should be understood by "intellectual property". What about personality rights, geographical indications, trade secrets? Furthermore, the fact that national provisions can only remain in place if they are more favourable to right holders than those contained in the directive may pose problems in a situation where the measures taken against an alleged infringer not only prove to be unfounded, but appear to have been instigated with an intention to harass and cause detriment. The directive only provides that the opposing party receive just compensation for damages, without mentioning the possibility that damages are claimed with respect to the moral prejudice caused, or that publication of the judgment is demanded. As a consequence of Art. 2, it might be generally prohibited in the future to impose such sanctions as may be available at present in national law.

Not being able to address and discuss all elements in the directive, it shall only be mentioned briefly that Arts. 6 and 7 contain rules on procurement and protection of evidence, with Art. 6 concerning the obligation to produce specific evidence under the control of the adverse party, while Art. 7 deals with the search for and protection of evidence, typically occurring in the pre-procedural stage, and being ordered, in cases of urgency, by way of preliminary measures without the alleged infringer being heard. Building heavily on Arts. 43 and 50 TRIPS, the impact of both articles on national law will at least partly depend on the question as to how diligently TRIPS has been implemented until now.

Provisional measures in general are regulated in Art. 9. The article comprises interlocutory injunctions, seizure of allegedly infringing goods so as to prevent their (further) commercialisation, and, in cases of infringement committed on a commercial scale, precautionary seizure of movable and immovable property or blocking of bank accounts. While there is no doubt that interlocutory injunctions are of central importance in intellectual property infringement proceedings, the beneficial effects of the provision remain doubtful.[1] Already at present, all member states provide for the possibility to claim for provisional measures of various kinds, including *ex-parte* preliminary injunctions. The fact that conspicuous differences exist in national practice with respect to the frequency of which use is made of these possibilities therefore does not have its roots in legal deficiencies but rather in factors such as the willingness of courts to grant preliminary injunction in cases typically involving complex assessments, as in patent law—a difference in attitude which can hardly be overcome by a directive.

The sanctions to be imposed on the basis of the directive comprise permanent injunctions (Art. 11), payment of damages (Art. 13), so-called corrective measures (Art. 10; destruction of goods, recall and definite removal from the channels of commerce), and publication of judgments (Art. 15). As a novel type of remedy for most member states, the directive further introduces the right to obtain information about the involvement of third parties (Art. 8)—as stated in the introduction, this is probably one of the core issues of the whole project.

Pending a more detailed analysis of these provisions, only the following aspects shall be highlighted briefly.

The list of corrective measures contained in Art. 10 shows quite clearly that, in spite of its applicability to all kinds of IP infringement cases, the spirit of the directive is still focussed on combating piracy and counterfeiting. Measures like destruction of goods and removal from the channels of commerce, appropriate as they are when counterfeit goods have been released on the market, are grossly disproportionate with respect to "ordinary" trade mark or patent infringement. It is true that paragraph 3 of the provision contains a safeguarding clause, according to which "the need for proportionality between the seriousness of the infringement and the remedies ordered as well as the interests of third parties" must be taken into account. However, it would have been preferable to limit those remedies expressly to obvious cases of piracy and counterfeiting. Otherwise, the risk exists that these measures are taken for the general rule, and are only set aside, or mitigated in their effects, under exceptional circumstances.

Another remarkable feature concerns the fact that the directive expressly leaves room for application of measures and sanctions against persons who are not found to be infringing an IP right themselves. This concerns preliminary as well as permanent injunctions which may be directed against "intermediates"; the same applies to the right of

---

[1]   If applied strictly, Art. 10 might give rise to problems for national law. For instance, the criterion of urgency *(Dringlichkeit),* which is generally required in Germany for the issuing of a preliminary injunction, is only mentioned as an aspect to be taken into account for *ex-parte* proceedings. For British law, the question might arise whether the fact that preliminary injunctions are declared to constitute a means to "prevent any infringement of intellectual property rights" puts an end to the practice of emphasising the balance of convenience rather than establishing a prima facie case of infringement, which was established in *American Cyanamid v. Ethicon,* [1975] A.C. 3%, [1975] R.P.C. 513.

information, and to corrective measures. The impact and practical relevance of this widening of the circle of potential addressees for measures and sanctions must be analysed critically. As the liability of ISPs seems to be confined in most of the crucial cases to what is set out in the e-commerce directive, the practical consequences may materialise primarily in the transport business.

2.   In Particular: Damages

As a general rule, it is stipulated in Art. 13 that damages should be appropriate to the actual prejudice suffered by the right holder as a result of the infringement. This is important not least because the Commission's proposal as well as the text adopted by the EP's Legal Committee had embraced the possibility to claim, at the choice of the plaintiff, double licence fees as regular damages. This feature could give rise to the impression that the concept of punitive damages was about to be secretly implanted in European law. Had it been so, the breach with principles heretofore firmly established in (continental) European law would indeed have been spectacular.

On the other hand, double licence fees are not necessarily alien to the legal systems presently applying in EU member states. For instance, according to German practice supported by case law, a 100% surcharge on top of the normal tariff is regularly due for certain infringements of copyright law asserted by collecting societies, the motivation being found in the increased efforts and expenses the collecting societies have to undergo to monitor the market. At least in part of the legal doctrine, it is argued that this practice should be extended to other areas of IP law, making it likely that the issue will become topical (again) within the framework of implementation.

In its mandatory part, Art. 13 provides for two methods to be applied by the courts for computing damages. The first method would be to take into account all aspects of the economic consequences resulting from the infringement on the part of the infringer as well as the right holder, including, in appropriate cases, also the moral prejudice caused. As an alternative damages may be set as a lump sum on the basis of factors such as at least the amount of royalties or fees that would have been due if the infringer had asked for authorisation.

It is unclear how the first of these options will change the practice of damage computation in member states that until now have distinguished between compensation for actual damages and recuperation of the infringer's profits. It is also difficult to see what kind of moral prejudice will be taken into account (apart from the obvious cases of copyright infringement where the author's moral rights were actually violated), and how it will be measured. The wording of the provision as well as the general spirit of the directive suggest that it is intended to provide for a better opportunity for courts to grant higher damages than on the basis of present national legislation, *e.g.* in Germany which is frequently accused by right holders of posing an overly high obstacle to the award of damages capable of functioning as a true deterrent against infringers. However, these problems are mostly due to the fact that courts are bound by procedural law as well as by general principles to require sufficient factual evidence to sustain damage claims, whereas in other countries judges are granted more freedom to estimate the amount due. Whether the directive can have a material impact on those fundamental differences appears doubtful.

Concerning the alternative mode of damage computation, it is interesting to note that the lump sum awarded should at least take account of the ordinary licence fees. This might be taken as an indication that in spite of the general confinement of sanctions to the actual prejudice suffered, the directive does not intend to discourage the application of double licence schemes such as the German case law referred to above, if they can be properly justified. This point is further confirmed by recital 26, where it is stated that the aim of the directive is not to introduce an obligation to provide for punitive damages, "but to allow for compensation based on an objective criterion while taking account of the expenses incurred by the right holder, such as the costs of identification and research". This reasoning is quite similar to, and may have been inspired by, the justification given by German courts for the 100% surplus added to the tariffs usually charged by collecting societies.

The question remains whether it will be possible and feasible within the framework of implementation to extend that scheme beyond its original scope of application. Until now, German jurisprudence has constantly rejected attempts to apply the same rule to infringements other than intangible communication of protected works or to other IP rights.

The reluctance of courts to apply a more generous standard with respect to double licence fees has met with critical comments in the literature. In his treatise on compensation and prevention, Thomas Dreier argues that double licence fees should be added as a general feature to the arsenal of available sanctions in cases of IP infringement knowingly undertaken *("vorsätzlich")*. Although contending that this could already be done under present German law, he recommends that this rule be expressly anchored in future legislation, possibly reinforced by an option for further enhancement of the amount due in case of repeated violation. As a motivation, reference is made to the objective of efficient prevention, to which all WTO member states are bound according to TRIPS.

The argumentation reflects the frequently stated view that if an infringer only has to pay licence fees, it will be more cost-efficient from an economic point of view to simply infringe than to apply for a licence, thus discouraging honest conduct of competitors. However, the picture is clearly mistaken, at least for cases of ordinary trade mark infringement: a trade mark licence will authorise the licensee actually to use a mark in its original shape for the goods or services to which it relates, whereas the ordinary trade mark infringer uses a sign which, although being held capable of creating a likelihood of confusion, remains a different trade mark. The argument referred to above therefore is only valid when the infringer puts himself in the same situation as a licensee, *i.e.* when—like in typical counterfeiting cases-identical marks are used for identical products. It remains to be investigated whether similar considerations also apply to other areas of IP law.

Another aspect to be considered in forthcoming debates about the introduction of double licence fees or other kinds of enhanced sanctions for IP infringement is the following. Tightening the regime of remedies will typically entail a chilling effect in the sense that, in order to avoid liability, cautious actors will tend to respect a broader security margin in areas where an infringement appears at least possible. This means that a *de-facto* expansion of IP rights will occur in those areas where doubts exist as to their exact scope—the "grey zones". The significance of this effect increases in proportion to the difficulties that even experts may experience when trying to make a safe ex-ante assessment of whether a certain sign, invention, or other protected item, or a specific mode of use, may be found to infringe another person's IP right. It hardly needs to be emphasised here that in all fields of contemporary IP law, difficulties of this kind are frequent and can be quite conspicuous.

This aspect is neglected in an argumentation that solely refers to the need to ensure protection and prevent further infringement of IP rights. Hence, the legislature should be aware that, in order to reach a full and responsible decision on these matters, it must also be considered whether the side-effect of *de-facto* expansion of IP rights is acceptable or even desirable from a general point of view. If that should be denied, the introduction of qualified sanctions, if undertaken at all, should be confined to infringements that overstep a red line that is obvious to everyone, as in clear cases of counterfeiting and piracy, when the infringer's intention to use and violate another party's intellectual property right is established beyond doubt.

Computer Associates International, Inc.v. Altai, Inc.

United States Court of Appeals for the Second Circuit, 1997.
126 F.3d 365, 44 U.S.P.Q.2d 1281.

WALKER, CIRCUIT JUDGE:

Defendant-appellant, Altai, Inc. ("Altai"), appeals from the order of the United States District Court for the Eastern District of New York (Dennis R. Hurley, District Judge) denying its motion for an injunction against Computer Associates International, Inc. ("Computer Associates"). The issue on appeal is whether, under a theory of either claim or issue preclusion, a federal court should enjoin Computer Associates from pursuing an action claiming copyright infringement of a computer program in a French forum where Computer Associates has previously brought and lost a United States copyright infringement action based on the same computer program in federal court. Because we agree with the district court that res judicata and collateral estoppel are inapplicable under the circumstances of this case, we affirm.

I.   BACKGROUND

A.   The United States Action

In August of 1988, Computer Associates brought a copyright infringement and trade secrets misappropriation action in the Eastern District of New York against Altai, alleging that Altai had copied substantial portions of Computer Associates's ADAPTER computer program into Altai's OSCAR 3.4 and OSCAR 3.5 computer programs in violation of Computer Associates's United States copyright (the "United States action"). On August 9, 1991, following a trial, the district court found that Altai's OSCAR 3.4 computer program infringed Computer Associates's copyright, but held that OSCAR 3.5 was not substantially similar to the ADAPTER portion of Computer Associates's SCHEDULER program and therefore did not infringe Computer Associates copyright. Computer Assocs. Int'l, Inc. v. Altai, Inc., 775 F. Supp. 544, 560–62 (E.D.N.Y. 1991) ("Altai I"). The district court dismissed Computer Associates's trade secrets claim as preempted by the federal Copyright Act. Id. at 565.

On December 17, 1992, the Second Circuit affirmed the district court's findings and judgment with regards to Computer Associates's copyright claims, but vacated the district court's preemption holding. Computer Assocs. Int'l, Inc. v. Altai, Inc., 982 F.2d 693, 715, 720 (2d Cir. 1992) ("Altai II"). On remand, the district court held that the trade secret claim was barred under Texas's two-year statute of limitations. Computer Assocs. Int'l, Inc. v. Altai, Inc., 832 F. Supp. 50, 54 (E.D.N.Y. 1993) ("Altai III"). Computer Associates appealed and the Second Circuit certified the issue to the Texas Supreme Court. Computer Assocs. Int'l, Inc. v. Altai, Inc., 22 F.3d 32, 37 (2d Cir. 1994) ("Altai IV"). On July 17, 1995, following a decision by the Texas Supreme Court, the Second Circuit issued a mandate affirming the district court's decision dismissing Computer Associates's trade secret claim. Computer Assocs. Int'l, Inc. v. Altai, Inc., 61 F.3d 6, 8 (2d Cir. 1995) (per curiam) ("Altai V").

B.   The French Action

On January 23, 1990, Computer Associates and L'Agence pour la Protection des Programmes ("L'Agence") secured an ex parte order from the President of the Tribunal de Grande Instance in Bobigny, France, authorizing seizure of computer programs and business records from the offices of Altai's French distributor, la Societe FASTER, S.A.R.L. ("FASTER"), and enjoining FASTER from distributing or marketing its products. On February 2, 1990, a raid of FASTER's offices yielded five object code tapes of Altai software that contained OSCAR 3.5 code.

On February 15, 1990, one month before trial commenced in the United States, Computer Associates and L'Agence filed an action in the Tribunal de Commerce in Bobigny, France (the "Commercial Court"), against Altai and FASTER, charging violations of Computer Associates's French copyright (the "French action"). The French action centered on Computer Associates's allegations that Altai's importation and FASTER's distribution of OSCAR 3.5 in France violated Computer Associates's French copyright.

On October 1, 1991, Altai brought to the Commercial Court's attention the district court's holding in Altai I that its OSCAR 3.5 computer program did not violate Computer Associates's United States copyright and of the status of Computer Associates's appeal to the Second Circuit. Trial in the French action was postponed until September 10, 1992.

On September 16, 1992, Altai requested a stay of the French proceeding from the Tribunal de Grande Instance in Paris (the "Tribunal"), pending disposition of Altai's request for an exequatur, which would make the judgment in Altai I enforceable in France and allow Altai to introduce the judgment during the course of the French action in the Commercial Court. On October 22, 1992, the Commercial Court issued a stay. The exequatur was issued by the Tribunal in June 1993.

On May 14, 1994, Computer Associates moved to resume the French proceedings, and on November 25, 1994, trial in the Commercial Court began. On January 20, 1995, the Commercial Court found that Altai's OSCAR 3.5 program did not violate Computer Associates's rights under French copyright law. The Commercial Court specifically rejected Altai's argument that the United States decision in Altai I governed the disposition of the French action. The Commercial Court stated:

> The United States decision was made with reference to United States law which, even if it is close to French law with regard to the protection of literary and artistic works, cannot be completely and immediately identified with French law without an analysis of the facts under French law. Jurisprudence on the matter of software protection is in flux, as the United States decision shows, with each case having to be considered individually. . . .

On April 25, 1995, Computer Associates appealed the decision to the Paris Court of Appeals which scheduled briefing for May 13, 1998, and oral argument for June 18, 1998.

C.   Motion To Enjoin French Copyright Infringement Action

On November 16, 1994, Altai moved in the Eastern District of New York to enjoin Computer Associates from continuing to litigate the action in France. On February 22, 1995, in light of the January 20, 1995 decision of the Commercial Court in its favor, Altai voluntarily withdrew this motion.

On April 11, 1995, after learning of Computer Associates's plan to appeal the decision of the Commercial Court, Altai reactivated its motion to enjoin Computer Associates from continuing to proceed with its French action. On June 17, 1996, the district court denied Altai's motion to enjoin Computer Associates from pursuing its French action. Computer Associates, Inc. v. Altai, Inc., 950 F. Supp. 48, 54 (E.D.N.Y. 1996) ("Altai VI"). This appeal followed.

On appeal, Altai contends: (i) that Computer Associates's United States action for violation of its United States copyright precludes, under the doctrine of res judicata, its French action for violation of its French copyright; (ii) that, alternatively, Computer Associates is collaterally estopped from claiming that OSCAR 3.5 violates its French copyright because, in the United States action, judgment was rendered to the effect that OSCAR 3.5 does not violate Computer Associates's United States copyright; and (iii) finally, an antisuit injunction is appropriate, because comity concerns which caution against enjoining parties to a parallel foreign proceeding are inapplicable when, as here, judgment has already been rendered in the United States action. We address each contention in turn.

We review a district court's application of the principles of res judicata and collateral estoppel de novo, accepting all factual findings of the district court unless clearly erroneous.

A.   Res Judicata

Altai argues that the doctrine of res judicata bars Computer Associates from litigating its French action because Computer Associates could have raised its French copyright claims during the course of its United States action on its United States copyright claims. We disagree.

Under the doctrine of res judicata, a final judgment on the merits in an action "precludes the parties or their privies from relitigating issues that were or could have been raised in that action." Federated Dep't Stores, Inc. v. Moitie, 452 U.S. 394, 398, 69 L.Ed. 2d 103, 101 S.Ct. 2424 (1981).

Simply put, the doctrine of res judicata provides that when a final judgment has been entered on the merits of a case, it is a finality as to the claim or demand in controversy, concluding parties and those in privity with them, not only as to every matter which was offered and received to sustain or defeat the claim or demand, but as to any other admissible matter which might have been offered for that purpose.

Res judicata therefore bars the subsequent litigation of any claims arising from the transaction or series of transactions which was the subject of the prior suit.

The burden is on the party seeking to invoke res judicata to prove that the doctrine bars the second action. Without a demonstration that the conduct complained of in the French action occurred prior to the initiation of the United States action, res judicata is simply inapplicable. . . .

In this case, Altai has failed to meet its burden of showing that the conduct which forms the basis of the French action—the unauthorized importation into France of Computer Associates's copyrighted work, and the subsequent distribution of the work in that country—occurred prior to August 1988 when the action was filed in New York. Altai simply asserts that the actions giving rise to the French action "took place prior to February 15, 1990, the date [the French action] was filed" and that they "took place well before [Computer Associates's] United States claims went to trial on March 28, 1990." Absent evidence that the French action is based on conduct by Altai and by FASTER that occurred prior to August 1988, res judicata will not bar Computer Associates from pursuing its claims in France.

Altai argues that res judicata bars the French action nonetheless, because Computer Associates could have amended its complaint in the United States action to assert its French copyright claims of which it became aware prior to the beginning of trial in the United States. We disagree.

For the purposes of res judicata, "the scope of litigation is framed by the complaint at the time it is filed." Los Angeles Branch NAACP v. Los Angeles Unified Sch. Dist., 750 F.2d 731, 739 (9th Cir. 1984). The res judicata doctrine does not apply to new rights acquired during the action which might have been, but which were not, litigated. Although a plaintiff may seek leave to file a supplemental pleading to assert a new claim based on actionable conduct which the defendant engaged in after a lawsuit is commenced, he is not required to do so. Altai was under no obligation to amend its complaint in the United States action, and res judicata does not bar litigation of claims arising from transactions which occurred after the United States action was brought.

Even if we were to assume that the French suit arose from transactions identical to those in the United States suit, there is a second reason why Altai may not invoke res judicata to bar the French action: the New York federal district court in the United States action could not have exercised personal jurisdiction over FASTER, a principal party to the French suit. Res judicata will not apply where " 'the initial forum did not have the power to award the full measure of relief sought in the later litigation.' " Burgos v. Hopkins, 14 F.3d 787, 790 (2d Cir. 1994) (quoting Davidson v. Capuano, 792 F.2d 275, 278 (2d Cir. 1986)). Even where a second action arises from some of the same factual circumstances that gave rise to a prior action, res judicata is inapplicable if formal jurisdictional or statutory barriers precluded the plaintiff from asserting its claims in the first action. Such a "formal barrier," the absence of personal jurisdiction over FASTER, precludes application of res judicata here. . . .

Altai has failed to show that the New York federal court adjudicating Computer Associates's United States copyright claims would have had jurisdiction over FASTER under New York's long arm statute, N.Y. C.P.L.R. § 302(a). That statute limits the jurisdiction of New York courts over non-domiciliaries to those that "transact[ ] any business" within New York, or "regularly do[ ] or solicit[ ] business, or engage[ ] in any other persistent course of conduct, or derive[ ] substantial revenue in the state." Id. There is no evidence in the record that FASTER either transacts business within New York or derives substantial revenue from the state.

Even if personal jurisdiction were allowed by New York's long arm statute, the Due Process Clause limits the exercise of personal jurisdiction to persons having certain "minimum contacts" with the forum state. A court may exercise personal jurisdiction only over a defendant whose " 'conduct and connection with the forum State are such that he should reasonably anticipate being haled into court there.' " Burger King Corp. v. Rudzewicz, 471 U.S. 462, 474, 85 L.Ed. 2d 528, 105 S.Ct. 2174 (1985) (quoting World-Wide Volkswagen Corp. v. Woodson, 444 U.S. 286, 297, 62 L.Ed. 2d 490, 100 S.Ct. 559 (1980)). Essential to the exercise of personal jurisdiction in each case is " 'some act by which the defendant purposely avails itself of the privilege of conducting activities within the forum State, thus invoking the benefits and protections of its laws.' " Burger King Corp., 471 U.S. at 475 (quoting Hanson v. Denckla, 357 U.S. 235, 253, 2 L.Ed. 2d 1283, 78 S.Ct. 1228 (1958)). In this case, Altai has failed to show that FASTER, a French company that distributed software in France, had any contacts with New York, much less "minimum" ones, sufficient to justify the exercise of personal jurisdiction.

On appeal, Altai claims that the essential minimum contacts with the Eastern District of New York exist by virtue of FASTER's 1988 distribution agreement with Altai wherein FASTER agreed to arbitration in Texas. From the record, we have no indication that this argument was raised in the district court; for that reason, we normally would disregard it on appeal. In any event, whether or not this agreement standing alone would provide the necessary minimum contacts with Texas, it is immaterial to the question of whether personal jurisdiction would be proper in New York.

In conclusion, there are two reasons why res judicata does not prevent Computer Associates from maintaining its action based on French copyright claims in France: (i) the infringing conduct which formed the basis of the French action occurred after the filing of the United States action; and (ii) the New York federal district court lacked personal jurisdiction over FASTER. We therefore affirm the district court.

B.   Collateral Estoppel

Altai argues, in the alternative, that Computer Associates is collaterally estopped from claiming that OSCAR 3.5 infringes its French copyright. We disagree.

The doctrine of collateral estoppel "bars a party from relitigating in a second proceeding an issue of fact or law that was litigated and actually decided in a prior proceeding, if that party had a full and fair opportunity to litigate the issue in the prior proceeding and the decision of the issue was necessary to support a valid and final judgment on the merits." Metromedia v. Fugazy, 983 F.2d 350 (2d Cir. 1992). For collateral estoppel to apply, the issues in each action must be identical, and issues are not identical when the legal standards governing their resolution are significantly different.

On appeal, Altai asserts that the French standard for copyrightability of computer programs is not "significantly different" from the standard applied in the United States because, as under United States copyright law, French law protects expression and not ideas. Such a superficial comparison begs key questions: What constitutes expression or ideas in the context of computer software, to what extent may expression be copied with impunity when it is necessary to the communication of the idea, how much expression is not original with the plaintiff or is in the public domain? Altai's argument is far from sufficient to show that the two copyright standards in France and the United States are "identical" as required for application of collateral estoppel. The Commercial Court arrived at a similar conclusion, refusing Altai's request to give the decision in the United States action dispositive effect. We, therefore, affirm the district court's decision that collateral estoppel does not bar litigation of the French action.

C.   Foreign Antisuit Injunction

It is well established that a federal court has the power to enjoin a foreign suit by persons subject to its jurisdiction; however, due regard for principles of international comity require that this power should be "used sparingly." China Trade & Dev. Corp. v. M.V. Choong Yong, 837 F.2d 33, 36 (2d Cir. 1987). Antisuit injunctions should be "granted only with care and great restraint." China Trade, 837 F.2d at 36. Ordinarily when the courts of two sovereigns have in personam jurisdiction, one court will not try to restrain proceedings before the other.

In determining whether to enjoin foreign litigation, a court must consider, as a threshold matter, whether (i) the parties to both suits are the same and (ii) resolution of the case before the enjoining court would be dispositive of the action to be enjoined.

Altai argues that the China Trade factors are inapplicable where a final judgment has been reached in the United States forum. We need not decide whether the China Trade factors are inapplicable when a final judgment issues in a United States action because we hold that, in this case, the injunction is not necessary to protect our jurisdiction or the integrity of our judgment. While Altai may experience as vexatious Computer Associates' decision to pursue its rights in France, the French action would in no way affect the decision rendered by a court of the United States. In short, the action in this country involved violations of Computer Associates's United States copyright, and the French action involves violations of Computer Associates's French copyright. We can discern no basis for enjoining Computer Associates from pursuing its French action; moreover, the interests of comity caution against such an injunction.

III. CONCLUSION

Based on the foregoing, we affirm the decision of the district court denying Altai's motion to enjoin Computer Associates from continuing to litigate its French copyright infringement action against Altai and FASTER in France, based on actions that occurred in France.

PROBLEM 5

FoodCable ultimately acquired from Ann Autry *all* of her rights in *all* countries of the world—and not just U.S. television rights—in *One-Hour Gourmet*, considered in Problem 4 at page 250. Since acquiring these rights, the following activities have come to FoodCable's attention:

Acme Accessories, with headquarters in Country *A*, has without FoodCable's permission printed 50,000 copies of 25 of the recipes collected in *One-Hour Gourmet* for distribution to kitchen supply stores in Country *A*. Country *A*'s copyright act expressly excludes protection for recipes and collections of recipes.

Under its "Public Lending Scheme," Country *B* pays reference book publishers 1% of a book's retail price each time their reference books are borrowed from a public library in Country *B*. Although the system counts recipe books as reference books, and although *One-Hour Gourmet* has been borrowed well in excess of the required minimum of 1,000 times, FoodCable has been denied compensation on the ground that the Public Lending Scheme compensates only nationals or domiciliaries of Country *B*.

Cathy Clark has, without FoodCable's permission, made 10 videotape copies of the first three programs in FoodCable's *One-Hour Gourmet* television series for distribution to members of a cooking group to which she belongs in Country *C*. She claims that this use comes under the "fair dealing" exception of Country *C's* copyright law. Research into case law in Country *C* reveals decisions of Country *C's* highest court that excuse comparable unauthorized copying under the fair dealing provision.

Please advise FoodCable of the rights and remedies that might be available to it in connection with the described activities in Countries *A*, *B* and *C*. Countries *A*, *B*, and *C* have all adhered to the Berne Convention (1971) and they treat the Berne Convention as self-executing.

b.   NEIGHBORING RIGHTS

Paul Goldstein, Copyright's Highway: From Gutenberg to the Celestial Jukebox*

155–159 (rev. ed. 2003).

Attacks on a treaty's minimum requirements are rarely as direct as the aborted Stockholm Protocol. The more subtle temptation to cheat emerges when a new kind of product, or a new technological use of a copyrighted work, creates the opportunity to have the best of both worlds: to collect royalties on the domestic use of both foreign and domestic products, but pay royalties only to one's own nationals. Starting in the mid-1960s, new technologies provided just such an opportunity—tape recording of cassettes on home audio equipment—and statutory systems for collecting royalties on homemade tapes provided the means. But this time it was not the United States, or traditional pirate countries or the developing countries of the Third World, that seized the opportunity. The new chiselers were the old European stalwarts of the Berne Union, who shrewdly manipulated the slogan of author's rights to achieve protectionist ends.

In the spring of 1993, Mihály Ficsor, director of the World Intellectual Property Organization's Copyright Department, went to Washington to testify before the House Intellectual Property Subcommittee about the vexed issue of national treatment. "Since 1971," he began, "no revision of the Berne Convention has taken place, although during the more than two decades since then, perhaps more important developments have taken place in the creation, dissemination and conditions of protection of works than between the adoption of the Convention and its last revision in 1971." He had in mind the digital and other technologies that were rapidly bringing copyrighted works into homes across the world. And by "conditions of protection," Ficsor evidently meant that substantial revenues from new home-taping charges were already being diverted away from the authors and owners of the copyrighted works and into the pockets of individuals and companies in the countries where the works were being copied.

Another witness at the hearings, Robert Hadl, vice president and general counsel of the entertainment conglomerate MCA, put it differently. "Economic protectionism is rearing its ugly head" he said, "in some countries where imports of copyrighted works are far exceeding exports. This new wave of protectionism has resulted in an abandonment of national treatment in those countries where payments to U.S. nationals, under newly created rights, would exceed payments to their own nationals. States have adopted reciprocity, new concepts of formalities such as 'first fixation' distinctions based on neighboring rights

---

versus copyright, cultural fund deductions, and 'quotas,' all designed to restrict payments to U.S. nationals."

Part of the problem was that while Berne and the Universal Copyright Convention require national treatment for author's rights and copyright, lawyers can—and do—disagree on whether a given right in fact is an author's right or copyright. Several European countries have a public lending right—Denmark adopted the first in 1946—to compensate writers for the potential income they lose when library patrons borrow rather than purchase their books. Is this public lending right part of the author's rights guaranteed by Berne? (Only Germany has concluded that it is.) If so, all nationals of Berne member states, wherever they reside, are entitled to share in public lending revenues. Or are the public lending fees merely a form of government subsidy to local authors? (Among other nations, the United Kingdom—which adopted such a right in 1979 after a long and bitter fight between authors and librarians—thinks they are.) If so, no obligation exists to share the proceeds with foreigners.

Rights that fall outside the definition of author's right or copyright are not the only sources of value that escape the national treatment requirement. The Berne Convention requires its members to protect only "works" and "authors." If, for some reason, a given product does not qualify as a "work" or if its creator does not qualify as an "author," it, too, may escape national treatment. Is a singer or musician an "author"? Is a recording of a performance a "work"? The United States Copyright Act says they are; continental author's right doctrine says they are not. The result of these discrepant characterizations is a lopsided allocation of international copyright revenues, with Country A getting protection for its nationals' goods in Country B, while Country B's nationals get no protection for the very same goods in Country A.

The difference in national approaches to products such as sound recordings stems from an important, residual difference between the two cultures of copyright. The essentially utilitarian American culture asks not whether there is an author or a work, but only whether copyright is needed to ensure the production and dissemination of information and entertainment products. United States copyright law thus tends to bring all literary and artistic creations, including sound recordings, within the scope of copyright; the principle of national treatment consequently makes the United States protect foreign sound recordings under copyright even though the nation where the recording was made—France, for example—may not extend copyright to sound recordings and thus is not obligated to protect them when they come from the United States.

The rejection of protection for products like sound recordings in nations that adhere to the doctrine of author's rights did not begin as a brazen strategy to avoid payments to foreign nationals. Rather, it emerged out of two principles of the author's rights doctrine: only flesh-and-blood authors, not corporate entities such as motion picture studios or record companies, qualify for copyright protection; and if a work is to get this protection, it must be truly creative, revealing the "impress of the author's personality." Although sound recordings or television or radio broadcasts might lack the creative personal element required for the invocation of author's rights, these nations still had an interest in nurturing their domestic recording and broadcast industries and wanted to give them some form of intellectual property protection. The answer was a new system of intellectual property, "neighboring rights" so called because these diluted, low-rise rights merely border on the cathedral of author's rights.

The evolution of the idea of neighboring rights—from being a doctrine intended to fill a gap left by the rigorous author's rights theory to being a protectionist canard—was gradual. It began with photography, the first technology to challenge the author's rights culture. Europeans ultimately finessed the question of whether these technically created images were "works" by simply calling the photographer an author and finding the impress of his personality in the photographic image. Motion pictures proved only slightly harder to bring within author's rights. Sound recordings finally pressed European lawmakers to the verge. Performers and studio musicians might in a pinch be called authors. But what of record producers and recording technicians? Live radio and television broadcasts, although they called for creativity in editing and production, also appeared to dwell outside the cathedral of author's rights. The solution was to declare that rights in sound recordings and broadcasts were not author's rights at all, but neighboring rights.

Once a nation characterizes a right in some product as a neighboring right, it is free to treat it as it wishes, with no obligations under either the Berne Convention or the Universal Copyright Convention. If, for example, a country requires a royalty to be paid on audio copying equipment and blank tapes, it can distribute the sound recording royalty revenues exclusively to its own nationals, even if most of the copies were of foreign recordings. It can also dip into the pot for its own ends—to subsidize its own authors and artists, for example. It will be constrained only by its sense of good domestic policy, by treaty restrictions other than those of Berne or the UCC, and by considerations of international comity. The Rome Convention for the Protection of Performers, Producers of Phonograms and Broadcasting Organizations (which the United States has not joined) is one source of international obligations.

France's 1985 home-taping law, which imposes a statutory royalty on the sale of blank audiotapes and videotapes, is a good example of how a nation can use the idea of neighboring rights to promote its domestic economy at the expense of foreign creators. The French law first deducts twenty-five percent of the royalties from the home-taping pool for French social and cultural purposes. (These might include subsidies to French filmmakers.) It then divides what is left in three, one-third each to the composer of the musical composition, the performers, and the producer.

Because musical compositions are Berne "works," American composers, as their "authors," are entitled under the Berne Convention to share in the third allocated to composers. But, since neither performers nor producers are "authors" and since the United States is not a party to the Rome Convention, Americans have no claim to the performers' or producers' thirds, which in France are the subject only of neighboring rights.

France's private copy law offers one narrow alternative to American performers and producers: they can share in the tape revenues if their sound recording or film was first "fixed"—*i.e.*, recorded—in France. The French domestic fixation requirement for films and records is the Gallic twin of the old American manufacturing clause in the copyright law. It is a blatantly protectionist measure aimed at supporting the local record and motion picture industry; like the American manufacturing requirement, it is so onerous that it is unlikely to attract many takers. A fixation requirement is, of course, a formality that Berne would not tolerate—except that, since it applies to a neighboring right, not an author's, right, Berne prohibitions do not apply.

From the American perspective—copyright pirate turned prince—the drama of international copyright protection is poignant, indeed. After a century with no foreign copyright relations, the United States grudgingly opened its doors to bilateral arrangements, but on onerous terms. Sixty years later, an accelerating, positive balance of copyright trade pushed it in the direction of Berne, while its formality-ridden copyright statute held it back. No sooner did the United States succeed in promoting the low-level Universal Copyright Convention than the Third World countries threatened to defect. And when, in 1989, the United States finally entered the Berne Union, it was only to discover some of Berne's oldest members assiduously sweeping the choicest morsels off the table.

Paul Goldstein & Bernt Hugenholtz, International Copyright: Principles, Law, and Practice*

§ 9.2 (4th ed. 2019).

As a rule, countries belonging to the common law tradition assimilate the rights granted to performers, phonogram producers, and broadcasters to the rights they grant to authors of literary and artistic works, while civil law countries protect these rights under the separate rubric of neighboring rights (*Leistungsschutzrechte* in German, *droits voisins* in French). Rights under both systems are, however, closely comparable. One reason is that copyright legislation in common law countries sometimes imposes limitations on these rights that it does not impose on traditional literary and artistic works. The U.S. Copyright Act withholds the public performance right from sound recordings except for rights in specified digital performances. At the same time, the civil law countries, particularly as spurred by E.C. Directives, have increased the protection that they grant to neighboring rights to a point at which these rights often approach author's rights in rigor and effect.

The principal treaties that govern one or more of the neighboring rights in performances, phonograms, and broadcasts are the International Convention for the Protection of Performers, Producers of Phonograms and Broadcasting Organizations, commonly called the Rome Convention, Article 14 of the TRIPs Agreement** and the WIPO Performances and Phonograms Treaty (WPPT). Most civil law countries—and all Member States of the European Union—are parties to these treaties and often offer protection at standards well exceeding the Rome, TRIPs, and WPPT minima. The United States has adhered to the WTO TRIPs Agreement and the WPPT, but not to the Rome Convention.

In the European Union, the 1992 Directive on Rental Right and Lending Right and on Certain Rights Related to Copyright in the Field of Intellectual Property harmonized the economic rights prescribed by the Rome Convention. The Directive protects not only the three traditional "Rome" categories (performing artists, phonogram producers, and broadcasting organizations) but adds film producers as a fourth category. Rights granted by the Directive generally follow the structure of the Rome Convention but tend to be more extensive, including, for example, a distribution right.

The E.C. Copyright in the Information Society Directive of 2001, implementing the European Union's obligations under the WIPO Treaties, consolidates and extends existing economic rights, such as the right of reproduction, and also introduces new rights, such as the right of making available online.

§ 9.2.1   Rights of Performers

National legislation on performers' rights stems from various legal sources. Besides laws on neighboring rights, protection may derive from rules on unfair competition and unjust enrichment, criminal sanctions, and—in the common law countries—from copyright. The governing treaties—the Rome Convention, the TRIPs Agreement, and the WIPO Performances and Phonograms Treaty—accommodate this variety by formulating the scope of guaranteed rights in the most general terms.

** The minimum standards of protection for performers, producers of phonograms and broadcasting organizations established by Article 14 of the TRIPs Agreement borrow heavily from the Rome Convention. Nonetheless, Article 3 of the TRIPs Agreement, providing that "in respect of performers, producers of phonograms and broadcasting organizations," the Agreement's national treatment obligation "only applies in respect of the rights provided under this Agreement," effectively excuses Rome Convention countries from giving Rome-level neighboring rights protection to nationals of non-Rome countries. *Ed.*

At the heart of the Rome Convention's promise to performers is that they will have the right to extract revenues from their work's first exploitation in any technological medium. Specifically, Article 7(1) obligates signatory countries to grant performers the "possibility of preventing" three discrete technological means of exploitation: *"(a)* the broadcasting and the communication to the public, without their consent, of their performance, except where the performance used in the broadcasting or the public communication is itself already a broadcast performance or is made from a fixation"; *"(b)* the fixation, without their consent, of their unfixed performance"; and *"(c)* the reproduction, without their consent, of a fixation of their performance: (i) if the original fixation itself was made without their consent; (ii) if the reproduction is made for purposes different from those for which the performers gave their consent; (iii) if the original fixation was made in accordance with the provisions of Article 15, and the reproduction is made for purposes different from those referred to in those provisions."

Like the Rome Convention, the 1996 WIPO Performances and Phonograms Treaty obligates member countries to protect performers against the unauthorized fixation, broadcast, or communication of their performances. However, the WIPO Performances and Phonograms Treaty extends the Rome formula to encompass new technological means of exploitation by adding new definitions of "broadcasting," "communication," and "fixation." Political rather than technological factors doubtless explain the decision to confine performers' fixation rights to audio fixation, leaving the question of audiovisual fixation to another day.

Article 6 of the Performances and Phonograms Treaty assures performers two exclusive rights in their unfixed performances: "(i) the broadcasting and communication to the public of their unfixed performances except where the performance is already a broadcast performance; and (ii) the fixation of their unfixed performances." Once a performance is fixed in a phonogram, performers are to have the exclusive right to authorize its "direct or indirect" reproduction "in any manner or form";[1] "the making available to the public of the original and copies" through "sale or other transfer of ownership"[2]; "the commercial rental to the public of the original and copies of their performances fixed in phonograms as determined in the national law of Contracting Parties, even after distribution of them by, or pursuant to, authorization by the performer";[3] and "the exclusive right of authorizing the making available to the public of their performances fixed in phonograms, by wire or wireless means, in such a way that members of the public may access them from a place and at a time individually chosen by them."[4]

---

[1]   WIPO Performances and Phonograms Treaty Art. 7.
[2]   WIPO Performances and Phonograms Treaty Art. 8(1).
[3]   WIPO Performances and Phonograms Treaty Art. 9(1).
[4]   WIPO Performances and Phonograms Treaty Art. 10.

Within the European Union, the E.C. Rental Right Directive obligates member states to grant performers the exclusive right to authorize or prohibit rental or lending of fixations of their performances.[5] This right may be freely transferred by the performer,[6] but the Directive provides that, where the performer has transferred the rental right to a phonogram or film producer, the performer retains, and cannot waive, the right to obtain an equitable remuneration for the rental.[7] The Directive also requires performers to receive the exclusive rights to authorize or prohibit the fixation of their performances;[8] to authorize or prohibit broadcast and communication of their performances to the public, "except where the performance is itself already a broadcast performance or is made from a fixation";[9] and to distribute fixations of their performances to the public.[10] The right to authorize or prohibit the direct or indirect reproduction of fixations of their performances that was initially required by the 1992 version of the Directive, has been consolidated in the E.C. Copyright in the Information Society Directive, which applies both to copyright owners and owners of neighboring rights. The latter Directive has increased the level of protection offered to performers in the E.U. by extending the reproduction right to include temporary digital copies and by adding a right of making available online.[11]

Before the Performances and Phonograms Treaty, some, but far from all, countries granted moral rights to performers. The French Intellectual Property Code, for example, provided that "[a] performer shall have the right to respect for his name, his capacity and his performance."[12] The German Copyright Act provided, "A performer shall have the right to prohibit any distortion or other alteration of his performance of such nature as to jeopardize his standing or reputation as a performer."[13] The Performances and Phonograms Treaty now makes moral rights protection mandatory on adherents.[14]

§ 9.2.2   Rights of Phonogram Producers

Both the Rome Convention and the Geneva Phonograms Convention protect record producers against the unauthorized reproduction of their phonograms—"direct" or "indirect reproduction" in the case of the Rome Convention,[15] and "making of duplicates" in the case of the Phonograms

---

[5]   E.C. Rental Right Directive Art. 3(1)(b).
[6]   E.C. Rental Right Directive Art. 3(3).
[7]   E.C. Rental Right Directive Art. 5(1),(2).
[8]   E.C. Rental Right Directive Art. 7(1).
[9]   E.C. Rental Right Directive Art. 8(1).
[10] E.C. Rental Right Directive Art. 9(1)(a).
[11] E.C. Copyright in the Information Society Directive, Arts. 2(b) and 3(2).
[12] France, Intellectual Property Code Art. L. 212–2.
[13] Germany, Copyright Act Art 83.
[14] WIPO Performances and Phonograms Treaty Art. 5.
[15] Rome Convention, Art. 10. See also TRIPs Agreement Art. 14(2).

Convention."[16] Unlike the Rome Convention, the Phonograms Convention provides for a public distribution right.[17] Unlike the Phonograms Convention, the Rome Convention provides for a performance right: "If a phonogram published for commercial purposes, or a reproduction of such phonogram, is used directly for broadcasting or for any communication to the public, a single equitable remuneration shall be paid by the user to the performers, or to the producers of the phonograms, or to both."[18]

The WIPO Performances and Phonograms Treaty extends the rights of phonogram producers to new technological uses, much as it does with the rights of performers.[19] Like the Rome Convention and the TRIPs Agreement, the Performances and Phonograms Treaty provides that phonogram producers "shall enjoy the exclusive right of authorizing the direct or indirect reproduction of their phonograms, in any manner or form."[20] Like the Phonograms Convention, the Performances, and Phonograms Treaty establishes a commercial rental right[21] and, though in far less cumbered terms, a distribution right.[22] Finally, as with performers, the Performances and Phonograms Treaty promises phonogram producers "the exclusive right of authorizing the making available to the public of their phonograms, by wire or wireless means, in such a way that members of the public may access them from a place and at a time individually chosen by them.[23] The E.C. Directive on Rental Rights and Related Rights requires member states to give phonogram producers an exclusive rental and lending right with respect to their phonograms[24] and an exclusive right to distribute their phonograms to the public.[25] As with performers, the E.C. Copyright in the Information Society Directive consolidates and extends the reproduction right of phonogram producers to include temporary digital copies and also introduces a right of making available online.[26]

§ 9.2.3 Rights of Broadcasting Organizations

Article 13 of the Rome Convention and Article 14(3) of the TRIPs Agreement prescribe, in roughly comparable terms, the minimum rights that member countries must give to broadcasting organizations in connection with their broadcasts. The TRIPs Agreement states the pivotal requirements in broader terms than does the Rome Convention, giving broadcasters "the right to prohibit the following acts when

---

[16]   Geneva Phonograms Convention Art. 2.

[17]   Geneva Phonograms Convention Art. 2. Compare TRIPs Agreement Art. 14(4).

[18]   Rome Convention Art. 12.

[19]   *See* Section 9.2.1, above.

[20]   WIPO Performances and Phonograms Treaty Art. 11.

[21]   WIPO Performances and Phonograms Treaty Art. 13.

[22]   WIPO Performances and Phonograms Treaty Art. 12.

[23]   WIPO Performances and Phonograms Treaty Art. 14.

[24]   E.C. Rental Rights Directive Art. 3(1)(c).

[25]   E.C. Rental Rights Directive Art. 9(1)(b).

[26]   E.C. Copyright in the Information Society Directive Arts. 2(c) and 3(2).

undertaken without their authorization: the fixation, the reproduction of fixations, and the rebroadcasting by wireless means of broadcasts, as well as the communication to the public of television broadcasts of the same."[27] The E.C. Rental and Related Rights Directive requires member states to grant broadcasting organizations the exclusive right to fix their broadcasts, "whether these broadcasts are transmitted by wire or over the air, including by cable or satellite."[28] The Directive also requires the grant of public rebroadcast and communication rights[29] and public distribution rights[30] to broadcasters. As with performers and phonogram producers, the E.C. Copyright in the Information Society Directive consolidates and extends the reproduction right of broadcasting organizations to include temporary digital copies and also introduces a right of making available online.[31]

§ 9.2.4   Other Neighboring Rights

Outside the neighboring rights of performers, phonogram producers, and broadcasters is a potpourri of rights that neighbor on copyright and author's right. The European continent offers the greatest profusion of such rights, in part because the European Union's harmonizing efforts have generally brought protection to the highest level reached in one or more states, rather than to the lowest common denominator. For example, drawing in part on earlier French and German practice, the E.C. Rental and Related Rights Directive and E.C. Copyright in the Information Society Directive jointly grant film producers the exclusive rights to rent and lend copies of their films,[32] to reproduce the films directly or indirectly,[33] and to distribute copies of the films to the public.[34] Article 4 of the E.C. Term Directive provides that anyone who, following the expiration of copyright in unpublished works such as private letters, publishes "or lawfully communicates [them] to the public" for the first time shall enjoy protection equivalent to author's economic rights, subject however to a shortened term, 25 years from publication. British law grants publishers copyright in the typographical arrangement of published editions principally as a means for protecting their investment in producing editions of public domain works.[35] The German Act grants rights comparable to copyright to authors who produce materially new editions of public domain works[36] and to publishers who publish previously unpublished works in which the copyright has expired.[37]

---

[27]   TRIPs Agreement Art. 14(3).

[28]   E.C. Rental Right Directive Art. 7(2).

[29]   E.C. Rental Right Directive Art. 8(3).

[30]   E.C. Rental Right Directive Art. 9(1)(d).

[31]   E.C. Copyright in the Information Society Directive Arts. 2(e) and 3(2).

[32]   E.C. Rental Right Directive Art. 3(1)(d).

[33]   E.C. Copyright in the Information Society Directive Art. 2(d).

[34]   E.C. Rental Right Directive Art. 9(1)(c).

[35]   United Kingdom, Copyright, Designs and Patents Act 1988 § 1(1)(c).

[36]   Germany, Copyright Act Art. 70.

[37]   Germany, Copyright Act Art. 71.

NOTE

Article 19 of the Rome Convention withholds Article 7's minimum rights for performers "once a performer has consented to the incorporation of his performance in a visual or audio-visual fixation." A half-century later, performers obtained minimum treaty standards for their contributions to audiovisual works with the June 24, 2012 adoption by the WIPO Beijing Diplomatic Conference of the Beijing Treaty on Audiovisual Performances. The terms of the Beijing Treaty closely parallel those of the WIPO Performances and Phonograms Treaty. Indeed, most of the countries that negotiated the 1996 WIPO Performances and Phonograms Treaty had been inclined at the time to include audiovisual performances within the 1996's treaty's scope, but stumbled on the issue of transferability of rights. As promulgated, the Beijing Treaty provides in Article 12 that "[a] contracting party may provide in its national law that once a performer has consented to fixation of his or her performance in an audiovisual fixation, the exclusive rights . . . [granted by the Treaty] shall be owned or exercised by or transferred to the producer . . . subject to any contract to the contrary between the performer and the producer. . . as determined by the national law."

On the Beijing Treaty, see Silke von Lewinski, The Beijing Treaty on Audiovisual Performances, 6 Auteurs & Media 539 (2012).

6. MORAL RIGHTS

John Henry Merryman, The Refrigerator of Bernard Buffet*

27 Hastings Law Journal 1023–1028 (1976).

The French artist Bernard Buffet was invited to decorate a refrigerator to be auctioned in Paris for the benefit of charity. He did so by painting a composition consisting of six panels: three on the front, one on the top, and one on each side of the refrigerator. He considered the six panels parts of one painting and signed only one of them. The refrigerator was duly auctioned along with nine others, decorated by nine other artists, at the Galerie Charpentier. Six months later the catalog for another auction included a "Still Life With Fruits" by Bernard Buffet, illustrated and described as a painting on metal. Inspection showed that the painting was one of the panels decorating the front of the refrigerator. The artist brought an action against the owner-consignor to prevent the separate sale of the panel, and the court so ordered.[1]

Guille, a painter, agreed to deliver to Colmant, a dealer, his entire future production for a period of ten years, at a rate of at least twenty

---

*   © 1976 by University of California, Hastings College of the Law. Reprinted by permission.

[1]   The judgment of the Tribunal de la grande instance de la Seine of June 7, 1960 is contained in the report of the appellate court decision. Buffet v. Fersing, [1962] Recueil Dalloz [D. Jur.] 570, 571 (cour d'appel, Paris).

paintings a month. The contract provided that the works furnished the dealer would be signed with a pseudonym and that the painter would not sign the earlier works still in his possession. There was no evidence that the artist entered the agreement under duress or that he lacked capacity to contract. A dispute eventually arose, and the dealer sued the artist for breach of contract. The court of appeals held the dealer could not prohibit the artist from using his real name in connection with works he created, despite the terms of the contract.[2]

In 1893 Lord Eden commissioned the American artist James McNeill Whistler, then living in Paris, to paint Lady Eden's portrait. Through intermediaries they agreed on a price "between" 100 and 150 guineas. Whistler eventually completed the portrait, which he exhibited (with Eden's approval) at the Salon du Champs de Mars with the title: *Brown and Gold, Portrait of Lady E.* . . . Meanwhile Lord Eden had sent Whistler a check for 100 guineas, which Whistler took as an insult (although he cashed it). On the return of the painting to his studio after the exhibition, Whistler painted out Lady Eden's head, painted in another, and refused to deliver the painting to Lord Eden, who sued to require restoration of the portrait, delivery, and damages. The trial court held for Eden on all counts,[3] but in the court of appeal that part of judgment ordering restoration and delivery was reversed. Lord Eden was entitled to restitution of the 100 guineas he had paid and damages for breach of contract, but he could not compel restoration of the portrait or its delivery. The Cour de Cassation agreed.[4]

These three decisions illustrate three principal components of "the moral right of the artist," a right that has had its major development in France but that is a part of the law of most European and some Latin American nations. The moral right of the artist is usually classified in civil law doctrine as a right of *personality,* and in particular is distinguished from patrimonial or property rights. Copyright, for example, which is available to artists in civil law countries as well as in the United States and other common law countries, is a patrimonial or property right which protects the artists pecuniary interest in the work of art. The moral right, on the contrary, is one of a small group of rights intended to recognize and protect the individual's personality. Rights of personality include the rights to one's identity, to a name, to one's reputation, one's occupation or profession, to the integrity of one's person, and to privacy.

It is interesting to note that the moral right of the artist in French law is entirely judicial in origin. This is in itself remarkable, since one of the most treasured tenets of the conventional wisdom about the civil law

---

[2]   *See* Guille v. Colmant, [1967] Recueil Dalloz-Sirey [D.S. Jur.] 284, [1967] Gazette du Palais [Gaz. Pal.] I. 17 (Cour d'appel, Paris).

[3]   The judgment of the Tribunal de la Seine of March 20, 1895 is set out in the judgment of the court of appeals. *See* Whistler v. Eden, [1898] Recueil Periodique et Critique [D.P.] II. 465 (Cour d'appel, Paris).

[4]   Eden v. Whistler, [1900] [D.P.] I. 497, [1900] Recueil Sirey [S. Jur.] I. 490 (Cass. civ.).

is that law is made by legislators and executives, not by judges. The development of the moral right of the artist is merely another example of the extent to which this tattered brocard is inapplicable to France. Although judicial in origin, the moral right of the artist has been put into statutory form in France and in many other civil law nations, and is regularly included in international conventions on the topic of copyright and related rights of authors and artists. Like other statutory rights, it continues to grow and develop through judicial interpretation and application, and it is probably accurate to say that the moral right of the artist, still comparatively young even in the nation of its origin, has not reached anything like its full development.

The moral right of the artist is actually a composite right. The *Buffet* case involved one of the components: the right of integrity (of the work of art), also sometimes called the right to respect of the work. The notion is that the work of art is an expression of the artist's personality. Distortion, dismemberment or misrepresentation of the work mistreats an expression of the artist's personality, affects his artistic identity, personality, and honor, and thus impairs a legally protected personality interest. To treat one of the six panels of the refrigerator painting as a separate work distorted and misrepresented the artist's intention. The owner of the refrigerator could keep and enjoy it. He could dispose of the entire painting. He was not permitted to take it apart and dispose of it piece by piece.

The *Guille* case involved a second component of the moral right, the right of paternity. This is the right of the artist to insist that his work be associated with his name. In France and in some other nations the artist cannot waive this right, so that, as in the *Guille* case, the artist can insist that his paintings be attributed to him even though he has contracted to the contrary. The artist can also insist that his name not be associated with works that are not his creation.

The *Whistler* case is an example of the artist's right to withhold the work, sometimes referred to as the right of divulgation. This component of the moral right gives the artist the absolute right to decide when (and whether) a work of art is complete, and when (and whether) to show it to the public. Even though knowledgeable third persons might conclude that a work of art is for all practical purposes complete and even if their judgment is supported by the artist's conduct with respect to the work, the artist still can insist that the work not be shown or treated as complete.

In addition to these three components (the right of integrity, right of paternity, and the right of divulgation) French commentators usually mention other interests commonly treated as aspects of the more general moral right. Of these the "right to repent or to retake" is the most important and consists of the right of the artist to withdraw the work from its owner on payment of an indemnity. Related to this right, and sometimes treated as an aspect of it, is the "right of modification." These rights are usually considered primarily applicable to literary works, although their potential utility in connection with works of visual art is apparent.

Gilliam v. American Broadcasting Companies, Inc.

United States Court of Appeals for the Second Circuit, 1976.
538 F.2d 14, 192 U.S.P.Q. 1.

LUMBARD, CIRCUIT JUDGE:

Plaintiffs, a group of British writers and performers known as "Monty Python," appeal from a denial by Judge Lasker in the Southern District of a preliminary injunction to restrain the American Broadcasting Company (ABC) from broadcasting edited versions of three separate programs originally written and performed by Monty Python for broadcast by the British Broadcasting Corporation (BBC). We agree with Judge Lasker that the appellants have demonstrated that the excising done for ABC impairs the integrity of the original work. We further find that the countervailing injuries that Judge Lasker found might have accrued to ABC as a result of an injunction at a prior date no longer exist. We therefore direct the issuance of a preliminary injunction by the district court.

Since its formation in 1969, the Monty Python group has gained popularity primarily through its thirty-minute television programs created for BBC as part of a comedy series entitled "Monty Python's Flying Circus." In accordance with an agreement between Monty Python and BBC, the group writes and delivers to BBC scripts for use in the television series. This scriptwriters' agreement recites in great detail the procedure to be followed when any alterations are to be made in the script prior to recording of the program. The essence of this section of the agreement is that, while BBC retains final authority to make changes, appellants or their representatives exercise optimum control over the scripts consistent with BBC's authority and only minor changes may be made without prior consultation with the writers. Nothing in the scriptwriters' agreement entitles BBC to alter a program once it has been recorded. The agreement further provides that, subject to the terms therein, the group retains all rights in the script.

Under the agreement, BBC may license the transmission of recordings of the television programs in any overseas territory. The series has been broadcast in this country primarily on non-commercial public broadcasting television stations, although several of the programs have been broadcast on commercial stations in Texas and Nevada. In each instance, the thirty-minute programs have been broadcast as originally recorded and broadcast in England in their entirety and without commercial interruption.

In October 1973, Time-Life Films acquired the right to distribute in the United States certain BBC television programs, including the Monty

Python series. Time-Life was permitted to edit the programs only "for insertion of commercials, applicable censorship or governmental . . . rules and regulations, and National Association of Broadcasters and time segment requirements." No similar clause was included in the scriptwriters' agreement between appellants and BBC. Prior to this time, ABC had sought to acquire the right to broadcast excerpts from various Monty Python programs in the spring of 1975, but the group rejected the proposal for such a disjoined format. Thereafter, in July 1975, ABC agreed with Time-Life to broadcast two ninety-minute specials each comprising three thirty-minute Monty Python programs that had not previously been shown in this country.

Correspondence between representatives of BBC and Monty Python reveals that these parties assumed that ABC would broadcast each of the Monty Python programs "in its entirety." On September 5, 1975, however, the group's British representative inquired of BBC how ABC planned to show the programs in their entirety if approximately 24 minutes of each 90 minute program were to be devoted to commercials. BBC replied on September 12, "we can only reassure you that ABC have decided to run the programmes 'back to back,' and that there is a firm undertaking not to segment them."

ABC broadcast the first of the specials on October 3, 1975. Appellants did not see a tape of the program until late November and were allegedly "appalled" at the discontinuity and "mutilation" that had resulted from the editing done by Time-Life for ABC. Twenty-four minutes of the original 90 minutes of recording had been omitted. Some of the editing had been done in order to make time for commercials; other material had been edited, according to ABC, because the original programs contained offensive or obscene matter.

In early December, Monty Python learned that ABC planned to broadcast the second special on December 26, 1975. The parties began negotiations concerning editing of that program and a delay of the broadcast until Monty Python could view it. These negotiations were futile, however, and on December 15 the group filed this action to enjoin the broadcast and for damages. Following an evidentiary hearing, Judge Lasker found that "the plaintiffs have established an impairment of the integrity of their work" which "caused the film or program . . . to lose its iconoclastic verve." According to Judge Lasker, "the damage that has been caused to the plaintiffs is irreparable by its nature." Nevertheless, the judge denied the motion for the preliminary injunction on the grounds that it was unclear who owned the copyright in the programs produced by BBC from the scripts written by Monty Python; that there was a question of whether Time-Life and BBC were indispensable parties to the litigation; that ABC would suffer significant financial loss if it were enjoined a week before the scheduled broadcast; and that Monty Python had displayed a "somewhat disturbing casualness" in their pursuance of the matter.

Judge Lasker granted Monty Python's request for more limited relief by requiring ABC to broadcast a disclaimer during the December 26 special to the effect that the group dissociated itself from the program because of the editing. A panel of this court, however, granted a stay of that order until this appeal could be heard and permitted ABC to broadcast, at the beginning of the special, only the legend that the program had been edited by ABC. We heard argument on April 13 and, at that time, enjoined ABC from any further broadcast of edited Monty Python programs pending the decision of the court.

I.

In determining the availability of injunctive relief at this early stage of the proceedings, Judge Lasker properly considered the harm that would inure to the plaintiffs if the injunction were denied, the harm that defendant would suffer if the injunction were granted, and the likelihood that plaintiffs would ultimately succeed on the merits. We direct the issuance of a preliminary injunction because we find that all these factors weigh in favor of appellants.

There is nothing clearly erroneous in Judge Lasker's conclusion that any injury suffered by appellants as a result of the broadcast of edited versions of their programs was irreparable by its nature. ABC presented the appellants with their first opportunity for broadcast to a nationwide network audience in this country. If ABC adversely misrepresented the quality of Monty Python's work, it is likely that many members of the audience, many of whom, by defendant's admission, were previously unfamiliar with appellants, would not become loyal followers of Monty Python productions. The subsequent injury to appellants' theatrical reputation would imperil their ability to attract the large audience necessary to the success of their venture. Such an injury to professional reputation cannot be measured in monetary terms or recompensed by other relief.

In contrast to the harm that Monty Python would suffer by a denial of the preliminary injunction, Judge Lasker found that ABC's relationship with its affiliates would be impaired by a grant of an injunction within a week of the scheduled December 26 broadcast. The court also found that ABC and its affiliates had advertised the program and had included it in listings of forthcoming television programs that were distributed to the public. Thus a last minute cancellation of the December 26 program, Judge Lasker concluded, would injure defendant financially and in its reputation with the public and its advertisers.

However valid these considerations may have been when the issue before the court was whether a preliminary injunction should immediately precede the broadcast, any injury to ABC is presently more speculative. No rebroadcast of the edited specials has been scheduled and no advertising costs have been incurred for the immediate future. Thus there is no danger that defendant's relations with affiliates or the public will suffer irreparably if subsequent broadcasts of the programs are enjoined pending a disposition of the issues.

We then reach the question whether there is a likelihood that appellants will succeed on the merits. In concluding that there is a likelihood of infringement here, we rely especially on the fact that the editing was substantial, *i.e.*, approximately 27 per cent of the original program was omitted, and the editing contravened contractual provisions that limited the right to edit Monty Python material. It should be emphasized that our discussion of these matters refers only to such facts as have been developed upon the hearing for a preliminary injunction. Modified or contrary findings may become appropriate after a plenary trial.

Judge Lasker denied the preliminary injunction in part because he was unsure of the ownership of the copyright in the recorded program. Appellants first contend that the question of ownership is irrelevant because the recorded program was merely a derivative work taken from the script in which they hold the uncontested copyright. Thus, even if BBC owned the copyright in the recorded program, its use of that work would be limited by the license granted to BBC by Monty Python for use of the underlying script. We agree.

Section 7 of the Copyright Law, 17 U.S.C. § 7, provides in part that "adaptations, arrangements, dramatizations . . . or other versions of . . . copyrighted works when produced with the consent of the proprietor of the copyright in such works . . . shall be regarded as new works subject to copyright. . . ." Manifestly, the recorded program falls into this category as a dramatization of the script, and thus the program was itself entitled to copyright protection. However, section 7 limits the copyright protection of the derivative work, as works adapted from previously existing scripts have become known, to the novel additions made to the underlying work, and the derivative work does not affect the "force or validity" of the copyright in the matter from which it is derived. Thus, any ownership by BBC of the copyright in the recorded program would not affect the scope or ownership of the copyright in the underlying script.

Since the copyright in the underlying script survives intact despite the incorporation of that work into a derivative work, one who uses the script, even with the permission of the proprietor of the derivative work, may infringe the underlying copyright.

If the proprietor of the derivative work is licensed by the proprietor of the copyright in the underlying work to vend or distribute the derivative work to third parties, those parties will, of course, suffer no liability for their use of the underlying work consistent with the license to the proprietor of the derivative work. Obviously, it was just this type of arrangement that was contemplated in this instance. The scriptwriters' agreement between Monty Python and BBC specifically permitted the latter to license the transmission of the recordings made by BBC to distributors such as Time-Life for broadcast in overseas territories.

One who obtains permission to use a copyrighted script in the production of a derivative work, however, may not exceed the specific purpose for which permission was granted. Most of the decisions that have reached this conclusion have dealt with the improper extension of the underlying work into media or time, *i.e.*, duration of the license, not covered by the grant of permission to the derivative work proprietor. Appellants herein do not claim that the broadcast by ABC violated media or time restrictions contained in the license of the script to BBC. Rather, they claim that revisions in the script, and ultimately in the program, could be made only after consultation with Monty Python, and that ABC's broadcast of a program edited after recording and without consultation with Monty Python exceeded the scope of any license that BBC was entitled to grant.

The rationale for finding infringement when a licensee exceeds time or media restrictions on his license—the need to allow the proprietor of the underlying copyright to control the method in which his work is presented to the public—applies equally to the situation in which a licensee makes an unauthorized use of the underlying work by publishing it in a truncated version. Whether intended to allow greater economic exploitation of the work, as in the media and time cases, or to ensure that the copyright proprietor retains a veto power over revisions desired for the derivative work, the ability of the copyright holder to control his work remains paramount in our copyright law. We find, therefore, that unauthorized editing of the underlying work, if proven, would constitute an infringement of the copyright in that work similar to any other use of a work that exceeded the license granted by the proprietor of the copyright.

If the broadcast of an edited version of the Monty Python program infringed the group's copyright in the script, ABC may obtain no solace from the fact that editing was permitted in the agreements between BBC and Time-Life or Time-Life and ABC. BBC was not entitled to make unilateral changes in the script and was not specifically empowered to alter the recordings once made; Monty Python, moreover, had reserved to itself any rights not granted to BBC. Since a grantor may not convey greater rights than it owns, BBC's permission to allow Time-Life, and hence ABC, to edit appears to have been a nullity.

ABC answers appellants' infringement argument with a series of contentions, none of which seems meritorious at this stage of the litigation. The network asserts that Monty Python's British representative, Jill Foster, knew that ABC planned to exclude much of the original BBC program in the October 3 broadcast. ABC thus contends that by not previously objecting to this procedure, Monty Python ratified BBC's authority to license others to edit the underlying script.

Although the case of Ilyin v. Avon Publications, Inc., 144 F.Supp. 368, 373 (S.D.N.Y. 1956), may be broadly read for the proposition that a holder of a derivative copyright may obtain rights in the underlying work through ratification, the conduct necessary to that conclusion has yet to be demonstrated in this case. It is undisputed that appellants did not have actual notice of the cuts in the October 3 broadcast until late November. Even if they are chargeable with the knowledge of their British representative, it is not clear that she had prior notice of the cuts or ratified the omissions, nor did Judge Lasker make any finding on the question. While Foster, on September 5, did question how ABC was to broadcast the entire program if it was going to interpose 24 minutes of commercials, she received assurances from BBC that the programs would not be "segmented." The fact that she knew precisely the length of material that would have to be omitted to allow for commercials does not prove that she ratified the deletions. This is especially true in light of previous assurances that the program would contain the original shows in their entirety. On the present record, it cannot be said that there was any ratification of BBC's grant of editing rights. ABC, of course, is entitled to attempt to prove otherwise during the trial on the merits. . . .

Aside from the question of who owns the relevant copyrights, ABC asserts that the contracts between appellants and BBC permit editing of the programs for commercial television in the United States. ABC argues that the scriptwriters' agreement allows appellants the right to participate in revisions of the script only prior to the recording of the programs, and thus infers that BBC had unrestricted authority to revise after that point. This argument, however, proves too much. A reading of the contract seems to indicate that Monty Python obtained control over editing the script only to ensure control over the program recorded from that script. Since the scriptwriters' agreement explicitly retains for the group all rights not granted by the contract, omission of any terms concerning alterations in the program after recording must be read as reserving to appellants exclusive authority for such revisions.

Finally, ABC contends that appellants must have expected that deletions would be made in the recordings to conform them for use on commercial television in the United States. ABC argues that licensing in the United States implicitly grants a license to insert commercials in a program and to remove offensive or obscene material prior to broadcast. According to the network, appellants should have anticipated that most of the excised material contained scatological references inappropriate for American television and that these scenes would be replaced with commercials, which presumably are more palatable to the American public.

The proof adduced up to this point, however, provides no basis for finding any implied consent to edit. Prior to the ABC broadcasts, Monty Python programs had been broadcast on a regular basis by both commercial and public television stations in this country without interruption or deletion. Indeed, there is no evidence of any prior broadcast of edited Monty Python material in the United States. These facts, combined with the persistent requests for assurances by the group and its representatives that the programs would be shown intact belie the argument that the group knew or should have known that deletions and commercial interruptions were inevitable.

Several of the deletions made for ABC, such as elimination of the words "hell" and "damn," seem inexplicable given today's standard television fare. If, however, ABC honestly determined that the programs were obscene in substantial part, it could have decided not to broadcast the specials at all, or it could have attempted to reconcile its differences with appellants. The network could not, however, free from a claim of infringement, broadcast in a substantially altered form a program incorporating the script over which the group had retained control.

Our resolution of these technical arguments serves to reinforce our initial inclination that the copyright law should be used to recognize the important role of the artist in our society and the need to encourage production and dissemination of artistic works by providing adequate legal protection for one who submits his work to the public. We therefore conclude that there is a substantial likelihood that, after a full trial, appellants will succeed in proving infringement of their copyright by ABC's broadcast of edited versions of Monty Python programs. In reaching this conclusion, however, we need not accept appellants' assertion that any editing whatsoever would constitute infringement. Courts have recognized that licensees are entitled to some small degree of latitude in arranging the licensed work for presentation to the public in a manner consistent with the licensee's style or standards. That privilege, however, does not extend to the degree of editing that occurred here especially in light of contractual provisions that limited the right to edit Monty Python material.

II.

It also seems likely that appellants will succeed on the theory that, regardless of the right ABC had to broadcast an edited program, the cuts made constituted an actionable mutilation of Monty Python's work. This cause of action, which seeks redress for deformation of an artist's work, finds its roots in the continental concept of droit moral, or moral right, which may generally be summarized as including the right of the artist to have his work attributed to him in the form in which he created it.

American copyright law, as presently written, does not recognize moral rights or provide a cause of action for their violation, since the law seeks to vindicate the economic, rather than the personal, rights of authors. Nevertheless, the economic incentive for artistic and intellectual creation that serves as the foundation for American copyright law, cannot be reconciled with the inability of artists to obtain relief for mutilation or misrepresentation of their work to the public on which the artists are financially dependent. Thus courts have long granted relief for misrepresentation of an artist's work by relying on theories outside the statutory law of copyright, such as contract law, or the tort of unfair competition. Although such decisions are clothed in terms of proprietary right in one's creation, they also properly vindicate the author's personal right to prevent the presentation of his work to the public in a distorted form.

Here, the appellants claim that the editing done for ABC mutilated the original work and that consequently the broadcast of those programs as the creation of Monty Python violated the Lanham Act § 43(a), 15 U.S.C. § 1125(a).[10] This statute, the federal counterpart to state unfair competition laws, has been invoked to prevent misrepresentations that may injure plaintiff's business or personal reputation, even where no registered trademark is concerned. It is sufficient to violate the Act that a representation of a product, although technically true, creates a false impression of the product's origin. *See* Rich v. RCA Corp., 390 F.Supp. 530 (S.D.N.Y. 1975) (recent picture of plaintiff on cover of album containing songs recorded in distant past held to be a false representation that the songs were new); Geisel v. Poynter Products, Inc., 283 F.Supp. 261, 267 (S.D.N.Y. 1968).

These cases cannot be distinguished from the situation in which a television network broadcasts a program properly designated as having been written and performed by a group, but which has been edited, without the writer's consent, into a form that departs substantially from the original work. "To deform his work is to present him to the public as the creator of a work not his own, and thus makes him subject to criticism for work he has not done." Roeder, [53 Harv. L. Rev.] at 569. In such a case, it is the writer or performer, rather than the network, who suffers the consequences of the mutilation, for the public will have only the final product by which to evaluate the work. Thus, an allegation that a defendant has presented to the public a "garbled," distorted version of plaintiff's work seeks to redress the very rights sought to be protected by the Lanham Act, 15 U.S.C. § 1125(a), and should be recognized as stating a cause of action under that statute.

During the hearing on the preliminary injunction, Judge Lasker viewed the edited version of the Monty Python program broadcast on December 26 and the original, unedited version. After hearing argument of this appeal, this panel also viewed and compared the two versions. We find that the truncated version at times omitted the climax of the skits to which appellants' rare brand of humor was leading and at other times deleted essential elements in the schematic development of a story line. We therefore agree with Judge Lasker's conclusion that the edited

---

[10] That statute provides in part:

Any person who shall affix, apply, or annex, or use in connection with any goods or services, . . . a false designation of origin, or any false description or representation . . . and shall cause such goods or services to enter into commerce . . . shall be liable to a civil action by any person . . . who believes that he is or is likely to be damaged by the use of any such false description or representation.

version broadcast by ABC impaired the integrity of appellants' work and represented to the public as the product of appellants what was actually a mere caricature of their talents. We believe that a valid cause of action for such distortion exists and that therefore a preliminary injunction may issue to prevent repetition of the broadcast prior to final determination of the issues. . . .

For these reasons we direct that the district court issue the preliminary injunction sought by the appellants.

GURFEIN, CIRCUIT JUDGE (concurring):

I concur in my brother Lumbard's scholarly opinion, but I wish to comment on the application of Section 43(a) of the Lanham Act, 15 U.S.C. § 1125(a).

I believe that this is the first case in which a federal appellate court has held that there may be a violation of Section 43(a) of the Lanham Act with respect to a common-law copyright. The Lanham Act is a trademark statute, not a copyright statute. Nevertheless, we must recognize that the language of Section 43(a) is broad. It speaks of the affixation or use of false designations of origin or false descriptions or representations, but proscribes such use "in connection with any goods or services." It is easy enough to incorporate trade names as well as trademarks into Section 43(a) and the statute specifically applies to common law trademarks, as well as registered trademarks.

In the present case, we are holding that the deletion of portions of the recorded tape constitutes a breach of contract, as well as an infringement of a common-law copyright of the original work. There is literally no need to discuss whether plaintiffs also have a claim for relief under the Lanham Act or for unfair competition under New York law. I agree with Judge Lumbard, however, that it may be an exercise of judicial economy to express our view on the Lanham Act claim, and I do not dissent therefrom. I simply wish to leave it open for the District Court to fashion the remedy.

The Copyright Act provides no recognition of the so-called droit moral, or moral right of authors. Nor are such rights recognized in the field of copyright law in the United States. If a distortion or truncation in connection with a use constitutes an infringement of copyright, there is no need for an additional cause of action beyond copyright infringement. An obligation to mention the name of the author carries the implied duty, however, as a matter of contract, not to make such changes in the work as would render the credit line a false attribution of authorship.

So far as the Lanham Act is concerned, it is not a substitute for droit moral which authors in Europe enjoy. If the licensee may, by contract, distort the recorded work, the Lanham Act does not come into play. If the licensee has no such right by contract, there will be a violation in breach of contract. The Lanham Act can hardly apply literally when the credit line correctly states the work to be that of the plaintiffs which, indeed it is, so far as it goes. The vice complained of is that the truncated version is not what the plaintiffs wrote. But the Lanham Act does not deal with artistic integrity. It only goes to misdescription of origin and the like.

The misdescription of origin can be dealt with, as Judge Lasker did below, by devising an appropriate legend to indicate that the plaintiffs had not approved the editing of the ABC version. With such a legend, there is no conceivable violation of the Lanham Act. If plaintiffs complain that their artistic integrity is still compromised by the distorted version, their claim does not lie under the Lanham Act, which does not protect the copyrighted work itself but protects only against the misdescription or mislabelling.

So long as it is made clear that the ABC version is not approved by the Monty Python group, there is no misdescription of origin. So far as the content of the broadcast itself is concerned, that is not within the proscription of the Lanham Act when there is no misdescription of the authorship.

I add this brief explanation because I do not believe that the Lanham Act claim necessarily requires the drastic remedy of permanent injunction. That form of ultimate relief must be found in some other fountainhead of equity jurisprudence.

Adolf Dietz, The Moral Right of the Author: Moral Rights and the Civil Law Countries

(Report to the ALAI Congress on Moral Rights,
Antwerp, Belgium, Sept. 19–24 (1993)).
19 Columbia-V.L.A. Journal of Law and the Arts 199, 213–227 (1995).

A.   Time Limit or Perpetuity of *Droit Moral*

French theory sees a clear consequence of the preeminence of moral rights over economic rights also in the fact that protection is declared perpetual by the law itself. It continues after protection of pecuniary rights has run out fifty years, or even seventy years, after the author's death. According to the French national report, this solution corresponds to the fundamental concept of moral right in French law, even if theoretically other solutions to the problem of duration were conceivable. The other solutions, however, would misunderstand the originality of moral rights as compared to other personality rights. Since, according to the French concept, the link between the author and his work exists as long as the work is capable of being communicated to the public, in a certain way, the personality of the author lives as long as the work itself exists. On the other hand, at first sight it also appears to be a consequence of the monistic or synthetic interpretation of copyright in German doctrine that moral rights, being an integral part of copyright as a whole, end together with it seventy years after the death of the author.* This result is confirmed by the majority interpretation of the legal situation in German copyright law.

A closer and, in particular, comparative look at this question, however, tells us that there is no necessary correlation of dualism and perpetuity, on the one hand, and monism and *droit moral* protection limited in time, on the other hand. If, apart from Germany (and perhaps—according to my own interpretation of its new law— Switzerland), almost all other countries covered by this analysis, namely Belgium, Denmark, Italy, Netherlands, Spain and Sweden, according to the relevant national reports, can be more or less counted as dualistic countries, there is no unanimity as to whether perpetuity of moral rights protection exists or should exist.

The French model, once more, is followed in Belgium, at least in the sense that moral rights protection, independently of the protection period of economic rights, exists as long as there are certain persons, normally members of the family of the author, who have the mission to protect the author's moral rights in nomine auctoris (exercise of the right to repent being excluded after the author's death). In Denmark, and to a certain degree also in Sweden, perpetuity of enforcement of one particular faculty of moral rights, the right of integrity, appears possible, if cultural interests are violated. But both national reports, in particular the Danish one, do not conceal a certain skepticism about the theory behind this rule. The case of the cancellation of a grant from the Danish Film Institute for the production of a film on the life of Jesus Christ on the ground that the film would be an infringement of the moral rights of the authors of the Bible, a case which finally was decided on other grounds, has demonstrated the danger of overdrawing certain arguments in this field.

That case in Denmark rather had the opposite result—as the Danish report states—that cultural interests are no longer taken into consideration in this way. The Danish report also notes that:

> Danish experience with the perpetual protection is not a good one, and . . . European law would perhaps be better off if the Moral Rights always ran out with copyright. Discussions about the "cultural interests" have shown to be futile and pointless, and modern society obviously cannot be forced by law to respect the integrity of works only because they are called works of art. Experience shows, however, that valuable works of art and literature do survive and are handed down to posterity even if there is no special legal protection in the Copyright Acts.

This point of view is also shared by the Dutch report, according to which "(t)he Netherlands decidedly does not belong to the group of

---

*   *Monist* theory, followed most prominently in Germany, fuses an author's personal and economic interests into a single doctrine and prescribes the same rules for both. *Dualist* theory, followed most prominently in France, separates the author's personal right from his economic rights, and treats the two interests differently. *Ed.*

countries which recognize an eternal moral right, with the State acting as a watchdog over the integrity of works, as well as with all the ensuing dangers for freedom of expression and information."

On the other hand, as underlined by the Spanish report, Spain expressly provides for perpetuity of moral rights, but restricts it to the right of paternity and of integrity of the work in its negative or defensive aspects. However, more precisely than in the case of France, there is also a general subsidiary competence of the State and of other public authorities—but not of private associations such as collecting societies— to enforce these rights. The Italian report also is more positive about perpetuity, since the copyright law itself (once more with the exception of the right to repent) grants moral rights protection after the author's death without time limit: they can be exercised by the members of the author's family as determined by the law, but in cases of public interest, public authorities can also intervene. The Italian report characteristically thinks that this could be particularly relevant for the utilization of the works of so-called "serious" music (lyric, opera, symphonic and other music), but gives no examples in case law.

It should, however, be mentioned that even the French report openly admits that the Ministry of Culture hesitates to use the possibility granted to it by Article L.121–3 of the Code in case of misuse in exercise or non-exercise of the divulgation right. In addition, still according to the French report, referring to the famous decision on "Les Liaisons dangereuses," courts were extremely reticent in accepting actions of persons other than the family members of the author, in particular collecting societies. Consequently, in spite of the recognized principle, the reduced number of persons able to sue for infringement of moral rights makes the perpetuity of its protection considerably less important. It is no surprise that, according to the new Swiss Copyright Act, which I personally would rather interpret as a monistic concept, moral rights do not exist longer than pecuniary rights; on the contrary, according to the relevant national report, the Swiss government has expressly avoided introduction of a sort of monument protection into copyright law.

If the German and, perhaps, also the Swiss example demonstrate that monistic or unitary interpretation of copyright shows a natural tendency to stop moral right protection together with copyright as a whole, there exists no necessary correlation. Duration of moral rights longer than the period of protection for the economic rights is rather a question of culture and policy. Of course, under public and administrative law, in Germany there are also certain possibilities to protect monuments and other cultural goods against destruction and misuse. However, according to Eugen Ulmer, whose opinion is widely shared in Germany, in cases of pure reproduction and public performance of works, public critique and discussion should prevail over the apparently problematic invocations and interpretations of the interests of an author who has been dead for more than fifty or seventy years. Is it really certain—to take the famous French case as an example—that the author of a frivolous novel of the 18th century, provocative in his own time, would not have himself liked its equally frivolous transposition into the 20th century, realized by so outstanding figures of modern film art like Roger Vadim and Jeanne Moreau? Perhaps there is no general answer to this problem and we should leave it to the legal and cultural traditions of the individual countries.

B.   Determination and Legal Position of the Author's Legal Successors in his Moral Rights

The problem of who shall decide, and in whose interest, about questions of moral right after the author's death is also of relevance during the normal period of protection of copyright. In some countries, in particular in France, but also in Belgium, Italy and Spain the legal successors of the author (his family members or other persons as determined by the laws) clearly have to enforce the moral rights in *nomine auctoris*—an expression used in the Belgian report. Consequently, the moral rights in their hands are subject to a total change of character. The legal successors receive droit moral only, as is stated in the French report, in order to respect the work and the person of the author. They must not exercise it in their own personal interests; this is why *droit moral* after the author's death is called a functional right (*droit-fonction*). This concept also explains why—as in other countries— the right to repent expires at the death of the author. In addition, misuse of moral rights by legal successors in the sense that they do not fulfill their duties in respecting the author's name and work could even be subject to judicial control in accordance with Article L.121–3 of the Code.

In the interest of such a concept, some countries even provide different rules for transmission of moral rights—as contrasted to economic rights—to the author's legal successors, since the family members or those persons whom the author has specifically entrusted with exercise of his moral rights normally are supposed to exercise them as the author himself would have. There is of course no legal guaranty for that, unless the law also provides for some means of control of those persons as the French Code does for the divulgation right.

German copyright law does not provide for specific rules on transmission of moral rights at the author's death, apart from the fact that, according to Section 28(2) of the Copyright Act, exercise of the copyright (and, of course, also of individual faculties of it) can be transmitted to an executor by testamentary disposition. That copyright as a whole, comprising its economic as well as its moral faculties, therefore passes over to the regular legal successors, also appears as a logical consequence of the monistic interpretation of copyright which always stresses its unity. But the true reason seems to be that German legal doctrine rejects a concept of *droit-fonction* or of special obligations of the legal successors as against the dead author. Accordingly, apart from concrete and legally binding testamentary dispositions of the author, the legal successors are able to exercise moral right protection as they think fit, even in their own interests. Of course in Germany, too, widows and widowers as well as children and other family members of dead authors de facto will normally act, to the best of their knowledge, in accordance with the dead author's interests and wishes. There is simply no control.

We also have to think of the realities of modern cultural industries where, for example, the question of whether a novel or a piece of theater can be filmed has to be decided by the legal successors of the author years after his death. Would it really make sense, in particular when there is certain actual or public interest in such a film production, to hinder the legal successors with the interference of state authorities simply because the author, many years ago, had expressed some doubts about such a filming? Think of Franz Kafka who, according to his friend Max Brod, wanted to have his work destroyed after his death. Would Max Brod have really rendered a service to mankind if he had followed this desperate decision and had not published it, as he finally did? *Tempora mutantur, nos et mutamur in illis*!

The concept of *droit-fonction*, or the express provision that the so-called positive faculties within moral rights end with the author's death, appears somewhat too narrow and impractical to me in view of the large variety of works and objects protected by copyright law, from the simplest solutions of design, advertising, functional literature and functional drawings to the top results of man's creativity in the field of belles lettres, music, film and art. Of course, we have to respect legal and cultural traditions in the individual countries. But in a world with growing internationalization and globalization of exploitation of copyright works, we should try to find convincing compromise solutions which can further worldwide acceptance of the fundamental legitimacy of moral right protection.

C.   Exercise of the Paternity and the Integrity Rights—Waiver of Rights and Balance of Interests

As stated at the beginning, there is no unanimity even within the group of civil law countries as to how far moral rights protection extends and what individual faculties it should cover. However, unanimity exists, at least in principle, as far as the paternity right and the integrity right are concerned. In all countries as reported here statutory provisions regulate these two faculties. In Belgium the provisions of Article 6*bis* of the Berne Convention are directly applied.

1.   Paternity Right

The reports generally state that the paternity right has two facets: the author can not only claim recognition of his authorship by third parties in a negative or defensive way, but also determine in a positive way whether a work is to bear an author's designation and what designation is to be used. The latter possibility also involves a right of non-paternity, which allows the author to opt for an anonymous form of publication of his work in the same way that he can decide to use a pseudonym instead of his true name. But, as most laws directly or indirectly recognize, the author always has the possibility of disclosing and claiming his paternity.

The real problem in the context of the paternity right therefore concerns the question of how far contractual arrangements concerning naming or not naming the author are enforceable and whether the right of attribution can be waived, in particular, within so-called ghostwriter agreements. The clearest provision that the author can always insist on an attribution of his name is contained in Article 21(2) of the Italian Act, whereas Article 25(3) of the Netherlands Act generally allows waiver of the right to be named (which itself is already granted only within the limits of reasonableness) as well as of the right to object to modification of the designation.

An intermediate position is taken by the Danish and Swedish Copyright Acts which, first, like the Dutch law, grant the right to be named only in accordance with the requirements of proper usage, but, second, exclude waiver of moral rights in a general way, while still allowing it in respect of a use of the work which is limited in nature and extent. In spite of a relatively strict formulation in Article 13 of its Copyright Act, German practice also allows waiver within certain limits, determined partly by proper usage and partly by a balancing of interests. Finally, a special situation exists under the new Swiss Act since there is no express exclusion of moral rights from the general rule in its Article 16(1) that copyright can be ceded and transmitted. The Swiss national report underlines, however, that a general waiver of the right to be named as author for all future creations would be judged as against honest practices.

As a result, the legal situation in the individual countries is far from being uniform. Against this background, the question of ghostwriter agreements also has to be judged. Since there is almost no relevant case law in most of the countries, one would cautiously conclude that if waiver of the right to be named, combined with consent to the naming of another person, could be possible, the legal status of the ghostwriter agreement remains a precarious one. Since the creational bond linking the author to his work as an empirical fact can never be totally disapproved, an author can always disclose the real facts of such a situation and publicly proclaim his authorship.

2.   Integrity Right

In the field of the integrity right, that is the right to object to distortion, mutilation or other modifications of the author's work, the question of admissibility of transfer or waiver is even more difficult to answer. There are countries such as France, Italy and Spain that strictly stress the inalienability of this special faculty of moral right. Legal provisions in other countries, on the contrary, admit at least some restrictions of the integrity right by contract or waiver. In addition, the question of whether modifications are absolutely forbidden without the author's consent, or whether infringement of this moral right depends on certain conditions or qualifications such as prejudice to the author's honor or reputation, is also answered differently in the individual countries.

Of course, in modern cultural industry and modern media, modification and adaptation of works in the framework of their exploitation is often more the rule than the exception. The laws themselves, when granting the author the economic right of adaptation, necessarily imply that the author who allows adaptation of his work must give the adaptor certain room to maneuver, as the French report rightly states. The very provisions concerning adaptation right and adaptation contract therefore demonstrate that a concept of absolute inalienability and of exclusion of waiver is not compatible with the laws of even the most fundamental moral rights countries.

In this context the French report also rightly notes that the question of whether an a priori waiver is allowed or not must not be mixed up with the question of how the author reacts to later modifications of his work made by third parties when he really gets knowledge of them. Since he is the only person to judge the critical character of these modifications, he can also ratify them. In many cases this would appear not so much as a waiver of his moral right of integrity, but as a continuation of the creational process itself. The true criterium for deciding whether a waiver is null and void, therefore, appears to be whether the author had to sign abstract and general clauses on (future) modifications of his work without having the possibility to ratify them, at least ex posteriori. There seems to be general agreement on this point in the national reports.

Totally different is the question of whether the exercise of the right of integrity has an unconditional or discretionary character or whether it is conditioned or qualified by certain elements. At least in theory, the protection of authors in France is the most absolute and unconditional; French law, according to Article L.121–1 of the Intellectual Property Code, does not make the right of respect for the author's name, authorship and work dependent on any condition. In the other countries the condition provided in Article 6*bis* of the Berne Convention, namely that modification of his work must be prejudicial to the author's honor or reputation, in one form or another is repeated in the provisions on moral rights, a result which in Belgium once more is obtained by direct application of the Berne Convention.

The French national report criticizes this approach, prefigured by the Berne Convention, as minimalist. This critique is based on the "personalistic" view of moral rights protection in French law which, without applying the criterium of honor or reputation, totally respects the subjectivity of the author, his aesthetic, moral and philosophic convictions. I think this critical position is right insofar as the formula of honor and reputation is too narrow; indeed, modification of an author's work can conflict with his fundamental artistic and moral convictions without, judging from outside, prejudicing his honor or reputation. This problem is avoided, to a certain extent, by the formulation in Section 14 of the German Act and in Article 14 (iv) of the Spanish Act, which applies the criterium of prejudice to the lawful (intellectual or personal) interests of the author in his work. Article 25 of the Dutch Copyright Act, which applies a rule of reason to modifications not amounting to distortions, applies the criterium of the value or dignity of the author in addition to prejudice to his honor or reputation in case of distortions of the work, and hence adopts a broader concept.

On the other hand, I do not agree with the French critique that all of these formulas would allow the author's aesthetic, moral or philosophic convictions and judgments to be replaced unacceptably by judgments of other persons, be it the general public or the courts. The question, in my view, is not whether the author's convictions are respected or replaced, but whether the author has to accept certain changes and modifications of his works in view of the counter-interests of the work users. This criterium, which finally leads to a concept of balancing of interests, is clearly recognizable in those countries like Germany, Spain, and the Netherlands, where the relevant provisions speak of "lawful" interests or apply a rule of reason.

As a consequence, changes or modifications in the process of exploitation of the work which would be solely dictated by artistic and aesthetic convictions and concepts of other persons, especially the work user, would not be acceptable, whereas those dictated by the concrete technical, financial, and circumstantial conditions of the exploitation of the work would have to be taken into consideration in this process of balancing of interests. This also is recognized in French law in the special case of adaptations of a work, a situation which, under modern conditions, exists more often than one would expect, since adaptation in the technical, but not necessarily creational, sense of the word, appears rather the rule than the exception. Since the situation in various fields, for example in the book sector, the periodic press, the film industry, theater and opera, design and architecture, are so different, ultimately the balance of interests would also have to differ in a case by case analysis.

Legislators themselves tell us that sometimes different rules have to be applied for different categories of works. Even French law introduced some restrictions on the exercise of moral rights in the film sector and in the field of computer programs: the film author's moral right of integrity can only be asserted when the final version of the film has been established, and the author of a computer program cannot oppose adaptation of the program or exercise his right to repent or to withdraw. In the same way, the German Copyright Act provides that authors of a cinematographic work may only prohibit gross distortions and other gross injuries of the work or of their contribution to it and, in addition, that in the exercise of their rights they must take into account the respective legitimate interests of the other film creators and of the producer. Finally, according to Article 20(2) of the Italian Act the author of a work of architecture cannot oppose modifications which become necessary in the course of or after its realization. This reduction of moral rights protection is itself restricted in cases of works of important artistic character.

A special problem within the integrity right is raised by the question of unauthorized destruction of works, especially in the field of visual arts and architecture. If in the past there was some controversy over whether destruction of a work could or could not amount to distortion of it, the opinion gains ground today that destruction of a work appears as the most intensive form of its distortion, depriving the author of the authentic means of proof for his artistic and professional skills and self-conscience. According to the report of Professors Kernochan and Ginsburg, the United States legislators of the Visual Artists Rights Act of 1990 played a pioneer role in introducing provisions barring intentional or grossly negligent destruction of a covered work "of recognized stature." We will not discuss further details of these very interesting provisions of the U.S. legislation, not being civil law legislation; however, they demonstrate, once more, how legislators try to find adequate solutions that will be viable also in the years to come by differentiating the rules according to categories or groups of works.

Surprisingly, the very recent Copyright Act of Switzerland, fulfilling a similar pioneer function for a civil law country, provided in its Article 15 that under certain circumstances the owner of the unique original exemplar of a work may not destroy it without first offering it to the author. In the case of a work of architecture, however, the author is only entitled to take photographs of it and to make copies of the architectural plans. On the other hand, similarly to the Italian law, a work of architecture may be modified by its owner as long as there is no distortion or mutilation of the work, meaning an attack on its author's personality. These bold, if nuanced provisions, once more show the necessity of differentiation in the delicate field of moral rights protection.

In a general way, all of these legislative solutions, in my view, only exemplify the concept that moral rights questions always have to be judged in their individual context and that correspondingly different solutions have to be found for different categories of works and manners of work uses. This is why German theory came to the result that, when judging moral rights questions in the field of integrity right (as well as of paternity right), a balancing of interests has to be applied in a general way. At the end of this report we will, therefore, try to make a proposal for a corresponding legal formula which could perhaps serve to clarify and elaborate the insufficient criterium of honor and reputation in Article 6*bis* of the Berne Convention.

3.   A Possible Compromise: Codifying the Criteria for a General Balance of Interests

It is generally known that the Anglo-American copyright law for a long time had to operate with the principle of fair use or fair dealing when it came to deciding whether a certain non-authorized use of a work was allowed or not. The new British Copyright, Designs and Patents Act of 1988 still leaves the concept of fair dealing undefined, so that "in these cases the courts are left to judge fairness in the light of all the circumstances." In the United States, however, the concept of fair use, having been developed first by case law, was incorporated in the Copyright Act of 1976 within Section 107 on limitations on exclusive rights. The most important element of Section 107 is a list of criteria intended as a guide for the court in finding the right decision. According to that provision, in determining whether the use made of a work in any particular case is a fair use, the factors to be considered shall include the purpose and character of use, including whether such use is of a commercial nature or is for non-profit educational purposes; the nature of the copyrighted work; the amount and substantiality of the portion used in relation to the copyrighted work as a whole; and the effect of the use on the potential for or value of the copyrighted work.

The question of the extent of moral right protection, in particular of the integrity right, finally is also a question of fundamental fairness between author and work user; consequently, a similar catalogue of criteria for that fairness could certainly help also in this field. It could contain the following elements: the nature and intensity of modifications of or other interference with the work, as well as its reversible or irreversible character; the number of people or the size of the public addressed by the use of the infringing work; whether the author created the work in an employment relationship or as a self-employed author, or whether a commissioning party had or had not decisive influence onto the final result of the creation; and the possible consequences for the professional life of the author, and, of course, his honor and reputation.

As we are accustomed to the rule that copyright protection is granted irrespective of the merit and destination of the work concerned, it may be a surprising proposition that one of the criteria within the balance of interests should also be the nature and the artistic rank or class of a work, not its aesthetic value, of course. If granting of copyright protection as such remains a yes or no decision, this does not hinder an interpretation that would allow the artistic rank or class of a work as well as its destination to influence the balance of interests in cases of alleged infringement of moral rights. We have already mentioned a number of cases, in particular in the fields of computer programs, film works and architecture, where legislators, also of civil law countries, have already introduced some specific provisions that take into consideration the specific, often utilitarian character of those works.

Since all of these criteria are only individual elements within the balance of interests, no single criterium—such as the existence of an employment relationship—can be applied or be decisive in an isolated manner. Consequently even employed authors or authors of functional works such as computer programs would not be without any chance to enforce moral rights when really grave infringements of their personal or intellectual interests are at stake. To take another famous example, we must acknowledge that colorization of a highly ambitious artistic movie, even a work made for hire, is much less acceptable than the same procedure as applied to a purely scientific film, colorized post festum simply in order to achieve a better contrasting effect. These few examples demonstrate why a list of criteria is preferable to other solutions that operate to totally exclude certain categories of authors (such as employed authors) or of works (such as computer programs) from moral right protection.

In view of its flexibility, such a concept could perhaps also serve as a bridge between civil law countries and common law countries, where a new interest in moral right questions exists, but where a fundamental skepticism still prevails. In the words of Professor Kernochan, one of the authors of the American national report, *droit moral* has "an important and enduring core of validity. One may hope it will continue to be viable . . . in the coming age of digitalization and other new technology. (But) (a)s the concept stands, it is still . . . insufficiently defined and insufficiently tailored to practical realities." It appears to him overly broad in the sense that, of the huge volume of works produced to which authors' rights have been granted, only a certain part really warrants the application of moral rights.

I do not totally agree with this very restrictive language since there are cases where moral rights protection can easily be realized even in more modest fields of creation. For example, in Germany, the attribution of the names of photographers in the daily press is better enforced now, with the help of the collecting society Bild/Kunst, than it was before. Nevertheless, if we want to stop the tendency to devalue and play down moral rights questions and regulations, we must be prepared to accept more flexibility and to take into consideration, within a balancing of interests, the counter-interests of work users and investors.

CONCLUSION

Copyright law from its historic beginnings centered around works of literature and art in the traditional sense of the word; moral rights have been developed with this in mind. If modern copyright law has a certain tendency to cover all and everything, in the very interest of authors of literature and art, music and film, we must adapt our positions to the new situation, in order to save the principle as such.

NOTES

1. *Moral Rights in International Treaties.* Moral rights did not emerge as a Berne Convention norm until the 1928 Rome Act, and the new Article 6*bis* guaranteed only two of the moral rights variously enforced on the European Continent—the right of paternity and the right of integrity. Article 6*bis* also falls short of requirements imposed in some countries making the rights inalienable and perpetual. (Article 6*bis*(1) provides only that the author retains rights even after the transfer of economic rights and Article 6*bis*(2) provides that the rights shall "be maintained at least until the expiry of the economic rights.")

Although the TRIPs Agreement expressly excludes Berne Article 6*bis* from the substantive Berne obligations incorporated in Article 9(1), the WIPO Performances and Phonograms Treaty, dealing with neighboring rights, provides in Article 5 for the protection of moral rights of performers under terms that closely parallel those of Article 6*bis*. Article 5(1) provides "Independently of a performer's economic rights, and even after the transfer of those rights, the performer shall, as regards his live aural performances or performances fixed in phonograms, have the right to claim to be identified as the performer of his performances, except where omission is dictated by the manner of the use of the performance, and to object to any distortion, mutilation or other modification of his performances that would be prejudicial to his reputation." Article 5 of the Beijing Treaty on Audiovisual Performances does much the same for performers' moral rights in their audiovisual performances.

The anomalous introduction of performers into the authorial pantheon of moral rights—the law historically treated performers as second class citizens entitled only to neighboring rights and not author's rights—is at least ostensibly connected to the new stresses that the Internet has placed on interests in attribution and integrity. *See* J. Carlos Fernández-Molina & Eduardo Peis, The Moral Rights of Authors in the Age of Digital Information, 52 J. Am. Soc'y for Inf. Science & Tech 109 (2001).

See generally Mira Rajan, Moral Rights: Principles, Practice and New Technology (2011); Gillian Davies & Kevin Garnett, Moral Rights (2d ed. 2016); Elizabeth Adeney, The Moral Rights of Authors and Performers: An International and Comparative Analysis (2006).

2. *Moral Rights and Common Law Systems.* Professor Gerald Dworkin begins his valuable survey of moral rights in the common law countries with the observation that there "is a widely held belief, particularly among civil lawyers, that the concept of moral rights is a relatively novel intruder into common law copyright systems; and that such systems, by dint of Article 6*bis* of the Berne Convention, are being compelled, kicking and screaming, to dilute their pure economic approach to copyright with alien personality rights. This is an over-stated, and to a large extent inaccurate, view." Gerald Dworkin, The Moral Right of the Author: Moral Rights and the Common Law Countries, 19 Colum.-VLA J.L. & Arts 229 (1995).

Dworkin cites no less an authority than Lord Mansfield, arguing for a perpetual copyright in the landmark decision, Millar v. Taylor, 98 Eng. Rep.

201, 252 (K.B. 1769): "The author may not only be deprived of any profit, but lose the expense he has been at. He is no more master of the use of his own name. He has no control over the correctness of his own work. He can not prevent additions. He can not retract errors. He can not amend; or cancel a faulty edition. Any one may print, pirate, and perpetuate the imperfections, to the disgrace and against the will of the author; may propagate sentiments under his name, which he disapproves, repents and is ashamed of. He can exercise no discretion as to the manner in which, or the persons by whom his work shall be published."

Canada was the first common law country to enact specific moral rights legislation, while other Commonwealth countries more or less complied with the requirements of Article 6*bis* through a patchwork of statutory and decisional law. Sections 77–85 of Britain's 1988 Copyright, Designs and Patents Act prescribe four express statutory moral rights—the rights of attribution and integrity required by Berne; a right against false attribution; and a special right of privacy in the case of certain photographs and films. The British Act subjects the integrity and paternity rights to several exceptions (employees enjoy no right of paternity; there are no rights of paternity or integrity in computer programs) and, although section 94 bars lifetime transfers, section 87 allows the rights to be waived. Article 78 of the British Act conditions the rights of attribution on the author's or director's express assertion of the right in writing. *See* generally, W.R. Cornish, Moral Rights Under the 1988 Act, 11 EIPR 449 (1989).

3. *Moral Rights in the United States: In General.* Noting that "Article 6*bis* of Berne has generated one of the biggest controversies surrounding United States adherence to Berne," the House Report on the Berne Implementation Amendments concluded that existing state and federal law satisfied the Convention's requirements: "According to this view, there is a composite of laws in this country that provides the kind of protection envisioned by Article 6*bis*. Federal laws include 17 U.S.C. § 106, relating to derivative works; 17 U.S.C. § 115(a)(2), relating to distortions of musical works used under the compulsory license respecting sound recordings; 17 U.S.C. § 203, relating to termination of transfers and licenses, and section 43(a) of the Lanham Act, relating to false designations of origin and false descriptions. State and local laws include those relating to publicity, contractual violations, fraud and misrepresentation, unfair competition, defamation, and invasion of privacy. In addition, eight states have recently enacted specific statutes protecting the rights of integrity and paternity in certain works of art. Finally, some courts have recognized the equivalent of such rights." H.R. Rep. No. 609, 100th Cong., 2d Sess. 32–34 (1988).

American protection of moral rights has shrunk, not expanded, since the country's adherence to the Berne Convention. Although *Gilliam* indicates the possible reach of section 43(a) in securing the right of integrity, the U.S. Supreme Court's decision in Dastar Corp. v. Twentieth Century Fox Film Corp., 539 U.S. 23, 37 (2003), sharply curtailed the provision's usefulness in protecting the right of attribution. Lower federal courts at one time held that it constituted reverse passing off, actionable under section 43(a)'s bar on misrepresentations in the sale of goods and services, to distribute a work with a false attribution of authorship because the representation implied that someone other than the actual author created the work. *Dastar,* however, held that the phrase "origin . . . of . . . goods" in section 43(a)(1)(A) "refers to the production of the tangible goods that are offered for sale, and not to the author of any idea, concept, or communication embodied in those goods." Consequently, the court ruled that the defendant, which had copied and edited plaintiff's public domain television series, was free to distribute the edited version under its own name without crediting plaintiff.

For the suggestion that, by undermining U.S. obligations under Berne Article 6*bis, Dastar* may violate the longstanding constructional principle that statutes should be interpreted consistently with a country's international obligations, see Graeme W. Austin, 61 NYU Annual Survey of American Law 111 (2005). *See* generally, Roberta Kwall, The Soul of Creativity: Forging a Moral Rights Law for the United States (2010).

4.   *Moral Rights in the United States: VARA.* One year after the United States adhered to the Berne Convention, Congress passed the Visual Artists Rights Act of 1990, Pub. L. No. 101–650, (tit. VI,) 603(a) 104 Stat. 5089 (1990), adding section 106A to the Copyright Act to give creators of qualifying "works of visual art" rights of attribution and integrity in their works. The Act essentially equates "works of visual art" with works of fine art—works that exist in only a single copy or are published in signed and numbered editions of no more than 200 copies. Although section 106A defines attribution and integrity broadly to include misattribution as well as nonattribution and destruction as well as distortion, it subjects the rights to sweeping limitations.

Section 106A's most significant limitation is its exemption from liability of virtually all significant commercial uses of artistic works, including reproduction in books, magazines, newspapers, motion pictures and works made for hire. *See* Carter v. Helmsley-Spear, Inc., 71 F.3d 77, 37 U.S.P.Q.2d 1020 (2d Cir. 1995) (vacating injunction against removal of sculpture installed in defendant's building because it was made as work for hire). For a work to enjoy the rights granted by section 106A, it is not enough that it qualifies as a "work of visual art;" the offending work, too, must be a "work of visual art." Thus, section 106A will give the artist a remedy against a gallery owner who fails to attribute a work of visual art to him. But a newspaper that reproduces the same work of art without attribution will escape liability since a newspaper does not itself qualify as a "work of visual art," and the copyright owner of a motion picture made for hire will be similarly exempt. As a practical matter, what scope does this leave for moral right protection of fine art?

5.   *Why Is Moral Right Protection in the United States So Retrograde?* The TRIPs Agreement's exclusion of Article 6*bis* from the substantive Berne obligations that it incorporates in Article 9(1) reflects the staunch resistance in the United States to any TRIPs measure that might require the adoption of express protection for rights of integrity and attribution under national law. Does the fact that motion pictures and other works continue to be produced with little interference in such stalwart moral right countries as France and Germany, as well as more recent adherents, such as Canada and

Britain, suggest that the rights of integrity and attribution can be adopted in the United States with similarly modest effect? Why would the various flexibilities in continental doctrine described by Adolf Dietz in his report, excerpted above, not also emerge in American practice?

B. PATENTS

The first known system for granting patents to inventions in the useful arts dates to Venice in the mid-fifteenth century. The Venetian system, codified into a general patent statute in 1474, sought to spur the introduction of new technologies by giving patentees the exclusive right to practice their art for a specified period, usually ranging from ten to fifty years. Some of these patents issued to new inventions, others to technologies that the patent applicant had imported into Venice from other regions. Other European states granted similar monopolies to innovations through the sixteenth and seventeenth centuries as part of sovereign privileges, licenses and franchises.

Early English patent practice followed the Venetian model, awarding durationally limited monopolies to importers of already established crafts and industries as well as to originators of new devices. The Statute of Monopolies, 21 Jac. 1 c. 3 (1624), the seminal document in the history of English patent law, generally ratified this system, but also laid the foundation for an independent system of patents for invention. The Statute, prohibiting monopolies "for the sole buying, selling, making, working, or using of anything within this Realm," was passed in response to the Crown's generous grants of monopolies to court favorites for the manufacture of such common items as vinegar and starch. While outlawing these commercial monopolies, the Statute allowed the Crown to grant patents for fourteen years or less "to the true and first inventor or inventors" for "the sole working or making of any manner of new manufactures within this realm" provided "they be not contrary to the law nor mischievous to the state, by raising prices of commodities at home, or hurt of trade, or generally inconvenient."

On the European continent the lasting effects of guild practices stifled the emergence of independent patents for invention until well into the eighteenth century. French legislation in 1791 basically followed the approach of the English Statute of Monopolies, as did legislation passed between 1810 and 1843 in Austria, Russia, Belgium, the Netherlands, Spain, Sweden, Portugal and the several German states.

In the middle of the nineteenth century an anti-patent reaction set in, casting substantial doubt over the future of patents in Europe. Fueled by free trade sentiments that targeted patents as baleful protectionist measures, the attack on patent legislation was particularly severe on the Continent. The Netherlands repealed its patent law in 1869. Switzerland, which had so far failed to adopt a patent law, consistently rejected proposals to enact patent legislation. In England, speakers in both Houses of Parliament proposed the abolition of patents, and a bill passed by the House of Lords proposed to cut back the patent term and to introduce compulsory licensing and working requirements. By the 1870's, the anti-patent movement had mostly dissipated. (However, Switzerland did not adopt a patent law until 1887 and the Netherlands did not re-introduce a patent law until 1910.) The residues of the anti-patent movement can be found in the compulsory license and working requirements in many national laws today. For an incisive review of the anti-patent movement in nineteenth-century Europe, see Fritz Machlup & Edith Penrose, The Patent Controversy in the Nineteenth Century, 10 J. Econ. Hist. 1 (1950).

The American colonies and, after the Revolution, the state legislatures, generally followed England's *ad hoc* patent system, awarding patents through private acts passed in response to individual petitions. The first federal patent law, Act of April 10, 1790, ch. 7, 1 Stat. 109–110, was a general, rather than a private act, authorizing patents for "any useful art, manufacture, engine, machine, or device, or any improvement therein not before known or used." Upon a showing that the claimed invention was "sufficiently useful and important," a patent board composed of the Secretary of State, the Secretary of War and the Attorney General was to grant a patent for a term of up to fourteen years. The burden of examining patent applications soon proved too heavy for these busy civil servants, and a new patent law, Act of February 21, 1793, ch. 11, 1 Stat. 318, substituted the simple act of registration for the previous examination system. The Act of July 4, 1836, ch. 357, 5 Stat. 117, reinstated the examination system and also fixed the patent term at fourteen years with a seven year renewal period.

Though patterned after the same general model, national patent laws diverged on important points. Germany, for example, excluded patent protection for chemical products, and most countries other than England and the United States denied protection to medical devices. Rules differed from country to country on the form and content of patent applications, on the acts that would defeat the novelty required of a patentable invention, and on whether examination for novelty and inventiveness was a condition to a patent's issuance (France, for example, issued patents upon registration, without examination). Although, as a rule, national patent laws imposed the same terms on foreigners as on the country's own nationals, these divergences in substantive requirements, most notably the novelty requirement, frequently eliminated opportunities to obtain protection in foreign countries; the very act of applying for a patent in Country *A* might defeat novelty under the requirements imposed by the patent law of Country *B*.

An 1873 international exhibition of inventions in Vienna became the springboard for international patent harmonization. When several foreign firms decided not to participate out of concern that by exhibiting their inventions they would jeopardize protection for them, the Austrian government passed a special law protecting foreign inventions for the duration of the exhibition. Looking to the longer term, the government initiated the Congress of Vienna for Patent Reform to formulate principles for international patent protection. This and subsequent congresses led to an 1883 diplomatic conference in Paris that produced the first international agreement on patent protection, the Paris Convention for the Protection of Industrial Property. The Convention, which is based on the principle of national treatment, came into effect on July 7, 1884, and has since been revised several times, most recently at Stockholm in 1967.

The Paris Convention has harmonized some national patent norms but not others. Under the Convention, an inventor must file and prosecute a patent application in each country where he seeks protection, with consequent duplication of application fees, translation costs and attorney's fees. Since, as a practical matter, a filing has to be made within the limited priority period prescribed by the Convention, the inventor must decide whether to undertake the substantial cost of multiple applications well before he has any clear idea of his invention's potential for commercial success.

Regional arrangements, such as the European Patent Convention, have alleviated some of these burdens by enabling nationals of member countries to obtain nationally-enforceable patents through a single application. The Patent Cooperation Treaty, which entered into force on January 24, 1978, economizes significantly, but by no means completely, on multinational patent filings.

The 1994 TRIPs Agreement brought existing international patent norms into the trade process, obligating member states to comply with the normative provisions of the Paris Convention, 1967 Act. Apart from Article 2(1)'s incorporation of Paris Convention norms, Articles 27–34 of the TRIPs Agreement establish new norms respecting patent subject matter, conditions, rights and term of protection. Part III of the TRIPs Agreement provides for minimum standards for enforcement of patents, including availability of fair and equitable procedures, measures for obtaining evidence, and injunctive and monetary relief.

Notwithstanding the existing international treaties that have harmonized some aspects of national patent laws, differences in the laws and their implementations persist and complicate harmonization. The Patent Law Treaty, concluded in 2000, enhances conditions favorable to patent applicants operating internationally by further aligning certain practices in the national patent offices; however, the Treaty does not advance the harmonization of substantive patent law. Differences in national patent laws and policies have prevented countries from agreeing on the Substantive Patent Law Treaty that was proposed in the early 2000s.

While substantive patent law harmonization has not progressed at the global level since the TRIPs Agreement, the European Patent Convention has contributed to the harmonization of national patent laws in European countries—signatories to the Convention. The well-functioning system of European patents based on the Convention has slowed the development of a unitary patent that was proposed for the European Union to a certain extent; nevertheless, after decades of discussions, most European Union member states agreed near the end of 2012 to create a European patent with unitary effect, together with a Unified Patent Court.

Bibliographic Note. See generally Jon Nelson, International Patent Treaties with Commentary (2007); Stephen Ladas, Patents, Trademarks, and Related Rights: National and International Protection (1975); G.H.C. Bodenhausen, Guide to the Application of the Paris Convention for the Protection of Industrial Property as Revised at Stockholm in 1967 (1968). On the European Patent Convention, see Romualde Singer & Margarete Singer, The European Patent Convention (rev. English ed., by Ralph Lunzer) (1995); Gerald Paterson, The European Patent System: The Law and Practice of the European Patent Convention (1992). On the European patent with unitary effect and the Unified Patent Court, see The Unitary EU Patent System (Justine Pila & Christopher Wadlow eds., 2015); Pieter Callens & Sam Granata, The Unitary Patent and the Unified Patent Court (2017).

Joseph Straus, Implications of the TRIPs Agreement in the Field of Patent Law

Friedrich-Karl Beier and Gerhard Schricker, (Eds.),
From GATT to TRIPs: The Agreement on Trade-Related Aspects of
Intellectual Property Rights 160, 170–175 (1996).

12. The tremendous significance of the TRIPs Agreement for patent law can best be appreciated by taking a glance at the two conventions that until [the TRIPs Agreement] governed patents at a universal level: the Paris Convention for the Protection of Industrial Property of 1883 (PC), in the Stockholm version of 1967, . . . , and the Patent Cooperation Treaty (PCT) of 1970 . . . On a regional level inventors had at their disposal the European Patent Convention of 1973 (EPC) and two African patent granting systems, the Libreville Agreement of 1962, as revised at Bangui in 1977 of the African Intellectual Property Organization (OAPI) in Yaunde (Cameroon) for the French-speaking African countries, and the 1976 Lusaka Agreement on the Creation of the African Regional Industrial Property Organization (ARIPO) domiciled in Harare.

13. Examination of the patent provisions laid down in the venerable Paris Convention renders absolutely understandable the necessity mentioned in the Preamble to the TRIPs Agreement of establishing new rules and disciplines with respect to "the availability, scope and use of trade-related intellectual property rights." The Paris Convention is based on a combination of the principles of national treatment and non-discrimination (Art. 2) together with certain guaranteed minimum rights; in relation to the grant of such minimum rights for patents the

text is extremely reserved. There is a total lack of minimum standards as regards the availability and scope of patent protection. Hence, for over 100 years the Paris Convention left it to the discretion of its member states to provide for patents for inventions in all fields of technology or to exclude certain fields, to protect all categories of inventions, *i.e.* product and process inventions and their specific variations, *e.g.* inventions of certain uses, to decide on the prerequisites for the patent grant, and to determine the content, scope and term of patent protection. Inequalities in protection that may result from a lack of reciprocity, *e.g.* where one member country grants a long term of patent protection and demands modest or no annual fees whilst other countries proceed far more restrictively, were already pointed out by the U.S. during the Revision Conference of The Hague held in 1925, yet were dismissed at the time with reference, among other things, to increasing harmonization tendencies in the countries party to the Convention.

14. The main and in practice most important, yet strictly speaking the only effective minimum right in the patent field that is laid down in the Paris Convention is the extensive and at the same time complicated regulation of Union priority in Art. 4. This provision will only be discussed to the extent to which individual TRIPs provisions influence the claiming of Union priority. Apart from this the Paris Convention establishes the following minimum rights for patent holders: Art. 4*bis* ensures the independence of patents that have been obtained for the same invention in different Union countries, and in Art. 4*bis*(5) it is established that claiming priority shall not affect the term of the patent. In addition, pursuant to Art. 4 *quater*, the Union countries are prohibited from refusing to grant a patent or from declaring a patent invalid on the ground that the sale of the patented product or of the product of a patented process is subject to restrictions or limitations under national law. Article 5 *quater* also refers to national legislatures in clarifying that Union countries that extend process patent protection to products manufactured directly by such processes must grant such protection to patentees who are nationals of other Union countries, for imported products as well, *i.e.* not only for products manufactured within the importing country's national territory.

15. If one disregards the very limited but nevertheless considerable practical implications of the provisions of Art. 5*bis*, according to which Union countries must allow holders of industrial property rights a grace period of at least 6 months to rectify a failure to pay patent maintenance fees, and of Art. 11 of the Paris Convention—temporary protection of patentable inventions at certain international exhibitions—then the only other provision of the Paris Convention affording protection to patent holders is Art. 5A. This provision limits the freedom to act of the Union countries as regards both the possibility of forfeiture of patents and the grant of compulsory licenses. Article 5A(1), Paris Convention, relates to the no longer current problem of the effect of the importation by the

patent holder of patented products that were manufactured in other countries of the Union, establishing that in the country of import such an importation shall not lead to forfeiture of the patent. The implications of paragraphs 2 to 4 of this same Article were much more significant, at least within the context of international controversies in connection with the revision of the Convention. Here the Convention text encroaches circumspectly upon the regulative authority of the national legislatures to provide for legal measures to prevent the abusive exercise of patent rights, *e.g.*, as a result of failure to work or insufficient working of the patent. Pursuant to Art. 5A(4) Union countries may not allow applications for compulsory licenses due to failure to work or insufficient working before a period of four years has passed after filing of the patent application or a period of three years after the patent grant, depending upon which period expires last. If the patent holder is able to justify "his inaction by legitimate reasons," *i.e.* "if he can prove that legal, economic or technical barriers prevented (sufficient) working of the patent in his country, then applications for compulsory licenses must be refused. Where compulsory licenses are granted, they shall not be exclusive and may only be transferred together with the part of the enterprise or business that is involved in their exploitation." The Union countries must also establish additional restrictions of term and scope if they provide for the forfeiture of patents in cases of abuse: pursuant to Art. 5A(3) proceedings for the forfeiture or revocation of a patent may not be initiated before a period of two years has passed after the grant of the first compulsory license; the patent may only be declared forfeited if the grant of compulsory licenses would not have been sufficient in order to prevent abuse of the former. Although Art. 5A(4), Paris Convention, only restricts the countries of the Union in respect of compulsory licenses granted as a result of failure to work or insufficient working of the patent, and does not tie them in respect of the grant of compulsory licenses in the public interest, including compulsory licenses for dependent patents, this paragraph comprised the actual bone of contention and the reason for one of the most fruitless and lengthy debates between the developing countries and the industrialized states in the course of the attempts to revise the Paris Convention during the 1970s and 1980s. Whereas the industrialized states held on to Art. 5A of the Convention, the developing countries demanded special treatment so that they would be in a position to curtail the waiting periods in cases of failure to work and to grant exclusive compulsory licenses in certain cases of abusive failure to work.

16. The gravest consequence of the lack of minimum standards of patent protection in the Paris Convention was the fact that in 1988 it was established that at that time, *e.g.*, pharmaceutical products were not patentable in 49, animal species in 45, methods for the treatment of the human or animal body in 44, plant varieties in 44, biological processes for the production of plant varieties or animal species in 42, food products in 35, computer programs in 32, chemical products in 22, pharmaceutical processes in 10, processes for the manufacture of food in 9, and micro-

organisms in 9 of a total of 92 Paris Union states. In addition, in several Latin-American countries and a number of so-called socialist countries the term of patents and the scope of the patent right were little more than symbolic.

17. In order to clarify this point it must be noted that the text of the Patent Cooperation Treaty (PCT) was not intended or able to alter this situation. At the same time it must be appreciated that the PCT did provide an impetus for harmonization efforts on the part of the contracting states in the field of substantive patent law as well. This applies to the prior art that is decisive for international search pursuant to Art. 15 and for the international preliminary examination pursuant to Art. 33, and which is defined in Rule 33 of the Regulations Under the PCT, and to the patent requirements of Art. 33(2–4) that are decisive for preliminary examination, which for the most part are identical to the patentability requirements of the EPC. However, as clarified in Art. 33(5) PCT, the criteria listed in paras. (2) to (4) are only of significance as regards international preliminary examination. This means that PCT contracting states that establish additional or divergent criteria for the patentability of inventions are acting in accordance with the Treaty. Consequently, the international preliminary examination report may not contain any determinations as to whether or not the invention claimed is patentable under any national law (Art. 35(2) PCT).

18. As far as Europe is concerned, the European Patent Convention (EPC) that was signed in 1973 and which entered into force in 1978 sparked a voluntary wave of harmonization efforts of substantive patent law that would not have been imaginable beforehand. From an economic perspective, certainly the most important initiative was the harmonization of the catalogue of patentable inventions, which led a number of EC states to introduce product protection for chemical and pharmaceutical inventions and for food, beverages and tobacco products immediately or after a transitional period. Yet at the same time the catalogue of unpatentable subject matter and the exceptions to patentability were also harmonized with the extremely far-reaching consequence that, *e.g.*, the exclusion of computer programs as such from the category of patentable inventions and the unpatentability of inventions relating to animal or plant varieties, or to essentially biological processes for the production of plants or animals were set down by law throughout Europe . . . Moreover, the patentability requirements of novelty, inventive step and industrial applicability were approximated to the EPC regulations by almost all European countries, leaving only marginal differences. In the area of the effects of patent rights, which was affected to a far lesser degree by harmonization initiatives, the most important result was the extension of the term of protection to 20 years. It has almost been forgotten within general "patent awareness" that in Germany the 20-year term of protection was not introduced until the 1976 Law on International Patent Conventions was enacted . . .

1.   TERRITORIAL REACH OF PATENT LAW

Microsoft Corporation v. AT&T Corporation
Supreme Court of the United States, 2007.
550 U.S. 437, 82 U.S.P.Q.2d 1400.

JUSTICE GINSBURG delivered the opinion of the Court, except as to footnote 14.

It is the general rule under United States patent law that no infringement occurs when a patented product is made and sold in another country. There is an exception. Section 271(f) of the Patent Act, adopted in 1984, provides that infringement does occur when one "supplies . . . from the United States," for "combination" abroad, a patented invention's "components." 35 U.S.C. § 271(f)(1). This case concerns the applicability of § 271(f) to computer software first sent from the United States to a foreign manufacturer on a master disk, or by electronic transmission, then copied by the foreign recipient for installation on computers made and sold abroad.

AT&T holds a patent on an apparatus for digitally encoding and compressing recorded speech. Microsoft's Windows operating system, it is conceded, has the potential to infringe AT&T's patent, because Windows incorporates software code that, when installed, enables a computer to process speech in the manner claimed by that patent. It bears emphasis, however, that uninstalled Windows software does not infringe AT&T's patent any more than a computer standing alone does; instead, the patent is infringed only when a computer is loaded with Windows and is thereby rendered capable of performing as the patented speech processor. The question before us: Does Microsoft's liability extend to computers made in another country when loaded with Windows software copied abroad from a master disk or electronic transmission dispatched by Microsoft from the United States? Our answer is "No."

The master disk or electronic transmission Microsoft sends from the United States is never installed on any of the foreign-made computers in question. Instead, copies made abroad are used for installation. Because Microsoft does not export from the United States the copies actually installed, it does not "suppl[y] . . . from the United States" "components" of the relevant computers, and therefore is not liable under § 271(f) as currently written.

Plausible arguments can be made for and against extending § 271(f) to the conduct charged in this case as infringing AT&T's patent. Recognizing that § 271(f) is an exception to the general rule that our patent law does not apply extraterritorially, we resist giving the language in which Congress cast § 271(f) an expansive interpretation. Our decision leaves to Congress' informed judgment any adjustment of § 271(f) it deems necessary or proper.

I

Our decision some 35 years ago in *Deepsouth Packing Co. v. Laitram Corp.,* 406 U.S. 518 (1972), a case about a shrimp deveining machine, led Congress to enact § 271(f). In that case, Laitram, holder of a patent on the time-and-expense-saving machine, sued Deepsouth, manufacturer of an infringing deveiner. Deepsouth conceded that the Patent Act barred it from making and selling its deveining machine in the United States, but sought to salvage a portion of its business: Nothing in United States patent law, Deepsouth urged, stopped it from making in the United States the *parts* of its deveiner, as opposed to the machine itself, and selling those *parts* to foreign buyers for assembly and use abroad. . . . We agreed.

Interpreting our patent law as then written, we reiterated in *Deepsouth* that it was "not an infringement to make or use a patented product outside of the United States." *Id.,* at 527, see 35 U.S.C. § 271(a) (1970 ed.) ("[W]hoever without authority makes, uses or sells any patented invention, within the United States during the term of the patent therefor, infringes the patent."). Deepsouth's foreign buyers did not infringe Laitram's patent, we held, because they assembled and used the deveining machines outside the United States. Deepsouth, we therefore concluded, could not be charged with inducing or contributing to an infringement. . . .[2] Nor could Deepsouth be held liable as a direct infringer, for it did not make, sell, or use the patented invention—the fully assembled deveining machine—within the United States. The parts of the machine were not themselves patented, we noted, hence export of those parts, unassembled, did not rank as an infringement of Laitram's patent. . . .

Laitram had argued in *Deepsouth* that resistance to extension of the patent privilege to cover exported parts "derived from too narrow and technical an interpretation of the [Patent Act]." *Id.,* at 529. . . . Rejecting that argument, we referred to prior decisions holding that "a combination patent protects only against the operable assembly of the whole and not the manufacture of its parts." *Id.,* at 528. . . . Congress' codification of patent law, we said, signaled no intention to broaden the scope of the privilege. . . . And we again emphasized that

> "[o]ur patent system makes no claim to extraterritorial effect; these acts of Congress do not, and were not intended to, operate beyond the limits of the United States; and we correspondingly reject the claims of others to such control over our markets." *Id.,* at 531, (quoting *Brown v. Duchesne,* 19 How. 183, 195, 15 L.Ed. 595 (1857)).

---

[2]   See 35 U.S.C. § 271(b) (1970 ed.) ("Whoever actively induces infringement of a patent shall be liable as an infringer."); § 271(c) (rendering liable as a contributory infringer anyone who sells or imports a "component" of a patented invention, "knowing the same to be especially made or especially adapted for use in an infringement of such patent, and not a staple article or commodity of commerce suitable for substantial non-infringing use").

Absent "a clear congressional indication of intent," we stated, courts had no warrant to stop the manufacture and sale of the parts of patented inventions for assembly and use abroad. . . .

Focusing its attention on *Deepsouth,* Congress enacted § 271(f). . . . The provision expands the definition of infringement to include supplying from the United States a patented invention's components:

> "(1) Whoever without authority supplies or causes to be supplied in or from the United States all or a substantial portion of the components of a patented invention, where such components are uncombined in whole or in part, in such manner as to actively induce the combination of such components outside of the United States in a manner that would infringe the patent if such combination occurred within the United States, shall be liable as an infringer.

> "(2) Whoever without authority supplies or causes to be supplied in or from the United States any component of a patented invention that is especially made or especially adapted for use in the invention and not a staple article or commodity of commerce suitable for substantial noninfringing use, where such component is uncombined in whole or in part, knowing that such component is so made or adapted and intending that such component will be combined outside of the United States in a manner that would infringe the patent if such combination occurred within the United States, shall be liable as an infringer." 35 U.S.C. § 271(f).

II

Windows is designed, authored, and tested at Microsoft's Redmond, Washington, headquarters. Microsoft sells Windows to end users and computer manufacturers, both foreign and domestic. Purchasing manufacturers install the software onto the computers they sell. Microsoft sends to each of the foreign manufacturers a master version of Windows, either on a disk or via encrypted electronic transmission. The manufacturer uses the master version to generate copies. Those copies, not the master sent by Microsoft, are installed on the foreign manufacturer's computers. Once assembly is complete, the foreign-made computers are sold to users abroad. . . .

AT&T's patent ('580 patent) is for an apparatus (as relevant here, a computer) capable of digitally encoding and compressing recorded speech. Windows, the parties agree, contains software that enables a computer to process speech in the manner claimed by the '580 patent. In 2001, AT&T filed an infringement suit in the United States District Court for the Southern District of New York, charging Microsoft with liability for domestic and foreign installations of Windows.

Neither Windows software (*e.g.,* in a box on the shelf) nor a computer standing alone (*i.e.,* without Windows installed) infringes AT&T's patent.

Infringement occurs only when Windows is installed on a computer, thereby rendering it capable of performing as the patented speech processor. Microsoft stipulated that by installing Windows on its own computers during the software development process, it directly infringed the '580 patent. Microsoft further acknowledged that by licensing copies of Windows to manufacturers of computers sold in the United States, it induced infringement of AT&T's patent. . . .

Microsoft denied, however, any liability based on the master disks and electronic transmissions it dispatched to foreign manufacturers, thus joining issue with AT&T. By sending Windows to foreign manufacturers, AT&T contended, Microsoft "supplie[d] . . . from the United States," for "combination" abroad, "components" of AT&T's patented speech processor; accordingly, AT&T urged, Microsoft was liable under § 271(f). . . . Microsoft responded that unincorporated software, because it is intangible information, cannot be typed a "component" of an invention under § 271(f). In any event, Microsoft urged, the foreign-generated copies of Windows actually installed abroad were not "supplie[d] . . . from the United States." Rejecting these responses, the District Court held Microsoft liable under § 271(f). On appeal, a divided panel of the Court of Appeals for the Federal Circuit affirmed. . . . We granted certiorari . . . , and now reverse.

III

A

This case poses two questions: First, when, or in what form, does software qualify as a "component" under § 271(f)? Second, were "components" of the foreign-made computers involved in this case "supplie[d]" by Microsoft "from the United States"? . . .

As to the first question, no one in this litigation argues that software can *never* rank as a "component" under § 271(f). The parties disagree, however, over the stage at which software becomes a component. Software, the "set of instructions, known as code, that directs a computer to perform specified functions or operations," *Fantasy Sports Properties, Inc. v. Sportsline.com, Inc.,* 287 F.3d 1108, 1118 (C.A.Fed. 2002), can be conceptualized in (at least) two ways. One can speak of software in the abstract: the instructions themselves detached from any medium. (An analogy: The notes of Beethoven's Ninth Symphony.) One can alternatively envision a tangible "copy" of software, the instructions encoded on a medium such as a CD-ROM. (Sheet music for Beethoven's Ninth.) AT&T argues that software in the abstract, not simply a particular copy of software, qualifies as a "component" under § 271(f). Microsoft and the United States argue that only a copy of software, not software in the abstract, can be a component. . . .

The significance of these diverse views becomes apparent when we turn to the second question: Were components of the foreign-made computers involved in this case "supplie[d]" by Microsoft "from the

United States"? If the relevant components are the copies of Windows actually installed on the foreign computers, AT&T could not persuasively argue that those components, though generated abroad, were "supplic[d] . . . from the United States" as § 271(f) requires for liability to attach. . . . If, on the other hand, Windows in the abstract qualifies as a component within § 271(f)'s compass, it would not matter that the master copies of Windows software dispatched from the United States were not themselves installed abroad as working parts of the foreign computers. . . .

With this explanation of the relationship between the two questions in view, we further consider the twin inquiries.

B

First, when, or in what form, does software become a "component" under § 271(f)? We construe § 271(f)'s terms "in accordance with [their] ordinary or natural meaning." *FDIC v. Meyer,* 510 U.S. 471, 476, 114 S.Ct. 996, 127 L.Ed.2d 308 (1994). Section 271(f) applies to the supply abroad of the "components of a patented invention, where *such components* are uncombined in whole or in part, in such manner as to actively induce the combination of *such components.*" § 271(f)(1) (emphasis added). The provision thus applies only to "such components" . . . as are combined to form the "patented invention" at issue. The patented invention here is AT&T's speech-processing computer.

Until it is expressed as a computer-readable "copy," *e.g.,* on a CD-ROM, Windows software—indeed any software detached from an activating medium—remains uncombinable. It cannot be inserted into a CD-ROM drive or downloaded from the Internet; it cannot be installed or executed on a computer. Abstract software code is an idea without physical embodiment, and as such, it does not match § 271(f)'s categorization: "components" amenable to "combination." Windows abstracted from a tangible copy no doubt is information—a detailed set of instructions—and thus might be compared to a blueprint (or anything containing design information, *e.g.,* a schematic, template, or prototype). A blueprint may contain precise instructions for thc construction and combination of the components of a patented device, but it is not itself a combinable component of that device. AT&T and its *amici* do not suggest otherwise. . . .

AT&T urges that software, at least when expressed as machine-readable object code, is distinguishable from design information presented in a blueprint. Software, unlike a blueprint, is "modular"; it is a stand-alone product developed and marketed "for use on many different types of computer hardware and in conjunction with many other types of software." . . . Software's modularity persists even after installation; it can be updated or removed (deleted) without affecting the hardware on which it is installed. . . . Software, unlike a blueprint, is also "dynamic." . . . After a device has been built according to a blueprint's instructions, the blueprint's work is done (as AT&T puts it, the blueprint's instructions have been "exhausted" . . .). Software's instructions, in contrast, are contained in and continuously performed by a computer. . . .

The distinctions advanced by AT&T do not persuade us to characterize software, uncoupled from a medium, as a combinable component. Blueprints too, or any design information for that matter, can be independently developed, bought, and sold. If the point of AT&T's argument is that we do not see blueprints lining stores' shelves, the same observation may be made about software in the abstract: What retailers sell, and consumers buy, are *copies* of software. Likewise, before software can be contained in and continuously performed by a computer, before it can be updated or deleted, an actual, physical copy of the software must be delivered by CD-ROM or some other means capable of interfacing with the computer. . . .

Because it is so easy to encode software's instructions onto a medium that can be read by a computer, AT&T intimates, that extra step should not play a decisive role under § 271(f). But the extra step is what renders the software a usable, combinable part of a computer; easy or not, the copy-producing step is essential. Moreover, many tools may be used easily and inexpensively to generate the parts of a device. A machine for making sprockets might be used by a manufacturer to produce tens of thousands of sprockets an hour. That does not make the machine a "component" of the tens of thousands of devices in which the sprockets are incorporated, at least not under any ordinary understanding of the term "component." Congress, of course, might have included within § 271(f)'s compass, for example, not only combinable "components" of a patented invention, but also "information, instructions, or tools from which those components readily may be generated." It did not. In sum, a copy of Windows, not Windows in the abstract, qualifies as a "component" under § 271(f). . . .

C

The next question, has Microsoft "supplie[d] . . . from the United States" components of the computers here involved? Under a conventional reading of § 271(f)'s text, the answer would be "No," for the foreign-made copies of Windows actually installed on the computers were "supplie[d]" from places outside the United States. The Federal Circuit majority concluded, however, that "for software 'components,' the act of copying is subsumed in the act of 'supplying.' " 414 F.3d, at 1370. A master sent abroad, the majority observed, differs not at all from the exact copies, easily, inexpensively, and swiftly generated from the master; hence "sending a single copy abroad with the intent that it be replicated invokes § 271(f) liability for th[e] foreign-made copies." *Ibid.* . . .

Judge Rader, dissenting, noted that "supplying" is ordinarily understood to mean an activity separate and distinct from any subsequent "copying, replicating, or reproducing—in effect manufacturing." 414 F.3d, at 1372–1373. . . . He further observed: "The only true difference between making and supplying software components and physical components [of other patented inventions] is that copies of software components are easier to make and transport." *Id.*, at 1374. But nothing in § 271(f)'s text, Judge Rader maintained, renders ease of copying a relevant, no less decisive, factor in triggering liability for infringement. . . . We agree.

Section 271(f) prohibits the supply of components "from the United States . . . in such manner as to actively induce the combination of *such components*." § 271(f)(1) (emphasis added). Under this formulation, the very components supplied from the United States, and not copies thereof, trigger § 271(f) liability when combined abroad to form the patented invention at issue. Here, as we have repeatedly noted . . . , the copies of Windows actually installed on the foreign computers were not themselves supplied from the United States.[14] Indeed, those copies did not exist until they were generated by third parties outside the United States. . . . Copying software abroad, all might agree, is indeed easy and inexpensive. But the same could be said of other items: "Keys or machine parts might be copied from a master; chemical or biological substances might be created by reproduction; and paper products might be made by electronic copying and printing." Brief for United States as *Amicus Curiae* 24. . . . Section 271(f) contains no instruction to gauge when duplication is easy and cheap enough to deem a copy in fact made abroad nevertheless "supplie[d] . . . from the United States." The absence of anything addressing copying in the statutory text weighs against a judicial determination that replication abroad of a master dispatched from the United States "supplies" the foreign-made copies from the United States within the intendment of § 271(f). . . .

D

Any doubt that Microsoft's conduct falls outside § 271(f)'s compass would be resolved by the presumption against extraterritoriality, on which we have already touched. . . . The presumption that United States law governs domestically but does not rule the world applies with particular force in patent law. The traditional understanding that our patent law "operate[s] only domestically and d[oes] not extend to foreign activities," Fisch & Allen, [25 U.Pa. J. Int'l Econ. L. 557] at 559, is embedded in the Patent Act itself, which provides that a patent confers exclusive rights in an invention within the United States. 35 U.S.C. § 154(a)(1) (patentee's rights over invention apply to manufacture, use, or sale "throughout the United States" and to importation "into the United States"). . . .

As a principle of general application, moreover, we have stated that courts should "assume that legislators take account of the legitimate

---

[14]   In a footnote, Microsoft suggests that even a disk shipped from the United States, and used to install Windows directly on a foreign computer, would not give rise to liability under § 271(f) if the disk were removed after installation. . . . We need not and do not reach that issue here.

sovereign interests of other nations when they write American laws." *F. Hoffmann-La Roche Ltd. v. Empagran S. A.,* 542 U.S. 155, 164 (2004). . . . Thus, the United States accurately conveyed in this case: "Foreign conduct is [generally] the domain of foreign law," and in the area here involved, in particular, foreign law "may embody different policy judgments about the relative rights of inventors, competitors, and the public in patented inventions." Brief for United States as *Amicus Curiae* 28. Applied to this case, the presumption tugs strongly against construction of § 271(f) to encompass as a "component" not only a physical copy of software, but also software's intangible code, and to render "supplie[d] . . . from the United States" not only exported copies of software, but also duplicates made abroad.

AT&T argues that the presumption is inapplicable because Congress enacted § 271(f) specifically to extend the reach of United States patent law to cover certain activity abroad. But as this Court has explained, "the presumption is not defeated . . . just because [a statute] specifically addresses [an] issue of extraterritorial application," *Smith v. United States,* 507 U.S. 197, 204 (1993); it remains instructive in determining the *extent* of the statutory exception. . . .

AT&T alternately contends that the presumption holds no sway here given that § 271(f), by its terms, applies only to domestic conduct, *i.e.,* to the supply of a patented invention's components "from the United States." AT&T's reading, however, "converts a single act of supply from the United States into a springboard for liability each time a copy of the software is subsequently made [abroad] and combined with computer hardware [abroad] for sale [abroad.]" Brief for United States as *Amicus Curiae* 29. . . . In short, foreign law alone, not United States law, currently governs the manufacture and sale of components of patented inventions in foreign countries. If AT&T desires to prevent copying in foreign countries, its remedy today lies in obtaining and enforcing foreign patents. . . .

IV

AT&T urges that reading § 271(f) to cover only those copies of software actually dispatched from the United States creates a "loophole" for software makers. Liability for infringing a United States patent could be avoided, as Microsoft's practice shows, by an easily arranged circumvention: Instead of making installation copies of software in the United States, the copies can be made abroad, swiftly and at small cost, by generating them from a master supplied from the United States. The Federal Circuit majority found AT&T's plea compelling:

> "Were we to hold that Microsoft's supply by exportation of the master versions of the Windows & reg. software—specifically for the purpose of foreign replication—avoids infringement, we would be subverting the remedial nature of § 271(f), permitting a technical avoidance of the statute by ignoring the advances in a field of technology—and its associated industry practices—

that developed after the enactment of § 271(f). . . . Section § 271(f), if it is to remain effective, must therefore be interpreted in a manner that is appropriate to the nature of the technology at issue." 414 F.3d, at 1371.

While the majority's concern is understandable, we are not persuaded that dynamic judicial interpretation of § 271(f) is in order. The "loophole," in our judgment, is properly left for Congress to consider, and to close if it finds such action warranted.

There is no dispute, we note again, that § 271(f) is inapplicable to the export of design tools—blueprints, schematics, templates, and prototypes—all of which may provide the information required to construct and combine overseas the components of inventions patented under United States law. . . . We have no license to attribute to Congress an unstated intention to place the information Microsoft dispatched from the United States in a separate category. . . .

* * *

For the reasons stated, the judgment of the Court of Appeals for the Federal Circuit is

Reversed.

THE CHIEF JUSTICE took no part in the consideration or decision of this case.

(The concurring opinion by Justice Alito with whom Justice Thomas and Justice Breyer joined, is omitted.)

NOTES

1.   *Microsoft v. AT&T.* Justice Alito, joined by Justices Thomas and Breyer, concurred with the majority as to all but footnote 14, and declined to reach the question whether shipping a disk from the United States, to be removed after its installation abroad, would avoid infringement. Agreeing with the Court that Microsoft supplied no components of the foreign-made computers from the United States, Justice Alito thought it significant that the foreign-made CD-ROMS, after being used to install the code in computers, are removed "without affecting the computer's implementation of the code," so that "[n]o physical aspect of a Windows CD-ROM—original disk or copy—is ever incorporated into the computer itself." Consequently, "[b]ecause no physical object originating in the United States was combined with these computers, there was no violation of § 271(f)." 127 S.Ct. at 1761–62.

Justice Stevens, dissenting, thought that code itself could be considered a "component" for purposes of the statute. "[I]f a disk with software inscribed on it is a 'component,' I find it difficult to understand why the most important ingredient of that component is not also a component." Also, "unlike a blueprint that merely instructs a user how to do something, software actually causes infringing conduct to occur. It is more like a roller that causes a player piano to produce sound than sheet music that tells a pianist what to do." 127 S.Ct. at 1763.

Was the difference between Justice Stevens and the majority that the majority thought that section 271(f) applies only to physical, mechanical inventions, while Stevens believed that it applied to virtual, electronic ones as well? Or was the difference that the majority—and not Stevens—believed that the principle of territoriality requires resolving any doubt about a statute's geographic scope against its extraterritorial application?

2. *Supplying Components of an Invention.* When the 1952 U.S. Patent Act extended protection to components of a patented invention in section 271(c), it codified then-existing case law on contributory infringement, which required an act of direct infringement in the United States, and thus was of no help to the patent owner in *Deepsouth*, where the final assembly occurred outside the United States.

Is it an unacceptable extraterritorial expansion of a country's patent law to render the supply of a component abroad a patent infringing act? Territoriality is a principle of prudence as well as of statutory interpretation. Even if Congress had the *power* to enact section 271(f), was it *correct* for it to do so in light of the requirements of comity and respect for foreign legal systems? The Supreme Court observed in *Deepsouth* that "[r]espondent holds foreign patents; it does not adequately explain why it does not avail itself of them." 406 U.S. 518, 531 (1972). Is it a sufficient explanation that American patent owners should not have to go to the expense of prosecuting infringement actions in far-off lands? Does the fact that U.S. courts do not treat patent infringement suits as transitory causes of action that can be filed outside the country in which the infringement occurred provide a rationale for this extension of U.S. patent rights? Is it an acceptable rationale that the law of the importing country gives inadequate protection to the patented invention? Even if the latter rationale may have been acceptable at one time in the past, is it valid now that the substantive and procedural norms of the TRIPs Agreement should have been implemented in most countries around the world?

3. *Making of Components of an Invention.* If the manufacture of a patented invention is divided between two or more countries, should the making of the components of the patented invention lead to liability for infringement regardless of where the final assembly occurs? In the United States, section 271(a) does not incorporate the joint tortfeasor liability principle, and neither section 271(c) nor section 271(f) covers the "making" of components. However, if a patent owner can obtain lost profits from sales abroad of products made from components supplied from the United States under section 271(f), does this result "modify the circumstances when the law . . . treat[s] an invention as having been made within the United States?" *See* Justice Gorsuch's dissenting opinion in WesternGeco LLC v. ION Geophysical Corp., 138 S.Ct. 2129, 2141 (2018). For a discussion of *WesternGeco* see note 6 on page 11, above.

In Germany courts have adopted the view that "the manufacturing of a patented invention encompasses the entire activity necessary for a production of the product from its very beginning." Reichsgericht, I 98/97, Sept. 18, 1897, RGZ 22, 79. Therefore, German courts have been able to stop the manufacture of components of the patented invention intended for assembly anywhere, including outside of Germany. One commentator has expressed concern over the extraterritorial expansion implicit in the German approach: "Even in situations where the facts indicate that the alleged infringer actively induces or even controls the ultimate step in the process of manufacture carried out abroad, it cannot be neglected that it is outside the territory of production where this ultimate step takes place, *i.e.* where the patented product is made." Rainer Moufang, The Extraterritorial Reach of Patent Law, in Patents and Technological Progress in a Globalized World— Liber Amicorum Joseph Straus 601, 607–608 (Wolrad Prinz zu Waldeck und Pyrmont, Martin J. Adelman, Robert Brauneis, Josef Drexl, & Ralph Nack eds., 2009).

4. *Territorially Divided Infringements (U.S.).* So-called divided infringements occur when the use of an invention consists of uses of individual parts of the invention by different users. Divided infringements can also occur when some parts of the invention are used inside the protecting country and other parts outside the protecting country. If under U.S. law the partial manufacture of an invention does not infringe a U.S. patent, can partial use of an invention infringe a U.S. patent?

In NTP, Inc. v. Research In Motion, Ltd., 418 F.3d 1282 (Fed.Cir. 2005), defendant, distributor of the BlackBerry system that allows out-of-office users to remain in constant contact with their email, argued that even if its system fell within plaintiff's patent claims, an important element of the system—the BlackBerry Relay—was located in Canada, so that it did not infringe plaintiff's patents under the U.S. Patent Act. Following an instruction from the district court that "the location of RIM's Relay in Canada does not preclude infringement," the jury found that RIM had committed direct, induced, and contributory infringement on all asserted claims.

The Court of Appeals for the Federal Circuit took a more discriminating approach. Starting with the plaintiff's claimed "system," the court held that "[t]he use of a claimed system under section 271(a) is [in] the place at which the system as a whole is put into service, *i.e.*, the place where control of the system is exercised and beneficial use of the system obtained." Since "RIM's customers located within the United States controlled the transmission of the originated information and also benefited from such an exchange of information," it "was proper for the jury to have found that use of NTP's asserted system claims occurred within the United States." 418 F.3d at 1317.

The Court of Appeals reached a different conclusion as to infringement of NTP's method claims. "A method or process consists of one or more operative steps," and "the use of a process necessarily involves doing or performing each of the steps recited. . . . We therefore hold that a process cannot be used 'within' the United States as required by section 271(a) unless each of the steps is performed in this country." Since the location of RIM's relay in Canada precluded a finding of direct infringement by RIM customers of the method claims reciting an "interface switch" or an "interface," RIM could not be held liable for induced or contributory infringement of these claims as a matter of law. 418 F.3d at 1317–1318.

The Federal Circuit also concluded that RIM could not have infringed the asserted method claims under the "sells," "offers to sell," or "imports" prongs of sections 271(a); nor "[b]y merely supplying to its customers in the United States," did RIM supply any "steps of a patented process invention for combination outside the United States" under section 271(f). Finally, "the district court erred in not holding as a matter of law that § 271(g) was inapplicable to the asserted method claims." 418 F.3d at 1318–1324.

5. *Territorially Divided Infringements (U.K.).* In Menashe Business Mercantile Ltd. v. William Hill Organisation Ltd., [2002] EWHC 397 (Patents), plaintiff, the owner of a British patent on a system for playing an interactive casino game consisting of a host computer, one or more player terminals, and communication means and software for interoperating the host and terminals, charged that defendant's system infringed its patent under section 60(2) of the 1977 U.K. Patents Act, which makes it an infringement for one to supply, or offer to supply, in the United Kingdom "any of the means, relating to an essential element of the invention, for putting the invention into effect" when he knows that the means are suited to putting the invention into effect in the United Kingdom. Defendant answered that it did not infringe because its host computer was situated in Antigua or Curacao, and not in the U.K.

Justice Jacob, in the Patents Court, had "no hesitation" in accepting plaintiff's argument because "[a]ny other result would be monstrous—allowing a defendant to use supposed cross-border problems to avoid infringement of a system anywhere." *Id.,* ¶ 20. Justice Jacob fastened his result on section 60(2)'s phrasing, which "looks to *effect* within the U.K. not *use within the U.K.,*" and, rejecting the argument that an effect test was too ambiguous, asserted that "[n]o businessman would think for [a] moment that the effect of the invention is not within the U.K. when the whole point of defendants' system is to get U.K. punters to play their system." *Id.,* ¶ 24.

On appeal, the Court of Appeal, noted that section 60(2) is concerned with putting something into effect, and "does not look to something which merely has an effect in the United Kingdom," but nonetheless affirmed, on different grounds.

> "The claimed invention requires there to be a host computer. In the age that we live in, it does not matter where the host computer is situated. It could be in the United Kingdom, on a satellite, or even on the border between two countries. Its location is not important to the user of the invention nor to the claimed gaming system. In that respect, there is a real difference between the claimed gaming system and an ordinary machine. For my part I believe that it would be wrong to apply the old ideas of location to inventions of the type under consideration in this case. A person who is situated in the United Kingdom who obtains in the United Kingdom a CD and then uses his terminal to address a host computer is not bothered where the host computer is located. It is of no relevance to him, the user, nor the patentee as to whether or not it is situated in the United Kingdom."

Menashe Business Mercantile Ltd. v. William Hill Organization Ltd., [2002] EWCA Civ 1702, ¶ 32.

To what extent does the approach taken by the Court of Appeal differ from the approach taken by the Federal Circuit in the *BlackBerry* case? Plaintiff had in the Patents Court used a simple example to illustrate the hole in patent infringement rules that would follow from a decision against it:

> Take the case of a someone who installs and sells a telecommunication apparatus which straddles the French-German border. Suppose the patent claim calls for integers A + B. Both are essential integers. But A is in France and B is in Germany. If [the defendants] are right, no infringement. We respectfully submit it obviously would be infringement—else it would offend common sense. [2002] EWHC 397 (Patents), par. [11]

To this, defendant answered that the hole was one "which if the claimant's patent agent had been more ingenious, could have been plugged . . . through separate claims to the terminal and the host computers." Would more astute drafting of claims have better resolved the territoriality problem in *Menashe*? In the *BlackBerry* case, above?

6. *Components of a Patented Method.* If the U.S. approach outlined in *NTP v. RIM* to territorially divided infringements of method claims were to be adopted by other countries, one result could be that a patent owner would have no remedy against someone using a patented method in several countries. German courts, by contrast, have found infringements of process patents even where some of the steps of the patented methods were performed outside of Germany. In *Rohrschweissverfahren* the Federal Supreme Court ruled that a "method to control the elevation of the temperature of electrically heated parts" was infringed when the initial steps of the process were performed in Switzerland and the remaining steps were performed in Germany. Rohrschweissverfahren, Bundesgerichtshof, X ZR 113/04, 2007.

Can the steps of a patented method be supplied and therefore infringe a patent under section 271(f)? In *NTP v. RIM* the Court of Appeals observed that "it is difficult to conceive of how one might supply or cause to be supplied all or a substantial portion of the steps of a patented method in the sense contemplated by the phrase 'components of a patented invention.' " 418 F.3d at 1322. Later, in Cardiac Pacemakers, Inc. v. St. Jude Medical, Inc., 576 F.3d 1348 (Fed.Cir. 2009) (en banc), the Court of Appeals held that section 271(f) does not cover method claims, reasoning that "[s]upplying an intangible step is . . . a physical impossibility." 576 F.3d at 1364.

Are process steps always entirely intangible? In Quanta Computer, Inc. v. LG Electronics, Inc., 553 U.S. 617 (2008), a decision concerning the exhaustion of method patents, the U.S. Supreme Court noted that methods may be substantially embodied in a product if the product "ha[s] no reasonable noninfringing use and include[s] all the inventive aspects of the patented methods." *Id.*, 638. In *Cardiac Pacemakers* the method at issue was a method of heart stimulation using an implantable heart stimulator, and

Cardiac Pacemakers argued that when its competitor supplied defibrillators abroad, it infringed the patent by supplying components of the patented method. In *NTP v. RIM* the method claim of the patent consisted of "a method for transmitting originated information from one of a plurality of originating processors in an *electronic mail system* to at least one of a plurality of destination processors in the *electronic mail system*." 418 F.3d at 1294.

7. *Secondary Liability Arising from Acts Committed Outside the Protecting Country.* Under U.S. law a finding of secondary liability requires proof of a related direct infringement. While the acts of direct infringement, such as the making or using of a patented invention, must occur in the protecting country, the acts of secondary infringement may take place outside the protecting country. Therefore, inducement under section 271(b) has been found even when the inducing activity occurred outside the United States. Until 1994, the provision of section 271(c) on contributory infringement concerning components could also be used against acts of secondary infringement abroad that led to direct infringements in the United States; however, a 1994 amendment added language that now limits contributory infringement to offers to sell or sales "within the United States" and importation "into the United States."

In other countries, general doctrines of aiding and abetting a tortious activity may provide a vehicle for a finding of secondary liability for acts committed outside a protecting country. In Germany, section 830 of the Civil Code has been used for this purpose. Aiding and abetting under the German Civil Code may even reach infringers whose connection to the protecting country is remote. For example, in *Funkuhr* a Dutch company was found to infringe a German patent by supplying devices to another Dutch company; the German Federal Supreme Court reasoned that the infringer "knew of the patent and knew of the country of destination and therefore willingly and willfully helped to cause the domestic distribution." Funkuhr, Bundesgerichtshof, X ZR 36/01, 2002, 2002 GRUR 599. When a 1980 amendment introduced a provision on secondary patent infringement into the German Patent Act, it limited the infringement to acts committed "within the territory of the application of the Act"—meaning within Germany. However, as the Federal Supreme Court explained in *Funkuhr II*, a defendant will be liable under the provision even when it supplies an essential element of a patented invention from Germany to a company abroad if the defendant thereby contributes to the manufacture abroad of a product that is intended to be supplied into Germany where the product will infringe a patent. Funkuhr II, Bundesgerichtshof, X ZR 53/04, 2007.

For a comparative analysis of contributory infringement provisions in the laws of the United Kingdom, the United States, and Germany, and in the 1975 Convention for the European Patent for the Common Market see Justice Jacob's judgment in Grimme Landmaschinenfabrik GmbH & Co KG v. Scott, [2010] EWCA Civ 1110. For a discussion of extraterritorial features of U.S. patent law see Timothy R. Holbrook, Extraterritoriality in U.S. Patent Law, 49 Wm. & Mary L. Rev. 2119 (2008).

2. REQUIREMENTS FOR PROTECTION

a. STATUTORY SUBJECT MATTER

Novartis AG v. Union of India
Supreme Court of India, 2013.
Civil Appeal Nos. 2706–2716 of 2013.

AFTAB ALAM, J.

. . .

31. At the time of Independence, India's patent regime was governed by the Patents and Designs Act, 1911, which had provisions both for product and process patents. It was, however, generally felt that the patent law had done little good to the people of the country. . . .

34. In 1957, [a] committee came to be appointed under the chairmanship of Justice N. Rajagopala Ayyangar to take a fresh look at the law of patent and to completely revamp and recast it to best sub-serve the (contemporary) needs of the country.

35. Justice Ayyangar . . . pointed out that during the period 1930–37, the grant of patents to Indians and foreigners was roughly in the ratio of 1:9. Even after Independence, though a number of institutions for post-graduate training were set up and several national laboratories were established to encourage a rapid growth of scientific education, the proportion of Indian and the foreign patents remained substantially the same, at roughly 1:9. Justice Ayyangar further pointed out that this ratio does not take into account the economic or industrial or scientific importance of the inventions. . . .

38. Justice Ayyangar observed that the provisions of the Patent law have to be designed, with special reference to the economic conditions of the country, the state of its scientific and technological advancement, its future needs and other relevant factors, and *so as to minimize, if not to eliminate, the abuses to which a system of patent monopoly is capable of being put.* Bearing in view the matters set above, he recommended retaining the patent system, but with a number of improvements.

39. One of the improvements suggested was to define, with precision, those inventions which should be patentable *and equally clearly identify certain inventions, the grant of patents to which would retard research, or industrial progress, or be detrimental to the national health or well-being, and to make those inventions non-patentable.*

40. Justice Ayyangar's report specially discussed (a) patents for chemical inventions; and (b) patents for inventions relating to food and medicine.

41. In regard to patents for chemical substances, he examined the history of the law in other countries and pointed out that Germany was the first to adopt the system of confining the patentability of inventions

relating to chemical products or substances to process claims. The law was then followed in many other countries in the world, for instance Austria, Brazil, Czechoslovakia, Holland, Hungary, Japan, Mexico, Norway, Poland and the U.S.S.R. Products produced by chemical process were not patentable though processes for making such products were patentable, if, of course, they satisfied the other tests of patentability, *e.g.* novelty, subject matter, etc. In light of the experience of the other countries, Justice Ayyangar recommended:

> "I have considered the matter with the utmost care and have reached the conclusion that the chemical and pharmaceutical industry of this country would be advanced and the tempo of research in that field would be promoted if the German system of permitting only process claims were adopted."

42. Coming next to the patents for inventions relating to food and medicine, Justice Ayyangar pointed out that barring the US, there was hardly any country that allowed unrestricted grant of patents in respect of articles of food and medicines, or as to the licensing and working of patents in this class. In none of the countries of Europe were patents granted for product claims for articles of food or medicine, and in a few (Denmark for articles of food; and Italy, under the law of 1957, for medicinal products) even claims for processes for producing them were non-patentable. He explained that the reason for this state of law is stated to be that the denial of product claims is necessary in order that important articles of daily use such as medicine or food, which are vital to the health of the community, should be made available to everyone at reasonable prices and that no monopoly should be granted in respect of such articles. It is considered that the refusal of product patents would enlarge the area of competition and thus result in the production of these articles in sufficient quantity and at the lowest possible cost to the public.

43. . . . [T]he Patents Act, 1970, came to be enacted mainly based on the recommendations of the report, and came into force on April 20, 1972, replacing the Patents and Designs Act, 1911. . . .

45. . . . Chapter II [of the Patents Act, 1970] was headed "Inventions not patentable". . . .

> "**Section 3. What are not inventions.**—The following are not inventions within the meaning of this Act,—. . .
>
> d) the mere discovery of any new property or new use for a known substance or of the mere use of a known process, machine or apparatus unless such known process results in a new product or employs at least one new reactant . . .
>
> **Section 5. Inventions where only methods or processes of manufacture patentable.**—In the case of inventions—
>
> a) claiming substances intended for the use, or capable of being used, as food or as medicine or drug . . .

no patent shall be granted in respect of claims for the substances themselves, but claims for the methods of processes of manufacture shall be patentable." . . .

47. . . . We may now take a look at how the Patent and Designs Act, 1911, and the Patents Act, 1970, impacted the pharmaceutical industry and the availability of drugs in the country. . . .

49. The fall and rise of the Indian pharmaceutical industry is explained as the result of certain factors, not the least important of which was the change in the patent law in the country, which made medicines and drugs and chemical substances non-patentable. Chaudhuri explains that before the introduction of sulfa drugs (1930s) and penicillin (1940) that brought about the therapeutic revolution, drugs of natural origin were more important than synthetic ones. Also, medicinal plants (that is, raw materials) for about three-fourths of the drugs mentioned in British and other pharmacopoeias actually grew in India.

50. By the time the Second World War started (1939), several indigenous firms were engaged in manufacturing drugs, and indigenous producers met 13 per cent of the medicinal requirements of the country. They still had a long way to go to attain self-sufficiency but in terms of the range of operations they were already manufacturing all types of drugs. By the early 1950s, because of the spread of manufacturing activities, the indigenous sector dominated the pharmaceutical industry in India. It accounted for about 62 per cent of the market in 1952 . . . However, the rise and growth of multinational corporations (MNCs) worldwide in the post-Second World War period, as well as the therapeutic revolution changed these dynamics. The MNCs started research for developing new drugs in the 1930s–40s. As a result, in the late 1940s and during the 1950s and even after that at a slower rate, new drugs discovered by the MNCs began to be available for medical use. The indigenous sector was not equipped for research for developing new drugs, that is, for developing a new chemical entity. With the introduction of new drugs at a rapid rate by the MNCs, the role of patents became important. Because of the patent regime under the 1911 Act and the unsupportive industrial policy, the indigenous sector lost its status in the 1950s and the 1960s. In contrast to 62 per cent of the market in the early 1950s, the market share of the indigenous sector declined to 32 per cent by 1970. In contrast, the market share of the MNCs increased from 38 per cent in 1952 to 68 per cent in 1970 . . .

51. However, according to Chaudhuri, the situation changed in the 1970s. Several official initiatives were taken in the 1970s, of which the most important one was the enactment of the Patents Act, 1970, which changed the environment in favour of the indigenous sector.

52. In regard to the Patents Act, 1970, Chaudhuri maintains that Patent "reforms" contributed directly to the transformation of the pharmaceutical industry. He points out that under the Patents Act, 1970, articles of food, medicines and drugs and chemical substances could be

patented only for a new method or process of manufacture, not for the products as such ... Further, unlike in the previous patent regime, for each particular drug only one method or process—the best known to the applicant—could be patented ...

54. Till the early 1970s the industry was dominated by MNCs who commanded 68% of the market share. India was dependent on imports for many essential bulk drugs. This import dependence constricted consumption in a country deficient in foreign exchange, and inhibited the growth of the industry. Drug prices in India were very high.

55. In the late 1970s and 1980s, Indian companies started large-scale production of bulk drugs. The development of the bulk drugs sector is actually the most important achievement of the pharmaceutical industry in India. This led to the transformation of the industry.

56. The most rapid growth of the Indian pharmaceutical industry took place from the 1990s onwards. Both production and exports grew remarkably fast. The production of both bulk drugs and formulations started increasing sharply and steadily.... The growth was most remarkable from 2000 to 2005, when production increased much more than it had in the last two decades. Indian companies further consolidated their domination in the domestic market. Their market share increased from 60 per cent in 1991 to 68 per cent in 1998 and 77 per cent in 2003.

57. The growth was also very fast in the export markets. India became a net exporter by 1988–89, and since then there has only been an increase in the Indian exports.... More than three-fourths of bulk drug production and almost one-fourth of the formulations production are exported. The USA, which has the toughest regulatory requirements, has emerged as India's largest export partner in pharmaceuticals....

59. Even as the country's pharmaceutical industry, helped by the basic changes made in the patent system by the Patent Act, 1970, was going from strength to strength, certain developments were taking place at the international level that would deeply impact the Patent system in the country. Following the Uruguay round of multilateral negotiations under the General Agreement on Tariffs and Trade (GATT), the Agreement on Trade-Related Aspects of Intellectual Property Rights (The TRIPS) was arrived at and it came into force on January 1, 1995. The TRIPS Agreement is the most comprehensive multilateral agreement to set detailed minimum standards for the protection and enforcement of intellectual property rights, and aims at harmonizing national intellectual property systems....

61. Article 65 (sub-articles 1 and 2) [of the TRIPS Agreement] allowed India to delay the application of the provisions of the Agreement for a period of 5 years, that is, till January 1, 2000; sub-Article 4 allowed India to delay for a further period of five years, that is, till January 1, 2005, the application of the provision relating to product patent, in respect of all

articles excluded by the Patent Act, 1970, which included pharmaceuticals and agricultural chemical products. But, Article 70 . . . enjoined that in the meanwhile it should provide for a means by which applications for patents for inventions in respect of pharmaceutical and agricultural chemical products could be filed and also for the grant of "exclusive marketing rights" for such products. In discharge of its obligations under the Agreement, the Government of India promulgated the Patents (Amendment) Ordinance, 1994 . . . , amending the Patents Act, 1970. The Ordinance provided for making "a claim for patent of an invention for **a substance itself intended for use, or capable of being used, as medicine or drug**" . . . and for the grant of exclusive marketing rights with respect to the product that is the subject matter of such a patent claim . . . The Ordinance, however, lapsed on March 26, 1995, . . . without being replaced by any corresponding Act. . . .

62. In this state of the patent law in the country, India was twice taken to the WTO panel, first on a complaint by the USA (WT/DS50/AB/R, dated December 19, 1997) and the second time on a complaint filed by the European Communities (WT/DS79/R, dated August 24, 1998). . . . By a decision dated December 19, 1997, the Appellate Body affirmed the panel's findings that India had not complied with its obligations under Article 70.8(a) and Article 70.9 of the TRIPS Agreement . . .

67. . . . Thus faced with the threat of trade sanctions, Parliament passed the Patents (Amendment) Act 1999 . . . on March 26, 1999, which amended the provisions of the Patents Act 1970 retrospectively, with effect from January 1, 1995, the date when the TRIPS Agreement came into force. By the Amendment Act of 1999, section 5 of the Patent Act was amended to provide for making "a claim for patent of an invention for **a substance itself intended for use or capable of being used, as medicine or drug**". The Amendment Act further incorporated in the Patent Act, Chapter IVA, which contained provisions for grant of exclusive marketing rights in respect of pharmaceutical substances for which a claim for patent was made under section 5 of the Act. The Amendment Act of 1999 thus complied with Article 70(8) and (9) of the TRIPS Agreement. . . .

76. Parliament had an absolutely unenviable task on its hands. It was required to forge, within a very limited time, an Act that would be TRIPS compliant without, in any way, compromising on public health considerations. . . . [T]he TRIPS Agreement had aroused grave concerns about its impact on public health. India had learnt from experience the inverse relationship between product patents and the indigenous pharmaceutical industry, and its effects on the availability of essential drugs at affordable prices. It is also seen above that after the patent system in India barred the grant of patents for pharmaceutical and chemical substances, the pharmaceutical industry in the country scaled great heights and became the major supplier of drugs at cheap prices to a number of developing and under developed countries. Hence, the

reintroduction of product patents in the Indian patent system through the TRIPS Agreement became a cause of alarm not only in this country but also for some international agencies. . . .

95. After the amendment with effect from Jan 1, 2005, section 3(d) stands as under:—

> **"Section 3. What are not inventions.**—The following are not inventions within the meaning of this Act,—
>
> (d) **the mere discovery of a new form of a known substance which does not result in the enhancement of the known efficacy of that substance** or the mere discovery of any new property or new use for a known substance or of the mere use of a known process, machine or apparatus unless such known process results in a new product or employs at least one new reactant.
>
> *Explanation.*—**For the purposes of this clause, salts, esters, ethers, polymorphs, metabolites, pure form, particle size, isomers, mixtures of isomers, complexes, combinations and other derivatives of known substance shall be considered to be the same substance, unless they differ significantly in properties with regard to efficacy."**
> . . .*

97. A perusal of the Parliamentary debate would further reveal that the whole debate centered on medicines and drugs. It would not be an exaggeration to say that eighty per cent of the debate was focused on medicines and drugs and the remaining twenty per cent on agricultural chemicals. . . .

NOTES

1. *Patentable Subject Matter.* TRIPs Article 27 aims to curtail national limitations on intellectual property protection. It provides that "patents shall be available for any inventions, whether products or processes, in all fields of technology, provided that they are new, involve an inventive step and are capable of industrial application." The "products or processes" clause obliterates the distinction once drawn in many countries, including India, between unpatentable pharmaceutical and chemical products and the patentable processes for making these products. The "all fields of technology" clause bars member states from denying protection to inventions in such broad fields as foods and beverages.

How much flexibility does TRIPs Article 27 give countries to adjust their patent system to local needs? Carlos Correa suggests that it is "[a]n important flexibility allowed to WTO members . . . to determine what is meant by 'invention,' a concept that is not defined in the TRIPs Agreement. In fact, there is significant diversity in national laws and practices around

---

* Section 5, quoted in ¶ 45, above, was omitted by the Patents (Amendment) Act, 2005. *Ed.*

the notion of invention." Carlos M. Correa, Guidelines for Pharmaceutical Patent Examination: Examining Pharmaceutical Patents from a Public Health Perspective, United Nations Development Programme, 2016, p. 18.

2.   *Novartis.* *Novartis* concerned the patentability of the beta crystalline form of Novartis's pre-existing cancer drug Glivec/Gleevec. The Supreme Court of India held that the new form was not patentable in India because the form failed to meet the requirement of enhanced efficacy included in section 3(d) of the Patents Act (quoted at the end of the excerpt, above). Does section 3(d)'s efficacy requirement run afoul of TRIPs Article 27(1)'s prohibition against discrimination based on the field of technology because it narrows the scope of patentable subject matter for medicines and other chemical substances by heightening the standard for what qualifies as an "invention?" *Novartis*, ¶ 104; Novartis AG v. Union of India, High Court of Judicature at Madras, W.P. Nos. 24759 and 24760 of 2006, 2007, ¶ 4.

For a discussion of the *Novartis* case and an analysis of post-*Novartis* developments in Indian patent law see Shamnad Basheer, Trumping TRIPS: Indian Patent Proficiency and the Evolution of an Evergreening Enigma, 18(1) Oxford University Commonwealth Law Journal 16 (2018). The requirement of enhanced efficacy and the *Novartis* decision are discussed further in note 6 on page 481, below.

3.   *Exclusions from Patentable Subject Matter*. The last two paragraphs of TRIPs Article 27 allow limited grounds for excluding subject matter from patent protection. Article 27(2) applies to all fields of invention but imposes stringent conditions on exclusion: the invention's commercial exploitation must be barred "to protect *ordre public* or morality," and the exclusion cannot be made "merely because the exploitation is prohibited by public law." (*Ordre public* means deep-seated public policy, not "public order.") Article 27(3), by contrast, allows exclusions for certain narrowly drawn subject matter categories without any required showing of pertinent public policy. What connection, if any, exists between the decision to prohibit exploitation of an invention and the decision to prohibit patents on the invention?

How likely is it that a WTO panel will, under Article 27(2), second-guess the motives of a sovereign nation in prohibiting the exploitation of a class of inventions? The EPO Technical Board of Appeal explained in the context of the European Patent Convention, which also includes *ordre public* and morality as possible grounds for exclusions from patentability, that "[t]he concept of morality is related to the belief that some behaviour is right and acceptable whereas other behaviour is wrong, this belief being founded on the totality of the accepted norms which are deeply rooted in a particular culture. For the purposes of the European Patent Convention, the culture in question is the culture inherent in European society and civilisation." Plant Cells, EPO Technical Board of Appeal, T 356/93 (1995), ¶ 6. Is there a single concept of morality shared among all of the thirty-eight member countries of the European Patent Organization?

For a historical and comparative discussion of the concepts of *ordre public* and morality in patent law see Joseph Straus, *Ordre Public* and

Morality Issues in Patent Eligibility, in Intellectual Property in Common Law and Civil Law (Toshiko Takenaka ed., 2013), pp. 19–49.

4.   *Pharmaceuticals.* The requirement of patent protection for medicines has been particularly problematic for countries such as India, where a significant portion of the population struggles with access to medicines. TRIPs Articles 65 and 66 provided for transitional periods that allowed developed and least-developed countries to delay the implementation of most of the provisions of the TRIPs Agreement, including Article 27(1), but critics argue that the eventual implementation impedes access to medicines in these countries. Is the internationally-mandated patent protection for medicines compatible with the constitutional right to health that many countries recognize? *See* Constitution of India, Articles 39(e) and (f), and 47; Constitution of the Federal Republic of Brazil, Article 196; Constitution of the Republic of South Africa, Article 27.

In 2012 a group of Kenyan citizens infected with HIV successfully challenged a Kenyan anti-counterfeiting law designed to protect patented products, including pharmaceuticals. The High Court of Kenya ruled that the law violated fundamental rights to life, human dignity, and health contained in Articles 26(1), 28, and 43 of the Constitution of Kenya because the law restricted access to cheaper, generic versions of patented drugs. Patricia Asero Ochieng v. Attorney General, High Court of Kenya, Petition No. 409 of 2009, Apr. 20, 2012, ¶ 87. The Court noted that "[w]hile . . . intellectual property rights should be protected, where there is the likelihood . . . that their protection will put in jeopardy fundamental rights such as the right to life of others, . . . they must give way to the fundamental rights of citizens." *Id.*, ¶ 86.

Recognizing the implementation challenges faced by least-developed countries, the TRIPs Council permitted these countries to delay TRIPs implementation for ten years and, in the case of pharmaceuticals, subsequently postponed the implementation deadline to 2016. With that deadline looming, Bangladesh in February 2015 submitted a request on behalf of the 34 least-developed countries for another extension of the transition period for pharmaceuticals. WTO members agreed to extend the deadline to 2033.

For general and comparative discussions of the intersection of patent law and access to medicines see Balancing Wealth and Health (Rochelle C. Dreyfuss & César Rodríguez-Garavito eds., 2014); Jennifer Sellin, Access to Medicines (2014); Duncan Matthews, When Framing Meets Law: Using Human Rights As a Practical Instrument to Facilitate Access to Medicines in Developing Countries, in TRIPS and Developing Countries: Towards a New IP World Order? (Gustavo Ghidini, Rudolph J.R. Peritz & Marco Ricolfi, 2014), pp. 12–38. For TRIPs accommodations that were requested and made with regard to pharmaceuticals see page 542, below.

5.   *Biotechnological Inventions.* Virtually since the inception of the biotechnology industry, the question of patent protection for products consisting of biological material—microorganisms, transgenic animals, human proteins—and processes for the use or production of biological materials, has stirred an ethical and technical debate. The ethical issues have centered on whether and to what extent the state, through its patent policies, should be complicit in the alteration of life forms, particularly humans. Some questions are peculiar to protection for living matter—for example, whether the subject matter is already encompassed by *sui generis* legislation on plant or animal varieties. Other questions are more routine— Is the subject matter no more than a discovery or principle of nature? What is the proper scope of the patent claim? What constitutes an enabling disclosure? The TRIPs Agreement captures these ambivalences not only in Article 27(2)'s exception for *ordre public* or public morality, but also in Article 27(3)(b)'s exception for "plants and animals other than microorganisms, and essentially biological processes for the production of plants or animals other than non-biological and microbiological processes."

In the United States, the Supreme Court's landmark decision in Diamond v. Chakrabarty, 447 U.S. 303, 206 U.S.P.Q. 193 (1980), held that a live, genetically-altered microorganism—the claim was for a new, genetically engineered bacterium to be used in the treatment of oil spills—was patentable subject matter and was not disqualified from protection either for being a living thing or a product of nature. The PTO Board of Patent Appeals and Interferences subsequently invoked *Chakrabarty* to hold that man-made, non-naturally occurring polyploid oysters constituted patentable subject matter, Ex parte Allen, 2 U.S.P.Q.2d 1425 (1987), and the next year the PTO issued its first animal patent, No. 4,736,866, for a mouse—called an oncomouse—genetically altered by researchers at Harvard University to facilitate cancer research.

Developments in other countries have also favored protection for biological products and processes. The German Federal Supreme Court early held that "biological forces and phenomena belong in principle to the area in which patentable inventions are possible," and that a method for breeding animals can represent a teaching to utilize natural biological forces and phenomena and therefore be patentable. Red Dove (Rote Taube), Bundesgerichtshof, X ZB 15/67, 1969, 1 IIC 136 (1970). In 1990 the European Patent Office's Technical Appeal Board set aside the rejection of Harvard's patent application for the oncomouse, and on reconsideration the Examining Division granted the patent, holding that the subject matter fell outside the European Patent Convention's prohibition on claims to animal varieties in Article 53(b), and, further that the subject matter was not contrary to *ordre public* or morality under Article 53(a). Harvard/Onco-mouse, 1991 EPO Reports 525 (1991).

Will the approach be different in cases of cloning—creating genetically identical living organisms? The U.S. Court of Appeals for the Federal Circuit held that Dolly the Sheep, "the first mammal ever cloned from an adult somatic cell," was not eligible for patent. In re Roslin Institute (Edinburgh), 750 F.3d 1333, 1334 and 1339 (2014). Referring to the 2013 U.S. Supreme Court decision in *Myriad*, the Court of Appeals explained that "Dolly's genetic identity to her donor parent renders her unpatentable." *Id.*, 1337.

6. *Biotechnological Inventions: The Human Body.* The ethical issues surrounding biotechnological inventions are even more pronounced for inventions that involve the human body and its elements. While the need for invention is particularly pressing when human lives are at stake, the prospect of a legal monopoly on elements of the human body is worrisome. In the United States, in line with the then-existing practice of the U.S. Patent and Trademark Office, section 33(a) of the 2011 Leahy-Smith America Invents Act formalized the rule that "no patent may issue on a claim directed to or encompassing a human organism." But questions have arisen about the patenting of human DNA sequences and inventions originating from stem cell research.

Patents concerning DNA sequences associated with breast and ovarian cancers were at the center of disputes testing the patentability of DNA sequences. The U.S. Supreme Court held that a naturally occurring DNA segment was not eligible for a patent because it fell within the "law of nature" exception to patentable subject matter, but that synthetically created DNA (so-called cDNA) was patent-eligible to the extent that it was not naturally occurring. Association for Molecular Pathology v. Myriad Genetics, Inc., 569 U.S. 576, 580 (2013).

The High Court of Australia took a different view, holding that DNA sequences, including cDNA sequences, are not patent-eligible under Australian law because they are not "manners of manufacture" and do not satisfy other factors that Australian courts consider when they assess patent eligibility. D'Arcy v. Myriad Genetics, Inc., [2015] HCA 35, ¶ 94.

In the end, the outcome in the United States and Australia for the particular Myriad patents was identical; because the cDNA at issue was identical to the naturally-occurring DNA, the U.S. courts held it unpatentable in the United States. In re BRCA1- and BRCA2-Based Hereditary Cancer Test Patent Litigation, 774 F.3d 755 (Fed. Cir. 2014). For a detailed comparative analysis of the U.S. and Australian decisions concerning DNA sequences see Jessica C. Li, *D'Arcy v. Myriad Genetics*: A Demand for the "Made" or "Non-Information" and Clear Subject Matter?, 47 IIC 537 (2016).

In the European Union, the patentability of inventions resulting from stem cell research came under scrutiny in light of Article 6(2)(c) of Directive 98/44/EC of the European Parliament and of the Council of 6 July 1998 on the legal protection of biotechnological inventions. The Directive, which took ten years to be approved, established a basis for biotechnology patents across the European Union, requiring member states to protect "biotechnological inventions" under national patent law. Article 3 of the Directive provides that inventions meeting the standard requirements of novelty, inventive step and utility "shall be patentable even if they concern a product consisting of or containing biological material"—defined as "[a]ny material containing genetic information and capable of reproducing itself or being reproduced in a biological system"—or "a process by means of which biological material is produced, processed or used." Article 6 contains an exception for *ordre public* or morality and Article 6(2) specifically identifies as unpatentable "(a) processes for cloning human beings; (b) processes for modifying the germ line genetic identity of human beings; (c) uses of human embryos for industrial or commercial purposes; (d) processes for modifying the genetic identity of animals which are likely to cause them suffering without any substantial medical benefit to man or animal, and also animals resulting from such processes."

Disputes concerning Article 6(2)(c) of the Directive have centered on the definition of "human embryos." In Brüstle v. Greenpeace, CJEU, C-34/10, 2011, the Greenpeace organization attacked the validity of a German patent for "isolated and purified neural precursor cells, processes for their production from embryonic stem cells and the use of neural precursor cells for the treatment of neural defects." *Id.*, ¶ 15. The Court of Justice of the European Union explained that the term "human embryo" covers even "non-fertilized ovum into which the cell nucleus from a mature human cell has been transplanted" or "whose division and further development have been stimulated by parthenogenesis." *Id.*, ¶ 38. In a later decision the Court clarified its holding in *Brüstle* by explaining that the prohibition on patentability does not apply when the human ovum "does not, in itself, have the inherent capacity of developing into a human being." International Stem Cell Corp. v. Comptroller General of Patents, Designs and Trade Marks, CJEU, C-364/13, 2014, ruling of the Court.

7. *Software Patents.* In the early years of the software industry, most countries that addressed the question whether computer programs were statutory patent subject matter either concluded that they were not or else put substantial hurdles in the way of protection. The European Patent Convention provides in Article 52(1) that "European patents shall be granted for any inventions, in all fields of technology, provided that they are new, involve an inventive step and are susceptible to industrial application," and Article 52(2) lists among the subject matter that does not constitute inventions, "schemes, rules and methods for performing mental acts, playing games or doing business, and programs for computers." (Comparable provisions appear in the laws of most member states.) The U.S. Patent Act does not expressly exclude protection for computer programs but, starting in the 1970's, the Patent and Trademark Office, abetted by ambiguous Supreme Court opinions, invoked such antique exceptions as the "mental steps" and "printed matter" doctrines to rule that computer programs were not statutory subject matter.

By the 1990's, obstacles to patent protection for software had begun to erode. A series of 1994 decisions of the U.S. Court of Appeals for the Federal Circuit effectively held that while a computer program alone was not protectible, a machine, such as a computer, whose operations were reconfigured by a computer program constituted statutory subject matter. Subsequent judicial decisions, such as State Street Bank & Trust Co. v. Signature Financial Group, Inc., 149 F.3d 1368, 47 U.S.P.Q.2d 1596 (Fed.Cir. 1998), opened the door to protection even wider, allowing any invention producing "a useful, concrete and tangible result" to be patentable. The U.S. Court of Appeals for the Federal Circuit developed a "machine-or-transformation" test to determine patentability but the U.S. Supreme Court in Bilski v. Kappos, 561 U.S. 593 (2010), rejected the exclusivity of the test without articulating another test.

In the early 2010s the United States experienced a backlash against patents on computer programs. Some of the ambivalence about computer programs as patentable subject matter can be traced to the "patent troll" phenomenon—the rise of entities that often create no inventions themselves but rather acquire patents from others and build their business model on the use of questionable practices to enforce the patents; so-called patent trolls have often focused on high-technology-related patents with broad claims. The 2014 U.S. Supreme Court decision in *Alice Corp. Pty Ltd v. CLS Bank Int'l* put the validity of many existing U.S. patents on computer programs in question with its holding that when patent claims are drawn to an abstract idea, "merely requiring generic computer implementation fails to transform that abstract idea into a patent-eligible invention." 134 S.Ct. 2347, 2352 (2014). Although the Court did not foreclose the possibility that some computer programs may be patent-eligible, the decision neither defined "abstract idea" nor specified the types of "element or combination of elements" that if claimed would be "sufficient to ensure that the patent in practice amounts to significantly more than a patent upon the [abstract idea] itself." *Id.*, 2355 (internal quotations omitted). *See also* page 481, below.

In Europe, the European Patent Office and some national courts ruled that because Article 52(3) of the European Convention denies protection only to computer programs "as such," programs could be protected if they exhibited an added "technical effect." In an early and influential opinion, VICOM/Computer Related Invention, T 208/84, O.J. EPO 14 (1987), the EPO Technical Board of Appeal ruled that while the mathematical method behind a program was not protectible, the program could qualify as statutory subject matter to the extent that it controlled and directed the steps in a technical process—digitally processing images. "Decisive [was] what technical contribution the invention . . . made to known art." *Id.*, ¶ 16. Later, in IBM, T 1173/97, O.J. EPO 609 (1999), the Board explained that a computer program has to have a "further technical effect" to be patentable, meaning "a technical effect going beyond those effects which occur inevitably when any program is run." Opinion G 3/08, Enlarged Board of Appeal, May 12, 2010, ¶ 10.8.4. In Microsoft, T 424/03 (2006), the Board of Appeal specified that "[a] computer system including a memory (clipboard) is a technical means, and consequently the claimed method [(having a clipboard for performing data transfer of data in a clipboard format)] has technical character." *Id.*, ¶ 5.1. In 2010 the Enlarged Board of Appeal confirmed that "a claim in the area of computer programs can avoid exclusion [from patentability] merely by explicitly mentioning the use of a computer or a computer-readable storage medium." Opinion G 3/08, May 12, 2010, ¶ 10.13.

Can Article 52(2) of the European Patent Convention, and comparable rules under national law that exclude patent protection for computer programs as such, be reconciled with EPC Article 52(1), and with TRIPs Article 27(1), which requires that patents "be available for any inventions, whether products or processes, in all fields of technology, provided that they are new, involve an inventive step and are capable of industrial application"? Is the answer that, like mental steps, games or business methods, computer programs are not "inventions"? That they occupy no "field of technology"?

Does a "further technical effect" test bring computer software into a field of technology?

For a comparison of approaches adopted for software patents in the United States, the United Kingdom, and Australia see Research Affiliates LLC v. Commissioner of Patents, Federal Court of Australia, [2014] FCAFC 150.

8. *Utility Models.* Some worthwhile inventions will fail to meet patent law's high inventive standard or will lack the market value to justify the lengthy rigors of the patent examination process. Rather than consign these more modest inventions to the public domain or leave them to the vagaries of unfair competition protection, many countries supplement utility patents with "petty patents" or "utility models" that operate on the basis of registration rather than examination, provide a significantly shorter term of protection and, though imposing patent law's traditional novelty requirement, withhold its high standard of inventiveness. Most of these statutes follow the example of the 1891 German *Gebrauchsmustergesetz.* Some form of utility model protection exists in many countries, including Brazil, China, a number of European Union member countries, Japan, and South Korea.

Debates over a proposed directive to harmonize utility model protection in the European Union addressed some of the more salient issues raised by these statutes. (Britain, which introduced the concept of the utility model in 1843, Act 6 & 7 Vict. ch. 65, dropped the system forty years later, and is one of the few EU countries without utility model legislation.) One issue was whether protection should be confined to physical devices or extended to processes and substances as well. (Only a handful of EU member states impose the requirement of a three-dimensional physical embodiment.) Another issue was whether computer programs, including particularized algorithms, should be protected. Discussions also focused on the precise level of invention to be required for protection. The proposal for the directive on utility model protection became moot in 2000 when it was decided that a proposal for a European Union patent should take priority, and in 2006 the utility model proposal was officially withdrawn from the legislative process. *See* Jose Antonio Gomez Segade, Utility Models—Lost in Translation, 39(2) IIC 135 (2008); Rudolf Krasser, Harmonization of Utility Model Law in Europe, 31 IIC 797 (2000).

The 1911 Washington Revision to the Paris Convention added utility models to the Convention's list of the objects of industrial property protection in Article 1(2). As a consequence, Article 2's national treatment obligation requires Country *A* to extend protection under its utility model law to nationals of Country *B*, a member of the Paris Union, even though Country *B*, not having a utility model law, offers no comparable protection to nationals of Country *A*.

NOTE: PLANT PATENTS AND PLANT VARIETY PROTECTION

Lawmakers first addressed the question of protection for plants and plant varieties in the 1930's, and since that time a perennial question for

intellectual property policy has been whether these newly-important
forms of subject matter should be protected under an existing intellectual
property law or under a new, *sui generis* regime. Doubts that plant
subject matter could meet traditional patent standards prompted the
proposals for *sui generis* protection, while the subsequently revealed
shortcomings of *sui generis* protection have increased the pressure for
more capacious protection under patent statutes. Among the
reservations expressed about plants as patent subject matter are that
plants are living organisms and products of nature; that they lack utility
or industrial application; that drafting an enabling disclosure for a plant
is difficult if not impossible; and that results are not replicable.

At the level of international policymaking, successive texts of the
International Convention for the Protection of New Varieties of Plants
have had a substantial impact on the formation of national law. TRIPs
Article 27(3)(b), which allows member countries to exclude patent
protection for plants and animals other than micro-organisms, but
specifically requires members to "provide for the protection of plant
varieties either by patents or by an effective *sui generis* system or by any
combination thereof," perpetuates the longstanding division.

In the United States, the 1930 Plant Patent Act, Pub. L. No. 71–245,
46 Stat. 376 (1930), added sections 161–164 to the Patent Act to provide
sui generis protection for asexually reproduced plants—"any distinct and
new variety of plant, including cultivated sports, mutants, hybrids and
newly found seedlings, other than a tuber-propagated plant or a plant
found in an uncultured state." Forty years later, Congress passed the
Plant Variety Protection Act, Pub. L. No. 91–577, 84 Stat. 1542 (1970),
protecting new varieties of plants that reproduce sexually through seeds.
A certificate of plant variety protection will issue if the applicant's variety
meets the statutory requirements of distinctness, uniformity and
stability, and passes novelty and other statutory bars comparable to
those imposed by section 102 of the Patent Act. Protection lasts for a
period of eighteen years from the date the certificate is issued. The Act is
administered by the Plant Variety Protection Office in the United States
Department of Agriculture. The Plant Variety Protection Act appears at
7 U.S.C. §§ 2321 *et seq.*

In Europe, where reservations about traditional patent protection
for plants were, if anything, deeper than in the United States, the first
sui generis statutes were enacted in the 1940's and 1950's. The 1961
International Convention for the Protection of New Varieties of Plants,
founded by several European countries (Belgium, Denmark, France,
Germany, Italy, the Netherlands, Switzerland and the United Kingdom)
triggered a second generation of plant variety legislation in Europe
modeled after the treaty's requirements. (After considering whether the
treaty should be a special agreement under the Paris Convention, the
organizing countries concluded that it should be a separate convention
with a union of its own, the *Union pour la Protection des Obtentions*

Végétales, or UPOV.) In the European Union, the Council Regulation (EC) No. 2100/94 of 27 July 1994 on Community plant variety rights created a European Union-wide plant variety right modeled in part on the 1991 text of the International Plant Variety Protection Treaty as an alternative to rights under national law.

Because *sui generis* plant protection statutes carved out exceptions from protection not present in mainstream patent laws, some U.S. and European breeders pressed for protection under the less circumscribed patent statutes. The U.S. Supreme Court's decision in Diamond v. Chakrabarty, 447 U.S. 303 (1980), holding that neither the 1930 Plant Patent Act nor the 1970 Plant Variety Protection Act intended to exclude living things from protection under the general Patent Act, laid the foundation for a ruling that plants could be patented. In 1985, the Board of Patent Appeals and Interferences ruled in Ex Parte Hibberd, 227 U.S.P.Q. 443, that plants, plant seeds, and plant tissue cultures were patentable subject matter. In Pioneer Hi-Bred International, Inc. v. J.E.M. Ag Supply, Inc., 200 F.3d 1374, 53 U.S.P.Q.2d 1440 (Fed.Cir. 2000), the Court of Appeals for the Federal Circuit ruled that seeds, as well as the plants grown from them, are patentable subject matter and that the Plant Variety Protection Act was not the exclusive means for obtaining federal protection against the sexual reproduction of plants.

Article 53(b) of the European Patent Convention presented a particular hurdle to patent protection for plants in its provision that a European patent shall not be granted in respect of "plant or animal varieties or essentially biological processes for the production of plants or animals"—*i.e.* subject matter that, with respect to plants, is protectible under the International Plant Variety Convention and national plant variety protection laws. Limiting the scope of the European Patent Convention's exclusion to subject matter that the plant variety statutes included, the Enlarged Board of Appeal of the European Patent Office ruled in Transgenic Plant NOVARTIS II, EPO Enlarged Board of Appeal, G 1/98, 1999, that "[a] claim wherein specific plant varieties are not individually claimed is not excluded from patentability under Article 53(b) EPC even though it may embrace plant varieties." In the European Union, Article 4(2) of the EU Biotech Directive affirmed the availability of patent protection for plants by allowing patent protection for inventions concerning plants (or animals) "if the technical feasibility of the invention is not confined to a particular plant or animal variety."

Although plants may be patentable, non-microbiological processes consisting of crossing and selecting plants are excluded from patentability under Article 53(b) of the European Patent Convention. The Enlarged Board of Appeal of the European Patent Office confirmed in 2010 that "a process for the production of plants which is based on the sexual crossing of whole genomes and on the subsequent selection of plants, in which human intervention, including the provision of a technical means, serves to enable or assist the performance of the process steps, remains excluded from patentability as being essentially biological within the meaning of Article 53(b) EPC." State of Israel/Tomatoes, EPO Enlarged Board of Appeal, G 1/08, 2010, point 6.4.2.3. In 2016 the Enlarged Board held that the exclusion from patentability applied to essentially biological processes but did not cover products directly obtained from such processes. Tomato II and Broccoli II, EPO Enlarged Board of Appeal, G 2/12 and G 2/13, 2016.

In an important decision in 2010 the Court of Justice of the European Union ruled that a patent on a plant gene does not cover the material that is made out of the plant "where [the gene] does not perform the function for which it was patented." Monsanto Technology LLC v. Cefetra BV and Others, CJEU, C-428/08, 2010, ¶ 50. Article 9 of the EU Biotech Directive extends patent protection to "all material . . . in which the patented product is incorporated and in which the genetic information is contained and performs its function;" however, under Article 10, the protection does "not extend to biological material obtained from the propagation or multiplication of biological material placed on the market in the territory of a Member State by the holder of the patent or with his consent."

The CJEU decision in *Monsanto* arose from a series of patent infringement suits filed by Monsanto Technology Ltd. in several countries, including the United States. In the CJEU case, which originated in the Netherlands, Monsanto argued that the importation of soy derivatives into Europe from Argentina infringed Monsanto's patents on modified DNA molecules because the molecules were included in the derivatives. In the United States, Monsanto prevailed in its dispute over a farmer who replanted seeds that were harvested from crops grown from patented Monsanto seeds. Bowman v. Monsanto Co., 569 U.S. 278 (2013). The U.S. Supreme Court held that "the exhaustion doctrine [did] not enable Bowman to make *additional* patented soybeans without Monsanto's permission." *Id.*, 1766.

As one commentator observed, Monsanto's technology has been surrounded by significant social tensions. The commentator warned that "while genetic modification in the food sector and the corresponding expectation to obtain patent protection for the modified products may have done a lot to stimulate development in this area, the balance between users and developers has notably shifted towards the latter." Christopher Heath, The Scope of DNA Patents in Light of the Recent Monsanto Decisions, 40(8) IIC 940, 956 (2009).

The United Nations International Treaty on Plant Genetic Resources for Food and Agriculture, adopted in 2001, directly confronts intellectual property's potential threat to access to food. The Treaty facilitates the study of 64 particular crops for the purposes of research, breeding, and training, but in Article 13(2)(d) provides that "[r]ecipients [of the genetic resources] shall not claim any intellectual property or other rights that limit the facilitated access for food and agriculture, or their genetic parts or components."

As discussed in Chapter I, above, intellectual property rights currently fail to provide mechanisms to compensate for genetic resources and traditional knowledge on which inventions and new varieties are based. For example, native plants and other genetic resources in biodiversity-rich developing and least-developed countries have been the targets of corporate bioprospecting, leading to patents and certificates of protection that fail to share the benefits of the bioprospecting with the countries of origin.

Nonetheless, efforts continue to be made to protect the countries and communities where genetic resources and traditional knowledge originate. The 2010 Protocol to the 1992 Convention on Biological Diversity—the Nagoya Protocol on Access to Genetic Resources and the Fair and Equitable Sharing of Benefits Arising from their Utilization—provides in Article 5(1) that "benefits arising from the utilization of genetic resources as well as subsequent applications and commercialization shall be shared in a fair and equitable way with the [country] providing such resources." In WIPO, the Intergovernmental Committee on Intellectual Property and Genetic Resources, Traditional Knowledge and Folklore has been negotiating an international legal instrument that would ensure the effective protection of genetic resources. The establishment of registries of genetic resources and traditional knowledge, and an obligation for a patent applicant to disclose the origin of an invention, have been promoted as two mechanisms that could help protect the interests of countries of origin.

For a comparative review of approaches to patenting plants and protecting plant varieties see Mark D. Janis et al., Intellectual Property Law of Plants (2014); Herman Tuhairwe, Farmers' Rights and Plant Variety Protection in Uganda: Considerations and Opportunities, 12(12) J. of Intell. Prop. Law & Practice 1004 (2017); Emmanuel Salami, Patent Protection and Plant Variety Rights for Plant Related Inventions in the EU and Selected Jurisdictions, 40(10) EIPR 630 (2018).

b.   STANDARDS

i.   *Priority, Novelty and Statutory Bars*

NOTE: FIRST-TO-INVENT AND FIRST-TO-FILE SYSTEMS

For an invention to be patented, it must not only fall within the definition of patentable subject matter; the invention must also be new, involve an inventive step (be non-obvious), and be capable of industrial application (be useful). Although TRIPs Article 27(1) includes these three requirements, their definitions and practical implementation vary among countries. U.S. novelty rules exhibited salient differences from those of the rest of the world until 2013 because, until that year, the

United States shaped its rules on principles different from those used in the rest of the world. While the first-to-file principle became the standard for patent systems, the U.S. patent system continued to operate based on the first-to-invent principle. After many years of contentious debates the United States joined the rest of the world with the 2011 Leahy-Smith America Invents Act ("AIA"), according to which U.S. patent applications filed on or after March 16, 2013, are subject to novelty rules that are based on the first-to-file principle.

Important reasons remain to be familiar with both principles: First, at least until 2033, U.S. patents will exist that were granted under the first-to-invent principle, and the old novelty rules will continue to apply when the validity of these patents is challenged. Second, the new U.S. rules of novelty, while generally consistent with the first-to-file principle, bear some marks of the first-to-invent principle. Familiarity with the first-to-invent principle is therefore important for understanding the persisting differences in national rules of novelty. Finally, elements of the novelty rules have been carefully calibrated under each principle to serve the goals of the patent systems. Studying the calibration of the elements under the two principles is important for an appreciation for the calibration, which should occur each time any changes to the novelty rules are contemplated.

Priority. In a first-to-file system the first inventor to file a patent application claiming a patentable invention is granted a patent. Therefore, under the AIA, the U.S. patent system, like other national patent systems, bases priority on the effective filing date.

In a first-to-invent system the inventor who first invented a product or process was granted a patent. Under U.S. patent law prior to the AIA the priority date was the date on which the inventor reduced the invention to practice; the date of the reduction to practice could have referred to either actual or constructive reduction to practice. An inventor could also claim the date of conception as the priority date as long as the inventor proceeded diligently toward the reduction to practice.

Grace Period. The two types of systems differ in the types of disclosures that do not defeat priority, and sometimes also in the length of the period during which such disclosures may occur without defeating priority. First-to-file systems prefer that disclosures be made in patent applications, and therefore these systems provide for a limited grace period. Few and narrow types of disclosures, made typically within six months prior to the filing of the patent application, are permissible for the priority to be preserved.

The U.S. first-to-invent system permitted more types of priority non-defeating disclosures. Before the AIA the U.S. grace period was formulated as a statutory bar to patentability, and section 102(b) of the Patent Act excluded from patentability any invention that was "patented or described in a printed publication in this or a foreign country or in public use or on sale in this country, more than one year prior to the date of the application for patent in the United States."

There was significant pressure to maintain the broad scope of the grace period in the United States even after the change to the first-to-file system. The 1992 Report of the Secretary of Commerce Advisory Commission noted that "[t]he grace period is . . . of critical importance to the scientific community in facilitating early dissemination of research results, while preserving the patenting opportunity of the inventor for a reasonable period."* Additionally, the Report pointed out that "[t]he grace period . . . is essential to protect entities which have limited financial resources for speculative patent application filing and prosecution. The U.S. grace period helps to ensure equal access for such entities to the benefits of U.S. patent rights during the initial period of testing or promotional activities."**

The AIA introduced in the United States a grace period that is narrower in scope than the pre-AIA grace period, but that is still more generous in scope and duration than the grace periods in many other countries. The AIA enlarged the scope of prior art that will defeat novelty by defining prior art as inventions "patented, described in a printed publication, or in public use, on sale, or otherwise available to the public before the effective filing date of the claimed invention"; descriptions of an invention in an issued U.S. patent or in a published U.S. patent application that was filed before the filing date will also defeat priority. 35 U.S.C. § 102(a). In section 102(b) the AIA excludes from prior art only disclosures that are made one year or less before the effective filing date by the inventor or "another who obtained the subject matter disclosed directly or indirectly from the inventor," and any other subsequent disclosures. 35 U.S.C. § 102(b). The AIA design of the grace period has led some commentators to call the new U.S. system a "first-inventor-to-disclose" system because the first disclosure, coupled with a timely filing of a patent application, will result in priority being given to the first inventor who disclosed the invention.

Patent Application. Because first-to-file systems promote early filings of patent applications, first-to-file systems impose lower requirements for patent applications than the first-to-invent systems did.

Before 1994, comparatively high requirements for U.S. patent applications disadvantaged U.S. patent applicants because their competitors outside the United States could easily secure priority by filing simpler patent applications. Therefore, Congress in 1994 introduced provisional applications into the U.S. patent system, and the AIA preserved provisional applications in the first-to-file system in the United States. As regular applications must, provisional applications must contain a specification and a drawing. Unlike regular applications,

---

*   Advisory Commission on Patent Law Reform, A Report to the Secretary of Commerce, 1992, p. 47.

**   Id.

provisional applications require neither a claim nor an oath by the applicant. Provisional applications require the payment of a lower fee than regular applications, and they are not subject to examination. The filing of a provisional application triggers a 12-month national priority period; the applicant has twelve months to file a regular U.S. patent application.

Prior User Rights. In first-to-file systems some inventors, even if they invented first, might not file their patent applications first. First-to-file systems afford such inventors rights to practice the patented invention, and the inventors may enjoy these rights under certain conditions if they independently developed the invention and began to use it (or undertook preparations for its use) before a patent application was filed by another inventor.

In first-to-invent systems no need for prior user rights existed; if the patent applicant was not the first to invent the invention, the first inventor could dispute inventorship, and the first inventor, rather than the patent applicant, would be granted the patent. An important difference between the two types of systems was that while the prior user right is a defense to patent infringement, a dispute regarding inventorship could have resulted in the invalidation of a patent in a first-to-invent system.

A prior user right, albeit extremely limited, first appeared in the U.S. Patent Act in 1999 when Congress provided in section 273(b)(1) that in cases of business method patents an alleged infringer had a defense to an infringement action if, acting in good faith, he actually reduced the invention to practice at least one year before the patent's filing date and commercially used the invention before the filing date. The AIA lifted the business method patent limitation and now gives the prior user right to any person who, "acting in good faith, commercially used the subject matter in the United States" at least one year before the effective filing date of a patent application or a disclosure to the public by the inventor or another who obtained the subject matter disclosed directly or indirectly from the inventor, whichever occurred earlier. 35 U.S.C. § 273(a).

NOTES

1.   *Objections to the Change to the First-to-File System in the United States.* By 1999 the United States was the only country in the world with a first-to-invent system; all other countries employed a first-to-file system. The last two countries to switch to the first-to-file system prior to the United States were Canada in 1989 and the Philippines in 1998. Nevertheless, critics in the United States voiced numerous objections to the change.

U.S. opponents of first-to-file were concerned that such a change could harm inventive activity in the United States. In the words of a number of organizations representing small inventors, "[c]hanging U.S. patent law to be like the less-successful patent systems of Europe and Asia [could] not be regarded as positive 'reform.'" Letter to Senate Majority Leader Harry Reid dated February 23, 2011, signed by several organizations, including the IEEE-USA, the National Association of Patent Practitioners, and the National Small Business Association. Is it the first-to-file principle or the first-to-invent principle that is more likely to promote inventive activity? To address concerns that the first-to-file principle may disadvantage small inventors, the AIA introduced special provisions to assist so-called micro-entities. 35 U.S.C. § 123.

Other concerns were that "a first-to-file system might tend to foster premature and sketchy disclosures in hastily-filed patent applications" with the result that "the USPTO could be burdened with an increased volume of patent applications filed for defensive purposes." Advisory Commission on Patent Law Reform, A Report to the Secretary of Commerce, 1992, p. 43.

2.   *Grace Period.* The grace period in the AIA is more generous than the grace period in some other countries, in both scope and duration. For example, Article 55 of the European Patent Convention carves out only two narrow exceptions if the disclosure occurred no earlier than six months before filing and was due to "an evident abuse in relation to the applicant or his legal predecessor," or the applicant displayed the invention at a qualifying international exhibition.

China narrowed its grace period in 2009. According to Article 24 of the Chinese Patent Act, priority will not be defeated if, within the six month period prior to the filing date, the invention is exhibited at a qualifying international conference, made public at an academic or technical conference, or disclosed without the consent of the applicant. Before the 2009 amendment, priority would also not be defeated by prior uses and other non-publication forms of disclosure outside of China. The 2009 amendment introduced the absolute novelty standard, under which any public disclosure prior to the filing date (except for the three grace period exceptions) will bar patentability in China.

Japan expanded the coverage of its grace period by a 2011 amendment to the Japanese Patent Act; the grace period now covers disclosures within six months prior to the filing of a patent application by "the person having the right to obtain a patent" and disclosures made by another "against the will of the person having the right to obtain a patent." Japanese Patent Act, Article 30. For a comparative analysis of grace periods see Shohei Ishimaru & Yuichiro Nakaya, International Harmonization of the Grace Period: The Experience of Japan, 9(1) J. of Intell. Property Law & Practice 61 (2014).

What qualifies as "obtaining" the subject matter from the inventor in the AIA grace period provision? How little information will suffice for a "disclosure" that will commence the grace period? According to the House Judiciary Committee Report on the America Invents Act, "the grace period benefits the public by encouraging early disclosure of new inventions, regardless of whether an application may later be filed for a patent on it." Rept. 112–98, June 1, 2011. Will inventors rush to disclose only the minimum information necessary to become the first to publish? Would the public or inventors be better served with an even more limited grace period?

3. *Prior User Right.* The prior user right is a regular feature of first-to-file patent systems. For example, section 79 of the Japanese Patent Law provides that if *B* independently makes, and undertakes to exploit an invention before *A* files an application for a patent on the same invention, *B* will be entitled to a compulsory non-exclusive license to continue to exploit the invention. Section 12 of the German Patent Act provides in part: "A patent shall have no effect in respect of a person who, at the time of the filing of the application, had already begun to use the invention in Germany or had made the necessary arrangements for so doing. Such person shall be entitled to use the invention for the needs of his own business in his own workshops or in the workshops of others."

4. *Harmonization.* An important argument in favor of the change in the United States from the first-to-invent to the first-to-file system was that the change would support efforts toward a deeper international harmonization of patent law. How do the persisting differences among countries' rules on novelty and the grace period affect U.S. inventors? How do the differences affect foreign inventors who are seeking patent protection in the United States? The 1992 Advisory Commission Report observed that "[t]he absence of parallel protection for the inventor who has published or otherwise publicly disclosed the invention abroad has caused many United States inventors to unnecessarily or inadvertently forfeit their patent rights in much of the rest of the world." *Id.*, p. 47.

After the failure to negotiate the Substantive Patent Law Treaty, what options does the United States have to influence the design of other countries' patent laws? The Free Trade Agreement that came into force in 2012 between the United States and the Republic of Korea contains the following provision in Article 18.8(7):

"Each Party shall disregard information contained in public disclosures used to determine if an invention is novel or has an inventive step if the public disclosure:

(a) was made or authorized by, or derived from, the patent applicant, and

(b) occurred within 12 months prior to the date of filing of the application in the territory of the Party."

Because of the Agreement, Korea extended its grace period from its original six to twelve months.

How do businesses shape their conduct in a world in which differences in patent laws, such as the differences in the scope and duration of grace periods, persist? Some commentators had argued that the implementation of the first-to-file system in the United States would not result in dramatic changes to the practice of many patent applicants who even before the implementation had to comply with the various rules applicable in the rest of the world in order to preserve their rights in other countries.

Stein Associates, Inc. v. Heat and Control, Inc.

United States Court of Appeals, Federal Circuit, 1984.
748 F.2d 653, 223 U.S.P.Q. 1277.

MARKEY, CHIEF JUDGE.

Appeal from an order of the United States District Court for the Northern District of California (district court) denying Stein Associates' (Stein's) motion for preliminary injunction. We *affirm*.

Background

In 1982, Heat and Control, Inc., (H & C) became aware that Stein was offering to sell its Counterflow Oven (CFO) to a British company, G.W. Padley Poultry Ltd. (Padley) and had installed a pilot CFO at Padley's factory in Lincolnshire, Great Britain. H & C was advised by its British patent counsel that the pilot oven infringed H & C's two British patents. Accordingly, a writ of infringement was issued against Padley on March 31, 1983. When Padley did not then actually purchase the CFO oven from Stein, the writ of infringement was withdrawn.

Having learned that Stein was selling its CFO oven through a British distributor, RHM Ingredient Supplies Ltd. (RHM), and believing that Stein and RHM intended to continue that activity in Great Britain, H & C initiated court proceedings against Stein and RHM on August 5, 1983 for infringement of H & C's two British patents.

In the interim, on July 6, 1983, Stein filed an action in Toledo, Ohio, for a declaratory judgment that H & C's U.S. patents are invalid and not infringed, that H & C unfairly competed with Stein, and that H & C violated Sections 1 and 2 of the Sherman Antitrust Act. H & C counterclaimed for infringement of its United States patents.

H & C's United States patents relate to apparatus and method for cooking solid food products in a continuously circulating steam laden atmosphere. The patents, one for the apparatus and one for the method, resulted from a parent application filed in the Patent and Trademark Office (PTO) on February 2, 1973. H & C filed a British application on May 9, 1973, claiming priority in view of the United States parent application under Article 4 of the Paris Convention.

On September 12, 1983, H & C moved to transfer the Toledo action to San Francisco, California. Stein reacted by moving in the Ohio district court for summary judgment that H & C's United States patents are invalid under 35 U.S.C. § 102(b), because of an alleged offer to sell more than one year before the filing date of H & C's parent application, and for an order enjoining H & C's enforcement of its British patents against Stein and RHM. Stein filed an affidavit of Richard Egan (one of Stein's attorneys) and an affidavit of Arthur Nilsen, a retired H & C employee.

On November 8, 1983, the Ohio district court granted H & C's motion to transfer, leaving the decision on Stein's motions to the district court in California. Stein's appeal of that action to this court (Appeal No. 84–654) was dismissed on December 21, 1983. Stein then noticed its motions for hearing relying on the same record (the Egan and Nilsen affidavits).

Stein's affidavits said that the oven and process originally claimed in the parent application were reduced to practice on September 16, 1971, when H & C tested an experimental oven for Kraft Foods, a potential customer, and that that oven was offered for sale to Kraft on January 2, 1972, more than one year before the February 2, 1973 filing date of the parent application.

H & C relied on testimony of inventors Andrew Caridis and Clark Benson, and of Nilsen, given at depositions on October 9, 10 and 11, 1983. That testimony was that the oven tested for Kraft Foods on September 16, 1971 was not that defined in the claims of the issued patents, and that the inventions claimed in the patents were not actually reduced to practice until after the critical date of February 2, 1972.

Specifically referring to the patent claims, Caridis, Benson, and Nilsen testified that the experimental oven tested on September 16, 1971 did not have means for excluding outside air from the cooking chamber and did not have means for measuring and regulating the moisture content of the circulating process vapor.

At a March 2, 1984 hearing, the district court denied Stein's motion for partial summary judgment because Stein failed to establish that there had been an invalidating offer for sale and because issues of material fact were present. The court denied Stein's motion to preliminarily enjoin H & C's effort to enforce its British patents in Great Britain.

Issue

Did the district court abuse its discretion in denying a preliminary injunction?

OPINION

(1) *The Paris Convention*

The denial of Stein's motion for partial summary judgment is not appealable . . . , and has not been appealed. That motion, however, serves as Stein's intended basis for its appeal from denial of its motion for an injunction.

Stein set forth to establish by way of summary judgment that H & C's United States patents are invalid under § 102(b), in the mistaken belief that H & C's British patents would thereupon lose their priority dates under the Paris Convention. Stein argues that without those priority dates the British patents are invalid under British law and that the district court should enjoin enforcement of those "invalid" British patents. Stein thus proceeded on a theory founded in twisted logic.

Stein employed the novel technique of attempting to show that H & C's United States patents are "void ab initio" by applying two of the thirteen claims in the parent application as *originally* filed to the oven allegedly on sale before the critical date. Those two claims, however, were amended during prosecution and are not found in the issued patents. Absent inequitable conduct in prosecution of the application, a patent is invalid under § 102(b) only if every element in every claim in the *issued* patent reads on the device offered for sale. . . . Stein cites only *In re Theis*, 610 F.2d 786, 204 USPQ 188 (CCPA 1979). That case was an *ex parte* appeal from a PTO rejection, and did not involve the validity of an issued patent.

Just as a patentee cannot prevail by proving infringement of claims originally filed but not in its patent, a patent challenger cannot prevail by proving invalidity of those claims. . . .

Stein's purpose in attempting to show that the oven set forth in originally filed claims had been on sale was to create a basis for showing that H & C's parent application was not a "regular national filing" under Article 4 of the Paris Convention, and that H & C could not therefore claim for its British patents the benefit of the filing date of its parent application in the PTO. Whether H & C may claim that benefit is a matter for determination by the British court before which the claim is asserted. To forestall efforts similar to Stein's, however, the flaw in its approach to the Paris Convention should be made clear.

Stein's attempt to convince this court that once a United States patent falls, all corresponding foreign patents lose their priority dates is totally without merit and is expressly refuted by the Paris Convention itself. Article 4 *bis* of the Paris Convention provides:

> (1) Patents applied for in the various countries of the Union by nationals of countries of the Union shall be independent of patents obtained for the same invention in other countries, whether members of the Union or not.

> (2) The foregoing provision is to be understood in an unrestricted sense, in particular, in the sense that patents applied for in the period of priority are independent, both as regards the grounds for nullity and forfeiture, and as regards their normal duration.

Article 4(A)(3) of the Paris Convention defines a "regular national filing":

> (3) By a regular national filing is meant any filing that is adequate to establish the date on which the application was filed in the country concerned, whatever may be the outcome of the application.

The key language in Article 4(A)(3) is "any filing that is adequate to establish the date on which the application was filed in the country concerned" and "whatever may be the outcome of the application."

35 U.S.C. § 111 defines the requirements for establishing a filing date for a patent application in the United States. . .

It would defeat the purpose of the Paris Convention if inventors filing applications in the PTO were required to prove that their original claims were patentable before establishing a filing date entitling them to claim a right of priority for their corresponding foreign applications.

Repeatedly referring to "invalid filing," Stein would construe 35 U.S.C. § 111 as including the conditions of patentability set forth in § 102 and § 103, a construction inconsistent with the statutory scheme. Whether the claims of a United States application as originally filed meet all patentability requirements is determined during prosecution. That determination is the "outcome" of the application and is not a prerequisite to the establishment of a filing date under § 111, nor is that determination a condition precedent to the creation of a "regular national filing" under the Paris Convention.

Stein cites dicta in *Eli Lilly & Co. v. Brenner*, 248 F.Supp. 402, 147 U.S.P.Q. 442 (D.D.C. 1965), *rev'd*, 375 F.2d 599, 153 USPQ 95 (D.C.Cir. 1967), but the court was there dealing with an entirely different issue, namely, whether a United States patent claiming priority based on an earlier filed foreign application acts as a § 102(e) reference as of its actual United States filing date or as of the foreign priority date. The citation aids H & C, not Stein, for the court specifically held that a right of priority in the United States arose when the requirements of the foreign country were met.

Stein cites the provision in 35 U.S.C. § 119 for determination of the § 102(a) and (b) bars as of the United States filing date. However, § 119 deals only with an application filed in the PTO and claiming priority based on a foreign application. It has no relation whatever to the determination by a British court under British law on whether H & C is entitled to claim for its British patents the priority benefit of the United States filing date of its parent application.

Stein's notion that it could establish a basis for its requested injunction by proving invalidity of H & C's United States patent is in direct conflict with the total independence of the patents of signatory countries, as set forth in Article 4 *bis* of the Paris Convention quoted above.

(2) *Preliminary Injunction*

On appeal, "one denied a preliminary injunction must meet the burden of showing that the district court abused its discretion, committed an error of law, or seriously misjudged the evidence." *Smith Int'l., Inc. v. Hughes Tool Co.*, 718 F.2d 1573, 1579, 219 USPQ 686, 691 (Fed.Cir.), cert. denied, 464 U.S. 996, 104 S.Ct. 493, 78 L.Ed.2d 687 (1983). Stein has not carried that burden.

The district court has the discretionary power to enjoin a party from pursuing litigation before a foreign tribunal but can exercise that power only if the parties and issues are the same, and resolution of the domestic action will dispose of the foreign action. . . .

Here, the issues are not the same, one action involving United States patents and the other involving British patents.

Further, resolution of the domestic action will not dispose of the British action. Only a British court, applying British law, can determine validity and infringement of British patents. British law being different from our own, and British and United States courts being independent of each other, resolution of the question of whether the United States patents are valid could have no binding effect on the British court's decision.

In each of the cases relied on by Stein, the court *refused* to enjoin a party from pursuing foreign litigation involving that party's foreign patents. . . .

In light of the foregoing, it is not necessary to explore in this case whether Stein has shown a likelihood of success, or irreparable harm, or whether harm to H & C or to the public interest should preclude a grant of the injunction sought.

The district court properly exercised its discretion in denying Stein's motion for preliminary injunction.

AFFIRMED.

NOTES

1. *Priority Under the Paris Convention.* Until the Paris Convention, two facts conspired to hobble patent protection outside the country in which the application was first made: the fact that it was difficult and costly to file simultaneously in two or more countries, and the fact that the failure to file simultaneously often deprived the invention of the required novelty in countries other than the first. Although work on the Paris Convention commenced in 1873, a right of priority that would enable patent applicants to surmount these hurdles was not formally proposed until the 1880 Paris Diplomatic Conference. As embodied in Article 4, the right of priority represents one of the major—if not *the* major—contributions of the Paris Convention to international patent practice. *See* generally, Stephen Ladas, 1 Patents, Trademarks and Related Rights: National and International Protection § 255 (1975).

In the United States, section 119 of the Patent Act implements the Paris Convention priority. Section 119(a) provides: "An application for patent for an invention filed in this country by any person who has, or whose legal representatives or assigns have, previously regularly filed an application for a patent for the same invention in a foreign country which affords similar privileges in the case of applications filed in the United States or to citizens of the United States, or in a WTO member country, shall have the same effect as the same application would have if filed in this country on the date on which the application for patent for the same invention was first filed in such foreign country, if the application in this country is filed within 12 months from the earliest date on which such foreign application was filed." 35 U.S.C. § 119(a).

2. *Provisional Applications and the Paris Convention Priority.* Article 4(A)(1) of the Paris Convention ties its requirement of patent priority to an "application for a patent . . . in one of the countries of the Union". Article 4(A)(2) provides that "[a]ny filing that is equivalent to a regular national filing under the domestic legislation of any country of the Union . . . shall be recognized as giving rise to the right of priority." Section 4(A)(3) adds that "[b]y a regular national filing is meant any filing that is adequate to establish the date on which the application was filed in the country concerned, whatever may be the subsequent fate of the application." Is a provisional application under section 111(b) of the U.S. Patent Act a "regular national filing" for purposes of obtaining the Paris Convention priority? *See* Todd Miller, "The Same Effect": United States Provisional Patent Applications and Paris Convention Priority Rights, 78 J. Pat. & Trademark Off. Soc'y 716 (1996).

3. *The Hilmer Rule.* Article 4 of the Paris Convention, as implemented by section 119 of the U.S. Patent Act, confers an *offensive* one-year priority on an application that derives from a qualifying foreign application. When the scope of prior art was limited geographically, as it used to be in the United States prior to the AIA, the question arose whether Article 4 also requires that a *defensive* priority be given to qualifying foreign applications, meaning whether it is the foreign priority date that triggers the patent-defeating reference.

Under the "Hilmer rule," it was the date of the U.S. filing that triggered the patent-defeating reference, not the priority date of the foreign filing that preceded the U.S. filing. In Application of Hilmer, 359 F.2d 859, 149 U.S.P.Q. 480 (CCPA 1966), Hilmer had filed an application in Germany on July 31, 1957, and in the United States on July 25, 1958. Habicht had filed in Switzerland on January 24, 1957, and in the United States on January 23, 1958. Hilmer argued that although his German application was filed after Habicht's Swiss application, it was nonetheless filed before Habicht filed his U.S. application, so that section 119 prevented use of Habicht's disclosure as a defeating reference. The court held that Habicht could not rely on his Swiss filing date to defeat Hilmer's priority in the United States, which was based on Hilmer's German filing date.

Did *Hilmer* contradict the purpose behind Article 4 of the Paris Convention, as some have argued? Did *Hilmer* violate Article 27(1) of the TRIPs Agreement, requiring that "patents shall be available and patent rights enjoyable without discrimination as to the place of invention"? Did Congress meliorate *Hilmer's* effect when, in 1999, it amended the Patent Act to provide that published patent applications constitute prior art under section 102(e)? Only applications filed in the United States before the invention were considered prior art, and foreign-filed international applications were prior art only if the applications designated the United States and were published in the English language. 35 U.S.C. § 102(e) (pre-AIA). Under the AIA, for the purposes of determining prior art, published applications for U.S. patents enjoy the benefit of their priority date that is based on an earlier foreign filing date. 35 U.S.C. § 102(a)(2) and (d).

For an analysis of *Hilmer* and its progeny in the context of international patent policy, see Toshiko Takenaka & Martin J. Adelman, First-inventor-to-file under the America Invents Act: A View of First-to-File Lawyer and A View of First-to-Invent Lawyer, in Intellectual Property in Common Law and Civil Law (Toshiko Takenaka ed., 2013), pp. 62–64.

4.   *TRIPs and Discrimination as to the Place of Invention.* Until passage of the Uruguay Round Agreements Act, Pub. L. No. 103–465, 108 Stat. 4809 (1994), section 104 of the U.S. Patent Act effectively provided that a patent applicant could not establish a date of invention by reference to activities that occurred outside the United States. As a practical matter, the rule discriminated against foreign inventors by preventing them from using a reduction to practice that occurred in their home countries to establish their date of invention. To implement Article 1709(7) of NAFTA and Article 27(1) of the TRIPs Agreement, which provide in part that patents shall be available and patent rights enjoyable without discrimination as to the place of invention, section 104 was amended to provide that "[i]n proceedings in the Patent and Trademark Office, in the courts, and before any other competent authority, an applicant for a patent, or a patentee, may not establish a date of invention by reference to knowledge or use thereof, or other activity with respect thereto, in a foreign country other than a NAFTA country or a WTO member country, except as provided in sections 119 and 365 of this title." Section 104 was finally repealed when the AIA was enacted.

See generally, Stephen Bodenheimer, Jr., Edward Kessler & Guy Gosnell, The Effect of the Interference Rule Revisions Enacted in Response to NAFTA and GATT, 36 IDEA 19 (1995).

PROBLEM 6

Software developers employed by your client, Vitek Ventures, have created a computer program that, when executed in a digital computer, enables a fully automated system of inventory control for products sold over the Internet. Specifically, when an order for a product is placed over the Internet with a retailer on whose server the program is installed, the program routes the order to the retailer's distribution facility and, at the same time, cumulates the order with previous orders for the same product until a predetermined number of orders—computed by the program according to a formula that accounts for seasonal sales profiles and delivery schedules—is reached. At this point, the program automatically routes an order for stock replacement to the product's manufacturer.

On January 8, within a week of the creation of a working version of the program, Vitek's patent counsel prepared, but did not file, a U.S. patent application with claims encompassing the developers' software-related invention. A week later, on January 15, Vitek installed the program in the computer systems of three Internet retailers to test the program's efficacy. After correcting a half-dozen bugs discovered in the course of these tests, Vitek started installing the program for customers on February 15.

On March 12 of the same year, software designers at Silicon Software, a Swiss software company, completed work on a program identical in all material respects to the Vitek program and, on the same day, Silicon filed a patent application containing claims materially identical to the Vitek claims in the Swiss Patent Office. On November 20 Vitek applied for a patent for the software-related invention in the U.S. Patent and Trademark Office and on December 21 it applied for a patent in the Swiss Patent Office. (The Vitek employees have assigned all their rights in the patent applications to Vitek.) On December 28 of the same year, Silicon applied for a patent on the identical invention in the U.S. Patent and Trademark Office.

Please advise Vitek on the likelihood that (a) it will obtain a patent from the U.S. Patent and Trademark Office; (b) it will obtain a patent from the Swiss Patent Office; (c) Silicon will obtain a patent from the U.S. Patent and Trademark Office; (d) Silicon will obtain a patent from the Swiss Patent Office.

ii. Inventive Step (Nonobviousness) and Industrial Application (Utility)

Friedrich-Karl Beier, The Inventive Step in Its Historical Development

17 International Review of Industrial Property and Copyright Law
301, 303–305, 307–310, 312–323 (1986).

The requirement of "inventive step," "nonobviousness" or "inventive level" being the crucial condition of patentability, stands in the center of every practitioner's daily work. Case law and literature on nonobviousness are so overwhelming that it is difficult to present something new on this topic. But the daily user of this term may be interested in reading how it all began, how this requirement with all its different names, now incorporated in most of our patent statutes and still the subject of controversy, has historically developed as a creation of examining practice and case law. This article is an attempt to illustrate this development using a comparative law approach. . . .

Now let us concentrate on the real development of the requirement of inventive step in the 19th and 20th century. It began around 1850, reached a first climax around 1880/90—in Germany a little later—and has still not ended.

The demand for inventive step emerged slowly from the practice of examining patent offices, was recognized in important court decisions and has been the subject of controversy in legal literature. The further development toward a statutory patentability requirement was not straightforward and continuous, but rather gradual, with peaks and valleys.

Let us begin with the development in the United States. Although the Germans coined the term *"Erfindungshöhe"* ("inventive level")—Richard Wirth, patent attorney in Frankfurt was the inventor—the so-called patentability requirement was invented by the Americans, in particular the Justices of the U.S. Supreme Court in the famous case *Hotchkiss v. Greenwood* in 1850.[7]

1.   The Development in the United States

In the *Hotchkiss* case, which became the basis of later case law and legislation, we find the often cited sentences:

> . . . unless more ingenuity and skill . . . were required . . . than were possessed by an ordinary mechanic acquainted with the business, there was an absence of that degree of skill and ingenuity which constitute essential elements of every invention. In other words, the improvement is the work of the skillful mechanic, not that of the inventor.[8]

With these words, in which for the first time the famous person with average skill in the art appears, the Supreme Court denied the patentability of a door knob made out of porcelain which had the same shape and was attached in the same way as previously known door knobs made out of wood or metal. The case thus dealt with a mere replacement of materials, which previous decisions also had found to be not worthy of a patent.

From that standpoint the *Hotchkiss* decision is not particularly revolutionary; the decision pursued thoughts which Thomas Jefferson— a founding father of the United States who was also the author of the first patent law and as Secretary of State one of the first three patent examiners of the United States (1790–1793), as well as being an important inventor—had articulated earlier. Jefferson realized that novelty and utility, the two historical requirements for patentability, would not be sufficient to prevent monopolies on insignificant actions from the prior art which were no more than small improvements. Thus, Jefferson proposed a provision for the statute of 1790 to the effect that invention should not be patented, if it is so "unimportant and obvious, that it does not deserve a monopoly." . . .

Congress, however, left novelty and utility as the only statutory criteria and the courts used Jefferson's ideas in the beginning only occasionally by denying so-called "patentable novelty" for unimportant or insignificant deviations from the prior art, particularly from already patented inventions. Even before 1850, prior to *Hotchkiss v. Greenwood*, the term "significant novelty" appears, which sometimes later served in Germany, Scandinavia, and the U.S.S.R. as an ersatz for the criterion of inventive step.

Hotchkiss v. Greenwood refers for the first time to the basic, albeit ambiguous term "invention," and the knowledge and ability of a person with average skill in the art is emphasized as the controlling test, in order to draw the line between the result of mere mechanical skills and the

---

[7]   Hotchkiss, et al. v. Greenwood et al., 11 Howard 248 (1850); 52 U.S. 261; Woodbury J., dissenting.

[8]   *Id.*

true patent-worthy invention. "Patentable invention" or simply "invention" from then on not only meant the mere discovery of something new and the immaterial or physical object of the new technical teaching, but simultaneously also a certain quality of the invention which was necessary for granting a patent, its inventive character. This ambiguous and at times tautological use of the term invention, which one finds in all countries, has caused confusion until the present day. . . .

The patent community in the United States regarded the thus increased standard for patentability in the early phase of its development as unquestionably necessary and justified in order to avoid abuses. The courts developed and refined the requirement, which initially was called "invention" or "standard of invention," in a large number of cases, based the requirement directly on the Constitution, and called it later "nonobvious," without causing any significant criticism from industry or the bar. The United States Patent Office, also accepted the new examination requirement using the person of average skill as the yardstick to sift the chaff from the wheat with no serious complaints being articulated.

Slowly, however, particularly from the mid-30's on—at the time of Roosevelt's "New Deal" and the huge antitrust litigations of the government—the courts tightened the screws.

While in the beginning only a little more than the skill in the art was required, later in ever new and flowery language "inventive faculty," "creative work of inventive faculty" or even "inventive genius" was required. . . .

This phraseology, centering more and more around the person of the inventor and the act of inventing, culminated in 1941 in the famous *Cuno Engineering v. Automatic Devices* decision[17] which asked for a "flash of the creative genius," a flash on which every invention had to be based to comply with the constitutional standard of patentability. A tempest of rage arose against this wording from Justice Douglas, who together with Justice Black, was one of the strongest enemies of monopolies and patents of the already not very pro-patent Supreme Court. The necessity of protecting even small steps which were the result of long and costly research activities in industrial laboratories was correctly pointed out, since these and not the rare flashes of genius "advance the art." The Supreme Court, however, and consequently most lower courts, did not abandon their hostile attitude toward patents and, for example, qualified almost all inventions resulting from laboratory teamwork, which were based on a number of experiments, as routine work of persons with average skill in the art and not as the result of a flash of genius. . . .

This went too far, so that the legislature, under massive pressure of the interested circles, felt obligated to conclude the work on a revision of the patent statute which had been under way since 1941.

---

[17]   314 U.S. 84 (1941).

One express goal of the reform was to abolish the subjective flash of genius test of the Supreme Court and to replace it by a reasonable yardstick for determining patentability, oriented to the concepts of the advance in the art and contribution to the public good. The new patent statute was enacted in 1952 and its central provision is the well-known definition of nonobviousness. This statutory definition, the first of its kind, has found many followers and it is therefore cited here:

> A patent may not be obtained though the invention is not identically disclosed or described as set forth in section 102 of this title, *if the differences between the subject matter sought to be patented and the prior art are such that the subject matter as a whole would have been obvious at the time the invention was made to a person having ordinary skill in the art to which said subject matter pertains.* Patentability shall not be negatived by the manner in which the invention was made (emphasis added).[20]

Although the entire provision, particularly, however, the second sentence with its specific prohibition of basing the decision on the genesis of the invention, as well as the materials and history of the section reflected the clear intention of Congress to abolish and overrule the flash of genius test of the Supreme Court and to instigate a milder measure of inventiveness, there was no agreement in case law and literature about the meaning of the new provision in the years following 1952. Some assumed the legislature only intended to codify existing case law, one faction meaning the mild *Hotchkiss* standard of the early days, the other faction meaning the tough *Cuno* standard prior to the enacting of 35 U.S.C. § 103. It was not until 1966 that this controversy was authoritatively decided by the Supreme Court in three cases swept by it for review, which were decided together and became known as the trilogy decisions, or simply *Graham v. John Deere.* . . . Much to everybody's surprise the Supreme Court found that the legislature only intended to codify the entire case law from *Hotchkiss* to *Cuno* and *A & P* but had no intention of mitigating it. The legislature could not have done so, said the Supreme Court, since applying a lower standard than the Supreme Court would be a violation of the Constitution. Besides, the formula of the "flash of genius" had been misunderstood. It had been only a play of words without legal significance, but not an expression of an intended tightening of the examination standard. . . .

2.   The Development in Great Britain

Perhaps I should have started in England, the home of modern patent law. However, if I am not mistaken, the inventive step, at least as a separate patentability requirement, was born a little later in England than in the United States, namely around 1890 in one of the many patent litigations of those days. Each development, of course, has its

---

[20]   35 U.S.C. § 103.

predecessors and this is also true of England. Particularly in the 18th through the beginning of the 19th century older cases can be found, in which the idea surfaces that in addition to novelty and utility there had to be something more in order to justify a patent monopoly. Thus in *Mitchell v. Reynolds*,[23] a patent case in 1711, it was held that a patent should not grant more than "a reasonable reward to ingenuity and uncommon industry."

In the beginning of the 19th century in several patent infringement cases the argument of the defendants occurs that not every novelty is an invention deserving protection under the Statute of Monopolies: "A new principle must be discovered—skill and ingenuity must be exerted to entitle an inventor to a patent."[24]

All these efforts, however, were initially rejected by the British courts and not only because the Statute of Monopolies, the venerable basis of British patent law of 1624, did not contain the word "invention," which could have been used as a basis, but referred to "any matter of new manufacture." In *Crane v. Price*,[25] a famous patent infringement case relating to a new iron smelter process, Chief Justice Tindal rejected the plea of insufficient inventive quality of the new process with the often cited phrase:

> For if the invention be new and useful to the public, it is not material whether it be the result of long experiments and profound research, or whether by some sudden and lucky thought, or mere accidental discovery.

He added that the new process for the first time filled a long existing need in industry; this was sufficient proof of the patentworthiness of the process.

This still often cited case, which maintains that novelty and utility are the only patentability requirements, is also remarkable for the fact that it rejects any consideration of the genesis of the invention, the manner of creative process. Inventions stemming from tedious experiments or diligent research work are recognized as just as deserving of a patent as an unexpected idea, a lucky chance or a purely accidental discovery. And finally, in this case one of our famous objective criteria for nonobviousness, the long felt want, appears for the first time. . . .

Although the fundamental British decisions relating to inventive step were handed down in a not exactly pro-patent era, they avoided demanding too much from the inventor. Not the inventive genius who crosses the frontiers of science and technology is the guide for the British decisions, but rather the brave, average inventor who accomplishes a

---

[23]   1 P. Wins. 181, 188; (1558–1774) All E. R. Rep. 26 (1711), quoted from Bochnovic, "The Inventive Step—Its Evolution in Canada, the United Kingdom and the United States" 12 (Weinheim, 1982), a very instructive treatise.

[24]   Walker v. Congreve (1816) 1 Carp. Pat. Cases 356, 361; see also Hall v. Jervis, [1822] 1 W.P.C. 100.

[25]   Crane v. Price & Others [1840] 1. W.P.C. 377.

little more than the average artisan. In England, the leading industrialized nation, it was known better than elsewhere what "ordinary skill" means and where inventing begins, and it was recognized earlier than elsewhere that small steps also advance the art.

This technical-practical and at the same time modest approach to the requirement of inventive step, which characterized the early decisions has continued in British decisions and examining practice until the present day. This can be seen, for example, in the famous test question worded by Mr. Cripps in 1928, which emphasizes right at the beginning: "Was it for all practical purposes obvious to any skilled chemist . . . that he could . . . do the invention?" thereby preventing speculation. Finally, the common sense of English judges is shown by the weight they attributed from the very outset to the technical and economic success of an invention as an objectively provable fact in the determination of inventive step. Allow me to support the latter by a particularly nice quote. It is by Justice Tomlin in the 1929 decision *Samuel Parkes & Co. Ld. v. Cocker Brothers Ld.*[29] and reads:

> Nobody has told me, and I do not suppose anybody ever will tell me, what is the precise characteristic or quality the presence of which distinguishes invention from a workshop improvement. Day is day, and night is night, but who shall tell where day ends or night begins?

After this slight resignation in the face of the difficulties of a reliable demarcation he emphasized that already 1 1/4 million of the patented apparatuses had been sold, that railroad companies had accepted it as standard equipment and that it had defeated all competing products. From that he drew the conclusion:

> The truth is that, when once it had been found, that the problem had waited solution for many years, and that the device is in fact novel and superior to what had gone before, and has been widely used, and used in preference to alternative devices, it is, I think, practically impossible to say that there is not present that *scintilla of invention* necessary to support the Patent (emphasis added).

In other words: If an invention fills a long existing need and the invention is new and better than known solutions and the invention has commercial success, nobody can deny the required sparklet of inventiveness.

As a believer in technical advance as the overall aim of patent protection (which is no longer generally accepted philosophy) these words based on the technical and economic reality find my full support. The same is true for the question Professor Cornish formulated to explain why technical progress should plead in arguing in favor of inventive step

---

[29]   46 R.P.C. 241, 248 (1929).

of an invention. He asks: "If the idea is a real step forward in technic, yet it is an obvious one, why was it not made before?"[30]

As to recent developments in England, I have to report that the requirement of an inventive step was introduced already in 1932 into the British patent statute, although initially only as a ground for revocation which was worded as follows:

> That the invention is obvious and does not involve any inventive step having regard to what was known or used prior to the date of the patent.

In the Patents Act of 1949 the obviously missing inventive step was also introduced by statute as a ground for opposition. In the Patent Act of 1977 the inventive step in its modern, European dress was finally fully introduced into the British patent statute. Will British practice change under this statute and approximate a more stringent European standard? Or, conversely, will the British practice influence the European? Personally I favor the latter. British practice as demonstrated in the case law appears to me highly reasonable, and that should be the ultimate yardstick.

3. The Development in France

Let us now—quasi as a counterpoint—address the development in France which has taken a route quite different from that of Anglo-American countries. I could do this very simply by following Maître Mathély, the authoritative mentor of French jurisprudence, and state: French patent law did not recognize inventive activity. The only requirements of patentability were novelty and industrial character. . . .

But things were not quite that simple in my opinion: Mâtre Mathély, is, of course, correct, if one interprets his statement in the sense that classical French patent law, which until the 1968 reform was based on the ancient Patent Act of 1844, did not recognize inventive step or inventive activity as prerequisite for patentability which had to be separately considered.

However, even in France there have been approaches in case law and literature toward not finding every invention patentable which is novel and leads to an industrial result. Both in earlier and more recent cases we find decisions requiring *essential* novelty or *functional* novelty, or which point to the *advantages* of the patented invention as compared to the prior art or to the difficulties surmounted by the inventor. . . . It is furthermore recognized, even by Mathély, that improvements of known products or processes which involve not more than a so-called *"tour de main"* the *"savoir faire"* of the person with average skill in the art, are not patentable. . . . In contrast to the so-called *"new application of known means"* (*"application nouvelle de moyens connus"*), the so-called *"emploi nouveau,"* the new use of known means, leading to the same result, is not

---

[30] W. Cornish, "Intellectual Property" 155 (London, 1981) with reference to British Vacuum v. L.S.W.R., 29 R.P.C. 309, 328–330, 333 (1912).

patentable. . . . A subcategory is the mere *exchange of materials*, which in France as in other countries is not regarded as patentable. The same applies to the mere *juxtaposition* of known means, which contrary to a real combination—do not functionally interact. . . . And finally more recent French case law denies patentability also in cases where the essential elements of an invention are not described identically but only in an equivalent way in the prior art. . . .

All these questions, which have been discussed and examined in Germany and in other countries, mainly under the auspices of inventive step or nonobviousness, were until recently part of the traditional novelty examination in France. Legal theory has created for this approach the term *"nouveauté brevetable,"* (patentable novelty), . . . meaning a qualified novelty which does not merely ask for the differences between the patented invention and the prior art, but implies both quantitative and qualitative reflections. The differing approach is certainly more than just terminological, but in practice the French case law is not all that different from the case law of other countries recognizing the requirement of inventive step. . . .

One important point needs emphasis, however. Based on a decision of the *Cour de Cassation* in 1845[40] and Pouillet,[41] French courts supported by the literature have unanimously refused to let the patentability depend upon the merits, the value and the importance of the invention, let alone the greater or smaller efforts of the inventor. This is done for the same reason why, not only in France, the judges refuse to evaluate the artistic quality of a literary or musical work. This aversion toward subjective, uncertain, basically non-justifiable evaluations is the main reason why the requirement of inventive activity or even inventive step has been rejected—even condemned—in France for such a long time. An article by Mathély and Lavoix begins with the simple statement *"La théorie du niveau inventif doit être condamnée* and they continue *car ce critérium est mauvais. Il est incertain, essentiellement subjectif et arbitraire, pratiquement inapplicable et fondamentalement contraire à la tradition juridique française, laquelle requiert des critères certains, objectifs et constants."** The hitherto prevailing French opinion . . . cannot be put better or more concisely.

An important exception was Paul Roubier, Professor of Law and longtime dean in Lyons, the probably most prominent French scholar in industrial property law. In his fundamental treatise "Le Droit de la Propriété Industrielle" (1952–1954) he analyzes the criterion of inventive activity, in an exhaustive chapter which even today is very worthwhile reading. . . . Similar to the Anglo-American and German case law and

---

40   *Cass.* decision of December 30, 1845, Dall. 46 1. 46.
41   Pouillet, "Traité des Brevets d'Invention" No. 15/16 (Paris, 5th ed., 1909).
*   "The theory of the inventive aspect must be rejected . . . because this criterium is bad. It is uncertain, essentially subjective and arbitrary, virtually inapplicable and fundamentally contrary to the French judicial tradition, which requires definite, objective, and constant criteria." *Ed.*

strongly influenced by German legal theory he derives the requirement of "inventive activity" from the concept and essence of the invention and from the necessity not to hinder the normal development of technology by patents for inventions, which based on nothing but the knowledge and ability of the person with average skill in the art, the "*homme du métier.*"

The *Tribunal civil de la Seine* had the courage to follow Roubier's theory in two 1956 decisions,[44] but encountered harsh criticism from Mathély and Lavoix, whom I have quoted above. Under the influence of this criticism both decisions were reversed one year later by the *Cour d'appel de Paris*.[45] The key phrases of these decisions read:

> If the patented apparatus unquestionably represents a technical result and the lack of novelty has not been sufficiently demonstrated, then the invalidity of the patent cannot be based solely on the alleged low merits of the invention and also not on the pretext that any person skilled in the art could have made it. Such a subjective criterion is in opposition to the words and spirit of the Patent Act of 1844.

And similarly in the second case:

> The validity of a patent which relates to a new technical product in accordance with Art. 2 Patent Act, cannot be subject to doubt because of the lack of sufficient inventive activity. Such a criterium, which makes the validity of the patent dependent on the practical and technical importance of the invention, is contrary to the principles of the Patent Act of 1844.

Thus Maître Mathély retrieved jurisprudence from its dangerous foray into modern life and put it back onto the correct path, *i.e.* the classic Pouillet-Mathély direction. And it stayed that way until 1968 when the French legislature decided—in accordance with the drafts for a European Patent—to introduce into French national patent law the requirement of inventive activity as the third requirement for patentability. . . . That was the end of the controversy, and the inventive step moved from its "sémi-clandestinité," in which it was hidden until that time in France (Robert Plaisant), . . . into the glare of legal reality. And now, like it or not, it must be applied as a statutory criterion with all its "ugly" features.

4.   The Development in Germany

The development in Germany is not exactly straightforward and is above all accompanied by a huge mass of mutually contradictory theories. A disentanglement of these twisted threads is not possible in this review; it would be a subject for a yet unwritten dissertation. . . .

a)   Fortunately, the development in Germany did not start until 1877, when the first uniform patent law for the German Empire was

---

[44]   *Trib. civ. Seine* of March 22, 1956, 1956 Ann. 304; *Trib. civ. Seine* of April 13, 1956, 1956 Ann. 308. . . .

[45]   *Cour d'appel de Paris* decision of March 31 and of May 31, 1957, 1957 GRUR Int. 435, 437 *Coq electrique.*

enacted—a difficult, belated outcome of the industrial revolution. . . . According to Sec. 1, Patents Act, which remained unchanged until recently, patents are granted for new inventions which are susceptible of industrial application. The preparatory documents do not explain what an invention is and give no indication that, in addition to the novelty requirement defined in Sec. 2 and that of industrial applicability, other patentability requirements such as "technical advance" or "inventive height" (*Erfindungshöhe*) are required.

However, in the examination practice of the Imperial Patent Office the need for such additional patentability criteria very soon appeared, in order to prevent a flood of technical innovations, which had accumulated over a long period of time due to the absence of any effective patent protection, and which then inundated the Patent Office and its poor examiners. In the heyday of industrial development and technical advance not only the great and important inventions of the time required the protection that had been missing for so long as an absolutely necessary instrument for the striving German industry. The Patent Office also had to fight an avalanche of technical gags and novelties, such as the hexagonal pencil, the nonsliding hernial support, the Haby's *moustache band à la Kaiser Wilhelm*, etc., which the inventors would like to advertise in family magazines like "Die Gartenlaube" equipped with the Imperial patent seal.

To sift this and other chaff from the patent-worthy wheat, the Patent Office tightened its examining practice right from the start, albeit initially without a clear direction and without mitigating the sorry state of affairs. Thus, only eight years after the Patent Office opened its doors an Investigation Commission for the revision of the patent statute was established, . . . the negotiations of which are very interesting for our topic. Here one finds the first indication of inventive level and technical advance as additional patentability criteria which were to be derived from the statutorily undefined concept of an invention. In the report, it is stated that industry deplored that, in decisions of the Patent Office and of the *Reichsgericht*, in addition to novelty and industrial applicability it was required that the subject of the application also comply with the additional requirement

> that the said represent itself as the result of an intellectual activity exceeding the average industrial ability—and thereby a decision on a case by case basis must be made to determine whether an "invention" existed. . . .

In a decision of December 12, 1889 it was held:

> In judging the inventive character of an innovation the main emphasis is by no means to be put on the fact, that it requires particularly difficult mental work, or that its application is remote from the path which the technology takes in its natural development. Decisive is to a much higher degree the technical success achieved by the innovation as compared to what has

been done heretofore. Not the size of the step from the known to the novel is of predominant significance but the utilitarian value of the innovation for economic purposes is of equal importance.[52]

It was said to be sufficient that the "inventor" had created an advance art in a conscious way by supplying the art with a new tool, and that he was the first who found this tool and used it in practice.

The *Reichsgericht* confirmed this opinion, but its definition of a patentable invention contained from the outset certain elements of inventive step:

> An innovation is patentable if it is technically unique, has a certain mental content not necessarily existing for every person skilled in the art, simultaneously, achieves industrial advantages and with these a qualitative progress. . . .

The Court, however, also emphasized that patentability should not be denied to an inventive idea, merely because it "was very simple and very obvious."

In another decision of the day[53] one reads:

> that the application of a known means to a known process can only be regarded as an invention, if the application would have faced *special difficulties* requiring an inventive thought to surmount them, or if the known means appeared to be a *qualitatively new means* with new technical effects.

This decision, too, requires inventive step *or* technical advance. I want to confess already here that this alternative test for the quality of invention, this *"either/or"* approach still appears to me to be the best of all possible solutions. Both the nonobvious, particularly difficult invention and the particularly advantageous, improved invention, each on its own, and not only both combined, further technical development and deserve a patent.

c) Development in Germany has, however, taken a different route. The Patent Office dismissed the too subjective, "individual-psychological" criterion of obviousness, and required instead not only a simple but also a significant or important advance, which it characterized as the only useful criterion of patentability. . . . The *Reichsgericht* approved this practice initially by emphasizing that in judging the inventive character it was not so much the obviousness of the invention but rather the success which could be achieved with the invention, that matters. . . . Soon, however, since about 1914, the *Reichsgericht* required that in addition to novelty and advance a *certain degree of inventive level* (*Erfindungshöhe*) must be reached. A merely objective enrichment of the art was declared to be insufficient; the invention must be based on "creative mental

---

[52]   1891 PBI. 65.

[53]   *Reichsgericht* decision of January 8, 1890, 1890 PBI. 49, 51—*Verfahren zur Herstellung von Walzdraht.*

activity," and must not have been obvious to a person skilled in the art. . . . On the contrary it was said to be unnecessary that the technical advance reach a particularly high level, *i.e.* be particularly important. . . .

This development was unquestionably influenced by the basic article of *Richard Wirth* on "The Measure of Inventive Level" ("*Das Maß der Erfindungshöhe*) published in 1906. . . . *Wirth* distinguishes between *difficult*, *ingenious* and *useful/advantageous* inventions and criticizes the practice of the Patent Office which overemphasizes the requirement of advance in the art by demanding significant technical progress" to be demonstrated in every case. He points out convincingly that it is the small advances which increasingly further the technical development and that these, too, have to be given an incentive by a patent, namely in cases, when they exceed the knowledge and ability of the person with average skill in the art, *i.e.* when they attain the "inventive level" (*Erfindungshöhe*).

The *Reichsgericht* followed this clear opinion and so did the commentaries written by the Supreme Court Judges Pietzeker . . . and Krausse. . . . The Patent Office initially stood by its position but in the early 30's it followed the Supreme Court, and since then in continuous practice it has required, both advance in the art and inventive level, with the proviso that in the case of a large advance the inventive level may be lower and vice versa. . . .

Hermann Isay in the 5th edition of his magnificent Patent Law commentary . . . stood by the earlier *"either/or" theory*, which he once more convincingly explained: In his opinion the value of an invention can reside both in the intellectual accomplishment and in its success. If, however, the value of the invention is justified by its success alone *i.e.* it means an important advance in the art, then the question whether the intellectual effort as such has an inventive value need not be posed. Only in a questionable case of advance should the intellectual effort be considered to tilt the scale. . . .

This opinion has, unfortunately, not been adopted in Germany. One of the sad reasons for that may have been that *Isay* and other Jewish authors from the mid-30's on were no longer allowed to be cited and lost all influence on the further development of the law. Instead, particularly after the enactment of the revised Patent Act of 1936, increasing emphasis was given to a line of thinking centering around the person of the inventor and his achievement. In an article "The creative achievement as prerequisite for the patent grant" in 1939 . . . the high-ranking author specifically referred to the words of the "*Führer*" Adolf Hitler in "*Mein Kampf*" from which he derived:

> that the new patent law makes the creative achievement of the inventor for the general public the foundation and prerequisite of patent protection as the means he has chosen to further the inventor.

From this ideological position the opinion is dismissed, that a large technical advance can replace the missing inventive level, and the inventive level is emphasized as an inalienable condition for patent protection. During this time terms like "creative achievement," "creative mental activity" . . . and the like appeared more and more in the decisions of the *Reichsgericht* and the Patent Office; the significant technical advance, which is accomplished by the invention, is degraded to a mere secondary consideration for demonstrating inventive level, . . . which has to exist in every case.

In doing so the *Reichsgericht* dismissed both the opinion that a large technical advance can replace the inventive height, as well as the opinion of the Patent Office that in such a case the degree of inventiveness may be less. In a decision of the *Reichsgericht* of 1940 the following nice circular logic can be found:

> The opinion that due to the unquestionable technical success of the patent in suit the requirements with respect to the inventor achievements could be less stringent cannot be followed. This opinion must be dismissed for the reason alone that a creative achievement is a necessary prerequisite for patentability.[68]

This is indeed not very convincing, but the courts including the Federal Supreme Court (*Bundesgerichtshof*) followed this opinion after the war. . . . I say frankly that I cannot agree with it and that I prefer a solution which in the case of a proven significant technical and economic advance assumes that the new invention is based on an "inventive activity," and at least has that "scintilla" of inventive step that is regarded sufficient in these cases by British courts. . . .

But with this we are no longer in the history of patent law developments, but have reached the present stage. What then happened from the beginning of 60's, namely the statutory introduction of the prerequisite of inventive step in form of the so inapt term "inventive *activity*" (which need not exactly be present because it is the *result* of that activity which counts), and the entire dismissal of the advance in the art (or technical progress) as a separate patentability requirement in the process of harmonizing European patent law—to all of that I have an opinion which I can, however, not elaborate in this article. . . .

NOTES

1.   *Inventive Step and Nonobviousness.* The requirement of an "inventive step," as it is called in most of the world—"nonobviousness" in the United States—implies some greater difference between the claimed art and the prior art than will satisfy the less demanding novelty requirement. Although the requirement is directed at patentability, it may also affect decisions on infringement when courts evaluate the distance not only between the

---

[68]   [*Reichsgericht* decision of February 9, 1940, 1940 GRUR 195, 196.]

patented subject matter and the accused subject matter, but between the patented subject matter, the accused subject matter, and the prior art.

The fact that an explicit inventive step requirement first emerged in industrializing countries toward the latter part of the nineteenth century is no coincidence: the industrial revolutions of that era underscored the need for a doctrine that would at once spur inventors to direct investment toward significant, but achievable, technological advances and at the same time define the resulting property right in a way that would not inhibit others from inventing around or improving on these advances.

2. *Inventive Step and Nonobviousness: Different Approaches.* Although TRIPs Article 27 includes inventive step as a requirement of patentability, TRIPs does not define the term. The basic concept seems to be identical across countries' patent systems: the invention must not be obvious to a person skilled in the art. However, countries' systems vary in the approaches they take to assessing the presence of an inventive step. In the United States, the U.S. Supreme Court has endorsed the following approach:

> "Under § 103, the scope and content of the prior art are to be determined; differences between the prior art and the claims at issue are to be ascertained; and the level of ordinary skill in the pertinent art resolved. Against this background, the obviousness or nonobviousness of the subject matter is determined. Such secondary considerations as commercial success, long felt but unsolved needs, failure of others, etc., might be utilized to give light to the circumstances surrounding the origin of the subject matter sought to be patented."

Graham v. John Deere Co., 383 U.S. 1, 17–18 (1966); KSR Int'l Co. v. Teleflex, Inc., 550 U.S. 398, 405 (2007).

Examiners may differ in how they approach prior art. U.S. examiners may in practice refer to the closest prior art, but their analyses encompass the entire body of prior art. In the European Patent Office, by contrast, the identification of the closest prior art is fundamental to the "problem-and-solution" approach under which an examiner (1) identifies the closest prior art, (2) determines the objective technical problem to be solved, and (3) considers "whether or not the claimed invention, starting from the closest prior art and the objective technical problem, would have been obvious to the skilled person." Guidelines for Examination in the EPO, 2018, Part G, Chapter VII-3, Guideline 5.

3. *Prior Art.* Outcomes of inventive step analyses may diverge because of differences in the definitions of the relevant prior art; these differences stem not only from the definitions of the grace period, as was discussed above at page 453, but also from other factors: National patent systems may differ in the subset of prior art that they consider pertinent to the inventive step analysis. For example, in the United States pertinent prior art includes not only prior art in the same field as the invention but also "analogous prior art"—prior art that is reasonably pertinent to the particular problem. Commentators consider the scope of potentially pertinent prior art under U.S. law to be larger than it is under the European Patent Convention. In the European Patent Office the "closest prior art" is "directed to a similar purpose or effect as the invention or at least belong[s] to the same or a closely related technical field as the claimed invention." Guidelines for Examination in the EPO, 2018, Part G, Chapter VII-3, Guideline 5.1.

Differences among national patent offices in the accessibility of search tools and databases, and examiners' language abilities can also effectively alter the prior art that examiners consider in the inventive step analysis. Stephen G. Kunin & Philippe J.C. Signore, A Comparative Analysis of the Inventive Step Standard in the European and Japanese Patent Offices from a US Perspective, IP Litigator, January/February 2008, pp. 17–18.

4. *Other Differences in Inventive Step/Nonobviousness Analyses.* Examiners, appeal boards, and courts may vary not only in their identification of the pertinent or closest prior art, but also in their assessment of the knowledge possessed by the person ordinarily skilled in the art. Procedural rules, such as the rules of burden of proof and the rules on admissibility of evidence, may also cause disparities in outcomes. Varying outcomes may result from the different circumstances of each proceeding and a different evaluation of the evidence. In *Astrazeneca AB v. Hexal AG* an English judge identified the following reasons for a Dutch court's different conclusion on the obviousness of an invention protected by an identical European patent: there was "different evidence; the Dutch court proceeded on the basis that the patent was not entitled to the priority date; different arguments were advanced; and different conclusions were reached on motivation and expectation of success." [2013] EWCA Civ 454, ¶ 48.

The different approaches might not always lead to different outcomes. In 2008 the European Patent Office, the Japan Patent Office, and the U.S. Patent and Trademark Office compared the results of their inventive step analyses in six specific cases. In only one of the six cases did the offices reach different results: "In that particular case, there [were] differences in the determination of the scope of the claim and that of the invention described in the prior art document, as well as in the way prior art documents may be combined." Comparative Study on Hypothetical/Real Cases: Inventive Step/Non-obviousness, November 2008, p. 55. In the *Astrazeneca AB v. Hexal AG* case mentioned above, The Hague Regional Court of Appeal ultimately reversed the decision of the lower Dutch court, with the result that the European patent was held invalid in both the United Kingdom and the Netherlands, as well as in Belgium and Germany.

For comparative discussions of inventive step and nonobviousness see also Amy L. Landers, The Inventive Step and Cooperative Harmonization, in Intellectual Property in Common Law and Civil Law (Toshiko Takenaka ed., 2013), pp. 81–98.

5. *Inventive Step/Nonobviousness and Patent Validity.* If lack of an inventive step is identified during the patent prosecution process, the patent applicant may be able to amend the patent application to correct the omission. However, once a patent is granted, a later finding of lack of inventive step will result in invalidation of the patent. The story of Amazon's

"1-Click" invention is an example of two different outcomes of findings concerning inventive step.

In 1998, Amazon.com, Inc. filed patent applications in several countries for the "1-Click" "method and system for placing a purchase order via a communication network." The applications came under attack in national patent offices for, among other reasons, a lack of an inventive step that was claimed in both the single-action ordering and the use of cookies to identify customers. The EPO Technical Board of Appeal, taking the problem-and-solution approach, identified a 1996 article in Dr. Dobbs Journal, a U.S. software developer journal, as the closest prior art; the article described an implementation of a shopping cart on the Internet. The Board noted that the article explicitly mentioned the problem of combining a simplification of the acts necessary to make a purchase on the Internet with the use of a secure client identifier. The Board further noted that the use of cookies to identify and track purchaser data was known on the claimed priority date of the invention. The Board concluded that "the skilled person would have realised that any sensitive data traditionally requiring a login could be accessed by cookies," and therefore "the invention was not a situation of a long felt want, but more an immediate application of [cookies] as soon as [they] had become available." The Board decided that "the subject-matter of claim 1 would have been obvious to a skilled person." 1-Click/Amazon, T 1244/07, EPO Technical Board of Appeal, 2011, ¶¶ 15, 20, and 22.

In Australia, an opposition proceeding concerning the "1-Click" patent resulted in a different finding on inventive step. The Delegate of the Commissioner of Patents first established the "common general knowledge" based on the opponent's submission. As for the single-action ordering, the Delegate noted that "it seem[ed] 'very plain' . . . and a matter of simple logic that one way . . . is to reduce the number of actions, with the ideal scenario being just one action," and that "[t]here would seem to be practically no doubt that the [person skilled in the art] would have been directly led to the present solution to the problem." While the Delegate thus found that the single-action ordering lacked the required inventive step, his decision was different for the use of cookies. Although the Delegate agreed that cookies were known before the priority date of the claimed invention, the Delegate found that the claims concerning the use of cookies fulfilled the requirement of the inventive step: "[T]he use to which server generated client identifiers are put in the present invention is both an elegant and inventive way of achieving one action ordering functionality." Telstra Corp. Ltd. v. Amazon.com, Inc., 2011 APO 28, ¶¶ 91 and 96.

In the United States, the validity of the "1-Click" patent was attacked in an infringement proceeding. The patent issued in September 1999 (U.S. 5,960,411), and less than a month later Amazon sued Barnes and Noble for infringement of the patent. Although a preliminary injunction was granted in the case, the U.S. Court of Appeals for the Federal Circuit vacated the grant of the injunction because Barnes and Noble "mounted a serious challenge to the validity of Amazon's patent," which questioned both the novelty and the nonobviousness of the invention. Amazon.com, Inc. v. Barnesandnoble.com, Inc., 239 F.3d 1343, 1360 (Fed.Cir. 2001). Following a re-examination in the U.S. Patent and Trademark Office, the U.S. patent was "allowed in essentially the same form albeit limited with additional features of a shopping cart." 1-Click/Amazon, T 1244/07, EPO Technical Board of Appeal, 2011, ¶ 27.

6. *Efficacy.* Novartis's attempt to patent the beta crystalline form of its existing cancer drug Glivec/Gleevec, which was the subject of the Supreme Court of India's *Novartis* judgment excerpted on page 436, above, was characterized by some as an example of "evergreening"—a patent owner's strategy to extend artificially the duration of the patent owner's time-limited monopoly beyond the existing term of the patent.

The enhanced efficacy requirement in section 3(d) of the Indian Patent Act (quoted in the *Novartis* excerpt and discussed in note 2 on page 442, above) seeks to prevent evergreening. According to the Supreme Court of India, "section 3(d) clearly sets up a second tier of qualifying standards for chemical substances/pharmaceutical products in order to leave the door open for true and genuine inventions but, at the same time, to check any attempt at repetitive patenting or extension of the patent term on spurious grounds." Civil Appeal Nos. 2706–2716 of 2013, ¶ 103. Is the enhanced efficacy requirement only a reiteration of the requirements of novelty and inventive step? And, if it is not, is India in compliance with TRIPs Article 27(1) when it imposes a requirement of patentability that goes beyond novelty, inventive step, and industrial application?

For a review of different evergreening strategies see Roberto Reis & Claudia Chamas, The Green, Green Grass of Evergreening Patents, in Intellectual Property Rights as Obstacles to Legitimate Trade? (Christopher Heath et al. eds. 2018), pp. 131–157.

7. *Inventive Step/Nonobviousness and Patentable Subject Matter.* Some critics noted that the validity of the patent in the *Alice* case (see page 447, above) should have been argued and decided as a question of obviousness rather than as a question of patentable subject matter. In *Alice* the U.S. Supreme Court elaborated on a test that the Court set out in an earlier decision: When patent claims are directed at a patent-ineligible concept, there must be an "inventive concept" present in the claims that "ensure[s] that the patent in practice amounts to significantly more than a patent upon the [ineligible concept] itself." Mayo Collaborative Services v. Prometheus Laboratories, Inc., 566 U.S. 66, 72 (2012); Alice Corp. Pty. Ltd. v. CLS Bank Intern., 573 U.S. 208, 218 (2014).

One commentator observed that "[t]he components of the *Alice Corp.* test bear comparison to reasoning from the European Patent Office that grapples with essentially the same problem." Dan L. Burk, The Inventive Concept in *Alice Corp. v. CLS Bank Int'l*, 45 IIC 865, 866 (2014). The European Patent Office sets a low bar for software as patentable subject matter (see the discussion at page 447, above) and focuses instead on the potential obviousness of software inventions. *See* Nicholas Fox & William Corbett, UK and EPO Approaches to Excluded Subject-Matter and Inventive Step: Are Aerotel and Pozzoli Heading for the Rocks?. 36(9) EIPR 569 (2014).

Does it matter whether it is an ineligible subject matter or obviousness that excludes an invention from patent protection? Justice Arden noted that "[i]t is deliberate legislative policy to exclude certain matters from patentability even if they would otherwise be patentable." Lantana Ltd v. The Comptroller General of Patents, Design and Trade Marks, [2014] EWCA Civ 1463, ¶ 19. How is the hindsight problem, which is inherent in all inventive step analyses, addressed when the "inventive concept" is a factor in determining whether an invention presents a protectible subject matter?

8. *Industrial Application and Utility.* The requirement that patentable subject matter be susceptible to industrial application—in the United States the requirement is that it be "useful"—implies at the very least that the claimed invention has some practical and tangible application. Article 57 of the European Patent Convention states that "[a]n invention shall be considered as susceptible of industrial application if it can be made or used in any kind of industry, including agriculture." One aim of the requirement is to exclude patents for abstract concepts that might undermine technological advances.

National practice variously supplements the industrial application test with other requirements. In the United States, the utility requirement requires that an invention must confer some social benefit and, at the least, cause no harm. *See* Donald Chisum, 1 Patents § 4.01 (1998). Other elaborations of the industrial application test will sometimes cross over into considerations of inventive step, and in fact, until recently, a lack of industrial applicability rarely served as the ground for a finding of patent invalidity. For example, in the United Kingdom an application for a flying saucer was rejected as incapable of industrial application because it contravened Newton's third law of motion and the first law of thermodynamics. Joseph Thompson v. The Comptroller General of Patents, Designs and Trademarks, [2005] EWHC 3065.

Canadian courts had developed a "promise doctrine" for pharmaceutical and biopharmaceutical patents that led to the invalidation of several patents based on their lack of utility. Under the doctrine, if a patent applicant made a promise in a patent application of a certain utility, the patent was assessed based on "whether there was sufficient evidence demonstrating that, at the date of filing, [the invention] would do what the patent promised, or, if not, that its utility could be soundly predicted." Eli Lilly v. Teva Canada Ltd., Federal Court of Appeal, 2011 FCA 220. Is the promise doctrine consistent with TRIPs Article 27(1)?

In an arbitration dispute brought by Eli Lilly against the Canadian government under the North American Free Trade Agreement, the arbitral tribunal concluded that Eli Lilly did not demonstrate that the introduction of the "promise doctrine" was "a fundamental or dramatic change in Canadian patent law" that would violate Eli Lilly's legitimate expectations protected by NAFTA. Eli Lilly and Co. v. Government of Canada, Final Award, No. UNCT/14/2, 2017, ¶ 387.

The "promise doctrine" did not survive the NAFTA arbitration for long; in a different dispute decided fewer than four months later, the Supreme

Court of Canada held that the "promise doctrine" was not the correct method of determining whether the utility requirement had been met. The Court did not, however, address arguments made by some interveners that the doctrine "put[. . .] Canada out of step with international standards" and "the utility standard should [have] reflect[ed] a low threshold that would [have] be[en] in accordance with Canada's international obligations." AstraZeneca Canada Inc. v. Apotex Inc., [2017] 1 R.C.S., ¶¶ 21 and 24. Does TRIPs Article 27(1) set a threshold for the requirement of industrial application? Can an internationally binding threshold be discerned from the practices of WTO countries?

9. *Sufficient Disclosure.* It is consistent with the notice function of the patent system for patent law to require that patent applicants sufficiently disclose their inventions in patent applications. TRIPs Article 29(1) requires that a disclosure be "sufficiently clear and complete for the invention to be carried out by a person skilled in the art." The requirement of "best mode for carrying out the invention" in TRIPs is optional for countries to implement. *Id.* In the United States, the "claims, read in light of the specification . . . , and the prosecution history" must "inform, with reasonable certainty, those skilled in the art about the scope of the invention." Nautilus Inc. v. Biosig Instruments, Inc., 572 U.S. 898, 901 (2014). For a discussion of the TRIPs provision and national requirements see Matthew Fisher, Enablement and Written Description, in Patent Law in Global Perspective (Ruth L. Okediji & Margo A. Bagley eds., 2014), pp. 243–283; Bingbin Lu, Disclosure Requirements for Patent Application: Article 29 of the TRIPS Agreement and a Dimensional Exploration, 34(5) EIPR 336 (2012).

A majority of WIPO member countries have supported proposals to introduce an obligation to disclose in a patent application any genetic resources on which the invention is based. The Patent Law of the People's Republic of China, for example, requires a patent applicant to include in the application information about "the direct and original source of . . . genetic resources" that the applicant relied on in his invention. *Id.*, Article 26. However, the United States, Canada, Japan, and South Korea have opposed the proposal for such a disclosure obligation.

Does a disclosure requirement address the concerns about bioprospecting that are discussed at pages 112 and 452, above? *See* generally Daniel Gervais, The TRIPS Agreement: Drafting History and Analysis (4th ed. 2012), pp. 76–100; The Protection of Traditional Knowledge: Draft Articles, Rev. 2, WIPO Intergovernmental Committee on Intellectual Property and Genetic Resources, Traditional Knowledge and Folklore, Mar. 28, 2014.

3.   PROSECUTION AND OWNERSHIP

a.   PATENT PROSECUTION

**Robert Benson, The Impact of the Patent
Cooperation Treaty (PCT) and the
European Patent Convention (EPC)
on U.S. Practitioners**

60 Journal of the Patent Office Society 118–126 (1978).

Back in the mid-1960s President Johnson appointed a special commission to study the United States patent system. One of the recommendations of this commission was that "the United States promote direct interim steps towards the ultimate goal—a universal patent including harmonization of patent practices." As a direct result of this recommendation, the United States Government, along with some other countries, asked the United International Bureau for the Protection of Intellectual Property (BIRPI) to develop a proposal that would meet the recommendation of the Presidential Commission. Specifically, they were asked to draft a proposal that would (a) simplify the procedures in filing foreign patent applications corresponding to the basic initially filed patent application, (b) reduce the cost of obtaining patents in foreign countries, (c) promote more uniform national laws relating to procurement and enforcement of patents and (d) improve the patent systems in countries that did not have a patent examination system.

The first proposal from BIRPI came out in February of 1967 and called for a system of international cooperation that included a uniform format for patent applications, a centralized searching system and a preliminary examination which could result in the issuance of what was then called "a certificate of patentability." This proposal then became the basic document from which the various drafts of the proposed Patent Cooperation Treaty, were drawn. The negotiations for the Patent Cooperation Treaty culminated in a diplomatic conference in June of 1970 at which conference the Patent Cooperation Treaty was signed by some 26 countries.

A lot has been written about the various provisions of the Patent Cooperation Treaty and I will not go into them in detail except to outline the principal provisions. First the form and content of the international applications would be accepted by all countries who participate in the Patent Cooperation Treaty. Secondly, the PCT called for searching authorities which would have to have minimum prior art documentation for their searches. The PCT defined minimum standards of patentability against which the applications would be examined. In the first phase, or Chapter I, of the Patent Cooperation Treaty a prior art search would be conducted and a search report issued to the applicant. In the second phase of the Patent Cooperation Treaty, referred to as Chapter II, a preliminary examination would be conducted with the prior art actually being applied to the claimed invention. The PCT applicant has the right to amend his application, including the claims, to distinguish from the art cited by the searching authority and as applied during the examination phase. At the end of this procedure, copies of the application together with the search report would be forwarded to the national offices of the countries the applicant had designated. The national patent offices of the designated countries are responsible for finally issuing a patent. After the patent is issued, it is to be enforced in each country strictly in accordance with the national laws of that country.

Immediately after the Patent Cooperation Treaty was signed, the common market countries reopened negotiations relative to a European patent and a common market patent. The Common Market Patent Convention providing for a single patent for all of the EEC countries has been signed but now must be ratified by all the member countries before coming into force. The negotiations leading to the European Patent Convention continued through 1973 at which time a number of European countries signed what is now known as the "European Patent Convention." The European Patent Convention contains a large number of clauses which were extracted almost verbatim from the Patent Cooperation Treaty and are completely compatible with that Treaty. In accordance with the European Patent Convention, initial proceedings take place in the European Patent Office in Munich, but the prior art searches are conducted in the branch of the European Patent Office at The Hague. The proceedings in the European Patent Convention include not only a preliminary search but a complete examination against a specific standard of invention for all applications filed in the European Patent Office. Upon completion of the examination stage and a determination of patentability, a copy of the patent application is transferred to the Patent Office in each of the individual countries that were designated in the original application. The application is then translated (if required) and issued as a patent. In effect, then, although you file a single patent application in the European Patent Office and prosecute it through to completion in that office, the result is that you have as many separate and distinct patents as the countries that were designated in the original application. As in the Patent Cooperation Treaty, patents in the European Patent Convention are enforced in each individual country strictly in accordance with the national laws of that country. A number of countries in the European community have amended or are planning to amend their patent laws to bring them into conformity with specific provisions set forth in the European Patent Convention.

Both the European Patent Convention and the Patent Cooperation Treaty become operational in June of 1978. As we look at it today, we will soon have two additional systems that we can utilize for obtaining patent protection for our clients' inventions. It will be interesting to measure the results from these treaties against the goal that was set forth in the mid-1960s. Have we really developed systems that will simplify the filing and obtaining of patents in various foreign countries at less cost? Will the new systems promote or encourage more uniform laws in various countries? Have we set up a system in which the less developed countries can participate and thereby significantly upgrade the patent systems in those countries? I think that we have met at least some of these goals, although only time will tell if there is sufficient use of the new system to achieve the goals. Furthermore, there is a good bit of controversy over whether or not the cost of obtaining patents through the new systems will be less than going the conventional country-by-country route.

A U.S. practitioner, especially those representing multinational companies who market their products or license their technology worldwide, must take a hard look at these systems to determine whether or not they are applicable to the inventions of his clients. . . .

Now let's look at some of the potential advantages of using the new systems.

The most significant advantage is the additional time provided before a final decision has to be made on the filing of individual applications in the different countries. In accordance with PCT, the applicant has eight additional months beyond the year provided by the Paris Convention, plus a preliminary search report on which to base the decision on whether to complete the filings in the designated countries. Under Article 27(7) and Rule 4.7, an applicant does not need to appoint a national attorney or agent until processing of the application has started in the designated national Patent Office. In practice, appointment of the associate attorney or agent can be delayed until the 20th month following the filing date of the international application. Under the European Patent Convention, you will not only have the preliminary search, but you will have a complete examination of the claimed invention against the prior art and the application will be prosecuted through to the point of allowance. In both PCT and the European Patent Convention, the applicant has the opportunity to amend the claims and the specification of the application.

If, under either system, the applicant decides that his invention is not patentable or that the protection he is likely to obtain is not valuable, he can withdraw his designations of countries and does not have to complete the filing of the applications in individually designated countries. Of course, if he has not yet appointed agents, he saves the initial "opening the file" type of charge that agents usually make. The possibility of changing the decision of filing additional applications has a very significant bearing on the potential cost of using either PCT or the European Patent Convention. For example, if in one case out of ten the applicant is able to make a better decision which results in not filing applications in initially designated countries, he could save more money than the additional costs he has incurred in using either the PCT or the European Patent Convention.

Another significant advantage is that the applications in the United States, the Patent Cooperation Treaty and the European Patent Convention can all be prepared in exactly the same format. The form and content of an application, if it meets the standards of the Patent Cooperation Treaty, must be accepted in the European Patent Convention and in all of the countries which have adhered to either the European Patent Convention or the Patent Cooperation Treaty. The format includes the drawings, the description of the invention, the claims and the typing which, in accordance with the new system, is 1-1/2 spaced typing. As you know, under the present system many countries have different requirements for drawings, formalities in the application, paper size and type spacing. Although this may appear to be trivia, it all takes time which increases costs.

The fact that PCT and European Patent Convention applications, in the initial stages, can all be prepared and prosecuted in the English language is an advantage for those of us who do not have good command of a second and third language. This avoids at least some of the problems encountered in translations.

Another significant advantage, at least from our point of view, is the savings in valuable attorney time by using the international system. Simply being able to prosecute a single patent application through to issuance, such as in the European Patent Convention, before having to embark on the prosecution of patent applications in other countries, is a significant advantage. For example, an amendment in a patent application in the European Patent Convention automatically applies to all of the patent applications that will be filed based on that international application thus eliminating the need to make duplicate amendments. Furthermore, the arguments made to distinguish the invention from the prior art will automatically be part of the file in all applications filed in the designated countries. Thus, instead of attempting to prosecute patent applications on the same invention in four or five or more countries simultaneously, the attorney will have the opportunity to go through one complete prosecution before he has to spend any time on the applications filed in other countries. Furthermore, assuming that the European Patent Convention operates as expected, there will be no requirement for further prosecution of a patent application when it is filed in the other countries. However, some countries may require a translation of the entire application into their native language. The present rules require that the claims in each patent be translated into the other official languages of the treaty.

Another advantage of both the PCT and the European Patent Convention which will be available to all of us, even those that do not use the system, is the periodic publication of an Official Journal containing an abstract of all patents issued through either the European Patent Convention or the Patent Cooperation Treaty.

Let's now consider some of the possible disadvantages of using either one of the international patent systems. First and foremost, of course, is the question of cost. There is no question, but the cost of filing and prosecuting a patent application in either the PCT or the European Patent Convention is going to be considerably more than in any individual country. At one time, it was projected that filing through the PCT would be a cost savings if the applicant intended to file patent applications in three or more countries. Later studies seem to indicate that the break even point is higher than that. Furthermore, some of the quotations of costs coming in from associates abroad indicate that the overall cost in the European Patent Office is going to be substantially more than we originally anticipated. However, the costs that are being quoted are primarily the Patent Office and associate fees and do not take into account the savings in attorney time or the potential savings due to the applicant being in a position to make a better judgment as to whether or not to finally file the applications in the designated countries. Therefore, any such study should be carefully scrutinized and the quoted costs of filing through either of the international systems should be measured against some of the other potential cost-saving features of the treaties before a final decision is made that the system is prohibitively expensive.

Other potential disadvantages of using the system is the argument that you are placing all of your eggs in a single basket. It is pointed out that if you go the individual country route in Europe, you are certain to get patents issued in some countries even if you can't get them in the difficult examination countries such as Switzerland and Germany. While this may be true, I think that you have to consider the potential value of such patents to your client. I am sure that when it comes to enforcing patents in the European Community, the courts are going to inquire as to whether or not the patent was prosecuted through the European Patent Office or whether or not it went directly through the national offices. Thus, even if the national standard of patentability is not harmonized with the European Patent Convention standard by national legislative action, the national courts of the European Patent Convention member countries are likely to achieve some harmonization. This will be especially true in countries that do not maintain an examination system.

NOTES

1. *Patent Cooperation Treaty*. Just as the patent priority established by Article 4 of the Paris Convention gives a patent applicant a year to assess the patentability and marketability of its invention before investing the resources required for application in other national systems, the Patent Cooperation Treaty—a special agreement under Article 19 of the Paris Convention, open only to Paris Convention parties—extends to as long as

thirty-four months the time an applicant can take before making other national applications. The period varies between thirty and thirty-four months depending on the country, and a few countries, such as Canada, allow an applicant to delay entry into the national phase even further upon payment of an additional fee. The purpose and method of this extended period are to enable the applicant to obtain further information on the prior art that bears on the invention and the scope of the claims that are likely to survive examination. The PCT can be viewed as a second-best alternative to a single, international patent office, disposing of important search and examination functions before applications are made to national offices.

For a U.S. patent applicant interested in exploiting its invention in foreign markets, the first step in the PCT process is, within twelve months, to refile its U.S. application as a PCT application with the request that a patentability search—at its election—be made by the U.S. Patent and Trademark Office under Chapter I of the PCT. (As of March 1, 2019 there were 22 patent offices designated as International Searching Authorities, including the Australian Patent Office, the Brazilian National Institute of Industrial Property, the Canadian Intellectual Property Office, the State Intellectual Property Office of the People's Republic of China, the European Patent Office, the Indian Patent Office, and the U.S. Patent and Trademark Office.) Six months later—typically eighteen months from the application priority filing date—WIPO will publish the PCT application in Geneva; the search results will be published at roughly the same time.

Not more than twenty-two months from the priority filing date, the applicant must choose whether to request ("demand," in PCT parlance) an international preliminary examination under Chapter II of the PCT, or to forgo the examination stage and enter the national phase of the process without the benefit of the international examination. (Designated International Preliminary Examining Authorities are the same patent offices as are designated as International Searching Authorities.) An international examination, if demanded, will usually occur within two to six months, resulting in a non-binding opinion on the patentability of the invention. The applicant has thirty to thirty-one months from the priority date (depending on the country, with a few countries permitting an even longer period) to convert its PCT application into national applications.

2.   *The PCT in Operation.* According to figures collected and analyzed by the World Intellectual Property Organization, whose International Bureau oversees the operation of the Patent Cooperation Treaty, two million international applications were filed under the treaty from June 1, 1978, when it became operational, through April, 2011. Of the approximately 243,500 PCT applications filed in 2017, the largest numbers originated in the United States, China, and Japan, with Huawei Technologies and ZTE Corp.—two China-based telecommunication companies—being the largest PCT application filers. WIPO IP Facts and Figures 2018, pp. 16–17.

Not all patent applicants use the PCT application for filing in foreign countries. Estimates of the "break even point" mentioned in the Benson article above vary, meaning estimates of the number of countries for which it is cost-effective to file a PCT application instead of filing individual direct national patent applications. Why would a patent applicant use a PCT application even though the applicant does not intend to apply for patents in a sufficient number of countries to reach the "break even point?"

3. *European Patent Convention.* The European Patent Convention, which was signed in 1973 and took effect in 1977, created the European Patent Office to serve member states consisting principally of the countries of the European Union. Headquartered in Munich, the European Patent Office is a designated International Searching Authority and Preliminary Examining Authority under the PCT and is also a regional patent-granting authority in its own right. The EPO is self-financed through fees levied on patent applications and renewal fees levied annually on issued patents.

The European Patent Convention provides an optional approach to national patent protection in Europe, enabling an applicant to obtain protection in one or more countries, either under a European patent through a filing in the EPO, or under one or more national patents by filings in one or more national patent offices with the aid of a European search report drawn up by the EPO. Under Article 2(2) of the Convention, a European patent has the same effect in each contracting state for which it is granted as a patent granted by that state. By default, all contracting states are deemed to be designated for protection unless a patent applicant withdraws one or more of the designations before the European patent is granted (Article 79).

The European patent takes on all of the characteristics and limitations imposed by national law and may be revoked through proceedings in the EPO or through proceedings in the individual countries. Although national courts generally strive to interpret the EPC, it is possible that a patent granted by the EPO will be revoked in one country and upheld in another. Actions for infringement of a European patent are brought in national courts, subject to the usual rules on choice of forum, and will typically be decided under the usual rules for choice of applicable law. *See* generally, Joseph Straus, The Present State of the Patent System in the European Union: As Compared with the Situation in the United States of America and Japan (1997).

4. *European (Union) Patent with Unitary Effect.* A Community Patent Convention that would have created a European Community-wide patent, though signed in 1975 and adopted in 1984, did not enter into force for lack of the necessary ratifications. After decades of debates and negotiations, most of the member countries of the European Union agreed toward the end of 2012 to create a "European patent with unitary effect" throughout the European Union ("unitary patent"). A proprietor of a European patent issued under the EPC will be able to request that the patent be registered by the EPO for unitary patent protection in most of the EU member states. The unitary patent will have equal effect in all participating European Union countries. Regulation (EU) 1257/2012 of the European Parliament and of the Council of 17 December 2012 implementing enhanced cooperation in the area of the creation of unitary patent protection, Article 3.

For the unitary patent system to be fully operational, countries must ratify the Agreement on a Unified Patent Court. The Agreement establishes a court structure with exclusive competence to decide disputes concerning European patents and European patents with unitary effect, including actions for infringement and for revocation of such patents. The Agreement envisages a court structure consisting of a Court of First Instance with a central division and local and regional divisions, a Court of Appeal, and a Registry. The central division of the Court of First Instance will be located in Paris and will have sections in two major European patent litigation venues. The panels of the courts will be composed of judges who are legally qualified and judges who are technically qualified, and the judges will be from multiple countries. The Court will apply the law of the European Union, the Agreement on a Unified Patent Court, the European Patent Convention, other international agreements, and national laws. Agreement on a Unified Patent Court, Feb. 19, 2013. Is the Unified Patent Court an indispensable component of the unitary patent system?

The creation of the unitary patent system has not been without controversy. The decision to limit the number of languages into which the unitary patent would have to be translated generated protests by Italy and Spain, which decided not to join the unitary patent system. The two countries brought an action against the decision of the Council of the European Union to allow member countries to proceed with the creation of the system notwithstanding the absence of some member states. The Court of Justice of the European Union dismissed Italy and Spain's action in April 2013, and in May 2015 the Court also dismissed a later action in which Spain claimed that the unitary patent system violated the principle of non-discrimination on the ground of language and other principles of European Union law. Spain and Italy v. Council, CJEU, C-274/11, 2013; Spain v. Council, CJEU, C-147/13, 2015. The ratification of the Agreement on the Unified Patent Court suffered setbacks because of constitutional complaints filed by its opponents in Germany and Hungary; the opponents challenged the Agreement's ratification process and the new Court system's compliance with national constitutional requirements. German Federal Constitutional Court, 2 BvR 739/17; Constitutional Court of Hungary, X/01514/2017.

For an insightful discussion of the system, including the historical and the U.S. perspectives, see The Unitary EU Patent System (Justine Pila & Christopher Wadlow eds., 2015).

5.   *Efficiency Considerations in the Issuance of Patents.* The U.S. Patent and Trademark Office's *ex parte* examination of all patent applications against all of the statutory standards of patentability—including novelty, nonobviousness and utility—has been criticized as economically wasteful. One effect of the *ex parte* examination should be that every holder or licensee of a U.S. patent can exploit the patented invention with the expectation that the patent, because it was earlier subjected to administrative scrutiny, will have a reasonable chance of surviving judicial scrutiny in an infringement action. But, from the standpoint of efficiency, the problem with an *ex parte* examination system is that it indiscriminately lavishes attention on the overwhelming proportion of inventions that are economically worthless, along with the relative few that are economically valuable. One alternative is to award patents simply on the basis of review for formal compliance alone, deferring substantive examination to later infringement litigation—*if* there is infringement litigation—respecting the few patents covering inventions that have achieved success in the marketplace.

A comparison of national patent systems reveals a rich variety of approaches to the efficiency tradeoffs between early determinations of patent validity for all inventions and deferred examinations limited to commercially worthwhile inventions. The first U.S. Patent Act, Act of April 10, 1790, ch. 7, 1 Stat. 109–110, called for an examination of sorts by a patent board composed of the Secretary of State, the Secretary of War and the Attorney General. Three years later, a new patent law replaced this with the simple act of registration, and an examination system was not reintroduced until the Act of July 4, 1836, ch. 357, 5 Stat. 117. Formal rather than substantive examination was long the administrative norm in many civil law countries, and still exists in some countries today, although several civil law countries have moved from formal registration to substantive examination systems. Can the preliminary examination report issued under the PCT meliorate some of the limitations of a strict registration system by giving the patent owner and its prospective licensees a basis for determining whether the patent will withstand substantive attack in litigation?

Many countries, both common law and civil law, provide for deferred examination for periods ranging from months to years; Rule 70(1) of the Implementing Regulations to the European Patent Convention gives an applicant up to six months following reference to publication of the European search report to request examination, while section 48*ter* of the Japanese Patent Act allows three years from filing of the patent application. A large number of countries winnow out invalid patents through an opposition procedure under which any interested party may oppose the grant of a patent on prescribed grounds of invalidity within a period that is usually measured in months from the application's passage to acceptance by the examiner. One popular technique for weeding out patents that have enjoyed little commercial success is to impose periodic levies—variously called renewal fees, maintenance fees or annuities—on the patent owner; in addition to clearing out undesired monopolies, the fees help to subvent patent office operations.

See generally J.W. Baxter, *et al.* 2 World Patent Law and Practice chapters 3, 7, 14 (1999).

6. *Cooperation Among Patent Offices.* Facing rapidly increasing numbers of patent applications, patent offices strive to economize patent prosecution processes in various ways, including by cooperating with patent offices in other countries. The Patent Prosecution Highway is one such cooperative project; it enables participating patent offices to share the results of their patent examinations, which increases the efficiency of the examinations and accelerates the prosecution process. After the office of the first filing rules on patentability, other offices can fast track subsequent examinations.

Economizing the prosecution process is not the only goal of the collaboration; a desire to improve the quality and consistency of searches is a goal as well. In 2018 WIPO launched the "Collaborative Search and Examination" program, which allows patent applicants to request that five major patent offices—the U.S., Chinese, Japanese, and Korean patent offices and the EPO—carry out prior art searches.

Some countries with limited institutional resources have chosen to recognize patents granted by well-established foreign patent offices: Morocco, Moldova, Tunisia, and Cambodia will validate European patents granted by the EPO. Applicants who obtain U.K. patents may apply, typically within three years from the date of the issue of their U.K. patents, to have their U.K. patents re-registered as national patents in a number of Commonwealth countries, such as Fiji, Guyana, and Vanuatu; the parallel patents then expire on the same date as the applicants' U.K. patents. Is this re-registration practice a victory for international patent harmonization? Or is it a sign of defeat for the small developing countries that have yielded to international patent harmonization because of the costs discussed in Primo Braga's article on page 95, above?

7. *Publication of a Patent Application.* One difference between the patent system in the United States and those in the rest of the world before the AIA was in the rules for publication of patent applications. In the United States, before the effective date of the AIA, a patent application was not published until a patent was granted, while other patent systems published patent applications 18 months after an application's effective filing date. What reason is there not to publish applications immediately upon filing? Is it likely that inventors will avoid a patent system that does not give them a period of secrecy during which, aided by a first office action on the merits, they can decide whether to abandon the application?

What is the public's interest in an early publication of patent applications? The 1992 Advisory Commission Report noted that "[e]arly publication of pending patent applications would primarily benefit the public, because it would accelerate access to information contained in the patent disclosure, and would permit identification of potential patent conflicts sooner. These benefits would, in turn speed technological progress by providing useful information to the public at an earlier stage after its discovery." Advisory Commission on Patent Law Reform, A Report to the Secretary of Commerce, 1992, p. 62.

In line with the recommendation of the Advisory Commission Report, Congress in 1999 amended section 122 of the Patent Act to establish the default rule that patent applications will be published "promptly after the expiration of a period of 18 months from the earliest filing date for which a benefit is sought under this title." An applicant may request earlier publication, or may request that there be no publication at all; in the latter case, the applicant must certify that no foreign application has been, or will be, filed for the invention under terms requiring publication eighteen months after filing. 35 U.S.C. § 122(b)(1)(A) and (b)(2)(B)(i). To give the applicant an incentive to elect eighteen-month publication, or to request earlier publication, section 154(d) provides that a patentee may recover a reasonable royalty for infringements occurring after publication if the infringer actually knew of the publication and if the patent claims ultimately granted are "substantially identical" to the claims published.

b.   INVENTORSHIP AND PATENT OWNERSHIP

Boston Scientific Scimed, Inc. v. Medtronic Vascular, Inc.

United States Court of Appeals for the Federal Circuit, 2007.
497 F.3d 1293, 83 U.S.P.Q.2d 1669.

MAYER, CIRCUIT JUDGE.

Boston Scientific Scimed, Inc. ("Scimed") appeals the district court's grant of summary judgment affirming the Board of Patent Appeals and Interferences' final decision, which denied Scimed the priority benefit of an earlier-filed European patent application for the subject matter at issue in Patent Interference Number 104,192 ("the '192 interference"). . . . We affirm.

Background

This appeal stems from an interference proceeding before the United States Patent and Trademark Office Board of Patent Appeals and Interferences. Scimed and Medtronic Vascular, Inc. ("Medtronic") are each assignees of different United States patent applications covering the same invention. Andrew Cragg and Michael Dake (collectively "Cragg") filed patent application 08/461,402 ("the '402 application") for the invention in question on June 5, 1995. Cragg then assigned all rights in the '402 application to Boston Scientific Technology, Inc., which later merged into Scimed, the plaintiff-appellant and current legal owner of the '402 application. Also on June 5, 1995, Thomas J. Fogarty, Timothy J. Ryan, and Kirsten Freislinger (collectively "Fogarty") filed patent application 08/463,836 ("the '836 application") for the same invention. Fogarty assigned their rights in the '836 application to a company that eventually became Medtronic, the defendant-appellee and current legal owner of the '836 application. Eric Martin, a third-party to the instant appeal, owns U.S. Patent No. 5,575,817 (the "Martin patent" or " '817 patent"), which resulted from an application filed on August 19, 1994.

On April 23, 1998, the board declared an interference between Scimed's '402 application, Medtronic's '836 application, and Martin's '817 patent. The purpose of the interference was to determine which party had priority of inventorship, thereby entitling it to the invention. . . .

The board initially gave Cragg the benefit of the filing dates of two European patent applications filed by MinTec SARL ("MinTec"), a French company. The earlier of these dates was February 9, 1994.* At the

---

* Cragg's U.S. application '402 was a divisional application of U.S. application 08/317,763, which was filed on October 4, 1994. The original application filed on October 4, 1994,

time these European applications were filed, no legal relationship existed between MinTec and Cragg, nor was MinTec acting on behalf of Cragg. Fogerty was granted the benefit of the filing date of U.S. patent application 08/255,681, which was June 8, 1994. Martin was accorded benefit of the application that led to the '817 patent, which was filed on August 19, 1994. Accordingly, the PTO initially designated Cragg as the senior party in the interference.

Fogarty responded by filing a motion attacking the priority benefit granted to Cragg. The board granted the motion, declaring Fogarty the senior party in the interference. After Cragg protested this decision, the board issued a final decision denying his request to be declared the senior party. The board ruled that Cragg was not entitled to priority benefit under 35 U.S.C. § 119 because neither Cragg nor Dake had assigned their rights to MinTec until after it had filed the European applications. . . .

Scimed, the assignee of Cragg's U.S. patent application, then brought an action in the United States District Court for the District of Columbia challenging the board's final decision in the '192 interference. The district court affirmed the board's final decision . . . , and Scimed filed this appeal. We have jurisdiction under 28 U.S.C. § 1295(a)(1).

Discussion

We review a district court's grant of summary judgment *de novo*. . . . We also apply a *de novo* standard when reviewing questions of law, including a trial court's interpretation of statutory language. . . .

At issue here is whether 35 U.S.C. § 119(a)** permits an applicant for a United States patent to benefit from the priority of a foreign application previously filed by an entity that was not acting on behalf of the U.S. applicant at the time of filing. We hold that it does not.

A similar issue was addressed by the Court of Customs and Patent Appeals in *Vogel v. Jones*, 486 F.2d 1068 (CCPA 1973), which, to the extent relevant here, is binding upon us. . . . According to *Vogel*, "§ 119 gives rise to a right of priority that is personal to the United States applicant." 486 F.2d at 1072. Due to the personal nature of this right, an applicant for a U.S. patent may only benefit from the priority of a foreign application if it was filed by the U.S. applicant or "on his behalf." *Id.*

---

was the application that received the benefit of the European patent application priority date of February 9, 1994. *Ed.*

**   35 U.S.C. § 119(a) reads in relevant part:

An application for patent for an invention filed in this country by any person who has, or whose legal representatives or assigns have, previously regularly filed an application for a patent for the same invention in a foreign country which affords similar privileges in the case of applications filed in the United States or to citizens of the United States, or in a WTO member country, shall have the same effect as the same application would have if filed in this country on the date on which the application for patent for the same invention was first filed in such foreign country, if the application in this country is filed within twelve months from the earliest date on which such foreign application was filed. . . . *Ed.*

Scimed argues that *Vogel* does not require the foreign applicant to have been acting on behalf of the U.S. applicant *at the time the foreign application was filed*. It points to the following passage in support:

> This practice [of allowing a U.S. applicant to claim priority from a foreign application filed by someone else] arose because it was recognized that in many foreign countries, unlike in the United States, the actual applicant for a patent can be other than the inventor, *e.g.*, an assignee. In light of this, we regard the language in § 119 referring to legal representatives and assigns to merely represent a codification of the actual practice under [the predecessor statute to § 119]. Since under United States law an application for patent must be made by the inventor, that practice was based on the requirement that the foreign application, regardless of the identity of the applicant, must have been filed for an invention actually made by the inventive entity seeking to rely upon it for priority purposes. We think § 119 must be construed to the same end.

Id. . . . Scimed attempts to construe this language as permitting a U.S. applicant to benefit from a foreign application's earlier filing date whenever "the invention described in the foreign application [is the same] one actually made by the U.S. applicant," " 'regardless of the identity of the applicant' of the foreign application." According to its interpretation, "the *Vogel* court did *not* hold that the foreign application must have been filed by a person who was an assignee or legal representative of the U.S. inventor *at the time the foreign application was filed*, or that the foreign application must have been filed on his behalf in order for there to be priority benefit." We disagree.

Vogel clearly held that the above-quoted passage "means that an applicant for a United States patent can rely for priority on the 'first filed' application by an assignee *on his behalf*." *Id.* (emphasis added). Moreover, "the existence of an application made by [the inventor's] assignee in a foreign country on behalf of one other than the United States inventor is irrelevant to his right of priority based on applications made on his behalf." *Id.* In other words, while the foreign application must obviously be for the same invention and may be filed by someone other than the inventor, section 119(a) also requires that a nexus exist between the inventor and the foreign applicant at the time the foreign application was filed. Indeed, as a matter of pure logic, an entity could not have filed a foreign application "on behalf of" an inventor without the inventor's knowledge or consent; that the foreign application may have been filed in accordance with the laws of the country in which it was filed has no bearing here. Therefore, to the extent that there may have been any uncertainty or ambiguity in *Vogel*, we now explicitly hold that a foreign application may *only* form the basis for priority under section 119(a) if that application was filed by either the U.S. applicant himself, or by someone acting on his behalf *at the time the foreign application was filed.* . . .

Conclusion

Accordingly, the judgment of the United States District Court for the District of Columbia is affirmed.

NOTES

1. *Inventorship.* One theme that shaped the debate in the United States about the change to the first-to-file system was a concern that the system would lead to "thefts" of inventions, as any first filer could obtain a patent even if the first filer did not invent the invention. However, as explained in the 1992 Advisory Commission Report, "[p]rotection for bona fide inventors against theft is a feature of all first-to-file patent systems throughout the world." For example, under Article 60 of the European Patent Convention, only "the inventor or his successor in title" has the right to a European patent. Similarly, Article 27(1) of the Canadian Patent Act allows only the inventor or the inventor's legal representative to be granted a patent.

Section 101 of the U.S. Patent Act continues to state that only "[w]hoever invents or discovers" a patentable subject matter may obtain a patent. The AIA replaced the interference procedure, in which the Board of Patent Appeals and Interferences determined the priority of an invention, with a derivation proceeding, in which a patent applicant may demonstrate that an identical or substantially identical invention described in an earlier-filed patent application was derived from the inventor named in the applicant's application, and that the earlier application was filed without the inventor's authorization. A petition to institute a derivation proceeding may be filed within one year of the first publication of the patent claim. 35 U.S.C. § 135.

Other first-to-file systems have mechanisms to remedy situations in which a patent application is filed by someone other than the inventor or his successor in title. For example, according to the European Patent Convention, if a national court decides that a person other than the applicant is entitled to the grant of a European patent, that person may prosecute the filed application as his own, file a new application, or request that the application be refused. EPC, Article 61; Unlawful applicant, EPO Board of Appeals, G 0003/92, June 13, 1994. As for the law applicable to a decision on who has the right to the grant of a European patent, the national court that has jurisdiction based on the EPC Protocol on Jurisdiction and the Recognition of Decisions in Respect of the Right to the Grant of a European Patent "appl[ies] the particular national law which governs determination of the case, which may or may not be its own national law, within the framework of its own legal system." "[W]hatever the result in that court," the Board explained, "its decision is recognised in all the other Contracting States." *Id.*, ¶ 3.4.

2. *The Right to a Patent and Employee Inventions.* Who is the initial patent holder when an employee makes an invention in the scope of employment, and which country's law should apply to determine who the right holder is?

Although possibilities for international regulation of rights of employers to employee inventions have been discussed, the discussions have not produced an international treaty, and rights to employee inventions continue to be regulated by national laws. According to Article 60(1) of the European Patent Convention, the law of the country "in which the employee is mainly employed" will determine who has the right to a European patent. If the country cannot be determined, the law of the country of "the place of business to which the employee is attached" will govern the right to a European patent.

If an employee-inventor's invention falls within the scope of the employment, either the employer has priority to acquire the rights to the invention (Germany, Sweden), or the employer owns the rights to the invention (France, Spain, the United Kingdom). In the United States, state statutes and common law apply to issues related to employee inventions. Employment contracts are customarily used to establish the rules for assignment of inventions resulting from employment.

A significant difference between the situation in the United States and other countries is that while in the United States, wages are usually considered to be the remuneration to an employee-inventor for his employment-related inventions, in other countries, such as Japan, Germany, France, and China, the inventor is entitled to an equitable remuneration. In the United Kingdom, the employee-inventor will receive compensation for the invention that belongs to the employer only if the invention has produced an "outstanding benefit" to the employer. U.K. Patent Act, Section 40(1). Very few cases have been brought under the provision because of the difficulties in establishing the outstanding nature of the benefit, the causal link between the patent and the benefit, and the just nature of the compensation demanded. *See* Joshua Marshall, Employee Compensation for Patented Inventions, 40(7) EIPR 421 (2018); Shanks v. Unilever PLC, [2017] EWCA Civ 2.

Does an employee's right to remuneration extend to remuneration for the right to file for a patent abroad? The question arose in Japan in *Yonezawa v. Hitachi Co. Ltd.*, where the employee sought equitable remuneration in exchange for the right to apply for patents abroad for his inventions, which were patented in several countries. The Japanese Supreme Court ruled that the employee was entitled to equitable remuneration under Japanese law for transferring to his employer his right to obtain a patent not only in Japan but also in other countries. The Court ruled that the right to equitable remuneration extends to the right to obtain a patent abroad and explained that while the question of the scope of the right transferred and the validity of the right are governed by the laws of the individual countries in which patent applications are filed, "[t]he question whether the [employee] can claim a remuneration for the transfer of the right to obtain a patent must be answered on the basis of the transfer contract that gives a right to remuneration for the transfer, and the applicable law is thus Japanese law." Christopher Heath, Japan: Patent Act, Sec. 35; Horei, Art. 7—"RW Laser Disk," 39(6) IIC 733 (2008); Yonezawa v. Hitachi Co. Ltd., Supreme Court of Japan, 2006. Similarly, the U.K. Patent Act extends the right to remuneration for employee inventions to cover any patents "whether under the law of the United Kingdom or the law in force in any other country or under any treaty or international convention." U.K. Patent Act, Section 43(4). For a comparative analysis of employee invention and remuneration systems see J. Tarr & A. McBratney, A Fork in the Australian Road? Ownership of Patented Employee Inventions, 35(4) EIPR 191 (2013).

For a comparative discussion of employee inventions see Toshiko Takenaka & Yves Reboul, Employee Invention System: Comparative Law Perspective, in Intellectual Property in Common Law and Civil Law (Toshiko Takenaka ed., 2013), pp. 365–400; Employees' Intellectual Property Rights (Sanna Wolk & Kacper Szkalej, 2d ed., 2018).

3. *Transferability of the Right to File, the Patent Application, and the Patent.* The right to file for a patent, the patent application, and the patent may be freely assigned. Assignment or licensing of a European patent application is possible for any of the countries that are parties to the European Patent Convention (Articles 71–73).

The timing of an assignment is important for maintaining the international priority date. Article 4A(1) of the Paris Convention effectuates the priority on a country by country basis by making it transferable to the patent applicant's successor in title. For example, *X*, an applicant in Country *A,* may transfer to *Y* his priority for Country *B* and to *Z* his priority for Country *C*. However, as indicated in *Boston Scientific*, under U.S. law a patent applicant cannot purchase a foreign priority after the event of foreign application.

In Edwards Lifesciences AG v. Cook Biotech Inc., [2009] EWHC 1304 (Pat), Cook Biotech filed a PCT application on January 31, 2001, claiming priority from a U.S. patent application filed not by Cook Biotech but by three inventors on January 31, 2000. Only one of the inventors was a Cook Biotech employee at the time of the U.S. filing; the other two inventors assigned their interests in the invention to Cook Biotech in September 2002. Justice Kitchin explained that "[a] person who files a patent application for an invention is afforded the privilege of claiming priority only if he himself filed the earlier application from which priority is claimed or if he is the successor in title to the person who filed that earlier application. If he is neither the person who filed the earlier application nor his successor in title then he is denied the privilege. Moreover, his position is not improved if he subsequently acquires title to the invention. It remains the case that he was not entitled to the privilege when he filed the later application and made his claim." *Id.*, ¶ 95.

4. *Foreign Filing.* In the 1800s countries limited the ability of inventors to file in foreign countries; in some countries, filing for a patent in a foreign country would cause the domestic patent to be cancelled. Even today, many countries require that applications be filed first domestically if the applications concern inventions made by those countries' own nationals or entities with their principal place of business in those countries (*e.g.*, Bulgaria, France, Portugal, Spain, and the United Kingdom). Some countries limit this requirement only to applications for inventions that concern national security or other state interests (*e.g.*, Belgium, Denmark, Finland,

Germany, the Netherlands, and Sweden). In some countries, such as the United Kingdom, permission may be obtained to make the initial filing abroad. National Law Relating to the EPC, 15th Edition, European Patent Office, May 2011.

In the United States, "a person shall not file or cause or authorize to be filed in any foreign country prior to six months after filing in the United States an application for patent . . . in respect to an invention made in [the United States]." 35 U.S.C. 184(a). A patent applicant may file solely abroad or may file abroad earlier if the applicant obtains a license from the Commissioner of Patents. *Id.* Filing abroad earlier than six months after filing in the United States may result in a denial of a patent grant or invalidation of the patent granted in the United States. 35 U.S.C. 184 and 185.

Is there a reason to maintain the obligation to file domestically first when patent applications are published and often accessible in online databases? What are countries' interests in having patent applicants file for patents domestically first? The Patent Law of the People's Republic of China previously required that all Chinese applicants file for patents in China first; the obligation did not apply to foreign applicants unless they were registered in China. After China's 2009 amendment of the Patent Law, any applicant who wishes to apply for a patent in a foreign country for an invention that was invented in China must first submit the invention to the Chinese State Intellectual Property Office for a "confidentiality examination." *Id.*, Article 20. Failure to submit to the examination before filing abroad will lead to a denial of the grant of a patent in China or invalidation of the existing Chinese patent. Stefan Luginbuehl, Thomas Pattloch, The Awakening of the Chinese Patent Dragon—The Revised Chinese Patent Law 2009, IIC 130 (2011).

For a general discussion of countries' historical approaches to foreign patent filings see Marketa Trimble, Global Patents: Limits of Transnational Enforcement (2012), pp. 18–23.

4. RIGHTS

Carlos Correa, The GATT Agreement on Trade-Related Aspects of Intellectual Property Rights: New Standards for Patent Protection
16 European Intellectual Property Review 327, 329–330 (1994).

Rights Conferred

Article 28 sets forth the right that a patent should confer to its title-holder by referring to the two traditional categories of inventions: products and processes. . . .

Patents relating to products confer the right to prevent third parties not having the patentee's consent from "making, using, offering for sale or importing for these purposes the product" (Article 28.1(a)). One significant aspect of this detailed provision is that it expressly refers to importation as one of the exclusive rights of the patent-holder. . . . In a footnote to the same Article a cross-reference is made, however, to Article 6 of the Agreement, which implicitly allows parties to provide for the exhaustion of intellectual property rights, subject to the national and most-favoured-nation treatment. . . . Exhaustion may be contemplated only for acts taking place within the country or extended to those occurring in a group of countries (for example, members of a common market) or in the international market at large. Several countries have manifested, in recent legislative proposals, their interest in a broad principle of international exhaustion, in order to introduce some degree of competition into the domestic market. . . . A point which merits further consideration is whether, given the territoriality of industrial property, the exhaustion principle could also be extended to cases where a product is imported from a country where the invention is in the public domain, because patent protection was not available, the patentee did not apply for protection, or the latter was lost due to revocation or other reasons.

Article 28.2(b) contemplates the extension of the protection conferred on a process to the product "obtained directly by that process". This extension, not recognised till now by a majority of countries, coupled with the reversal of burden of proof (Article 34), will lead in many cases to a significant strengthening of the patent rights concerning process inventions.

Finally, Article 28.2 confirms what most laws in the world allow with regard to the right to assign the patent or transfer it by succession or to grant licences for its use.

Transocean Offshore Deepwater Drilling, Inc. v. Maersk Contractors USA, Inc.

United States Court of Appeals for the Federal Circuit, 2010.
617 F.3d 1296.

MOORE, CIRCUIT JUDGE.

Transocean Offshore Deepwater Drilling, Inc. (Transocean) appeals from a final judgment of the U.S. District Court for the Southern District of Texas. . . .

BACKGROUND

Transocean asserted claims 10–13 and 30 of U.S. Patent No. 6,047,781 ('781 patent), claim 17 of U.S. Patent No. 6,068,069 ('069 patent), and claim 10 of U.S. Patent No. 6,085,851 ('851 patent) against Maersk USA. The patents-in-suit share a common specification. The patents relate to an improved apparatus for conducting offshore drilling. . . .

Transocean appeals the district court's grant of summary judgment of (1) invalidity of all asserted claims based on obviousness and lack of enablement, (2) noninfringement, and (3) no willfulness. We have jurisdiction under 28 U.S.C. § 1295(a)(1).

DISCUSSION

We review a district court's grant of summary judgment de novo. ICU Med., Inc. v. Alaris Med. Sys. Inc., 558 F.3d 1368, 1374 (Fed.Cir. 2009). Summary judgment is appropriate when, drawing all justifiable inferences in the nonmovant's favor, there exists no genuine issue of material fact and the movant is entitled to judgment as a matter of law. Fed.R.Civ.P. 56(c); Anderson v. Liberty Lobby, Inc., 477 U.S. 242, 255, 106 S.Ct. 2505, 91 L.Ed.2d 202 (1986). . . .

II.   Infringement

The infringement issues in this case are unusual and require a discussion of the factual background. Transocean accused Maersk USA's DSS–21 rig of infringement. Maersk USA's Danish parent company, Maersk A/S, contracted with Keppel FELS Ltd. in 2005 to build the accused rig in Singapore. Later, Maersk A/S negotiated with Statoil ASA (a Norwegian company) for Statoil's use of the accused rig. The companies came to an agreement for use of the rig and Maersk USA and Statoil Gulf of Mexico LLC (Statoil), a Texas Corporation, signed a contract in Norway. The contract specified that the "Operating Area" for the rig was the U.S. Gulf of Mexico but that Statoil had the right to use the rig outside the Operating Area with certain limitations. . . .

The contract also included mention of Transocean's U.S. patents. Maersk USA specifically retained the right to make "alterations" to the accused rig "in view of court or administrative determinations throughout the world." . . . One of these "determinations" came when Transocean asserted the same patent claims in this case against another competitor, GlobalSantaFe Corp. (GSF). Transocean prevailed in that case and the court issued an injunction requiring GSF to install a "casing sleeve" on one of its two advancing stations. Transocean Offshore Deepwater Drilling, Inc. v. GlobalSantaFe Corp., No. H-03-2910, 2006 WL 3813778, 2006 U.S. Dist. LEXIS 93408 (S.D.Tex. Dec. 27, 2006). This casing sleeve prevents the auxiliary advancing station from lowering a drill string into the water. Id. 2006 WL 3813778, *8–9, 2006 U.S. Dist. LEXIS 93408 at *32–34. The district court in GSF held that this avoids infringement because the cased advancing station can no longer advance tubes to the seabed as the independent claims require. Before delivering the rig to the U.S., Maersk USA learned of the injunction against GSF and modified the accused rig with the same casing sleeve to prevent one of the stations from advancing pipes to the seabed.

The district court granted summary judgment of noninfringement after determining that there was no sale or offer to sell under 35 U.S.C. § 271(a). . . . Transocean Offshore Deepwater Drilling, Inc. v. Maersk Contractors USA, No. 07–2392, D.I. 148, *8–9 (S.D.Tex. May 15, 2009) (Willfulness Order). The court relied on the undisputed facts that the negotiation and signing of the contract took place outside the U.S. and that the contract gave Maersk the option to alter the rig to avoid infringement. *Id.* The district court also held that Transocean was collaterally estopped from arguing that the modified rig that Maersk USA delivered to Statoil (that included the casing sleeve to prevent advancing tubular members to the seabed) infringed the patent claims because this design was adjudicated as noninfringing in the GSF litigation. Noninfringement/Invalidity Order at *12.

A.   Offer to Sell

Section 271(a) defines infringing conduct: "whoever without authority makes, uses, offers to sell, or sells any patented invention, within the United States . . . infringes the patent." 35 U.S.C. § 271(a). An offer to sell is a distinct act of infringement separate from an actual sale. An offer to sell differs from a sale in that an offer to sell need not be accepted to constitute an act of infringement. *See* MEMC Elec. Materials, Inc. v. Mitsubishi Materials Silicon Corp., 420 F.3d 1369, 1376 (Fed.Cir. 2005). Moreover, the damages that would flow from an unaccepted offer to sell and an actual sale would likely be quite different. *See* Timothy R. Holbrook, Liability for the "Threat of Sale": Assessing Patent Infringement for Offering to Sell an Invention and Implications for the On-Sale Patentability Bar and Other Forms of Infringement, 43 Santa Clara L.Rev. 751, 791–92 (2003). We analyze an offer to sell under § 271(a) using traditional contract principles. Rotec Indus., Inc. v. Mitsubishi Corp., 215 F.3d 1246 (Fed.Cir. 2000). There is no dispute that there was an offer to sell in this case, but Maersk USA argues that the offer was made in Norway, not the United States, thereby absolving it of § 271(a) liability.

Maersk A/S (a Danish company) and Statoil ASA (a Norwegian company) negotiated the contract that is the subject of this alleged offer to sell. Their U.S. affiliates, Maersk USA and Statoil executed the contract in Norway. The contract included an "Operating Area" of the U.S. Gulf of Mexico. The district court held that because the negotiations and execution took place outside the U.S., this could not be an offer to sell within the United States under § 271(a).

Transocean argues that to hold that this contract between two U.S. companies for performance in the U.S. is not an offer to sell within the U.S. simply because the contract was negotiated and executed abroad would be inconsistent with Litecubes, LLC v. Northern Light Products, Inc., 523 F.3d 1353 (Fed.Cir. 2008) (holding that a foreign company cannot avoid liability for a sale by delivering the product outside the U.S. to a U.S. customer for importation). Transocean argues that a contract between two U.S. companies for delivery or performance in the U.S. must be an offer to sell within the United States under § 271(a).

Maersk USA argues that Rotec, 215 F.3d 1246 and MEMC, 420 F.3d 1369 require that, for there to be an offer to sell within the U.S., the offer activities must occur within the U.S. It argues that the negotiations and execution outside the U.S. preclude offer to sell liability in this case.

This case presents the question whether an offer which is made in Norway by a U.S. company to a U.S. company to sell a product within the U.S., for delivery and use within the U.S. constitutes an offer to sell within the U.S. under § 271(a). We conclude that it does. Section 271(a) states that "whoever . . . offers to sell . . . within the United States any patented invention . . . infringes." In order for an offer to sell to constitute infringement, the offer must be to sell a patented invention within the United States. The focus should not be on the location of the offer, but rather the location of the future sale that would occur pursuant to the offer.

The offer to sell liability was added to the patent statute to conform to the April 1994 Uruguay Round's Trade-Related Aspects of Intellectual Property Agreement (TRIPS). The underlying purpose of holding someone who offers to sell liable for infringement is to prevent "generating interest in a potential infringing product to the commercial detriment of the rightful patentee." 3D Sys., Inc. v. Aarotech Labs., Inc., 160 F.3d 1373, 1379 (Fed.Cir. 1998). The offer must be for a potentially infringing article. *Id.* We are mindful of the presumption against extraterritoriality. Microsoft Corp. v. AT&T Corp., 550 U.S. 437, 441, 127 S.Ct. 1746, 167 L.Ed.2d 737 (2007). "It is the general rule under United States patent law that no infringement occurs when a patented product is made and sold in another country." *Id.* This presumption has guided other courts to conclude that the contemplated sale would occur within the United States in order for an offer to sell to constitute infringement. See, *e.g.,* Semiconductor Energy Lab. Co. v. Chi Mei Optoelectronics Corp., 531 F.Supp.2d 1084, 1110–11 (N.D.Cal. 2007). We agree that the location of the contemplated sale controls whether there is an offer to sell within the United States.

The statute precludes "offers to sell . . . within the United States." To adopt Maersk USA's position would have us read the statute as "offers made within the United States to sell" or "offers made within the United States to sell within the United States." First, this is not the statutory language. Second, this interpretation would exalt form over substance by allowing a U.S. company to travel abroad to make offers to sell back into the U.S. without any liability for infringement. *See* 3D Sys., 160 F.3d at 1379. This company would generate interest in its product in the U.S. to the detriment of the U.S. patent owner, the type of harm that offer to sell within the U.S. liability is meant to remedy. *Id.* These acts create a real harm in the U.S. to a U.S. patentee.

Neither Rotec nor MEMC preclude our determination that an offer by a U.S. company to sell a patented invention to another U.S. company for delivery and use in the U.S. constitutes an offer to sell within the U.S. First, SEB S.A. v. Montgomery Ward & Co., 594 F.3d 1360, 1375 (Fed.Cir. 2010) contemplated whether the territorial reach of the offer to sell language had been decided by Rotec and concluded that it had not. The defendants in Rotec did argue that because the offer was made in China, not the U.S., they did not infringe. Rotec, 215 F.3d at 1251. And the Rotec court discussed the evidence regarding meetings and communications made in the United States. *Id.* at 1255. The Rotec court held that there was no offer to sell, not because of the location of the offer or of the ultimate sale, but rather because there was no evidence that an offer was communicated or conveyed by the defendants. *Id.* at 1255 ("None of this evidence, however, establishes any communication by Defendants with any third party."). In concurrence, Judge Newman indicates that she would have instead decided the case on the ground that there was no offer which contemplated a sale within the U.S. *Id.* at 1259 (Newman, J., concurring). The MEMC case is even further attenuated as it did not even consider location of the offer or the contemplated sale, but instead held there was no offer to sell because the emails at issue, which contained only technical data and no price terms, cannot constitute an offer that could be made into a binding contract by acceptance. 420 F.3d at 1376.

We conclude that neither Rotec nor MEMC control this case. We hold that the district court erred because a contract between two U.S. companies for performance in the U.S. may constitute an offer to sell within the U.S. under § 271(a). The fact that the offer was negotiated or a contract signed while the two U.S. companies were abroad does not remove this case from statutory liability. We therefore vacate the district court's summary judgment of noninfringement.[4]

B.   Sale

The parties begin with the same territoriality argument presented in the context of an offer to sell. Transocean argues that a contract between two U.S. companies for performance in the U.S. constitutes a sale under § 271(a). Maersk USA responds that this cannot be a sale within the U.S. because all negotiations and execution of the contract took place in Norway and the contract did not provide for performance only in the U.S.

The parties further dispute whether the device that was sold was "the patented invention." Transocean argues that we should analyze infringement based on the schematics that accompanied the contract. Maersk USA argues that this was not an infringing sale because it reserved the right to alter the rig to avoid infringement. Finally, Maersk USA argues this cannot be a sale under § 271(a) because the rig was not

---

[4]   We note that because the district court held that the location of the offer in this case removed it from the statute as a matter of law, it never reached the factual issue of whether the subject of the offer to sell was of a "patented invention" by analyzing the design of the rig. Of course, in this analysis, the district court must determine what was offered for sale, not what was ultimately delivered. See Holbrook, supra, at 753. In other words, it does not affect this analysis that Maersk USA eventually altered the design prior to delivery; the subject of the offer to sell was the unmodified rig. The district court must determine whether this unmodified rig was "the patented invention." We decline to perform this analysis in the first instance on appeal.

complete at the time of contracting. It argues that "in order for there to have been a sale within the meaning of 35 U.S.C. § 271(a), the entire apparatus must have been constructed and ready for use," citing Ecodyne Corp. v. Croll-Reynolds Engineering, 491 F.Supp. 194, 197 (D. Conn. 1979).

As with the offer to sell, we hold that a contract between two U.S. companies for the sale of the patented invention with delivery and performance in the U.S. constitutes a sale under § 271(a) as a matter of law. Maersk USA's first argument, that the location of negotiation and contracting should control is contrary to our precedent in Litecubes. There, we held that a sale does not only occur at a "single point where some legally operative act took place." Litecubes, 523 F.3d at 1369–70. We may also consider other factors such as the place of performance. Id. at 1371. Maersk USA's argument that Statoil could use the rig outside the U.S. ignores the plain language of the contract, which includes an "Operating Area" of the U.S. Gulf of Mexico. J.A. 7167. It also ignores the fact that Maersk did in fact deliver the rig to U.S. waters. Maersk USA's remaining arguments regarding the right to alter the final design and the fact that the rig was not complete at the time of contracting do not change the result. Maersk USA and Statoil signed a contract and the schematics that accompanied that contract could support a finding that the sale was of an infringing article under § 271(a). The fact that Maersk USA, after the execution of the contract, altered the rig in response to the GSF injunction is irrelevant to this infringement analysis. The potentially infringing article is the rig sold in the contract, not the altered rig that Maersk USA delivered to the U.S.

Finally, we reject Maersk USA's claim that the entire apparatus must have been constructed and ready for use in order to have been sold. Our precedent establishes that a contract can constitute a sale to trigger infringement liability. See NTP, Inc. v. Research in Motion, Ltd., 418 F.3d 1282, 1319 (Fed.Cir. 2005). A "sale" is not limited to the transfer of tangible property; a sale may also be the agreement by which such a transfer takes place. Id. In this case, there was a contract to sell a rig that included schematics. On summary judgment, we must draw all justifiable inferences in favor of the nonmovant, Transocean. Transocean argues that these schematics show sale of the patented invention. This is a genuine issue of material fact sufficient to withstand summary judgment.

We conclude that the district court erred in granting summary judgment that there was no sale within the U.S. in this case. As with the offer to sell, there remains a dispute over whether the unmodified rig that was sold was the patented invention, a question not reached by the district court thus far. . . .

CONCLUSION

Because there remain genuine issues of material fact regarding objective evidence of nonobviousness and undue experimentation, the grant of summary judgment relating to obviousness and enablement is reversed. Because the contract between Statoil and Maersk USA is both an offer to sell and a sale, we vacate the district court's summary judgment of noninfringement and remand for further findings on infringement based on the rig that was the subject of this contract. We affirm the district court's holding of summary judgment of no willfulness.

REVERSED-IN-PART, VACATED-IN-PART, AFFIRMED-IN-PART, and REMANDED

NOTES

1. *TRIPs Standards and U.S. Rights.* Section 271(a) and related provisions of the Patent Act historically conferred three exclusive rights on patent owners: the rights to make, use, and sell the patented invention. As indicated in *Transocean Offshore*, to conform the Act to the requirements of TRIPs Article 28(1), the Uruguay Round Agreements Act added to these three exclusive rights the rights to "offer to sell" and to "import into the United States." Pub. L. No. 103–465 §§ 532(a)(1), 533(a)(1)–(4), 108 Stat. 4809 (Dec. 8, 1994). What limits does the territoriality principle place on this new right? Will an offer telephoned from abroad into the United States satisfy the Patent Act's territoriality requirement? Will an advertisement for patented goods or services run afoul of the new right? If so, and if the advertisement is communicated to the United States from abroad, will its receipt in the United States satisfy the territoriality requirement?

2. *The "Offer" in the Offer to Sell.* What constitutes an infringing offer to sell? The possibilities range from the kind of offer it takes to form a contract to a mere advertisement. TRIPs Article 28(1), which mandates that countries introduce an exclusive right to prevent offers to sell a patented invention, neither defines the term "offer" nor instructs countries where they should seek guidance to define the term.

In Rotec Industries, Inc. v. Mitsubishi Corp., 215 F.3d 1246 (Fed.Cir. 2000), the U.S. Court of Appeals for the Federal Circuit decided that contract law should be used to determine whether a patent infringing offer to sell was made. Referring to a 1998 U.S. Supreme Court decision on the on-sale bar, according to which only a commercial offer for sale more than one year prior to the filing of a patent application in the United States barred patentability, the Court of Appeals defined "offer to sell . . . according to the norms of traditional contractual analysis." *Id.*, 1254–1255. The defendants in *Rotec* made preparations to submit a bid to supply five units of a concrete placing system for the Three Gorges Dam project on the Yangtze River in China. Although negotiations related to the planned transaction took place, and various documents were prepared, in the United States, there were no communications between the defendants and the potential buyers. Therefore, the court held that there was no infringing offer to sell.

In analyzing the meaning of the term "offer" in the context of a patent-infringing offer to sell, the *Rotec* court pointed to the English decision in Gerber Garment Tech. Inc. v. Lectra Sys. Ltd., [1995] RPC 383, to show that other countries had adopted a broader definition of the term "offer" in the context of a patent-infringing offer to sell. In *Gerber* Justice Jacob explained that "[a] party who approaches potential customers individually or by advertisement saying he is willing to supply a machine, terms to be agreed, is offering it or putting it on the market. If that happens during the life of the patent he infringes. He is disturbing the patentee's monopoly which he ought not to do."

In Germany, the mere exhibition of a patented invention at a trade fair without authorization was deemed an offer for the purposes of the German Patent Act. *See* Zeitlagenmultiplexverfahren, Landgericht Düsseldorf, 4a O 124/05, Feb. 13, 2007. In the United States, the act of exhibiting at a trade fair would not be considered an offer and therefore could not constitute an infringing offer to sell under the U.S. Patent Act. Medical Solutions, Inc. v. C Change Surgical LLC, 541 F.3d 1136 (Fed.Cir. 2008).

3.   *Localization of an Offer to Sell.* Because in *Rotec* no "offer" was found, the majority did not need to address the issue of the territorial limitations of an infringing offer to sell. *Transocean Offshore* provided an opportunity to answer the question that remained open after Rotec, and Halo Elecs., Inc. v. Pulse Elecs., Inc., 831 F.3d 1369 (Fed. Cir. 2016), confirmed that an offer to sell that contemplates a sale outside the United States does not directly infringe a U.S. patent. 831 F.3d at 1380.

By making the location of the offered sale dispositive, did the Court render the liability for an "offer to sell" merely a species of secondary liability? Does the provision on inducement in section 271(b) of the U.S. Patent Act provide adequate protection against the same acts committed abroad? In *Transocean Offshore* the absence of inducement was evidenced by the language in the sales contract that "allowed Maersk USA to make changes to the rig pending the outcome of any 'court or administrative determinations that favour the validity or infringement arguments of Transocean' related to Transocean's patents." 617 F.3d 1296, 1312 (2010).

What is the policy reason behind limiting the territorial scope of an infringing offer to sell to instances when the intended sale is to occur in the United States? What might be the arguments for or against adopting the opposite approach—making an offer in the United States an act of infringement of a U.S. patent regardless of where the intended sale takes place? In Germany, for example, an offer to sell is considered infringing even if the sale is to occur outside of Germany.

4.   *Localization of a Sale.* Negotiations conducted in the United States of a sale occurring outside the United States will not be sufficient to localize an infringing sale in the United States. In *Halo Elecs., Inc. v. Pulse Elecs., Inc.* the U.S. Court of Appeals for the Federal Circuit concluded that "when substantial activities of a sales transaction, including the final formation of a contract for sale encompassing all essential terms as well as the delivery and performance under that sales contract, occur entirely outside the United States, pricing and contracting negotiations in the United States alone do not constitute or transform those extraterritorial activities into a sale within the United States for purposes of § 271(a)." Halo Elecs., Inc. v. Pulse Elecs.,

Inc., 831 F.3d 1369, 1378 (Fed. Cir. 2016). Would "pricing and contracting negotiations in the United States" suffice to find an infringing offer to sell?

On extraterritorial reaches of national patent rights generally see Marketa Trimble, Global Patents: Limits of Transnational Enforcement (2012).

5. *Products Made by Patented Processes.* Consider the plight of a producer with a patent in Country *A* on a process for making a product, but not on the product itself, when a competitor in Country *B*, which denies patent protection to such processes, employs the process to produce the identical product which it then exports into Country *A*. The producer's chance for relief would be good if Country *A* were one of the many civil law countries that traditionally define rights in process patents to include the right to sell and to use a product obtained directly by the patented process. *See* Stephen Ladas, 1 Patents, Trademarks and Related Rights 392 (1975).

The United States adopted this approach only in 1988 when the Omnibus Trade and Competitiveness Act, Pub. L. No. 100–418, § 9003, 102 Stat. 1564, added section 271(g) to the Patent Act, providing in part: "[w]hoever without authority imports into the United States or sells or uses within the United States a product which is made by a process patented in the United States shall be liable as an infringer, if the importation, sale, or use of the product occurs during the term of such process patent." Section 295 buttresses this right by creating a presumption that a product was made by a patented process where the court finds "(1) that a substantial likelihood exists that the product was made by the patented process, and (2) that the plaintiff has made a reasonable effort to determine the process actually used in the production of the product and was unable to so determine. . . ."

Efforts to establish this approach as an international norm faltered at the 1958 Lisbon Conference on Revision of the Paris Convention, where objections from a handful of countries—most notably the United States—resulted in the entirely noncontroversial Article *5quater*. An international norm was finally achieved in Article 28(1)(b) of the TRIPs Agreement, providing that rights in a patented process include "using, offering for sale, selling, or importing for these purposes at least the product obtained directly by that process." According to one commentary on the TRIPs Agreement, "the inclusion of products obtained by a patented process in the scope of protection of process patents was the result of a long and difficult debate." Daniel Gervais, The TRIPs Agreement: Drafting History and Analysis 154 (1998).

Merck & Co., Inc. v. Stephar B.V.
Court of Justice of the European Communities, 1981.
Case C-187/80.

Decision

1   By a judgement of 2 July 1980 which was received at the Court on 15 September 1980 the President of the Arrondissementsrechtbank Rotterdam referred to the Court for a preliminary ruling under Article 177 of the EEC Treaty a question on the relationship between the

provisions of the Treaty concerning free movement of goods, in particular Article 36, and the protection of industrial and commercial property afforded by national laws.

2   In the judgement making the reference the President of the Arrondissementsrechtbank described the elements of fact and national law constituting the background to the question substantially as follows:

— Merck & Co. Inc. (hereinafter referred to as "Merck") is the proprietor of two Netherlands patents protecting a drug, Moduretic, and its manufacturing process, by virtue of which pursuant to Netherlands law it has a legal remedy against the protected product's being marketed in that country by other persons, even when that product has been marketed in a different Member State by or with the consent of the holder of the patent.

— The company markets the drug in Italy where it has not been able to patent it owing to the fact that at the time when the drug was sold in Italy the Italian Patent Law (Regio Decreto [Royal Decree] No. 1127 of 29 June 1939)—which was subsequently declared unconstitutional by a judgment of the Italian Corte Costituzionale [Constitutional Court] delivered on 20 March 1978—prohibited the grant of patents for drugs and their manufacturing processes.

— Stephar imports the drug from Italy into the Netherlands and markets it there in competition with Merck.

3   On the basis of those facts the court has asked whether in such circumstances the general rules of the Treaty concerning the free movement of goods, notwithstanding the provisions of Article 36, prohibit the proprietor of a patent who sells a drug protected by that patent in a Member State (The Netherlands) from preventing, as he may under the national legislation of that Member State, the drug which he himself sells freely in another Member State where no patent protection exists (Italy), from being imported from that other Member State and marketed by other persons in the first Member State (The Netherlands).

4   The parties to the proceedings commenced their discussion of the question by emphasizing that the Court has already stated, in its judgment of 31 October 1974 (*Sterling Drug*, Case 15/74 [1974] ECR 1147), that inasmuch as it provides an exception, for reasons concerned with the protection of industrial and commercial property rights, to one of the fundamental principles of the Common Market, Article 36 admits of such a derogation only in so far as it is justified for the purpose of safeguarding rights which constitute the specific subject-matter of that property, which as far as patents are concerned is in particular to guarantee "that the patentee, to reward the creative effort of the inventor, has the exclusive right to use an invention with a view to manufacturing industrial products and putting them into circulation for the first time, either directly or by the grant of licences to third parties, as well as the right to oppose infringements".

5   In the same judgment the Court declared that an obstacle to the free movement of goods may be justified on the ground of protection of industrial property where such protection is invoked against a product coming from a Member State where it is not patentable and has been manufactured by third parties without the consent of the patentee.

6   The parties are in agreement as to the fact that the situation under consideration in the present instance differs from that which was the subject of that decision because, although it concerns a Member State where the product in question is not patentable, that product has been marketed not by third parties but by the proprietor of the patent and manufacturer of the product himself; however, from that statement they draw opposite conclusions.

7   Stephar and the Commission conclude that once the proprietor of the patent has himself placed the product in question on the open market in a Member State in which it is not patentable, the importation of such goods into the Member State in which the product is protected may not be prohibited because the proprietor of the patent has placed it on the market of his own free will.

8   In contrast Merck, supported by the French Government and the Government of the United Kingdom, maintains that the purpose of the patent, which is to reward the inventor, is not safeguarded if owing to the fact that the patent right is not recognized by law in the country in which the proprietor of the patent has marketed his product he is unable to collect the reward for his creative effort because he does not enjoy a monopoly in first placing the product on the market.

9   In the light of that conflict of views, it must be stated that in accordance with the definition of the specific purpose of the patent, which has been described above, the substance of a patent right lies essentially in according the inventor an exclusive right of first placing the product on the market.

10   That right of first placing a product on the market enables the inventor, by allowing him a monopoly in exploiting his product, to obtain the reward for his creative effort without, however, guaranteeing that he will obtain such a reward in all circumstances.

11   It is for the proprietor of the patent to decide, in the light of all the circumstances, under what conditions he will market his product, including the possibility of marketing it in a Member State where the law does not provide patent protection for the product in question. If he decides to do so he must then accept the consequences of his choice as regards the free movement of the product within the Common Market, which is a fundamental principle forming part of the legal and economic circumstances which must be taken into account by the proprietor of the patent in determining the manner in which his exclusive right will be exercised.

12 That is borne out, moreover, by the statements of the Court in its judgments of 22 June 1976 (*Terrapin*, Case 119/75 [1976] ECR 1039) and 20 January 1981 (*Musik Vertrieb Membran and K-Tel*, Joined Cases 55 and 57/80 [1981] 2 CMLR 44) inasmuch as "the proprietor of an industrial or commercial property right protected by the law of a Member State cannot rely on that law to prevent the importation of a product which has been lawfully marketed in another Member State by the proprietor himself or with his consent".

13 Under those conditions to permit an inventor, or one claiming under him, to invoke a patent held by him in one Member State in order to prevent the importation of the product freely marketed by him in another Member State where that product is not patentable would bring about a partitioning of the national markets which would be contrary to the aims of the Treaty.

14 The reply to the question which has been raised therefore should be that the rules contained in the EEC Treaty concerning the free movement of goods, including the provisions of Article 36, must be interpreted as preventing the proprietor of a patent for a medicinal preparation who sells the preparation in one Member State where patent protection exists, and then markets it himself in another Member State where there is no such protection, from availing himself of the right conferred by the legislation of the first Member State to prevent the marketing in that State of the said preparation imported from the other Member State. . . .

On those grounds,

THE COURT,

in answer to the question referred to it by the President of the Arrondissementsrechtbank Rotterdam by an order dated 2 July 1980,

HEREBY RULES:

The rules contained in the EEC Treaty concerning the free movement of goods, including the provisions of Article 36, must be interpreted as preventing the proprietor of a patent for a medicinal preparation who sells the preparation in one Member State where patent protection exists, and then markets it himself in another Member State where there is no such protection, from availing himself of the right conferred by the legislation of the first Member State to prevent the marketing in that State of the said preparation imported from the other Member State.

NOTES

1. *Exhaustion*. Courts in all countries hold that the first sale of a patented good inside the country's borders will terminate the patent owner's right to control the good's resale in that country. Countries differ, however, on the impact of the first sale of a patented good outside the country's borders. Most, but not all, industrialized countries follow the rule of "national exhaustion," under which the patented good's sale outside the country will not terminate

the patent owner's right to control the good's resale inside the country. The United States followed the rule of national exhaustion until the U.S. Supreme Court's decision in *Lexmark*, discussed in note 2, below.

Other countries, including India, Japan, and since 2009 China, follow the rule of "international exhaustion" and extend the effect of exhaustion globally, holding that, once a patent owner allows the good to be sold anywhere in the world, it terminates its right to control resale of the patented good inside the country. Although patent owners in international exhaustion countries will sometimes try to circumvent exhaustion by contractually imposing territorial limitations on their distributors, contracts generally bind only those who make them, and a reseller from the distributor will typically not be constrained by the distributor's undertaking.

Exhaustion was one of the most divisive issues in the TRIPs negotiations and was ultimately addressed in the Agreement's noncommittal Article 6 providing that "[f]or the purpose of dispute settlement under this Agreement, subject to the provisions of Articles 3 and 4 above [dealing with national treatment and most-favored nation treatment, respectively] nothing in the agreement shall be used to address the issue of the exhaustion of intellectual property rights."

2. *Exhaustion in the United States.* The U.S. position on international exhaustion had at best been unclear until 2017 when the U.S. Supreme Court clarified the exhaustion rule in Impression Products, Inc. v. Lexmark International, Inc., 137 S.Ct. 1523 (2017). An earlier decision of the Court of Appeals for the Federal Circuit, Jazz Photo Corp. v. International Trade Commission, 264 F.3d 1094 (Fed.Cir. 2001), *cert. denied*, 536 U.S. 950 (2002), suggested that the United States adhered to the principle of national exhaustion; the court concluded in *Jazz Photo* that "[t]o invoke the protection of the first sale doctrine, the authorized first sale must have occurred under the United States patent." 264 F.3d at 1105. The Supreme Court disagreed and held in *Lexmark* that "[a]n authorized sale outside the United States, just as one within the United States, exhausts all rights under the Patent Act." 137 S.Ct. 1536.

As she did on the issue of copyright exhaustion in *Kirtsaeng*, discussed in note 3 on pages 291–292, above, Justice Ginsburg dissented in *Lexmark*, rejecting the majority's reasoning that the exhaustion rule in patent law should follow the rule in copyright law; the two "are not identical twins," the U.S. Patent Act does not contain a first sale provision analogous to section 109(a) of the U.S. Copyright Act, and, as opposed to copyright law, patent law is not harmonized internationally. 137 S.Ct. 1539. Should the choice of the exhaustion principle be different in patent law because "[t]he copyright protections one receives abroad are . . . likely to be similar to those received at home, even if provided under each country's separate copyright regime?" 137 S.Ct. 1539.

For a critical analysis of rules of patent exhaustion pre-*Lexmark,* see Sarah Wasserman Rajec, Free Trade in Patented Goods: International Exhaustion for Patents, 29 Berkeley Technology L. J. 317 (2014). For comparative reviews of exhaustion rules see Shubha Ghosh & Irene Calboli,

Exhausting Intellectual Property Rights: A Comparative Law and Policy Analysis (2018); Research Handbook on Intellectual Property Exhaustion and Parallel Imports (Irene Calboli & Edward Lee eds., 2016).

3. *Exhaustion in the European Union.* The general rule in the European Union on exhaustion of intellectual property rights is that once a product is sold with the right owner's authority in one country of the Union, the exclusive distribution right is exhausted and the product may be freely resold in any country of the Union. Consider whether the European Court of Justice in *Merck v. Stephar* gave an unnecessary twist to this rule by holding that the EEC Treaty prevents "the proprietor of a patent for a medicinal preparation who sells the preparation in one Member State where patent protection exists, *and then* markets it himself in another Member State where there is no such protection, from availing himself of the right conferred by legislation of the first Member State to prevent the marketing in that State of the said preparation imported from the other Member State." (Emphasis supplied.) The holding in *Merck v. Stephar* was challenged, but ultimately upheld, in Merck & Co. v. Primecrown Ltd., ECJ, C-267/95 and C-268/95, 1995.

Following the decision in *Merck v. Stephar*, what reason would Merck have to continue marketing its pharmaceuticals in Italy, or in any other Union country that did not give them patent protection? From a policy perspective, is there a difference between price discrimination where all relevant countries provide patent protection and price differentials reflect only different patterns of demand, and price discrimination where goods are protected by some countries but not others, and the price differential reflects the presence of competitors who can sell the good without paying any patent tribute? Discrepant treatment of patent subject matter, such as gave rise to *Merck v. Stephar*, is not a relic of the pre-TRIPs era in which countries were free to withhold patent protection from entire classes of goods and processes. Even after TRIPs Article 27 harmonized minimum national obligations respecting patentable subject matter, cases will arise in which different national standards of nonobviousness, novelty and *ordre public* will result in a product being protected in one WTO country but not another.

Once it is ratified, will the Agreement on a Unified Patent Court change the exhaustion rule in the European Union for European patents? According to Article 29 of the Agreement, the rights "shall not extend to acts concerning a product covered by [the] patent after that product has been placed on the market in the Union by, or with the consent of, the patent proprietor, unless there are legitimate grounds for the patent proprietor to oppose further commercialisation of the product."

4. *Exhaustion of Method Patents.* Are rights arising from patents on methods (process patents) subject to exhaustion? An authorized sale of a product made by a patented method exhausts the patent rights in the method with regard to that particular product, but does a sale of a product exhaust the rights in the patent on the method of *using* the product? In Germany, the Federal Supreme Court held that method patents are not subject to exhaustion, but in the United States, the U.S. Supreme Court held that the exhaustion doctrine applies to method patents; according to the Court, an authorized sale of a product that substantially embodies a method patent exhausts the rights in the method patent. Quanta Computer, Inc. v. LG Electronics, Inc., 553 U.S. 617, 635 (2008).

How do differences in the rules of patent exhaustion affect the legal frameworks for global supply chains involving products, such as computer chips, that substantially embody methods and are patented in multiple countries? In some countries where the exhaustion doctrine does not apply to method patents, courts may recognize the existence of an implied license to practice the patented method.

5.   *Patent Term.* Article 33 of the TRIPs Agreement, providing that "[t]he term of protection available shall not end before the expiration of twenty years counted from the filing date," required dramatic legislative changes around the world. In some developing countries, the patent term could be as short as five, seven or ten years; even in economically developed countries the term often fell short of the twenty-year minimum. In the United States, Congress implemented TRIPs Article 33 by altering the patent term from seventeen years counted from the date the patent issued to a "term beginning on the date on which the patent issues and ending twenty years from the date on which the application for the patent was filed in the United States." 35 U.S.C. § 154(a)(2).

National patent laws sometimes provide for extensions of the patent term to compensate for delays in patent prosecution or regulatory review. For example, section 154 of the Patent Act allows extensions in order to compensate for specified delays in the Patent and Trademark Office. *See* Joseph Straus, Implications of the TRIPs Agreement in the Field of Patent Law, in Friedrich-Karl Beier & Gerhard Schricker, (eds.), From GATT to TRIPs—The Agreement on Trade-Related Aspects of Intellectual Property Rights 160, 197–201 (1996).

6.   *Extending Protection Beyond the Patent Term.* Mechanisms from outside patent law may prolong a patent owner's monopoly. "Data exclusivity" provisions ensure that test data submitted by a new drug applicant in the regulatory approval process will not be used to evaluate a competitor's application for the registration of a generic equivalent of the same drug. Data exclusivity in the United States may last up to five years. Does TRIPs Article 39(3) require members to grant "data exclusivity?" Not all countries provide this exclusivity, and the United States has exported its "data exclusivity" provisions by including them in its free trade agreements with other countries.

The European Union has included in its free trade agreements with other countries an obligation to provide for an "extension [of up to five years] of the duration of rights conferred by the patent protection to compensate the patent owner for the reduction in the effective patent life as a result of the first authorization to place the product on their respective markets." European Union-Korea Free Trade Agreement, Article 10.35(2). In the European Union, patent owners may obtain the extension through a supplementary protection certificate. Regulation (EC) No 469/2009 of the European Parliament and of the Council of 6 May 2009 concerning the supplementary protection certificate for medicinal products; Regulation (EC) No 1610/96 of the European Parliament and of the Council of 23 July 1996 concerning the creation of a supplementary protection certificate for plant protection products.

What are the advantages and disadvantages of providing rights extensions through *sui generis* mechanisms rather than patents? Do TRIPs Article 33 and EPC Article 63 require or prohibit *sui generis* mechanisms for rights extensions? In the United States, the Hatch-Waxman Act provides for a patent term extension to account for the regulatory approval process. 35 U.S.C. § 156.

For a discussion of "data exclusivity" provisions see Brook K. Baker, Ending Drug Registration Apartheid: Taming Data Exclusivity and Patent/ Registration Linkage, 34 Am. J.L. & Med. 303 (2008); Carlos M. Correa, Protecting Test Data for Pharmaceutical and Agrochemical Products Under Free Trade Agreements, 2004, https://www.ictsd.org/sites/default/files/ event/2008/12/report31.pdf.

7. *Evergreening.* Although a patent should expire at the end of the existing patent term and any available extensions, patent owners often attempt to extend their monopoly beyond the patent term by employing various "evergreening" strategies. In *Novartis AG v. Union of India* the Supreme Court of India explained that " '[e]vergreening' is a term used to label practices that have developed in certain jurisdictions wherein a trifling change is made to an existing product, and claimed as a new invention. The coverage/protection afforded by the alleged new invention is then used to extend the patentee's exclusive rights over the product, preventing competition." Civil Appeal Nos. 2706–2716 of 2013, ¶ 100.

One evergreening strategy employing this tactic is to use a small chemical modification of a known structure, a new formulation or a new concentration of a pharmaceutical, or a different polymorphic structure to support a claim that a different product has been created. As discussed in note 2 on page 442, above, the *Novartis* case involved a patent on a minor modification.

Some pharmaceutical patent owners conclude agreements with their competitors—generic drug manufacturers—under which the patent owner makes so-called "reverse payments" to the generic manufacturer for delaying the launch of generic versions of the patented pharmaceuticals whose patents are about to expire. The U.S. Supreme Court has held that reverse payment settlements may sometimes violate U.S. antitrust laws. Federal Trade Commission v. Actavis, Inc., 570 U.S. 136, 141 (2013). On several occasions the European Commission has found that settlement agreements between patent owners and generic drug manufacturers have violated EU competition rules when the agreements resulted in a delayed market entry for generic drugs.

For a comparative review of pay-for-delay agreements in light of antitrust rules see Joseph Straus, "Pay for Delay"—A Subtly Hidden, Overlooked or Ignored Transatlantic Divide: Exemplified on the *Actavis* Decision of the US Supreme Court and the *Servier* Decision of the EU

Commission, 76 Zbornik znanstvenih razprav 197 (2016). For EU developments in this area see Vilhelm Schröder, Pay-for-delay Settlements in the EU: Did the Commission Go Too Far?, 38(12) EIPR 726 (2016).

5. LIMITATIONS ON RIGHTS

Carlos Correa, The GATT Agreement on Trade-Related Aspects of Intellectual Property Rights: New Standards for Patent Protection

16 European Intellectual Property Review 327, 330–333 (1994).

Exceptions to Rights Conferred

The very general wording of Article 30 indicates how difficult it was for the negotiating parties to agree on the nature and extent of the exceptions to the patent rights. . . . Three conditions need to be met by the exceptions. First, they must be "limited", but it is unclear whether in scope, duration or otherwise. Second, they should not "unreasonably conflict with a normal exploitation of the patent". And, third, the exceptions should not "unreasonably prejudice the legitimate interests of the patent owner". All these three conditions are to be applied, however, "taking account of the legitimate interests of third parties."

This text necessarily leads to a case by case assessment of the exceptions that can be granted. Based on the present status of comparative patent law and on other proposals, . . . the following exceptions may be deemed legitimate within the scope of Article 30:

(1) importation of a product that has been put in the market elsewhere by the patentee or with his consent;

(2) acts done privately and on a non-commercial scale or for a non-commercial purpose;

(3) using the invention for research and experimentation and for teaching purposes;

(4) preparation of medicines for individual cases according to a prescription;

(5) compulsory licensing (see next section);

(6) use of the invention by a third party who started or undertook serious preparatory acts before the application for the patent (or its publication).

A particular case that also deserves attention concerns experiments made for the purpose of seeking regulatory approval for the marketing of a product. Some legislations explicitly authorise such acts. . . .

Compulsory Licensing

The TRIPs Agreement does not refer to the widely accepted notion of "non-voluntary" or "compulsory" licensing. Ninety-six countries—or 71 per cent of all the countries in the world—allow for one form or another of compulsory licences. . . . Nevertheless, Article 31 on "Other use without the authorisation of the right holder" contains a detailed set of conditions and limitations for the granting of such licences. Through this Article industrialised countries have tried to limit the room for the use of the compulsory licensing system, even though its actual application has been rather limited in the past. . . . Different aspects need to be considered here.

Grounds for granting compulsory licences

Article 31 allows national legislations to determine the grounds for granting compulsory licensing. Although it refers to some specific grounds (national emergency, anticompetitive practices, public non-commercial use, dependent patents), it does not limit, in principle, the members' right to establish such a remedy for different situations. The text only sets out the conditions to be met "where the law of a Party allows for other use" without the authorisation of the rightholder. The only exception relates to "semi-conductor technology", which can only be subject to compulsory licences for public non-commercial use and to remedy anti-competitive practices.

Compulsory licences may, therefore, be contemplated for grounds other than those explicitly referred to such as:

(1) Public health and nutrition or other reasons of public interest

Article 8 ("Principles") of the TRIPs Agreement states the right of parties to "adopt measures necessary to protect public health and nutrition, and to promote public interest in sectors of vital importance to their socio-economic and technological development, provided that such measures are consistent with the provisions of this Agreement". Based on this provision, and subject to the condition set forth by Article 31, compulsory licences could be granted, for instance, for reasons of "public interest" (as under German law), or to satisfy objectives of public health.

(2) Lack or insufficiency of working

The obligation to work a patented invention has historically been together with disclosure requirements—one of the foundations of the patent system. During this century—as evidenced by the successive amendments to the Paris Convention—industrialised countries have tended to make such an obligation flexible in order to facilitate transnational activities of large corporations in increasingly globalised markets. For most developing countries, however, such an obligation (understood as actual industrial application and not just as importation of the protected product) has been one of the essential counterbalances of the patent system, and viewed as an important incentive for the transfer of technology.

Not surprisingly, the extent of the working obligation was one of the most controversial issues in the TRIPs negotiations. The difficulties encountered to reach an agreement are evidenced by the language of the compromise contained in Article 27.1. It states, as indicated before, that "patent rights [shall be] enjoyable without discrimination as to . . . whether products are imported or locally produced". According to one interpretation, this clause would ban working obligations that require industrial execution of the invention in a particular country: working could be satisfied through importation. A second interpretation would be that the requirement of that provision is met if the compulsory licensing rules do not treat differently imported and locally produced products. If, for instance, compulsory licences are granted for lack of production or of importation on an equal footing, no contradiction with Article 27.1 would exist. . . .

(3)   Environmental protection

One of the most pressing problems in the world today is the degradation of the environment. Important efforts are under way at international and national levels to prevent harmful activities and to develop effective measures of environment protection. In the patent field, compulsory licensing may contribute to the expansion of the use of environmentally sound technologies as well as of technologies available for environmental protection, in line with the international proposals to promote the transfer to and use of such technologies in developing countries. . . .

(4)   Dependent patents

A very detailed provision on compulsory licences grounded on the dependency of patents is contained in Article 31.1. It contains a number of conditions for its granting relating to the technical and economic importance of the "second patent" (it shall involve "an important technical advance of considerable economic significance"), the granting of "a cross licence on reasonable terms" to the owner of the "first patent", and the non-assignability of the licence (except with the assignment of the "second patent"). These conditions tend to limit the ways in which improvement patents have been used in some countries in order to promote access to patent technology by national enterprises. Crucial in the actual operation of the system will be the interpretation of the economic and technical importance of the second invention.

(5)   Other grounds

As mentioned before, Article 31 is not limitative as to the grounds for compulsory licensing, with the exception of the case of semi-conductor technology. A limitation is imposed by Article 27.1 insofar as it prohibits to discriminate the enjoyance of the patent rights on the basis of the "field of technology". This provision may outlaw systems of compulsory licences focused on a particular type of processes or products belonging to a precise area of technology. However, such systems may be provided under the general exception of Article 30, to the extent that the conditions set forth therein are met. It seems clear, in any case, that Article 27.1 would not restrict compulsory licence systems defined on the basis of a determined goal (for example, to protect public health or the environment), the achievement of which would normally require the use of inventions belonging to different technological fields (for example, chemistry, biotechnology, mechanical engineering, X-ray technology, and so on).

Conditions for the granting of compulsory licences

The TRIPs Agreement has paid particular attention to the conditions under which a compulsory licence may be granted. They include the following:

(1) Such a licence should be granted taking into consideration "its individual merits" (Article 31a). This means that decisions need to be taken for each individual application and that they cannot involve a certain type of patent defined by its subject-matter, title-holder or otherwise.

(2) Prior to the granting of the licence, the proposed licensee should have made "efforts to obtain authorisation from the right holder on reasonable terms and conditions" and if "such efforts have not been successful within a reasonable period of time", he may then apply for a compulsory licence. This provision makes compulsory the existence of prior commercial negotiations with the titleholder, a requirement that many legislations have omitted, particularly in cases of licences granted on grounds of public interest. Article 31 allows, nevertheless, for exceptions in cases of national emergency or other circumstances of extreme urgency as well as in cases of "public noncommercial use" . . . and where a licence is granted to remedy anti-competitive practices.

(3) The scope and duration of the authorisation "shall be limited to the purpose for which it was authorized" (Article 31c). This clause may imply the limitation of the licence, both in terms of scope (for example, to certain claims or kind of products) and of duration. In exchange, nothing will prevent a potential licensee from asking for a comprehensive licence extending until the expiration of the patent. This has been, in fact, the generally accepted practice under the Paris Convention until now. For a licensee that has to undertake investments in production or marketing it will often be essential to obtain a licence for the lifetime of the patent.

Another important point is that the Agreement does not limit the purpose for which a compulsory licence can be granted. In other words, it can be conferred to import or to locally produce a patented product. In some cases—licences to remedy abuses of market dominant positions or to protect public health—importation may, in fact, be the sole or main way to comply with the purposes for which the authorisation is given.

(4) Any authorisation shall be—as is established in most legislations—non-exclusive and non-assignable, except with that part of

the enterprise or goodwill that uses it. The non-exclusive character of the licence means that the title-holder could import or industrially execute the invention, in parallel with the compulsory licensee, by himself or by means of other voluntary licensees. It also means that more than one compulsory licence can be granted for a given patent.

(5) The licences should be granted "predominantly for the supply of the domestic market" (Article 31f). This provision—which may not be applied in connection with licences to remedy anti-competitive practices—will conflict with national laws allowing for compulsory licences to satisfy solely export markets.

(6) One important change is introduced into the system of compulsory licensing as generally applied today with regard to the term of the licence. Article 31g sets forth the principle that a compulsory licence is liable to be terminated when "the circumstances which led to it cease to exist and are unlikely to recur". Competent authorities shall have, therefore, the authority to review, on motivated request, the continued existence of such circumstances. The eventual termination is subject, however, to "adequate protection of the legitimate interests of the persons" authorised to use the invention. Without this proviso, this provision would have completely diluted the potential of any system of compulsory licensing. The protection of the legitimate interests of the licensee means that he could not be deprived of his right to the licence once he has made serious preparations for putting the invention into use, or established productive or marketing capabilities. If a reasonable degree of certainty is not assured, nobody would be interested in applying for a licence that could be terminated at any time. Paradoxically, the most and more immediately affected licensee could be precisely the one who more efficiently contributed to remedy the situation that gave rise to the granting of a licence.

(7) The title-holder shall be paid "adequate remuneration in the circumstances of each case, taking into account the economic value of the authorisation" (Article 31h). This provision would apply, in principle, to any kind of compulsory licence. . . .

Considerable room is left for interpretation at the national level on the criteria to determine when a remuneration is to be deemed "adequate". . . . The same provision provides two elements for this interpretation: on the one hand, the adequateness is to be judged in the circumstances of each case and, on the other, it is necessary to take into account—as one but not the sole or determining factor—"the economic value of the authorisation". Thus, the circumstances of the licensee and of the country where it operates, as well as the purpose of the licence should be considered to establish the remuneration due. A licence conferred to satisfy public health or other social needs may be subject to parameters different from those applicable when purely commercial and industrial interests are involved. The "economic value" will differ depending, *inter alia,* on the size of the market to be supplied (generally the domestic one), the age of the technology, the rate of obsolescence in the respective sector, the degree of competition of substitute products and the coverage of the patent.

The word "adequate" also needs to be clarified in order to give more precise guidance to national judicial and administrative authorities. One possible understanding is that it simply means the remuneration that the title-holder should be able to obtain in an arm's length transaction. This would not be, however, the natural meaning of the word in English. . . . An alternative interpretation would take into account factors such as the subsidies or other contributions that the title-holder eventually received to develop the invention, the degree to which development costs have been amortised and the R & D commitment of the patent-owner.

(8)   Finally, the title-holder should be given the possibility of review, by a judicial or other authority, of the "legal validity" of any decision relating to the granting of a licence as well as of the determined remuneration (Article 31i and g). Such a right will not prevent a member, however, from giving immediate effect to a decision conferring a licence, subject to a later review. This will be particularly important for cases involving public interests or the correction of anti-competitive practices.

Canada, Patent Protection of Pharmaceutical Products

Report of the Panel, World Trade Organization, WT/DS114/R, March 17, 2000.

. . . VII. FINDINGS

A.   MEASURES AT ISSUE

7.1 At issue in this dispute is the conformity of two provisions of Canada's *Patent Act* with Canada's obligations under the *Agreement on Trade-Related Aspects of Intellectual Property Rights* ("the TRIPS Agreement"). The two provisions in dispute, Sections 55.2(1) and 55.2(2) of the Patent Act, create exceptions to the exclusive rights of patent owners. Under Article 28.1 of the TRIPS Agreement, patent owners shall have the right to exclude others from making, using, selling, offering for sale or importing the patented product during the term of the patent. According to Article 33 of the TRIPS Agreement, the term of protection available shall not end before the expiration of a period of 20 years counted from the filing date of the application against which the patent was granted. Sections 55.2(1) and 55.2(2) allow third parties to make, use or sell the patented product during the term of the patent without the consent of the patent owner in certain defined circumstances.

(1) SECTION 55.2(1): THE REGULATORY REVIEW EXCEPTION

7.2 Section 55.2(1) provides as follows:

"It is not an infringement of a patent for any person to make, construct, use or sell the patented invention solely for uses reasonably related to the development and submission of information required under any law of Canada, a province or a country other than Canada that regulates the manufacture, construction, use or sale of any product."

Section 55.2(1) is known as the "regulatory review exception". It applies to patented products such as pharmaceuticals whose marketing is subject to government regulation in order to assure their safety or effectiveness. The purpose of the regulatory review exception is to permit potential competitors of the patent owner to obtain government marketing approval during the term of the patent, so that they will have regulatory permission to sell in competition with the patent owner by the date on which the patent expires. Without the regulatory review exception, the patent owner might be able to prevent potential competitors from using the patented product during the term of the patent to comply with testing requirements, so that competitors would have to wait until the patent expires before they could begin the process of obtaining marketing approval. This, in turn, would prevent potential competitors from entering the market for the additional time required to complete the regulatory approval process, in effect extending the patent owner's period of market exclusivity beyond the end of the term of the patent.

7.3 ... Since patent applications are generally filed as quickly as possible after the invention has been made, actual marketing of the patented product is frequently delayed for a certain period of time because time is required for development of the product in commercial form, after which additional time is required to complete the testing required for government approval. According to the information supplied by Canada, the process of development of the drug and regulatory approval for new patented pharmaceuticals normally takes approximately eight to 12 years. The long development and approval process means that, for most patented pharmaceuticals, the 20-year patent term results in an actual period of market exclusivity of only some 12 to eight years. After a pharmaceutical patent expires, it is common for other producers to enter the market supplying copies of the patented product at lower prices. These lower-priced copies, known as "generic" pharmaceuticals, often constitute a large part of the supply of pharmaceuticals in national markets. Generic pharmaceuticals must also comply with the government approval process. According to Canada's information, for generic producers the process of developing their version of the drug and obtaining regulatory approval takes approximately three to six-and-a-half years, with development taking some two to four years and the regulatory process itself one to two-and-a-half years. If none of the development process could be performed during the term of the patent, generic producers could be forced to wait the full three to six-and-a-half years after the patent expires before being able to enter the market in competition with the patent owner. To the extent that some development activity might be permitted, consistently with Article 30 of the TRIPS Agreement, under other exceptions such as the traditional exception for experimental use of the patented product, the delay in entering the market would be correspondingly less. The regulatory review exception in Section 55.2(1) would allow generic producers to complete both development and regulatory approval during the term of the patent, thus allowing them to enter the market as soon as the patent expires.

7.4 The structure of the generic pharmaceutical industry illustrates the actual operation of the regulatory review exception. Production of generic pharmaceuticals often involves a two-tier production arrangement. The firm that assembles and markets the final generic product often does not have the technological capacity/expertise or the commercial motivation to produce the so-called "active ingredient"—the chemical product that generates the desired medicinal effect. The active ingredient is thus often manufactured by a specialized producer of fine chemicals, and then sold to the generic producer which assembles the active ingredient with other agents to create the final product in a form that can be used by the ultimate consumer. In such cases, both producers must engage in conduct that, in the absence of a regulatory review exception, would be potentially infringing, if they are to satisfy the requirements of the regulatory review process—the fine chemical producer in developing, making and selling the necessary amounts of the active ingredient to the generic producer, and the generic producer in combining the various elements to make the final product and then demonstrating its safety, stability and effectiveness by appropriate tests. The regulatory review exception applies to these activities of both producers.

7.5 To qualify for exemption under Section 55.2(1), such activities by either fine chemical producers or generic producers must be "solely for uses reasonably related to the development and submission of information required" by any law, Canadian or non-Canadian, that "regulates the manufacture, construction, use or sale of any product". In answer to a question from the Panel, Canada stated that, although Canadian marketing regulations for generic producers did not require production runs to demonstrate the applicant's ability to maintain quality production in commercial volumes . . . , the statute would allow either fine chemical manufacturers or generic producers to undertake such production runs if they were required by regulations in other countries.

7.6 With regard to the enforcement of these conditions, Canada explained that these exceptions were part of the general law of infringement, under which it is up to the patent owner to enforce his patent rights in a civil action for infringement. . . . Patent owners who believed that actions by generic producers did not comply with the requirements of Section 55.2(1) would have to bring an infringement action against such conduct. . . . Patent owners would merely be required to prove conduct inconsistent with the owner's exclusive patent rights, after which persons claiming the benefit of the Section 55.2(1) exemptions would then be required to prove their compliance with the conditions of that provision as a defence. . . .*

B.   CLAIMS OF THE PARTIES

7.11   The EC asked the Panel to find that Sections 55.2(1) and 55.2(2) of Canada's Patent Act are inconsistent with Canada's obligations under Articles 27.1 and 28.1 of the TRIPS Agreement and, to the extent that Section 55.2(2) violates Article 28.1, it is also inconsistent with Article 33 of the TRIPS Agreement. . . .

7.12   Canada argued that neither Section 55.2(1) nor Section 55.2(2) violate any of the three TRIPS provisions cited. With regard to the claimed violation of Article 28.1 of the TRIPS Agreement, Canada acknowledged that Sections 55.2(1) and 55.2(2) permit conduct that conflicts with the patent rights granted in accordance with Article 28.1, but Canada claimed that each of these two provisions is an exception authorized by Article 30 of the Agreement. With regard to the claimed violation of Article 27.1, Canada presented two defences: first, that Article 27.1 does not apply to measures authorized by Article 30 of the Agreement and second, that, even if Article 27.1 does apply to measures authorized by Article 30, the two provisions of the Patent Act in question do not discriminate in violation of Article 27.1. With regard to the claimed violation of Article 33, Canada maintained that Section 55.2(2) does not violate Article 33.

C.   PRINCIPLES OF INTERPRETATION

7.13   The legal issues in this dispute primarily involve differences over interpretation of the key TRIPS provisions invoked by the parties, chiefly Articles 27.1, 30 and 33. The rules that govern the interpretation of WTO agreements are the rules of treaty interpretation stated in Articles 31 and 32 of the Vienna Convention.[378] The starting point is the rule of Article 31(1) which states:

> "A treaty is to be interpreted in good faith in accordance with the ordinary meaning to be given to the terms of the treaty in their context and in the light of its object and purpose."

The parties have submitted arguments on each of these elements, as well as further arguments based on subsequent practice by certain WTO

---

*   This excerpt omits the Panel's discussion of section 55.2(2) of the Canadian Patent Act, the "stockpiling exception," which allows competitors to manufacture and stockpile patented goods during a prescribed period before the patent expires, but does not allow the goods to be sold until the patent expires. *Ed.*

[378] Vienna Convention on the Law of Treaties 1969, entered into force on 27 January 1980.

Members, thus relying on Article 31(3)(b), which reads in relevant part as follows:

> "There shall be taken into account, together with the context: (a) . . . ; (b) any subsequent practice in the application of the treaty which establishes the agreement of the parties regarding its interpretation."

The parties have also advanced arguments based on the negotiating history of the TRIPS provisions in dispute. Negotiating history falls within the category of "Supplementary Means of Interpretation" and is governed by the rule of Article 32 of the Vienna Convention, which provides as follows:

> "Recourse may be had to supplementary means of interpretation, including the preparatory work of the treaty and the circumstances of its conclusion, in order to confirm the meaning resulting from the application of Article 31, or to determine the meaning when the interpretation according to Article 31:
>
> (a) leaves the meaning ambiguous or obscure; or
>
> (b) leads to a result which is manifestly absurd or unreasonable."

7.14   The Panel noted that, in the framework of the TRIPS Agreement, which incorporates certain provisions of the major pre-existing international instruments on intellectual property, the context to which the Panel may have recourse for purposes of interpretation of specific TRIPS provisions, in this case Articles 27 and 28, is not restricted to the text, Preamble and Annexes of the TRIPS Agreement itself, but also includes the provisions of the international instruments on intellectual property incorporated into the TRIPS Agreement, as well as any agreement between the parties relating to these agreements within the meaning of Article 31(2) of the Vienna Convention on the Law of Treaties. Thus, as the Panel will have occasion to elaborate further below, Article 9(2) of the Berne Convention for the Protection of Literary and Artistic Works (1971) (hereinafter referred to as the Berne Convention) is an important contextual element for the interpretation of Article 30 of the TRIPS Agreement.

7.15   As a consequence of the extended context that has to be taken into account when interpreting provisions of the TRIPS Agreement, the Panel, in considering the negotiating history of the TRIPS Agreement, concluded that interpretation may go beyond the negotiating history of the TRIPS Agreement proper and also inquire into that of the incorporated international instruments on intellectual property.

D.   BURDEN OF PROOF

7.16   The legal issues in the present dispute turn primarily on questions of legal interpretation—the meaning of the TRIPS provisions under which the two provisions of Canada's Patent Act have been challenged. The basic facts pertaining to these issues of interpretation are essentially undisputed. However, a small number of factual issues have been raised with regard to the meaning of certain aspects of the Canadian law, and about the actual impact of that law in practice. Moreover, application of legal standards frequently involves mixed questions of law and fact, and disagreements over the application of such standards sometimes therefore involve disagreement over factual premises. To the extent that such factual disagreements do exist, rules pertaining to burden of proof are potentially relevant whenever the weight of the evidence does not permit conclusive judgements. . . .

[I]t was the Panel's view that the EC bears the burden to present evidence and argument sufficient to establish a prima facie case that Canada has violated Articles 27.1, 28.1 and 33 of the TRIPS Agreement. It would be up to Canada to advance sufficient argument and evidence to rebut such a prima facie case. Canada has, for all practical purposes, conceded the violation of Article 28, because it has resorted to the exception of Article 30 of the TRIPS Agreement in this case. Since Article 30 is an exception to the obligations of the TRIPS Agreement, it would be up to Canada to demonstrate that the provisions of Sections 55.2(1) and 55.2(2) comply with the criteria laid down in Article 30. It is on this basis that the Panel approached the analysis of the claims submitted to it. . . .

F.   SECTION 55.2(1) (THE REGULATORY REVIEW EXCEPTION)

(1) APPLICATION OF ARTICLE 28.1 AND ARTICLE 30 OF THE TRIPS AGREEMENT

7.39   Both parties agreed that, if the regulatory review exception of Section 55.2(1) met the conditions of Article 30 of the TRIPS Agreement, the acts permitted by that Section would not be in violation of Article 28.1 of the TRIPS Agreement. Canada argued that Section 55.2(1) complies with each of the three conditions of Article 30. The European Communities argued that Section 55.2(1) fails to comply with any of the three conditions. We now turn to the respective arguments for applying these three Article 30 conditions to Section 55.2(1).

(a)   "Limited Exceptions" . . .

7.44   In the previous part of this Report dealing with the stockpiling exception of Section 55.2(2), the Panel concluded that the words "limited exception" express a requirement that the exception make only a narrow curtailment of the legal rights which Article 28.1 requires to be granted to patent owners, and that the measure of that curtailment was the extent to which the affected legal rights themselves had been impaired. As was made clear by our conclusions regarding the stockpiling exception, the Panel could not accept Canada's contention that an exception can be regarded as "limited" just so long as it preserves the patent owner's exclusive right to sell to the ultimate consumer during the patent term.

7.45   In the Panel's view, however, Canada's regulatory review exception is a "limited exception" within the meaning of TRIPS Article 30. It is "limited" because of the narrow scope of its curtailment of Article 28.1 rights. As long as the exception is confined to conduct needed to comply with the requirements of the regulatory approval process, the extent of the acts unauthorized by the right holder that are permitted by it will be small and narrowly bounded. Even though regulatory approval processes may require substantial amounts of test production to demonstrate reliable manufacturing, the patent owner's rights themselves are not impaired any further by the size of such production runs, as long as they are solely for regulatory purposes and no commercial use is made of resulting final products. . . .

7.48   A final objection to the Panel's general conclusion remains to be addressed. Although the point was raised only briefly in the parties' legal arguments, the Panel was compelled to acknowledge that the economic impact of the regulatory review exception could be considerable. According to information supplied by Canada itself, in the case of patented pharmaceutical products approximately three to six-and-a-half years are required for generic drug producers to develop and obtain regulatory approval for their products. If there were no regulatory review exception allowing competitors to apply for regulatory approval during the term of the patent, therefore, the patent owner would be able to extend its period of market exclusivity, de facto, for some part of that three to six-and-half year period, depending on how much, if any, of the development process could be performed during the term of the patent under other exceptions, such as the scientific or experimental use exception. The Panel believed it was necessary to ask whether measures having such a significant impact on the economic interests of patent owners could be called a "limited" exception to patent rights.

7.49   After analysing all three conditions stated in Article 30 of the TRIPS Agreement, the Panel was satisfied that Article 30 does in fact address the issue of economic impact, but only in the other two conditions contained in that Article. As will be seen in the analysis of these other conditions below, the other two conditions deal with the issue of economic impact, according to criteria that relate specifically to that issue. Viewing all three conditions as a whole, it is apparent that the first condition ("limited exception") is neither designed nor intended to address the issue of economic impact directly.

7.50   In sum, the Panel found that the regulatory review exception of Section 55.2(1) is a "limited exception" within the meaning of Article 30 of the TRIPS Agreement.

(b)   "Normal Exploitation"

7.51   The second condition of Article 30 prohibits exceptions that "unreasonably conflict with a normal exploitation of the patent". Canada took the position that "exploitation" of the patent involves the extraction of commercial value from the patent by "working" the patent, either by selling the product in a market from which competitors are excluded, or by licensing others to do so, or by selling the patent rights outright. . . . The European Communities also defined "exploitation" by referring to the same three ways of "working" a patent. . . . The parties differed primarily on their interpretation of the term "normal". . . .

7.54   The Panel considered that "exploitation" refers to the commercial activity by which patent owners employ their exclusive patent rights to extract economic value from their patent. The term "normal" defines the kind of commercial activity Article 30 seeks to protect. The ordinary meaning of the word "normal" is found in the dictionary definition: "regular, usual, typical, ordinary, conventional".[411] As so defined, the term can be understood to refer either to an empirical conclusion about what is common within a relevant community, or to a normative standard of entitlement. The Panel concluded that the word "normal" was being used in Article 30 in a sense that combined the two meanings.

7.55   The normal practice of exploitation by patent owners, as with owners of any other intellectual property right, is to exclude all forms of competition that could detract significantly from the economic returns anticipated from a patent's grant of market exclusivity. The specific forms of patent exploitation are not static, of course, for to be effective exploitation must adapt to changing forms of competition due to technological development and the evolution of marketing practices. Protection of all normal exploitation practices is a key element of the policy reflected in all patent laws. Patent laws establish a carefully defined period of market exclusivity as an inducement to innovation, and the policy of those laws cannot be achieved unless patent owners are permitted to take effective advantage of that inducement once it has been defined.

7.56   Canada has raised the argument that market exclusivity occurring after the 20-year patent term expires should not be regarded as "normal". The Panel was unable to accept that as a categorical proposition. Some of the basic rights granted to all patent owners, and routinely exercised by all patent owners, will typically produce a certain period of market exclusivity after the expiration of a patent. For example, the separate right to prevent "making" the patented product during the term of the patent often prevents competitors from building an inventory needed to enter the market immediately upon expiration of a patent. There is nothing abnormal about that more or less brief period of market exclusivity after the patent has expired.

7.57   The Panel considered that Canada was on firmer ground, however, in arguing that the additional period of de facto market exclusivity created by using patent rights to preclude submissions for regulatory authorization should not be considered "normal". The additional period of market exclusivity in this situation is not a natural or normal

---

[411]   The New Shorter Oxford English Dictionary, p. 1940.

consequence of enforcing patent rights. It is an unintended consequence of the conjunction of the patent laws with product regulatory laws, where the combination of patent rights with the time demands of the regulatory process gives a greater than normal period of market exclusivity to the enforcement of certain patent rights. It is likewise a form of exploitation that most patent owners do not in fact employ. For the vast majority of patented products, there is no marketing regulation of the kind covered by Section 55.2(1), and thus there is no possibility to extend patent exclusivity by delaying the marketing approval process for competitors.

7.58   The Panel could not agree with the EC's assertion that the mere existence of the patent owner's rights to exclude was a sufficient reason, by itself, for treating all gains derived from such rights as flowing from "normal exploitation". In the Panel's view, the EC's argument contained no evidence or analysis addressed to the various meanings of "normal"—neither a demonstration that most patent owners extract the value of their patents in the manner barred by Section 55.2(1), nor an argument that the prohibited manner of exploitation was "normal" in the sense of being essential to the achievement of the goals of patent policy. To the contrary, the EC's focus on the exclusionary rights themselves merely restated the concern to protect Article 28 exclusionary rights as such. This is a concern already dealt with by the first condition of Article 30 ("limited exception") and the Panel found the ultimate EC arguments here impossible to distinguish from the arguments it had made under that first condition. . . .

7.59   In sum, the Panel found that the regulatory review exception of Section 55.2(1) does not conflict with a normal exploitation of patents, within the meaning of the second condition of Article 30 of the TRIPS Agreement. The fact that no conflict has been found makes it unnecessary to consider the question of whether, if a conflict were found, the conflict would be "unreasonable". Accordingly, it is also unnecessary to determine whether or not the final phrase of Article 30, calling for consideration of the legitimate interests of third parties, does or does not apply to the determination of "unreasonable conflict" under the second condition of Article 30.

(c)   "Legitimate Interests"

7.60   The third condition of Article 30 is the requirement that the proposed exception must not "unreasonably prejudice the legitimate interests of the patent owner, taking into account the legitimate interests of third parties". Although Canada, as the party asserting the exception provided for in Article 30, bears the burden of proving compliance with the conditions of that exception, the order of proof is complicated by the fact that the condition involves proving a negative. One cannot demonstrate that no legitimate interest of the patent owner has been prejudiced until one knows what claims of legitimate interest can be made. Likewise, the weight of legitimate third party interests cannot be fully appraised until the legitimacy and weight of the patent owner's legitimate interests, if any, are defined. Accordingly, without disturbing the ultimate burden of proof, the Panel chose to analyse the issues presented by the third condition of Article 30 according to the logical sequence in which those issues became defined.

7.61   The ultimate issue with regard to the regulatory review exception's compliance with the third condition of Article 30 involved similar considerations to those arising under the second condition ("normal exploitation")—the fact that the exception would remove the additional period of de facto market exclusivity that patent owners could achieve if they were permitted to employ their rights to exclude "making" and "using" (and "selling") the patented product during the term of the patent to prevent potential competitors from preparing and/or applying for regulatory approval during the term of the patent. The issue was whether patent owners could claim a "legitimate interest" in the economic benefits that could be derived from such an additional period of de facto market exclusivity and, if so, whether the regulatory review exception "unreasonably prejudiced" that interest. . . .

   (ii) Definition of "legitimate interests"

7.68   The word "legitimate" is commonly defined as follows:

   (a) Conformable to, sanctioned or authorized by, law or principle: lawful; justifiable; proper;

   (b) Normal, regular, conformable to a recognized standard type.

Although the European Communities' definition equating "legitimate interests" with a full respect of legal interests pursuant to Article 28.1 is within at least some of these definitions, the EC definition makes it difficult to make sense of the rest of the third condition of Article 30, in at least three respects. First, since by that definition every exception under Article 30 will be causing "prejudice" to some legal rights provided by Article 28 of the Agreement, that definition would reduce the first part of the third condition to a simple requirement that the proposed exception must not be "unreasonable". Such a requirement could certainly have been expressed more directly if that was what was meant. Second, a definition equating "legitimate interests" with legal interests makes no sense at all when applied to the final phrase of Article 30 referring to the "legitimate interests" of third parties. Third parties are by definition parties who have no legal right at all in being able to perform the tasks excluded by Article 28 patent rights. An exceptions clause permitting governments to take account of such third party legal interests would be permitting them to take account of nothing. And third, reading the third condition as a further protection of legal rights would render it essentially redundant in light of the very similar protection of legal rights in the first condition of Article 30 ("limited exception").

7.69   To make sense of the term "legitimate interests" in this context, that term must be defined in the way that it is often used in legal discourse—as a normative claim calling for protection of interests that are "justifiable" in the sense that they are supported by relevant public policies or other social norms. This is the sense of the word that often appears in statements such as "X has no legitimate interest in being able to do Y". We may take as an illustration one of the most widely adopted Article 30-type exceptions in national patent laws—the exception under which use of the patented product for scientific experimentation, during the term of the patent and without consent, is not an infringement. It is often argued that this exception is based on the notion that a key public policy purpose underlying patent laws is to facilitate the dissemination and advancement of technical knowledge and that allowing the patent owner to prevent experimental use during the term of the patent would frustrate part of the purpose of the requirement that the nature of the invention be disclosed to the public. To the contrary, the argument concludes, under the policy of the patent laws, both society and the scientist have a "legitimate interest" in using the patent disclosure to support the advance of science and technology. While the Panel draws no conclusion about the correctness of any such national exceptions in terms of Article 30 of the TRIPS Agreement, it does adopt the general meaning of the term "legitimate interests" contained in legal analysis of this type.

7.70   The negotiating history of the TRIPS Agreement itself casts no further illumination on the meaning of the term "legitimate interests", but the negotiating history of Article 9(2) of the Berne Convention, from which the text of the third condition was clearly drawn, does tend to affirm the Panel's interpretation of that term. With regard to the TRIPS negotiations themselves, the meaning of several important drafting changes turns out to be equivocal upon closer examination. The negotiating records of the TRIPS Agreement itself show that the first drafts of the provision that was to become Article 30 contemplated authorizing "limited exceptions" that would be defined by an illustrative list of exceptions—private use, scientific use, prior use, a traditional exception for pharmacists, and the like. . . . Eventually, this illustrative list approach was abandoned in favour of a more general authorization following the outlines of the present Article 30. The negotiating records of the TRIPS Agreement give no explanation of the reason for this decision.

7.71   The text of the present, more general version of Article 30 of the TRIPS Agreement was obviously based on the text of Article 9(2) of the Berne Convention. Berne Article 9(2) deals with exceptions to the copyright holder's right to exclude reproduction of its copyrighted work without permission. The text of Article 9(2) is as follows:

> "It shall be a matter for legislation in the countries of the Union to permit the reproduction of [literary and artistic] works in certain special cases, provided that such reproduction does not conflict with a normal exploitation of the work and does not

unreasonably prejudice the legitimate interests of the author."

. . .

The text of Berne Article 9(2) was not adopted into Article 30 of the TRIPS Agreement without change. Whereas the final condition in Berne Article 9(2) ("legitimate interests") simply refers to the legitimate interests of the author, the TRIPS negotiators added in Article 30 the instruction that account must be taken of "the legitimate interests of third parties". Absent further explanation in the records of the TRIPS negotiations, however, the Panel was not able to attach a substantive meaning to this change other than what is already obvious in the text itself, namely that the reference to the "legitimate interests of third parties" makes sense only if the term "legitimate interests" is construed as a concept broader than legal interests.

7.72   With regard to the meaning of Berne Article 9(2) itself, the Panel examined the drafting committee report that is usually cited as the most authoritative explanation of what Article 9(2) means. The drafting committee report states:

> "If it is considered that reproduction conflicts with the normal exploitation of the work, reproduction is not permitted at all. If it is considered that reproduction does not conflict with the normal exploitation of the work, the next step would be to consider whether it does not unreasonably prejudice the legitimate interests of the author. Only if such is not the case would it be possible in certain special cases to introduce a compulsory license, or to provide for use without payment. A practical example may be photocopying for various purposes. If it consists of producing a very large number of copies, it may not be permitted, as it conflicts with a normal exploitation of the work. If it implies a rather large number of copies for use in industrial undertakings, it may not unreasonably prejudice the legitimate interests of the author, provided that, according to national legislation, an equitable remuneration is paid. If a small number of copies is made, photocopying may be permitted without payment, particularly for individual or scientific use."[421]

The Panel recognized that the drafting committee's examples concern the area of copyright as opposed to patents, and that, even further, they deal with the situation as it was in 1967, and accordingly the Panel was reluctant to read too much into these examples as guides to the meaning of Article 30. But the Panel did find that the concepts of "normal exploitation" and "legitimate interests" underlying the three examples

---

[421] Report on the Work of Main Committee I (Substantive Provisions of the Berne Convention: Articles 1 to 20), paragraph 85, in "Records of the Intellectual Property Conference of Stockholm, June 11–July 14, 1967", World Intellectual Property Organization (WIPO), Geneva, 1971, Vol. II, pp. 1145–1146.

used by the drafting committee were consistent with the Panel's definitions of these concepts and of the differences between them.

7.73   In sum, after consideration of the ordinary meaning of the term "legitimate interests", as it is used in Article 30, the Panel was unable to accept the EC's interpretation of that term as referring to legal interests pursuant to Article 28.1. Accordingly, the Panel was unable to accept the primary EC argument with regard to the third condition of Article 30. It found that the EC argument based solely on the patent owner's legal rights pursuant to Article 28.1, without reference to any more particular normative claims of interest, did not raise a relevant claim of non-compliance with the third condition of Article 30.

(iii) Second claim of "legitimate interest"

7.74   After reaching the previous conclusion concerning the EC's primary argument under the "legitimate interests" condition of Article 30, the Panel then directed its attention to another line of argument raised in statements made by the EC and by one third party. This second line of argument called attention to the fact that patent owners whose innovative products are subject to marketing approval requirements suffer a loss of economic benefits to the extent that delays in obtaining government approval prevent them from marketing their product during a substantial part of the patent term. According to information supplied by Canada, regulatory approval of new pharmaceuticals usually does not occur until approximately eight to 12 years after the patent application has been filed, due to the time needed to complete development of the product and the time needed to comply with the regulatory procedure itself. The result in the case of pharmaceuticals, therefore, is that the innovative producer is in fact able to market its patented product in only the remaining eight to 12 years of the 20-year patent term, thus receiving an effective period of market exclusivity that is only 40–60 per cent of the period of exclusivity normally envisaged in a 20-year patent term. The EC argued that patent owners who suffer a reduction of effective market exclusivity from such delays should be entitled to impose the same type of delay in connection with corresponding regulatory requirements upon the market entry of competing products. According to the EC,

> "[T]here exists no reason why the research based pharmaceutical enterprise is obliged to accept the economic consequence of patent term erosion because of marketing approval requirements which reduce their effective term of protection to 12–8 years while the copy producer should be entirely compensated for the economic consequence of the need of marketing approval for his generic product, and at the expense of the inventor and patent holder". . . .

Applied to the regulatory review exception, this argument called for the removal of such exceptions so that patent owners may use their exclusionary patent rights to prevent competitors from engaging in product development and initiating the regulatory review process until the patent has expired. The result of removing the exception would be to allow patent owners to create a period of further, de facto market exclusivity after the expiration of the patent, for the length of time it would take competing producers to complete product development and obtain marketing approval. . . .

7.82   On balance, the Panel concluded that the interest claimed on behalf of patent owners whose effective period of market exclusivity had been reduced by delays in marketing approval was neither so compelling nor so widely recognized that it could be regarded as a "legitimate interest" within the meaning of Article 30 of the TRIPS Agreement. Notwithstanding the number of governments that had responded positively to that claimed interest by granting compensatory patent term extensions, the issue itself was of relatively recent standing, and the community of governments was obviously still divided over the merits of such claims. Moreover, the Panel believed that it was significant that concerns about regulatory review exceptions in general, although well known at the time of the TRIPS negotiations, were apparently not clear enough, or compelling enough, to make their way explicitly into the recorded agenda of the TRIPS negotiations. The Panel believed that Article 30's "legitimate interests" concept should not be used to decide, through adjudication, a normative policy issue that is still obviously a matter of unresolved political debate.

7.83   Consequently, having considered the two claims of "legitimate interest" put forward by the EC, and having found that neither of these claimed interests can be considered "legitimate interests" within the meaning of the third condition of Article 30 of the TRIPS Agreement, the Panel concluded that Canada had demonstrated to the Panel's satisfaction that Section 55.2(1) of Canada's Patent Act did not prejudice "legitimate interests" of affected patent owners within the meaning of Article 30.

   (iv) Conclusion with regard to compliance of Section 55.2(1) with Article 30

7.84   Having reviewed the conformity of Section 55.2(1) with each of the three conditions for an exception under Article 30 of the TRIPS Agreement, the Panel concluded that Section 55.2(1) does satisfy all three conditions of Article 30, and thus is not inconsistent with Canada's obligations under Article 28.1 of the TRIPS Agreement.

   (2) APPLICATION OF ARTICLE 27.1 OF THE TRIPS AGREEMENT

7.85   The EC claimed that Section 55.2(1) of the Canada Patent Act is also in conflict with the obligations under Article 27.1 of the TRIPS Agreement. Article 27.1 provides:

"Article 27
Patentable Subject Matter

1.   Subject to the provisions of paragraphs 2 and 3, patents shall be available for any inventions, whether products or processes, in all fields of technology, provided that they are new, involve an inventive step and are capable of industrial application. Subject to paragraph 4 of Article 65, paragraph 8 of Article 70 and paragraph 3 of this Article, *patents shall be available and patent rights enjoyable without discrimination as to the place of invention, the field of technology and whether products are imported or locally produced.*" (emphasis added)

7.86   The EC argued that the anti-discrimination rule stated in the italicized language in the text of Article 27.1 above not only requires that the core patent rights made available under Article 28 be non-discriminatory, but also requires that any exceptions to those basic rights made under Articles 30 and 31 must be non-discriminatory as well. Thus, the EC concluded, Article 27.1 requires that the exception made by Section 55.2(1) must be non-discriminatory. The EC contended that Section 55.2(1) does not comply with the obligations of Article 27.1, because it is limited, both *de jure* and de facto, to pharmaceutical products alone, and thus discriminates by field of technology.

7.87   Canada advanced two defences to the EC's claim of an Article 27.1 violation. First, Canada argued that the non-discrimination rule of Article 27.1 does not apply to exceptions taken under Article 30. Second, Canada argued that Section 55.2(1) does not discriminate against pharmaceutical products. The Panel examined these two defences in order.

(a)   Applicability of Article 27.1 to Article 30 Exceptions

7.88   Canada took the position that Article 27.1's reference to "patent rights" that must be enjoyable without discrimination as to field of technology refers to the basic rights enumerated in Article 28.1 subject to any exceptions that might be made under Article 30. In other words, governments may discriminate when making the "limited" exceptions allowed under Article 30, but they may not discriminate as to patent rights as modified by such exceptions. . . .

7.91   The Panel was unable to agree with Canada's contention that Article 27.1 did not apply to exceptions granted under Article 30. The text of the TRIPS Agreement offers no support for such an interpretation. Article 27.1 prohibits discrimination as to enjoyment of "patent rights" without qualifying that term. Article 30 exceptions are explicitly described as "exceptions to the exclusive rights conferred by a patent" and contain no indication that any exemption from non-discrimination rules is intended. A discriminatory exception that takes away enjoyment of a patent right is discrimination as much as is discrimination in the basic rights themselves. The acknowledged fact that the Article 31 exception for compulsory licences and government use is understood to be subject to the non-discrimination rule of Article 27.1, without the need for any textual provision so providing, further strengthens the case for treating the non-discrimination rules as applicable to Article 30. Articles 30 and 31 are linked together by the opening words of Article 31 which define the scope of Article 31 in terms of exceptions not covered by Article 30. Finally, the Panel could not agree with Canada's attempt to distinguish between Articles 30 and 31 on the basis of their mandatory/permissive character; both provisions permit exceptions to patent rights subject to certain mandatory conditions. Nor could the Panel understand how such a "mandatory/permissive" distinction, even if present, would logically support making the kind of distinction Canada was arguing. In the Panel's view, what was important was that in the rights available under national law, that is to say those resulting from the basic rights and any permissible exceptions to them, the forms of discrimination referred to in Article 27.1 should not be present.

7.92   Nor was the Panel able to agree with the policy arguments in support of Canada's interpretation of Article 27. To begin with, it is not true that being able to discriminate against particular patents will make it possible to meet Article 30's requirement that the exception be "limited". An Article 30 exception cannot be made "limited" by limiting it to one field of technology, because the effects of each exception must be found to be "limited" when measured against each affected patent. Beyond that, it is not true that Article 27 requires all Article 30 exceptions to be applied to all products. Article 27 prohibits only discrimination as to the place of invention, the field of technology, and whether products are imported or produced locally. Article 27 does not prohibit bona fide exceptions to deal with problems that may exist only in certain product areas. Moreover, to the extent the prohibition of discrimination does limit the ability to target certain products in dealing with certain of the important national policies referred to in Articles 7 and 8.1, that fact may well constitute a deliberate limitation rather than a frustration of purpose. It is quite plausible, as the EC argued, that the TRIPS Agreement would want to require governments to apply exceptions in a non-discriminatory manner, in order to ensure that governments do not succumb to domestic pressures to limit exceptions to areas where right holders tend to be foreign producers.

7.93   The Panel concluded, therefore, that the anti-discrimination rule of Article 27.1 does apply to exceptions of the kind authorized by Article 30. We turn, accordingly, to the question of whether Section 55.2(1) of the Canadian Patent Act discriminates as to fields of technology.

   (b)   <u>Discrimination as to the Field of Technology</u>

7.94   The primary TRIPS provisions that deal with discrimination, such as the national treatment and most-favoured-nation provisions of Articles 3 and 4, do not use the term "discrimination". They speak in more precise terms. The ordinary meaning of the word "discriminate" is potentially broader than these more specific definitions. It certainly extends beyond the concept of differential treatment. It is a normative term, pejorative in connotation, referring to results of the unjustified imposition of differentially disadvantageous treatment. Discrimination may arise from explicitly different treatment, sometimes called *"de jure discrimination"*, but it may also arise from ostensibly identical treatment which, due to differences in circumstances, produces differentially disadvantageous effects, sometimes called "de facto discrimination". The standards by which the justification for differential treatment is measured are a subject of infinite complexity. "Discrimination" is a term to be avoided whenever more precise standards are available, and, when employed, it is a term to be interpreted with caution, and with care to add no more precision than the concept contains.

7.95   The European Communities acknowledged that the words of the regulatory review exception of Section 55.2(1) do not limit its application to pharmaceutical products. The terms of the exception protect potentially infringing conduct:

> "solely for uses reasonably related to the development and submission of information required under any law ... that regulates the manufacture, construction, use or sale of any product".

Applied literally, these words apply to any of a wide range of products that require regulatory approval for marketing. The EC itself mentioned agricultural chemicals, foodstuffs, cosmetics, automobiles, vessels and aircraft as products that often require regulatory approval. . . .

7.105   In sum, the Panel found that the evidence in record before it did not raise a plausible claim of discrimination under Article 27.1 of the TRIPS Agreement. It was not proved that the legal scope of Section 55.2(1) was limited to pharmaceutical products, as would normally be required to raise a claim of *de jure* discrimination. Likewise, it was not proved that the adverse effects of Section 55.2(1) were limited to the pharmaceutical industry, or that the objective indications of purpose demonstrated a purpose to impose disadvantages on pharmaceutical patents in particular, as is often required to raise a claim of de facto discrimination. Having found that the record did not raise any of these basic elements of a discrimination claim, the Panel was able to find that Section 55.2(1) is not inconsistent with Canada's obligations under Article 27.1 of the TRIPS Agreement. Because the record did not present issues requiring any more precise interpretation of the term "discrimination" in Article 27.1, none was made. . . .

VIII.   CONCLUSIONS

8.1 In light of the findings above, the Panel has concluded as follows:

> (1) Section 55.2(1) of Canada's *Patent Act* is not inconsistent with Canada's obligations under Article 27.1 and Article 28.1 of the TRIPS Agreement.

(2)   Section 55.2(2) of Canada's *Patent Act* is not consistent with the requirements of Article 28.1 of the TRIPS Agreement.

Accordingly, the Panel recommends that the Dispute Settlement Body request that Canada bring Section 55.2(2) into conformity with Canada's obligations under the TRIPS Agreement.

NOTES

1. *Relationship Between TRIPs Articles 30 and 31.* As indicated in the Panel Report, *Canada—Patent Protection for Pharmaceutical Products*, Article 30 of the TRIPs Agreement closely tracks Article 9(2) of the Berne Convention, 1971 Paris Act, which prescribes a formula for permitted exceptions from copyright's exclusive reproduction right. Berne Article 9(2) is generally thought to encompass private uses that fall outside the normal markets for copyrighted works. If the copying is limited and discrete, it is presumed that there will be no unreasonable prejudice to the copyright owner's interests, so that the use may be subject to a complete exemption; where the copying is on a larger scale, an exemption is not allowed but a compulsory license is. Against the background of Berne Article 9(2), what kinds of exemptions or compulsory licenses does TRIPs Article 30 contemplate? Would each of the six examples given by Carlos Correa in the excerpt above fit into this formula?

TRIPs Article 31 refers to laws allowing "for other use" of the subject matter of a patent, and footnote 7 to Article 31 states that "other use" refers "to use other than that allowed under Article 30." This appears to mean that, to the extent a compulsory license meets the requirements of Article 30, it need not comply with the conditions imposed by Article 31. Another difference is that where Article 30 contemplates complete exemptions from liability as well as compulsory licenses, Article 31 with its requirement, of "adequate remuneration," contemplates only compulsory licenses.

2. *Experimental Use Exceptions.* In the United States, the applicability of the experimental use exception is limited to non-commercial purposes, which is why in *Roche Products v. Bolar Pharmaceutical* a court held that testing for the purposes of obtaining an FDA approval and marketing the drug was not covered by the exception. 733 F.2d 858 (Fed.Cir. 1984). The Hatch-Waxman Act, adopted shortly after the *Bolar* decision, introduced section 271(e) into the U.S. Patent Act to provide an exception covering testing for purposes of FDA approval.

On the European Union version of the so-called "Bolar" exception that allows testing for purposes of regulatory approval see Joseph Straus, The Bolar Exemption and the Supply of Patented Active Pharmaceutical Ingredients to Generic Drug Producers: An Attempt to Interpret Article 10(6) of Directive 2004/27, 9(11) J. of Intell. Property Law & Practice 895 (2014). For developments concerning the Bolar exception in India see Sandeep K. Rathod, The Curious Case of India's Bolar Provision, 14(1) Journal of Generic Medicines 16 (2018).

The data exclusivity, discussed in note 6 on page 515, above, which proprietary drug manufacturers enjoy in some countries, became a significant point of controversy in post-TRIPs developments. Data exclusivity contributes to delays in the market entry of generics and thereby extends the protection of proprietary manufacturers. Are the data exclusivity provisions consistent with the non-discrimination principle of TRIPs Article 27? *See* Australia—United States Free Trade Agreement, Article 17.10.

3. *Dependent Patents.* What if the patent owner of invention *A* declines to license elements that are essential to exploiting later invention *B*, that builds upon invention *A*? Statutory provisions in many countries—but not the United States—attack such blockages by authorizing compulsory licenses for so-called dependent patents.

Compulsory licenses for dependent patents have historically imposed two of the three conditions established in TRIPs Agreement Article 31(1). First, the improvement for which a license is sought must not only be covered by a patent, but must also be more than trivial; Article 31(1)(i) uses the term, "important technical advance." (Presumably this requirement seeks to prevent improvement patentees from using patents on trivial inventions as leverage for obtaining compulsory licenses.) Second, to avoid giving the improvement patentee a market advantage over the initial patentee, these provisions also commonly condition the compulsory license on the grant by the improvement patentee to the initial patentee of a cross license to practice the improvement. The prospect of a compulsory license doubtless spurs many patent owners to privately negotiate cross licenses between basic and improvement patents.

4. *Compulsory Licenses: Public Interest.* Even actively worked patents may fall short of meeting the national interest in the invention's exploitation—typically because output of the patented products is too low or license terms are too onerous. Subject to the limitations imposed on WTO members by TRIPs Article 31, national governments may subject patents to compulsory licenses for any number of public purposes.

Compulsory licensing for public purposes may be assimilated into the sovereign's power of eminent domain. In Pfizer Corp. v. Ministry of Health, [1965] R.P.C. 261, the House of Lords ruled that hospital services administered by the British National Health Service were "services of the Crown" under applicable patent legislation, so that the Health Ministry acted within its powers in authorizing the purchase of certain drugs from unlicensed sources on the ground that the price offered by the patentee was unreasonably high.

The question of compulsory licenses was a significant flashpoint in failed efforts to revise the Paris Convention, and the substantial limitations imposed by TRIPs Article 31 on the use of compulsory licenses were principally aimed at the perception that economically developing countries employed the device to expropriate foreign inventions. Although many of the recent compulsory licenses have been issued by developing countries, developed countries also employ compulsory licenses for public purposes, as the English case above demonstrates. In what commentators have called a milestone in German patent law, the German Federal Supreme Court in

2017 granted a compulsory license to an active compound used in the treatment of AIDS. Raltegravir, Bundesgerichtshof, X ZB 2/17, 2017.

Although the U.S. Government has been one of the main opponents of compulsory licensing in international discussions, the United States, as well as contractors working for it, effectively enjoy a compulsory license under 28 U.S.C. § 1498 which provides that "[w]henever an invention described in and covered by a patent of the United States is used or manufactured by or for the United States without license of the owner thereof . . . the owner's remedy shall be by action against the United States in the United States Court of Federal Claims for the recovery of his reasonable and entire compensation for such use and manufacture."

5.   *Compulsory Licenses: Pharmaceuticals.* With pharmaceutical products and processes now guaranteed protection under TRIPs Article 27, and compulsory licensing now constrained under Article 31, what practical options, if any, are available to a developing country that wishes to make life-saving pharmaceuticals available to its citizens at prices lower than market prices?

What effects do compulsory licenses have, if any, on pharmaceutical research and development? How do compulsory licenses affect the operations of proprietary drug manufacturers and generic drug manufacturers? Starting in 2001, Brazil threatened to issue a compulsory license for Efavirenz, an HIV medicine; after the Brazilian government failed to negotiate a reduced price for the patented medicine, it issued a compulsory license for Efavirenz in 2007. Based on the compulsory license the government could buy an Indian generic version of the medicine for about one third of the price of the Merck medicine.

India issued its first compulsory license under TRIPs in 2012; the license was granted to Natco Pharma Ltd. for Bayer's cancer medicine Nexavar. Natco had been in licensing negotiations with Bayer since 2010, at which time Natco had proposed selling a monthly treatment for under Rs. 10,000 rather than the Rs. 280,428 charged by Bayer. The 2012 compulsory license provided for a 6% royalty to be paid to Bayer from net sales of the patented drug, and the price was set at Rs. 8,800 for a monthly treatment. Bayer Corp. v. Union of India, High Court of Judicature at Bombay, Writ petition No. 1323, 2013, ¶ 3(g). The compulsory license survived Bayer's challenge at the Intellectual Property Appellate Board, the High Court of Judicature at Bombay, and the Supreme Court of India. Bayer Corp. v. Union of India, Supreme Court of India, Appeal No. 30145, Dec. 12, 2014 (dismissing the petition for special leave).

For a comprehensive and comparative discussion of compulsory licenses see Compulsory Licensing: Practical Experiences and Ways Forward (Reto M. Hilty & Kung-Chung Liu eds., 2015); Compulsory Licensing in Europe: A Country-by-Country Overview (EPO, 2018).

6.   *Compulsory Licenses: Least Developed Countries.* Article 31(f) of the TRIPs Agreement requires as a condition to the Article's exceptions from exclusive rights that "any such [excepted] use shall be authorized predominantly for the supply of the domestic market of the Member authorizing such use." One effect of the provision is to limit the availability of needed drugs in countries that, though hard pressed by the ravages of HIV/AIDS, tuberculosis, malaria and other epidemics, lack the manufacturing capacity to produce them.

In November 2001, at the beginning of the Doha Round, the Ministerial Conference issued a Declaration on the TRIPs Agreement and Public Health, recognizing in Paragraph 6 "that WTO Members with insufficient or no manufacturing capacities in the pharmaceutical sector could face difficulties in making effective use of compulsory licensing under the TRIPs Agreement" and instructing the Council for TRIPs "to find an expeditious solution to this problem" by the end of 2002. (WTO, WT/MIN(01)/DEC/2, November 20, 2001). Subsequent decisions of the WTO Council in 2003 and 2005 created a framework—respectively, through a waiver and an amendment to TRIPs— for allowing compulsory licenses in countries that wish to produce drugs for export to countries that need them to supply the domestic market.

The 2005 agreement inserted the framework into a new TRIPs Article 31*bis*, but it was not until 2017 that the required two-thirds of all WTO member countries ratified the amendment and the TRIPs article came into effect.

As of March 2019 only one country, Rwanda, had notified the WTO (in 2007) that it intended to use the system to import one particular drug from Canada, and correspondingly, Canada had notified the WTO that Canada's Commissioner of Patents was authorizing the drug to be manufactured in Canada and exported to Rwanda. What might be the reasons for the underutilization of the system and for the delay in the countries' ratification of Article 31*bis*? High transaction costs associated with the use of the system and the significant administrative delay in the Rwanda case caused the drug to be unavailable in Rwanda until one year after the Rwandan notification to the WTO. *See* Jenny Wakely, Compulsory Licensing Under TRIPs: An Effective Tool to Increase Access to Medicines in Developing and Least Developed Countries?, 33(5) EIPR 299, 304 and 307 (2011).

Commentators have suggested a number of reasons for the underutilization of Article 31*bis* and other TRIPs flexibilities in the least developed countries. The 2012 *Managing Drug Supply* study by the World Health Organization identified several "constraints to establishing health-sensitive intellectual property laws": insufficient expertise to utilize the flexibilities, lack of information concerning best practices, insufficient domestic research and manufacturing capacity, and insufficient capacity for medicine registration, regulation, and procurement. MDS-3: Managing Access to Medicines and Health Technologies, WHO, 2012, Chapter 3.3. The Pat-INFORMED database, launched in 2018 as an initiative of WIPO, the International Federation of Pharmaceutical Manufacturers and Associations, and leading biopharmaceutical industries, is designed to improve access to patent information concerning medicines. Pat-INFORMED—The Gateway to Medicine Patent Information, WIPO.

For detailed and insightful analyses of the background to the Decision on Implementation of Paragraph 6 of the Doha Declaration on the TRIPs

Agreement and Public Health, see Daniel Gervais, The TRIPS Agreement: Drafting History and Analysis (4th ed. 2012), pp. 54–75; Frederick M. Abbott, The WTO Medicines Decisions: World Pharmaceutical Trade and the Protection of Public Health, 99 Am. J. Int'l L. 317 (2005). For EU legislation establishing a compulsory licensing system see Regulation (EC) No 816/2006 of the European Parliament and of the Council of 17 May 2006 on compulsory licensing of patents relating to the manufacture of pharmaceutical products for export to countries with public health problems.

Huawei Technologies Co. Ltd v ZTE Corp.

Court of Justice of the European Union, Fifth Chamber, 2015.
Case C-170/13.

Judgment

1   This request for a preliminary ruling concerns the interpretation of Article 102 TFEU.

2   The request has been made in proceedings between Huawei Technologies Co. Ltd ('Huawei Technologies'), on the one hand, and ZTE Corp. and ZTE Deutschland GmbH ('ZTE'), on the other hand, concerning an alleged infringement of a patent which is essential to a standard established by a standardisation body ('standard-essential patent' or 'SEP').

Legal context . . .

The ETSI rules

12   The European Telecommunications Standards Institute ('ETSI') is a body the objective of which, according to Clause 3.1 of Annex 6 to the ETSI Rules of Procedure, which annex is entitled 'ETSI Intellectual-Property Rights Policy', is to create standards which meet the technical objectives of the European telecommunications sector and to reduce the risk to ETSI, its members and others applying ETSI standards, that investment in the preparation, adoption and application of standards could be wasted as a result of an essential intellectual-property right for those standards being unavailable. To that end, Annex 6 seeks a balance between the needs of standardisation for public use in the field of telecommunications and the rights of the owners of intellectual-property rights.

13   Clause 3.2 of that annex provides that owners of intellectual-property rights should be adequately and fairly rewarded for the use of their intellectual-property rights.

14   Under Clause 4.1 of Annex 6, each of the members of ETSI is required to use reasonable endeavours, in particular during the development of a standard in the establishment of which it participates, to inform ETSI of that member's intellectual-property rights which are essential to that standard, in a timely fashion.

15   Clause 6.1 of Annex 6 to the ETSI Rules of Procedure provides that, when an intellectual-property right essential to a standard is brought to the attention of ETSI, the Director-General of ETSI must immediately request the owner of that right to give, within three months, an irrevocable undertaking that it is prepared to grant licences on fair, reasonable and non-discriminatory terms ('FRAND terms') in relation to that right.

16   Under Clause 6.3 of that annex, for so long as such an undertaking has not been given, ETSI is to assess whether work on the relevant parts of the standard should be suspended.

17   Clause 8.1 of Annex 6 provides that, if the owner of the intellectual-property rights refuses to give that undertaking, ETSI is to seek an alternative technology and, if no such technology exists, to stop work on the adoption of the standard in question.

18   Under Clause 14 of Annex 6 to the ETSI Rules of Procedure, any violation of the provisions of that annex by a member of ETSI is deemed to be a breach of that member's obligations to ETSI.

19   Clause 15.6 of that annex provides that an intellectual-property right is regarded as essential where, in particular, it is not possible on technical grounds to make equipment which complies with the standard without infringing the intellectual-property right ('essential patent'). . . .

The dispute in the main proceedings and the questions referred for a preliminary ruling

21   Huawei Technologies, a multinational company active in the telecommunications sector, is the proprietor of, inter alia, the European patent registered under the reference EP 2 090 050 B 1, bearing the title 'Method and apparatus of establishing a synchronisation signal in a communication system', granted by the Federal Republic of Germany, a Contracting State of the EPC ('patent EP 2 090 050 B 1').

22   That patent was notified to ETSI on 4 March 2009 by Huawei Technologies as a patent essential to the 'Long Term Evolution' standard. At the same time, Huawei Technologies undertook to grant licences to third parties on FRAND terms.

23   The referring court states, in the order for reference, that that patent is essential to that standard, which means that anyone using the 'Long Term Evolution' standard inevitably uses the teaching of that patent.

24   Between November 2010 and the end of March 2011, Huawei Technologies and ZTE Corp., a company belonging to a multinational group active in the telecommunications sector and which markets, in Germany, products equipped with software linked to that standard, engaged in discussions concerning, inter alia, the infringement of patent EP 2 090 050 B 1 and the possibility of concluding a licence on FRAND terms in relation to those products.

25   Huawei Technologies indicated the amount which it considered to be a reasonable royalty. For its part, ZTE Corp. sought a cross-licensing agreement. However, no offer relating to a licensing agreement was finalised.

26   None the less, ZTE markets products that operate on the basis of the 'Long Term Evolution' standard, thus using patent EP 2 090 050 B 1, without paying a royalty to Huawei Technologies or exhaustively rendering an account to Huawei Technologies in respect of past acts of use.

27   On 28 April 2011, on the basis of Article 64 of the EPC and Paragraph 139 et seq. of the German Law on Patents, as amended most recently by Paragraph 13 of the Law of 24 November 2011, Huawei Technologies brought an action for infringement against ZTE before the referring court, seeking an injunction prohibiting the infringement, the rendering of accounts, the recall of products and an award of damages.

28   That court considers that the decision on the substance in the main proceedings turns on whether the action brought by Huawei Technologies constitutes an abuse of that company's dominant position. It thus observes that it might be possible to rely on the mandatory nature of the grant of the licence in order to dismiss the action for a prohibitory injunction—in particular, on the basis of Article 102 TFEU—if, by its action, Huawei Technologies were to be regarded as abusing its dominant position. According to the referring court, the existence of that dominant position is not in dispute. . . .

39   In those circumstances, the Landgericht Düsseldorf decided to stay the proceedings and to refer the following questions to the Court of Justice for a preliminary ruling. . . .

Consideration of the questions referred

40   A preliminary point to note is that the present request for a preliminary ruling has arisen in the context of an action concerning infringement of a patent between two operators in the telecommunications sector, which are holders of numerous patents essential to the 'Long Term Evolution' standard established by ETSI, which standard is composed of more than 4 700 SEPs, in respect of which those operators have undertaken to grant licences to third parties on FRAND terms.

41   In the context of that dispute, the referring court raises the question whether the action for infringement seeking an injunction prohibiting that infringement, the rendering of accounts, the recall of products and damages, brought by the proprietor of an SEP—in this case, Huawei Technologies—against the alleged infringer of that SEP—ZTE, which requested the conclusion of a licensing agreement—is to be characterised as an 'abuse of a dominant position', within the meaning of Article 102 TFEU, and, accordingly, whether the action must be dismissed.

42   For the purpose of providing an answer to the referring court and in assessing the lawfulness of such an action for infringement brought by the proprietor of an SEP against an infringer with which no licensing agreement has been concluded, the Court must strike a balance between maintaining free competition—in respect of which primary law and, in particular, Article 102 TFEU prohibit abuses of a dominant position— and the requirement to safeguard that proprietor's intellectual-property rights and its right to effective judicial protection, guaranteed by Article 17(2) and Article 47 of the Charter [of Fundamental Rights of the European Union], respectively.

43   As the referring court states in the order for reference, the existence of a dominant position has not been contested before it by the parties to the dispute in the main proceedings. Given that the questions posed by the referring court relate only to the existence of an abuse, the analysis must be confined to the latter criterion.

> . . . *[L]egal proceedings brought with a view to obtaining the recall of products*

44   . . . [T]he referring court asks, essentially, in what circumstances the bringing of an action for infringement, by an undertaking in a dominant position and holding an SEP, which has given an undertaking to the standardisation body to grant licences to third parties on FRAND terms, seeking an injunction prohibiting the infringement of that SEP or seeking the recall of products for the manufacture of which the SEP has been used, is to be regarded as constituting an abuse contrary to Article 102 TFEU.

45   First of all, it must be recalled that the concept of an abuse of a dominant position within the meaning of Article 102 TFEU is an objective concept relating to the conduct of a dominant undertaking which, on a market where the degree of competition is already weakened precisely because of the presence of the undertaking concerned, through recourse to methods different from those governing normal competition in products or services on the basis of the transactions of commercial operators, has the effect of hindering the maintenance of the degree of competition still existing in the market or the growth of that competition. . .

46   It is, in this connection, settled case-law that the exercise of an exclusive right linked to an intellectual-property right—in the case in the main proceedings, namely the right to bring an action for infringement— forms part of the rights of the proprietor of an intellectual-property right, with the result that the exercise of such a right, even if it is the act of an undertaking holding a dominant position, cannot in itself constitute an abuse of a dominant position. . .

47   However, it is also settled case-law that the exercise of an exclusive right linked to an intellectual-property right by the proprietor may, in

exceptional circumstances, involve abusive conduct for the purposes of Article 102 TFEU.

48 Nevertheless, it must be pointed out ... that the particular circumstances of the case in the main proceedings distinguish that case from the cases which gave rise to the case-law cited in paragraphs 46 and 47 of the present judgment.

49 It is characterised, first, as the referring court has observed, by the fact that the patent at issue is essential to a standard established by a standardisation body, rendering its use indispensable to all competitors which envisage manufacturing products that comply with the standard to which it is linked.

50 That feature distinguishes SEPs from patents that are not essential to a standard and which normally allow third parties to manufacture competing products without recourse to the patent concerned and without compromising the essential functions of the product in question.

51 Secondly, the case in the main proceedings may be distinguished by the fact ... that the patent at issue obtained SEP status only in return for the proprietor's irrevocable undertaking, given to the standardisation body in question, that it is prepared to grant licences on FRAND terms.

52 Although the proprietor of the essential patent at issue has the right to bring an action for a prohibitory injunction or for the recall of products, the fact that that patent has obtained SEP status means that its proprietor can prevent products manufactured by competitors from appearing or remaining on the market and, thereby, reserve to itself the manufacture of the products in question.

53 In those circumstances, and having regard to the fact that an undertaking to grant licences on FRAND terms creates legitimate expectations on the part of third parties that the proprietor of the SEP will in fact grant licences on such terms, a refusal by the proprietor of the SEP to grant a licence on those terms may, in principle, constitute an abuse within the meaning of Article 102 TFEU.

54 It follows that, having regard to the legitimate expectations created, the abusive nature of such a refusal may, in principle, be raised in defence to actions for a prohibitory injunction or for the recall of products. However, under Article 102 TFEU, the proprietor of the patent is obliged only to grant a licence on FRAND terms. In the case in the main proceedings, the parties are not in agreement as to what is required by FRAND terms in the circumstances of that case.

55 In such a situation, in order to prevent an action for a prohibitory injunction or for the recall of products from being regarded as abusive, the proprietor of an SEP must comply with conditions which seek to ensure a fair balance between the interests concerned.

56 In this connection, due account must be taken of the specific legal and factual circumstances in the case. . .

57   Thus, the need to enforce intellectual-property rights, covered by, inter alia, Directive 2004/48, which—in accordance with Article 17(2) of the Charter—provides for a range of legal remedies aimed at ensuring a high level of protection for intellectual-property rights in the internal market, and the right to effective judicial protection guaranteed by Article 47 of the Charter, comprising various elements, including the right of access to a tribunal, must be taken into consideration. . .

58   This need for a high level of protection for intellectual-property rights means that, in principle, the proprietor may not be deprived of the right to have recourse to legal proceedings to ensure effective enforcement of his exclusive rights, and that, in principle, the user of those rights, if he is not the proprietor, is required to obtain a licence prior to any use.

59   Thus, although the irrevocable undertaking to grant licences on FRAND terms given to the standardisation body by the proprietor of an SEP cannot negate the substance of the rights guaranteed to that proprietor by Article 17(2) and Article 47 of the Charter, it does, none the less, justify the imposition on that proprietor of an obligation to comply with specific requirements when bringing actions against alleged infringers for a prohibitory injunction or for the recall of products.

60   Accordingly, the proprietor of an SEP which considers that that SEP is the subject of an infringement cannot, without infringing Article 102 TFEU, bring an action for a prohibitory injunction or for the recall of products against the alleged infringer without notice or prior consultation with the alleged infringer, even if the SEP has already been used by the alleged infringer.

61   Prior to such proceedings, it is thus for the proprietor of the SEP in question, first, to alert the alleged infringer of the infringement complained about by designating that SEP and specifying the way in which it has been infringed.

62   . . . [I]n view of the large number of SEPs composing a standard such as that at issue in the main proceedings, it is not certain that the infringer of one of those SEPs will necessarily be aware that it is using the teaching of an SEP that is both valid and essential to a standard.

63   Secondly, after the alleged infringer has expressed its willingness to conclude a licensing agreement on FRAND terms, it is for the proprietor of the SEP to present to that alleged infringer a specific, written offer for a licence on FRAND terms, in accordance with the undertaking given to the standardisation body, specifying, in particular, the amount of the royalty and the way in which that royalty is to be calculated.

64   . . . [W]here the proprietor of an SEP has given an undertaking to the standardisation body to grant licences on FRAND terms, it can be expected that it will make such an offer. Furthermore, in the absence of a public standard licensing agreement, and where licensing agreements already concluded with other competitors are not made public, the

proprietor of the SEP is better placed to check whether its offer complies with the condition of non-discrimination than is the alleged infringer.

65   By contrast, it is for the alleged infringer diligently to respond to that offer, in accordance with recognised commercial practices in the field and in good faith, a point which must be established on the basis of objective factors and which implies, in particular, that there are no delaying tactics.

66   Should the alleged infringer not accept the offer made to it, it may rely on the abusive nature of an action for a prohibitory injunction or for the recall of products only if it has submitted to the proprietor of the SEP in question, promptly and in writing, a specific counter-offer that corresponds to FRAND terms.

67   Furthermore, where the alleged infringer is using the teachings of the SEP before a licensing agreement has been concluded, it is for that alleged infringer, from the point at which its counter-offer is rejected, to provide appropriate security, in accordance with recognised commercial practices in the field, for example by providing a bank guarantee or by placing the amounts necessary on deposit. The calculation of that security must include, inter alia, the number of the past acts of use of the SEP, and the alleged infringer must be able to render an account in respect of those acts of use.

68   In addition, where no agreement is reached on the details of the FRAND terms following the counter-offer by the alleged infringer, the parties may, by common agreement, request that the amount of the royalty be determined by an independent third party, by decision without delay.

69   Lastly, having regard, first, to the fact that a standardisation body such as that which developed the standard at issue in the main proceedings does not check whether patents are valid or essential to the standard in which they are included during the standardisation procedure, and, secondly, to the right to effective judicial protection guaranteed by Article 47 of the Charter, an alleged infringer cannot be criticised either for challenging, in parallel to the negotiations relating to the grant of licences, the validity of those patents and/or the essential nature of those patents to the standard in which they are included and/or their actual use, or for reserving the right to do so in the future.

70   It is for the referring court to determine whether the above-mentioned criteria are satisfied in the present case, in so far as they are relevant, in the circumstances, for the purpose of resolving the dispute in the main proceedings.

71   It follows from all the foregoing considerations that the answer . . . in so far as that question concerns legal proceedings brought with a view to obtaining the recall of products, is that Article 102 TFEU must be interpreted as meaning that the proprietor of an SEP, which has given an irrevocable undertaking to a standardisation body to grant a licence

to third parties on FRAND terms, does not abuse its dominant position, within the meaning of Article 102 TFEU, by bringing an action for infringement seeking an injunction prohibiting the infringement of its patent or seeking the recall of products for the manufacture of which that patent has been used, as long as:

> — prior to bringing that action, the proprietor has, first, alerted the alleged infringer of the infringement complained about by designating that patent and specifying the way in which it has been infringed, and, secondly, after the alleged infringer has expressed its willingness to conclude a licensing agreement on FRAND terms, presented to that infringer a specific, written offer for a licence on such terms, specifying, in particular, the royalty and the way in which it is to be calculated, and

> — where the alleged infringer continues to use the patent in question, the alleged infringer has not diligently responded to that offer, in accordance with recognised commercial practices in the field and in good faith, this being a matter which must be established on the basis of objective factors and which implies, in particular, that there are no delaying tactics.

. . . [L]egal proceedings brought with a view to obtaining the rendering of accounts or an award of damages

72   . . . [I]n so far as . . . legal proceedings brought with a view to obtaining the rendering of accounts or an award of damages, the referring court asks, in essence, whether Article 102 TFEU must be interpreted as prohibiting an undertaking in a dominant position and holding an SEP, which has given an undertaking to the standardisation body to grant licences for that patent on FRAND terms, from bringing an action for infringement against the alleged infringer of its SEP and seeking the rendering of accounts in relation to past acts of use of that SEP or an award of damages in respect of those acts of use.

73   As is apparent from paragraphs 52 and 53 above, the exercise by the proprietor of the SEP of its intellectual-property rights, by bringing actions for a prohibitory injunction or for the recall of products, may be characterised, in circumstances such as those in the main proceedings, as an abuse, where those proceedings are liable to prevent products complying with the standard in question manufactured by competitors from appearing or remaining on the market.

74   In the present case, according to the description set out in the order for reference, the actions for infringement brought by the proprietor of an SEP, seeking the rendering of accounts in relation to past acts of use of that SEP or an award of damages in respect of those acts of use, do not have a direct impact on products complying with the standard in question manufactured by competitors appearing or remaining on the market.

75 Consequently, in circumstances such as those in the main proceedings, such actions cannot be regarded as an abuse under Article 102 TFEU.

76 In the light of the foregoing considerations, the answer . . ., in so far as . . . legal proceedings brought with a view to obtaining the rendering of accounts or an award of damages, is that Article 102 TFEU must be interpreted as not prohibiting, in circumstances such as those in the main proceedings, an undertaking in a dominant position and holding an SEP, which has given an undertaking to the standardisation body to grant licences for that SEP on FRAND terms, from bringing an action for infringement against the alleged infringer of its SEP and seeking the rendering of accounts in relation to past acts of use of that SEP or an award of damages in respect of those acts of use. . . .

NOTES

1. *Working Requirements.* Most countries require a patent owner to work its invention inside the country. In some countries it will suffice if the patent owner shows that it has offered licenses to practice the invention on reasonable terms; other countries require the patent owner or licensee to manufacture the patented product or practice the patented process unless doing so would be unreasonable under the circumstances. For example, under Article L613–11 of the French Intellectual Property Code, the non-working of a patent for three years after the grant of the patent or four years after the filing of the patent application may result in the issuance of a compulsory license. For purposes of the French law, importation is considered to be a working of a patent only if the imported goods are manufactured in a WTO member country. Similarly, Article 48 of the Chinese Patent Act allows the grant of a compulsory license if a patent has not been exploited for three years after its issuance or four years after the filing of the patent application.

Patent forfeiture was at one time the common remedy for nonworking; later, countries began to impose compulsory licenses instead. Article 5A of the Paris Convention prescribes the conditions for imposing compulsory licenses (and forfeitures) for nonworking or insufficient working of a patented invention. Historically, the main rationale for the working requirement was that in return for granting a patent, with its prospect of monopoly rents, a country is entitled to the economic benefits of industrialization that flow from the product's manufacture. For many products, however, manufacture in every country in the world will not be profitable, a fact that at least partially explains the abandonment of the forfeiture sanction and the turn to compulsory licenses; no one will seek a compulsory license unless there is profit to be earned from local manufacture.

Are working requirements consistent with Article 27(1) of the TRIPs Agreement, which prohibits "discrimination as to the place of invention, the field of technology and whether products are imported or locally produced?" In 2000 the United States filed a complaint with the WTO against the

Brazilian local working requirement, which had been used by the Brazilian government to secure affordable AIDS medication. The dispute was resolved by a mutually agreed solution in 2001, in which the United States, under pressure of public opinion, agreed to an arrangement whereby the Brazilian government would notify the United States in advance of the issuance of compulsory licenses for failure to work a patent. Measures Affecting Patent Protection, WT/DS199/1.

For a discussion of the WTO dispute and an analysis of the issue of the consistency of working requirements with Article 27(1) of the TRIPs Agreement see Bryan Mercurio & Mitali Tyagi, Treaty Interpretation in WTO Dispute Settlement: The Outstanding Question on the Legality of Local Working Requirements, 19 Minn. J. Int'l L. 275 (2010). For the history and present state of the requirements in different countries see Marketa Trimble, Patent Working Requirements: Historical and Comparative Perspectives, 6 UC Irvine L. R. 483 (2016); Jorge L. Contreras et al., Patent Working Requirements and Complex Products, 7(1) NYU J. Intell. Prop. & Entertainment L. 1 (2017).

2. *Abuse of Patent Rights.* The Hague Revision Conference in 1925 added Article 5A to the Paris Convention, which allowed for compulsory licenses to be granted "to prevent the abuses which might result from the exercise of the exclusive rights conferred by the patent." In addition to failure to work, the 1925 Conference considered the following to be abuses of patent rights: insufficient working, refusal to grant licenses on reasonable terms to the detriment of industrial development, insufficient supplying of the national market with the patented product, and demanding excessive prices for the product. Georg Hendrik Christiaan Bodenhausen, Guide to the Application of the Paris Convention for the Protection of Industrial Property as Revised at Stockholm in 1967, 71 (WIPO 2004) (1969). Can compulsory licenses be granted under Article 31 of the TRIPs Agreement for the abuses that the 1925 Conference contemplated?

Article 5A of the Paris Convention leaves it to each country's national law to define what kinds of conduct constitute patent abuse. The U.S. Patent Act lists several practices that are not considered to be patent "misuse"; among the practices are "refus[al] to license or use any rights to the patent" and "condition[ing] the license of any rights to the patent or the sale of the patented product on the acquisition of a license to rights in another patent or purchase of a separate product, unless, in view of the circumstances, the patent owner has market power in the relevant market for the patent or the patented product on which the license or sale is conditioned." 35 U.S.C. § 271(d).

3. *Patent Rights and Competition Law.* Competition law may place constraints on the exercise of intellectual property rights, as demonstrated in the *Magill* decision on page 334, above. Are the abuses that competition laws seek to eliminate different from the abuses of patent rights in Article 5A of the Paris Convention? Is there any reason to maintain a separate patent misuse doctrine that does not require a finding of dominant position and anticompetitive effect? In the United States the patent misuse doctrine was originally developed independently of antitrust law, but eventually antitrust law began to influence patent misuse case law, and in 1986 the U.S. Court of Appeals for the Federal Circuit included anticompetitive effects as a requirement for a finding of patent misuse. Windsurfing International, Inc. v. AMF, Inc., 782 F.2d 995, 1001 (Fed. Cir. 1986), cert. denied; Marshall Leaffer, Patent Misuse and Innovation, 10 J. High Tech. L. 142 (2010).

In *Huawei v. ZTE* the CJEU did not question the existence of the patent owner's dominant position on the market. Does the ownership of an SEP always result in a dominant position? Is the relevant market the market for licenses under the SEP, as courts in the U.K. have held, or is it the market for the products and services using the SEP, as the German courts have held? *See* Unwired Planet v. Huawei, [2018] EWCA Civ 2344, ¶¶ 213–229; Oberlandesgericht Düsseldorf, I-15 U 66/15, 2017, ¶ 182.

For a review of court approaches to the interface of FRAND issues and competition law see The Cambridge Handbook of Technical Standardization Law: Competition, Antitrust, and Patents (Jorge L. Contreras ed. 2018); Complications and Quandaries in the ICT Sector (Ashish Bharadwaj eds. 2018). For a commentary on *Huawei v. ZTE* and later developments see Matthias Leistner, FRAND Patents in Europe in the Post-Huawei Era: A Recent Report from Germany, in SEPs, SSOs and FRAND—Asian and Global Perspectives on Fostering Innovation in Interconnectivity (Hilty & Liu eds., forthcoming).

4. *The "Huawei Etiquette."* As Lord Justice Kitchen observed in *Unwired Planet*, excerpted on page 568, below, "the negotiation of licences for SEPs on FRAND terms may be far from straightforward." Valuation of patents and patent licenses is complex, and whoever moves first in SEP licensing negotiations can significantly influence the outcome of the negotiations, given the information disparity between the SEP holder and the prospective licensee. Courts and legislators may influence the process by setting the conditions under which the SEP owner may obtain an injunction against the prospective licensee.

Before the CJEU established in *Huawei v. ZTE* the approach that some commentators have termed the "Huawei etiquette," different approaches led to inconsistent decisions in the European Union: In 2014 the European Commission held that Motorola, an SEP owner, infringed European antitrust rules when Motorola sought to enforce an injunction against Apple in a German court at the same time that Apple was willing to accept a license on FRAND terms. Commission Decision of 29 April 2014 addressed to Motorola Mobility LLC, C(2014) 2892 final. The German court had issued the injunction because it had considered the several offers that Apple had made to be insufficient. It was this type of inconsistency that prompted the Düsseldorf Landgericht to refer the questions in *Huawei v. ZTE* to the CJEU.

Other courts may prefer a less formulaic approach than the approach adopted by the CJEU. For example, in 2017 the Beijing Intellectual Property Court granted an SEP owner an injunction against a prospective SEP licensee after the court had assessed the reasonableness of the conduct of the prospective licensee and found a lack of good faith on the part of the prospective licensee. Xian Xidian Jietong Wireless Comm. Co. Ltd.

(IWNComm) v. Sony Mobile Comm, Products (China) Co. Ltd., Beijing Intellectual Property Court, 2017. German and U.K. courts have also articulated the requirement that an SEP owner and a prospective licensee act in good faith. On the developments in German jurisprudence see Maximilian Haedicke, Lessons from the *Huawei v. Unwired Planet* Decision for German Patent Law, 13(7) J. of Intell. Prop. Law & Practice 581 (2018).

5.   *Injunctive Relief.* In the United States, the Supreme Court in 2006 held that injunctions in patent infringement cases are, like injunctions in other cases, subject to a four-factor test. Application of the test may lead to a denial of an injunction even when the patent in suit was infringed. The four-factor test requires that a plaintiff demonstrate "(1) that it has suffered an irreparable injury; (2) that remedies available at law are inadequate to compensate for that injury; (3) that considering the balance of hardships between the plaintiff and defendant, a remedy in equity is warranted; and (4) that the public interest would not be disserved by a permanent injunction." eBay Inc. v. MercExchange, L.L.C., 547 U.S. 388, 391 (2006).

Does a FRAND commitment automatically render an injunction unavailable under U.S. law? In *Apple, Inc. v. Motorola, Inc.*, a case involving the same technology that was at issue in the European Commission antitrust decision in note 4, above, a U.S. judge declined to issue an injunction against Apple and observed that "[b]y committing to license its patents on FRAND terms, Motorola committed to license the [patent] to anyone willing to pay a FRAND royalty and thus implicitly acknowledged that a royalty is adequate compensation for a license to use that patent." 869 F.Supp.2d 901, 914 (N.D.Ill. 2012), *aff'd on this point by* 757 F.3d 1286 (Fed.Cir. 2014).

For an insightful comparative analysis of remedies in the context of FRAND licenses see Thomas F. Cotter, The Comparative Law and Economics of Standard-Essential Patents and FRAND Royalties, 22 Texas Intell. Prop. L. J. 311 (2014). For a further discussion of injunctions see note 4 on page 577, below.

PROBLEM 7

On September 17 a U.S. patent encompassing the subject matter and claims described in Problem 6, at page 464, issued and was promptly assigned by the patent owner to Consumer Corp., a major U.S. consumer goods retailer. Consumer Corp. incorporated the program into its web-based international retail sales and inventory control operations through servers located in the United States. On October 23, Best Buy, a Belgian-based international retailer acting without authority from Consumer Corp., incorporated into its web server in Brussels a computer program identical in all material respects to the Consumer Corp. program, and uses this program in its web-based sales and inventory control operations.

Consumer Corp. would like to bring an action for infringement of the U.S. patent. On the assumption that it can obtain personal jurisdiction over Best Buy in the United States, please advise Consumer Corp. on the likelihood of its success in an action against Best Buy, making any assumptions you think appropriate about the scope of the claims in its U.S. patent.

6. INFRINGEMENT AND REMEDIES

Actavis UK Limited v. Eli Lilly

United Kingdom Supreme Court, 2017.
[2017] UKSC 48.

LORD NEUBERGER:

1.   The issue raised on this appeal and cross-appeal is whether three products manufactured by the Actavis group of companies ("Actavis") would infringe a patent whose proprietor is Eli Lilly & Company ("Lilly"), namely European Patent (UK) No 1 313 508 ("the Patent"), and its corresponding designations in France, Italy and Spain. . . .

The factual and technical background

The factual background

3.   Pemetrexed is a chemical which has been known for some time to have therapeutic effects on cancerous tumours. However, when used for that purpose on its own, pemetrexed can often have seriously damaging, sometimes even fatal, side-effects. Accordingly, its use as an anti-cancer drug was effectively precluded in practice. The essential disclosure of the Patent was that the damaging side-effects could largely be avoided if a compound called pemetrexed disodium was administered together with vitamin B12. This has enabled pemetrexed disodium to be used for treatment in the form of a medicament which includes the vitamin. Such a medicament has been successfully marketed, under the brand name Alimta, by Lilly since 2004.

4.   The Patent primarily claims the use of pemetrexed disodium in the manufacture of a medicament for use in combination with vitamin B12 (and, optionally, folic acid) for the treatment of cancer. . . .

8.   Actavis's proposed products involve pemetrexed compounds being used together with vitamin B12 for cancer treatment. However, rather than pemetrexed disodium, the active ingredient in those products ("the Actavis products") is (a) pemetrexed diacid, (b) pemetrexed ditromethamine, or (c) pemetrexed dipotassium. . . . Actavis contend that, because they intend to use the Actavis products which do not include pemetrexed disodium, the claims of the Patent, which are expressed as involving the use of pemetrexed disodium, would not be infringed. By contrast, Lilly contends that there would be either direct or indirect infringement of the Patent if Actavis launch any of the Actavis products on the market in the UK or in France, Italy, or Spain. . . .

10.   [T]he appeal raises the issue of the correct approach under UK law (and the law of the three other states) to the interpretation of patent

claims, and in particular the requirement of EPC 2000* to take account of "equivalents", and also the extent to which it is permissible to make use of the prosecution history of a patent when determining its scope. . . .

The specification and claims in the Patent

12. The Patent is entitled "Combination containing an antifolate and methylmalonic acid lowering agent" . . .

21. Turning to the claims, it is only necessary for present purposes to refer to claims 1 and 12, which are in these terms:

> "1. Use of pemetrexed disodium in the manufacture of a medicament for use in combination therapy for inhibiting tumour growth in mammals wherein said medicament is to be administered in combination with vitamin B12 or a pharmaceutical derivative thereof [which it then specifies]."

> "12. A product containing pemetrexed disodium, vitamin B12 or a pharmaceutical derivative thereof said pharmaceutical derivative [which it again specifies], and, optionally, a folic binding protein binding agent selected from [a specified group of chemicals including folic acid], as a combined preparation for the simultaneous, separate or sequential use in inhibiting tumour growth." . . .

Direct infringement . . .

The legislative context

28. The domestic provision governing direct patent infringement is section 60(1) of the Patents Act 1977. However, section 130(7) declares that certain provisions of that Act, including section 60, are "so framed as to have, as nearly as practicable, the same effects in the United Kingdom as the corresponding provisions of the European Patent Convention . . . have in the territories to which [that Convention applies]". Accordingly, it is common ground that it is appropriate to consider the present case by reference to the EPC 2000.

29. Article 69(1) EPC 2000 provides that "[t]he extent of the protection conferred by a European patent . . . shall be determined by the claims", although it is followed by another sentence, namely "[n]evertheless, the description and drawings shall be used to interpret the claims".

30. As a matter of ordinary language, it is quite clear that the only type of pemetrexed compound to which the Patent's claims expressly extend is pemetrexed disodium. One only needs to read claim 1 and claim 12 to justify that: as a matter of ordinary language, "pemetrexed disodium" means that particular salt, and no other salt, let alone the free acid. . . .

31. In these circumstances, The Protocol on the Interpretation of article 69 as amended in 2000 ("the Protocol") is crucial to Lilly's contention that

---

*   "EPC 2000" refers to the European Patent Convention as revised by the Act from November 29, 2000. The revised version of the Convention entered into force in 2007. *Ed.*

the scope of protection afforded by the Patent extends to the Actavis products. The Protocol provides:

"*Article 1*

General principles

Article 69 should not be interpreted as meaning that the extent of the protection conferred by a European patent is to be understood as that defined by the strict, literal meaning of the wording used in the claims, the description and drawings being employed only for the purpose of resolving an ambiguity found in the claims. Nor should it be taken to mean that the claims serve only as a guideline and that the actual protection conferred may extend to what, from a consideration of the description and drawings by a person skilled in the art, the patent proprietor has contemplated. On the contrary, it is to be interpreted as defining a position between these extremes which combines a fair protection for the patent proprietor with a reasonable degree of legal certainty for third parties.

Article 2

Equivalents

For the purpose of determining the extent of protection conferred by a European patent, due account shall be taken of any element which is equivalent to an element specified in the claims." . . .

32.   The drafting of the Protocol bears all the hallmarks of the product of a compromise agreement. This is unsurprising. There is an inevitable conflict between the desirability of giving an inventor an appropriate degree of protection in a particular case and the need for clarity of principle as to the extent of such protection generally; and, of course, there is an unavoidable tension between the appropriateness of giving an inventor a monopoly and the public interest in maximising competition. In addition, the EPC 2000 and the Protocol apply in many different states which have different traditions and approaches in relation to the law of patents. . . .

34.   The question of how far one can go outside the wording of a claim to enable the patentee to enjoy protection against products or processes which are not within the ambit of the actual language, construed in accordance with ordinary principles of interpretation, has been considered in three significant UK cases and in a number of significant cases decided in the courts of other Convention states.

The domestic case law

38.   [In *Improver Corpn v Remington Consumer Products Ltd* [1990] FSR 181], 189, Hoffmann J suggested the following approach, largely based on his reading of the reasoning in *Catnic* [1982] RPC 183, 242 to 243:

"If the issue was whether a feature embodied in an alleged infringement which fell outside the primary, literal or a contextual meaning of a descriptive word or phrase in the claim ('a variant') was nevertheless within its language as properly interpreted, the court should ask itself the following three questions:

(1) Does the variant have a material effect upon the way the invention works? If yes, the variant is outside the claim. If no—

(2) Would this (ie that the variant had no material effect) have been obvious at the date of publication of the patent to a reader skilled in the art? If no, the variant is outside the claim. If yes—

(3) Would the reader skilled in the art nevertheless have understood from the language of the claim that the patentee intended that strict compliance with the primary meaning was an essential requirement of the invention? If yes, the variant is outside the claim.

On the other hand, a negative answer to the last question would lead to the conclusion that the patentee was intending the word or phrase to have not a literal, but a figurative meaning (the figure being a form of synecdoche or metonymy) denoting a class of things which included the variant and the literal meaning, the latter being perhaps the most perfect, best-known or striking example of the class." . . .

40. Thereafter, for the next 15 years or so, this three-stage approach was almost routinely applied by judges in UK patent infringement cases, where the three "*Improver* questions" were subsequently renamed the three "Protocol questions."

42. Lord Hoffmann . . . turned to the doctrine of equivalents, which he explained [in *Kirin-Amgen Inc v Hoechst Marion Roussel Ltd* [2005] RPC 9,] 37 had been developed in the United States courts and "allow[ed] the patentee to extend his monopoly beyond his claims", so as to prevent "the unscrupulous copyist [from making] unimportant and insubstantial changes and substitutions in the patent which, though adding nothing, would be enough to take the copied matter outside the claim, and hence outside the reach of law", quoting Jackson J in *Graver Tank & Manufacturing Co Inc v Linde Air Products Co* 339 US 605, 607 (1950). Lord Hoffmann expressed concern that "once the monopoly had been allowed to escape from the terms of the claims, it is not easy to know where its limits should be drawn", and concluded that, rather than adhering to literalism and adopting the doctrine, the solution was "to adopt a principle of construction which actually gave effect to what the person skilled in the art would have understood the patentee to be claiming" . . . He also said that article 69 EPC 2000 "firmly shuts the door on any doctrine which extends protection outside the claims."

The approach in the courts of other EPC states . . .

46. French law, according to the expert witnesses in this case, applies the doctrine of equivalents where the variant is "different in form but perform[s] the same function" as the invention, but only where "the function [claimed in the patent] is a new one". This seems to be supported by *Azéma and Galloux, Droit de la propriété industrielle*, 7th ed (2012), which distinguishes at p 442 between two categories of patents. The first category is those which "in general terms claim the means that provide for a particular function" (*moyens généraux*), or . . . claims which cover "general means". The second category is patents "which indicate the particular means which infer such function" (*moyens particuliers*), or claims which are "narrowly worded to cover specific means". . . . The doctrine is only normally applicable to the first category of claims. . . .

49. At any rate at local appellate level, Spanish courts appear to have effectively adopted the approach embodied in the three questions suggested by Hoffmann J in *Improver* [1990] FSR 181. . . .

52. It may be of some significance that the product which Hoffmann J concluded in *Improver* [1990] FSR 181 was non-infringing was held by the German, Italian and Dutch courts to infringe. Of course, the fact that courts of two states reach different conclusions on the same issue does not of itself mean that there is a difference in the law of those states, let alone that one court is wrong and the other right: the evidence may be different, and there may be issues of judgment on which reasonable judges could differ. . . .

The proper approach to infringement claims

53. Any patent system must strike a balance between the two competing factors referred to at the end of article 1 of the Protocol, namely "a fair protection for the patent proprietor [and] a reasonable degree of legal certainty for third parties". The balance cannot be struck on an *ad hoc* case-by-case basis without any guiding principles, as that would mean that there was no legal certainty. On the other hand, striking the balance by adopting a normal approach to interpretation would risk depriving patentees of a proper measure of protection . . . But, if one departs from ordinary language, it is necessary to have some guidance or to draw some lines . . .

66. [G]iven the weight that has been given by courts in this jurisdiction (and indeed in some other jurisdictions) to the three "*Improver* questions", I think it must be right for this court to express in our own words our reformulated version of those questions. . . . While the language of some or all of the questions may sometimes have to be adapted to apply more aptly to the specific facts of a particular case, the three reformulated questions are as follows:

> i) Notwithstanding that it is not within the literal meaning of the relevant claim(s) of the patent, does the variant achieve

substantially the same result in substantially the same way as the invention, ie the inventive concept revealed by the patent?

ii)   Would it be obvious to the person skilled in the art, reading the patent at the priority date, but knowing that the variant achieves substantially the same result as the invention, that it does so in substantially the same way as the invention?

iii)   Would such a reader of the patent have concluded that the patentee nonetheless intended that strict compliance with the literal meaning of the relevant claim(s) of the patent was an essential requirement of the invention?

In order to establish infringement in a case where there is no literal infringement, a patentee would have to establish that the answer to the first two questions was "yes" and that the answer to the third question was "no".

Provisional conclusion on direct infringement in the UK

67. Given that the Actavis products do not infringe on the basis of a normal interpretation of claim 1 of the Patent, it is necessary to consider whether they represent an immaterial variation on that claim. I propose to address that issue initially disregarding the prosecution history, and having reached a provisional conclusion, I will then address that history and its effect on the provisional conclusion.

68. In my view, application in the present case of the three questions just identified results in the conclusion that the Actavis products infringe. So far as the first question is concerned, there can be no doubt but that those products work in the same way as the invention: they all ultimately involve a medicament containing the pemetrexed anion and vitamin B12. Thus, they achieve substantially the same result in substantially the same way as the invention. . . .

69. As to the second question, it seems to me clear that the notional addressee of the Patent would appreciate (and would have appreciated as at the priority date) that each of the Actavis products would work in precisely the same way as pemetrexed disodium when included in a medicament with vitamin B12. . . . Furthermore, the notional addressee of the Patent would regard investigating whether pemetrexed free acid, pemetrexed ditromethamine or pemetrexed dipotassium worked as a purely routine exercise . . .

70. Turning to the third question, the Court of Appeal considered that the notional addressee "would understand that the patent was clearly limited to the disodium salt, and did not extend to the diacid, or the dipotassium or ditromethamine salts". They based this conclusion on the fact that the specification of the Patent contains a number of passages . . . which refer to "anti-folates" and the like and other passages which refer to pemetrexed disodium, which is "a highly specific chemical compound", and the fact that the claim is limited to pemetrexed disodium

would therefore lead the notional addressee to conclude that the claim is indeed intended to be so limited . . .

74. Looking at matters more broadly, the addressee of the Patent would, as I see it, understand that the reason why the claims were limited to the disodium salt was because that was the only pemetrexed salt on which the experiments described in the specification had been carried out. However, it does not follow that the patentee did not intend any other pemetrexed salts to infringe . . .

75. Accordingly, I would conclude that, subject to considering the prosecution history, the Actavis products infringe claim 1 of the Patent.

The effect of the prosecution history

81. Actavis contends that the prosecution history . . . makes it clear that the claims of the Patent should be interpreted as being limited to pemetrexed disodium not only as a matter of language, but in the sense that the use of any other pemetrexed compound, including other pemetrexed salts and the free acid, could not infringe. This contention gives rise to two issues. The first is one of relatively general application, namely whether and if so when it is permissible to have recourse to the prosecution history of a patent when considering whether a variant infringes that patent. The second issue is whether the prosecution history of the Patent in this case alters the provisional conclusion reached in para 75 above.

82. So far as the first issue is concerned, Lord Hoffmann said in *Kirin-Amgen* [2005] RPC 9, para 35:

> "The courts of the United Kingdom, the Netherlands and Germany certainly discourage, if they do not actually prohibit, use of the patent office file in aid of construction. There are good reasons: the meaning of the patent should not change according to whether or not the person skilled in the art has access to the file and in any case life is too short for the limited assistance which it can provide. It is however frequently impossible to know without access, not merely to the file but to the private thoughts of the patentee and his advisors as well, what the reason was for some apparently inexplicable limitation in the extent of the monopoly claimed."

83. In the absence of good reason to the contrary, it would be wrong to depart from what was said by the House of Lords. It is said by Actavis that there is good reason to depart from what Lord Hoffmann said on the ground that he was wrong in his description of the German and Dutch approaches to this issue, and that anyway he failed to have regard to the jurisprudence of other European courts.

84. In my view, Lord Hoffmann was right about the approach of the German and Dutch courts to this issue. Thus, the Bundesgerichtshof, in a decision involving the German equivalent of the instant Patent, Case No X ZR 29/15 (*Eli Lilly v Actavis Group PTC*), paras 39–40, stated that

"it is permissible . . . to use statements made by the applicant [and the examiner] during the grant procedure as an indication of how the person skilled in the art understands the subject matter of the patent" but "such indications cannot be readily used as the sole basis for construction". And in *Ciba-Geigy AG v Oté Optics BV* (1995) 28 IIC 748, the Dutch Supreme Court said that "a court will only be justified in using clarifying information from the public part of the granting file, when it holds that even after the average person skilled in the art has considered the description and the drawings, it is still open to question how the contents of the claims must be interpreted".

85. It is argued by Actavis that this limited approach to the circumstances in which reference can be made to the prosecution file may be more restrictive than the approach adopted in France, Italy, and Spain . . .

86. While the French courts appear to be more ready to refer to the prosecution file on issues of interpretation or scope than the German or Dutch courts, it is unclear how much, if any, difference there is in outcome. The position in relation to the Italian courts is more unclear, and it may well be that the effect of the approach of the Spanish courts is the same in outcome as that of the German and Dutch courts. . . .

87. In my judgment, it is appropriate for the UK courts to adopt a sceptical, but not absolutist, attitude to a suggestion that the contents of the prosecution file of a patent should be referred to when considering a question of interpretation or infringement, along substantially the same lines as the German and Dutch courts. It is tempting to exclude the file on the basis that anyone concerned about, or affected by, a patent should be entitled to rely on its contents without searching other records such as the prosecution file, as a matter of both principle and practicality. However, given that the contents of the file are publicly available (by virtue of article 128 EPC 2000) and (at least according to what we were told) are unlikely to be extensive, there will be occasions when justice may fairly be said to require reference to be made to the contents of the file. However, not least in the light of the wording of article 69 EPC 2000, which is discussed above, the circumstances in which a court can rely on the prosecution history to determine the extent of protection or scope of a patent must be limited.

88. While it would be arrogant to exclude the existence of any other circumstances, my current view is that reference to the file would only be appropriate where (i) the point at issue is truly unclear if one confines oneself to the specification and claims of the patent, and the contents of the file unambiguously resolve the point, or (ii) it would be contrary to the public interest for the contents of the file to be ignored. . . .

89. Turning to the second issue, I do not consider that the contents of the prosecution file in this case justify departing from the provisional conclusion expressed in para 75 above. It seems to me clear that the reason why the examiner considered that the claims in the patent should

be limited to pemetrexed disodium was because the teaching in the specification did not expressly extend to any other anti-folates. It is unnecessary to decide the issue, but, at least as at present advised, I am inclined to think that the examiner was wrong in taking that view. Indeed, in the course of his well-presented argument for Actavis, Mr Alexander QC seemed to accept that Lilly could have expressed its claims more widely than it did . . . However, even if the examiner was right or at least justified in taking the stance that he did, I do not consider that that consideration can have any bearing on the question whether any pemetrexed salts other than pemetrexed disodium should be within the scope of the patent pursuant to the doctrine of equivalents. The whole point of the doctrine is that it entitles a patentee to contend that the scope of protection afforded by the patent extends beyond the ambit of its claims as construed according to normal principles of interpretation. . . .

91. I draw comfort from the fact that neither party was able to refer to a case where a French or Spanish Court had relied upon the patentee's response to a disclosure or added matter objection by the examining officer as being relevant to the scope of claim. . . . I draw even greater comfort from the fact that the Bundesgerichtshof reached the same conclusion on this very issue in relation to the German equivalent of the Patent in this case in Case No X ZR 29/15 (*Eli Lilly v Actavis Group PTC*) . . .

Direct infringement in France, Italy and Spain

92. Having concluded that the Actavis products directly infringe the Patent as a matter of UK law, it is necessary to consider whether the same result obtains under French, Italian and Spanish law. In my judgment, direct infringement is established in those jurisdictions as well.

93. Turning first to French law, it appears to me that the answer to the question of direct infringement ultimately turns on whether the Patent in this case falls into the *moyens généraux* category or the *moyens particuliers* category, because, as discussed in para 46 above, the doctrine of equivalents is apparently only applicable to patent claims in the former category. With some diffidence, I have . . . concluded that the Patent in this case falls into the former category. . . .

94. The Judge considered that the Patent in this case represents a *moyen particulier*, because pemetrexed disodium was the relevant means and the Patent did not reveal it having a novel function: it merely revealed a new and better way in which its function could be achieved. To my mind the better analysis is that the Patent discloses that pemetrexed disodium could be used for a function for which it could not previously have been satisfactorily or safely used in practice; specifically, that pemetrexed disodium could be used with vitamin B12 to achieve an end which could not have been achieved by either chemical on its own, pemetrexed disodium because of its harmful side-effects and vitamin B12 because it would not have worked. The essential point, as I see it, is that

the Patent revealed for the first time the existence of a combined means which functioned in a certain way, namely to alleviate certain cancers without serious side-effects. It would be different if the overall function of the combination of the two chemicals had not been new.

95. Support for this conclusion appears in the book referred to in para 46 above, *Droit de la propriété industrielle*, whose two authors were the expert witnesses on French law in this case. At para 719, p 443, they wrote "when the claim is over a combination of means for which global function is novel, any combination of means with a different structure but achieving the same global function is a priori equivalent and thus infringing". . . .

97. So far as Spanish law is concerned, it is common ground that the Spanish courts have followed the United Kingdom approach, which leads to the difficult question whether one should assume that they would follow this decision in modifying the *Improver* questions and in particular the second question. I incline to the view that judicial comity would tend to suggest that the Spanish courts would follow this court in modifying the *Improver* questions, not least because this appears to render the UK courts and therefore the Spanish courts more consistent with the German and Dutch courts, and no more inconsistent with the French and Italian courts. . . .

102. Accordingly, I would hold that the French, Italian and Spanish designations of the Patent are also directly infringed by the Actavis products.

[The discussion of infringement under Italian law and discussion of indirect infringement are omitted.]

NOTES

1.   *The Scope of a Patent.* National rules on the scope of equivalents, if any, to be admitted in patent infringement litigation reflect some of the most fundamental assumptions about the purposes and limits of the patent grant. Historically, common law patent systems derived from the British Statute of Monopolies, 21 Jac. 1 C. 3 (1624), have inclined to keep the scope of equivalents relatively close to the literal patent claims. In part this reflects a wariness about monopolies—all that is not expressly claimed belongs to the public—and in part it reflects a concern for efficiency—ensuring competitors who closely studied a patent's claims, in order to avoid them, that their inventions will not later be ensnared by elements omitted from the claims. Civil law patent systems, by contrast, incline in the direction of liberally interpreting claims, to the point even of ignoring the claims and interpreting instead the general description of the invention. This tendency reflects an emphasis on equity over efficiency—rewarding the patentee for his inventive concept and curbing the competitor who would seek to escape by the deft circumvention of literal claims. This approach also vests greater confidence in courts than in patent offices as arbiters of the patent monopoly.

In a 2009 article the late Justice Laddie suggested that the protocol to the European Patent Convention "appears to settle for a compromise which involves finding an extent of protection which is somewhere between the scope which would be arrived at by a literal interpretation of the claims and the scope determined by a process which downgrades the function of the claims to mere guidelines. It is determining where that middle ground is which has led to the differences between national courts." Hugh Laddie, Kirin Amgen—The End of Equivalents in England?, 40(1) IIC 3, 7 (2009).

See generally, Daehwan Koo, Comparisons of the First Requirement of the Doctrine of Equivalents Between Korea and Japan, 44(2) IIC 178 (2013); Paul England, Towards A Single Pan-European Standard—Common Concepts in UK and "Continental European" Patent Law: Part 1: Scope of Patent Protection and Inventive Concept, 32(5) EIPR 195 (2010).

2. *Doctrine of Equivalents.* As is illustrated in the review of the English, French, and Spanish approaches in the *Actavis* decision, above, courts in different countries have developed different tests to assess equivalents. Are the approaches to the determination of the scope of a patent converging? In the United States, where the doctrine of equivalents has its roots in the 1850s, the doctrine of equivalents applies when a device "performs substantially the same function in substantially the same way to obtain the same result." Union Paper-Bag Machine Co. v. Murphy, 97 U.S. 120, 125 (1877).

In Japan the doctrine of equivalents was first recognized in the 1998 Japanese Supreme Court decision in *Ball Spline*. Five requirements must be met for the doctrine to apply:

1) The Part of the claim differing from the allegedly infringing product is not the essential part of the patented invention;

2) The purpose of the patented invention can still be achieved in the case of replacing this part, and an identical function and effect can be obtained;

3) A person of ordinary skill in the art could easily come up with the idea of such replacement at the time of the production of the product;

4) The product after the replacement is neither identical to the technology in the public domain nor could have been easily conceived by the person of ordinary skill in the art;

5) There were no special circumstances that the product had been intentionally excluded from the scope of the patent claim in the patent application process.

Johann Pitz, Atsushi Kawada, & Jeffrey A. Schwab, Patent Litigation in Germany, Japan and the United States (2015), p. 29.

In the decision concerning the German patent on pemetrexed, which Justice Neuberger mentions in paragraphs 84 and 91 of the *Actavis* decision, above, the German Federal Supreme Court clarified its jurisprudence concerning the doctrine of equivalents. Pemetrexed, Bundesgerichtshof, X ZR 29/15, 2016. Earlier cases had established that an infringement through an equivalent exists when (i) the embodiment solves the same problem as the invention and with the same effect, (ii) a person skilled in the art would consider the modified embodiment as having the same effect, and (iii) the person skilled in the art would consider the modified embodiment to be an equivalent solution. If the patentee made a selection between different embodiments during patent prosecution and included only one of the embodiments in its patent claims while mentioning the other embodiments only in the patent specification, the scope of the patent should not be interpreted to cover any embodiments not included in the patent claims. *Id.*, ¶ 52. In *Pemetrexed* the Court found that the general references in the patent specification to "anti-folates" did not amount to the disclosure of additional embodiments that was envisioned by the earlier decisions, and that there was no evidence that the patentee limited its claim to one embodiment in order to satisfy patentability requirements; the Court therefore concluded that the scope of the patent could have been extended to cover equivalents.

For the decisions on the national parallel patents on pemetrexed by courts in Switzerland and Italy see Eli Lilly and Co. v. Actavis Switzerland AG, Bundesgericht, 4A_208/2017, 2017; Eli Lily & Co. v. Fresenius Oncology PLC, Court of Milan, No. 45209/2017, 2018.

3. *The Scope of a Patent and Requirements of Patentability.* Is there a link between the scope of a patent and requirements of patentability? In the United Kingdom, a defendant in a patent infringement suit may raise a "*Gillette* defense," according to which no patent infringement will be found if interpreting the patent claims to cover the allegedly infringing product or method would result in the claims being so broad that a patent that included such claims would have been invalidated due to existing prior art. Gillette Safety Razor v. Anglo-American Trading, [1913] UKHL, 30 R.P.C. 465.

Does the defense apply when infringement is claimed not by equivalents but by literal means? In Germany, under the "*Formstein* defense," there can be no infringement if the product or method allegedly infringing by equivalents would not be patentable because of existing prior art. Formstein, Bundesgerichtshof, X ZR 28/85, 1986, 28 IIC 795 (1987). However, the *Formstein* defense is not available in cases of literal infringement. Luftkappensystem, Bundesgerichtshof, X ZR 74/14, 2015, ¶ 30, 47 IIC 843 (2016). In the United States, the U.S. Court of Appeals for the Federal Circuit explained that "a patentee should not be able to obtain, under the doctrine of equivalents, coverage which he could not lawfully have obtained from the PTO by literal claims." Wilson Sporting Goods v. David Geoffrey & Assoc., 904 F.2d 677, 684 (Fed.Cir. 1990), cert. denied.

4. *Bifurcated Versus Non-Bifurcated Patent Litigation Systems.* In the United States, infringement and validity issues may be assessed within one court proceeding, but other countries divide the tasks. Germany, for example, has a bifurcated patent litigation system in which patent validity is not adjudicated by infringement courts but by specialized patent courts. German courts operate on the presumption that the patent in suit is valid, and unless the presumption is defeated, the courts will adjudicate infringement—often long before the Federal Patent Court or (on appeal) the Federal Supreme Court decide whether or not the patent is valid. If the presumption is defeated in the infringement proceedings the courts will stay the infringement proceedings until a decision on validity is issued; however, such stays are apparently rarely granted.

In Italy, patent validity may be attacked either in the patent office or in court; in court, validity may be raised as a counterclaim in a patent infringement case or in a separate case concerning patent validity. In 2016 the Italian Supreme Court discontinued a long-standing practice when it held that a court that is hearing a patent infringement case must stay its proceedings if a separate validity case is pending. Panotec S.r.l. v. L.C.R. Macchine Automatiche S.r.l., Corte Suprema di Cassazione, 2016. One commentator observed that the change may encourage defendants—alleged infringers—to bifurcate patent cases. Agata Sobol, The Italian Supreme Court's Revirement on Bifurcated Cases . . ., 38(12) EIPR 765 (2016).

For analyses of the functioning of the systems in Japan, Germany, and the United States see Toshiko Takenaka, Merging Civil and Common Law Traditions in the Patent Validity Challenge System: Japanese Experiences, in Nourriture de l'Esprit: Festschrift für Dieter Stauder zum 70. Geburtstag (Horst-Petter Gotting & Claudia Schluter eds., 2011), p. 271; Peter Mes, Reflections on the German Patent Litigation System, in Patents and Technological Progress in a Globalized World, Liber Amicorum Joseph Straus (W. Prinz zu Waldeck und Pyrmont, M.J. Adelman, R. Brauneis, J. Drexl, R. Nack eds., 2009), 401.

5. *Post-Infringement Invalidity Findings.* One problem with bifurcated systems arises when infringement of a patent is found in the infringement proceedings and later the same patent is held invalid. Following the finding that the patent is invalid, the party that was held to be infringing must bring an action to set aside the earlier decision on infringement. In Germany, either the plaintiff will be estopped from executing the judgment from the earlier decision, or the defendant will be granted a retrial. Similarly, in Japan a retrial and an action for unjust enrichment (if infringement damages were paid or other infringement remedies effectuated) will be possible.

Even in non-bifurcated systems problems will arise when a patent is found invalid after it has been found to be infringed, and multiple patent validity proceedings can even be pending simultaneously. Non-bifurcated systems attempt to prevent at least some inconsistent results by setting the order in which certain types of challenges to patent validity may be launched by the same challenger. In India, for example, the Supreme Court ruled that a revocation petition takes precedence over a counterclaim of invalidity filed in a patent infringement suit if the petition is filed with the Intellectual Property Appellate Board before the infringement complaint is filed. However, a revocation petition may not be filed after a validity issue has been raised as a counterclaim in an infringement suit. Dr. Aloys Wobben v. Yogesh Mehra, Supreme Court, Civil Appeal No. 6718, June 2, 2014.

In the United States, a petitioner may not petition for an inter partes review or post grant review after the petitioner has filed a court action for a declaration of non-infringement. 37 C.F.R. 42.101(a) and 42.201(a). The petitioner also may not petition for an inter partes review more than one year after the petitioner has been served with a complaint of patent infringement. 37 C.F.R. 42.101(b). What should the rule be when the inter partes review is initiated by a third party and not the petitioner? In considering whether to stay the court proceedings, courts consider three factors: "(1) the impact of inter partes review, to include whether a stay would simplify the issues in question and streamline the trial; (2) how far the litigation has progressed . . . ; and (3) whether a stay would unduly prejudice or present a clear tactical disadvantage to the non-moving party." CANVS Corp. v. U.S., 118 Fed.Cl. 587, 592 (Fed.Cl. 2014).

In the member countries of the European Patent Organization, where the validity of a patent may be attacked in national courts, court decisions on the validity of the national patent stemming from the European patent may be in conflict with a later decision on validity rendered by the European Patent Office. English courts were reluctant to stay their proceedings in favor of validity proceedings before the European Patent Office. In Justice Jacob's words "one does not have to wait to find out who has won until the slowest horse in the race gets there." Unilin Beheer BV v. Berry Floor NV, [2007] EWCA Civ 364, ¶ 88. The U.K. Supreme Court changed the practice of English courts in *Virgin Atlantic Airways Ltd v. Zodiac Seats UK Ltd.*, at least with respect to cases in which courts have not yet awarded damages. [2013] UKSC 46, ¶¶ 35 and 36. In the decision Lord Sumption also said that English courts should stay their proceedings while validity proceedings are pending in the European Patent Office. *Id.*, ¶ 38.

For an analysis of conflicts between decisions on infringement and later decisions on invalidity see Katrin Cremers, Fabian Gaessler, Dietmar Harhoff & Christian Helmers, Invalid but Infringed? An Analysis of Germany's Bifurcated Patent Litigation System, Max Planck Institute for Innovation & Competition Research Paper No. 14-14, Aug. 1, 2014. For excellent introductions to comparative infringement litigation procedure, see Stuart J.H. Graham & Nicolas Van Zeebroeck, Comparing Patent Litigation across Europe: A First Look, 17 Stan. Tech. L. Rev. 655 (2014); David W. Hill, Patent Litigation in Japan, 1 Akron Int. Prop. J. 141 (2007); Jan Klink, Cherry Picking in Cross Border Infringement Actions: A Comparative Overview of German and U.K. Procedure and Practice, 26 EIPR 493 (2004).

Unwired Planet Intl. Ltd. v. Huawei Techn. Co. Ltd.

Court of Appeal (Civil Division).
[2018] EWCA Civ 2344.

LORD KITCHIN: . . .

2.   This appeal raises a number of important points of principle concerning the obligation upon the owner of a patent which protects a technology which its owner has declared to be essential to the implementation of one or more of the telecommunications standards such as 2G-GSM, 3G-UMTS and 4G-LTE. A patent of this kind is called a standard essential patent (a "SEP").

3. It is generally accepted that the publication of such a standard supports innovation and growth by ensuring the interoperability of the digital technologies to which it relates. It leads to an increase in the range and volume of products which meet the standard and it allows consumers to switch more easily between the products of different manufacturers. Standards are set by standard setting organisations ("SSOs"). SSOs bring together industry participants to evaluate technologies for inclusion in a new standard, encourage those participants to contribute their most advanced technologies to that standard and promote the standard once it has been agreed. There are various SSOs around the world and each of them operates in much the same way. The SSO with which these proceedings are most concerned is the European Telecommunications Standards Institute ("ETSI").

4. As the European Commission has recognised, SEPs can be of great value to their holders. These holders can expect a substantial revenue stream from their SEPs as the standard for which they are essential is implemented in products sold to millions of consumers. This revenue stream is supported by the fact that alternative technologies which do not meet the standard may well disappear from the market. But the potential for anti-competitive behaviour is obvious. The owner of a SEP has the potential ability to "hold-up" users after the adoption and publication of the standard either by refusing to license the SEP or by extracting excessive royalty fees for its use, and in that way to prevent competitors from gaining effective access to the standard and the part of the telecommunications market to which it relates. ETSI and other SSOs therefore require the owners of SEPs to give an irrevocable undertaking in writing that they are prepared to grant licences of their SEPs on fair, reasonable and non-discriminatory ("FRAND") terms. This undertaking is designed to ensure that any technology protected by a SEP which is incorporated into a standard is accessible to users of that standard on fair and reasonable terms and that its owner cannot impede the implementation of the standard by refusing to license it or by requesting unfair, unreasonable or discriminatory licence fees.

5. . . . [T]he negotiation of licences for SEPs on FRAND terms may be far from straightforward, however. The owner of a SEP may still use the threat of an injunction to try to secure the payment of excessive licence fees and so engage in hold-up activities. Conversely, the infringer may refuse to engage constructively or behave unreasonably in the negotiation process and so avoid paying the licence fees to which the SEP owner is properly entitled, a process known as "hold-out".

6. In these proceedings, the claimant ("UP International") sued the Huawei defendants (together "Huawei"), Samsung and Google for infringement of five SEPs in the UK. . . . [W]e are now concerned only with the proceedings against Huawei. The SEPs in issue formed part of a worldwide patent portfolio which UP International and its associated companies had acquired from Ericsson. UP International contended that

the five SEPs had been infringed and were essential, and that Huawei, having refused to take a FRAND licence, should be restrained by injunction from further infringement. Huawei responded that the SEPs were neither essential nor valid. It also raised defences and counterclaims based on breaches of competition law, aspects of which were founded upon the contention that UP International and its associated companies had not made an offer to license these patents on FRAND terms. . . .

The FRAND framework . . .

25. Article 4.1 of the ETSI IPR Policy requires members of ETSI to inform ETSI of any "ESSENTIAL" intellectual property right ("IPR") in a timely fashion. An ESSENTIAL IPR is defined as an IPR which is necessary from a technical perspective for the implementation of a standard. A SEP is necessarily an ESSENTIAL IPR. Once an ESSENTIAL IPR has been declared by its owner to ETSI then, irrespective of whether that owner is a member of ETSI, it will be requested by ETSI, pursuant to clause 6.1 of the ETSI IPR Policy, to give an irrevocable undertaking in writing that it is prepared to grant irrevocable licences on FRAND terms. . . .

26. It is important to mention four further points at this stage. First, an undertaking given to ETSI pursuant to clause 6.1 has international effect. This is because the standards supported by the ETSI undertaking are themselves of international effect so that businesses can make and supply, and members of the public can use, products which comply with the standard all over the world. To this end clause 6.2 provides that an undertaking given pursuant to clause 6.1 in respect of a member of a patent family shall apply to all existing and future ESSENTIAL IPRs of that patent family unless there is an explicit written exclusion of specified IPRs at the time the undertaking is given. . . .

27. Secondly, it was common ground at the trial that UP was bound in law to license its ESSENTIAL IPR on FRAND terms. The ETSI IPR Policy is governed by French law and the judge found (and there is no appeal against his finding) that the FRAND undertaking given by UP was binding upon UP and enforceable by Huawei and, indeed, any third party. The nature of that obligation did not mean that either UP or Huawei could be compelled to enter into a contract against its will, however. It meant that if UP refused to enter into a FRAND licence then the court could and normally should refuse to grant it relief for patent infringement. Conversely, if Huawei declined to enter into a FRAND licence then the relief available for infringement should normally follow.

28. Thirdly, there was no real dispute at trial as to how FRAND terms should be assessed, at least in general terms. . . . It was also agreed that it is appropriate to start by assessing a global rate, effectively as a benchmark, and then, if and so far as it may be necessary and appropriate to do so, to adjust it upwards to arrive at a UK rate.

29. Fourthly, one of the questions which arose before the judge was whether, for any given set of circumstances, there is only one FRAND rate and, by parity of reasoning, only one set of FRAND licence terms. The judge concluded that there is indeed only one set of terms, including one rate or set of rates, which are truly FRAND. . . .

Ground 1—global licensing . . .

The rival approaches

47. Counsel for Huawei submit that the obligation on the owner of a SEP is to be prepared to grant licences on FRAND terms. But they say there is nothing in the FRAND undertaking which either creates a global portfolio right or which alters the basic legal characteristics of a SEP which is a territorially limited intellectual property right.

48. Counsel for Huawei accept that SEP owners and implementers may negotiate a licence which suits their requirements in accordance with FRAND principles, and that such a licence will often be of worldwide scope. But, they continue, we are concerned with a different case for it is one in which UP elected to pursue Huawei in the UK and Germany before any negotiations could begin. In these circumstances the issue became one of national patent enforcement. A UK court can only properly determine the infringement and validity of UP's UK SEPs. . . .

52. We should say straight away that we accept without question that a UK SEP has limited territorial scope and that courts in this jurisdiction will generally only determine disputes concerning the infringement and validity of UK or EP UK patents. If a UK SEP is found valid and infringed, a UK court will only grant relief in respect of the infringement of that patent. As Aldous LJ explained in Coflexip SA v Stolt Comex [2001] RPC 9 at [18], the injunction must equate to the statutory right given; a right which has been held to have been validly granted and infringed. So the court will only grant an injunction to restrain infringement of the SEP in issue in the proceedings. The same applies to a claim for damages: they will only be awarded for infringement of that SEP.

53. The position in relation to a FRAND undertaking is rather different, however. As we have seen, ETSI is the SSO for the EU but its standards are of international effect. So too, the FRAND undertaking given by a patent owner to ETSI in return for the incorporation into the standard of the technology protected by the patent is also of international effect. It applies to all patents which belong to the same family irrespective of the territory in which they subsist. This is necessary to protect implementers whose equipment may be sold in a number of different jurisdictions and then used by members of the public who may travel with that equipment from one jurisdiction to another. These implementers must be able to use the technology embodied in and required by the standard provided they are prepared to pay a FRAND rate for doing so, for otherwise the owner of the relevant patent rights would be able to charge excessive licensing

fees. So any implementer must be able to secure a licence on FRAND terms under all the SEPs it needs to produce and market its products which meet the standard.

54. But there is another side to the coin which needs some elaboration at this point. Just as implementers need protection, so too do the SEP owners. They are entitled to an appropriate reward for carrying out their research and development activities and for engaging with the standardisation process, and they must be able to prevent technology users from free-riding on their innovations. It is therefore important that implementers engage constructively in any FRAND negotiation and, where necessary, agree to submit to the outcome of an appropriate FRAND determination.

55. It therefore comes as no surprise to us that Huawei accepts, through counsel, that, outside the litigation process, SEP owners and implementers will often negotiate a licence which best suits their respective needs in accordance with FRAND principles and further, that this licence will often be global or at least cover a number of different territories. It may be wholly impractical for a SEP owner to seek to negotiate a licence of its patent rights country by country, just as it may be prohibitively expensive for it to seek to enforce those rights by litigating in each country in which they subsist. . . .

56. In our judgment these considerations point strongly to the conclusion that, depending on all the relevant circumstances, a global licence between a SEP owner and an implementer may be FRAND. Indeed, on the face of it, it is very hard to see how a contrary view could be justified. Assuming such a licence is not discriminatory, it would be the product of two undertakings acting fairly and reasonably. What is more, it seems to us, at least as a matter of principle, that there may be circumstances in which it would not be fair and reasonable to expect a SEP owner to negotiate a licence or bring proceedings territory by territory and that in those circumstances only a global licence or at least a multi-territorial licence would be FRAND.

57. Now we must consider the position of a SEP owner who brings proceedings for infringement against an implementer in one jurisdiction in respect of the SEPs which it owns there and makes good its case. If we assume, as Huawei invites us to, that the defendant establishes that a willing licensor and a willing licensee in the position of the parties would agree a FRAND licence in respect of that jurisdiction but the SEP owner refuses to offer it such a licence then we agree that no injunction should be granted. If, on the other hand, the implementer refuses to enter into the FRAND licence for that jurisdiction then the SEP owner can properly seek an injunction to restrain further infringement.

58. This is only part of the picture, however. We must also consider the position on the basis that a willing licensor and a willing licensee in the position of the parties to the proceedings would agree a global FRAND licence, that such a licence would conform to industry practice and that

it would not be discriminatory. If the SEP owner were to refuse to grant such a licence to the implementer then once again it should be denied an injunction. If, on the other hand, the implementer were to refuse to enter into such a licence then, as a matter of principle, we think the SEP owner should be entitled to an injunction in that jurisdiction to restrain infringement of the particular SEPs in issue in those proceedings. Were the position otherwise then the SEP owner seeking to recover the FRAND licence monies for all of the SEPs in the same family from an uncooperative implementer who is acting unreasonably would be required to bring proceedings in every jurisdiction in which those rights subsist, which might be prohibitively expensive for it to do. This result would not involve any alteration of the territorially limited characteristics of any SEP; nor would it involve any jurisdictional expansionism. To the contrary, it would amount to a recognition by the court (i) that the SEP owner has complied with its undertaking to ETSI to offer a licence on FRAND terms; (ii) that the implementer has refused or declined to accept that offer without any reasonable ground for so doing; and (iii) that in these circumstances the SEP owner is entitled to the usual relief available for patent infringement including an injunction to restrain further infringement of the particular SEPs in issue in the proceedings.

83. It may be true that the approaches of courts around the world to the assessment of royalties under a worldwide licence are not at present wholly aligned but this is not surprising given the developing nature of this jurisdiction. . . .

84. Huawei's second point under this head is that the judge's approach necessarily and wrongly presumes infringement of at least some valid SEPs in territories other than the UK. It contends that a party that agrees to a global licence or the assessment of such a licence may have effectively consented to forgo its right to challenge the validity and essentiality of the patents owned by the prospective licensor. But a court ought not to compel a party to do so, particularly since it is well known that courts in different jurisdictions have different approaches to issues of infringement and validity and in any event do not always come to the same conclusion.

85. Counsel for Huawei have developed this point by focusing on the position in China and Germany. As for China, they say, entirely fairly, that UP only has five relevant SEP families in China and yet it is of critical importance to Huawei. It is not only Huawei's largest market but, in addition, it is where Huawei manufactures the products it sells in China and around the world, including territories where UP has no patent rights at all. Indeed, they continue, the total proportion of Huawei's sales in respect of which UP's claim to a royalty depends on infringement by manufacture or sale in China is about 64%; and correspondingly, if Huawei does not infringe any valid Chinese SEPs, there is no basis for demanding a royalty on those sales.

86. The same point can be made about Germany, argue Huawei's counsel. Thus far, the outcome of the proceedings in Germany is that UP has failed to establish infringement by Huawei of any German SEP for 4G. But the effect of the licence settled by the judge is that Huawei must pay licence fees for Germany at the rate the judge has determined. . . .

88. We do not accept that the judge's approach wrongly assumes validity and infringement of UP's foreign SEPs or that a licensee is required to forgo its right to challenge the validity and essentiality of those SEPs. To the contrary and as we have explained, the judge stated in terms that a FRAND licence should not prevent a licensee from challenging the validity and essentiality of licensed patents and should make provision for sales in non-patent countries. It is of course true that the licence provides for payment of royalties in respect of the use by Huawei of UP's whole portfolio of SEPs but the alternative would be to require UP to bring proceedings in each territory in which its SEPs subsist. That is not how a reasonable and willing licensor and licensee in the position of, respectively, UP and Huawei would behave; it would be a blue print for hold-out; and, as Mr Cheng[, the Deputy Director of Huawei's IP Department,] accepted, the costs of such litigation for UP would be prohibitively high. So the outcome would be that, as a result of its FRAND undertaking, UP would not be able to secure an injunction in any jurisdiction and would not be able to secure payment of royalties for those jurisdictions in which it could not afford to bring proceedings.

89. As for the position in China and Germany, we have no difficulty accepting that China is a territory of particular importance to Huawei and that Germany too is a significant market. But here it is important to have firmly in mind that the mechanism arrived at by the judge for dealing with the position in different countries is not challenged on this appeal. Counsel for UP helpfully summarised that mechanism in the following terms which we do not understand to be contentious:

i)   The royalty rate is tied to the country where Huawei sells its equipment.

ii)   The rate applicable will be at one of two levels (either at a higher or lower rate) which depends on the extent of patent protection in a given territory.

iii) China receives special treatment and the royalty rate is the lower tier regardless of the extent of patent protection in China.

iv)   Adjustments are made annually to which territories are in the upper and lower tiers to take account of any change in the patent landscape.

v)   Royalties are payable in respect of sales in territories where there are no patents at the lower (Chinese) rate because the equipment is manufactured in China.

90. We agree that the effect of the licence is that Huawei must pay royalties in respect of manufacture and sales in China and sales in

Germany in accordance with this mechanism. But this provides no foundation for the submission that the judge has erred in principle in deciding that a willing licensor and licensee in the position of the parties would have agreed a global licence. . . .

Does the judge's approach create significant practical problems?

100. Huawei contends that the judge's approach will lead to significant practical problems and inconsistencies and that many of these are illustrated by the global licence he has settled.

101. Counsel for Huawei have developed this contention as follows. In summary, they submit: if any court can set a global rate then there will be a race between the SEP owner and the implementer to choose what each perceives to be the most favourable jurisdiction, with the likelihood of anti-suit injunction applications; there may be a divided system with some courts settling global licences and others not; the position of the parties in relation to cross-licensing will become impossible; implementers may be faced with the threat of injunctions which effectively deprive them of their ability to defend their FRAND positions before the courts of the territories where the relevant SEPs subsist; courts will set rates for SEPs over which they have no jurisdiction; the judgment of a single court in a jurisdiction in which an implementer does not wish to litigate may create a res judicata as between it and the SEP owner in relation to the terms of a global licence, and this might be very unfair; SEP owners will be able to choose which SEPs to include in a global licence to be settled by the court as it suits them; and the judge's approach will increase the costs of implementers doing business in the UK. . . .

104. We do not find these arguments persuasive. The judge was required to determine the meaning and effect of the FRAND undertaking which UP had given and Huawei was seeking to enforce. That is what he proceeded to do. He found that, having regard to the parties and in all the circumstances of this case, UP's undertaking to ETSI would be met by offering Huawei a global licence in respect of all of its SEPs on the terms he settled. We do not accept that this approach is likely to cause any problems of a kind with which commercial courts around the world are not familiar or which might impact upon the meaning and effect of the undertaking UP has given to ETSI. It is true that a court in one country will decide, as between the parties, whether a global or multi-territorial licence is FRAND but that is inevitable and we see nothing unfair about it, and it most certainly does not deprive a licensee from challenging the validity and essentiality of the SEPs in any jurisdiction where it may choose to do so. . . .

Conclusion on ground 1

129. The judge was entitled to find that in all the circumstances only a global licence would be FRAND. He fell into error in one aspect of his

reasoning but this had no material effect on the conclusion to which he came. Ground one must therefore be dismissed.[*]

Overall conclusion

291. For all of the reasons we have given, this appeal must be dismissed.

NOTES

1. *Global Enforcement.* In *Unwired Planet* the values of efficiency, expediency, and judicial economy appear to drive the court's decision to adjudicate the global dispute and set global FRAND licensing fees. Should comity and respect for the sovereignty of foreign countries have played a role in the court's decision? What is the greater affront to another country's sovereignty—to adjudicate the validity of its patents or to set licensing fees for the country's patents, irrespective of whether the patents are valid? Does the judgment preempt the courts of other countries from adjudicating the validity and infringement of their own national patents that form the same standard and are covered by the English judgment?

If only one court should adjudicate a global FRAND license, what country's court should do the adjudicating? In Huawei Tech. v. Conversant Wireless Licensing S.A.R.L., [2019] EWCA Civ 38, Conversant, a Luxembourg company that is a part of a Canadian group managed from the United States, sued Huawei and ZTE, two telecommunications groups based in China, for infringement of Conversant's SEPs. Huawei argued that the English court should have dismissed the case based on *forum non conveniens*; Huawei pointed out that China was an available forum and that a license set by a Chinese court with reference to Conversant's Chinese patents "could in fact be global because the Chinese patents were controlling in the place of manufacture." *Id.*, ¶ 59. The English court disagreed; Lord Justice Floyd explained that the disputes before the English and Chinese courts were not identical, as they concerned the patents of different countries, and he rejected Huawei's characterization of the claim at issue as "one for enforcement of a global portfolio right," concluding that "[n]o such right exists." *Id.*, ¶ 103.

Could the SSO's IPR Policy set the venue and applicable law for any SEP disputes concerning FRAND undertakings made under the Policy? Would such a forum selection clause, and choice-of-law clause, be binding upon third parties seeking to obtain a FRAND license from an SEP owner?

2. *Judicial Competition.* Notwithstanding Lord Justice Kitchin's conclusion in *Unwired Planet*, will the approach taken by his court with respect to SEP disputes inevitably lead to the race to court that Huawei's counsel predicted in *Unwired Planet*? In *Huawei v. Conversant* Lord Justice Floyd noted that a Chinese court had already invalidated seven of the eleven patents in Conversant's Chinese patent portfolio. *Id.*, ¶ 12.

Will SEP disputes result in competing antisuit injunctions by courts that target parties' conduct in each other's proceedings? In 2016, Huawei

---

[*] The discussions of Ground 2 concerning non-discrimination and Ground 3 concerning the abuse of dominant position are omitted. *Ed.*

filed suit against Samsung in the U.S. District Court for the Northern District of California for infringements of Huawei's U.S. patents on 4G LTE technology, and the next day Huawei filed another suit in the Intermediate People's Court of Shenzhen for infringements of Huawei's parallel Chinese patents. The Shenzhen court held that Samsung infringed Huawei's patents and issued an injunction prohibiting Samsung from manufacturing and selling its 4G LTE smartphones in China. In the space of a week, Samsung both appealed the Shenzhen court decision in China and filed a motion in the U.S. court for an antisuit injunction to enjoin Huawei from enforcing the Shenzhen Court order in China.

The U.S. court granted the antisuit injunction. The court considered the issues in the two litigations not as identical, but "functionally the same" because the parallel patents were part of Huawei's global portfolio of patents that were subject to the same obligation that required Huawei to license them on FRAND terms, and both parties asserted breach of contract claims in both countries. Huawei Technologies, Co., Ltd. v. Samsung Electronics Co., Ltd., 2018 WL 1784065, *1–2 (N.D.Cal. 2018). The U.S. court concluded that other factors also weighed in favor of the antisuit injunction, including the injunction's impact on comity, which the court described as "tolerable" and "negligible" because the U.S. action preceded the Chinese action, even if only by one day, and the antisuit injunction was to be in effect only until the U.S. court made its own decision on the merits. In February 2019 the parties agreed to settle the dispute.

3. *Monetary Remedies.* In *Unwired Planet* the lower-court judge concluded that there can be only one FRAND license. However, remedies awarded in patent cases may vary among countries; Part III of the TRIPs Agreement, prescribing minimum remedies for intellectual property cases, leaves room for differences in the administration of remedies by WTO member countries. These differences may not only offset the substantive harmonization achieved by other provisions of the Agreement; they may also affect a patent litigant's preference for one national forum over another.

Following U.S. industry complaints about the relatively modest damage awards granted under the Japanese Patent Act, section 102 of the Act, dealing with computation of damages, was amended in 1998 to increase the recovery possible under the "reasonable royalty" measures of damages and to provide for recovery of lost profits, requiring a prevailing patentee only to prove its own profits, the number of infringing products, and its capacity to make the lost sales itself. *See* Toshiko Takenaka, Recent Legislative Updates in Japan, 6 CASRIP Newsletter 11 (Summer 1999). *See* also, Thomas F. Cotter, Comparative Patent Remedies (2013); Toshiko Takenaka, Patent Infringement Damages in Japan and the United States: Will Enhanced Patent Infringement Damage Awards Revive Japanese Economy? 2 Wash. U. J. L. & Policy 309 (2000).

4. *Injunctions.* As discussed in note 5 on page 554, above, U.S. courts may decline to issue an injunction, even if a patent is valid and infringed, if the four factors weigh against the issuance of the injunction. As opposed to the U.S. courts, German courts have no discretion to refuse to issue a permanent injunction if they find a patent valid and infringed. Even in Germany, however, circumstances can arise in which courts may decline to issue or enforce an injunction in a patent infringement case; for example, a court may conclude that a patent owner forfeited its rights by not acting against an infringement for an extended period, or an infringer may raise the competition law defense (see the *Huawei v. ZTE* decision, above).

Is the denial of injunctive relief to a patent owner whose patent was infringed compatible with the TRIPs Agreement? Article 44(1) requires that countries' "judicial authorities . . . have the authority to order a party to desist from an infringement," and Article 44(2) maintains that the conditions in Article 31 must be complied with in cases when injunctive relief is denied. One commentator noted that, at least in some cases, the refusal of an injunction under U.S. law "while in line with the weak language of Art. 44 of the TRIPs Agreement will in substance amount to a new kind of compulsory licence, which would violate the letter (and the spirit) of Art. 31 of the TRIPs Agreement." Alexander von Muhlendahl, Enforcement of Intellectual Property Rights—Is Injunctive Relief Mandatory?, 38(4) IIC 377, 380 (2007).

For a comparative discussion of injunctions see Christoph Rademacher, Injunctive Relief in Patent Cases in the US, Germany and Japan: Recent Developments and Outlook, in Intellectual Property in Common Law and Civil Law (Toshiko Takenaka ed., 2013), pp. 325–346.

5.   *Territorial Scope of Patent Remedies.* Does the territorial scope of remedies strictly correspond to the territorial scope of the right, as suggested in *Unwired Planet* at ¶ 52? In so-called *kort geding* proceedings, Dutch courts have granted a form of interim relief to enjoin alleged patent infringements occurring inside, as well as outside, the Netherlands. The remedy is essentially pan-European, implicating Article 36 of the Brussels Regulation I (recast), which makes a judgment rendered in one member state enforceable in all other states.

In the United States, the Court of Appeals for the Federal Circuit held that "[a]n injunction [. . .] can reach extraterritorial activities [. . .], even if these activities do not themselves constitute infringement," as long as the injunction is designed to "prevent infringement of a United States patent." Johns Hopkins University v. CellPro, Inc., 152 F.3d 1342, 1366–1367 (Fed. Cir. 1998). Could U.S. courts award damages to cover an infringer's sales outside the United States if the sales stemmed from a predicate act of infringement in the United States? In light of the U.S. Supreme Court decision in *WesternGeco*, discussed in note 6 on page 11, above, is the availability of such remedies limited to cases of patent infringement under section 271(f) of the Patent Act? *See* Power Integrations, Inc. v. Fairchild Semiconductor Intern., Inc., D.Del., No. 04-1371-LPS (Oct. 4, 2018).

6.   *Importation and Customs Measures.* TRIPs Article 28 introduced at the international level the right to prevent the importation of a patented invention. Under TRIPs Article 50(1)(a), judicial authorities have the authority to grant provisional measures to prevent the importation of infringing goods. Additionally, under TRIPs Article 51, national customs authorities may suspend the release of goods if the right holder "has valid grounds for suspecting" that the goods are infringing the right holder's intellectual property rights; however, Article 51 does not mandate that countries provide for the suspension of goods by customs with regard to patent infringing goods. What are the reasons for treating pirated copyrighted goods and counterfeit trademarked goods, for which border measures under TRIPs are mandatory, differently from patent infringing goods?

Free trade in goods may be impaired if countries permit patent holders to stop goods in transit. Is it a barrier to "legitimate trade" if country A's authorities seize goods that are being shipped from country B to country C through country A if the goods are legally produced and distributed in B and C but patent-infringing in country A? Under TRIPs Article 41, enforcement "procedures shall be applied in such a manner as to avoid the creation of barriers to legitimate trade." What is the difference between legal and legitimate trade? *See* Matthew Kennedy, Avoiding Barriers to Legitimate Trade: Objectives and Obligations, in Intellectual Property Rights as Obstacles to Legitimate Trade? (Christopher Heath et al. eds. 2018), pp. 3–30.

In 2008 and 2009 Dutch customs authorities seized several consignments of generic drugs that were being shipped from India to Brazil and other South American countries. The consignments were destroyed, returned to India, or in a few instances allowed to proceed to the countries of their destination, but with a substantial delay. India and Brazil filed requests for consultations with the WTO; India argued, inter alia, that TRIPs and the Doha Declaration should be interpreted to require that "the rights conferred on the owner of a patent cannot be extended to interfere with the freedom of transit of generic drugs lawfully manufactured within, and exported from, India." European Union and a Member State—Seizure of Generic Drugs in Transit, WT/DS408/1, May 19, 2010, p. 3.

The disputes became moot when the Court of Justice of the European Union held in 2011 that goods in pure transit through the European Union are not to be deemed to infringe intellectual property rights in the European Union. However, the Court explained that intellectual property rights "may be infringed where, during their placement under a suspensive procedure in the customs territory of the European Union, or even before their arrival in that territory, goods coming from non-member States are the subject of a commercial act directed at European Union consumers, such as a sale, offer for sale or advertising." Koninklijke Philips Electronics NV v. Lucheng Meijing Industrial Company Ltd., CJEU, C-446/09, 2011, ¶ 59.

For detailed discussions of the problems involving seizures of patent infringing goods and seizures of goods in transit see Christopher Heath, Customs Seizures, Transit and Trade—In Honour of Dieter Stauder's 70th Birthday, IIC 381 (2010); Shashank P. Kumar, Border Enforcement of Intellectual Property Rights Against In-Transit Generic Pharmaceuticals: An Analysis of Character and Consistency, 32(10) EIPR 506 (2010). For further developments in the EU law on transit in the trademark law context see page 735, below.

C. TRADEMARKS AND GEOGRAPHICAL INDICATIONS

Guild practices requiring craftsmen to affix production marks to their goods may be the most direct precursor of modern trademark laws, ensuring honesty and consistency in indications of the source of goods. But even before the guilds, merchants used marks to indicate the ownership or source of goods. Archaeologists have unearthed Greek vases of the fifth and sixth centuries B.C. bearing the potter's mark, and merchants in the Middle Ages affixed distinctive marks to their goods before shipment to identify them in the event of shipwreck or piracy.

Systematic legal protection of trademarks in the common law world began to take shape in the early years of the nineteenth century. The starting point was the common law of deceit, from which courts in both England and the United States gradually evolved a distinct tort of "passing off" under which the plaintiff would prevail if it could prove that defendant had used its mark to deceive consumers into thinking that plaintiff was the source of defendant's goods. Intent to deceive was the gravamen of passing off and remains so today in unfair competition cases in which the plaintiff's symbol is descriptive or otherwise nondistinctive. Over time, in cases where the plaintiff's symbol was arbitrary or otherwise highly distinctive, courts began to relax the required proof of fraudulent intent; the fact that defendant copied a distinctive mark was itself evidence of intent to deceive. Courts eventually came to categorize disputes over distinctive symbols as trademark infringement cases rather than unfair competition cases and conclusively removed any requirement that fraudulent intent be proved. The next step was for the legislature—in 1862 in England and 1870 in the United States—to provide a registry for such trademarks and to extend discrete rights and remedies for registered marks.

Unfair competition principles in civil law countries evolved out of the Civil Code and the evolution was more gradual and episodic than in the common law countries. In countries like France, where close analogues existed in the Code, courts developed rules against unfair competition with relative speed and completeness; in countries like Germany, with no comparably close Code provisions, the development was slower. In some civil law countries legislatures supplemented unfair competition protection with specific provisions covering trade names and geographic indications of origin. Unlike unfair competition law, civil law protection for trademarks closely paralleled developments in the common law countries, and by the end of the nineteenth century all the economically important countries on the European continent, as well as many in Latin America, had adopted trademark registration statutes.

Differences in national rules on trademark formalities, procedures and rights—not only between civil law and common law countries, but also between countries within each tradition—disrupted cross-border trade and effectively discriminated against foreigners. Also, reciprocity was the governing norm for trademark relations between countries. Country *A* would often condition protection of marks first used and acquired in Country *B*, on reciprocity of protection between Country *B* and Country *A*.

The 1883 Paris Convention for the Protection of Industrial Property materially reduced discrepant international treatment of trademarks by establishing priorities and prescribing protection for famous marks; it also required member countries of the Paris Union to ensure effective protection against unfair competition. The United States adhered to the Paris Convention in 1887, but declined to sign the 1891 Madrid Agreement Concerning the International Registration of Marks, which aims at harmonizing and rationalizing trademark registration procedures, principally because of its disadvantages for U.S. applicants. (The reasons for the decision not to join the Madrid Agreement stem in significant part from the relatively lengthy trademark examination period in the United States and the relative vulnerability of registered marks to cancellation.) However, after initial opposition, the United States did adhere to the 1989 Protocol to the Madrid Agreement, which materially reduced the disadvantages to American applicants. The Protocol first came into effect in the United States on November 2, 2003. The Madrid Agreement and Protocol are discussed at page 667, below.

The Trademark Law Treaty, aimed at harmonizing application and registration procedures, was ratified by the United States in June, 1998 and implemented by the Trademark Law Treaty Implementation Act, P.L. 105–330 (Oct. 30, 1998). The United States signed the Trademark Registration Treaty in 1973, but has not yet ratified it. (The treaty entered into force in 1980.) The Singapore Treaty on the Law of Trademarks, adopted by WIPO member states in 2006, mirrors the Trademark Law Treaty but extends the international framework for application and registration procedures to all types of marks that might be registered under the law of a contracting state. It also addresses the possibilities of electronic communications with trademark offices. The United States ratified the Treaty in 2008 and it has been in force since March 16, 2009. The Trademark Law Treaty, the Trademark Registration Treaty, and the Singapore Treaty on the Law of Trademarks are discussed at page 669, below.

Under the European Union Trademark system, which has been in effect since April 1, 1996, only a single application need be made in the designated registry in Alicante, Spain, to obtain a European Union trademark (formerly a Community trademark); the resulting registration can be enforced throughout the countries of the European Union. The significant efficiencies of the EU trademark can be of benefit to EU trademark owners who are based in the United States, as well as to EU trademark owners based in European Union countries. The EU trademark is discussed at page 669, below. The EU trademark system did not replace the national trademark regimes in the European Union, which have been harmonized since 1989 by EU directives and which co-exist with the EU trademark system.

International trademark norms are incorporated in the TRIPs Agreement through Article 2(1)'s imposition of the Paris Convention's normative provisions on member countries, and through specific new norms added in Articles 15–21 respecting trademark subject matter, conditions for protection, rights and term of protection. Articles 22–24 introduce important rules on geographical indications. Part III of the TRIPs Agreement concerns measures of enforcement of intellectual property rights, including trademarks.

The Internet poses new challenges for the protection of trademarks. Conflicts over the use of trademarks in Internet domain names and in meta tags, keywords, and adwords used on websites evidence the struggle of trademark owners to protect their rights against infringers and suggest a need to find reasonable resolutions to conflicts among rights arising from territorially-limited trademarks that exist under different national and regional laws and seek to coexist with each other on the Internet.

Bibliographic Note. See generally, Stephen Ladas, Patents, Trademarks, and Related Rights: National and International Protection (1975); Alexander von Mühlendahl et al., Trade Mark Law in Europe (3d ed. 2016); Graeme Dinwoodie, Territorial Overlaps in Trademark Law: The Evolving European Model, 92 Notre Dame L. Rev. 1669 (2017); Guide to the International Registration of Marks under the Madrid Agreement and the Madrid Protocol, WIPO (2018).

For a superb study of the evolution of trademark law from its earliest origins, see Frank Schechter, The Historical Foundations of the Law Relating to Trade-Marks (1925). *See* also, John Burrell, Two Hundred Years of English Trademark Law, and Beverly Pattishall, Two Hundred Years of American Trademark Law, in American Bar Association, Two Hundred Years of English and American Patent, Trademark and Copyright Law 35, 51 (1977).

1. TERRITORIAL REACH OF TRADEMARK LAW

McBee v. Delica Co., Ltd.
United States Court of Appeals for the First Circuit, 2005.
417 F.3d 107, 75 U.S.P.Q.2d 1609.

LYNCH, CIRCUIT JUDGE.

It has long been settled that the Lanham Act can, in appropriate cases, be applied extraterritorially. *See Steele v. Bulova Watch Co.,* 344 U.S. 280, 73 S.Ct. 252, 97 L.Ed. 319 (1952). This case, dismissed for lack of subject matter jurisdiction, requires us, as a matter of first impression for this circuit, to lay out a framework for determining when such extraterritorial use of the Lanham Act is proper.

In doing so, we choose not to adopt the formulations used by various other circuits. *See, e.g., Reebok Int'l, Ltd. v. Marnatech Enters.,* 970 F.2d 552, 554–57 (9th Cir. 1992); *Vanity Fair Mills v. T. Eaton Co.,* 234 F.2d 633, 642–43 (2d Cir. 1956). The best-known test, the *Vanity Fair* test, asks (1) whether the defendant is an American citizen, (2) whether the defendant's actions have a substantial effect on United States commerce, and (3) whether relief would create a conflict with foreign law. . . . These three prongs are given an uncertain weight. Based on *Steele* and subsequent Supreme Court case law, we disaggregate the three prongs of the *Vanity Fair* test, identify the different types of "extraterritorial" application questions, and isolate the factors pertinent to subject matter jurisdiction.

Our framework asks first whether the defendant is an American citizen; that inquiry is different because a separate constitutional basis for jurisdiction exists for control of activities, even foreign activities, of an American citizen. Further, when the Lanham Act plaintiff seeks to enjoin sales in the United States, there is no question of extraterritorial application; the court has subject matter jurisdiction.

In order for a plaintiff to reach foreign activities of foreign defendants in American courts, however, we adopt a separate test. We hold that subject matter jurisdiction under the Lanham Act is proper only if the complained-of activities have a substantial effect on United States commerce, viewed in light of the purposes of the Lanham Act. If this "substantial effects" question is answered in the negative, then the court lacks jurisdiction over the defendant's extraterritorial acts; if it is answered in the affirmative, then the court possesses subject matter jurisdiction.

We reject the notion that a comity analysis is part of subject matter jurisdiction. Comity considerations, including potential conflicts with foreign trademark law, are properly treated as questions of whether a court should, in its discretion, decline to exercise subject matter jurisdiction that it already possesses. Our approach to each of these issues is in harmony with the analogous rules for extraterritorial application of the antitrust laws. *See Hartford Fire Ins. Co. v. California,* 509 U.S. 764, 795–99, 113 S.Ct. 2891, 125 L.Ed.2d 612 (1993).

The plaintiff, Cecil McBee, an American citizen and resident, seeks to hold the defendant, Delica Co., Ltd. (Delica), responsible for its activities in Japan said to harm McBee's reputation in both Japan and the United States and for Delica's purported activities in the United States. McBee is a well-known American jazz musician; Delica is a Japanese corporation that adopted the name "Cecil McBee" for its adolescent female clothing line. McBee sued for false endorsement and dilution under the Lanham Act. The district court dismissed all of McBee's Lanham Act claims, concluding that it lacked subject matter jurisdiction. . . .

We affirm, albeit on different reasoning. We conclude that the court lacked jurisdiction over McBee's claims seeking (1) an injunction in the United States barring access to Delica's Internet website, which is written in Japanese, and (2) damages for harm to McBee due to Delica's sales in Japan. McBee has made no showing that Delica's activities had a substantial effect on United States commerce. As to McBee's claim for (3) an injunction barring Delica from selling its goods in the United States, we hold that the district court had jurisdiction but conclude that this claim is without merit because the only sales Delica has made into the United States were induced by McBee for purposes of this litigation, and there is no showing that Delica plans on selling into the United States again.

I.

The relevant facts are basically undisputed. McBee, who lives in both Maine and New York, is a jazz bassist with a distinguished career spanning over forty-five years. He has performed in the United States and worldwide, has performed on over 200 albums, and has released six albums under his own name (including in Japan). He won a Grammy Award in 1989, was inducted into the Oklahoma Jazz Hall of Fame in 1991, and teaches at the New England Conservatory of Music in Boston. McBee has toured Japan several times, beginning in the early 1980s, and has performed in many major Japanese cities, including Tokyo. He continues to tour in Japan. McBee has never licensed or authorized the use of his name to anyone, except of course in direct connection with his musical performances, as for example on an album. In his own words, he has sought to "have [his] name associated only with musical excellence."

Delica is a Japanese clothing retailer. In 1984, Delica adopted the trade name "Cecil McBee" for a line of clothing and accessories primarily marketed to teen-aged girls. Delica holds a Japanese trademark for "Cecil McBee," in both Japanese and Roman or English characters, for a variety of product types. Delica owns and operates retail shops throughout Japan under the brand name "Cecil McBee"; these are the only stores where "Cecil McBee" products are sold. There are no "Cecil McBee" retail shops outside of Japan. Delica sold approximately $23 million worth of "Cecil McBee" goods in 1996 and experienced steady growth in sales in subsequent years; in 2002, Delica sold $112 million worth of "Cecil McBee" goods.

Delica puts out a "style book" or catalog that includes pictures and descriptions of the products in its "Cecil McBee" line; this style book is written in Japanese with some English words for effect. The style book is available in Japan at the retail stores and in certain other locations; sometimes it is included with shipped packages of "Cecil McBee" products. The style book contains telephone and fax numbers which allow a customer to order "Cecil McBee" merchandise from another company, Opus M. Co., Ltd., and have it shipped directly to the customer. Opus M. Co. buys the goods from Delica for this purpose, and then uses yet another company, Hamasho Co., Ltd., to do the shipping. It is undisputed that Hamasho Co. has never shipped any "Cecil McBee" goods outside of Japan. As described later, Delica's policy generally is to decline orders from the United States.

Delica operates a website, http://www.cecilmcbee.net, which contains pictures and descriptions of "Cecil McBee" products, as well as locations and telephone numbers of retail stores selling those products. The website is created and hosted in Japan, and is written almost entirely in Japanese, using Japanese characters (although, like the style book, it contains some English words). The website contains news about the "Cecil McBee" line, including promotions. Customers can log onto the site to access their balance of bonus "points" earned for making past "Cecil McBee" purchases, as well as information about how to redeem those points for additional merchandise. However, the site does not allow purchases of "Cecil McBee" products to be made online. The website can be viewed from anywhere in the Internet-accessible world.

McBee produced evidence that, when searches on Internet search engines (such as Google) are performed for the phrase "Cecil McBee," Delica's website (www.cecilmcbee.net) generally comes up as one of the first few results, and occasionally comes up first, ahead of any of the various websites that describe the musical accomplishments of the plaintiff. Certain other websites associated with Delica's "Cecil McBee" product line also come up when such searches are performed; like www.cecilmcbee.net, it is evident from the search results page that these websites are written primarily in Japanese characters.

In 1995, plaintiff McBee became aware that Delica was using his name, without his authorization, for a line of clothing in Japan. He contacted an American lawyer, who advised him that Delica was unlikely to be subject to personal jurisdiction in the United States. McBee retained a Japanese attorney, who sent a letter to Delica asking it to cease using the "Cecil McBee" name. When Delica declined, McBee petitioned the Japanese Patent Office to invalidate Delica's English-language trademark on "Cecil McBee."

On February 28, 2002, the Japanese Patent Office ruled Delica's trademark in Japan invalid. However, Delica appealed to the Tokyo High Court, which on December 26, 2002, vacated the decision of the Japanese Patent Office. On remand, the Japanese Patent Office found for Delica and reinstated Delica's registration of the "Cecil McBee" trademark. McBee appealed that ruling to the Tokyo High Court and lost; the trademark reinstatement has become final.[1]

---

[1]   The Japanese courts' rationale for finding in favor of Delica was (1) while Japanese law protects a person's full name from exploitation, McBee's full name, including his middle name, was "Cecil Leroy McBee," and thus the "Cecil McBee" line of products was not an exact copy of McBee's full name; and (2) McBee received no protection for the abbreviated version of his name, "Cecil McBee," because the name had not received sufficient recognition in general Japanese society.

In early 2002, Delica formulated a policy not to sell or ship "Cecil McBee" brand products to the United States and informed its managers throughout the company. Delica's admitted reason for this policy was to prevent McBee from being able to sue Delica in the United States.

McBee was beginning to consider just such a strategy. From December 2001 through early 2003, McBee retained three Japanese-speaking investigators to attempt to purchase "Cecil McBee" products from Delica and have them shipped to Maine. They met with mixed success. One initially, in December 2001, contacted the webmaster of http://www.cecilmcbee.net by email, asking about certain jewelry displayed on the website; that webmaster referred the investigator to the "Cecil McBee" retail shops in Japan for further information, but noted that at that time only domestic shipping was available.

The investigators then used the telephone numbers on the http://www.cecilmcbee.net website to contact various "Cecil McBee" retail stores in Japan directly. The investigators made it clear that they were residents of the United States inquiring about purchasing "Cecil McBee" goods. When the investigators requested an opportunity to buy merchandise and have it shipped to them in Maine, some stores stated that this could not be done, some of the stores worked out an arrangement whereby they would ship to an address in Japan but the investigator would then arrange to have the products forwarded to Maine, and some of the stores, at various times, shipped directly to the investigators in Maine. The total value of "Cecil McBee" merchandise purchased by these three investigators—including both goods shipped directly to Maine by Delica and goods shipped via the indirect method—was approximately $2,500. As counsel for McBee has conceded, there is no evidence of any other "Cecil McBee" sales by Delica to the United States.

Further, there is virtually no evidence of "Cecil McBee" brand goods entering the United States after being sold by Delica in Japan. McBee stated in affidavit that "[f]riends, fellow musicians, fans, students, and others . . . have reported seeing [his] name on clothing, shopping bags [and] merchandise (whether worn or carried by a young girl walking on the street in Boston or New York or elsewhere). . . ." But no further evidence or detail of these sightings in the United States was provided. McBee also provided evidence that Cecil McBee goods have occasionally been sold on eBay, an auction website that allows bids to be placed and items sold anywhere in the world. Most of the sellers were not located in the United States, and there is no evidence that any of the items were purchased by American buyers. . . .

II.

McBee's complaint, filed October 1, 2002, alleged trademark dilution and unfair competition claims under the Lanham Act as well as various pendent Maine state law claims. McBee requested injunctive relief, damages, and attorney's fees. The core of McBee's Lanham Act claims is false endorsement: that the unlicensed use of his name has "made a misleading and false inference" that McBee endorses, approves, or sponsors Delica's product, and that inference has caused McBee harm. . . .

Delica first moved to dismiss the complaint, under Fed.R.Civ.P. 12(b)(2), on the ground that the Maine federal district court lacked personal jurisdiction over it. A magistrate judge recommended that the motion be denied, emphasizing the existence of Delica's website and the $2,500 in sales to McBee's investigators in Maine; the district court adopted the magistrate judge's recommendation on July 9, 2003. Discovery proceeded. Delica then moved to dismiss McBee's complaint under Fed.R.Civ.P. 12(b)(1), asserting that the court lacked subject matter jurisdiction over McBee's Lanham Act claims because Delica's actions constituted extraterritorial conduct outside the ambit of the Act. Delica also moved for summary judgment under Fed.R.Civ.P. 56 based on laches, collateral estoppel due to the Japanese court decision against McBee, and various merits issues, including McBee's alleged failure to make a sufficient showing of likelihood of confusion to sustain his Lanham Act claims. McBee opposed but not on grounds of insufficient discovery, nor did he file a Rule 56(f) affidavit.

The magistrate judge issued a recommended decision on these motions on August 19, 2004. . . . On the subject matter jurisdiction question, the magistrate judge first noted that the Supreme Court had held, in *Steele v. Bulova Watch Co.,* 344 U.S. 280 (1952), that the Lanham Act could, in some circumstances, be applied to reach extraterritorial conduct. . . . The magistrate judge also noted that this circuit has never laid out a test for when such extraterritorial application is appropriate. . . . The magistrate judge thus utilized the test stated by the Second Circuit in *Vanity Fair Mills, Inc. v. T. Eaton Co.,* 234 F.2d 633, 642 (2d Cir. 1956), described earlier. However, the magistrate judge accepted the Fifth Circuit's modification of the first prong in *Am. Rice, Inc. v. Arkansas Rice Growers Co-op. Ass'n,* 701 F.2d 408, 414 n. 8 (5th Cir. 1983), and required a showing of only "some" effect on United States commerce. . . . The magistrate judge recommended that all of McBee's Lanham Act claims for injunctive relief be dismissed because they failed two of the three *Vanity Fair* factors, but that all of his Lanham Act damages claims be allowed to go forward because they met two prongs of the test. . . .

Delica filed an objection, arguing that all of McBee's Lanham Act claims—and not just those claims requesting injunctive relief—failed the *Vanity Fair* test for extraterritorial application. McBee moved that the recommended decision be modified. He conceded that American courts had no extraterritorial jurisdiction to enjoin sales that occurred in Japan, but argued that there was jurisdiction for his damages claim against those sales. McBee also stated that he sought an injunction against Delica's sales of "Cecil McBee" goods in the United States and against

Delica's use of the "Cecil McBee" website to reach United States consumers; these forms of relief, he argued, did not constitute extraterritorial applications of the Lanham Act at all and therefore the court should assert subject matter jurisdiction over them.

The district court amended the magistrate judge's recommended decision by holding that it lacked subject matter jurisdiction over all of McBee's Lanham Act claims, including both those for injunctive relief and damages. . . . The district court, like the magistrate judge, applied essentially the test laid out by the Second Circuit in *Vanity Fair*. . . . But the district court disagreed with the magistrate judge's application of that test, finding that a claim for damages, like a claim for injunctive relief, would create a conflict with Japanese trademark law. . . . Finding two of the three factors unsatisfied, the court ordered McBee's Lanham Act claims dismissed for lack of subject matter jurisdiction without considering the effect of Delica's actions on United States commerce. . . . With respect to this factor, however, the court noted that Delica's only sales into the United States "appear to have been made for purposes of this lawsuit alone." . . . After dismissing McBee's Lanham Act claims, the court declined to exercise supplemental jurisdiction over his pendent state law claims. . . . This made it unnecessary for the court to consider Delica's summary judgment motion on other bases.

On appeal, McBee renews his argument that his claims for a domestic injunction, both against Delica's sales into the United States and against its broadcasting of its website in the United States, do not constitute extraterritorial applications of the Lanham Act at all. Further, while McBee concedes that United States courts lack jurisdiction over his Lanham Act claim for an injunction against Delica's sales in Japan, he argues that the district court had extraterritorial jurisdiction over damages claims against those same sales. Delica responds by arguing that United States courts lack extraterritorial jurisdiction over all of McBee's Lanham Act claims, and further urges lack of personal jurisdiction, preclusion due to collateral estoppel based on the Japanese judgment, and laches as alternative grounds for affirmance.

III.

A. *Framework for Assessing Extraterritorial Use of the Lanham Act*

By extraterritorial application of the Lanham Act, we mean application of the Act to activity (such as sales) of a defendant outside of the territorial boundaries of the United States. In addressing extraterritorial application of the Lanham Act, we face issues of Congressional intent to legislate extraterritorially, undergirded by issues of Congressional power to legislate extraterritorially. Usually in addressing questions of extraterritoriality, the Supreme Court has discussed Congressional intent, doing so by employing various presumptions designed to avoid unnecessary international conflict. . . .

The parties characterize the extraterritoriality issue as, at least in part, one of subject matter jurisdiction under the Act, and it is often viewed that way. . . .

The Supreme Court has long since made it clear that the Lanham Act could sometimes be used to reach extraterritorial conduct, but it has never laid down a precise test for when such reach would be appropriate. . . . The circuit courts have established a variety of tests for determining when extraterritorial application of the Lanham Act is appropriate, treating different factual contexts as all subject to the same set of criteria. . . . This court has not previously addressed the question.

Steele found that there was Lanham Act jurisdiction over a defendant, selling watches in Mexico, who was a United States citizen and whose "operations and their effects were not confined within the territorial limits of a foreign nation." . . . 344 U.S. at 286. Defendant made no sales within the United States. The Court held that the Lanham Act conferred broad jurisdiction in that its purpose was to regulate "commerce within the control of Congress." . . . The Act prohibits the use of certain infringing marks "in commerce." . . . Importantly, commerce is defined in the Act as "all commerce which may lawfully be regulated by Congress." . . .

The *Steele* Court did not define the outer limits of Congressional power because it was clear that the facts presented a case within those limits. The *Steele* Court explicitly and implicitly relied on two different aspects of Congressional power to reach this conclusion. First, it explicitly relied on the power of Congress to regulate "the conduct of its own citizens," even extraterritorial conduct. *Steele,* 344 U.S. at 285–86. This doctrine is based on an idea that Congressional power over American citizens is a matter of domestic law that raises no serious international concerns, even when the citizen is located abroad. . . .

Second, *Steele* also implicitly appears to rely on Congressional power over foreign commerce, although the Foreign Commerce clause is not cited—the Court noted that the defendant's actions had an impact on the plaintiff's reputation, and thus on commerce within the United States. . . . The *Steele* Court concluded that an American citizen could not evade the thrust of the laws of the United States by moving his operations to a "privileged sanctuary" beyond our borders. . . .

For purposes of determining subject matter jurisdiction, we think certain distinctions are important at the outset. The reach of the Lanham Act depends on context; the nature of the analysis of the jurisdictional question may vary with that context. *Steele* addressed the pertinent Lanham Act jurisdictional analysis when an American citizen is the defendant. In such cases, the domestic effect of the international activities may be of lesser importance and a lesser showing of domestic effects may be all that is needed. We do not explore this further because our case does not involve an American citizen as the alleged infringer.

When the purported infringer is not an American citizen, and the alleged illegal activities occur outside the United States, then the analysis is different, and appears to rest solely on the foreign commerce power. Yet it is beyond much doubt that the Lanham Act can be applied against foreign corporations or individuals in appropriate cases; no court has ever suggested that the foreign citizenship of a defendant is always fatal. . . . Some academics have criticized treating the Lanham Act differently from patent and copyright law, which generally are not applied extraterritorially. . . . Nonetheless, the Supreme Court recently reaffirmed the *Steele* approach to extraterritorial jurisdiction under the Lanham Act by distinguishing it in *Arabian American Oil Co. See* 499 U.S. at 252–53. . . . The question becomes one of articulating a test for Lanham Act jurisdiction over foreign infringing activities by foreign defendants.

The decisions of the Supreme Court in the antitrust context seem useful to us as a guide. The Court has written in this area, on the issue of extraterritorial application, far more recently than it has written on the Lanham Act, and thus the decisions reflect more recent evolutions in terms of legal analysis of extraterritorial activity. As the Court noted in *Steele,* Lanham Act violations abroad often radiate unlawful consequences into the United States. . . . One can easily imagine a variety of harms to American commerce arising from wholly foreign activities by foreign defendants. There could be harm caused by false endorsements, passing off, or product disparagement, or confusion over sponsorship affecting American commerce and causing loss of American sales. Further, global piracy of American goods is a major problem for American companies: annual losses from unauthorized use of United States trademarks, according to one commentator, now amount to $200 billion annually. . . . In both the antitrust and the Lanham Act areas, there is a risk that absent a certain degree of extraterritorial enforcement, violators will either take advantage of international coordination problems or hide in countries without efficacious antitrust or trademark laws, thereby avoiding legal authority.

In *Hartford Fire Ins. Co. v. California,* 509 U.S. 764 (1993), the Supreme Court addressed the issue of when a United States court could assert jurisdiction over Sherman Act claims brought against foreign defendants for a conspiracy that occurred abroad to raise reinsurance prices. It held that jurisdiction over foreign conduct existed under the antitrust laws if that conduct "was meant to produce and did in fact produce some substantial effect in the United States." *Id.* at 796, 113 S.Ct. 2891. . . . The *Hartford Fire* Court also held that comity considerations, such as whether relief ordered by an American court would conflict with foreign law, were properly understood not as questions of whether a United States court possessed subject matter jurisdiction, but instead as issues of whether such a court should decline to exercise the jurisdiction that it possessed. . . .

The framework stated in *Hartford Fire* guides our analysis of the Lanham Act jurisdictional question for foreign activities of foreign defendants. We hold that the Lanham Act grants subject matter jurisdiction over extraterritorial conduct by foreign defendants only where the conduct has a substantial effect on United States commerce. . . . Absent a showing of such a substantial effect, at least as to foreign defendants, the court lacks jurisdiction over the Lanham Act claim. Congress has little reason to assert jurisdiction over foreign defendants who are engaging in activities that have no substantial effect on the United States, and courts, absent an express statement from Congress, have no good reason to go further in such situations. . . .

The substantial effects test requires that there be evidence of impacts within the United States, and these impacts must be of a sufficient character and magnitude to give the United States a reasonably strong interest in the litigation. . . . The "substantial effects" test must be applied in light of the core purposes of the Lanham Act, which are both to protect the ability of American consumers to avoid confusion and to help assure a trademark's owner that it will reap the financial and reputational rewards associated with having a desirable name or product. . . . The goal of the jurisdictional test is to ensure that the United States has a sufficient interest in the litigation, as measured by the interests protected by the Lanham Act, to assert jurisdiction.

Of course, the *Vanity Fair* test includes a "substantial effects" inquiry as part of its three-part test. . . . We differ from the *Vanity Fair* court in that we disaggregate the elements of its test: we first ask whether the defendant is an American citizen, and if he is not, then we use the substantial effects test as the sole touchstone to determine jurisdiction.

If the substantial effects test is met, then the court should proceed, in appropriate cases, to consider comity. We also transplant for Lanham Act purposes *Hartford Fire's* holding that comity considerations are properly analyzed not as questions of whether there is subject matter jurisdiction, but as prudential questions of whether that jurisdiction should be exercised. . . . Our analysis differs again from *Vanity Fair* on this point. . . . *Vanity Fair* and other cases have considered as part of the basic jurisdictional analysis whether the defendant acted under color of protection of the trademark laws of his own country. We disagree and do not see why the scope of Congressional intent and power to create jurisdiction under the Lanham Act should turn on the existence and meaning of foreign law.

Congress could, of course, preclude the exercise of such Lanham Act jurisdiction by statute or by ratified treaty. Or it could by statute define limits in Lanham Act jurisdiction in such international cases, as it has chosen to do in the antitrust area. . . . It has not done so.

B.   *Application of the Framework . . .*

1.   *Claim for Injunction Barring Delica's United States Sales*

McBee contends that his claim for an injunction against Delica's sales to consumers inside the United States does not constitute an extraterritorial application of the Lanham Act, and therefore the district court should have taken jurisdiction over this claim without pausing to consider whether there was a substantial effect on United States commerce. The factual predicate for this argument is the $2,500 of "Cecil McBee" brand goods that Delica sold to McBee's investigators in Maine; there is no evidence of any other sales made by Delica to United States consumers. McBee is correct that the court had subject matter jurisdiction over this claim.

There can be no doubt of Congress's power to enjoin sales of infringing goods into the United States, and as a matter of Congressional intent there can be no doubt that Congress intended to reach such sales via the Lanham Act. Courts have repeatedly distinguished between domestic acts of a foreign infringer and foreign acts of that foreign infringer; the extraterritoriality analysis to determine jurisdiction attaches only to the latter. . . . Since sales in the United States are domestic acts, McBee need not satisfy the "substantial effect on United States commerce" test for this claim; jurisdiction exists because, under the ordinary domestic test, the $2,500 worth of goods sold by Delica to McBee's investigators in the United States were in United States commerce, at least insofar as some of those goods were shipped directly by Delica to the buyers in the United States. . . .

The district court thus had subject matter jurisdiction over McBee's claim for an injunction against Delica's sales of "Cecil McBee" goods in the United States. Nonetheless, dismissal of the claim was appropriate for reasons stated later. . . .

2.   *Claim for Injunction Barring Access to Internet Website*

McBee next argues that his claim for an injunction against Delica's posting of its Internet website in a way that is visible to United States consumers also does not call for an extraterritorial application of the Lanham Act. Here McBee is incorrect: granting this relief would constitute an extraterritorial application of the Act, and thus subject matter jurisdiction would only be appropriate if McBee could show a substantial effect on United States commerce. . . . McBee has not shown such a substantial effect from Delica's website.

We begin with McBee's argument that his website claim, like his claim for Delica's sales into the United States, is not an extraterritorial application of the Lanham Act. McBee does not seek to reach the website because it is a method, by Delica, for selling "Cecil McBee" goods into the United States. In such a case, if a court had jurisdiction to enjoin sales of goods within the United States, it might have jurisdiction to enjoin the website as well, or at least those parts of the website that are necessary to allow the sales to occur. . . . Rather, the injury McBee complains about from the website is that its mere existence has caused him harm, because United States citizens can view the website and become confused about McBee's relationship with the Japanese clothing company. In particular, McBee argues that he has suffered harm from the fact that Delica's website often comes up on search engines ahead of fan sites about McBee's jazz career.

Delica's website, although hosted from Japan and written in Japanese, happens to be reachable from the United States just as it is reachable from other countries. That is the nature of the Internet. The website is hosted and managed overseas; its visibility within the United States is more in the nature of an effect, which occurs only when someone in the United States decides to visit the website. To hold that any website in a foreign language, wherever hosted, is automatically reachable under the Lanham Act so long as it is visible in the United States would be senseless. The United States often will have no real interest in hearing trademark lawsuits about websites that are written in a foreign language and hosted in other countries. McBee attempts to analogize the existence of Delica's website, which happens to be visible in any country, to the direct mail advertising that the *Vanity Fair* court considered to be domestic conduct and so held outside the scope of the extraterritoriality analysis. . . . The analogy is poor for three reasons: first, the advertising in *Vanity Fair* was closely connected with mail-order sales; second, direct mail advertising is a far more targeted act than is the hosting of a website; and third, Delica's website, unlike the advertising in *Vanity Fair*, is in a foreign language.

Our conclusion that McBee's website claim calls for extraterritorial application of the Lanham Act is bolstered by a consideration of the now extensive case law relating to treatment of Internet websites with respect to personal jurisdiction. We recognize that the contexts are distinct, but the extraterritorial application of jurisdiction under the Lanham Act evokes concerns about territorial restraints on sovereigns that are similar to concerns driving personal jurisdiction. To put the principle broadly, the mere existence of a website that is visible in a forum and that gives information about a company and its products is not enough, by itself, to subject a defendant to personal jurisdiction in that forum. . . .

Something more is necessary, such as interactive features which allow the successful online ordering of the defendant's products. . . . The mere existence of a website does not show that a defendant is directing its business activities towards every forum where the website is visible; as well, given the omnipresence of Internet websites today, allowing personal jurisdiction to be premised on such a contact alone would "eviscerate" the limits on a state's jurisdiction over out-of-state or foreign defendants. . . .

Similarly, allowing subject matter jurisdiction under the Lanham Act to automatically attach whenever a website is visible in the United

States would eviscerate the territorial curbs on judicial authority that Congress is, quite sensibly, presumed to have imposed in this area.

Our conclusion does not make it impossible for McBee to use the Lanham Act to attack a Japan-based website; it merely requires that McBee first establish that the website has a substantial effect on commerce in the United States before there is subject matter jurisdiction under the Lanham Act. We can imagine many situations in which the presence of a website would ensure (or, at least, help to ensure) that the United States has a sufficient interest. The substantial effects test, however, is not met here.

Delica's website is written almost entirely in Japanese characters; this makes it very unlikely that any real confusion of American consumers, or diminishing of McBee's reputation, would result from the website's existence. In fact, most American consumers are unlikely to be able to understand Delica's website at all. Further, McBee's claim that Americans looking for information about him will be unable to find it is unpersuasive: the Internet searches reproduced in the record all turned up both sites about McBee and sites about Delica's clothing line on their first page of results. The two sets of results are easily distinguishable to any consumer, given that the Delica sites are clearly shown, by the search engines, as being written in Japanese characters. Finally, we stress that McBee has produced no evidence of any American consumers going to the website and then becoming confused about whether McBee had a relationship with Delica.

3. Claim for Damages for Delica's Japanese Sales

McBee's claim for damages due to Delica's sales in Japan fares no better, because these sales as well have no substantial effect on commerce in the United States. McBee seeks damages for Delica's sales in Japan to Japanese consumers based on (a) tarnishing of McBee's image in the United States, and (b) loss of income in the United States due to loss of commercial opportunity as a jazz musician in Japan, stemming from the tarnishing of McBee's reputation there. The alleged tarnishing—both in the United States and Japan—is purportedly caused by the confusion of McBee's name with a brand selling (sometimes provocative) clothing to young teenage girls in Japan. McBee presents essentially no evidence that either type of tarnishing has occurred, much less that it has any substantial effect on United States commerce.

McBee's first argument, that *American* consumers are being confused and/or led to think less of McBee's name because of Delica's Japanese sales, cuts very close to the core purposes of the Lanham Act. . . . Such confusion and reputational harm in the eyes of American consumers can often—although not always—be inferred from the fact that American consumers have been exposed to the infringing mark. But no inference of dilution or other harm can be made in situations where American citizens are not exposed at all to the infringing product. The trouble with McBee's argument is that there is virtually no evidence that American consumers are actually seeing Delica's products.

Quite commonly, plaintiffs in these sorts of cases can meet their burden by presenting evidence that while the initial sales of infringing goods may occur in foreign countries, the goods subsequently tend to enter the United States in some way and in substantial quantities. . . . McBee has presented essentially no evidence that Delica's products have been brought into the United States after their initial sale in Japan. McBee's own statement, without more, that people have seen women wearing Delica clothing in the United States does not show very much; likewise, McBee's evidence that Delica's goods are occasionally sold on eBay shows little, given particularly that such goods need not have been auctioned to buyers in the United States. The evidence indicates only one incident in which an American citizen saw McBee advertisements while traveling in Japan and demonstrated confusion upon returning to the United States.

Beyond that, there is also nothing that indicates any harm to McBee's career in the United States due to Delica's product sales. McBee's argument that there has potentially been harm to McBee's career as a product endorser is most unlikely, especially given his own disinterest in performing such endorsements. Further, McBee's statement that his teaching career may have been hindered by Delica is speculation.

McBee's second argument is that Delica's sales have confused Japanese consumers, hindering McBee's record sales and touring career in Japan. Evidence of economic harm to McBee in Japan due to confusion of Japanese consumers is less tightly tied to the interests that the Lanham Act intends to protect, since there is no United States interest in protecting *Japanese consumers*. American courts do, however, arguably have an interest in protecting American commerce by protecting *McBee* from lost income due to the tarnishing of his trademark in Japan. Courts have considered sales diverted from American companies in foreign countries in their analyses. . . .

Assuming *arguendo* that evidence of harm to an American plaintiff's economic interests abroad, due to the tarnishing of his reputation there, might sometimes meet the substantial effects test, McBee has presented no evidence of such harm in this case. McBee has presented no evidence of economic harm due to losses in record sales or touring opportunities in Japan. McBee's statement that he might have expected more Japanese touring opportunities by now, and may have had such opportunities absent Delica's sales, is wholly speculative. There is no probative evidence of any decline in McBee's touring revenue as compared to past patterns, nor is there any evidence of any decline in McBee's Japanese record sales.

McBee has not shown that Delica's Japanese sales have a substantial effect on United States commerce, and thus McBee's claim for damages based on those sales, as well as McBee's claim for an injunction against Delica's website, must be dismissed for lack of subject matter jurisdiction. We need not reach the issue of whether we should decline jurisdiction because of comity. . . . Were we to assert jurisdiction in this case, where there is no evidence of any harm to American commerce beyond the facts that the plaintiff is an American citizen and that the allegedly infringing goods were sold and seen in a foreign country, we would be forced to find jurisdiction in almost all false endorsement or trademark cases involving an American plaintiff and allegedly infringing sales abroad.

C.   *Frivolousness of Claim Based on Delica's Product Sales in the United States*

Because we do have subject matter jurisdiction over McBee's claim for an injunction against Delica's sales in the United States, . . . we proceed on that claim. . . .

As to the merits, there is no evidence of existing confusion or dilution due to Delica's past sales, since these few sales were all made to McBee's own investigators, who were brought in to assist in this litigation and therefore fully understood McBee's lack of any relationship with Delica. . . . There is no evidence of any other sales, nor any evidence that Delica has any desire to sell into the United States in the future. All the evidence, in fact, is to the contrary. Thus, there is no justification for injunctive relief, and summary judgment must enter for Delica on this claim.

Absent any viable federal claim, the district court's dismissal of all of McBee's pendent state law claims (without prejudice to their being refiled in state court) was fully appropriate and was not an abuse of discretion—McBee has not argued otherwise. . . . We need not reach Delica's laches or collateral estoppel arguments.

IV.

The district court's decision ordering judgment for the defendant Delica is affirmed. Costs are awarded to Delica.

NOTES

1.   *Territorial Scope of the Lanham Act.* Although U.S. circuit court tests for assessing the territorial applicability of the Lanham Act vary, "[m]ost circuits apply some version of a three-part test that considers the effects of the defendant's conduct on U.S. commerce, the citizenship of the defendant, and the likelihood of a conflict between U.S. law and foreign law." *See* Curtis Bradley's article excerpted on page 6, above. A difference among the tests is in the effects that the tests require the infringing acts to have; while in *McBee* the court looked for "a substantial effect on U.S. commerce," in the Ninth Circuit, courts inquire about "some effects on American foreign commerce" combined with "a cognizable injury to the plaintiffs under the

Lanham Act." *See* the *Timberlane* test quoted in Curtis Bradley's article on page 6, above.

Do the different tests lead to different outcomes? In Trader Joe's Co. v. Hallatt, 835 F.3d 960 (9th Cir. 2016), the plaintiff alleged that a Canadian retailer's resale of Trader Joe's-branded goods in Canada, which the retailer purchased in Trader Joe's stores in the United States, infringed Trader Joe's rights under the Lanham Act. The court concluded that all three *Timberlane* test prongs were met when Trader Joe's sufficiently alleged some effects on American foreign commerce, a cognizable injury under the Lanham Act, and sufficiently strong links to American foreign commerce "in relation to those of other nations to justify the assertion of extraterritorial authority." 835 F.3d at 969.

Would the different tests satisfy the second step of the extraterritoriality analysis that the U.S. Supreme Court outlined in RJR Nabisco, Inc. v. European Cmty., 136 S.Ct. 2090 (2016)? According to *RJR Nabisco*'s second step, "if the conduct relevant to the [statute's] focus occurred in a foreign country, then the case involves an impermissible extraterritorial application regardless of any other conduct that occurred in U.S. territory." 136 S.Ct. at 2101. For a discussion of the territorial scope of the Lanham Act see also note 2 on page 8.

2. *Prescriptive Jurisdiction and Adjudicatory Jurisdiction.* Is the territorial scope of the application of the Lanham Act a question of subject matter jurisdiction, or rather the merits of the case? The *McBee* court discussed the territorial scope in its analysis of subject matter jurisdiction and declined to consider comity issues arising from a potential conflict with Japanese trademark law. Should potential conflicts with foreign trademark laws limit a country's prescriptive jurisdiction or adjudicatory jurisdiction? In *Trader Joe's*, where the court held that the issue of the territorial scope of the Lanham Act was a question on the merits, the court noted the fact that there was no ongoing proceeding in Canada between Trader Joe's and the Canadian retailer concerning Trader Joe's Canadian trademarks and considered that fact as weighing in favor of extraterritorial application of the Lanham Act. 835 F.3d at 973.

On the links among personal jurisdiction, subject matter jurisdiction, and the territorial scope of applicable law see note 11 on page 51, above.

3. *Trademark Law and the Internet.* Under what circumstances will the United States have a "real interest in hearing trademark lawsuits about websites that are written in a foreign language and hosted in other countries" (which the *McBee* court mentioned)? Does it matter how widespread the knowledge of a website's foreign language is in the United States? Should courts give different weight to the mere accessibility of a website if only the website itself is displaying an infringing trademark—as opposed to a website that offers for sale products that bear the infringing trademark?

Was McBee correct when he stated that the injunction that he was requesting against Delica's "broadcasting of its website in the United States" was a "domestic injunction?" Do the developments in geolocation and geoblocking technologies suggest that such injunctions could target websites in a strictly territorial manner and therefore courts can design purely domestic injunctions? On geolocation and geoblocking see note 10 on page 50, above.

2.   PROTECTED SUBJECT MATTER

a.   TRADEMARKS

Agreement on Trade-Related Aspects of Intellectual Property Rights

33 International Legal Materials Journal 1, 89 (1994).

Article 15
Protectable Subject Matter

1.   Any sign, or any combination of signs, capable of distinguishing the goods or services of one undertaking from those of other undertakings, shall be capable of constituting a trademark. Such signs, in particular words including personal names, letters, numerals, figurative elements and combinations of colours as well as any combination of such signs, shall be eligible for registration as trademarks. Where signs are not inherently capable of distinguishing the relevant goods or services, Members may make registrability depend on distinctiveness acquired through use. Members may require, as a condition of registration, that signs be visually perceptible.

2.   Paragraph 1 shall not be understood to prevent a Member from denying registration of a trademark on other grounds, provided that they do not derogate from the provisions of the Paris Convention (1967).

3.   Members may make registrability depend on use. However, actual use of a trademark shall not be a condition for filing an application for registration. An application shall not be refused solely on the ground that intended use has not taken place before the expiry of a period of three years from the date of application.

4.   The nature of the goods or services to which a trademark is to be applied shall in no case form an obstacle to registration of the trade mark.

5.   Members shall publish each trademark either before it is registered or promptly after it is registered and shall afford a reasonable opportunity for petitions to cancel the registration. In addition, Members may afford an opportunity for the registration of a trademark to be opposed.

Otokoyama Co. Ltd. v. Wine of Japan Import, Inc.

United States Court of Appeals for the Second Circuit, 1999.
175 F.3d 266, 50 U.S.P.Q.2d 1626.

LEVAL, CIRCUIT JUDGE:

This is a trademark dispute between two importers of Japanese sake. Otokoyama Co. Ltd., the registered owner of four U.S. trademarks for the word "otokoyama" and Japanese language pictograms signifying that word, filed suit against Wine of Japan Import, Inc., alleging, *inter alia*, that defendant infringed its trademark in violation of the Lanham Act . . . by importing a brand of sake labelled "Mutsu Otokoyama." Defendant counterclaimed, seeking to cancel plaintiff's trademarks under § 14 of the Lanham Act, 15 U.S.C. § 1064. Defendant contended that 1) otokoyama is a generic term signifying a type of sake and is therefore ineligible for trademark protection, and 2) plaintiff's trademarks were "obtained fraudulently" within the meaning of 15 U.S.C. § 1064(3).

After a hearing, the district court granted plaintiff's motion for a preliminary injunction. On appeal from that order, defendant argues that the district court erred when it refused to consider evidence of the meaning and usage of otokoyama in Japan and refused to consider a ruling of the Japanese trademark office denying plaintiff's application for trademark protection on the ground that otokoyama is generic. We agree that the district court erred in both respects. Applying the correct legal standard and crediting defendant with the improperly excluded evidence, we find that defendant raises sufficient doubt as to the validity of plaintiff's trademark to overcome plaintiff's showing of likelihood of success. We therefore vacate the preliminary injunction.

BACKGROUND

Plaintiff, a Japanese corporation, has been brewing sake—a Japanese wine made from fermented rice—on the northern island of Hokkaido since the 1930s. In Japan, its sake is sold under the name "Hokkai Otokoyama," Hokkai being a reference to the island of Hokkaido. Since 1984, plaintiff has imported its sake into the U.S., where it is marketed and sold as "Otokoyama" brand sake. Plaintiff registered the English transliteration of otokoyama and three trademarks of Japanese pictograms comprising otokoyama with the U.S. Trademark Office.

Defendant is a domestic corporation, which imports various brands of sake into the U.S. Defendant's importation and sale of sake under the designation "Mutsu Otokoyama," begun in or around 1997, is the subject of this suit. As noted, plaintiff claims the defendant's use of otokoyama infringes plaintiff's trademark, while defendant claims that because otokoyama is a generic word for a type of sake, it is not eligible for use as a trademark for sake.

In Japanese pictograms, the word otokoyama is comprised of the characters for "man" and "mountain." The parties dispute the meaning and history of the word in relation to sake, but they agree that its use in Japan in relation to sake dates back at least to the Edo period, which began in the seventeenth century. Paintings from the period show samurai warriors drinking from sake barrels displaying the characters for otokoyama. In Japan, between ten and twenty brewers in addition to plaintiff designate sake as "otokoyama," often (like plaintiff) adding a geographical modifier.

Plaintiff has been unsuccessful in its attempts to obtain trademark rights in Japan for otokoyama. In 1962 (then doing business under the name Yamazaki Shuzo K.K.) plaintiff sought to register the characters for "Hokkai Otokoyama" as a trademark in Japan. The application was rejected, and in 1966 the Japanese Patent Office ("JPO") affirmed the rejection. The JPO issued a written decision, whose exact translation is disputed, . . . but which apparently signified that the word otokoyama was not eligible for trademark protection because of its longstanding use as a designation for sake by other traders in the industry.

In 1984, plaintiff became the first company to market sake labelled otokoyama in the United States. Two years later, plaintiff petitioned the United States Patent and Trademark Office ("USPTO") to register the Kanji characters for otokoyama. In processing plaintiff's application, the USPTO asked plaintiff to provide an English translation of the characters. Plaintiff responded with a sworn statement that "to applicant's knowledge, the mark is an arbitrary, fanciful term. Accordingly, the mark cannot be translated." The USPTO granted plaintiff's request to register the mark in 1988.

Between 1992 and 1995, plaintiff sought and obtained U.S. registrations for three other otokoyama trademarks: one each for the Katakana and Hiragana[2] characters for otokoyama, and one for the English transliteration. Again the USPTO asked for English translations, to which plaintiff again responded in sworn declarations that otokoyama is "an arbitrary, fanciful" term that "has no meaning and cannot be translated."

In April, 1997, plaintiff wrote to defendant demanding that it cease importation, distribution, advertisement and sale of "Mutsu Otokoyama." Defendant replied that it believed plaintiff's trademarks were invalid, and refused.

Plaintiff filed suit, alleging trademark infringement, unfair competition, and false designation of origin under the Lanham Act, as well as state law violations, and moved for a preliminary injunction. As noted, defendant challenged the validity of plaintiff's trademarks on two grounds: first, that otokoyama is a generic term for a type of sake, and second, that plaintiff secured its U.S. registrations by fraudulent

---

[2]   Katakana, Hiragana, and Kanji are apparently three different writing systems in the Japanese language.

misrepresentations that concealed from the USPTO otokoyama's usage as a generic term in Japan.

At the preliminary injunction hearing, the court declined to consider any meaning the word otokoyama might have outside the United States, stating that "the meaning of a term outside of the United States is irrelevant" to a determination of entitlement to the protection of the U.S. trademark laws. . . . The court also declined to consider defendant's proffer of the 1966 decision of the Japanese Patent Office which denied plaintiff's request to register otokoyama in Japan. . . . Concluding that plaintiff had shown both irreparable harm and likelihood of success on the merits, the court granted the preliminary injunction. . . .

DISCUSSION

A party seeking a preliminary injunction must establish that 1) absent injunctive relief, it will suffer irreparable harm, and 2) either a) that it is likely to succeed on the merits, or b) that there are sufficiently serious questions going to the merits to make them a fair ground for litigation, and that the balance of hardships tips decidedly in favor of the moving party. . . . The plaintiff in a trademark infringement action establishes a likelihood of success by showing both 1) a legal, exclusive right to the mark, and 2) a likelihood that customers will be confused as to the source of the infringing product. . . . To prove likelihood of success below, plaintiff showed that since 1984 it had been importing and selling its sake in the United States under the label "otokoyama," that it had registered this trademark with the USPTO, and that it had successfully protected the mark against unauthorized use by others.

We review a district court's decision to grant or deny a preliminary injunction for abuse of discretion, which is shown if, *inter alia*, the district court applies the incorrect legal standard. . . . Because the court applied the wrong legal standard and excluded relevant evidence favorable to the defendant's claim, we vacate the injunction.

Defendant contends the district court erred in refusing to consider evidence that otokoyama is a generic term for sake, or a type of sake, in the Japanese language as spoken in Japan, and that the district court erred in excluding the decision of the Japanese Patent Office. . . . We agree with defendant that the district court was mistaken in its understanding of the potential significance of the meaning of otokoyama in the Japanese language. We also agree with the defendant that the ruling of the Japanese Patent Office may have been admissible for certain relevant purposes.

I.

It is a bedrock principle of the trademark law that no trader may acquire the exclusive right to the use of a term by which the covered goods or services are designated in the language. Such a term is "generic." Generic terms are not eligible for protection as trademarks; everyone may use them to refer to the goods they designate. . . . This rule protects the interest of the consuming public in understanding the nature of goods offered for sale, as well as a fair marketplace among competitors by insuring that every provider may refer to his goods as what they are. . . .

The same rule applies when the word designates the product in a language other than English. This extension rests on the assumption that there are (or someday will be) customers in the United States who speak that foreign language. Because of the diversity of the population of the United States, coupled with temporary visitors, all of whom are part of the United States marketplace, commerce in the United States utilizes innumerable foreign languages. No merchant may obtain the exclusive right over a trademark designation if that exclusivity would prevent competitors from designating a product as what it is in the foreign language their customers know best. Courts and the USPTO apply this policy, known as the doctrine of "foreign equivalents," . . . to make generic foreign words ineligible for private ownership as trademarks. . . .

This rule, furthermore, does not apply only to words that designate an entire species. Generic words for sub-classifications or varieties of a good are similarly ineligible for trademark protection. . . . A word may also be generic by virtue of its association with a particular region, cultural movement, or legend. . . .

The defendant contended in the district court that the word "otokoyama" falls within the generic category. It claimed that in Japanese, otokoyama has long been understood as designating a variety of "dry, manly sake" that originated more than 300 years ago. . . . The district court, however, declined to accord any significance to the Japanese meaning of the word. The court stated that the Japanese meaning of otokoyama is "irrelevant to the U.S. PTO's determination of [plaintiff's] trademark rights. . . . [T]he meaning of the term 'otokoyama' in Japan is not relevant to this action." . . .

For the reasons explained above, this was error. If otokoyama in Japanese signifies a type of sake, and one United States merchant were given the exclusive right to use that word to designate its brand of sake, competing merchants would be prevented from calling their product by the word which designates that product in Japanese. Any Japanese-speaking customers and others who are familiar with the Japanese terminology would be misled to believe that there is only one brand of otokoyama available in the United States. . . .

The meaning of otokoyama in Japanese, and particularly whether it designates sake, or a type or category of sake, was therefore highly relevant to whether plaintiff may assert the exclusive right to use that word as a mark applied to sake. Defendant should have been allowed to introduce evidence of otokoyama's meaning and usage in Japan to support its claim that the mark is generic and therefore ineligible for protection as a trademark. In light of this error, the district court's finding that plaintiff is likely to succeed on the merits cannot be sustained.

II.

Defendant also challenges the district court's exclusion of the ruling of the Japanese Patent Office denying plaintiff trademark rights in Japan. The district court, citing *Vanity Fair Mills, Inc. v. T. Eaton Co.*, 234 F.2d 633, 639 (2d Cir. 1956), ruled that the JPO decision was irrelevant. . . . We disagree.

We disagree first with the district court's understanding of the precedent it cited. It is true that a claimant's rights (or lack of rights) to a trademark in the United States cannot be established by the fact that the claimant was found by a foreign court to have (or not to have) rights over the same mark in a foreign country. That is what the *Vanity Fair* opinion meant by its broad statement to the effect that "the decisions of foreign courts concerning the respective trade-mark rights of the parties are irrelevant and inadmissible." *Id.* at 639. It does not follow, however, that foreign court decisions are *never* relevant or admissible for any purpose in a U.S. trademark dispute. Indeed, as authority for the quoted proposition, the *Vanity Fair* opinion cited our ruling in *George W. Luft Co. v. Zande Cosmetic Co.*, 142 F.2d 536, 539 (2d Cir. 1944), which ruled that foreign decisions *were* relevant and admissible. In *Luft*, the defendant offered various foreign registrations of the disputed mark to prove that the defendants might lawfully use the mark within the foreign country that granted the registration. The district court had excluded them in reliance on *City of Carlsbad v. Kutnow*, 68 F. 794 (S.D.N.Y.), *aff'd*, 71 F. 167 (2d Cir. 1895). The *Luft* Court pointed out that in *Carlsbad*, "the purpose of introducing the English registration was to prove that the defendants were privileged to use [the mark] on sales in the United States. *On this issue* a foreign trade-mark was rightly held irrelevant, for clearly the English law could not confer [a trademark right] which our courts were bound to recognize." 142 F.2d at 539 (emphasis added). The opinion goes on, however, to say "We do not think that the *Carlsbad* case controls the case at bar." *Id.* Because "the purpose of offering the foreign registrations was not to establish the privilege of using the [mark] in the United States but to prove that the defendants might lawfully use it within the foreign country which granted the registration," *id.*, the court found that the foreign decisions were relevant and admissible and the district court had erred in failing to consider them.

Whether a foreign decision is relevant in a trademark case in our courts depends on the purpose for which it is offered. The fact that a litigant has been awarded or denied rights over a mark in a foreign country ordinarily does not determine its entitlement to the mark in the United States. The foreign court decision is not admissible if that is the purpose of the offer. But if, as in *Luft*, the foreign decision is competent evidence of a relevant fact, it is relevant and admissible to prove that fact.

Defendant offered the decision of the JPO for two purposes. First, it was offered to prove the fact assertedly found by the JPO that the word otokoyama in Japanese refers to a type or class of sake. Second, it was offered as evidence supporting defendant's claim that plaintiff committed fraud on the trademark office in the prosecution of its application for registration. . . . The theory of this offer was to show plaintiff's awareness that the word otokoyama was not an "arbitrary, fanciful term . . . [that] cannot be translated," as plaintiff represented to the trademark examiner. Both purposes are relevant to defendant's claims. It was error to exclude the JPO decision on grounds of relevance.

Our reversal of the preliminary injunction awarded to plaintiff should not be construed as an indication that defendant should necessarily prevail on the merits. The question whether otokayama is a generic term for sake or a type of sake in the Japanese language will turn on the strength of the evidence defendant presents at trial once given the opportunity. The evidence defendant sought unsuccessfully to introduce at the preliminary injunction hearing was sufficient to undermine plaintiff's likelihood of success on the merits, but was not necessarily sufficient to carry the defendant's burden of proving that otokoyama is generic. . . . Whether otokoyama is generic in Japanese as defendant contends remains to be seen based on the evidence that will be presented at trial. We hold only that the improperly excluded evidence casts sufficient doubt on the validity of plaintiff's trademark, and on plaintiff's likelihood of success, to require that we vacate the preliminary injunction.

CONCLUSION

The preliminary injunction in plaintiff's favor is hereby vacated. The case is remanded for trial.

NOTES

1.   *Telle Quelle.* National practice respecting the scope of subject matter registrable as trademarks has varied widely, often leaving consumer product companies uncertain about whether their marks will receive protection in foreign markets. Article 6*quinquies* A(1) of the Paris Convention, the so-called *telle quelle* ("as is") provision, has meliorated national differences somewhat by requiring member states to register "as is" any mark that has been properly registered in a Paris Union country of origin. For example, Germany, which at one time barred registration of numbers and letters as trademarks, relaxed these domestic bars for number and letter marks originating in other Paris Union countries. However, exceptions to the *telle quelle* requirement, such as for marks lacking distinctive character, have limited the requirement's effectiveness in achieving international trademark harmony.

In re Rath, 402 F.3d 1207 (Fed.Cir. 2005), affirmed the rejection of an application by a German citizen, Dr. Matthias Rath, to secure registration of the marks "Dr. Rath" or "Rath" for goods and services. According to the trademark examiner, each mark was "primarily merely a surname" and, so, disqualified from registration under Lanham Act section 2(e)(4) in the absence of proof that they had acquired secondary meaning. Dr. Rath, who had earlier obtained German registration for the marks, argued that the *telle quelle* provision of Paris Convention Article 6*quinquies* required the U.S. Patent and Trademark Office to register the marks because his surname did not fall within any of the three exceptions allowed by the provision. The Patent and Trademark Office answered that surnames are descriptive, and thus "devoid of any distinctive character," under the second exception of 6*quinquies*, so that there was no conflict between the Lanham Act and the Paris Convention.

Ultimately, the Court of Appeals concluded that it did not have to decide the issue because "we find that the Paris Convention is not a self-executing treaty and requires congressional implementation." 402 F.3d at 1209. Nor, according to the court was there any evidence that Lanham Act section 44(e), providing that "[a] mark duly registered in the country of origin of the foreign applicant may be registered on the principal register if eligible . . ." effectively implements the *telle quelle* provision. "Congress did not simply adopt language incorporating the requirements of the convention in the Lanham Act. Rather it provided for registration of a foreign mark 'if eligible.' A mark is not 'eligible' for registration on the principal register under the statute unless it satisfies the section 2 requirements, including the surname rule." 402 F.3d at 1211.

The *telle-quelle* provision concerns the form but not the ownership of a trademark. As the WTO Appellate Body held in *United States—Section 211 Omnibus Appropriations Act*, "the obligation of countries of the Paris Union under Article 6*quinquies*(A)(1) to accept for filing and protect a trademark duly registered in the country of origin 'as is' does not encompass matters related to ownership." WT/DS176/AB/R, Jan. 2, 2002, ¶ 147. In the dispute, known as the "Havana Club Rum" dispute, the Appellate Body did not find the U.S. statute at issue contrary to Article 6*quinquies*; the statute prohibited the registration or renewal of trademarks "used in connection with a business or assets that were confiscated unless the original owner of such mark . . . or the bona fide successor-in-interest has expressly consented." Section 211(1)(a) of the Department of Commerce Appropriations Act, 1999, Public Law 105–277, 112 Stat. 2681. (However, the Appellate Body did find the statute to be inconsistent with U.S. national treatment obligations under the Paris Convention and the TRIPs Agreement, and the most-favored-nation obligation under the TRIPs Agreement "to the extent that they concern the treatment of original owners." *Id.*, ¶¶ 296 and 319.)

2.   *Registrable Subject Matter.* All national trademark systems embody the fundamental principle that a sign or symbol should be registered if, either inherently or through continued exclusive use, it signifies a product's source. The difference between national systems lies in the rate at which they assimilate newer forms of marks to this principle. All countries accept word marks for registration, but some have been quicker than others to accept such other possible indicators of source as surnames, letters, numerals,

signatures, portraits and colors. For example, it was only in 2015 that the Japanese trademark law and the Japan Patent Office began to provide for registration of non-traditional marks, including colors and sounds. Act No. 36 on the Partial Revision of the Patent Law and Other Laws, 2014.

TRIPs Article 15(1) should presumably accelerate acceptance of these newer forms of marks in member states, but it will not entirely harmonize national practice. Article 15(1)'s last sentence leaves member states free to deny registration to sound marks and fragrance marks. Do Article 15(1)'s first two sentences also allow member states to deny registration to three-dimensional configurations, such as the classic Coca-Cola bottle? Newer non-traditional marks that have been registered by some trademark offices include position marks, holograms, and animated sequences. The requirement for a graphic representation of a trademark may pose difficulties for some non-traditional marks and, to better serve non-traditional marks, EU trademark legislation eliminated the requirement in 2015. *See* Directive (EU) 2015/2436 of the European Parliament and of the Council of 16 December 2015 to approximate the laws of the Member States relating to trade marks (EU Trademark Directive), recital 13; Regulation (EU) 2015/2424, recital 9; currently Commission Implementing Regulation (EU) 2018/626, Article 3(3). EU trademarks are discussed further in note 5 at page 669, below.

Generally see Annette Kur, TRIPs and Trademark Law, in Friedrich-Karl Beier & Gerhard Schricker, eds., From GATT to TRIPs—The Agreement on Trade-Related Aspects of Intellectual Property Rights 93, 98–100 (1996); The Protection of Non-Traditional Trademarks (Irene Calboli & Martin Senftleben, eds., 2018).

3. *Service Marks.* Historically, trademark legislation has restricted registration to trade marks—marks affixed to goods such as food products or photographic film—and left to unfair competition law the protection of service marks—marks indicating the source of services such as restaurants or film processing. The United States was the first country to provide for registration of service marks; the Lanham Act, signed into law on July 5, 1946, put service marks on an equal footing with trademarks. Many—but by no means all—countries have since provided for service mark registration.

The 1958 Lisbon Revision Conference rejected a proposal to give service marks the same status as trademarks and Article 6*sexies*, added to the Paris Convention that year, provided only that, "[t]he countries of the Union undertake to protect service marks," an obligation that a Union member could meet not only by registering service marks, but also by protecting them under unfair competition law. Article 16 of the 1994 Trademark Law Treaty and Article 16 of the 2006 Singapore Treaty on the Law of Trademarks require contracting states to register service marks and to apply to service marks "the provisions of the Paris Convention which concern marks," and Article 15(1) of the TRIPs Agreement, which in its first sentence refers to any "sign or combination of signs capable of distinguishing . . . goods or services," definitively brings the registration of service marks within the obligations of member states.

4. *Generic Terms.* Trademark law denies protection to generic terms—"Oats," say, as an indication for cereal—on the twin premises that competitors—other cereal producers—must be free to use the term if they are to stay in business, and that consumers will usually not associate such terms with a single source. Accordingly, Article 6*quinquies*(B)(2) of the Paris Convention prohibits the registration of generic terms. How international is the concept of genericism? The term "Pilsner" stands in many countries for a type of beer, but in the Czech Republic the word mark "Pilsner Bier" has been a registered trademark since 1933 for a beer that claims its origin in a beer first brewed in 1842 in the city of Pilsen, located in today's Czech Republic. A sign mark bearing the words "Pilsner Bier" claims its priority in the Czech Republic since 1859. *See* page 630, below, for a discussion of genericism and geographical indications.

5. *Morality.* Article 6*quinquies*(B)(3) of the Paris Convention allows countries to prohibit the registration of marks that are contrary to morality or public order. The U.S. Supreme Court held first that the Lanham Act's bar to registration of disparaging marks was invalid because it violated First Amendment free speech protections; later the Supreme Court held that the same reasoning barred the prohibition of registration of immoral and scandalous marks. Matal v. Tam, 137 S.Ct. 1744 (2017); Iancu v. Brunetti, 139 S.Ct. 2294 (2019); 15 U.S.C. § 1052(a). Does prohibition of registration of immoral marks violate U.S. obligations under international law? The Paris Convention's provision is optional—it does not mandate that countries deny registration to immoral marks; NAFTA Article 1708(14) required the signatory countries to provide for a refusal to register immoral marks, but the U.S.-Mexico-Canada Agreement does not include this requirement.

How do the concepts of morality and public order differ among countries? In 2010 the Board of Appeal of the European Union's Office for Harmonisation in the Internal Market (now the European Union Intellectual Property Office) dismissed an appeal concerning the rejection of a registration of a Community trademark that would have consisted of the coat of arms of the former Soviet Union. In its rejection the Board relied on legislation and administrative practices in Hungary, Latvia, and the Czech Republic—three European Union member states that had been under Soviet control. The Court of Justice of the European Union rejected the applicant's argument that the Office should have considered "the public policy and accepted principles of morality of the European Union" as a whole and held that "the assessment of whether a sign is contrary to public policy or to accepted principles of morality must be carried out with reference to the perception of that sign, when being used as a trade mark, by the relevant public within the European Union or part of the Union. That part may, in some circumstances, be comprised of a single Member State." Couture Tech Ltd v. OHIM, CJEU (General Court), T-232/10, 2011, ¶ 50. *See* also La Mafia Franchises SL v. EUIPO, CJEU (General Court), T-1/17, 2018 (on the invalidation, based on an application from Italy, of an EU trademark including the word element "Mafia"); Constantin Film Produktion GmbH v. EUIPO, CJEU (General Court), T-69/17, 2018 (on the Office's refusal to register the word mark "Fack Ju Göhte").

In addition to historical experiences, what other factors may affect countries' concepts of morality and public order? Switzerland's Supreme Court affirmed the decision of a lower court that held that the registration of the trademark "Madonna" would be contrary to morality in Switzerland. Bundesgericht, 4A 302/2010, 2010. By 2010 the word "Madonna" had been registered multiple times as a trademark by the U.S. Trademark Office; although the Office refused to register the mark for wine in 1938 and 1959, the Office eventually registered "Madonna" for brandy in 2008.

6. *Foreign Equivalents.* In the United States, "[u]nder the doctrine of foreign equivalents, foreign words from common languages are translated into English to determine genericness, descriptiveness, as well as similarity of connotation in order to ascertain confusing similarity with English word marks." Palm Bay Imports Inv. v. Veuve Clicquot Ponsardin Maison Fondee En 1772, 396 F.3d 1369, 1377 (Fed.Cir. 2005).

What are "common languages?" Are all words to be treated equally for purposes of this analysis? According to the U.K. Trade Marks Manual, "[w]hilst the majority of UK consumers cannot be assumed to be fluent in [the most commonly understood European languages], most of them will have an appreciation of some of their more common words." Additionally, "[t]he average UK consumer will be familiar with the non-English names of certain products and/or services, and the local name for their geographical origin." Trade Marks Manual, Intellectual Property Office, 2019, Part B. *See* also Matratzen Concord AG v. Hukla Germany SA, ECJ, C-421/04, 2006.

7. *Trademarks in Different Scripts.* The *Otokoyama* trademark was a transliteration of a Japanese word. Would the mark be registerable if the applicant had applied for a sign mark consisting of the word in Japanese script? At one time, the U.K. Intellectual Property Office considered foreign-script marks to be distinctive; even if the marks were descriptive in another language, the Office would conclude that the average U.K. consumer would not recognize the descriptiveness of the marks. But the view of the Office evolved, and according to the 2019 version of its Manual, "[c]haracters in script such as Chinese, Japanese, Arabic, or a non-Roman alphabet language are not assumed to be acceptable prima facie. They must be transliterated to find out their meaning. If the words transliterate into something which is descriptive for the goods/services, an objection must be raised." Trade Marks Manual, Intellectual Property Office, 2019, Part B.

How should trademark law treat transliterations in scripts that consist of ideograms—characters that convey meanings on their own? There might be multiple options for transliterations but some might be more appealing and valuable than others. For example, 必胜客 is pronounced in Cantonese closely to "Pizza Hut," and at the same time, in Chinese the characters mean "the person that must win." How should the law treat combined marks that consist of a translation and a transliteration? For example, should Starbucks have rights in China against the registrant of 星巴克—"xingbake," where "xing" stands for "star," while the pronunciation of "bake" resembles "buck?"

For an illuminating discussion of translations and transliterations in Chinese trademark law and the struggle of multinational corporations, such as Pfizer and Apple, to protect their brands in China see Daniel C.K. Chow, Trademark Squatting and the Limits of the Famous Marks Doctrine in China, 47 Geo. Wash. Int'l L. Rev. 57 (2015).

b.   GEOGRAPHICAL INDICATIONS

Agreement on Trade-Related Aspects of Intellectual Property Rights

33 International Legal Materials Journal 1, 91 (1994).

Article 22
Protection of Geographical Indications

1.   Geographical indications are, for the purposes of this Agreement, indications which identify a good as originating in the territory of a Member, or a region or locality in that territory, where a given quality, reputation or other characteristic of the good is essentially attributable to its geographical origin.

2.   In respect of geographical indications, Members shall provide the legal means for interested parties to prevent:

(a)   the use of any means in the designation or presentation of a good that indicates or suggests that the good in question originates in a geographical area other than the true place of origin in a manner which misleads the public as to the geographical origin of the good;

(b)   any use which constitutes an act of unfair competition within the meaning of Article 10*bis* of the Paris Convention (1967).

3.   A Member shall, *ex officio* if its legislation so permits or at the request of an interested party, refuse or invalidate the registration of a trademark which contains or consists of a geographical indication with respect to goods not originating in the territory indicated, if use of the indication in the trademark for such goods in that Member is of such a nature as to mislead the public as to the true place of origin.

4.   The protection under paragraphs 1, 2 and 3 shall be applicable against a geographical indication which, although literally true as to the territory, region or locality in which the goods originate, falsely represents to the public that the goods originate in another territory.

Molly Torsen, Apples and Oranges: French and American Models of Geographic Indications Policies Demonstrate an International Lack of Consensus*

95 Trademark Reporter 1415, 1416, 1421–1424 (2005).

As the individual regions and cities of the world begin to share more and more commercial similarities, it is natural that producers will strive to protect products and foodstuffs that are somehow singular or noted for their quality or rarity. Two forms of protection are trademarks and geographic indications (GIs). Trademark law protects the names and symbols associated with products that have attained a certain reputation for particular qualities. For example, trademark law provides a consumer with the ability to choose between Chateau Ste. Michelle and Columbia Winery wines, trusting that the label of each indicates a certain level of quality based on that consumer's past experience or knowledge of those brands. However, where the uniqueness or attributes of a certain geographic area lend a product special traits, the related concept of geographic indications governs. GIs ostensibly enable a consumer to choose between a Bordeaux and a Chianti with some assurance as to the taste of those wines.

The laws and policies of GIs offer the potential for "re-linking production to the social, cultural and environmental aspects of particular places, further distinguishing them from anonymous mass produced goods, and opening the possibility of increased responsibility to place,"[1] but whether the law should regulate such "re-linking" is a contentious issue in the international community. France's laws offer some certainty that a product comes from a specific place if the place's name is included in the product's name; as explored below, France's winemaking industry historically has depended upon the protection provided by GIs. The United States has provided much weaker protection for GIs unless the indication is also registered as another type of mark, such as a certification mark. . . . Today, as products move across borders with greater frequency, an inevitable debate has arisen concerning the level of protection that GIs should be afforded. For example, both Bordeaux and Chianti are regions in Europe, and the degree to which their names have come to signify types of red wine is something that Europeans and Americans, in particular, are struggling to regulate, qualify and quantify. . . .

A. The TRIPS Agreement

. . . Articles 22 through 24 of the TRIPS Agreement govern GIs. Article 22 defines a standard level of protection for all products: GIs

---

[1]   Elizabeth Barham, *Translating Terroir: The Global Challenge of French AOC Labeling*, Journal of Rural Studies 19 (2003) 127, 129.

should be protected to avoid misleading the public and to prevent unfair competition. Article 23 provides enhanced protection for GIs for wines and spirits. Article 24 specifies how international negotiations concerning GIs should take place and enumerates exceptions to the general rules, such as allowing "generic" terms in one country that are classified as GIs elsewhere to escape that classification. . . . One example is "cheddar cheese," which may refer to a particular variety type of cheese that is not necessarily produced only in Cheddar, United Kingdom. . . . A similar exception from GI classification is appropriate if a term has already been registered as a trademark, such as PARMA ham. In Italy, that term denotes ham from the region of the city of Parma, but in Canada, it has long been a registered trademark for ham made by a particular Canadian company. . . .

The Parma ham example highlights some of the difficult issues raised by the GIs debate. A valid trademark such as PARMA can be an irreplaceable asset to a company. On the other hand, as Gregor Kreuzhueber, the agriculture spokesman for the European Commission, has observed: "Italian Parma ham producers cannot sell their Parma ham under that name in Canada because there is a Canadian trademark on it, which means a Canadian producer is selling his Canadian ham under the trademark Parma ham in Canada. And this is, of course, a major problem."[36] Indeed, Franz Fischler, the European Farm Commissioner, has stated that it is "simply not acceptable that the EU cannot sell its genuine Parma ham in Canada because the trademark 'Parma Ham' is reserved for a ham produced in Canada."[37] Two current debates in the TRIPS Council are whether and how to create a multilateral register for wines and spirits, and whether to extend the higher-level Article 23 protection to other goods aside from wine and spirits. . . . Although this article focuses on the first issue, the second is also very contentious; several parties are opposed to the idea that wine and spirits deserve special treatment and propose that the value of GIs in general would be harmed by inconsistent application.

The TRIPS Agreement tries to account for the fact that different countries use a variety of legal means to protect GIs, ranging from specific GI statutes to parts of trademark statutes to purely common law. These differences, however, coupled with ideological differences, account for the inability of many countries to reach agreement regarding the strength and breadth of GI protection. Indeed, the TRIPS Agreement requires that its signatories negotiate to create a multilateral register for wines and spirits. A WTO Panel, in an interim decision in December of 2004, found that the existing European rules on GIs were

---

[36]   Breffni O'Rourke, *EU: What's In a Name? Plenty, When It Comes to Famous Brands*, Truth News, Sept. 2, 2003, available at http://truthnews.com/world/2003090013.htm (last visited Feb. 4, 2005).

[37]   *A Ham and Cheese Sandwich by Any Other Name*, Deutsche Welle, Aug. 29, 2003, available at http://www.dw-world.de/dw/article/0,1564,958339,00.html (last visited Feb. 5, 2005).

discriminatory. . . . In the final ruling on the same issue, which came out in March 2005, . . . the WTO Panel upheld claims from the United States and Australia insofar as their claim that provisions under a 1992 EU framework regulation on GI protection are in violation of WTO national treatment rules. . . . The decision has several ramifications, one of which would arguably permit situations, albeit under limited circumstances, where the owner of a valid EU trademark must tolerate the use of a GI registered later, even if there is a subsequent likelihood of confusion, despite the fact that TRIPS does not condone general coexistence of an identical trademark and GI. . . . Upon closer scrutiny, however, the Panel clearly favored the idea that all intellectual property rights are private and equal rights and endorsed the idea that the owner of a prior mark must be able to challenge the registration or use of an identical GI and that, in the event that a high likelihood of confusion would ensue, the challenge should succeed. . . .

There are two main schools of thought on the issue. The United States, among others, supports a system whereby GIs would be voluntarily registered in a database that individual countries would be encouraged to contribute to and consult. . . . By contrast, the "EU Proposal" . . . suggests that registration of a GI should create the presumption that the GI is entitled to protection in all other countries and that, once it has been registered, no country should refuse protection after an 18-month grace period. . . . Because the European Union already has specific regulations in place governing GIs, . . . it stands to "benefit substantially from the economic gains derived from protecting its intellectual property rights in geographical indications."[48] Even so, the European regulations are not universally praised in Europe. There are different levels of understanding of the strength of a GI and, by streamlining the various laws into one, those countries with stronger GI regulations than the European Union regulations may find that their GIs are diluted by weaker standards of protection. . . .

Federal Republic of Germany v. Commission of the European Communities

Court of Justice of the European Communities, 2005.
Joined Cases C-465/02 and C-466/02, 2005.

1   The Federal Republic of Germany and the Kingdom of Denmark have applied for annulment of Commission Regulation (EC) No 1829/2002 of 14 October 2002 amending the Annex to Regulation (EC) No 1107/96 with regard to the name 'Feta' (OJ 2002 L 277, p. 10) ('the contested regulation').

---

[48]   [Stacy D. Goldberg, Who Will Raise the White Flag? The Battle Between the United States and the European Union over the Protection of Geographical Indications, 22 U.Pa. J. Int'l Econ. L. 107, 145.]

Legal framework

2   Article 2(1) to (3) of Council Regulation (EEC) No 2081/92 of 14 July
1992 on the protection of geographical indications and designations of
origin for agricultural products and foodstuffs ('the basic regulation')
provides:

> 1.   Community protection of designations of origin and of
> geographical indications of agricultural products and foodstuffs
> shall be obtained in accordance with this Regulation.

> 2.   For the purposes of this Regulation:

> (a)   designation of origin: means the name of a region, a specific
> place or, in exceptional cases, a country, used to describe an
> agricultural product or a foodstuff:

>> —   originating in that region, specific place or country, and

>> —   the quality or characteristics of which are essentially
>> or exclusively due to a particular geographical environment
>> with its inherent natural and human factors, and the
>> production, processing and preparation of which take place
>> in the defined geographical area;

> (b)   geographical indication: means the name of a region, a
> specific place or, in exceptional cases, a country, used to describe
> an agricultural product or a foodstuff:

>> —   originating in that region, specific place or country, and

>> —   which possesses a specific quality, reputation or other
>> characteristics attributable to that geographical origin and
>> the production and/or processing and/or preparation of
>> which take place in the defined geographical area.

> 3.   Certain traditional geographical or non-geographical
> names designating an agricultural product or a foodstuff
> originating in a region or a specific place, which fulfil the
> conditions referred to in the second indent of paragraph 2(a)
> shall also be considered as designations of origin.

3   Article 3(1) of the same regulation provides:

'Names that have become generic may not be registered.

For the purposes of this Regulation, a "name that has become generic"
means the name of an agricultural product or a foodstuff which, although
it relates to the place or the region where this product or foodstuff was
originally produced or marketed, has become the common name of an
agricultural product or a foodstuff.

To establish whether or not a name has become generic, account shall be
taken of all factors, in particular:

> —   the existing situation in the Member State in which the
> name originates and in areas of consumption,

—   the existing situation in other Member States,

—   the relevant national or Community laws. . . .' . . .

Facts

11   By letter of 21 January 1994, the Greek Government applied under Article 17(1) of the basic regulation for registration of the word 'feta' as a designation of origin.

12   On 12 June 1996, the Commission adopted Commission Regulation (EC) No 1107/96 of 12 June 1996 on the registration of geographical indications and designations of origin under the procedure laid down in Article 17 of Regulation No 2081/92 (OJ 1996 L 148, p. 1). Under the first paragraph of Article 1 of that regulation, the name 'feta' in the Annex thereto in Part A, under the heading 'cheeses' and the country 'Greece', was registered as a protected designation of origin ('PDO').

13   By judgment of 16 March 1999 in Joined Cases C-289/96, C-293/96 and C-299/96 *Denmark and Others* v *Commission* [1999] ECR I-1541, the Court of Justice annulled Regulation No 1107/96 in so far as it registered the name 'feta' as a protected designation of origin.

14   In paragraph 101 of that judgment, the Court held that, when registering the name 'feta', the Commission had not taken any account whatsoever of the fact that that name had been used for a considerable time in certain Member States other than the Hellenic Republic.

15   In paragraph 102 of the judgment, the Court found that the Commission, in considering the question of whether 'feta' was a generic name, had not taken due account of all the factors which the third indent of Article 3(1) of the basic regulation required it to take into consideration.

16   Following that judgment, on 25 May 1999 the Commission adopted Commission Regulation (EC) No 1070/1999 of 25 May 1999 amending the Annex to Regulation (EC) No 1107/96 . . . , which deleted the name 'feta' from the Register of protected designations of origin and geographical indications and from the Annex to Regulation No 1107/96.

17   By letter of 15 October 1999, the Commission sent the Member States a questionnaire on the manufacture and consumption of cheeses known as 'feta' and on how well known that name was amongst consumers in each of the States.

18   The information received in response to that questionnaire was presented to the scientific committee, which gave its opinion on 24 April 2001 ('the scientific committee's opinion'). In that opinion, the committee concluded unanimously that the name 'feta' was not generic in nature.

19   On 14 October 2002, the Commission adopted the contested regulation. Under that regulation, the name 'feta' was once again registered as a protected designation of origin.

20   Article 1 of that regulation provides:

> 1.   The name "Φέτα" (Feta) shall be included in the register of protected designations of origin and geographical indications provided for in Article 6(3) of Regulation (EEC) No 2081/92 as a protected designation of origin (PDO).
>
> 2.   The name "Φέτα" shall be added to part A of the Annex to Regulation (EC) No 1107/96 under the heading "Cheeses", "Greece".

21   According to the 20th recital in the preamble to the contested regulation:

> '(20) According to the information sent by the Member States, those cheeses actually bearing the name "Feta" on Community territory generally make explicit or implicit reference to Greek territory, culture or tradition, even when produced in Member States other than Greece, by adding text or drawings with a marked Greek connotation. The link between the name "Feta" and Greece is thus deliberately suggested and sought as part of a sales strategy that capitalises on the reputation of the original product, and this creates a real risk of consumer confusion. Labels for "Feta" cheese not originating in Greece but actually marketed in the Community under that name without making any direct or indirect allusion to Greece are in the minority and the quantities of cheese actually marketed in this way account for a very small proportion of the Community market.'

22   According to the 33rd to 37th recitals in the preamble to that regulation:

> '(33) The Commission has taken note of the advisory opinion of the Scientific Committee. It takes the view that the exhaustive overall analysis of the legal, historical, cultural, political, social, economic, scientific and technical information notified by the Member States or resulting from investigations undertaken or sponsored by the Commission leads to the conclusion that in particular none of the criteria required under Article 3 of Regulation (EEC) No 2081/92 to show that a name is generic have been met, and that consequently the name "Feta" has not become "the name of an agricultural product or a foodstuff which, although it relates to the place or the region where this product or foodstuff was originally produced or marketed, has become the common name of an agricultural product or a foodstuff".
>
> (34) Since the term "Feta" has not been established as generic, the Commission has verified, in accordance with Article 17(2) of Regulation (EEC) No 2081/92, that the application by the Greek authorities for the name "Feta" to be registered as a protected designation of origin complies with Articles 2 and 4 thereof.

(35) The name "Feta" is a traditional non-geographical name within the meaning of Article 2(3) of Regulation (EEC) No 2081/92. The terms "region" and "place" mentioned in that provision may be interpreted only from a geomorphological and non-administrative viewpoint, in so far as the natural and human factors inherent in a given product are likely to transcend administrative borders. Under the above Article 2(3), however, the geographical area inherent in a designation may not cover an entire country. In the case of the name "Feta", it has therefore been noted that the defined geographical area referred to in the second indent of Article 2(2)(a) of Regulation (EEC) No 2081/92 covers only the territory of mainland Greece and the department of Lesbos; all other islands and archipelagos are excluded because the necessary natural and/or human factors do not apply there. Moreover, the administrative definition of the geographical area has been refined and developed, since the product specification submitted by the Greek authorities contains mandatory cumulative requirements: in particular, the area of origin of the raw material has been substantially limited since the milk used to produce "Feta" cheese must come from ewes and goats of local breeds reared traditionally, whose feed must be based on the flora present in the pastures of eligible regions.

(36) The geographical area covered by the administrative definition and meeting the requirements of the product specification is sufficiently uniform to meet the requirements of Articles 2(2)(a) and 4(2)(f) of Regulation (EEC) No 2081/92. Extensive grazing and transhumance, central to the method of keeping the ewes and goats used to provide the raw material for making "Feta" cheese, are the result of an ancestral tradition allowing adaptation to climate changes and their impact on the available vegetation. This has led to the development of small native breeds of sheep and goats which are extremely tough and resistant, fitted for survival in an environment that offers little food in quantitative terms but, in terms of quality, is endowed with an extremely diversified flora, thus giving the finished product its own specific aroma and flavour. The interplay between the above natural factors and the specific human factors, in particular the traditional production method, which requires straining without pressure, has thus given "Feta" cheese its remarkable international reputation.

(37) Since the product specification submitted by the Greek authorities includes all the information required under Article 4 of Regulation (EEC) No 2081/92, and the formal analysis of that specification has not revealed any obvious error of

assessment, the name "Feta" should be registered as a protected designation of origin.' . . .

41 Accordingly, the first plea must be rejected.

The second plea

42 The German Government submits that there has been infringement of Article 2(3) of the basic regulation. The word 'feta' comes from Italian and means 'slice'. It entered the Greek language in the seventeenth century. The name 'feta' is used not only in Greece but also in other countries in the Balkans and the Middle East to refer to a cheese in brine. The Commission was wrong to consider, in the recitals in the preamble to the contested regulation, whether 'feta' had become a generic name. Since the word is, first of all, a non-geographical term, the Commission should have established that it has acquired a geographic meaning and has done so in a way which does not extend to the whole of the territory of a Member State. Next, the sub-region indicated by the Greek Government in its application for registration is artificially created; it is not based on tradition or on generally-accepted views. Moreover, feta does not owe its quality and characteristics essentially or exclusively to a geographical environment; the statements in the 36th recital in the preamble to the contested regulation are not supported by either the Greek Government's application for registration or by the scientific committee's findings. Lastly, there is no correlation between the geographical area of production and the area of preparation, as is shown by the Greek legal provisions and the fact that the Community grants aid for the production of feta in the Aegean Islands.

43 The Danish Government submits that the name 'feta' does not fulfil the conditions required for registration as a traditional non-geographical name pursuant to Article 2(3) of the basic regulation. The Danish Government states that it is first for the applicant State, and then for the Commission, to establish that the conditions for registration of a designation of origin as a traditional non-geographical name are fulfilled. It states that the geographical area indicated for the purposes of registration in the present case, namely mainland Greece and the department of Lesbos, covers almost all Greece and that no objective reason has been put forward to explain in what respect the regions which have been excluded are any different. The Danish Government states that the exclusive link required between feta cheese and the geographical area indicated in the application does not exist, quite simply because feta comes from throughout the Balkans and not just Greece. The designated geographical area displays considerable climatic and morphological differences and there are many different varieties of Greek fetas, all with different tastes. The international reputation of feta cannot be clearly and directly attributed to the designated geographical area, but rather is largely due to the considerable production and exports of other States, including the Kingdom of Denmark, during the second half of the twentieth century. . . .

46   It is common ground in the present proceedings that the term 'feta' is derived from the Italian word 'fetta', meaning 'slice', which entered the Greek language in the seventeenth century. It is also common ground that 'feta' is not the name of a region, place or country within the meaning of Article 2(2)(a) of the basic regulation. Accordingly, the term cannot be registered as a designation of origin pursuant to that provision. At most, it may be registered under Article 2(3) of the basic regulation, which extends the definition of designation of origin, in particular, to certain traditional non-geographical names.

47   It was on that basis that the term 'feta' was registered as a designation of origin by the contested regulation. According to the 35th recital in the preamble thereto, 'the name "Feta" is a traditional non-geographical name within the meaning of Article 2(3) of [the basic regulation]'.

48   In order to be protected under that provision, a traditional non-geographical name must, inter alia, designate an agricultural product or a foodstuff 'originating in a region or a specific place'.

49   Article 2(3) of the basic regulation, moreover, in referring to the second indent of Article 2(2)(a) of the same regulation, requires that the quality or characteristics of the agricultural product or foodstuff be essentially or exclusively due to a particular geographical environment with its inherent natural and human factors, and that the production, processing and preparation of that product take place in the defined geographical area.

50   It follows from a combined reading of those two provisions that the place or region referred to in Article 2(3) must be defined as a geographical environment with specific natural and human factors and which is capable of giving an agricultural product or foodstuff its specific characteristics. The area of origin referred to must, therefore, present homogenous natural factors which distinguish it from the areas adjoining it. . . .

51   The issue of whether the definition of the region of origin used in the contested regulation complies with the requirements of Article 2(3) of the basic regulation falls to be examined in the light of those various criteria.

52   As the Commission based itself on the Greek legislation governing the matter, it is appropriate to consider Article 1 of Ministerial Order No 313025/1994 of 11 January 1994 recognising the protected designation of origin (PDO) of feta cheese, which provides:

> '1.   The name "feta" is recognised as a protected designation of origin (PDO) for white cheese soaked in brine traditionally produced in Greece, more specifically ("syngekrimena") in the regions mentioned in paragraph 2 of this article, from ewes' milk or a mixture of ewes' milk and goats' milk.
>
> 2.   The milk used for the manufacture of "feta" must come exclusively from the regions of Macedonia, Thrace, Epirus,

Thessaly, Central Greece, Peloponnese and the department (*Nomos*) of Lesbos.'

53 The geographical area thus defined for the production of feta covers only mainland Greece and the department of Lesbos. It does not include the island of Crete or certain Greek archipelagos, namely the Sporades, the Cyclades, the Dodecanese Islands and the Ionian Islands.

54 These areas which have been excluded from this geographical area cannot be considered as negligible. Thus the area defined by the national legislation for the production of cheese bearing the name 'feta' does not cover the entire territory of the Hellenic Republic. It is therefore not necessary to consider whether Article 2(3) of the basic regulation allows the geographical area connected with a name to cover the entire territory of a country.

55 It is nevertheless appropriate to consider whether the area in question was determined in an artificial manner.

56 Article 2(1)(e) of Ministerial Order No 313025 states: 'the milk used for the manufacture of feta must come from breeds of ewes and goats raised using traditional methods and adapted to the region of manufacture of the feta and the flora of that region must be the basis of their feed'.

57 According to the information submitted to the Court, and particularly to the specifications sent by the Greek Government to the Commission on 21 January 1994 with a view to registering the name 'feta' as a designation of origin, the effect of that provision, read together with Article 1 of the same Ministerial Order, is to define the geographical area covered by reference, inter alia, to geomorphology, that is, the mountainous or semi-mountainous nature of the terrain; to the climate, that is, mild winters, hot summers and a great deal of sunshine; and to the botanical characteristics, namely the typical vegetation of the Balkan medium mountain range.

58 Those factors adequately indicate that the area has homogenous natural features which distinguish it from the adjoining areas. The case-file indicates that the areas of Greece which are excluded from the defined area do not display the same natural features as the area in question. It is thus apparent that the area in question in the present case was not determined in an artificial manner. . . .

64 It follows that Article 6(2) of Regulation No 2019/93 is consistent with the definition of the geographical area for the manufacture of feta laid down by the national legislation and included in the application for registration of that name, and that the argument to the contrary put forward by the German Government is unfounded.

65 The applicants submit that the quality and characteristics of feta are not essentially or exclusively due to a particular geographical environment, as required by the second indent of Article 2(2)(a) of the basic regulation.

66   However, the 36th recital in the preamble to the contested regulation refers to a series of factors which indicate that the characteristics of feta are essentially or exclusively due to a particular geographical environment. Contrary to the submissions of the German Government, that statement is supported by the specifications submitted by the Greek Government, which list in detail the natural and human factors which give feta its specific characteristics.

67   Those factors include the amount of sunshine, temperature changes, the practice of transhumance, extensive grazing and vegetation.

68   The applicants have not demonstrated that the Commission's assessment on this point is unfounded.

69   The plea alleging infringement of Article 2(3) of the basic regulation must therefore be dismissed as unfounded.

The third plea

70   The German Government submits that the contested regulation infringes Article 3(1) of the basic regulation. 'Feta' is a generic name within the meaning of Article 3(1). The Commission did not take due account of all the factors, such as the manufacture of feta in Member States other than Greece, the consumption of feta outside Greece, consumer perception, national and Community legislation and previous assessments by the Commission. The likelihood of consumer confusion referred to in the 20th recital in the preamble to the contested regulation cannot serve as a basis for the protection of the name 'feta', because the misleading presentation of a product has no bearing on the issue of whether a name is generic or whether it is a designation of origin.

71   The German Government adds that the finding that the name 'feta' has not become generic is not supported by a sufficient statement of reasons for the purposes of Article 253 EC; the reference to the advisory opinion of a committee is inadequate for this purpose.

72   The Danish Government submits that the Commission adopted the contested regulation in violation of Article 3(1) and Article 17(2) of the basic regulation, since the term 'feta' is a generic name. In its view, when a name is generic in nature from the beginning, or has subsequently become so, it remains so permanently and irrevocably. It is for the applicant State, and secondly for the Commission, to prove that a name other than a geographical one is not generic.

73   The Danish Government further submits that feta does not specifically originate from Greece, either as a name or as a product. The traditional area of consumption and production is spread over several Balkan countries. The Hellenic Republic itself has imported, produced, consumed and exported cheese under the name 'feta', including feta produced using cow's milk. It is probable that Greek consumers, after a number of years, also consider it to be a generic name. Likewise, in other States where feta is consumed and produced in large quantities, whether within the Community or not, consumers consider feta to be a generic

name. Outside its area of origin, feta has been lawfully produced and marketed in many Member States and non-member countries.

74   The Danish Government also submits that Danish production and marketing of feta is in no way contrary to long-standing practices and traditions and does not give rise to any real likelihood of confusion because, since as early as 1963, the Danish legislation has required the name 'Danish feta' to be on the product. The fact that feta is a generic name is evident from a series of provisions and measures emanating from the Community legislature, which includes the Commission.

The generic nature of the name

75   It must be recalled that the third subparagraph of Article 3(1) of the basic regulation provides:

> 'To establish whether or not a name has become generic, account shall be taken of all factors, in particular:
>
> — the existing situation in the Member State in which the name originates and in areas of consumption,
>
> — the existing situation in other Member States,
>
> — the relevant national or Community laws.'

76   As to the argument put forward by the Danish Government to the effect that the term 'feta' refers to a type of cheese originating from the Balkans, it is common ground that white cheeses soaked in brine have been produced for a long time, not only in Greece but in various countries in the Balkans and the southeast of the Mediterranean basin. However, as noted in point B(a) of the scientific committee's opinion, those cheeses are known in those countries under other names than 'feta'.

77   As regards the production situation in the Hellenic Republic itself, the Danish Government submits, without being contradicted on this point, that, until 1988, cheese produced from cow's milk according to methods other than the traditional Greek methods was imported into Greece under the name 'feta' and that, until 1987, feta cheese was produced in Greece using non-traditional methods, in particular from cow's milk.

78   It must be recognised that, if such operations were to persist, they would tend to confer a generic nature on the name 'feta'. The Court nevertheless notes that, by Ministerial Order No 2109/88 of 5 December 1988 approving the replacement of Article 83 'Cheese products' in the Food Code, the definition of the geographical area of production based on traditional practices was established. In 1994, Ministerial Order No 313025 codified all of the rules applicable to feta cheese. Furthermore, all of that legislation created a new situation in which such operations should no longer take place.

79   As to the production situation in the other Member States, the Court notes that it held in paragraph 99 of the judgment in *Denmark and Others* v *Commission*, cited above, that the fact that a product has been

lawfully marketed under a name in some Member States may constitute a factor which must be taken into account in the assessment of whether that name has become generic within the meaning of Article 3(1) of the basic regulation.

80   The Commission acknowledges, moreover, that feta is produced in Member States other than the Hellenic Republic, namely the Kingdom of Denmark, the Federal Republic of Germany and the French Republic. According to the 13th to the 17th recitals in the preamble to the contested regulation, the Hellenic Republic produces approximately 115 000 tonnes annually. In 1998, almost 27 640 tonnes were produced in Denmark. From 1988 to 1998, production in France varied between 7 960 tonnes and 19 964 tonnes. Production in Germany has varied between 19 757 and 39 201 tonnes since 1985.

81   According to those same recitals, the production of feta commenced in 1972 in Germany, in 1931 in France and in the 1930s in Denmark.

82   Moreover, it is common ground that the cheese thus produced could be lawfully marketed, even in Greece, at least until 1988.

83   Although the production in the other countries has been relatively large and of substantial duration, the Court notes, as pointed out by the scientific committee in the first indent of the conclusion in its opinion, that the production of feta has remained concentrated in Greece.

84   The fact that the product has been lawfully produced in Member States other than the Hellenic Republic is only one factor of several which must be taken into account pursuant to Article 3(1) of the basic regulation.

85   As regards the consumption of feta in the various Member States, as opposed to its production, the Court notes that the 19th recital in the preamble to the contested regulation indicates that more than 85% of Community consumption of feta, per capita and per year, takes place in Greece. As noted by the scientific committee, the consumption of feta is therefore concentrated in Greece.

86   The information provided to the Court indicates that the majority of consumers in Greece consider that the name 'feta' carries a geographical and not a generic connotation. In Denmark, by contrast, the majority of consumers believe that the name is generic. The Court does not have any conclusive evidence regarding the other Member States.

87   The evidence adduced to the Court also shows that, in Member States other than Greece, feta is commonly marketed with labels referring to Greek cultural traditions and civilisation. It is legitimate to infer therefrom that consumers in those Member States perceive feta as a cheese associated with the Hellenic Republic, even if in reality it has been produced in another Member State.

88 Those various factors relating to the consumption of feta in the Member States tend to indicate that the name 'feta' is not generic in nature.

89 As to the German Government's argument referring to the second sentence of the 20th recital in the preamble to the contested regulation, it follows from paragraph 87 of this judgment that it is not incorrect to state, with respect to consumers in Member States other than the Hellenic Republic, that 'the link between the name "Feta" and Greece is thus deliberately suggested and sought as part of a sales strategy that capitalises on the reputation of the original product, and this creates a real risk of consumer confusion'.

90 The argument put forward by the German Government maintaining the contrary is, therefore, unfounded.

91 As to the national legislation, it must be borne in mind that, according to the 18th and 31st recitals in the preamble to the contested regulation, the Kingdom of Denmark and the Hellenic Republic were the only Member States at the time which had legislation specifically relating to feta.

92 The Danish legislation does not refer to 'feta' but to 'Danish feta', which would tend to suggest that in Denmark the name 'feta', by itself, has retained a Greek connotation.

93 Furthermore, as the Court noted in paragraph 27 of *Denmark and Others* v *Commission*, cited above, the name 'feta' was protected by a convention between the Republic of Austria and the Kingdom of Greece, concluded on 20 June 1972 pursuant to the agreement of 5 June 1970 between those two States relating to the protection of indications of provenance, designations of origin and names of agricultural, craft and industrial products (BGBl. Nos 378/1972 and 379/1972). Since then, the use of the name in Austria has been reserved exclusively for Greek products.

94 It follows that, as a whole, the relevant national legislation tends to indicate that the name 'feta' is not generic.

95 As to the Community legislation, it is true that the name 'feta' is used without further specification as to the Member State of origin in the combined customs nomenclature and in the Community legislation relating to export refunds.

96 However, the latter legislation and the customs nomenclature apply to customs matters and are not intended to regulate industrial property rights. Their provisions are, therefore, not conclusive in this context.

97 As to earlier assessments made by the Commission, it is true that, on 21 June 1985, it responded to written question No 13/85 from an MEP as follows: 'feta describes a type of cheese and is not a designation of origin'. . . .

98 It should be borne in mind, however, that, at that time, there was not yet Community protection in place for designations of origin and geographical indications, which was established for the first time in the basic regulation. At the date of that response, the name 'feta' was protected in Greece only by traditional custom.

99 It follows from the foregoing that several relevant and important factors indicate that the term has not become generic.

100 In the light of the foregoing, the Court finds that the Commission could lawfully decide, in the contested regulation, that the term 'feta' had not become generic within the meaning of Article 3 of the basic regulation. . . .

107 The Commission clearly set out, in the 11th to the 33rd recitals in the preamble to the contested regulation, the essential factors which led it to the conclusion that the name 'feta' was not generic within the meaning of Article 3 of the basic regulation. That discussion constitutes a sufficient statement of reasons for the purposes of Article 253 EC.

108 It follows that the argument that the statement of reasons contained in the contested regulation is insufficient for a finding that the name 'feta' is not generic lacks foundation.

109 It follows that the plea alleging infringement of Article 3(1) of the basic regulation and of Article 253 EC must be dismissed as unfounded.

110 In the light of all of the foregoing considerations, the present action must be dismissed. . . .

On those grounds, the Court (Grand Chamber) hereby:

1. Dismisses the actions;

2. Orders the Federal Republic of Germany to pay the costs in relation to Case C-465/02 and the Kingdom of Denmark to pay the costs in relation to Case C-466/02;

3. Orders the Hellenic Republic, the French Republic and the United Kingdom of Great Britain and Northern Ireland to bear their own costs.

NOTES

1. *National Traditions for Protecting Geographical Indications.* Geographical indications differ fundamentally from trademarks for goods. Geographical indications are inherently descriptive ("Swiss" watch, for example) with the result that, if considered as trademarks, they would have to acquire secondary meaning in order to be protected. In many cases, geographic indications will be generic ("Roquefort" cheese), which means that, if treated as trademarks, they would not be protected at all. U.S. law brings some otherwise possibly unregistrable geographical indications into the trademark system by allowing them to be registered as certification marks or collective marks, granting the collective that administers the mark the authority to enjoin its use by non-members. For example, use of the geographic name "Vidalia" to indicate that onions come from a particular locale would support registration of a certification mark, while its use by members of a collective to indicate that the onions come from the collective would support registration as a collective mark. *See* 15 U.S.C. § 1127 (definitions of certification and collective marks).

National legislation historically categorized geographical indications as *indications of source*, which are names or signs indicating a product's geographic origin ("Swiss" for watches), and as *appellations of origin*, which indicate not only a product's geographic origin but also qualities attributable to manufacturing processes or environmental factors that prevail in the region ("Roquefort" for cheese). Although the inherently descriptive qualities of appellations of origin generally prevent their registration as trademarks, some countries—France was the first—provide for registration of appellations of origin and impose quality controls on goods bearing the appellation. Originally, appellations of origin were limited to wines and spirits, but the category has since been expanded to encompass food products such as cheese, butter and poultry, and lately even other, non-agricultural products.

2.   *International Protection of Geographical Indications Before TRIPs.*

Paris Convention. Article 1(2) of the Paris Convention includes "indications of source or appellations of origin" among the objects of the treaty's protection, effectively subjecting them to the principle of national treatment under Article 2. Article 10(1) of the Convention enlists Article 9's remedy of seizure upon importation for cases of "direct or indirect use of a false indication of the source of the goods," and Article 10(2) defines the "interested party" entitled to request seizure under Article 9(3) to include producers, manufacturers or merchants established in the locality, region or country falsely indicated, "or in the country where the false indication of source is used." Deceptive use of geographic indications may also be repressed under the provision of Article 10*bis* respecting unfair competition. The Paris Convention provides no specific norms for deceptive conduct, leaving that to the law of the protecting country.

Madrid Agreement for the Prevention of False or Misleading Indications of Source on Goods. Articles 1 and 2 of this Agreement provide extensive seizure remedies, comparable to those prescribed in Article 9 of the Paris Convention, for goods bearing false or misleading indications of geographical origin. Article 3*bis* adds the substantive norm that member countries shall "undertake to prohibit the use, in connection with the sale or display or offering for sale of any goods, of all indications in the nature of publicity capable of deceiving the public as to the source of goods and appearing on signs, advertisements, invoices, wine lists, business letters or papers or any other commercial communication." Under Article 4, national courts may decide which appellations, because generic, are to be denied protection, except in the case of "regional appellations concerning the source of products of the vine."

Lisbon Agreement for the Protection of Appellations of Origin and Their International Registration. The 1958 Lisbon Agreement prescribes a higher level of protection for geographical indications than the Madrid Agreement but, in Article 2(1), limits protection to a narrowly-defined class of appellations of origin—"the geographical name of a country, region, or locality, which serves to designate a product originating therein, the quality and characteristics of which are due exclusively or essentially to the geographical environment, including natural and human factors." The appellation must be specifically recognized and protected in its country of origin and registered at the WIPO International Bureau. Under Article 3, appellations meeting these stringent requirements enjoy protection against a wide range of nondeceptive uses—"any usurpation or imitation, even if the true origin of the product is indicated or if the appellation is used in translated form or accompanied by terms such as 'kind', 'type', 'make,' 'imitation,' or the like." The 2015 Geneva Act of the Lisbon Agreement, once in effect, will formally extend the scope of the Lisbon System to geographical indications in their broadest definition.

Inter-American Convention for Trademark and Commercial Protection. Article 23 of the Convention, which was signed in 1929 and has been ratified by ten countries, including the United States, provides that "[e]very indication of geographical origin or source which does not actually correspond to the place in which the article, product or merchandise was fabricated, manufactured, produced or harvested, shall be considered fraudulent and illegal, and therefore prohibited." While the Convention recognizes an exception for terms which "have come to form the name or designation itself of the article," the Convention does not recognize this exception in cases of "regional indications of origin of industrial or agricultural products the quality and reputation of which to the consuming public depend on the place of production or origin." Additionally, Article 3(5) of the Convention prohibits the registration or deposit of trademarks "[w]hich contain representations of racial types or scenes typical or characteristic of any of the Contracting States, other than that of the origin of the mark."

For a discussion of the international treaty framework for geographical indications see Intellectual Property and Geographical Indications (Dev S. Gangjee ed., 2016), pp. 95–201.

3. *TRIPs Agreement.* Article 22 of the TRIPs Agreement defines "geographical indications" in terms narrower than the reference to indications of source in the Paris Convention and the Madrid Agreement, but broader than the Lisbon Agreement's reference to appellations of origin. Unlike the Lisbon Agreement, TRIPs Article 22(1) clearly encompasses industrial as well as agricultural products, reputation as well as quality of goods, and any indication of geographic origin, not just geographical names. Article 22(2)'s prescription of minimum rights for geographical indications is less rigorous than the rights guaranteed by the Lisbon Agreement, and requires the interested party to demonstrate that the defendant's conduct is either deceptive with respect to geographic origin or constitutes unfair competition under the terms of Paris Convention Article 10*bis*.

What conduct does Article 22(4) cover in its provision respecting "a geographical indication which, although literally true as to the territory, region or locality in which the goods originate, falsely represents to the public that the goods originate in another territory?" Would Article 22(4) require the United States to bar a pork processor in Parma, Ohio from labeling its product as "Parma Ham"?

4. *Wines and Spirits.* Article 23 of the TRIPs Agreement, which together with Article 24 was the subject of intense negotiations, establishes a higher level of protection for wines and spirits than for other classes of geographical indications, requiring member states to protect geographical indications for wines or spirits apart from any deception of the public or other form of unfair competition. (Wines, historically the focus of appellations of origin, shaped the TRIPs debate; spirits were only added at the end of the negotiations.) *See* generally Daniel Gervais, The TRIPs Agreement: Drafting History and Analysis 129–130 (1998).

Article 24 carves out three important exceptions to Article 23's otherwise extensive minimum protection for wines and spirits: Clause (4) allows member states to exempt nationals or domiciliaries who have continuously used a geographical indication for wines or spirits in good faith, or for at least ten years, before the conclusion of the Uruguay Round; clause (5) grandfathers trademarks acquired in good faith under prescribed conditions; and clause (6) exempts a member country from any obligation to protect indications "with respect to products of the vine for which the relevant indication is identical with the customary name of a grape variety existing in the territory of that Member as of the date of entry into force of the WTO Agreement."

Regulations of the U.S. Alcohol and Tobacco Tax and Trade Bureau provide that a name of geographic significance that is also the designation of a class or type of wine, and that is found to be "semi-generic" by the Bureau's Administrator, may be used to designate wines of some other origin if the true origin is disclosed and if the wine is of the same general quality as wine from the indicated origin. Among examples of such semi-generic names are Burgundy, Claret, Chablis, Champagne and Moselle. 27 C.F.R. § 4.24(b)(1), (b)(2) (2015). Would this provision withstand attack under Articles 23 and 24 of the TRIPs Agreement? Is the factual determination whether a term has become a "customary name of a grape variety" to be made by the member state in which the challenged use is made—as would typically be the case for generic marks—or ultimately by a WTO panel? *See* generally Paul Heald, Trademarks and Geographic Indications: Exploring the Contours of the TRIPs Agreement, 29 Vand. J. Trans. L. 635 (1996).

U.S. "Standards of Identity for Distilled Spirits" limit the uses of certain names, such as Scotch whisky, Irish whisky, and Canadian whisky to products made in those regions and countries. The Standards also provide that "[g]eographical names for distinctive types of distilled spirits," such as "Eau de Vie de Dantzig (Danziger Goldwasser), Ojen, [and] Swedish punch," "shall not be applied to distilled spirits produced in any other place than the particular region indicated by the name, unless (i) in direct conjunction with the name there appears the word 'type' or the word 'American' or some other adjective indicating the true place of production, in lettering substantially as conspicuous as such name, and (ii) the distilled spirits to which the name is applied conform to the distilled spirits of that particular region." "Geographical names that are not names for distinctive types of distilled spirits and that have not become generic," such as "Armagnac, Greek brandy, Jamaica rum, [and] Puerto Rico rum," "shall not be applied to distilled spirits produced in any other place than the particular place or region indicated in the name." 27 C.F.R. 5.22 (2013).

5. *The European Union System of Protection.* The European Union recognizes three degrees of protection for geographical designations of agricultural products and foodstuffs. In addition to "designations of origin" and "geographical indications," the EU Regulation also recognizes protection for "traditional specialties guaranteed," which are registered in the European Union for products that "(a) result from a mode of production, processing or composition corresponding to traditional practice for that product or foodstuff; or (b) [are] produced from raw materials or ingredients that are those traditionally used." Regulation (EU) No 1151/2012 of the European Parliament and of the Council of 21 November 2012 on quality schemes for agricultural products and foodstuffs, Article 18(1). In 2009 the Court of Justice of the European Communities observed that the EU system is "a uniform and exhaustive system of protection for such indications" and that it precludes any parallel national protection in the individual EU member states. Budějovický Budvar v. Rudolf Ammersin GmbH, ECJ, C-478/07, 2009, ¶ 114.

In addition to Feta, other EU-registered designations of origin are, for example, Roquefort, Noord-Hollandse Edammer, Blue Stilton, Parmigiano Reggiano, Mozzarella di Bufala Campana, and Prosciutto di Parma. Registered geographical indications include Emmental de Savoie, Lübecker Marzipan, and, since 2003, Budějovické Pivo (Budweiser beer). Examples of registered traditional specialties guaranteed are Mozzarella, Pizza Napoletana, and Traditionally Farmed Gloucestershire Old Spots Pork.

6. *Geographical Indications in U.S. Trademark Law.* The United States, though one of the most active proponents of increased levels of intellectual property protection in the TRIPs Agreement, was notably reticent in the campaign for more rigorous protection of geographical indications. U.S. law has historically treated indications of geographic origin as descriptive and consequently unprotectible absent secondary meaning. In addition to the Lanham Act's provision for registration of geographic certification marks or collective marks, protection against the misleading use of geographic terms is available under the Lanham Act's section 43(a), 15 U.S.C. § 1125(a), outlawing false designations of origin, and under section 42, 15 U.S.C. § 1124, which bars the importation of goods bearing a false indication that the good "is manufactured in any foreign country or locality other than the country or locality in which it is in fact manufactured." *See* generally J. Thomas McCarthy, Trademarks and Unfair Competition, chap. 14 (1999).

International obligations have shaped parts of U.S. trademark law dealing with geographical indications. To implement the North American Free Trade Agreement's requirement that member governments refuse registration to "geographically deceptively misdescriptive marks," Congress in 1993 amended Lanham Act section 2, 15 U.S.C. § 1052(f), to bar registration of these marks. P.L. 103–182, 107 Stat. 2114 (Dec. 8, 1993). To implement Art. 23(2) of the TRIPs Agreement, Congress amended 15 U.S.C. § 1052(a) to bar registration under prescribed conditions of "a geographical indication which, when used on or in connection with wines or spirits, identifies a place other than the origin of the goods."

These amendments did not, however, expressly implement the requirement in TRIPs Article 22 that member states provide legal means for interested parties to prevent "the use of any means in the designation or presentation of a good that indicates or suggests that the good in question originates in a geographical area other than the true place of origin in a manner which misleads the public as to the geographical origin of the good."

Are existing provisions of U.S. trademark law sufficient to comply with this obligation? In the United States, geographically misdescriptive marks for wine and spirits are excluded from registration. Outside of wine and spirits, the U.S. Trademark Office will grant registration to a geographically misdescriptive mark unless "the primary significance of [the mark] is a generally known geographic location," "purchasers would be likely to believe that the goods or services originate in the geographic place identified in the mark," and "the misrepresentation is a material factor in a significant portion of the relevant consumer's decision to buy the goods or use the services." Trademark Manual of Examining Procedure, USPTO, 2018, § 1210.01(b).

7. *The "Old" World v. the "New."* Many countries have valuable geographical indications within their borders, and some of the most valuable of these indications are situated in the "Old World" of Europe. Not surprisingly, the conflict between Old World and New has surfaced at the WTO. In European Communities—Protection of Trademarks and Geographical Indications for Agricultural Products and Foodstuffs, WT/DS174/R, 15 March 2005, a WTO panel ruled in favor of the United States and Australia on their complaint that a 1992 EU Regulation violated applicable national treatment rules, including Article 3 of the TRIPs Agreement, by requiring other WTO members to extend EU-level protection to European geographical indications as a condition to their own nationals receiving registration for their geographical indications in the European Union.

The United States and Australia enjoyed less success in their complaint that, by allowing registration for a geographical indication that is identical or similar to a pre-existing trademark, the same EU Regulation violated TRIPs Article 16(1)'s guarantee against the use of confusingly similar marks. Although the WTO panel agreed that the coexistence of geographical indications and prior trademarks can in principle violate Article 16(1), it concluded that, under the present facts, the EU provision came within the fair use exception of TRIPs Article 17.

The complaint respecting prior trademark use of a geographical indication was triggered by an extended global conflict between American beer producer Anheuser-Busch and Czech brewer Budějovický Budvar (named after its location in a Southern Bohemian town long known by its

German-speaking citizens as Budweis) that has since the early 1900s brought the Budweiser brand and Budweis geographical indication before the courts of no fewer than fifty countries. The WTO panel specifically noted that the EU registrations of the geographical indications were expressly limited to apply without prejudice to any beer trademark or other rights existing in the European Union on the date of the Czech Republic's accession to the Union in 2004, thus meeting Article 17's standard that the exception "take account of the legitimate interests of the owner of the trademark and of third parties." On the tortuous history the Budweiser-Budvar dispute, see Paul Goldstein, Intellectual Property: The Tough New Realities That Could Make or Break Your Business (2007), 192–193; Christopher Heath, A Hungarian Chapter to the Budweiser Saga, 40(3) IIC 328 (2009).

8. *Geographical Indications and Developing and Least-Developed Countries.* A desire to protect local production, guard the quality of goods associated with particular localities, achieve global recognition of local brands, and charge premiums that are associated with reputable brands has led a number of developing and least-developed countries to explore the protection afforded by geographical indications. Organizations and agencies representing producers have tried to protect their indications outside their home countries. For example, the Tea Board of India has pursued protection for "Darjeeling Tea" in multiple countries, and other examples are discussed in Kremer's article excerpted in Chapter I, above.

In colonial times, some countries had systems of protection in certain sectors, such as Algeria in the wine sector, but in general these countries have only recently embarked on developing comprehensive systems for the protection of geographical indications. For example, in 2008 Morocco implemented *sui generis* protection for geographical indications, which it modeled after the EU system, and in 2015 Morocco concluded an agreement with the European Union for the mutual recognition of geographical indications. In Africa, ARIPO and OAPI have pledged their support for development of the protection of geographical indications in their respective member countries.

On the cases concerning "Darjeeling Tea" see Benedetta Ubertazzi, EU Geographical Indications and Intangible Cultural Heritage, 48(5) IIC 562 (2017). On the protection of geographical indications in Africa and its challenges see Getachew Mengistie & Michael Blakeney, Geographical Indications in Africa—Opportunities, Experiences and Challenges, 38(5) EIPR 290 (2016); Obi Chinedu et al., Protected Geographical Indication in Sub-Saharan Africa: Issues and Implications, 1(2) The African Journal of Intell. Property 79 (2017).

9. *Generic Geographical Terms.* Should generic geographical indications be treated any differently than trademarks? What successful geographical indication is *not* generic, at least in the sense that it describes goods of a particular quality? Does the line drawn in *Germany v. EC*, the principal case, make sense in terms of standard trademark principles? General principles of consumer welfare?

Outside the sensitive area of wine, Article 4 of the Madrid Agreement leaves it to national law to determine whether an appellation is generic and consequently unprotected. Article 6 of the Lisbon Agreement provides that a registered appellation cannot be deemed generic under national law so long as it is still protected as an appellation in its country of origin. For example, in 1967 Czechoslovakia requested the registration of "Pilsner" and related terms including "Pilsener" and "Pilsen Beer Pils" as appellations of origin under the Lisbon Agreement. However, following the registration, several countries, including France, filed declarations of refusal under Article 5(3) of the Agreement. *See* also page 607, above.

For a discussion of genericism and geographical indications see Dev S. Gangjee, Genericide: The Death of a Geographical Indication?, in Intellectual Property and Geographical Indications (Dev S. Gangjee ed., 2016), pp. 508–548.

10. *Protection of Geographical Names by Trademark Law.* Can trademark law and unfair competition law sufficiently protect geographical indications? In the EU trademark system, marks indicating the geographical origin of goods or services may be registered after they have acquired distinctivess; marks that are deceptive or protected under *sui generis* legislation on geographical indications will not be registered as EU trademarks. Regulation (EU) 2017/1001 of the European Parliament and of the Council of 14 June 2017 on the European Union trade mark (EU Trademark Regulation), Article 7(1). Indications of the geographical origin of goods and services may be registered as collective marks that distinguish the goods and services of the members of an association, but not as certification marks. *Id.*, Articles 74(2) and 83(1). *See* also Martina Repas & Tomaz Kerestes, The Certification Mark as A New EU-Wide Industrial Property Right, 49(3) IIC 299 (2018).

The tort of so-called "extended passing off" may protect a geographical term in England. In FAGE UK Ltd. v. Chobani UK Ltd., [2014] EWCA Civ 5. FAGE sued Chobani, a U.S.-based manufacturer, in an English court alleging that Chobani committed passing off when it described its U.S.-made yoghurt as "Greek Yoghurt." FAGE contended that the phrase denotes a type of yoghurt made in Greece, while Chobani argued that the phrase was a general term covering a variety of products, including its U.S.-made yoghurt. Lord Justice Kitchin agreed with the finding of the lower-court judge that there was a passing off, noting that "contrary and notwithstanding that few know how or why Greek yoghurt has its distinctive thick and creamy texture, a substantial proportion of the relevant public not only believe that Greek yoghurt comes from Greece but also believe it to be special." *Id.*, ¶ 70.

Responding to Chobani's argument that EU law on the protection of geographical indications precludes national systems of protection for geographical indications, Lord Justice Kitchin pointed out that "[EU] law does not preclude the application of national rules for the protection of geographical denominations which do not fall within the material scope of the 2012 Regulation." *Id.*, ¶ 90. The judge concluded that "Greek yoghurt" fell outside the scope of the Regulation: "It cannot be said that its quality or characteristics are essentially due to any aspect of the environment in

[Greece]." Additionally, the Justice observed that "the fundamental difficulty facing any applicant to register Greek yoghurt in Greece is that the phrase has never been used in any language in Greece to describe yoghurt sold there on the open market." *Id.*, ¶¶ 90 and 106.

11. *Geographical Indications for Non-Agricultural Products.* Should the protection of geographical indications extend to products other than wine, spirits, agricultural products, and foodstuffs? The concept of *terroir* refers to the link between a product's characteristics and the environment in which the product is produced, but consider whether Carrara marble and Solingen knives also enjoy a link between their characteristics and the environment in which they are produced.

Discussions regarding the protection of folklore and traditional knowledge have propelled interest in expanding the protection of geographical indications to cover some aspects of folklore and traditional knowledge. However, as the examples above suggest, the interest is far from being limited to the developing and least-developed countries. The European Commission and the EU Parliament recommended in 2014 and 2015, respectively, that a geographical indications system for handicrafts be adopted in the European Union.

Some countries, such as Croatia, the Czech Republic, Estonia, India, Thailand, Tunisia, and Uganda, have created sui generis protection for non-agricultural products. For example, under a Ugandan law that introduced protection of geographical indications in 2013, protection is available to any "natural or agricultural product or animal product or a product of handicraft or industry" whose "quality, reputation or other characteristics [are] essentially attributable to its geographical origin." Geographical Indications Act No. 8 of 2013, Section 2. Specific laws protect particular products in some countries. For example, a special regulation protects the use of the word "Solingen" on knives and other products in Germany. Regulation for the Protection of the Name Solingen, 1994.

In 2014 France added a new section on geographical indications to its Intellectual Property Code on protecting industrial and handicraft products. According to Article L721-2, a geographical indication protected under the section is "a name of a geographical area or of a specific place that is used to describe a product, other than agricultural, forestry, food, or sea product, which originates there and has a specific quality, reputation, or other characteristic that is essentially attributable to its geographical origin." Law No. 2014-344 of 2014 on Consumer Protection. The first application filed under the law was for "Marseille soap." On the French law of 2014 see Giancarlo Moretti, The Registration of Geographical Indications for Non-Agricultural Products in France and Its Impact on Proposed EU Legislation, 38(11) EIPR 686 (2016).

Do current international intellectual property treaties apply to non-agricultural geographical indications? As of March 1, 2019, there were 129 geographical indications for non-agricultural products registered under the Lisbon Agreement, including "Poterie de Vallauris" pottery from Vallauris, France, and "Lepenica" marble from Lepenica, Bulgaria.

For a general discussion of geographical indications for non-agricultural products see Delphine Marie-Vivien, A Comparative Analysis of GIs for Handicrafts: The Link to Origin in Culture as well as Nature?, Intellectual Property and Geographical Indications (Dev S. Gangjee ed., 2016), pp. 292–326.

12. *Geographical Indications and Migration.* Wars, acts of violence, and economic struggle trigger movements of entire populations. How should the law view descriptions of products that are produced only by people who no longer live in an area to which the designations of origin refer? Königsberger Bärenfang is a liquor that was originally made by German inhabitants of Königsberg, which is now called Kaliningrad and is now part of Russia. After the German inhabitants of Kaliningrad left Kaliningrad for Germany, should Germany be able to claim Königsberger Bärenfang as a geographical indication for the liquor now produced in Germany? Regulation (EC) No 110/2008 of the European Parliament and of the Council of 15 January 2008 on the definition, description, labelling and the protection of geographical indications of spirit drinks.

Should the country from which a population migrates be permitted to register a geographical indication for a product once associated with the population? Austria and Germany objected to the registration of the Czech name "Karlovarské oplatky" ("Carlsbad Wafers" in English, "Karlsbader Oblaten" in German) as a protected geographical indication for wafers made in Karlovy Vary in the Czech Republic (known as Karlsbad in German). Germany argued that German consumers perceived the term, describing wafers made in the part of the Czech Republic that used to be inhabited primarily by a German population before 1945, as a term describing a certain type of wafer. Additionally, trademarks including "Karlsbader Oblaten" had been registered in Germany by producers originating from Karlovy Vary. Commission Regulation (EU) No 744/2011 of 28 July 2011 entering a name in the register of protected designations of origin and protected geographical indications (Karlovarské oplatky (PGI)).

3. REGISTRATION, USE AND PRIORITIES

a. USE AND USE PRIORITIES

Paris Convention for the Protection of Industrial Property
Stockholm Text, 1967.

Article 6*bis*

(1) The countries of the Union undertake, ex officio if their legislation so permits, or at the request of an interested party, to refuse or to cancel the registration, and to prohibit the use, of a trademark which constitutes a reproduction, an imitation, or a translation, liable to create confusion, of a mark considered by the competent authority of the country of registration or use to be well known in that country as being

already the mark of a person entitled to the benefits of this Convention and used for identical or similar goods. These provisions shall also apply when the essential part of the mark constitutes a reproduction of any such well-known mark or an imitation liable to create confusion therewith.

(2)   A period of at least five years from the date of registration shall be allowed for requesting the cancellation of such a mark. The countries of the Union may provide for a period within which the prohibition of use must be requested.

(3)   No time limit shall be fixed for requesting the cancellation or the prohibition of the use of marks registered or used in bad faith.

i.   *Famous Marks*

McDonald's Corporation v. Joburgers Drive-Inn Restaurant (Pty) Ltd.

1997 South African Law Reports 1.
Supreme Court of South Africa, Appellate Division, Case No. 547/95, 1996.

E M Grosskopf JA: This is a dispute about the use and continued registration of the appellant's trade marks. The appellant, to which I shall refer as McDonald's, is a corporation incorporated in the state of Delaware in the United States of America. It is one of the largest franchisers of fast food restaurants in the world, if not the largest. It first commenced business in the United States of America in 1955 and has carried on business internationally since 1971. It operates its own restaurants and also franchises others to do so. It sells hamburgers and other fast foods. The McDonald's trade mark is widely used in relation to restaurants owned by McDonald's as well as those that are franchised.

McDonald's obtained registration of its trade marks in South Africa in 1968, 1974, 1979, 1980, 1984 and 1985. It is now the registered proprietor of 52 marks. Of these, 27 consist of or incorporate the word McDonald or McDonald's. Also used is the letter 'M' in the form of so-called golden arches, with or without the word McDonald's. Others consist of the words Big Mac, Egg McMuffin and McMuffin. There are also two clown devices. The trade marks are registered in respect of goods, mainly in classes 29 and 30, and for services in class 42.

When the present proceedings commenced, McDonald's had not traded in South Africa nor, we may assume for present purposes, had it used any of its trade marks here.

Joburgers Drive-Inn Restaurant (Pty) Ltd ('Joburgers') is a South African company with its principal place of business in Johannesburg. Its managing director is Mr. George Sombonos. Mr. Sombonos has been engaged in the fast food industry since 1968. In 1979 he registered a company called Golden Fried Chicken (Pty) Ltd ('Chicken Licken'). He holds 90% of the shares in the company and is its managing director. In

1979 Chicken Licken applied for the registration of a number of trade marks, including Chicken Licken. Since then it has franchised the Chicken Licken business so that today there are more than 177 stores throughout South Africa. Mr. Sombonos says that Chicken Licken is the biggest fried chicken fast food franchise chain in the world not having its origins in the United States of America.

During 1992 Mr. Sombonos on behalf of Joburgers decided to establish fast food outlets and restaurants using the trade marks McDonald's, Big Mac and the golden arches design. In 1993 Mr. Sombonos applied for the registration of these and some other McDonald's marks. At the same time he applied to the Registrar of Trade Marks in terms of s 36(*l*)(a) and (b) of the Trade Marks Act 62 of 1963 ('the old Act') for the expungement of the trade marks which are held by McDonald's. McDonald's opposed these applications and filed its counter-statements in the expungement applications during August 1993. During the same period McDonald's applied again for the registration of all the trade marks in its name.

On 29 August 1993 there appeared an article in the Sunday Times newspaper, reading *inter alia* as follows:

'Big Macs may soon be eaten all over South Africa, but not because American hamburger giant McDonald's is entering the market. Nor will they be on sale before judgment in which could be SA's biggest trade mark battle.

Chicken Licken franchise owner George Sombonos plans to start his own national McDonald's hamburger chain. Sites have been chosen and an advertising campaign is being prepared.

Mr. Sombonos's lawyer, Shaun Ryan of Ryans Attorneys, says the first restaurant will open in Johannesburg "as soon as physically possible".

The chain will serve McMuffins and Big Mac burgers. Restaurants will also be decorated with a large M device similar to two joined arches.'

In response to this article McDonald's wrote through its attorneys to Joburgers' attorney, *inter alia*, as follows:

'We are instructed that the intended use of McDonald's trade marks (which were listed in an annexure to the letter) constitutes an infringement of our client's trade mark rights. Your client has unequivocally expressed a clear intention to use such trade marks.

We have been instructed to demand as we hereby do that your client unequivocally undertake that it will not use our client's registered trade marks or any other marks which are deceptively or confusingly similar to our client's registered trade marks.'

Failing an undertaking as demanded in this letter, McDonald's threatened legal proceedings.

Joburgers' reply was uncompromising. It read, *inter alia*:

'We are aware that your client is the registrant for the trade marks listed in the annexure to your letter. Your client is not the proprietor of these trade marks. The true proprietor of the subject-matter of these registrations is Joburgers Drive-Inn Restaurant (Pty) Ltd. You may take it that it is our client's intention to both use and register its trade marks in the Republic of South Africa. . . . Your client is invited to take legal proceedings as threatened.'

On 23 September 1993 McDonald's launched an urgent application against Joburgers in the Transvaal Provincial Division for relief on the grounds of infringement of its trade marks, passing-off and unlawful competition. I shall refer to this application as the Joburgers application. On 28 September 1993 Swart J granted an order by agreement, the relevant part of which read as follows:

'The respondent undertakes, pending the determination of this application and the proposed counter-application, not to infringe the applicant's registered trade marks . . . which undertaking is made an order of Court.'

It came to Joburgers' notice that there was a fast food outlet in Durban trading under the name (or names) Asian Dawn and MacDonalds. MacDonalds, it is pointed out in passing, is spelt differently from McDonald's. On 15 October 1993 Mrs. A. T. Pead, a director of Joburgers, and Mr. S F Ryan, Joburgers' attorney, travelled to Durban from Johannesburg to buy the outlet. It is not quite clear from the papers who exactly owned the business, but the interested parties were a close corporation called Asian Dawn Investments CC, its sole member, Miss Sajee Bibi Farid Khan, and her brother, Mr. Rafique Khan. According to an affidavit by Mrs. Pead, she approached Mr. Rafique Khan in the shop and offered to buy it as a going concern. She said she wanted it for her son to encourage him not to leave the country. (In fact she was acting for Joburgers and wanted to secure the trade mark for use in the present proceedings.) Mr. Khan was prepared to sell if the price was right, but first wanted to speak to his sister as, he said, they were joint owners. Later he informed Mrs. Pead that he had spoken to his sister and that they were willing to sell the business as a going concern for R250 000. The Joburgers contingent were not happy with the price, but asked for an option to give them time to think about it. The parties then executed and signed a written option at a price of R250 000. Some days later, after further negotiations, the parties agreed telephonically on a price of R225 000. The Khans' attorney was to draw up a written contract.

The contract was not forthcoming. Mrs. Pead phoned Mr. Khan to find out what was happening. He told her that he had been approached by attorneys acting for McDonald's and that the price he had agreed with Mrs. Pead was made to look 'not only like peanuts but dried peanuts'. He now wanted offers that were 'telephone figures'. No amount of persuasion could change his attitude, and Joburgers brought an urgent application to restrain Mr. and Miss Khan and her close corporation from selling, alienating or otherwise disposing of the business. An order to this effect was granted. Ultimately, on 22 November 1993, the parties entered into a new contract of sale at a price of R350 000.

In the meantime the proceedings between McDonald's and Joburgers were continuing. On 15 November 1993 Joburgers served answering affidavits and a counter-application. The main relief sought in the counter-application was the expungement of the McDonald's trade marks in terms of s 36(1)(a) and (b) of the old Act, *i.e.* on the grounds, broadly stated, that the marks were registered without any *bona fide* intention on the part of McDonald's that they should be used and that they had in fact not been used for the periods required by the section.

Early in 1994 McDonald's became aware that Joburgers was conducting the business in Durban under the name MacDonalds. McDonald's immediately launched proceedings for relief on the grounds that Joburgers was in contempt of Court—it was contravening the order granted by consent on 28 September 1993 in terms of which Joburgers undertook (and was ordered) not to infringe the registered McDonald's trade marks. The matter came before Nugent J. On 15 March 1994 he declared that Joburgers was in contempt of the earlier order and that all proceedings in respect of its counter-application to expunge the McDonald's trade marks be stayed until it had purged its contempt.

On the very next day Joburgers' attorney wrote to the attorneys for McDonald's to say that Joburgers had disposed of the business. Requests by McDonald's for further information about the disposal proved fruitless.

In May 1994 it came to the notice of McDonald's that the MacDonald's business in Durban was being conducted by Dax Prop CC ('Dax'). The sole member of Dax is Mr. George Charalambous. He has worked as a baker and hotelier. In 1988 he gave up his employment to commence his own business as a franchisee of Chicken Licken. He is now the sole director and shareholder of a company which has six Chicken Licken franchises and a member of a close corporation which also has several franchises. These are all in KwaZulu/Natal. Mr. Charalambous is responsible for the management of all these businesses.

On 17 May 1994 McDonald's wrote through its attorneys to Dax asking, *inter alia*, for an undertaking that Dax cease forthwith to use the trade mark MacDonalds or any other trade mark which is deceptively or confusingly similar to McDonald's, failing which proceedings would be instituted.

No such undertaking was given.

On 25 May 1994 Dax applied to register the mark MacDonald's in classes 29, 30, and 42. On 9 August 1994 Dax launched an application, also in the Transvall Provincial Division, against McDonald's, seeking expungement from the register of the trade marks relied upon by

McDonald's in its letter of 17 May 1994. Dax also sought some additional relief which need not be set out. McDonald's brought a counter-application for an interdict preventing Dax from infringing its trade marks.

At this stage the position then was that, in the Joburgers application, McDonald's applied against Joburgers for an interdict to restrain trade mark infringement and Joburgers sought, in a counter-application, expungement of the marks, whereas in the Dax application, Dax asked for expungement and McDonald's, in the counter-application, asked for an interdict.

On 1 May 1995 the Trade Marks Act 194 of 1993 ('the new Act') came into force. Section 35 of the new Act provides for the protection of 'well-known' trade marks emanating from certain foreign countries. On 20 June 1995 McDonald's brought an application against Joburgers and Dax under s 35 of the new Act. It claimed that all 52 of its trade marks are well-known marks in terms of the section, and sought an order that Joburgers and Dax be interdicted and restrained from imitating, reproducing or transmitting those marks in the Republic of South Africa. I shall call this the 'well-known marks application'.

Section 71 of the new Act repealed the old Act. However, s 3(2) of the new Act provides that all applications and proceedings commenced under the repealed Act shall be dealt with in accordance with the provisions of that Act as if it had not been repealed. The Joburgers and Dax applications must therefore be dealt with in accordance with the old Act. The well-known marks application, on the other hand, must be decided according to the new Act.

The three applications were heard together by Southwood J. He found in favour of Joburgers and Dax. Accordingly, in the Joburgers application, the application by McDonald's for an interdict was dismissed and Joburgers's counter-application for expungement granted; in the Dax application, Dax's application for expungement was granted and the counter-application by McDonald's for an interdict was refused; and the well-known marks application by McDonald's was refused. In all cases appropriate costs orders were made.

With the leave of the Court *a quo* McDonald's now appeals against these orders. . . .

I turn now to the arguments on the merits. For convenience I start with the well-known marks application. Section 35 of the new Act reads as follows:

'(1) References in this Act to a trade mark which is entitled to protection under the Paris Convention as a well-known trade mark, are to a mark which is well known in the Republic as being the mark of—

(a)   a person who is a national of a convention country; or

(b)   a person who is domiciled in, or has a real and effective industrial or commercial establishment in, a convention country, whether or not such person carries on business, or has any goodwill, in the Republic.

(2)   A reference in this Act to the proprietor of such a mark shall be construed accordingly.

(3)   The proprietor of a trade mark which is entitled to protection under the Paris Convention as a well-known trade mark is entitled to restrain the use in the Republic of a trade mark which constitutes, or the essential part of which constitutes, a reproduction, imitation or translation of the well-known trade mark in relation to goods or services which are identical or similar to the goods or services in respect of which the trade mark is well known and where the use is likely to cause deception or confusion.'

There was a large area of agreement between the parties about the meaning and application of this section. Thus it was common cause that McDonald's in fact is a person such as is described in paras (a) and (b) of s (1). The parties were also agreed on what it is that has to be 'well known' in the Republic. In this regard the Court *a quo* had said:

'. . . (I)t is not sufficient that the mark simply be well known in the Republic. It must be established that the mark is well known as the mark of a person who is (a) a national of, or (b) is domiciled in, or (c) has a real and effective industrial or commercial establishment in, a convention country: *i.e.* it must also be well known that there is a connection between the mark and some person falling in categories (a), (b) or (c).'

This seems to suggest that the section only applies if what is well known is not only the mark itself, but also the nationality, domicile or place of business of the mark's owner, and moreover the fact that the relevant country is a convention country. Before us counsel were *ad idem* that such an interpretation could not be supported. If it were correct the section would be a dead letter. It is difficult to imagine any mark, however well known, in respect of which such further facts would be common knowledge. The parties accordingly accepted (I think correctly) that it would be enough for a plaintiff to prove that the mark is well known as a mark which has its origin in some foreign country, provided that as a fact the proprietor of the mark is a person falling within ss (1)(a) or (b).

The essential dispute between the parties was what level of awareness in the public mind is required for a mark to qualify as 'well known' in terms of s 35. In this regard it is useful to look at the background to the section. . . .

Also in South Africa it has been held that a goodwill existing within the country is necessary to found a claim in respect of passing-off. See, for instance, Slenderella Systems Incorporated of America v. Hawkins and Another 1959 (1) SA 519 (W) at 52 IA–522B, Lorimar Productions Inc and Others v Sterling Clothing Manufacturers (Pty) Ltd; Lorimar Productions Inc and Others v OK Hyperama Ltd and Others; Lorimar Productions Inc and Others v Dallas Restaurant 1981 (3) SA 1129 M at 11 38H–1 140A and Tie Rack plc v Tie Rack Stores (Pty) Ltd and Another 1989 (4) SA 427 (T) at 442G–445D. In the last-mentioned case the applicant conducted in the United Kingdom and elsewhere, but not in South Africa, either by itself or through franchisees, a number of shops under the name 'Tie Rack'. It sought to interdict the respondents from doing likewise in this country. This attempt failed. The basic reason was stated by Kriegler J as follows (at 445C–D):

> 'The simple truth is that applicant has no goodwill, no attractive force in this country. The fact that people in this country—and accepting that there may be many—know of applicant's business abroad and may be misled into believing first respondent's shops are in some way associated therewith, does not afford applicant a proprietary right in this country. Put differently, applicant has no business of any kind in South Africa and nothing first respondent has done can or is likely to do any harm to applicant in the patrimonial sense in this country.'

For present purposes it is not necessary to determine whether these cases were correctly decided either in the United Kingdom or in South Africa. In Australia, for instance, the Federal Court went the other way. *See* Conagra Inc v McCain Foods (Aust) Ay Ltd 23 IPR 193. However, whether the above cases were right or wrong, they demonstrate that the Courts in this country and the United Kingdom have in fact not protected the owners of foreign trade marks who did not have a goodwill within the country. To that extent the common law of passing-off has not been sufficient to constitute compliance with art 6*bis* of the Paris Convention.

It seems clear that s 35 of the new Act and the corresponding provision in the United Kingdom were intended to remedy this lack. Thus, s 35(1) pertinently extends protection to the owner of a foreign mark, 'whether or not such person carries on business, or has any goodwill, in the Republic'. And the type of protection which is granted by ss (3) is typical of that which is available under the common law of passing-off: a prohibition on the use of the mark in relation to goods or services in respect of which the mark is well known and where the use is likely to cause deception or confusion.

It is against this background that the expressions 'well-known trademark' and 'well known in the Republic' must be interpreted. Counsel for McDonald's contended that the Legislature intended to impose no more than the ordinary requirement for passing-off actions, namely that the reputation must extend to a substantial number of members of the public or persons in the trade in question. . . .

Of course, the mere fact that the Legislature intended to provide some protection for a foreign trader who does not have a goodwill or a business inside the country does not necessarily mean that such protection must be coterminous with that afforded to local businessmen. It is accordingly conceivable that, in order to receive protection, the foreigner might have to prove a greater public awareness of his mark than is required of a local businessman claiming a remedy against passing-off. And, indeed, the respondents argued that the Legislature, in giving protection only to well-known marks, did impose a higher standard. On the ordinary meaning of language, so the argument went, a mark is well known in the Republic only when known to a large part of the population as a whole.

This argument raises two questions, namely

(a) must the mark be well known to all sectors of the population; and

(b) whatever the relevant sector of the population may be, what degree of awareness within that sector is required before a mark can properly be described as well known.

The answer to question (a) is, I think, clear. Section 35 of the new Act was intended to provide a practical solution to the problems of foreign businessmen whose marks were known in South Africa but who did not have a business here. The South African population is a diverse one in many respects. There are wide differences—in income, education, cultural values, interests, tastes, personal life styles, recreational activities, etc. This was obviously known to the Legislature when it passed the new Act. If protection is granted only to marks which are known (not to say well known) to every segment of the population (or even to most segments of the population), there must be very few marks, if any, which could pass the test. The legislation would therefore not achieve its desired purpose. Moreover, there would not appear to be any point in imposing such a rigorous requirement. In argument we were referred as an example to a mark which might be very well known to all persons interested in golf. Why should it be relevant, when deciding whether or not to protect such a mark, that non-golfers might never have heard of it? I consider therefore that a mark is well known in the Republic if it is well known to persons interested in the goods or services to which the mark relates.

The next question then is: how well should it be known to such persons? (Question (b) above.) On behalf of McDonald's it was argued that the test in this regard is a qualitative and not a quantitative one. The question is not, it was argued, how many of the relevant persons know the mark, but how profound the knowledge of the mark is among those who do know it. In my view this argument is untenable. I suppose that knowledge of a mark could be so vague or superficial as hardly to count as knowledge at all, but apart from that I would not have thought that there would normally be great differences in the degree of knowledge of the mark by members of the public, or that such differences, if they existed, would be of any relevance. In the present context the important practical question is not whether a few people know the mark well but rather whether sufficient persons know it well enough to entitle it to protection against deception or confusion.

How many people are sufficient? The only guideline provided by the Legislature lies in the expression 'well known'. This is in itself so vague as hardly to provide any assistance at all. It is certainly capable of bearing the meaning urged upon us by counsel for McDonald's, namely a substantial number as used in the law of passing-off generally. In this regard the judge *a quo* commented that if it was the object of the subsection to require knowledge only of a substantial number of persons, 'it is strange that this was not simply stated to be the requirement instead of merely adopting the terminology of section (*sic*) 6*bis* (1) of the Paris Convention'. With respect, I do not agree. The purpose of the Legislature clearly was to give legislative force to article 6*bis* of the Convention. To this end it was natural to repeat the language of the Convention, leaving it to the Courts to give practical effect to the vague expressions used.

On behalf of the respondents it was contended that a greater extent of public knowledge is required. The difficulty here is one of definition and practical application. If a substantial number is not sufficient, what is? To require one hundred percent would clearly be excessive, but how much less would suffice? Seventy-five percent, fifty percent? What logical basis is there for laying down any such requirement? And how does one prove any such arbitrary percentage?

It seems to me that McDonald's contention must be sustained. The Legislature intended to extend the protection of a passing-off action to foreign businessmen who did not have a business or enjoy a goodwill inside the country, provided their marks were well known in the Republic. It seems logical to accept that the degree of knowledge of the marks that is required would be similar to that protected in the existing law of passing-off. The concept of a substantial number of persons is well established. It provides a practical and flexible criterion which is consistent with the terms of the statute. No feasible alternative has been suggested. . . .

I turn now to the evidence concerning the extent to which the McDonald's trade marks are known in the Republic. As I have stated earlier, McDonald's is one of the largest, if not the largest, franchiser of fast food restaurants in the world. At the end of 1993 there were 13,993 McDonald's restaurants spread over 70 countries. The annual turnover of McDonald's restaurants amounts to some $23, 587 million. McDonald's trade marks are used extensively in relation to its own restaurants as well as to those that are franchised. The level of advertising and promotion which has been carried out by McDonald's, its subsidiaries, affiliates and franchisees in relation to McDonald's restaurants exceeds the sum of $900 million annually. Their international marketing campaigns have included sponsorship of the 1984 Los Angeles and 1992 Barcelona Olympics. McDonald's has also been a sponsor of the 1990 soccer World Cup Tournament in Italy and the 1994 World Cup Soccer Tournament in the United States of America. Mr. Paul R Duncan, the vice president and general counsel of McDonald's, stated on affidavit that, in view of the vast scale of his organisation's operations, the McDonald's trade marks are in all probability some of the best known trade marks in the world. This was not denied. Although there was no evidence on the extent to which the advertising outside South Africa spilled over into this country through printed publications and television, it must, in all probability, be quite extensive. In addition, the McDonald's trade marks would be known to many South Africans who have travelled abroad. This again would not be an insignificant number.

Spontaneous acts by South Africans have confirmed that there is a general level of knowledge in this country about the operations of McDonald's. Thus McDonald's disclosed that, between 1975 and 1993 it received 242 requests from South Africans to conclude franchising agreements. Some of these applicants were prominent companies. For reasons which are not relevant at present, none of these applications were acceded to.

The conduct of Joburgers and Dax in the present case confirms the reputation attaching to the McDonald's marks. Intrinsically the word McDonald has no attractive force. It is a fairly common surname. Had it not been for the reputation it has acquired over the years nobody would wish to appropriate it. It is therefore significant that Joburgers and Dax have gone to considerable trouble and expense to obtain control over the McDonald's marks. . . .

The evidence adduced by McDonald's leads, in my view, to the inference that its marks, and particularly the mark McDonald's, are well known amongst the more affluent people in the country. People who travel, watch television, and who read local and foreign publications, are likely to know about it. They would have seen McDonald's outlets in other countries, and seen or heard its advertisements there or its spillover here in foreign journals, television shows, etc. Although the extent of such spillover has not been quantified, it must be substantial. Moreover, as has been shown, McDonald's has also received publicity in the local media. The market survey evidence specifically related to two groups of adult white persons living in relatively affluent suburbs of Gauteng and KwaZulu/Natal. It is reasonable to suppose that much the same results would be achieved elsewhere among persons of all races who have a similar financial and social background. These are also the type of people who would have heard about McDonald's and its marks from Collins, or who would have discussed these matters with him, or would have written to McDonald's to solicit a franchise agreement.

By the same token, people who are poor, do not travel abroad, do not read foreign publications or, possibly, do not read at all, and are not exposed to television, are likely not to have heard of McDonald's or its marks. It is accordingly not surprising that market surveys commissioned by Joburgers and Dax showed a low awareness of McDonald's and its marks among black persons generally.

These conclusions must be applied to the relevant categories among the public. Potential franchisees, I consider, would be the type of persons who would almost without exception have heard of McDonald's and know its marks. Among potential customers the level of awareness would be lower. Many people who would be interested in buying a hamburger would not have heard of McDonald's. However, a certain degree of financial well-being is required for the purchase of prepared food. Extremely poor people are not likely to patronise McDonald's establishments. Of the persons who are likely to do so, at least a substantial portion must be of the category who would probably have heard of McDonald's and know its marks, or some of them. This inference is supported by the zeal shown by Joburgers and Dax to appropriate these marks for themselves.

I consider therefore that at least a substantial portion of persons who would be interested in the goods or services provided by McDonald's know its name, which is also its principal trade mark. At least this mark is in my view well known for the purposes of s 35 of the new Act. Since McDonald's has not in fact carried on business in South Africa, people who know its mark will also know it as a foreign (and, more particularly, American) business. It almost goes without saying that if the McDonald's mark is used as contemplated by Joburgers and Dax in relation to the same type of fast food business as that conducted by McDonald's, it would cause deception or confusion within the meaning of s 35(3) of the new Act. In the result McDonald's has in my view satisfied all the requirements of this subsection. . . .

I now turn to the Joburgers application and the Dax application. As stated above, these applications have to be decided in accordance with the terms of the old Act.

It will be recalled that each of these matters involved an application for the removal from the register of the McDonald's trade marks and an application by McDonald's for an interdict restraining the use of its marks. It was common cause that the decisive issue related to removal— if the applications for removal were granted, the applications for interdicts would fall away. Per contra, if removal was refused, the interdicts had to be granted.

The applications for removal from the register were brought under s 36(*l*) of the old Act. This subsection provides, *inter alia*, that

'. . . a registered trade mark may, on application to the court . . . by any person aggrieved, be taken off the register in respect of any of the goods or services in respect of which it is registered, on the ground either—

(a) that the trade mark was registered without any *bona fide* intention on the part of the applicant for registration that it should be used in relation to those goods or services by him, and that there has in fact been no *bona fide* use of the trade mark in relation to those goods or services by any proprietor thereof for the time being up to the date one month before the date of the application; or

(b) that up to the date one month before the date of the application a continuous period of five years or longer elapsed during which the trade mark was a registered trade mark and during which there was no *bona fide* use thereof in relation to those goods, or services by any proprietor thereof for the time being; . . . .'

A great deal of evidence and argument was presented to us on whether Joburgers and Dax have established a case for removal under these provisions and, if they have, whether McDonald's has succeeded in showing that, as far as the application under s 36(*l*)(b) was concerned, its non-use of the marks was excusable as being 'due to special circumstances in the trade' for the purposes of s 36(2). In my view it is not necessary to consider these aspects. The position now is that the well-known marks application has succeeded, at least as far as the mark 'McDonald's' is concerned. Although, as stated above, there are some McDonald's marks which do not incorporate the name McDonald's, we were assured that the marks were all in some way associated with one another. Moreover, the case was fought on a winner take all principle. It was not suggested by Joburgers or Dax that, even if the marks containing the name McDonald's were well known, they would still be entitled to use, say, the clown device. The prize at issue is the mark McDonald's. The well-known marks application has effectively awarded it to McDonald's.

In these circumstances it seems anomalous and even futile to proceed with the applications for removal from the register. Even if these applications succeeded it would not benefit Joburgers or Dax. They would still be interdicted from using the mark McDonald's. . . .

In the result the following order is made.

(A) McDonald's application to adduce further evidence is dismissed with costs, including the costs of two counsel.

(B) The appeals in all three matters are allowed with costs, including the costs of two counsel. The orders of the Court *a quo* are set aside and the following substituted:

(1)   In the well-known marks application (case No 11700/95):

The first and second respondents are hereby interdicted and restrained, with costs, from imitating, reproducing or translating in the Republic of South Africa any of the applicant's trade marks in which the word McDonald or McDonald's appears.

(2)   In the Joburgers application (case No 19719/93):

(a)   An order is granted in terms of prayers 5.1 and 6 of the notice of motion.

(b)   The counter-application is dismissed with costs.

(3)   In the Dax application (case No 16493/94):

(a)   The application is dismissed with costs.

(b)   An order is granted in terms of paras 119.2.1 and 119.2.2 of the counter-application set out in the document headed 'first respondent's founding affidavit'.

(4)   All costs orders are to include the costs of two counsel.

NOTES

1.   *Well-Known Marks.* Article 6*bis* of the Paris Convention mediates between the interests of global marketers and local consumers by treating a mark's fame, like its use, as an index of consumer identification of source. Does the provision adequately serve contemporary marketing realities? Cross-national registration will rarely pose a problem for a global consumer products company like McDonald's. However, for a company to continue using a mark everywhere it is registered—which may be required to sustain the registration—will sometimes be problematic. In the case of McDonald's, the company's failure to use its marks in South Africa evidently stemmed from the country's apartheid practices and the economic and political sanctions of the time. *See* Charles Webster, The *McDonald's* Case: South Africa Joins the Global Village, 86 Trademark Rep. 576 (1986).

Did the facts and law of the *McDonald's* case involve goods—the subject of trademarks—or services—the subject matter of service marks? Article 16(2) of the TRIPs Agreement provides that Article 6*bis* of the Paris Convention (1967) shall apply, *mutatis mutandis*, to services.

2.   *Comparative Treatment of Well-Known/Famous Marks.* At one time, common law and civil law systems differed in their treatment of unregistered famous marks. Common law countries, with their robust passing off jurisprudence, generally treated secondary meaning as the pivot on which protection turned and gave famous unregistered marks protection comparable to the protection they gave famous registered marks. By contrast, civil law countries, where registration is usually the pivot of protection, gave registered marks—famous or not—a wider scope of protection than even unregistered marks with strong secondary meaning. Many national laws have since brought registered and unregistered marks closer to parity. For example, section 4 of the German Trademark Act provides: "Trade mark protection shall accrue (1) by registration of a sign as a trade mark in the Register kept by the German Patent and Trade Mark Office (2) through the use of a sign in the course of trade, insofar as the sign has acquired secondary meaning as a trade mark within the affected trade circles; or (3) by notoriety as a well-known mark within the meaning of Article 6*bis* of the Paris Convention for the Protection of Industrial Property."

See generally Leah Chan Grinvald, A Tale of Two Theories of Well-Known Marks, 13 Vand. J. Ent. & Tech. L. 1 (2010); Annette Kur, Not Prior in Time, But Superior in Right—How Trademark Registrations Can Be Affected By Third-Party Interests in a Sign, 44(7) IIC 790 (2013); Marshall A. Leaffer, Protection of Well-Known Marks: A Transnational Perspective, in Trademark Protection and Territoriality Challenges in the Global Economy (Irene Calboli & Edward Lee eds., 2014), pp. 15–36.

3. *Well-Known Mark Status.* What factors should weigh in favor of a finding that a mark is well-known? According to a Joint Recommendation adopted by the Paris Union Assembly and the WIPO General Assembly, the factors should include "any circumstances from which it may be inferred that the mark is well-known." The Joint Recommendation lists several factors that should be considered in particular:

"1.   The degree of knowledge or recognition of the mark in the relevant sector of the public;

2.   the duration, extent and geographical area of any use of the mark;

3.   the duration and geographical area of any promotion of the mark. . . ;

4.   the duration and geographical area of any registrations, and/or any applications for registration, of the mark, to the extent that they reflect use or recognition of the mark;

5.   the record of successful enforcement of rights in the mark, in particular, the extent to which the mark was recognized as well known by competent authorities;

6.   the value associated with the mark."

Joint Recommendation Concerning Provisions on the Protection of Well-Known Marks, 1999, Article 2(1)(b).

TRIPs Article 16(2) also provides that "[i]n determining whether a trademark is well-known, account shall be taken of the knowledge of the trademark in the relevant sector of the public, including knowledge in that Member obtained as a result of the promotion of the trademark." Did the court's assessment of the mark's fame in South Africa in the *McDonald's* case include the "relevant sector of the public" as contemplated by Article 16(2)?

4. *Use in the Country as a Condition of the Status of the Well-Known Mark.* Can a court or legislature decide as a matter of national law that a mark must be used inside the country before it can qualify as a famous mark? According to the leading commentary on the Paris Convention, the 1958 Lisbon Conference to revise the Convention "rejected a proposal according to which *use* of a well-known mark in the country in which its protection is claimed would *not* be necessary for such protection. This means that a member State is not *obliged* to protect well-known trademarks which have not been used on its territory, but it will be free to do so." G.H.C. Bodenhausen, Guide to the Application of the Paris Convention for the Protection of Industrial Property 91 (1968). Is a requirement of the use inside the country dictated by the principle of territoriality?

In ITC Ltd. v. Punchgini, Inc., 482 F.3d 135 (2d Cir. 2007), the court ruled that plaintiff, which had through nonuse abandoned its registered U.S. mark "Bukhara" for restaurant services, could not invoke the famous marks doctrine to bar defendant from operating the restaurant "Bukhara Grill" in New York City. Plaintiff argued that the continued operation and international renown of its Bukhara restaurants in India and elsewhere in Asia gave it the requisite fame. The court rested its decision on the territoriality principle: "absent some use of its mark in the United States, a foreign mark holder generally may not assert priority rights under federal law."

The court acknowledged that some American authorities in some contexts have treated famous marks as an exception to the territoriality principle: New York trial courts in certain cases under New York law; the federal Trademark Trial and Appeal Board in decisions barring registration of marks that would be confused with a famous foreign mark; and a decision of the Ninth Circuit Court of Appeals, Grupo Gigante SA de CV v. Dallo & Co., 391 F.3d 1088 (9th Cir. 2004), holding that there is a famous mark exception to the territoriality principle. 482 F.3d at 157–161. Indeed, the court recognized "that a persuasive policy argument can be advanced in support of the famous marks doctrine," quoting from the *Grupo Gigante* opinion: "[a]n absolute territoriality rule without a famous-mark exception would promote consumer confusion and fraud. Commerce crosses borders. In this nation of immigrants, so do people. Trademark is, at its core, about protecting against consumer confusion and 'palming off.' There can be no justification for using trademark law to fool immigrants into thinking that they are buying from the store they liked back home." 391 F.3d at 1094.

But, ultimately, territoriality won the day. Responding to ITC's argument that Paris Convention Article 6*bis* and TRIPs Article 16(2) supported its famous marks claim, the *Punchgini* court observed that while *dicta* in Vanity Fair Mills, Inc. v. T. Eaton Co., 234 F.2d 633 (2d Cir. 1956), might support a claim that the Paris Convention was self-executing in the United States, "no similar conclusion can extend to Article 16(2) protection of service marks because TRIPs is plainly not a self-executing treaty." Nor in the court's view did sections 44(b) and (h) of the Lanham Act implement protection for famous marks; the Paris Convention, as incorporated by the Act, requires only national treatment. 482 F.3d at 161–162.

Since, however, ITC asserted claims under New York law, the court certified to the New York Court of Appeals the questions whether New York "recognizes the famous marks doctrine" and, if so, "how famous must a mark be to come within the famous marks doctrine?" 482 F.3d 166–167. In response, the New York Court of Appeals explained that, although New York does not recognize "the 'famous' or 'well-known' marks doctrine," it does protect a business from misappropriation under state unfair competition law "whether the business is domestic or foreign." ITC Ltd. v. Punchgini, Inc., 9 N.Y.3d 467, 471, 479, 880 N.E.2d 852 (2007). The court stated that the existence of actual goodwill of a foreign business in New York must be assessed by considering various factors, including a foreign business's use of its mark in New York. "[A]t a minimum," the court stated, "consumers of the good or service provided under a certain mark by a defendant in New York must primarily associate the mark with the foreign plaintiff." 9 N.Y.3d 467, 479 (2007). Ultimately, the U.S. Court of Appeals for the Second Circuit held that ITC failed to adduce sufficient evidence of goodwill in New York. ITC Ltd. v. Punchgini, Inc., 518 F.3d 159, 162–163 (2d Cir. 2008).

In India, under Article 11(9)(i) of the Trade Marks Act, use is not required for finding a trademark to be well-known in India. But consider whether the Supreme Court of India changed this rule in its decision in *Toyota Jidosha Kabushiki Kaisha v. Prius Auto Industries Ltd.* When in 2009 Toyota launched its "Prius" cars in India, it had found that Prius Industries Ltd. had already obtained the registration for and had used the mark "Prius" in India, allegedly as an adaptation of the Hindi words "pehela prayas," meaning "first attempt." Toyota filed for cancellation of Prius Industries' registered trademark in the Indian Trademark Registry and simultaneously filed suit against Prius Industries alleging passing off.

The lower-court judge ruled in favor of Toyota, finding the mark "Prius" to be well-known because of its "excellent global goodwill" that had spilled over into India due to the global sales of Prius cars, its advertisements in the international press, exhibitions of the cars in India and elsewhere, and information about the cars on the Internet. The Supreme Court of India overturned the decision holding that Toyota had enjoyed no goodwill in India with respect to its Prius cars prior to the launch of the Prius in India because the car had had no customers in India before the launch. In the Supreme Court's view, in 2001 when Prius Industries began using the trademark, the Toyota Prius's online exposure, its advertisements, and its sales in India were insufficient for a finding of goodwill in India. Toyota Jidosha Kabushiki Kaisha v. Prius Auto Industries Ltd., Supreme Court of India, Nos. 5375-5377/2017, 2017.

5. *Registration and Certification of Famous Marks.* What challenges does the protection of famous marks pose to businesses? Some countries address the inefficiencies that stem from the protection of unregistered famous marks by registering or certifying marks as famous. For example, Japan offers well-known mark holders the option of registering their marks without requiring that they use or intend to use the marks in Japan. In Russia, well-known mark holders may request that their marks be recognized as well-known and placed on a special list. Since 2007, famous and notorious marks (which receive different levels of protection) may be registered in Mexico.

On famous marks registration systems see Kung-Chung Liu, Xinliang Tao & Eric Wang, The Use and Misuse of Well-Known Marks Listings, 40(6) IIC 685 (2009); Kaiyu Xiao et al., The New Legal Framework for Acquiring

Well-Known Status in China: Signalling a More Coherent Phase of Enhanced Trade Mark Protection?, 48(3) IIC 305 (2017).

6.   *Recognition of Foreign Marks Outside the Well-Known Mark Doctrine.* The 1929 Inter-American Convention for Trademark and Commercial Protection mentioned at page 626, above, provides for recognition of certain foreign marks even if they have not achieved the status of a well-known mark. Under Article 3(6) of the Convention, "[r]egistration or deposit may be refused or cancelled of marks: . . . [w]hich have as a principal distinguishing element, phrases, names or slogans which constitute the trade name or an essential or characteristic part thereof, belonging to some person engaged in any of the other Contracting States in the manufacture, trade or production of articles or merchandise of the same class as that to which the mark is applied." For a discussion of the Convention see Christine Haight Farley, The Pan-American Trademark Convention of 1929: A Bold Vision of Extraterritorial Meets Current Realities, in Trademark Protection and Territoriality: Challenges in the Global Economy (Irene Calboli & Edward Lee eds., 2014), pp. 57–76.

ii.   *Good Faith Adoption*

Person's Co. Ltd. v. Christman

United States Court of Appeals, Federal Circuit, 1990.
900 F.2d 1565, 14 U.S.P.Q. 2d 1477.

EDWARD S. SMITH, SENIOR CIRCUIT JUDGE.

Person's Co., Ltd. appeals from the decision of the Patent and Trademark Office Trademark Trial and Appeal Board (Board) . . . which granted summary judgment in favor of Larry Christman and ordered the cancellation of appellant's registration . . . for the mark "PERSON'S" for various apparel items. Appellant Person's Co. seeks cancellation of Christman's registration . . . for the mark "PERSON'S" for wearing apparel on the following grounds: likelihood of confusion based on its prior foreign use, abandonment, and unfair competition within the meaning of the Paris Convention. We affirm the Board's decision.

Background

The facts pertinent to this appeal are as follows: In 1977, Takaya Iwasaki first applied a stylized logo bearing the name "PERSON'S" to clothing in his native Japan. Two years later Iwasaki formed Person's Co., Ltd., a Japanese corporation, to market and distribute the clothing items in retail stores located in Japan.

In 1981, Larry Christman, a U.S. citizen and employee of a sportswear wholesaler, visited a Person's Co. retail store while on a business trip to Japan. Christman purchased several clothing items bearing the "PERSON'S" logo and returned with them to the United States. After consulting with legal counsel and being advised that no one had yet established a claim to the logo in the United States, Christman developed designs for his own "PERSON'S" brand sportswear line based on appellant's products he had purchased in Japan. In February 1982, Christman contracted with a clothing manufacturer to produce clothing articles with the "PERSON'S" logo attached. These clothing items were sold, beginning in April 1982, to sportswear retailers in the northwestern United States. Christman formed Team Concepts, Ltd., a Washington corporation, in May 1983 to continue merchandising his sportswear line, which had expanded to include additional articles such as shoulder bags. All the sportswear marketed by Team Concepts bore either the mark "PERSON'S" or a copy of appellant's globe logo; many of the clothing styles were apparently copied directly from appellant's designs.

In April 1983, Christman filed an application for U.S. trademark registration in an effort to protect the "PERSON'S" mark. Christman believed himself to be the exclusive owner of the right to use and register the mark in the United States and apparently had no knowledge that appellant soon intended to introduce its similar sportswear line under the identical mark in the U.S. market. Christman's registration issued in September 1984 for use on wearing apparel.

In the interim between Christman's first sale and the issuance of his registration, Person's Co., Ltd. became a well known and highly respected force in the Japanese fashion industry. The company, which had previously sold garments under the "PERSON'S" mark only in Japan, began implementing its plan to sell goods under this mark in the United States. According to Mr. Iwasaki, purchases by buyers for resale in the United States occurred as early as November 1982. This was some seven months subsequent to Christman's first sales in the United States. Person's Co. filed an application for U.S. trademark registration in the following year, and, in 1985, engaged an export trading company to introduce its goods into the U.S. market. The registration for the mark "PERSON'S" issued in August 1985 for use on luggage, clothing and accessories. After recording U.S. sales near 4 million dollars in 1985, Person's Co. granted California distributor Zip Zone International a license to manufacture and sell goods under the "PERSON'S" mark in the United States.

In early 1986, appellant's advertising in the U.S. became known to Christman and both parties became aware of confusion in the marketplace. Person's Co. initiated an action to cancel Christman's registration on the following grounds: (1) likelihood of confusion; (2) abandonment; and (3) unfair competition within the meaning of the Paris Convention. Christman counterclaimed and asserted prior use and likelihood of confusion as grounds for cancellation of the Person's Co. registration.

After some discovery, Christman filed a motion with the Board for summary judgment on all counts. In a well reasoned decision, . . . the Board held for Christman on the grounds that Person's use of the mark in Japan could not be used to establish priority against a "good faith" senior user in U.S. commerce. The Board found no evidence to suggest that the "PERSON'S" mark had acquired any notoriety in this country at the time of its adoption by Christman. Therefore, appellant had no reputation or goodwill upon which Christman could have intended to trade, rendering the unfair competition provisions of the Paris Convention inapplicable. The Board also found that Christman had not abandoned the mark, although sales of articles bearing the mark were often intermittent. The Board granted summary judgment to Christman and ordered appellant's registration cancelled.

The Board held in its opinion on reconsideration that Christman had not adopted the mark in bad faith despite his appropriation of a mark in use by appellant in a foreign country. The Board adopted the view that copying a mark in use in a foreign country is not in bad faith unless the foreign mark is famous in the United States or the copying is undertaken for the purpose of interfering with the prior user's planned expansion into the United States. Person's Co. appeals and requests that this court direct the Board to enter summary judgment in its favor.

Issues

1.   Does knowledge of a mark's use outside U.S. commerce preclude good faith adoption and use of the identical mark in the United States prior to the entry of the foreign user into the domestic market?

2.   Did the Board properly grant summary judgment in favor of Christman on the issue of abandonment?

Cancellation

The Board may properly cancel a trademark registration within five years of issue when, *e.g.* (1) there is a valid ground why the trademark should not continue to be registered and (2) the party petitioning for cancellation has standing. . . . Such cancellation of the marks' registrations may be based upon any ground which could have prevented registration initially. . . . The legal issue in a cancellation proceeding is the right to register a mark, . . . which may be based on either (1) ownership of a foreign registration of the mark in question or (2) use of the mark in United States commerce. . . .

Priority

The first ground asserted for cancellation in the present action is § 2(d) of the Lanham Act; . . . each party claims prior use of registered marks which unquestionably are confusingly similar and affixed to similar goods.

Section 1 of the Lanham Act . . . states that "[t]he owner of a trademark *used in commerce* may register his trademark. . . ." . . . The term "commerce" is defined in Section 45 of the Act as ". . . all commerce which may be lawfully regulated by Congress." . . . No specific Constitutional language gives Congress power to regulate trademarks, so the power of the federal government to provide for trademark registration comes only under its commerce power. The term "used in commerce" in the Lanham Act refers to a sale or transportation of goods bearing the mark in or having an effect on: (1) United States interstate commerce; (2) United States commerce with foreign nations; or (3) United States commerce with the Indian Tribes. . . .

In the present case, appellant Person's Co. relies on its use of the mark in Japan in an attempt to support its claim for priority in the United States. Such foreign use has no effect on U.S. commerce and cannot form the basis for a holding that appellant has priority here. . . . The concept of territoriality is basic to trademark law; trademark rights exist in each country solely according to that country's statutory scheme. . . . Christman was the first to use the mark in United States commerce and the first to obtain a federal registration thereon. Appellant has no basis upon which to claim priority and is the junior user under these facts. . . .

Bad Faith

Appellant vigorously asserts that Christman's adoption and use of the mark in the United States subsequent to Person's Co.'s adoption in Japan is tainted with "bad faith" and that the priority in the United States obtained thereby is insufficient to establish rights superior to those arising from Person's Co.'s prior adoption in a foreign country. Relying on *Woman's World Shops, Inc. v. Lane Bryant, Inc.*,[17] Person's Co. argues that a "remote junior user" of a mark obtains no right superior to the "senior user" if the "junior user" has adopted the mark with knowledge of the "senior user's" prior use. . . . In *Woman's World*, the senior user utilized the mark within a limited geographical area. A junior user from a different geographical area of the United States sought unrestricted federal registration for a nearly identical mark, with the exception to its virtually exclusive rights being those of the known senior user. The Board held that such an appropriation with knowledge failed to satisfy the good faith requirements of the Lanham Act and denied the concurrent use rights sought by the junior user. . . . Person's Co. cites *Woman's World* for the proposition that a junior user's adoption and use of a mark with knowledge of another's prior use constitutes bad faith. It is urged that this principle is equitable in nature and should not be limited to knowledge of use within the territory of the United States.

While the facts of the present case are analogous to those in *Woman's World*, the case is distinguishable in one significant respect. In *Woman's World*, the first use of the mark by both the junior and senior users was in United States commerce. In the case at bar, appellant Person's Co., while first to adopt the mark, was not the first user in the United States. Christman is the senior user, and we are aware of no case where a senior user has been charged with bad faith. The concept of bad faith adoption applies to remote junior users seeking concurrent use registrations; in

---

[17]   5 U.S.P.Q.2d 1985 (TTAB 1985).

such cases, the likelihood of customer confusion in the remote area may be presumed from proof of the junior user's knowledge. . . . In the present case, when Christman initiated use of the mark, Person's Co. had not yet entered U.S. commerce. The Person's Co. had no goodwill in the United States and the "PERSON'S" mark had no reputation here. Appellant's argument ignores the territorial nature of trademark rights.

Appellant next asserts that Christman's knowledge of its prior use of the mark in Japan should preclude his acquisition of superior trademark rights in the United States. The Board found that, at the time of registration, Christman was not aware of appellant's intention to enter the U.S. clothing and accessories market in the future. Christman obtained a trademark search on the "PERSON'S" mark and an opinion of competent counsel that the mark was "available" in the United States. Since Appellant had taken no steps to secure registration of the mark in the United States, Christman was aware of no basis for Person's Co. to assert superior rights to use and registration here. Appellant would have us infer bad faith adoption because of Christman's awareness of its use of the mark in Japan, but an inference of bad faith requires something more than mere knowledge of prior use of a similar mark in a foreign country. . . .

As the Board noted below, Christman's prior use in U.S. commerce cannot be discounted solely because he was aware of appellant's use of the mark in Japan. While adoption of a mark with knowledge of a prior actual *user* in U.S. commerce may give rise to cognizable equities as between the parties, no such equities may be based upon knowledge of a similar mark's existence or on a problematical intent to use such a similar mark in the future. . . . Knowledge of a foreign use does not preclude good faith adoption and use in the United States. While there is some case law supporting a finding of bad faith where (1) the foreign mark is famous here . . . or (2) the use is a nominal one made solely to block the prior foreign user's planned expansion into the United States, . . . as the Board correctly found, neither of these circumstances is present in this case.

We agree with the Board's conclusion that Christman's adoption and use of the mark were in good faith. Christman's adoption of the mark occurred at a time when appellant had not yet entered U.S. commerce; therefore, no prior user was in place to give Christman notice of appellant's potential U.S. rights. Christman's conduct in appropriating and using appellant's mark in a market where he believed the Japanese manufacturer did not compete can hardly be considered unscrupulous commercial conduct. . . . Christman adopted the trademark being used by appellant in Japan, but appellant has not identified any aspect of U.S. trademark law violated by such action. Trademark rights under the Lanham Act arise solely out of use of the mark in U.S. commerce or from ownership of a foreign registration thereon; "[t]he law pertaining to registration of trademarks does not regulate all aspects of business morality."[26] When the law has been crafted with the clarity of crystal, it also has the qualities of a glass slipper: it cannot be shoe-horned onto facts it does not fit, no matter how appealing they might appear.

The Paris Convention

Appellant next claims that Christman's adoption and use of the "PERSON'S" mark in the United States constitutes unfair competition under Articles 6*bis* and 10*bis* of the Paris Convention. . . . It is well settled that the Trademark Trial and Appeal Board cannot adjudicate unfair competition issues in a cancellation or opposition proceeding. . . . The Board's function is to determine whether there is a right to secure or to maintain a registration. . . .

Conclusion

In *United Drug Co. v. Rectanus Co.*,[35] the Supreme Court of the United States determined that "there is no such thing as property in a trademark except as a right appurtenant to an established business or trade in connection with which the mark is employed. . . . [I]ts function is simply to designate the goods as the product of a particular trader and to protect his goodwill against the sale of another's product as his; and it is not the subject of property except in connection with an existing business."[36] In the present case, appellant failed to secure protection for its mark through use in U.S. commerce; therefore, no established business or product line was in place from which trademark rights could arise. Christman was the first to use the mark in U.S. commerce. This first use was not tainted with bad faith by Christman's mere knowledge of appellant's prior foreign use, so the Board's conclusion on the issue of priority was correct. Appellant also raises no factual dispute which is material to the resolution of the issue of abandonment. Accordingly, the grant of summary judgment was entirely in order, and the Board's decision is affirmed.

NOTES

1. *Use as a Condition of Trademark Ownership.* It is not uncommon for businesses to explore expansion to other countries, particularly since the Internet now makes such expansion easier. What steps could Person's Co. have taken to ensure protection for its trademark in the United States before Christman began marketing goods under the "Person's" mark?

Both in civil law and common law countries, trademark ownership originally turned on trademark use. A merchant could not reserve a mark for future use in connection with its goods, and rights would attach to the mark only in those territories where the merchant used it. Applied strictly, this requirement undercut the demands of commerce, confronting a trademark owner with the constant risk that an interloper would begin using

---

[26] *Selfway*, 579 F.2d at 79, 198 U.S.P.Q. at 275.
[35] 248 U.S. 90, 39 S.Ct. 48, 63 L.Ed. 141 (1918).
[36] 248 U.S. at 97, 39 S.Ct. at 50–51.

its mark—and acquiring rights of its own—in corners of the country the merchant had not yet entered. The standard legislative response was to enact a trademark statute under which a mark's registration would establish the owner's exclusive rights throughout the country. While early trademark legislation conditioned registration on the mark's prior use, most countries today have detached registration—and ownership—from a requirement of prior use. *See* generally, Stephen Ladas, Patents, Trademarks and Related Rights 598–599 (1975).

In a footnote to its opinion, the *Person's* court observed that section 44 of the Lanham Act, 15 U.S.C. § 1126, allows foreign applicants who own a registered mark in their country of origin to register the mark in the United States without alleging use. (Also, under section 44(c) the U.S. application will receive the foreign filing date if the application is made within six months of the foreign filing.) In the court's view, "[t]he statutory scheme set forth in § 44 is no place to lower barriers to entry and assist foreign applicants in establishing business good will in the United States." 900 F.2d at 1569, n. 16.

2. *Intent to Use Applications in the United States.* Until the 1988 Trademark Law Revision Act, Pub. Law No. 100–667, 102 Stat. 3935, which allowed an application for registration—but not registration itself—to be made upon a showing of a *bona fide* intention to use the mark, the United States was the only industrialized country to require prior trademark use as a condition to application, a position that often gave commercial rivals from other Paris Union countries an advantage over U.S. trademark claimants because other countries allowed registration without prior use, and because section 44 of the Lanham Act, 15 U.S.C. § 1126, required the U.S. Patent and Trademark Office to honor these registrations as part of the country's Paris Convention obligations. *See* SCM Corp. v. Langis Foods Ltd., 539 F.2d 196, 190 U.S.P.Q. 288 (D.C.Cir. 1976).

The 1988 intent-to-use amendments reduced the disparity between domestic and foreign applicants by entitling U.S. nationals to apply for registration on the basis of an intent to use, rather than an actual use of the mark and, under section 44(e) of the 15 U.S.C. § 1126(e), by requiring foreign applicants to state their intention to use the mark. Unlike U.S. nationals, qualifying foreign nationals may under section 44(e) obtain registration without use, but the foreign applicant must as a practical matter use the mark within three years of registration or face a presumption that it has abandoned the mark. Article 15(3) of the TRIPs Agreement reflects U.S. practice in providing that "Members may make registrability depend on use," but the "actual use of a trademark shall not be a condition for filing an application for registration."

3. *Good Faith Adoption and Well-Known Marks.* What role is there in an international trademark system for the famous mark doctrine applied in *McDonald's* and the good faith doctrine applied in *Person's*? Presumably both rules aim to relax the rigors of a strict registration system by carving out protection, for producers and consumers alike, where a producer has invested in exploiting a mark but has failed to register it in all countries where it will be used. However, as both *McDonald's* and *Person's* indicate, the doctrines introduce a degree of uncertainty into international trademark planning. Is this imprecision inevitable in any event because of the concurrent availability of unfair competition rules in most if not all jurisdictions to bar the confusing use of names and symbols that have acquired secondary meaning?

See, generally, Annette Kur, Not Prior in Time, But Superior in Right—How Trademark Registrations Can Be Affected by Third-Party Interests in a Sign, 44(7) IIC 790 (2013); Frederick Mostert & Gloria Wu, The Importance of the Element of Bad Faith in International Trade Mark Law and Its Relevance under the New Chinese Trade Mark Law Provisions, 12(8) J. Intell. Property Law & Practice 650 (2017).

4. *Elements of Bad Faith.* Should knowledge or presumed knowledge of a foreign mark suffice for a finding of bad faith registration? The Court of Justice of the European Communities interpreted "bad faith" in the context of the EU Trademark Regulation in a case that involved a three-dimensional Community trademark for a chocolate bunny. The alleged infringer argued that the Community trademark should be invalidated because the trademark owner acted in bad faith when it applied for registration of the mark because the applicant was aware of the use of the mark by a competitor in at least one EU member state and because the applicant applied for registration of the trademark to eliminate its competitors. The Court held that knowledge or presumption of knowledge by the applicant is not sufficient for a finding of bad faith; additional factors must be considered, in particular "the applicant's intention to prevent [the competitor] from continuing to use such sign; and the degree of legal protection enjoyed by the [competitor's] sign and by the sign for which registration is sought." Chocoladenfabriken Lindt & Sprüngli AG v. Franz Hauswirth GmbH, ECJ, C-529/07, 2009, ruling of the Court. The Court explained that an intent to exclude competitors may be an element of bad faith in some circumstances, for example when "the applicant applied for registration of a sign as a Community trademark without intending to use it, his sole objective being to prevent a third party from entering the market." *Id.*, ¶ 44.

The concept of bad faith in *Chocoladenfabriken Lindt* differed from the concept used in Denmark and the Benelux countries, where trademark statutes explicitly equated "bad faith" with "knowledge." In 2013 the Court confirmed that Danish law did not comply with the Court's definition of "bad faith," which the Court extended to the corresponding provision of the EU Trademark Directive that harmonizes the national trademark laws of the EU member states. Malaysia Dairy Industries Pte. Ltd v. Ankenævnet for Patenter og Varemærker, CJEU, C-320/12, 2013. For a discussion of the impact of the decision on national trademark laws see Alexander Tsoutsanis, Trade Mark Applications in Bad Faith: Righting Wrong in Denmark and Why the Benelux Is Next, 9(2) JIPLP 118 (2014).

5. *Extraterritorial Use.* Can use outside the protecting country be sufficient to establish the required goodwill to obtain protection for a foreign-used trademark? In Starbucks (HK) Ltd. v. British Sky Broadcasting Group PLC, [2015] UKSC 31, the U.K. Supreme Court clarified the rule that, under English law, a "claimant must show that it has a significant goodwill, in the form of customers, in the jurisdiction, but it is not necessary that the claimant actually has an establishment or office in this country. In order to establish goodwill, the claimant must have customers within the jurisdiction, as opposed to people in the jurisdiction who happen to be customers elsewhere. Thus, where the claimant's business is carried on abroad, it is not enough for a claimant to show that there are people in this jurisdiction who happen to be its customers when they are abroad. However, it could be enough if the claimant could show that there were people in this jurisdiction who, by booking with, or purchasing from, an entity in this country, obtained the right to receive the claimant's service abroad." *Id.*, ¶ 52.

Use in U.S. interstate commerce is required to infringe a trademark under the Lanham Act. Does section 43(a) of the Lanham Act, 15 U.S.C. § 1125, provide protection for marks that are not used in U.S. interstate commerce, including foreign-used trademarks? In Belmora LLC v. Bayer Consumer Care AG, 819 F.3d 697 (4th Cir. 2016), Bayer owned the registered trademark "Flanax" in Mexico, where it had used the trademark since the 1970s; however, Bayer never registered and never used the mark in the United States. Belmora owned the trademark in the United States, where it had used the trademark since 2004. Bayer petitioned the U.S. Trademark Trial and Appeal Board to cancel Balmora's registration and also brought suit in a U.S. district court against Belmora for false designation of origin, false advertising, and misrepresentation of source under section 43(a) of the Lanham Act.

The U.S. Court of Appeals for the Fourth Circuit held that because section 43(a) does not require a plaintiff to use its mark in U.S. commerce, the district court erred in requiring Bayer to plead prior use of its mark in U.S. commerce. The Fourth Circuit Court further found that Bayer had the right to bring suit under 43(a) because its interests fell within the protected zone of interest and it had pleaded proximate causation of a cognizable injury: "Mexican-Americans may forego purchasing the FLANAX they know when they cross the border to visit Mexico because Belmora's alleged deception led them to purchase the Belmora product in the United States." 819 F.3d at 711. Will *Belmora* open a floodgate of cases seeking protection for foreign-used marks through 43(a), or does *Belmora*'s reasoning apply only in cases with similar facts?

Why did Bayer choose not to use the mark "Flanax" in U.S. commerce? Why did Bayer register the trademark in Mexico and not in the United States? Marketing of identical goods under different trademarks in different countries may support a trademark owner's market partitioning efforts, particularly when the trademark owner cannot rely on other market partitioning tools, such as patent protection.

b.   REGISTRATION AND REGISTRATION PRIORITIES

Imperial Tobacco Limited v. Philip Morris

United States Court of Appeals, Federal Circuit, 1990.
899 F.2d 1575, 14 U.S.P.Q. 2d 1390.

NIES, CIRCUIT JUDGE.

Imperial Tobacco Limited appeals from the final decision of the Trademark Trial and Appeal Board of the United States Patent and Trademark Office, in Cancellation No. 16,024, granting the petition of Philip Morris, Incorporated, for cancellation of Imperial's Registration No. 1,160,229 on a motion for summary judgment. We affirm.

I

Imperial Tobacco Limited, a United Kingdom corporation, owns Registration No. 1,160,229 issued on July 7, 1981, on the Principal Register for the trademark shown below for cigarettes:

The registration in issue was obtained on the basis of its prior United Kingdom registration in accordance with section 44(e) of the Lanham Act, . . . 15 U.S.C. § 1126(e) (1982). No use of the mark in commerce in or with the United States was alleged.

Philip Morris filed a petition to cancel Imperial's registration on the ground that the registered mark was abandoned. *See* sections 14 and 45, 15 U.S.C. §§ 1064 and 1127 (1982). At the close of discovery, cross-motions for summary judgment were made. In support of its motion, Philip Morris relied on the undisputed fact that there had been no United States sales of cigarettes under the registered mark from the date of registration up to the date of Philip Morris' petition filed November 3, 1986. Philip Morris acknowledged Imperial made sales of approximately 50,000 *JPS* cigarettes after May 1987, apparently to support the filing of a declaration of use under section 8, 15 U.S.C. § 1058 (1982),[2] but argued that neither such use nor Imperial's activities during the period of nonuse raised a genuine issue of material fact that the mark had been previously abandoned.

Imperial maintains that in this case the period of nonuse is insufficient in itself to establish abandonment of the mark. In opposing

---

[2]   By the terms of the statute, a registration must be cancelled unless an affidavit or declaration of use is filed in accordance with this section during the sixth year of registration.

Philip Morris' motion, Imperial submitted affidavits and evidence purporting to show that it had no intention to abandon the mark because during that period it had been trying to open the United States market. Per Imperial, its activities excuse its delay in introducing in the United States cigarettes bearing the *JPS* mark and negate an inference of intent to abandon the mark, or at least raise a genuine issue with respect to its intent to abandon the mark, thereby precluding summary judgment.

The board ruled that Philip Morris had demonstrated its entitlement to prevail on the issue of Imperial's abandonment as a matter of law. It found no genuine issue of material fact underlying that issue and concluded that more evidence, obtained by trial, could not reasonably be expected to change the result. Specifically, it held the undisputed facts show that, although Imperial commenced actual use in the United States in May of 1987, abandonment had occurred before that date. The board rejected Imperial's position that the prima facie case of abandonment arising from an extended period of nonuse of the mark was overcome or in doubt. Per the board, none of the proffered reasons for Imperial's nonuse had the effect of precluding Imperial from selling cigarettes under the *JPS* mark at any time in the United States. Imperial simply chose not to do so for various business reasons that did not excuse its nonuse. Further, the board held that the affidavits of Imperial's personnel that it did not intend to abandon its rights in the mark were insufficient to create a genuine issue of material fact. We agree.

II

This appeal requires interpretation of the statutory provision under which a registration for a mark may be cancelled on the ground that such mark has been abandoned. Specifically, the question relates to abandonment of a mark covered by a U.S. registration which was obtained on the basis of a foreign registration, where no use has been made of the mark in the United States from the date of registration up to the time the petition was filed, a period here of at least five years. The issue is one of first impression in this court.

Under section 1 of the Lanham Act, as it existed prior to recent amendments, 15 U.S.C. § 1051 (1982), an applicant for registration of a trademark in the United States was not entitled to file an application until the applicant actually used the mark in U.S. commerce in connection with particular goods or services.[3] However, an exception was provided to this general rule. Pursuant to section 44(e), a foreign applicant of a country with whom the United States maintained certain

---

[3]   In the Trademark Law Revision Act of 1988, Pub.L. No. 100–667, § 103(3), 102 Stat. 3935 (codified at 15 U.S.C. § 1051(b) (1988)), Congress added a new basis for the filing of an application, namely, a bona fide intention to use a mark in commerce in relation to specific goods or services. However, for these "intent-to-use" applications, actual use of the mark in commerce is a prerequisite to the issuance of a registration. The same declaration of intent-to-use must now be made in connection with section 44 applications, 15 U.S.C. § 1126(e) (1988), but such registration may issue without actual use. See Pegram, J., Section 44 Revision: After the 1988 Act, 79 Trademark Reporter 220–223 (1989).

treaty rights was entitled to obtain a U.S. registration for a mark based on ownership of a registration in its home country without any use in the United States. . . . Section 44(e) gave such foreign applicant a significant advantage over other applicants in procuring a registration in this country. However, the statute gave no similar advantage in the *maintenance* of a section 44(e) registration. On the contrary, section 44(f) provided, and still provides, that a registration obtained under section 44(e) "shall be independent of the registration in the country of origin and the duration, validity, or transfer in the United States of such registration shall be governed by the provisions of this chapter." Thus, after registration, a section 44(e) registrant is entitled only to the same national treatment as any other registrant.

When a petition for cancellation of a registration is filed more than five years after the date of registration, the statute provides limited grounds for cancellation. One basis that continues, after the five-year period, is abandonment of the mark which is the subject of the registration. As provided in section 14(c), abandonment is a basis for cancellation "at any time." . . . Thus, a section 44(e) registration, like any other registration, may be cancelled on the ground of abandonment of the mark at any time. As stated in *P.A.B. Produits et Appareils de Beaute v. Satinine Societa in Nome Collettivo di S.A. e.M. Usellini*, 570 F.2d 328, 196 U.S.P.Q. 801 (CCPA 1978):

> Having obtained a registration, the foreign registrant is subject to our national law; it is subject to the same treatment and conditions which prevail in connection with domestic registrations based on use in the United States, including the possibility of cancellation on the ground of abandonment. 570 F.2d at 330, 196 USPQ 802–03.

Under the statute, an abandoned mark is not entitled to continued registration regardless of the basis on which the registration was originally obtained. Thus, the question on summary judgment here is whether the undisputed facts establish as a matter of law that the *JPS* mark has been "abandoned" within the meaning of the statute.

III

Under section 45, a mark shall be deemed to be abandoned *inter alia*:

(a) When its use has been discontinued with intent not to resume. Intent not to resume may be inferred from circumstances. Nonuse for two consecutive years shall be prima facie abandonment.

Under the above provision, *prima facie* abandonment of a mark is established by proof of its nonuse for two consecutive years. . . .* The terms "use" and "nonuse" mean use and nonuse in the United States. . . . To overcome that *prima facie* case, the registrant must come forth with

---

*   The 1994 Uruguay Round Agreements Act extended the period of nonuse from two to three consecutive years. Pub. L. No. 103-465, 108 Stat 4809. *Ed.*

evidence that it "discontinued" use of a mark without an "intent not to resume" use.

At common law there was no similar presumption of abandonment of a mark simply from proof of nonuse. A challenger had to prove not only nonuse of the mark but also that the former user *intended to abandon* the mark. . . . However, with respect to rights under the Lanham Act, proof of abandonment was facilitated by the creation of the above statutory presumption.

In effect, the presumption eliminates the challenger's burden to establish the intent element of abandonment as an initial part of its case. Thus, statements from opinions under the common law of abandonment concerning the nature of the element of intent and who had the burden of proof cannot be applied indiscriminately to an abandonment case under the Lanham Act concerned with a party's entitlement to continued registration. In the instant case, Philip Morris proved that Imperial did not use the mark *JPS* for cigarettes in the United States for more than two years immediately preceding the filing of its petition for cancellation. Such proof established a *prima facie* case of abandonment of the *JPS* mark under section 45(a), including the element of intent.

As an initial matter, Imperial asserts that the finding of abandonment is inconsistent with the finding of Philip Morris' standing to bring this case. On the standing issue, Philip Morris alleged *inter alia* that the *JPS* mark was likely to be known to some potential customers in this country by reason of their having travelled abroad where the mark was used. . . . Imperial argues that because its mark was alleged to be known here, it could not at the same time be abandoned. While superficially appealing, the argument is without merit. The question here is a right to registration. . . . A foreign trademark may be known by reputation in this country and may even be protectable under concepts of unfair competition, but such mark is not entitled to either initial or continued *registration* where the *statutory requirements* for registration cannot be met. . . .

Imperial next argues that the board erred as a matter of law by imposing a new and unreasonable burden on a registrant to prove it possessed an intent to use the mark in the United States at some definite time. The statutory provision, per Imperial, does not require evidence of such intent. Technically, Imperial is correct that the statutory definition for abandonment of a mark does not use the words "intent to use" or "intent to begin use." The statutory language is "intent not to resume" use. Those words are appropriate for the usual situation in which a registered mark has been used at some time in this country. Where there is use, followed by a period of nonuse, the question is whether the registrant "discontinued" use with an "intent not to resume." In contrast, the subject registration, as indicated, was obtained without allegations of use of the mark in the United States and, during the pertinent time frame, the mark has never been used in the United States. The statutory language "discontinued" and "intent not to resume," as applied to the present situation, is inapt.

Imperial solves this language problem by arguing that the statutory language "intent not to resume" use of the mark should be interpreted to mean "intent to abandon" the mark. Under Imperial's interpretation, it asserts it would then have raised a genuine issue of material fact as to its intent by the submission of affidavits averring that Imperial had no intent to abandon its rights in the mark *JPS*.

Imperial is correct that in some post-Lanham Act opinions, "intent not to resume" and "intent to abandon" have been used interchangeably. However, as more precisely analyzed by Judge Higginbotham in *Exxon Corp. v. Humble Exploration Co.*, 695 F.2d 96, 102, 217 USPQ 1200, 1204 (5th Cir. 1983), in the factual context of those cases, . . . the substitution of one phrase for the other made no difference. On the other hand, as Judge Higginbotham explains in *Exxon Corp.*:

> There is a difference between intent not to abandon or relinquish and intent to resume use in that an owner may not wish to abandon its mark but may have no intent to resume its use. . . . In the context of a challenge strictly under the Lanham Act to an alleged warehousing program, as the facts of this case present, the application of the statutory language is critical.

695 F.2d at 102, 217 USPQ at 1204–05.

As in the *Exxon* case, we also conclude that an affirmative desire by the registrant not to relinquish a mark is not determinative of the intent element of abandonment under the Lanham Act. Nothing in the statute entitles a registrant who has formerly used a mark to overcome a presumption of abandonment arising from subsequent nonuse by simply averring a subjective affirmative "intent not to abandon." As indicated in the quotation from *Exxon*, the Lanham Act was not intended to provide a warehouse for unused marks. . . .

Intent to resume use in abandonment cases has been equated with a showing of special circumstances which excuse a registrant's nonuse. . . . While not expressly stated in other cases, the analysis has been comparable. . . . Thus, whether one characterizes the "intent" element of abandonment as an intent not to resume use or an intent to abandon is not significant. If a registrant's nonuse is excusable, the registrant has overcome the presumption that its nonuse was coupled with an "intent not to resume use," or, as Imperial would have it, an "intent to abandon." If the activities are insufficient to excuse nonuse, the presumption is not overcome. . . .

We see no justification to adopt a different or more liberal interpretation of the statute in connection with a mark of a section 44(e) registrant which has *never* been used in this country. Such registrant has no right to maintain a registration except in accordance with the statute, and nothing in the statute suggests that the registration of a never-used mark can be maintained indefinitely simply because the registrant does not have an affirmative intent to relinquish the mark. A section 44(e) registrant is merely granted a dispensation from actual use prior to registration, but after registration, there is no dispensation of use requirements. If the registrant fails to make use of the registered mark for two years, the presumption of abandonment may be invoked against that registrant, as against any other.

We do not find the board's reference to an "intent to begin use" or "intent to use" to be legal error here. Indeed, these words are an appropriate adaptation of the statutory language in the situation of a never-used mark. In any event, the significant question is whether the board imposed a heavier burden on Imperial than other registrants must shoulder, which would be contrary to the requirement for national treatment. We conclude it did not. The board simply required Imperial, like any other registrant who admits to at least two years of nonuse, to put forth sufficient evidence in response to a motion for summary judgment to at least raise a genuine issue that its nonuse was excusable.

In a thorough and complete analysis, the board reviewed Imperial's proffered evidence and found it was not sufficient to raise a viable defense of excusable nonuse. Imperial maintains that from 1981 to 1987 "steps were taken each year towards introduction in the United States of cigarettes bearing the 'JPS' design mark." However, its evidence belies that assertion. The board carefully analyzed and rejected that evidence, and we must agree that Imperial's activities from 1981 to 1986, either separately or combined, were insufficient to raise a genuine issue of fact precluding summary judgment.

Imperial's principal argument is that during the six-year period, it was engaged in the development of a "marketing strategy." However, much of that strategy was not for the purpose of introducing cigarettes into the United States bearing the *JPS* mark. Rather, it was directed to marketing "incidental" products, such as whisky, pens, watches, sunglasses and food under the *JPS* mark. In addition, the "strategy" included, for example, seeking federal trademark registrations covering the *JPS* mark (alone and together with "JOHN PLAYER SPECIAL") on these incidental products. We agree with the board that Imperial's concern with marketing incidental products did not excuse nonuse of *JPS* for cigarettes. The board noted that when Imperial finally made sales of *JPS* cigarettes in 1987, there was no implementation of a complex marketing strategy to introduce them. As the board pointed out, Imperial simply began selling cigarettes in 1987, as it could have all along.

Imperial also maintains that it did not use the registered mark because it was concerned with potential legal problems with Philip Morris. Although the board recognized that suspension of actual use, or plans to use a mark pending resolution of litigation, may serve to justify nonuse, . . . it held that this case did not present such facts. The undisputed facts point to a conclusion entirely different from that which

Imperial asserts. The record shows that Imperial's ongoing and major litigation concern was over its desire to use *JPS in combination with* JOHN PLAYER SPECIAL as used abroad,[11] and to use the mark on packaging having a distinctive black and gold trade dress similar to that used by Philip Morris on its BENSON AND HEDGES cigarettes. Its unsuccessful efforts to license *JPS* for cigarettes were also directed to the use of *JPS* in this manner. The board inferred that litigation fears and licensing efforts were attributable to Imperial's desire to sell *JPS* cigarettes in a particular display, not because it could not use *JPS* as registered for cigarettes. We see no other reasonable inference. . . .

Imperial's other evidence of licensing efforts pertained to the use of the *JPS* mark only on goods other than cigarettes. Other evidence pertained to licensing use of the mark outside the United States. In any event, Imperial has not asserted any reason why it could not use its mark without a licensee. Indeed, when Imperial did make shipments in 1987, it was not through a licensee. We agree with the board that none of Imperial's licensing efforts justify its nonuse of the registered mark.

Imperial proffered no other evidence which might support any additional reason for its nonuse. The evidence which it did offer does not create a genuine issue which requires resolution at trial. Imperial simply has proffered no viable excuse for nonuse of the mark for over five years. The *prima facie* case of abandonment of the mark arising from that nonuse was, therefore, not overcome.

IV

For the foregoing reasons we conclude that the Trademark Trial and Appeal Board did not err in granting Philip Morris' motion for summary judgment on its petition for cancellation of Registration No. 1,160,229. Imperial has shown no reversible error in the standard the board applied to determine whether the mark had been abandoned within the meaning of the statute. Nor has Imperial raised a genuine issue of material fact. Accordingly, the decision of the board cancelling Registration No. 1,160,229 is affirmed.

AFFIRMED.

NOTES

1.   *Registration and Use.* At one time, national trademark systems divided between those that centered trademark ownership on use, with registration conferring only limited procedural advantages, and those that centered trademark ownership on registration, with use at most a condition

---

[11]   Philip Morris owns rights in the mark PLAYERS in the United States. The board noted that Imperial's use of JOHN PLAYER SPECIAL was held to infringe those rights in *Philip Morris, Inc. v. Imperial Tobacco Co., Ltd.*, 282 F.Supp. 931, 937, 156 USPQ 239, 244 (E.D.Va. 1967) (Imperial's use of JOHN PLAYER'S & SONS in connection with the sale of tobacco products infringes Philip Morris' trademark PLAYER'S), aff'd, 401 F.2d 179, 180–81, 158 USPQ 561, 562 (4th Cir. 1968), cert. denied, 393 U.S. 1094, 89 S.Ct. 875, 21 L.Ed.2d 784 (1969).

subsequent for protection. The trend since the latter part of the twentieth century has been for each camp to borrow features from the other.

In the United States, where the Lanham Act has consistently required trademark use as a condition to registration by U.S. applicants, amendments in 1988 made it possible for the first time to apply for registration on the basis of a *bona fide* intention to use a mark. Although registration still requires use—and an *ex parte* examination for distinctiveness and noninfringement—once the mark is registered, the filing of the application "shall constitute constructive use of the mark, conferring a right of priority, nationwide in effect, on or in connection with the goods or services specified in the registration." 15 U.S.C. § 1057(c).

France, a member of the registration camp, at one time registered marks without any showing of trademark use or other than a strictly formal examination. Ownership of marks under French law is still acquired by registration, not use, but French legislation in 1964 and 1991 deepened the examination process to require some showing that the mark in issue is distinctive and noninfringing. *See* France, Law on Trademarks and Service Marks, §§ 1–2, 4–5 [No. 91–7 of January 4, 1991] Industrial Prop. 3–002 (May 1991). *See* generally, Daniel C. Schulte, The Madrid Agreement's Basis in Registration-Based Systems: Does the Protocol Overcome Past Biases? (Part II) 77 J. Patent and Trademark Off. Soc'y 729, 735–738 (1995).

Use-centered registration systems are commonly thought to favor equity over efficiency, giving rights to the first to use a mark (and to invest resources in exploiting the mark) rather than to the first to file (and to give other potential users notice of its prior claim). Registration systems suffer their own inefficiencies, however, one of which is a register clogged with owned, but unused marks. *Imperial Tobacco* illustrates one procedural technique—cancellation—for introducing efficiency into use-centered registration systems. What other techniques might optimally balance equity and efficiency in both use-centered and registration-centered systems? Would Imperial Tobacco have prevailed if it had been able to show that, though unused in the United States, its mark was a famous mark?

2.   *Registration and Priority Under the Paris Convention.* The Paris Convention for the Protection of Industrial Property, though not a registration treaty like the Madrid Agreement, discussed in note 4, below, establishes several norms that affect national registration practice. One is Article 4's priority right which gives any one who has filed an application for trademark registration in one Union country a six-month right of priority for purposes of filing in other member countries. Like the one-year priority for patent applications, discussed at page 462, above, Article 4's trademark priority gives a trademark applicant a grace period within which to determine in which countries it will exploit its mark and to prepare applications for those countries. The effect of the priority is to insulate the later-filed application from events, such as third-party use, that occur during the priority period.

Article 6 of the Paris Convention anchors registration for foreign marks in domestic law. Article 6(1) makes the conditions for trademark filing and registration a matter of domestic law; Article 6(2) adds that registration for the mark of a Union national may neither be refused nor invalidated "on the ground that filing, registration, or renewal, has not been effected in the country of origin"; and Article 6(3) makes marks registered in one Union country independent of marks registered in other Union countries, including the country of origin, so that, for example, the mark's cancellation in its country of origin will not of itself undermine registrations in other countries.

Article 6*quinquies*, the so-called *telle quelle* provision, obligates Union countries to accept for filing and to protect "as is" (*telle quelle*) any trademark duly registered in the mark's country of origin so long as that country is also a Union member. The provision, as amended over several acts of the Paris Convention, excepts from this obligation marks that "infringe rights acquired by third parties in the country where protection is claimed"; nondistinctive marks; and marks that "are contrary to morality or public order and, in particular [are] of such a nature as to deceive the public." The effect of these exceptions was to relieve countries such as the United States, with relatively rigorous examination systems, of the obligation to register nondistinctive or infringing marks originating in countries such as France with weak or nonexistent examination systems.

3. *Registration and Priority Under U.S. Practice.* Section 44 of the Lanham Act, 15 U.S.C. § 1126, implements U.S. obligations under the Paris Convention. As discussed at page 656, above, before the 1988 intent-to-use amendments, section 44 created a harsh disparity between U.S. and foreign applicants. Section 44 of the Lanham Act continues to distinguish between U.S. and foreign nationals by requiring U.S. nationals actually to use their marks—even those subject to an intent to use application—before the mark will be registered while, in the case of foreign applications under section 44(e), "use in commerce shall not be required prior to registration." In light of *Imperial Tobacco's* application of the Act's cancellation provisions, how significant is this advantage to foreign applicants? (Note that U.S. intent-to-use applicants can typically extend their applications, without alleging use, for as long as three years). Does section 44(e)'s requirement that foreign applicants state an intention to use their marks violate the *telle quelle* provision of Paris Convention Article 6*quinquies*?

4. *Registration and Classification Treaties.*

The 1891 Madrid Agreement Concerning the International Registration of Marks. The Madrid Agreement, last revised at Stockholm in 1967, greatly simplifies the international registration process by enabling a trademark owner that is a national of a Madrid Union country to apply for trademark registration in other member countries through a single filing in its home country designating the other countries of its choice; the filing is to be made in a single language and with payment of a single fee. The World Intellectual Property Organization administers the Madrid Agreement, receiving international applications from trademark offices in member countries, transmitting them to the designated countries for examination, and issuing international registrations.

Several features of the Madrid Agreement explain the decision of the United States not to adhere to it. Article 1 of the Agreement requires registration to be completed in the home country before an international application can be filed. Since, unlike many other countries, U.S. law requires extended, substantive examination before a registration issues, U.S. applicants would, in the race to file first, invariably lag behind nationals of countries that treat registration as a formality. Article 5 of the Madrid Agreement provides that, unless a country designated by the applicant rejects the applicant's international application within one year, the mark will be deemed to be registered in that country. Since examination in the U.S. Patent and Trademark Office often consumes more than a year, the PTO would be forced to put these foreign applications at the head of the line—further protracting examination of domestic applications—or suffer their enrollment on the Principal Register by default.

Yet another reason the United States has not adhered to the Madrid Agreement is Article 6 providing for "central attack": if the home country registration is cancelled or otherwise invalidated at any time during the first five years of the international registration, registrations in all designated foreign countries will fall with it. Since the Lanham Act provides more grounds for cancellation than other national trademark laws, U.S. registrants would again suffer a comparative disadvantage. (Other U.S. objections to the Madrid Agreement are that it provides a lower fee schedule than does the PTO and that its official language is French.)

The Madrid Protocol. The Protocol Relating to the Madrid Agreement Concerning the International Registration of Marks, adopted at Madrid in 1989, modified the most objectionable features of the Madrid Agreement in an effort to win new members. Unlike the Madrid Agreement, which requires registration as a condition to filing an international application, Article 2 of the Madrid Protocol requires only a trademark application. Article 5 of the Protocol extends the default period for registration from twelve to eighteen months at the option of the member country. Article 9*quinquies* meliorates the effects of central attack by allowing an owner of an international registration that has suffered cancellation of its home registration to make individual applications in its designated countries and, at the same time, retain its international filing priority in those countries. The principal obstacle to U.S. adherence to the Madrid Protocol, ultimately resolved through negotiations between the United States and the European Union, was structural rather than substantive—specifically, a provision that would have effectively given voting rights not only to individual members of the European Union but also to the Union itself. *See* U.S. and EU Reach Agreement in the Madrid Protocol, 59 Patent, Copyright, Trademark, J. 573 (June 2, 2000). The U.S. legislation implementing the Protocol took effect in 2003. The Madrid Protocol Implementation Act, Pub. L. No. 107–273, Tit. III, subtit. D, 116 Stat. 1913–1921.

See generally Jeffrey Samuels & Linda Samuels, The Changing Landscape of International Trademark Law, 27 Geo. Wash. J. Int'l L. & Econ. 433 (1993–94); Roger Schechter, Facilitating Trademark Registration

Abroad: The Implication of U.S. Ratification of the Madrid Protocol, 25 Geo. Wash. J. Int'l L. & Econ. 419 (1991).

Trademark Law Treaty. Just months after stating its initial opposition to the Madrid Protocol in May 1994, the United States signed the Trademark Law Treaty which aims to harmonize member countries' trademark laws, mainly application and registration procedures, over a six to eight year period—six years for developed countries, eight for developing countries. Articles 3(5) and (6) of the Treaty, for example, break ground in some member countries by allowing a single trademark or service mark application to include goods or services belonging to more than one class of goods and services. The TLT was ratified by the United States in 1998, and implemented by the Trademark Law Treaty Implementation Act, P.L. 105–330, 112 Stat. 3064 (Oct. 30, 1998). The United States has also ratified the 2006 Singapore Treaty on the Law of Trademarks, which extends the provisions of the Trademark Law Treaty to all types of marks that can be registered as marks under the law of a contracting state, and updates the procedures for application and registration by taking into account modern communications technologies.

Trademark Registration Treaty. Although the United States signed the Trademark Registration Treaty in 1973—and although the treaty entered into force in 1980—the United States has not yet ratified the treaty, and there seems little likelihood that it ever will. One stumbling block in the way of ratification was the treaty's insulation of registered marks from cancellation for nonuse during the first three years of the registration. Another was the possibility that examination delays in the Patent and Trademark Office would exceed the TRT's permitted fifteen-month examination period. On the TRT generally, see Symposium, The Trademark Registration Treaty (TRT), 63 Trademark Rep. 421 (1973); David Allen, The Trademark Registration Treaty: Its Implementing Legislation, 21 IDEA 161 (1980); Beverly Pattishall, The Proposed Trademark Registration Treaty and its Domestic Import, 62 Trademark Rep. 125 (1972).

5. *The European Union Trademark.* In 1996 the European Union's Office for Harmonization in the Internal Market, now called the European Union Intellectual Property Office (EUIPO), began accepting applications for Community trademarks, now called European Union trademarks. The Office, which is located in Alicante, Spain, administers the unitary trademark system. The system, the product of efforts dating to the early 1960's, is unitary in virtually every conceivable respect. Only a single application need be made in the Alicante Office; a single registration will be enforced throughout the countries of the European Union through a single lawsuit in a designated court; and renewal and maintenance fees have to be paid only on the single registration. Owners based in European Union countries are not the only beneficiaries of the efficiencies of the EU trademark system. According to statistics from EUIPO, between January 2016 and January 2019, applicants from the United States filed 34% of all EU trademark applications; only applicants from Germany filed more applications than did U.S. applicants.

On the EU trademark see Martina Repas & Tomaz Kerestes, The Certification Mark as A New EU-Wide Industrial Property Right, 49(3) IIC 299 (2018); Eric Raciti, The Harmonization of Trademarks in the European Community, 78 J. Patent & Trademark Off. Soc'y 51 (1996); David Wilkinson, The Community Trademark Regulation and its Role in European Economic Integration, 80 Trademark Rep. 107 (1990).

6.   *The Use Requirement.* National laws typically require that following registration, trademarks be used in commerce. In the United States, the Lanham Act requires that trademark owners regularly file affidavits of use of their marks in commerce. 15 U.S.C. 1058. Nonuse of a trademark for three consecutive years constitutes prima facie evidence of trademark abandonment. 15 U.S.C. 1127. Where must the use in commerce occur? How is the use to be localized? Under what conditions does the use of a trademark on a trademark owner's website satisfy the "use in commerce" requirement?

The EU Trademark Regulation requires "genuine use in the [European] Union." EU Trademark Regulation, Article 18(1). Non-use for five consecutive years will lead to revocation of the trademark. *Id.*, Articles 18(1) and 58(1). Affixing an EU trademark to goods in the European Union "solely for export purposes" will satisfy the use requirement in the European Union. *Id.*, Article 18(1)(b). Must an owner of an EU trademark maintain use of the trademark in all EU member states? The Court of Justice of the European Union explained that "it is not necessary that the [EU] mark should be used in an extensive geographic area for the use to be deemed genuine, since such a qualification will depend on the characteristics of the product or service concerned on the corresponding market." Leno Merken BV v. Hagelkruis Beheer BV, CJEU, C-149/11, 2012, ¶ 54. What should the sufficient geographical scope of use be in the case of a trademark used for artisanal pralines? *See* Reber Holding GmbH & Co. KG v. OHIM, CJEU, C-141/13 P, 2014.

PROBLEM 8

Your client, Tonawanda Thread Co. (TTC), a Nebraska corporation with headquarters in Omaha, manufactures a line of sewing thread to which, in the course of the manufacturing process, it applies a distinctive floral scent. On January 15, TTC obtained a registration on the Principal Register in the U.S. Patent and Trademark Office for a "high impact, fresh floral fragrance reminiscent of plumeria blossoms as applied to sewing thread." On the advice of its intellectual property counsel that no other country would register a fragrance as a trademark, TTC decided not to seek trademark registration for the fragrance in the 24 other countries in which it markets its thread.

One of these 24 countries, Country *X*, amended its trademark act on May 12 of the same year to allow registration of distinctive fragrances as trademarks. Four months later, the Trademark Office of Country *X* granted a trademark registration to Net Notions (NN) for "a high impact, fresh floral fragrance reminiscent of plumeria blossoms" as applied to sewing thread manufactured by it. NN has also applied to register the fragrance in Country *Y*, which is not one of the 24 countries in which TTC markets its thread, and is considering applying for registration in Country *Z* which also is not one of these 24 countries.

Please advise TTC of the likelihood that it can obtain trademark registration for its fragrance as applied to sewing thread in Countries *X*, *Y*, and *Z*, all of which have adhered to the Paris Convention (1967).

c.   REGISTRATION OF DOMAIN NAMES

Uniform Domain Name Dispute Resolution Policy*
(As Approved by ICANN on October 24, 1999).

1.   *Purpose.* This Uniform Domain Name Dispute Resolution Policy (the "Policy") has been adopted by the Internet Corporation for Assigned Names and Numbers ("ICANN"), is incorporated by reference into your Registration Agreement, and sets forth the terms and conditions in connection with a dispute between you and any party other than us (the registrar) over the registration and use of an Internet domain name registered by you. Proceedings under Paragraph 4 of this Policy will be conducted according to the Rules for Uniform Domain-Name Dispute Resolution Policy (the "Rules of Procedure"), which are available at http://www.icann.org/en/dndr/udrp/uniform-rules.htm, and the selected administrative-dispute-resolution service provider's supplemental rules.

2.   *Your Representations.* By applying to register a domain name, or by asking us to maintain or renew a domain name registration, you hereby represent and warrant to us that (a) the statements that you made in your Registration Agreement are complete and accurate; (b) to your knowledge, the registration of the domain name will not infringe upon or otherwise violate the rights of any third party; (c) you are not registering the domain name for an unlawful purpose; and (d) you will not knowingly use the domain name in violation of any applicable laws or regulations. It is your responsibility to determine whether your domain name registration infringes or violates someone else's rights.

3.   *Cancellations, Transfers, and Changes.* We will cancel, transfer or otherwise make changes to domain name registrations under the following circumstances:

---

*   NOTES:

   1.   This policy is now in effect. See https://www.icann.org/resources/pages/help/dndr/udrp-en for the implementation schedule.

   2.   This policy has been adopted by all accredited domain-name registrars for domain names ending in .com, .net, and .org. It has also been adopted by certain managers of country-code top-level domains (*e.g.*, .nu, .tv, .ws).

   3.   The policy is between the registrar (or other registration authority in the case of a country-code top-level domain) and its customer (the domain-name holder or registrant). Thus, the policy uses "we" and "our" to refer to the registrar and it uses "you" and "your" to refer to the domain-name holder.

a.   subject to the provisions of Paragraph 8, our receipt of written or appropriate electronic instructions from you or your authorized agent to take such action;

b.   our receipt of an order from a court or arbitral tribunal, in each case of competent jurisdiction, requiring such action; and/or

c.   our receipt of a decision of an Administrative Panel requiring such action in any administrative proceeding to which you were a party and which was conducted under this Policy or a later version of this Policy adopted by ICANN. (*See* Paragraph 4(i) and (k) below.)

We may also cancel, transfer or otherwise make changes to a domain name registration in accordance with the terms of your Registration Agreement or other legal requirements.

4.   *Mandatory Administrative Proceeding.*

This Paragraph sets forth the type of disputes for which you are required to submit to a mandatory administrative proceeding. These proceedings will be conducted before one of the administrative-dispute-resolution service providers listed at www.icann.org/udrp/approved-providers.htm (each, a "Provider").

a.   *Applicable Disputes.* You are required to submit to a mandatory administrative proceeding in the event that a third party (a "complainant") asserts to the applicable Provider, in compliance with the Rules of Procedure, that

(i)   your domain name is identical or confusingly similar to a trademark or service mark in which the complainant has rights; and

(ii)   you have no rights or legitimate interests in respect of the domain name; and

(iii)   your domain name has been registered and is being used in bad faith.

In the administrative proceeding, the complainant must prove that each of these three elements are present.

b.   *Evidence of Registration and Use in Bad Faith.* For the purposes of Paragraph 4(a)(iii), the following circumstances, in particular but without limitation, if found by the Panel to be present, shall be evidence of the registration and use of a domain name in bad faith:

(i)   circumstances indicating that you have registered or you have acquired the domain name primarily for the purpose of selling, renting, or otherwise transferring the domain name registration to the complainant who is the owner of the trademark or service mark or to a competitor of that complainant, for valuable consideration in excess of your documented out-of-pocket costs directly related to the domain name; or

(ii) you have registered the domain name in order to prevent the owner of the trademark or service mark from reflecting the mark in a corresponding domain name, provided that you have engaged in a pattern of such conduct; or

(iii) you have registered the domain name primarily for the purpose of disrupting the business of a competitor; or

(iv) by using the domain name, you have intentionally attempted to attract, for commercial gain, Internet users to your web site or other on-line location, by creating a likelihood of confusion with the complainant's mark as to the source, sponsorship, affiliation, or endorsement of your web site or location or of a product or service on your web site or location.

c.   How to Demonstrate Your Rights to and Legitimate Interests in the Domain Name in Responding to a Complaint. When you receive a complaint, you should refer to Paragraph 5 of the Rules of Procedure in determining how your response should be prepared. Any of the following circumstances, in particular but without limitation, if found by the Panel to be proved based on its evaluation of all evidence presented, shall demonstrate your rights or legitimate interests to the domain name for purposes of Paragraph 4(a)(ii):

(i) before any notice to you of the dispute, your use of, or demonstrable preparations to use, the domain name or a name corresponding to the, domain name in connection with a bona fide offering of goods or services; or

(ii) you (as an individual, business, or other organization) have been commonly known by the domain name, even if you have acquired no trademark or service mark rights; or

(iii) you are making a legitimate noncommercial or fair use of the domain name, without intent for commercial gain to misleadingly divert consumers or to tarnish the trademark or service mark at issue.

d.   Selection of Provider. The complainant shall select the Provider from among those approved by ICANN by submitting the complaint to that Provider. The selected Provider will administer the proceeding, except in cases of consolidation as described in Paragraph 4(f).

e.   Initiation of Proceeding and Process and Appointment of Administrative Panel. The Rules of Procedure state the process for initiating and conducting a proceeding and for appointing the panel that will decide the dispute (the "Administrative Panel").

f.   Consolidation. In the event of multiple disputes between you and a complainant, either you or the complainant may petition to consolidate the disputes before a single Administrative Panel. This petition shall be made to the first Administrative Panel appointed to hear a pending dispute between the parties. This Administrative Panel may consolidate before it any or all such disputes in its sole discretion, provided that the disputes being consolidated are governed by this Policy or a later version of this Policy adopted by ICANN.

g.   *Fees.* All fees charged by a Provider in connection with any dispute before an Administrative Panel pursuant to this Policy shall be paid by the complainant, except in cases where you elect to expand the Administrative Panel from one to three panelists as provided in Paragraph 1, (b)(iv) of the Rules of Procedure, in which case all fees will be split evenly by you and the complainant.

h.   *Our Involvement in Administrative Proceedings.* We do not, and will not, participate in the administration or conduct of any proceeding before an Administrative Panel. In addition, we will not be liable as a result of any decisions rendered by the Administrative Panel.

i.   *Remedies.* The remedies available to a complainant pursuant to any proceeding before an Administrative Panel shall be limited to requiring the cancellation of your domain name or the transfer of your domain name registration to the complainant.

j.   *Notification and Publication.* The Provider shall notify us of any decision made by an Administrative Panel with respect to a domain name you have registered with us. All decisions under this Policy will be published in full over the Internet, except when an Administrative Panel determines in an exceptional case to redact portions of its decision.

k.   *Availability of Court Proceedings.* The mandatory administrative proceeding requirements set forth in Paragraph 4 shall not prevent either you or the complainant from submitting the dispute to a court of competent jurisdiction for independent resolution before such mandatory administrative proceeding is commenced or after such proceeding is concluded. If an Administrative Panel decides that your domain name registration should be canceled or transferred, we will wait ten (10) business days (as observed in the location of our principal office) after we are informed by the applicable Provider of the Administrative Panel's decision before implementing that decision. We will then implement the decision unless we have received from you during that ten (10) business day period official documentation (such as a copy of a complaint, file-stamped by the clerk of the court) that you have commenced a lawsuit against the complainant in a jurisdiction to which the complainant has submitted under Paragraph 3(b)(xiii) of the Rules of Procedure. (In general, that jurisdiction is either the location of our principal office or of your address as shown in our Whois database. *See* Paragraphs 1 and 3 b xiii of the Rules of Procedure for details.) If we receive such documentation within the ten (10) business day period, we will not implement the Administrative Panel's decision, and we will take no further action, until we receive (i) evidence satisfactory to us of a resolution between the parties; (ii) evidence satisfactory to us that your lawsuit has been dismissed or withdrawn; or (iii) a copy of an order from such court dismissing your lawsuit or ordering that you do not have the right to continue to use your domain name.

5. *All Other Disputes and Litigation.* All other disputes between you and any party other than us regarding your domain name registration that are not brought pursuant to the mandatory administrative proceeding provisions of Paragraph 4 shall be resolved between you and such other party through any court, arbitration or other proceeding that may be available.

6. *Our Involvement in Disputes.* We will not participate in any way in any dispute between you and any party other than us regarding the registration and use of your domain name. You shall not name us as a party or otherwise include us in any such proceeding. In the event that we are named as a party in any such proceeding, we reserve the right to raise any and all defenses deemed appropriate, and to take any other action necessary to defend ourselves.

7. *Maintaining the Status Quo.* We will not cancel, transfer, activate, deactivate, or otherwise change the status of any domain name registration under this Policy except as provided in Paragraph 3 above.

8. *Transfers During a Dispute.*

a. *Transfers of a Domain Name to a New Holder.* You may not transfer your domain name registration to another holder (i) during a pending administrative proceeding brought pursuant to Paragraph 4 or for a period of fifteen (15) business days (as observed in the location of our principal place of business) after such proceeding is concluded; or (ii) during a pending court proceeding or arbitration commenced regarding your domain name unless the party to whom the domain name registration is being transferred agrees, in Writing, to be bound by the decision of the court or arbitrator. We reserve the right to cancel any transfer of a domain name registration to another holder that is made in violation of this subparagraph.

b. *Changing Registrars.* You may not transfer your domain name registration to another registrar during a pending administrative proceeding brought pursuant to Paragraph 4 or for a period of fifteen (15) business days (as observed in the location of our principal place of business) after such proceeding is concluded. You may transfer administration of your domain name registration to another registrar during a pending court action or arbitration, provided that the domain name you have registered with us shall continue to be subject to the proceedings commenced against you in accordance with the terms of this Policy. In the event that you transfer a domain name registration to us during the pendency of a court action or arbitration, such dispute shall remain subject to the domain name dispute policy of the registrar from which the domain name registration was transferred.

9.   *Policy Modifications.* We reserve the right to modify this Policy at any time with the permission of ICANN. We will post our revised Policy at <URL> at least thirty (30) calendar days before it becomes effective. Unless this Policy has already been invoked by the submission of a complaint to a Provider, in which event the version of the Policy in effect at the time it was invoked will apply to you until the dispute is over, all such changes will be binding upon you with respect to any domain name registration dispute, whether the dispute arose before, on or after the effective date of our change. In the event that you object to a change in this Policy, your sole remedy is to cancel your domain name registration with us, provided that you will not be entitled to a refund of any fees you paid to us. The revised Policy will apply to you until you cancel your domain name registration.

Barcelona.com, Incorporated v. Excelentisimo Ayuntamiento de Barcelona

United States Court of Appeals, Fourth Circuit, 2003.
330 F.3d 617, 67 U.S.P.Q.2d 1025.

NIEMEYER, CIRCUIT JUDGE:

Barcelona.com, Inc. ("Bcom, Inc."), a Delaware corporation, commenced this action under the Anticybersquatting Consumer Protection Act against Excelentisimo Ayuntamiento de Barcelona (the City Council of Barcelona, Spain) for a declaratory judgment that Bcom, Inc.'s registration and use of the domain name <barcelona.com> is not unlawful under the Lanham Act (Chapter 22 of Title 15 of the United States Code). The district court concluded that Bcom, Inc.'s use of <barcelona.com> was confusingly similar to Spanish trademarks owned by the City Council that include the word "Barcelona." Also finding bad faith on the basis that Bcom, Inc. had attempted to sell the <barcelona.com> domain name to the City Council for a profit, the court ordered the transfer of the domain name to the City Council.

Because the district court applied Spanish law rather than United States law and based its transfer order, in part, on a counterclaim that the City Council never filed, we reverse the judgment of the district court denying Bcom, Inc. relief under the Anticybersquatting Consumer Protection Act, vacate its memorandum opinion and its order to transfer the domain name <barcelona.com> to the City Council, and remand for further proceedings consistent with this opinion.

I

In 1996, Mr. Joan Nogueras Cobo ("Nogueras"), a Spanish citizen, registered the domain name <barcelona.com> in the name of his wife, also a Spanish citizen, with the domain registrar, Network Solutions, Inc., in Herndon, Virginia. In the application for registration of the domain name, Nogueras listed himself as the administrative contact. When Nogueras met Mr. Shahab Hanif, a British citizen, in June 1999, they developed a business plan to turn <barcelona.com> into a tourist portal for the Barcelona, Spain, region. A few months later they formed Bcom, Inc. under Delaware law to own <barcelona.com> and to run the website, and Nogueras, his wife, and Hanif became Bcom, Inc.'s officers. Bcom, Inc. was formed as an American company in part because Nogueras believed that doing so would facilitate obtaining financing for the development of the website. Although Bcom, Inc. maintains a New York mailing address, it has no employees in the United States, does not own or lease office space in the United States, and does not have a telephone listing in the United States. Its computer server is in Spain.

Shortly after Nogueras registered the domain name <barcelona.com> in 1996, he placed some Barcelona-related information on the site. The site offered commercial services such as domain registry and web hosting, but did not offer much due to the lack of financing. Before developing the business plan with Hanif, Nogueras used a web-form on the City Council's official website to e-mail the mayor of Barcelona, Spain, proposing to "negotiate" with the City Council for its acquisition of the domain name <barcelona.com>, but Nogueras received no response. And even after the development of a business plan and after speaking with potential investors, Nogueras was unable to secure financing to develop the website.

In March 2000, about a year after Nogueras had e-mailed the Mayor, the City Council contacted Nogueras to learn more about Bcom, Inc. and its plans for the domain name <barcelona.com>. Nogueras and his marketing director met with City Council representatives, and after the meeting, sent them the business plan that was developed for Bcom, Inc.

On May 3, 2000, a lawyer for the City Council sent a letter to Nogueras demanding that Nogueras transfer the domain name <barcelona.com> to the City Council. The City Council owned about 150 trademarks issued in Spain, the majority of which included the word Barcelona, such as "Teatre Barcelona," "Barcelona Informacio I Grafic," and "Barcelona Informacio 010 El Tlefon Que Ho Contesta Tot." Its earlier effort in 1995 to register the domain name <barcelona.es>, however, was unsuccessful. The City Council's representative explained, "It was denied to Barcelona and to all place names in Spain." This representative also explained that the City Council did not try also to register <barcelona.com> in 1995 even though that domain name was available because "[a]t that time . . . the world Internet that we know now was just beginning and it was not seen as a priority by the City Council."

The City Council now took the position with Bcom, Inc. that its domain name <barcelona.com> was confusingly similar to numerous trademarks that the City Council owned.

A couple of days after the City Council sent its letter, Nogueras had the domain name <barcelona.com> transferred from his wife's name to Bcom, Inc., which he had neglected to do in 1999 when Bcom, Inc. was formed.

Upon Bcom, Inc.'s refusal to transfer <barcelona.com> to the City Council, the City Council invoked the Uniform Domain Name Dispute Resolution Policy ("UDRP") promulgated by the Internet Corporation for Assigned Names and Numbers ("ICANN") to resolve the dispute. Every domain name issued by Network Solutions, Inc. is issued under a contract, the terms of which include a provision requiring resolution of disputes through the UDRP. In accordance with that policy, the City Council filed an administrative complaint with the World Intellectual Property Organization ("WIPO"), an ICANN-authorized dispute-resolution provider located in Switzerland. The complaint sought transfer of the domain name <barcelona.com> to the City Council and relied on Spanish law in asserting that Bcom, Inc. had no rights to the domain name while the City Council had numerous Spanish trademarks that contained the word "Barcelona." As part of its complaint, the City Council agreed "to be subject to the jurisdiction of the registrant[']s residence, the Courts of Virginia (United States), only with respect to any challenge that may be made by the Respondent to a decision by the Administrative Panel to transfer or cancel the domain names that are [the] subject of this complaint."

The administrative complaint was resolved by a single WIPO panelist who issued a ruling in favor of the City Council on August 4, 2000. The WIPO panelist concluded that <barcelona.com> was confusingly similar to the City Council's Spanish trademarks, that Bcom, Inc. had no legitimate interest in <barcelona.com>, and that Bcom, Inc.'s registration and use of <barcelona.com> was in bad faith. To support his conclusion that Bcom, Inc. acted in bad faith, the WIPO panelist observed that the only purpose of the business plan was "to commercially exploit information about the City of Barcelona ... particularly ... the information prepared and provided by [the City Council] as part of its public service." The WIPO panelist ordered that Bcom, Inc. transfer the domain name <barcelona.com> to the City Council.

In accordance with the UDRP's provision that required a party aggrieved by the dispute resolution process to file any court challenge within ten business days, Bcom, Inc. commenced this action on August 18, 2000 under the provision of the Anticybersquatting Consumer Protection Act (the "ACPA") that authorizes a domain name owner to seek recovery or restoration of its domain name when a trademark owner has overstepped its authority in causing the domain name to be suspended, disabled, or transferred. Bcom, Inc.'s complaint sought a declaratory judgment that its use of the name <barcelona.com> "does not infringe upon any trademark of defendant or cause confusion as to the origin, sponsorship, or approval of the website <barcelona.com>; . . . [and] that [the City Council] is barred from instituting any action against [Bcom, Inc.] for trademark infringement." While the City Council answered the complaint and stated, as an affirmative defense, that the court lacked jurisdiction over the City Council for any cause of action other than Bcom, Inc.'s "challenge to the arbitrator's Order issued in the UDRP domain name arbitration proceeding," the City Council filed no counterclaim to assert any trademark rights.

Following a bench trial, the district court entered a memorandum opinion and an order dated February 22, 2002, denying Bcom, Inc.'s request for declaratory judgment and directing Bcom, Inc. to "transfer the domain name barcelona.com to the [City Council] forthwith." 189 F.Supp.2d 367, 377 (E.D.Va. 2002). Although the district court concluded that the WIPO panel ruling "should be given no weight and this case must be decided based on the evidence presented before the Court," the court proceeded in essence to apply the WIPO panelist opinion as well as Spanish law. *Id.* at 371. The court explained that even though the City Council did not own a trademark in the name "Barcelona" alone, it owned numerous Spanish trademarks that included the word Barcelona, which could, under Spanish law as understood by the district court, be enforced against an infringing use such as <barcelona.com>. *Id.* Adopting the WIPO panelist's decision, the court stated that "the WIPO decision was correct in its determination that [Bcom, Inc.] took 'advantage of the normal confusion' of an Internet user by using the 'Barcelona route' because an Internet user would 'normally expect to reach some official body . . . for . . . the information.' " *Id.* at 372. Referring to the facts that Bcom, Inc. engaged in little activity and attempted to sell the domain name to the City Council, the court concluded that "these factors clearly demonstrate a bad faith intent on the part of the Plaintiff and its sole shareholders to improperly profit from their registration of the domain name barcelona.com." At bottom, the court concluded that Bcom, Inc. failed to demonstrate, as required by 15 U.S.C. § 1114(2)(D)(v), that its use of <barcelona.com> was "not unlawful." *Id.* at 373.

In addition to concluding that Bcom, Inc. failed to establish its claim, the court stated that it was also deciding the City Council's counterclaim for relief under 15 U.S.C. § 1125 and determined that "the Spanish trademark 'Barcelona' is valid for purposes of the ACPA." *Id.* at 374. Applying the factors of 15 U.S.C. § 1125(2)(d)(1)(B)(i), the court found that Nogueras and his wife acted with "bad faith intent" in registering <barcelona.com> as a domain name. *Id.* at 374–76. The court also found that <barcelona.com> "is confusingly similar to the defendant's mark." *Id.* at 376.

From the district court's order of February 22, 2002, Bcom, Inc. filed this appeal.

II

Bcom, Inc. contends that when it "sought a declaration under 15 U.S.C. § 1114(2)(D)(v), it was entitled to have its conduct judged by U.S. trademark law, not Spanish trademark law." It argues that even if Spanish law applies, however, a party cannot, under Spanish law, "get a registration for a term that is only geographically descriptive, such as the word 'Barcelona.'" Finally, it maintains that its use of the domain name was not unlawful under United States trademark law because it could not be found to have acted in bad faith under § 1125, as the district court concluded.

The City Council contends that the WIPO panelist's decision, including its reference to Spanish law, must be considered to decide this case. It argues:

> [T]rial courts may consider rights in foreign trademarks which were asserted in the transfer decision under review. The [WIPO] administrative transfer proceeding itself gives the district court both subject matter and personal jurisdiction; jurisdiction is not dependent upon allegations of U.S. trademark rights. Therefore, failure to consider the basis for the administrative decision would remove the basis for jurisdiction, and require dismissal of the case. The statute language does not limit the marks considered to U.S. marks. To hold otherwise would be to strip a trademark owner of its foreign rights whenever it is haled into court by a U.S. domain name owner who has lost a UDRP administrative proceeding. Without the ability to assert their rights, foreign trademark owners would automatically lose such proceedings, creating an unintended and unjust result.

The City Council also maintains that the district court's conclusions of confusing similarity and bad faith were factually supported and justified.

In light of the City Council's argument that "failure to consider the basis for the [WIPO] decision would remove the basis for [this court's] jurisdiction," we will review first the basis for our jurisdiction and the role of the WIPO panelist's administrative decision.

Bcom, Inc.'s complaint, brought in the Eastern District of Virginia where the domain name <barcelona.com> was registered with Network Solutions, Inc., originally asserted three claims in three separate counts: a claim for declaratory judgment and injunctive relief under 15 U.S.C. § 1114(2)(D)(v); a claim for fraud and unfair competition; and a claim for tortious interference with prospective economic advantage. In response to the City Council's motion to dismiss on various jurisdictional grounds, Bcom, Inc. voluntarily dismissed all claims except its claim under § 1114(2)(D)(v). After the district court denied the City Council's motion to dismiss, the City Council filed an answer, stating as one of its affirmative defenses:

This court lacks jurisdiction over Defendant regarding any cause of action other than Plaintiff's challenge to the arbitrator's Order issued in the UDRP domain name arbitration proceeding.

This statement reflects the City Council's stipulation that when it filed the WIPO administrative claim in Switzerland, "the City Council agreed to be subject to the jurisdiction of 'the Courts of Virginia (United States), only with respect to any challenge that may be made by the Respondent to a decision by the Administrative Panel to transfer or cancel the domain names that are [the] subject of this complaint.'" Accordingly, at least with respect to a claim brought under § 1114(2)(D)(v), the City Council agrees that the district court had personal jurisdiction over the City Council.

The district court had subject matter jurisdiction based on the fact that this case was brought under the Lanham Act, as amended by the ACPA, and that §§ 1331 and 1338 of Title 28 confer jurisdiction over such claims.

Apparently, the City Council does not dispute these jurisdictional observations as far as they go. It contends, however, that jurisdiction to hear a claim under § 1114(2)(D)(v) rests on a recognition of the WIPO proceeding and the law that the WIPO panelist applied. Although we agree with the City Council that the WIPO proceeding is relevant to a claim under § 1114(2)(D)(v), it is not jurisdictional; indeed, the WIPO panelist's decision is not even entitled to deference on the merits. . . .

In sum, domain names are issued pursuant to contractual arrangements under which the registrant agrees to a dispute resolution process, the UDRP, which is designed to resolve a large number of disputes involving domain names, but this process is not intended to interfere with or modify any "independent resolution" by a court of competent jurisdiction. Moreover, the UDRP makes no effort at unifying the law of trademarks among the nations served by the Internet. Rather, it forms part of a contractual policy developed by ICANN for use by registrars in administering the issuance and transfer of domain names. Indeed, it explicitly anticipates that judicial proceedings will continue under various nations' laws applicable to the parties.

The ACPA recognizes the UDRP only insofar as it constitutes a part of a policy followed by registrars in administering domain names, and the UDRP is relevant to actions brought under the ACPA in two contexts. First, the ACPA limits the liability of a registrar in respect to registering, transferring, disabling, or cancelling a domain name if it is done in the "implementation of *a reasonable policy*" (including the UDRP) that prohibits registration of a domain name "identical to, confusingly similar to, or dilutive of another's mark." 15 U.S.C. § 1114(2)(D)(ii)(II) (emphasis added). Second, the ACPA authorizes a suit by a domain name registrant whose domain name has been suspended, disabled or transferred *under that reasonable policy* (including the UDRP) to seek a declaration that the registrant's registration and use of the domain name involves no violation of the Lanham Act as well as an injunction returning the domain name.

Thus, while a decision by an ICANN-recognized panel might be a condition of, indeed the reason for, bringing an action under 15 U.S.C. § 1114(2)(D)(v), its recognition *vel non* is not jurisdictional. Jurisdiction to hear trademark matters is conferred on federal courts by 28 U.S.C. §§ 1331 and 1338, and a claim brought under the ACPA, which amended the Lanham Act, is a trademark matter over which federal courts have subject matter jurisdiction.

Moreover, any decision made by a panel under the UDRP is no more than an agreed-upon administration that is *not* given any deference under the ACPA. To the contrary, because a UDRP decision is susceptible of being grounded on principles foreign or hostile to American law, the ACPA authorizes reversing a panel decision if such a result is called for by application of the Lanham Act.

In sum, we conclude that we have jurisdiction over this dispute brought under the ACPA and the Lanham Act. Moreover, we give the decision of the WIPO panelist no deference in deciding this action under § 1114(2)(D)(v). . . . Thus, for our purposes, the WIPO panelist's decision is relevant only to serve as the reason for Bcom, Inc.'s bringing an action under § 1114(2)(D)(v) to reverse the WIPO panelist's decision.

III

Now we turn to the principal issue raised in this appeal. Bcom, Inc. contends that in deciding its claim under § 1114(2)(D)(v), the district court erred in applying the law of Spain rather than the law of the United States. Because the ACPA explicitly requires application of the Lanham Act, not foreign law, we agree.

Section 1114(2)(D)(v), the reverse domain name hijacking provision, states:

> A domain name registrant whose domain name has been suspended, disabled, or transferred under a policy described under clause (ii)(II) may, upon notice to the mark owner, file a civil action to establish that the registration or use of the domain name by such registrant is not unlawful under this chapter. The court may grant injunctive relief to the domain name registrant, including the reactivation of the domain name or transfer of the domain name to the domain name registrant.

15 U.S.C. § 1114(2)(D)(v). Thus, to establish a right to relief against an "overreaching trademark owner" under this reverse hijacking provision, a plaintiff must establish (1) that it is a domain name registrant; (2) that its domain name was suspended, disabled, or transferred under a policy implemented by a registrar as described in 15 U.S.C. § 1114(2)(D)(ii)(II); (3) that the owner of the mark that prompted the domain name to be suspended, disabled, or transferred has notice of the action by service or

otherwise; and (4) that the plaintiff's registration or use of the domain name is not unlawful under the Lanham Act, as amended.

The parties do not dispute that the first two elements are satisfied. Bcom, Inc. is a domain name registrant, and its domain name was suspended, disabled, or transferred under Network Solutions' policy, *i.e.*, the UDRP incorporated into the domain name registration agreement for <barcelona.com>. Although the domain name had not actually been transferred from Bcom, Inc. as of the time that Bcom, Inc. commenced this action, the WIPO panelist had already ordered the transfer, and as a result of this order the transfer was certain to occur absent the filing of this action to stop it. By filing this suit, Bcom, Inc. obtained an automatic stay of the transfer order by virtue of paragraph 4(k) of the UDRP, which provides that the registrar will stay implementation of the administrative panel's decision if the registrant commences "a lawsuit against the complainant in a jurisdiction to which the complainant has submitted" under the applicable UDRP rule of procedure. . . . Moreover, this suit for declaratory judgment and injunctive relief under § 1114(2)(D)(v) appears to be precisely the mechanism designed by Congress to empower a party whose domain name is subject to a transfer order like the one in the present case to prevent the order from being implemented. . . .

There also can be no dispute that Bcom, Inc. provided notice of this § 1114(2)(D)(v) action to the City Council.

It is the last element that raises the principal issue on appeal. Bcom, Inc. argues that the district court erred in deciding whether Bcom, Inc. satisfied this element by applying Spanish law and then by concluding that Bcom, Inc.'s use of the domain name violated Spanish law.

It appears from the district court's memorandum opinion that it indeed did resolve the last element by applying Spanish law. Although the district court recognized that the City Council did not have a registered trademark in the name "Barcelona" alone, either in Spain or in the United States, it observed that "[u]nder Spanish law, when trademarks consisting of two or more words contain one word that stands out in a predominant manner, that dominant word must be given decisive relevance." *Barcelona.com, Inc.,* 189 F.Supp.2d at 371–72. The court noted that "the term 'Barcelona' has been included in many trademarks consisting of two or more words owned by the City Council of Barcelona. In most of these marks, the word 'Barcelona' is clearly the dominant word which characterizes the mark." *Id.* at 372. These observations regarding the substance and effect of Spanish law led the court to conclude that the City Council of Barcelona "owns a legally valid Spanish trademark for the dominant word 'Barcelona.' " The district court then proceeded to determine whether Bcom's "use of the Barcelona trademark is 'not unlawful.' " *Id.* In this portion of its analysis, the district court determined that there was a "confusing similarity between the barcelona.com domain name and the marks held by the Council," *id.,* and that "the circumstances surrounding the incorporation of [Bcom, Inc.] and the actions taken by Nogueras in attempting to sell the domain name evidence[d] a bad faith intent to profit from the registration of a domain name containing the Council's mark," *id.* Applying Spanish trademark law in this manner, the court resolved that Bcom, Inc.'s registration and use of <barcelona.com> were unlawful.

It requires little discussion to demonstrate that this use of Spanish law by the district court was erroneous under the plain terms of the statute. The text of the ACPA explicitly requires application of the Lanham Act, not foreign law, to resolve an action brought under 15 U.S.C. § 1114(2)(D)(v). Specifically, it authorizes an aggrieved domain name registrant to "file a civil action to establish that the registration or use of the domain name by such registrant is *not unlawful under this chapter.*" 15 U.S.C. § 1114(2)(D)(v) (emphasis added). . . . It is thus readily apparent that the cause of action created by Congress in this portion of the ACPA requires the court adjudicating such an action to determine whether the registration or use of the domain name violates the Lanham Act. Because the statutory language has a plain and unambiguous meaning that is consistent with the statutory context and application of this language in accordance with its plain meaning provides a component of a coherent statutory scheme, our statutory analysis need proceed no further. . . .

By requiring application of United States trademark law to this action brought in a United States court by a United States corporation involving a domain name administered by a United States registrar, 15 U.S.C. § 1114(2)(D)(v) is consistent with the fundamental doctrine of territoriality upon which our trademark law is presently based. Both the United States and Spain have long adhered to the Paris Convention for the Protection of Industrial Property. Section 44 of the Lanham Act, 15 U.S.C. § 1126, incorporates the Paris Convention into United States law, but only "to provide foreign nationals with rights under United States law which are coextensive with the substantive provisions of the treaty involved." *Scotch Whisky Ass'n v. Majestic Distilling Co.,* 958 F.2d 594, 597 (4th Cir. 1992). . . . The relevant substantive provision in this case is Article 6(3) of the Paris Convention, which implements the doctrine of territoriality by providing that "[a] mark duly registered in a country of the [Paris] Union shall be regarded as independent of marks registered in the other countries of the Union, including the country of origin." Paris Convention, *supra,* art. 6(3). As one distinguished commentary explains, "the Paris Convention creates nothing that even remotely resembles a 'world mark' or an 'international registration.' Rather, it recognizes the principle of the territoriality of trademarks [in the sense that] a mark exists only under the laws of each sovereign nation." 4 J. Thomas McCarthy, *McCarthy on Trademarks and Unfair Competition* § 29:25 (4th ed. 2002).

It follows from incorporation of the doctrine of territoriality into United States law through Section 44 of the Lanham Act that United States courts do not entertain actions seeking to enforce trademark rights that exist only under foreign law. . . . Yet the district court's application of foreign law in this declaratory judgment action did precisely this and thereby neglected to apply United States law as required by the statute.

When we apply the Lanham Act, not Spanish law, in determining whether Bcom, Inc.'s registration and use of <barcelona.com> is unlawful, the ineluctable conclusion follows that Bcom, Inc.'s registration and use of the name "Barcelona" is not unlawful. Under the Lanham Act, and apparently even under Spanish law, the City Council could not obtain a trademark interest in a purely descriptive geographical designation that refers only to the City of Barcelona. Under United States trademark law, a geographic designation can obtain trademark protection if that designation acquires secondary meaning. . . . On the record in this case, however, there was no evidence that the public—in the United States or elsewhere—associates "Barcelona" with anything other than the City itself. Indeed, the Chief Director of the City Council submitted an affidavit stating that "[t]he City does not own and is not using any trademarks in the United States, to identify any goods or services." Therefore, under United States trademark law, "Barcelona" should have been treated as a purely descriptive geographical term entitled to no trademark protection. . . . It follows then that there was nothing unlawful about Nogueras' registration of <barcelona.com>, nor is there anything unlawful under United States trademark law about Bcom, Inc.'s continued use of that domain name. . . .

For these reasons, we conclude that Bcom, Inc. established entitlement to relief under 15 U.S.C. § 1114(2)(D)(v) with respect to the domain name <barcelona.com>, and accordingly we reverse the district court's ruling in this regard. . . .

V

For the foregoing reasons, we reverse the district court's ruling that denied Bcom, Inc. relief under 15 U.S.C. § 1114(2)(D)(v); we vacate its Memorandum Opinion and Order of February 22, 2002; and we remand for further proceedings to determine and grant the appropriate relief under § 1114(2)(D)(v).

REVERSED, VACATED, AND REMANDED

NOTES

1. *Use of Domain Names and the Territoriality Principle.* Can the use of domain names be reconciled with the territoriality principle? The court in *Barcelona.com* emphasized that "[b]y requiring application of United States trademark law to this action brought in a United States court by a United States corporation involving a domain name administered by a United States

registrar," the ACPA "is consistent with the fundamental doctrine of territoriality upon which our trademark law is presently based." Under traditional principles of private international law, the location of the forum in which a case is brought should not affect the choice of applicable law or the outcome of a case. Why, then, should the fact that a domain name was administered by a U.S. registrar have been material to the application of U.S. trademark law in deciding the case?

2. *Trademarks and Domain Names.* The use of trademarks as domain names adds a layer of complexity to choice of law and subject matter jurisdiction in trademark cases. Consider, for example, the plight of two companies, one French the other American, that have registered and used worldwide the mark "Why"—the American company in connection with jeans, the French company in connection with perfume—when the American company registers "why.com" as its domain name. Presumably the law of the protecting country will govern questions of trademark infringement, with the probable result that the domain name will be considered confusingly similar under the laws of some countries but not others. Can a remedy be fashioned that will at once bar use of the domain name in countries where it infringes, but permit it in countries where it does not? What would be the appropriate resolution of the conflict under the UDRP? Do internationalized domain names, such as domain names in Arabic or Chinese script, or top-level domains referring to particular goods or services, such as .clothing or .beauty, offer suitable solutions?

Although the unauthorized use of a trade or service mark in a domain name may seriously undermine the mark's merchandising value, traditional requirements of competition and trademark use previously constrained some courts from granting trademark relief against these uses. Later decisions have applied the trademark dilution doctrine and broad interpretations of trademark law's confusion requirement to curb these uses.

In British Telecommunications plc v. One in a Million Ltd., [1999] F.S.R. 1, the English Court of Appeal ruled against defendant, which had registered such well-known British trade names as sainsbury.com, bt.org, marksandspencer.co.uk and virgin.org, on grounds of trademark infringement and passing off. The court rejected the argument that domain name registration alone could not give rise to a cause of action and that actual use or sale was required before trademark infringement or passing off could be found. The court held that, apart from creating an enjoinable instrument of fraud, registration of the names in issue constituted both passing off and trademark infringement. In the case of Marks & Spencer, "the placing on a register of a distinctive name such as marksandspencer makes a representation to persons who consult the register that the registrant is connected or associated with the name registered and thus the owner of the goodwill in the name. Such persons would not know of One In A Million Ltd. and would believe that they were connected or associated with the owner of the goodwill in the domain name they had registered. Further, registration of the domain name including the words Marks & Spencer is an erosion of the exclusive goodwill in the name which damages or is likely to damage Marks & Spencer plc." *See* also Yoyo.Email Ltd. v. Royal Bank of Scotland Group Plc [2016] F.S.R. 18.

In Panavision Int'l v. Toeppen, 141 F.3d 1316, 46 U.S.P.Q.2d (9th Cir. 1998), the U.S. Court of Appeals for the Ninth Circuit ruled that the unauthorized domain name registration of plaintiff's "Panavision" and "Panaflex" marks violated the Federal Trademark Dilution Act, 15 U.S.C. § 1125(c). The court rejected defendant's argument that its registration neither constituted the required "commercial use" of the Panavision marks nor diluted the capacity of the marks to identify goods or services. Recognizing precedential support for the first argument, the court nonetheless concluded it did not matter that defendant had not attached the mark to goods. Also, a domain name is more than an address. "It marks the location of the site within cyberspace, much like a postal address in the real world, but it may also indicate to users some information as to the content of the site, and, in instances of well-known trade names or trademarks, may provide information as to the origin of the contents of the site. Moreover, potential customers of Panavision will be discouraged if they cannot find its Web page by typing in Panavision.com, but instead are forced to wade through hundreds of Web sites. This dilutes the value of Panavision's trademark." 141 F.3d at 1327.

See generally Torsten Bettinger, Trademark Law in Cyberspace—the Battle for Domain Names, 28 IIC 508 (1997); Assafa Endeshaw, The Threat of Domain Names to the Trademark System, 3 J. World Int. Prop. 323 (2000); Tony Willoughby, Domain Name Disputes: The UDRP 10 Years On, 4(10) J. Intell. Property L. & Practice 714 (2009).

3. *Sui Generis Legislation.* As indicated in the *Barcelona.com* case, the Anticybersquatting Consumer Protection Act, Pub. L. No. 106–113, 113 Stat. 1501, was passed by Congress in 1999 to bar the abusive use of marks and personal names in situations that traditional trademark law might not reach. The Act gives owners of a mark, including a personal name used as a mark, rights against anyone who, with "a bad faith intent to profit from the mark," registers, traffics in or uses a domain name that is confusingly similar to a distinctive mark, that is "confusingly similar to or dilutive" of a famous mark, or that is specifically protected by statutes protecting marks of the Red Cross and the U.S. Olympic Committee. 15 U.S.C. § 1125(d)(1)(A). The mark need not be registered to be protected, and protection is "without regard to the goods or services of the parties."

The Act lists several factors that a court may weigh in determining whether the defendant had the required bad faith intent. Among the factors are: the fact that defendant itself had trademark or other intellectual property rights in the domain name, or made prior use of the domain name in connection with the bona fide offering of goods or services; "the person's intent to divert consumers from the mark owner's online location to a site accessible under the domain name that could harm the goodwill represented by the mark, either for commercial gain or with the intent to tarnish or disparage the mark, by creating a likelihood of confusion as to the source, sponsorship, affiliation, or endorsement of the site"; and "the person's offer to transfer, sell, or otherwise assign the domain name to the mark owner or any third party for financial gain without having used, or having an intent to use, the domain name in the bona fide offering of any goods or services, or the person's prior conduct indicating a pattern of such conduct." 15 U.S.C. § 1125(d)(1)(B).

The anticybersquatting amendments also prescribe remedies, including actual or statutory damages and costs, and forfeiture of the domain name or its cancellation or transfer to the owner of the mark. Of particular significance in the context of cross-border uses, section 43(d)(2)(A), 15 U.S.C. § 1125(d)(2)(A), authorizes an *in rem* civil action against the domain name itself in situations where the owner is unable to obtain *in personam* jurisdiction over the offender or was unable to find the offender. The situs for *in rem* actions includes the judicial district in which the domain name registry is located. Remedies in *in rem* cases are limited to forfeiture, cancellation or transfer of the domain name to the owner of the mark.

4.   *Domain Name Registrations, Dispute Resolution, and Applicable Law.* Domain name registry operators (also referred to as "registries"), that are designated by the Internet Corporation for Assigned Names and Numbers (ICANN) to operate top-level domain registries, can promulgate rules for registration of domain names on their domains. Sometimes the registration rules make a particular national law apply to some or all registration issues, and registries' versions of dispute resolution policies, though typically modelled after the UDRP, sometimes include choice-of-law provisions that make national law supplement the policies' other rules.

The UDRP, which ICANN adopted, does not prescribe a choice-of-law rule for domain name disputes, and according to the Rules for the Policy "[a] Panel shall decide a complaint [concerning a domain name registration] on the basis of the statements and documents submitted and in accordance with the Policy, [the] Rules and any rules and principles of law that it deems applicable." *Id.*, section 15(a). What issues does the UDRP not regulate, and what laws should apply to those issues? Consider whether it should be the law of the place of (1) the ICANN-approved dispute resolution service provider (there were five providers as of March 2019); (2) the domain name registry (which operates the registry for the domain); (3) the domain name registrar (who registered the domain name); (4) one or both of the parties to the dispute; or (5) the registration of the trademark right.

Some UDRP panelists have promoted the development and use of autonomous UDRP principles; other panelists prefer to supplement the UDRP with national law, particularly in light of the overriding force of national law in any subsequent court proceedings, such as U.S. law in *Barcelona*. Which approach is more likely to lead to consistency and legal certainty in UDRP proceedings? "Inconsistencies can arise either (1) among UDRP decisions if they are based on different countries' laws, or (2) between a UDRP decision and a national court decision if the UDRP decision is based on autonomous UDRP law and the national court decision on national law." Marketa Trimble, Territorialization of the Internet Domain Name System, 45(4) Pepperdine L. Rev. 623, 650 (2018).

For an analysis of the functioning of the UDRP system see Andrew F. Christie, Online Dispute Resolution: The Phenomenon of the UDRP, in Research Handbook on Cross-Border Enforcement of Intellectual Property (Paul Torremans ed., 2014), pp. 642–681.

5. *Competing Trademarks and the UDRP.* How should a dispute over a domain name be resolved between the holders of the same mark registered in different countries? Gibson Brands Inc. owns the trademark Epiphone in numerous countries, including in the United States and Taiwan, and claims its use on amplifiers since 1939. Gibson filed a UDRP complaint against a Chinese respondent who registered the domain name epiphoneamps.com. The respondent registered the trademark Epiphone in China with a 2009 priority date. Notwithstanding the duration of Gibson's use of the mark and its registration of the mark in the United States, a UDRP panel ruled in favor of the respondent. The panel found that the domain name was confusingly similar to Gibson's trademark, but the panel also found that the respondent had rights in respect of the domain name. Gibson Brands, Inc. v. Zong Wen, National Arbitration Forum, Claim No. FA1501001602037, Mar. 9, 2015.

In *Gibson* the panel also made a reverse domain name hijacking finding against Gibson. Under the Rules, "[i]f after considering the submissions the Panel finds that the complaint was brought in bad faith, for example in an attempt at Reverse Domain Name Hijacking, or was brought primarily to harass the domain name holder, the Panel shall declare in its decision that the complaint was brought in bad faith and constitutes an abuse of the administrative proceeding." Rules for Uniform Domain Name Dispute Resolution Policy, ICANN, Oct. 30, 2009, ¶ 15(e). The panel considered it "inconceivable" that Gibson was not aware of the respondent's trademark registration in China. Is it consistent with the principle of territoriality that Gibson did not prevail in the dispute notwithstanding the fact that the dispute concerned a .com domain name? Would the outcome have been different if Epiphone was a well-known mark?

6. *Domains, Domain Names, and Geographical Indications.* What do users expect to find under the domain name barcelona.com? Or barcelona.es or barcelona.eu? Do users perceive domain names, including geographical names or domains including country name abbreviations, as indicators of the geographical source of information or of goods or services offered on the website with the domain name or on websites with the domain?

Should trademark protection trump protection of geographical indications or other geographical descriptions in domain names? In conflicts over domain names consisting of geographical names, most UDRP panels have denied complaints that claimed rights based on geographical names. For example, the city of Heidelberg was unsuccessful in disputing registration of heidelberg.net by a U.S. registrant because the city failed to show that it had any rights to a trademark or service mark with which the domain name would be identical or confusingly similar. Stadt Heidelberg v. Media Factory, WIPO Arbitration and Mediation Center, Case No. D2001-1500, Mar. 6, 2002.

In a dispute concerning the domain name champagne.ie, a WIPO panel ordered the domain name to be transferred to Comité interprofessionel du Vin de Champagne, a body responsible for managing, promoting, and protecting the Champagne appellation of origin. The dispute was governed by the .IE Dispute Resolution Policy which, in contrast to UDRP, includes geographical indications in the category of "protected identifiers" to which a domain name must not be identical or misleadingly similar. .IE Dispute Resolution Policy, 1.1.1. and 1.3.3. Therefore, the registrant did not prevail in the dispute notwithstanding the fact that the registrant was a licensed champagne distributor and importer. Comité interprofessionel du Vin de Champagne (CIVC) v. Richard Doyle, WIPO Arbitration and Mediation Center, Case No. DIE2007-0005, Feb. 5, 2008.

Should different rules govern in the case of top-level domains that refer to particular products with which geographical indications may be associated? Applications for the top-level domains .wine and .vin generated discussions between U.S. and Australian governments on one side, and the European Union and 36 other countries on the other. Eventually, wine industry representatives reached a private agreement with the registry. "Champagne" and "Prosecco" were among the first domain names registered on the .wine and .vin domains. Scott Gerien & Christopher Passarelli, Challenges for Geographical Indications (GIs) in the Context of the ICANN New Generic Top-Level Domains (gTLDs), Organization for an International Geographical Indications Network, 2016, p. 41.

7.   *Geographical Top-Level Domains.* When ICANN created two-character country code top level domains, such as .us, .uk, and .jp, ICANN reserved the domains for the country or territory using the abbreviation. Principles for the Delegation and Administration of Country Code Top Level Domains, Feb. 23, 2000. A new top-level domains program has permitted registration of words consisting of multiple characters, including geographical names, as domains. Rules for registrations of domain names on country code top-level domains and other geographical domains often, though not always, require registrants to be linked to the country, territory, or location by citizenship, residence, incorporation, establishment, or linguistic or cultural ties. On the territorial connections of the domain name system see Marketa Trimble, Territorialization of the Internet Domain Name System, 45(4) Pepperdine L. Rev. 623 (2018).

Should geographical names as top level domains be reserved for "the relevant communities where they belong" or be delegated only "after a specific authorization given by the government or community to the applicant?" The Protection of Geographic Names in the New gTLDs Process, Sub-Working Group for Protection of Geographic Names in Next Rounds of New gTLDs, Aug. 29, 2014. Should .paris be delegated to Paris, France, or to Paris, Texas? When the U.S. corporation Amazon.com, Inc. applied for .amazon as a new top level domain, representatives of the Amazon region in South America raised objections to the application. ICANN rejected Amazon.com, Inc.'s application for .amazon after considering an expert opinion that stated that ICANN was not obligated by any rule of international, regional, or national law to decide one way or another. Expert

Analysis by Professor Jérôme Passa, Mar. 31, 2014; Resolution 2014.05.14.NG02, ICANN, May 14, 2014.

8. *The Uniform Rapid Suspension System.* Responding to concerns about potential abuses associated with the introduction of new top level domains, ICANN launched in 2013 the Uniform Rapid Suspension System ("URS")— a mechanism to achieve a rapid and less costly suspension (a "lock") of a domain name. A registrant may file a response to a URS complaint, which is then forwarded together with the complaint to an examiner for a decision. If the examiner finds for the complainant, the domain name is suspended for the balance of the registration period. The suspension, which may be extended for an additional period of time, is the sole remedy available under the URS. Uniform Rapid Suspension (URS) Rules, Effective 28 June 2013, ¶ 14(a).

What are the differences between the UDRP and the URS? As one commentator noted, the URS "has a higher burden of proof as it requires 'clear and convincing evidence' and the complainant must also prove use for instance." David Taylor, ICANN Offers Rapid Relief to Trade Mark Holders in Clear Cases of Infringement, 9(5) JIPLP 357 (2014). The URS is suitable for complainants who are trademark owners but who do not want the domain name at issue to be transferred to them.

Does the URS address the problem of territoriality? In a complaint, the complainant has to "specify the trademark(s) or service mark(s) on which the complaint is based and the goods and services with which the mark is used including evidence of use. . . ." Uniform Rapid Suspension (URS) Rules, Effective 28 June 2013, ¶ 3(b)(v).

9. *ICANN Trademark Clearinghouse.* Another response to concerns about the introduction of new top-level domains was the creation of the Trademark Clearinghouse. Trademark owners may submit their trademarks to be included in a Clearinghouse database that will streamline their participation in the sunrise (launch) periods of new top-level domains, during which time the trademark owners may obtain priority registration of domain names. The Clearinghouse accepts and verifies "registered trademarks, marks protected by a statute or treaty, or court validated marks as well as any other marks that constitute Intellectual Property (IP) rights in accordance with the registry's policies and that meet the eligibility requirements of the Trademark Clearinghouse." Accepted Trademarks, Trademark Clearinghouse, https://www.trademark-clearinghouse.com/. How should the Clearinghouse handle competing national trademarks? Or a well-known mark and another earlier-registered trademark?

4. OWNERSHIP

IHT Internationale Heiztechnik GmbH v. Ideal Standard GmbH

Court of Justice of the European Communities, 1994.
Case C-9/93.

1   By order of 15 December 1992, received at the Court on 12 January 1993, the Oberlandesgericht (Higher Regional Court) Düsseldorf referred to the Court for a preliminary ruling under Article 177 EEC a question on the interpretation of Articles 30 and 36 EEC in order to assess the compatibility with Community law of restrictions on the use of a name where a group of companies held, through subsidiaries, a trade mark consisting of that name in several Member States of the Community and where that trade mark was assigned, for one Member State only and for some of the products for which it had been registered, to an undertaking outside the group.

2   That question arose in a dispute between Ideal-Standard GmbH and IHT, both German companies, regarding the use in Germany of the trade mark Ideal Standard for heating equipment manufactured in France by IHT's parent, Compagnie Internationale de Chauffage ("CICh").

3   Until 1984 the American Standard group held, through its German and French subsidiaries—Ideal-Standard GmbH and Ideal-Standard SA—the trade mark Ideal Standard in Germany and in France for sanitary fittings and heating equipment.

4   In July 1984 the French subsidiary of that group, Ideal-Standard SA, sold the trade mark for the heating equipment sector, with its heating business, to Société Générale de Fonderie ("SGF"), a French company with which it had no links. That trade mark assignment related to France (including the overseas departments and territories), Tunisia and Algeria.

5   The background to that assignment was the following. From 1976 Ideal-Standard SA had been in financial difficulties. Insolvency proceedings were opened. A management agreement was concluded between the trustees and another French company set up by, *inter alios*, SGF. That company carried on Ideal-Standard SA's production and sales activities. The management agreement came to an end in 1980. The business of Ideal-Standard SA's heating equipment division remained unsatisfactory. In view of SGF's interest in maintaining the heating equipment division and its marketing in France under the device "Ideal Standard," Ideal-Standard SA assigned the trade mark and transferred the production plants for the heating division referred to in [the preceding] paragraph to SGF. SGF later assigned the trade mark to another French company, CICh, which, like SGF, is part of the French Nord-Est group and has no links with the American Standard group.

6   Ideal-Standard GmbH brought proceedings against IHT for infringement of its trade mark and its commercial name by marketing in Germany heating equipment bearing the trade mark Ideal Standard manufactured in France by CICh. Ideal-Standard GmbH was still the owner of the trade mark Ideal Standard in Germany both for sanitary fittings and for heating equipment although it had stopped manufacturing and marketing heating equipment in 1976.

7   The action seeks an injunction against IHT from marketing in Germany heating equipment bearing the trade mark "Ideal Standard" and from using that trade mark on various commercial documents.

8   At first instance the proceedings were heard by the Landgericht (Regional Court) Düsseldorf which, by judgment of 25 February 1992, upheld the claim.

9   The Landgericht held first that there was risk of confusion. The device used—the name "Ideal Standard"—was identical. Moreover, the products were sufficiently close for the relevant users, seeing the same device on the products, to be led to believe that they came from the same undertaking.

10   The Landgericht further held that there was no reason for it to avail itself of its power to refer a question to the Court of Justice under Article 177 of the Treaty on the interpretation of Articles 30 and 36 of the Treaty. It reviewed the judgments in Case 192/73 *Van Zuylen v HAG* [1974] ECR 731 (*HAG I*) and Case C-10/89 *CNL-SUCAL v HAG* [1990] ECR I-3711 (*HAG II*) and held that the reasoning of the Court in *HAG II* "suffices to show that there is no longer any foundation for the doctrine of common origin, not only in the context of the facts underlying that decision, that is cases of expropriation in a Member State, but also in cases of voluntary division of ownership of a trade mark originally in single ownership, which is the position in this case".

11   IHT appealed against that judgment to the Oberlandesgericht Düsseldorf which, referring to *HAG II*, considered whether this case should, as the Landgericht had held, be decided in the same way pursuant to Community law.

12   Accordingly, the Oberlandesgericht referred the following question to the Court of Justice for a preliminary ruling:

> Does it constitute an unlawful restriction of intra-Community trade, within the meaning of Articles 30 and 36 EEC, for an undertaking carrying on business in Member State A which is a subsidiary of a manufacturer of heating systems based in Member State B to be prohibited from using as a trade mark the name "Ideal Standard" on the grounds of risk of confusion with a mark having the same origin, where the name "Ideal Standard" is lawfully used by the manufacturer in its home country by virtue of a trade mark registered there which it has acquired by means of a legal transaction and which was

originally the property of a company affiliated to the undertaking which is opposing, in Member State A, the importation of goods marked "Ideal Standard"?

13   It is common ground that a prohibition on the use in Germany by IHT of the name "Ideal Standard" for heating equipment would constitute a measure having equivalent effect to a quantitative restriction under Article 30. The question is, therefore, whether that prohibition may be justified under Article 36 of the Treaty.

14   It is appropriate first of all to review certain key features of trade-mark law and the case-law of the Court on Articles 30 and 36 of the Treaty in order to identify the precise legal context of the national court's question.

The similarity of the products and the risk of confusion

15   The *HAG II* case, whose bearing on the main proceedings is the point of the question put by the national court, related to a situation where it was not just the name that was identical but also the products marketed by the parties to the dispute. This dispute, by contrast, relates to the use of an identical device for different products since Ideal-Standard GmbH is relying on its registration of the trade mark "Ideal Standard" for sanitary fittings in order to oppose the use of that device for heating equipment.

16   It is common ground that the right of prohibition stemming from a protected trade mark, whether protected by registration or on some other basis, extends beyond the products for which the trade mark has been acquired. The object of trade-mark law is to protect owners against contrivances of third parties who might seek, by creating a risk of confusion amongst consumers, to take advantage of the reputation accruing to the trade mark. . . . That risk may arise from the use of an identical device for products different from those for which a trade mark has been acquired (by registration or otherwise) where the products in question are sufficiently close to induce users seeing the same device on those products to conclude that the products come from the same undertaking. Similarity of the products is thus part of the concept of risk of confusion and must be assessed in relation to the purpose of trade-mark law.

17   In its observations the Commission warned against taking the broad view of the risk of confusion and similarity of products taken by the German courts, since it is liable to have restrictive effects, not covered by Article 36 EEC, on the free movement of goods.

18   As regards the period before the entry into force of the First Council Directive (89/104) . . . to approximate the laws of the Member States relating to trade marks . . . , which was postponed to 31 December 1992 by Article 1 of Council Decision 92/10 . . . , that being the material period for the main dispute, the Court held in Case C-317/91 *Deutsche Renault v. Audi* . . . that "the determination of the criteria allowing the conclusion

to be drawn that there is a risk of confusion is part of the detailed rules for protection of trade marks, which ... are a matter for national law" ... and "Community law does not lay down any criterion requiring a strict interpretation of the risk of confusion". ...

19   However, as was held in the *Deutsche Renault* case, application of national law continues to be subject to the limits set out in the second sentence of Article 36 of the Treaty: there must be no arbitrary discrimination or disguised restriction on trade between Member States. There would, in particular, be a disguised restriction if the national court were to conduct an arbitrary assessment of the similarity of products. As soon as application of national law as to similarity of the products led to arbitrary discrimination or a disguised restriction, the obstacle to imports could not anyway be justified under Article 36. Moreover, if the competent national court were finally to hold that the products in question were not similar, there would be no obstacle to imports susceptible of justification under Article 36.

20   Subject to those reservations, it is for the court hearing the main proceedings to assess the similarity of the products in question. Since that is a question involving determination of the facts of which only the national court can have direct knowledge and so, to that extent, is outside the Court's jurisdiction under Article 177, the Court must proceed on the assumption that there is a risk of confusion. The problem therefore arises on the same basis as if the products for which the trade mark was assigned and those covered by the registration relied on in Germany were identical.

The territorial nature and independence of national trade mark rights

21   Since this case concerns a situation where the trade mark has been assigned for one State only and the question whether the solution in *Hag II* regarding the splitting of a mark as a result of sequestration also applies in the event of splitting by voluntary act, it should be noted first, as the United Kingdom pointed out, that national trade-mark rights are not only territorial but also independent of each other.

22   National trade-mark rights are first of all territorial. This principle of territoriality, which is recognised under international treaty law, means that it is the law of the country where protection of a trade mark is sought which determines the conditions of that protection. Moreover, national law can only provide relief in respect of acts performed on the national territory in question.

23   Article 36 EEC itself, by allowing certain restrictions on imports on grounds of protection of intellectual property, presupposes that in principle the legislation of the importing State applies to acts performed in that State in relation to the imported product. A restriction on importation permitted by that legislation will of course escape Article 30 only if it is covered by Article 36.

24   National trade-mark rights are also independent of each other.

25   The principle of the independence of trade marks is expressed in Article 6(3) of the Paris Union Convention for the Protection of Industrial Property of 20 March 1883, as last revised at Stockholm on 14 July 1967 . . . which provides: "A mark duly registered in a country of the Union shall be regarded as independent of marks registered in other countries of the Union . . .".

26   That principle has led to recognition that a trade mark right may be assigned for one country without at the same time being assigned by its owner in other countries.

27   The possibility of independent assignments is first of all implicit in Article 6*quater* of the Paris Union Convention.

28   Some national laws permit the transfer of the trade mark without a concomitant transfer of the undertaking whilst others continue to require that the undertaking should be transferred with the trade mark. In some countries the requirement of the concomitant transfer of the undertaking was even interpreted as necessitating the transfer of the whole undertaking even if certain parts of it were situated in countries other than that for which the transfer was proposed. The transfer of a trade mark for one country therefore almost necessarily entailed the transfer of the trade mark for other countries.

29   That is why Article 6*quater* of the Paris Union Convention provided: "When, in accordance with the law of a country of the Union, the assignment of a mark is valid only if it takes place at the same time as the transfer of the business or goodwill to which the mark belongs, it shall suffice for the recognition of such validity that the portion of the business or goodwill located in that country be transferred to the assignee, together with the exclusive right to manufacture in the said country, or to sell therein the goods bearing the mark assigned."

30   By thus making possible the assignment of a trade mark for one country without the concomitant transfer of the trade mark in another country, Article 6*quater* of the Paris Union Convention presupposes that such independent assignments may be made.

31   The principle of the independence of trade marks is, moreover, expressly enshrined in Article 9*ter*(2) of the Madrid Agreement concerning the International Registration of Marks of 14 April 1891, as last revised at Stockholm in 1967 . . . , which provides: "The International Bureau shall likewise record the assignment of an international mark in respect of one or several of the contracting countries only."

32   Unified laws, which bring the territory of several States into a single territory for purposes of trade-mark law, such as the Uniform Benelux Act on Trade Marks for Goods (annexed to the Convention Benelux en Matiere de Marques de Produits . . .), or Council Regulation 40/94 . . . on the Community trade mark . . . render void transfers of trade marks for only one part of the territory to which they apply. . . . However, those unified laws do not, any more than national laws, make the validity of a

trade-mark assignment for the territory to which they apply conditional on the concomitant assignment of the trade mark for the territory of third States.

The case law on Articles 30 and 36 trade mark law and parallel imports

33   On the basis of the second sentence of Article 36 of the Treaty the Court has consistently held:

> "Inasmuch as it provides an exception to one of the fundamental principles of the Common Market, Article 36 in fact only admits of derogations from the free movement of goods where such derogations are justified for the purpose of safeguarding rights which constitute the specific subject-matter of this property.
>
> In relation to trade marks, the specific subject-matter of the industrial property is the guarantee that the owner of the trade mark has the exclusive right to use that trade mark, for the purpose of putting products protected by the trade mark into circulation for the first time, and is therefore intended to protect him against competitors wishing to take advantage of the status and reputation of the trade mark by selling products illegally bearing that trade mark.
>
> An obstacle to the free movement of goods may arise out of the existence, within a national trade mark legislation concerning industrial and commercial property, of provisions laying down that a trade mark owner's right is not exhausted when the product protected by the trade mark is marketed in another Member State, with the result that the trade mark owner can [oppose] importation of the product into his own Member State when it has been marketed in another Member State.
>
> Such an obstacle is not justified when the product has been put onto the market in a legal manner in the Member State from which it has been imported, by the trade mark owner himself or with his consent, so that there can be no question of abuse or infringement of the trade mark.
>
> In fact, if a trade mark owner could prevent the import of protected products marketed by him or with his consent in another Member State, he would be able to partition off national markets and thereby restrict trade between Member States, in a situation where no such restriction was necessary to guarantee the essence of the exclusive right flowing from the trade mark". . . .

34   So, application of a national law which would give the trade-mark owner in the importing State the right to oppose the marketing of products which have been put into circulation in the exporting State by him or with his consent is precluded as contrary to Articles 30 and 36. This principle, known as the exhaustion of rights, applies where the owner of the trade mark in the importing State and the owner of the trade

mark in the exporting State are the same or where, even if they are separate persons, they are economically linked. A number of situations are covered: products put into circulation by the same undertaking, by a licensee, by a parent company, by a subsidiary of the same group, or by an exclusive distributor.

35   There are numerous instances in national case-law and Community case-law where the trade mark had been assigned to a subsidiary or to an exclusive distributor in order to enable those undertakings to protect their national markets against parallel imports by taking advantage of restrictive approaches to the exhaustion of rights in the national laws of some States.

36   Articles 30 and 36 defeat such manipulation of trade-mark rights since they preclude national laws which enable the holder of the right to oppose imports.

37   In the situations described above . . . the function of the trade mark is in no way called in question by freedom to import. As was held in *Hag II*: "For the trade mark to be able to fulfil [its] role, it must offer a guarantee that all goods bearing it have been produced under the control of a single undertaking which is accountable for their quality". . . . In all the cases mentioned, control was in the hands of a single body: the group of companies in the case of products put into circulation by a subsidiary; the manufacturer in the case of products marketed by the distributor; the licensor in the case of products marketed by a licensee. In the case of a licence, the licensor can control the quality of the licensee's products by including in the contract clauses requiring the licensee to comply with his instructions and giving him the possibility of verifying such compliance. The origin which the trade mark is intended to guarantee is the same: it is not defined by reference to the manufacturer but by reference to the point of control of manufacture (see the statement of grounds for the Benelux Convention and the Uniform Act . . .).

38   It must further be stressed that the decisive factor is the possibility of control over the quality of goods, not the actual exercise of that control. Accordingly, a national law allowing the licensor to oppose importation of the licensee's products on grounds of poor quality would be precluded as contrary to Articles 30 and 36: if the licensor tolerates the manufacture of poor quality products, despite having contractual means of preventing it, he must bear the responsibility. Similarly if the manufacture of products is decentralised within a group of companies and the subsidiaries in each of the Member States manufacture products whose quality is geared to the particularities of each national market, a national law which enabled one subsidiary of the group to oppose the marketing in the territory of that State of products manufactured by an affiliated company on grounds of those quality differences would also be precluded. Articles 30 and 36 require the group to bear the consequences of its choice.

39   Articles 30 and 36 thus debar the application of national laws which allow recourse to trade-mark rights in order to prevent the free movement of a product bearing a trade mark whose use is under unitary control.

The situation where unitary control of the trade mark has been severed following assignment for one or several Member States only

40   The problem posed by the Oberlandesgericht's question is whether the same principles apply where the trade mark has been assigned, for one or several Member States only, to an undertaking which has no economic link with the assignor and the assignor opposes the marketing, in the State in which he has retained the trade mark, of products to which the trade mark has been affixed by the assignee.

41   That situation must be clearly distinguished from the case where the imported products come from a licensee or a subsidiary to which ownership of the trade mark right has been assigned in the exporting State: a contract of assignment by itself, that is in the absence of any economic link, does not give the assignor any means of controlling the quality of products which are marketed by the assignee and to which the latter has affixed the trade mark.

42   The Commission has submitted that by assigning in France the trade mark "Ideal Standard" for heating equipment to a third company, the American Standard group gave implied consent to that third company putting heating equipment into circulation in France bearing that trade mark. Because of that implied consent, it should not be possible to prohibit the marketing in Germany of heating equipment bearing the assigned trade mark.

43   That view must be rejected. The consent implicit in any assignment is not the consent required for application of the doctrine of exhaustion of rights. For that, the owner of the right in the importing State must, directly or indirectly, be able to determine the products to which the trade mark may be affixed in the exporting State and to control their quality. That power is lost if, by assignment, control over the trade mark is surrendered to a third party having no economic link with the assignor.

44   The insulation of markets where, for two Member States of the Community, there are separate trade-mark owners having no economic links is a result that has already been accepted by the Court in *Hag II*. However, since that was a case where unitary ownership was divided following sequestration, it has been submitted that the same result does not have to be adopted in the case of voluntary division.

45   That view cannot be accepted because it is contrary to the reasoning of the Court in *HAG II*. The Court began by noting that trade-mark rights are an essential element in the system of undistorted competition which the Treaty seeks to establish. . . . It went on to recall the identifying function of trade marks, and in a passage cited in paragraph 37 above, the conditions for trade marks to be able to fulfil that role. The Court

further noted that the scope of the exclusive right which is the specific subject-matter of the trade mark must be determined having regard to its function. . . . It stressed that in that case the determinant factor was absence of consent of the proprietor of the trade mark in the importing State to the putting into circulation in the exporting State of products marketed by the proprietor of the right in the latter State. . . . It concluded that free movement of the goods would undermine the essential function of the trade mark: consumers would no longer be able to identify for certain the origin of the marked goods and the proprietor of the trade mark could be held responsible for the poor quality of goods for which he was in no way accountable. . . .

46   Those considerations apply, as was rightly stressed by the United Kingdom and Germany and was held by the Landgericht Düsseldorf at first instance, whether the splitting of the trade mark originally held by the same owner is due to an act of public authority or a contractual assignment.

47   IHT in particular has submitted that the owner of a trade mark who assigns the trade mark in one Member State, while retaining it in others, must accept the consequences of the weakening of the identifying function of the trade mark flowing from that assignment. By a territorially limited assignment, the owner voluntarily renounces his position as the only person marketing goods bearing the trade mark in question in the Community.

48   That argument must be rejected. It fails to take account of the fact that, since trade-mark rights are territorial, the function of the trade mark is to be assessed by reference to a particular territory. . . .

49   IHT has further argued that the French subsidiary, Ideal-Standard SA, has adjusted itself in France to a situation where products (such as heating equipment and sanitary fittings) from different sources may be marketed under the same trade mark on the same national territory. The conduct of the German subsidiary of the same group which opposes the marketing of the heating equipment in Germany under the trade mark "Ideal Standard" is therefore abusive.

50   That argument cannot be upheld either.

51   First of all, the assignment was made only for France. The effect of that argument, if it were accepted, would, as the German Government points out, be that assignment of the right for France would entail permission to use the device in Germany, whereas assignments and licences always relate, having regard to the territorial nature of national trade-mark rights, to a specified territory.

52   Moreover, and most importantly, French law, which governs the assignment in question here, permits assignments of trade marks confined to certain products, with the result that similar products from different sources may be in circulation on French territory under the same trade mark, whereas German law, by prohibiting assignments of

trade marks confined to certain products, seeks to prevent such co-existence. The effect of IHT's argument, if it were accepted, would be to extend to the importing State whose law opposes such co-existence the solution prevailing in the exporting State despite the territorial nature of the rights in question.

53 Starting from the position that assignment to an assignee having no links with the assignor would lead to the existence of separate sources within a single territory and that, in order to safeguard the function of the trade mark, it would then be necessary to allow prohibition of export of the assignee's products to the assignor's territory and vice versa, unified laws, to avoid creating such obstacles to the free movement of goods, render void assignments made for only part of the territory covered by the rights they create. By limiting the right to dispose of the trade mark in this way, such unified laws ensure single ownership throughout the territory to which they apply and guarantee free movement of the product.

54 Thus, the Uniform Benelux Act on Trade Marks for Goods, whose objective was to unify the territory of the three States for trade mark purposes (statement of grounds . . .), provided that, from the date of its entry into force, a trade mark could be granted only for the whole of Benelux (statement of grounds . . .). To that end it further provided that trade-mark assignments not effected for the whole of Benelux were void.

55 The regulation on the Community trade mark referred to above also creates a right with a unitary character. Subject to certain exceptions (see in this respect Article 106 on the prohibition of use of Community trade marks and Article 107 on prior rights applicable to particular localities), the Community trade mark "shall have equal effect throughout the Community: it shall not be registered, transferred or surrendered or be the subject of a decision revoking the rights of the proprietor or declaring it invalid, nor shall its use be prohibited, save in respect of the whole Community" (Article 1(2)).

56 However, unlike the Benelux Act, "the Community law relating to trade marks . . . does not replace the laws of the Member States on trade marks" (fifth recital in the preamble to the regulation on the Community trade mark). The Community trade mark is merely superimposed on the national rights. Undertakings are in no way obliged to take out Community trade marks (fifth recital). Moreover, the existence of earlier national rights may be an obstacle to the registration of a Community trade mark since, under Article 8 of the regulation, the owner of a trade mark in a single Member State may oppose the registration of a Community trade mark by the proprietor of national rights for identical or similar products in all the other Member States. That provision cannot be interpreted as precluding the assignment of national trade marks for one or more States of the Community only. It is therefore apparent that the regulation on the Community trade mark does not render void

assignments of national marks which are confined to certain States of the Community.

57   That sanction cannot be introduced through case-law. To hold that the national laws are measures having equivalent effect which fall under Article 30 and are not justified by Article 36, in that, given the independence of national rights they do not, at present, make the validity of assignments for the territories to which they apply conditional on the concomitant assignment of the trade mark for the other States of the Community, would have the effect of imposing on the States a positive obligation, namely to embody in their laws a rule rendering void assignments of national trade marks made for part only of the Community.

58   It is for the Community legislature to impose such an obligation on the Member States by a directive adopted under Article 100a of the EEC Treaty, elimination of the obstacles arising from the territoriality of national trade marks being necessary for the establishment and functioning of the internal market, or itself to enact that rule directly by a regulation adopted under the same provision.

59   It should be added that, where undertakings independent of each other make trade mark assignments following a market-sharing agreement, the prohibition of anti-competitive agreements under Article 85 applies and assignments which give effect to that agreement are consequently void. However, as the United Kingdom rightly pointed out, that rule and the accompanying sanction cannot be applied mechanically to every assignment. Before a trade-mark assignment can be treated as giving effect to an agreement prohibited under Article 85, it is necessary to analyse the context, the commitments underlying the assignment, the intention of the parties and the consideration for the assignment.

60   In view of the foregoing, the answer to the Oberlandesgericht Düsseldorf's question must be that there is no unlawful restriction on trade between Member States within the meaning of Articles 30 and 36 where a subsidiary operating in Member State A of a manufacturer established in Member State B is to be enjoined from using as a trade mark the name "Ideal Standard" because of the risk of confusion with a device having the same origin, even if the manufacturer is lawfully using that name in his country of origin under a trade mark protected there, he acquired that trade mark by assignment and the trade mark originally belonged to a company affiliated to the undertaking which, in Member State A, opposes the importation of goods bearing the trade mark "Ideal Standard".

Costs

61   The costs incurred by the German Government, the United Kingdom and the European Commission, which have submitted observations to the Court, are not recoverable. Since these proceedings are, for the

parties to the main proceedings, a step in the action pending before the national court, the decision on costs is a matter for that court.

On those grounds,

THE COURT,

in answer to the question referred to it by the Oberlandesgericht Düsseldorf, by order of 15 December 1992,

HEREBY RULES:

There is no unlawful restriction on trade between Member States within the meaning of Articles 30 and 36 where a subsidiary operating in Member State A of a manufacturer established in Member State B is to be enjoined from using as a trade mark the name "Ideal Standard" because of the risk of confusion with a device having the same origin, even if the manufacturer is lawfully using that name in his country of origin under a trade mark protected there, he acquired that trade mark by assignment and the trade mark originally belonged to a company affiliated to the undertaking which, in Member State A, opposes the importation of goods bearing the trade mark "Ideal Standard".

NOTES

1. *Ideal-Standard.* If *A* owned the registered mark "Ideal" for bicycles in France and *B*, an entirely unrelated company, owned the registered mark "Ideal" for bicycles in Germany, *A* could obtain relief against *B*'s use of the mark in France, just as *B* could obtain relief against *A*'s use of the mark in Germany. The issue in *Ideal-Standard* was whether, for purposes of determining the existence of an unlawful restriction of intra-Community trade, the common corporate origin of the marks in issue—but the absence of economic links between plaintiff and defendant—should change this result. Was the court correct to follow the analogy of exhaustion cases, tying the legitimacy of the complaining trademark owner's actions to its ability to control the quality of the defendant's goods? Would it—and should it—have made a difference if French or German law prohibited a trademark owner from transferring its mark without the simultaneous imposition of quality control measures?

See generally, Gregory Hotaling, *Ideal Standard v. IHT*: In the European Union, Must a Company Surrender Its National Trademark Rights When it Assigns Its Trademark?, 19 Ford. Int'l L. J. 1178 (1996).

2. *Early and Contemporary Theories of Trademark Transfer.* Until well into the twentieth century, legislation and judicial decisions in most countries allowed a trademark to be transferred only as part of the business in which it was used. The legal theory behind this rule was that a trademark signified the source of goods to consumers, and that once a mark was detached from its source it could no longer serve to guarantee quality. Applied rigorously, the rule could prevent a firm in Country *A* from transferring a mark it had registered in Country *B* to a firm that might exploit the mark more efficiently in Country *B* without at the same time also transferring its business to the same firm.

Through the first half of the twentieth century, courts in many civil law countries and some common law countries adjusted their rules on trademark transfer to new marketing realities. For example, the early rules on trademark transfer made it difficult for trademark owners to exploit their marks across product boundaries. Not only did the rules bar a trademark owner that had acquired goodwill in the mark "Ideal" for bicycles from licensing another firm to produce and market bicycles under the "Ideal" mark; it also inhibited licensing of the mark to a manufacturer of scooters. The newer rules allowed trademark owners to grant licenses apart from any underlying business so long as the license embodied sufficient controls to ensure that consumers would not be deceived as to the quality of goods. In some countries these licenses were allowed only on identical products, while in others they were allowed on different products as well.

In the United States, section 5 of the Lanham Act, 15 U.S.C. § 1055, validates licensing apart from transfer of a business or goodwill, by providing that "[w]here a registered mark or a mark sought to be registered is or may be used legitimately by related companies, such use shall inure to the benefit of the registrant or applicant for registration, and such use shall not affect the validity of such mark or of its registration, provided such mark is not used in such manner as to deceive the public." Section 45 of the Lanham Act, 15 U.S.C. § 1127, defines "related company" as "any person whose use of a mark is controlled by the owner of the mark with respect to the nature and quality of the goods or services on or in connection with which the mark is used." U.S. courts have been less than rigorous in imposing quality control as a condition of continued trademark ownership. *See, e.g.,* Dawn Donut Co. v. Hart's Food Stores, Inc., 267 F.2d 358, 121 U.S.P.Q. 430 (2d Cir. 1959). *See generally,* J. Thomas McCarthy, Trademarks and Unfair Competition § 18:48 (1999).

Are the contemporary rules on trademark transfer any better grounded in commercial realities than the earlier rules which prohibited trademark transfers apart from sale of the underlying business? The premise of the earlier rules was that consumer expectations of consistent product quality could be secured only if the underlying business was transferred along with the mark. But, as a strictly legal matter, what would prevent the new owner of the underlying business—or, for that matter, the original business owner itself—from letting the quality of its goods decline? The contemporary insistence on quality controls in trademark licenses might appear to address the issue of consumer expectations more directly. But, again strictly as a legal matter, what would prevent a licensor from altering its prescribed quality criteria? Consider whether, entirely apart from legal rules, a firm that has invested in, and wishes to maintain, the goodwill associated with its marks will as a matter of good business practice have an interest in maintaining a consistent level of quality for its goods and services.

For a particularly insightful analysis of applicable doctrine, see Irene Calboli, Trademark Assignment "With Goodwill": A Concept Whose Time Has Gone, 57 Fla. L. Rev. 771 (2005). On national laws governing trademark transactions see The Law and Practice of Trademark Transactions: A Global and Local Outlook (Irene Calboli & Jacques de Werra, 2016), pp. 327–586.

3. *Paris Convention Art. 6quater and TRIPs Art. 21.* Attempts were made in the 1930s to revise the Paris Convention to enable assignment of trademarks apart from their underlying business, but the 1934 London Revision Conference only produced a compromise in the form of Article *6quater*. The new provision partially ameliorated the plight of foreign registrants by providing that if a member country's law would validate the assignment of a mark "only if it takes place at the same time as the transfer of the business or goodwill to which the mark belongs, it shall suffice for the recognition of such validity that the portion of the business or goodwill located in that country be transferred to the assignee, together with the exclusive right to manufacture in the said country, or to sell therein, the goods bearing the mark assigned." The second part of the provision added the important qualification that a member country's obligation to enforce the assignment will not apply if the mark's use by the assignee would "in fact, be of such a nature as to mislead the public, particularly as regards the origin, nature, or essential qualities, of the goods to which the mark is applied." *See* generally, Stephen Ladas, 2 Patents, Trademarks and Related Rights § 617 (1975).

Notwithstanding Article *6quater,* some countries continued to require transfer of the entire business. *See* G.H.C. Bodenhausen, Guide to the Application of the Paris Convention for the Protection of Industrial Property 105 (1968). Article 21 of the TRIPs Agreement advances international norms on the alienability of trademark interests a step beyond Article *6quater* of the Paris Convention. The provision allows member countries to prescribe conditions for the assignment and licensing of trademarks but nonetheless provides that "the owner of a registered trademark shall have the right to assign the trademark with or without the transfer of the business to which the trademark belongs."

4. *Registration of Transfers.* The 1938 Trade Marks Act in the United Kingdom charted a distinctive approach to validating trademark licenses with a "registered user" system under which, upon an administrative authority's examination and approval of a license, the licensee would be registered as a user of the trademark. (A license would be acceptable only if it was part of a patent license or intra-company license, or subject to quality control by the licensor.) The system was widely adopted in common law countries—with the notable exception of the United States—and in some civil law countries as well. Though initially viewed as mandatory, the U.K. registered user system was subsequently viewed as permissive, and courts declined to invalidate unregistered trademark licenses so long as the licensor and licensee maintained adequate quality controls. *See* generally, Neil Wilkof, Trade Mark Licensing 57–77 (1995).

The registered user system has more recently been modified or abolished in some common law countries. In the United Kingdom, the 1994 Trade Marks Act replaced examination of licenses for quality control with a simple recordation function to put third parties on notice of the trademark transfer. In Canada, the 1993 Intellectual Property Law Improvement Act,

S.C. 1993 c. 15, abolished the registered user system and replaced it with rules comparable to those employed in the U.S. Trademark Act's provisions for use by related companies: "For the purposes of this Act, if an entity is licensed by or with the authority of the owner of a trade-mark to use the trade-mark in a country and the owner has, under the licence, direct or indirect control of the character or quality for the wares or services, then the use, advertisement or display of the trade-mark in that country as or in a trade-mark, trade-name or otherwise by that entity has, and is deemed always to have had, the same effect as such a use, advertisement or display of the trade-mark in that country by the owner." R.S.C. 1985, c. T–13, § 50(1).

See generally, Sheldon Burshtein, The First Five Years of the New Canadian Trademark Licensing Regime, 38 1DEA 569 (1998).

5. RIGHTS AND LIMITATIONS ON RIGHTS

Agreement on Trade-Related Aspects of Intellectual Property Rights

33 International Legal Materials Journal 1, 89–90 (1994).

Article 16

Rights Conferred

1.   The owner of a registered trademark shall have the exclusive right to prevent all third parties not having the owner's consent from using in the course of trade identical or similar signs for goods or services which are identical or similar to those in respect of which the trademark is registered where such use would result in a likelihood of confusion. In case of the use of an identical sign for identical goods or services, a likelihood of confusion shall be presumed. The rights described above shall not prejudice any existing prior rights, nor shall they affect the possibility of Members making rights available on the basis of use.

2.   Article 6*bis* of the Paris Convention (1967) shall apply, *mutatis mutandis*, to services. In determining whether a trademark is well-known, Members shall take account of the knowledge of the trademark in the relevant sector of the public, including knowledge in the Member concerned which has been obtained as a result of the promotion of the trademark.

3.   Article 6*bis* of the Paris Convention (1967) shall apply, *mutatis mutandis*, to goods or services which are not similar to those in respect of which a trademark is registered, provided that use of that trademark in relation to those goods or services would indicate a connection between those goods or services and the owner of the registered trade mark and provided that the interests of the owner of the registered trademark are likely to be damaged by such use.

Article 17

Exceptions

Members may provide limited exceptions to the rights conferred by a trademark, such as fair use of descriptive terms, provided that such exceptions take account of the legitimate interests of the owner of the trademark and of third parties.

Lever Brothers Company v. United States

United States Court of Appeals for the District of Columbia Circuit, 1993.
981 F.2d 1330, 25 U.S.P.Q.2d 1579.

SENTELLE, CIRCUIT JUDGE:

The District Court entered a judgment invalidating the "affiliate exception" of 19 C.F.R. § 133.21(c)(2) (1988) as inconsistent with the statutory mandate of the Lanham Act of 1946, 15 U.S.C. § 1124 (1988), prohibiting importation of goods which copy or simulate the mark of a domestic manufacturer, and issued a nationwide injunction barring enforcement of the regulation with respect to *any* foreign goods bearing a valid United States trademark but materially and physically differing from the United States version of the goods. The United States . . . appeals. We conclude that the District Court, obedient to our limited remand in a prior decision in this same cause, properly determined that the regulation is inconsistent with the statute.

However, because we conclude that the remedy the District Court provided is overbroad, we vacate the judgment and remand for entry of an injunction against allowing the importation of the foreign-produced Lever Brothers brand products at issue in this case.

I.   BACKGROUND . . .

Lever Brothers Company ("Lever US" or "Lever"), an American company, and its British affiliate, Lever Brothers Limited ("Lever UK"), both manufacture deodorant soap under the "Shield" trademark and hand dishwashing liquid under the "Sunlight" trademark. The trademarks are registered in each country. The products have evidently been formulated differently to suit local tastes and circumstances. The U.S. version lathers more, the soaps smell different, the colorants used in American "Shield" have been certified by the FDA whereas the colorants in British "Shield" have not, and the U.S. version contains a bacteriostat that enhances the deodorant properties of the soap. The British version of "Sunlight" dishwashing soap produces less suds, and the American version is formulated to work best in the "soft water" available in most American cities, whereas the British version is designed for "hard water" common in Britain.

The packaging of the U.S. and U.K. products is also somewhat different. The British "Shield" logo is written in script form and is packaged in foil wrapping and contains a wave motif, whereas the

American "Shield" logo is written in block form, does not come in foil wrapping and contains a grid pattern. There is small print on the packages indicating where they were manufactured. The British "Sunlight" comes in a cylindrical bottle labeled "Sunlight Washing Up Liquid." The American "Sunlight" comes in a yellow, hourglass-shaped bottle labeled "Sunlight Dishwashing Liquid."

Lever asserts that the unauthorized influx of these foreign products has created substantial consumer confusion and deception in the United States about the nature and origin of this merchandise, and that it has received numerous consumer complaints from American consumers who unknowingly bought the British products and were disappointed.

Lever argues that the importation of the British products was in violation of section 42 of the Lanham Act, 15 U.S.C. § 1124 which provides that with the exception of goods imported for personal use:

> [N]o article of imported merchandise which shall copy or simulate the name of the [sic] any domestic manufacture, or manufacturer . . . or which shall copy or simulate a trademark registered in accordance with the provisions of this chapter . . . shall be admitted to entry at any customhouse of the United States.

Id. The United States Customs Service ("Customs"), however, was allowing importation of the British goods under the "affiliate exception" created by 19 C.F.R. § 133.21(c)(2), which provides that foreign goods bearing United States trademarks are not forbidden when "the foreign and domestic trademark or tradename owners are parent and subsidiary companies or are otherwise subject to common ownership or control."[3]

In *Lever I,* we concluded that "the natural, virtually inevitable reading of section 42 is that it bars foreign goods bearing a trademark identical to the valid U.S. trademark but physically different," without regard to affiliation between the producing firms or the genuine character of the trademark abroad. . . .

After reviewing the submissions of the parties, the District Court found that Customs' administrative practice was "at best inconsistent" and, in any event, had "never addressed the specific question of physically different goods that bear identical trademarks." . . . The District Court concluded that "section 42 . . . prohibits the importation of foreign goods that . . . are physically different, regardless of the validity of the foreign trademark or the existence of an affiliation between the U.S. and foreign markholders." *Id.* The court accordingly concluded that "[n]either the legislative history of the statute nor the administrative practice of the Customs Service clearly contradicts the plain meaning of section 42" and granted summary judgment against the government. . . .

---

[3]   This case does not involve a dispute between corporate affiliates. Neither Lever U.S. nor Lever UK has authorized the importation which is being conducted by third parties. . . .

By way of remedy, the District Court enjoined Customs "from enforcing 19 C.F.R. § 133.21(c)(2) as to foreign goods that bear a trademark identical to a valid United States trademark but which are materially, physically different." . . .

B. Legislative History of Section 42 of Lanham Act

In the late 1930s and early 1940s, Congress considered a wholesale revision and codification of the United States trademark laws, resulting in the Lanham Trade-Mark Act of 1946. In 1944, the Tariff Commission submitted a memorandum to the Senate Subcommittee on Patents which, after discussing the legislative and administrative history of section 27, stated that "in the light of the Supreme Court's decision in the *Bourjois* case, . . . Section 27 of the Trade-Mark Act of 1905 prohibits the entry of all articles bearing marks which infringe registered trademarks." *Hearings on H.R. 82 Before the Subcomm. of the Senate Comm. on Patents*, 78th Cong., 2d Sess. 86 (1944) (hereinafter "*1944 Hearings*"). The memorandum explicitly stated that the 1905 Act's phrase "all articles" included "articles identical with those sold by the registrant under his mark and bearing identical trade-marks." *Id*. The memorandum then added: "However, section 27 does not apply to the registrant's own merchandise, *i.e.*, merchandise of the registrant bearing the registrant's mark, which mark has been applied by or for the account of the registrant." *Id*.

In *Lever I*, we concluded that the Tariff Commission's memorandum "falls far short of ratification of the affiliate exception, at least in the broad form applied by Customs here." We noted two shortcomings with reliance on this memorandum. First, the memorandum refers to "articles identical to those sold by the registrant," but "makes no mention of the situation presented here, where a third party imports foreign goods bearing a valid foreign trademark identical to a U.S. trademark but covering physically different goods." Customs failed to respond to this point on remand, and for good reason: the 1944 memorandum does not address the distinction between identical and materially different merchandise.

Second, we stated that "we can find no indication that a single member of Congress, much less the committee, much less members speaking on the floor of either house, ever excavated these paragraphs from the mass in which they lay embedded." The United States responds to this by noting that Senator Pepper, Chairman of the Subcommittee, requested the memorandum to be made part of the record, . . . from which it infers congressional awareness of Customs' policy. We conclude that this evidence is insufficient to meet our earlier stated objection. The routine insertion into the record of an agency's prepared hearing testimony is at best minuscule evidence that this testimony reflected shared congressional intent at the time of enactment.

It is also noteworthy that the 1944 memorandum does not refer to "affiliates" or "closely affiliated" companies, but only to the importation of one's "own" merchandise. In short, there is nothing in the record concerning the Lanham Act indicating that Congress contemplated much less intended to allow—an affiliate exception. More to the point, there is no evidence that Congress intended to allow third parties to import physically different trademarked goods that are manufactured and sold abroad by a foreign affiliate of the American trademark holder.

C.   *Legislative History and Developments Since Passage of Lanham Act*

The Treasury Department's administrative practice after passage of the Lanham Act has been inconsistent. The 1936 regulations remained in effect until 1953, when the Department briefly adopted a "related companies" exception. There was no indication that this regulation took cognizance of physically different goods. In any event, Treasury abandoned the related-companies exception in 1959 because it was inconsistent with section 42. There is some evidence that Customs continued to apply the related-companies exception, even after the Customs regulations were returned to their earlier formulation, although apparently only to identical "gray market" goods. *See K Mart Corp. v. Cartier, Inc.*, 486 U.S. 281, 311, 100 L.Ed. 2d 313, 108 S.Ct. 1811 (1988).

In the 1950s, several attempts were made to enact the affiliate exception into law. . . . None of these bills were passed; furthermore, none of them suggest that physically different infringing imports would be permitted.

After Congress repeatedly considered and failed to enact the affiliate exception, the Treasury Department revived the exception. In 1972 the affiliate exception was adopted in the form at issue here. . . . Under the 1972 regulations, section 42's protections were rendered inapplicable where:

(1)   Both the foreign and the U.S. trademark or trade name are owned by the same person or business entity;

(2)   The foreign and domestic trademark or trade name owners are parent and subsidiary companies or are otherwise subject to common ownership or control;

(3)   The articles of foreign manufacture bear a recorded trademark or trade name applied under authorization of the U.S. owner.

19 C.F.R. § 133.21(c). . . .[5]

---

[5]   In *K Mart Corp. v. Cartier, Inc.*, 486 U.S. 281, 100 L.Ed. 2d 313, 108 S.Ct. 1811 (1988), the Supreme Court struck down 19 C.F.R. § 133.21(c)(3), which allowed the importation of foreign-made goods where the United States trademark owner has authorized the use of the mark, as in conflict with the unequivocal language of section 526 of the Tariff Act. Section 526 prohibits the importation of "any merchandise of foreign manufacture" bearing a trademark "owned by" a citizen of, or by a "corporation . . . organized within, the United States" unless written consent of the trademark owner is produced at the time of entry. 19 U.S.C. § 1526. By a different majority, the Supreme Court upheld 19 C.F.R. § 133.21(c)(2), the regulation at issue here, as consistent with section 526. As we noted above, the *Kmart* case did not address the validity of these regulations under the Lanham Act. . . .

Neither the notice proposing the regulations, . . . nor the final notice adopting them, . . . explained their rationale. The statement accompanying the final rule contained no response to objections raised by several companies and associations.

Customs has not even adhered consistently to its own 1972 regulations. In *Bell & Howell: Mamiya Co. v. Masel Supply Co.*, 719 F.2d 42 (2d Cir. 1983), the Department of Justice and Customs filed an *amicus curiae* brief urging that import protection be provided to exclude parallel imports of identical foreign goods made by a company affiliated with the U.S. trademark owner. At that time, Customs took the position that "neither the legislative reports nor the congressional debate contain any clear evidence of a legislative intent to deny trademark protection where the owner of the U.S. mark is owned or controlled by the foreign manufacturer of the trademarked goods." Brief of the United States as *Amicus Curiae* at 8, *Bell & Howell: Mamiya Co. v. Masel Supply Co.*, 719 F.2d 42 (2d Cir. 1983).

The United States denounces its *Bell & Howell* brief now on the grounds that Customs signed the brief without the knowledge or approval of the Treasury Department, and deems it irrelevant because it never resulted in a change to the regulations at issue in this case. We stress that monumental inferences cannot be drawn from inconsistent litigating positions taken by a large agency, but the Customs Service's position in favor of excluding imports in *Bell & Howell* is evidence of Lever's claim that Customs' administrative policy has been inconsistent. And Customs' assertion in the *Bell & Howell* brief that the legislative history of the Lanham Act contains no clear evidence in support of the affiliate exception is undeniably relevant given that Customs defends the opposite position here.

In 1978, Congress added an exception to section 42 for goods imported for personal consumption. . . . However, neither the 1978 amendment nor the accompanying legislative history sheds any light on the application of section 42 in general, or the affiliate exception in particular. . . .

In 1984, Congress enacted the Trademark Counterfeiting Act of 1984, 18 U.S.C. § 2320 (1984). That statute, however, was a criminal statute and did not take the form of an amendment to section 42. Thus, any views expressed in the legislative history of that statute "form a hazardous basis for inferring the intent" of the Congress that enacted section 42. *Consumer Prod. Safety Comm'n v. GTE Sylvania, Inc.*, 447 U.S. 102, 117, 64 L.Ed. 2d 766, 100 S.Ct. 2051 (1980). In any event, the legislative history accompanying the 1984 Act does not address the question of the importation of physically different trademarked goods manufactured by affiliated companies.

Customs' main argument from the legislative history is that section 42 of the Lanham Act applies only to imports of goods bearing trademarks that "copy or simulate" a registered mark. Customs thus draws a distinction between "genuine" marks and marks that "copy or simulate." A mark applied by a foreign firm subject to ownership and control common to that of the domestic trademark owner is by definition "genuine," Customs urges, regardless of whether or not the goods are identical. Thus, any importation of goods manufactured by an affiliate of a U.S. trademark owner cannot "copy or simulate" a registered mark because those goods are *ipso facto* "genuine."

This argument is fatally flawed. It rests on the false premise that foreign trademarks applied to foreign goods are "genuine" in the United States. Trademarks applied to physically different foreign goods are not genuine from the viewpoint of the American consumer. As we stated in *Lever I*:

> On its face . . . section [42] appears to aim at deceit and consumer confusion; when identical trademarks have acquired different meanings in different countries, one who imports the foreign version to sell it under that trademark will (in the absence of some specially differentiating feature) cause the confusion Congress sought to avoid. The fact of affiliation between the producers in no way reduces the probability of that confusion; it is certainly not a constructive consent to importation. . . .

There is a larger, more fundamental and ultimately fatal weakness in Customs' position in this case. Section 42 on its face appears to forbid importation of goods that "copy or simulate" a United States trademark. Customs has the burden of adducing evidence from the legislative history of section 42 and its administrative practice of an exception for materially different goods whose similar foreign and domestic trademarks are owned by affiliated companies. At a minimum, this requires that the specific question be addressed in the legislative history and administrative practice. The bottom line, however, is that the issue of materially different goods was not addressed either in the legislative history or the administrative record. It is not enough to posit that silence implies authorization, when the authorization sought runs counter to the evident meaning of the governing statute. Therefore, we conclude that section 42 of the Lanham Act precludes the application of Customs' affiliate exception with respect to physically, materially different goods.

IV. SCOPE OF INJUNCTION

The United States alternatively argues that this Court should vacate the District Court's injunction that applies to materially different goods other than those directly at issue in this case. The District Court's injunction provides that the Customs Service is "enjoined from enforcing [the common ownership or control provision] as to foreign goods that bear a trademark identical to a valid United States trademark but which are materially, physically different." . . .

The United States points out that this suit was brought by a single company, proceeding solely on its own behalf, to protect two specific trademarks. Lever never asked the District Court to enjoin Customs from applying the affiliate exception to other trademarks or other companies, nor did Lever seek to certify this suit as a class action. In its prayer for relief, Lever asked only that the Customs Service be permanently enjoined "from enforcing said regulations with respect to plaintiff's 'Shield' and 'Sunlight' trademarks, and directing defendants to exclude from entry into the United States any foreign-manufactured merchandise and material bearing said trademarks. To be sure, Lever did include boilerplate language requesting that the court award "such other and further relief as the Court may deem just and proper," but this is too slender a reed upon which to rest a nationwide injunction under the facts of this case. We therefore conclude that Lever is entitled only to that relief specifically sought in its complaint, namely, that Customs be enjoined from allowing the importation of Lever's "Shield" and "Sunlight" trademarks.

V. CONCLUSION

For the foregoing reasons, we affirm the District Court's ruling that section 42 of the Lanham Act, . . . bars the importation of physically different foreign goods bearing a trademark identical to a valid U.S. trademark, regardless of the trademark's genuine character abroad or affiliation between the producing firms. Injunctive relief, however, is limited to the two products which were the subject of this action. We therefore vacate the District Court's prior order to the extent that it renders global relief and remand for the entry of an injunction consistent with this opinion.

So ordered.

Silhouette International Schmied GmbH & Co. KG v. Hartlauer Handelsgesellschaft mbH

Court of Justice of the European Communities, 1998.
Case C-355/96.

1   By order of 15 October 1996, received at the Court on 30 October 1996, the Oberster Gerichtshof referred to the Court for a preliminary ruling under Article 177 of the EC Treaty two questions on the interpretation of Article 7 of the First Council Directive 89/104/EEC of 21 December 1988 to approximate the laws of the Member States relating to trade marks ("the Directive"), as amended by the Agreement on the European Economic Area of 2 May 1992. ("the EEA Agreement").

2   Those questions were raised in proceedings between two Austrian companies, Silhouette International Schmied GmbH & Co. KG ("Silhouette") and Hartlauer Handelsgesellschaft mbH ("Hartlauer").

3   Article 7 of the Directive, concerning exhaustion of the rights conferred by a trade mark, provides:

(1)   The trade mark shall not entitle the proprietor to prohibit its use in relation to goods which have been put on the market in the Community under that trade mark by the proprietor or with his consent.

(2)   Paragraph 1 shall not apply where there exist legitimate reasons for the proprietor to oppose further commercialisation of the goods, especially where the condition of the goods is changed or impaired after they have been put on the market.

4   In accordance with Article 65(2), in conjunction with Annex XVII, point 4, of the EEA Agreement, Article 7(1) has been amended for the purposes of the Agreement so that the expression "in the Community" has been replaced by "in a Contracting Party."

5   Article 7 of the Directive was transposed into Austrian law by Paragraph 10a of the Markenschutzgesetz (Law on the Protection of Trade Marks), the first subparagraph of which provides: "The right conferred by the trade mark shall not entitle the proprietor to prohibit a third party from using it in relation to goods which have been put on the market in the European Economic Area under that trade mark by the proprietor or with his consent."

6   Silhouette produces spectacles in the higher price ranges. It markets them worldwide under the trade mark "Silhouette", registered in Austria and most countries of the world. In Austria, Silhouette itself supplies spectacles to opticians; in other States it has subsidiary companies or distributors.

7   Hartlauer sells *inter alia* spectacles through its numerous subsidiaries in Austria, and its low prices are its chief selling point. It is not supplied by Silhouette because that company considers that distribution of its products by Hartlauer would be harmful to its image as a manufacturer of top-quality fashion spectacles.

8   In October 1995 Silhouette sold 21 000 out-of-fashion spectacle frames to a Bulgarian company, Union Trading, for the sum of USD 261 450. It had directed its representative to instruct the purchasers to sell the spectacle frames in Bulgaria or the states of the former USSR only, and not to export them to other countries. The representative assured Silhouette that it had so instructed the purchaser. However, the Oberster Gerichtshof noted that it had not proved possible to ascertain whether that had actually been done.

9   In November 1995 Silhouette delivered the frames in question to Union Trading in Sofia. Hartlauer bought those goods—it has not, according to the Oberster Gerichtshof, been possible to find out from whom—and offered them for sale in Austria from December 1995. In a press campaign Hartlauer announced that, despite not being supplied by Silhouette, it had managed to acquire 21 000 Silhouette frames abroad.

10 Silhouette brought an action for interim relief before the Landesgericht Steyr, seeking an injunction restraining Hartlauer from

offering spectacles or spectacle frames for sale in Austria under its trade mark, where they had not been put on the market in the European Economic Area ("EEA") by Silhouette itself or by third parties with its consent. It claims that it has not exhausted its trade mark rights, since, in terms of the Directive, trade-mark rights are exhausted only when the products have been put on the market in the EEA by the proprietor or with his consent. It based its claim on Paragraph 10a of the Markenschutzgesetz and on Paragraphs 1 and 9 of the Gesetz gegen den Unlauteren Wettbewerb (Law against Unfair Competition) and Paragraph 43 of the Allgemeines Bürgerliches Gesetzbuch (General Civil Code, the "ABGB").

11 Hartlauer contended that the action should be dismissed since Silhouette had not sold the frames subject to any prohibition of reimportation into the Community. In its view Paragraph 43 of the ABGB was not applicable. Moreover, it observed that the Markenschutzgesetz does not grant a right to seek prohibitory injunctions and that, given that the legal position was unclear, its conduct was not contrary to established customs.

12 Silhouette's action was dismissed by the Landesgericht Steyr and, on appeal, by the Oberlandesgericht Linz. Silhouette appealed to the Oberster Gerichtshof on a point of law.

13 The Gerichtshof noted, first, that the case before it concerned the reimportation of goods originally produced by the proprietor of the trade mark and put on the market by the proprietor in a non-member country. It went on to point out that before Paragraph 10a of the Markenschutzgesetz entered into force Austrian courts applied the principle of international exhaustion of the right conferred by a trademark (the principle that the proprietor's rights are exhausted once the trade-marked product has been put on the market, no matter where that takes place). Finally, the Oberster Gerichtshof stated that the explanatory memorandum to the Austrian law implementing Article 7 of the Directive indicated that it was intended to leave the resolution of the question of the validity of the principle of international exhaustion to judicial decision.

14 Accordingly, the Oberster Gerichtshof decided to stay proceedings and refer the following questions to the Court for a preliminary ruling:

(1) Is Article 7(1) of the First Council Directive 89/104/EEC of 21 December 1988 to approximate the laws of the Member States relating to trade marks to be interpreted as meaning that the trade mark entitles its proprietor to prohibit a third party from using the mark for goods which have been put on the market under that mark in a State which is not a Contracting State?

(2) May the proprietor of the trade mark on the basis of Article 7(1) of the Trade Marks Directive alone seek an order that the

third party cease using the trade mark for goods which have been put on the market under that mark in a State which is not a Contracting State?

Question 1

15   By its first question the Oberster Gerichtshof is in substance asking whether national rules providing for exhaustion of trade-mark rights in respect of products put on the market outside the EEA under that mark by the proprietor or with his consent are contrary to Article 7(1) of the Directive.

16   It is to be noted at the outset that Article 5 of the Directive defines the "rights conferred by a trade mark" and Article 7 contains the rule concerning "exhaustion of the rights conferred by a trade mark."

17   According to Article 5(1) of the Directive, the registered trade mark confers on the proprietor exclusive rights therein. In addition, Article 5(1)(a) provides that those exclusive rights entitle the proprietor to prevent all third parties not having his consent from use in the course of trade of, *inter alia*, any sign identical with the trade mark in relation to goods or services which are identical to those for which the trade mark is registered. Article 5(3) sets out a non-exhaustive list of the kinds of practice which the proprietor is entitled to prohibit under paragraph 1, including, in particular, importing or exporting goods under the trade mark concerned.

18   Like the rules laid down in Article 6 of the Directive, which set certain limits to the effects of a trade mark, Article 7 states that, in the circumstances which it specifies, the exclusive rights conferred by the trade mark are exhausted, with the result that the proprietor is no longer entitled to prohibit use of the mark. Exhaustion is subject first of all to the condition that the goods have been put on the market by the proprietor or with his consent. According to the text of the Directive itself, exhaustion occurs only where the products have been put on the market in the Community (in the EEA since the EEA Agreement entered into force).

19   No argument has been presented to the Court that the Directive could be interpreted as providing for the exhaustion of the rights conferred by a trade mark in respect of goods put on the market by the proprietor or with his consent irrespective of where they were put on the market.

20   On the contrary, Hartlauer and the Swedish Government have maintained that the Directive left the Member States free to provide in their national law for exhaustion, not only in respect of products put on the market in the EEA but also of those put on the market in non-member countries.

21   The interpretation of the Directive proposed by Hartlauer and the Swedish Government assumes, having regard to the wording of Article 7, that the Directive, like the Court's case-law concerning Articles 30 and

36 of the EC Treaty, is limited to requiring the Member States to provide for exhaustion within the Community, but that Article 7 does not comprehensively resolve the question of exhaustion of rights conferred by the trade mark, thus leaving it open to the Member States to adopt rules on exhaustion going further than those explicitly laid down in Article 7 of the Directive.

22   As Silhouette, the Austrian, French, German, Italian and United Kingdom Governments and the Commission have all argued, such an interpretation is contrary to the wording of Article 7 and to the scheme and purpose of the rules of the Directive concerning the rights which a trade mark confers on its proprietor.

23   In that respect, although the third recital in the preamble to the Directive states that "it does not appear to be necessary at present to undertake full-scale approximation of the trade mark laws of the Member States," the Directive none the less provides for harmonisation in relation to substantive rules of central importance in this sphere, that is to say, according to that same recital, the rules concerning those provisions of national law which most directly affect the functioning of the internal market, and that that recital does not preclude the harmonisation relating to those rules from being complete.

24   The first recital in the preamble to the Directive notes that the trade mark laws applicable in the Member States contain disparities which may impede the free movement of goods and freedom to provide services and may distort competition within the common market, so that it is necessary, in view of the establishment and functioning of the internal market, to approximate the laws of Member States. The ninth recital emphasises that it is fundamental, in order to facilitate the free movement of goods and services, to ensure that registered trade marks enjoy the same protection under the legal systems of all the Member States, but that this should not prevent Member States from granting at their option extensive protection to those trade marks which have a reputation.

25   In the light of those recitals, Articles 5 to 7 of the Directive must be construed as embodying a complete harmonisation of the rules relating to the rights conferred by a trade mark. That interpretation, it may be added, is borne out by the fact that Article 5 expressly leaves it open to the Member States to maintain or introduce certain rules specifically defined by the Community legislature. Thus, in accordance with Article 5(2), to which the ninth recital refers, the Member States have the option to grant more extensive protection to trade marks with a reputation.

26   Accordingly, the Directive cannot be interpreted as leaving it open to the Member States to provide in their domestic law for exhaustion of the rights conferred by a trade mark in respect of products put on the market in non-member countries.

27 This, moreover, is the only interpretation which is fully capable of ensuring that the purpose of the Directive is achieved, namely to safeguard the functioning of the internal market. A situation in which some Member States could provide for international exhaustion while others provided for Community exhaustion only would inevitably give rise to barriers to the free movement of goods and the freedom to provide services.

28 Contrary to the arguments of the Swedish Government, it is no objection to that interpretation that since the Directive was adopted on the basis of Article 100a of the EC Treaty, which governs the approximation of the laws of the Member States concerning the functioning of the internal market, it cannot regulate relations between the Member States and non-member countries, with the result that Article 7 is to be interpreted as meaning that the Directive applies only to intra-Community relations.

29 Even if Article 100a of the Treaty were to be construed in the sense argued for by the Swedish Government, the fact remains that Article 7, as has been pointed out in this judgment, is not intended to regulate relations between Member States and non-member countries but to define the rights of proprietors of trade marks in the Community.

30 Finally, the Community authorities could always extend the exhaustion provided for by Article 7 to products put on the market in non-member countries by entering into international agreements in that sphere, as was done in the context of the EEA Agreement.

31 In the light of the foregoing, the answer to be given to the first question must be that national rules providing for exhaustion of trade-mark rights in respect of products put on the market outside the EEA under that mark by the proprietor or with his consent are contrary to Article 7(1) of the Directive, as amended by the EEA Agreement.

Question 2

32 By its second question the Oberster Gerichtshof is in substance asking whether Article 7(1) of the Directive can be construed as meaning that the proprietor of a trade mark is entitled, on the basis of that provision alone, to obtain an order restraining a third party from using its mark for products which have been put on the market outside the EEA under that mark by the proprietor or with his consent.

33 In its order for reference, as clarified subsequently by letter, the Oberster Gerichtshof has pointed out:

> — that the second question was put because the Markenschutzgesetz does not provide for any right to obtain a prohibitory injunction, nor does it contain any provision corresponding to Article 5(1)(a) of the Directive. A prohibitory injunction may be sought in respect of a trade mark infringement only if there is at the same time a breach of Paragraph 9 of the UWG, the application of which presupposes the risk of confusion, which is

not the case where the original products of the trade-mark proprietor are concerned;

— in Austrian law, at least according to current academic legal writing, the proprietor of a trade mark has no right to obtain a prohibitory injunction against a person who makes parallel imports or reimports of trade-marked goods, unless the right to a prohibitory injunction is already available under Paragraph 10a(1) of the Markenschutzgesetz. The question thus arises, under Austrian law, whether Article 7(1) of the Trade Marks Directive, which has the same content as Paragraph 10a(1) of the Markenschutzgesetz, provides for such a right to apply for a prohibitory injunction and whether the proprietor of the trade mark can therefore seek, solely on the basis of that provision, an order that a third party cease using the trade mark for goods which have been put on the market under that mark outside the EEA.

34 Under the scheme of the Directive the rights conferred by a trade mark are defined by Article 5, while Article 7 contains an important qualification with respect to that definition, in that it provides that the rights conferred by Article 5 do not entitle the proprietor to prohibit the use of the trade mark where the conditions laid down in that provision are satisfied.

35 Accordingly, while it is undeniable that the Directive requires Member States to implement provisions on the basis of which the proprietor of a trade mark, when his rights are infringed, must be able to obtain an order restraining third parties from making use of his mark, that requirement is imposed, not by Article 7, but by Article 5 of the Directive.

36 That being so, it is to be remembered, first, that, according to settled case-law of the Court, a directive cannot of itself impose obligations on an individual and cannot therefore be relied upon as such against an individual. Second, according to the same case-law, when applying domestic law, whether adopted before or after the directive, the national court that has to interpret that law must do so, as far as possible, in the light of the wording and the purpose of the directive so as to achieve the result it has in view and thereby comply with the third paragraph of Article 189 of the Treaty.

37 The answer to be given to the second question must therefore be that, subject to the national court's duty to interpret, so far as possible, domestic law in conformity with Community law, Article 7(1) of the Directive cannot be interpreted as meaning that the proprietor of a trade mark is entitled, on the basis of that provision alone, to obtain an order restraining a third party from using his trade mark for products which have been put on the market outside the EEA under that mark by the proprietor or with his consent. . . .

NOTES

1. *Rights.* The first sentence of Article 16(1) of the TRIPs Agreement effectively codifies longstanding national rules as an international norm, ensuring owners of registered trademarks exclusive rights against the unauthorized use of identical or similar marks on identical or similar goods or services with a consequent likelihood of confusion among consumers. TRIPs Article 16(3) makes trademark dilution an international norm. Under the provision, for dilution to occur the use of the registered mark on dissimilar goods or services must indicate a connection between the goods or services and the owner of the trademark, and also that the owner's interests "are likely to be damaged by such use."

What are the implications of importing concepts from Paris Convention Article 6*bis*, dealing with famous marks, into TRIPs Article 16(3)? Article 6*bis* deals with marks that have not been registered in the protecting country. What reason was there to limit the benefits of Article 16(3) to owners of registered marks? Dr. Annette Kur has observed that "the linking together of two basically different problems and concepts—protection for unregistered marks belonging to foreign trademark owners on one hand and protection for reputed or famous marks against dilution or abuse on the other—in addition to the somewhat unclear wording of Art. 16(2) and (3), is most likely to give rise to further problems." Annette Kur, TRIPs and Trademark Law, in Friedrich-Karl Beier & Gerhard Schricker, eds, From GATT to TRIPs—The Agreement on Trade-Related Aspects of Intellectual Property Rights 93, 105–106 (1996). For a comparative analysis of dilution see Martin Senftleben, The Trademark Tower of Babel—Dilution Concepts in International, US and EC Trademark Law, 40(1) IIC 45 (2009).

2. *Exceptions to Rights.* National laws have historically allowed few exceptions to trademark rights. If the purpose of trademark law is to secure consumer expectations respecting the source of goods and services, exceptions to the right, no matter how well motivated, would inevitably disserve that purpose by increasing the risk of consumer confusion. One widely-followed exception, for fair use, allows competitors to describe their goods or services accurately, even though the description may overlap elements of a protected trademark. National legislation and judicial decisions may also permit two other exceptions: the continued use of the original mark on goods that have been reconditioned or repackaged, so long as the quality of the goods is not materially altered; and allusion to the trademark of a manufactured product—"Porsche" for automobiles, say—to indicate that another product—parts produced by an independent manufacturer—can be used in the product. *See* Stephen Ladas, 2 Patents, Trademarks and Related Rights 1109–1113 (1975).

Article 17 of the TRIPs Agreement, which allows limited exceptions to trademark rights, probably encompasses the few exceptions generally allowed under national law. The provision's express reference to "fair use of descriptive terms" clearly validates the fair use exception, but may require continuing recalibration in the context of other uses, such as use in connection with repackaged and reconditioned good or spare parts, to ensure that they "take account of the legitimate interests of the owner of the trademark and of third parties."

3. *Trademark Exhaustion.* With the exception of the countries of the European Union, which apply the rule of EU-wide exhaustion, trademark rights typically exhaust internationally. Why do countries generally agree on the international exhaustion principle for trademarks when countries traditionally disagree on whether the principle of national or international exhaustion should apply to copyright and patent?

Mauritius adheres to the principle of national exhaustion of trademark rights, and in 2012 the Mauritian Supreme Court confirmed that importation of genuine products into the country without the consent of the trademark owner was a violation of the owner's trademark rights. Two commentators referred to "the system of national exhaustion [as] a blessing for local distributors." Mauritius, the commentators explained, "with its 1.3 million inhabitants is a very small market[,] and the system of national exhaustion ... helps to safeguard [local distributors'] investments in negotiating distributorships and bringing internationally renowned products to Mauritius." Surishta Chetamun & Marius Schneider, Mauritian Supreme Court Confirms National Exhaustion of IP Rights, 13(8) J. Intell. Property Law & Practice 599 (2018).

What possible harm may a national exhaustion rule inflict on consumers? In 2018 the Russian Constitutional Court explained, in the context of the regional trademark exhaustion principle that Russia applies within the Eurasian Economic Union, that in cases involving gray market goods, as opposed to counterfeit goods, courts should not order seizure and destruction of goods and should grant lower damages than the courts would in cases involving counterfeit goods. The Court instructed lower courts to exercise their discretion in order to refuse to grant any remedies to a trademark owner against a parallel importer of gray market goods "if, due to the unfair practices of a trade mark owner, such remedies may create a threat to citizens' lives and health or affect other significant public interest." Alexandra Bakhtiozina, Russian Constitutional Court Adopts New Approach to Parallel Imports, 13(8) J. Intell. Property Law & Practice 600, 601 (2018). The Court referred specifically to "establishing unfair price policies or imposing a ban on the import of goods jeopardizing the interests of ... Russian consumers, especially if it concerns vital goods (medicines, medical devices)." *Id.* A trade mark owner's compliance with international sanctions against Russia "may be deemed an unfair practice *per se*" if the sanctions are imposed "without due international legal procedure and in contradiction with international treaties." *Id.* The Eurasian Economic Union consists of Russia, Armenia, Belarus, Kzakhstan, and Kyrgyzstan.

One commentator has suggested that after the U.S. Supreme Court clarified in *Kirtsaeng* that the principle of international exhaustion applies to copyright in the United States, copyright owners may turn to their U.S. trademarks as a means to prevent parallel importation into the United States. Mary LaFrance, A Material World: Using Trademark Law to Override Copyright's First Sale Rule for Imported Copies, 21 Mich. Telecomm. & Tech. L. Rev. 43 (2014). Given the discussion in *Lever Bros.*, above, what would copyright owners have to do to use their U.S. trademarks to prevent the importation of copies into the United States that the copyright owners placed on the market in countries outside the United States?

For arguments in favor of and against international exhaustion of trademark rights see Ioannis Avgoustis, Parallel Imports and Exhaustion of Trade Mark Rights: Should Steps Be Taken Towards an International Exhaustion Regime?, 34(2) EIPR 108 (2012).

4. *European Union-Wide Exhaustion.* The 1988 Trademark Directive considered in *Silhouette* (replaced by EU Directive 2015/2436) binds not only EU member states, but European Free Trade Area countries as well. In MAG Instrument Inc. v. California Trading Co., EFTA Court, E-2/97, 29 IIC 316 (1998), decided six months before *Silhouette*, the EFTA Court ruled that Article 7 of the Directive did not preempt national rules providing for international exhaustion, so that the trademark law of EFTA member Norway, which provided for international exhaustion, continued to apply. Anticipating a contrary decision in the *Silhouette* case, the EFTA Court cited material differences between the EC Treaty and the EEA Agreement, but also rested its decision on policy grounds that sharply diverged from the premises of *Silhouette*: "[t]he principle of international exhaustion is in the interest of free trade and competition and thus in the interest of consumers. Parallel imports from countries outside the European Economic Area lead to a greater supply of goods bearing a trade mark on the market. As a result of this situation, price levels of products will be lower than in a market where only importers authorized by the trade mark holder distribute their products." Further, the Court noted, "the principle of international exhaustion is in line with the main function of a trade mark, which is to allow the consumer to identify with certainty the origin of the products."

Article 15(1) of the current EU Trademark Directive (formerly Article 7(1) of the 1988 Trademark Directive) requires that, for exhaustion to apply, the goods in issue must "have been put on the market . . . by the [trade mark] proprietor or with his consent." Can a national court in an EU member country escape *Silhouette*'s bar on international exhaustion by finding that the trademark owner's sale of goods outside the European Economic Area implied its consent to their sale in the EEA? In Zino Davidoff SA v. A & G Imports Ltd, ECJ, Joined Cases C-414/99 to C-416/99, 2001, the European Court of Justice, observing that it was the Court's responsibility "to supply a uniform interpretation of the concept of consent to the placing of goods on the market within the EEA," acknowledged the possibility of implied consent, but emphasized that "the factors taken into consideration in finding implied consent must unequivocally demonstrate that the trademark proprietor has renounced any intention to enforce his exclusive rights," and that implied consent "cannot be inferred from the mere silence of the trademark proprietors." ¶¶ 43, 53, 55.

See generally Ioannis Avgoustis, Parallel Imports and Exhaustion of Trade Mark Rights: Should Steps Be Taken Towards an International Exhaustion Regime?, 34(2) EIPR 108 (2012); Gill Grassie, Parallel Imports and Trademarks—Where Are We? Parts 1 & 2, 28 EIPR 474, 28 EIPR 513 (2006); Irini Stamatoudi & Paul Torremans, International Exhaustion in the

European Union in the Light of "Zino Davidoff": Contract Versus Trade Mark Law? 31 IIC 123 (2000).

5. *Relabelled and Repackaged Products.* Article 15(2) of the current EU Trademark Directive (formerly Article 7(2) of the 1988 Trademark Directive) excludes from exhaustion those cases "where there exist legitimate reasons for the proprietor to oppose further commercialisation of the goods, especially where the condition of the goods is changed or impaired after they have been put on the market." Should differences of the sort involved in *Lever Brothers* justify application of Article 15(2)'s exception? Or should the exception be limited to instances of used, repackaged, or reconditioned goods? In Bristol-Myers Squibb v. Paranova, ECJ, C-427/93, 1996, the European Court of Justice set out five requirements for parallel importers who re-package and re-apply a manufacturer's trademark: the repackaging must be necessary to market the product; the repackaging cannot affect the original condition of the product and must include proper instructions; the new packaging must identify the manufacturer and importer; the packaging cannot damage the reputation of the trademark or its owner; and the importer must give notice—and, on demand, a specimen of the repackaged product—to the trademark owner before sale. ¶ 79.

In Boehringer Ingelheim KG v. Swingward Ltd, ECJ, C-348/04, 2007, the European Court of Justice elaborated on these conditions and ruled that they applied to relabelled as well as repackaged products. For purposes of the first condition, the Court ruled, "necessity" related exclusively to the need to repackage, and not to its manner. The Court also listed several practices that might be held to damage the trademark's reputation—among them, failure to affix the trademark to the new packaging, "co-branding" by adding the importer's brand to the trademark owner's, and giving greater prominence to the name of the parallel importer than to the trademark. ¶¶ 28, 39, 47.

6. *Trademarks and Competition Law.* TRIPs Article 40(2) allows countries to determine the circumstances under which particular conduct constitutes "an abuse of intellectual property rights having an adverse effect on competition in the relevant market," including abuse of trademark rights, and to adopt "appropriate measures to prevent or control such practices." The EU Trademark Directive and the EU Trademark Regulation do not exclude the application of unfair competition rules. EU Trademark Directive, Recital 40; EU Trademark Regulation, Article 17(2). However, unlike copyright and patent law, trademark law has only rarely admitted the possibility of compulsory licenses, and TRIPs Article 21 makes this norm explicit in providing that members "may determine conditions on the licensing and assignment of trademarks, it being understood that the compulsory licensing of trademarks shall not be permitted."

The CJEU has explained that under EU trademark law "a national court may impose a penalty on the proprietor of a trade mark or order it to pay compensation for the damage suffered if it finds that that proprietor has unlawfully withdrawn the consent by which it allowed a third party to use signs which are identical to its marks. However, . . . a finding that there has been such conduct cannot have the effect of prolonging, by a court decision and for an unspecified period, the shared use of those marks where the companies concerned no longer have the joint intention of sharing their use." Martin Y Paz Diffusion SA v. David Depuydt, CJEU, C-661/11, 2013, ¶ 61.

A rare example of the intersection of trademark law and competition law is the *Green Dot Logo* case. In 2001 the European Commission held that the German company Duales System Deutschland AG (DSD) abused its dominant position on the market in the supply of collection and recycling services when DSD charged fees to manufacturers and distributers who participated in its recycling services that were based on the amount of manufacturers' and distributors' packaging bearing DSD's Green Dot logo, rather than fees based on their actual use of the DSD system. DSD's license obligated manufacturers and distributors to affix the DSD logo to all packaging. The Commission ordered DSD not to charge a licensing fee for the use of its logo on packaging that its manufacturers and distributors collected and recycled in a different manner.

DSD appealed, arguing that the decision deprived it of its right to prevent third parties from using its trademark. The European Court of Justice affirmed the Commission's holding on the abuse of dominant position and held that the trademark retained its exclusive character because DSD permitted, and actually required, the use of the Green Dot on all manufacturer packaging. The Court acknowledged that "the possibility cannot be ruled out that the affixing of the [Green Dot] logo to packaging, whether part of the DSD system or not, may have a price which, even if it cannot represent the actual price of the collection and recovery service, should be able to be paid to DSD in consideration for the use of the mark alone." Der Grüne Punkt-Duales System Deutschland GmbH v. European Commission, ECJ, C-385/07 P, 2009, ¶ 131.

7.   *Keywords and Adwords.* Businesses often use keywords to assist search engines in locating their websites. Some Internet search engines and other referencing services sell these keywords as "adwords" to ensure that a link to the business's website will appear as a "sponsored link" once a user searches for the keyword. Can a trademark owner bar the sale of a keyword that is identical to its trademark? Can it stop a web business from using the keyword as an adword?

In Playboy Enterprises, Inc. v. Netscape Communications Corp., 354 F.3d 1020 (9th Cir. 2004), the U.S. Court of Appeals for the Ninth Circuit ruled that Internet search engines may be directly or contributorily liable for trademark infringement when they "key" advertisements to trademarks. The court held that such use is a use in commerce and, if the use creates a likelihood of confusion, the search engines are liable for trademark infringement. The court explained that the keying practice could lead to initial interest confusion, and "[a]lthough dispelled before an actual sale occurs, initial interest confusion impermissibly capitalizes on the goodwill associated with a mark." *Id.*, 1025. According to the court, the likelihood of initial confusion was more likely to exist where the search engines did not label the "sponsored links" as such.

Whether Google's AdWords system creates a likelihood of confusion has been disputed. In Network Automation, Inc. v. Advanced Systems Concepts, Inc., 638 F.3d 1137, 1154 (9th Cir. 2011), the court suggested that, as opposed to the Netscape and Excite systems that were at issue in *Playboy*, Google's AdWords system might have sufficiently labeled the ads to avoid consumer confusion. In Rosetta Stone Ltd. v. Google Inc., 730 F.Supp.2d 531 (E.D.Va. 2010), a judge of the U.S. District Court for the District of Virginia held that Google was not liable for trademark infringement when it auctioned adwords that were trademarks to third party advertisers. The Court of Appeals for the Fourth Circuit affirmed that Google was not liable for vicarious trademark infringement but remanded the case with respect to direct infringement, contributory infringement, and dilution claims. Rosetta Stone Ltd. v. Google, Inc., 676 Fed.3d 144 (4th Cir. 2012). In October 2012 the two companies settled the dispute.

In Europe, where French courts initially held Google liable for selling keywords for use as adwords when the keywords were identical to the trademarks of others, the Court of Justice of the European Union has held that in the context of adwords, Internet referencing services do not use trademarks in the course of trade. Google France SARL and Google, Inc. v. Louis Vuitton, CJEU, Joined Cases C-236/08 and 238/08, 2010, ¶ 99. The court explained that "[t]he fact of creating the technical conditions necessary for the use of a [mark] and being paid for that service does not mean that the party offering the service itself uses the [mark]." *Id.*, ¶ 57. Following the CJEU judgment, the French Supreme Court in 2010 reversed the judgments of the French lower courts and held that Google was not liable for trademark infringement.

While, according to CJEU jurisprudence, Internet referencing services will not be liable for trademarks used as adwords, a business that uses a trademark as a keyword for an adword may still be liable for trademark infringement. In a series of decisions rendered in 2009–2011 the Court of Justice of the European Union clarified EU law on advertisers' liability for the use of keywords as adwords. The Court held that when an advertiser uses a trademark as a keyword for an adword, it is a use in the course of trade within the meaning of the EU Trademark Directive and the EU Trademark Regulation. However, the Court also held that the use of an identical mark for identical goods, by itself, is not sufficient for trademark infringement, as the "double identity" rule of EU trademark law would suggest. The Court held that the use of the keyword must adversely affect one of the functions of trademarks. The function of a trademark as an indication of origin is not adversely affected if an advertisement that appears as a "sponsored link" enables an average Internet user to ascertain without difficulty that the goods or services do not originate from the trademark owner. Google France SARL v. Louis Vuitton Malletier SA, CJEU, C-236/08 and C-238/08, 2010, holding of the Court.

In addition to the origin function (also referred to as the "essential function") of trademarks, the Court of Justice identified the advertising, investment, and communication functions of trademarks. L'Oréal SA v. Bellure NV, ECJ, C-487/07, 2009, ¶ 58. Although the advertising function might not be adversely affected by the use of a trademark as a keyword, the investment function of the trademark may still be adversely affected "if it substantially interferes with the proprietor's use of its trade mark to acquire or preserve a reputation capable of attracting consumers and retaining their loyalty." Interflora, Inc. v. Marks & Spencer plc, CJEU, C-323/09, 2011, ¶ 66. The trademark owner may be able to prevent the business from using the trademark as a keyword even if the goods and services offered by the business are not identical to the goods or services for which the trademark is registered, if it is a trademark with a reputation and its use as a keyword constitutes free-riding, dilution, or tarnishment. *Id.*, holding, ¶ 2. For definitions of trademark functions under CJEU case law see Andrew Bailey, Trade Mark Functions and Protection for Marks with a Reputation, 8(11) JIPLP 868 (2013).

8. *Plain Packaging.* With the aim of improving public health, Australia in 2011 adopted the Tobacco Plain Packaging Act, placing restrictions on the packaging used by tobacco product manufacturers; it dictated, for example, the standard style, color, and size of font for the packaging. In response, tobacco companies launched cases against Australia and other countries that followed Australia's lead with their own plain packaging legislation.

Do the restrictions imposed by such legislation comply with TRIPs Article 17 on limited exceptions to trademark rights? Does TRIPs Article 17 apply only to exceptions to the negative right formulated in TRIPs Article 16? In R. v. Secretary of State for Health, [2016] EWCA Civ 1182, the English Court of Appeal held that U.K.'s Standardised Packaging of Tobacco Products Regulations 2015 "were not *a priori* incompatible with TRIPs." *Id.*, ¶ 149.

In 2012, Ukraine, Honduras, the Dominican Republic, Cuba, and Indonesia filed complaints against Australia in the WTO. Australia— Certain Measures Concerning Trademarks and Other Plain Packaging Requirements Applicable to Tobacco Products and Packaging, WTO, DS434, DS435, DS441, DS458, and DS467. In 2018 a WTO panel ruled in favor of Australia because, inter alia, the complainants had not demonstrated that the measures violated Articles 6*quinquies* and 10*bis* of the Paris Convention, and TRIPs Articles 15(4), 16(1), 16(3), 20, 22(2)(b), and 24(3). Report of the Panels, WT/DS435/R, 2018. Honduras and the Dominican Republic appealed the decision. The International Trademark Association has argued that Australia's measures do violate TRIPs Article 20 and warned that "by eliminating the source function served by trademarks, the . . . measures open up the market for counterfeits (often backed by organized crime or terrorist organizations)." Brief of Amicus Curiae, INTA, 2019, ¶ 41.

The state-to-state disputes in the WTO were preceded by the tobacco companies' launch of a constitutional challenge to the Australian law in the Australian courts and Philip Morris' filing of two investor-state disputes against Uruguay and Australia under bilateral agreements between Switzerland and Uruguay, and between Hong Kong and Australia, respectively. The investor-state dispute tribunal in the first dispute decided in Uruguay's favor, rejecting, inter alia, arguments claiming that Uruguay's actions expropriated Philip Morris' intellectual property and unreasonably and discriminatorily denied the company the use and enjoyment of its intellectual property rights. Philip Morris Brands Sàrl v. Uruguay, ICSID, Case No. ARB/10/7, 2016. In the second dispute the tribunal found that Philip Morris Asia's claim was an abuse of process and an abuse of rights because Philip Morris has changed its corporate structure to gain protection under the investment treaty. Philip Morris Asia Ltd. v. Australia, PCA, Case No. 2012-12, 2015.

On intellectual property rights in investor-state disputes see Rochelle Dreyfuss & Susy Frankel, Reconceptualizing ISDS: When Is IP An Investment and How Much Can States Regulate It?, 21 Vand. J. Ent. & Tech. L. 377 (2018); Pratyush Nath Upreti, Philip Morris v Uruguay: A Breathing Space for Domestic IP Regulation, 40(4) EIPR 277 (2018).

6. REMEDIES

United States v. Lozano

United States Court of Appeals, Eleventh Circuit, 2007.
490 F.3d 1317, 83 U.S.P.Q.2d 1527.

STAGG, DISTRICT JUDGE:

I.   FACTUAL AND PROCEDURAL BACKGROUND

Suplimet Corporation was a Miami-based company acting as a wholesale distributor of cell phone parts and accessories. In January of 2003, police received information that Suplimet was selling counterfeit items, and on that basis, conducted a controlled purchase of counterfeit cell phone parts. Following the purchase, the authorities requested permission to search Suplimet's warehouse. Xavier Lozano, who was present, advised police that he could not authorize a search, as he was only Suplimet's sales manager. Instead, he contacted his brother Herman, the owner of Suplimet, for permission to search and obtained Herman's consent. The search yielded forty-one boxes of counterfeit goods. However, no criminal charges were filed at this time. . . .

During 2004, authorities conducted two controlled purchases of counterfeit cell phone parts from two Miami retailers. They discovered that the counterfeit items originated from Suplimet. In September of 2004, agents purchased fifty counterfeit cell phone batteries from Suplimet. Armed with a warrant, agents again searched Suplimet's warehouse and seized approximately 85,000 pieces of counterfeit cell phone parts. On October 21, 2004, Herman and Xavier were indicted for conspiracy to traffic in counterfeit goods and trafficking in counterfeit goods, in violation of 18 U.S.C. §§ 371 and 2320(a). In May of 2005, both defendants pled guilty.

At the sentencing hearing, both Herman and Xavier agreed that United States Sentencing Guidelines ("U.S.S.G.") § 2B5.3 applied to their sentence calculations. Section 2B5.3 is used to calculate the offense level for a conviction stemming from the counterfeiting and/or infringement of a trademark or copyright. This provision provides for a base offense level of 8, which is then enhanced on the basis of the amount of the infringement, pursuant to U.S.S.G. § 2B1.1 . . . The Presentence Report ("PSR") attributed a loss amount of $10,177,485 to the Lozanos, which resulted in a 20-level enhancement under section 2B1.1. It also recommended a 2-point enhancement for both Herman and Xavier for their aggravating roles in the offenses, pursuant to section 3B1.1(c). After 3-level reductions for acceptance of responsibility, the total offense level for both defendants was 27. With a criminal history category of I for each defendant, both computations resulted in a recommended sentencing range of 70 to 87 months.

The Lozanos objected to the PSR's recommendation of the 20-level enhancement. Instead, they argued that the correct computations should have reflected the value of the counterfeit or infringing[3] items in the market in which those goods were sold, which in this case was Latin America, as opposed to the Manufacturer's Suggested Retail Price in the United States, which the PSR recommended. Under the Lozanos' calculations, their offense levels would have been 8.

The government, on the other hand, asserted that the retail value . . . of the legitimate or infringed item in the United States was the proper valuation method under section 2B5.3. However, it conceded that the total loss amount should be reduced to $3,700,000, which resulted in an 18-level enhancement, as opposed to the 20-level enhancement recommended in the PSR. Agreeing with the government, the district court overruled the Lozanos' objections, finding that the retail value of the infringed items in the United States was the appropriate valuation method because (1) the Lozanos operated a business in the United States, (2) they sold a portion of the counterfeit goods in the United States, and (3) the counterfeit items were seized in the United States. In addition, the court overruled Xavier's objection to the enhancement for his role in the offense. Further, at sentencing the government refused to move for the additional 1-point reduction for acceptance of responsibility; thus, the court only applied a 2-point reduction, rather than the 3-point reduction recommended in the PSR. In all, the total offense level dropped from 27 to 26, which yielded a sentencing range of 63 to 78 months.

After considering the Guidelines range and the factors set forth in 18 U.S.C. § 3553(a), the court sentenced both Herman and Xavier to 72 months. . . .

On appeal, the Lozanos argue that the district court's use of the MSRP created a grossly inflated infringement amount, far beyond the profits they realized or the pecuniary loss they caused the trademark holders to suffer. Instead, they contend the court should have used the sale price of the counterfeit items in the market in which they were sold—

[3] "Infringing items" are distinguishable form "infringed items." Infringed items are the legitimate items that are infringed upon by the infringing item. *See* U.S.S.G. § 2B5.3 at comment. n.1.

Latin America—because the retail value of the trademarked items in the United States market over-represents their culpability. The Lozanos argue that the MSRPs reflect prices above those normally charged for such items. In support of this, they point out that none of the trademark holders submitted a victim impact statement, such that the court had no evidence of pecuniary loss. They further maintain that the prices of the goods in the Latin American market should have been considered, as they intended the products to be sold in that market and the products were much cheaper there. In all, they assert that the court's infringement computation resulted in a fictional loss amount far beyond that actually caused by their fraud. In addition, Xavier asserts that the section 3B1.1 enhancement he received for his role in the offense was improper, as he had no authority or control either in the company or over other employees. Finally, the Lozanos contend that their sentences were unreasonable. We address each of these issues in turn.

A. Application of the Guidelines.

In reviewing a sentence, the court must first determine whether the district court correctly calculated the Guidelines range. The parties disagree about whether the district court properly applied section 2B5.3, which provides that the infringement amount is the retail value of the infringing item, except in the following enumerated situations that necessitate use of the infringed item's value:

> (i) The infringing item (I) is, or appears to a reasonably informed purchaser to be, identical or substantially equivalent to the infringed item; . . . or (v) The retail value of the infringed item provides a more accurate assessment of the pecuniary harm to the copyright or trademark owner than does the retail value of the infringing item.

U.S.S.G. § 2B5.3 at comment. n.2(A). The court is directed to use the retail value of the infringing item in any case not covered by the aforementioned provisions. . . .

In the case at bar, the language providing that the infringing item "is, or appears to a reasonably informed purchaser to be, identical or substantially equivalent to the infringed item" is critical. The district court found that the infringing and infringed items were essentially indistinguishable and thus concluded that use of the retail value of the infringed item was appropriate. . . .

Nonetheless, the Lozanos contend that use of the infringed item's retail value over-represents their culpability and ignores the "nature and magnitude of the pecuniary harm." The Lozanos assert that because the majority of their sales occurred in Latin America—a market in which the trademark holders did not operate—the trademark holders thus suffered minimal pecuniary injury. In support of their argument, the Lozanos unconvincingly refer to *United States v. Yi,* 460 F.3d 623 (5th Cir. 2006).

In *Yi*, the Fifth Circuit Court of Appeals reversed the district court's use of the retail value of the infringed items because "[t]he lack of record evidence on pecuniary harm to the victim companies weighs against the district court's decision to use the infringed item value." *Yi*, 460 F.3d at 637. In doing so, it clearly disagreed with the district court's contention that the retail value of the infringed items provided "a more accurate assessment of the pecuniary harm to the trademark owners." Crucial to the Fifth Circuit's reversal of the lower court was the fact that the infringing and infringed items were distinguishable to a reasonably informed purchaser. The same cannot be said in the case at bar. Accordingly, *Yi* cannot be interpreted to mean that the retail value of the infringing item should *always* be considered. Rather, based on the specific facts of that case, the Fifth Circuit found inapplicable the enumerated provisions regarding retail value of the infringed item and therefore applied the "catch-all" provision, in which the retail value of the infringing item is used. However, on the facts presented here, it would be inappropriate to follow *Yi*.

The Lozanos next argue that the district court erred in applying the retail value of the products in the United States, as opposed to Latin America. The parties do not dispute that the retail value of both trademarked and counterfeit items in Latin America is drastically less than the retail value in the United States. However, the Lozanos argue that the court should have used the Latin American market because the majority of Suplimet's sales occurred there. The government asserts that because undercover purchases were made in Miami, the district court correctly used the retail market for the United States. Under section 2B5.3, retail value is defined as the retail price of an item in the market in which it is sold. . . . Here, it is undisputed that the Lozanos sold counterfeit items in Miami. Though they may have shipped the majority of their products to Latin America for sale, that does not render the district court's decision to use the United States market clearly erroneous. To the contrary, use of the products' retail value in the United States was supported by the evidence and appropriate under our reading of the Guidelines. . . .

The counterfeiting operation was expansive, expensive, and extensive. The Lozanos, located in Miami, had contacts in China who manufactured and shipped to them the counterfeit phone parts. They then had their father in Colombia sell the counterfeited material to retailers in Latin America. It was an international undertaking.

Given the length, breadth, and depth of the Lozanos counterfeiting scheme, the 72-month prison sentences are not unreasonable. It follows that if there was any error in calculating the retail value of the goods under section 2B5.3, that error did not affect the sentences that were imposed. It was harmless. No purpose would be served by a remand. *See Keene*, 470 F.3d at 1350.

AFFIRMED.

CARNES, CIRCUIT JUDGE, concurring:

I concur in all of the Court's opinion except for the first six paragraphs of Part II. A. In those paragraphs the Court holds that the district court did not err in its application of U.S.S.G. § 2B5.3(b)(1) by calculating the infringement amount using the retail value in the United States of the infringed item, instead of using the retail value in Latin America of the infringing item. I see no need to decide this issue in order to dispose of the appeal.

The district court explicitly stated that even if it had decided the infringing amount issue the other way, which would have resulted in a lower offense level, it would have imposed the same sentence after considering the 18 U.S.C. § 3553(a) factors. And, as the Court concludes in Part II B. of our opinion, the final sentence is reasonable. That means, under *United States v. Keene,* 470 F.3d 1347 (11th Cir. 2006), we can affirm regardless of whether the district court was correct in its interpretation and application of § 2B5.3(b)(1). On that basis I concur in the affirmance.

A M Moolla Group Limited v. The Gap, Inc.

The Supreme Court of Appeal of South Africa.
Case No 543/03, 2004.

HARMS JA:

[1] This appeal concerns the interpretation of some provisions of the Counterfeit Goods Act 37 of 1997 ('the Act'). The factual background is simple. The trade mark GAP is registered in 110 countries in the name of one or more of the respondents [The Gap, Inc. *et al.*] (a group of affiliated companies to whom I shall refer in the singular since their individual corporate identities are not relevant). In South Africa the respondent holds registrations for the mark in classes 3 and 30 while the marks THE GAP, THE GAP device and GAP device are registered in the name of the third appellant [Salt of the Earth Creations] in class 25 in respect of clothing. In related litigation the TPD has expunged the third appellant's trade marks and simultaneously dismissed an application for expunging the respondent's marks. That judgment is presently on appeal and for present purposes it will be assumed that the registrations in the name of the third appellant are valid.*

[2] The respondent sources clothing carrying the GAP trade mark in Lesotho, Swaziland, Zimbabwe, Mauritius and Madagascar (countries where it holds registrations for the mark) destined for marketing in other countries where it also holds registrations. In other words, the source and destination of the goods are countries where the goods are genuine and

---

*   "TPD" refers to the Transvaal Provincial Division of the High Court of South Africa. In a subsequent decision, A M Moolla v. The Gap (Supreme Court of Appeal of South Africa, 123/2004, 2005) the court expunged the trademarks of A M Moola from the register due to non-use. *Ed.*

not counterfeit (*i.e.* fraudulent imitations). The goods from Mauritius and Madagascar have to be transhipped via South African harbours and goods from the landlocked countries mentioned have to be transported through South Africa to a harbour. Relying on the third appellant's registered trade marks, the appellants (a group of related companies) have used, attempted to use and threatened to use the provisions of the Act to have the goods in transit impounded by the SA Police Services or the Commissioner of Customs and Excise. To prevent further interference with these 'transhipments', the respondent sought and obtained an order from the Durban High Court (Magid J) declaring that it is not unlawful under the Act (or the Trade Marks Act 194 of 1993) for the respondent to export through or to import through (*i.e.*, tranship through) the Republic goods bearing the GAP marks in circumstances where such marks are placed on the goods outside of the Republic and where such goods are not for sale in the Republic.

[3] The appellants allege that transhipment (by which I include the transportation of goods in transit) is hit by the provisions of s 2(1)(f) of the Act which provide that goods that are 'counterfeit goods' may not be imported into or through or exported from or through the Republic except if so imported or exported for the private and domestic use of the importer or exporter, respectively.[1] (The exception is not applicable and will be ignored in the discussion that follows.) A person who performs or engages in such an act is guilty of an offence if certain requirements are present. The respondent, on the other hand, submits that its actions are not hit by these provisions.

[4] Before entering into a detailed analysis of the relevant provisions of the Act, it is necessary to say something about its background and genesis. Counterfeiting of trade marks has, historically and imperfectly, been dealt with by different Merchandise Marks Acts. . . . Piracy, which concerns copyright infringement committed knowingly, was criminalised by Copyright Acts and still is. . . . International concern about counterfeiting and piracy led to certain provisions in the TRIPs

---

[1]   The full text of § 2(1) reads:

'(1) Goods that are counterfeit goods, may not—

(a) be in the possession or under the control of any person in the course of business for the purpose of dealing in those goods;

(b) be manufactured, produced or made except for the private and domestic use of the person by whom the goods were manufactured, produced or made;

(c) be sold, hired out, bartered or exchanged, or be offered or exposed for sale hiring out, barter or exchange;

(d) be exhibited in public for purposes of trade;

(e) be distributed—

(i) for purposes of trade; or

(ii) for any other purpose to such an extent that the owner of an intellectual property right in respect of any particular protected goods suffers prejudice;

(f) be imported into or through or exported from or through the Republic except if so imported or exported for the private and domestic use of the importer or exporter, respectively;

(g) in any other manner be disposed of in the course of trade.'

agreement, the preamble of which speaks of the desire of member states—

> 'to reduce distortions and impediments to international trade, and taking into account the need to promote effective and adequate protection of intellectual property rights, and to ensure that measures and procedures to enforce intellectual property rights do not themselves become barriers to legitimate trade.'

The agreement requires of member states to provide certain minimum measures for the protection of intellectual property rights but leaves it to them to grant more should they wish to do so. . . . As far as border measures are concerned, art 51 is of significance for present purposes:

> 'Members shall, in conformity with the provisions set out below, adopt procedures to enable a right holder, who has valid grounds for suspecting that <u>the importation of counterfeit trademark or pirated copyright goods</u> may take place, to lodge an application in writing with competent authorities, administrative or judicial, for the suspension by the customs authorities of the release into free circulation of such goods. . . . Members may also provide for corresponding procedures concerning the suspension by the customs authorities of the release of infringing goods destined for exportation from their territories.'

(My underlining.). . . .

[8] . . . Reverting then to s 2(1)(f), it may be useful to quote the salient wording again:

> 'goods that are counterfeit goods, may not be imported into or through or exported from or through the Republic . . .'.

For purposes of the present debate it will be assumed that should the respondent, for instance, import GAP clothing into this country, it would amount to a contravention of the provision. The first question is whether 'transhipment' is included in the words 'imported into' the Republic. Transhipment (also spelt transshipment) is a concept well known to the legislature and in ordinary legislative language a distinction is drawn between the two concepts. . . . Interpreting a 1918 statutory provision requiring that a person who 'imports' wheat flour into the country must submit immediately 'after the importation' certain returns and mix it with other flour, our courts have held that the intention of the legislature could not have been to include flour in transit to another country to fall under 'import'. . . . Magid J relied on these judgments to conclude that the same applied in this case. This court, too, has held that goods in transit are not 'imported' into the country for purposes of the Customs and Excise Act 91 of 1963. . . .

[10] In a local context there may be good reason to wish to provide for remedies to impound counterfeit goods in transit as there would be to impound illegal drugs or weapons in transit. On the other hand, is there any reason to impound goods, which are not in the ordinary sense of the word 'counterfeit', that have to be transhipped through this country from island and landlocked countries, especially if no local rights holder is thereby affected and no intellectual property right infringed? Counsel could not suggest any and I cannot conceive of any. One has to assume that this country would not wish to interfere with the legitimate trade of countries that, due to their particular geographical location, are dependent for access and egress on this country. In the light of the preamble of TRIPs quoted above, it is not lightly to be presumed that legislation based on it would 'become barriers to legitimate trade'.

[11] The Act is intended to criminalise a particular species of fraud. What the respondent does can by no stretch of the imagination be considered as fraudulent. Would the Act then wish to criminalise its actions? Since this Act is a penal statute it must be interpreted restrictively without doing violence to the wording. . . . Where, as indicated, the word 'import' need not include transhipment, as the cases referred to indicate, I do not believe that the interpretation contended for by the appellants should prevail. . . .

[12] The appellants relied additionally on the phrase 'be imported . . . through . . . or . . . exported through the Republic' in s 2(1)(f), but immediately conceded that it has no discernable meaning. The respondent suggested that it might refer to a case where the goods are landed in, say, Durban to be cleared by customs at City Deep, Johannesburg; in such a case there would be a reason to criminalise the importation through the country en route to City Deep. Whether that is the meaning we need not to decide. What we have to is whether the respondent imports 'through' this country. It does not and, once again, if the legislature intended otherwise it was obliged to make its intention clear.

The judge below was consequently correct in his finding and the following order is made:

The appeal is dismissed with costs, including the costs of two counsel.

NOTES

1.   *Enforcement and Extraterritoriality.* Did the court in *United States v. Lozano* observe the general rule that statutes should be interpreted to avoid their extraterritorial application? Exception (I) of section 2B5.3 presumably contemplates a domestic U.S. sale in which the fact that the infringed and infringing goods are identical will lead a reasonable consumer to pay the same price for the infringing good as he would have for the infringed good. Since even genuine goods will command lower prices in less affluent markets, would it have been a preferable—because strictly territorial—

interpretation of section 2B5.3 to equate the price of infringed and infringing goods in the Latin American markets to which the goods were to be shipped for sale, rather than in the U.S. market?

The question presented in the *Gap* case is precisely the obverse of the question presented in *Lozano*: when should a statute that has no extraterritorial purport be interpreted to exonerate conduct—transhipment—that in fact takes place on national territory? Is it a premise of territoriality that acts of commission inside a country's territory are not enough, and that some local injury must be shown before the lawmaking power arises? In light of the economic premises of the territoriality principle, which approach to transhipment makes sense?

2. *U.S. Border Measures.* Section 42 of the Lanham Act, 15 U.S.C. § 1124, provides in part that "no article of imported merchandise which shall copy or simulate the name of any domestic manufacture, or manufacturer, or trader, or of any manufacturer or trader located in any foreign country which, by treaty, convention, or law affords similar privileges to citizens of the United States, or which shall copy or simulate a trademark registered in accordance with the provisions of this chapter or shall bear a name or mark calculated to induce the public to believe that the article is manufactured in the United States, or that it is manufactured in any foreign country or locality other than the country or locality in which it is in fact manufactured, shall be admitted to entry at any customhouse of the United States. . . ."

To prevent importation of infringing articles, the trademark or trade name owner must record the mark or name with the United States Customs Service. The Customs Service will then seize any goods bearing a confusingly similar mark or name. *See* 19 C.F.R. § 133.21 (2011). One strategic advantage of Customs exclusion is that it saves the trademark owner the effort of tracking down, and bringing infringement actions against, distributors who have purchased the imported goods for resale in the United States. *See* also section 526 of the Tariff Act of 1930, 19 U.S.C. § 1526 (2006). Trademark owners may also initiate proceedings before the International Trade Commission (ITC) under 19 U.S.C. § 1337, and thereby obtain either a general or limited exclusion order, enforceable by the U.S. Customs Service. *See* generally, Timothy Trainer, Border Enforcement of Intellectual Property (2000).

3. *EU Border Measures.* Though not foreclosed by Article 51 of the TRIPs Agreement, are seizures of counterfeit goods in transit contrary to WTO rules? Some EU member states interpreted the now-replaced EC Customs Regulation (EC) No 3295/94 in combination with the *Polo/Lauren* decision from 2000 to permit seizures of goods in transit any time the goods would infringe intellectual property rights in the countries of transit. The Polo/Lauren Co LP v PT Dwidua Langgeng Pramata International Freight Forwarders, ECJ, C-383/98, 2000.

A need for a clarification of the EU transit rules became particularly pressing in 2010 after India and Brazil filed requests for consultations with the WTO alleging that the practice of seizing goods in transit was contrary to GATT and TRIPs. In a judgment that concerned seizures of allegedly patent and trademark infringing goods, the Court of Justice of the European Union explained that goods cannot be seized in transit unless they "are the subject of a commercial act directed at European Union consumers, such as a sale, offer for sale or advertising." Koninklijke Philips Electronics NV v. Lucheng Meijing Industrial Company Ltd., CJEU, C-446/09, 2011, ¶ 59.

The 2015 version of the EU Trademark Directive and the 2015 amendment of the EU Trademark Regulation introduced a new right enabling trademark owners to request that goods in transit from third countries be detained by customs in the European Union if the goods bear a sign that is identical or essentially identical to the trademark owner's registered trademark. It is then the burden of the holder of the goods to prove, in the country of transit, that the trademark owner has no grounds "to prohibit the placing of the goods on the market in the country of final destination." EU Trademark Regulation, Article 9(4); EU Trademark Directive, Article 10(4).

Is the new rule compatible with the freedom of transit rule in GATT? Is it compatible with the Canada-European Union free trade agreement, which requires that a trademark owner provide adequate evidence that there is an infringement of the owner's trademark under the law of the country of the customs measures (of transit)? How difficult will it be for a court in the country of transit to assess trademark infringement under the law of the country of destination?

On post-*Koninklijke Philips* changes in EU legislation concerning border measures see Martin Senftleben, Wolf in Sheep's Clothing? Trade Mark Rights against Goods in Transit and the End of Traditional Territorial Limits, 47(8) IIC 941 (2016); Hesham M. Abdelgawad, Detention of 'Non-Union Goods in Transit' at the EU Borders . . ., 13(6) J. Intell. Property Law & Practice 469, 473 (2018). For a discussion of seizures of goods in transit see also page 579, above.

4. *Border Measures and Private Imports.* TRIPs Article 60 allows countries to "exclude from the application of the [customs] provision small quantities of goods of a non-commercial nature contained in travellers' personal luggage or sent in small consignments." Has the character of *de minimis* imports changed since 1994, when the TRIPs Agreement was signed? The 2013 EU Customs Regulation excludes from customs measures "goods of a non-commercial nature contained in travellers' personal luggage" but the exclusion does not cover small consignments, such as shipments of products purchased on the Internet. *See* Martin Blomqvist v. Rolex SA, CJEU, C-98/13, 2014. Does it make sense to distinguish between the two types of imports? Where does the sale occur in each case? In 2008 the Swiss Trade Mark Protection Act removed its earlier distinctions between goods imported in personal luggage and small consignments. Federal Act of 2007, AS 2008, Article 13(2bis).

5. *Border Measures and the Internet.* Do TRIPs provisions concerning border measures apply on the Internet? Improved geolocation technologies have made the borderless Internet practically obsolete, but are countries equipped to replicate on the Internet the same border measures that they have implemented in the physical world?

In the United States, Align Technology, Inc. filed a complaint with the ITC alleging that importation of orthodontic aligners infringed their patent because the unauthorized imports were created through a series of steps that involved electronic transmissions of data from the United States (where scans were taken) to Pakistan (where digital models were adjusted) and back to the United States (where 3D physical models were printed from files transmitted from Pakistan). The ITC found that ClearCorrect Pakistan infringed Align's patent, and because the ITC had jurisdictional authority over electronically imported data under 19 U.S.C. § 1337, it issued a cease and desist order.

The U.S. Court of Appeals for the Federal Circuit disagreed with the ITC's assertion of jurisdiction over electronic data; under section 1337 the ITC's "jurisdiction to remedy unfair international trade practices is limited to unfair acts involving the importation of 'articles'," and according to the court, the term " 'articles' is defined as 'material things,' and thus does not extend to electronic transmission of digital data." Clearcorrect Operating, LLC v. ITC, 810 F.3d 1283, 1290 (Fed. Cir. 2015). Will it violate TRIPs if the ITC denies the issuance of an order prohibiting importations over the Internet of goods with counterfeit trademarks?

D. UNFAIR COMPETITION AND TRADE SECRETS

1. UNFAIR COMPETITION

Paris Convention for the Protection of Industrial Property

Stockholm Text, 1967.

Article 10*bis*

Unfair Competition

(1)   The countries of the Union are bound to assure to nationals of such countries effective protection against unfair competition.

(2)   Any act of competition contrary to honest practices in industrial or commercial matters constitutes an act of unfair competition.

(3)   The following in particular shall be prohibited:

1.   all acts of such a nature as to create confusion by any me whatever with the establishment, the goods, or the industria commercial activities, of a competitor;

2.   false allegations in the course of trade of such a natur to discredit the establishment, the goods, or the industria commercial activities, of a competitor;

3.   indications or allegations the use of which in the cours trade is liable to mislead the public as to the nature,

manufacturing process, the characteristics, the suitability for their purpose, or the quantity, of the goods.

Aidan Robertson & Audrey Horton, Does the United Kingdom or the European Community Need an Unfair Competition Law?*

17 European Intellectual Property Review 568–569, 574–578 (1995).

UK Law

It is accepted that there is at present no general right to restrain unfair competition. An attempt to persuade the Privy Council to develop such a concept in *Pub Squash* was met with judicial indifference.[1] English law is difficult to summarise succinctly, as it depends on the interaction of a number of torts, each of which has been developed in largely piecemeal fashion. As a broad generalisation, it could be said that English law prevents unfair competition in three principal ways.

(1) *Passing off.* A may be restrained from misappropriating B's reputation in its goods by misleading B's customers, for example, by suggesting a connection or association with B's business. This is done by B bringing an action for passing off against A. The essence of this action is customer confusion. Unless B can show that its customers have been or are likely to be misled into confusing A's for B's goods or into making a false connection or association with B's business, it will not succeed.

(2) *Inducing breach of contract and unlawful interference with contractual relations.* A may be restrained from acquiring B's customers through unlawful means. This applies where A induces B's customers to break their contracts with B or otherwise unlawfully interferes with B's contractual relations.

(3) *Defamation and injurious falsehood.* A may be restrained from acquiring B's customers by telling lies to B's customers about B or B's goods. In the case of lies about B, there is an action for defamation. In the case of lies about B's goods, there are actions for slander of goods and injurious falsehood.

Seen in this way, the law emphasises the role of the customer. It is unfair competition to acquire customers by causing them to transfer their custom by (1) confusing them as to with whom they are doing business; (2) inducing them to break existing contracts with competitors, or (3) lying to them about competitors. Beyond these limits, attempts to attract customers from other competitors are considered legal.

---

*   Reprinted with permission of the authors.

1   [1981] RPC 429. The Privy Council chose to state that their Lordships expressed no opinion on the development of a tort of unfair competition by the US Supreme Court in *International News Service v. Associated Press* (1918) 248 U.S. 215.

Indeed these categories may be further rationalised, and it may be seen that there are two underlying assumptions at work here. First, lying is a means of confusing customers as to reality. Hence, the essence of the law is that customers should not be confused. Secondly, the prohibition against inducing breach of contract should be seen as part of English law's regard for the 'sanctity' of contract.

The focus of English law relevant to unfair competition (as distinct from contract law) is to prevent customers being confused. Provided customers have available correct information about what and with whom they are dealing, and that bargains once struck are adhered to, the law is prepared to leave the proper functioning of the market to the free play of market forces. A similar attitude is taken by U.S. federal and state laws.

In continental Europe, while civil law jurisdictions also prevent customer confusion, unfair competition law starts from the basis that its rationale is to enforce the "honest usages" of the market-place. Beier summarises this as meaning that a trader was granted "the right to restrain his competitors from causing him injury by unfair conduct". Thus the focus is not just on customer confusion, but on what is fair or ethical commercial conduct. English law has eschewed this approach, and continues to focus on customer confusion . . .

Unfair Competition Laws in Europe

European unfair competition laws must be considered at two levels. First, there are national laws in most states, and, secondly, laws in those states which are now members of the European Union must be examined for their compatibility with European Community laws. While there is no EC law specifically addressing substantive unfair competition law, certain aspects of EC law can alter national unfair competition laws. Accordingly, this article will first summarise national laws before going on to consider the impact of EC law.

National unfair competition laws in Europe

It is not proposed to present a comprehensive survey of national unfair competition laws. Rather the authors seek to present some general observations about civil unfair competition laws, illustrated by case law examples, as a means of giving common lawyers a flavour of what they typically involve. They then seek to draw a contrast with English law.

A survey of unfair competition cases reported in English reveals much apparent activity in most jurisdictions under this name. Most attention in the literature available on this topic in English is focused on German unfair competition law, owing principally to the fact that it is seemingly often the most strict and rigid and therefore is the most eye-catching, not to say startling, for a common lawyer. However, it is possible to summarise more generally the content of civil unfair competition laws.

Ulmer[2] identified a coherent body of unfair competition law across Europe, which despite national differences, could be said to have a unifying objective. This is described by Beier as being the interest:

> of the honest trader in having the right to restrain his competitors from causing him injury by unfair conduct. The test was whether a competitor's conduct complied with "honest usages" of the trade, the "usages honntes" (Article 10*bis* Paris Convention), the "correttezza professionale" (Article 2598 Codice Civile) or "the bonos mores" ("gute Sitten") in the course of trade (Article 1, German Law against Unfair Competition 1909).

Beier takes the view that this "classical" unfair competition law has, in more recent times, been "shattered as unfair competition law has become a playground for special interests and competences, uncoordinated and lacking any clear vision". However, from a common law perspective the similarities in the civil law approach remain more striking than the differences and while there are undeniably very distinct national differences, the following common elements of unfair competition law can be identified:

Prohibition on unfair conduct

This includes laws regulating comparative advertising, special offers, low prices (including loss-leading), prohibiting disparaging competitors, and a general prohibition on discriminatory sales conditions, including price discounting.

In France, it was held that a supermarket is permitted to advertise its prices as against those of competitors only in relation to identical products and under precisely similar conditions. Thus it would not be possible to have a price comparison between a supermarket and a small shop. In Germany, Ford was held to have contravened unfair competition law by inviting Opel drivers to trade in their "good old Opels" for a "well-designed Sierra, a sports Capri or a comfortable Granada". This was regarded as comparative advertising, implicitly denigrating a competitor's products.

Low prices were condemned as unfair competition in Italy, where a court held that sale is not fair if the seller does not charge all costs plus a reasonable profit. Similarly, the Hague Appeal Court condemned as unfair competition an attempt by Dutch daily newspapers to queer the pitch of a new weekly sports newspaper which was to come out on Monday mornings by distributing free their normal Monday evening sports sections some hours earlier on Monday mornings. Such sports sections, it was held, could only be legitimately distributed at a reasonable price.

---

[2]   Referred to in F. Beier, "The law of unfair competition in the European Community—its development and present status" [1985] EIPR 284.

Its capacity for novel applications is illustrated by a case in France in which a software company was restrained from selling software which would enable users to evade anticopying protection included in other software. Enabling infringement of copyright was considered an act of unfair competition. Similarly, a Dutch court held that sales of pirate decoders for subscription television was an act of unfair competition, even though not an infringement of any intellectual property right. Importing bootleg compact discs into the Netherlands, though not an infringement under Dutch intellectual property law nor in the country of manufacture, was held to be unfair competition.

An example of the German courts' extensive interpretation of what contravenes "bonos mores" is afforded by the Federal Supreme Court's condemnation on this ground of telephone solicitation, without prior approval from the person concerned to be phoned. Similar condemnation has also been made of telex or fax solicitation methods.

Prohibition on deceptive advertising and marketing

A classic example of deceptive marketing of goods was condemned as unfair competition by a Swedish court which ordered a spaghetti importer not to sell its product in a packet larger than was necessary for its contents. Beier notes that the suppression of deceptive advertising still poses great difficulties in Italy, as courts refer to the principle of Roman law *omnis mercator mendax*, viewing the Italian consumer as suspicious and vigilant enough to exclude the possibility of deception. The Italian judiciary's view of its consumers is to be contrasted with that of the German judges with their concern to protect, in Schricker's words, "purchasers with below average talent".

The German Federal Supreme Court has condemned, for example, the sort of promotional advertising which requires returning a lucky winning ticket for a prize, if potential participants are excessively enticed by being misled as to the chances of winning a prize. Indeed, it was held in the same case that the distribution of money off coupons as a promotional tool can infringe the law on rebates which forbids discounts on goods and services of more than 3 per cent. The Federal Supreme Court regarded as unfair competition anything that tied a prize to the purchase of a product. In another case, it was held that a promotional game which required contestants to enter the defendant's shops to collect a sticker required to play the game would make them feel morally obliged to buy something and thus was contrary to fair competition. Similar promotional devices such as restaurant guides including vouchers for two main courses for the price of one, and American Express card air miles points in return for expenditure charged to the card account' have also been held to be in contravention of this law.

An advertising description of a mineral water as "A Champagne among Mineral Waters" was condemned by the German Federal Supreme Court as *contra bonos mores*, since the defendant was devaluing the plaintiff champagne producers' product by comparing champagne to water (the ultimate in trade mark dilution perhaps?), unless the slogan was permitted under French law, since this was the country of origin of both products. This can be compared with an Italian Supreme Court decision in which a Champagne producer failed to prevent a bath foam producer using champagne shaped bottles, on the basis that it had not shown either that there would be confusion between customers nor that use of the same type of bottle would cause customers to think less of the Champagne producer's product. Similarly, in France, the same producer failed to stop a publicity campaign advertising its product as a prize to winners of a draw, on the basis that it was disparagement of their trade mark.

Prohibition on false indications of origin

In Belgium, a Scotch whisky producer was able to obtain an injunction preventing a Belgian blend of Scotch whisky and Belgian alcohol from using a name and get-up suggestive of Scottish origin.

In France, a perfume company was restrained by injunction from calling its perfume "Champagne", the action being brought by two French state-controlled organisations, the Institut National des Appellations d'Origine and the Comite Interprofessionel du Vin de Champagne.

Prohibition on slavish copying

In Denmark, slavish copying of an item not protected by copyright or patent may be an act of unfair competition.

In Italy, protection against slavish copying has been granted to protect colours used in packaging a product in circumstances which might well not amount to passing off under English law, although it was stressed that protection depended on evidence of customer confusion.

Confusingly similar packaging (*in casu* a petroleum additive packaged in a way similar to beer and soft drinks cans) was condemned as unfair competition in a German court on the grounds of consumer protection. However, in another Italian case, an injunction was granted to prevent slavish copying (*in casu* an opera libretto copied from the original score, now out of copyright) even though it was specifically found that there was no risk of customer confusion.

In the Netherlands, the style of a particular artist in illustrating children's books was protected under unfair competition even in the absence of copyright infringement.

Protection for distribution networks

This is illustrated by two Greek cases. In one, an injunction was ordered against an unauthorised trader refilling the plaintiff's butane gas cylinders, this being held to give an unfair advantage over the appointed agent who had to bear costs of repairing damaged cylinders. In the second, an injunction was granted to the exclusive distributor of "Lacoste" products in Greece preventing parallel imports of genuine Dutch Lacoste goods. However, the Italian courts reached the opposite conclusion in a case involving parallel imports of "Christian Dior" perfumes, applying notions of privity of contract familiar to the common law.

However, German unfair competition law did not prevent a German importer of computer games from Japan selling them in the absence of an authorised German distributor.

German law seemingly goes further than other civil laws in two principal ways. First, it allows a wider class of plaintiffs to enforce unfair competition laws. Competitors and trade associations may sue even without proof of direct injury. Secondly, in assessing deceptiveness, German courts place great reliance on the public's opinion of whether something would be false or misleading, rather than judging such issues on the basis of legislative intent or on an assessment of competing interests.

Conclusions on the relationship between UK law and European unfair competition laws

It appears that European unfair competition laws go further than English and federal U.S. laws in the following areas by including:

(1) general prohibitions on unfair conduct, such as disparagement of competitors;

(2) prohibitions on making special offers, low prices (including loss-leading) and discounting;

(3) prohibitions on slavish copying; and

(4) protection for distribution networks.

Moreover, the rules on who may sue frequently allow competitors to bring actions to restrain unfair competition in the civil courts. Therefore, while applying a false trade description is a criminal offence in the United Kingdom, it may be restrained by way of an action brought by a competitor in many continental European systems.

EC Law and Unfair Competition Law

There is no Community law on unfair competition. Rather, national laws have to be reconciled with the Community rules on free movement of goods contained in Articles 30 to 36 and the equivalent rules on services in Articles 59 to 66 of the Treaty of Rome. The competition rules set out in Articles 85 and 86, when read in conjunction with Articles 3(g) and 5(2) and/or 90, may also be relevant. In addition, there is now some specific legislation which is relevant. The impact of the Treaty and the specific legislation will be considered in turn. But first some cases will illustrate the way in which the application of national laws may raise problems for Community law.

The scope for conflict between EC law and national laws

In Greece, an injunction was granted to the exclusive distributor of "Lacoste" products in Greece preventing parallel imports of genuine

Dutch Lacoste goods. No such injunction would be available under English law. In Italy, the Supreme Court held that it did have jurisdiction under the Brussels Convention to hear an unfair competition case against a British company alleged to be spreading false information on foreign markets about an Italian manufacturer's products. It is likely that the same result would be achieved were an injurious falsehood or slander of goods case to be brought in equivalent circumstances before an English court. In Germany, an injunction was ordered against a German company distributing advertising pamphlets in the United States making false statements as to its circulation, in an attempt to attract advertising from the United States. On its facts, this case did not raise any wider issues for EC law, but now that Austria has acceded to the Community, it would be possible that this magazine would also circulate in Austria and thus the German court's prohibition would have an impact on the circulation of goods within the Community.

In considering the impact of Community law on national unfair competition laws, it is convenient to look first at the application of the Treaty rules on free movement of goods, then at Community competition law, before finally considering the legislative developments that have taken place.

EC law on free movement of goods

Article 30 EC ensures free movement of goods within the EC. The Court of Justice has developed this Article into a means of ensuring that Member States' trading rules do not place disproportionate restrictions on trading goods across borders. Hence in *Cassis de Dijon* itself, minimum alcoholic content rules were declared to be contrary to Article 30, since equivalent consumer protection could be achieved through labelling requirements. In *Prantl*, German law restricting use of a traditional shape of wine bottle was held not to comply with Article 30, since it prevented imports of another wine also traditionally produced in this shape of bottle.

On the other hand a Dutch law restricting promotional gifts was held to be compatible with Article 30 since it pursued legitimate objectives of consumer protection and fair trading.

The *Cassis de Dijon* principle has been qualified by the Court of Justice in *Keck*[3] to provide an exception to this principle that selling arrangements are not caught by Article 30 EC, provided they apply equally as between domestically produced and imported products:

> In *Cassis de Dijon* it was held that, in the absence of harmonisation of legislation, measures of equivalent effect prohibited by Article 30 included obstacles to the free movement of goods where they were the consequence of applying rules that laid down requirements to be met by such goods (such as requirements as to designation, form, size, weight, composition,

---

3   C-267 & 268/91 *Keck* [1995] 1 CMLR 101.

presentation, labelling, packaging) to goods from other Member States where they were lawfully manufactured and marketed, even if those rules applied without distinction to all products unless their application could be justified by a public interest objective taking precedence over the free movement of goods.

However, contrary to what had previously been decided, the application to products from other Member States of national provisions restricting or prohibiting certain selling arrangements was not such as to hinder directly or indirectly, actually or potentially trade between Member States within the meaning of the *Dassonville* judgment, provided that those provisions applied to all affected traders operating within the national territory and provided that they affected in fact, the marketing of domestic products and of those from other Member States.

It is not clear how this ruling applies to unfair competition law. Do such rules constitute marketing arrangements, potentially within the ambit of Article 30, or are they selling arrangements falling beyond Article 30's jurisdictional scope? Some guidance may be obtained from the Court of justice's judgment in *Clinique*.[4]

German law on packaging of goods prevented Clinique being used by Estée Lauder as a trade mark for cosmetics on ground that it could mislead consumers into thinking that the products had medicinal qualities. Este Lauder wanted to relaunch the product in Germany and to cease repacking it as "Linique" (*sic*) in Germany.

On an Article 177 reference, the court cited *Keck* as support for the proposition that a rule relating to requirements such as presentation and labelling was prohibited by Article 30 unless justified by a "public interest objective taking precedence over free movement of goods". It was held that as the products were not presented as medicinal, were not sold in pharmacies but in cosmetic and perfume departments and the use of the name Clinique had not apparently misled other consumers in the EC, the German law could not be enforced. Thus provisions of national unfair competition laws relating to the packaging of goods would seem not to be classified as selling arrangements.

This may be contrasted with the *Yves Rocher* case.[5] In this case, decided prior to *Keck*, a German law prohibiting eye-catching advertisements on price, even where the price information was correct, was struck down as being contrary to Article 30 EC. Advertising can now be seen as a selling arrangement falling outside Article 30 and thus German controls on what is permitted in advertisements would remain a matter exclusively for German unfair competition law. The only way of escaping this conclusion would be to recognise that advertising price is a

---

[4]   C-315/92 *Clinique* [1994] ECR I-317.
[5]   C-126/91 *Yves Rocher* [1993] ECR I-236.

way of promoting cross-border trade and therefore while advertisements may be seen as selling arrangements, they should not be included in the class of "certain" selling arrangements referred to by the court in *Keck*. The goal of the single market should enable some selling arrangements necessary to make the market function to remain within the ambit of Article 30. However, this argument appears not to have succeeded in *Leclerc Siplec*, III where the Court of Justice held that Article 30 did not apply to a restriction on television advertisements which affected all products and distributors in the same way.

Thus a case like *Yves Rocher* could be contrasted with the *American Express Air Miles* case. German unfair competition law prevented American Express from granting air miles as a reward for use of their card. American Express' promotional exercise was designed to promote use of their charge card within Germany, but did not form part of a wider plan to encourage cross-border trade, and therefore remained a matter for German regulation. It seems, following the *Keck* judgment, that American Express would now find it more difficult to invoke Article 30 to challenge the German law.

More generally, one can hazard a classification of unfair competition laws into those involving selling arrangements outside Article 30 and those to which Article 30, as interpreted by *Cassis de Dijon*, still applies:

(1) *Selling arrangements outside Article 30*
— general prohibitions on unfair conduct;
— laws regulating comparative advertising;
— prohibitions on making special offers, low prices (including loss-leading) and discounting;
— prohibitions on disparaging competitors; and
— prohibitions on deceptive advertising.

(2) *Unfair competition laws subject to Article 30 (ceteris paribus)*
— prohibitions on deceptive packaging;
— prohibitions on false indications of origin;
— prohibitions on slavish copying; and
— rules on distribution networks.

Despite the attempt at clarification in *Keck*, the classification suggested above is difficult to make and the authors are not confident that it would be followed by the court. It seems that the overall picture remains confused and in need of rationalisation specifically addressed to the problem of unfair competition law.

NOTES

1. *National Traditions of Unfair Competition and Article 10bis of the Paris Convention.* As indicated in the article by Robertson and Horton excerpted above, common law countries generally define unfair competition more narrowly than civil law countries, which usually employ the term to encompass all forms of dishonest or otherwise unfair competitive conduct. In one sense, the distinction is only nominal since conduct that is governed by unfair competition rules on the European continent may in common law countries be regulated by discrete doctrines such as trade secret law and tortious interference with contracts. In another sense, however, the unfair competition label has substantive consequence as it may well determine whether regulation of the conduct in issue comes within a country's Paris Convention obligations under Article 10*bis*.

The 1900 Brussels Additional Act introduced Article 10*bis* into the Paris Convention in the form of a national treatment obligation respecting the repression of unfair competition. The 1911 Washington Act added a substantive norm of effective protection against unfair competition and subsequent revisions of Article 10*bis* in 1925, 1934 and 1958 bolstered the provision's obligations and added a definition and examples of unfair competition. *See* G.H.C. Bodenhausen, Guide to the Application of the Paris Convention for the Protection of Industrial Property 142–143 (1968). According to Professor Bodenhausen, Article 10*bis* implies that "[a]ny act of unfair competition will have to be considered unfair if it is contrary to honest practices existing in the country where protection against unfair competition is sought. The judicial or administrative authorities of such country will therefore also have to take into account honest practices established in international trade." *Id.* at 144.

Open-ended as it is, Article 10*bis* played an important role in shaping the unfair competition law of Paris Union countries through the early part of the twentieth century. In those countries that treat intellectual property treaties as self-executing, Article 10*bis* could be invoked directly by nationals of other Union countries; many countries also extended the provision's coverage to their own nationals. The evolution of universal legal norms slowed toward the middle and latter parts of the century, hampered by the heterogeneity of national approaches to unfair competition, not only between civil law and common law countries, but also among countries in each group. Local norms nonetheless continue to evolve through national legislation in both economically developed and developing countries.

See generally Frauke Henning-Bodewig, International Protection Against Unfair Competition—Art. 10*bis* Paris Convention, TRIPS and WIPO Model Provisions, 30 IIC 166 (1999); Gerhard Schricker, Twenty-Five Years of Protection Against Unfair Competition, 26 IIC 782 (1995).

2. *Does U.S. Law Embody International Unfair Competition Norms?* Most, but not all, U.S. courts hold that the Paris Convention is not a self-executing treaty that can be directly invoked by foreign nationals. *Compare* La Republique Francaise v. Saratoga Vichy Spring Co., 191 U.S. 427, 439 (1903) (not self-executing) *with* Master, Wardens, Searchers v. Cribben & Sexton Co., 202 F.2d 779, 97 U.S.P.Q. 153 (C.C.P.A. 1953) (self-executing). As indicated in the next principal case, *BP Chemicals v. Jiangsu Sopo Corp.*, some courts have held that section 44(b) and (h) of the Lanham Act, 15 U.S.C. § 1126(b), (h), incorporate the substantive unfair competition norms of Paris

Convention Article 10*bis*, while others hold that the provision only effectuates U.S. national treatment obligations under the Convention. There is a surprising paucity of authority directly on point, and most decisions taking the national treatment approach involve a U.S. national, not a foreign national, seeking to invoke the terms of Article 10*bis*, either against a foreign national or another U.S. national. *See* generally, Patricia Norton, The Effect of Article 10*bis* of the Paris Convention in American Unfair Competition Law, 68 Fordham L. Rev. 225 (1999).

Article 10*bis* prescribes norms, not a detailed code of competitive conduct. If a U.S. court follows the line of cases holding that section 44 incorporates the substantive norms of Article 10*bis*, what law should the court apply in a case where section 44 is properly invoked? Presumably, the starting point is the law of the protecting country, including its implementation of Article 10*bis*. Under rules governing transitory causes of action, page 29, above, would a U.S. court accept jurisdiction over a case involving foreign acts? Does section 44 alter the existing decisional rules on transitory causes of action? What connection, if any, is there between rules on extraterritoriality in intellectual property cases and the question whether section 44 of the Lanham Act incorporates the substantive norms of Article 10*bis*?

PROBLEM 9

TTC, your client in Problem 8, at page 670, above, has applied for trademark registration for its scented thread in Countries *X*, *Y*, and *Z*. While it is awaiting the disposition of its applications, TTC would like to obtain injunctive relief barring NN from further sales of its scented thread. Please advise TTC of its likelihood of success in unfair competition actions against NN.

2. TRADE SECRETS

Agreement on Trade-Related Aspects of Intellectual Property Rights

33 International Legal Materials Journal 1, 98 (1994).

SECTION 7: PROTECTION OF UNDISCLOSED INFORMATION

Article 39

1.   In the course of ensuring effective protection against unfair competition as provided in Article 10*bis* of the Paris Convention (1967), Members shall protect undisclosed information in accordance with paragraph 2 below and data submitted to governments or governmental agencies in accordance with paragraph 3 below.

2.   Natural and legal persons shall have the possibility of preventing information lawfully within their control from being disclosed

to, acquired by, or used by others without their consent in a manner contrary to honest commercial practices[1] so long as such information:

— is secret in the sense that it is not, as a body or in the precise configuration and assembly of its components, generally known among or readily accessible to persons within the circles that normally deal with the kind of information in question;

— has commercial value because it is secret; and

— has been subject to reasonable steps under the circumstances, by the person lawfully in control of the information, to keep it secret.

3. Members, when requiring, as a condition of approving the marketing of pharmaceutical or of agricultural chemical products which utilize new chemical entities, the submission of undisclosed test or other data, the origination of which involves a considerable effort, shall protect such data against unfair commercial use. In addition, Members shall protect such data against disclosure, except where necessary to protect the public, or unless steps are taken to ensure that the data are protected against unfair commercial use.

Holly Emrick Svetz, Japan's New Trade Secret Law: We Asked for It—Now What Have We Got?

26 George Washington Journal of International Law and Economics
413, 417–442 (1992).

A. *Background on Trade Secret Law*

1. *United States*

English common law, which recognized medicinal formulae as trade secrets, was the basis for the development of early U.S. case law in this area. Trade-related topics may be additionally covered by federal statutes enacted under the Commerce Clause power of Congress. Trade secret protection, however, is governed by state law rather than federal law, as it is traditionally considered to be part of the laws governing unfair competition. The 1939 definition of a trade secret in the Restatement of Torts gained widespread acceptance and is still the standard in several jurisdictions. Trade secrets were not included in the Restatement (Second) of Torts because the American Law Institute felt that trade secrets had become incorporated in unfair competition law, which the Institute considered to be a field separate from tort law.

At common law, trade secrets are protected under multiple, concurrently applicable theories: misappropriation under tort law,

---

[1]   For the purpose of this provision, "a manner contrary to honest commercial practices" shall mean at least practices such as breach of contract, breach of confidence and inducement to breach, and includes the acquisition of undisclosed information by third parties who knew, or were grossly negligent in failing to know, that such practices were involved in the acquisition.

breach of a confidential relationship under contract or agency law, and theft under criminal law. To remedy the excision of the Restatement definition, the Uniform Law Institute proposed the Uniform Trade Secrets Act (UTSA) as a new standard in 1979. To date this act has been adopted with little or no modifications by thirty-six jurisdictions, while four states have adopted variants of the UTSA provisions.

2. Japan

Japan operates under a civil law system where the judicial function involves mainly code interpretation, rather than obtaining results consistent with prior case precedent. Case reports are not distributed commercially for precedential value as they are in the United States, and scholarly research is often necessary to determine the courts' position in an area of law. Most aspects of modern business and trade law contained in the Japanese Commercial Code were imported piecemeal from Western countries in response to foreign pressure. As a result, Japanese courts have to confront and deal with numerous inconsistencies between Japanese cultural norms, a U.S.-influenced Constitution, and the European-model substantive and procedural codes.

Japan's 1990 trade secret provisions were incorporated into Japan's Unfair Competition Prevention Law. The Unfair Competition Prevention Law was originally enacted in 1934 following Japan's participation in the Hague amendments to the Paris Convention for the Protection of Industrial Property. Patterned, in the words of a commentator, after the 1909 German Act Against Unfair Competition, the Japanese law differed from the German model in one fundamental respect—the Japanese law omitted all references to trade secrets, leaving the task to the Civil, Commercial and Penal Codes. In the 1930s, Japan did not feel the need to imitate this aspect of the German law for several reasons: first, it was unnecessary because of the relatively underdeveloped nature of industry in Japan at that time; second, the practice of lifetime employment at many of the larger Japanese companies made the improper transfer of trade secrets by employees to their new employers rare; and third, for sociocultural reasons such as the importance placed upon loyalty to the group and the protection of personal and familial reputations.

In the absence of an express statutory right, Japanese courts were unwilling to grant substantial relief that would bar third parties from making use of misappropriated trade secrets. Like at common law in the United States, coverage was inferred from the Civil Code if a tort, the Commercial Code if a breach of contract, or—in limited circumstances— the Penal Code when an official duty was breached. Before the new amendments were passed, attempts were made by trade secret owners to sue misappropriators using Japanese tort law, but such cases were scant. Now that a cause of action has been established by statute, an increase in litigation can be expected.

3. United States Pressure for Japanese Trade Secret Protection

As U.S. trade secret law matured in the 1980s, U.S. businesses began to demand intellectual property protection in Japan and other foreign markets. Japan failed to respond to a 1988 U.S. request that it set up trade secret rules similar to those in the United States. Japan's reasoning was that trade secret rights were too complicated for government intervention, and that protection of trade secrets should be left to the private sector.

As a result of mounting foreign and domestic pressure, Japan soon changed its official position to support formal protection for trade secrets. Former President Bush attributed this change to the strong international actions of the United States, noting the bilateral and multilateral pressure put on the Japanese government to adopt improved intellectual property protection.

On the unilateral front, Congress passed the Omnibus Trade and Competitiveness Act of 1988, placing pressure on both Japanese government and industry to change their positions on intellectual property standards. The 1988 Trade Act empowers the United States Trade Representative (USTR) to apply trade sanctions against any nation whose intellectual property laws do not adequately protect U.S. interests. Section 1342 of the 1988 Trade Act defines unfair trade methods and specifies the relief that may be provided. The 1988 Trade Act also lowered the quantum of proof required of a plaintiff in order to gain relief through the United States International Trade Commission (ITC). New amendments incorporated with Section 1301 of the 1988 Trade Act, commonly referred to as the "Special 301" provisions, require the USTR to generate an annual report listing countries "that have the most onerous or egregious acts, policies, or practices that . . . deny adequate and effective [protection of] intellectual property rights."[61] The purpose of the annual report requirement is to provide public pressure within the international community on violators, and each year its release receives substantial media attention.

In bilateral negotiations through the Intellectual Property Rights Working Group of the United States-Japan Trade Committee, the United States did not succeed in convincing Japan to strengthen its level of trade secret protection. Prior to the negotiations, the United States Commissioner of Patents and Trademarks had expressed his concern over Japanese reluctance to extend adequate protection to trade secrets.

The focus of multilateral efforts is centered on the ongoing Uruguay Round of the GATT negotiations. The 1990 proposed agreement by the Japanese on Trade Related Aspects of Intellectual Property Rights (TRIPs) did not include trade secret protection, because the Japanese did not then consider it to be appropriate subject matter for GATT. The draft

---

[61] 1988 Trade Act, sec. 1303, § 182(b)(1)(A)(i), 102 Stat. 1107, 1179 (codified at 19 U.S.C. § 2242(b)(1)(A)(i) (1992)).

agreement proposed by the United States in 1990, however, included trade secret protection. United States industry had earlier lobbied Japanese and European businesses to present a united front of developed nations in support of strong intellectual property laws in order to discourage developing countries from misappropriating technology. By 1988, a formal joint position had evolved between the U.S., European, and Japanese business communities to protect trade secrets under the general category of proprietary information. Largely due to the efforts of the Intellectual Property Committee, a U.S. industry lobby, TRIPs proposals have been included in the Uruguay Round of GATT negotiations.

4.   Japanese Action in Response to U.S. Pressure

In Japan, it is industry, usually through trade associations, that generally drafts trade legislation and submits it to an administrative agency such as the Ministry of International Trade and Industry (MITI). The agency then presents the legislation for consideration by the Diet, the Japanese legislature. The Industrial Structure Council of MITI set up a Proprietary Information Committee (PIC), and in October 1989, the Industrial Structure Council instructed the PIC to study the feasibility of protecting trade secrets under the Unfair Competition Prevention Law. In March 1990, the PIC published a report noting that Japan was the only major industrial country lacking statutory authorization for injunctive relief against trade secret misappropriation. As a solution, the PIC suggested amendments to the Japanese Unfair Competition Prevention Law that would consolidate the remedies available under that law with those already available for trade secrets under the Civil, Commercial, and Penal Codes. The PIC gave several reasons for the new legislation: 1) pressure from the United States in the Uruguay Round of the GATT negotiations to bring Japanese trade secret law into conformity with U.S. and European norms; 2) the current lack of protection in Japan for information-oriented technology and marketing fields; and 3) the trend toward increased mobility in the Japanese labor market. MITI prepared a draft bill to follow the report's recommendations. After soliciting comments, MITI submitted the final draft of the bill to the Diet. The new amendments for trade secret protection were enacted and became effective on June 1, 1991.

B.   Comparison of Current U.S. and Japanese Trade Secret Laws

In this section, elements of trade secret protection such as subject matter restrictions and the requirement of secrecy are discussed, as are remedies. Current U.S. law is used as the benchmark for comparison with corresponding provisions of Japanese law.

1.   Eligible Subject Matter

In Japan, the subject matter eligible for trade secret protection is defined as "technical or business information . . . useful in commercial activities, such as manufacturing or marketing methods, which is kept secret and not publicly known."[84] The new amendments do not set any threshold economic value requirement for a trade secret. The information need only possess commercial utility. The subject matter covered by the Japanese law is substantially similar to the UTSA, but has a wider scope because of its explicit protection of business information.

2.   *Unfair Acts or Improper Means*

The illegal act of misappropriation involves direct or third-party acquisition of a trade secret through improper means. UTSA defines the term "improper means" to include "theft, bribery, misrepresentation, breach or inducement of a breach of a duty to maintain secrecy, or espionage through electronic or other means."[89]

With the 1990 amendments, Japanese law now proscribes six kinds of unfair acts that are similar to the description of improper means under the UTSA. The six acts fall into three main categories: 1) acquiring trade secrets by unfair means such as stealing or cheating; 2) misusing a legitimately acquired trade secret for committing acts of unfair competition or for unfair gain; and 3) willful or gross negligence in acquiring, using or disclosing trade secrets tainted by an intervening unfair act.

Because the U.S. and Japanese laws are conceptually similar, the scope of proscribed acts would be familiar to U.S. businesses that seek to enforce the Japanese law in Japanese courts.

3.   *Secrecy Requirement*

In the United States, a holder of a trade secret is required to provide such protection for the trade secret as would be considered reasonable under a totality of circumstances analysis. To be considered reasonable, the possessor of a trade secret is not required to guard against unanticipated, undetectable or unpreventable methods of espionage. The commissioner's comment to the UTSA provides the following examples of reasonable efforts to protect a trade secret: advising employees of the existence of a trade secret; limiting access to a trade secret on a "need to know" basis; and controlling plant access. However, public disclosure of a trade secret through display, publication in a trade journal, advertising or other acts of carelessness can nullify any protection that may otherwise be available.

The new Japanese amendments define a trade secret as qualified subject matter "that is kept secret and not publicly known."[98] Professor Doi states that MITI submitted an explanatory note to accompany the 1990 Trade Secret Amendments when they were presented to the Diet that clarified the degree of secrecy required to maintain confidential

---

[84]   Revised Unfair Competition Law, art. 1, ¶ 3.

[89]   UTSA, § 1(1), 14 U.L.A. at 437.

[98]   Revised Unfair Competition Law, art. 1, ¶ 3.

information as a trade secret.[99] The note apparently emphasized that a holder's intention of maintaining secrecy was not sufficient. A trade secret holder was required to have "an objective secrecy administration," a term that suggests that the holder was also expected to design and implement procedural safeguards to protect the secret.[101] Thus a trade secret may be disclosed as necessary to an employee or licensee, but in order for it to maintain its status as a trade secret, an express or implied obligation of secrecy must be imposed on the employee or licensee.

As shown above, the standard of secrecy required to maintain trade secret status under Japanese law is stricter than the U.S. standard, which requires security measures to be "reasonable under the circumstances."[103] In *E.I. du Pont de Nemours & Co. v. Christopher*,[104] a leading case that typifies the U.S. approach, the Fifth Circuit held that DuPont had sufficiently protected its trade secrets. In this case, during the construction of a DuPont chemical processing plant, trade secrets concerning chemical processes used in the plant were obtained by aerial photography. The Fifth Circuit, adopting the Restatement of Torts view that the means of discovery used could not be improper, held that it would have been unreasonable to require DuPont to put a temporary roof on a half-constructed plant just to protect trade secrets from aerial surveillance. Explaining the policy reasons behind the decision, the court held that "tolerance of the espionage game must cease when the protections required to prevent another's spying cost so much that the spirit of inventiveness is dampened."[108] A Japanese court faced with the same facts may have required DuPont to demonstrate an "active secrecy administration" geared towards preventing aerial espionage. This would seem to imply that more expensive and extensive efforts may be required by any company doing business in Japan to ensure its trade secrets are legally protected.

4.   Third-Party Liability

In Japan, trade secret misappropriation occurs every time a third party knowingly or with gross negligence acquires, uses or discloses a trade secret tainted by a prior act of improper acquisition. This post-1990 standard under Japanese law is the same as the UTSA standard. In contrast, the Restatement of Torts holds third parties liable only when they have actual knowledge of prior improper acts.

Third-party liability and the availability of injunctive relief are the two most important elements of trade secret law that were added by the 1990 amendments. This liability is frequently associated with the disclosure of trade secrets by former employees or licensees. Japan

---

[99]   [Teruo Doi, The New Trade Secret Statute of Japan (2), Pat. & Licensing (Japan) Aug. 1990, at 6.]

[101]   Id.

[103]   UTSA § 1(4)(ii), 14 U.L.A. at 438.

[104]   431 F.2d 1012 (5th Cir. 1970), *cert. denied*, 400 U.S. 1024 (1971).

[108]   Id. [at 1016.]

licenses a great deal of technology from the United States. Whenever a trade secret is licensed, the contractual relationship that is created places an affirmative duty on the licensee not to disclose the trade secret. Prior to the 1990 amendments, a licensee's subcontractor, employee or joint venture partner was not bound by the licensee's contractual duties.

The leading case on trade secret law prior to the 1990 amendments is *Deutsche Werft A.G. v. Waukesha Chūetsu Yūgen Kaisha*.[115] In this case, a German company had granted an exclusive license to a Wisconsin-based corporation for the manufacture and sale of high-technology products in the United States and Canada. The U.S. partner, in violation of the contract, transferred the technology to a joint venture that it had set up in Japan with a Japanese partner. In the ensuing action, the Tokyo High Court affirmed the denial of an injunction requested by the German company against the U.S. corporation and the joint venture on the grounds that the Japanese joint venture was merely a third party to the licensing agreement. Under the new trade secret provisions, the Japanese joint venture, even though only a third party to the licensing agreement, would have been enjoined because it had knowingly used an improperly acquired trade secret.

5. *Remedies*

a. Injunctions

The primary remedy granted in trade secret misappropriation cases is a permanent injunction. This is because damages fail to compensate a trade secret holder for the loss of many unquantifiable competitive advantages such as control over the direction and marketing of a new technology; unfettered use of the trade secrets in other fields; the right to be the first to market; a reputation for innovation; customer loyalty and the respect of peers; and the absence of any need to be entangled in continuous litigation. State legislatures in the United States, recognizing that monetary damages are generally inadequate, have often provided for injunctive remedies by statute, thus relieving the trade secret holder of the burden of proving such inadequacy on a case-by-case basis.

Under the UTSA, actual or threatened misappropriation may be enjoined. A trade secret holder has the burden of proving an actual or threatened misappropriation; this is a lesser standard than the usual burden of proving that the movant would suffer "immediate and irreparable injury" before injunctive relief is granted.[122]

The duration of an injunction against trade secret misappropriation is also limited. Such an injunction may be terminated by a court when the trade secret loses its secret status because of intentional or inadvertent public disclosure. An injunction, however, may be extended beyond the life of the trade secret to negate any commercial advantage that a misappropriating party might receive over good faith competitors.

---

[115] Judgment of Sept. 5, 1966, [Tokyo] Kōsai [High Court], 464 HANJI 34 (Japan).

[122] Fed. R. Civ. p. 65(b).

For this purpose, the life of a trade secret is often taken to be equal to the time it would take a competitor to reach the same level of technology by reverse engineering or independent development. A court may also compel affirmative acts, such as the return or destruction of copies or samples of trade secret material. If a wrongdoer ignores an injunction, the injured party may request the court to hold the wrongdoer in contempt.

The new Japanese trade secret provisions permit injunctive relief against misappropriation, for the first time allowing a trade secret holder to recover against third parties with whom it lacks any contractual relationship. In addition to a prohibitory injunction, Japanese courts now have the authority to order the destruction of the trade secret material (such as a computer disk or a printout), the items produced using misappropriated trade secrets, and the facilities used for prohibited acts of trade secret misappropriation. Following the civil law tradition, Japanese law does not allow courts to enforce an injunction using contempt orders.

The addition of injunctive relief in the new 1990 amendments to the Unfair Competition Prevention Law overrules the landmark Japanese trade secret decision in Deutsche Werft A.G. v. Waukesha Chūetsu Yūgen Kaisha. As a general principle, Japanese courts did not award injunctive relief unless it was expressly authorized by the governing substantive law. The 1990 Trade Secret Amendments to the Unfair Competition Prevention Law added trade secrets to the list of laws—such as those governing patents, trademarks, and real estate—that expressly authorize courts to provide injunctive relief.

b.   Damages

United States law allows recovery for a complainant's actual loss from any misappropriation, but limits the recovery to the damages for the time period prior to the issuance of an injunction so as to avoid any double recovery by the complainant. The UTSA, by limiting a complainant's recovery to either the loss to the complainant or the unjust benefit to the misappropriator, whenever combining them would result in double recovery, explicitly rejected the Tenth Circuit decision in *Telex Corp. v. International Business Machines Corp.*,[136] which allowed awards of both the full actual loss to a complainant and the unjust enrichment of the misappropriator. The trial court has the discretion to award up to twice the amount of actual damages as punitive damages for misappropriation of trade secrets. As a result, the amount of damages awarded is not likely to be reversed on appeal unless the trial court's action was clearly erroneous.

In Japan, only actual damages may be awarded. There is no provision for punitive damages in the Unfair Competition Prevention Law since such damages are not, in general, part of Japanese law. Even

---

[136]   510 F.2d 894 (10th Cir.) (*per curiam*), *cert. dismissed*, 423 U.S. 802 (1975).

prior to the enactment of the new law, Japanese courts had been willing to award monetary damages in trade secret cases. In a recent trade secret case, however, a Japanese court awarded monetary damages without explaining whether the award was based on tort or unfair competition law. Under the 1990 amendments, the courts now have clear statutory authority to award monetary damages in cases of trade secret misappropriation.

c. Other Available Remedies

In the United States, when exceptional circumstances arise, a court may issue a conditional injunction that conditions further use of the trade secret upon the payment of a reasonable royalty, instead of prohibiting outright all further unauthorized use of the trade secret. The period for which a royalty has to be paid should be no longer than the period for which any use of the trade secret could have been prohibited by an injunction. In addition, a court may award reasonable attorney costs to the prevailing party if a claim of misappropriation is made in bad faith; if a motion to terminate an injunction is made or resisted in bad faith; or if willful or malicious misappropriation is found.

In Japan, measures to restore business goodwill, usually by means of a public apology, may be ordered by the court in lieu of or in addition to damages. For example, in *Athena K.K. v. Nagano-ken Keisanki Center K.K.*, a computer tape containing the subscription list for Nikkei Business, a biweekly journal, was illegally copied and sold by someone while in the possession of the computer center to Japan Reader's Digest, Inc. Although the Nikkei Business distributor filed criminal charges, a settlement was reached. The criminal charges were withdrawn and the parties agreed not to file a civil suit. As a condition of the settlement, Japan Reader's Digest, Inc. published a letter of apology in major newspapers. The concept and use of apology is deeply rooted in the Japanese culture, and is often utilized in every phase of litigation.

6. *Preservation of Secrecy During Litigation*

In order to protect trade secrets during the litigation process, the UTSA instructs courts to take such preventive measures as granting protective orders during discovery, holding *in camera* hearings, and sealing the records of the action. In federal courts, the Federal Rules of Civil Procedure permit a person from whom discovery is sought or a party, upon showing good cause, to seek a protective order "that a trade secret or other confidential research, development, or commercial information not be disclosed or be disclosed only in a designated way." A newly amended Federal Rule of Civil Procedure explicitly makes any trade secret disclosure a proper basis for a court to quash or modify a subpoena.

Under Rule 26, the good cause needed to resist discovery must be demonstrated by specific examples of substantial competitive harm that would result from disclosure. There is no absolute privilege protecting trade secrets from discovery—any protection is limited and qualified. Courts encourage the use of "umbrella" protective orders in order to avoid repetitive litigation during discovery regarding the trade secret status of each document. The violation of a protective order is punishable by civil or criminal contempt of court proceedings, and may result in jail sentences or substantial fines.

In addition to protection afforded to trade secrets during discovery, U.S. courts may receive evidence *in camera*, seal all or parts of the trial record, or close all or part of the trial itself so as to protect trade secrets. However, a court-ordered seal may be broken in a later proceeding if the litigants demonstrate a sufficient need for disclosure. Alternatives used by courts to protect the trade secrets in written records include the use of arbitrary symbols to indicate secret ingredients, or asterisks to indicate redacted portions of an opinion.

One U.S. commentator has noted that even after the 1990 amendments, Japanese law does not expressly provide for the protection of trade secrets during litigation. Under the new Japanese legislation, only limited procedural protection is available. Rather, the risk of disclosure of trade secrets during litigation in Japanese courts is lessened by systemic factors. For example, there are no pretrial discovery procedures in the Japanese system. The Japanese Constitution requires all trials to be open to the public except when publicity would be dangerous to public order or morality. As a consequence, Japanese civil procedure lacks administrative devices analogous to protective orders, *in camera* proceedings, and the sealing of the trial record.

One protective provision of the Japanese Code of Civil Procedure allows a witness to refuse to reveal trade secrets in testimony. In some circumstances, evidence may also be examined *in camera* under a separate provision of the Japanese Code of Civil Procedure. The benefit to the trade secret owner is limited, however, because the transcript of an *in camera* hearing is required to be submitted to the court for inclusion in the public record.

7. *Alternative Dispute Resolution Methods*

A public trial and a public record may be avoided by resolving disputes through negotiation, conciliation or arbitration. It must be noted that in Japan, negotiation, conciliation, and arbitration efforts are practically obligatory. As a result, courts expect every alternative be exhausted before litigation is initiated. For example, in 1985, the means by which trial level proceedings were resolved in the district courts of Japan were as follows: conciliation—31.2%; default judgments—25.2%; voluntary dismissals of claim by plaintiff—18.6%; settlements in favor of plaintiffs—1.3%; court orders for relief—0.5%; court rulings on liability on the merits—0.4%; abandonment of claim by plaintiff—0.1%; and other—22.7%.

The first level of dispute resolution involves negotiation between the parties. When these negotiations break down, neutral outside parties are then added to the process as the dispute enters either arbitration or conciliation.

Conciliation is the most common way of resolving disputes in Japan. There are two types of conciliation: in-court compromise and post-action conciliation. In post-action conciliation, two nonjudicial conciliators negotiate until the parties agree on a solution, which is then examined by a judge for legality. This method allows all parties to save face, as each side can partially accommodate the other without having to assign blame. Unlike arbitration, any solution reached through conciliation becomes an executable court judgment simply by being recorded in a protocol by a court clerk. Further, conciliation cannot be agreed to as a form of dispute resolution at the time a contract or other relationship is formed. Both conciliation and arbitration are informal, private methods of dispute resolution.

Arbitration is well established in the rules of the American Arbitration Association and the Japan Commercial Arbitration Association and is frequently stipulated in contracts as the principal means of dispute resolution.

8. *Employee Nondisclosure Agreements and Covenants Not to Compete*

In Japan, statutory law forbids directors, managers, and commercial agents from appropriating the corporate opportunities of their companies. However, all other employees are not so restricted, except through contractual agreements between the employer and the employee. Similar to U.S. law requiring restrictive covenants to be reasonable, employee agreements not to compete or disclose trade secrets may be held invalid in Japan if they unreasonably restrict an employee's right to continued employment or to choose a future occupation. In a 1970 case, an employee argued that the restrictive agreement at issue was against "public order and good morals."[191] The employee further argued that the agreement was void because it was not limited geographically, paid no compensation during the period of the restriction, and prevented the employee from earning a living by not allowing employment in any business of the same kind for two years. However, the court refused to invalidate the agreement, finding the two year duration of the restriction to be sufficiently limited, the business preclusion narrow as it covered only the employer's field, and the unlimited geographical reach of the agreement necessary due to the nature of the trade secrets being protected. The consideration of temporal and geographical limits in an agreement not to compete or disclose is in accord with U.S. common law.

---

[191] [Teruo Doi, The Intellectual Property Law of Japan 91–92 (citing Judgment of Oct. 23, 1970 (Yūgen Kaisha Forseco Japan, Ltd. v. Okuno), [Nara] Chisai [District Court], 624 HANJI 78 (Japan)).]

9. *Criminal Sanctions*

Trade secret misappropriation is not commonly prosecuted through criminal sanctions in either Japan or the United States, as such prosecution is considered ineffective. Criminal punishment of misappropriating individuals, without also prosecuting or enjoining the users or buyers of the trade secrets, is an inadequate remedy for industrial espionage.

In the United States, while trade secrets are recognized in every state as property that may be protected from theft, the manner in which legislatures chose to protect them varies according to the state. Fourteen states have statutes specifically covering theft of trade secrets; eight states include trade secrets as valuable property in their statutes governing crimes against property; two states include trade secrets in their computer crime statutes; two states list trade secrets separately from other property in their larceny statutes; and twenty-four states and the District of Columbia make no explicit mention of trade secrets in their penal statutes. In these last twenty-five jurisdictions, a plaintiff must convince a court that trade secrets fit within the definition of property before being able to prosecute misappropriation of trade secrets using general theft of property statutes.

At present, there is no explicit provision under Japanese law for criminal sanctions for trade secret misappropriation. Like courts in the United States, Japanese courts have ordered criminal sanctions for willful trade secret violations under legal theories such as embezzlement, breach of trust, larceny, and receiving stolen property. Two sections of the draft act for amending the Japanese Criminal Code which were proposed in 1974 provided for limited criminal sanctions against officers, employees, and persons who were in breach of a confidential relationship. These proposals called for up to three years imprisonment and a fine of up to ¥500,000 (approximately $4000). These draft provisions faced strong opposition and were never enacted.

10. *Statute of Limitations*

The UTSA sets a three year statute of limitations for bringing an action for misappropriation of a trade secret. Under the amended Japanese law, a similar cause of action expires three years after the discovery of an unfair act or ten years after the initial unfair act in cases of continuing violations.

BP Chemicals Limited v. Jiangsu
Sopo Corporation

United States District Court, E.D. Missouri, Eastern Division, 2006.
429 F.Supp.2d 1179.

PERRY, DISTRICT JUDGE.

Defendant Jiangsu Sopo Corporation ("SOPO") seeks dismissal of this case on the grounds of international comity and *forum non conveniens,* or a stay on the grounds of international abstention. SOPO also seeks a judgment on the pleadings or summary judgment on plaintiff BP Chemicals's Lanham Act and Missouri Uniform Trade Secrets Act claims.

I previously denied SOPO's motion to dismiss for *forum non conveniens,* but SOPO argues that things have changed since that decision. Specifically, SOPO argues that BP's filing suit against it in a Chinese court shows that the Chinese forum is adequate and more convenient. I disagree, and continue to hold that the courts of China would not provide an adequate forum for BP's claims against SOPO. Nor do I find that the circumstances of this case justify a stay of this proceeding on the grounds of international abstention.

I agree with SOPO, however, that the Lanham Act, even in conjunction with the Paris Convention, does not provide a federal cause of action for trade secret misappropriation, and so I will grant SOPO's motion for judgment on Counts II and VI. I also agree with SOPO that BP's claim under the Missouri Uniform Trade Secrets Act must fail because it is based on allegations of misappropriation that began before MUTSA was effective. I will therefore grant the motion for judgment on the pleadings as to Count III.

I. *Background*

This case has twice already gone to the Court of Appeals, and the reported decisions, *BP Chemicals Ltd. v. Jiangsu Sopo Corp.,* 285 F.3d 677 (8th Cir. 2002) *(BP I)* and *BP Chemicals, Ltd. v. Jiangsu SOPO Corp. (Group),* 420 F.3d 810 (8th Cir. 2005) *(BP II),* set out its factual and procedural background.

Plaintiff BP Chemicals Ltd. is a British corporation with its principal place of business in London, England. Among other businesses, BP is involved in the design and construction of commercial plants used to manufacture acetic acid through a process known as methanol carbonylation. Since BP acquired the rights in 1986, it has licensed rights to use its methanol carbonylation process to other acetic acid plants in numerous countries. BP has taken extensive steps to maintain the proprietary nature of its acetic acid technology.

Defendant Jiangsu SOPO Corporation (Group) Ltd. is a Chinese state-owned petrochemical company. SOPO is the owner of the "921 plant," which is an acetic acid plant located in Zhenjiang City, Jiangsu

Province, People's Republic of China. Production at the 921 plant began in 1998. SOPO is a large enterprise which has significant ties to the local Chinese Communist Party.

BP alleges that SOPO, acting with others, unlawfully obtained access to BP's acetic acid technology and that SOPO copied the specifications for its 921 plant from one of BP's licensed plants in Asia. According to BP, SOPO disclosed the wrongfully acquired trade secrets to a number of vendors in the United States, who used BP's stolen trade secrets to fabricate and provide items for SOPO's use in the 921 plant.

In March 2004, I denied SOPO's motion to dismiss, which alleged immunity under the Foreign Sovereign Immunities Act and lack of personal jurisdiction. I also denied SOPO's request for dismissal on grounds of *forum non conveniens*. Based on an extensive evidentiary record, I concluded that the courts of China would not provide an adequate forum for BP's claims and that, even if China were an adequate alternative forum, the balance of public and private interests weighed in BP's favor. SOPO appealed the jurisdictional ruling, and the Eighth Circuit, in *BP II*, affirmed my ruling on both FSIA immunity and personal jurisdiction, and remanded for further proceedings. The *forum non conveniens* decision was not considered in the appeal.

While the appeal was pending, BP filed suit in the Shanghai High People's Court in the People's Republic of China against SOPO and others. The bill of indictment requests the court to order defendants to: (1) immediately stop infringing BP's business secrets; (2) immediately stop infringing BP's copyright; (3) pay compensation for BP's loss; (4) publicly apologize to BP; and (5) bear the legal costs and attorney's fees of the Chinese court action. On September 8, 2005, the Chinese court accepted the case and issued a Notice of Response to Action.

After this case had been remanded from the Eighth Circuit, SOPO moved to dismiss on international comity or *forum non conveniens* grounds, citing BP's recent filing in China. Alternatively, SOPO seeks a stay on the grounds of international abstention, pending the conclusion of the Shanghai suit.

II.   *Motion to Dismiss or Stay*

A.   International Comity

SOPO argues that I should defer to the Chinese court that is now considering BP's new case. It contends that international comity requires this Court to show respect to foreign nations and to avoid litigation in two court systems that could lead to conflicting judgments.

The Supreme Court has explained international comity as "the recognition which one nation allows within its territory to the legislative, executive, or judicial acts of another nation, having due regard both to international duty and convenience, and to the rights of its own citizens, or of other persons who are under the protection of its laws." *Hilton v. Guyot,* 159 U.S. 113, 164, 16 S.Ct. 139, 40 L.Ed. 95 (1895). " 'Comity refers to deference to another sovereign's definite law or judicial decision' and not to pending proceedings." *Abdullah Sayid Rajab Al-Rifai & Sons W.L.L. v. McDonnell Douglas Foreign Sales Corp.,* 988 F.Supp. 1285, 1290 n. 3 (E.D.Mo. 1997)

Because no definite judicial decision has been reached in the Shanghai Court action, international comity does not apply. Even the case cited by SOPO in its memorandum in support, *Turner Entm't Co. v. Degeto Film GmbH* [25 F.3d 1512 (11th Cir. 1994)], discussed comity in the context of deference to a judgment on the merits that had been reached in a foreign court. International comity suggests deference to judicial decisions, not to pending actions.

B. Forum Non Conveniens

The doctrine of *forum non conveniens* requires a balancing of "the plaintiff's privilege of choosing his forum . . . against that forum's convenience for the parties and the court." 5B Charles Alan Wright & Arthur R. Miller, *Federal Practice and Procedure* § 1352 (3d ed. 2004). The balance must be strongly in favor of the defendant in order to upset plaintiff's choice of forum. Based on the presumption that an alternative adequate forum exists, the *forum non conveniens* decision requires analysis of private and public factors.

In my March 29, 2004 Order I examined in great detail the application of the doctrine of *forum non conveniens* to the facts of this case. Most of SOPO's newly-filed evidence is redundant of evidence submitted earlier and presents little change to the analysis of the public and private interest factors. The only new information that is material to this analysis is the notice of a parallel proceeding, voluntarily filed by BP and currently pending in Shanghai High People's Court.

SOPO argues that BP is estopped from challenging the adequacy of the Chinese court system since it voluntarily filed suit there. SOPO cites cases where the foreign proceeding was filed before the U.S. court proceeding. The cases SOPO cites are unlike this one because here suit was originally filed in the United States, and the Chinese suit was not filed until six years later.

One of the private interest factors in the *forum non conveniens* analysis is the level of deference due to the plaintiff's choice of forum. According to the Supreme Court, "unless the balance is strongly in favor of the defendant, the plaintiff's choice of forum should rarely be disturbed." *Gulf Oil,* 330 U.S. at 508, 67 S.Ct. 839. Some cases decided after *Gulf Oil* have held that foreign plaintiffs are entitled to less deference in their choice of forum than plaintiffs who are citizens or residents of the United States. As I noted in footnote 1 of my March 29, 2004 Order, however, and as is discussed in more detail *infra,* the Paris Convention requires that foreign nationals be given the same rights as citizens in bringing suits such as this, and BP's choice is entitled to the same deference as a U.S. citizen's would receive.

BP's filing suit against SOPO in a Chinese court after arguing to this Court that it could not get a fair trial there could be interpreted as forum shopping. The Supreme Court has pointed out that one of many attractive factors of American courts to foreign plaintiffs is that generally "discovery is more extensive in American than in foreign courts." *Piper,* 454 U.S. at 252 n. 18, 102 S.Ct. 252. According to the Second Circuit's sliding-scale method for evaluating the level of deference, the more it appears that plaintiff's choice of forum is based on forum-shopping reasons, the less deference should be given to that choice. SOPO argues that BP is now simply using this case to obtain discovery it could not get in China. I do not know BP's motivation for filing the new Chinese suit, but its actions in this case convince me that it is vigorously seeking to enforce its rights under American law, and that it is not improperly forum shopping.

The parallel proceeding in China does not change the inadequacy of the Chinese forum for a trial of BP's claims. No matter how the *forum non conveniens* public and private factors are affected, this case continued to present one of the rare situations where no adequate alternative forum exists. SOPO carries the burden of persuasion in proving "all elements necessary for the court to dismiss a claim based on *forum non conveniens.*" *Reid-Walen,* 933 F.2d at 1393. SOPO has not met that burden, and I will deny the motion to dismiss.

C.   International Abstention

As an alternative to dismissal, SOPO seeks a stay of this matter on the grounds of international abstention, pending a resolution of the dispute filed by BP in China.[1] Generally, parallel proceedings on the same claims should be allowed to proceed simultaneously. *See Abdullah,* 988 F.Supp. at 1291. However, a federal court may stay an action in favor of pending foreign litigation "in the interests of judicial economy and international relations." *Id.* Multiple factors should be evaluated in determining whether a stay based on international abstention is appropriate, including: "the similarity of the two actions, the degree of progress already made in the [foreign] action, the adequacy and appropriateness of the [foreign] forum, and notions of international comity and judicial efficiency." *Boushel v. Toro Co.,* 985 F.2d 406, 410 n. 2 (8th Cir. 1993).

1.   The Similarity of the Two Actions

SOPO argues that BP's Chinese claims fully encompass those at issue here. BP responds that the claims brought in this case are "U.S.-based claims" that arise under U.S. law and are founded on the wrongful disclosure of trade secrets to U.S. vendors. It argues that the claims brought in the Shanghai Court are "China-based claims" that are

---

[1]   Dismissal on the grounds of international abstention would not be appropriate here because BP seeks monetary relief, not equitable or discretionary relief. *See Abdullah,* 988 F.Supp. at 1290–91 ("The Eighth Circuit has recognized that in actions at law, the court does not have power to dismiss an action based on abstention principles.")

founded on the wrongful acquisition of trade secrets, including the theft of the secrets and the ongoing misuse of them.

In both cases, foreign and domestic, BP seeks relief for the injury it has suffered as a result of the alleged misappropriation of trade secrets used in the creation of the 921 plant. The Bill of Indictment from the Shanghai Court action states claims based on the misappropriation of the same trade secrets. These lawsuits are sufficiently similar actions for purposes of international abstention. The issues and parties are substantially similar such that this factor of the analysis favors the granting of a stay.

2. Degree of Progress Already Made in the Other Action

SOPO submitted a declaration from a Chinese law professor familiar with China's judicial system who states that most cases involving foreign parties are adjudicated within one year of acceptance by a Chinese court. If this is correct, the Shanghai Court would rule by Fall of 2006 on BP's claims, while the case here is not set for trial until September of 2007. However, the law professor admits that there is *no* time limit under China's laws of civil procedure for cases involving a foreign party. The previous proceeding in Zhenjiang Intermediate Court, filed by SOPO against BP, took over three years for resolution. Additionally, the only reason this case is set for the Fall of 2007 is that the parties indicated they needed that amount of time for discovery and trial preparation. My trial docket is not at all congested, and I could reach the case for trial much sooner if the parties were ready.

The Shanghai Court action was filed on July 25, 2005. The action pending in this Court was filed on February 26, 1999. Despite the Chinese law professor's declaration, there is no reason for this Court to believe that the proceeding in China has progressed further than has this case. This factor does not favor a stay.

3. The Adequacy and Appropriateness of the Foreign Forum

As stated in my analysis of *forum non conveniens,* the courts in China are not an adequate forum for the adjudication of BP's stated claims. Just because a court in China may resolve a matter more expeditiously does not make it the more adequate and appropriate forum. This factor weighs against a stay of this case.

4. Judicial Efficiency and Deference to Foreign Proceedings

As stated above, principles of international comity do not apply here because no formal judgment has been reached in the Shanghai Court action. A stay of this action will not promote judicial efficiency. Although the actions are similar, resolution of the issues in the Chinese court would not resolve the issue here of wrongful disclosure of trade secrets to U.S. vendors. Additionally, there are no complex issues of local Chinese law present in this case that would suggest this Court should defer to the Chinese court for evaluation. The claims here are based on U.S., not Chinese, law.

Overall three of the four factors for international abstention suggest that a stay is not appropriate in this case. SOPO's motion to dismiss or stay will be denied.

III. *Motion for Judgment on the Pleadings or Summary Judgment*

A.   Lanham Act Claims

. . . Count II of BP's complaint alleges that SOPO's misappropriation of trade secrets is actionable unfair competition under the Lanham Act and the Paris Convention. SOPO moves for judgment on this claim and on the related claim for attorneys' fees in Count VI.

BP argues that the combination of Section 44 of the Lanham Act and the Paris Convention confers a federal right to sue for acts of unfair competition and "invoke[s] federal and state law rights and remedies in pursuing a federal cause of action in federal court." BP goes on to allege that misappropriation of trade secrets in violation of Missouri law constitutes an act "contrary to honest practices" covered by the Paris Convention. Understanding how BP can argue that the Lanham Act gives it the right to sue for misappropriation of trade secrets requires following a somewhat confusing statutory path.

Section 44(b) of the Lanham Act refers to foreign nationals whose country is party to a convention or treaty with the United States:

> Any person whose country of origin is a party to any convention or treaty relating to trademarks, trade or commercial names, or the repression of unfair competition, to which the United States is also a party, or extends reciprocal rights to nationals of the United States by law, shall be *entitled to the benefits of this section* under the conditions expressed herein *to the extent necessary to give effect to any provision of such convention,* treaty or reciprocal law, *in addition to* the rights to which any owner of a mark is otherwise entitled by this chapter.

15 U.S.C. § 1126(b) (emphasis added). Section 44(h) then refers back to subsection (b): Any person designated in subsection (b) of this section as entitled to the benefits and subject to the provisions of this chapter shall be entitled to *effective protection against unfair competition,* and the remedies provided in this chapter for infringement of marks shall be available so far as they may be appropriate in repressing acts of unfair competition. 15 U.S.C. § 1126(h) (emphasis added).

The Paris Convention for the Protection of Industrial Property, to which the United States and the United Kingdom are parties, requires signatory nations to prohibit unfair competition:

> (1) The countries of the Union are bound to assure to nationals of such countries effective protection against unfair competition.

(2) Any act of competition *contrary to honest practices* in industrial or commercial matters constitutes an act of unfair competition.

July 14, 1967, art. 10*bis*, 21 U.S.T. 1583 (emphasis added).

The argument that the combination of the Paris Convention and the Lanham Act creates a federal claim for unfair competition has been considered by a number of different courts, and, depending on the context of the cases, those courts have reached different results. Having reviewed the cases, arguments, and—most importantly—the statutory language, I conclude that the Lanham Act incorporates the substantive law of the treaties to which it refers, in this case the Paris Convention, and provides foreign nationals the rights available under that treaty. The Paris Convention, however, does not create a general tort of unfair competition, and it therefore provides BP no protection against trade secret misappropriation. Additionally, to the extent that BP argues that the Paris Convention somehow incorporates the state law of unfair competition, which can then be brought as a Lanham Act claim, I disagree.

According to its plain terms, the Lanham Act's protections only extend to infringement of registered trademarks, false designation of the origin of goods, and false advertising. In the decade or two after the Lanham Act was initially passed, courts defined the scope of the Act by rejecting a variety of arguments that it created a federal claim for unfair competition, providing protection beyond the express terms of the Act. . . . The cases involved only domestic litigants. Later cases involving foreign national parties required courts to examine the interplay between the Lanham Act and international treaties, and to determine if together they create a federal cause of action for unfair competition.

For example, in a case relied on by both parties in their briefs, *Toho Co., Ltd. v. Sears, Roebuck & Co.*, the Ninth Circuit analyzed the relationship between § 44 of the Lanham Act and the Treaty of Friendship, Commerce and Navigation entered into between the United States and Japan. 645 F.2d 788, 792 (9th Cir. 1981). *Toho* was a suit by the Japanese owner of "Godzilla" movies and merchandise against an American company who marketed "Bagzilla" garbage bags. The Ninth Circuit held that there was no likelihood that consumers would be confused about the origin of the goods. It dismissed the plaintiff's claims under § 43(a) of the Lanham Act, and also held that the defendant had not violated California's anti-dilution statute or California's common-law prohibition on misappropriation. In terms of the relationship between § 44 of the Lanham Act and the Treaty of Friendship, Commerce and Navigation, the court concluded that the treaty required "only that Japanese companies be treated as favorably as domestic companies." It then went on to hold that since domestic companies have protection under state laws of unfair competition, "the practical effect of section 44 and this treaty is to provide a federal forum in which Toho can pursue its state claims." 645 F.2d at 793. Because the plaintiff could not recover under California law, however, it had no remedy under the Lanham Act.

The language of *Toho* supports the positions of both parties in this case, although both also seek to distinguish it, and even the Ninth Circuit has limited its application to its facts. To the extent that *Toho* interprets and applies the Lanham Act alone, it has relevance to this case. Its analysis of the interaction of the Treaty of Friendship with the Lanham Act is not applicable to this case however, because this case involves the Paris Convention. More recent cases have looked at whether § 44 provides "national treatment"—giving the foreign national the same rights afforded U.S. citizens—or creates new federal rights for foreign nationals and/or U.S. citizens, and many of those cases have specifically considered the Paris Convention.

According to the cases following the national treatment approach, the Lanham Act incorporates the provisions of the Paris Convention, but only to give foreign nationals the same rights that U.S. citizens have under the Act. All of these cases cite to an earlier Second Circuit case, *Vanity Fair Mills, Inc. v. T. Eaton Co.,* 234 F.2d 633 (2d Cir. 1956), for their underlying interpretation of the Paris Convention.

According to *Vanity Fair,* the Paris Convention's purpose was to require signatory nations to provide the same treatment to foreign nationals as they provide their own citizens:

> The [Paris] Convention is essentially a compact between the various member countries to accord in their own countries to citizens of the other contracting parties trade-mark and other rights comparable to those accorded their own citizens by their domestic law. The underlying principle is that foreign nationals should be given the same treatment in each of the member countries as that country makes available to its own citizens.

234 F.2d at 640. This underlying principle is derived from the Convention's provision establishing equal treatment for foreign nationals: Nationals of any country of the Union shall, as regards the protection of industrial property, enjoy in all the other countries of the Union the advantages that their respective laws now grant, or may hereafter grant, to nationals . . . Consequently, they shall have the same protection as the latter, and the same legal remedy against any infringement of their rights . . .

Courts following *Vanity Fair* have concluded that the "Paris Convention does not provide substantive rights but ensures 'national treatment.'" *Mattel,* 296 F.3d at 908. So if the Lanham Act alone does not provide protection against misappropriation of trade secrets for U.S. citizens, it does not provide any greater protection for foreign nationals under the Paris Convention.

A few courts have applied the new federal rights approach, and have held that substantive rights are created by the Paris Convention's broad statement that signatories must provide "effective protection against unfair competition." Article 10bis.

The language of § 44(b) of the Lanham Act gives foreign nationals whose countries are parties to treaties rights "in addition to" the rights to which they would otherwise be entitled under the Lanham Act. This "in addition to" language, along with § 44(h), must have been intended to give foreign nationals something more than regular rights under the Lanham Act. So to the extent that the new federal rights approach finds that the protections of the Lanham Act could be expanded by a treaty or convention, I agree. But on the next analytical step, I agree with the national treatment cases' conclusion that the Paris Convention does not create new rights; it only requires equal treatment.

Section 44 provides a new federal cause of action only to the extent the Paris Convention or some other treaty would provide such a right. The "unfair competition" language contained in both the Paris Convention and in § 44(h) does not specify what types of unfair competition are referred to, and there is no reference to misappropriation of trade secrets. Although the Convention refers to "any act contrary to honest practices," this language is too general to include all possible torts of unfair competition recognized by any state's common or statutory law. Neither the Lanham Act nor the Paris Convention makes any reference to state law, and again, the reference simply to "unfair competition" is not sufficient to incorporate all fifty states' laws of unfair competition into the Lanham Act. The Paris Convention forbids national discrimination, but it does not give foreign nationals or those suing them greater rights than domestic litigants have.

I conclude that the Lanham Act and Paris Convention do not create a cause of action for misappropriation of trade secrets, and so I will grant judgment on the pleadings to SOPO on Counts II and VI, which are BP's claims arising under the Lanham Act.

B. MUTSA Claims

[The court's judgment for SOPO on BP's Missouri Uniform Trade Secrets Act claim is omitted.]

IV. Conclusion

Dismissal based on *forum non conveniens* continues to be inappropriate in this case. The courts of China are an inadequate alternative forum and the balance of public and private interests are not strongly in favor of SOPO. Also, dismissal based on international comity is not suitable here because formal judgment has not been rendered in the alternative forum. Based on a weighing of the factors for international abstention, I will not enter a stay in this case. This Court has already invested significant time and resources into this case, while the Shanghai action has only recently been filed. However, I will grant SOPO's request for judgment on the pleadings as to BP's Lanham Act and MUTSA claims.

Notes

1. *TRIPs.* Historically, civil law countries have protected interests in undisclosed information under the general rubric of unfair competition and the Paris Convention standard of "honest practices in industrial or commercial matters." Common law countries protect undisclosed information under theories of contract and property. Contract theory typically governs cases involving appropriation of trade secrets in violation of a confidential relationship, while property theory covers trade secret appropriations by unrelated parties. The difference between civil law and common law approaches will sometimes be consequential. For example, in common law countries that treat undisclosed information as property, a trade secret owner can obtain relief not only against the thief or spy himself, but also against third parties who come into possession of the information from him. Civil law countries typically bar relief in these circumstances because the third party has not itself engaged in dishonest practices.

TRIPs Article 39's minimum standards of protection significantly trims the robust, property-based standard that the United States initially proposed for trade secrets in the TRIPs Agreement and effectively strikes a balance between the civil law and common law positions. Footnote 10, defining "a manner contrary to honest commercial practices," significantly limits third-party liability to those "who knew, or were grossly negligent in failing to know," that dishonest practices were involved in acquiring the information in issue. Several developing countries invoked the civil law theory of protection to argue that, because it was not property, undisclosed information could not be the subject of intellectual property and for that reason fell outside the scope of the TRIPs Agreement. The compromise, which tied Article 39's legitimacy as a source of intellectual property norms to Article 10*bis* of the Paris Convention, also underscored the lack of a property dimension to the provision's protection of undisclosed information.

See generally, Rudolf Krasser, The Protection of Trade Secrets in the TRIPs Agreement, in Friedrich-Karl Beier & Gerhard Schricker, eds., From GATT to TRIPs—The Agreement on Trade-Related Aspects of Intellectual Property Rights 216 (1996). *See* also Nathan Greene, Enforceability of the People's Republic of China's Trade Secret Law: Impact on Technology Transfer in the PRC and Preparing for Successful Licensing, 44 IDEA 437 (2004); Robin J. Effron, Secrets and Spies: Extraterritorial Application of the Espionage Act and the TRIPs Agreement, 78 N.Y.U. L. Rev. 1475 (2003).

2. *Trade Secrets in the U.S.* Trade secret protection in the United States, long the preserve of state law—first under the Restatement of Torts and subsequently under the widely-adopted Uniform Trade Secrets Act—has more recently been fortified by federal legislation. The Economic Espionage Act of 1996 outlawed trade secret thefts committed "with intent to convert a trade secret, that is related to or included in a product that is produced or placed in interstate or foreign commerce, to the economic benefit of anyone other than the owner thereof, and intending or knowing that the offense will injure any owner of that trade secret." The 2016 Defend Trade Secrets Act added civil remedies to the criminal penalties specified in the 1996 legislation and introduced provisions dealing with some more contemporary concerns such as *ex parte* seizure of secret information and protection for corporate whistleblowers.

3. *Trade Secrets in the European Union.* Directive 2016/943 on the protection of undisclosed know-how and business information (trade secrets) against their unlawful acquisition, use and disclosure generally harmonizes minimum standards for national trade secret protection in the European Union around the framework of TRIPs Article 39, including provision for rights against third parties. The Directive prescribes civil, but not criminal, remedies and in Article 1 carves out important exceptions for "the exercise of the right to freedom of expression and information as set out in the Charter [of Fundamental Rights]" and the "application of Union or national rules requiring trade secret holders to disclose, for reasons of public interest, information, including trade secrets, to the public or to administrative or judicial authorities for the performance of the duties of those authorities." Further, "[n]othing in this Directive shall be understood to offer any ground for restricting the mobility of employees," including "limiting employees' use of experience and skill honestly acquired in the normal course of their employment."

See Sharon K. Sandeen, Implementing the EU Trade Secret Directive: A View from the United States, 39 EIPR 4 (2017).

4. *See* generally, Elizabeth A. Rowe & Sharon K. Sandeen, Trade Secrecy and International Transactions (2015); Rudolf Krasser, The Protection of Trade Secrets in the TRIPs Agreement, in Friedrich-Karl Beier & Gerhard Schricker, eds., From GATT to TRIPs—The Agreement on Trade-Related Aspects of Intellectual Property Rights 216 (1996). *See* also Nathan Greene, Enforceability of the People's Republic of China's Trade Secret Law: Impact on Technology Transfer in the PRC and Preparing for Successful Licensing, 44 IDEA 437 (2004); Robin J. Effron, Secrets and Spies: Extraterritorial Application of the Espionage Act and the TRIPs Agreement, 78 N.Y.U. L. Rev. 1475 (2003).

E. INDUSTRIAL DESIGN

Industrial design—the design, for a chair, say, or for a pair of running shoes—is the contested child of intellectual property law. Article 1(2) of the Paris Convention, 1967 Stockholm Act, identifies "industrial designs" as an object of industrial property protection subject to national treatment under Article 2 and, in Article 5 *quinquies,* specifically requires that "[i]ndustrial designs shall be protected in all countries of the Union." Articles 25–26 of the TRIPs Agreement also provide for the protection of industrial design.

Article 2(7) of the Berne Convention, 1971 Paris Act contemplates the possibility of copyright protection for industrial design, but reflects the ambivalence of many countries on the subject by providing that "it shall be a matter for legislation in the countries of the Union to determine the extent of the application of their laws to works of applied art and industrial designs and models, as well as the conditions under which such works, designs and models shall be protected. Works protected in the country of origin solely as designs and models shall be entitled in another country of the Union only to such special protection as is granted in that country to designs and models; however, if no such special protection is granted in that country, such works shall be protected as artistic works."

Historically, protection for industrial design was first connected to protection for artistic works. The first design legislation was a 1787 British Act "for the encouragement of the acts of designing and printing linens, cottons, calicoes and muslins," and was roughly modelled after copyright legislation of the day, though with a severely abbreviated term. Then, through what Stephen Ladas has characterized as a series of historical accidents, design protection evolved as a specialized branch of industrial property. According to Ladas, it was an 1806 French law aimed at complaints that copyright law insufficiently protected manufacturers—and that, as interpreted by French courts, separated industrial design from artistic design—that became the model for national legislation patterned after patent statutes. An historical accident in the United States, where until 1870 there was no centralized office for copyright deposits, contributed to Congress's decision in 1842 to lodge protection for industrial designs under the Patent Act, with deposits to be made in the U.S. Patent Office. Stephen Ladas, 2 Patents, Trademarks and Related Rights 829–830 (1975).

Many countries today protect industrial designs under registration statutes based on rudimentary patent law concepts. In the United States, the Design Patent Act, 35 U.S.C. §§ 171–173, authorizes design patents for anyone who "invents any new, original and ornamental design for an article of manufacture," subject to other provisions of the Patent Act generally; the term of protection is fifteen years from the date of the grant. Other design registration statutes impose only a novelty standard on protectible design, and many—unlike the U.S. statute—do not require examination as a condition to registration.

Despite the enactment of registration-based design legislation in many countries, industrial designs continue to be protected in these as well as other countries under copyright, trademark and unfair competition laws. In the United States, for example, industrial designs are protected to varying degrees under design patent law, copyright law and trademark and unfair competition law.

The Hague Agreement Concerning the International Deposit of Industrial Designs, which was adopted on November 6, 1925 and entered into force on June 1, 1928, enables nationals of Hague Union member countries to make a single design deposit with the International Bureau of the World Intellectual Property Organization in Geneva instead of making individual deposits—with the attendant applications, national fees and translation expenses—in each state in which it seeks protection.

The Locarno Agreement Establishing an International Classification for Industrial Designs, which entered into force on April 27, 1971, provides for a system of classifying designs to expedite novelty and infringement searches. Only members of the Paris Union may belong to the Hague Union or the Locarno Union.

Bibliographic Note. Katrine A. Levin & Monica B. Richman, A Survey of Industrial Design Protection in the European Union and the United States, 25 EIPR 111 (2003) provides a concise overview. Anne Marie Greene, Designs and Utility Models Throughout the World (1989), compiles summaries of design laws in force around the world. Uma Suthersanen, Design Law: European Union and United States of America (2d ed. 2010) is a comprehensive study. A dated, but still valuable, bibliography appears in U.S. Copyright Office, Bibliography on Design Protection (1955 & Supp. 1976). *See* also W.I.P.O., Guide to the International Deposit of Industrial Designs (under the Hague Agreement Concerning the International Deposit of Industrial Designs) (1994); A.L.A.I., The Protection of Designs and Models (1985); Design Protection (Herman Cohen Jehoram, ed. 1976); Christine Fellner, The Future of Legal Protection for Industrial Design (1985).

J.H. Reichman, Design Protection in Domestic and Foreign Copyright Law: From the Berne Revision of 1948 to the Copyright Act of 1976

1983 Duke Law Journal 1143, 1153–1170.

1.   *The Unity of Art Thesis in France.* The copyright approach to industrial art rests on the notion that ornamental designs of useful articles should not be denied protection as artistic works merely because of their industrial character. A cultural and political bias in favor of gratuitous art or "art for art's sake" fueled resistance to this proposition. It is now clear, however, that copyright protection of aesthetic designs affects competition between useful articles whose legal status is otherwise determined by the laws of industrial property. The laws governing industrial property, including patent, trademark and, since the eighteenth century, sui generis design laws, obey different legal principles that drive most useful articles toward free competition. As Madame Perot Morel observed in 1968, industrial art is a legal hybrid that different legal subcultures subject to conflicting and sometimes irreconcilable demands.

During the nineteenth century, French courts recognized that "art applied to industry" could aspire to legal protection as art. *Sui generis* design protection was also established in France at a very early date. For nearly a century, French courts and commentators struggled to establish a strict line of demarcation between designs that deserved protection as "pure art" under the French copyright law of 1793 and those that deserved only the protection afforded by the special design law of 1806. Between 1806 and 1902 France experimented with five different criteria for distinguishing the subject matter of these two regimes: 1) the method of reproduction, 2) the purpose or end use of the design, 3) the secondary or accessory character of the aesthetic features, 4) the status of the creator, and 5) the relative artistic value of the candidate design. French courts found all of these criteria difficult to apply; in the end, their inconsistent and increasingly arbitrary decisions paved the way for Pouillet's attack on the validity of drawing any line of demarcation whatsoever.

Pouillet and his followers argued that there could be no discrimination as to the degree of legal protection accorded different forms of aesthetic creativity, and that all creations were entitled to protection in the law of literary and artistic property:

> Whence comes the difficulty that is found in clearly defining the nature and character of the industrial design and model? It comes . . . from the fact that we have got it in our heads that art and industry, two things made to be allied and united, should be separated, and because we have dreamed of establishing a line of demarcation between them.

Pouillet therefore rejected all such distinctions as necessarily based on judges' subjective assessments of aesthetic merit:

> It is a remarkable thing that as long as the question is that of appreciating a work conceived through the inspiration of purely abstract and speculative thought, everyone is in agreement concerning the principle of the unity of art . . . but as soon as an application of art is involved, as soon as an immediate and direct use of the object appears indicated, then the most disparate opinions emerge and, with the help of strong feelings, the result is the worst inconsistencies and the most unexpected contradictions.

Pouillet's "theory of the unity of art" gained legislative recognition in both France and Belgium. Viewing attempts to establish a rational line of demarcation between the design law and the copyright law as futile, Pouillet maintained that decorators, painters, sculptors, and fashion designers were all artists whose works uniformly deserved to be governed by the copyright paradigm. Under Pouillet's influence, French copyright law, as amended in 1902, extended protection to "designers of ornaments, whatever may be the merit and the purpose of the work." By the 1930's, despite pockets of judicial resistance, French law had rejected every test of aesthetic creation that "would allow industrial art to be separated from real art." Consequently, originators of "all creations of form, even the most modest," obtain a generous bundle of economic and moral rights for a term of life plus fifty years from creation, and need not comply with any formal prerequisites whatsoever, such as notice, registration, or deposit.

Despite the triumph of the unity of art thesis, the French legislature did not repeal the special design law of 1806. Instead, the legislature passed the design law of July 14, 1909, still in force, which further refined the advantages conferred by sui generis legislation with respect to establishing proof of ownership, facilitating transfers of title, and restricting competition. The unity of art principle, expressly confirmed by the law of 1909 and later by the copyright law of March 11, 1957, gave designers and manufacturers the opportunity to cumulate the advantages of both acts without penalizing them for failing to take one route or the other in any given case. Provided that a design were registered under the design law of 1909, the provisions of this law might fully satisfy the owner's legal needs. If, for one reason or another, his attempt to invoke the design law proved abortive or otherwise insufficient, the owner could simultaneously invoke the protection of copyright law in the very action for infringement under the design law. If, finally, the creator had ignored the design law altogether, his entitlement to copyright protection from the date of creation would not suffer merely because special design protection might have been available had he taken the pains to meet the requirements of registration and deposit.

The unity of art thesis in France produced two results of primary importance from the comparative standpoint. First, it led France to extend copyright protection to all industrial art, including commercial designs "on the lower frontier of applied art" that "depend on what is called industrial aesthetics." Second, it led to gradual integration of the copyright law and the special design law into what is technically described as *a regime of absolute or total cumulation.*

2. *Revival of the Sui Generis Regime of Design Protection.* If Pouillet's "simple but seminal" idea eventually prevailed in France, the soundest writers caution that it was a victory by default rather than by persuasion. The chief virtue of this position was that it eliminated arbitrary distinctions between pure and industrial art that French jurisprudence found unworkable and then intolerable. Nevertheless, the "unity of art" theory continues to elicit skepticism even in France. Many of those moved by Pouillet's evocation of Bellini were dismayed to see the laws of literary and artistic property expand to protect the designs of such articles as plastic salad bowls, drinking glasses, fireplace grates, a hair brush, the luggage rack of a motor scooter, and the hexagonal head of a lubricating pump.

The unity of art doctrine glossed over the affinity of ornamental designs of useful articles to industrial property, an affinity recognized by the Paris Union at the International Convention for the Protection of Industrial Property in 1883. Arguably, France and Belgium, which had sought to rescue artistic designs from the exigencies of patent law, were now converting copyright law into a de facto industrial property law without the characteristic safeguards of the industrial property paradigm. Moreover, critics observed that many of the items that French copyright law protected displayed no aesthetic creativity whatsoever. Such claims, though open to debate in individual cases, reinforced suspicion that applied art suffered from a chronically low degree of creative content, due in part to the subordination of aesthetic features to technical exigencies and to the marketing methods characteristic of a consumer economy.

Other members of the Berne Union viewed with increasing diffidence this expansion of predictability in France and Belgium under the unity of art thesis. Opponents of the copyright approach intensified efforts to distinguish applied art from noncopyrightable "industrial designs" on conceptually tenable grounds. Two dominant positions emerged. One, typified by Italy, insisted on the "duality of art." On this view, ornamental designs were normally ineligible for copyright protection because their dependence on useful articles made them primarily objects of commerce and deprived them of the independent existence deemed a basic attribute of true works of art. The second position, typified by Germany, conceded copyright protection to a limited number of exceptional designs but rejected the rest as lacking the requisite degree of artistic intensity or value.

It should be stressed that countries opposed to the unity of art thesis did not automatically relegate designs excluded from copyright law to the public domain. Both Germany and Italy, while subscribing to different exclusionary criteria, agreed in principle that designs of useful articles should be regulated by sui generis design laws modeled on the French design law of 1806. These sui generis design laws placed ornamental designs within a hybrid legal framework, heavily influenced by patent law, that seemed consistent with the industrial character of the useful articles in which any artistic components were embodied.

The legal status of industrial art thus varied from country to country, despite the broad multilateral conventions that otherwise regulated artistic property on the one hand and industrial property on the other. The 1948 Brussels Conference to Revise the Berne Convention did not eliminate either the tension or the impediments to trade caused by such inconsistent treatment. Participants in the Conference were unable to reach a consensus regarding the unity of art thesis promoted by France. Consequently, their attempt to systematize the international regulation of industrial art ended in an awkward compromise.

Legitimation of applied art within the Berne Convention was a key element of this compromise. Works of applied art were expressly incorporated within the broad list of protectible subject matter set forth in article 2 of the 1948 revision. From the French perspective, this left no doubt that works of applied art were henceforth to be "viewed broadly as artistic works."

Adherents of other views succeeded in imposing two major reservations. Each country in which protection was sought acquired the right to limit the duration of copyrights in applied art. In addition, national governments retained authority to define the applied art to be protected by domestic copyright law, and to distinguish between this category of applied art and a subcategory of "designs and models" that could be subjected to more restrictive regimes. States electing to exercise this option could then deny copyright protection to a foreign design protected as applied art in the country of origin by finding that the design did not qualify as applied art under the territorial law of the receiving state. Moreover, in derogation of the basic right of national treatment under the Convention, a receiving state that might otherwise have recognized foreign designs as applied art under territorial law would nonetheless deny copyright protection if the designs were protectible only as "industrial designs or models" in the country of origin. In short, the 1948 text of the Berne Convention admitted applied art to full standing as copyrightable subject matter but authorized—or indeed invited— members to curb the excesses of the copyright approach by recourse to the kind of subsidiary legal framework that the Paris Convention for the Protection of Industrial Property had long recognized.

The decisions of the Brussels Conference in 1948 profoundly influenced the evolution of design protection law in both member and non-member countries. Within the Berne Union, the movement to absorb industrial designs and models into the law of artistic property lost a momentum it never regained. Sui generis design laws, long the "neglected relative" of industrial property law, were assigned a new role. The growing economic importance of design, the high costs of development and promotion, and the enormous losses from misappropriation in a field in which "counterfeiting is endemic" elicited pressures for more effective protection in every country, pressures that partly account for the spread of the copyright approach in the first instance. Special design laws could alleviate fears of overprotection and excessive restraints of trade evoked by this approach, and could provide legal safeguards lacking in copyright law. This, however, presupposed both modernization of these laws and their universal adoption.

The Lisbon Conference to Revise the Paris Convention took the first step in this direction in 1958 by adopting a new article providing that "industrial designs shall be protected in all the countries of the Union." All member countries were thereafter obliged to ensure a reasonable degree of design protection within the framework of the Paris Convention, although each country remained free to determine the nature, subject matter, and conditions of such protection. The second step was taken on November 28, 1960, with the revision and simplification of the Hague Arrangement of 1925, which permits a single international deposit of protected designs. The third step was to try to standardize national design legislation through a world-wide effort to develop a model design law, or at least an agreed set of principles that would further the goals of uniformity and modernization.

This reform movement culminated in the Tokyo Resolution of the International Association for the Protection of Industrial Property (AIPPI) in 1966 and in a new generation of design laws enacted in many countries. As late as 1968, Mme. Pérot-Morel pointed out that many important countries had no special design laws at all while most countries retained inadequate legislation. By 1978, Mme. Englert found the protection of industrial designs "in a state of radical change," as a result of which leading countries in all political and economic blocs, including the centrally planned economies and the developing countries, had either enacted new design laws or given high priority to the reform of existing laws.

It cannot be said, however, that these reform efforts have led to the coherent system of design regulation anticipated after the decisions of the Paris Union in 1958. The number of designs deposited under domestic design laws has been relatively small in relation to the number of designs launched on the market each year. Further, the technical solutions devised by various committees of experts have not succeeded in eliminating the drawbacks of the "patent approach" that traditionally make design protection costly, slow, and administratively inconvenient. as well as of uncertain legal effectiveness. Above all, the Berne Union's inability to establish a clear line of demarcation between applied art protectible in copyright law and industrial designs protectible in sui generis design law has undermined even those achievements that did emerge from twenty-five years of reform efforts.

3.   *The Intractable Problem of Cumulation.* The legal history of industrial art in the twentieth century may be viewed as a continuing effort to establish special regimes of design protection without unduly derogating from the general principles of copyright law. The difficulty of this task becomes apparent when it is recalled that, within the Berne Union, works of art original in the copyright sense obtain long-term protection without formalities, whereas under special design laws, only short-term protection is normally available for novel and qualitatively original designs deposited or registered prior to divulgation. Even the most technically refined design laws can govern only those designs that fall within their jurisdictional sweep. The harder a country makes it to obtain copyright protection for industrial art, the more that country's special design law may determine the scope of the design protection actually available within that system. If a country makes it easy for industrial art to qualify for copyright protection as applied art, designers will have less incentive to make use of a special design law and design protection will increasingly be characterized by the copyright approach. The true scope and effectiveness of any given design law will therefore depend on the extent to which the scope of protection it affords, and the conditions it imposes, are undermined by the concurrent availability of copyright protection for industrial art. At the same time, measures

needed to limit concurrent protection are likely to derogate from general principles of copyright law.

Hindsight suggests that the reform of sui generis design laws after 1958 was thwarted by the decisions made at Brussels in 1948, which hardened the preexisting attitudes toward applied art and converted cumulation into "the biggest problem of all for the protection of designs and models." *Cumulation* means that concurrent protection is available for ornamental designs of useful articles in copyright and special design law. When concurrent protection is always possible, as in the French regime of absolute cumulation, special design laws serve as optional methods of augmenting manufacturers' rights, without forfeiting protection against copying under the law of artistic property. When, as in the Italian regime of noncumulation, there is virtually no possibility of concurrent protection for ornamental designs and models, short-term protection in a special design law becomes the only safe route regardless of the degree of artistic content. Italian manufacturers locked into the design law can lose all protection if they fail to meet its formal and substantive prerequisites, which reflect a modified patent law paradigm. When partial cumulation is practiced, as in the Federal Republic of Germany, the Benelux countries, and the Scandinavian countries, manufacturers occasionally obtain copyright protection for designs and models that manifest exceptional creativity. As a rule, however, systems that allow partial cumulation attempt to relegate most industrial art to special design laws despite general principles of copyright law that prohibit legal discrimination on the basis of artistic merit.

Three options—cumulation, noncumulation and partial cumulation—have thus continued to exist in the Berne Union's intellectual property law system after the Brussels Conference of 1948. Some countries have shifted allegiance over the course of time, notably the United Kingdom and the Benelux group. The choices among these options made by different countries reflect more than domestic self-interest; they also reflect fundamental differences of principle concerning both the nature of art and the proper limits of protection for intellectual property, which differences are exacerbated by the hybrid nature of industrial art. Until they are resolved or tempered by compromise, no international system of design protection can fulfill its goals, despite continuing efforts at harmonization and reform. . . .

J.H. Reichman, Design Protection After the Copyright Act of 1976: A Comparative View of the Emerging Interim Models

31 Journal of the Copyright Society of the U.S.A. 267, 268–271, 365–373 (1983).

At the Brussels Revision Conference of 1948, the Berne Union Countries extended the Berne Convention's coverage of copyrightable subject matter to "works of applied art," but allowed member countries to distinguish between this category and a subcategory of "designs and models." Under the Revised Convention, works of applied art enter the domestic copyright laws of member states without formalities; they obtain moral rights and, as a rule, the long term of protection accorded other forms of artistic property. Non-copyrightable ornamental designs can obtain short-term protection under sui generis design laws. However, the Brussels Conference could not agree upon a criterion to determine the line of demarcation between "works of applied art" and non-copyrightable "designs and models." The leading member countries are still divided into three camps according to their willingness to tolerate *cumulation*, that is, concurrent protection in copyright law for ornamental designs otherwise subject to sui generis design laws. France, faithful to a unity of art philosophy, allows total cumulation between the two protective schemes; hence, ornamental designs routinely acquire copyright protection. Italy, following a theory of dissociation, maintains a regime of *non-cumulation* in which a criterion of *scindibiltà* or "separability" excludes virtually all modern designs from any protection in copyright law. The Federal Republic of Germany, and more recently the Benelux countries, have pursued regimes of partial cumulation that permit some exceptionally creative designs to obtain protection under copyright law while confining the rest to sui generis design laws.

In the United States, after the Supreme Court had recognized applied art in the 1954 case of *Mazer v. Stein*, Register Arthur Fisher endorsed a proposal, in 1959, that would have confined virtually all ornamental designs to a sui generis regime built mainly on copyright principles. This approach yielded to a compromise in which the Copyright Office accepted a version of the Italian model, based on the criterion of separability, as articulated in Regulation Section 202.10(c) of 1959. This compromise was part of an effort to expedite passage of a sui generis design bill that would have operated side by side with the existing design patent law. By the 1970s, when no such bill had been passed, the evidence suggests that the Copyright Office was prepared to switch to a regime of partial cumulation made possible, from 1969 on by the integration of the copyright bill (Title I) and the design bill (Title II) into a single revision bill.

However, district court decisions in 1976 attacked the criterion of separability still operative in Regulation Section 202.10(c). These and other decisions, by combining *Bleistein v. Donaldson Lithographing Co.* with a broad reading of *Mazer v. Stein,* threatened to establish the unity of art thesis in United States laws copyright law on the eve of the 1976 Act. In order to block this development, the Copyright Office asked Congress to codify the criterion of separability in Sections 101 and 102(a)(5) of the pending revision bill. Thus, in 1976, the Copyright Office had embraced the Italian position of non-cumulation, as it had in 1959, in order to forestall a regime of total cumulation in the French tradition. When the general revision bill emerged from the various committees preparing the Final Act, it still subjected ornamental designs of useful articles to the criterion of separability; but the sui generis design bill, pending since 1959, had been deleted at the last minute. Congressional enactment of the Copyright Act of 1976 in this truncated form sanctioned an American regime of non-cumulation, built on the criterion of separability, without the special design law that was the natural complement of such regime.

This article describes the principal responses of courts and administrators to this dilemma from 1976 to the present day. In assessing these responses, it should be noted that a circular pattern can be discerned in the treatment of ornamental designs both here and abroad:

> Traditionally, the right to copyright protection is premised on a claim that certain industrial designs are entitled to legal recognition as art in the historical sense. The economic repercussions of such recognition flow principally from the industrial character of the material support in which ornamental designs are embodied. The incidence of these repercussions upon any given system vary with the extent to which the claim to recognition as art is itself given effect. As copyright protection for designs of useful articles expands, the economic effects of this expansion on the general products market induces countervailing pressures to reduce the scope of protection acquired in the name of art. As protection in copyright law correspondingly contracts, pressures for recognition of industrial art as a legally protectable form of industrial property normally increase. The tendency of industrial property law to breed still further instances of under-protection or over-protection then fosters renewed pressures for the regulation of industrial art within the framework of the laws governing literary and artistic property.

These insights serve to place the evolution of the copyright approach to ornamental designs in a world perspective and provide a unifying theme to account for what otherwise appear to be a series of actions and reactions in domestic law with no clear logic of their own. They also provide a basis for short term predictions and recommendations to assist the courts in dealing with the failure of the 1976 Act to adopt a coherent position concerning the protection of ornamental designs of useful articles. . . .

It has been demonstrated that neither the budding regime of partial cumulation in the Second Circuit nor the regime of non-cumulation established by the District of Columbia Circuit can be considered a legal anomaly. Both positions are grounded in legislative history and in logic; both share a common opposition to the unity of art thesis that flourished only yesterday in the United States and both correspond to major factions in foreign intellectual property law. Were the United States wholeheartedly to embrace one regime or another, it might indirectly influence the delicate and so far unsuccessful attempts to harmonize the treatment of applied art in the domestic copyright laws of the European Community. The question is, which, if any, of these regimes has the most to recommend it?

A.   *Inconclusive Lessons of the Competing Foreign Models*

While the division of the Berne Union into regimes of non-cumulation, partial cumulation, and total cumulation continues to reflect fundamental differences of principle concerning an appropriate legal response to the hybrid nature of industrial art, these differences have become more methodological than substantive with the passage of time. Supporters of the Italian regime of non-cumulation, for example, seek to reconcile their opposition to protecting ornamental designs of useful articles in copyright law with the disinclination to sit in judgment of art that all Berne members share to some extent. A systemic judgment about the dependent status of non-representational forms of industrial art, expressed in terms of "separability," shields Italian courts from having to adjudicate the degree of unjust enrichment that victims of copying might otherwise seek to evidence in particular cases. Most designs and models stand or fall in accordance with the grant of positive rights under sui generis legislation.

Supporters of the regime of partial cumulation in the Federal Republic of Germany also seek to reconcile the principle of non-discrimination with their opposition to protecting ornamental designs and models in copyright law. A concern for the exceptionally artistic design includes a disposition to evaluate unjust enrichment in particular cases and to objectify judgments about art when necessary. This is balanced by a formal unwillingness to discriminate against any single category of ornamental designs *a priori*, and by a concomitant disinclination to view industrial art as exceptional in all but a very limited number of cases. Once again the legal status of most designs and models is determined by the grant of positive rights under sui generis legislation.

Even present-day supporters of total cumulation in France seek to reconcile traditional antipathy towards sitting in judgment of art with growing opposition to the protection of ornamental designs under a copyright law that confers moral rights, strong remedies, and the long duration meant to reward individual creators of works of art. A systemic disposition to repress unjust enrichment in particular cases inhibits French courts and commentators from establishing a threshold of artistic or creative content that ought generally to be required for purposes of copyright protection. Yet, the protection that ensues is so broad and the potential restraints on trade so great that judicial resistance in particular cases, either at the infringement stage or more recently at the subject matter stage, may gradually re-introduce judgments about art through the back door. Recent commentators in France would prefer to limit the protection accorded ornamental designs of useful articles if a solution could be found that inspired more confidence than the sui generis regimes operating elsewhere at the present time.

When these methodological preferences are evaluated empirically, the distance between the different regimes further recedes for the reason that each is potentially subject to expansive or restrictive phases that can greatly affect the scope of protectibility at any given period. To maintain the integrity of their regime of non-cumulation, for example, Italian courts dealing with ornamental designs must steadfastly refuse to see artistic values capable of independent existence for copyright purposes despite mounting pressures for an effective doctrine of conceptual separability. If the judicial response to these pressures were to become more indulgent, the regime of non-cumulation would begin to drift towards the regimes of partial cumulation. This follows because judicial determination of conceptual separability inherently reflects a judgment about the intensity of the artistic values in question. At least one author thinks that a drift towards a regime of partial cumulation is the natural path for the Italian regime of non-cumulation to take; and the Commission of the European Communities has recommended that member countries accept the principle of partial cumulation as a basis for harmonizing their domestic copyright laws with respect to applied art.

Yet, experience further shows that regimes of partial cumulation, however exclusionary in principle, are subject to even more intense protectionist pressures than those exerted against the unaccommodating regime of non-cumulation. If the threshold to copyright protection is set at arbitrarily high levels, as occurs in the Federal Republic of Germany, efforts to distinguish between protectible and non-protectible aesthetic designs may degenerate into mere preferences or value judgements that elicit inconsistent and arbitrary results over time. Periodic fluctuations in taste and economic outlook add new inconsistencies while compounding the old. Inconsistent decisions, if prolonged over time, pull towards the unity of art position, as occurred in France prior to 1902 and Belgium prior to 1935. Downward pressures are already being exerted on the newest criterion in use among regimes of partial cumulation—the "marked artistic character"—test that the Uniform Benelux Designs Law introduced in 1975—and the ability of Benelux courts to muster sufficient resistance looks doubtful.

When, conversely, partisans of a regime of partial cumulation do resist downward pressures of this kind, the threshold of copyrightability for applied art must logically be set at a very high level in order to limit the zone in which subjective value judgments can effectively influence the outcome of litigation. In the Federal Republic of Germany, copyrightable works of applied art must amount to creative achievements as measured by the kinds of tests ordinarily used in industrial property law. This elevation of the requisite level of originality calls into question a basic purpose of the law of literary and artistic property, namely, to reward living artists and creators and to protect their works. It also strains the principle of non-discrimination to the breaking point since ornamental designs of useful articles will then receive treatment, for purposes of copyright law, inferior to that accorded minimalist works of modern art, to commercial paintings sold as household decorations, and even to the address books, directories, and instruction manuals that constitute the small change of copyright law.

Defenders of the Italian regime of non-cumulation therefore argue that the criterion of *scindibiltà* does less overt violence to general principles of copyright law than an arbitrarily high threshold of originality, such as courts have established in the Federal Republic of Germany. Whatever validity, if any, this argument may have possessed in 1941, when Italian copyright law first codified the theory of dissociation, it seems less persuasive today when both regimes must routinely deal with modernistic designs of useful articles that rely on simplicity of line and form rather than extrinsic ornamentation. Behind the rhetoric that supports one regime or the other, the end result is that both arbitrarily exclude the bulk of ornamental designs of useful articles from their respective copyright laws by means that are discriminatory in fact, if not in law. In so doing, both the regimes of partial cumulation and the regime of noncumulation rely on the common functional justification that special design laws exist to protect designs exiled from copyright law.

This reliance may be misplaced. Arguably, a primary function of a special design law today is to reduce the scale, but not the scope, of protection that would be available in copyright law. Thus, one might expect the special design laws of the European Community to be miniature versions of the Berne Union's basic copyright paradigm with a shorter term of protection and with perhaps the addition of some of the formalities otherwise abolished by the Convention. Design laws of this stamp would resemble the regime nearly enacted into United States law as the former Title II. Indeed, the 1975 Hearings on Title II may have conveyed the impression that foreign design laws provided better protection than the United States design patent law because they were constructed along the lines of the proposed Title II.

In reality, the evidence suggests that foreign design laws retain the characteristic features of the basic industrial property paradigm, with its insistence on non-divulgation, priority, novelty, qualitative originality, and even, in the case of Italy, forfeiture for non-exploitation. Although modern design laws normally operate without a formal search of the prior art that would be required under the full patent paradigm, the substantive requirements of objective novelty and qualitative originality may nonetheless exclude a significant number of ornamental designs ostensibly entitled to protection. For example, the requirement of qualitative originality in the design law of the Federal Republic of

Germany is surprisingly high and may become even higher under the pending reform. Where courts have lowered the qualitative originality standard in administering a design law, as in Italy, or where the government has abolished it altogether, as in the Benelux countries, the standard of objective novelty, whether absolute or relative, remains a formidable barrier. Absent timely and costly steps to satisfy formal requirements of, deposit and registration, a proprietor who divulges his ornamental design through direct commercial exploitation may thereby destroy novelty for purposes of most special design laws.

For these and other reasons, foreign design laws have not in fact provided the breadth of protection conjured up when the existence of such laws is claimed as a justification for excluding industrial art from copyright law. The criteria that exclude ornamental designs from protection as applied art in foreign copyright laws lead to another set of exclusionary criteria in special design laws heavily influenced by the industrial property paradigm. Sometimes the substantive tests used to exclude ornamental designs from either legal subculture seem functional equivalents of the same basic criteria serving two different but parallel goals. In copyright law, doctrines of quantitative and qualitative creativity serve to filter and limit the number of industrial designs entitled to long-term protection, without formalities, against copying only. In design law, doctrines of objective novelty and qualitative originality, coupled with obligatory requirements of registration and deposit, serve to restrict the number of industrial designs entitled to protection for a much shorter period of time.

When the legal machinery of the special regimes fails to deliver the rights officially made available to stimulate and reward innovation in industrial art the twice-excluded design must then either supplicate at the door of unfair competition law or seek to enter copyright through the back door as a marginal case. To the extent that unfair competition law intervenes against misappropriation in the form of servile imitation, it tends to recreate the excesses of the copyright approach without providing the minimum safeguards built into the machinery of copyright law. To the extent that unfair competition law declines to intervene or fails to intervene with sufficient vigour, the proliferation of design piracy, increasingly conducted on a world scale, forces harried designers and manufacturers to batter on the door to copyright law. Sooner or later this door may open in order to redress a particularly grievous case of unjust enrichment. In this event, an apparently isolated decision becomes a fertile source of inconsistent and arbitrary results for the future as tensions between worthiness of protection and unjust enrichment begin to tug in opposite directions.

Only in France would the door to copyright law open as a matter of course. The classic regime of absolute cumulation that Pouillet sired constitutes a response not only to the discriminatory nature of the criteria used to exclude ornamental designs from copyright law in other systems, but also to the rigidity of the sui generis design laws themselves—including the French design law of 1909. To avoid the kind of technical forfeitures produced elsewhere, France allows ornamental designs of useful articles to obtain concurrent protection against copying in the law of artistic property without any formal prerequisites whatsoever. This applies even to designs registered under the 1909 law whose term of absolute protection has run out.

However, the evidence shows that the French regime of total cumulation, in seeking to clear distortions that occur in the copyright laws of other regimes, actually creates so many distortions of its own that countries such as Belgium, the Netherlands, Italy and the Federal Republic of Germany have all rejected this approach after flirtations of varying degrees of intensity. If the chief virtue of a regime premised on the "unity of art" theory is indeed its ability to avoid the vices of competing regimes, its chief vice may be that, by broadly protecting designs of low creative content, it stimulates courts, commentators, and governments to invent the very exclusionary criteria that have caused so many difficulties in the first instance. This search for valid exclusionary criteria continues even in present-day France, where some courts have recently begun to insist on a more substantial creative effort as a prerequisite for copyright protection.

Neither legal theory nor empirical results thus provide any clear answer when the models competing within the European Community are critically evaluated in the abstract. At a recent international symposium, exponents of all three regimes expressed disenchantment with their respective national systems without recognizing the extent to which courts and governments seem slowly to be converging upon some intermediate and perhaps still rudimentary regime of partial cumulation. If continued, this trend would be consistent with the direction that the Commission of the European Communities proposed to follow in 1977 as a matter of expedience.

For the present, as each system clings to its own vices in preference to those of the others, the prospects for rapid harmonization of foreign law in this area remain poor. A logical question this impasse prompts is, which of the competing models under review may prove most beneficial to the United States pending a more definitive solution at the international level.

Karen Millen Fashions Ltd v. Dunnes Stores (Limerick) Ltd

Court of Justice of the European Union, Second Chamber, 2014.
Case C-345/13.

Judgment

1 This request for a preliminary ruling concerns the interpretation of Articles 6 and 85(2) of Council Regulation (EC) No 6/2002 of 12 December 2001 on Community designs (OJ 2002 L 3, p. 1).

2 The request has been made in proceedings between Karen Millen Fashions Ltd ('KMF'), on the one hand, and Dunnes Stores and Dunnes Stores (Limerick) Ltd ('Dunnes'), on the other, concerning an application made by KMF to restrain the use of designs by Dunnes.

Legal context

The TRIPS Agreement

3 The Agreement on Trade-Related Aspects of Intellectual Property Rights ('the TRIPs Agreement') constitutes Annex 1C to the Agreement establishing the World Trade Organisation (WTO), which was signed in Marrakesh on 15 April 1994 and approved by Council Decision 94/800/EC of 22 December 1994 concerning the conclusion on behalf of the European Community, as regards matters within its competence, of the agreements reached in the Uruguay Round multilateral negotiations.

4 In section 4, entitled 'Industrial Designs', of Part II of that agreement, entitled 'Standards concerning the availability, scope and use of Intellectual Property Rights', Article 25, itself entitled 'Requirements for Protection', provides:

'1. Members shall provide for the protection of independently created industrial designs that are new or original. Members may provide that designs are not new or original if they do not significantly differ from known designs or combinations of known design features. Members may provide that such protection shall not extend to designs dictated essentially by technical or functional considerations. . . .'

Regulation No 6/2002

5 Recitals 9, 14, 16, 17, 19 and 25 in the preamble to Regulation No 6/2002 state:

'(9) The substantive provisions of this Regulation on design law should be aligned with the respective provisions in Directive 98/71/EC.

(14) The assessment as to whether a design has individual character should be based on whether the overall impression produced on an informed user viewing the design clearly differs from that produced on him by the existing design corpus, taking into consideration the nature of the product to which the design

is applied or in which it is incorporated, and in particular the industrial sector to which it belongs and the degree of freedom of the designer in developing the design.

(16) Some of those sectors produce large numbers of designs for products frequently having a short market life where protection without the burden of registration formalities is an advantage and the duration of protection is of lesser significance. On the other hand, there are sectors of industry which value the advantages of registration for the greater legal certainty it provides and which require the possibility of a longer term of protection corresponding to the foreseeable market life of their products.

(17) This calls for two forms of protection, one being a short-term unregistered design and the other being a longer term registered design. . . .

(19) A Community design should not be upheld unless the design is new and unless it also possesses an individual character in comparison with other designs.

(25) Those sectors of industry producing large numbers of possibly short-lived designs over short periods of time of which only some may be eventually commercialized will find advantage in the unregistered Community design. Furthermore, there is also a need for these sectors to have easier recourse to the registered Community design. Therefore, the option of combining a number of designs in one multiple application would satisfy that need. However, the designs contained in a multiple application may be dealt with independently of each other for the purposes of enforcement of rights, licensing, rights in rem, levy of execution, insolvency proceedings, surrender, renewal, assignment, deferred publication or declaration of invalidity.'

6   Under Article 1 of Regulation No 6/2002:

1.   A design which complies with the conditions contained in this Regulation is hereinafter referred to as a "Community design".

2.   A design shall be protected:

(a) by an "unregistered Community design", if made available to the public in the manner provided for in this Regulation;

7   Article 4(1) of that regulation provides that a design is to be protected by a Community design to the extent that it is new and has individual character.

8   Article 5 thereof states:

'1.   A design shall be considered to be new if no identical design has been made available to the public:

(a) in the case of an unregistered Community design, before the date on which the design for which protection is claimed has first been made available to the public;

(b) in the case of a registered Community design, before the date of filing of the application for registration of the design for which protection is claimed, or, if priority is claimed, the date of priority.

2.   Designs shall be deemed to be identical if their features differ only in immaterial details.'

9   Article 6 of that regulation provides:

'1.   A design shall be considered to have individual character if the overall impression it produces on the informed user differs from the overall impression produced on such a user by any design which has been made available to the public:

(a) in the case of an unregistered Community design, before the date on which the design for which protection is claimed has first been made available to the public;

(b) in the case of a registered Community design, before the date of filing the application for registration or, if a priority is claimed, the date of priority.

2.   In assessing individual character, the degree of freedom of the designer in developing the design shall be taken into consideration.'

10   Article 11 of Regulation No 6/2002 provides:

'1.   A design which meets the requirements under Section 1 shall be protected by an unregistered Community design for a period of three years as from the date on which the design was first made available to the public within the Community.

2.   For the purpose of paragraph 1, a design shall be deemed to have been made available to the public within the Community if it has been published, exhibited, used in trade or otherwise disclosed in such a way that, in the normal course of business, these events could reasonably have become known to the circles specialised in the sector concerned, operating within the Community. The design shall not, however, be deemed to have been made available to the public for the sole reason that it has been disclosed to a third person under explicit or implicit conditions of confidentiality.'

11   Article 19 of that regulation provides:

1.   A registered Community design shall confer on its holder the exclusive right to use it and to prevent any third party not having his consent from using it. The aforementioned use shall cover, in particular, the making, offering, putting on the market, importing, exporting or using of a product in which the design is incorporated or to which it is applied, or stocking such a product for those purposes.

2.   An unregistered Community design shall, however, confer on its holder the right to prevent the acts referred to in paragraph 1 only if the contested use results from copying the protected design. The contested use shall not be deemed to result from copying the protected design if it results from an independent work of creation by a designer who may be reasonably thought not to be familiar with the design made available to the public by the holder.

12   According to Article 85(2) of that regulation:

'In proceedings in respect of an infringement action or an action for threatened infringement of an unregistered Community design, the Community design court shall treat the Community design as valid if the right holder produces proof that the conditions laid down in Article 11 have been met and indicates what constitutes the individual character of his Community design. However, the defendant may contest its validity by way of a plea or with a counterclaim for a declaration of invalidity.'

The dispute in the main proceedings and the questions referred for a preliminary ruling

13   KMF is a company incorporated under the law of England and Wales which carries on the business of producing and selling women's clothing.

14   Dunnes is a substantial retailing group in Ireland which, among other things, sells women's clothing.

15   In 2005 KMF designed and placed on sale in Ireland a striped shirt (in a blue and a stone brown version) and a black knit top ('the KMF garments').

16   Examples of the KMF garments were purchased by representatives of Dunnes from one of KMF's Irish outlets. Dunnes subsequently had copies of the garments manufactured outside Ireland and put them on sale in its Irish stores in late 2006.

17   Asserting itself to be the holder of unregistered Community designs relating to the garments, on 2 January 2007, KMF commenced proceedings in the High Court in which it claimed, inter alia, injunctions restraining Dunnes from using the designs, and damages.

18   The High Court upheld that action.

19   Dunnes brought an appeal against the judgment of the High Court before the Supreme Court.

20   That court states that Dunnes does not dispute that it copied the KMF garments and acknowledges that the unregistered Community designs of which KMF claims to be the holder are new designs.

21   However, it is clear from the order for reference that Dunnes disputes that KMF is the holder of an unregistered Community design for each of the KMF garments on the grounds, first, that the garments do not have individual character within the meaning of Regulation No 6/2002 and, secondly, that that regulation requires KMF to prove, as a matter of fact, that the garments have individual character.

22   It was in those circumstances that the Supreme Court decided to stay the proceedings and to refer two questions to the Court for a preliminary ruling:

> '1.   In consideration of the individual character of a design which is claimed to be entitled to be protected as an unregistered Community design for the purposes of [Regulation No 6/2002], is the overall impression it produces on the informed user, within the meaning of Article 6 of that Regulation, to be considered by reference to whether it differs from the overall impression produced on such a user by:
>
>> (a)   any individual design which has previously been made available to the public, or
>>
>> (b)   any combination of known design features from more than one such earlier design?
>
> 2.   Is a Community design court obliged to treat an unregistered Community design as valid for the purposes of Article 85(2) of [Regulation No 6/2002] where the right holder merely indicates what constitutes the individual character of the design or is the right holder obliged to prove that the design has individual character in accordance with Article 6 of that Regulation?'

The questions referred

The first question

23   By its first question, the referring court asks, in essence, whether Article 6 of Regulation No 6/2002 must be interpreted as meaning that, in order for a design to be considered to have individual character, the overall impression which that design produces on the informed user must be different from that produced on such a user by one or more earlier designs, taken individually, or by a combination of features taken in isolation and drawn from a number of earlier designs.

24   There is nothing in the wording of Article 6 of Regulation No 6/2002 to support the view that the overall impression referred to therein must be produced by such a combination.

25   The reference to the overall impression produced on the informed user by 'any design' which has been made available to the public indicates that Article 6 must be interpreted as meaning that the assessment as to whether a design has individual character must be conducted in relation to one or more specific, individualised, defined and identified designs from among all the designs which have been made available to the public previously.

26   As observed by the United Kingdom Government and the European Commission, that interpretation is in keeping with the case-law in which it has been held that, when possible, the informed user will make a direct comparison between the designs at issue because that type of comparison actually relates to the impression produced on that user by earlier individualised and defined designs, as opposed to an amalgam of specific features or parts of earlier designs.

27   It is true that the Court also held that it cannot be ruled out that a direct comparison might be impracticable or uncommon in the sector concerned, in particular because of specific circumstances or the characteristics of the items which the earlier mark and the design at issue represent. It observed in that context that, in the absence of any precise indications to that effect in Regulation No 6/2002, the EU legislature cannot be regarded as having intended to limit the assessment of potential designs to a direct comparison.

28   It should be remembered, however, that although the Court acknowledged the possibility of an indirect comparison of the designs at issue, it went on to hold merely that the General Court had not erred in basing its reasoning on an imperfect recollection of the overall impression produced by those designs.

29   Moreover, and as observed by the Advocate General in points 48 to 50 of his Opinion, such an indirect comparison, which is based on an imperfect recollection, is not based on a recollection of specific features from several different earlier designs but of specific designs.

30   The arguments put forward by Dunnes do not cast any doubt on the foregoing considerations.

31   Thus, regarding, first, the arguments based on recitals 14 and 19 in the preamble to Regulation No 6/2002, which use the expressions 'the existing design corpus' and 'in comparison with other designs', it should be borne in mind that the preamble to a Community act has no binding legal force and cannot be relied on either as a ground for derogating from the actual provisions of the act in question or for interpreting those provisions in a manner clearly contrary to their wording.

32   It should be noted in any event that although recital 14 in the preamble to Regulation No 6/2002 refers to the impression produced on an informed user by the 'existing design corpus', those terms are not used in any of the provisions of that regulation.

33   Moreover, neither the use of those terms nor of the wording 'in comparison with other designs' in recital 19 in the preamble to Regulation No 6/2002 means that the relevant impression for the purpose of the application of Article 6 of that regulation is the one produced not by one or more earlier designs, taken individually, but by a combination of features taken in isolation and drawn from a number of earlier designs.

34   Furthermore, as regards the reference to 'combinations of known design features' in the second sentence of Article 25(1) of the TRIPS Agreement, suffice it to note that that provision is worded in optional terms and that, consequently, the parties to that agreement are not required to provide for the novel character or originality of a design to be assessed in comparison with such combinations.

35   In those circumstances, the answer to the first question is that Article 6 of Regulation No 6/2002 must be interpreted as meaning that, in order for a design to be considered to have individual character, the overall impression which that design produces on the informed user must be different from that produced on such a user not by a combination of features taken in isolation and drawn from a number of earlier designs, but by one or more earlier designs, taken individually.

The second question

36   By its second question, the referring court asks, in essence, whether Article 85(2) of Regulation No 6/2002 must be interpreted as meaning that, in order for a Community design court to treat an unregistered Community design as valid, the right holder of that design is required to prove that it has individual character within the meaning of Article 6 of that regulation, or need only indicate what constitutes the individual character of that design.

37   It is apparent from the very wording of Article 85(2) of Regulation No 6/2002 that, in order for an unregistered Community design to be treated as valid, the right holder of that design is required, first of all, to prove that the conditions laid down in Article 11 of that regulation have been met and, secondly, to indicate what constitutes the individual character of that design.

38   Under Article 11(1) of Regulation No 6/2002, a design which meets the requirements under Section 1 of that regulation is to be protected by an unregistered Community design for a period of three years as from the date on which the design was first made available to the public within the European Union.

39   As indicated by the very heading of Article 85 of Regulation No 6/2002, paragraph 1 thereof establishes a presumption of validity of registered Community designs and, in paragraph 2, a presumption of validity of unregistered Community designs.

40   The implementation of that presumption of validity is, by its very nature, incompatible with the interpretation of Article 85(2) of Regulation No 6/2002 advocated by Dunnes, to the effect that the proof

which the holder of a design must make out under that provision, namely that the conditions laid down in Article 11 of that regulation have been met, includes the proof that the design concerned also satisfies all of the conditions laid down in Section 1 of Title II of that regulation, that is to say, Articles 3 to 9 thereof.

41   Similarly, the interpretation of 85(2) of Regulation No 6/2002, read in conjunction with Article 11 of that regulation, as proposed by Dunnes, would have the effect of rendering meaningless and nugatory the second condition, laid down in Article 85(2), that the holder of a design must indicate what constitutes the individual character of that design.

42   Nor would that interpretation be compatible with the objective of simplicity and expeditiousness which, as evidenced by recitals 16 and 17 in the preamble to Regulation No 6/2002, underpins the idea of protection of unregistered Community designs.

43   In that context, it should be noted that the different procedures provided for in Article 85 of Regulation No 6/2002 with regard to a registered Community design and an unregistered Community design arise from the need to determine, with regard to the latter, the date as from which the design at issue is covered by the protection under that regulation and specifically what is covered, which, as there are no registration formalities, may be more difficult to identify in the case of an unregistered design than for a registered design.

44   Moreover, if Article 85(2) of Regulation No 6/2002 were to be interpreted as meaning that an unregistered Community design may be treated as valid only if its holder proves that all of the conditions laid down in Section 1 of Title II of that regulation have been met, the possibility for the defendant to contest the validity of that design by way of a plea or with a counterclaim for a declaration of invalidity, as provided for in the second sentence of Article 85(2), would be rendered largely meaningless and nugatory.

45   As regards the second condition set out in Article 85(2) of Regulation No 6/2002, suffice it to note that the wording of that provision, in merely requiring the holder of an unregistered Community design to indicate what constitutes the individual character of that design, is unambiguous and cannot be interpreted as entailing an obligation to prove that the design concerned has individual character.

46   Although, given the lack of registration formalities for this category of design, it is necessary for the holder of the design at issue to specify what he wants to have protected under that regulation, it is sufficient for him to identify the features of his design which give it individual character.

47   In those circumstances, the answer to the second question is that Article 85(2) of Regulation No 6/2002 must be interpreted as meaning that, in order for a Community design court to treat an unregistered Community design as valid, the right holder of that design is not required

to prove that it has individual character within the meaning of Article 6 of that regulation, but need only indicate what constitutes the individual character of that design, that is to say, indicates what, in his view, are the element or elements of the design concerned which give it its individual character.

Costs

48   Since these proceedings are, for the parties to the main proceedings, a step in the action pending before the national court, the decision on costs is a matter for that court. Costs incurred in submitting observations to the Court, other than the costs of those parties, are not recoverable.

On those grounds, the Court (Second Chamber) hereby rules:

1.   Article 6 of Council Regulation (EC) No 6/2002 of 12 December 2001 on Community designs is to be interpreted as meaning that, in order for a design to be considered to have individual character, the overall impression which that design produces on the informed user must be different from that produced on such a user not by a combination of features taken in isolation and drawn from a number of earlier designs, but by one or more earlier designs, taken individually.

2.   Article 85(2) of Regulation No 6/2002 must be interpreted as meaning that, in order for a Community design court to treat an unregistered Community design as valid, the right holder of that design is not required to prove that it has individual character within the meaning of Article 6 of that regulation, but need only indicate what constitutes the individual character of that design, that is to say, indicates what, in his view, are the element or elements of the design concerned which give it its individual character.

NOTES

1.   *Community Design Regulation.* As indicated in the *Karen Millen Fashions* decision, the EU Community Design Regulation offers two tiers of protection. Registered designs receive five years of protection measured from the date of application, with four optional five-year renewal terms; registration is made in the European Union Intellectual Property Office. Unregistered designs receive automatic protection, but only against the unauthorized use of copies, for three years from first public distribution. Protection for both registered and unregistered designs under the Community Design Regulation co-exists with protection for designs— whether under copyright, trademark, or specific design laws—provided by national law in EU member countries. The 1998 EC Design Directive, 98/71/EC, aims to harmonize aspects of these national laws with respect to registered designs.

On design protection in the European Union, see Uma Suthersanen, Design Law: European Union and United States of America (2d ed. 2010); David Stone, European Union Design Law: A Practitioner's Guide (2012).

2.   *The Paris Convention and the TRIPs Agreement.* Article 1(2) of the Paris Convention identifies industrial design as an object of industrial property protection; Article 5*quinquies*, introduced by the 1958 Lisbon Act, adds the requirement that "industrial designs shall be protected in all the countries of the Union." The language originally proposed at Lisbon included a definition of industrial design and a minimum term of protection, but both elements were rejected in favor of an open-ended obligation that member countries could meet through specialized design legislation or through their copyright or unfair competition laws. *See* G.H.C. Bodenhausen, Guide to the Application of the Paris Convention for the Protection of Industrial Property 86 (1968). Article 4 of the Paris Convention gives industrial designs the same six-month filing priority as trademarks, and Article 5B provides that "protection of industrial designs shall not, under any circumstances, be subject to any forfeiture, either by reason of failure to work or by reason of the importation of articles corresponding to those which are protected."

Although, like Article 5*quinquies* of the Paris Convention, Article 25 of the TRIPs Agreement leaves it to member states to determine how to protect industrial designs, Article 25(1)'s formulation of standards for protectible subject matter tilts in the direction of copyright and registration-based design legislation. The requirement that the design be "independently created" is taken from both copyright and design laws, while the additional requirement that the design be original or that it be new stems from copyright and design law respectively. The TRIPs negotiators did not adopt a proposal, drawn from U.S. design patent legislation, that would have required the design to be "ornamental and non-obvious." However, by allowing member states to provide that a design is not new or original if it does "not significantly differ from known designs or contributions of known design features," Article 25(1) leaves room for tests of nonobviousness and inventive step applied under some design registration systems and the creativity standard applied under some copyright systems. *See* Daniel Gervais, The TRIPs Agreement, Drafting History and Analysis 140 (1998).

3.   *Hague Agreement.* The 1925 Hague Agreement Concerning the International Deposit of Industrial Designs, which entered into force on June 1, 1928 and has since been revised several times, aims to simplify and lower the cost of multinational design registration filings. Through the deposit of a single application, in a single language, and for a single fee, a design owner in a Hague member country may obtain registration for its design in any member countries that it designates. Each member country decides for itself, however, whether the design meets the standards of its design law.

The Hague procedures are oriented toward registered design systems that require only cursory examination, a fact that was an obstacle to adherence by countries like the United States that require a substantive, and consequently time-consuming, examination before a design patent or registration will issue. Revision efforts, initiated in 1991 to accommodate the needs of countries with substantive examination systems, culminated in a

New Act Concerning the International Registration of Industrial Designs, adopted in Geneva on July 2, 1999, with the United States as one of the twenty-three signatories. In December 2006, the Council of the European Union approved the EU's accession to the Geneva Act and the accession took effect as of January 1, 2008. In February 2015 the United States deposited its instrument of ratification, and the Geneva Act went into effect for the United States on May 13, 2015.

4. *Berne Convention Article 2(7).* Article 2(1) of the Berne Convention, Paris Text includes applied art among its classes of protected works and Article 2(7) coordinates the obligations of member countries that variously follow the cumulative, partial cumulative and non-cumulative approaches to protection of industrial design. Article 2(7) provides:

> Subject to the provisions of Article 7(4) of this Convention, it shall be a matter for legislation in the countries of the Union to determine the extent of the application of their laws to works of applied art and industrial designs and models, as well as the conditions under which such works, designs and models shall be protected. Works protected in the country of origin solely as designs and models shall be entitled in another country of the Union only to such special protection as is granted in that country to designs and models; however, if no such special protection is granted in that country, such works shall be protected as artistic works.

The 1967 Stockholm Revision added the last clause, requiring a country that lacks a design registration statute to give copyright protection to works of applied art coming from a country that gives them only noncumulative design protection. This approach might appear to impose an undue burden on copyright countries, particularly countries that take a partial cumulative approach. Nonetheless, because most countries today have some form of industrial design statute, the disparity may be more apparent than real.

5. *U.S. Design Protection and the Berne Convention.* The U.S. Copyright Act approximates the noncumulative approach to industrial design by withholding protection from a design's utilitarian elements. Section 101 of the Act defines protectible "pictorial, graphic, and sculptural works" to include "works of artistic craftsmanship insofar as their form but not their mechanical or utilitarian aspects are concerned," and provides that the design of a useful article "shall be considered a pictorial, graphic, or sculptural work only if, and only to the extent that, such design incorporates pictorial, graphic, or sculptural features that can be identified separately from, and are capable of existing independently of, the utilitarian aspects of the article."

Section 101's line between copyrightable and uncopyrightable industrial design has proved to be highly elusive in practice. It also presents a difficult interpretational question under Berne Convention Article 2(7) which limits a protecting country's obligations with respect to works "protected in the country of origin solely as designs and models." Can a protecting country that grants both copyright protection and special protection to works of applied art deny copyright protection to an industrial design where the country of origin (the United States, say) would deny copyright protection to the particular design in issue, but not to the general class of applied art to which the work belongs? For example, under the U.S. Copyright Act, courts will protect the design of lamp bases in general, but will deny protection to any lamp base whose artistic features lack the separability required by section 101 of the Act. Will a lamp base that lacks the required, separable elements be entitled to copyright protection, or only to design protection, in the protecting country?

6. *Functionality and the Problem of Spare Parts.* Article 25(1) of the TRIPs Agreement, obligating members to protect new or original industrial designs, expressly allows them to "provide that such protection shall not extend to designs dictated essentially by technical or functional considerations." (Article 7(1) of the EC Design Directive, for example, provides: "A design right shall not subsist in features of appearance of a product which are solely dictated by its technical function.") The TRIPs provision reflects the premise, widely followed in design registration legislation around the world, that for functional subject matter to qualify for intellectual property protection, it must meet utility patent law's comparatively higher standards of novelty and nonobviousness or inventive step.

The question of spare parts as functional features has been particularly vexing. Should design laws have a "must-fit" exception, or should an automobile manufacturer be able to monopolize the market for spare fenders that are configured to fit onto automobile bodies produced by the manufacturer? Is a must-fit exception enough, or is a "must-match" exception also necessary, so that competitors can produce and sell fenders that will not only attach to the automobile body but will also aesthetically match the fender on the other side of the car? Do the principles that support a must-fit exception also support a must-match exception?

The constantly shifting patterns of protection for industrial design and of negotiating the boundaries of functionality shifted once again when the EC Design Directive required EU countries, most notably Italy, to depart from the rule of non-cumulation that effectively excluded industrial design from copyright protection. Article 17 of the Directive provides that "[a] design protected by a design right registered in or in respect of a Member State in accordance with this Directive shall also be eligible for protection under the law of copyright of that State as from the date on which the design was created or fixed in any form."

For a thoughtful appraisal of these issues in the context of EU policymaking, see Graeme Dinwoodie, Federalized Functionalism: The Future of Design Protection in the European Union, 24 AIPLA Q.J. 611 (1996).

7. *Trademark and Unfair Competition Law.* The packaging for a product, or the design of the product itself, may be as effective an indicator of the product's source as more traditional trademarks such as words, symbols and slogans. Although many countries at one time excluded industrial designs from trademark protection, the overwhelming trend today is to grant them protection on the same terms as other forms of trademark subject matter.

For example, section 4 of the 1993 EC Regulation on the Community Trademark, Council Regulation (EC) No. 40/94, includes among the "signs" in which a community trademark may subsist "not only words or letters, but also 'the shape of goods or of their packaging'." The Regulation also adopts the principle, evident in design registration statutes as well, that trademarks not be allowed to substitute for patents in protecting an article's functional features. Section 7(1)(e) of the Regulation provides as an absolute ground for refusal of registration that a sign consists exclusively of "(i) the shape which results from the nature of the goods themselves; or (ii) the shape of goods which is necessary to obtain a technical result; or (iii) the shape which gives substantial value to the goods."

8. *Layout-Designs (Topographies) of Integrated Circuits.* Following failed efforts to bring the design of the intricate stencils used in manufacturing semiconductor chips under copyright law, the U.S. Congress in 1984 passed the Semiconductor Chip Protection Act, P.L. 98–620 Tit. III § 302, 98 Stat. 3347, 17 U.S.C. §§ 901 *et seq.*, to protect original "mask works" fixed in "semiconductor chip products." Under the Act, a mask work first becomes eligible for protection when it is fixed in a semiconductor chip product. The mask work owner will forfeit protection if it fails to apply for registration within two years of the work's first commercial exploitation. The Act prescribes a ten-year term of protection and grants exclusive reproduction, importation and distribution rights; it also carves out exceptions for reverse engineering, first sale and innocent infringement under prescribed conditions. The hotly-contested reverse engineering exception permits "the 'unauthorized' creation of a second mask work whose layout, in substantial part, is similar to the layout of the protected mask work—if the second mask work was the product of substantial study and analysis, and not the mere result of plagiarism accomplished without such study or analysis." H.R. Rep. No. 781, 98th Cong., 2d Sess. 22 (1984).

The difference between semiconductor chip designs and traditional copyright subject matter was only one reason the U.S. Congress decided on a *sui generis* statute. Another reason was doubtless that, by bringing mask works under a *sui generis* regime rather than under copyright, U.S. protection could be freed from the national treatment obligation imposed by the Universal Copyright Convention (the only multilateral copyright treaty to which the United States had adhered at the time) and could be rested instead on a requirement of reciprocity.

Section 902(a)(1)(A) extends protection not only to U.S. nationals and domiciliaries, but also to nationals or domiciliaries of foreign nations that are party to a mask work treaty to which the United States is also a party, and section 902(a)(2) empowers the President by proclamation to extend mask work protection to foreign works upon finding that the foreign nation protects United States works on substantially the same basis as the Semiconductor Chip Protection Act or "on substantially the same basis as that on which the foreign nation extends protection to mask works of its own nationals and domiciliaries and mask works first exploited in that nation. . . ." Many countries received interim protection under this power, including Japan—which in 1985 enacted legislation that closely followed the terms of the U.S. Act, but did not require reciprocity—Canada and countries of the European Community. *See* generally, Charles McManis, International Protection for Semiconductor Chip Designs and the Standard of Judicial Review of Presidential Proclamations Issued Pursuant to the Semiconductor Chip Protection Act of 1984, 22 Geo. Wash. J. Int'l L. & Econ 331 (1988). For an overview and analysis of national laws, see Thomas Dreier, Development of the Protection of Semiconductor Integrated Circuits, 19 IIC 427 (1988).

In 1989, countries meeting in Washington, D.C. adopted a Treaty on the Protection of Intellectual Property in Respect of Integrated Circuits (IPIC) prepared under the auspices of the World Intellectual Property Organization. However, opposition from the world's two largest producers of integrated circuits—the United States and Japan—doomed the IPIC Treaty to failure. (Objectionable features included provision for compulsory licensing.) Nonetheless, Articles 35–38 of the TRIPs Agreement expressly borrow from the IPIC Treaty in establishing minimum standards for protection of layout-designs of integrated circuits. Among the provisions of the IPIC Treaty established as norms by the TRIPs provision is Article 4 providing that "[e]ach Contracting Party shall be free to implement its obligations under this Treaty through a special law on layout-designs (topographies) or its law on copyright, patents, utility models, industrial designs, unfair competition or any other law or a combination of any of those laws."

PROBLEM 10

On April 2, 1988 Acme Appliances, which has its headquarters in Country *X*, began distributing a portable, battery-powered toaster to retail customers in Countries *X* and *Y*, the designer of the toaster having previously assigned to Acme "all intellectual property rights in the toaster design throughout the world in perpetuity." On December 15, 1991, counterfeit copies of the toaster appeared on the market in Country *Z*. Country *X*, which on April 2, 1988, was a member of the Paris Convention (1967) but not of the Berne Convention (1971), protects designs such as the toaster design under design patent and unfair competition law and also under its copyright law, but only if and to the extent that the design "incorporates pictorial, graphic or sculptural features that can be identified separately from, and are capable of existing independently of, the utilitarian aspects of the article itself." Country *Y*, protects designs exclusively under design patent law, and Country *Z* protects them under both design patent and copyright law. Countries *Y* and *Z* are members of both the Berne (1971) and Paris (1967) Conventions.

Please advise Acme on the protection it is likely to receive for the design in Country *Z*. If Acme began distributing the toaster not in 1988, but on April 2, 1989, after Country *X* had adhered to the Berne Convention (1971), would this fact change your earlier answer?

INDEX

References are to Pages

Components of a patented method, 434
Secondary liability, 435
Territoriality
Generally, 1
Statutory extraterritoriality, 8
Trademark law compared, 7
Timely prosecution, 489
Trademark law compared, territoriality, 7
Transfer rights of holders, 501
Transferability
Patents, 499
Right to file, 499
TRIPs Agreement
Compulsory licenses, 518, 520
Discrimination as to the place of invention, 464
Historical background, 417
Limitations on rights, 517
Petty patents, 448
Remedies of holders, 500, 515
Rights of holders
Generally, 500, 507
Limitations, 517
Use rights, 507
Utility models, 448
Utility requirements for protection, 482
Validity
Choice of forum
European Union, 29
Policy considerations, 31
U.S. law, 32
Collateral estoppel, 72
European Union, 29
Policy considerations, 32
Post-infringement invalidity findings, 567
U.S. law, 32
Working requirement
Generally, 519
Compulsory licenses remedies, 552

PERSONAL JURISDICTION
See Jurisdiction, this index

PESTICIDES
Trade secret protections, 749

PHARMACEUTICALS
Compulsory licenses
Generally, 522 et seq.
Developing countries, 152, 541
Least developed countries, 541
Patent protection
Generally, 500
Compulsory licenses, above
Trade secret protections, 749
TRIPs Agreement, 133

PHONOGRAMS
Generally, 190
See also Sound Recordings, this index

PHONORECORDS
Generally, 290
See also Sound Recordings, this index

PHOTOCOPIES
Copyright
Limitations on rights, 317
Secondary liability of photocopying services providers, 348

PHOTOGRAPHS
Copyright
Protection, European Union, 223

PHOTOGRAPHY
Copyright
Neighboring rights, 382
Neighboring rights, 382

PIRACY
Anti-Counterfeiting Trade Agreement
Generally, 134, 184
Negotiation, 138
Criminal prosecutions, trademark piracy, 727
Economic considerations, North-South debate, 97
Havens, 13
North-South debate piracy issues
Generally, 92
Economic considerations, 97
Personal jurisdiction, pirate havens, 49
Territoriality, 11
Trademarks remedies, 727
Watch List, United States Trade Representative, 185

PLANT PATENTS
European Patent Convention, 449
Requirements for protection, 448

PLANT VARIETY PROTECTION
Generally, 448

POLICY CONSIDERATIONS
Generally, 90 et seq.
Authorship, 247, 380
Choice of forum, patent validity, 31
Collateral estoppel, patents, 73
Copyright, this index
Developing Countries, this index
European Union, unfair competition law, 739
Exhaustion of rights
Generally, 291
International exhaustion, 722
First sale doctrine, 291
Folklore protection, developing countries, 108 et seq.
Foreign direct investment, developing countries, 104, 128
Genetic resources protection, developing countries, 108 et seq.
Geographical indications, Old-World conflicts, 629
Global technological dynamism, 103
Harmonization of National Laws, this index
Industrial design protection, 778
Intellectual property protections, trade considerations, 104
International exhaustion of rights, 722

**TRADE-RELATED ASPECTS OF
    INTELLECTUAL PROPERTY
    RIGHTS**

**TRADITIONAL KNOWLEDGE
    PROTECTION**

TRANSFERS OF RIGHTS

TRANSITORY CAUSES OF ACTION

TRANSLATIONS

TREATIES

**TREATY ON INTELLECTUAL
    PROPERTY IN RESPECT OF
    INTEGRATED CIRCUITS**

TRIPS AGREEMENT

**UNDERSTANDING ON DISPUTE
SETTLEMENT (DSU)**

UNFAIR COMPETITION

**UNIFORM DOMAIN NAME DISPUTE
RESOLUTION POLICY (UDRP)**

**UNIFORM FOREIGN MONEY
JUDGMENTS RECOGNITION
ACT**

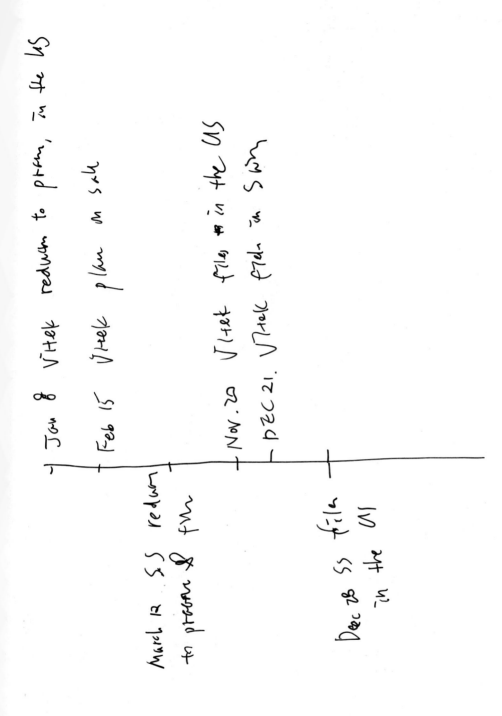

Jan 8   Vitek return to plan, in the US

Feb 15   Vitek plan on sale

March 12   SS return
to prepare of file

Nov. 20   Vitet files # in the US

DEC 21. Vitek files in Switz

Dec 28   SS files
in the US

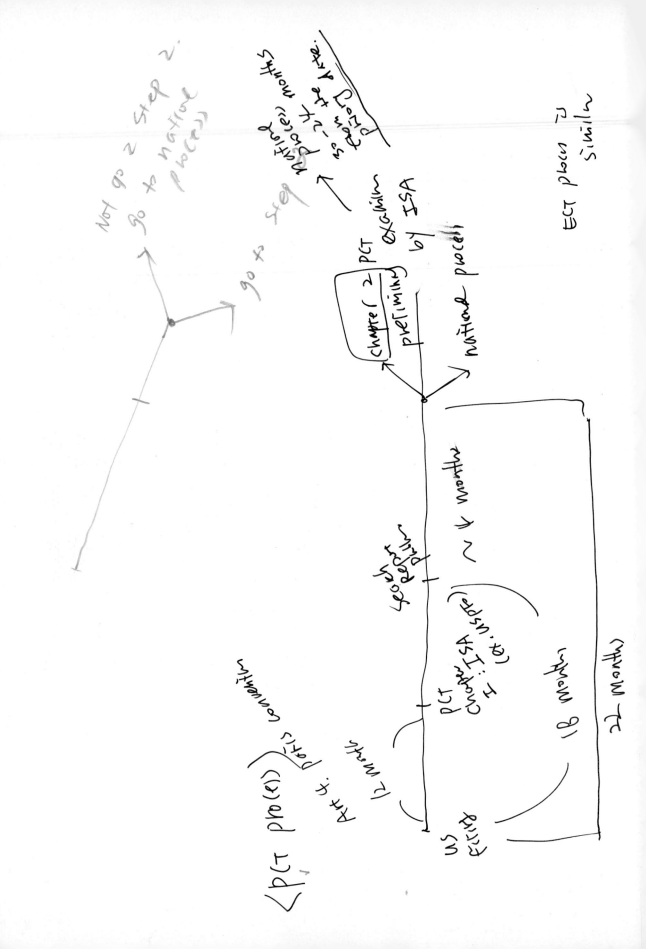

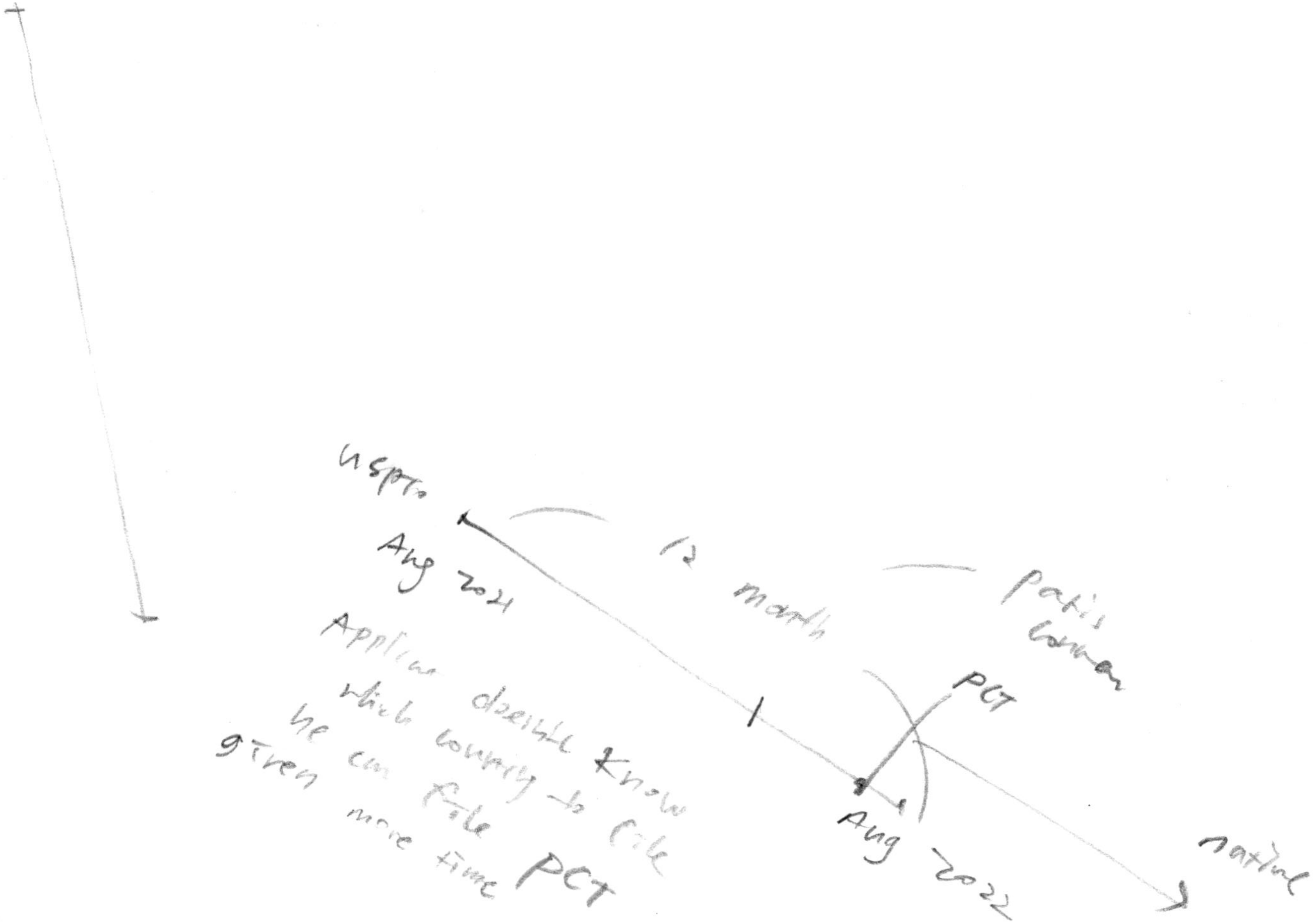

Patis
Conner

PCT

12 month

Aug 2022

Aug 2021

Upto

Applian describe know
whit country to file
he can rate
given more time PCT

natul